Computer Vision: Principles

Rangachar Kasturi
and
Ramesh C. Jain

1951-1991
40 YEARS OF SERVICE

IEEE COMPUTER SOCIETY
A member society of the
Institute of Electrical and Electronics Engineers, Inc.

IEEE Computer Society Press
Los Alamitos, California

Washington • Brussels • Tokyo

IEEE Computer Society Press Tutorial

Library of Congress Cataloging-in-Publication Data

Computer Vision / [edited by] Rangachar Kasturi and Ramesh C. Jain.
    p. cm. — (IEEE Computer Society Press tutorial)
Includes bibliographical references.
Contents: v. 1. Principles — v. 2. Advances and Applications.
ISBN 0-8186-9102-6
1. Computer vision.
I. Kasturi, Rangachar, 1949-. II. Jain, Ramesh. III. Series.
TA1632.C6582 1991
621.39'9 — dc20   91-13117
                                                                   CIP

Published by the
IEEE Computer Society Press
10662 Los Vaqueros Circle
PO Box 3014
Los Alamitos, CA 90720-1264

IEEE Computer Society Press Order Number 2102
Library of Congress Number 91-13117
IEEE Catalog Number 91EH0339-2
ISBN 0-8186-6102-X (microfiche)
ISBN 0-8186-9102-6 (case)

Additional copies can be ordered from

IEEE Computer Society Press
Customer Service Center
10662 Los Vaqueros Circle
PO Box 3014
Los Alamitos, CA 90720-1264

IEEE Service Center
445 Hoes Lane
PO Box 1331
Piscataway, NJ 08855-1331

IEEE Computer Society
13, avenue de l'Aquilon
B-1200 Brussels
BELGIUM

IEEE Computer Society
Ooshima Building
2-19-1 Minami-Aoyama
Minato-ku, Tokyo 107
JAPAN

Third printing, 1993

Technical Editor: Fred Petry
Production Editors: Lisa O'Conner and Mary E. Kavanaugh
Copy Editor: Phyllis Walker
Cover Image: Karen Brady
Cover Design: Alex Torres
Printed in the United States of America by Braun-Brumfield, Inc.

 THE INSTITUTE OF ELECTRICAL AND ELECTRONICS ENGINEERS, INC.

Preface

Designing intelligent computer-based systems with scene interpretation capabilities comparable to those of humans has attracted the attention of researchers for more than two decades. Initially, the memory and processing limitations of computers constrained computer vision research. But recent advances in computer hardware have opened the door for the design of systems that analyze and interpret complex three-dimensional scenes.

Like other evolving technologies, computer vision is based on certain fundamental principles and techniques. For example, models of image formation and techniques for pixel-level image processing are reasonably well developed. Several commercial machine vision systems, notably in the area of industrial inspection, have been successfully developed and installed. However, designing a general-purpose natural-scene interpretation system that operates in an unconstrained domain remains an elusive and challenging task.

To design successful practical computer vision systems requires a thorough understanding of all system aspects, from initial image formation to final scene interpretation. To convert raw data at the sensors to meaningful information about objects in the scene being interpreted, typical vision systems use the following processing-step sequence:

- Image capture and enhancement;
- Segmentation;
- Feature extraction;
- Matching of features to models;
- Exploitation of constraints and image cues to recover information lost during the imaging process; and
- Application of domain knowledge to recognize objects in the scene and their attributes.

In each of these steps, many factors influence the choice of algorithms and techniques. The system designer should be knowledgeable about the issues and design trade-offs inherent in the realization of a practical system. For example, careful choice of factors influencing image formation — such as imaging modality — could greatly simplify subsequent image analysis problems.

This book, together with its companion book *Computer Vision: Advances and Applications* (IEEE Computer Society Press), is (1) a tutorial, (2) a guide to practical applications, and (3) a reference source on recent advances in computer vision research. The tutorial component will benefit students and professionals who are relatively new to the computer vision field. The description of practical applications of machine vision technology will act as a guide to practicing engineers. And the collection of papers on recent research advances will be an excellent reference source for active researchers in the computer vision field.

The seven chapters in this book introduce the following fundamental topics in computer vision:

- Image formation;
- Segmentation;
- Feature extraction and matching;
- Constraint exploitation and shape recovery
- Three-dimensional object recognition;
- Dynamic vision; and
- Knowledge-based vision.

The order of topic presentation is generally the same as that followed in vision systems that generate scene interpretation from image data, with some overlapping between chapters. Each chapter begins with an introductory tutorial, followed by a collection of key papers covering the topics presented in the tutorial. We have chosen papers that are tutorial in nature or that describe a fundamental principle, concept, or commonly used algorithm. The Epilogue presents current research trends and future directions for computer vision. The Bibliography, at the end of the book, lists selected papers. The large volume of published literature in the computer vision field precludes the Bibliography from being comprehensive; we have generally limited the selection to papers published since 1980. It is intended to function as a pointer to related literature.

The organization of the companion book, *Computer Vision: Advances and Applications*, is the same as that followed in this book, with chapter titles being the same in the two. The papers included therein describe recent research advances in the topics covered in each of the chapters in this book. Also included in the companion book is a representative set of papers describing the following five machine vision application areas:

- Aerial image analysis;
- Document image analysis;
- Medical image analysis;
- Industrial inspection and robotics; and
- Autonomous navigation.

We believe that the ideas and techniques that are described in the two companion books, *Computer Vision: Principles* and *Computer Vision: Advances and Applications*, will continue to influence vision system research and design for many years to come.

The contributions of a large number of researchers have enriched the computer vision field. Unfortunately, due to space constraints, we could not include in these two companion books all papers containing significant contributions. The 77 papers selected for inclusion in these two books include frequently cited reference papers and recent papers that we believe represent significant contributions to the literature.

To identify papers that are frequently cited in current literature, we compiled a list of papers cited in about 275 relevant papers published in the *Proceedings of the IEEE International Conference on Computer Vision, Proceedings of IEEE Conference on Computer Vision and Pattern Recognition, and IEEE Transactions on Pattern Analysis and Machine Intelligence*. The resulting list comprised 1,740 papers, excluding references such as books and reports. Out of this list of 1,740 papers, 280 were cited more than once and 40 of these were cited at least five times. We selected only papers that are relevant to the topics covered in these two books. (Papers were replaced with their most recent versions, whenever available.) To this list of relevant, frequently cited papers, we added papers from recent journals and conferences to obtain the final list of 77 papers. Most of the papers selected were published within the past five years. Earlier papers were included only if they are key papers describing a particular topic.

We appreciate the assistance provided by Thawach Sripradisvarakul, Yuan-liang Tang, Jayant Kattepur, Chan-pyng Lai, Erliang Yeh, and Chia-hong Chen in compiling the Bibliography. We would like to thank Professor Mohan Trivedi and anonymous reviewers for their helpful comments and suggestions; Professors Jon Butler and Fred Petry for their help and encouragement; Kathy Dewitt, Elaine Smiles, and Dolores Bolsenga for secretarial assistance; Karen Brady for cover art; Alex Torres for cover design, Phyllis Walker for copyediting, IEEE Computer Society Press Editorial Director Henry Ayling for his comments, and Lisa O'Conner and Catherine Harris of the IEEE Computer Society Press for their help in assembling all of the material in a short time to ensure timely publication of these books. We would also like to thank the many authors who provided reprints of their articles for reproduction and gave us permission to use their work. We hope that the readers find that these books meet their expectations and welcome any comments, corrections, and suggestions.

September 27, 1991: Rangachar Kasturi and Ramesh C. Jain

Table of Contents

Chapter 1: Image Formation

An image is formed when a sensor records received radiation as a two-dimensional function. The brightness or intensity values in an image may represent different physical entities. For example, in a typical image obtained using a video camera, the intensity values represent the reflectance of light from various object surfaces in the scene; in a thermal image, they represent the temperature of corresponding regions in the scene; and in a range image, they represent the distance from the camera to various points in the scene. Multiple images of the same scene are often captured using different types of sensors to facilitate more robust and reliable interpretation of scene than the interpretation based on a single image. Selecting an appropriate image formation system plays a key role in the design of practical computer vision systems. Principles of image formation are described in this chapter.

Intensity images

Intensity images of scenes formed using visible light are widely used in computer vision systems. The primary challenge in computer vision is the analysis of two-dimensional images of scenes to generate a three-dimensional interpretation. Construction of a model of image formation, which encapsulates knowledge of imaging geometry, the projection process, and the reflectance properties of objects, is essential for image analysis and interpretation.

Imaging geometry. A simple camera-centered imaging model is shown in Figure 1.1.[1] The coordinate system is chosen such that the X,Y-plane coincides with the image plane and the Z-axis passes through the lens center, which is at a distance of f, the focal length from the image plane. The image of a scene point (X,Y,Z) forms at a point (x,y) on the image plane where

$$x = \frac{fX}{(f - Z)},$$

$$y = \frac{fY}{(f - Z)}. \tag{1.1}$$

These are the perspective projection equations for an imaging system. (Note that an abstract frontal image plane that is located at a distance of f in front of the lens center is often used to model imaging. In such a model, the signs of coordinates of scene points are preserved in their corresponding image point coordinates.) When f is very large, the perspective projection equations can be approximated by the orthographic projection equations $x = X$ and $y = Y$. In a typical imaging situation, the camera may have several degrees of freedom, such as translation, pan, and tilt. Also, more than one camera may be imaging the same scene from different points, in which case it is convenient to adopt a world coordinate system in reference to which the scene coordinates and camera coordinates are defined. For example, the camera shown in Figure 1.2[1] is translated by (X_0,Y_0,Z_0), panned by an angle θ (the angle between the x- and X-axes), and tilted by an angle α (the angle between the z- and Z-axes). In addition, there is a displacement of the image plane with respect to the gimbal center by vector $r = (r_1,r_2,r_3)$. The image coordinates (x,y) of a point (X,Y,Z) in the world coordinate system are then obtained by applying appropriate transformations, yielding[1]

$$x = f \frac{(X - X_0)\cos\theta + (Y - Y_0)\sin\theta - r_1}{-(X - X_0)\sin\theta\sin\alpha + (Y - Y_0)\cos\theta\sin\alpha - (Z - Z_0)\cos\alpha + r_3 + f} \tag{1.2}$$

and

$$y = f \frac{-(X - X_0)\sin\theta\cos\alpha + (Y - Y_0)\cos\theta\cos\alpha + (Z - Z_0)\sin\alpha - r_2}{-(X - X_0)\sin\theta\sin\alpha + (Y - Y_0)\cos\theta\sin\alpha - (Z - Z_0)\cos\alpha + r_3 + f}. \tag{1.3}$$

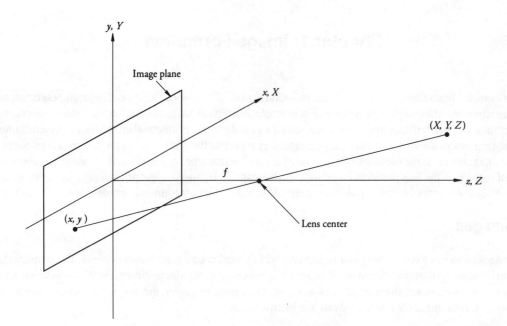

Figure 1.1: A camera-centered imaging model (from R.C. Gonzalez and P. Wintz, *Digital Image Processing*, © 1977 by Addison-Wesley Publishing Company. Reprinted with permission of the publisher).[1]

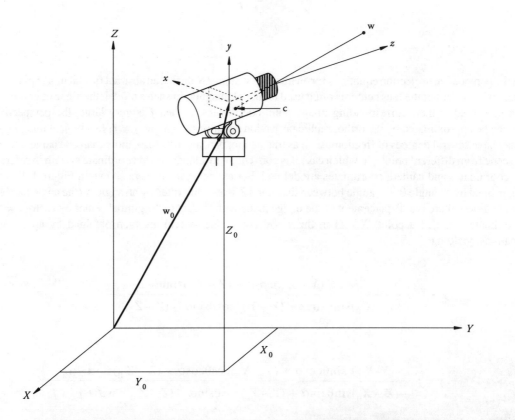

Figure 1.2: Imaging geometry to determine the relationship between scene points defined in world coordinates and image coordinates (from R.C. Gonzalez and P. Wintz, *Digital Image Processing*, © 1977 by Addison-Wesley Publishing Company. Reprinted with permission of the publisher).[1]

Often, the exact location, orientation, and focal length of the camera are not known. Then, the parameters of transformations must be computed, using known scene and image coordinates of a set of points. For example, the perspective transformation relationship between the world coordinates of a point (X, Y, Z) and its image coordinates (x, y) for a camera system with an arbitrary location and orientation is given by[1]

$$a_{11}X + a_{12}Y + a_{13}Z - a_{41}xX - a_{42}xY - a_{43}xZ - a_{44}x + a_{14} = 0,$$
$$a_{21}X + a_{22}Y + a_{23}Z - a_{41}yX - a_{42}yY - a_{43}yZ - a_{44}y + a_{24} = 0, \tag{1.4}$$

The unknown coefficients in these two equations can be computed — using a process called "camera calibration" — when the scene and image coordinates of a set of at least six points are known. The image coordinates of any other scene point can then be easily computed using these coefficients.

Image intensity. While the imaging geometry uniquely determines the relationship between scene coordinates and image coordinates, the brightness or intensity at each point is determined not only by the imaging geometry but also by several other factors, including scene illumination, reflectance properties and surface orientations of objects in the scene, and radiometric properties of the imaging sensor.

The reflectance properties of a surface are characterized by the Bidirectional Reflectance Distribution Function (BRDF)[2]. BRDF is the ratio of the radiance in the direction of the observer to the irradiance due to a source from a given direction. It captures how bright a surface will appear when viewed from a given direction and illuminated by another direction. For example, for a Lambertian surface, BRDF is a constant; hence, the surface appears equally bright from all directions. For a specular (mirrorlike) surface, BRDF is an impulse function, as determined by the laws of reflection. The scene illumination, together with BRDF, determine the scene radiance (flux density emitted into a unit solid angle in a given direction) at a point. The relationship between the image irradiance E (flux density incident on the image plane at a given point), the scene radiance L, the diameter d and focal length f of the imaging lens, and the angle α between the camera axis and the line connecting the scene point to the lens center (see Figure 1.3[3]) is given by[2,3]

$$E = L\,\frac{\pi}{4}\left(\frac{d}{f}\right)^2\cos^4\alpha. \tag{1.5}$$

Note that although the image irradiance is directly proportional to the scene radiance, the sensitivity of the system is not constant over the entire image plane; rather, it diminishes as the fourth power of the cosine of the off-axis angle α. However, this diminishment can be ignored when the angular field of view of the imaging system is small. Image intensity is related to the image irradiance by the relative luminous efficiency function of the sensor.[4] Sensors with spectral responses at different bands of the electromagnetic spectrum are often used to obtain multispectral image data.

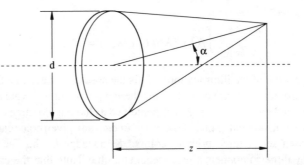

Figure 1.3: Geometry to find the relationship between image irradiance and scene radiance
(from B.K.P. Horn, *Robot Vision*, © 1986 McGraw-Hill, Inc., reprinted with permission.).[3]

Reflectance map. The scene radiance at a point on the surface of an object depends on the reflectance properties of the surface, as well as on the intensity and direction of the illuminating sources. For example, for a Lambertian surface illuminated by a point source, the scene radiance is proportional to the cosine of the angle between the surface normal and the direction of illumination.

The relationship between surface orientation and brightness is captured in the reflectance map. In the reflectance map for a given surface and illumination, contours of constant brightness [$R(p,q) = constant$] are plotted as a function of surface orientation specified by the gradient space coordinates (p,q). A typical reflectance map for a Lambertian surface illuminated by a point source of light is shown in Figure 1.4.[3] In this figure, the brightest point [$R(p,q) = maximum$] corresponds to the surface orientation such that its normal points in the direction of the source. Since image brightness is proportional to scene radiance, a direct relationship exists between the image intensity at a point and the orientation of the surface at the corresponding scene point. Shape-from-shading algorithms exploit this relationship between image intensity and surface orientation to recover three-dimensional object shape. An alternative method, photometric stereo, exploits the same principles to recover object shape from multiple images obtained by illuminating the object from different directions.[3] These methods are discussed in detail in Chapter 4.

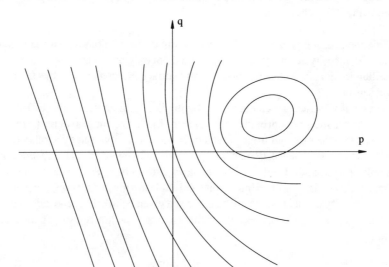

Figure 1.4: Typical reflectance map for a Lambertian surface illuminated by a point source (from B.K.P. Horn, *Robot Vision*, © 1986 McGraw-Hill, Inc., reprinted with permission.).[3]

Color vision

Perception of color by humans is attributed to differences in the spectral responses of photoreceptors — rods and cones — in the retina. Rods are responsible for monochromatic vision. The human visual system consists of three types of cones, each with a different spectral response. Assuming a simple multiplicative model, the total response of each of the cones is given by the integral

$$\int f(\lambda)r(\lambda)h_i(\lambda)d\lambda, \quad i=1,2,3 \tag{1.6}$$

where $f(\lambda)$ is the spectral composition of the illumination, $r(\lambda)$ is the spectral reflectance function of the reflecting surface, and $h_i(\lambda)$, where $i = 1,2,3$ is the spectral response of each of the three types of cones.[5] Note that two surfaces with reflectance functions $r_1(\lambda)$ and $r_2(\lambda)$ illuminated by $f_1(\lambda)$ and $f_2(\lambda)$ are perceived as having the same color if the total response for each sensor, as given by the above integral, is equal to that of the other. In fact, any given color can be matched by using a weighted combination of a suitably chosen set of three primary colors.[4] Knowledge of this fact leads to the familiar notion of representing color in images by three components: red, green, and blue. Note that the choice of the three primary colors determines the range of possible colors that can be realized as a weighted combination of the primary colors. The CIE (Commission Internationale de l'Eclairage) standard primary system uses the following spectral primaries: red [700 nanometers (nm)], green (546.1 nm), and blue (435.8 nm). All colors that are within the triangle drawn on a chromaticity diagram with vertices at these three points can be matched by a weighted combination of these colors. Matching colors that are outside this triangle would require choosing a different set of primary colors.

Although color plays an important role in scene interpretation by humans, the bulk of computer vision research has been limited to processing monochromatic images. Exceptions are applications — such as remote sensing — in which multispectral data are used for classification. A threefold increase in processing and memory requirements, compared to those of monochromatic images, has been the principal inhibiting factor in color image processing. But with recent advances in computer hardware, activity in exploiting the additional dimensionality provided by color images has increased. An important first step toward designing color vision systems is obtaining an accurate model for color image formation.

Light reflection model for color images. Color in images is determined primarily by

- Light source chromaticity;
- Spectral reflection properties of object surfaces; and
- Sensor spectral responsivity of the imaging system.

Light reflected from surfaces is modeled as consisting of

- An interface reflection component and
- A body reflection component.[6]

The spectral composition of the interface reflection component is assumed to be the same as that of the illuminating source, whereas the spectral composition of the body reflection component is determined by the pigments in the object. Using this assumption, the Bidirectional Spectral Reflectance Distribution Function (BSRDF) — which includes both spectral and directional dependence of the reflectivity function — can be written as

$$f_r(\theta_i, \phi_i; \theta_r, \phi_r; \lambda) = a(\lambda)g(\theta_i, \phi_i; \theta_r, \phi_r) + sh(\theta_i, \phi_i; \theta_r, \phi_r), \tag{1.7}$$

where (θ_i, ϕ_i) and (θ_r, ϕ_r) are the direction of the source and the direction of the observer, respectively. The first term represents the body reflection component (which is wavelength selective) and the second term represents the interface reflection component.[7] Lee, et al., have shown that this neutral-interface-reflection model is appropriate for polychromatic collimated light sources that illuminate surfaces whose BSRDFs have separable spectral and geometric factors. Also, they have presented experimental results evaluating the accuracy of this model for surfaces made up of different materials.[7]

Color constancy. The human perceptual system has the remarkable ability to assign stable colors to object surfaces despite changes in the spectral distribution of illuminating sources. This well-known ability is called "color constancy." However, the spectral distribution of received radiation at the sensor is a function of both the spectral reflectance properties of the object surfaces in the scene and the spectral composition of the illuminating sources. Maloney and Wandell[8] describe an algorithm for estimating the spectral reflectance functions of surfaces even when information about the spectral distribution of ambient light is incomplete. Funt and Ho[9] describe a technique that exploits the chromatic aberration in an optical-imaging system to separate the reflectance component from the illumination component. This method, in principle, solves the color constancy problem.

Range images

Extraction of the three-dimensional structure of objects from images is an important task for a computer vision system. Although three-dimensional information can be extracted from images with two-dimensional intensity — using image cues such as shading, texture, and motion — the problem is greatly simplified by range imaging. Range imaging is acquiring images for which the value at each pixel is a function of the distance of the corresponding point of the object from the sensor. Besl[10] describes in detail various methods of range imaging and compares their relative merits. An earlier survey by Jarvis[11] includes not only direct range-measuring techniques, but also techniques in which the range is calculated from two-dimensional image cues. Range-image sensing, processing, interpretation, and applications are described in detail in Jain and Jain.[12] Two of the most commonly used principles for range imaging — imaging radar and triangulation — are briefly described in the following sections.

Imaging radar. In a time-of-flight pulsed radar, the distance to the object is computed by observing the time difference between the transmitted and received electromagnetic pulses. Range information can also be obtained by detecting the phase difference between the transmitted and received waves of an amplitude-modulated beam or by detecting the beat frequency in a coherently mixed transmitted-and-received signal in a frequency-modulated beam. Several commercial laser beam imaging systems have been built using these principles.

Triangulation. In an active triangulation-based range-imaging system, a light projector and a camera aligned along the z-axis are separated by a baseline distance b, as shown in Figure 1.5.[10] The object coordinates (X,Y,Z) are related to the measured image coordinates (x,y) and the projection angle θ by

$$[X\ Y\ Z] = \frac{b}{f\ \cot\theta - x}\ [x\ y\ f].\tag{1.8}$$

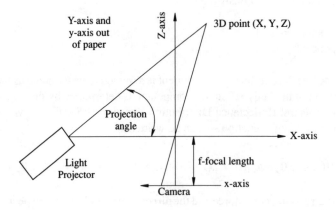

Figure 1.5: Camera-centered triangulation geometry (from Besl).[10]

The accuracy with which the angle θ and the horizontal position x can be measured determines the range resolution of such a triangulation system. This system of active triangulation using a point source of light is an example of structured lighting, a technique that is described in more detail in the following section.

Structured lighting

Imaging using structured lighting refers to systems in which the scene is illuminated by a known geometric pattern of light. In a simple point projection system — like the triangulation system discussed above — the scene is illuminated, one point at a time, at each point in a two-dimensional grid pattern. The depth at each point is then calculated using equation 1.8 above to obtain a two-dimensional-range image. Because of the sequential nature of this system, it is slow and not suitable for use with dynamically changing scenes.

In a typical structured-lighting system, either planes of light or two-dimensional patterns of light are projected on the scene. A camera (displaced spatially from the source of illumination) observes the patterns of light projected on object surfaces. The observed images of the light patterns contain distortions that are determined by the shape and orientation of surfaces of objects on which the patterns are projected, as illustrated in Figure 1.6.[11] Note that the light pattern as seen by the camera contains discontinuities and changes in orientation and curvature. The three-dimensional object coordinate corresponding to any point in the image plane can be calculated by computing the intersection of the line-of-sight with the light plane. To obtain the complete object description, parallel planes of light are projected in sequence, and the corresponding stripe images are acquired. Different surfaces in the object are detected by clustering stripes of light having similar spatial attributes. In dynamically changing situations in which projecting light stripes in sequence is not practical, a set of multiple stripes of light — in which each stripe is uniquely encoded — is projected. For example, using a binary-encoding scheme, a complete set of data can be acquired by projecting only $\log_2 N$ patterns, where $(N-1)$ is the total number of stripes. Boyer and Kak[13] describe a method in which color coding is used to acquire the range information using a single image. The classical paper by Will and Pennington[14] describes using grid coding and Fourier domain processing techniques to locate different planar surfaces in a scene.

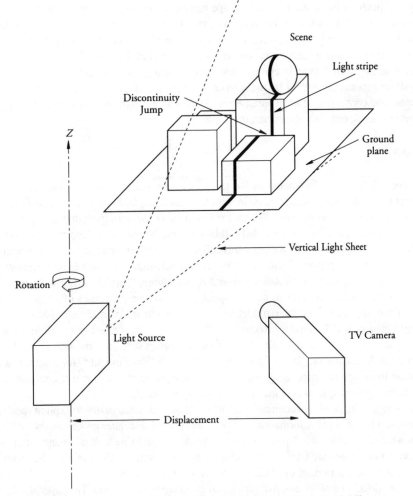

Figure 1.6: Illustration of striped lighting technique (from Jarvis).[11]

Structured-lighting techniques have been used extensively in industrial vision applications in which the illumination of the scene can be easily controlled. In a typical application, objects on a conveyor belt pass through a plane of light, creating a distortion in the image of the light stripe. The profile of the object at the plane of the light beam is then calculated. This process is repeated at regular intervals to recover the shape of the object. The primary drawback of structured-lighting systems is that data cannot be obtained for object points that are not visible to either the light source or the imaging camera.

Structured lighting is useful in binocular stereopsis of surfaces that contain few dominant features, thereby making the finding of corresponding points in a stereo pair of images difficult. In such a structured-lighting system, the stereo pair of images of a projected pattern are matched to find the disparity between the images and hence calculate the depth.

Active vision

Most computer vision systems rely on data captured by systems with fixed characteristics. These systems include passive sensing systems — such as video cameras — and active sensing systems — such as laser range finders. Bajcsy[15] has argued that, in contrast to these systems of data capture, an active vision system — in which the parameters and characteristics of data capture are dynamically controlled by the scene interpretation system — is crucial for perception. Active vision systems may employ either passive or active sensors; however, in an active vision system, the state parameters of the sensors — such as focus, aperture, vergence, and illumination — are controlled to acquire data that will facilitate scene interpretation. The concept of active vision is not new. Biological systems routinely acquire data in an active fashion. The advantages of accommodation in acquiring images for computer vision tasks were elaborated by Tenenbaum.[16] Aloimonos et al.[17] described the advantages of active vision systems for performing many computer vision tasks, including shape recovery from image cues. Krotkov[18] described a stereo-image-capture system in which the focus, zoom, aperture, vergence, and illumination are actively controlled to obtain depth maps. In this system, information from several low-level-vision modules is combined to control the parameters of the imaging system. Control strategies for an active vision system are based on both local and global models.[15] Local models contain physical and geometric properties, whereas global models contain interaction among local models. Active perception is essentially an intelligent data acquisition process controlled by the measured and calculated parameters and errors from the scene. Precise definition of these scene- and context-dependent parameters requires a thorough understanding of not only the properties of the imaging and processing systems, but also of their interdependence.

Research trends

Computer vision research has been dominated by the study of imaging and image analysis techniques for monochromatic intensity images (except for multispectral images used in remote-sensing applications). Analyses of true color images and range images have become more common only recently. We have selected a set of seven papers that are representative of papers dealing with the topics covered in this chapter. Two are included in this book and the remaining five can be found in the companion book, *Computer Vision: Advances and Applications*. We begin this collection with the classic paper, "Understanding Image Intensities," by Horn in *Principles*. Relationships between image intensity, surface reflectance properties and orientation, and illumination are derived in this paper. In our companion book *Advances and Applications*, "Modeling Light Reflection for Computer Color Vision," by Lee et al., extends these concepts to include spectral reflectance properties of surfaces. This paper also contains experimental results of the application of their model to surfaces made up of different materials. Also in *Advances and Applications*, in "Color Constancy: A Method for Recovering Surface Spectral Reflectance," Maloney and Wandell describe an algorithm for estimating the spectral reflectance functions of surfaces even when information about the spectral distribution of ambient light is incomplete. In *Advances*, "Color From Black and White," by Funt and Ho, describes a technique that exploits the chromatic aberration in an optical-imaging system in order to separate the reflectance component from the illumination component. This technique, in principle, solves the color constancy problem.

In the last few years, range images (like structured light earlier) have been popular due to explicit specification of depth values. At one time, it was believed that if depth information were explicitly available, later processing would be easy. Research in the last few years has shown that — although depth information helps — the basic task of image interpretation retains all of its problems. Nevertheless, range images are finding increasing applications in many industrial applications, particularly in surface inspection.[12] The next three papers pertain to obtaining depth information. In *Principles*, "Active, Optical Range-Imaging Sensors," by Besl describes principles of operation of various range-imaging techniques. The paper also includes a comprehensive survey and an objective comparison of sensing methodologies and sensors, many of which are commercially available. Will and Pennington[14] introduced to computer vision the concept of structured lighting and many systems have been built using the basic principles they describe. In *Advances and Applications*, "Color-Encoded Structured Light for Rapid Active Ranging," by Boyer and Kak describes a range measurement system that exploits the additional degree of freedom provided by color to obtain a depth map from a single color-encoded structured light image.

Remote-sensing[19,20] and medical-imaging engineers have implemented many computer vision techniques to interpret images obtained using different sensors. Basic techniques, developed in computer vision for processing in early stages, can be applied to disparate sensory data used in various applications. Later processing stages require the embedding of image formation knowledge in interpretation programs. Current computer vision systems embed image formation knowledge implicitly during interpretation, making these programs ineffective for any other sensor. The trend to represent image formation knowledge explicitly is increasing, as shown by so-called "active vision approaches."[15] We conclude this chapter in *Advances and Applications* with "Active Perception," by Bajcsy, which strongly advocates integrating image acquisition and image interpretation within the framework of a cooperating control strategy. Bajcsy argues that such a system would simplify many difficult problems encountered by computer vision systems that operate upon data acquired by passive systems.

Many applications require that properties be represented in three-dimensional space. In such applications, three-dimensional sensory information is obtained. Such information differs from that obtained from range images, which are really two-dimensional. Three-dimensional information is common in various applications, including medical imaging,[21] oceanography, space, and fluid flow. The increasing use of computer vision techniques in these applications is sure to result in many new early-processing techniques in computer vision. Also, representation and processing of multisensory information will become more commonplace in computer vision research in the next decade. The current trend suggests that computer vision is fast becoming computer perception.

References Cited
Chapter 1

1. R.C. Gonzalez and P. Wintz, *Digital Image Processing,* second edition, Addison-Wesley, Reading, Mass., 1987.
2. B.K.P. Horn and R.W. Sjoberg, "Calculating the Reflectance Map," *Applied Optics,* Vol. 18, No. 11, 1979, pp. 1770-1779.
3. B.K.P. Horn, *Robot Vision,* McGraw-Hill, New York, N.Y., 1986.
4. A.K. Jain, *Fundamentals of Digital Image Processing,* Prentice-Hall, Englewood Cliffs, N.J., 1989.
5. D.H. Ballard and C.M. Brown, *Computer Vision,* Prentice-Hall, Englewood Cliffs, N.J., 1982.
6. S.A. Shafer, "Using Color to Separate Reflection Components," *Color: Research and Applications,* Vol. 10, No. 4, 1985, pp. 210-218.
7. H.C. Lee, E.J. Breneman, and C.P. Schulte, "Modeling Light Reflection for Computer Color Vision," *IEEE Trans. Pattern Analysis and Machine Intelligence,* Vol. 12, No. 4, 1990, pp. 402-409.
8. L.T. Maloney and B.A. Wandell, "Color Constancy: A Method for Recovering Surface Spectral Reflectance," *J. Opt. Soc. Am. A,* Vol. 3, No. 1, 1986, pp. 29-33.
9. B. Funt and J. Ho, "Color from Black and White," *Int'l. J. Computer Vision,* Vol. 3, No. 2, 1989, pp. 109-117.
10. P.J. Besl, "Active, Optical Range Imaging Sensors," *Machine Vision and Applications,* Vol. 1, No. 2, 1988, pp. 127-152.
11. R.A. Jarvis, "A Perspective on Range Finding Techniques for Computer Vision," *IEEE Trans. Pattern Analysis and Machine Intelligence,* Vol. 5, No. 2, 1983, pp. 122-139.
12. R.C. Jain and A.K. Jain, eds., *Analysis and Interpretation of Range Images,* Springer-Verlag, New York, N.Y., 1990.
13. K.L. Boyer and A.C. Kak, "Color-Encoded Structured Light for Rapid Active Ranging," *IEEE Trans. Pattern Analysis and Machine Intelligence,* Vol. 9, No. 1, 1987, pp. 14-28.
14. P.M. Will and K.S. Pennington, "Grid Coding: A Novel Technique for Image Processing," *Proc. IEEE,* Vol. 60, No. 6, IEEE Press, New York, N.Y., 1972, pp. 669-680.
15. R. Bajcsy, "Active Perception," *Proc. IEEE,* Vol. 76, No. 8, IEEE Press, New York, N.Y., 1988, pp. 996-1005.
16. J.M. Tenenbaum, *Accommodation in Computer Vision,* PhD thesis, Stanford University, 1970.
17. J.Y. Aloimonos, I. Weiss, and A. Bandyopadhyay, "Active Vision," *Int'l. J. Computer Vision,* Vol. 1, 1988, pp. 333-356.
18. E. Krotkov, *Exploratory Visual Sensing for Determining Spatial Layout with an Agile Stereo Camera System,* PhD thesis, University of Pennsylvania, 1987.
19. R. Bernstein, *Digital Image Processing for Remote Sensing,* IEEE Press, New York, N.Y., 1978.
20. R.M. Hord, *Remote Sensing Methods and Applications,* John Wiley & Sons, New York, N.Y., 1986.
21. A.C. Kak and M. Slaney, eds., *Principles of Computerized Tomographic Imaging,* IEEE Press, New York, N.Y., 1988.

ARTIFICIAL INTELLIGENCE

Understanding Image Intensities[1]

Berthold K. P. Horn

Artificial Intelligence Laboratory, Massachusetts Institute of Technology, Cambridge, MA 02139, U.S.A.

Recommended by Max Clowes

ABSTRACT

Traditionally, image intensities have been processed to segment an image into regions or to find edge-fragments. Image intensities carry a great deal more information about three-dimensional shape, however. To exploit this information, it is necessary to understand how images are formed and what determines the observed intensity in the image. The gradient space, popularized by Huffman and Mackworth in a slightly different context, is a helpful tool in the development of new methods.

0. Introduction and Motivation

The purpose of this paper is to explore some of the puzzling phenomena observed by researchers in computer vision. They range from the effects of mutual illumination to the characteristic appearance of metallic surfaces—subjects which at first glance may seem to take us away from the central issues of artificial intelligence. But surely if artificial intelligence research is to claim victory over the vision problem, then it has to embrace the whole domain, understanding not only the problem solving aspects, but also the physical laws that underlie image formation and the corresponding symbolic constraints that enable the problem solving.

One reason for previous neglect of the image itself was the supposition that the work must surely already have been done by researchers in image processing, pattern recognition, signal processing and allied fields. There are several reasons why this attitude was misadvised:

Image processing deals with the conversion of images into new images, usually for human viewing. Computer image understanding systems, on the other hand, must work toward symbolic descriptions, not new images.

[1] This report describes research done at the Artificial Intelligence Laboratory of the Massachusetts Institute of Technology. Support for the laboratory's research is provided in part by the Advanced Research Projects Agency of the Department of Defence under Office of Naval Research contract N00014-75-C-0643.

Pattern recognition, when concerned with images, has concentrated on the classification of images of characters and other two-dimensional input, often of a binary nature. Yet the world we want to understand is three-dimensional and the images we obtain have many grey-levels.

Signal processing studies the characteristics of transformations which are amenable to mathematical analysis, not the characteristics imposed on images by nature. Yet in the end, the choice of what to do with an image must depend on it alone, not the character of an established technical discipline.

Although we can borrow some of the techniques of each of these approaches we must still understand how the world forms an image if we are to make machines see. Yet I do not mean to suggest analysis by synthesis. Nothing of the sort! I propose only that if we are to solve the problem of creating computer performance in this domain, we must first thoroughly understand that domain.

This is, of course, not without precedent. The line of research beginning with Guzman and continuing through Clowes, Huffman, Waltz, Mackworth and others, was a study of how the physical world dictates constraints on what we see—constraints that once understood can be turned around and used to analyze what is seen with great speed and accuracy relative to older techniques which stressed problem solving expertise at the expense of domain understanding.

1. Developing the Tools for Image Understanding

An understanding of the visual effects of edge imperfections and mutual illumination will be used to suggest interpretations of image intensity profiles across edges, including those that puzzled researchers working in the blocks world. We shall see that a "sharp peak" or edge-effect implies that the edge is convex, a "roof" or triangular profile suggests a concave edge, while a step-transition or discontinuity accompanied by neither a sharp peak nor a roof component is probably an obscuring edge. This last hypothesis is strengthened significantly if an "inverse peak" or negative edge-effect is also present. (See Section 3.)

Next, it will be shown that the image intensities of regions meeting at a joint corresponding to an object's corner determine fairly accurately the orientation of each of the planes meeting at the corner. Thus we can establish the three-dimensional structure of a polyhedral scene without using information about the size or, support or nature of the objects being viewed. (See Section 3.4.)

Finally, we will turn to curved objects and show that their shape often can be determined from the intensities recorded in the image. The approach given here is supported by geometric arguments and does not depend on methods for solving first-order non-linear partial differential equations. It combines my previous shape-from-shading method [4, 2] with geometric arguments in gradient-space (Huffman and Mackworth [1, 2, 3, 9]). This approach to the image analysis problem enables us to establish whether or not certain features can be extracted from images. (See Sections 4 and 5.)

1.1. Image formation

The visual world consists of opaque bodies immersed in a transparent medium. The dimensionality of the two domains match: since only the object's surfaces are important for recognition and description purposes. On one hand we have two-dimensional surfaces plus depth and on the other, a two-dimensional image plus intensity. There are two parts to the problem of exploiting this observation to understand what is being imaged: one deals with the geometry of projection, the other with the intensity of light recorded in the image.

Artificial Intelligence 8 (1977), 201–231

The relation between object coordinates and image coordinates is given by the well-known perspective projection equations derived from a diagram such as Fig. 1, where f if the focal length and,

$$x' = (x/z)f \quad \text{and} \quad y' = (y/z)f$$

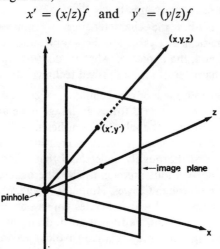

FIG. 1. Image projection geometry.

For the development presented here it will be convenient to concentrate on the case where the viewer is very far from the objects relative to their size. The resultant scene occupies a small visual angle as if viewed by a telephoto lens. This corresponds to orthographic projection, where z is considered constant in the equations above.

1.2. Surface orientation

We must understand the geometry of the rays connecting the lightsource(s), the object and the viewer in order to determine the light flux reflected to the viewer from a particular element of the object. The surface orientation in particular, plays a major role. There are, of course, various ways of specifying the surface orientation of a plane. We can give, for example, the equation defining the plane or the direction of a vector perpendicular to the surface. If the equation for the plane is $ax+by+cz = d$, then a suitable surface normal is (a, b, c).

We extend this method to curved surfaces simply by applying it to tangent planes. A local normal to a smooth surface is $(z_x, z_y, -1)$, where z_x and z_y are the first partial derivatives of z with respect to x and y. It is convenient to use the abbreviations p and q for these quantities. The local normal then becomes $(p, q, -1)$. It is clear then that the surface orientation thus defined has but two degrees to freedom. The quantity (p, q) is called the *gradient* (Fig. 2).

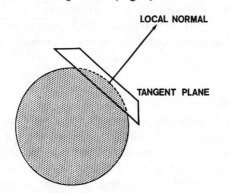

FIG. 2. Definition of surface orientation for curved objects.

Artificial Intelligence **8** (1977), 201–231

1.3. Image intensity

The amount of light reflected by a surface element depends on its micro-structure and the distribution of incident light. Constructing a tangent plane to the object's surface at the point under consideration, we see that light may be arriving from directions distributed over a hemisphere. We first consider the contributions separately, from each of these directions and then superimpose the results.

For most surfaces there is a *unique value of reflectance and hence image intensity for a given surface orientation*. No matter how complex the distribution of light sources. We shall spend some time exploring this and develop the reflectance map in the process.

The simplest case is that of a single point-source where the geometry of reflection is governed by three angles: the incident, the emittance and the phase angles (Fig. 3). The incident angle, i, is the angle between the incident ray and the local normal,

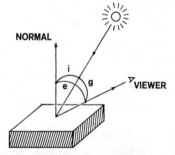

FIG. 3. The reflectivity is a function of the incident, emittance, and phase angles.

the emittance angle, e, is the angle between the ray to the viewer and the local normal, while the phase angle, g, is the angle between the incident and the emitted ray [4]. The reflectivity function is a measure of how much of the incident light is reflected in a particular direction. Superficially, it is the fraction of the incident light reflected per unit surface area, per unit solid angle in the direction of the viewer. More precisely:

Let the illumination be E (flux/area) and the resulting surface luminance in the direction of the viewer by B (flux/steradian/projected area). (The projected area is the equivalent foreshortened area as seen by the viewer.) *The reflectivity is then defined to be B/E*. It may be written $\phi(i, e, g)$, to indicate its dependence on the three angles involved.

Note that an infinitesimal surface element, dA, captures a flux $E \cos(i)\, dA$, since its surface normal is inclined i relative to the incident ray. Similarly, the intensity I(flux/steradian) equals $B \cos(e)\, dA$, since the projected area is foreshortened by the inclination of the surface normal relative to the emitted ray.

1.4 Reflectivity function

For some surfaces, mathematical models have been constructed that allow an analytical determination of the reflectivity function. Since such techniques have rarely proved successful, reflectivity functions are usually determined empirically. Often there will be more than one source illuminating the object. In this case one has to integrate the product of reflectivity and the incident light intensity per unit solid angle over the hemisphere visible from the point under consideration. This determines the total light flux reflected in the direction of the viewer.

The normal to the surface relates object geometry to image intensity because it is defined in terms of the surface geometry, yet it also appears in the equation for the reflected light intensity. Indeed two of the three angles on which the reflectivity function depends are angles between the normal and other rays. Although we could now proceed to develop a partial differential equation based on this observation, it is more fruitful to introduce first another tool—gradient space.

1.5. Gradient space

Gradient-space can be derived as a projection of dual-space or of the Gaussian sphere but it is easier here to relate it directly to surface orientation [2]. We will concern ourselves with orthographic projection only, although some of the methods can be extended to deal with perspective projection as well.

The mapping from surface orientation to gradient-space is made by constructing a normal $(p, q, -1)$ at a point on an object and mapping it into the point (p, q) in gradient-space. Equivalently, one can imagine the normal placed at the origin and find its intersection with a plane at unit distance from the origin.)

We should look at some examples in order to gain a feel for gradient-space. Parallel planes map into a single point in gradient-space. Planes perpendicular to the view-vector map into the point at the origin of gradient-space. Moving away from the origin in gradient-space, we find that the distance from the origin equals the tangent of the emittance angle e, between the surface normal and the view-vector.

If we rotate the object-space about the view-vector, we induce an equal rotation of gradient-space about the origin. This allows us to line up points with the axes and simplify analysis. Using this technique, it is easy to show that the angular position of a point in gradient-space corresponds to the direction of steepest descent on the original surface.

Let us call the orthogonal projection of the original space the image-plane. Usually this is all that is directly accessible. Now consider two planes and their intersection. Let us call the projection of the line of intersection the image-line. The two planes, of course, also correspond to two points in gradient space. Let us call the line connecting these two points the gradient-line. Thus, a line maps into a line. The perpendicular distance of the gradient-space line from the origin equals the tangent of the inclination of the original line of intersection with respect to the image plane. We show by superimposing gradient-space on the image-space [2, 11] that the gradient-space line and the image-line are *mutually perpendicular*. Mackworth's scheme for scene analysis of line drawings of polyhedra depends on this observation [2].

1.6. Trihedral corners

The points in gradient-space corresponding to the three planes meeting at a trihedral corner must satisfy certain constraints. The lines connecting these points must be perpendicular to the corresponding lines in the image-plane (Fig. 4). This provides us with three constraints but that is not enough to fix the position of three points in gradient-space. Three degrees of freedom—the *position* and *scale* of the triangle—remain undetermined. We see later that measurement of image intensities for the three planes provides enough information to specify their orientations, thus allowing a determination of the three-dimensional structure of a polyhedral scene.

Artificial Intelligence **8** (1977), 201–231

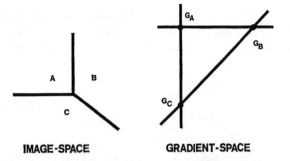

G_A

G_B

A B

G_C

C

IMAGE-SPACE **GRADIENT-SPACE**

FIG. 4. Constraints on the gradient-space points corresponding to the planes meeting at a trihedral corner. The gradient-lines must be perpendicular to the image-lines.

2. The Reflectance Map

The amount of light reflected by a given surface element depends on the orientation of the surface and the distribution of light sources around it, as well as on the nature of the surface. For a given type of surface and distribution of light sources, there is a fixed value of reflectance for every orientation of the surface normal and hence for every point in *gradient-space*. Thus image intensity is a single-valued function of p and q. We can think of this as a map in gradient-space. This is *not* a transform of the image seen by the viewer. It is, in fact, independent of the scene and instead, only a function of the surface properties and the light source distribution (but see Section 2.6).

What can we do with this strange "image" of the world surrounding the object? If we measure a certain intensity at a given point on the object, we know that the orientation of the surface at that point is restricted to a subset of all possible orientations; we cannot, however, uniquely determine the orientation. The one constraint is that it be one of the points in gradient-space where we find this same value of intensity.

The use of the gradient-space diagram is analogous to the use of the hodogram or velocity-space diagram. The latter provides insight into the motion of particles in force field that is hard to obtain by algebraic reasoning alone. Similarly, the gradient-space allows geometric reasoning about surface orientation and image intensities.

2.1. Matte surfaces and a point-source near the viewer

A perfect lambertian surface or diffuser looks equally bright from all directions; the amount of light reflected depends only on the cosine of the incident angle. In order to postpone the calculation of incident, emittance and phase angles from p and q, we first place a single light source near the viewer. The incident angle then equals the emittance angle, the angle between the surface normal and the view-vector. The cosine of the incident angle is the dot product of the corresponding unit vectors:

$$\cos(i) = \frac{(p, q, -1) \cdot (0, 0, -1)}{|(p, q, -1)|\,|(0, 0, -1)|} = \frac{1}{\sqrt{1 + p^2 + q^2}}.$$

We obtain the same result by remembering that the distance from the origin in gradient-space is the tangent of the angle between the surface normal and the view-vector:

$$\sqrt{p^2 + q^2} = \tan(e),$$

$$\cos(e) = \frac{1}{\sqrt{1 + \tan^2(e)}},$$

and

$$e = i.$$

If we plot reflectance as a function of p and q, we obtain a central maximum of 1 at the origin and a circularly symmetric function that falls smoothly to 0 as we approach infinity in gradient-space. This is a nice, smooth reflectance map, typical of matte surfaces (Fig. 5).

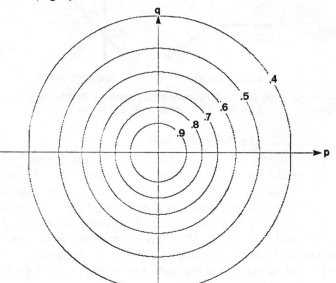

FIG. 5. Contours of $E = \cos(e)$. This is the reflectance map for objects with lambertian surfaces when there is a single light source and the light source is near the viewer.

A given image intensity corresponds to a simple locus in gradient-space, in this case a circle centered on the origin. A measurement of image intensity tells us that the surface gradient falls on a certain circle in gradient-space.

Since the light-source is not always likely to be near the viewer we now explore the more complicated geometry of incident and emitted rays for arbitrary directions of incident light at the object.

2.2. Incident, emittance, and phase angles

For many surfaces the reflectance is a smooth function of the angles of incidence, emittance and phase. It is convenient to work with the cosines of these angles, $I = \cos(i)$, $E = \cos(e)$, and $G = \cos(g)$. (These can be obtained easily from the dot products of the unit vectors.) If we have a single distant light source whose direction is given by a vector $(p_s, q_s, -1)$, and note that the view-vector is $(0, 0, -1)$, then,

$$G = \frac{1}{\sqrt{1+p_s^2+q_s^2}}, \qquad E = \frac{1}{\sqrt{1+p^2+q^2}},$$

and

$$I = \frac{(1+p_s p+q_s q)}{\sqrt{1+p^2+q^2}\sqrt{1+p_s^2+q_s^2}} = (1+p_s p+q_s q)EG.$$

It is simple to calculate I, E, and G for any point in gradient-space. In fact G is *constant* given our assumption of orthogonal projection and distant light source. We saw earlier that the contours of constant E are circles in gradient-space centered on the origin. Setting I constant gives us a second-order polynomial in p and q and suggests that loci of constant I may be conic sections. The terminator—the line separating lighted from shadowed regions, for example, is a straight line obtained by setting $i = \pi/2$. That is, $I = 0$; or $1+p_s p+q_s q = 0$. Similarly, the locus of $I = 1$ is the single point $p = p_s$ and $q = q_s$.

A geometrical way of constructing the loci of constant I is to develop the cone generated by all directions that have the same incident angle. The axis of the cone is the direction to the light-source $(p_s, q_s, -1)$. We find the corresponding points in gradient-space by intersecting this cone with a plane at unit distance from the origin. Varying values of I produce cones with varying angles. The cones form a nested sheaf. The intersection of this nested sheaf with the unit plane is a nested set of conic sections (Fig. 6). Note that our previous example (Fig. 5) is merely a special case in which the axis of the sheaf of nested cones points directly at the viewer.

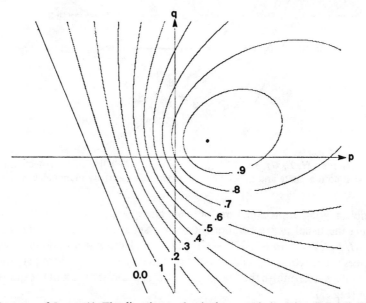

FIG. 6. Contours of $I = \cos(i)$. The direction to the single source is $(p_s, q_s) = (0.7, 0.3)$. This is the reflectance map for objects with lambertian surfaces when the light source is not near the viewer.

If we measure a particular image intensity, we know that the gradient of the corresponding surface element must fall on a particular conic section. The possible normals are confined to a cone—in this case, merely a circular cone. In the case of more general reflectivity functions, the locus of possible normals constitutes a more general figure called the *Monge cone*.

2.3. Specularity and glossy surfaces

Many surfaces have some specular or mirror-like reflection from the outermost layers of their surface, and thus are not completely matte. This is particularly true of surfaces that are smooth on a microscopic scale. For specular reflection $i = e$, and the incident, emitted, and normal vectors are all in the same plane. Alternatively, we can say that $i + e = g$. In any case, only one surface orientation is correct for reflecting the light source towards the viewer. That is, a perfect specular reflection contributes an impulse to the gradient-space image at a particular point.

In practice, few surfaces are perfectly specular. Glossy surfaces reflect some light in directions slightly away from the geometrically correct direction [8]. It can be shown that the cosine of the angle between the direction for perfectly specular reflection and any other direction is $(2IE - G)$ [11]. This clearly equals 1 in the ideal direction and falls off towards 0 as the angle increases to a right-angle. By taking various functions of $(2IE - G)$, such as high powers, one can construct more or less compact specular contributions.

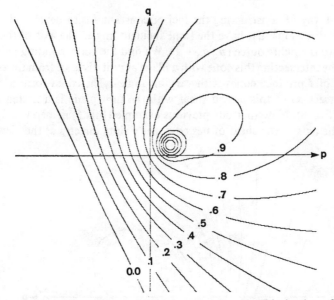

FIG. 7. Contours for $\phi(I, E, G) = \frac{1}{2}s(n+1)(2IE-G)^n+(1-s)I$. This is the reflectance map for a surface with both a matte and a specular component of reflectivity illuminated by a single point-source.

For example, a good approximation for some glossy white paint can be obtained by combining the usual matte component with a specular component defined in this way—$\phi(I, E, G) = \frac{1}{2}s(n+1)(2IE-G)^n+(1-s)I$. Here s lies between 0 and 1 and determines the fraction of incident light reflected specularly before penetrating the surface, while n determines the sharpness of the specularity peak in the gradient-space image (Fig. 7).

2.4. Finding the gradient from the angles

In order to further explore the relation between the specification of surface orientation in gradient-space and the angles involved, we solve for p and q, given I, E, and G. We have already shown that the opposite operation is simple to perform. One approach to this problem is to solve the polynomial equations in p and q derived from the equations for I, E, and G. It can be shown that [11]:

$$p = p' \cos(\theta) - q' \sin(\theta),$$
$$q = p' \sin(\theta) + q' \cos(\theta),$$

where

$$p' = \frac{(I/E-G)}{\sqrt{1-G^2}} \quad \text{and} \quad q' = \frac{(\Delta/E)}{\sqrt{1-G^2}},$$

$$\Delta^2 = 1+2IEG-(I^2+E^2+G^2),$$

$$\cos(\theta) = \frac{p_s}{\sqrt{p_s^2+q_s^2}} \quad \text{and} \quad \sin(\theta) = \frac{q_s}{\sqrt{p_s^2+q_s^2}}.$$

It is immediately apparent that there are two solution points in gradient space for most values of I, E, and G. Notice that θ is the direction of the light source in gradient-space, that is, the line connecting (p_s, q_s) to the origin makes an angle θ with the p-axis. So p' and q' are coordinates in a new gradient-space obtained after

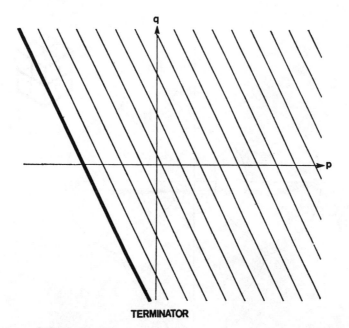

TERMINATOR

FIG. 8. Contours of $\phi(I, E, G) = I/E$. Contour intervals are 0.2 units wide. The reflectivity function for the material in the maria of the moon is constant for constant I/E (constant luminance longitude).

simplifying matters by rotating the axes until $q_s = 0$. The light source is then in the direction of the x'-axis. Notice that p' is constant if I/E is constant (remembering that G is constant anyway.) Hence the loci of constant I/E are straight lines. These lines are all parallel to the terminator, for which $I = 0$. This turns out to be important since some surfaces have constant reflectance for constant I/E (Fig. 8).

2.5. Smooth metallic surfaces

Consider a smooth metallic surface: a surface with a purely specular or mirror-like reflectance. Each point in gradient-space corresponds to a particular direction of the surface normal and defines a direction from which incident light has to approach the object in order to be reflected towards the viewer. In fact, we can produce a complete map of the sphere of possible directions as seen from the object. At the origin, for example, we have the direction towards the viewer. Now for each incident direction there is a certain light-intensity depending on what objects lie that way. Consider recording these intensities at the corresponding points in gradient-space. Clearly one obtains some kind of image of the world surrounding the given metallic object. In fact, one develops a stereographic projection, a plane projection of a sphere with one of the poles as the center of projection. Another way of looking at it is that the image we construct in this fashion is like one we obtain by looking into a convex mirror—a metallic paraboloid to be precise (Fig. 9).

In order to construct reflectance maps for various surfaces and distributions of light sources, we superimpose the results in gradient-space for each light source in turn. We now examine a flaw in this approach and attempt a partial analysis of mutual illumination.

2.6. Mutual illumination

The reflectance map is based on the assumption that the viewer and all light sources are distant from the object. Only under these assumptions can we associate a

Artificial Intelligence **8** (1977), 201–231

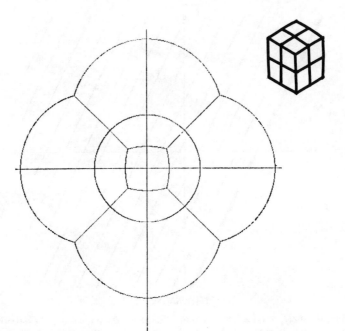

Fig. 9. Reflectance map for a metallic object in the center of a very large wire cube. Equivalently one can think of it as the reflection of the wire cube in a paraboloid with a specularly-reflecting surface.

unique value of image intensity with every surface orientation. If the scene consists of a single convex object these assumptions will be satisfied, but when there are several highly reflective objects placed near one another, mutual illumination may become important. That is, the distribution of incident light no longer depends only on direction, but is a function of position as well. The general case is very difficult, and we shall only study some idealized situations applicable to scenes consisting of polyhedra.

Two important effects of mutual illumination are a reduction in *contrast* between faces, and the appearance of *shading* or gradation of light on images of plane surfaces. In the absence of this effect, we would expect plane surfaces to give rise to images of uniform intensity since all points on a plane surface have the same orientation.

2.7. Two semi-infinite planes

First, let us consider a highly idealized situation of two semi-infinite planes joined at right angles and a distant light source. Let the incident rays make an angle α with respect to one of the planes (Fig. 10). Assume further that the surfaces reflect

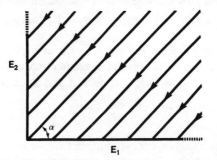

Fig. 10. Mutual illumination of two infinite lambertian planes of reflectance r, when illuminated by a single distant source.

Artificial Intelligence **8** (1977), 201–231

a fraction r of the light falling on them, and that the illumination provided by the source is E (light flux/unit area). Picking any point on one of the half-planes, we find that one-half of its hemisphere of directions is occupied by the other plane, one-half of the light radiated from this point hits the other plane, while one-half is lost. Since both planes are semi-infinite, the geometry of this does not depend on the distance from the corner. The light incident at any point is made up of two components: that received directly from the source and that reflected from the other plane. The intensity on one plane does not vary with distance from the corner—a point receives light from one-half of its hemisphere of directions no matter what its distance from the corner. Put another way, there is no natural scale factor for a fluctuation in intensity. Let the illumination of the plane be E_1 and E_2 (light flux/unit area); then,

$$E_1 = \tfrac{1}{2}rE_2 + E\cos(\alpha),$$
$$E_2 = \tfrac{1}{2}rE_1 + E\sin(\alpha).$$

Solving for E_1 and E_2, we get:

$$E_1 = E[\cos(\alpha) + \tfrac{1}{2}r\sin(\alpha)]\frac{1}{[1 - (\tfrac{1}{2}r)^2]},$$

$$E_2 = E[\sin(\alpha) + \tfrac{1}{2}r\cos(\alpha)]\frac{1}{[1 - (\tfrac{1}{2}r)^2]}.$$

Had we ignored the effects of mutual illumination we would have found $E_1 = E\cos(\alpha)$ and $E_2 = E\sin(\alpha)$. Clearly the effect increases as reflectance r increases (it is not significant for dark surfaces). When the planes are illuminated equally, for $\alpha = \pi/4$, we find

$$E_1 = E_2 = (E/\sqrt{2})/(1 - \tfrac{1}{2}r).$$

When $r = 1$, we obtain *twice* the illumination and hence twice the brightness than that obtained in the absence of mutual illumination. If the angle between the two planes varies, we find that the effect becomes larger and larger as the angle becomes more and more acute. By choosing the angle small enough, we can obtain arbitrary "amplification". Conversely, for angles larger than $\pi/2$, the effect is less pronounced.

In the derivation above, we did not make very specific assumptions about the angular distribution of reflected light, just that it is symmetrical about the normal and that it does not depend on the direction from which the incident ray comes. Hence, a lambertian surface is included, while a highly specular one is not. The effect is indeed less pronounced for surfaces with a high specular component of reflection, since most of the light is bounced back to the source after two reflections. Another important thing to note is that even if the planes are not infinite, the above calculations are approximately valid close to the corner. For finite planes we expect a variation of intensity as a function of distance from the corner; the results derived here apply asymptotically as one approaches the corner.

2.8. Two truncated planes

The geometry becomes quite complex if the planes are of finite extent, but we can develop an integral equation if we allow the planes to be infinite along their line of intersection and truncate them only in the direction perpendicular to this. Suppose two perpendicular planes extend a distance L from the corner, and that $\alpha = \pi/4$. This produces a particularly simple integral equation [11]; nevertheless I have been unable to solve it analytically. Numerical methods show that the resultant illumination falls off monotonically from the corner (Fig. 11), that the value at the corner is

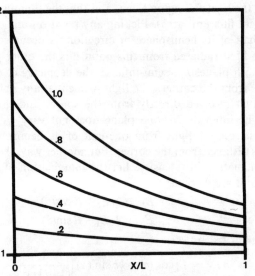

FIG. 11. Surface luminance plotted versus fractional distance from a right-angle corner. The curves are for reflectances of 0.2, 0.4, 0.6, 0.8, and 1.0.

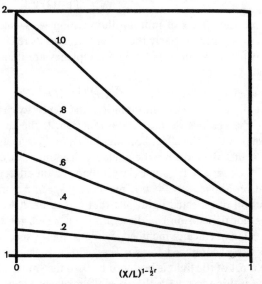

FIG. 12. Surface luminance plotted versus $(x/L)^{(1-\frac{1}{2}r)}$ to illustrate asymptotic behavior near the corner. The curves correspond to reflectances of 0.2, 0.4, 0.6, 0.8, and 1.0.

indeed what was predicted in the previous section, and the fall-off near the corner is governed by a term in $-(x/L)^{(1-\frac{1}{2}r)}$ (Fig. 12). A good approximation appears to be $1 + E_{2/r}(x/L)$, where $E_n(x)$ is the elliptical integral and x is the distance along the plane measured from the edge where the planes meet.

3. The Semantics of Edge-Profiles

We are now ready to apply the tools developed so far. First let us consider the interpretation of intensity profiles taken across edges. If polyhedral objects and image sensors were perfect, if there were no mutual illumination, and if light sources were distant from the scene, images of polyhedral objects would be divided into polygonal areas, each of uniform intensity. It is well known that in real images, image intensity varies within the polygonal areas and that an intensity profile taken across an edge separating two such polygonal regions does not have a simple step-shaped intensity transition. Herskovits and Binford determined experimentally that the most common edge transitions are step-, peak-, and roof-shaped [7] (Fig. 13). So

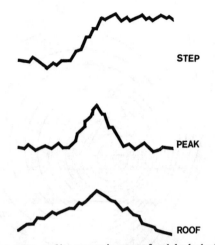

FIG. 13. Most common intensity profiles across images of polyhedral edges.

far this has been considered no more than a nuisance, because it complicates the process of finding edges. We now discuss the interpretation of these profiles in terms of the three-dimensional aspects of the scene.

3.1. Imperfections of polyhedral edges

A perfect polyhedron has a discontinuity in surface normal at an edge. In practice, edges are somewhat rounded off. A cross-section through the object's edge show that the surface normal varies smoothly from one value to the other and takes on values that are linear combinations of the surface normals of the two adjoining planes (Fig. 14). What does this mean in terms of reflected light intensity? Intensity varies smoothly at the edge, instead of jumping from one surface normal value to

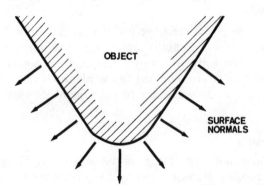

FIG. 14. The normals at an imperfect, rounded off edge are positive linear combinations of the normals of the two adjoining faces.

another. The important point is that it may take on values *outside* the range of those defined by the two planes. The best way to see this is to consider the situation in gradient-space. The two planes defined two points in gradient-space. Tangent planes on the corner correspond to points on the line connecting these two points. If the image intensity is higher for a point somewhere on this line, we will see a peak in the intensity profile across the edge. (Fig. 15.)

Artificial Intelligence **8** (1977), 201–231

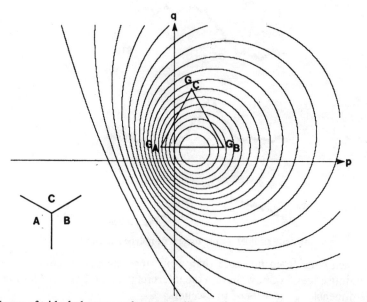

FIG. 15. Image of tri-hedral corner and corresponding gradient-space diagram. The image intensity profile across the edge between face A and face B will have a peak or highlight. The others will not.

If we find an edge profile with a peak shape or step with a peak superimposed, it is most likely that the corresponding edge is convex. The converse is not true (an edge may be convex and not give rise to a peak) if the line connecting the two points in gradient space has intensity varying monotonically along its length. The identification is also not completely certain since under peculiar lighting conditions with objects that have acute angles between adjacent faces, a peak may appear at an obscuring edge. Notice that the peak is quite compact, since it extends only as far as the rounded-off edge.

At a corner, where the planes meet, we find that surface imperfections provide surface normals that are linear combinations of the three normals corresponding to the three planes. In gradient space, this corresponds to points in the triangle connecting the three points corresponding to the planes. If this triangle contains a maximum in image intensity we expect to see a highlight right on the corner (Fig. 15).

3.2. Mutual illumination

We have seen that mutual illumination gives rise to intensity variations on planar surfaces—intensity roughly decreases linearly away from the corner. Notice that this affects the intensity profile over a large distance from the edge, quite unlike the sharp peak found due to edge imperfections. Clearly, if we find a roof-shaped profile or step with a roof-shaped superimposed we should consider labelling the edge concave.

The identification is, however, partly unreliable since some imaging device defects can produce a similar effect. Image dissectors, for example suffer from a great deal of scattering—areas further from a dark background appear brighter. So we may see a smoothed version of a roof-shape in the middle of a bright scene against a dark background. Experimentation with high quality image input devices such as a PIN-diode mirror-deflection system has confirmed that this is an artifact introduced by the image dissector. When the light source is close to the scene, significant gradients can appear on planar surfaces as pointed out by Herskovitz and Binford [7]. Lastly, the roof-shaped profiles on the two surfaces may be due to mutual illumination with other surfaces, not each other. Nevertheless, a roof-shaped profile usually suggests a concave edge.

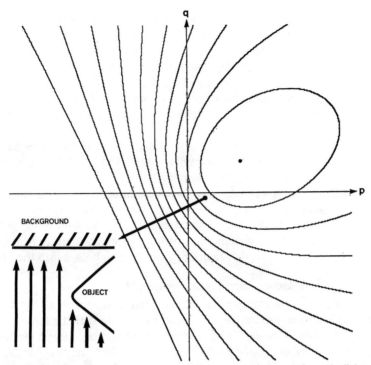

Fig. 16. Generation of a negative peak at an obscuring edge facing away from the light source.

3.3. Obscuring edges

Although they can be found with both convex and concave edges, step-shaped intensity profiles occur most often when objects obscure one another. If the obscuring surface adjoins a self-shadowed surface however, edge imperfections will produce a negative peak on the profile, since the line connecting the points corresponding to the two surfaces of the object passes through the terminator in gradient-space. Hence a negative peak or a step with a superimposed negative peak strongly suggests obscuration. Unfortunately it is difficult to tell on which side the obscuring plane lies (Fig. 16).

3.4. Determining the three-dimensional structure of polyhedral scenes

Mackworth's approach to understanding line drawings of polyhedra allows us to take into account some of the quantitative aspects of the three-dimensional geometry of scenes [2]. It does not, however, allow us to fully determine the orientation of all the planes. The scale and position of the gradient space diagram is undetermined by his technique. To illustrate this, consider a single trihedral corner. Here we know that the three points in gradient space representing the three planes meeting at the corner have to satisfy certain constraints: they must lie on three lines perpendicular to the image lines (see fig. 4).

It takes six parameters to specify the position of three points on a plane, leaving three degrees of freedom after the introduction of these constraints. Measuring the three image intensities of the planes supplies another three. The constraints are due to the fact that the points in gradient-space have to lie on the correct contours of image intensity. The triangle can be stretched and moved until the points correspond to the correct image intensities as measured for the three planes.

Since this process corresponds to solving three non-linear equations for three unknowns, we can expect a finite number of solutions. Often there are but one or two—prior knowledge often eliminates some. (For a numerical example, see Appendix).

When more than three planes meet at a corner, the equations are over-determined, and the situation is even more constraint. Conversely, we cannot determine much with just two planes meeting at an edge—there are too few equations and an infinite number of solutions. The possible ambiguity at a trihedral corner is not very serious when we consider that in a typical scene there are many "connect" edges, either convex or concave as determined by Mackworth's program. In such a case the overall constraints may allow only one consistent interpretation. A practical difficulty is that it is unclear which search strategy leads most efficiently to this interpretation.

Measurements of image intensity are not very precise and surfaces have properties that vary from point to point as well as with handling. We cannot expect this method to be extremely accurate in pinning down surface orientation. In general, the equations for a typical scene are over-determined; a least-squares approach may improve matters slightly. The idea of stretching and shifting can be generalized to smooth surfaces. We know that the image of a paraboloid is the same as the reflectance map. If we can stretch and shift the reflectance map to fit the image of some object, then the same deformations turn the paraboloid into the object.

4. Determining Lunar Topography

When viewed from a great distance, the material in the maria of the moon has a particularly interesting reflectivity function. First, note that the lunar phase is the angle at the moon between the light source (sun) and the viewer (earth). This is clearly the angle we call g, and explains why we use the term phase angle. For constant phase angle, detailed measurements using surface elements whose projected area as seen from the source is a constant multiple of the projected area as seen by the viewer have shown that all such surface elements have the same reflectance. But the area appears foreshortened by $\cos(i)$ and $\cos(e)$ as seen by the source and the viewer respectively. Hence the reflectivity function is constant for constant $\cos(i)/\cos(e) = I/E$.

In this case each surface element scatters light uniformly into its hemisphere of directions, quite unlike the lambertian surface which favors directions normal to its surface. This is not an isolated incident. The surfaces of other rocky, dusty objects when viewed from great distances appear to have similar properties. For example, the surface of the planet Mercury and perhaps Mars as well as some asteroids and atmosphere-free satellites fit this pattern. Surfaces with reflectance a function of I/E thus form a third species we should add to matte surfaces where the reflectance is a function of I and glossy surfaces where the reflectance is a function of $(2IE - G)$.

4.1. Lunar reflectivity function

Returning to the lunar surface, we find an early formula due to Lommel Seelinger [6].

$$\phi(I, E, G) = \frac{\Gamma_0(I/E)}{(I/E) + \lambda(G)}.$$

Here Γ_0 is a constant and the function $\lambda(G)$ is defined by an empirically determined table. A somewhat more satisfactory fit to the data is provided by a formula of Fesenkov's [6]:

$$\phi(I, E, G) = \frac{\Gamma_0(I/E)[1 + \cos^2(\alpha/2)]}{(I/E) + \lambda_0[1 + \tan^2(\lambda/2)]}.$$

Where Γ_0 and λ_0 are constants and $\tan(\alpha) = -p' = -(I/E-G)/\sqrt{1-G^2}$. This formula is also supported by a theoretical model of the surface due to Hapke. Note that given I, E, and G, it is straightforward to calculate the expected reflectance. We need to go in the reverse direction and solve for I/E given G and the reflectance as measured by the image intensity. While it may be hard to invert the above equation analytically, it should be clear that by some iterative, interpolation, or hill-climbing scheme one can solve for I/E. We shall ignore for now the ambiguities that arise if there is more than one solution.

4.2. Lunar reflectance map

Next, we ask what the reflectance map looks like for the lunar surface illuminated by a single point source. The contours of constant intensity in gradient-space will be lines of constant I/E. But the contours of constant I/E are straight lines! So the gradient-space image can be generated from a single curve by shifting it along a straight-line—the shadow-line, for example (see Fig. 8). The contour lines are perpendicular to the direction defined by the position of the source (that is, the line from the origin to p_s, q_s).

Now what information does a single measurement of image intensity provide? It tells us that the gradient has to be on a particular straight line. Again, we ignore for the moment the possible existence of more than one contour for a given intensity.

What we would like to know, of course, is the orientation of the surface element. We cannot completely determine the local orientation, but we *can* determine its component in the direction perpendicular to the contour lines in gradient-space.

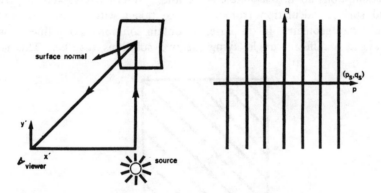

FIG. 17. Rotation of coordinate system to simplify gradient-space geometry.

We can tell nothing about it in the direction at right angles. That is, knowing I/E and G determines p', as previously defined, and tells us nothing about q'.

This favored direction lies in the plane defined by the source, the viewer, and the surface element under consideration. If we wish, we can simplify matters by rotating the viewer's coordinate system until the x axis lies in this plane as well. Then $q_s = 0$, and the contours of constant intensity in gradient-space are all vertical lines. Evidently, an image intensity measurement determines the slope of the surface in the x' direction, without telling us anything about the slope in the y' direction (Fig. 17). We are now ready to develop the surface by advancing in the direction in which we can determine locally the surface slope.

4.3. Finding a surface profile by integration

We have:

$$p' = \frac{dz}{ds} = \frac{I/E-G}{\sqrt{1-G^2}}.$$

The distance s from some starting point is measured in the object coordinate system and is related to the distance along the curve's projection in the image by $s' = s(f/z_0)$.

$$\frac{dz}{ds'} = \frac{f}{z_0} \frac{I/E - G}{\sqrt{1-G^2}}.$$

Integrating, we get:

$$z(s') = z_0 + \frac{f}{z_0} \int_0^{s'} \frac{I/E - G}{\sqrt{1-G^2}} \, ds',$$

where I/E is found from G and the image intensity $b(x', y')$. Starting anywhere in the image, we can integrate along a particular line and find the relative elevation of the corresponding points on the object.

The curves traced out on the object in this fashion are called *characteristics*, and their projections in the image-plane are called *base characteristics*. It is clear that here the base characteristics are parallel straight lines in the image, independent of the object's shape.

4.4. Finding the whole surface

We can explore the whole image by choosing sufficient starting points along a line at an angle to the favored direction. In this way we obtain the surface shape over the whole area recorded in the image (Fig. 18). Since we cannot determine the gradient at right angles to the direction of the characteristics, there is nothing to relate adjacent characteristics in the image. We have to know an initial curve, or use assumptions about reasonable smoothness. Alternatively, we can perform a second surface calculation from an image taken with a different source-surface-observer geometry. In this case, we obtain solutions along lines crossing the surface at a different angle, tying the two solutions together. This is not

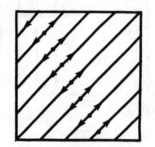

FIG. 18. Finding the shape of the surface by integrating along several base characteristics starting from different initial points.

quite as useful as one might first think, because it does not apply to pictures taken from earth. The plane of the sun, moon and earth varies little from the ecliptic plane. The lines of integration in the image vary little in inclination. This idea however *does* work for pictures taken from near the moon.

4.5. Ambiguity in local gradient

What if more than one contour in gradient-space corresponds to a given intensity? Then we cannot tell locally which gradient to apply. If we are integrating along some curve however, this is no problem, since we may assume that there is little change in gradient over small distances, and pick one close to the gradient last used. This assumption of smoothness leaves us with one remaining problem: what happens if we approach a maximum of intensity in gradient-space and then enter areas of lower intensity (Fig. 19). Which side of the local maximum do we slide down?

Artificial Intelligence **8** (1977), 201–231

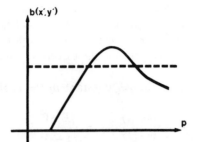

FIG. 19. Problem of ambiguity caused by non-uniqueness of slope for a particular observed image intensity.

This is an ambiguity which cannot be resolved locally, and the solution has to be terminated at this point. Under certain lighting conditions the image is divided into regions inside each of which we can find a solution. The regions are separated by ambiguity edges, which cannot be crossed without making an arbitrary choice [4].

4.6. Low sun angles

This problem can be avoided entirely if one deals only with pictures taken at low sun angles, where the gradient is a single-valued function of image intensity. This is a good idea in any case, since the accuracy of the reconstruction depends on how accurately one can determine the gradient, which in turn depends on the spacing of the contour lines in gradient-space. If they are close together, this accuracy is high (near a maximum, on the other hand, it is low). It is easy to convince oneself that pictures taken at low sun angle have "better contrast," show the "relief in more detail," and are "easier to interpret." An additional reason for interest in low sun angle images is that the contours of constant intensity near the shadow-line in gradient-space are nearly straight lines even if we are *not* dealing with the special reflectivity function for the lunar material! An early solution to the problem of determining the shape of lunar hills makes use of this fact by integrating along lines perpendicular to the terminator [5].

Working at low sun angles introduces another problem, of course, since shadows are likely to appear. Fortunately, they are easy to deal with since we simply trace the line in the image until we see a lighted area again. Knowing the direction of the source's rays, we easily determine the position of the first lighted point. The integration is then continued from there (Fig. 20). In fact, no special attention to this

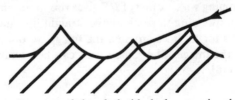

FIG. 20. Geometry of grazing ray needed to deal with shadow gaps in solution.

problem is needed since a surface element oriented for grazing incidence of light already has the correct slope. Thus, simply looking up the slope for zero intensity and integrating with this value will do. Some portion of the surface, of course, is not explored because of shadows. If we take one picture just after "sunrise" and one just before "sunset," most of this area is covered.

4.7. Generalization to perspective projection

All along we have assumed orthographic projection—looking at the surface from a great distance with a telephoto lens. In practice, this is an unreasonable assumption for pictures taken by artificial satellites near the surface. The first thing that changes in the more general case of perspective projection is that the sun-surface-viewer plane is no longer the same for all portions of the surface images. Since it is this plane which determines the integration lines, we expect that these lines are no longer parallel. Instead they all converge on the anti-solar point in the image which corresponds to a direction directly opposite the direction towards the source (Fig. 21).

The next change is that z is no longer constant in the projection equation. So $s' = f(s/z)$. Hence,

$$p' = \frac{dz}{ds} = \frac{f}{z}\frac{dz}{ds'} = \frac{I/E - G}{\sqrt{1 - G^2}}.$$

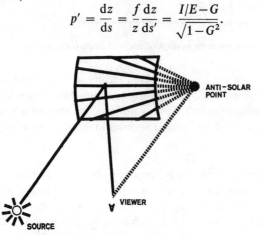

ANTI-SOLAR POINT

VIEWER

SOURCE

Fig. 21. The base-characteristics converge on the anti-solar point.

We can no longer simply integrate. It is easy, however, to solve the above differential equation for z by separating terms:

$$\log(z) = \frac{1}{f}\int \frac{I/E - G}{\sqrt{1 - G^2}}\,ds',$$

and so

$$z(s') = z_0 \exp\left(\frac{1}{f}\int_0^{s'} \frac{I/E - G}{\sqrt{1 - G^2}}\,ds'\right).$$

Finally, note that the phase angle g is no longer constant. This has to be taken into account when calculating I/E from the measured image intensity. On the whole, the process is still very simple. The paths of integration are predetermined straight lines in the image radiating from the anti-solar point. At each point we measure the image intensity, determining which value of I/E gives rise to this image intensity. Then we calculate the corresponding slope along the straight line and take a small step. Repeating the process for all lines crossing the image we obtain the surface elevation at all points in the image. The same result can be obtained by a very complex algebraic method [6].

4.8. A note on accuracy

Since image intensities are determined only with rather limited precision, we must expect the calculation of surface coordinates to suffer from errors that accumulate along characteristics. A "sharpening" method that relates adjacent characteristics reduces these errors somewhat [4].

It also appears that an object's shape is better described by the orientations of its surface normals than by the distances from the viewer to points on its surface. In part, this may be because distances to the surface undergo a more complicated transformation when the object is rotated than do surface normal directions. Note that the calculation of surface normals is *not* subject to the cumulative errors mentioned.

Artificial Intelligence **8** (1977), 201–231

Finally, we should point out that the precise determination of the surface is not the main impetus for the development presented here. The understanding of how image intensities are determined by the object, the lighting, and the image forming system is of more importance and may lead to more interesting heuristic methods.

5. The Shape of Surfaces with Arbitrary Reflectance Maps

The simple method developed for lunar topography is inapplicable if the contours of constant intensity in gradient-space are not parallel straight lines. We will still be able to trace along the surface, but the direction we take at each point now depends on the image and changes along the profile. The base characteristics no longer are predetermined straight lines in the image. At each point on a characteristic curve we find that the solution can be continued only in a particular direction. It also appears that we need more information to start a solution and will have to carry along more information to proceed. Reasoning from the gradient-space diagram is augmented here by some algebraic manipulation.

Let $a(p, q)$ be the intensity corresponding to a surface element with a gradient (p, q). Let $b(x, y)$ be the intensity recorded in the image at the point (x, y). Then, for a particular surface element, we must have:

$$a(p, q) = b(x, y).$$

Now suppose we want to proceed in a manner analogous to the method developed earlier by taking a small step (dx, dy) in the image. It is clear that we can calculate the corresponding change in z as follows:

$$dz = z_x dx + z_y d_y = p\, dx + q\, dy.$$

To do this we need the values of p and q. We have to keep track of the values of the gradient as we integrate along the curve. We can calculate the increments in p and q by:

$$dp = p_x\, dx + p_y\, dy \quad \text{and} \quad dq = q_x\, dx + q_y\, dy.$$

At first, we appear to be getting into more difficulty, since now we need to know $p_x, p_y = q_x$ and q_y. In order to determine these unknowns we will differentiate the basic equation $a(p, q) = b(x, y)$ with respect to x and y:

$$a_p p_x + a_q q_x = b_x \quad \text{and} \quad a_p p_y + a_q q_y = b_y.$$

While these equations contain the right unknowns, there are only two equations, not enough to solve for three unknowns. Note, however, that we do not really need the individual values! We are only after the linear combinations $(p_x\, dx + p_y\, dy)$ and $(q_x\, dx + q_y\, dy)$.

We have to properly choose the direction of the small step (dx, dy) to allow the determination of these quantities. There is only one such direction. Let $(dx, dy) = (a_p, a_q)\, ds$, then $(dp, dq) = (b_x, b_y)\, ds$. This is the solution we were after. Summarizing, we have five ordinary differential equations:

$$\dot{x} = a_p, \quad \dot{y} = a_q, \quad \dot{z} = a_p p + a_q q, \quad \dot{p} = b_x \quad \text{and} \quad \dot{q} = b_y.$$

Here the dot denotes differentiation with respect to s, a parameter that varies along the solution curve.

5.1. Interpretation in terms of the gradient-space

As we solve along a particular characteristic curve on the object, we simultaneously trace out a base characteristic in the image and a curve in gradient-space. At each point in the solution we know to which point in the image and to which point in the gradient-space the surface element under consideration corresponds.

The intensity in the real image and in the gradient space image must, of course, be the same. The paths in the two spaces are related in a peculiar manner. The step we take in the image is perpendicular to the contour in *gradient-space* and the step we take in gradient-space is perpendicular to the intensity contour in the *image-plane*. (See Fig. 22.)

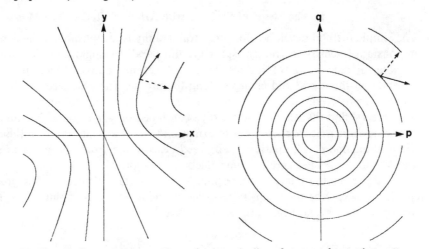

FIG. 22. The solution curve in image-space is along the line of steepest descent in gradient-space and the solution curve in gradient-space is along the line of steepest descent in image-space.

5.2. Generalization to source and viewer near the object

The last solution method, while correct for arbitrary reflectivity functions, still assumes orthographic projection and a distant source. This is a good approximation for many practical cases. In order to take into account the effects of the nearness of the source and the viewer, we discard the gradient-space diagram, since it is based on the assumption of constant phase angle. The problem can still be tackled by algebraic manipulation, much as the last solution. It turns out that we are really trying to solve a first order non-linear partial differential equation in two independent variables. The well-known solution involves converting this equation into five ordinary differential equations, quite like the ones we obtain in the last Section [4].

Appendix

Using the reflectance map to determine three-dimensional structure of polyhedral scenes

What follows is a simple numerical example to illustrate the idea that information about surface reflectance can augment the gradient-space diagram and lead to a solution for the orientation of three planes meeting at a vertex. We will assume a lambertian reflectance for the object and assume that the light-source and viewer are far removed from the object, but close to each other. Suppose now that we are given the partial line-drawing as in Fig. 23 showing edges separating three planes

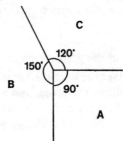

FIG. 23. Image-lines of a tri-hedral vertex. The orientations of the planes *A*, *B* and *C* are to be found.

A, B and C. The gradient-space diagram showing the three points G_A, G_B and G_C corresponding to these three planes will be as in Fig. 24. The scale and position of the indicated triangle are not yet determined. In fact the whole diagram could be flipped around if the scale is negative.

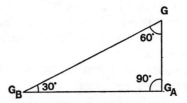

FIG. 24. The gradient-space diagram corresponding to the previous figure. The planes A, B and C map into the points G_A, G_B and G_C. The scale and position of this triangle is as yet undetermined.

Nevertheless, we now have available three linear constraints on the coordinates (p_a, q_a), (p_b, q_b) and (p_c, q_c) of the points G_A, G_B, G_C.

$$p_a = p_c, \quad q_a = q_b, \quad \text{and} \quad (q_c - q_a) = (p_a - p_b)t.$$

Where $t = \tan(30°) = 1/\sqrt{3}$. We are now told that image measurements suggest reflectances of 0.707, 0.807 and 0.577 for the three faces respectively. From the information about the position of the source and viewer, we know that $G = 1$ and that $I = E$. Next, since we are dealing with a lambertian surface we calculate the reflectance from $\phi(I, E, G) = I$, which here equals $E = \cos(e) = 1/\sqrt{1 + p^2 + q^2}$. We immediately conclude that the surface normals of the three planes are inclined 45°, 36.2° and 54.8° respectively with respect to the view vector.

It also follows that the points G_A, G_B and G_C must lie on circles of radii 1.0, 0.732 and 1.415 in gradient-space, since distance from the origin in gradient space $\sqrt{p^2 + q^2}$ equals $\tan(e)$. That is, the points have to lie on the appropriate contours of reflectance in the reflectance map as in Fig. 25.

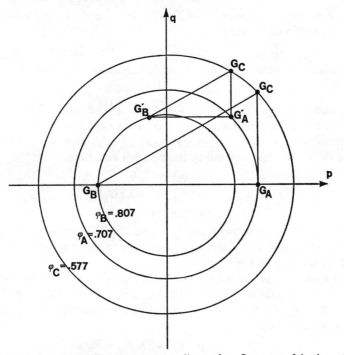

FIG. 25. Contours of constant reflectance corresponding to the reflectances of the three planes. Two solutions are superimposed on the reflectance map.

This gives us three further constraints, unfortunately non-linear ones. Let us call the radii r_a, r_b and r_c respectively, then

$$p_a^2 + q_a^2 = r_a^2, \qquad p_b^2 + q_b^2 = r_b^2 \quad \text{and} \quad p_c^2 + q_c^2 = r_c^2.$$

If the source had *not* been near the viewer, these equations would have involved linear terms in p and q as well, since then the contours of equal reflectance would have been conic sections other than circles. In the general case these three equations could be more complicated and in fact it is possible that the reflectance map is only known numerically. Then one will have to proceed iteratively from here. In our simple example however it is possible to solve the three linear equations and the three non-linear ones we have developed directly. As usual one proceeds by judiciously eliminating variables.

Let us use the three linear equations to eliminate the unknowns p_c, q_b and q_c from the three non-linear equations, then,

$$p_a^2 + q_a^2 = r_a^2, \qquad p_b^2 + q_a^2 = r_b^2 \quad \text{and} \quad p_a^2 + [q_a + t(p_a - p_b)]^2 = r_c^2.$$

We now have three non-linear equations in three unknowns. First note that

$$(p_a - p_b)(p_a + p_b) = p_a^2 - p_b^2 = r_a^2 - r_b^2.$$

Then expand the last of the three equations to get:

$$p_a^2 + q_a^2 + 2tq_a(p_a - p_b) + t^2(p_a - p_b)^2 = r_c^2.$$

Now using $p_a^2 + q_a^2 = r_a^2$ and the previous equation for $(p_a - p_b)$:

$$[2tq_a + t^2(p_a - p_b)](r_a^2 - r_b^2) = (p_a + p_b)(r_c^2 - r_a^2).$$

This last question is linear! It is of the form $ap_a + bp_b + cq_a = 0$, where a, b and c can be evaluated and found to be -0.845, -1.155 and 0.536.

The simplest next operation is the elimination of p_a and p_b, using the equations for r_a^2 and r_b^2.

$$-a\sqrt{r_a^2 - q_a^2} - b\sqrt{r_b^2 - q_a^2} = cq_a.$$

A single equation in a single unknown, at last. Squaring both sides leads to:

$$2ab\sqrt{(r_a^2 - q_a^2)(r_b^2 - q_a^2)} = (a^2 + b^2 + c^2)q_a^2 - (a^2 r_a^2 + b^2 r_b^2).$$

Letting $e = (a^2 + b^2 + c^2)/(2ab)$ and $f = (a^2 r_a^2 + b^2 r_b^2)/(2ab)$ and squaring again to get rid of the square-root:

$$(q_a^2)^2(1 - d^2) + (q_a^2)[2de - (r_a^2 + r_b^2)] + (r_a^2 r_b^2 - e^2) = 0.$$

This quadratic equation in q_a^2 can be further simplified by evaluating the terms to:

$$(q_a^2)^2 - 0.5(q_a^2) = 0.0.$$

The solutions are $q_a = 0.0$, -0.7071 and $+0.7071$. Not all of these may be solutions of the original equations, so we will have to check the results. Trying $q_a = 0$, leads to $q_b = 0$, $p_a = \pm 1$, $p_c = \pm 1$, $p_b = \pm 0.732$, and $q_c = 0.577(\pm 1 \pm 0.732)$. Two of these combinations satisfy the original equations.

$$(p_a, q_a) = (1, 0)$$
$$(p_b, q_b) = (-0.732, 0)$$
$$(p_c, q_c) = (1, 1).$$

The other solution is the mirror image of this one, with the same numerical values, but reversed signs. One of these solutions is seen superimposed on the contours of the reflectance map in Fig. 25.

If one tries the other possible set of values for q_a, ± 0.7071 one finds, $p_a = q_b = \pm 0.7071$, $p_b = \pm 0.1895$, $p_c = \pm 0.1895$, and $q_c = \pm 0.7071 + 0.577(\pm 0.7071 \pm 0.1895)$. As before only two combinations satisfy the original equations. One of these is the following:

$$(p_a, q_a) = (0.707, 0.707),$$
$$(p_b, q_b) = (-0.189, 0.707),$$
$$(p_c, q_c) = (0.707, 1.225).$$

The other solution again simply has the signs reversed. One of these solutions is also shown in figure 25. The symmetry of the problem here contributes to the plethora of solutions, more usually one finds but two.

Clearly it would be desirable to avoid this tedious solution of simultaneous non-linear equations. Graphical techniques work and iterative Newton–Raphson techniques are appropriate for computer implementations of this method. For a numerical example see [11].

ACKNOWLEDGMENTS

I wish to thank Blenda Horn and Eva Kampitts for help in the preparation of the paper, Karen Prendergast for the drawings and Kathy Van Sant for an early version of the numerical solution for the truncated-plane mutual-illumination problem. David Marr and Patrick Winston provided much appreciated stimulation and discussion.

REFERENCES

1. Huffman, D. A., Impossible objects as nonsense sentences, *Machine Intelligence* 6, Meltzer, R., and Michie, D. (Eds.), (Edinburgh University Press, 1971) 295–323.
2. Mackworth, A. K., Interpreting pictures of polyhedral scenes, *Artificial Intelligence* 4 (1973), 121–137.
3. Huffman, D. A., Curvature and creases: a primer on paper, *Proc. Conf. Computer Graphics, Pattern Recognition and Data Structures* (May 1975) 360–370.
4. Horn, B. K. P., Obtaining shape from shading information, in: Winston, P. H., (Ed.), *The Psychology of Machine Vision* (McGraw-Hill, NY, 1975) 115–155.
5. Van Diggelen, J., A photometric investigation of the slopes and heights of the ranges of hills in the maria of the moon, *Bull. Astron. Inst. Netherlands* 11 (1951) 283–289.
6. Rindfleisch, T., Photometric method for lunar topography, *Photogrammetric Eng.* 32 (1966) 262–276.
7. Herskovits, A. and Binford, T. O., On boundary detection, MIT Artificial Intelligence Memo 183 (July 1970) 19, 55, 56.
8. Phong, Bui Tuong, Illumination for Computer Generated Pictures, *CACM* 18 (1975) 311–317.
9. Hilbert, D. and Cohn-Vossen, S., *Geometry and the Imagination* (Chelsea Publishers, New York, 1952).
10. Hildebrand, F. D., *Methods of Applied Mathematics* (Prentice-Hall, New Jersey, 1952) 222–294.
11. Horn, B. K. P., Image intensity understanding, MIT Artificial Intelligence Memo 335 (August 1975).

Received January 1976; final version received August 1976

Machine Vision and
Applications
© 1988 Springer-Verlag New York Inc.

Active, Optical Range Imaging Sensors

Paul J. Besl
Computer Science Department, General Motors Research Laboratories, Warren, Michigan 48090-9055 USA

Abstract: Active, optical range imaging sensors collect
three-dimensional coordinate data from object surfaces
and can be useful in a wide variety of automation applications, including shape acquisition, bin picking, assembly, inspection, gaging, robot navigation, medical diagnosis, and cartography. They are unique imaging devices in
that the image data points explicitly represent scene surface geometry in a sampled form. At least six different
optical principles have been used to actively obtain range
images: (1) radar, (2) triangulation, (3) moire, (4) holographic interferometry, (5) focusing, and (6) diffraction.
In this survey, the relative capabilities of different sensors and sensing methods are evaluated using a figure of
merit based on range accuracy, depth of field, and image
acquisition time.

Key Words: range image, depth map, optical measurement, laser radar, active triangulation

1. Introduction

Range-imaging sensors collect large amounts of
three-dimensional (3-D) coordinate data from visible surfaces in a scene and can be used in a wide
variety of automation applications, including object
shape acquisition, bin picking, robotic assembly, inspection, gaging, mobile robot navigation, automated cartography, and medical diagnosis (biostereometrics). They are unique imaging devices in
that the image data points explicitly represent scene
surface geometry as sampled points. The inherent
problems of interpreting 3-D structure in other
types of imagery are not encountered in range imagery although most low-level problems, such as
filtering, segmentation, and edge detection, remain.

Most active optical techniques for obtaining
range images are based on one of six principles: (1)
radar, (2) triangulation, (3) moire, (4) holographic
interferometry, (5) lens focus, and (6) Fresnel diffraction. This paper addresses each fundamental
category by discussing example sensors from that

class. To make comparisons between different sensors and sensing techniques, a performance figure
of merit is defined and computed for each representative sensor if information was available. This
measure combines image acquisition speed, depth
of field, and range accuracy into a single number.
Other application-specific factors, such as sensor
cost, field of view, and standoff distance are not
compared.

No claims are made regarding the completeness
of this survey, and the inclusion of commercial sensors should not be interpreted in any way as an
endorsement of a vendor's product. Moreover, if
the figure of merit ranks one sensor better than another, this does not necessarily mean that it is better
than the other for any given application.

Jarvis (1983b) wrote a survey of range-imaging
methods that has served as a classic reference in
range imaging for computer vision researchers. An
earlier survey was done by Kanade and Asada
(1981). Strand (1983) covered range imaging techniques from an optical engineering viewpoint. Several other surveys have appeared since then (Kak
1985, Nitzan et al. 1986, Svetkoff 1986, Wagner
1987). The goal of this survey is different from previous work in that it provides a simple example
methodology for quantitative performance comparisons between different sensing methods which may
assist system engineers in performing evaluations.
In addition, the state of the art in range imaging
advanced rapidly in the past few years and is not
adequately documented elsewhere.

This survey is structured as follows. Definitions
of range images and range-imaging sensors are
given first. Different forms of range images and generic viewing constraints and motion requirements
are discussed next followed by an introduction to
sensor performance parameters, which are then
used to define a figure of merit. The main body
sequentially addresses each fundamental ranging
method. The figure of merit is computed for each
sensor if possible. The conclusion consists of a sen-

sor comparison section and a final summary. An introduction to laser eye safety is included in the appendix. This paper is an abridged version of Besl (1988), which was derived from sections of Besl (1987). Tutorial material on range-imaging techniques may be found in both as well as in the references.

2. Preliminaries

A *range-imaging sensor* is any combination of hardware and software capable of producing a *range image* of a real-world scene under appropriate operating conditions. A *range image* is a large collection of *distance measurements* from a known reference coordinate system to *surface points* on object(s) in a *scene*. If scenes are defined as collections of physical objects and if each *object* is defined by its mass density function, then surface points are defined as the 3-D points in the half-density level set of each object's normalized mass-density function as in Koenderink and VanDoorn (1986). Range images are known by many other names depending on context: range map, depth map, depth image, range picture, rangepic, 3-D image, 2.5-D image, digital terrain map (DTM), topographic map, 2.5-D primal sketch, surface profiles, *xyz* point list, contour map, and surface height map.

If the distance measurements in a range image are listed relative to three orthogonal coordinate axes, the range image is in *xyz* form. If the distance measurements indicate range along 3-D direction vectors indexed by two integers (i, j), the range image is in r_{ij} form. Any range image in r_{ij} form can be converted directly to *xyz* form, but the converse is not true. Since no ordering of points is required in the *xyz* form, this is the more general form, but it can be more difficult to process than the r_{ij} form. If the sampling intervals are consistent in the *x*- and *y*-directions of an *xyz* range image, it can be represented in the form of a large matrix of scaled, quantized range values r_{ij} where the corresponding *x*, *y*, *z* coordinates are determined implicitly by the row and column position in the matrix and the range value. The term "image" is used because any r_{ij} range image can be displayed on a video monitor, and it is identical in form to a digitized video image from a TV camera. The only difference is that pixel values represent distance in a range image whereas they represent irradiance (brightness) in a video image.

The term "large" in the definition above is relative, but for this survey, a range image must specify more than 100 (x, y, z) sample points. In Figure 1, the 20×20 matrix of heights of surface points above a plane is a small range image. If r_{ij} is the pixel value at the *i*th row and the *j*th column of the matrix, then the 3-D coordinates would be given as

$$x = a_x + s_x i \qquad y = a_y + s_y j \qquad z = a_z + s_z r_{ij} \quad (1)$$

where the s_x, s_y, s_z values are scale factors and the a_x, a_y, a_z values are coordinate offsets. This matrix of numbers is plotted as a surface viewed obliquely in Figure 2, interpolated and plotted as a contour map in Figure 3, and displayed as a black and white image in Figure 4. Each representation is an equally valid way to look at the data.

The affine transformation in equation (1) is appropriate for *orthographic* r_{ij} range images where depths are measured along parallel rays orthogonal to the image plane. Nonaffine transformations of (i, j, r_{ij}) coordinates to Cartesian (x, y, z) coordinates are more common in active optical range sensors. In the spherical coordinate system shown in Figure

```
171 160 163 163 166 166 168 166 168 166 163 160 163 163 160 163 166 163 166 163
168 166 166 163 166 163 168 166 166 166 163 163 166 163 166 163 166 160 163 163
168 168 166 166 166 163 160 166 166 171 166 168 168 166 160 163 166 160 160 166
166 163 166 166 163 163 160 163 179 174 185 177 185 179 212 196 185 204 196 185
163 166 160 166 163 163 166 190 174 168 168 182 185 190 201 196 199 182 196 199
166 163 163 163 168 160 163 166 166 163 168 177 190 188 199 188 190 196 193 185
163 166 166 157 160 160 160 171 160 168 168 182 199 199 199 193 199 188 193 193
160 160 160 166 157 160 168 166 166 163 163 182 201 199 190 188 190 190 193 193
163 166 157 163 160 157 160 177 166 160 171 201 215 199 196 201 190 190 188 188
155 160 160 163 160 163 160 166 166 163 163 204 207 207 190 185 193 190 196 196
157 155 163 160 157 157 168 166 168 163 177 188 201 199 196 196 201 182 210 196
157 157 155 157 160 157 163 171 163 157 155 204 185 196 193 188 196 188 193 201
157 160 155 155 157 157 168 168 163 166 166 190 201 201 196 188 190 193 185 193
157 155 160 160 157 157 163 157 160 157 182 204 190 185 190 190 188 185 188
157 157 157 160 157 157 152 166 160 163 166 193 196 193 199 190 190 185 190 185
155 157 160 160 160 152 166 152 163 152 168 171 212 212 193 190 188 182 188 185
152 157 155 155 152 155 149 163 160 155 157 185 210 210 212 215 210 185 204 193
155 155 157 152 152 155 155 171 174 166 171 188 188 199 188 204 188 185 215 207
155 157 152 157 149 157 157 168 179 204 182 221 174 193 182 179 212 188 201 182
155 155 155 155 152 149 146 174 188 193 168 185 168 179 171 190 190 193 190 179
```

Figure 1. 20×20 matrix of range measurements: r_{ij} form of range image.

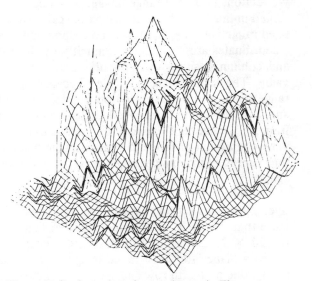

Figure 2. Surface plot of range image in Figure 1.

5, the (i, j) indices correspond to elevation (latitude) angles and azimuth (longitude) angles respectively. The spherical to Cartesian transformation is

$$x = a_x + s_r r_{ij} \cos(is_\phi)\sin(js_\theta) \quad (2)$$
$$y = a_y + s_r r_{ij} \sin(is_\phi)$$
$$z = a_z + s_r r_{ij} \cos(is_\phi)\cos(js_\theta)$$

where the s_r, s_ϕ, s_θ values are the scale factors in range, elevation, and azimuth and the a_x, a_y, a_z values are again the offsets. The "orthogonal-axis" angular coordinate system, also shown in Figure 5, uses an "alternate elevation angle" ψ with the

spherical azimuth definition θ. The transformation to Cartesian coordinates is

$$x = a_x + s_r r_{ij} \, tan(js_\theta)/\sqrt{1 + \tan^2(is_\theta)} + \tan^2(js_\psi) \quad (3)$$
$$y = a_y + s_r r_{ij} \tan(is_\psi)/\sqrt{1 + \tan^2(is_\theta) + \tan^2(js_\psi)}$$
$$z = a_z + s_r r_{ij}/\sqrt{1 + \tan^2(is_\theta) + \tan^2(js_\psi)}.$$

The alternate elevation angle ψ depends only on y and z whereas ϕ depends on x, y, and z. The differences in (x, y, z) for equations (2) and (3) for the same values of azimuth and elevation are less than 4% in x and z and less than 11% in y, even when both angles are as large as ± 30 degrees.

2.1 Viewing Constraints and Motion Requirements

The first question in range imaging requirements is *viewing constraints*. Is a single view sufficient, or are multiple views of a scene necessary for the given application? What types of sensors are compatible with these needs? For example, a mobile robot can acquire data from its on-board sensors only at its current location. An automated modeling system may acquire multiple views of an object with many sensors located at different viewpoints. Four basic types of range sensors are distinguished based on the viewing constraints, scanning mechanisms, and object movement possibilities:

1. A *Point Sensor* measures the distance to a single visible surface point from a single viewpoint along a single ray. A point sensor can create a range image if (1) the scene object(s) can be physically moved in two directions in front of the point-ranging sensor, (2) if the point-ranging sensor can be scanned in two directions over the scene, or (3) the scene object(s) are stepped in

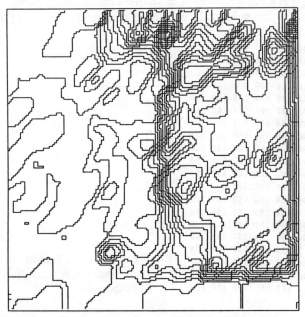

Figure 3. Contour plot of range image in Figure 1.

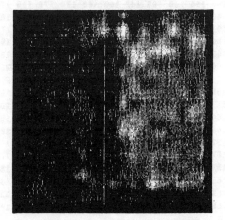

Figure 4. Gray level representation of range image in Figure 1.

one direction while the point sensor is scanned in the other direction.

2. A *Line* or *Circle Sensor* measures the distance to visible surface points that lie in a single 3-D plane or cone that contains the single viewpoint or viewing direction. A line or circle sensor can create a range image if (1) the scene object(s) can be moved orthogonal to the sensing plane or cone or (2) the line or circle sensor can be scanned over the scene in the orthogonal direction.

3. A *Field of View Sensor* measures the distance to many visible surface points that lie within a given field of view relative to a single viewpoint or viewing direction. This type of sensor creates a range image directly. No scene motion is required.

4. A *Multiple View Sensor System* locates surface points relative to more than one viewpoint or viewing direction because all surface points of interest are not visible or cannot be adequately measured from a single viewpoint or viewing direction. Scene motion is not required.

These sensor types form a natural hierarchy: a point sensor may be scanned (with respect to one sensor axis) to create a line or circle sensor, and a line or circle sensor may be scanned (with respect to the orthogonal sensor axis) to create a field of view sensor. Any combination of point, line/circle, and field of view sensors can be used to create a multiple view sensor by (1) rotating and/or translating the scene in front of the sensor(s); (2) maneuvering the sensor(s) around the scene with a robot; (3) using multiple sensors in different locations to capture the appropriate views; or any combination of the above.

Accurate sensor and/or scene object positioning is achieved via commercially available translation stages, $xy(z)$-tables, and $xy\theta$ tables (translation repeatability in submicron range, angular repeatabil-

ity in microradians or arc-seconds). Such methods are preferred to mirror scanning methods for high precision applications because these mechanisms can be controlled better than scanning mirrors. Controlled 3-D motion of sensor(s) and/or object(s) via gantry, slider, and/or revolute joint robot arms is also possible, but is generally much more expensive than table motion for the same accuracy. Scanning motion internal to sensor housings is usually rotational (using a rotating mirror), but may also be translational (using a precision translation stage). Optical scanning of lasers has been achieved via (1) motor-driven rotating polygon mirrors, (2) galvanometer-driven flat mirrors, (3) acoustooptic (AO) modulators, (4) rotating holographic scanners, or (5) stepper-motor-driven mirrors (Gottlieb 1983, Marshall 1985). However, AO modulators and holographic scanners significantly attenuate laser power, and AO modulators have a narrow angular field of view ($\approx 10° \times 10°$), making them less desirable for many applications.

2.2   Sensor Performance Parameters

Any measuring device is characterized by its measurement resolution or precision, repeatability, and accuracy. The following definitions are adopted here. *Range resolution* or *range precision* is the smallest change in range that a sensor can report. *Range repeatability* refers to statistical variations as a sensor makes repeated measurements of the exact same distance. *Range accuracy* refers to statistical variations as a sensor makes repeated measurements of a known *true value*. Accuracy should indicate the largest expected deviation of a measurement from the true value under normal operating conditions. Since range sensors can improve accuracy by averaging multiple measurements, accuracy should be quoted with measurement time. For our comparisons, a range sensor is characterized by its accuracy over a given measurement interval (the depth of field) and the measurement time. If a sensor has good repeatability, we assume that it is also calibrated to be accurate. Loss of calibration over time (drift) is a big problem for poorly engineered sensors but is not addressed here.

A range-imaging sensor measures point positions (x, y, z) within a specified accuracy or error tolerance. The method of specifying accuracy varies in different applications, but an accuracy specification should include one or more of the following for each 3-D direction given N observations: (1) the mean absolute error (MAE) ($\pm \delta_x$, $\pm \delta_y$, $\pm \delta_z$) where $\delta_x = (1/N)\Sigma|x_i - \mu_x|$ and $\mu_x = (1/N)\Sigma x_i$ (or $\mu_x =$ median (x_i)); (2) RMS (root-mean-square) error ($\pm \sigma_x$, $\pm \sigma_y$, $\pm \sigma_z$) where $\sigma_x^2 = (N - 1)^{-1}\Sigma(x_i - \mu_x)^2$ and $\mu_x =$

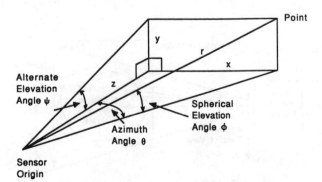

Figure 5. Cartesian, spherical, and orthogonal-axis coordinates.

$(1/N)\Sigma x_i$; or (3) maximum error ($\pm\epsilon_x$, $\pm\epsilon_y$, $\pm\epsilon_z$) where $\epsilon_x = \max_i |x_i - \mu_x|$. (Regardless of the measurement error probability distribution, $\delta \leq \sigma \leq \epsilon$ for each direction.) Some specify range accuracy (σ) with $\pm\sigma$ for RMS error as above; others specify $\pm 3\sigma$; others specify the positive width of the normal distribution as 2σ; and others do not say, if any of the above. Whatever specification is used, the sensor should ideally meet the specified error tolerance for any measured point within the working volume V of size $L_x \times L_y \times L_z$.

The foregoing parameters specify the spatial properties of the sensor. The pixel dwell time T is the time required for a single pixel range measurement. For points acquired *sequentially*, the total time to take N_p points in an image frame is N_pT, the frame rate is $1/N_pT$ frames/second, and the pixel data rate is $1/T$ pixels/second. If all points are acquired in *parallel* in time T, the frame rate is $1/T$ and the pixel rate N_p/T.

A system figure of merit maps several system parameters to a single number for comparing different systems. An application independent performance figure of merit M is defined to measure the spatial and temporal performance of range imaging sensors. For *xyz*-form range imaging, the figure of merit M is defined as

$$M = \frac{1}{\sqrt{T}}\left(\frac{L_xL_yL_z}{\sigma_x\sigma_y\sigma_z}\right)^{1/3}. \qquad (4)$$

For r_{ij}-form range imaging, there is usually very little relative uncertainty in the direction of a ray specified by the interger i and j indices compared to the uncertainty in the measured range r. Thus, the uncertainty in the resulting x, y, z coordinates is dominated by the uncertainty in the r_{ij} values. The working volume is a portion of a pyramid cut out by spherical surfaces with the minimum and maximum distance radii. The figure of merit for r_{ij}-form range-imaging sensors is given by the simpler expression

$$M \approx \frac{L_r}{\sigma_r\sqrt{T}} \qquad (5)$$

where L_r is the *depth of field* and σ_r is the *RMS range accuracy*. Both quantities are defined along rays emanating from the sensor. The factors of standoff distance, angular field of view, and field of view are other important parameters for range sensors that do not enter into the figure of merit calculations directly, but should be considered for each application. These parameters are shown in Figure 6.

The dimensions of M may be thought of roughly as the amount of good quality range data per second, and of course, the higher the number the better, other things being equal. A doubling of the depth-of-field to range-accuracy ratio is reflected by a doubling of the figure of merit. However, a quadrupling of image acquisition speed is required to double the figure of merit. This expresses a bias for accurate measurement over fast measurement, but also maintains an invariant figure of merit under internal sensor averaging changes. Suppose a system does internal averaging of normally distributed measurement errors during the pixel dwell time T. If T is quartered, the σ-value should only double. If the square root of time T were not used, the figure of merit would double as the data became noisier and the sensor got faster. This was considered undesirable.

The figures of merit quoted in this survey should be taken as examples of the rough order of magnitude of sensor performance, not exact numbers. First, it is difficult to know the actual accuracy for a given application without testing a sensor on typical scenes. Second, it is difficult to know whether quoted accuracy means 1, 2, 3, or 4σ or something else. Third, even if the quoted figure is a valid test result, the surface reflectance, absorption, and transmission properties for the test are not always stated. Sensor performance is often quoted under the most favorable conditions. Fourth, several sensors, especially sensors from conservative commercial companies, are underrated because of conservative accuracy figures. They know about the vast difference between measurements in the lab and in the customer's plant and about customer disappointment. In fact, some sensors are conservatively rated 10 to 20 times less accurate than they would be in the lab. Finally, only resolution is given for some sensors and accuracy had to be estimated.

The sensor cost C can be combined with the performance figure of merit to create a cost-weighted

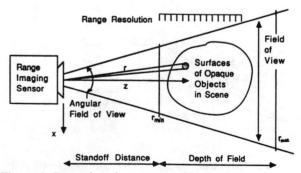

Figure 6. Range imaging sensor with angular scan.

figure of merit $M' = M/C$ where the dimensions are roughly range data per second per unit cost. Cost estimates are not included here because actual costs can vary significantly from year to year depending upon technical developments and market forces, not to mention customized features that are often needed for applications. Cost estimates were also not available for many sensors.

It is likely that these figures of merit M and M' may place no importance on factors that dominate decisions for a particular application. The figures of merit given here are application independent. No figure of merit can represent all factors for all applications. For example, some triangulation or moire range sensors with large source/detector separations may have a significant "missing parts" problem (shadowing problem) for certain applications and not for others. Figures of merit cannot easily reflect this limitation.

Neither can the "scene materials" problem be easily factored into a figure of merit. There are materials in many scenes that almost completely reflect, absorb, or transmit optical radiation. For example, mirrors and shiny metal or plastic surfaces reflect light, black paint may absorb infrared, and glass is transparent. These materials cause scene geometry interpretation problems for optical sensors. Hence, the physical/chemical composition of matter in a scene determines the quality and the meaning of range values. Even though optical range sensors are designed for determining scene geometry directly, a priori information about the optical properties of scene materials is needed for accurate interpretation.

3.   Imaging Radars

Bats (Griffin 1958) and porpoises (Kellogg 1961) are equipped by nature with ultrasonic "radars." Electromagnetic radar dates back to 1903 when Hulsmeyer (1904) experimented with the detection of radio waves reflected from ships. The basic time/ range equation for radars is

$$v\tau = 2r = \text{round-trip distance} \qquad (6)$$

where v is the speed of signal propagation, r is the distance to a reflecting object, and τ is the transit time of the signal traveling from the radar transmitter to the reflecting object and back to the radar receiver. For imaging laser radars, the unknown scene parameters at a reflecting point are the (1) range r, (2) the surface reflection coefficient

(albedo) ρ, and (3) the angle $\theta = \cos^{-1}(\hat{n} \cdot \hat{l})$ between the visible surface normal $\hat{n}$ and the direction $\hat{l}$ of the radar beam. Ignoring atmospheric attenuation, all other relevant physical parameters can be lumped into a single function $K(t)$ that depends only on the radar transceiver hardware. The received power $P(t)$ is

$$P(t, \theta, \rho, r) = K(t - \tau)\rho \cos\theta/r^2 \qquad (7)$$

This laser radar equation tells us that if 10 bits of range resolution are required on surfaces that may tilt away from the sight line by as much as 60 deg, and if surface reflection coefficients from 1 to 0.002 are possible on scene surfaces, then a radar receiver with a dynamic range of 90 dB is required.

3.1   Time of Flight, Pulse Detection

In this section, several pulse detection imaging laser radars are mentioned. A figure of merit M is assigned to each sensor.

Lewis and Johnston at JPL built an imaging laser radar beginning in 1972 for the Mars rover (Lewis and Johnston 1977). Their best range resolution was 20 mm over a 3-m depth of field and the maximum data rate possible was 100 points per second. It took about 40 seconds to obtain 64 × 64 range images ($M = 1520$).

Jarvis (1983a) built a similar sensor capable of acquiring a 64 × 64 range image with ±2.5 mm range resolution over a 4 m field of view in 40 s ($M = 16,160$).

Heikkinen et al. (1986) and Ahola et al. (1985) developed a pulsed time-of-flight range sensor with a depth of field of 1.5 m at a standoff of 2.5 m. The range resolution is about 20 mm at its maximum data rate (10,000 points/s) at a range of 3.5 m ($M = 7500$).

Ross (1978) patented a novel pulsed, time-of-flight imaging laser radar concept that uses several fast camera shutters instead of mechanical scanning. For a range sensor with 30 cm resolution over a 75-m depth of field, the least significant range-bit image is determined by a 2-ns shutter (the fastest shutter required). Assuming a conservative frame rate of 15 Hz and eight, 512 × 512 cameras, $M = 500,000$ if constructed.

An imaging laser radar is commercially available for airborne hydrographic surveying (Banic et al. 1987). The system can measure water depths down to 40 m with an accuracy of 0.3 m from an aerial standoff of 500 m. Two hundred scan lines were acquired covering 2000 km^2 with two million "soundings" in 30 h ($M = 596$). This number is low because *application specific capabilities* (e.g., standoff) are not included.

3.2 Amplitude Modulation

Rather than sending out a short pulse, waiting for an echo, and measuring transit time, a laser beam can be amplitude-modulated by varying the drive current of a laser diode at a frequency $f_{AM} = c/\lambda_{AM}$. An electronic phase detector measures the phase difference $\Delta\phi$ (in radians) between the transmitted signal and the received signal to get the range: $r(\Delta\phi) = c\Delta\phi/4\pi f_{AM} = \lambda_{AM}\Delta\phi/4\pi$. Since relative phase differences are only determined modulo 2π, the range to a point is only determined within a range ambiguity interval r_{ambig}. In the absence of any ambiguity-resolving mechanisms, the depth of field of an AM laser radar is the ambiguity interval: $L_r = r_{ambig} = c/2f_{AM} = \lambda_{AM}/2$ which is divided into $2^{N_{bits}}$ range levels where N_{bits} is the number of bits of quantization at the output of the phase detector. Finer depth resolution and smaller ambiguity intervals result from using higher modulating frequencies.

The ambiguity interval problem in AM CW radars can be resolved either via software or more hardware. If the imaged scene is limited in surface gradient relative to the sensor, it is possible in software to unwrap phase ambiguities because the phase gradient will always exceed the surface gradient limit at phase wraparound pixels. This type of processing is done routinely in moire sensors (see Halioua and Srinivasan 1987). In hardware, a system could use multiple modulation frequencies simultaneously. In a simple approach, each range ambiguity is resolved by checking against lower modulation frequency measurements. Other methods are possible, but none are commercially available at the current time.

Nitzan et al. (1977) built one of the first nonmilitary AM imaging laser radars. It created high-quality registered range and intensity images. With a 40-dB signal-to-noise ratio (SNR), a range accuracy of 4 cm in an ambiguity interval of 16.6 m was obtained. With a 67 dB SNR, the accuracy improved to 2 mm. The pixel dwell time was variable: 500 ms per pixel dwell times were common and more than 2 h was needed for a full 128×128 image ($M = 3770$ at 67 dB). The system insured image quality by averaging the received signal until the SNR was high enough.

The Environmental Research Institute of Michigan (ERIM) developed three AM imaging laser radars: (1) the Adaptive Suspension Vehicle (ASV) system, (2) the Autonomous Land Vehicle (ALV) system, and (3) the Intelligent Task Automation (ITA) system. Zuk and Dell'Eva (1983) described the ASV sensor. The range accuracy is about 61 mm over 9.75 m at a frame rate of two 128×128 images per second ($M = 28,930$). The ALV sensor generates two 256×64 image frames per second. The ambiguity interval was increased to 19.5 m, but $M = 28930$ is identical to the ASV sensor since pixel dwell time and depth of field to range accuracy ratios stayed the same. The new ERIM navigation sensor (Sampson 1987) uses lasers with three different frequencies and has 2-cm range resolution ($M = 353,000$ assuming depth of field is doubled). The ERIM ITA sensor is programmable for up to 512×512 range images (Svetkoff et al. 1984). The depth of field can change from 150 mm to 900 mm. As an inspection sensor, the laser diode is modulated at 720 MHz. The sensor then has a range accuracy of 100 μ at a standoff of 230 mm in a 76-mm $\times$ 76-mm field of view over a depth of field of 200 mm. The latest system of this type claims a 100-kHz pixel rate ($M = 632,500$).

A commercially available AM imaging laser radar is built by Odetics (Binger and Harris 1987). Their sensor has a 9.4-m ambiguity interval with 9-bit range resolution of 18 mm per depth level. The pixel dwell time is 32 μsec ($M = 71,720$). This sensor features an *auto-calibration feature* that calibrates the system *every frame* avoiding thermal drift problems encountered in other sensors of this type. It is currently the smallest ($9 \times 9 \times 9$ in.), lightest weight (33 lbs.), and least power hungry (42 W) sensor in its class. Class I CDRH eye safety requirements (see the appendix) are met except within a 0.4 m radius of the aperture.

Another commercially available AM imaging laser radar is built by Boulder Electro-Optics (1986). The ambiguity interval is 43 m with 8-bit resolution (about 170 mm). The frame rate was 1.4 256×256 frames/sec ($M = 27,360$).

Perceptron (1987) reports they are developing an AM imaging laser radar with a 360-kHz data rate, a 1.87-m ambiguity interval, a 3-m standoff, and 0.45-mm (12-bit) range resolution ($M = 153,600$ assuming 8-bit accuracy).

Cathey and Davis (1986) designed a system using multiple laser diodes, one for each pixel, to avoid scanning. They obtained a 15-cm range accuracy at a range of 13 m with a 2-diode system. For N^2 laser diodes fired four times a second, $M = 512N$. If the sensor cost is dominated by N^2 laser diode cost, the cost-weighted figure of merit M' would decrease as $1/N$. A full imaging system has not been built.

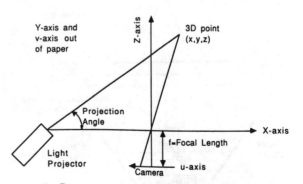

Miller and Wagner (1987) built an AM radar unit using a modulated infrared LED. The system scans 360 deg in azimuth, digitizing about 1000 points in a second. The depth of field is about 6 m with a range accuracy of about 25 mm ($M = 7590$). This system is very inexpensive to build and is designed for mobile robot navigation.

The Perkin-Elmer imaging airborne laser radar (Keyes 1986) scans 2790 pixels per scan line in 2 ms ($M = 302,360$ assuming 8-bit range accuracy). Aircraft motion provides the necessary scanning motion in the flight direction of the aircraft.

Wang et al. (1984) and Terras (1986) discussed the imaging laser radar developed at General Dynamics. The 12 × 12-deg angular field of view is scanned by dual galvanometers. It ranges out to 350 m, but the ambiguity interval is 10 m yielding lots of phase transition stripes in uncorrected range images.

Other work in AM imaging laser radars has been done at Hughes Aircraft, MIT Lincoln Labs (Quist et al. 1978), Raytheon (Jelalian and McManus 1977), as well as United Technologies and other defense contractors.

3.3 Frequency Modulation, Heterodyne Detection

The optical frequency of a laser diode can also be tuned thermally by modulating the laser diode drive current (Dandridge 1982). If the transmitted optical frequency is repetitively swept linearly between $v \pm \Delta v/2$ to create a total frequency deviation of Δv during the period $1/f_m$ (f_m is the linear sweep modulation frequency), the reflected return signal can be mixed coherently with a reference signal at the detector (Teich 1968) to create a beat frequency f_b signal that depends on the range to the object r (Skolnick 1962). This detection process is known as FM coherent heterodyne detection. Range is proportional to the beat frequency in an FM CW radar: $r(f_b) = cf_b/4f_m\Delta v$. One method for measuring the beat frequency is counting the number of zero-crossings N_b of the beat signal during a ramp of the linear sweep frequency modulation. This zero-crossing count must satisfy the relationship $2N_b = \lfloor f_b/f_m \rfloor$ which yields the range equation $r(N_b) = cN_b/2\Delta v$. The range values in this method are determined to within $\delta r = \pm c/4\Delta v$ since N_b must be an integer. The maximum range should satisfy the constraint that $r_{max} \ll c/f_m$. Since it is difficult to ensure the exact optical frequency deviation Δv of a laser diode, it is possible to measure range indirectly by comparing the N_b value with a known reference count N_{ref} for an accurately known reference distance r_{ref} using the relationship $r(N_b) = N_b r_{ref}/N_{ref}$. Hersman et al. (1987) reported results

for two commercially available FM imaging laser radars: a vision system and a metrology system (Digital Optronics 1986). The vision system measures a 1-m depth of field with 8-bit resolution at four 256 × 256 frames/second ($M = 3770$ using a quoted value of 12 mm for RMS depth accuracy after averaging 128 frames in 32 s). A new receiver is being developed to obtain similar performance in 0.25 s. The metrology system measures to an accuracy of 50 μ in 0.1 s over a depth of field of 2.5 m ($M = 30,430$). Better performance is expected when electronically tunable laser diodes are available.

Beheim and Fritsch (1986) reported results with an in-house sensor. Points were acquired at a rate of 29.3/s. The range accuracy varied with target to source distance. From 50 to 500 mm, the range accuracy was 2.7 mm; from 600 to 1000 mm, $\sigma_z = 7.4$ mm; and from 1100 to 1500 mm, $\sigma_z = 15$ mm (approximately $M = 1080$).

4. Active Triangulation

Triangulation based on the law of sines is certainly the oldest method for measuring range to remote points and is also the most common. A simple geometry for an active triangulation system is shown in Figure 7. A single camera is aligned along the z-axis with the center of the lens located at $(0, 0, 0)$. At a baseline distance b to the left of the camera (along the negative x-axis) is a light projector sending out a beam or plane of light at a variable angle θ relative to the x-axis baseline. The point (x, y, z) is projected into the digitized image at the pixel (u, v) so $uz = xf$ and $vz = yf$ by similar triangles where f is the focal length of the camera in pixels. The measured quantities (u, v, θ) are used to compute the (x, y, z) coordinates:

$$[x \ y \ z] = \frac{b}{f\cot\theta - u}[u \ v \ f] \quad (8)$$

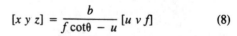

Figure 7. Camera-centered active triangulation geometry.

4.1 Structured Light: Point

It is commonly believed that a large baseline distance b separating the light source and the detector is necessary for accurate ranging. However, for any fixed focal length f and baseline distance b, the range resolution of a triangulation system is only limited by the ability to accurately measure the angle θ and the horizontal position u.

Rioux (1984) has patented a synchronized scanner concept for active triangulation in which the horizontal position detector and the beam projector are *both* scanned. The angle θ is coupled with the u measurement yielding high-range resolution with a small baseline by making more efficient use of the finite resolution of the horizontal position detector. The basic concept is that if one uses the available resolution to measure differences from the mean rather than absolute quantities, the effective resolution can be much greater. As shown in Figure 8, the beam leaves the source, hits the mirror currently rotated at a position θ, bounces off a fixed (source) mirror and impinges on an object surface. The illuminated bright spot is viewed via the opposite side of the mirror (and a symmetrically positioned fixed detector mirror). The average range is determined by the angular positioning of the fixed mirrors. The sensor creates a 128×256 range image in less than a second. The angular separation of the fixed mirrors is only 10 deg. For a total working volume of 250 mm $\times$ 250 mm $\times$ 100 mm, the x, y, z resolutions are 1, 2, and 0.4 mm, respectively ($M = 45,255$).

Servo-Robot (1987) manufactures the Saturn and the Jupiter line scan range sensors. Both are based on synchronous scanning. The Saturn system measures a 60 mm $\times$ 60 mm $\times$ 60 mm working volume from a standoff of 80 mm. The volume-center resolution is 0.06 mm in x and 0.05 mm in z ($M = 32,860$ for 3000 points/s). The Jupiter system measures a 1 m $\times$ 1 m $\times$ 1 m volume from a standoff of 0.1 m. The volume-center resolution is 1 mm in x and 0.3 mm in z ($M = 91,290$ for 3000 points/s).

Hymarc (1987) also makes a line scan sensor based on synchronous scanning. The sensor is accurate to 0.25 mm in a 500 mm $\times$ 500 mm $\times$ 500 mm working volume at a 600-mm standoff with a 3000 point per second data rate ($M = 109,540$).

Photonic Automation, Inc. (1987) is developing a commercially available sensor for fast ranging in a shallow depth of field. They claim a range accuracy of 25 μ over a depth of field of 6.25 mm at a speed of 10 million pixels per second ($M = 790,570$). The angular separation between source and detector is about 5 deg. Synthetic Vision Systems of Ann Arbor, Michigan has a competing unit.

Bickel et al. (1984) independently developed a mechanically coupled deflector arrangement for spot scanners similar in concept to the Rioux (1984) design. Bickel et al. (1985) addressed depth of focus problems inherent in triangulation systems for both illumination and detection. They suggest a tele-axicon lens and a laser source can provide a 25-μ spot that is in focus over a 100-mm range at a 500-mm standoff. Detection optics should be configured to satisfy the Scheimpflug (tilted detector plane) condition (Slevogt 1974) shown in Figure 9: $\tan \theta_{tilt} = 1/M \tan \theta_{sep}$ where θ_{sep} is the separation angle of the illumination direction and the detector's viewing direction, θ_{tilt} is the tilt angle of the photosensitive surface in the focusing region of the lens relative to the viewing direction, and $M = (w_c - f)/w_c$ is the on-axis magnification of the lens where w_c is the distance from the center of the lens to the center of the detector plane and f is the focal length of the lens. All points in the illumination plane are in exact focus in the detector plane. Using a 4000-element linear array detector, they get 25-μ range resolution, 13-μ lateral resolution, over a depth of field of 80 mm ($M = 17,530$ assuming 30 points/s rate). Tilted detector planes are used by some commercial

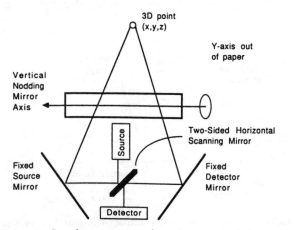

Figure 8. Synchronous scanning of source and detector.

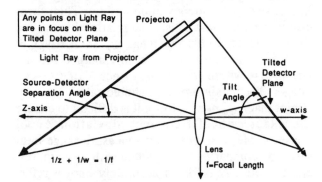

Figure 9. Scheimpflug condition: tilted detector to maintain focus for all depths.

vendors. Hausler and Maul (1985) examined the use of telecentric scanning configurations for point scanners. A telecentric system positions optical components at the focal length of the lens (or mirror).

Faugeras and Hebert (1986) used an in-house laser scanner. Their sensor uses a laser spot projector and two horizontal position detectors. Objects are placed on a turntable, and points are digitized as the object rotates. Scans are taken at several different heights to define object shape. No numbers were available to compute the figure of merit.

CyberOptics Corp. (1987) manufactures a series of point range sensors. For example, the PRS-30 measures a 300 μ depth of field from a standoff of 5 mm with 0.75-μ accuracy (1 part in 400). A precision xy-table (0.25 μ) provides object scanning under a stationary sensor at a rate of 15 points/s ($M = 1550$).

Diffracto, Ltd. (1987) also makes a series of point range sensors. Their Model 300 LaserProbe measures a depth of field of 2 mm from a standoff of 50 mm with an accuracy of 2.5 μ in 5 ms ($M = 11,300$). The detector handles a 50,000:1 dynamic range of reflected light intensities and works well for a variety of surfaces.

Kern Instruments (1987) has developed the System for Positioning and Automated Coordinate Evaluation (SPACE) using two automated Kern theodolites. This system measures points in a 3 m × 3 m × 3 m working volume to an accuracy of 50 μ (1 part in 60,000) at a rate of about 7.5 s per point ($M = 21,910$).

Lorenz (1984, 1986) has designed an optical probe to measure range with a repeatability of 2.5 μ over a depth of field of 100 mm (1 part in 40,000). He uses split-beam illumination and optimal estimation theory. The probe was tested on the z-axis of a CNC machining center. Even at one point per second, $M = 40000$.

The Selcom Opticator (1987) series are among the highest performance commercially available ranging point probes. They measure with one part in 4000 resolution at 16,000 points/s ($M = 126,490$ for 1 part in 1000 accuracy). The resolution of different models ranges from 2 to 128 μ in powers of two.

Pipitone and Marshall (1983) documented their experience in building a point scanning system. They measured with an accuracy of about 1 part in 400 over a depth of field of about 7.6 m ($M = 8940$ for 500 pts/s).

Haggren and Leikas (1987) have developed a four-camera photogrammetric machine-vision system with accuracy of better than 1 part in 10,000.

The system generates one 3-D point every 1.5 s ($M = 8160$). Earlier similar photogrammetry work is found in Pinckney (1978) and Kratky (1979).

4.2 Structured Light: Line
Passing a laser beam through a cylindrical lens creates a line of light. Shirai (1972) and Will and Pennington (1972) were some of the first researchers to use light striping for computer vision. Nevatia and Binford (1973), Rocker (1974), and Popplestone et al. (1975) also used light striping. The General Motors Consight System (Holland et al. 1979) was one of the first industrial systems to use light stripe principles.

Technical Arts Corp. (1987) produces the 100X White Scanner. The camera and laser are typically separated by 45 deg or more. The system can measure up to a range of 2.4 m with a resolution of about 0.5 mm ($M = 87,640$ for 3000 pts/s and accuracy of 1.5 mm).

The IMAGE Lab at ENST in France developed a light stripe laser ranging system (Schmitt et al. 1985), commercially available from Studec. Schmitt et al. (1986) show a range image of a human head sculpture obtained with this sensor.

Cotter and Batchelor (1986) describe a depth map module (DMM) based on light striping techniques that produces 128 × 128 range images in about 4 s ($M = 8192$ assuming 7-bit resolution).

Silvaggi et al. (1986) describe a very inexpensive triangulation system (less than $1000 in component cost) that is accurate to 0.25 mm over a 50-mm depth of field at a standoff of 100 mm. A photosensitive RAM chip is used as the camera.

CyberOptics Corp. (1987) also manufactures a series of line range sensors. The LRS-30-500 measures a 300 μ depth of field and an 800-μ field of view from a standoff of 15 mm with 0.75 μ range accuracy (1 part in 400). A precision xy-table (0.25 μ) provides object scanning under the stationary sensor head at a rate of 5 lines/s ($M = 7155$ assuming only 64 points per line).

Perceptron (1987) makes a contour sensor that uses light striping and the Scheimpflug condition to obtain 25-μ accuracy over a 45-mm depth of field at a rate of 15 points/s ($M = 6970$).

Diffracto, Ltd. (1987) manufactures a Z-Sensor series of light stripe range sensors. Their Z-750 can measure a 19 mm depth of field with an accuracy of 50 μ from a standoff of 762 mm ($M = 6100$ assuming one 256 point line/s).

Landman and Robertson (1986) describe the capabilities of the Eyecrometer system available from Octek. This system is capable of 25 μ 3σ accuracy in the narrow view mode with a 12.7 mm depth of field. The time for a high-accuracy scan is 9.2 s ($M = 2680$ assuming 256 pixels/scan).

Harding and Goodson (1986) implemented a prototype optical guillotine system that uses a high-precision translation stage with 2-μ resolution to obtain an accuracy of 1 part in 16,000 over a range of 150 mm. The system generates a scan in about 1 s ($M = 256,000$ assuming a 256-point scan).

The APOMS (Automated Propeller Optical Measurement System) built by RVSI (Robotic Vision Systems, Inc.) (1987) uses a high precision point range sensor mounted on the arm of a 5-axis inspection robot arm. The large working volume is 3.2 m × 3.5 m × 4.2 m. The accuracy of the optical sensor (x, y, z) coordinates is 64 μ in an 81 mm × 81 mm field of view. The linear axes of the robot are accurate to 2.5 μ, and the pitch and roll axes are accurate to 2 arc-seconds. The system covers 60 square feet per hour. Assuming 4 points per square millimeter, the data rate is about 6000 points/s ($M = 3,485,700$). The RVSI Ship Surface Scanner is a portable tripod mounted unit that has a maximum 70 deg × 70 deg field of view. The line scanner scans at an azimuthal rate of 8 deg/s. The range accuracy is about 1 part in 600 or about 5.7 mm at 3.66 m. The RVSI RoboLocator sensor can measure depths to an accuracy of 50 μ in a 25 mm × 25 mm field of view and a 50 mm depth of field. The RVSI RoboSensor measures about 1 part in 1000 over up to a 1-m depth of field in a 500 mm × 500 mm field of view. Assuming 3000 points/s, $M = 54,000$.

4.3 Structured Light: Miscellaneous
Kanade and Fuhrman (1987) developed an 18 LED light-source optical proximity sensor that computes 200 local surface points in 1 s with a precision of 0.1 mm over a depth of field of 100 mm ($M = 14,140$). Damm (1987) has developed a similar but smaller proximity sensor using optical fibers.

Labuz and McVey (1986) developed a ranging method based on tracking the multiple points of a moving grid over a scene. Lewis and Sopwith (1986) used the multiple-point-projection approach with a static stereo pair of images.

Jalkio et al. (1985) use multiple light stripes to obtain range images. The field of view is 60 mm × 60 mm with at least a 25-mm depth of field. The range resolution is about 0.25 mm with a lateral sampling interval of 0.5 mm. The image acquisition time was dominated by software processing of 2 min ($M = 1170$).

Mundy and Porter (1987) describe a system designed to yield 25-μ range resolution within 50 μ × 50 μ pixels at a pixel rate of 1 MHz while tolerating

a 10 to 1 change in surface reflectance. The goals were met except the data acquisition speed is about 16 kHz ($M = 32,380$ assuming 8-bit accuracy).

Range measurements can be extracted from a single projected grid image, but if no constraints are imposed on the surface shapes in the scene, ambiguities may arise. Will and Pennington (1972) discussed grid-coding methods for isolating planar surfaces in scenes based on vertical and horizontal spatial frequency analysis. Hall et al. (1982) described a grid-pattern method for obtaining sparse range images of simple objects. Potmesil (1983) used a projected grid method to obtain range data for automatically generating surface models of solid objects. Stockman and Hu (1986) examined the ambiguity problem using relaxation labeling. Wang et al. (1985) used projected grids to obtain local surface orientation.

Wei and Gini (1983) proposed a structured light method using circles. They propose a spinning mirror assembly to create a converging cone of light that projects to a circle on a flat surface and an ellipse on a sloped surface. Ellipse parameters determine the distance to the surface as well as the surface normal (within a sign ambiguity).

If the light source projects two intersecting lines (X), it is easier to achieve subpixel accuracy at the point. The cross is created by a laser by using a beamsplitter and two cylindrical lenses. Pelowski (1986) discusses a commercially available Perceptron sensor that guarantees a ±3σ accuracy in (x, y, z) of 0.1 mm over a depth of field of 45 mm in less than 0.25 s. Nakagawa and Ninomiya (1987) also uses the cross structure.

Asada et al. (1986) project thick stripes to obtain from a single image a denser map of surface normals than is possible using grid projection. The thickness of the stripes limits ambiguity somewhat because of the signed brightness transitions at thick stripe edges.

4.4 Structured Light: Coded Binary Patterns
Rather than scan a light stripe over a scene and process N separate images or deal with the ambiguities possible in processing a single gray scale multistripe image, it is possible to compute a range image using $N' = \lceil\log_2 N\rceil$ images where the scene is illuminated with binary stripe patterns. In an appropriate configuration, a range image can be computed from intensity images using lookup tables. This method is fast and relatively inexpensive.

Solid Photography, Inc. (1977) made the first use of gray-coded binary patterns for range imaging. A gantry mounted system of several range cameras acquired range data from a 2π solid angle around an object. The system was equipped with a milling machine so that if a person had his or her range picture taken, a 3-D bust could be machined in a matter of minutes. The point accuracy of the multisensor system was about 0.75 mm in a 300 mm × 300 mm × 300 mm volume ($M = 100,000$ assuming 64K points/s).

Altschuler et al. (1981) and Potsdamer and Altschuler (1983) developed a numerical stereo camera consisting of a laser and an electrooptic shutter synchronized to a video camera. They used standard binary patterns and also performed experiments using two crossed electrooptic shutters (grid-patterns).

Inokuchi et al. (1984) and Sato and Inokuchi (1985) showed results from their system based on the gray-code binary pattern concept. More recently, Yamamoto et al. (1986) reported another approach based on binary image accumulation. A variation on the binary pattern scheme is given in Yeung and Lawrence (1986).

Rosenfeld and Tsikos (1986) built a range camera using 10 gray-code patterns on a 6-in. dia disk that rotates at 5 revolutions per second. Their system creates a 256 × 256 8-bit range image with 2-mm resolution in about 0.7 s ($M = 78,330$).

Vuylsteke and Oosterlinck (1986) developed another binary coding scheme. They use a projection of a specially formulated binary mask where each local neighborhood of the mask has its own signature. A 64 × 64 range image was computed from a 604 × 576 resolution intensity image in about 70 CPU s (VAX 11/750) ($M = 1260$ assuming 7-bit accuracy).

4.5 Structured Light: Color Coded Stripes

Boyer and Kak (1987) developed a real-time light striping concept that requires only one image frame from a color camera (no mechanical operations). If many stripes are used to illuminate a scene and only one monochrome image is used, ambiguities arise at depth discontinuities because it is not clear which image stripe corresponds to which projected stripe. However, when stripes are color coded, unique color subsequences can be used to establish the correct correspondence for all stripes. Although no figures are given, 128 × 128 images with 8-bit accuracy at a 7.5-Hz frame rate would yield $M = 89,000$.

4.6 Structured Light: Intensity Ratio Sensor

The intensity ratio method, invented by Schwartz (1983), prototyped by Bastuschek and Schwartz (1984), researched by Carrihill (1986), and documented by Carrihill and Hummel (1985), determines range unambiguously using the digitization and analysis of only three images: an ambient image, a projector-illuminated image, and a projected lateral attenuation filter image. The depth of field was 860 mm with a range resolution of 12 bits at a standoff of 80 cm, but an overall range repeatability of 2 mm. The total acquisition and computation time for a 512 × 480 image with a Vicom processor was about 40 s ($M = 33,700$).

4.7 Structured Light: Random Texture

Schewe and Forstner (1986) developed a precision photogrammetry system based on random texture projection. A scene is illuminated by a texture projector and photographed with stereo metric cameras onto high-resolution glass plates. Registered pairs of subimages are digitized from the plates, and a manually selected starting point initializes automated processing. The range accuracy of the points is about 0.1 mm over about a 1-m depth of field and a several-meter field of view. A complete wireframe model is created requiring a few seconds per point on a microcomputer ($M = 10,000$).

5. Moire Techniques

A moire pattern is a low spatial frequency interference pattern created when two gratings with regularly spaced patterns of higher spatial frequency are superimposed on one another. Mathematically, the interference pattern $A(x)$ from two patterns A_1, A_2 is

$$A(x) = A_1\{1 + m_1 \cos[\omega_1 x + \phi_1(x)]\}$$
$$\cdot A_2\{1 + m_2 \cos[\omega_2 x + \phi_2(x)]\} \qquad (9)$$

where the A_i are amplitudes, the m_i are modulation indices, the ω_i are spatial frequencies, and the $\phi_i(x)$ are spatial phases. When this signal is low-pass filtered (LPF) (blurred), only the difference frequency and constant terms are passed:

$$A'(x) = \text{LPF}[A(x)]$$
$$= A_1 A_2(1 + m_1 m_2 \cos\{[\omega_1 - \omega_2]x + \phi_1(x) - \phi_2(x)]\}) . \qquad (10)$$

For equal spatial frequencies, only the phase difference term remains. In moire range-imaging sensors, surface depth information is encoded in and recovered from the phase difference term. Reviews and bibliographies of moire methods may be found in Pirodda (1982), Sciammarella (1982), and Oster (1965). Theocaris (1969) provides some history of moire techniques (e.g., Lord Rayleigh 1874).

Moire range-imaging methods are useful for measuring the *relative distance* to surface points on a smooth surface $z(x, y)$ that does not exhibit depth discontinuities. The magnitude of surface slope as viewed from the sensor direction should be bounded $\|\nabla z\| < K$. Under such constraints, absolute range for an entire moire image can be determined if the distance to one reference image point is known.

Moire methods for surface measurement use line gratings of alternating opaque and transparent bars of equal width (Ronchi gratings). The *pitch P* of a grating is the number of opaque/transparent linepairs per millimeter (LP/mm). The period $p = 1/P$ of the grating is the distance between the centers of two opaque lines.

5.1 Projection Moire
Khetan (1975) gives a theoretical analysis of projection moire. In a projection moire system, a precisely matched pair of gratings is required. The projector grating is placed in front of the projector and the camera grating is placed in front of the camera as shown in Figure 10. The projector is located at an angle θ_l and the camera is located at an angle θ_v relative to the z-axis. The projected light is spatially amplitude modulated by the pitch of the projector grating, creating a spatial "carrier" image. When the projected beam falls on the smooth surface, the surface shape modulates the phase of the spatial carrier. By viewing these stripes through the camera grating, interference fringes are created at the camera. The camera grating "demodulates" the modulated carrier yielding a "baseband" image signal whose fringes carry information about surface shape. If p_o is the period of the projected fringes at the object surface, then the change in z between the centers of the interference fringes viewed by the camera is given by

$$\Delta z = \frac{p_o}{\tan(\theta_l) + \tan(\theta_v)}. \qquad (11)$$

The angular separation of source and detector is

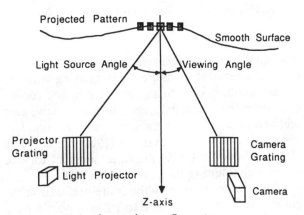

Figure 10. Projection moire configuration.

critical to range measurement and thus, moire may be considered a triangulation method (Perrin and Thomas 1979).

It is relatively inexpensive to set up a moire system using commercially available moire projectors, moire viewers, matched gratings, and video cameras (Newport Corp. 1987). The problem is accurate calibration and automated analysis of moire fringe images. Automated fringe analysis systems are surveyed in Reid (1986). The limitations of projection moire automated by digital image processing algorithms are addressed by Gasvik (1983). The main goal of such algorithms is to track the ridges or valleys of the fringes in the intensity surface to create 1-pixel wide contours. Phase unwrapping techniques are used to order the contours in depth assuming adequate spacing between the contours. It is not possible to correctly interpolate the phase (depth) between the fringes because between-fringe gray level variations are a function of local contrast, local surface reflectance, and phase change due to distance.

5.2 Shadow Moire
If a surface is relatively flat, shadow moire can be used. A single grating of large extent is positioned near the object surface. The surface is illuminated through the grating and viewed from another direction. Everything is the same as projection moire except that two matched gratings are not needed. Cline et al. (1982, 1984) show experimental results where 512×512 range images of several different surfaces were obtained automatically using shadow moire methods.

5.3 Single frame moire with reference
The projected grating on a surface can be imaged directly by a camera without a camera grating, digitized, and "demodulated" via computer software provided that a reference image of a flat plane is also digitized. As a general rule of thumb, single frame systems of this type are able to resolve range proportional to about 1/20 of a fringe spacing. Idesawa et al. (1977, 1980) did early work in automated moire surface measurement.

Electro-Optical Information Systems, Inc. (1987) has a commercially available range-imaging sensor of this type. On appropriate surfaces, the system creates a 480×512 range image in about 2 s using two array processors and has 1 part in 4000 resolution ($M = 350,540$ assuming accuracy of 1 part in 1000).

5.4 Multiple-frame phase-shifted moire
Multiple-frame (N-frame) phase-shifted moire is similar to single-frame moire except that after the

first frame of image data is acquired, the projector grating is precisely shifted laterally in front of the projector by a small distance increment that corresponds to a phase shift of $360/N$ degrees and subsequent image frames are acquired. This method, similar to quasi-heterodyne holographic interferometry, allows for an order of magnitude increase in range accuracy compared to conventional methods. Halioua and Srinivasan (1987) present a detailed description of the general moire concept. Srinivasan et al. (1985) show experimental results for a mannequin head using $N = 3$. They obtained 0.1-mm range accuracy over a 100-mm depth of field ($M = 46,740$ assuming 2 min. computation time for 512×512 images). Other research in this area has been reported by Andersen (1986).

Boehnlein and Harding (1986) implemented this approach on special hardware. The computations take less than 3.5 s for a 256×256 image, but the high-accuracy phase-shifting translation device (accurate to 0.1 μ) limited them to about 10 s for complete range image acquisition. The range resolution of the system is 11 μ over a 64-mm depth of field ($M = 121,430$ assuming 1 part in 1500 accuracy).

6.   Holographic Interferometry

Holography was introduced in 1961 by Leith and Upatnieks (1962). The principles of holographic interferometry were discovered soon after (see Vest 1979, Schuman and Dubas 1979). Holographic interferometers use coherent light from laser sources to produce interference patterns due to the optical-frequency phase differences in different optical paths. If two laser beams (same polarization) meet at a surface point $\mathbf{x}$, then the electric fields *add* to create the net electric field:

$$E(\mathbf{x}, t) = E_1 \cos(\omega_1 t - \mathbf{k}_1 \cdot \mathbf{x} + \phi_1(\mathbf{x}))$$
$$+ E_2 \cos(\omega_2 t - \mathbf{k}_2 \cdot \mathbf{x} + \phi_2(\mathbf{x})) \quad (12)$$

where the $\mathbf{k}_i$ are 3-D wave vectors pointing in the propagation directions with magnitude $\|\mathbf{k}_i\| = 2\pi/\lambda_i$, the $\omega_i = \|\mathbf{k}_i\|c$ are the radial optical frequencies, and $\phi_i(\mathbf{x})$ are the optical phases. Since photodetectors respond to the square of the electric field, the detectable irradiance (intensity) is $I(\mathbf{x}, t) = E^2(\mathbf{x}, t)$. Photodetectors themselves act as low-pass filters of the irradiance function I to yield the detectable interference signal $I'(\mathbf{x}, t) = \text{LPF}[I(\mathbf{x}, t)]$, or

$$I'(\mathbf{x}, t) = E_a\{1 + E_b\cos[\Delta\omega t + \Delta\mathbf{k} \cdot \mathbf{x} + \Delta\phi(\mathbf{x})]\} \quad (13)$$
where

$$E_a = E_1^2 + E_2^2/2 \text{ and}$$
$$E_b = 2E_1E_2/(E_1^2 + E_2^2),$$

$\Delta\omega = \omega_1 - \omega_2$ is the difference frequency, $\Delta\mathbf{k} = \mathbf{k}_2 - \mathbf{k}_1$ is the difference wave vector, and $\Delta\phi(\mathbf{x}) = \phi_1 - \phi_2$ is the phase difference. This equation is of the exact same form as the moire equation (10) above for $A'(x)$ except that a time-varying term is included. Since phase changes are proportional to optical path differences in holographic interferometry, fraction of a wavelength distances can be measured. For equal optical frequencies and equal (wave vector) spatial frequencies, only the phase difference term remains. In holographic interferometric range sensors, surface depth information is encoded in and recovered from the phase difference term. Just as the z-depth spacing of moire fringes is proportional to the period of grating lines, the z-depth spacing of holographic interference fringes is proportional to the wavelength of the light. Measured object surfaces must be very flat and smooth.

6.1   Conventional Holography

Conventional interferometry is somewhat like conventional projection moire in that the frequencies of the interfering beams are equal and between-fringe ranging is not possible. There are three types of conventional holographic interferometry used in industrial applications: (1) real-time holography, which allows observers to see instantaneous microscopic changes in surface shape, (2) double-exposure holographic systems, which provide permanent records of surface shape changes, (3) time-average holography, which produces vibration mode maps useful for verifying finite element analyses.

Conventional holographic interferometry is used to visualize stress, thermal strains, pressure effects, erosion, microscopic cracks, fluid flow, and other physical effects in nondestructive testing. Tozer et al. (1985), Mader (1985), Wuerker and Hill (1985), and Church et al. (1985) provide a sampling of industrial uses of holographic interferometry. The Holomatic 8000 (Laser Technology 1986) and the HC1000 Instant Holographic Camera (10-s development time on erasable thermoplastic film) (Newport Corp. 1987) are commercially available holographic camera systems.

6.2   Heterodyne Holography

Heterodyne holographic interferometers cause two coherent beams of slightly different optical frequencies (less than 100 MHz generates RF beat frequencies) to interfere creating time-varying holographic fringes in the image plane. Optical frequency shifts are achieved by acoustooptic modulators, rotating quarter wave plates, rotating gratings, and other methods. Optical phase measurements corresponding to optical path differences are made at each point by electronically measuring the phase of the beat frequency signal relative to a reference using a phasemeter. The time-varying interference fringe image is mechanically scanned with a high-speed detector to obtain a range image. Heterodyne holographic interferometers can make out-of-plane surface measurements with nanometer resolution over several microns, but they are typically slow. The general rule of thumb is that $\lambda/1000$ resolution is possible using heterodyne methods.

Pantzer et al. (1986) built a heterodyne profilometer that has a mechanical-vibration–limited range resolution of 5 nm and a lateral resolution of 3 μ. The theoretical resolution of this method is 0.4 nm if mechanical instabilities were removed. It took about 20 s to linearly scan 1 mm to get 330 points. ($M = 2450$ assuming a 3-μ depth of field).

Dandliker and Thalman (1985) obtained 0.2-nm range resolution over a depth of field of 3 μ at a rate of 1 point per second over a lateral range of 120 mm using a double-exposure heterodyne interferometer ($M = 7500$ assuming 0.4 nm accuracy).

Pryputniewicz (1985) used heterodyne interferometry to study the load-deformation characteristics of surface mount components on a printed circuit board. The reported 3σ range accuracy was 2 nm.

Sasaki and Okazaki (1986) developed a variation on frequency-shift heterodyne methods. The reference path mirror is mounted on a piezoelectric transducer (PZT) modulated at about 220 Hz. This phase modulation provides the needed small frequency shift for heterodyne accuracy. This is slow enough that image sensors can be used to collect the video signals. They obtained repeatable range measurements at less than 1 nm resolution. Over a 250 × 250 μ field of view, the lateral resolution is about 5 μ.

6.3   Quasi-Heterodyne (Phase-Shifted) Methods

Phase-shifted holographic interferometers are referred to as quasi-heterodyne since their $\lambda/100$ range resolution is not quite heterodyne performance, but is much better than conventional. Quasi-heterodyne systems can be much simpler, much cheaper, and much faster than heterodyne systems by trading off some range resolution. Standard video cameras can be used to image several frames of holographic fringes. Phase-shifts can be achieved at every pixel in parallel in real-time using a piezoelectric translator to move a mirror. (Compare this to the lateral shifting of a grating in front of a projector in phase-shifted moire.) Other phase-shifting methods are possible. The computations are very similar to those described in the previous section on multiple frame phase-shifted moire.

Hariharan (1985) used a 100 × 100 camera to digitize the holographic fringes needed to compute the range image. The measurement cycle for each fringe image was about 150 ms, and the total computation time was 10 s using a machine-language program. They used the same formulas as Boehnlein and Harding (1986) discussed above. Results are shown for a large 50 mm × 100 mm field of view ($M = 8095$ assuming 8-bit accuracy).

Thalman and Dandliker (1985) and Dandliker and Thalmann (1985) examine two-reference beam interferometry and two-wavelength contouring for quasi-heterodyne and heterodyne systems.

Chang et al. (1985) did experiments in digital phase-shifted holographic interferometry to eliminate the need to calibrate the phase shifter as in Hariharan et al. (1983). They claim an accuracy of 2 nm over a 300-nm depth of field.

6.4   Microscopic Interferometry

Peterson et al. (1984) measured VHS video tape surfaces with an interferometer obtaining 1 μ lateral resolution and 1 nm range repeatability.

Matthews et al. (1986) describe a phase-locked loop interferometric method where the two arms of a confocal interference microscope are maintained in quadrature by using an electrooptic phase modulator. Results are shown where the system scanned a 3-μ × 3-μ field of view over a depth of field of 300 nm in 2 s with a range accuracy of 1 nm ($M = 27,150$).

7.   Focusing

Horn (1968), Tenenbaum (1970), Jarvis (1976), and Krotkov (1986) have discussed focusing for range determination. Figure 11 shows basic focusing relationships. Pentland (1987), Grossman (1987), Krotkov and Martin (1986), Schlag et al. (1983), Jarvis (1976), and Harvey et al. (1985) discuss passive methods to determine range from focus.

The autofocus mechanisms in cameras act as range sensors (Denstman 1980, Goldberg 1982), but most commercially available units do not use focusing principles to determine range. The Canon "Sure-Shot" autofocusing mechanism is an active triangulation system using a frequency modulated infrared beam. Jarvis (1982) used this Canon sensor

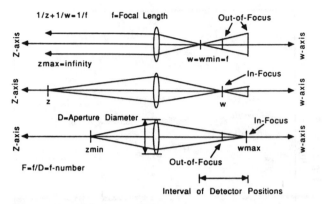

$$1/z + 1/w = 1/f \qquad f = \text{Focal Length}$$

Out-of-Focus

$z_{max} = \text{infinity}$

$w = w_{min} = f$

In-Focus

In-Focus

z

w

D=Aperture Diameter

z_{min}

w_{max}

F=f/D=f-number

Out-of-Focus

Interval of Detector Positions

Figure 11: Thin lens relationships.

module to create a 64 × 64 range image in 50 min. The Honeywell Visitronic module for Konica, Minolta, and Yashica cameras is a passive triangulation system that correlates photocell readouts to achieve a binocular stereomatch and the corresponding distance. The Polaroid autofocusing mechanism is a broad beam sonar unit.

Rioux and Blais (1986) developed two techniques based on lens focusing properties. In the first technique, a grid of point sources is projected onto a scene. The range to each point is determined by the radius of the blur in the focal plane of the camera. The system was capable of measuring depths to 144 points with 1-mm resolution over a 100-mm depth of field. The second technique uses a multistripe illuminator. If a stripe is not in focus, the camera sees split lines where the splitting distance between the lines is related to the distance to the illuminated surface. Special purpose electronics process the video signal (Blais and Rioux 1986) and detect peaks to obtain line splitting distances on each scan line and hence range. The system creates a 256 × 240 range image in less than 1 s by analyzing 10 projected lines in each of 24 frames. The projected lines are shifted between each frame. A resolution of 1 mm over a depth of 250 mm is quoted at a 1-m standoff for a small robot-mountable unit ($M = 63,450$).

Kinoshita et al. (1986) developed a point range sensor based on a projected conical ring of light and focusing principles. A lens is mechanically focused to optimize the energy density at a photodiode. The prototype system measured range with a repeatability of 0.3 mm over a depth of field of 150 mm (9 bits) with a standoff distance of 430 mm.

Corle et al. (1987) measured distances with accuracies as small as 40 nm over a 4-μ depth of field using a type II confocal scanning optical microscope.

8. Fresnel Diffraction

Talbot (1836) first observed that if a line grating $T(x, y) = T(x + p, y)$ with period p is illuminated with coherent light, exact in-focus images of the grating are formed at regular periodic (Talbot) intervals D. This is the self-imaging property of a grating. Lord Rayleigh (1881) first deduced that $D = 2p^2/\lambda$ when $p \gg \lambda$. The Talbot effect has been analyzed more recently by Cowley and Moodie (1957) and Winthrop and Worthington (1965). For cosine gratings, grating images are also reproduced at $D/2$ intervals with a 180-deg phase shift. Thus, the ambiguity interval for such a range sensor is given by $I_r = p^2/2\lambda = D/4$. Ambiguity resolving techniques are needed for larger depths of field. The important fact is that the grating images are out of focus in a predictable manner in the ambiguity interval such that local contrast depends on the depth z. Figure 12 shows the basic configuration for measuring distance with the Talbot effect.

The Chavel and Strand (1984) method illuminates an object with laser light that has passed through a cosine grating. A camera views the object through a beam-splitter so that the grating image is superimposed on the returned object image that is modulated by (1) the distance to object surface points and by (2) the object surface reflectivity. The contrast ratio of the power in the fundamental frequency p^{-1} to the average (dc) power is proportional to depth and can be determined in real-time by analog video electronics. The analog range-image signal was digitized to create an 8-bit 512 × 512 image representing a 20 mm × 20 mm field of view approximately. The ambiguity interval was 38 mm. The digitizer averaged 16 frames so that the frame time is about 0.5 s ($M = 92,680$ assuming 7-bit accuracy).

Leger and Snyder (1984) developed two techniques for range imaging using the Talbot effect.

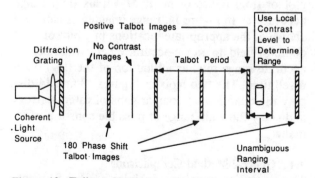

Positive Talbot Images

Use Local Contrast Level to Determine Range

Diffraction Grating

No Contrast Images

Talbot Period

Coherent Light Source

180 Phase Shift Talbot Images

Unambiguous Ranging Interval

Figure 12. Talbot effect or self-imaging property of gratings for ranging.

The first method used two gratings crossed at right angles to provide two independent channels for depth measurement. The second method uses a modulated grating created by performing optical spatial filtering operations on the original signal emanating from a standard grating. Two prototype sensors were built to demonstrate these methods. The ambiguity intervals were 7.3 mm and 4.6 mm. The figure of merit is similar to the Chavel and Strand sensor. Speckle noise (Goodman 1986, Leader 1986) is a problem with coherent light in these methods, and good range resolution is difficult to obtain from local contrast measures. Other research in this area has been pursued by Hane and Grover (1985).

9. Sensor Comparisons

The key performance factors of any range-imaging sensor are listed in the following table:

Depth of field	L_r
Range accuracy	σ_r
Pixel dwell time	T
Pixel rate	$1/T$
Range resolution	N_{bits}
Image size	$N_x \times N_y$
Angular field of view	$\theta_x \times \theta_y$
Lateral resolution	$\theta_x/N_x \times \theta_y/N_y$
Standoff distance	L_s
Nominal field of view	$(L_s + L_r/2)\theta_x \times$
	$(L_s + L_r/2)\theta_y$
Frame time	$T \times N_x \times N_y$
Frame rate	$1/(T \times N_x \times N_y)$

The figure of merit M used to evaluate sensors in this survey only uses the first three values. A full evaluation for a given application should consider all sensor parameters.

Different types of range imaging sensors are compared by showing the rated sensors in the survey in two scatterplots. In Figure 13, range-imaging sensors are shown at the appropriate locations in a plot of (log) figure of merit M versus (log) range accuracy σ. In Figure 14, range imaging sensors are shown at the appropriate locations in a plot of (log) depth-of-field to range-accuracy ratio (number of accurate range bits) as a function of the (log) pixel dwell time. The two plots in Figures 13 and 14 display the quantitative comparisons of rated sensors and show the wide range of possible sensor performance.

9.1 General Method Comparisons
The six optical ranging principles are briefly summarized below. Imaging laser radars are capable of

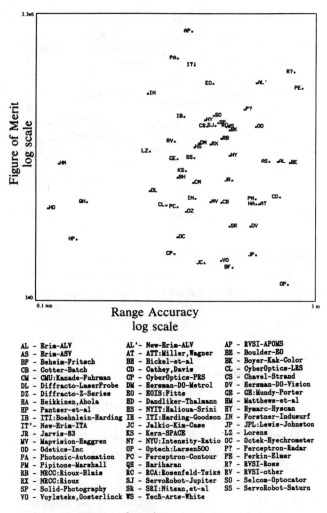

Figure 13. Figure of merit vs. range accuracy.

range accuracies from about 50 μ to 5 m over depths of field 250 to 25,000 times larger. They benefit from having very small source to detector separations and operate at higher speeds than many other types of range-imaging sensors because range is determined electronically. They are usually quite expensive, with commercially available units starting at around $100,000. Existing laser radars are sequential in data acquisition (they acquire one point at a time) although parallel designs have been suggested.

Triangulation sensors are capable of range accuracies beginning at about 1 μ over depths of field from 250 to 60,000 times larger. In the past, some have considered triangulation systems to be inaccurate or slow. Many believe that large baselines are required for reasonable accuracy. However, triangulation systems have shown themselves to be accurate, fast, and compact mainly owing to the advent of synchronous scanning approaches. Simple triangulation systems start between $1000 and

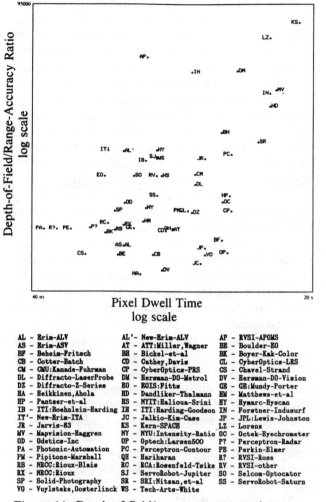

AL - Erim-ALV	AL'- New-Erim-ALV	AP - RVSI-APOMS
AS - Erim-ASV	AT - ATT:Miller,Wagner	BE - Boulder-EO
BF - Beheim-Fritsch	BH - Bickel-et-al	BK - Boyer-Kak-Color
CB - Cotter-Batch	CD - Cathey,Davis	CL - CyberOptics-LRS
CM - CMU:Kanade-Fuhrman	CP - CyberOptics-PRS	CS - Chavel-Strand
DL - Diffracto-LaserProbe	DM - Hersman-DO-Metrol	DV - Hersman-DO-Vision
DZ - Diffracto-Z-Series	EO - EOIS:Fitts	GE - GE:Mundy-Porter
HA - Heikkinen,Ahola	HD - Dandliker-Thalmann	HM - Matthews-et-al
HP - Pantser-et-al	HS - NYIT:Halioua-Srini	HY - Hymarc-Hyscan
IB - ITI:Boehnlein-Harding	IH - ITI:Harding-Goodson	IN - Forstner-Indusurf
IT'- New-Erim-ITA	JC - Jalkio-Kim-Case	JP - JPL:Lewis-Johnston
JR - Jarvis-83	KS - Kern-SPACE	LZ - Lorens
MV - Mapvision-Haggren	NY - NYU:Intensity-Ratio	OC - Octek-Eyechrometer
OD - Odetics-Inc	OP - Optech:Larsen500	P? - Perceptron-Radar
PA - Photonic-Automation	PC - Perceptron-Contour	PE - Perkin-Elmer
PM - Pipitone-Marshall	QH - Hariharan	R? - RVSI-other
RB - NRCC:Rioux-Blais	RC - RCA:Rosenfeld-Tsiks	RV - RVSI-other
RX - NRCC:Rioux	SJ - ServoRobot-Jupiter	SO - Selcom-Optocator
SP - Solid-Photography	SR - SRI:Nitzan,et-al	SS - ServoRobot-Saturn
VO - Vuylsteke,Oosterlinck	WS - Tech-Arts-White	

Figure 14. Depth-of-field/range-accuracy ratio versus pixel dwell time.

$10,000 depending on how much you put together yourself and how much needed equipment you already have. Commercially available turnkey systems can easily run upwards of $50,000, and fancier systems can run into the hundreds of thousands if there are requirements for fine accuracy over large working volumes. Triangulation systems go from totally sequential as in point scanners to almost parallel as in the intensity ratio scheme or the color encoded stripe scheme. Triangulation systems have been the mainstay of range imaging and promise to remain so.

Moire systems are limited to about the same accuracies as triangulation sensors (a few microns) and are not applicable unless surface slope constraints are satisfied. The depth of field of a moire system depends on the camera resolution and the object grating period p_o. For a 512×512 camera and a minimum of about 5 pixels per fringe, 100 phase transitions can be unwrapped yielding a depth of field on the order of $100 \, p_o$. Optical moire

components are a small part of the total system cost if fast computer hardware is used to carry out the necessary computations. Image array processors vary in cost, but a complete moire system with reasonable speed will probably run more than $50,000. Moire techniques are inherently parallel and will benefit from the development of parallel computing hardware.

Holographic interferometer systems can measure with accuracies of less than half a nanometer over as many wavelengths of light as can be disambiguated. Surface slope and smoothness constraints must be met before holographic methods are valid. The most accurate heterodyne methods are also the slowest and the most expensive. The quasi-heterodyne methods are faster and cheaper, but give up about an order of magnitude in accuracy compared to heterodyne. Holographic techniques are also inherently parallel and should benefit from the development of parallel computing hardware. Holographic systems are generally much more specialized than other optical techniques, and are applicable to fine grain surface inspection and nondestructive testing.

The Fresnel diffraction techniques based on the Talbot effect offer video frame rate range images using special-purpose analog video electronics. The range resolution of these systems is limited by the resolution of local contrast measures; it appears to be difficult to get more than seven or eight bits of range. Diffraction ranging is also inherently parallel.

Active focusing methods have great potential for compact, inexpensive range-imaging sensors, but high-precision systems are not likely.

Tactile methods still dominate many potential range-imaging applications where industry needs to exactly specify the shape of a prototype object. The reliability and accuracy of coordinate measuring machines (CMM's) over very large working volumes are hard to beat, but they are inherently slow and very expensive. If flexible noncontact optical methods can provide similar performance with reliability and ease of use, then a significant cost savings will be realized in applications currently requiring CMM's. At very fine scales, the (nonoptical) scanning tunneling microscope (Binnig and Rohrer 1985) is the state-of-the-art in very accurate (0.01 nm) surface studies. It is clear that active, optical ranging sensors have competition from other techniques.

Comments from this section and the survey are summarized in Figure 15. The first range value for each method in this table (ACC) is a good nominal accuracy rounded to the nearest power of ten

Category	ACC/DOF	Notes
Radar (Pulse,AM,FM)	0.1 mm 100 m	Detect Time, Phase, or Frequency Differences Signal Depends on Range, Surface Normal, Reflectance Beam Scanning Usually Required, No Computation History: Since 1903, Well known since 40's, Lasers since 70's Cost: Inexpensive to Extremely Expensive
Triangulation	1 μm 100 m	1 or More Cameras, 1 or more Projectors Scanned Point, Scanned Stripe, Multi-Stripe, Grid Binary Pattern, Color, Texture, Intensity Ratio Terms: Synchronous Scan, Scheimpflug Condition History: Since 200 B.C., Most Popular Method Cost: Inexpensive to Very Expensive
Moire Techniques	1 μm 10 m	Projector, Grating(s), Camera, Computer Fringe Tracking: Projection, Shadow Reference: Single-Frame, Multi-Frame (Phase-Shifted) Surface Slope Constraint, Non-coherent Light Computation Required, No Scanning History: Since 1859, Used Since 1950's in Mech.Eng. Cost: Inexpensive (excluding Computer)
Holographic Interferometry	0.1 nm 100 μm	Detector, Laser, Optics, Electronics, Computer Conventional: Real-Time, 2-Exposure, Time-Avg. Quasi-Heterodyne (Phase-Shifted), Heterodyne Surface Slope Constraint, Coherent Light Computation/Electronics Required, No Scanning History: Not Practical until Laser 1961, Big in NDT Cost: Inexpensive to Expensive
Focusing	1 mm 10 m	Measure Local Contrast, Blur, Displacement Limited Depth-of-Field to Accuracy Ratio History: Since 1800's, Gauss thin lens law Computation/Electronics Required, No Scanning Potential for Inexpensive Systems
Fresnel Diffraction (Talbot Effect)	0.1 mm 10 m	Laser, Grating, Camera / Not Explored by Many Video Rates, Limited Accuracy, Uses Local Contrast Electronics Required, No Scanning History: Discovered 1836, Used 1983 Potential for Inexpensive Systems

Figure 15. General comments on fundamental categories.

whereas the second value is the maximum nominal depth of field. Figure 16 indicates in a brief format the types of applications where the different ranging methods are being used or might be used.

10. Emerging Themes

As in any field, people always want equipment to be faster, more accurate, more reliable, easier to use, and less expensive. Range-imaging sensors are no exception. But compared to the state of the art 10 years ago, range imaging has come a long way. An image that took hours to acquire now takes less than a second. However, the sensors are only one part of the technology needed for practical automated systems. Algorithms and software play an even bigger role, and although research in range-image analysis and object recognition using range images (Besl and Jain 1985) has come a long way in recent years, there is still much to be done to achieve desired levels of performance for many applications.

Application	Radar	Trian	Moire	Holog	Focus	Diffr
Cartography	X	X				
Navigation	X	X			X	
Medical	X	X	X			
Shape Definition	X	X	X	X		
Bin Picking	X	X			X	X
Assembly	X	X	X	X	X	X
Inspection	X	X	X	X		X
Gauging	X	X	X	X		X

Figure 16. Methods and applications of range-imaging sensors.

Image acquisition speed is a critical issue. Since photons are quantized, the speed of data acquisition is limited by the number of photons that can be gathered by a pixel's effective photon collecting area during the pixel dwell time. Greater accuracy or faster frame times are possible using higher energy lasers since more photons can be collected reducing shot noise and improving signal-to-noise ratio. But today's higher-power laser diodes are difficult to focus to a small point size because of irregularities in the beam shapes. Moreover, higher-power lasers are a greater threat to eye safety if people will be working close to the range-imaging sensors (see appendix). Longer wavelengths (1.3–1.55 μ) are desirable for better eye safety, but not enough power is available from today's laser diodes at these wavelengths to obtain reasonable quality range images. The fiber optics communications industry is driving the development of longer wavelength laser diodes, and hopefully this situation will soon be remedied.

Another issue in the speed of data acquisition is scanning mechanisms. Many sensors are limited by the time for a moving part to move from point A to point B. Image dissector cameras are being explored by several investigators to avoid mechanical scanning. Mechanical scanning is a calibration and a reliability problem because moving parts do eventually wear out or break. However, today's mechanical scanners can offer years of reliable service.

Once considered state-of-the-art, 8-bit resolution sensors are giving way to sensors with 10 to 12 bits or more of resolution and possibly accuracy. Processing this information with inexpensive image processing hardware designed for 8-bit images is inappropriate. A few commercial vendors provide 16-bit and floating point image processing hardware, but it is generally more expensive.

Reliable subpixel image location is being achieved in many single light stripe triangulation sensors. It is commonly accepted that a fourth, a fifth, an eighth, or a tenth of a pixel accuracy can realistically be obtained with intensity weighted averaging techniques. Moreover, Kalman filtering (recursive least squares) algorithms (see e.g. Smith and Cheeseman 1987) are beginning to be used in vision algorithms for optimally combining geometric information from different sensing viewpoints or different range sensors. Such efforts will continue to increase the accuracy of sensors and systems.

Although not specifically mentioned, many range sensors also acquire registered intensity images at the same time. Although there is little 3-D metrology information in these images, there is a great deal of other useful information that is important for automated systems. A few researchers have addressed methods for using this additional information, but commercially available software solutions are more than several years away.

Range-imaging sensors are the data-gathering components of range-imaging systems, and ranging imaging systems are machine perception components of application systems. Algorithms, software, and hardware are typically developed in isolation and brought together later, but there are trends toward developing hardware that can incorporate programmability features that expedite operations common to many applications.

Acknowledgments. The author would like to express his appreciation to R. Tilove and W. Reguiro for their thorough reviews, and to G. Dodd, S. Walter, R. Khetan, J. Szczesniak, M. Stevens, S. Marin, R. Hickling, W. Wiitanen, R. Smith, T. Sanderson, M. Dell'Eva, H. Stern, and J. Sanz.

References

Agin GJ, Highnam, PT (1983) Movable light stripe sensor for obtaining 3D coordinate measurements. Proceedings SPIE Conference on 3-D Machine Perception (360):326

Ahola R, Heikkinen T, Manninen M (1985) 3D image acquisition by scanning time of flight measurements. Proceedings International Conference on Advances in Image Processing and Pattern Recognition

Altschuler MD, Altschuler BR, Toboada J (1981) Laser electro-optic system for rapid 3D topographic mapping of surfaces. Optical Engineering 20(6):953–961

Andresen K (1986) The phase shift method applied to moire image processing. Optik 72:115–119

ANSI 1986. American National Standard for the safe use of lasers. (ANSI Z136.1-1986) American National Standards Institute, New York

Asada M, Ichikawa H, Tsuji S (1986) Determining surface property by projecting a stripe pattern. Proceedings International Conference on Pattern Recognition IEEE-CS, IAPR: 1162–1164

Banic J, Sizgoric S, O'Neill R (1987) Airborne scanning lidar bathymeter measures water depth. Laser Focus/Electro-Optics: 48–52

Bastuschek CM, Schwartz JT (1984) Preliminary implementation of a ratio image depth sensor. Robotics Research Report No. 28, Courant Institute of Mathematical Sciences, New York University, New York

Beheim G, Fritsch K (1986) Range finding using frequency-modulated laser diode. Applied Optics, 25(9):1439–1442

Besl PJ (1987) Range imaging sensors. Tech. Report GMR-6090. Computer Science Dept., General Motors Research Labs, Warren, MI

Besl PJ (1988) Active optical range imaging sensors. In: Advances in Machine Vision: Architectures and Applications. J. Sanz (Ed.), Springer-Verlag, New York

Besl PJ, Jain RC (1985) Three dimensional object recognition. ACM Computing Surveys 17(1):75–145

Bickel G, Hausler G, Maul M (1984) Optics in Modern Science and Technology, Conf. Dig. ICO-13:534

Bickel G, Hausler G, Maul M (1985) Triangulation with expanded range of depth. Optical Engineering 24(6):975–979

Binger N, Harris SJ (1987) Applications of laser radar technology. Sensors 4(4):42–44

Binnig G, Rohrer H (1985) The scanning tunneling microscope. Scientific American 253,2 (Aug), 50–69

Blais F, Rioux M (1986) Biris: a simple 3D sensor. Proceedings SPIE Conference on Optics, Illumination, and Image Sensing for Machine Vision, 728:235–242

Boehnlein AJ, Harding KG (1986) Adaptation of a parallel architecture computer to phase-shifted moire interferometry. Proceedings SPIE Conference on Optics, Illumination, and Image Sensing for Machine Vision, 728:132–146

Boulder Electro-Optics (1986) Product information, Boulder, Colorado. (now Boulder Melles Griot)

Boyer KL, Kak AC (1987) Color encoded structured light for rapid active ranging. IEEE Transactions Pattern Analysis Machine Intelligence PAMI-9, 1:14–28

Brou P (1984) Finding the orientation of objects in vector maps. International Journal of Robot Research 3:4

Bumbaca F, Blais F, Rioux M (1986) Real-time correction of 3D nonlinearities for a laser rangefinder. Optical Engineering 25(4):561–565

Carrihill B (1986) The intensity ratio depth sensor. Ph.D. dissertation, Courant Institute of Mathematical Sciences, New York University, New York

Carrihill B, Hummel R (1985) Experiments with the intensity ratio depth sensor. Computer Vision, Graphics, Image Processing 32:337–358

Case SK, Jalkio JA, Kim RC (1987) 3D vision system analysis and design. In: Three-Dimensional Machine Vision, T. Kanade (Ed.), Kluwer Academic, Boston, pp. 63–96

Cathey WT, Davis WC (1986) Vision system with ranging for maneuvering in space. Optical Engineering 24(7):821–824. See also Imaging system with range to each pixel. Journal of the Optical Society of America A 3(9):1537–1542

CDRH 1985. Federal Register, Part III, Dept. of Health and Human Services, 21 CFR Parts 1000 and 1040 [Docket No. 80N-0364], Laser Products; Amendments to Performance Standard; Final Rule. For further info, Contact Glenn Conklin, Center for Devices and Radiological Health (HFZ-84), U.S. Food and Drug Administration, 5600 Fishers Lane, Rockville, MD 20857

Chang M, Hu CP, Lam P, Wyant JC (1985) High precision deformation measurement by digital phase shifting holographic interferometry. Applied Optics 24(22):3780–3783

Chavel P, Strand TC (1984) Range measurement using Talbot diffraction imaging of gratings. Applied Optics 23(6):862–871

Church EL, Vorburger TV, Wyant JC (1985) Direct comparison of mechanical and optical measurements of the finish of precision machined optical surfaces. Optical Engineering 24(3):388–395

Cline HE, Holik AS, Lorenson WE (1982) Computer-aided surface reconstruction of interference contours. Applied Optics 21(24):4481–4489

Cline HE, Lorenson WE, Holik AS (1984) Automated moire contouring. Applied Optics 23(10):1454–1459

Corle TR, Fanton JT, Kino GS (1987) Distance measurements by differential confocal optical ranging. Applied Optics 26(12):2416–2420

Cotter SM, Batchelor BG (1986) Deriving range maps at real-time video rates. Sensor Review 6(4):185–192

Cowley JM, Moodie AF (1957) Fourier images: I—the point source. Proceedings Physical Society 70:486–496

Cunningham R (1986) Laser radar for the space conscious. Lasers and Applications July: 18–20

Cyberoptics (1987) Product information. Minneapolis, MN

Damm L (1987) A minimum-size all purpose fiber optical proximity sensor. Proceedings Vision'87 Conference: 6-71—6-91

Dandliker R, Ineichen B, Mottier F (1973) Optics Communications 9:412

Dandliker R (1980) Heterodyne holography review. Progress in Optics 17:1

Dandliker R, Thalmann R (1985) Heterodyne and quasi-heterodyne holographic interferometry. Optical Engineering 24(5):824–831

Dandridge A (1982) Current induced frequency modulation in diode lasers. Electron. Letters 18:302

Denstman H (1980) State-of-the-art optics: Automated image focusing. Industrial Photography, July: 33—37

Dereniak EL, Crowe DG (1984) Optical Radiation Detectors. Wiley, New York

Diffracto (1987) Product Literature. Laser probe digital ranging sensor. Diffracto, Ltd., Windsor, Canada

Digital Optronics (1986) Product literature. Springfield, VA

Dimatteo PL, Ross JA, Stern HK (1979) Arrangement for sensing the geometric characteristics of an object. (RVSI) U.S. Patent 4175862

Electro-Optical Information Systems (1987) Product Information. EOIS, Santa Monica, CA

Faugeras OD, Hebert M (1986) The representation, recognition, and locating of 3-D objects. International Journal of Robotic Research 5(3):27–52

Froome KD, Bradsell RH (1961) Distance measurement by means of a light ray modulated at a microwave frequency. Journal of Scientific Instrumentation 38:458–462

Gasvik KJ (1983) Moire technique by means of digital image processing. Applied Optics 22(23):3543–3548

Goldberg N (1982) Inside autofocus: How the magic works. Popular Photography, Feb: 77–83

Goodman JW (1986) A random walk through the field of speckle. Optical Engineering 25(5):610–612

Gottlieb M (1983) Electro-Optic and Acousto-Optic Scanning and Deflection. Marcel-Dekker, New York

Griffin DR (1958) Listening in the dark: The acoustic orientation of bats and men. Yale University Press, New Haven, CT

Grossman P (1987) Depth from Focus. Pattern Recognition Letters 5(1):63–69

Haggren H, Leikas E (1987) Mapvision—The photogrammetric machine vision system. Proceedings Vision'87 Conference: 10-37–10-50

Halioua M, Srinivasan V (1987) Method and apparatus for surface profilometry. New York Institute of Technology, Old Westury, NY. U.S. Patent 4,641,972

Halioua M, Krishnamurthy RS, Liu H, Chiang FP (1983) Projection moire with moving gratings for automated 3D topography. Applied Optics 22(6):850–855

Hall EL, Tio JBK, McPherson CA, Sadjadi FA (1982) Measuring curved surfaces for robot vision. Computer 15(12):42–54

Hane K, Grover CP (1985) Grating imaging and its application to displacement sensing. Journal of Optical Society of America A 2(13):9

Harding KG (1983) Moire interferometry for industrial inspection. Lasers and Applications Nov.: 73

Harding KG, Goodson K (1986) Hybrid high accuracy structured light profiler. Proceedings SPIE Conference on Optics, Illumination, and Image Sensing for Machine Vision 728:132–145

Harding KG, Tait R (1986) Moire techniques applied to automated inspection of machined parts. Proceedings Vision'86 Conference, SME, Dearborn, MI

Hariharan P (1985) Quasi-heterodyne hologram interferometry. Optical Engineering 24(4):632–638

Hariharan P, Oreb BF, Brown N (1983) Applied Optics 22(6):876

Harvey JE, MacFarlane MJ, Forgham JL (1985) Design and performance of ranging telescopes: Monolithic vs. synthetic aperture. Optical Engineering 24(1):183–188

Hausler G, Maul M (1985) Telecentric scanner for 3D sensing. Optical Engineering 24(6):978–980

Heikkinen T, Ahola R, Manninen M, Myllyla R (1986) Recent results of the performance analysis of a 3D sensor based on time of flight. Proceedings SPIE Quebec International Symposium on Optical and Opto-electronic Applied Sciences and Engineering.

Hersman M, Goodwin F, Kenyon S, Slotwinski A (1987) Coherent laser radar application to 3D vision and metrology. Proceedings Vision'87 Conference 3-1–3-12

Holland SW, Rossol L, Ward MR (1979) Consight-1: A vision controlled robot system for transferring parts from belt conveyors. In: Computer Vision and Sensor-Based Robots G.G. Dodd and L. Rossol (Eds.), Plenum Press, New York, pp. 81–97

Horn BKP (1968) Focusing. MIT, Project MAC, AI Memo 160

Hulsmeyer C (1904) Hertzian wave projecting and receiving apparatus adapted to indicate or give warning of the presence of a metallic body, such as a ship or a train, in the line of projection of such waves. U.K. Patent 13,170

HYMARC (1987) Product information. Ottawa, Ontario Canada

Idesawa M, Yatagai Y, Soma T (1976) A method for the automatic measurement of 3D shapes by new type of moire topography. Proceedings 3rd International Conference Pattern Recognition: 708

Idesawa M, Yatagai Y, Soma T (1977) Scanning moire method and automatic measurement of 3D shapes. Applied Optics 16(8):2152–2162

Idesawa M, Yatagai Y (1980) 3D shape input and processing by moire technique. Proceedings 5th International Conference Pattern Recognition, IEEE-CS: 1085–1090

Idesawa M, Kinoshita G (1986) New type of miniaturized optical range sensing methods RORS and RORST. Journal of Robotic Systems 3(2):165–181

Inokuchi S, Sato K, Matsuda F (1984) Range imaging system for 3-D object recognition. Proceedings 7th International Conference Pattern Recognition: 806–808

Jalkio J, Kim R, Case S (1985) 3D inspection using multistripe structured light. Optical Engineering 24(6):966–974

Jalkio J, Kim R, Case S (1986) Triangulation based range sensor design. Proceedings SPIE Conference on Optics, Illumination, and Image Sensing for Machine Vision, 728:132–146

Jarvis RA (1976) Focus optimization criteria for computer image processing. Microscope 24(2):163–180

Jarvis RA (1982) Computer vision and robotics laboratory. IEEE Computer 15(6):9–23

Jarvis RA (1983a) A laser time-of-flight range scanner for robotic vision. IEEE Transactions Pattern Analysis Machine Intelligence PAMI-5, 5:505–512

Jarvis RA (1983b) A perspective on range finding techniques for computer vision. IEEE Transactions Pattern Analysis Machine Intelligence PAMI-5, 2:122–139

Jelalian AV, McManus RG (1977) AGARD Panel Proceeding No. 77. June, Sec. 2.1, pp 1–21

Johnson M (1985) Fiber displacement sensors for metrology and control. Optical Engineering 24(6):961–965

Kak AC (1985) Depth perception for robot vision. In: Handbook of Industrial Robotics, S. Nof (Ed.) Wiley, New York, pp 272–319

Kanade T, Asada H (1981) Noncontact visual 3D rangefinding devices. In: Proceedings SPIE 3D Machine Perception, B.R. Altschuler (Ed.):48–53

Kanade T, Fuhrman M (1985) A noncontact optical proximity sensor for measuring surface shape. In: Three-Dimensional Machine Vision, T. Kanade (Ed.), Kluwer Academic Boston, pp 151–194

Karara HM (1985) Close-range photogrammetry: where are we and where are we heading? Photogrammetric Engineering and Remote Sensing 51(5):537–544

Kawata H, Endo H, Eto Y (1985) A study of laser radar. Proceedings 10th International Technical Conference on Experimental Safety Vehicles

Kellogg WN (1961) Porpoises and sonar. University of Chicago Press, Chicago, IL

Kern Instruments (1987) Product Information. Gottwald, R. and Berner, W., The new Kern system for positioning and automated coordinate evaluation; advanced technology for automated 3D coordinate determination. Brewster, NY. and Aarau, Switzerland

Keyes RJ (1986) Heterodyne and nonheterodyne laser transceivers. Review of Scientific Instrumentation 57(4):519–528

Khetan RP (1975) The theory and application of projection moire methods. Ph.D. dissertation. Dept. of Engineering Mechanics, State University of New York, Stony Brook

Kingslake R (1983) Optical system design, Academic Press, New York

Kinoshita G, Idesawa M, Naomi S (1986) Robotic range sensor with projection of bright ring pattern. Journal of Robotic Systems 3(3):249–257

Koenderink JJ, Van Doorn AJ (1986) Dynamic shape. Biological Cybernetics 53:383–396

Kratky V (1979) Real-time photogrammetric support of dynamic 3D control. Photogrammetric Engineering and Remote Sensing 45(9):1231–1242

Krotkov EP (1986) Focusing. Ph.D. Dissertation, U. Penn, Phila, PA

Krotkov E, Martin JP (1986) Range from focus. Proceedings IEEE International Conference on Robotics and Automation, IEEE-CS: 1093–1098

Kurahashi A, Adachi M, Idesawa M (1986) A prototype of optical proximity sensor based on RORS. Journal of Robotic Systems 3(2):183–190

Labuz J, McVey ES (1986) Camera and projector motion for range mapping. Proceedings SPIE Conference on Optics, Illumination, and Image Sensing for Machine Vision 728:227–234

Lamy F, Liegeois C, Meyrueis P (1981) 3D automated pattern recognition using moire techniques. Proceedings SPIE 360:345–351

Landman MM, Robertson SJ (1986) A flexible industrial system for automated 3D inspection. Proceedings SPIE Conference on Optics, Illumination, and Image Sensing for Machine Vision, 728:203–209

Laser Technology (1986) Product information. Norristown, PA

Leader JC (1986) Speckle effects on coherent laser radar detection efficiency. Optical Engineering 25(5):644–650

Leger JR, Snyder MA (1984) Real-time depth measurement and display using Fresnel diffraction and white-light processing. Applied Optics 23(10):1655–1670

Leith E, Upatnieks J (1962) Reconstructed wavefronts and communication theory. Journal of Optical Society America 54:1123–1130

Lewis RA, Johnston AR (1977) A scanning laser rangefinder for a robotic vehicle. Proceedings 5th International Joint Conference on Artificial Intelligence: 762–768

Lewis JRT, Sopwith T (1986) 3D surface measurement by microcomputer. Image and Vision Computing 4(3):159–166

Livingstone FR, Tulai AF, Thomas MR (1987) Application of 3-D vision to the measurement of marine propellers. Proceedings Vision'87 Conference: 10-25–10-36

Livingstone FR, Rioux M (1986) Development of a large field of view 3D vision system. Proceedings SPIE 665

Lord Rayleigh (JW Strutt) (1874) On the manufacture and theory of diffraction gratings. Phil. Mag. 47(81):193

Lord Rayleigh (JW Strutt) (1881) Phil. Mag. 11:196

Lorenz RD (1984) Theory and design of optical/electronic probes for high performance measurement of parts. Ph.D. dissertation, Univ. of Wisconsin-Madison

Lorenz RD (1986) A novel, high-range-to-resolution ratio, optical sensing technique for high speed surface geometry measurements. Proceedings SPIE Conference on Optics, Illumination, and Image Sensing for Machine Vision 728:152–146

Macy WW (1983) Two-dimensional fringe pattern analysis. Applied Optics 22(22):3893–3901

Mader DL (1985) Holographic interferometry of pipes: precision interpretation by least squares fitting. Applied Optics 24(22):3784–3790

Marshall G (1985) Laser Beam Scanning, Marcel-Dekker, New York

Matsuda R (1986) Multifunctional optical proximity sensor using phase modulation. Journal of Robotic Systems 3(2):137–147

Matthews HJ, Hamilton DK, Sheppard CJR (1986) Surface profiling by phase-locked interferometry. Applied Optics 25(14):2372–2374

Mersch SH, Doles JE (1985) Cylindrical optics applied to machine vision. Proceedings Vision'85 Conference, SME, 4-53–4-63

Mertz L (1983) Real-time fringe pattern analysis. Applied Optics 22(10):1535–1539

Miller GL, Wagner ER (1987) An optical rangefinder for autonomous robot cart navigation. Proceedings SPIE Industrial Electronics, Cambridge, MA, (November)

Moore DT, Traux BE (1979) Phase-locked moire fringe analysis for automated contouring of diffuse surfaces. Applied Optics 18(1):91–96

Mundy JL, Porter GB (1986) A three-dimensional sensor based on structured light. In: Three-Dimensional Machine Vision, T. Kanade (Ed.), Kluwer Academic, Boston, pp 3–62

Nakagawa Y, Ninomiya T (1987) Three-dimensional vision systems using the structured light method for inspecting solder joints and assembly robots. Three-Dimensional Machine Vision, T. Kanade (Ed.), Kluwer Academic, Boston, pp 543–565

Nevatia R, Binford TO (1973) Structured descriptions of complex objects. Proceedings 3rd International Joint Conference on Artificial Intelligence: 641–647

Newport Corp (1987) Product Information. Design and testing with holography. Machine vision components. Fountain Valley, CA

Nitzan D, Brain AE, Duda RO (1977) The measurement and use of registered reflectance and range data in scene analysis. Proceedings IEEE 65(2):206–220.

Nitzan D, Bolles R, Kremers J, Mulgaonkar P (May 1986) 3D vision for robot applications. NATO Workshop on Knowledge Engineering for Robotic Applications, Maratea, Italy

Oboshi T (1976) Three-Dimensional Imaging Techniques. Academic Press, New York

Oster G (1965) Moire optics: a bibliography. Journal of Optical Society America 55:1329

Ozeki O, Nakano T, Yamamoto S (1986) Real-time range measurement device for 3D object recognition. IEEE Trans. Pattern Analysis Machine Intelligence. PAMI-8, 4, 550–553

Pantzer D, Politch J, Ek L (1986) Heterodyne profiling instrument for the angstrom region. Applied Optics 25(22):4168–4172

Parthasarathy S, Birk J, Dessimoz J (1982) Laser rangefinder for robot control and inspection. Proceedings SPIE Robot Vision 336:2–11

Pelowski KR (1986) 3D measurement with machine vision. Proceedings Vision'86 Conference: 2-17–2-31

Pentland AP (1987) A new sense of depth of field. IEEE Transaction Pattern Analysis Machine Intelligence PAMI-9, 4:523–531

Perceptron (1987) Product information. Farmington Hills, MI

Perrin JC, Thomas A (1979) Electronic processing of moire fringes: application to moire topography and comparison with photogrammetry. Applied Optics 18(4):563–574

Peterson RW, Robinson GM, Carlsen RA, Englund CD, Moran PJ, Wirth WM (1984) Interferometric measurements of the surface profile of moving samples. Applied Optics 23(10):1464–1466

Photonic Automation, Inc. (1987) Product literature. Improving automated SMT inspection with 3D vision. M. Juha and J. Donahue. Santa Ana, CA

Pipitone FJ, Marshall TG (1983) A wide-field scanning triangulation rangefinder for machine vision. International Journal of Robotics Research 2(1):39–49

Pinckney HFL (1978) Theory and development of an on-line 30 Hz video photogrammetry system for real-time 3D control. International Archives of Photogrammetry, Vol. XXII, Part V. 2:38 pages

Pirodda L (1982) Shadow and projection moire techniques for absolute and relative mapping of surface shapes. Optical Engineering 21:640

Popplestone RJ, Brown CM, Ambler AP, Crawford GF (1975) Forming models of plane-and-cylinder faceted bodies from light stripes. Proceedings 4th International Joint Conference on Artificial Intelligence: 664–668

Potmesil M (1983) Generating models of solid objects by matching 3D surface segments. Proceedings 8th International Joint Conference on Artificial Intelligence: 1089–1093

Potsdamer J, Altschuler M (1982) Surface measurement by space-encoded projected beam system. Computer Graphics Image Processing 18:1–17

Pryputniewicz RJ (1985) Heterodyne holography applications in studies of small components. Optical Engineering 24(5):849–854

Quist TM, Bicknell WE, Bates DA (1978) ARPA Semiannual report: optics research, Lincoln Laboratory, MIT

Reid GT (1986) Automatic fringe pattern analysis: A review. Optics and Lasers in Engineering 7:37–68

Rioux M (1984) Laser range finder based upon synchronized scanners. Applied Optics 23(21):3837–3844

Rioux M, Blais F (1986) Compact 3-D camera for robotic applications. Journal of Optical Society of America A 3(9):1518–1521

Robotic Vision Systems, Inc (1987) Product literature. RVSI, Hauppage, NY

Rocker F (1974) Localization and classification of 3D objects. Proceedings 2nd International Conference Pattern Recognition: 527–528

Rosenfeld JP, Tsikos CJ (1986) High-speed space encoding projector for 3D imaging. Proceedings SPIE Conference on Optics, Illumination, and Image Sensing for Machine Vision, 728:146–151

Ross JA (1978) Methods and systems for 3D measurement. U.S. Patent 4,199,253. (RVSI, Hauppage, NY)

Sampson RE (1987) 3D range sensor via phase shift detection (Insert). IEEE Computer 20(8):23–24

Sasaki O, Okazaki H (1986) Sinusoidal phase modulating interferometry for surface profile measurement. And Analysis of measurement accuracy in sinusoidal phase modulating interferometry. Applied Optics 25(18): 3137–3140,3152–3158

Sato Y, Kitagawa H, Fujita H (1982) Shape measurement of curved objects using multiple-slit ray projection. IEEE Transactions Pattern Analysis Machine Intelligence PAMI-4, 6:641–649

Sato K, Inokuchi S (1985) 3D surface measurement by space encoding range imaging. Journal of Robotic Systems 2(1):27–39

Schewe H, Forstner W (1986) The program PALM for automatic line and surface measurement using image matching techniques. Proceedings Symposium International Society for Photogrammetry and Remote Sensing, Vol. 26, Part 3/2:608–622

Schlag JF, Sanderson AC, Neumann CP, Wimberly FC (1983) Implementation of automatic focusing algorithms for a computer vision system with camera control. CMU-RI-TR-83-14

Schmitt F, Maitre H, Clainchard A, Lopez-Krahm J (1985) Acquisition and representation of real object surface data. SPIE Proceedings Biostereometrics Conf., Vol. 602

Schmitt F, Barsky B, Du W (1986) An adaptive subdivision method for surface-fitting from sampled data. Computer Graphics 20(4):179–188

Schuman W, Dubas M (1979) Holographic Interferometry. Springer-Verlag, Berlin

Schwartz J (1983) Structured light sensors for 3D robot vision. Robotics Research Report No. 8, Courant Institute of Mathematical Sciences, New York University, New York

Sciammarella CA (1982) The moire method—A review. Exp. Mech. 22:418–433

SELCOM (1987) Optocator product information. Valdese, NC, US; Partille, Sweden; Krefeld, West Germany

Servo-Robot (1987) Product information. Boucherville, Quebec, Canada

Shirai Y, Suwa (1972) Recognition of polyhedra with a range finder, Pattern Recognition 4:243–250

Silvaggi C, Luk F, North W (1986) Position/dimension by structured light. Experimental Techniques: 22–25

Skolnick MI (1962) Introduction to Radar Systems. McGraw-Hill, New York

Slevogt H (1974) Technische Optik. Walter de Gruyter, Berlin, pp 55–57

Smith RC, Cheeseman P (1987) On the representation and estimation of spatial uncertainty. International Journal of Robotics Res. 5(4):56–68

Solid Photography, Inc. (1977) (now Robotic Vision Systems, Inc. (RVSI), Hauppage, NY)

Srinivasan V, Liu HC, Halioua M (1985) Automated phase measuring profilometry: A phase-mapping approach. Applied Optics 24(2):185–188

Stockman G, Hu G (1986) Sensing 3D surface patches using a projected grid. Proceedings Computer Vision Pattern Recognition Conference: 602–607

Strand T (1983) Optical three-dimensional sensing. Optical Engineering 24(1):33–40

Svetkoff DJ (Oct. 1986) Towards a high resolution, video rate, 3D sensor for machine vision. Proceedings SPIE Conference on Optics, Illumination, and Image Sensing for Machine Vision, 728:216–226

Svetkoff DJ, Leonard PF, Sampson RE, Jain RC (1984) Techniques for real-time feature extraction using range information. Proceedings SPIE—Intelligent Robotics and Computer Vision 521:302–309

Talbot H (1836) Facts relating to optical science No. IV. Phil. Mag. 9:401–407

Technical Arts Corp (1987) Product Literature. Redmond, WA

Teich MC (1968) Infrared heterodyne detection. Proceedings IEEE 56(1):37–46

Tenenbaum J (1970) Accommodation in computer vision. Ph.D. dissertation, Stanford University, Stanford, CA

Terras R (1986) Detection of phase in modulated optical signals subject to ideal Rayleigh fading. Journal of Optical Society of America A 3(11):1816–1825

Thalmann R, Dandliker R (1985) Holographic contouring using electronic phase measurement. Optical Engineering 24(6):930–935

Theocaris PS (1969) Moire fringes in strain analysis. Pergamon Press, New York

Tozer BA, Glanville R, Gordon AL, Little MJ, Webster JM, Wright DG (1985) Holography applied to inspection and measurement in an industrial environment. Optical Engineering 24(5):746–753

Tsai R (1986) An efficient and accurate camera calibration technique for 3D machine vision. Proceedings Computer Vision Pattern Recognition Conference IEEE-CS:364–374

Vest CM (1979) Holographic interferometry. Wiley, New York

Vuylsteke P, Oosterlinck A (1986) 3D perception with a single binary coded illumination pattern. Proceedings SPIE Conference on Optics, Illumination, and Image Sensing for Machine Vision, 728:195–202

Wagner JW (1986) Heterodyne holographic interferometry for high-resolution 3D sensing. Proceedings SPIE Conference on Optics, Illumination, and Image Sensing for Machine Vision, 728:173–182

Wagner JF (June 1987) Sensors for dimensional measurement. Proceedings Vision'87 Conference, pp 13-1–13-18

Wang JY (1984) Detection efficiency of coherent optical radar. Applied Optics 23(19):3421–3427

Wang JY, Bartholomew BJ, Streiff ML, Starr EF (1984) Imaging CO_2 radar field tests. Applied Optics 23(15):2565–2571

Wang JY (1986) Lidar signal fluctuations caused by beam translation and scan. Applied Optics 25(17):2878–2885

Wang YE, Mitiche A, Aggarwal JK (1985) Inferring local surface orientation with the aid of grid coding. IEEE Workshop on Computer Vision: Representation and Control: pp 96–104

Wei D, Gini M (1983) The use of taper light beam for object recognition. In: Robot Vision, R. Pugh (Ed.), IFS Publications, Springer-Verlag, Berlin

Will PM, Pennington KS (1972) Grid coding: a novel technique for image processing. Proceedings IEEE 60(6):669–680

Winthrop JT, Worthington CR (1965) Theory of fresnel images I. Plane periodic objects in monochromatic light. Journal of the Optical Society of America 55(4):373–381

Wuerker RF, Hill DA (1985) Holographic microscopy. Optical Engineering 24(3):480–484

Yamamoto H, Sato K, Inokuchi S (1986) Range imaging system based on binary image accumulation. Proceedings International Conference on Pattern Recognition IEEE:233–235

Yatagai T, Idesawa M, Yamaashi Y, Suzuki M (1982) Interactive fringe analysis system: Applications to moire contourogram and interferogram. Optical Engineering 21(5):901

Yeung KK, Lawrence PD (1986) A low-cost 3D vision system using space-encoded spot projections. Proceedings SPIE Conference on Optics, Illumination, and Image Sensing for Machine Vision, 728:160–172

Zuk DM, Dell'Eva ML (1983) Three-dimensional vision system for the adaptive suspension vehicle. Final Report No. 170400-3-F, ERIM, DARPA 4468, Defense Supply Service-Washington

Note added in proofs: Several uncited references have been included to provide a more complete bibliography.

Appendix: Eye Safety

Lasers are used in all types of active optical range imaging sensors. When people are exposed to laser radiation, eye safety is critical. An understanding of eye safety issues is important to the range imaging applications engineer.

Concerning the *sale of laser products* across state lines in the United States, vendors of end-user equipment containing lasers must comply with the requirements of the Food and Drug Administration's Center for Devices and Radiological Health (CDRH). Concerning the *use of laser products,* most organizations follow the ANSI Z136.1 Standard regulations. The ANSI and CDRH regulations are essentially the same except for some fine points. A simplified version of the regulations is given below. The applications engineer should consult the CDRH (1985) regulations or the ANSI (1986) regulations for complete details.

Lasers emit electromagnetic radiation that is either visible (light) or invisible (infrared or ultraviolet). When laser radiation is received by the human eye, damage may occur in the retina or the cornea depending upon the wavelength if the radiation levels exceed the maximum permissible exposure. Visible light regulations are different from invisible regulations because of the aversion response. People will blink or look away in less than 0.25 s when exposed to intense visible radiation. With invisible radiation, no such aversion response occurs although broad spectrum near-infrared laser diodes are visible to many people. Although not listed separately in official documents, the regulations may be viewed as two distinct sets of safety classes, one set for visible and another set for invisible. Within each class, two requirements must be met: (1) the average power through a standard aperture (usually 7-mm dia) must be less than the maximum average power for that class laser at every point in the field of view of the laser, and (2) the energy in any pulse received by the standard aperture must be less than the maximum energy level for that class. One subtlety important to range-imaging sensors is that the pulse repetition frequency (PRF) factor is included in ANSI regulations, but not in CDRH regulations.

For visible light (400–700 nm wavelengths), there are really five classes of lasers. Actual ratings are wavelength dependent, but the following list gives a reasonable indication of allowable average powers through the standard 7 mm diameter aperture with a 5 diopter lens.

- Class I (No Risk, Eye Safe)
  Average Power < 0.4 µW.
- Class II (Low Power, Caution)
  0.4 µW < Average Power < 1 mW
- Class IIIa (Medium Low Power, Caution)
  1mW < Average Power < 5mW
- Class IIIb (Medium Power, Danger)
  5 mW < Average Power < 500 mW
- Class IV (High Power, Danger)
  Average Power > 500 mW

Pulse requirements are more complicated and must be computed from equations and tables listed in CDRH and ANSI regulations based on wavelength.

For invisible lasers (UV:200–400 nm, IR:700 nm–1 mm wavelengths), there are three classes:

- Class I (No Risk, Eye Safe)
  Wavelength-Dependent Regulations
- Class IIIb (Medium Power, Danger)
  Average Power < 500 mW, Not Class I

- Class IV (High Power, Danger)
  Average Power > 500 mW

Again, pulse requirements must be computed from equations and tables listed in CDRH and ANSI regulations based on wavelength. There are no low or medium low power categories here. However, ANSI regulations vary slightly from CDRH regulations in that they allow a Class IIIa (Caution) for infrared lasers with powers that exceed the Class I limit by less than a factor of five (Sec. 3.3.3.2, ANZI Z136.1, 1986).

About the Authors

PAUL J. BESL graduated *summa cum laude* in physics from Princeton University in 1978 and received the M.S. and Ph.D. degrees in electrical engineering and computer science from the University of Michigan, Ann Arbor, in 1981 and 1986, respectively. In 1987, he received a Rackham Distinguished Dissertation Award from the University of Michigan for his dissertation on range image understanding.

From 1979 to 1981, he did computer simulations for Bendix Aerospace Systems in Ann Arbor, MI, and from 1981 to 1983, worked on the Geomod solid modeling system at Structural Dynamics Research Corp. in Cincinnati, OH. Since 1986, he has been a research scientist at General Motors Research Laboratories in Warren, MI, where his primary research interest is computer vision, especially range image analysis and geometric modeling for image understanding. Dr. Besl is a member of the Institute of Electrical and Electronics Engineers, the Association for Computing Machinery, the American Association for Artificial Intelligence, and the Machine Vision Association of the Society of Manufacturing Engineers.

YORAM BRESLER received the B.Sc. and M.Sc. degrees from the Technion, Israel Institute of Technology, Haifa, Israel in 1974 and 1981, respectively, and the Ph.D. degree from Stanford University, Stanford, CA, in 1985, all in electrical engineering.

From 1974 to 1979 he served as an electronics engineer in the Israeli Defense Force. From 1979 to 1981 he worked on algorithms for autonomous TV aircraft guidance at the Flight Control Lab, Department of Aeronautical Engineering, Technion, Israel. From 1985 to 1987, he was a Research Associate at the Information Systems Laboratory at Stanford University, where his research involved array signal processing and medical imaging. Since 1987, he has been an Assistant Professor at the Department of Electrical and Computer Engineering at the University of Illinois at Urbana-Champaign. Dr. Bresler's research interests include statistical methods in imaging and in array signal processing.

JEFFREY A. FESSLER received the B.S. degree from Purdue University, West Lafayette, IN, in 1985 and the M.S. degree from Stanford University, Stanford, CA, in 1986, both in electrical engineering.

Since 1986, he has been a National Science Foundation Graduate Fellow at Stanford, working toward the Ph.D. degree in electrical engineering. His research interests include estimation theory and its applications to medical imaging and bioengineering.

LESTER A. GERHARDT holds a joint professorship with RPI's Electrical, Computer, and Systems Engineering and Computer Science Departments and is Director of the RPI CIM Program.

WILLIAM I. KWAK is a research assistant with the RPI CIM Program and a Ph.D. candidate with the RPI Electrical, Computer, and Systems Engineering Department.

ALBERT MACOVSKI received the B.E.E. degree from C.C.N.Y. in 1950, the M.E.E. degree from the Polytechnic Institute of Brooklyn in 1953, and the Ph.D. degree in electrical engineering from Stanford University in 1968.

From 1950–1957 Dr. Macovski was a member of the technical staff at R.C.A. Laboratories. From 1957–1960 he was an Assistant and then Associate Professor at the Polytechnic Institute of Brooklyn, NY. From 1960–1971 Dr. Macovski was a staff scientist at the Stanford Research Institute. Following one year as a special NIH fellow at the U.C. Medical Center in San Francisco, he joined the Stanford Faculty as an Adjunct Professor and then full Professor of Electrical Engineering and Radiology, his present position.

Dr. Macovski's research has been in a variety of imaging systems including television, facsimile, holography, and interferometry. During the past five years he has been particularly involved with diagnostic imaging techniques in ultrasound, radiography, and magnetic resonance.

Dr. Macovski is a Fellow of the Institute of Electrical and Electronics Engineers and Optical Society of America. He is a member of the American Association of Physicists in Medicine, Eta Kappa Nu, and Sigma Xi. In 1958 he received the award from the IRE professional group on broadcast and television receivers. In 1973 he received the IEEE Zworykin Award.

Dr. Macovski has approximately 150 issued U.S. Patents and 150 publications in the fields of optics, electronics, television, imaging, radiography, and ultrasonics.

CHARLES B. MALLOCH is a resident engineer from United Technologies Corporation with the RPI Computer Integrated Manufacturing Program and a Ph.D. candidate with the RPI Electrical, Computer, and Systems Engineering Department.

RICHARD A. ROBB received the Ph.D. degree in computer science and biophysics from the University of Utah in 1971. He is Professor of Biophysics in the Mayo Graduate School of Medicine and Director of the Mayo Biotechnology Computer Resource. He has been involved in the development and application of computer systems for processing, analysis, and display of biomedical image data for over fifteen years. He is principal investigator on several NIH research grants and has over 150 publications in the field of multi-dimensional biomedical image processing. He is one of the developers of the Dynamic Spatial Reconstructor, an advanced high temporal resolution 3-D image scanner at the Mayo Clinic. His current interests are in development of comprehensive, efficient workstations and networks for biomedical image analysis.-

Chapter 2: Segmentation

An image must be analyzed and the features it contains extracted before more abstract representations and descriptions are generated. Careful selection of algorithms for these so-called "low-level-vision" operations is critical for the success of higher level scene interpretation algorithms. One of the first operations that a computer vision system must perform is the separation of objects from the background. This operation, commonly called "segmentation," is approached as either

- An edge-based method for locating discontinuities in certain properties in the image or
- A region-based method of grouping of pixels according to certain similarities.

Success of a segmentation technique is measured by the utility of descriptions of resulting objects. Although many segmentation techniques have been proposed, a general solution still eludes researchers. By introducing enough additional knowledge about a particular application domain, the problem may be solvable. That this additional knowledge is necessary is hardly surprising, since philosophers and psychologists have known for centuries that what we sense when we view an object is a very minor fraction of the information required to see that object. For example, in Figure 2.1, most people do not see the dalmatian dog.

Figure 2.1: A difficult image for segmentation. Can you separate the object from the background?

In an edge-based approach, the boundaries of objects are used to partition an image. Points that lie on the boundaries of an object must be marked. Such points, called "edge points," can often be detected by analyzing the neighborhood of the point. By definition, the regions on either side of an edge point (i.e., the object and the background) have dissimilar characteristics. Thus, in edge detection, the emphasis is on detecting dissimilarities in the neighborhoods of points. Most edge detectors use only intensity characteristics; however, more sophisticated characteristics, which can be derived from intensity values such as texture and motion, may also be used.

In a region-based approach, all pixels corresponding to a single object are grouped together and are marked to indicate that they belong to the same object. The grouping of the points is based on some criterion that distinguishes points belonging to the same object from all other points. Two very important considerations in such a grouping are spatial proximity and intensity similarity. Without any domain-dependent information, we can assume that all points that belong to a given surface of an object will be spatially close and will have similar reflectance characteristics. Clearly, the second assumption is not satisfied in many real situations. But we can initially group points using these simple considerations, and then use domain-dependent knowledge to refine the results of this first grouping operation. Complex images may require the use of more rigorous techniques to perform the grouping operation.

In an ideal image, the edges of each object will define a closed region, and a region will be bounded by connected edge points. Theoretically, both edge-based and region-based approaches should give identical information. When an edged-based approach is used, regions could be obtained from edges using a simple region-filling algorithm; similarly, when a region-based approach is used, the edges could be obtained by using a simple boundary follower. Unfortunately, in real images, correct edges can rarely be obtained from region information, and vice versa. Due to noise and other factors, neither the dissimilarity measures used by edge detectors nor the similarity measures used by region growers give anywhere near perfect results.

Edge detection techniques are described next, followed by region-growing techniques. Finally, other methods for segmentation — methods that use features such as texture and color — are not described, but references to literature are given. Techniques for representation and description of regions and boundaries, feature extraction, and matching are described in Chapter 3.

Edge-based segmentation

Edge detection has been a very active research area for about two decades, and many edge detectors have been developed. Several types of edges are commonly found in an image. One-dimensional profiles of some of the common edge types are shown in Figure 2.2. The step edge is a good model only in those situations in which (1) objects and the background have very good contrast and (2) the intensity changes at the boundaries are crisp. However, step edges are rare in most real images; rather, ramp edges are common. Because of low-frequency components or the smoothing introduced by most sensing devices, sharp discontinuities rarely exist in real signals. Roof edges and line edges may occur if narrow objects are present in the scene. A line usually becomes a roof in the sensed image.

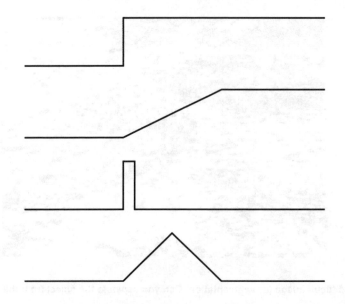

Figure 2.2: One-dimensional profile of edges

Gradient. Edges in an image are detected by computing the gradient at each pixel and then identifying those pixels with gradient magnitudes larger than a threshold. The magnitude of the gradient is used to represent the strength of the edge at each point and the direction of the gradient is used to link points belonging to the same physical edge. The magnitude $E(x,y)$ and the direction $\theta(x,y)$ of the edge at pixel (x,y) in terms of the first partial derivatives of intensities E_x and E_y (along the x- and y-directions) are given by the following equations:

$$E(x,y) = \sqrt{E_x^2(x,y) + E_y^2(x,y)} \qquad (2.1)$$

$$\theta = \tan^{-1}\left(\frac{E_y}{E_x}\right) \qquad (2.2)$$

In most applications, the following computationally simpler expressions are used to approximate the gradient:

$$E(x,y) = |E_x| + |E_y|$$

or

$$E(x,y) = Max\ (|E_x|, |E_y|) \tag{2.3}$$

Many approximations have been used to compute the partial derivatives in the x- and y-directions. One of the earliest edge detectors used, called "Roberts' cross operator," computes the partial derivatives by taking the difference in intensities of the diagonal pixels in a two-by-two pixel window. One of the most commonly used approximations, defined over a three-by-three window, is attributable to Sobel.[22] Using the following notation to identify neighboring pixels:

A_0	A_1	A_2
A_7	$f(x,y)$	A_3
A_6	A_5	A_4

this approximation is given by

$$E_x = (A_2 + 2A_3 + A_4) - (A_0 + 2A_7 + A_6)$$
$$E_y = (A_0 + 2A_1 + A_2) - (A_6 + 2A_5 + A_4) \tag{2.4}$$

Occasionally, operators that compute the edge strength in a number of different directions are used in computer vision. These directional operators are defined over three-by-three or larger neighborhoods.[23]

Laplacian. The operators we have just discussed require that E_x and E_y be computed separately and then combined to obtain the edge strength. The Laplacian operator, which responds to changes in intensity in an image, requires much less computation. The Laplacian is defined in terms of the second partial derivatives, as follows:

$$\nabla^2 f = \frac{\partial^2 f}{\partial x^2} + \frac{\partial^2 f}{\partial y^2} \tag{2.5}$$

The second derivatives along the x- and y-directions are approximated using the difference equations

$$\frac{\partial^2 f}{\partial x^2} = (f(x+1,y) - f(x,y)) - (f(x,y) - f(x-1,y))$$
$$= (f(x+1,y) - 2f(x,y) + f(x-1,y)) \tag{2.6}$$

and

$$\frac{\partial^2 f}{\partial y^2} = (f(x,y+1) - 2f(x,y) + f(x,y-1)) \tag{2.7}$$

Thus, the following three-by-three mask can be used to compute the Laplacian:

0	1	0
1	−4	1
0	1	0

The response of the Laplacian operator can be computed in one step by convolving the image with this mask. Nevertheless, since the Laplacian is an approximation to the second derivative, it reacts more strongly to lines, line ends, and noise pixels than it does to edges, and it generates two responses to each edge — one on either side of the edge. However, the zero-crossings in the output of the Laplacian are useful to localize the edges.

Every edge detector that uses the neighborhood of a point to compute edgeness is prone to responding incorrectly to intensity changes that are attributable to noisy pixels. This problem with such edge detectors occurs because they compute the property of a point, while an edge is actually a property of a region. Edge points of interest are not isolated points, but rather segments of boundaries between regions. Several suggestions have been made to include characteristics of regions in edge detection.

Multiresolution edge detectors. A multiresolution detector detects edges by computing characteristics of the areas of different sizes on either side of a point. In the simplest case, the edge strength may be defined as the difference in the average intensities of the areas on either side of a point. For small neighborhoods, such a detector gives high values close to the actual edge point. For larger neighborhoods, major edges are detected, including texture edges. Many variations on this approach to edge detection exist. That intensity changes in an image may occur at several levels is a very important implicit assumption in this approach. If we are interested in the detection of edges due to disparate physical phenomena in an image, we may need operators of different sizes. Also, several neighborhoods of a point can be considered and their characteristics combined to detect edges.

Natural images contain assorted objects of different sizes; the intensity changes in these images occur over a wide range of scales. Selection of appropriate filters allows an edge detector to respond to edges at different scales. The Marr and Hildreth[24] edge detector is an example of an edge detector in which different smoothing filters are applied to an image at various resolutions and smoothed by different amounts. Then, intensity changes are detected in each smoothed image. Intensity changes at a given resolution will indicate edges that are significant at that level of resolution. The intensity changes detected at multiple levels are combined to allow edges attributable to physical changes in a scene to be detected.

A Gaussian filter is used to average an image. The use of a Gaussian filter, as opposed to some other filter, results in good spatial- and spectral-localization characteristics; it is the only filter that has this capability. The Gaussian filter, excluding the constant multiplicative factor, is given by

$$G(x,y) = e^{-\left(\frac{x^2 + y^2}{2\sigma^2}\right)} \tag{2.8}$$

In many edge detection methods, if the first derivative of the image is above a certain threshold, an edge point is assumed. The result is too many edge points. A better approach is to find the image gradient and to consider as edge points only those points with a gradient value that is a local maximum. Then, a peak will be in the first derivative and, equivalently, a zero-crossing will be in the second derivative at edge points. Thus, edge points are detected by finding the zero-crossings of the second derivative of image intensity.

A first step in edge detection is convolution with a Gaussian filter. This smooths the image by removing structures that are smaller than the Gaussian window. Isolated noise points and small structures can be filtered out, making the response of the edge detector more reliable. Since the filtering will result in the blurring of edges, the edge detector only considers to be edge points those points that have a locally maximum gradient. This is accomplished by taking the zero-crossing of the second derivative. The second derivative in two dimensions is approximated by the Laplacian. Thus, zero-crossings are detected in $F(x,y)$, where $F(x,y)$ is given by

$$F(x,y) = \nabla^2(G(x,y) * f(x,y)) \tag{2.9}$$

where ∇^2 and $*$ denote the Laplacian and convolution operators, respectively. Since the Laplacian is an isotropic operator, it will detect edges in all directions.

The two operations — Gaussian smoothing and computation of the Laplacian — can be combined into a single operation: convolving the image with a Laplacian of Gaussian (LOG) function, which is given by

$$\nabla^2 G(x,y) = \left(\frac{x^2 + y^2 - 2\sigma^2}{\sigma^4}\right) e^{-\left(\frac{x^2 + y^2}{2\sigma^2}\right)} \tag{2.10}$$

The cross section of the LOG function (inverted) is shown in Figure 2.3. For discrete implementation of this operator, the size of the mask depends on the value of σ. Clearly, the performance of the operator also depends on the value of σ.

In the approach just described, edges are detected at a particular resolution. Determination of the real edges in an image may require that information from operators of several sizes be combined. Real edges in an image are due to a discontinuity in a physical variable in a scene; such edges should survive for more than one resolution of the operator.

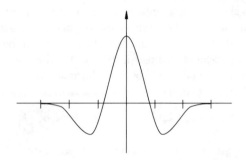

Figure 2.3: One-dimensional profile of Laplacian of Gaussian Operator

Witkin[25] applied the zero-crossing detector using different values of σ and created a scale-space. Such a scale-space for the one-dimensional function *f(x)* is shown in Figure 2.4,[25] where the horizontal axis represents *x*, the vertical axis represents σ, and the lines are contours of zero-crossings. Fewer edges are detected at larger values of σ, as can be seen by the decrease in the number of zero-crossings. The presence of edges at a particular resolution is found at the appropriate scale, and the exact location of edges is obtained by following the corresponding contours through lower values of σ. No new zero-crossings are created as σ is increased; this is a desirable property of the Gaussian smoothing function.

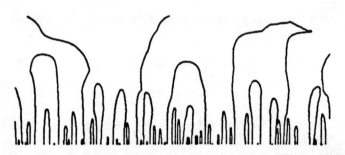

Figure 2.4: Typical contours of zero-crossings in scale-space (from Witkin).[25]

Using detection, localization, and uniqueness (single response to one edge) criteria, Canny[26] designed an edge detector that is optimum at any scale. He showed that the first derivative of the Gaussian is a good approximation to his optimal edge detector for detecting step edges. He presented a thresholding technique to eliminate streaking of edge contours and proposed a method for obtaining directional masks with oblong support.

The size of the operators causes a major problem in using multiresolution operators. The response of an operator at a point is the sum of the weighted responses at all points in its support. In an ideal situation, the response at a point is the result of the contributions from points on the two sides of the same edge point. Thus, it is desirable that only one edge pass through the support of the operator. However, in a complex image, as the size of the support increases, the number of edges in the support also increases, resulting in mutual influence of edges. This mutual influence may result in unpredictable behavior of detected edges: the edges may be dislocated, false edges may be generated, and real edges may be missing at different scale sizes.[27]

Surface fitting. Most ideas for analyzing images are relative to a continuous domain, while a digital image is actually a sampling of a continuous function of two-dimensional spatial variables. Desired properties must then be computed using discrete approximations of their continuous domain counterparts. If the continuous spatial function can be approximately reconstructed, then image properties can be more precisely computed. Computation of localization to subpixel accuracy may be possible. This concept leads to an interesting approach.

The intensity values in the neighborhood of a point can be used to obtain the underlying continuous intensity surface, which then can be used as a best approximation from which properties in the neighborhood of the point can be computed. An image function can be described by

$$z = f(x,y) \tag{2.11}$$

That intensity values at a point satisfy some analytical characteristics is assumed. Clearly, if the image represents one surface, the preceding equation will correctly characterize the image. However, an image generally contains several surfaces, in which case this equation would be satisfied only at local surface points. In other words, the intensity values in the neighborhood of a point usually belong to one surface; hence, they should show the structure of the surface. This will not be true at surface discontinuities. The Haralick's[28] facet model of an image is the result of this idea. In the facet model, the neighborhood of a point is approximated by the cubic surface patch that best fits the area. Thus, the intensity values in the neighborhood of the point are approximated by

$$f(r,c) = k_1 + k_2 r + k_3 c + k_4 r^2 + k_5 rc + k_6 c^2 + k_7 r^3 + k_8 r^2 c + k_9 rc^2 + k_{10} c^3 \tag{2.12}$$

where r and c are coordinates, along the x- and y-directions, respectively, relative to the point in the image whose neighborhood is being approximated. The k_i coefficients in the preceding equation can be computed using the least squares method.

Edge points are relative extrema in the first directional derivative of the function that approximates the surface in the neighborhood of a pixel. This fact can be used to detect edge points. Relative extrema in the first derivative will result in a zero-crossing in the second derivative, occurring in the direction of the first derivative. If θ is the edge direction, the second directional derivative at a point (r_0, c_0) is given by

$$f''_\theta (r,c) = 6(k_7 \sin^3\theta + k_8 \sin^2\theta\cos\theta + k_9 \sin\theta\cos^2\theta + k_{10}\cos^3\theta)\rho + 2(k_4 \sin^2\theta + k_5 \sin\theta\cos\theta + k_6\cos^2\theta)$$

$$= A\rho + B \tag{2.13}$$

where $r_0 = \rho \sin\theta$ and $c_0 = \rho \cos\theta$. Thus, (r_0, c_0) is an edge point if, for some ρ, $|\rho| < \rho_0$ (where ρ_0 is the length of the side of a pixel)

$$f''_\theta (r_0, c_0; \rho) = 0$$
$$and$$
$$f'_\theta (r_0, c_0; \rho) \neq 0 \tag{2.14}$$

Nalwa and Binford[29] used one-dimensional surfaces to detect edgels — short, linear edge elements. (A typical one-dimensional surface is shown in Figure 2.5.[29]) In Nalwa and Binford's method, the direction of the edgel is estimated initially by fitting a planar patch in a least squares sense; this estimate is refined using a one-dimensional cubic surface. Finally, a one-dimensional *tanh* surface is fitted, and the edgel characteristics are calculated.

Grimson and Pavlidis[30] used statistical properties of the differences between intensity values in a region and the planar approximation to detect discontinuities. If the differences are randomly distributed, then the underlying surface is assumed to be smooth; on the other hand, if the differences are distributed systematically, discontinuities are implied. Detecting discontinuities in an early stage permits more accurate surface fitting in a subsequent stage, since oscillations due to Gibb's phenomena are avoided.

Edge linking. Detection of edge pixels is only a part of the segmentation task. The outputs of typical edge detectors must be linked to form the boundaries of objects. Edge pixels seldom form closed boundaries; missed edge points will result in breaks in the boundaries. Thus, edge linking is an extremely important, but difficult, step in image segmentation.[31] Several methods have been suggested to improve the performance of edge detectors. In the relaxation-based edge-linking method, information from the neighborhood of an edge point is used to improve edge detector performance.[32,33] The basic idea behind this approach is to use the magnitude and direction of the edge at a point to detect other edges in the neighborhood. If the direction of an edge is compatible with its neighboring edges, the edges are linked; incompatible edges are removed. Looking at larger neighborhoods allows missing edges to be filled in. In a sequential edge detector — also called an "edge tracker" — the image is scanned to find a so-called "strong" edge point, which is considered to be a starting point for the boundary of an object. Starting at this point, all possible boundaries are grown by considering edge strength and directions. The tracking operation is computationally simplified by extending the boundary segment in a direction that depends on the current direction of the edge. Even very weak edge segments can be detected using this approach.

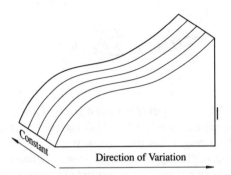

Constant

Direction of Variation

Figure 2.5: A one-dimensional surface (from Nalwa and Binford).[29]

Region-based segmentation

In region-based segmentation, points that have similar characteristics are identified and grouped into regions. Such points usually belong to a single object. A set of connected points that belong to the same object is called a "region." Several techniques are available for segmenting an image using this region-based approach.

Region formation. The segmentation process usually begins with a simple region formation step. In this step, intrinsic characteristics of the image are used to form initial regions. Thresholds obtained from a histogram of the image intensity are commonly used to perform this grouping. In general, an image will have several regions, each of which may have different intrinsic characteristics. In such cases, the intensity histogram of the image will show several peaks; each peak may correspond to one or more regions. Several thresholds are selected using these peaks. After thresholding, a connected-component algorithm can be used to find initial regions. This thresholding approach usually produces too many regions. Improvement can be obtained by performing some simple operations on the image to obtain better behaved histograms. One such operation uses the average of the differences between each pixel $f(x,y)$ and its neighbors. Let $g(x,y)$ represent this average. Then a new image is formed by multiplying h(x,y) and f(x,y), where

$$h(x,y) = 1, \quad if\ g(x,y) < H$$
$$= 0, \quad otherwise. \tag{2.15}$$

where H is a threshold. Peak selection in the histogram of this new image is simplified because the contribution of border points of regions is removed from the histogram. Border points generally have intermediate values and tend to fill in the "valley" between two peaks in the histogram that correspond to the gray levels of two separate regions. Elimination of the border points results in a better behaved histogram, which produces better thresholds for determining the initial regions.

These thresholding techniques may still produce too many regions. Since they were formed based only on first-order characteristics, the regions obtained are usually simplistic and do not correspond to complete objects. The regions obtained via thresholding may be considered to be only the first stage in segmentation. After the initial histogram-based segmentation, more sophisticated techniques are used to refine the segmentation.

Functional approximation. The intensity values in an image may be treated as representing a three-dimensional surface. The aim of segmentation is to find or approximate regular surfaces. The many approaches to partitioning an image using this approach assume that a region Y satisfies a similarity predicate if, at every point in Y,

$$\left[f(x,y) - \sum_{k=1}^{M} a_k \cdot b_k(x,y) \right] \le h \tag{2.16}$$

where h is a threshold, b_k represents a finite family of linearly independent functions and a_k represents parameters chosen to minimize the maximum pointwise error. Instead of this uniform approximation, the following least integral square error approximation can be used:

71

$$\sum_{Y}\left[f(x,y) - \sum_{k=1}^{M} a_k \cdot b_k(x,y)\right]^2 \leq \tau$$

(2.17)

where τ is a threshold. In the above model, if we select $M = 1$ and $b_1(x,y) = 1$, then the image is approximated using horizontal planes. This scheme then becomes the same as thresholding. In the last few years, this approach to image modeling, where the intensity value is considered to be a height, has received increasing attention. (The facet model for edge detection, discussed earlier, is based on this approach.) The approach is good for modeling objects whose surfaces do not have a strong texture component, while modeling of textured surfaces is somewhat tedious using this approach.

Besl and Jain[34] described an iterative algorithm for fitting variable-order bivariate surfaces to image data. Every pixel in the image is initially labeled as belonging to one of eight possible surface types, depending on the surface curvature sign computed using an approximating surface that best fits the image data surrounding that point. Pixels with similar labels are aggregated using a connected-component procedure to obtain initial regions. Pixels that are interior to these regions are chosen as seed regions for iterative surface fitting and a region-growing algorithm. The order of the function fitting the region is incremented from planar to biquartic, as necessary, until convergence criteria are satisfied. This algorithm has been applied to both range and intensity images.

Split and merge. The major problem with the results from a simple intensity-based segmentation is that there are usually too many regions. Even in images where most human observers will report very clear, uniform-intensity regions, the output of a thresholding algorithm will contain many spurious regions. The main reasons for this problem are high-frequency noise and smooth transition between uniform regions. In most applications, after initial intensity-based region formation, a method for refining or reforming the regions is needed. Several approaches have been proposed for processing such regions. Some of these approaches use domain-dependent knowledge, while others use knowledge about imaging. The refinement may be done interactively—by a person—or automatically—by a computer. In an automatic system, the segmentation will have to be refined based on object characteristics and general knowledge about the images.

Automatic refinement is done using a combination of split and merge operations. Split and merge operations eliminate false boundaries and spurious regions by either splitting a region that contains pieces from more than one object or merging adjacent regions that actually belong to the same object. Some possible approaches for this refinement are to

- Merge similar "adjacent" regions;
- Remove questionable edges;
- Use topological properties of the regions;
- Use shape information about objects in the scene; and
- Use semantic information about the scene.

The last two approaches require domain-dependent information, while the first three approaches use only intensity values and other domain-independent characteristics of regions.

Split. If some "property" of a region is not uniform, the region should be split. Segmentation based on the split approach starts with large regions. In many cases, the whole image may be used as the starting region. Several decisions must be made before a region is split. One is to decide when a property is nonuniform over a region; another is how to split a region so that the property for each of the resulting components is uniform. These decisions usually are not easy to make. In some applications, the variance of the intensity values is used as a measure of uniformity; in other applications, the error in the best functional approximation is used. More difficult than determining property uniformity is deciding where to split a region. Splitting regions based on property values is very difficult. One approach used when trying to determine the best boundaries with which to divide a region is to consider edgeness values within the region. The easiest schemes for splitting regions are those that divide the region into a fixed number of equal regions; such methods are called "regular decomposition methods." For example, in the quadtree approach, the region is split into four quadrants in each step.

Clearly, because of the numerous ways in which a region may be split, splitting regions is generally more difficult than merging them.

Merge. Many approaches have been proposed to judge similarity of regions. Broadly, the approaches to judge region similarity are based on either the characteristics of regions or the weakness of edges between them. Two approaches to judging the similarity of adjacent regions are to

(1)   Compare their mean intensities. In this approach, if the mean intensities do not differ by more than some predetermined value, the regions are considered to be similar. The regions are then candidates for merging. A modified form of this approach uses surface fitting to determine if the regions can be approximated by one surface.

(2)   Assume that the intensity values are drawn from a probability distribution. In this approach, the decision of whether or not to merge adjacent regions is based on considering the probability that they will have the same statistical distribution of intensity values. This approach uses hypothesis testing to judge the similarity of adjacent regions.

The first approach is easy to implement. The second approach is more powerful than the first. A description of the second approach follows.

Suppose that two adjacent regions R_1 and R_2 contain points m_1 and m_2, respectively. The two possible hypotheses are listed below.

- H_0: Both regions belong to the same object $\equiv$ the intensities are all drawn from a single Gaussian distribution with parameters (μ_0, σ_0).
- H_1: The regions belong to different objects $\equiv$ the intensities of each region are drawn from separate Gaussian distributions with parameters (μ_1, σ_1), (μ_2, σ_2).

Assuming that the intensities of different points are independent, it can be shown that the likelihood ratio is given by

$$L = \frac{Probability\ that\ there\ are\ two\ regions}{Probability\ there\ is\ one\ region}$$

$$= \frac{P_1 \cdot P_2}{P}$$

$$= \frac{\left(\sigma_0{}^2\right)^{m_1 + m_2}}{\left(\sigma_1{}^2\right)^{m_1} \cdot \left(\sigma_2{}^2\right)^{m_2}} \tag{2.18}$$

A likelihood ratio L that is below a threshold value indicates strongly that the existence of only one region is more likely than that of two regions. These two regions may be merged. This approach can be used for edge detection also. Since the likelihood ratio indicates when two regions should be considered to be separate, it also indicates when a boundary should be between two regions. For edge detection, the likelihood ratio between fixed neighborhoods on either side of a point can be used to detect the presence of edges. Other possible modifications to this ratio exist; these can play an important role in many applications.

Another approach to merging is to combine two regions if the boundary between them is weak. This approach attempts to remove weak edges between adjacent regions by considering not only the intensity characteristics, but also the length of the common boundary. The common boundary is dissolved if the boundary is "weak" and the resulting boundary (of the merged region) does not grow too fast. (A weak boundary is one for which the intensities on either side differ by less than an amount T.) Other criteria, such as edgeness values, can be used to determine strength of an edge point that is on the boundary separating two regions.

Split and merge operations may be used together. After a presegmentation based on thresholding, a succession of splits and merges may be applied as dictated by the properties of the regions. Such schemes have been proposed for segmentation of complex scenes. Domain knowledge with which the split and merge operations can be controlled may be introduced.

Other segmentation methods

In the preceding discussion, the primary concern was with intensity images. Segmentation techniques that are based on color,[35-37] texture,[38-42] and motion (described in more detail in Chapter 6) have also been developed. Segmentation based on spectral pattern classification techniques is extensively used in remote-sensing applications.

Research trends

After more than two decades of research efforts, segmentation still remains a problem. Many approaches to computer vision do not use any domain-specific information in the early stages.[43] On the other hand, some psychophysicists believe that every aspect of perception uses domain information extensively.[44] Computer vision research has been influenced by both of these views. Haralick and Shapiro[45] provide an excellent review of early segmentation techniques. The authors classify and define several segmentation techniques and illustrate them with examples.

Nine papers were selected for inclusion in this chapter: five are in this book and the remaining four in its companion book, *Computer Vision: Advances and Applications*. Edge detection still remains one of the most active areas of research in computer vision. Scale-space has been attracting increasing attention in the last few years.[25,27,46-48] Although most scale-space research has been concerned with possible reconstruction of signals, approaches are being developed for combining information at different scales.[27,49] The idea of using procedural reasoning, like that proposed by Georgeff and Lansky,[50] is likely to become increasingly important in computer vision; this will be the obvious next step after researchers have tried knowledge-based approaches for segmentation.[51,52] The first paper presented in *Principles,* "Theory of Edge Detection," by Marr and Hildreth, describes the Laplacian of Gaussian (LOG) operator for detecting edge segments. This paper is followed by "Scale-Space Filtering," by Witkin, and "A Computational Approach to Edge Detection," by Canny. Continuing in *Principles*, "Discontinuity Detection for Visual Surface Reconstruction," by Grimson and Pavlidis introduces a technique in which the statistical distribution of error in approximation of intensity values by a planar surface is used to detect discontinuities. Nalwa and Binford[29] discuss how groups of edge pixels — or edgels — are detected by fitting a one-dimensional surface to data. In *Advances*, Eichel et al. describe in their paper entitled "A Method for a Fully Automatic Definition of Coronary Arterial Edges From Cineangiograms," an algorithm for edge linking and its performance on angiogram images.

Though many edge detectors have been developed, no well-defined metric helps researchers select the appropriate edge detector for a given application. This lack of a performance measure makes judicious selection of an edge detector for a given application a difficult problem.

In the early days of computer vision, region-growing and other region-based approaches received the attention of researchers.[45] In the last few years, region-oriented segmentation approaches have once again become increasingly popular because of the availability of range images.[34,53-55] These approaches are usually more robust than edge-detection based segmentation techniques. In *Principles*, in the paper entitled "Segmentation Through Variable-Order Surface Fitting," Besl and Jain describe a functional approximation method in which image data are represented by piecewise smooth surfaces. It appears obvious that features of edge detection and region growing should be combined to yield good early segmentation; however, only little attention has been given in this direction.[56,57]

In many region-based image analysis methods, texture plays an important role. Van Gool et al.[39] present a review of methods used for texture analysis. Many techniques have been developed to model texture using statistical,[58,59] structural,[60,61] and spectral[62] methods. With the use of the models described in "Markov Random Field Texture Models," by Cross and Jain in *Advances*, blurry, sharp, linelike, and bloblike textures can be generated. This paper gives methods for estimating the parameters of the models to approximate various natural textures and a comparison of the generated synthetic texture and natural textures. The paper by Malik and Perona, "Preattentive Texture Discrimination With Early Vision Mechanisms" in *Advances*, is the latest, and the most convincing, model of human preattentive texture perception. A recent book, *A Taxonomy of Texture Description and Identification*, by Rao,[63] gives a good overview of approaches for texture classification and their applications.

We conclude *Advances* with "Using Color for Geometry-Insensitive Segmentation," by Healey which describes representative segmentation techniques that use color information.

Explicit application of knowledge for segmentation has been addressed in many systems.[50,51,64,65] Many of these systems showed promise, but had limited success because of poor performance of operators in domain-independent early processing. Model-based reasoning can help in this direction.[66] The literature has clearly started showing a strong trend toward using explicit, mostly geometric, models that help operators in early processing. Model-based reasoning will likely emerge as a powerful theme in the near future.

References Cited
Chapter 2

22. Sobel, I., "Camera Models and Machine Perception," *Stanford AI Memo 121*, Department of Computer Science, Stanford University, Stanford, Calif., May 1970.

23. R. Kirsch, "Computer Determination of the Constituent Structure of Biological Images," *Computers and Biomedical Research*, Vol. 4, No. 3, 1971, pp. 315-328.

24. D. Marr and E. Hildreth, "Theory of Edge Detection," *Proc. R. Soc. Lond. B*, Vol. 207, 1980, pp. 187-217.

25. A.P. Witkin, "Scale-Space Filtering," *Int'l Joint Conf. Artificial Intelligence*, Morgan Kaufmann Publishers, Inc., San Mateo, Calif., 1983, pp. 1019-1022.

26. J.F. Canny, "A Computational Approach to Edge Detection," *IEEE Trans. Pattern Analysis and Machine Intelligence*, Vol. 8, No. 6, 1986, pp. 679-698.

27. Y. Lu and R.C. Jain, "Behavior of Edges in Scale Space," *IEEE Trans. Pattern Analysis and Machine Intelligence*, Vol. 11, No. 3, 1989, pp. 337-356.

28. R.M. Haralick, "Digital Step Edges from Zero Crossing f Second Directional Derivatives," *IEEE Trans. Pattern Analysis and Machine Intelligence*, Vol. 6, No. 1, 1984, pp. 58-68.

29. V.S. Nalwa and T.O. Binford, "On Detecting Edges," *IEEE Trans. Pattern Analysis and Machine Intelligence*, Vol. 8, No. 6, 1986, pp. 699-714.

30. W.E.L. Grimson and T. Pavlidis, "Discontinuity Detection for Visual Surface Reconstruction," *Computer Vision, Graphics, and Image Processing*, Vol. 30, 1985, pp. 316-330.

31. P.H. Eichel et al, "A Method for a Fully Automatic Definition of Coronary Arterial Edges from Cineangiograms," *IEEE Trans. Medical Imaging*, Vol. 7, No. 4, Dec. 1988, pp. 313-320.

32. S.W. Zucker, R.A. Hummel, and A. Rosenfeld, "An Application of Relaxation Labeling to Line and Curve Enhancement" *IEEE Trans. Computers*, Vol. 26, 1977, pp. 394-403.

33. J.M. Prager, "Extracting and Labeling Boundary Segments in Natural Scenes," *IEEE Trans. Pattern Analysis and Machine Intelligence*, Vol. 2, No. 1, 1980, pp. 16-27.

34. P. Besl and R. Jain, "Segmentation through Variable-Order Surface Fitting," *IEEE Trans. Pattern Analysis and Machine Intelligence*, Vol. 10, No. 2, 1988, pp. 167-192.

35. R. Ohlander, K. Price, and D.R. Reddy, "Picture Segmentation Using a Recursive Splitting Method," *Comp. Graph. and Image Processing*, Vol. 8, 1978, pp. 313-333.

36. Y. Ohta, T. Kanade, and T. Sakai, "Color Information for Region Segmentation," *Comp. Graph. and Image Processing*, Vol. 13, 1980, pp. 222-241.

37. G. Healey, "Using Color for Geometry-Insensitive Segmentation," *J. Opt. Soc. Am. A*, Vol. 6, No. 6, 1989, pp. 920-937.

38. K.S. Fu, and J.K. Mui, "A Survey on Image Segmentation," *Pattern Recognition*, Vol. 13, 1981, pp. 3-16.

39. L. Van Gool, P. Dewaele, and O. Oosterlinck, "Texture Analysis Anno 1983," *Computer Vision, Graphics, and Image Processing*, Vol. 29, 1985, pp. 336-357.

40. H. Voorhees and T. Poggio, "Computing Texture Boundaries from Images," *Nature*, Vol. 333, 1988, pp. 364-367.

41. R.L. Kashyap and K.B. Eom, "Texture Boundary Detection Based on the Long Correlation Model," *IEEE Trans. Pattern Analysis and Machine Intelligence*, Vol. 11, No. 1, 1989, pp. 58-67.

42. J. Malik and P. Perona, "Preattentive Texture Discrimination with Early Vision Mechanisms," *J. Opt. Soc. Am. A*, Vol. 7, No. 5, May 1990, pp. 923-932.

43. D. Marr, *Vision: A Computational Investigation into the Human Representation and Processing of Visual Information*, W.H. Freeman & Co., San Francisco, Calif., 1982.

44. I. Rock, *The Logic of Perception*, MIT Press, Cambridge, Mass., 1983.

45. R.M. Haralick and L.G. Shapiro, "Image Segmentation Techniques," *Computer Vision, Graphics, and Image Processing*, Vol. 29, 1985, pp. 100-133.

46. V. Torre and T.A. Poggio, "On Edge Detection," *IEEE Trans. Pattern Analysis and Machine Intelligence*, Vol. 8, No. 2, 1986, pp. 147-163.

47. A.L. Yuille and T. Poggio, "Scaling Theorems for Zero Crossings," *IEEE Trans. Pattern Analysis and Machine Intelligence*, Vol. 8, No. 1, 1986, pp. 15-25.

48. L. Wu and Z. Xie, "Scaling Theorems for Zero Crossings," *IEEE Trans. Pattern Analysis and Machine Intelligence*, Vol. 12, No. 1, 1990, pp. 46-54.

49. F. Bergholm, "Edge Focusing," *IEEE Trans. Pattern Analysis and Machine Intelligence*, Vol. 9, No. 6, 1987, pp. 726-741.

50. M.P. Georgeff and A.L. Lansky, "Procedural Knowledge," *Proc. IEEE*, Vol. 74, IEEE Press, New York, N.Y., 1986, pp. 1383-1398.

51. A.M. Nazif and M.D. Levine, "Low Level Image Segmentation: An Expert System," *IEEE Trans. Pattern Analysis and Machine Intelligence*, Vol. 6, No. 5, 1984, pp. 555-577.

52. J.R. Beveridge et al, "Segmenting Images Using Localized Histograms and Region Merging," *Int'l J. Computer Vision*, Vol. 2, No. 3, 1989, pp. 311-347.

53. F. Solina and R. Bajcsy, "Recovery of Parametric Models from Range Images: The Case for Superquadrics with Global Deformations," *IEEE Trans. Pattern Analysis and Machine Intelligence*, Vol. 11, No. 1, 1990, pp. 131-148.

54. R. Hoffman and A.K. Jain "Segmentation and Classification of Range Images," *IEEE Trans. Pattern Analysis and Machine Intelligence*, Vol. 9, No. 5, 1987, pp. 608-620.

55. T.-J. Fan, G. Medioni, and R. Nevatia, "Segmented Descriptions of 3-D Surfaces," *IEEE Trans. Robotics and Automation,* Vol. 3, No. 6, 1987, pp. 527-538.

56. T. Pavlidis and Y.-T. Liow, "Integrated Region Growing and Edge Detection," *IEEE Trans. Pattern Analysis and Machine Intelligence,* Vol. 12, No. 3, 1990, pp. 225-233.

57. S.P. Liou and R.C. Jain, "A Parallel Technique for Three-Dimensional Scene Segmentation," *Proc. Tenth Int'l Conf. Pattern Recognition,* IEEE CS Press, Los Alamitos, Calif., 1990, pp. 201-203.

58. R.M. Haralick, "Statistical and Structural Approaches to Texture," *Proc. IEEE,* IEEE Press, Vol. 67, No. 5, New York, N.Y., 1979, pp. 786-804.

59. G.R. Cross and A.K. Jain, "Markov Random Field Texture Models," *IEEE Trans. Pattern Analysis and Machine Intelligence,* Vol. 5, No. 1, 1983, pp. 25-39.

60. S.Y. Lu and K.S. Fu, "A Syntactic Approach to Texture Analysis," *Computer Graphics and Image Processing,* Vol. 7, 1978, pp. 303-330.

61. F. Tomita, Y. Shirai, and S. Tsuji, "Description of Texture by Structural Analysis," *IEEE Trans. Pattern Analysis and Machine Intelligence,* Vol. 4, No. 2, 1982, pp. 183-191.

62. R. Bajcsy and L. Lieberman, "Texture Gradient as a Depth Cue," *Computer Graphics and Image Processing,* Vol. 5, 1977, pp. 52-67.

63. A. R. Rao, *Taxonomy for Texture Description and Identification,* Springer-Verlag, New York, N.Y., 1990.

64. T. Matsuyama, "Expert Systems for Image Processing: Knowledge-Based Composition of Image Analysis Processes," *Computer Vision, Graphics, and Image Processing,* Vol. 48, 1989, pp. 22-49.

65. V.S.S. Hwang, L.S. Davis, and T. Matsuyama, "Hypothesis Integration in Image Understanding Systems," *Computer Vision, Graphics, and Image Processing,* Vol. 36, 1986, pp. 321-371.

66. R.A. Brooks, "Model-Based Three-Dimensional Interpretations of Two-Dimensional Images," *IEEE Trans. Pattern Analysis and Machine Intelligence,* Vol. 5, No. 2, 1983, pp. 140-150.

Proc. R. Soc. Lond. B **207**, 187–217 (1980)

Printed in Great Britain

Theory of edge detection

By D. Marr and E. Hildreth

M.I.T. Psychology Department and Artificial Intelligence Laboratory,
79 Amherst Street, Cambridge, Massachusetts 02139, U.S.A.

(*Communicated by S. Brenner, F.R.S. – Received 22 February* 1979)

A theory of edge detection is presented. The analysis proceeds in two parts. (1) Intensity changes, which occur in a natural image over a wide range of scales, are detected separately at different scales. An appropriate filter for this purpose at a given scale is found to be the second derivative of a Gaussian, and it is shown that, provided some simple conditions are satisfied, these primary filters need not be orientation-dependent. Thus, intensity changes at a given scale are best detected by finding the zero values of $\nabla^2 G(x, y) * I(x, y)$ for image I, where $G(x, y)$ is a two-dimensional Gaussian distribution and ∇^2 is the Laplacian. The intensity changes thus discovered in each of the channels are then represented by oriented primitives called zero-crossing segments, and evidence is given that this representation is complete. (2) Intensity changes in images arise from surface discontinuities or from reflectance or illumination boundaries, and these all have the property that they are spatially localized. Because of this, the zero-crossing segments from the different channels are not independent, and rules are deduced for combining them into a description of the image. This description is called the raw primal sketch. The theory explains several basic psychophysical findings, and the operation of forming oriented zero-crossing segments from the output of centre–surround $\nabla^2 G$ filters acting on the image forms the basis for a physiological model of simple cells (see Marr & Ullman 1979).

Introduction

The experiments of Hubel & Wiesel (1962) and of Campbell & Robson (1968) introduced two rather distinct notions of the function of early information processing in higher visual systems. Hubel & Wiesel's description of simple cells as linear with bar- or edge-shaped receptive fields led to a view of the cortex as containing a population of feature detectors (Barlow 1969, p. 881) tuned to edges and bars of various widths and orientations. Campbell & Robson's experiments, showing that visual information is processed in parallel by a number of independent orientation and spatial-frequency-tuned channels, suggested a rather different view, which, in its extreme form, would describe the visual cortex as a kind of spatial Fourier analyser (Pollen *et al.* 1971; Maffei & Fiorentini 1977).

Protagonists of each of these views are able to make substantial criticisms of the other. The main points against a Fourier interpretation are: (1) The bandwidth of the channels is not narrow (1.6 octaves, Wilson & Bergen 1979). The corresponding receptive fields have a definite spatial localization. (2) As Campbell & Robson found, early visual information processing is not linear (e.g. probability summation (Graham 1977; Wilson & Giese 1977), and failure of superposition (Maffei & Fiorentini 1972a)). (3) Only rudimentary phase information is apparently encoded (Atkinson & Campbell 1974).

The main point against the linear feature-detector idea is that if a simple cell truly signals either the positive or the negative part of the linear convolution of its bar-shaped receptive field with the image intensity, it can hardly be thought of as making some symbolic assertion about the presence of a bar in the image (Marr 1976a, p. 648). Such a cell would necessarily respond to many stimuli other than a bar, more vigorously, for example, to a bright edge than to a dim bar, and thus would not be specific enough in its response to warrant being called a feature detector.

Perhaps the greatest difficulty faced by both camps is that neither approach can give direct information about the goals of the early analysis of an image. This motivated a new approach to vision, which enquired directly about the information processing problems inherent in the task of vision itself (Marr 1976a, b; and see Marr 1978 for the overall scheme). According to this scheme, the purpose of early visual processing is to construct a primitive but rich description of the image that is to be used to determine the reflectance and illumination of the visible surfaces, and their orientation and distance relative to the viewer. The first primitive description of the image was called the primal sketch (*Marr* 1976b) and it is formed in two parts. First, a description is constructed of the intensity changes in an image, using a primitive language of edge-segments, bars, blobs and terminations. This description was called the raw primal sketch (Marr 1976b, p. 497). Secondly, geometrical relations are made explicit (using virtual lines), and larger, more abstract tokens are constructed by selecting, grouping and summarizing the raw primitives in various ways. The resulting hierarchy of descriptions covers a range of scales, and is called the full primal sketch of an image.

Although the primal sketch was inspired by findings about mammalian visual systems, we were until recently unable to make it the basis of a detailed theory of human early vision. Three developments have made this possible now: (a) the emergence of quantitative information about the channels present in early human vision (Cowan 1977; Graham 1977; Wilson & Giese 1977; Wilson & Bergen 1979); (b) Marr & Poggio's (1979) theory of human vision (especially the framework within which it was written); and (c) the related observations of Marr et al. (1979) about the relevance of a result like Logan's (1977) theorem to early vision.

These advances have made possible the formulation of a satisfactory computational theory. This article deals with the first part, the derivation of the raw primal sketch. The theory itself is given in two sections, the first dealing with the analysis within each channel, and the second, with combining information from different channels. Each computational section discusses algorithms for implementing the theory, and gives examples.

The second half of the article examines the implications for biology. The behaviour of the algorithms is shown to account for a range of basic psychophysical findings, and a specific neural implementation is presented. Our model is not intended as a complete proposal for a physiological mechanism, because it ignores the attribute of directional selectivity that so pervades cortical simple cells. The model does, however, make explicit certain nonlinear features that we regard as critical, and it forms the starting point for the more complete proposal of Marr & Ullman (1979), which incorporates directional selectivity.

DETECTING AND REPRESENTING INTENSITY CHANGES IN AN IMAGE

A major difficulty with natural images is that changes can and do occur over a wide range of scales (Marr 1976*a*, *b*). No single filter can be optimal simultaneously at all scales, so it follows that one should seek a way of dealing separately with the changes occurring at different scales. This requirement, together with the findings of Campbell & Robson (1968), leads to the basic idea, illustrated in figure 1, in which one first takes local averages of the image at various resolutions and then detects the changes in intensity that occur at each one. To realize this idea, we need to determine (*a*) the nature of the optimal smoothing filter, and (*b*) how to detect intensity changes at a given scale.

The optimal smoothing filter

There are two physical considerations that combine to determine the appropriate smoothing filter. The first is that the motivation for filtering the image is to reduce the range of scales over which intensity changes take place. The filter's spectrum should therefore be smooth and roughly band-limited in the frequency domain. We may express this condition by requiring that its variance there, $\Delta\omega$, should be small.

The second consideration is best expressed as a constraint in the spatial domain, and we call it the constraint of spatial localization. The things in the world that give rise to intensity changes in the image are: (1) illumination changes, which include shadows, visible light sources and illumination gradients; (2) changes in the orientation or distance from the viewer of the visible surfaces; and (3) changes in surface reflectance. The critical observation here is that, at their own scale, these things can all be thought of as spatially localized. Apart from the occasional diffraction pattern, the visual world is not constructed of ripply, wave-like primitives that extend and add together over an area (c.f. Marr 1970, p. 169), but of contours, creases, scratches, marks, shadows and shading.

The consequence for us of this constraint is that the contributions to each

D. Marr and E. Hildreth

(a)

(b)

FIGURE 1. A local-average filtered image. In the original image (a), intensity changes can take place over a wide range of scales and no single operator will be very efficient at detecting all of them. The problem is much simplified in a Gaussian band-limited filtered image because there is effectively an upper limit to the rate at which changes can take place. The first part of our scheme can be thought of as decomposing the original image into a set of copies, each filtered like this, and detecting the intensity changes separately in each. In (b) the image is filtered with a Gaussian having $\sigma = 8$ picture elements, and, in (c), $\sigma = 4$. The image is 320×320 picture elements.

The raw primal sketch

point in the filtered image should arise from a smooth average of nearby points, rather than any kind of average of widely scattered points. Hence the filter that we seek should also be smooth and localized in the spatial domain, and in particular its spatial variance, Δx, should also be small.

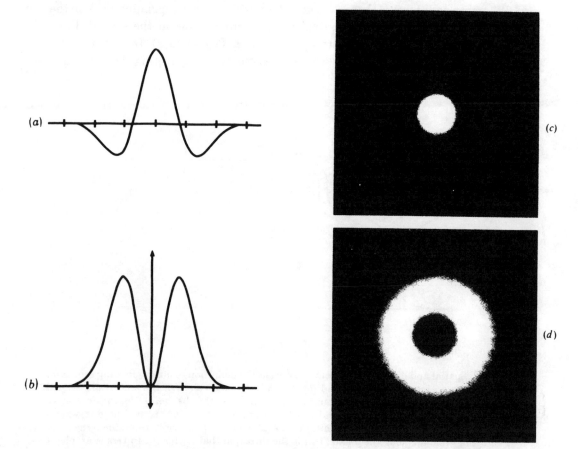

FIGURE 2. The operators G'' (equation 5) and $\nabla^2 G$: (a) shows G'', the second derivative of the one-dimensional Gaussian distribution; (c) shows $\nabla^2 G$, its rotationally symmetric two-dimensional counterpart; (b) and (d) exhibit their Fourier transforms.

Unfortunately, these two localization requirements, the one in the spatial and the other in the frequency domain, are conflicting. They are, in fact, related by the uncertainty principle, which states that $\Delta x\, \Delta \omega \geqslant \frac{1}{4}\pi$ (see, for example, Bracewell 1965, pp. 160–163). There is, moreover, only one distribution that optimizes this relation (Leipnik 1960), namely the Gaussian

$$G(x) = [1/\sigma(2\pi)^{\frac{1}{2}}] \exp(-x^2/2\sigma^2), \text{ with Fourier transform} \tag{1}$$

$$\tilde{G}(\omega) = \exp(-\tfrac{1}{2}\sigma^2 \omega^2). \tag{2}$$

In two dimensions, $G(r) = (\frac{1}{2}\pi\sigma^2) \exp(-r^2/2\sigma^2)$.

The filter G thus provides the optimal trade-off between our conflicting requirements.

Detecting intensity changes

Wherever an intensity change occurs, there will be a corresponding peak in the first directional derivative, or equivalently, a zero-crossing in the second directional derivative of intensity (Marr 1976b; Marr & Poggio 1979). In fact, we may define an intensity change in this way, so that the task of detecting these changes

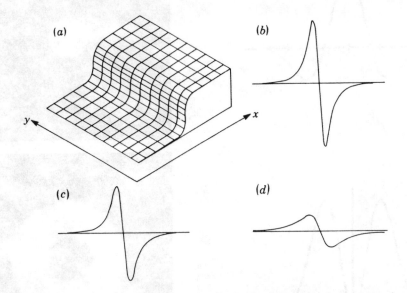

FIGURE 3. Spatial and directional factors interact in the definition of a zero-crossing segment; (a) shows an intensity change, and (b), (c) and (d) show values of the second directional derivative near the origin at various orientations across the change. In (b), the derivative is taken parallel to the x-axis, and in (c) and (d), at 30° and 60° to it. There is a zero-crossing at every orientation except for $\partial^2 I/\partial y^2$, which is identically zero. Since the zero-crossings line up along the y-axis, this is the direction that is chosen. In this example, it is also the direction that maximizes the slope of the second derivative.

can be reduced to that of finding the zero-crossings of the second derivative D^2 of intensity, in the appropriate direction. That is to say, we seek the zero-crossings in

$$f(x, y) = D^2[G(r) * I(x, y)], \tag{3}$$

where $I(x, y)$ is the image, and $*$ is the convolution operator. By the derivative rule for convolutions,

$$f(x, y) = D^2 G * I(x, y). \tag{4}$$

We can write the operator $D^2 G$ as G'', and in one dimension

$$G''(x) = [-1/\sigma^3(2\pi)^{\frac{1}{2}}] (1 - x^2/\sigma^2) \exp(-x^2/2\sigma^2). \tag{5}$$

$G''(x)$ looks like a Mexican hat operator (see figure 2), it closely resembles Wilson & Giese's (1977) difference of two Gaussians (DOG), and it is, in fact, the limit of the DOG function as the sizes of the two Gaussians tend to one another (see figure 11 and appendix B). It is an approximately bandpass operator, with a half-power bandwidth of about 1.2 octaves, and so it can be thought of as looking at the information contained in one particular part of the spectrum of the image.

These arguments establish that intensity changes at one scale may, in principle, be detected by convolving the image with the operator D^2G and looking for zero-crossings in its output. Only one issue is still unresolved, and it concerns the orientation associated with D^2. It is not enough to choose zero-crossings of the second derivative in *any* direction. To understand this, imagine a uniform intensity change running down the y-axis, as shown in figure 3. At the origin, the second directional derivative is zero in every direction, but it is non-zero nearby in every direction except along the y-axis.

In which direction should the derivative be taken?

To choose which directional derivative to use, we observe that the underlying motivation for detecting changes in intensity is that they will correspond to useful properties of the physical world, like changes in reflectance, illumination, surface orientation, or distance from the viewer. Such properties are spatially continuous and can almost everywhere be associated with a direction that projects to an orientation in the image. The orientation of the directional derivative that we choose to use is therefore that which coincides with the orientation formed locally by its zero-crossings. In figure 3, this orientation is the y-axis, and so the directional derivative we would choose there is $\partial^2 I/\partial x^2$.

Under what conditions does this direction coincide with that in which the zero-crossing has maximum slope? The answer to this is given by theorem 1 (see appendix A), and we call it the *condition of linear variation*:

> the intensity variation near and parallel to the line of zero-crossings should locally be linear.

This condition will be approximately true in smoothed images, and in the rest of this article we shall assume that the condition of linear variation holds.

This direction can be found by means of the Laplacian

There are three main steps in the detection of zero-crossings. They are: (1) a convolution with D^2G, where D^2 stands for a second directional derivative operator; (2) the localization of zero-crossings; and (3) checking of the alignment and orientation of a local segment of zero-crossings. Although it is possible to implement this scheme directly (Marr 1976b, p. 494), one immediate question that can be asked is, are directional derivatives of critical importance here? Convolutions are relatively expensive, and it would much lessen the computational burden if their number could be reduced, for example, by using just one orientation-independent operator.

The only orientation-independent second-order differential operator is the Laplacian ∇^2, and theorem 2 (see appendix A) makes explicit the conditions under which it can be used. They are weaker than the condition of linear variation, which we met in theorem 1, and they state that provided the intensity variation in $(G * I)$ is linear along but not necessarily near to a line of zero-crossings, then the zero-crossings will be detected and accurately located by the zero values of the Laplacian. Again, because in our application the condition of linear variation is approximately satisfied, so will be this condition. It follows that the detection of intensity changes can be based on the filter $\nabla^2 G$, illustrated in figure 2. It is, however, worth remembering that in principle, if intensity varies along a segment in a very non-linear way, the Laplacian, and hence the operator $\nabla^2 G$ will see the zero-crossing displaced to one side.

Summary of the argument

The main steps in the argument so far are, therefore, these.

(1) To limit the rate at which intensities can change, we first convolve the image I with a two-dimensional Gaussian operator G.

(2) Intensity changes in $G * I$ are then characterized by the zero-crossings in the second directional derivative $D^2(G * I)$. This operator is roughly bandpass, and so it examines only a portion of the spectrum of the image.

(3) The orientation of the directional derivative should be chosen to coincide with the local orientation of the underlying line of zero-crossings.

(4) Provided that the condition of linear variation holds, this orientation is also the one at which the zero-crossing has maximum slope (measured perpendicular to the orientation of the zero-crossing).

(5) By theorem 1 of appendix A, if the condition of linear variation holds, the lines of zero-crossings defined by (3) are precisely the zero-crossings of the orientation-independent differential operator, the Laplacian ∇^2.

(6) The loci of zero-crossings defined by (3) may therefore be detected economically in the image at each given scale by searching for the zero values of the convolution $\nabla^2 G * I$. In two dimensions,

$$\nabla^2 G(r) = -1/\pi\sigma^4[1 - r^2/2\sigma^2]\exp\left(-r^2/2\sigma^2\right).$$

We turn now to the question of how to represent the intensity changes thus detected.

Representing the intensity changes

In a band-limited image, changes take place smoothly, so it is always possible to divide a line of zero-crossings into small segments, each of which approximately obeys the condition of linear variation. This fact allows us to make the following definitions.

The raw primal sketch

(1) *A zero-crossing segment* in a Gaussian filtered image consists of a linear segment l of zero-crossings in the second directional derivative operator whose direction lies perpendicular to l.

(2) We can also define an *amplitude* ν associated with a zero-crossing segment, as the slope of the directional derivative taken perpendicular to the segment. To see why this is an appropriate measure, observe that a narrow bandpass channel near a zero-crossing at the origin can be described approximately by $\nu \sin \omega x$, which has slope $\nu\omega$ at the origin. Hence, if s is the measured slope of the zero-crossing, $\nu = s/\omega$. The factor $1/\omega$ is a space constant, and scales linearly with the sampling interval required.

The set of zero-crossing segments together with their amplitudes, constitutes a primitive symbolic representation of the changes taking place within one region of the spectrum of an image. Full coverage of the spectrum can now be had simply by applying the analysis over a sufficient number of channels simultaneously.

Finally, there are grounds for believing that this representation of the image is complete. Marr *et al.* (1979) noted that Logan's (1977) recent theorem, about the zero-crossings of one-octave bandpass signals, shows that the set of such zero-crossing segments is extremely rich in information. If the filters had bandwidth of an octave or less, they would in fact contain complete information about the filtered image. In practice, the $\nabla^2 G$ filter has a half-sensitivity bandwidth of about 1.75 octaves, which puts it outside the range in which Logan's theorem applies. On the other hand, if we add information about the slopes of the zero-crossings, the situation may be more congenial. In the standard sampling theorem, if the first derivative, as well as the value, is given, the sampling density can be halved (see, for example, Bracewell 1978, pp. 198–200). It seems likely than an analogous extension holds for Logan's (1977) theorem. If this were true, the zero-crossing segments, whose underlying motivation is physical, would in fact provide a sufficient basis for the recovery of arbitrary intensity profiles.

In summary, then, we have shown how intensity changes at one scale may be detected by means of the $\nabla^2 G$ operator and that they may be represented, probably completely, by oriented zero-crossing segments and their amplitudes. To detect changes at all scales, it is necessary only to add other channels, like the one described above, and to carry out the same computation in each. These representations are precursors of the descriptive primitives in the raw primal sketch, and mark the transition from the 'analytic' to the 'symbolic' analysis of an image. The remaining step is to combine the zero-crossings from the different channels into primitive 'edge' elements, and this task is addressed later in the article.

Examples and comments

Figure 4 shows some examples of zero-crossings. The top row shows images and the second shows their convolutions with the operator $\nabla^2 G$, exhibited in figure 2. Zero is represented here by an intermediate grey, so that very positive values

7-2

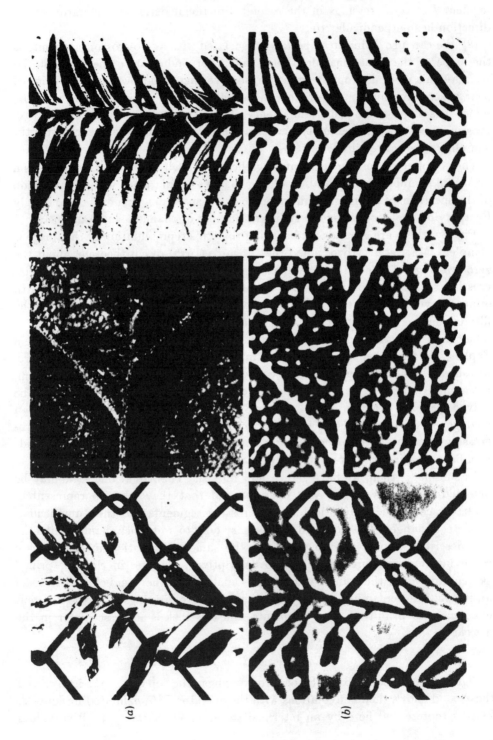

(a)
(b)

FIGURE 4. Examples of zero-crossing detection by means of $\nabla^2 G$. Row (a) shows three images and row (b) shows their convolutions with the $\nabla^2 G$ filter of figure 2 ($w = 2\sigma = 8$), zero being represented by an intermediate grey. In row (c), positive values are shown white, and negative, black; and in row (d) only the zero-crossings appear.

FIGURE 5. Comparison of the performance of $\nabla^2 G$ with that of similar filters. Column (a) shows an image, its convolution with $\nabla^2 G$ and the resulting signed zero-crossings. Column (b) contains the same sequence, but for the pure one-octave bandpass filter shown, with its Fourier transform, at the top of the column. The zero-crossing array contains echoes of the strong edges in the image. Columns (c) and (d) exhibit the same

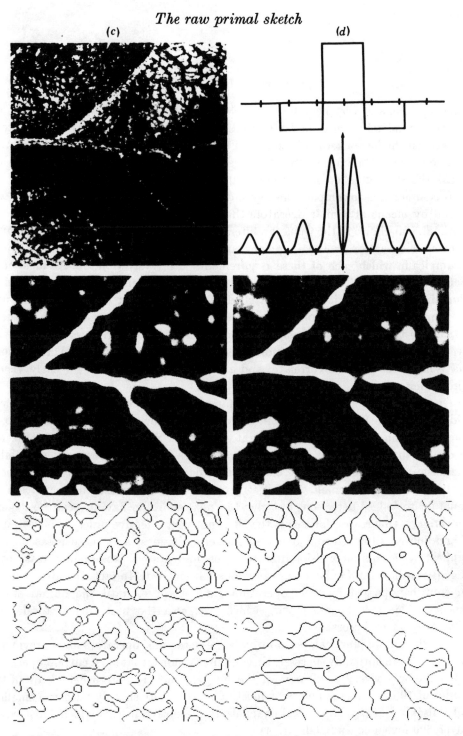

analysis of another image, except that here, $\nabla^2 G$ is compared with a square-wave approximation to the second derivative. The widths of the central excitatory regions of the filters are the same for each comparison pair, being 12 for (*a*) and (*b*), and 18 for (*c*) and (*d*). The square-wave filter sees relatively few zero-crossings.

appear white, and very negative ones, black. In the third row, all positive values appear completely white, and all negative ones are black, and the fourth row shows just the loci of zero values. It will be observed that these delineate well the visible edges in the images. (See the legend for more details.) It remains only to break the zero value loci into oriented line segments.

It is interesting to compare the zero-crossings found by means of $\nabla^2 G$ with those found by means of similar operators that, according to our arguments, are not optimal. Our choice of the Gaussian filter was based on the requirements of simultaneous localization in the frequency and spatial domains. We therefore show examples in which each of these requirements is severely violated. An ideal one-octave bandpass filter satisfies the localization requirement in the frequency domain, but violates it in the spatial domain. The reason is that strict band-limiting gives rise to sidelobes in the spatial filter, and the consequence of these is that, in the zero-crossing image, strong intensity changes give rise to echoes as well as to the directly corresponding zero-crossings (see figure 5). These echoes have no direct physical correlate, and are therefore undesirable for early visual processing.

On the other hand, if one cuts off the filter in the spatial domain, one acquires sidelobes in the frequency domain. Figure 5 also shows a square-wave approximation to the second derivative operator, together with an example of the zero-crossings to which it gives rise. This operator sees fewer zero-crossings, essentially because it is averaging out the changes that occur over a wider range of scales.

Interestingly, Rosenfeld & Kak (1976, pp. 281–4) discuss the Laplacian in relation to 'edge' detection, but they do not report its having been used very effectively. One reason for this is that it is not very effective unless it is used in a band-limited situation and one uses its zero-crossings, and these ideas do not appear in the computer vision literature (see, for example, Rosenfeld & Kak 1976, fig. 10, for how the Laplacian has previously been used). In fact, the idea of using narrow bandpass differential operators did not appear until the human stereo theory of Marr & Poggio (1979), which was also the first theory to depend primarily on zero-crossings.

Another, more practical, reason why 'edge-detecting' operators have previously been less than optimally successful in computer vision is that most current operators examine only a very small part of the image, their 'receptive fields' are of the order of 10 to 20 image points at most. This contrasts sharply with the smallest of Wilson's four psychophysical channels, the receptive field of which must cover over 500 foveal cones (see figure 4).

Finally, notice that G'', and hence $\nabla^2 G$, is approximately a second derivative operator, because its Fourier transform is $-4\pi^2\omega^2 \exp(-\sigma^2\omega^2)$, which behaves like $-\omega^2$ near the origin.

FIGURE 6. The image (*a*) has been convolved with $\nabla^2 G$ having $w = 2\sigma = 6$, 12 and 24 pixels. These filters span approximately the range of filters that operate in the human fovea. In (*b*), (*c*) and (*d*) are shown the zero-crossings thus obtained. Notice the fine detail picked up by the smallest. This set of figures neatly poses our next problem: how does one combine all this information into a single description?

COMBINING INFORMATION FROM DIFFERENT CHANNELS

The signals transmitted through channels that do not overlap in the Fourier domain will be generally unrelated unless the underlying signal is constrained. The critical question for us here is, therefore (and we are indebted to T. Poggio for conversations on this point), what additional information needs to be taken into account when we consider how to combine information from the different channels to form a primitive description of the image? In other words, are there any general physical constraints on the structure of the visual world that allow us to place valid restrictions on the way in which information from the different channels may be combined? Figure 6 illustrates the problem that we have to solve.

The spatial coincidence assumption

The additional information that we need here comes from the constraint of spatial localization, which we defined in the previous section. It states that the physical phenomena that give rise to intensity changes in the image are spatially localized. Since it is these changes that produce zero-crossings in the filtered images, it follows that if a discernible zero-crossing is present in a channel centred on wavelength λ_0, there should be a corresponding zero-crossing at the same spatial location in channels for wavelengths $\lambda > \lambda_0$. If this ceases to be true at some wavelength $\lambda_1 > \lambda_0$, it will be for one of two reasons: either (a) two or more local intensity changes are being averaged together in the larger channel; or (b) two independent physical phenomena are operating to produce intensity changes in the same region of the image but at different scales. An example of situation (a) would be a thin bar, whose edges will be accurately located by small channels but not by large ones. Situations of this kind can be recognized by the presence of two nearby zero-crossings in the smaller channels. An example of situation (b) would be a shadow superimposed on a sharp reflectance change, and it can be recognized if the zero-crossings in the larger channels are displaced relative to those in the smaller. If the shadow has exactly the correct position and orientation, the locations of the zero-crossings may not contain enough information to separate the two physical phenomena, but, in practice, this situation will be rare.

We can therefore base the parsing of sets of zero-crossing segments from different $\nabla^2 G$ channels on the following assumption, which we call the *spatial coincidence assumption*:

If a zero-crossing segment is present in a set of independent $\nabla^2 G$ channels over a contiguous range of sizes and the segment has the same position and orientation in each channel, then the set of such zero-crossing segments may may be taken to indicate the presence of an intensity change in the image that is due to a single physical phenomenon (a change in reflectance, illumination, depth or surface orientation).

In other words, provided that the zero-crossings from independent channels of adjacent sizes coincide, they can be taken together. If they do not, they probably arise from distinct surfaces or physical phenomena. It follows that the minimum number of channels required is two, and that provided the two channels are reasonably separated in the frequency domain, and their zero-crossings agree, the combined zero-crossings can be taken to indicate the presence of an edge in the image.

The parsing of sets of zero-crossing segments

Figure 6 shows the zero-crossings obtained from two channels whose dimensions are approximately the same as the two sustained channels present at the fovea in the human visual system (Wilson & Bergen 1979). We now derive the parsing rules needed for combining zero-crossings from the different channels.

Case (1): *isolated edges*

For an isolated, linearly disposed intensity change, there is a single zero-crossing present at the same orientation in all channels above some size that depends upon the channel sensitivity and the spatial extent of the edge. This set of zero-crossings may, therefore, be combined into a symbol that we shall call an edge-segment, with the attributes of edge-amplitude and width, which we may obtain as follows.

Calculation of edge-amplitude. Because the assumptions that we have made mean that the type of intensity change involved is a simple one, we can, in fact, use what Marr (1976 figure 1) called the selection criterion, according to which one

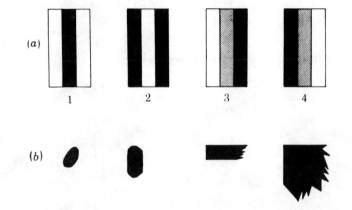

FIGURE 7. Parsing of sets of zero-crossing segments. (*a*) If zero-crossing segments lie close and roughly parallel (as in profile (*a*) of column 3 above), larger masks cannot be used, only the smaller masks. There are four possible configurations, shown in (1)–(4), and the figure represents the way in which the contrast changes across the edge. Each of these cases needs to be detected separately. (*b*) If the bar- or edge-segments are terminated, special descriptors are required. Doubly terminated bars, with $l \leqslant 3w$, are called *blobs* and the other assertions are labelled *terminations*. These are illustrated here for one contrast sign. Termination assertions may mark only a discontinuity in edge orientation, but it is often useful later on to have such positions explicitly available.

selects the smallest channel to which the intensity change is essentially indistinguishable from a step function, and uses that channel alone to estimate the contrast by means of the amplitude ν derived above. If one has just two independent channels with amplitudes ν_1 and ν_2, an approximation to the edge amplitude is $\sqrt{(\nu_1^2 + \nu_2^2)}$.

Calculation of width. The *width* of the edge in this case can also be estimated from the channel selected according to the selection criterion. For a narrow channel with central wavelength λ, the physical notion of width corresponds to the distance over which intensity increases. This distance is $\frac{1}{2}\lambda$, which is approximately w, the width of the central excitatory region of the receptive field associated with the most excited channel (in fact, $\lambda = \pi w$).

Case (2): bars

If two parallel edges with opposite contrast lie only a small distance d apart in the image, zero-crossings from channels with associated wavelength that exceeds about $2d$ cannot be relied upon to provide accurate information about the positions

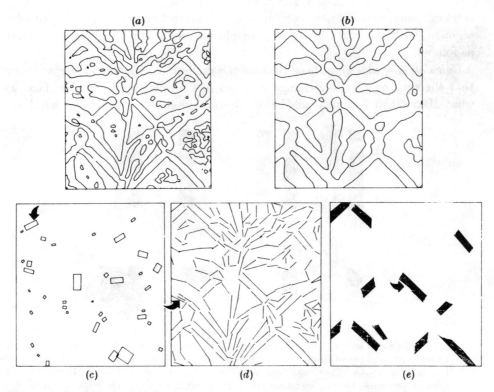

FIGURE 8. Combination of information from two channels. In (a) and (b) are shown the zero-
crossings obtained from one of the images of figure 4, by means of masks with $w = 9$
and 18. Because there are no zero-crossings in the larger channel that do not correspond
to zero-crossings in the smaller channel, the locations of the edges in the combined
description also correspond to (a). In (c), (d) and (e) are shown symbolic representations
of the descriptors attached to the locations marked in (a): (c) shows the blobs; (d), the
local orientations assigned to the edge segments; and (e), the bars. These diagrams show
only the spatial information contained in the descriptors. Typical examples of the full
descriptors are as follows.

(BLOB (POSITION 146 21)   (EDGE (POSITION 104 23)   (BAR (POSITION 118 134)
    (ORIENTATION 105)   (ORIENTATION 120)   (ORIENTATION 120)
    (CONTRAST 76)   (CONTRAST −25)   (CONTRAST −25)
    (LENGTH 16)   (LENGTH 25)   (LENGTH 25)
    (WIDTH 6))   (WIDTH 4))   (WIDTH 4))

The descriptors to which these correspond are marked with arrows. The resolution of
this analysis of the image of figure 4 roughly corresponds to what a human would see
when viewing it from a distance of about 6 ft (1.83 m).

or contrasts of the edges. In these circumstances, the larger channels must be
ignored, and the description formed solely from small channels of which the zero-
crossing segments do superimpose. An edge can have either positive or negative
contrast, and so two together give us the four situations shown in figure 7a. There
is, of course, no reason why the two edges should have the same contrast, and the
contrast of each edge must be obtained individually from the smallest channels

($w < d$). Two other parameters are useful; one is the average orientation of the two zero-crossing segments, and the other is their average separation.

Our case (2) applies only to situations in which neither zero-crossing segment terminates and they both remain approximately parallel (w or less apart). When the two edges are closer together than w for the smallest available channel, the zero-crossings associated with even the smallest channel will not accurately reflect the positions of the two edges, they will over estimate the distance between them. If the two edges have opposite contrasts that are not too different in absolute magnitude, the position of the centre of the 'line segment' so formed in the image will be the midpoint of the two corresponding zero-crossings. In these circumstances, the parameters associated with the line segment will be more reliable than those associated with each individual edge.

Case (3): *blobs and terminations*

It frequently happens that the zero-crossing segments do not continue very far across the image. Two parallel segments can merge, or be joined by a third segment, and in textured images they often form small closed curves (see figure 6), which are quite small compared to the underlying field size. Both situations can give rise to anomalous effects at larger channel sizes, and so are best made explicit early on. Following Marr (1976 *b*), the closed contours we call BLOBS, and assign to them a length, width, orientation and (average) contrast; and the terminations are assigned a position and orientation (see figure 7 *c*).

Remarks

Two interesting practical details have emerged from our implementation. First, the intensity changes at each edge of a bar are, in practice, rarely the same, so it is perhaps more proper to think of the BAR descriptor as a primitive grouping predicate that combines two edges the contrasts of which are specified precisely by the smallest channel. Brightness within the area of the bar will, of course, be constant. Secondly, it is often the case that the zero-crossings from the small and from the large masks roughly coincide, but those from the small mask weave around much more, partly because of the image structure and partly because of noise and the image tesselation. Local orientation has little meaning over distances shorter than the width w of the central excitatory region of the $\nabla^2 G$ filter, so if the zero-crossings from the smaller filter are changing direction rapidly locally, the orientation derived from the larger mask can provide a more stable and more reliable measure.

IMPLICATIONS FOR BIOLOGY

We have presented specific algorithms for the construction of the raw primal sketch, and we now ask whether the human visual system implements these algorithms or something close to them. There are two empirically accessible characteristics of our scheme. The first concerns the underlying convolutions and zero-crossing segments, and the second, whether zero-crossing segments from the different channels are combined in the way that we have described.

Detection of zero-crossing segments

According to our theory, the most economical way of detecting zero-crossing segments requires that the image first be filtered through at least two independent $\nabla^2 G$ channels, and that the zero-crossings then be found in the filtered outputs. These zero-crossings may be divided into short, oriented zero-crossing segments.

The empirical data

Recent psychophysical work by Wilson & Giese (1977), Wilson & Bergen (1979) (see also Macleod & Rosenfeld 1974), has led to a precise quantitative model of the orientation-dependent spatial-frequency-tuned channels discovered by Campbell & Robson (1968). At each point in the visual field, there are four such channels spanning about three octaves, and their peak sensitivity wavelength increases linearly with retinal eccentricity. The larger two channels at each point are transient and the smaller two are sustained. These channels can be realized by linear units with bar-shaped receptive fields made of the difference of two Gaussian distributions, with excitatory to inhibitory space constants in the ratio of 1:1.75 for the sustained, and 1:3.0 for the transient, channels (Wilson & Bergen 1979). The largest receptive field at each point is about four times the smallest.

This state of affairs is consistent with the neurophysiology since Hubel & Wiesel (1962) originally defined simple cells by the linearity of their response, and they reported many bar-shaped receptive fields. In addition, simple cell receptive field sizes increase linearly with eccentricity (Hubel & Wiesel 1974, fig. 6a), and the scatter in size at each location seems to be about 4:1 (Hubel & Wiesel 1974, fig. 7). It is therefore tempting to identify at least some of the simple cells with the psychophysical channels. If so, the first obvious way of making the identification is to propose that the simple cells measure the second directional derivatives, thus perhaps providing the convolution values from which zero-crossing segments are subsequently detected.

There are, however, various reasons why this proposal can probably be excluded. They are:

(1) If the simple cells are essentially performing a linear convolution that approximates the second directional derivative, why are they so orientation sensitive? Three measurements, in principle, suffice to characterize the second derivative completely and, in practice, the directional derivatives measured along four orientations are apparently enough for this stage (see Marr 1976b; Hildreth, in preparation), and yet simple cells divide the domain into about 12 orientations.

(2) Schiller et al. (1976b, pp. 1324–5) found that the orientation sensitivity of simple cells is relatively independent of the strength of flanking inhibition, and

of the separation and lengths of the positive and negative subfields of the receptive field of the cell. In addition, tripartite receptive fields did not appear to be more orientation sensitive than bipartite ones. These points provide good evidence that simple cells are not linear devices.

(3) If the simple cells perform the convolution, what elements find the zero-crossings and implement the spatial part of the computation, lining the zero-crossings up with the convolution orientations, for example?

Wilson's channel data is consistent with $\nabla^2 G$

Wilson's DOG functions are very similar to $\nabla^2 G$, and probably indistinguishable by means of his experimental technique, which yields about 10% accuracy (H. G. Wilson, personal communication). In appendix B, we show: (*a*) that $\nabla^2 G$ is the limit of the DOG function as σ_i/σ_e, the ratio of the inhibitory to excitatory space constants, tends to unity; and (*b*) that if an approximation to $\nabla^2 G$ is to be constructed out of the difference of two Gaussian distributions, one excitatory and the other inhibitory, the optimal choice on engineering grounds for σ_i/σ_e is about 1.6:

A specific proposal: lateral geniculate X-cells carry $\nabla^2 G * I$, and some simple cells detect and represent zero-crossing segments

It is known that retinal ganglion X-cells have receptive fields that are accurately described by the difference of two Gaussian distributions (Rodieck & Stone 1965; Ratliff 1965; Enroth-Cugell & Robson 1966). The positive and negative parts are not quite balanced (there is a response to diffuse illumination and it increases with intensity), and since the ganglion cells have a spontaneous resting discharge, they signal somewhat more than just the positive or just the negative part of such a convolution. Interestingly, there is little scatter in receptive field sizes of X-cells at a given location in the retina (Peichl & Wässle 1979).

There is some controversy about the way in which lateral geniculate receptive fields are constructed (cf. Maffei & Fiorentini 1972*b*), but it seems most likely that the on-centre geniculate X-cell fields are formed by combining a small number of on-centre retinal ganglion X-cell fields of which the centres approximately coincide (Cleland *et al.* 1971). It seems likely that the scatter in receptive field size arises in this way, since the amount of scatter required to account for the psychophysical findings is only a factor of two in both the X and the Y channels. Finally, lateral geniculate cells give a smaller response to diffuse illumination than do retinal ganglion cells, sometimes giving no response at all (Hubel & Wiesel 1961).

These facts lead us to a particularly attractive scheme, which, for simplicity, we present in idealized form.

(1) *Measurement of $\nabla^2 G$.* The sustained, or X-cell, geniculate fibres can be thought of as carrying either the positive or the negative part of $\nabla^2 G * I$, where the filter $\nabla^2 G$ of figure 2 is, in practice, approximated by a difference

D. Marr and E. Hildreth

of Gaussian convolution operator with centre-to-surround space constants in the ratio 1 : 1.75. (One should probably think of this as being a convolution on linear intensity values, rather than on their logarithms. The reason for this is that although the nerve signal in the retina is an adaptation term multiplied by $I/(I+K)$, where I is the incident illumination and $K = 800$ quanta per receptor per second (Alpern *et al.* 1970), in any given image the ratio of the darkest to the brightest portion rarely exceeds 25 (a local ratio of around

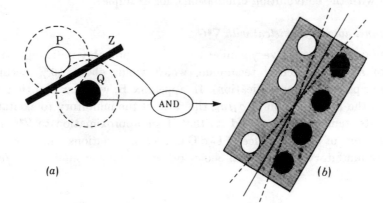

FIGURE 9. Proposed mechanism whereby some simple cells detect zero-crossing segments. In (*a*), if P represents an on-centre geniculate X-cell receptive field, and Q, an off-centre one, then if both are active, a zero-crossing Z in the Laplacian passes between them. If they are connected to a logical AND gate, as shown, then the gate will 'detect' the presence of the zero-crossing. If several are arranged in tandem, as in (*b*), and also connected by logical ANDs, the resulting operation detects an oriented zero-crossing segment within the orientation bounds given roughly by the dotted lines. This gives our most primitive model for simple cells. Ideally, one would like gates such that there is a response only if all (P, Q) inputs are active, and the magnitude of the response then varies with their sum. Marr & Ullman (1979) extend this model to include directional selectivity.

30 is seen as a light source (Ullman 1976)), and over such ranges this function does not depart far from linearity.) At each point in the visual field, there are two sizes of filter (the minimum required for combining zero-crossings between channels), and these correspond to Wilson & Bergen's (1979) N and S channels. The one-dimensional projection of the widths w of the central excitatory regions of these two channels scales linearly with eccentricity from 3.1′ and 6.2′ at the central fovea.

The basic idea behind our model for the detection of zero-crossings rests on the following observations: if an on-centre geniculate cell is active at location P and an off-centre cell is active at nearby location Q, then the value of $\nabla^2 G * I$ passes through zero between P and Q (see figure 9*a*). Hence, by combining the signals from P and Q through a logical AND operation, one can construct an operator for detecting when a zero-crossing segment (at some unknown orientation) passes between P and Q (figure 9*a*). By adding nonlinear AND operations in the longitudinal direction, one can, in a similar way, construct an operator that detects oriented zero-crossing segments. It is easy to see that the pure logical operator of figure 9*b* will respond only to zero-crossing segments whose orientations lie within its sensitivity range (shown roughly dotted). We therefore propose:

(2) *Detection and representation of zero-crossing segments.* Part of the function of one subclass of simple cells is to detect zero-crossing segments. Their receptive fields include the construction shown in figure 9*b*, with the proviso that the non-linearities may be weaker than the pure logical ANDs shown there. It is, however, a critical feature of this model that the (P AND Q) interaction (figure 9*a*) across the zero-crossing segment should contain a strong nonlinear component and that the longitudinal interaction (e.g. between the ends in figure 9*b*) contains at least a weak nonlinear component. Marr & Ullman's (1979) full model for simple cells contains this organization, but includes additional machinery for detecting the direction of movement of the zero-crossing segment, and it is this that provides a role for the two larger transient channels.

(3) *Signalling amplitude.* Ideally, the output of the cell should be gated by the logical AND function of (2), but its value should be the average local amplitude ν associated with the zero-crossings along the segment. As we saw earlier, this may be found by measuring the average local value of the slope of the zero-crossings, which (in suitable units) is equal to the sum of the inputs to the cell.

(4) *Sampling density.* Finally, for this scheme to be successful, the sampling density of the function $\nabla^2 G * I$ must be great enough to ensure that the zero-crossings may subsequently be localized accurately enough to account for the findings about hyperacuity (see, for example, Westheimer & McKee 1977), which means roughly to within 5'. This implies an extremely high precision of representation, but in layer IV of the monkey's striate cortex, there apparently exists a myriad of small, centre–surround, non-oriented cells (Hubel & Wiesel 1968). Barlow (1979) and Crick *et al.* (1980) have suggested that these cells may be involved in the reconstruction of the $\nabla^2 G$ function to an adequate precision for hyperacuity.

The empirical consequences of this overall scheme are set out by Marr & Ullman (1979).

Combination of zero-crossings

Empirical predictions for psychophysics

There are several aspects of our algorithm, for combining zero-crossings from different channels, that are accessible to psychophysical experiment. They are: (*a*) the phase relations; (*b*) combination of zero-crossings from different channels, and (*c*) the special cases that arise when zero-crossings lie close to one another.

(1) *Phase relations.* Our theory predicts that descriptors need exist only for sets

of zero-crossings, from different channels, that coincide spatially (i.e. have a phase relation of 0 or π). Interestingly, Atkinson & Campbell (1974) superimposed 1 and 3 cycles/deg sinusoidal gratings of the same orientation, and found that the number of perceptual fluctuations per minute (which they called rate of monocular rivalry) was low near the in-phase, 0, and out-of-phase, π, positions, but reached a high plateau for intermediate phase positions. They concluded (p.161) that the visual system contains a device that 'seems to be designed to respond only to 0 and π phase relation. When ... [it] ... is active, it gives rise to a stable percept that is the sum of the two spatial frequency selective channels' (cf. also Maffei & Fiorentini 1972a). Our theory would predict these results, if the additional assumption were made that units exist that represent explicitly the edge segment descriptor formed by combining appropriately arranged zero-crossing segments.

(2) *The parsing process.* The main point here is that the description of an edge (its width, amplitude and orientation) can be obtained from the (smallest) channel whose zero-crossing there has maximum slope. As Marr (1976b, pp. 496–497) observed, this is consistent with Harmon & Julesz's (1973) finding that noise bands spectrally adjacent to the spectrum of a picture are most effective at suppressing recognition, since these have their greatest effect on mask response amplitudes near the important mask sizes. It also explains why removal of the middle spatial frequencies from such an image leaves a recognizable image of Lincoln behind a visible graticule (see Harmon & Julesz 1973). The reason is that the zero-crossings from different mask sizes fail to coincide, and the gap in the spectrum means that the small bar descriptors fail to account for this discrepancy. Hence, the assumption of spatial coincidence cannot be used, and the outputs from the different mask sizes are assumed to be due to different physical phenomena. Accordingly, they give rise to independent descriptions.

There is another possible but weaker consequence. If one makes the extra assumption, that the selection criterion is implemented by inhibitory connections between zero-crossing segment detectors that are spatially coincident and lying adjacent in the frequency domain, then one would expect to find an inhibitory interaction between channels at the cortical, orientation-dependent level. There is, in fact, evidence that this occurs (see, for example, Tolhurst 1972; de Valois 1977a).

(3) *Bar-detectors.* Case (2) of our parsing algorithm requires the specific detection of close, parallel, zero-crossing segments. This requires the existence of units sensitive, at each orientation, to one of the four cases (black bar, white bar, two dark edges, two light edges) and sensitive to their width (i.e. the distance separating the edges) rather than to spatial frequency characteristics of the whole pattern. Adaptation studies that lead to these conclusions for white bars and for black bars have recently been published (Burton *et al.* 1977; de Valois 1977b). If our algorithm is implemented by the human visual system, the analogous result should hold for the remaining two cases (see figure 7a).

(4) *Blob-detectors and terminations.* Case (3) of our parsing algorithm requires

the explicit representation of (oriented) blobs and terminations. Units that represent them should be susceptible to psychophysical adaptation, and, in fact, Nakayama & Roberts (1972) and Burton & Ruddock (1978) have found evidence for units that are sensitive to bars whose length does not exceed three times the width.

Consequences for neurophysiology

There are several ways of implementing the parsing process that we have described, but it is probably not worth setting them out in detail until we have good evidence from psychophysics about the parsing algorithm that is actually used and we know whether simple cells, in fact, implement the detection of zero-crossing segments. Without these pieces of information firm predictions cannot be made, but we offer the following suggestions as a possible framework for the neural implementation. (1) The four types of 'bar' detectors could be implemented at the very first, simple cell level (along the lines of figure 9, but being fed by three rows of centre–surround cells instead of two). (2) For relatively isolated edges, there should exist oriented edge-segment–detecting neurons that combine zero-crossing segment detectors (simple cells) from different channels when, and only when, the segments are spatially coincident. (3) Detectors for terminations and blobs (doubly-terminated oriented bars) seem to have been found already (Hubel & Wiesel 1962, 1968). Interestingly, Schiller *et al.* (1976 *a*) found that even some simple cells are stopped. Our scheme is consistent with this since it requires such detectors at a very early stage.

DISCUSSION

The concept of an 'edge' has a partly visual and partly physical meaning. One of our main purposes in this article is to make explicit this dual dependence: our definition of an edge rests lightly on the early assumptions of theorem 1 about directional derivatives and heavily on the constraint of spatial localization.

Our theory is based on two main ideas. First, one simplifies the detection of intensity changes by dealing with the image separately at different resolutions. The detection process can then be based on finding zero-crossings in a second derivative operator, which, in practice, can be the (non-oriented) Laplacian. The representation at this point consists of zero-crossing segments and their slopes. This representation is probably complete and is, therefore, in principle, invertible. This had previously been given only an empirical demonstration by Marr and by R. Woodham (see Marr 1978, fig. 7).

The subsequent step, of combining information from different channels into a single description, rests on the second main idea of the theory, which we formulated as the spatial coincidence assumption. Physical edges will produce roughly coincident zero-crossings in channels of nearby sizes. The spatial coincidence assumption asserts that the converse of this is true, that is the coincidence of zero-crossings is sufficient evidence for the existence of a real physical edge. If the zero-crossings in one channel are not consistent with those in the others, they are probably caused by different physical phenomena, so descriptions need to be formed from both sources and kept somewhat separate.

Finally, the basic idea, that some simple cells detect and represent zero-crossing segments and that this is carried out simultaneously at different scales, has some implications for Marr & Poggio's (1979) stereo theory. According to various neuro-physiological studies (Barlow *et al.* 1967; Poggio & Fischer 1978; von der Heydt *et al.* 1978), there exist disparity sensitive simple cells. The existence of such cells is consistent with our suggestion that they detect zero-crossing segments, but not with the idea that they perform a linear convolution equivalent to a directional derivative, since it is the primitive symbolic descriptions provided by zero-crossing segments that need to be matched between images, not the raw convolution values.

We thank K. Nishihara, T. Poggio and S. Ullman for their illuminating and helpful comments. This work was conducted at the Artificial Intelligence Laboratory, a Massachusetts Institute of Technology research program supported in part by the Advanced Research Projects Agency of the Department of Defence and monitored by the Office of Naval Research, under contract number N00014-75-C-0643. D. M. was also supported by N.S.F. contract number 77-07569-MCS.

REFERENCES

Alpern, M., Rushton, W. A. H. & Torii, S. 1970 The size of rod signals. *J. Physiol., Lond.* **206**, 193–208.

Atkinson, J. & Campbell, F. W. 1974 The effect of phase on the perception of compound gratings. *Vision Res.* **14**, 159–162.

Barlow, H. B. 1969 Pattern recognition and the responses of sensory neurons. *Ann. N.Y. Acad. Sci.* **156**, 872–881.

Barlow, H. B. 1979 Reconstructing the visual image in space and time. *Nature, Lond.* **279**, 189–190.

Barlow, H. B., Blakemore, C. & Pettigrew, J. D. 1967 The neural mechanism of binocular depth discrimination. *J. Physiol., Lond.* **193**, 327–342.

Bracewell, R. 1965 *The Fourier transform and its applications.* New York: MacGraw-Hill.

Burton, G. J., Nagshineh, S. & Ruddock, K. H. 1977 Processing by the human visual system of the light and dark contrast components of the retinal image. *Biol. Cybernetics* **28**, 1–9.

Burton, G. J. & Ruddock, K. H. 1978 Visual adaptation to patterns containing two-dimensional spatial structure. *Vision Res.* **18**, 93–99.

Campbell, F. W. & Robson, J. G. 1968 Applications of Fourier analysis to the visibility of gratings. *J. Physiol., Lond.* **197**, 551–556.

Cleland, B. G., Dubin, M. W. & Levick, W. R. 1971 Sustained and transient neurones in the cat's retina and lateral geniculate nucleus. *J. Physiol., Lond.* **217**, 473–496.

Cowan, J. D. 1977 Some remarks on channel bandwidths for visual contrast detection. *Neurosci. Res. Prog. Bull.* **15**, 492–517.

Crick, F. H. C., Marr, D. & Poggio, T. 1980 An information processing approach to understanding the visual cortex. To appear in the N.R.P. symposium *The cerebral cortex* (ed. F. O. Schmidt & F. G. Worden).

De Valois, K. K. 1977a Spatial frequency adaptation can enhance contrast sensitivity. *Vision Res.* **17**, 1057–1065.

De Valois, K. K. 1977b Independence of black and white: phase-specific adaptation. *Vision Res.* **17**, 209–215.

Enroth-Cugell, C. & Robson, J. G. 1966 The contrast sensitivity of retinal ganglion cells of the cat. *J. Physiol., Lond.* **187**, 517–552.

Graham, N. 1977 Visual detection of aperiodic spatial stimuli by probability summation among narrowband channels. *Vision Res.* **17**, 637–652.

Harmon, L. D. & Julesz, B. 1973 Masking in visual recognition: effects of two-dimensional filtered noise. *Science N.Y.* **180**, 1194–1197.

von der Heydt, R., Adorjani, Cs., Hanny, P. & Baumgartner, G. 1978 Disparity sensitivity and receptive field incongruity of units in the cat striate cortex. *Exp. Brain Res.* **31**, 523–545.

Hubel, D. H. & Wiesel, T. N. 1961 Integrative action in the cat's lateral geniculate body. *J. Physiol., Lond.* **155**, 385–398.

Hubel, D. H. & Wiesel, T. N. 1962 Receptive fields, binocular interaction and functional architecture in the cat's visual cortex. *J. Physiol., Lond.* **160**, 106–154.

Hubel, D. H. & Wiesel, T. N. 1968 Receptive fields and functional architecture of monkey striate cortex. *J. Physiol., Lond.* **195**, 215–243.

Hubel, D. H. & Wiesel, T. N. 1974 Uniformity of monkey striate cortex: a parallel relationship between field size, scatter, and magnification factor. *J. comp. Neurol.* **158**, 295–306.

Kulikowski, J. J. & King-Smith, P. E. 1973 Spatial arrangement of line, edge, and grating detectors revealed by subthreshold summation. *Vision Res.* **13**. 1455–1478.

Leipnik, R. 1960 The extended entropy uncertainty principle. *Inf. Control* **3**, 18–25.

Logan, B. F. Jr 1977 Information in the zero-crossings of bandpass signals. *Bell Syst. tech. J.* **56**. 487–510.

Macleod, I. D. G. & Rosenfeld, A. 1974 The visibility of gratings: spatial frequency channels or bar-detecting units? *Vision Res.* **14**, 909–915.

Maffei, L. & Fiorentini, A. 1972a Process of synthesis in visual perception. *Nature, Lond.* **240**, 479–481.

Maffei, L. & Fiorentini, A. 1972b Retinogeniculate convergence and analysis of contrast. *J. Neurophysiol.* **35**, 65–72.

Maffei, L. & Fiorentini, A. 1977 Spatial frequency rows in the striate visual cortex. *Vision Res.* **17**, 257–264.

Marr, D. 1970 A theory for cerebral neocortex. *Proc. R. Soc. Lond.* B **176**, 161–234.

Marr, D. 1976a Analyzing natural images: a computational theory of texture vision. *Cold Spring Harbor Symp. quant. Biol.* **40**, 647–662.

Marr, D. 1976b Early processing of visual information. *Phil. Trans. R. Soc. Lond.* B **275**, 483–524.

Marr, D. 1978 Representing visual information. A.A.A.S. 143rd Annual Meeting, Symposium on: Some mathematical questions in biology, February 1977. Published in *Lectures on mathematics in the life sciences* **10**, 101–180. Also available as *M.I.T A.I. Lab. Memo* 415.

Marr, D. & Poggio, T. 1979 A computational theory of human stereo vision. *Proc. R. Soc. Lond.* B **204**, 301–328.

Marr, D., Poggio, T. & Ullman, S. 1979 Bandpass channels, zero-crossings, and early visual information processing. *J. opt. Soc. Am.* **69**, 914–916.

Marr, D. & Ullman, S. 1979 Directional selectivity and its use in early visual processing. (In preparation.)

Mayhew, J. E. W. & Frisby, J. P. 1978 Suprathreshold contrast perception and complex random textures. *Vision Res.* **18**, 895–897.

Nakayama, K. & Roberts, D. J. 1972 Line-length detectors in the human visual system: evidence from selective adaptation. *Vision Res.* **12**, 1709–1713.

Peichl, L. & Wässle, H. 1979 Size, scatter and coverage of ganglion cell receptive field centres in the cat retina. *J. Physiol., Lond.* **291**, 117–141.

Poggio, G. F. & Fischer, B. 1978 Binocular interaction and depth sensitivity of striate and prestriate neurons of the behaving rhesus monkey. *J. Neurophysiol.* **40**, 1392–1405.

D. Marr and E. Hildreth

Pollen, D. A., Lee, J. R. & Taylor, J. H. 1971 How does the striate cortex begin the reconstruction of the visual world? *Science N.Y.* **173**, 74–77.

Ratliff, F. 1965 *Mach bands: quantitative studies on neural networks in the retina.* San Francisco: Holden-Day.

Rodieck, R. W. & Stone, J. 1965 Analysis of receptive fields of cat retinal ganglion cells. *J. Neurophysiol.* **28**, 833–849.

Rosenfeld, A. & Kak, A. C. 1976 *Digital picture processing.* New York: Academic Press.

Sachs, M. B., Nachmias, J. & Robson, J. G. 1971 Spatial-frequency channels in human vision. *J. opt. Soc. Am.* **61**, 1176–1186.

Shapley, R. M. & Tolhurst, D. J. 1973 Edge detectors in human vision. *J. Physiol., Lond.* **229**, 165–183.

Schiller, P. H., Finlay, B. L. & Volman, S. F. 1976a Quantitative studies of single-cell properties in monkey striate cortex. I. Spatiotemporal organization of receptive fields. *J. Neurophysiol.* **39**, 1288–1319.

Schiller, P. H., Finlay, B. L. & Volman, S. F. 1976b Quantitative studies of single-cell properties in monkey striate cortex. II. Orientation specificity and ocular dominance. *J. Neurophysiol.* **39**, 1320–1333.

Ullman, S. 1976 On visual detection of light sources. *Biol. Cybernetics* **21**, 205–212.

Westheimer, G. & McKee, S. P. 1977 Spatial configurations for visual hyperacuity. *Vision Res.* **17**, 941–947.

Wilson, H. R. & Bergen, J. R. 1979 A four mechanism model for spatial vision. *Vision Res.* **19**, 19–32.

Wilson, H. R. & Giese, S. C. 1977 Threshold visibility of frequency gradient patterns. *Vision Res.* **17**. 1177–1190.

APPENDIX A

THEOREM 1

Let l be an open line segment of the y-axis, containing the origin O. Suppose that $f(x, y)$ is twice continuously differentiable and that $N(l)$ is an open two-dimensional neighbourhood of l. Assume that $\partial^2 f/\partial x^2 = 0$ on l. Then, if $\partial f/\partial y$ is constant in $N(l)$, the slope of the second directional derivative taken perpendicular to l (i.e., the slope of $\partial^2 f/\partial x^2$) is greater than the slope of the zero-crossing along any other line through O.

Proof

Consider the line segment $\Omega = (r \cos \theta, r \sin \theta)$ for fixed θ and values of r sufficiently small that Ω lies entirely within $N(l)$ (see figure 10). Now writing f_{xx} for $\partial^2 f/\partial x^2$ etc., we have

$$(\partial^2 f/\partial \Omega^2)_{r, \theta} = (f_{xx} \cos^2 \theta + f_{xy} 2 \sin \theta \cos \theta + f_{yy} \sin^2 \theta)_{r, \theta}$$
$$= (f_{xx} \cos^2 \theta)_{r, \theta},$$

since the condition of the theorem that f_y be constant implies that f_{xy} and f_{yy} are both zero. As required, therefore, the above quantity is zero at $r = 0$ and has maximum slope when $\theta = 0$.

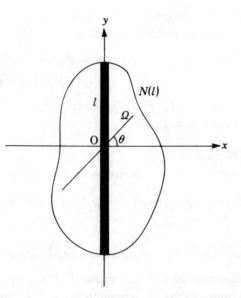

FIGURE 10. Diagram for theorems 1 and 2: l is a segment of the y-axis, containing the origin; $N(l)$ is a neighbourhood of it. Provided that $\partial f/\partial y$ is constant in $N(l)$, theorem 1 states that the orientation of the line of zero-crossings is perpendicular to the orientation at which the zero-crossings have maximum slope.

THEOREM 2

Let $f(x, y)$ be a real-valued, twice continuously differentiable function on the plane. Let l be an open line segment along the axis $x = 0$. Then the two conditions

$$\text{(i)} \quad \nabla^2 f = 0 \text{ on } l$$

$$\text{and (ii)} \quad \partial^2 f/\partial x^2 = 0 \text{ on } l$$

are equivalent if and only if $f(0, y)$ is constant or linear on l.

Proof

If $f(0, y)$ is linear on l, $\partial^2 f/\partial y^2 = 0$ on l. Hence, $\nabla^2 f = 0$ there implies that $\partial^2 f/\partial x^2 = 0$ on l too.

Conversely, if $\partial^2 f/\partial x^2 = \nabla^2 f = 0$ on l, then $\partial^2 f/\partial y^2 = 0$ on l, and so $f(0, y)$ varies at most linearly on l.

APPENDIX B
DOGS *and* $\nabla^2 G$

$\nabla^2 G$ *is the limit of a* DOG

Wilson's *DOG* function may be written

$$\text{DOG}\,(\sigma_{\mathrm{e}}, \sigma_1) = [1/(2\pi)^{\frac{1}{2}}\,\sigma_{\mathrm{e}}]\exp\left(-x^2/2\sigma_{\mathrm{e}}^2\right) - [1/(2\pi)^{\frac{1}{2}}\,\sigma_1]\exp\left(-x^2/2\sigma_1^2\right), \quad (3)$$

D. Marr and E. Hildreth

where σ_e and σ_i are the excitatory and inhibitory space constants. Writing $\sigma_e = \sigma$, and $\sigma_i = \sigma + \delta\sigma$, the right hand side varies with

$$(1/\sigma)\exp(-x^2/2\sigma^2) - [1/(\sigma + \delta\sigma)]\exp[-x^2/2(\sigma + \delta\sigma)^2]$$
$$= \delta\sigma\,(\partial/\partial\sigma)\,(1/\sigma\exp[-x^2/2\sigma^2]). \qquad (4)$$

This derivative is equal to $-(1/\sigma^2 - x^2/\sigma^4)\exp(-x^2/2\sigma^2)$, which equals G'' up to a constant (text equation 5).)

Approximation of $\nabla^2 G$ by a DOG

The function

$$\text{DOG}\,(\sigma_e, \sigma_1) = [1/(2\pi)^{\frac{1}{2}}\sigma_e]\exp(-x^2/2\sigma_e^2) - [1/(2\pi)^{\frac{1}{2}}\sigma_1]\exp(-x^2/2\sigma_i^2) \qquad (5)$$

has Fourier transform

$$\widetilde{DOG}\,(\omega) = \exp(-\sigma_e^2\,\omega^2/2) - \exp(-\sigma_i^2\,\omega^2/2) \qquad (6)$$

Notice that $\widetilde{DOG}\,(\omega)$ behaves like ω^2 for values of ω that are small compared with σ_e and σ_i, so that these filters, in common with $\nabla^2 G$, approximate a second derivative operator.

The problem with using a DOG to approximate $\nabla^2 G$ is to find a space constant that keeps the bandwidth of the filter small and yet allows the filter adequate sensitivity: for, clearly, as the space constants approach one another, the contributions of the excitatory and inhibitory components become identical and the sensitivity of the filter is reduced.

The bandwidths at half sensitivity and at half power and the peak sensitivity all depend together on the value of σ_i/σ_e in a way that is shown in figure 11. From this we see that: (i) the bandwidth at half sensitivity increases very slowly up to about $\sigma_i/\sigma_e = 1.6$, increases faster from there to $\sigma_i/\sigma_e = 3.0$, and is thereafter approximately constant; (ii) the peak sensitivity of the filter is desultory for small σ_i/σ_e, reaching about 33 % at $\sigma_i/\sigma_e = 1.6$. Since our aim is to create a narrow bandpass differential operator, we should choose σ_i/σ_e to minimize the bandwidth. Since the bandwidth is approximately constant for $\sigma_i/\sigma_e < 1.6$, and since sensitivity is low there, the minimal value one would in practice choose for σ_i/σ_e is around 1.6, giving a half-sensitivity bandwidth of 1.8 octaves and a half power bandwidth of 1.3 octaves.

The raw primal sketch

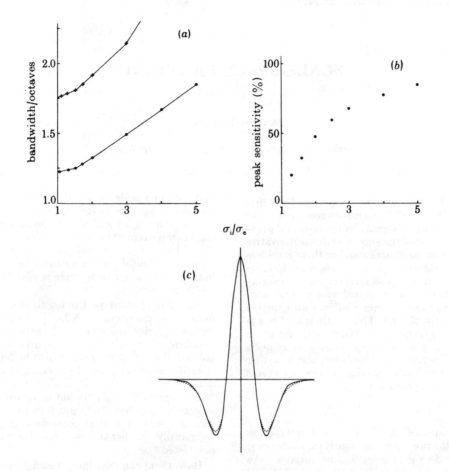

FIGURE 11. The values of certain parameters associated with difference-of-Gaussian (DOG) masks, with excitatory and inhibitory space constants σ_e and σ_i. (a) For various values of σ_e/σ_i, we show the half-sensitivity bandwidth ($+$) and the half-power bandwidth ($\bullet$) of the filter. In (b) is shown its peak sensitivity in the Fourier plane. (The peak sensitivity of the excitatory component alone equals 100 % on this scale.) (c) The arguments in the appendix show that the best engineering approximation to $\nabla^2 G$ using a DOG occurs with σ_i/σ_e around 1.6. In figure (c), this particular DOG is shown dotted against the operator $\nabla^2 G$ with the appropriate σ. The two profiles are very similar.

107

SCALE-SPACE FILTERING

Andrew P. Witkin

Fairchild Laboratory for Artificial Intelligence Research

ABSTRACT—The extrema in a signal and its first few derivatives provide a useful general-purpose qualitative description for many kinds of signals. A fundamental problem in computing such descriptions is scale: a derivative must be taken over some neighborhood, but there is seldom a principled basis for choosing its size. Scale-space filtering is a method that describes signals qualitatively, managing the ambiguity of scale in an organized and natural way. The signal is first expanded by convolution with gaussian masks over a continuum of sizes. This "scale-space" image is then collapsed, using its qualitative structure, into a tree providing a concise but complete qualitative description covering all scales of observation. The description is further refined by applying a stability criterion, to identify events that persist of large changes in scale.

1. Introduction

Hardly any sophisticated signal understanding task can be performed using the raw numerical signal values directly; some description of the signal must first be obtained. An initial description ought to be as compact as possible, and its elements should correspond as closely as possible to meaningful objects or events in the signal-forming process. Frequently, local extrema in the signal and its derivatives—and intervals bounded by extrema—are particularly appropriate descriptive primitives: although local and closely tied to the signal data, these events often have direct semantic interpretations, e.g. as edges in images. A description that characterizes a signal by its extrema and those of its first few derivatives is a *qualitative* description of exactly the kind we were taught to use in elementary calculus to "sketch" a function.

A great deal of effort has been expended to obtain this kind of primitive qualitative description (for overviews of this literature, see [1,2,3].) and the problem has proved extremely difficult. The problem of *scale* has emerged consistently as a fundamental source of difficulty, because the events we perceive and find meaningful vary enormously in size and extent. The problem is not so much to eliminate fine-scale noise, as to separate events at different scales arising from distinct physical processes.[4] It is possible to introduce a *parameter of scale* by smoothing the signal with a mask of variable size, but with the introduction of scale-dependence comes ambiguity: every setting of the scale parameter yields a different description; new extremal points may appear, and existing ones may move or disappear. How can we decide which if any of this continuum of descriptions is "right"?

There is rarely a sound basis for setting the scale parameter. In fact, it has become apparent that for many tasks no one scale of description is categorically correct: the physical processes that generate signals such as images act at a variety of scales, none intrinsically more interesting or important than another. Thus the ambiguity introduced by scale is inherent and inescapable, so the goal of scale-dependent description cannot be to eliminate this ambiguity, but rather to manage it effectively, and reduce it where possible.

This line of thinking has led to considerable interest in multi-scale descriptions [5,2,6,7]. However, merely computing descriptions at multiple scales does not solve the problem; if anything, it exacerbates it by increasing the volume of data. Some means must be found to organize or simplify the description, by relating one scale to another. Some work has been done in this area aimed at obtaining "edge pyramids" (e.g. [8]), but no clear-cut criteria for constructing them have been put forward. Marr [4] suggested that zero-crossings that coincide over several scales are "physically significant," but this idea was neither justified nor tested.

How, then, can descriptions at different scales be related to each other in an organized, natural, and compact way? Our solution, which we call *scale-space filtering,* begins by continuously varying the scale parameter, sweeping out a surface that we call the *scale-space image.* In this representation, it is possible to track extrema as they move continuously with scale changes, and to identify the singular points at which new extrema appear. The scale-space image is then collapsed into a tree, providing a concise but complete qualitative description of the signal over all scales of observation.[1]

2. The Scale-Space Image

Descriptions that depend on scale can be computed in many ways. As a primitive scale-parameterization, the gaussian convolution is attractive for a number of its properties, amounting to "well-behavedness": the gaussian is symmetric and strictly decreasing about the mean, and therefore the weighting assigned to signal values decreases smoothly with distance. The gaussian convolution behaves well near the limits of the scale parameter, σ, approaching the un-smoothed signal for small σ, and approaching the signal's mean for large σ. The gaussian is also readily differentiated and integrated.

The gaussian is not the only convolution kernel that meets these criteria. However, a more specific motivation for our choice is a property of the gaussian convolution's

---

[1] A complementary approach to the "natural" scale problem has been developed by Hoffman [9].

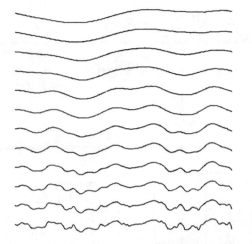

Figure 1. A sequence of gaussian smoothings of a waveform, with σ decreasing from top to bottom. Each graph is a constant-σ profile from the scale-space image.

zero-crossings (and those of its derivatives): as σ decreases, additional zeroes may appear, but existing ones cannot in general disappear; moreover, of convolution kernels satisfying "well behavedness" criteria (roughly those enumerated above,) the gaussian is the *only* one guaranteed to satisfy this condition [12]. The usefulness of this property will be explained in the following sections.

The gaussian convolution of a signal $f(x)$ depends both on x, the signal's independent variable, and on σ, the gaussian's standard deviation. The convolution is given by

$$F(x,\sigma) = f(x) * g(x,\sigma) = \int_{-\infty}^{\infty} f(u) \frac{1}{\sigma\sqrt{2\pi}} e^{-\frac{(x-u)^2}{2\sigma^2}} \, du,$$

(1)

where "$*$" denotes convolution with respect to x. This function defines a surface on the (x,σ)-plane, where each profile of constant σ is a gaussian-smoothed version of $f(x)$, the amount of smoothing increasing with σ. We will call the (x,σ)-plane *scale space*, and the function, F, defined in (1), the *scale-space image* of f.[2] Fig. 1 graphs a sequence of gaussian smoothings with increasing σ. These are constant-σ profiles from the scale-space image.

At any value of σ, the extrema in the nth derivative of the smoothed signal are given by the zero-crossings in the $(n+1)$th derivative, computed using the relation

$$\frac{\partial^n F}{\partial x^n} = f * \frac{\partial^n g}{\partial x^n},$$

where the derivatives of the gaussian are readily obtained. Although the methods presented here apply to zeros in any derivative, we will restrict our attention to those in the second. These are extrema of slope, i.e. inflection points. In terms of the scale-space image, the inflections at *all* values of σ are the points that satisfy

$$F_{xx} = 0, F_{xxx} \neq 0,$$

(2)

[2]It is actually convenient to treat $\log \sigma$ as the scale parameter, uniform expansion or contraction of the signal in the x-direction will cause a translation of the scale-space image along the $\log \sigma$ axis.

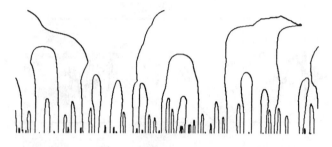

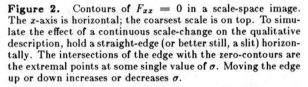

Figure 2. Contours of $F_{xx} = 0$ in a scale-space image. The x-axis is horizontal; the coarsest scale is on top. To simulate the effect of a continuous scale-change on the qualitative description, hold a straight-edge (or better still, a slit) horizontally. The intersections of the edge with the zero-contours are the extremal points at some single value of σ. Moving the edge up or down increases or decreases σ.

using subscript notation to indicate partial differentiation.[3]

3. Coarse-to-fine Tracking

The contours of $F_{xx} = 0$ mark the appearance and motion of inflection points in the smoothed signal, and provide the raw material for a qualitative description over all scales, in terms of inflection points. Next, we will apply two simplifying assumptions to these contours: (1) the *identity* assumption, that extrema observed at different scales, but lying on a common zero-contour in scale space, arise from a single underlying event, and (2) the *localization* assumption, that the true location of an event giving rise to a zero-contour is the contour's x location as $\sigma \to 0$.

Referring to fig. 2, notice that the zero contours form arches, closed above, but open below. The restriction that zero-crossings may never disappear with with decreasing σ (see section 2) means that the contours may *never* be closed below. Note that at the apexes of the arches, $F_{xxx} = 0$, so by eq. (2), these points do not belong to the contour. Each arch consists of a pair of contours, crossing zero with opposite sign.

The *localization assumption* is motivated by the observation that linear smoothing has two effects: qualitative simplification—the removal of fine-scale features—and spatial distortion—dislocation, broadening and flattening of the features that survive. The latter undesirable effect may be overcome, by tracking coarse extrema to their fine-scale locations. Thus, a coarse scale may be used to *identify* extrema, and a fine scale, to *localize* them. Each zero-contour therefore reduces to an (x,σ) pair, specifying its fine-scale location on the x-axis, and the coarsest scale at which the contour appears.

A coarse-to-fine tracking description is compared to the

[3]Note that the second condition in (2) excludes zero-crossings that are parallel to the x-axis, because these are not zero-crossings in the convolved signal.

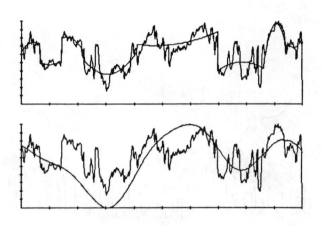

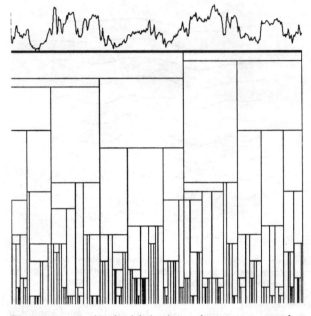

Figure 3. Above is shown a signal with a coarse-to-fine tracking approximation superimposed. The approximation was produced by independent parabolic fits between the localized inflections. Below is shown the corresponding (qualitatively isomorphic) gaussian smoothing.

corresponding linear smoothing in Fig. 3.[4]

4. The Interval Tree

While coarse-to-fine tracking solves the problem of localizing large-scale events, it does not solve the multi-scale integration problem, because the description still depends on the choice of the continuous global scale parameter, σ, just as simple linear filtering does. In this section, we reduce the scale-space image to a simple tree, concisely but completely describing the qualitative structure of the signal over all scales of observation.

This simplification rests on a basic property of the scale-space image: as σ is varied, extremal points in the smoothed signal appear and disappear at singular points (the tops of the arches in fig. 2.) Passing through such a point with decreasing σ, a pair of extrema of opposite sign appear in the smoothed signal. At these points, and only these points, the *un*distinguished interval (i.e. an interval bounded by extremal points but containing none) in which the singularity occurs splits into three subintervals. In general, each undistinguished interval, observed in scale space, is bounded on each side by the zero contours that define it, bounded above by the singular point at which it merges into an enclosing interval, and bounded below by the singular point at which it divides into sub-intervals.

Consequently, to each interval, I, corresponds a node in a (generally ternary-branching) tree, whose parent node denotes the larger interval from which I emerged, and whose offspring represent the smaller intervals into which I subdivides. Each interval also defines a rectangle in scale-space, denoting its location and extent on the signal (as defined by coarse-to-fine tracking) and its location and extent on the scale dimension. Collectively, these rectangles

Figure 4. A signal with its interval tree, represented as a rectangular tesselation of scale-space. Each rectangle is a node, indicating an interval on the signal, and the scale interval over which the signal interval exists.

tesselate the (x, σ)-plane. See fig. 4 for an illustration of the tree.

This *interval tree* may be viewed in two ways: as describing the signal simultaneously at all scales, or as generating a family of single-scale descriptions, each defined by a subset of nodes in the tree that cover the x-axis. On the second interpretation, one may move through the family of descriptions in orderly, local, discrete steps, either by choosing to subdivide an interval into its offspring, or to merge a triple of intervals into their parent.[5]

We found that it is in general possible, by moving interactively through the tree and observing the resulting "sketch" of the signal, to closely match observers' spontaneously perceived descriptions. Thus the interval tree, though tightly constrained, seems flexible enough to capture human perceptual intuitions. Somewhat surprisingly, we found that the tree, rather than being too constraining, is not constrained enough. That is, the perceptually salient descriptions can in general be duplicated within the tree's constraints, but the tree also generates many descriptions that plainly have no perceptual counterpart. This observation led us to develop a *stability* criterion for further pruning or ordering the states of the tree, which is described in the next section.

5. Stability

Recall that to each interval in the tree corresponds a rectangle in scale space. The x boundaries locate the interval on the signal. The σ boundaries define the scale range over which the interval exists, its *stability* over scale changes. We have observed empirically a marked correspondence between the stability of an interval and its perceptual salience: those intervals that survive over a broad range of scales

---

[4]In this and all illustrations, approximations were drawn by fitting parabolic arcs independently to the signal data on each interval marked by the description. This procedure is crude, particularly because continuity is not enforced across inflections. Bear in mind that this procedure has been used only to display the qualitative description.

[5]For previous uses of hierarchic signal descriptions see e.g. [10,11,2].

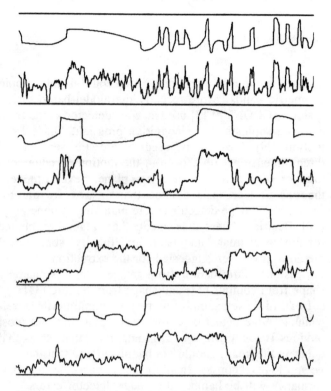

Figure 5. Several signals, with their maximum-stability descriptions. These are "top-level" descriptions, generated automatically and without thresholds. You should compare the descriptions to your own first-glance "top-level" percepts. (the noisy sine and square waves are synthetic signals.)

tend to leap out at the eye, while the most ephemeral are not perceived at all. To capture this relation, we have devised several versions of a stability criterion, one of which picks a "top-level" description by descending the tree until a local maximum in stability is found. Another iteratively removes nodes from the tree, splicing out nodes that are less stable than any of their parents and offspring. Both of these radically improve correspondence between the interval tree's descriptions and perceptual features (see fig. 5.)

6. Summary

Scale-space filtering is a method that describes signals qualitatively, in terms of extrema in the signal or its derivatives, in a manner that deals effectively with the problem of scale—precisely localizing large-scale events, and effectively managing the ambiguity of descriptions at multiple scales, without introducing arbitrary thresholds or free parameters. The one-dimensional signal is first expanded into a two-dimensional *scale-space image*, by convolution with gaussians over a continuum of sizes. This continuous surface is then collapsed into a discrete structure, using the connectivity of extremal points tracked through scale-space, and the singular points at which new extrema appear. The resulting tree representation is a a concise but complete qualitative description of the signal over all scales of observation. The tree is further constrained using a maximum-stability criterion to favor events that persist over large changes in scale.

We are currently developing applications of scale-space filtering to several signal matching and interpretation problems, and investigating its ability to explain perceptual grouping phenomena. The method is also being extended to apply to two-dimensional images: the scale-space image of a 2-D signal occupies a volume, containing zero-crossing surfaces.[6]

REFERENCES

[1] A. Rosenfeld and A. C. Kak Digital Picture Processing. *Academic Press, New York, New York*, 1976.

[2] D. H. Ballard and C. M. Brown Computer Vision. *Prentice Hall, Englewood Cliffs, New Jersey*, 1982.

[3] Pavlidis, T. *Structural Pattern Recognition*. Springer, 1977

[4] D. Marr Vision, *W. H. Freeman, San Fransisco*, 1982.

[5] Rosenfeld, A. and Thurston, M. "Edge and curve detection for visual scene analysis." *IEEE Transactions on computers, Vol C-20 pp. 562–569*. (May 1971).

[6] Marr, D and Poggio, T. "A computational theory of human stereo vision." *Proc. R. Soc. Lond.*, B. 204 (1979) pp. 301–328

[7] D. Marr and E. C. Hildreth Theory of Edge Detection. *M.I.T. Artificial Intelligence Memo Number 518, Cambridge, Massachusetts*, April 1979.

[8] Hong, T. H., Shneier, M. and Rosenfeld, A. Border Extraction using linked edge pyramids. *TR-1080, Computer Vision Laboratory, U. Maryland*, July 1981

[9] Hoffman, D. Representing Shapes For Visual Recognition *Ph.D. Thesis, MIT, forthcoming.*

[10] Erich, R. and Foith, J., "Representation of random waveforms by relational trees," *IEE Trans. Computers, Vol C-26, pp. 725–736*, (July 1976).

[11] Blumenthal A., Davis, L., and Rosenfeld, R., "Detecting natural 'plateaus' in one-dimensional patterns." *IEEE Transactions on computers*, (Feb. 1977)

[12] J. Babaud, R. Duda, and A. Witkin, *in preparation.*

[6]**Acknowledgments**—I thank my colleagues at FLAIR, particularly Richard Duda and Peter Hart, as well as J. Babaud of Schlumberger, ltd., for their help and encouragement.

Reprinted from *IEEE Transactions on Pattern Analysis and Machine Intelligence*, Volume PAMI-8, Number 6, November 1986, pages 679-698. Copyright © 1986 by The Institute of Electrical and Electronics Engineers, Inc. All rights reserved.

A Computational Approach to Edge Detection

JOHN CANNY, MEMBER, IEEE

Abstract—This paper describes a computational approach to edge detection. The success of the approach depends on the definition of a *comprehensive* set of goals for the computation of edge points. These goals must be precise enough to delimit the desired behavior of the detector while making minimal assumptions about the form of the solution. We define detection and localization criteria for a class of edges, and present mathematical forms for these criteria as functionals on the operator impulse response. A third criterion is then added to ensure that the detector has only one response to a single edge. We use the criteria in numerical optimization to derive detectors for several common image features, including step edges. On specializing the analysis to step edges, we find that there is a natural uncertainty principle between detection and localization performance, which are the two main goals. With this principle we derive a single operator shape which is optimal at any scale. The optimal detector has a simple approximate implementation in which edges are marked at maxima in gradient magnitude of a Gaussian-smoothed image. We extend this simple detector using operators of several widths to cope with different signal-to-noise ratios in the image. We present a general method, called feature synthesis, for the fine-to-coarse integration of information from operators at different scales. Finally we show that step edge detector performance improves considerably as the operator point spread function is extended along the edge. This detection scheme uses several elongated operators at each point, and the directional operator outputs are integrated with the gradient maximum detector.

Index Terms—Edge detection, feature extraction, image processing, machine vision, multiscale image analysis.

I. INTRODUCTION

EDGE detectors of some kind, particularly step edge detectors, have been an essential part of many computer vision systems. The edge detection process serves to simplify the analysis of images by drastically reducing the amount of data to be processed, while at the same time preserving useful structural information about object boundaries. There is certainly a great deal of diversity in the applications of edge detection, but it is felt that many applications share a common set of requirements. These requirements yield an abstract edge detection problem, the solution of which can be applied in any of the original problem domains.

We should mention some specific applications here. The Binford–Horn line finder [14] used the output of an edge

detector as input to a program which could isolate simple geometric solids. More recently the model-based vision system ACRONYM [3] used an edge detector as the front end to a sophisticated recognition program. Shape from motion [29], [13] can be used to infer the structure of three-dimensional objects from the motion of edge contours or edge points in the image plane. Several modern theories of stereopsis assume that images are preprocessed by an edge detector before matching is done [19], [20]. Beattie [1] describes an edge-based labeling scheme for low-level image understanding. Finally, some novel methods have been suggested for the extraction of three-dimensional information from image contours, namely shape from contour [27] and shape from texture [31].

In all of these examples there are common criteria relevant to edge detector performance. The first and most obvious is low error rate. It is important that edges that occur in the image should not be missed and that there be no spurious responses. In all the above cases, system performance will be hampered by edge detector errors. The second criterion is that the edge points be well localized. That is, the distance between the points marked by the detector and the "center" of the true edge should be minimized. This is particularly true of stereo and shape from motion, where small disparities are measured between left and right images or between images produced at slightly different times.

In this paper we will develop a mathematical form for these two criteria which can be used to design detectors for arbitrary edges. We will also discover that the first two criteria are not "tight" enough, and that it is necessary to add a third criterion to circumvent the possibility of multiple responses to a single edge. Using numerical optimization, we derive optimal operators for ridge and roof edges. We will then specialize the criteria for step edges and give a parametric closed form for the solution. In the process we will discover that there is an uncertainty principle relating detection and localization of noisy step edges, and that there is a direct tradeoff between the two. One consequence of this relationship is that there is a single unique "shape" of impulse response for an optimal step edge detector, and that the tradeoff between detection and localization can be varied by changing the spatial width of the detector. Several examples of the detector performance on real images will be given.

Manuscript received December 10, 1984; revised November 27, 1985. Recommended for acceptance by S. L. Tanimoto. This work was supported in part by the System Development Foundation, in part by the Office of Naval Research under Contract N00014-81-K-0494, and in part by the Advanced Research Projects Agency under Office of Naval Research Contracts N00014-80-C-0505 and N00014-82-K-0334.

The author is with the Artificial Intelligence Laboratory, Massachusetts Institute of Technology, Cambridge, MA 02139.

IEEE Log Number 8610412.

II. ONE-DIMENSIONAL FORMULATION

To facilitate the analysis we first consider one-dimensional edge profiles. That is, we will assume that two-

112

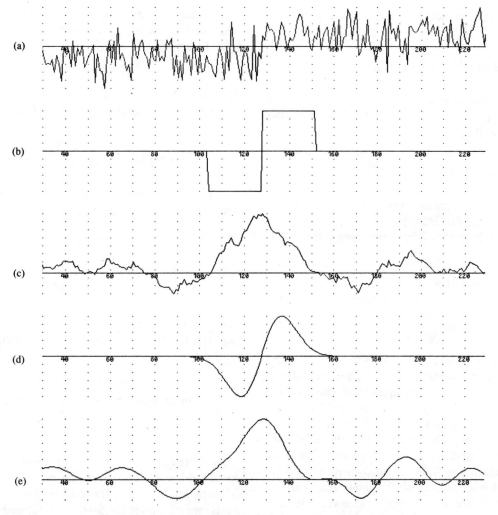

Fig. 1. (a) A noisy step edge. (b) Difference of boxes operator. (c) Difference of boxes operator applied to the edge. (d) First derivative of Gaussian operator. (e) First derivative of Gaussian applied to the edge.

dimensional edges locally have a constant cross-section in some direction. This would be true for example, of smooth edge contours or of ridges, but not true of corners. We will assume that the image consists of the edge and additive white Gaussian noise.

The detection problem is formulated as follows: We begin with an edge of known cross-section bathed in white Gaussian noise as in Fig. 1(a), which shows a step edge. We convolve this with a filter whose impulse response could be illustrated by either Fig. 1(b) or (d). The outputs of the convolutions are shown, respectively, in Fig. 1(c) and (e). We will mark the center of an edge at a local maximum in the output of the convolution. The design problem then becomes one of finding the filter which gives the best performance with respect to the criteria given below. For example, the filter in Fig. 1(d) performs much better than Fig. 1(b) on this example, because the response of the latter exhibits several local maxima in the region of the edge.

In summary, the three performance criteria are as follows:

1) Good detection. There should be a low probability of failing to mark real edge points, and low probability of falsely marking nonedge points. Since both these probabilities are monotonically decreasing functions of the output signal-to-noise ratio, this criterion corresponds to maximizing signal-to-noise ratio.

2) Good localization. The points marked as edge points by the operator should be as close as possible to the center of the true edge.

3) Only one response to a single edge. This is implicitly captured in the first criterion since when there are two responses to the same edge, one of them must be considered false. However, the mathematical form of the first criterion did not capture the multiple response requirement and it had to be made explicit.

A. Detection and Localization Criteria

A crucial step in our method is to capture the intuitive criteria given above in a mathematical form which is readily solvable. We deal first with signal-to-noise ratio and localization. Let the impulse response of the filter be $f(x)$, and denote the edge itself by $G(x)$. We will assume that the edge is centered at $x = 0$. Then the response of the filter to this edge at its center H_G is given by a convolution integral:

$$H_G = \int_{-W}^{+W} G(-x) f(x) \, dx \qquad (1)$$

assuming the filter has a finite impulse response bounded by $[-W, W]$. The root-mean-squared response to the noise $n(x)$ only, will be

$$H_n = n_0 \left[\int_{-W}^{+W} f^2(x) \, dx \right]^{1/2} \qquad (2)$$

where n_0^2 is the mean-squared noise amplitude per unit length. We define our first criterion, the output signal-to-noise ratio, as the quotient of these two responses.

$$\text{SNR} = \frac{\left| \int_{-W}^{+W} G(-x) f(x) \, dx \right|}{n_0 \sqrt{\int_{-W}^{+W} f^2(x) \, dx}} \qquad (3)$$

For the localization criterion, we want some measure which increases as localization improves, and we will use the reciprocal of the root-mean-squared distance of the marked edge from the center of the true edge. Since we have decided to mark edges at local maxima in the response of the operator $f(x)$, the first derivative of the response will be zero at these points. Note also that since edges are centered at $x = 0$, *in the absence of noise there should be a local maximum in the response at $x = 0$*.

Let $H_n(x)$ be the response of the filter to noise only, and $H_G(x)$ be its response to the edge, and suppose there is a local maximum in the total response at the point $x = x_0$. Then we have

$$H_n'(x_0) + H_G'(x_0) = 0. \qquad (4)$$

The Taylor expansion of $H_G'(x_0)$ about the origin gives

$$H_G'(x_0) = H_G'(0) + H_G''(0) x_0 + O(x_0^2). \qquad (5)$$

By assumption $H_G'(0) = 0$, i.e., the response of the filter in the absence of noise has a local maximum at the origin, so the first term in the expansion can be ignored. The displacement x_0 of the actual maximum is assumed to be small so we will ignore quadratic and higher terms. In fact by a simple argument we can show that if the edge $G(x)$ is either symmetric or antisymmetric, all even terms in x_0 vanish. Suppose $G(x)$ is antisymmetric, and express $f(x)$ as a sum of a symmetric component and an antisymmetric component. The convolution of the symmetric component with $G(x)$ contributes nothing to the numerator of the SNR, but it does contribute to the noise component in the denominator. Therefore, if $f(x)$ has any symmetric component, its SNR will be worse than a purely antisymmetric filter. A dual argument holds for symmetric edges, so that if the edge $G(x)$ is symmetric or antisymmetric, the filter $f(x)$ will follow suit. The net result of this is that the response $H_G(x)$ is always symmet-

ric, and that its derivatives of odd orders [which appear in the coefficients of even order in (5)] are zero at the origin. Equations (4) and (5) give

$$H_G''(0) x_0 \approx -H_n'(x_0). \qquad (6)$$

Now $H_n'(x_0)$ is a Gaussian random quantity whose variance is the mean-squared value of $H_n'(x_0)$, and is given by

$$E[H_n'(x_0)^2] = n_0^2 \int_{-W}^{+W} f'^2(x) \, dx \qquad (7)$$

where $E[y]$ is the expectation value of y. Combining this result with (6) and substituting for $H_G''(0)$ gives

$$E[x_0^2] \approx \frac{n_0^2 \int_{-W}^{+W} f'^2(x) \, dx}{\left[\int_{-W}^{+W} G'(-x) f'(x) \, dx \right]^2} = \delta x_0^2 \qquad (8)$$

where δx_0 is an approximation to the standard deviation of x_0. The localization is defined as the reciprocal of δx_0.

$$\text{Localization} = \frac{\left| \int_{-W}^{+W} G'(-x) f'(x) \, dx \right|}{n_0 \sqrt{\int_{-W}^{+W} f'^2(x) \, dx}}. \qquad (9)$$

Equations (3) and (9) are mathematical forms for the first two criteria, and the design problem reduces to the maximization of both of these simultaneously. In order to do this, we maximize the product of (3) and (9). We could conceivably have combined (3) and (9) using any function that is monotonic in two arguments, but the use of the product simplifies the analysis for step edges, as should become clear in Section III. For the present we will make use of the product of the criteria for arbitrary edges, i.e., we seek to maximize

$$\frac{\left| \int_{-W}^{+W} G(-x) f(x) \, dx \right|}{n_0 \sqrt{\int_{-W}^{+W} f^2(x) \, dx}} \frac{\left| \int_{-W}^{+W} G'(-x) f'(x) \, dx \right|}{n_0 \sqrt{\int_{-W}^{+W} f'^2(x) \, dx}}. \qquad (10)$$

There may be some additional constraints on the solution, such as the multiple response constraint (12) described next.

B. Eliminating Multiple Responses

In our specification of the edge detection problem, we decided that edges would be marked at local maxima in the response of a linear filter applied to the image. The detection criterion given in the last section measures the effectiveness of the filter in discriminating between signal and noise at the center of an edge. It does not take into account the behavior of the filter *nearby* the edge center. The first two criteria can be trivially maximized as follows. From the Schwarz inequality for integrals we can show that SNR (3) is bounded above by

$$n_0^{-1} \sqrt{\int_{-W}^{+W} G^2(x)\, dx}$$

and localization (9) by

$$n_0^{-1} \sqrt{\int_{-W}^{+W} G'^2(x)\, dx}.$$

Both bounds are attained, and the product of SNR and localization is maximized when $f(x) = G(-x)$ in $[-W, W]$.

Thus, according to the first two criteria, the optimal detector for step edges is a truncated step, or difference of boxes operator. The difference of boxes was used by Rosenfeld and Thurston [25], and in conjunction with lateral inhibition by Herskovits and Binford [11]. However it has a very high bandwidth and tends to exhibit many maxima in its response to noisy step edges, which is a serious problem when the imaging system adds noise or when the image itself contains textured regions. These extra edges should be considered erroneous according to the first of our criteria. However, the analytic form of this criterion was derived from the response at a single point (the center of the edge) and did not consider the interaction of the responses at several nearby points. If we examine the output of a difference of boxes edge detector we find that the response to a noisy step is a roughly triangular peak with numerous sharp maxima in the vicinity of the edge (see Fig. 1).

These maxima are so close together that it is not possible to select one as the response to the step while identifying the others as noise. We need to add to our criteria the requirement that the function f will not have "too many" responses to a single step edge in the vicinity of the step. We need to limit the number of peaks in the response so that there will be a low probability of declaring more than one edge. Ideally, we would like to make the distance between peaks in the noise response approximate the width of the response of the operator to a single step. This width will be some fraction of the operator width W.

In order to express this as a functional constraint on f, we need to obtain an expression for the distance between adjacent noise peaks. We first note that the mean distance between adjacent maxima in the output is twice the distance between adjacent zero-crossings in the derivative of the operator output. Then we make use of a result due to Rice [24] that the average distance between zero-crossings of the response of a function g to Gaussian noise is

$$x_{\text{ave}} = \pi \left(\frac{-R(0)}{R''(0)} \right)^{1/2} \tag{11}$$

where $R(\tau)$ is the autocorrelation function of g. In our case we are looking for the mean zero-crossing spacing for the function f'. Now since

$$R(0) = \int_{-\infty}^{+\infty} g^2(x)\, dx \quad \text{and} \quad R''(0) = -\int_{-\infty}^{+\infty} g'^2(x)\, dx$$

the mean distance between zero-crossings of f' will be

$$x_{zc}(f) = \pi \left(\frac{\int_{-\infty}^{+\infty} f'^2(x)\, dx}{\int_{-\infty}^{+\infty} f''^2(x)\, dx} \right)^{1/2} \tag{12}$$

The distance between adjacent maxima in the noise response of f, denoted $x_{\max}$, will be twice x_{zc}. We set this distance to be some fraction k of the operator width.

$$x_{\max}(f) = 2x_{zc}(f) = kW. \tag{13}$$

This is a natural form for the constraint because the response of the filter will be concentrated in a region of width $2W$, and the expected number of noise maxima in this region is N_n where

$$N_n = \frac{2W}{x_{\max}} = \frac{2}{k}. \tag{14}$$

Fixing k fixes the number of noise maxima that could lead to a false response.

We remark here that the intermaximum spacing (12) scales with the operator width. That is, we first define an operator f_w which is the result of stretching f by a factor of w, $f_w(x) = f(x/w)$. Then after substituting into (12) we find that the intermaximum spacing for f_w is $x_{zc}(f_w) = w x_{zc}(f)$. Therefore, if a function f satisfies the multiple response constraint (13) for fixed k, then the function f_w will also satisfy it, assuming W scales with w. For any fixed k, the multiple response criterion is invariant with respect to spatial scaling of f.

III. Finding Optimal Detectors by Numerical Optimization

In general it will be difficult (or impossible) to find a closed form for the function f which maximizes (10) subject to the multiple response constraint. Even when G has a particularly simple form (e.g., it is a step edge), the form of f may be complicated. However, if we are given a candidate function f, evaluation of (10) and (12) is straightforward. In particular, if the function f is represented by a discrete time sequence, evaluation of (10) requires only the computation of four inner products between sequences. This suggests that numerical optimization can be done directly on the sampled operator impulse response.

The output will not be an analytic form for the operator, but an implementation of a detector for the edge of interest will require discrete point-spread functions anyway. It is also possible to include additional constraints by using a *penalty method* [15]. In this scheme, the constrained optimization is reduced to one, or possibly several, unconstrained optimizations. For each constraint we define a penalty function which has a nonzero value when one

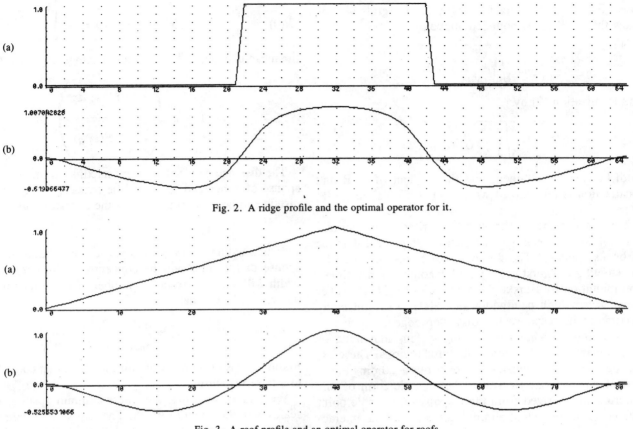

Fig. 2. A ridge profile and the optimal operator for it.

Fig. 3. A roof profile and an optimal operator for roofs.

of the constraints is violated. We then find the f which maximizes

$$\text{SNR}(f) * \text{Localization }(f) - \sum \mu_i P_i(f) \qquad (15)$$

where P_i is a function which has a positive value only when a constraint is violated. The larger the value of μ_i the more nearly the constraints will be satisfied, but at the same time the greater the likelihood that the problem will be ill-conditioned. A sequence of values of μ_i may need to be used, with the final form of f from each optimization used as the starting form for the next. The μ_i are increased at each iteration so that the value of $P_i(f)$ will be reduced, until the constraints are ''almost'' satisfied.

An example of the method applied to the problem of detecting ''ridge'' profiles is shown in Fig. 2. For a ridge, the function G is defined to be a flat plateau of width w, with step transitions to zero at the ends. The auxiliary constraints are

• The multiple response constraint. This constraint is taken directly from (12), and does not depend on the form of the edge.

• The operator should have zero dc component. That is it should have zero output to constant input.

Since the width of the operator is dependent on the width of the ridge, there is a suggestion that several widths of operators should be used. This has not been done in the present implementation however. A wide ridge can be considered to be two closely spaced edges, and the im-

plementation already includes detectors for these. The only reason for using a ridge detector is that there are ridges in images that are too small to be dealt with effectively by the narrowest edge operator. These occur frequently because there are many edges (e.g., scratches and cracks or printed matter) which lie at or beyond the resolution of the camera and result in contours only one or two pixels wide.

A similar procedure was used to find an optimal operator for roof edges. These edges typically occur at the concave junctions of two planar faces in polyhedral objects. The results are shown in Fig. 3. Again there are two subsidiary constraints, one for multiple responses and one for zero response to constant input.

A roof edge detector has not been incorporated into the implementation of the edge detector because it was found that ideal roof edges were relatively rare. In any case the ridge detector is an approximation to the ideal roof detector, and is adequate to cope with roofs. The situation may be different in the case of an edge detector designed explicitly to deal with images of polyhedra, like the Binford–Horn line-finder [14].

The method just described has been used to find optimal operators for both ridge and roof profiles and in addition it successfully finds the optimal step edge operator derived in Section IV. It should be possible to use it to find operators for arbitrary one-dimensional edges, and it should be possible to apply the method in two dimensions to find optimal detectors for various types of corner.

IV. A Detector for Step Edges

We now specialize the results of the last section to the case where the input $G(x)$ is step edge. Specifically we set $G(x) = Au_{-1}(x)$ where $u_n(x)$ is the nth derivative of a delta function, and A is the amplitude of the step. That is,

$$u_{-1}(x) = \begin{cases} 0, & \text{for } x < 0; \\ 1, & \text{for } x \geq 0; \end{cases} \qquad (16)$$

and substituting for $G(x)$ in (3) and (9) gives

$$\text{SNR} = \frac{A \left| \int_{-W}^{0} f(x)\, dx \right|}{n_0 \sqrt{\int_{-W}^{+W} f^2(x)\, dx}} \qquad (17)$$

$$\text{Localization} = \frac{A|f'(0)|}{n_0 \sqrt{\int_{-W}^{+W} f'^2(x)\, dx}}. \qquad (18)$$

Both of these criteria improve directly with the ratio A/n_0 which might be termed the signal-to-noise ratio of the image. We now remove this dependence on the image and define two performance measures Σ and Λ which depend on the filter only:

$$\text{SNR} = \frac{A}{n_0}\Sigma(f) \qquad \Sigma(f) = \frac{\left| \int_{-W}^{0} f(x)\, dx \right|}{\sqrt{\int_{-W}^{+W} f^2(x)\, dx}} \qquad (19)$$

$$\text{Localization} = \frac{A}{n_0}\Lambda(f') \qquad \Lambda(f') = \frac{|f'(0)|}{\sqrt{\int_{-W}^{+W} f'^2(x)\, dx}}. \qquad (20)$$

Suppose now that we form a spatially scaled filter f_w from f, where $f_w(x) = f(x/w)$. Recall from the end of Section II that the multiple response criterion is unaffected by spatial scaling. When we substitute f_w into (19) and (20) we obtain for the performance of the scaled filter:

$$\Sigma(f_w) = \sqrt{w}\,\Sigma(f) \quad \text{and} \quad \Lambda(f_w') = \frac{1}{\sqrt{w}}\Lambda(f'). \quad (21)$$

The first of these equations is quite intuitive, and implies that a filter with a broad impulse response will have better signal-to-noise ratio than a narrow filter when applied to a step edge. The second is less obvious, and it implies that a narrow filter will give better localization than a broad one. What is surprising is that the changes are inversely related, that is, both criteria either increase or decrease by $\sqrt{w}$. There is an uncertainty principle relating the detection and localization performance of the step edge detector. Through spatial scaling of f we can trade off detection performance against localization, but we cannot improve both simultaneously. This suggests that a natural choice for the composite criterion would be the product of (19) and (20), since this product would be invariant under changes in scale.

$$\Sigma(f)\,\Lambda(f') = \frac{\left| \int_{-W}^{0} f(x)\, dx \right|}{\sqrt{\int_{-W}^{+W} f^2(x)\, dx}} \frac{|f'(0)|}{\sqrt{\int_{-W}^{+W} f'^2(x)\, dx}}. \quad (22)$$

The solutions to the maximization of this expression will be a *class of functions* all related by spatial scaling. In fact this result is independent of the method of combination of the criteria. To see this we assume that there is a function f which gives the best localization Λ for a particular Σ. That is, we find f such that

$$\Sigma(f) = c_1 \quad \text{and} \quad \Lambda(f') \text{ is maximized.} \quad (23)$$

Now suppose we seek a second function f_w which gives the best possible localization while its signal-to-noise ratio is fixed to a different value, i.e.,

$$\Sigma(f_w) = c_2 \quad \text{while} \quad \Lambda(f_w') \text{ is maximized.} \quad (24)$$

If we now define $f_1(x)$ in terms of $f_w(x)$ as $f_1(x) = f_w(xw)$ where

$$w = c_2^2/c_1^2$$

then the constraint on f_w in (24) translates to a constraint on f_1 which is identical to (23), and (24) can be rewritten as

$$\Sigma(f_1) = c_1 \quad \text{and} \quad \frac{1}{\sqrt{w}}\Lambda(f_1') \text{ is maximized} \quad (25)$$

which has the solution $f_1 = f$. So if we find a single such function f, we can obtain maximal localization for any fixed signal-to-noise ratio by scaling f. The design problem for step edge detection has a *single unique* (up to spatial scaling) solution regardless of the absolute values of signal to noise ratio or localization.

The optimal filter is implicitly defined by (22), but we must transform the problem slightly before we can apply the calculus of variations. Specifically, we transform the maximization of (22) into a constrained minimization that involves only integral functionals. All but one of the integrals in (22) are set to undetermined constant values. We then find the extreme value of the remaining integral (since it will correspond to an extreme in the total expression) as a function of the undetermined constants. The values of the constants are then chosen so as to maximize the original expression, which is now a function only of these constants. Given the constants, we can uniquely specify the function $f(x)$ which gives a maximum of the composite criterion.

A second modification involves the limits of the integrals. The two integrals in the denominator of (22) have

117

limits at $+W$ and $-W$, while the integral in the numerator has one limit at 0 and the other at $-W$. Since the function f should be antisymmetric, we can use the latter limits for all integrals. The denominator integrals will have half the value over this subrange that they would have over the full range. Also, this enables the value of $f'(0)$ to be set as a boundary condition, rather than expressed as an integral of f''. If the integral to be minimized shares the same limits as the constraint integrals, it is possible to exploit the *isoperimetric constraint* condition (see [6, p. 216]). When this condition is fulfilled, the constrained optimization can be reduced to an unconstrained optimization using Lagrange multipliers for the constraint functionals. The problem of finding the maximum of (22) reduces to the minimization of the integral in the denominator of the SNR term, subject to the constraint that the other integrals remain constant. By the principle of reciprocity, we could have chosen to extremize any of the integrals while keeping the others constant, and the solution should be the same.

We seek some function f chosen from a space of *admissible* functions that minimizes the integral

$$\int_{-W}^{0} f^2(x)\, dx \qquad (26)$$

subject to

$$\int_{-W}^{0} f(x)\, dx = c_1 \qquad \int_{-W}^{0} f'^2(x)\, dx = c_2$$

$$\int_{-W}^{0} f''^2(x)\, dx = c_3 \qquad\qquad f'(0) = c_4. \quad (27)$$

The space of admissible functions in this case will be the space of all continuous functions that satisfy certain boundary conditions, namely that $f(0) = 0$ and $f(-W) = 0$. These boundary conditions are necessary to ensure that the integrals evaluated over finite limits accurately represent the infinite convolution integrals. That is, if the nth derivative of f appears in some integral, the function must be continuous in its $(n-1)$st derivative over the range $(-\infty, +\infty)$. This implies that the values of f and its first $(n-1)$ derivatives must be zero at the limits of integration, since they are zero outside this range.

The functional to be minimized is of the form $\int_a^b F(x, f, f', f'')$ and we have a series of constraints that can be written in the form $\int_a^b G_i(x, f, f', f'') = c_i$. Since the constraints are isoperimetric, i.e., they share the same limits of integration as the integral being minimized, we can form a composite functional using Lagrange multipliers [6]. The functional is a linear combination of the functionals that appear in the expression to be minimized and in the constraints. Finding a solution to the unconstrained maximization of $\Psi(x, f, f', f'')$ is equivalent to finding the solution to the constrained problem. The composite functional is

$$\Psi(x, f, f', f'') = F(x, f, f', f'') + \lambda_1 G_1(x, f, f', f'')$$

$$+ \lambda_2 G_2(x, f, f', f'') + \cdots$$

Substituting,

$$\Psi(x, f, f', f'') = f^2 + \lambda_1 f'^2 + \lambda_2 f''^2 + \lambda_3 f. \quad (28)$$

It may be seen from the form of this equation that the choice of which integral is extremized and which are constraints is arbitrary, the solution will be the same. This is an example of the *reciprocity* that was mentioned earlier. The choice of an integral from the denominator is simply convenient since the standard form of variational problem is a minimization problem. The Euler equation that corresponds to the functional Ψ is

$$\Psi_f - \frac{d}{dx}\Psi_{f'} + \frac{d^2}{dx^2}\Psi_{f''} = 0 \qquad (29)$$

where Ψ_f denotes the partial derivative of Ψ with respect to f, etc. We substitute for Ψ from (28) in the Euler equation giving:

$$2f(x) - 2\lambda_1 f''(x) + 2\lambda_2 f''''(x) + \lambda_3 = 0. \quad (30)$$

The solution of this differential equation is the sum of a constant and a set of four exponentials of the form $e^{\gamma x}$ where γ derives from the solution of the corresponding homogeneous differential equation. Now γ must satisfy

$$2 - 2\lambda_1 \gamma^2 + 2\lambda_2 \gamma^4 = 0$$

so

$$\gamma^2 = \frac{\lambda_1}{2\lambda_2} \pm \frac{\sqrt{\lambda_1^2 - 4\lambda_2}}{2\lambda_2}. \qquad (31)$$

This equation may have roots that are purely imaginary, purely real, or complex depending on the values of λ_1 and λ_2. From the composite functional Ψ we can infer that λ_2 is positive (since the integral of f''^2 is to be minimized) but it is not clear what the sign or magnitude of λ_1 should be. The Euler equation supplies a necessary condition for the existence of a minimum, but it is not a sufficient condition. By formulating such a condition we can resolve the ambiguity in the value of λ_1. To do this we must consider the second variation of the functional. Let

$$J[f] = \int_{x_0}^{x_1} \Psi(x, f, f', f'')\, dx.$$

Then by Taylor's theorem (see also [6, p. 214]),

$$J[f + \epsilon g] = J[f] + \epsilon J_1[f, g] + \tfrac{1}{2}\epsilon^2 J_2[f + \rho g, g]$$

where ρ is some number between 0 and ϵ, and g is chosen from the space of admissible functions, and where

$$J_1[f, g] = \int_{x_0}^{x_1} \Psi_f g + \Psi_{f'} g' + \Psi_{f''} g''\, dx$$

$$J_2[f, g] = \int_{x_0}^{x_1} \Psi_{ff} g^2 + \Psi_{f'f'} g'^2 + \Psi_{f''f''} g''^2$$

$$+ 2\Psi_{ff'} g g' + 2\Psi_{f'f''} g' g'' + 2\Psi_{ff''} g g''\, dx.$$

$$(32)$$

118

Note that J_1 is nothing more than the integral of g times the Euler equation for f (transformed using integration by parts) and will be zero if f satisfies the Euler equation. We can now define the second variation $\delta^2 J$ as

$$\delta^2 J = \frac{\epsilon^2}{2} J_2[f, g].$$

The necessary condition for a minimum is $\delta^2 J \geq 0$. We compute the second partial derivatives of Ψ from (28) and we get

$$J_1[f + g] = \int_{x_0}^{x_1} 2g^2 + 2\lambda_1 g'^2 + 2\lambda_2 g''^2 \, dx \geq 0.$$

$$(33)$$

Using the fact that g is an admissible function and therefore vanishes at the integration limits, we transform the above using integration by parts to

$$2\int_{x_0}^{x_1} g^2 - \lambda_1 gg'' + \lambda_2 g''^2 \, dx \geq 0$$

which can be written as

$$2\int_{x_0}^{x_1} \left(g^2 - \frac{\lambda_1}{2} g''\right)^2 + \left(\lambda_2 - \frac{\lambda_1^2}{4}\right) g''^2 \, dx \geq 0.$$

The integral is guaranteed to be positive if the expression being integrated is positive for all x, so if

$$4\lambda_2 > \lambda_1^2$$

then the integral will be positive for all x and for arbitrary g, and the extremum will certainly be a minimum. If we refer back to (31) we find that this condition is precisely that which gives complex roots for γ, so we have both guaranteed the existence of a minimum and resolved a possible ambiguity in the form of the solution. We can now proceed with the derivation and assume four complex roots of the form $\gamma = \pm\alpha \pm i\omega$ with α, ω real. Now $\gamma^2 = \alpha^2 - \omega^2 \pm 2i\alpha\omega$ and equating real and imaginary parts with (31) we obtain

$$\alpha^2 - \omega^2 = \frac{\lambda_1}{2\lambda_2} \quad \text{and} \quad 4\alpha^2\omega^2 = \frac{4\lambda_2 - \lambda_1^2}{4\lambda_2^2} \quad (34)$$

The general solution in the range $[-W, 0]$ may now be written

$$f(x) = a_1 e^{\alpha x} \sin \omega x + a_2 e^{\alpha x} \cos \omega x + a_3 e^{-\alpha x}$$

$$\sin \omega x + a_4 e^{-\alpha x} \cos \omega x + c. \quad (35)$$

This function is subject to the boundary conditions

$$f(0) = 0 \quad f(-W) = 0 \quad f'(0) = s \quad f'(-W) = 0$$

where s is an unknown constant equal to the slope of the function f at the origin. Since $f(x)$ is asymmetric, we can extend the above definition to the range $[-W, W]$ using $f(-x) = -f(x)$. The four boundary conditions enable us to solve for the quantities a_1 through a_4 in terms of the unknown constants α, ω, c, and s. The boundary conditions may be rewritten

$$a_2 + a_4 + c = 0$$

$$a_1 e^{\alpha} \sin \omega + a_2 e^{\alpha} \cos \omega + a_3 e^{-\alpha} \sin \omega$$

$$+ a_4 e^{-\alpha} \cos \omega + c = 0$$

$$a_1 \omega + a_2 \alpha + a_3 \omega - a_4 \alpha = s$$

$$a_1 e^{\alpha}(\alpha \sin \omega + \omega \cos \omega) + a_2 e^{\alpha}(\alpha \cos \omega$$

$$- \omega \sin \omega) + a_3 e^{-\alpha}(-\alpha \sin \omega + \omega \cos \omega)$$

$$+ a_4 e^{-\alpha}(-\alpha \cos \omega - \omega \sin \omega) = 0. \quad (36)$$

These equations are linear in the four unknowns a_1, a_2, a_3, a_4 and when solved they yield

$$a_1 = c(\alpha(\beta - \alpha) \sin 2\omega - \alpha\omega \cos 2\omega + (-2\omega^2 \sinh \alpha$$

$$+ 2\alpha^2 e^{-\alpha}) \sin \omega + 2\alpha\omega \sinh \alpha \cos \omega$$

$$+ \omega e^{-2\alpha}(\alpha + \beta) - \beta\omega)/4(\omega^2 \sinh^2 \alpha - \alpha^2 \sin^2 \omega)$$

$$a_2 = c(\alpha(\beta - \alpha) \cos 2\omega + \alpha\omega \sin 2\omega - 2\alpha\omega \cosh \alpha$$

$$\cdot \sin \omega - 2\omega^2 \sinh \alpha \cos \omega + 2\omega^2 e^{-\alpha} \sinh \alpha$$

$$+ \alpha(\alpha - \beta))/4(\omega^2 \sinh^2 \alpha - \alpha^2 \sin^2 \omega)$$

$$a_3 = c(-\alpha(\beta + \alpha) \sin 2\omega + \alpha\omega \cos 2\omega + (2\omega^2 \sinh \alpha$$

$$+ 2\alpha^2 e^{\alpha}) \sin \omega + 2\alpha\omega \sinh \alpha \cos \omega$$

$$+ \omega e^{2\alpha}(\beta - \alpha) - \beta\omega)/4(\omega^2 \sinh^2 \alpha - \alpha^2 \sin^2 \omega)$$

$$a_4 = c(-\alpha(\beta + \alpha) \cos 2\omega - \alpha\omega \sin 2\omega + 2\alpha\omega \cosh \alpha$$

$$\cdot \sin \omega + 2\omega^2 \sinh \alpha \cos \omega - 2\omega^2 e^{\alpha} \sinh \alpha$$

$$+ \alpha(\alpha - \beta))/4(\omega^2 \sinh^2 \alpha - \alpha^2 \sin^2 \omega) \quad (37)$$

where β is the slope s at the origin divided by the constant c. On inspection of these expressions we can see that a_3 can be obtained from a_1 by replacing α by $-\alpha$, and similarly for a_4 from a_2.

The function f is now parametrized in terms of the constants α, ω, β, and c. We have still to find the values of these parameters which maximize the quotient of integrals that forms our composite criterion. To do this we first express each of the integrals in terms of the constants. Since these integrals are very long and uninteresting, they are not given here but may be found in [4]. We have reduced the problem of optimizing over an infinite-dimensional space of functions to a nonlinear optimization in three variables α, ω, and β (not surprisingly, the combined criterion does not depend on c). Unfortunately the resulting criterion, which must still satisfy the multiple response constraint, is probably too complex to be solved analytically, and numerical methods must be used to provide the final solution.

The shape of f will depend on the multiple response constraint, i.e., it will depend on how far apart we force the adjacent responses. Fig. 5 shows the operators that result from particular choices of this distance. Recall that there was no single best function for arbitrary ω, but a class of functions which were obtained by scaling a pro-

119

totype function by ω. We will want to force the responses further apart as the signal-to-noise ratio in the image is lowered, but it is not clear what the value of signal-to-noise ratio will be for a single operator. In the context in which this operator is used, several operator widths are available, and a decision procedure is applied to select the smallest operator that has an output signal-to-noise ratio above a fixed threshold. With this arrangement the operators will spend much of the time operating close to their output Σ thresholds. We try to choose a spacing for which the probability of a multiple response error is comparable to the probability of an error due to thresholding.

A rough estimate for the probability of a spurious maximum in the neighborhood of the true maximum can be formed as follows. If we look at the response of f to an ideal step we find that its second derivative has magnitude $|Af'(0)|$ at $x = 0$. There will be only one maximum near the center of the edge if $|Af'(0)|$ is greater than the second derivative of the response to noise only. This latter quantity, denoted s_n, is a Gaussian random variable with standard deviation

$$n_0 \sigma_s = n_0 \left(\int_{-W}^{+W} f''^2(x)\, dx \right)^{1/2}.$$

The probability p_m that the noise slope s_n exceeds $Af'(0)$ is given in terms of the normal distribution function Φ

$$p_m = 1 - \Phi\left(\frac{A|f'(0)|}{n_0 \sigma_s} \right). \tag{38}$$

We can choose a value for this probability as an acceptable error rate and this will determine the ratio of $f'(0)$ to σ_s. We can relate the probability of a multiple response p_m to the probability of falsely marking an edge p_f which is

$$p_f = 1 - \Phi\left(\frac{A}{n_0} \Sigma \right) \tag{39}$$

by setting $p_m = p_f$. This is a natural choice since it makes a detection error or a multiple response error equally likely. Then from (38) and (39) we have

$$\frac{|f'(0)|}{\sigma_s} = \Sigma. \tag{40}$$

In practice it was impossible to find filters which satisfied this constraint, so instead we search for a filter satisfying

$$\frac{|f'(0)|}{\sigma_s} = r\Sigma \tag{41}$$

where r is as close as possible to 1. The performance indexes and parameter values for several filters are given in Fig. 4. The a_i coefficients for all these filters can be found from (37), by fixing c to, say, $c = 1$. Unfortunately, the largest value of r that could be obtained using the constrained numerical optimization was about 0.576 for filter number 6 in the table. In our implementation, we have

Filter Parameters						
n	x_{max}	$\Sigma\Lambda$	r	α	ω	β
1	0.15	4.21	0.215	24.59550	0.12250	63.97566
2	0.3	2.87	0.313	12.47120	0.38284	31.26860
3	0.5	2.13	0.417	7.85869	2.62856	18.28800
4	0.8	1.57	0.515	5.06500	2.56770	11.06100
5	1.0	1.33	0.561	3.45580	0.07161	4.80684
6	1.2	1.12	0.576	2.05220	1.56939	2.91540
7	1.4	0.75	0.484	0.00297	3.50350	7.47700

Fig. 4. Filter parameters and performance measures for the filters illustrated in Fig. 5.

approximated this filter using the first derivative of a Gaussian as described in the next section.

The first derivative of Gaussian operator, or even filter 6 itself, should not be taken as the final word in edge detection filters, even with respect to the criteria we have used. If we are willing to tolerate a slight reduction in multiple response performance r, we can obtain significant improvements in the other two criteria. For example, filters 4 and 5 both have significantly better $\Sigma\Lambda$ product than filter 6, and only slightly lower r. From Fig. 5 we can see that these filters have steeper slope at the origin, suggesting that the performance gain is mostly in localization, although this has not been verified experimentally. A thorough empirical comparison of these other operators remains to be done, and the theory in this case is unclear on how best to make the tradeoff.

V. AN EFFICIENT APPROXIMATION

The operator derived in the last section as filter number 6, and illustrated in Fig. 6, can be approximated by the first derivative of a Gaussian $G'(x)$, where

$$G(x) = \exp\left(-\frac{x^2}{2\sigma^2} \right).$$

The reason for doing this is that there are very efficient ways to compute the two-dimensional extension of the filter if it can be represented as some derivative of a Gaussian. This is described in detail elsewhere [4], but for the present we will compare the theoretical performance of a first derivative of a Gaussian filter to the optimal operator. The impulse response of the first derivative filter is

$$f(x) = -\frac{x}{x^2} \exp\left(-\frac{x^2}{2\sigma^2} \right) \tag{42}$$

and the terms in the performance criteria have the values

$$|f'(0)| = \frac{1}{\sigma_s}$$

$$\int_{-\infty}^{0} f(x)\, dx = 1 \qquad \int_{-\infty}^{+\infty} f^2(x)\, dx = \frac{\sqrt{\pi}}{2\sigma}$$

$$\int_{-\infty}^{+\infty} f'^2(x)\, dx = \frac{3\sqrt{\pi}}{4\sigma^3} \qquad \int_{-\infty}^{+\infty} f''^2(x)\, dx = \frac{15\sqrt{\pi}}{8\sigma^5}. \tag{43}$$

The overall performance index for this operator is

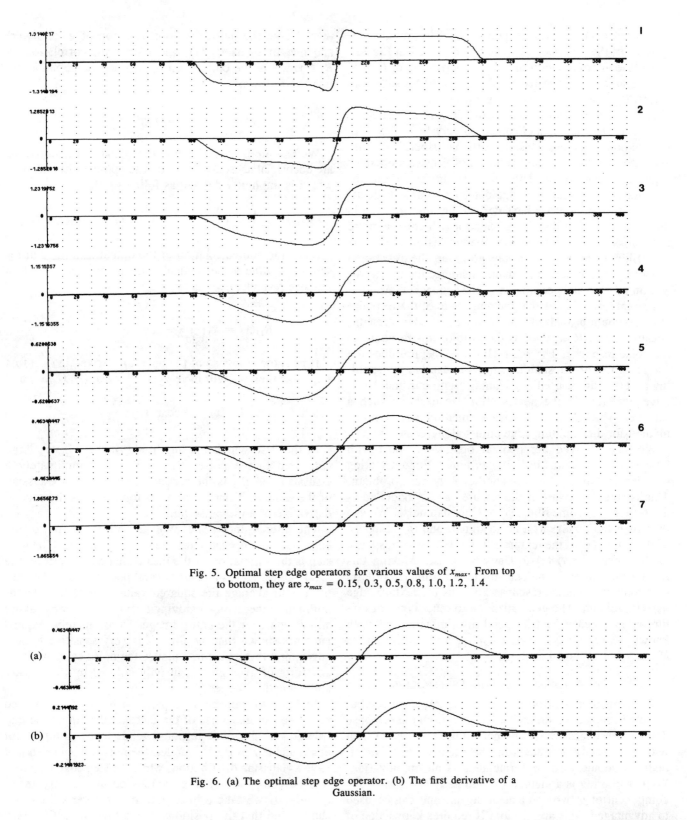

Fig. 5. Optimal step edge operators for various values of x_{max}. From top to bottom, they are $x_{max} = 0.15, 0.3, 0.5, 0.8, 1.0, 1.2, 1.4$.

Fig. 6. (a) The optimal step edge operator. (b) The first derivative of a Gaussian.

$$\Sigma\Lambda = \sqrt{\frac{8}{3\pi}} \approx 0.92 \qquad (44)$$

while the r value is, from (41),

$$r = \sqrt{\frac{4}{15}} \approx 0.51.$$

The performance of the first derivative of Gaussian operator above is worse than the optimal operator by about 20 percent and its multiple response measure r, is worse by about 10 percent. It would probably be difficult to detect a difference of this magnitude by looking at the performance of the two operators on real images, and because the first derivative of Gaussian operator can be computed with much less effort in two dimensions, it has

121

been used exclusively in experiments. The impulse responses of the two operators can be compared in Fig. 6.

A close approximation of the first derivative of Gaussian operator was suggested by Macleod [16] for step edge detection. Macleod's operator is a difference of two displaced two-dimensional Gaussians. It was evaluated in Fram and Deutsch [7] and compared very favorably with several other schemes considered in that paper. There are also strong links with the Laplacian of Gaussian operator suggested by Marr and Hildreth [18]. In fact, a one-dimensional Marr–Hildreth edge detector is almost identical with the operator we have derived because maxima in the output of a first derivative operator will correspond to zero-crossings in the Laplacian operator as used by Marr and Hildreth. In two dimensions however, the directional properties of our detector enhance its detection and localization performance compared to the Laplacian. Another important difference is that the amplitude of the response at a maximum provides a good estimate of edge strength, because the SNR criterion is the ratio of this response to the noise response. The Marr–Hildreth operator does not use any form of thresholding, but an adaptive thresholding scheme can be used to advantage with our first derivative operator. In the next section we describe such a scheme, which includes noise estimation and a novel method for thresholding edge points along contours.

We have derived our optimal operator to deal with known image features in Gaussian noise. Edge detection between textured regions is another important problem. This is straightforward if the texture can be modelled as the response of some filter $t(x)$ to Gaussian noise. We can then treat the texture as a noise signal, and the response of the filter $f(x)$ to the texture is the same as the response of the filter $(f * t)(x)$ to Gaussian noise. Making this replacement in each integral in the performance criteria that computes a noise response gives us the texture edge design problem. The generalization to other types of texture is not as easy, and for good discrimination between known texture types, a better approach would involve a Markov image model as in [5].

VI. Noise Estimation and Thresholding

To estimate noise from an operator output, we need to be able to separate its response to noise from the response due to step edges. Since the performance of the system will be critically dependent on the accuracy of this estimate, it should also be formulated as an optimization. Wiener filtering is a method for optimally estimating one component of a two-component signal, and can be used to advantage in this application. It requires knowledge of the autocorrelation functions of the two components and of the combined signal. Once the noise component has been optimally separated, we form a global histogram of noise amplitude, and estimate the noise strength from some fixed percentile of the noise signal.

Let $g_1(x)$ be the signal we are trying to detect (in this case the noise output), and $g_2(x)$ be some disturbance (paradoxically this will be the edge response of our filter),

then denote the autocorrelation function of g_1 as $R_{11}(\tau)$ and that of g_2 as $R_{22}(\tau)$, and their cross-correlation as $R_{12}(\tau)$, where the correlation of two real functions is defined as follows:

$$R_{ij}(\tau) = \int_{-\infty}^{+\infty} g_i(x)\, g_j(x + \tau)\, dx.$$

We assume in this case that the signal and disturbance are uncorrelated, so $R_{12}(\tau) = 0$. The optimal filter is $K(x)$, which is implicitly defined as follows [30]:

$$R_{11}(\tau) = \int_{-\infty}^{+\infty} (R_{11}(\tau - x) + R_{22}(\tau - x))\, K(x)\, dx.$$

Since the autocorrelation of the output of a filter in response to white noise is equal to the autocorrelation of its impulse response, we have

$$R_{11}(x) = k_3 \left(\frac{x^2}{2\sigma^2} - 1 \right) \exp\left(-\frac{x^2}{4\sigma^2} \right)$$

If g_2 is the response of the operator derived in (42) to a step edge then we will have $g_2(x) = k \exp(-x/2\sigma^2)$ and

$$R_{22}(x) = k_2 \exp\left(-\frac{x^2}{4\sigma^2} \right)$$

In the case where the amplitude of the edge is large compared to the noise, $R_{22} + R_{11}$ is approximately a Gaussian and R_{11} is the second derivative of a Gaussian of the same σ. Then the optimal form of K is the second derivative of an impulse function.

The filter K above is convolved with the output of the edge detection operator and the result is squared. The next step is the estimation of the mean-squared noise from the local values. Here there are several possibilities. The simplest is to average the squared values over some neighborhood, either using a moving average filter or by taking an average over the entire image. Unfortunately, experience has shown that the filter K is very sensitive to step edges, and that as a consequence the noise estimate from any form of averaging is heavily colored by the density and strength of edges.

In order to gain better separation between signal and noise we can make use of the fact that the amplitude distribution of the filter response tends to be different for edges and noise. By our model, the noise response should have a Gaussian distribution, while the step edge response will be composed of large values occurring very infrequently. If we take a histogram of the filter values, we should find that the positions of the low percentiles (say less than 80 percent) will be determined mainly the noise energy, and that they are therefore useful estimators for noise. A global histogram estimate is actually used in the current implementation of the algorithm.

Even with noise estimation, the edge detector will be susceptible to streaking if it uses only a single threshold. Streaking is the breaking up of an edge contour caused by the operator output fluctuating above and below the

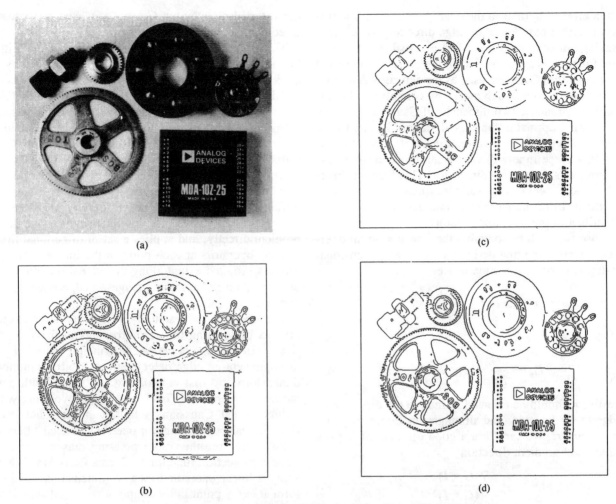

(a)

(c)

(b)

(d)

Fig. 7. (a) Parts image, 576 by 454 pixels. (b) Image thesholded at T_1. (c) Image thresholded at 2 T_1. (d) Image thresholded with hysteresis using both the thresholds in (a) and (b).

threshold along the length of the contour. Suppose we have a single threshold set at T_1, and that there is an edge in the image such that the response of the operator has mean value T_1. There will be some fluctuation of the output amplitude due to noise, even if the noise is very slight. We expect the contour to be above threshold only about half the time. This leads to a broken edge contour. While this is a pathological case, streaking is a very common problem with edge detectors that employ thresholding. It is very difficult to set a threshold so that there is small probability of marking noise edges while retaining high sensitivity. An example of the effect of streaking is given in Fig. 7.

One possible solution to this problem, used by Pentland [22] with Marr–Hildreth zero-crossings, is to average the edge strength of a contour over part of its length. If the average is above the threshold, the entire segment is marked. If the average is below threshold, no part of the contour appears in the output. The contour is segmented by breaking it at maxima in curvature. This segmentation is necessary in the case of zero-crossings since the zero-crossings always form closed contours, which obviously do not always correspond to contours in the image.

In the current algorithm, no attempt is made to presegment contours. Instead the thresholding is done with hysteresis. If any part of a contour is above a high threshold, those points are immediately output, as is the entire connected segment of contour which contains the points and which lies above a low threshold. The probability of streaking is greatly reduced because for a contour to be broken it must now fluctuate above the high threshold and below the low threshold. Also the probability of isolated false edge points is reduced because the strength of such points must be above a higher threshold. The ratio of the high to low threshold in the implementation is in the range two or three to one.

VII. Two or More Dimensions

In one dimension we can characterize the position of a step edge in space with one position coordinate. In two dimensions an edge also has an orientation. In this section we will use the term ''edge direction'' to mean the direction of the tangent to the contour that the edge defines in two dimensions. Suppose we wish to detect edges of a particular orientation. We create a two-dimensional mask for this orientation by convolving a linear edge detection function aligned normal to the edge direction with a projection function parallel to the edge direction. A substantial savings in computational effort is possible if the projection function is a Gaussian with the same σ as the (first derivative of the) Gaussian used as the detection function. It is possible to create such masks by convolving the image with a symmetric two-dimensional Gaussian and then differentiating normal to the edge direction. In fact we do not have to do this in every direction because the slope of a smooth surface in any direction can be determined exactly from its slope in two directions. This form of directional operator, while simple and inexpensive to compute, forms the heart of the more elaborate detector which will be described in the next few sections.

Suppose we wish to convolve the image with an operator G_n which is the first derivative of a two-dimensional Gaussian G in some direction n, i.e.,

$$G = \exp\left(-\frac{x^2 + y^2}{2\sigma^2}\right)$$

and

$$G_n = \frac{\partial G}{\partial n} = n \cdot \nabla G. \tag{45}$$

Ideally, n should be oriented normal to the direction of an edge to be detected, and although this direction is not known a priori, we can form a good estimate of it from the smoothed gradient direction

$$n = \frac{\nabla(G * I)}{|\nabla(G * I)|} \tag{46}$$

where $*$ denotes convolution. This turns out to be a very good estimator for edge normal direction for steps, since a smoothed step has strong gradient normal to the edge. It is exact for straight line edges in the absence of noise, and the Gaussian smoothing keeps it relatively insensitive to noise.

An edge point is defined to be a local maximum (in the direction n) of the operator G_n applied to the image I. At a local maximum, we have

$$\frac{\partial}{\partial n} G_n * I = 0$$

and substituting for G_n from (45) and associating Gaussian convolution, the above becomes

$$\frac{\partial^2}{\partial n^2} G * I = 0. \tag{47}$$

At such an edge point, the edge strength will be the magnitude of

$$|G_n * I| = |\nabla(G * I)|. \tag{48}$$

Because of the associativity of convolution, we can first convolve with a symmetric Gaussian G and then compute directional second derivative zeros to locate edges (47), and use the magnitude of (48) to estimate edge strength. This is equivalent to detecting and locating the edge using

the directional operator G_n, but we need not know the direction n before convolution.

The form of nonlinear second derivative operator in (47) has also been used by Torre and Poggio [28] and by Haralick [10]. It also appears in Prewitt [23] in the context of edge enhancement. A rather different two-dimensional extension is proposed by Spacek [26] who uses one-dimensional filters aligned normal to the edge direction but without extending them along the edge direction. Spacek starts with a one-dimensional formulation which maximizes the product of the three performance criteria defined in Section II, and leads to a step edge operator which differs slightly from the one we derived in Section IV. Gennert [8] addresses the two-dimensional edge detector problem directly, and applies a set of directional first derivative operators at each point in the image. The operators have limited extent along the edge direction and produce good results at sharp changes in edge orientation and corners.

The operator (47) actually locates either maxima or minima by locating the zero-crossings in the second derivative in the edge direction. In principle it could be used to implement an edge detector in an arbitrary number of dimensions, by first convolving the image with a symmetric n-dimensional Gaussian. The convolution with an n-dimensional Gaussian is highly efficient because the Gaussian is separable into n one-dimensional filters.

But there are other more pressing reasons for using a smooth projection function such as a Gaussian. When we apply a linear operator to a two-dimensional image, we form at every point in the output a weighted sum of some of the input values. For the edge detector described here, this sum will be a difference between local averages on different sides of the edge. This output, before nonmaximum suppression, represents a kind of moving average of the image. Ideally we would like to use an infinite projection function, but real edges are of limited extent. It is therefore necessary to window the projection function [9]. If the window function is abruptly truncated, e.g., if it is rectangular, the filtered image will not be smooth because of the very high bandwidth of this window. This effect is related to the Gibbs phenomenon in Fourier theory which occurs when a signal is transformed over a finite window. When nonmaximum suppression is applied to this rough signal we find that edge contours tend to "wander" or that in severe cases they are not even continuous.

The solution is to use a smooth window function. In statistics, the Hamming and Hanning windows are typically used for moving averages. The Gaussian is a reasonable approximation to both of these, and it certainly has very low bandwidth for a given spatial width. (The Gaussian is the unique function with minimal product of bandwidth and frequency.) The effect of the window function becomes very marked for large operator sizes and it is probably the biggest single reason why operators with large support were not practical until the work of Marr and Hildreth on the Laplacian of Gaussian.

It is worthwhile here to compare the performance of

this kind of directional second derivative operator with the Laplacian. First we note that the two-dimensional Laplacian can be decomposed into components of second derivative in two arbitrary orthogonal directions. If we choose to take one of the derivatives in the direction of principal gradient, we find that the operator output will contain one contribution that is essentially the same as the operator described above, and also a contribution that is aligned along the edge direction. This second component contributes nothing to localization or detection (the surface is roughly constant in this direction), but increases the output noise.

In later sections we will describe an edge detector which incorporates operators of varying orientation and aspect ratio, but these are a superset of the operators used in the simple detector described above. In typical images, most of the edges are marked by the operators of the smallest width, and most of these by nonelongated operators. The simple detector performs well enough in these cases, and as detector complexity increases, performance gains tend to diminish. However, as we shall see in the following sections, there are cases when larger or more directional operators should be used, and that they do improve performance when they are applicable. The key to making such a complicated detector produce a coherent output is to design effective decision procedures for choosing between operator outputs at each point in the image.

VIII. THE NEED FOR MULTIPLE WIDTHS

Having determined the optimal shape for the operator, we now face the problem of choosing the width of the operator so as to give the best detection/localization tradeoff in a particular application. In general the signal-to-noise ratio will be different for each edge within an image, and so it will be necessary to incorporate several widths of operator in the scheme. The decision as to which operator to use must be made dynamically by the algorithm and this requires a local estimate of the noise energy in the region surrounding the candidate edge. Once the noise energy is known, the signal-to-noise ratios of each of the operators will be known. If we then use a model of the probability distribution of the noise, we can effectively calculate the probability of a candidate edge being a false edge (for a given edge, this probability will be different for different operator widths).

If we assume that the *a priori* penalty associated with a falsely detected edge is independent of the edge strength, it is appropriate to threshold the detector outputs on probability of error rather than on magnitude of response. Once the probability threshold is set, the minimum acceptable signal-to-noise ratio is determined. However, there may be several operators with signal-to-noise ratios above the threshold, and in this case the smallest operator should be chosen, since it gives the best localization. We can afford to be conservative in the setting of the threshold since edges missed by the smallest operators may be picked up by the larger ones. Effectively the global tradeoff between error rate and localization remains, since choosing a high

signal-to-noise ratio threshold leads to a lower error rate, but will tend to give poorer localization since fewer edges will be recorded from the smaller operators.

In summary then, the first heuristic for choosing between operator outputs is that *small operator widths should be used whenever they have sufficient* Σ. This is similar to the selection criterion proposed by Marr and Hildreth [18] for choosing between different Laplacian of Gaussian channels. In their case the argument was based on the observation that the smaller channels have higher resolution, i.e., there is less possibility of interference from neighboring edges. That argument is also very relevant in the present context, as to date there has been no consideration of the possibility of more than one edge in a given operator support. Interestingly, Rosenfeld and Thurston [25] proposed exactly the opposite criterion in the choice of operator for edge detection in texture. The argument given was that the larger operators give better averaging and therefore (presumably) better signal-to-noise ratios.

Taking the fine-to-coarse heuristic as a starting point, we need to form a local decision procedure that will enable us to decide whether to mark one or more edges when several operators in a neighborhood are responding. If the operator with the smallest width responds to an edge and if it has a signal-to-noise ratio above the threshold, we should immediately mark an edge at that point. We now face the problem that there will almost certainly be edges marked by the larger operators, but that these edges will probably not be exactly coincident with the first edge. A possible answer to this would be to suppress the outputs of all nearby operators. This has the undesirable effect of preventing the large channels for responding to ''fuzzy'' edges that are superimposed on the sharp edge.

Instead we use a ''feature synthesis'' approach. We begin by marking all the edges from the smallest operators. From these edges, we synthesize the large operator outputs than would have been produced if these were the only edges in the image. We then compare the actual operator outputs to the synthetic outputs. We mark additional edges only if the large operator has significantly greater response than what we would predict from the synthetic output. The simplest way to produce the synthetic outputs is to take the edges marked by a small operator in a particular direction, and convolve with a Gaussian normal to the edge direction for this operator. The σ of this Gaussian should be the same as the σ of the large channel detection filter.

This procedure can be applied repeatedly to first mark the edges from the second smallest scale that were not marked by at the first, and then to find the edges from the third scale that were not marked by either of the first two, etc. Thus we build up a cumulative edge map by adding those edges at each scale that were not marked by smaller scales. It turns out that in many cases the majority of edges are picked up by the smallest channel, and the later channels mark mostly shadow and shading edges, or edges between textured regions.

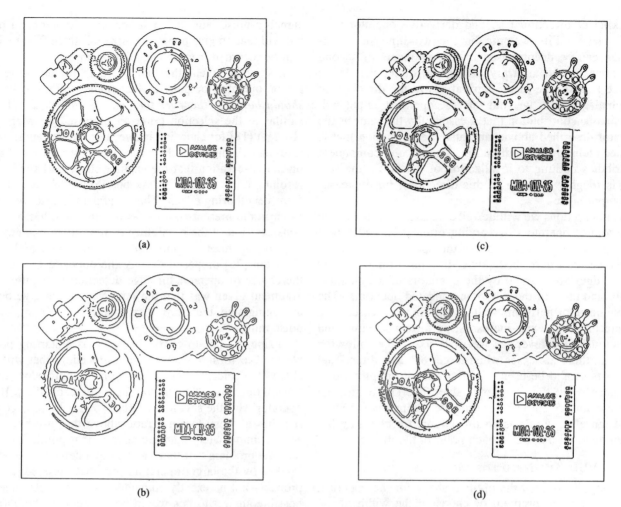

Fig. 8. (a) Edges from parts image at $\sigma = 1.0$. (b) Edges at $\sigma = 2.0$. (c) Superposition of the edges. (d) Edges combined using feature synthesis.

Some examples of feature synthesis applied to some sample images are shown in Figs. 8 and 9. Notice that most of the edges in Fig. 8 are marked by the smaller scale operator, and only a few additional edges, mostly shadows, are picked up by the coarser scale. However when the two sets of edges are superimposed, we notice that in many cases the responses of the two operators to the same edge are not spatially coincident. When feature synthesis is applied we find that redundant responses of the larger operator are eliminated leading to a sharp edge map.

By contrast, in Fig. 9 the edges marked by the two operators are essentially independent, and direct superposition of the edges gives a useful edge map. When we apply feature synthesis to these sets of edges we find that most of the edges at the coarser scale remain. Both Figs. 8 and 9 were produced by the edge detector with exactly the same set of parameters (other than operator size), and they were chosen to represent opposing extremes of image content across scale.

IX. The Need for Directional Operators

So far we have assumed that the projection function is a Gaussian with the same σ as the Gaussian used for the detection function. In fact both the detection and localization of the operator improve as the length of the projection function increases. We now prove this for the operator signal-to-noise ratio. The proof for localization is similar. We will consider a step edge in the x direction which passes through the origin. This edge can be represented by the equation

$$I(x, y) = Au_{-1}(y)$$

where u_{-1} is the unit step function, and A is the amplitude of the edge as before. Suppose that there is additive Gaussian noise of mean squared value n_{00}^2 per unit area. If we convolve this signal with a filter whose impulse response is $f(x, y)$, then the response to the edge (at the origin) is

$$\int_{-\infty}^{0} \int_{-\infty}^{+\infty} f(x, y)\, dx\, dy.$$

The root mean squared response to the noise only is

$$n_{00} \left(\int_{-\infty}^{+\infty} \int_{-\infty}^{+\infty} f^2(x, y)\, dx\, dy \right)^{1/2}$$

The signal-to-noise ratio is the quotient of these two

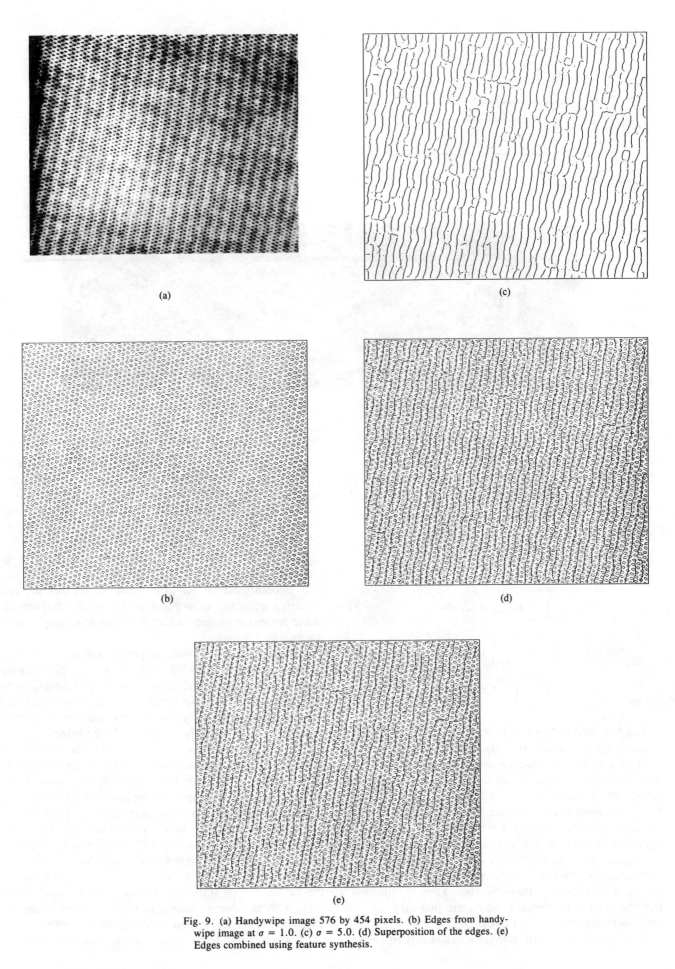

Fig. 9. (a) Handywipe image 576 by 454 pixels. (b) Edges from handywipe image at $\sigma = 1.0$. (c) $\sigma = 5.0$. (d) Superposition of the edges. (e)
Edges combined using feature synthesis.

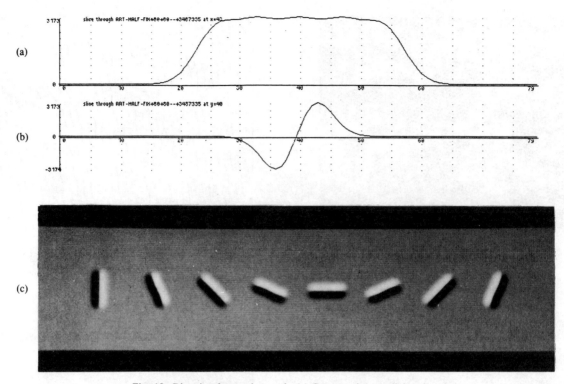

Fig. 10. Directional step edge mask. (a) Cross section parallel to the edge direction. (b) Cross section normal to edge direction. (c) Two-dimensional impulse responses of several masks.

integrals, and will be denoted by Σ. We have already seen what happens if we scale the function normal to the edge (21). We now do the same to the projection function by replacing $f(x, y)$ by $f_l(x, y) = f(x, (y/l))$. The integrals become

$$\int_{-\infty}^{0} \int_{-\infty}^{+\infty} f\left(x, \frac{y}{l}\right) dx\, dy$$

$$= \int_{-\infty}^{0} \int_{-\infty}^{+\infty} f(x, y_1)l\, dx\, dy_1$$

$$n_{00}\left(\int_{-\infty}^{+\infty} \int_{-\infty}^{+\infty} f^2\left(x, \frac{y}{l}\right) dx\, dy\right)^{1/2}$$

$$= n_{00}\left(\int_{-\infty}^{+\infty} \int_{-\infty}^{+\infty} f^2(x, y_1)l\, dx\, dy_1\right)^{1/2} \quad (49)$$

And the ratio of the two is now $\sqrt{l}\Sigma$. The localization Λ also improves as $\sqrt{l}$. It is clearly desirable that we use as large a projection function as possible. There are practical limitations on this however, in particular edges in an image are of limited extent, and few are perfectly linear. However, most edges continue for some distance, in fact much further than the 3 or 4 pixel supports of most edge operators. Even curved edges can be approximated by linear segments at a small enough scale. Considering the advantages, it is obviously preferable to use directional operators whenever they are applicable. The only proviso is that the detection scheme must ensure that they are used only when the image fits a linear edge model.

The present algorithm tests for applicability of each di-

rectional mask by forming a goodness-of-fit estimate. It does this at the same time as the mask itself is computed. An efficient way of forming long directional masks is to sample the output of nonelongated masks with the same direction. This output is sampled at regular intervals in a line parallel to the edge direction. If the samples are close together (less than 2σ apart), the resulting mask is essentially flat over most of its range in the edge direction and falls smoothly off to zero at its ends. Two cross sections of such a mask are shown in Fig. 10. In this diagram (as in the present implementation) there are five samples over the operator support.

Simultaneously with the computation of the mask, it is possible to establish goodness of fit by a simple squared-error measure. The mask is computed by summing some number of circular mask outputs (say 5) in a line. If the mask lies over a step edge in its preferred direction, these 5 values will be roughly the same. If the edge is curved or not aligned with the mask direction, the values will vary. We use the variance of these values as an estimate of the goodness of fit of the actual edge to an ideal step model. We then suppress the output of a directional mask if its variance is greater than some fraction of the squared output. Where no directional operator has sufficient goodness of fit at a point, the algorithm will use the output of the nonelongated operator described in Section VII. This simple goodness-of-fit measure is sufficient to eliminate the problems that traditionally plague directional operators, such as false responses to highly curved edges and extension of edges beyond corners; see Hildreth [12].

This particular form of projection function, that is a

function with constant value over some range which decays to zero at each end with two roughly half-Gaussians, is very similar to a commonly used extension of the Hanning window. This latter function is flat for some distance and decays to zero at each end with two half-cosine bells [2]. We can therefore expect our function to have good properties as a moving average estimator, which as we saw in Section VII, is an important role fulfilled by the projection function.

All that remains to be done in the design of directional operators is the specification of the number of directions, or equivalently the angle between two adjacent directions. To determine the latter, we need to determine the angular selectivity of a directional operator as a function of the angle θ between the edge direction and the preferred direction of the operator. Assume that we form the operator by taking an odd number $2N + 1$ of samples. Let the number of a sample be n where n is in the range $-N \cdots +N$. Recall that the directional operator is formed by convolving with a symmetric Gaussian, differentiating normal to the preferred edge direction of the operator, and then sampling along the preferred direction. The differentiated surface will be a ridge which makes an angle θ to the preferred edge direction. Its height will vary as $\cos \theta$, and the distance of the nth sample from the center of the ridge will be $nd \sin \theta$ where d is the distance between samples. The normalized output will be

$$O_n(\theta) = \frac{\cos \theta}{2N + 1} \left[\sum_{n=-N}^{N} \exp \left(-\frac{(nd \sin \theta)^2}{2\sigma^2} \right) \right]. \quad (50)$$

If there are m operator directions, then the angle between the preferred directions of two adjacent operators will be $180/m$. The worst case angle between the edge and the nearest preferred operator direction is therefore $90/m$. In the current implementation the value of d/σ is about 1.4 and there are 6 operator directions. The worst case for θ is 15 degrees, and for this case the operator output will fall to about 85 percent of its maximum value. Directional operators very much like the ones we have derived were suggested by Marr [17], but were discarded in favor of the Laplacian of Gaussian [18]. In part this was because the computation of several directional operators at each point in the image was thought to require an excessive amount of computation. In fact the sampling scheme described above requires only five multiplications per operator. An example of edge detection using five-point directional operators is given in Fig. 11.

X. Conclusions

We have described a procedure for the design of edge detectors for arbitrary edge profiles. The design was based on the specification of detection and localization criteria in a mathematical form. It was necessary to augment the original two criteria with a multiple response measure in order to fully capture the intuition of good detection. A mathematical form for the criteria was presented, and nu-

(a)

(b)

(c)

Fig. 11. (a) Dalek image 576 by 454 pixels. (b) Edges found using circular operator. (c) Directional edges (6 mask orientations).

merical optimization was used to find optimal operators for roof and ridge edges. The analysis was then restricted to consideration of optimal operators for step edges. The result was a class of operators related by spatial scaling. There was a direct tradeoff in detection performance versus localization, and this was determined by the spatial width. The impulse response of the optimal step edge operator was shown to approximate the first derivative of a Gaussian.

A detector was proposed which used adaptive thresholding with hysteresis to eliminate streaking of edge contours. The thresholds were set according to the amount of noise in the image, as determined by a noise estimation scheme. This detector made use of several operator widths to cope with varying image signal-to-noise ratios, and operator outputs were combined using a method called feature synthesis, where the responses of the smaller operators were used to predict the large operator responses. If the actual large operator outputs differ significantly from the predicted values, new edge points are marked. It is therefore possible to describe edges that occur at different scales, even if they are spatially coincident.

In two dimensions it was shown that marking edge points at maxima of gradient magnitude in the gradient direction is equivalent to finding zero-crossings of a certain nonlinear differential operator. It was shown that when edge contours are locally straight, highly directional operators will give better results than operators with a circular support. A method was proposed for the efficient generation of highly directional masks at several orientations, and their integration into a single description.

Among the possible extensions of the work, the most interesting unsolved problem is the integration of different edge detector outputs into a single description. A scheme which combined the edge and ridge detector outputs using feature synthesis was implemented, but the results were inconclusive. The problem is much more complicated here than for edge operators at different scales because there is no clear reason to prefer one edge type over another. Each edge set must be synthesized from the other, without a bias caused by overestimation in one direction.

The criteria we have presented can be used with slight modification for the design of other kinds of operator. For example, we may wish to design detectors for nonlinear two-dimensional features (such as corners). In this case the detection criterion would be a two-dimensional integral similar to (3), while a plausible localization criterion would need to take into account the variation of the edge position in both the x and y directions, and would not directly generalize from (9). There is a natural generalization to the detection of higher-dimensional edges, such as occur at material boundaries in tomographic scans. As was pointed out in Section VII, (47) can be used to find edges in images of arbitrary dimension, and the algorithm remains efficient in higher dimensions because n-dimensional Gaussian convolution can be broken down into n linear convolutions.

ACKNOWLEDGMENT

The author would like to thank Dr. J. M. Brady for his influence on the course of this work and for comments on early drafts of this paper. Thanks to the referees for their suggestions which have greatly improved the presentation of the paper. In particular thanks to the referee who suggested the simple derivation based on the Schwarz inequality that appears on p. 682.

REFERENCES

[1] R. J. Beattie, "Edge detection for semantically based early visual processing," Ph.D. dissertation, Univ. Edinburgh, 1984.
[2] C. Bingham, M. D. Godfrey, and J. W. Tukey, "Modern techniques of power spectrum estimation," IEEE Trans. Audio Electroacoust., vol. AU-15, no. 2, pp. 56–66, 1967.
[3] R. A. Brooks, "Symbolic reasoning among 3-D models and 2-D images," Dep. Comput. Sci., Stanford Univ., Stanford, CA, Rep. AIM-343, 1981.
[4] J. F. Canny, "Finding edges and lines in images," M.I.T. Artificial Intell. Lab., Cambridge, MA, Rep. AI-TR-720, 1983.
[5] F. S. Cohen, D. B. Cooper, J. F. Silverman, and E. B. Hinkle, "Simple parallel hierarchical and relaxation algorithms for segmenting textured images based on noncasual Markovian random field models," in Proc. 7th Int. Conf. Pattern Recognition and Image Processing, Canada, 1984.
[6] R. Courant and D. Hilbert, Methods of Mathematical Physics, vol. 1. New York: Wiley-Interscience, 1953.
[7] J. R. Fram and E. S. Deutsch, "On the quantitative evaluation of edge detection schemes and their comparison with human performance," IEEE Trans. Comput., vol. C-24, no. 6, pp. 616–628, 1975.
[8] M. Gennert, "Detecting half-edges and vertices in images," in IEEE Conf. Comput. Vision and Pattern Recognition, Miami Beach, FL, June 24–26, 1986.
[9] R. W. Hamming, Digital Filters. Englewood Cliffs, NJ: Prentice-Hall, 1983.
[10] R. M. Haralick, "Zero-crossings of second directional derivative edge operator," in SPIE Proc. Robot Vision, Arlington, VA, 1982.
[11] A. Herskovits and T. O. Binford, "On boundary detection," M.I.T. Artificial Intell. Lab., Cambridge, MA, AI Memo 183, 1970.
[12] E. C. Hildreth, "Implementation of a theory of edge detection," M.I.T. Artificial Intell. Lab., Cambridge, MA, Rep. AI-TR-579, 1980.
[13] ——, The Measurement of Visual Motion. Cambridge, MA: M.I.T. Press, 1983.
[14] B. K. P. Horn, "The Binford–Horn line-finder," M.I.T. Artificial Intell. Lab., Cambridge, MA, AI Memo 285, 1971.
[15] D. G. Luenberger, Introduction to Linear and Non-Linear Programming. Reading, MA: Addison-Wesley, 1973.
[16] I. D. G. Macleod, "On finding structure in pictures," in Picture Language Machines, S. Kaneff, Ed. New York: Academic, 1970, p. 231.
[17] D. C. Marr, "Early processing of visual information," Phil. Trans. Roy. Soc. London, vol. B 275, pp. 483–524, 1976.
[18] D. C. Marr and E. Hildreth, "Theory of edge detection," Proc. Roy. Soc. London., vol. B 207, pp. 187–217, 1980.
[19] D. C. Marr and T. Poggio, "A theory of human stereo vision," Proc. Roy. Soc. London., vol. B 204, pp. 301–328, 1979.
[20] J. E. W. Mayhew and J. P. Frisby, "Psychophysical and computational studies toward a theory of human stereopsis," Artificial Intell. (Special Issue on Computer Vision), vol. 17, 1981.
[21] T. Poggio, H. Voorhees, and A. Yuille, "A regularized solution to edge detection," M.I.T. Artificial Intell. Lab., Cambridge, MA, Rep. AIM-833, 1985.
[22] A. P. Pentland, "Visual inference of shape: Computation from local features," Ph.D. dissertation, Dep. Psychol., Massachusetts Inst. Technol., Cambridge, MA, 1982.
[23] J. M. S. Prewitt, "Object enhancement and extraction," in Picture Processing and Psychopictorics, B. Lipkin and A. Rosenfeld, Eds. New York: Academic, 1970, pp. 75–149.
[24] S. O. Rice, "Mathematical analysis of random Noise," Bell Syst. Tech. J., vol. 24, pp. 46–156, 1945.
[25] A. Rosenfeld and M. Thurston, "Edge and curve detection for visual scene analysis," IEEE Trans. Comput., vol. C-20, no. 5, pp. 562–569, 1971.
[26] L. Spacek, "The computation of visual motion," Ph.D. dissertation, Univ. Essex at Colchester, 1984.
[27] K. A. Stevens, "Surface perception from local analysis of texture and contour," M.I.T. Artificial Intell. Lab., Cambridge, MA, Rep. AI-TR-512, 1980.

[28] V. Torre and T. Poggio, "On edge detection," M.I.T. Artificial Intell. Lab., Cambridge, MA, Rep. AIM-768, 1984.
[29] S. Ullman, *The Interpretation of Visual Motion.* Cambridge, MA: M.I.T. Press, 1979.
[30] N. Wiener, *Extrapolation, Interpolation and Smoothing of Stationary Time Series.* Cambridge, MA: M.I.T. Press, 1949.
[31] A. P. Witkin, "Shape from contour," M.I.T. Artificial Intell. Lab., Cambridge, MA, Rep. AI-TR-589, 1980.

John Canny (S'81-M'82) was born in Adelaide, Australia, in 1958. He received the B.Sc. degree in computer science and the B.E. degree from Adelaide University in 1980 and 1981, respectively, and the S.M. degree from the Massachusetts Institute of Technology, Cambridge, in 1983.

He is with the Artificial Intelligence Laboratory, M.I.T. His research interests include low-level vision, model-based vision, motion planning for robots, and computer algebra.

Mr. Canny is a student member of the Association for Computing Machinery.

COMPUTER VISION, GRAPHICS, AND IMAGE PROCESSING **30**, 316–330 (1985)

Discontinuity Detection for Visual Surface Reconstruction

W. ERIC L. GRIMSON*

Artificial Intelligence Laboratory, M.I.T., Cambridge, Massachusetts 02139

AND

THEO PAVLIDIS

AT & T Bell Laboratories (2C-456), Murray Hill, New Jersey 07974

Received February 22, 1984; accepted February 5, 1985

A method is described for discontinuity detection in pictorial data. It computes at each point a planar approximation of the data and uses the statistics of the differences between the actual values and the approximations for detection of both steps and creases. The use of local statistical properties in the residuals provides a detection method that is sensitive to the local context of the data, and avoids the use of arbitrary thresholds. The subsequent reconstruction, bounded by the detected discontinuities, avoids Gibbs effects and provides reliable surface measurements. © 1985 Academic Press, Inc.

INTRODUCTION

This papers suggests a new approach to the detection of discontinuities in pictorial data: the use of the distribution of the error in local approximations of the data by a smooth surface. (The common practice now is to use the size of an error norm.) While similar approaches have been used before for spline approximations (Powell [10], Ichida, Kiyono, and Yoshimoto [6], this is the first application of the idea in image processing. It is based on the following observation. If the data have been generated by adding noise to a smooth surface, then the errors of approximation of the data by such a surface should exhibit the statistical properties of the noise. Any deviations from such a behavior (i.e., the appearance of systematic errors) indicates that the smoothness assumption is false. A similar reasoning may be used for data that are sampled from a Gibbs distribution (or a Markov field) [3]. The potential functions of the Gibbs distribution could be used to design approximating surfaces.

While the basic approach is quite general we shall use it here in connection with the fitting of smooth surfaces to scattered samples in the presence of noise. Thus the detection of discontinuities is only an intermediate step. Smooth interpolation is a recurrent problem in image analysis, and indeed in other types of signal processing. Recently, a solution to this problem for the case of stereo and motion data has been developed, relying on a surface reconstruction from 2-dimensional data [4, 11]. One of the difficulties of smooth surface reconstruction illuminated by these investigations is that it gives rise to oscillations (Gibbs effects) when applied around discontinuities in the data (see Fig. 1). This is not surprising since such smooth reconstructions make sense only over coherent parts of the signal, and applying a smooth reconstruction across a discontinuity implies that the shape of one surface

---

*Consultant to AT & T Bell Laboratories.

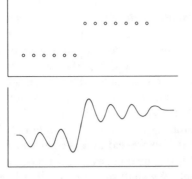

FIG. 1. Fitting a smooth curve (continuous with continuous derivatives) in the data shown at the top results in the oscillating curve shown at the bottom. The practically desirable interpolation is two horizontal lines with a discontinuity.

can influence the shape of a second, distinct surface, an implication which is clearly incorrect. The identification of such discontinuities has been the focus of considerable research in image processing and computer vision in general and we shall review such earlier approaches shortly.

Direct edge detection is a well-developed technique and can be found in any text on image processing. Its major disadvantage is that it is sensitive to noise, like any other method based on differentiation. Prefiltering the data may help in some cases but in general, the resulting smoothing introduces ambiguities in the location of the edges. Region growing or partition building techniques [8, 12] have been proposed as alternatives to edge detection but they also suffer from certain limitations. First they insist on finding coherent regions even if they do not exist. For example, Fig. 2 illustrates a case where $f(x, y)$ is continuous everywhere except along the line L. While finding discontinuities is equivalent to domain segmentation in the case of functions of a single variable, this is not the case for functions of two variables and partition building techniques tend to ignore that fact. Even where segmentation is feasible, it may be difficult when the form of the function in two adjacent regions is similar. In all these cases, partition building tends to produce regions whose shape reflects more the search strategy used than the true shape of regions. For example, segmentation using quad trees produces regions of square shape. (See Fig. 5.14 in [8].)

More recently, a third technique for detecting discontinuities in depth data has been proposed. If the surface reconstruction process is modeled as that of fitting a

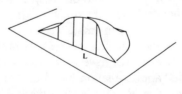
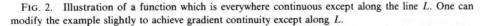

FIG. 2. Illustration of a function which is everywhere continuous except along the line L. One can modify the example slightly to achieve gradient continuity except along L.

thin, elastic plate to a set of known depth constraints [4, 1, 11], then it has been suggested [11] that the discontinuities in the data are associated with places of high tension in the plate. While this method does detect discontinuities, it is not completely error-free because there is no one-to-one correspondence between the two. It is possible to have many locations of high tension for a single discontinuity, because of Gibbs effects, or failure to detect high tension if the data points around a discontinuity are sparse.

Our approach to discontinuity detection is a hypothesis testing technique. While such techniques have been used before in image processing (see, e.g., [5, 2] etc.), our approach is novel because it focuses on the distribution of the error. We will fit locally simple surfaces (planes) to the data and then examine the distribution of residual error. If it appears to be "random," then we accept the hypothesis that there is no discontinuity. If there are systematic trends, then these imply discontinuities of various types. Once a discontinuity is detected, it is not necessary to worry about tracking edges or finding closed regions. The method of [4] computes the surface reconstructions by minimizing a particular functional, where the effect of the neighbors on a given point is expressed by a weight matrix $w(i, j)$ [4, pp. 183–184]. This matrix takes special forms near edges and corners, and such forms may be used near discontinuities as well. We shall say more on that later.

One of the advantages of detecting discontinuities first and fitting surfaces afterwards is that it is unlikely to have any oscillations due to Gibbs effects. Thus we may compute with confidence not only gradients of that surface but also higher order derivatives. We can then use these derivatives to detect changes in the form that correspond to different objects, in a manner similar to that used for 1-dimensional analysis by McClure [7].

METHODS

Let $\mathbf{x} = (x_1, x_2)$ be a point on the plane and $x(\mathbf{x})$ the value of the data there. For example, $z(\mathbf{x})$ could be depth or illumination intensity. Let $N(\mathbf{x}_0)$ be a neighborhood around $\mathbf{x}_0$ consisting of all points within a given distance from $\mathbf{x}_0$. (The exact manner in which $N(\mathbf{x}_0)$ is defined is not essential. For example, we could select the k nearest points to $\mathbf{x}_0$ in each quadrant for some selected value k.) Let S be a family of smooth functions defined over the plane and let $s(\mathbf{x}_0, \mathbf{x})$ be a member of S that is a good approximant to $z(\mathbf{x})$ over $N(\mathbf{x}_0)$. Again, the exact manner in which $s(\mathbf{x}_0, \mathbf{x})$ is selected is not essential.

We define the residual at a point x as

$$e(\mathbf{x}) = z(\mathbf{x}) - s(\mathbf{x}_0, \mathbf{x}). \tag{1}$$

Roughly speaking, $e(\mathbf{x})$ is the difference between the given value at $\mathbf{x}$ and a filtered, or expected, value there. We justify the use of the distribution of $e(\mathbf{x})$ for detection of discontinuities on the following grounds. Suppose that

$$z(\mathbf{x}) = q(\mathbf{x}) + n(\mathbf{x}), \tag{2}$$

where $q(\mathbf{x})$ is a smooth function of $\mathbf{x}$ and $n(\mathbf{x})$ is a zero-mean, high-frequency (relative to the signal $q(\mathbf{x})$) noise distribution. If $q(\mathbf{x})$ is a member of S, then for sufficiently large neighborhoods $N(\mathbf{x}_0)$, the function $s(\mathbf{x}_0, \mathbf{x})$ will be a good estimate of $q(\mathbf{x})$ and the residual $e(\mathbf{x})$ will approximately equal $n(\mathbf{x})$. Then the distribution of $e(\mathbf{x})$ will be determined by the statistics of $n(\mathbf{x})$. However, if $q(\mathbf{x})$ is a function outside S then the residual $e(\mathbf{x})$ will have properties that differ from those of the noise. Algorithms for spline approximation based on this idea have been proposed by Powell [10] and by Ichida et al. [6]. We shall discuss soon how these properties relate to discontinuities but first we would like to point out a connection with Bayesian methods for image restoration (e.g., [3]).

These techniques rely on estimates of the probability distribution of the values $z(\mathbf{x}_0)$ given the values of $N(\mathbf{x}_0)$. However, that density can be evaluated only when all the points in the neighborhood have values generated by the same stochastic process. Points where this is not true must be treated in a different way. Thus one is faced with two problems: first detecting such points, and second estimating a distribution for them. The proposed method can be seen as a test for checking the validity of the assumption that the points in $N(\mathbf{x}_0)$ have been generated by the same process.

In our present development we insist that $s(\mathbf{x}_0, \mathbf{x})$ be a plane. This is one of the simplest possible interpolants and its main justification is a posteriori: we shall show that it allows an easy detection of discontinuities without breaking quadratic surfaces. We feel that it is important not to segment quadratic surfaces for the following reasons. If the data are from a depth map, then surfaces correspond directly to object shapes and spherical or cylindrical objects are far too common to be ignored. If the data represent light intensities, then we know that Lambertian reflection produces intensities that are not constant but vary in ways that can be approximated by quadratics. The selection of a plane for the approximant implies that if $q(\mathbf{x})$ is also a plane, $e(\mathbf{x})$ will follow the noise distribution. We consider now several special cases.

(1) $q(\mathbf{x})$ is a convex (concave) function. Then, if there is no noise, $e(\mathbf{x})$ will always be negative (positive). Moreover, not only will the sign of $e(\mathbf{x})$ not change, but its magnitude should vary little among adjacent points. If $q(\mathbf{x})$ is a parabolic surface and if the error norm to be minimized is the maximum error (uniform approximation), then $e(\mathbf{x})$ is a constant (see Appendix). The presence of noise will modify these conclusions only slightly (see below).

(2) $q(\mathbf{x})$ is a crease, i.e., an intersection of two planes. If a point $\mathbf{x}$ is far enough from the (projection of the) intersection, then all of the data points corresponding to $N(\mathbf{x})$ will be within a single plane, and $e(\mathbf{x})$ will approximately equal $n(\mathbf{x})$. If $N(\mathbf{x})$ includes the intersection of the planes, then $e(\mathbf{x})$ will, for the most part, have a fixed sign, but not fixed magnitude. It can be shown that for a neighborhood that is symmetric with respect to the projection of the intersection of the planes, the residual will be proportional to the difference in the slopes of the planes along the direction perpendicular to their intersection (see Appendix).

(3) $q(\mathbf{x})$ is a step function. Then $e(\mathbf{x})$ will be a pulse with amplitude one quarter that of the step and changing from a positive to a negative value in the case of a step increasing to the right and vice versa for a step decreasing to the right (see Appendix).

(4) $q(\mathbf{x})$ is a filtered step function. For example, $q(\mathbf{x}) = 0$ is x_1 is less than $-\delta$ (δ is a given small number), $q(\mathbf{x}) = 1$ if x_1 is greater than δ, and $q(\mathbf{x})$ varies linearly over $[-\delta, \delta]$. Then $q(\mathbf{x})$ can be considered as a superposition of neighboring creases and $e(\mathbf{x})$ will again be a pulse, but triangular, rather than rectangular, as in the step case.

These special cases reveal that a data discontinuity will manifest itself as a change in the sign of the residuals (a zero-crossing) with the values on either side having size proportional to the step size. A crease will appear as a high value surrounded by linearly decreasing values of the same sign. Thus all we need is an algorithm for detecting extrema in the residuals. If an extremum is isolated, then we decide in favor of a crease. If it is paired with another extremum of opposite sign, then we decide in favor of a discontinuity. This allows a smooth degradation from step discontinuities into creases as the discontinuity is stretched out.

How can we distinguish "true" steps from those due to noise? If the variance of the noise is σ and the distribution is Gaussian, then the amplitude will not exceed 2σ with probability better than 95%. Since steps are attenuated by a factor of 4 (see Appendix), we can detect all steps whose size exceeds 8σ as being distinct from noise. Since the noise statistics may not be known a priori, we can estimate them from the residuals obtaining an estimate $\hat{\sigma}$ for the variance σ. If we select steps where the size exceeds $2\hat{\sigma}$, then we can assume that they are "true" steps, since $\hat{\sigma}$ will be an overestimation of σ because of the presence of systematic errors in the sample.

EXAMPLES

We demonstrate the method on a series of examples, and indicate its limiting behavior under a variety of circumstances. In all the cases illustrated, the surface reconstruction technique used was a least-square fit to the k nearest neighbors on either side, although this is not critical.

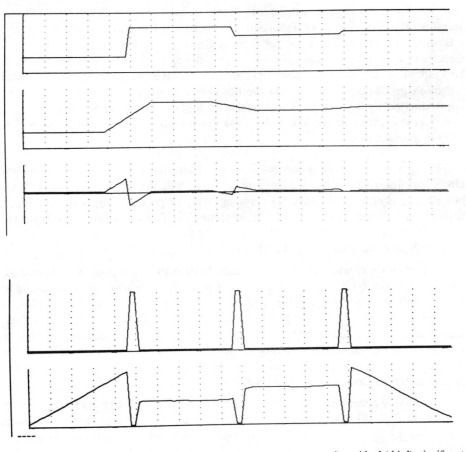

FIG. 3. Traces of plots of function (top), smooth approximation (second), residual (third), significant residual (fourth), and approximation after discontinuity detection (last).

Figure 3 shows the basic steps of the method. The first graph indicates the initial data, in this case a series of ideal, parallel planes. In the second graph, the filtered surface obtained by a point-wise, least-squares fit is shown. The third graph indicates the residuals of the surface under this filtering, and the fourth graph marks the points at which a step discontinuity is detected, based on the local distributions of the residuals. Finally, the fifth graph shows the final, segmented, least-squares reconstruction, in which the curve fitting is not propagated across marked discontinuities. The plotted approximation does not attempt to interpolate between different parts of the function. Whether this is desirable or not depends on the application and it can be easily accomplished.

In Fig. 4, zero-mean, high frequency noise has been added to the initial data, which consisted of four parallel planes, separated by increasingly larger step discontinuities. When the step size is large compared to the noise, then discontinuities are still detected but smaller steps are not. This is to be expected, since the magnitude of the noise has essentially reached the size of the step discontinuity. Thus, the method shows a graceful degradation in the presence of increasing corruptive noise.

An example of a quadratic surface with noise added to the data, is shown in Fig. 5. Note the form of the residuals. It can be seen that in this case, the connections between the cylindrical surface and the surrounding planes are detected as step discontinuities, since both the positive and negative extrema in the residuals around those points are detected as significant. As the gradient of the cylindrical surface is decreased, however, it is clear that the negative portion of the residual would eventually drop below detection range, leaving only positive extrema in the residuals. Hence, the connection between the two surfaces would gracefully degrade from a step discontinuity into a crease, as would be expected.

Figure 6 shows a series of arbitrary planes with noise in the data. Note that while the initial smoothed surface has extreme deviations from the data around the

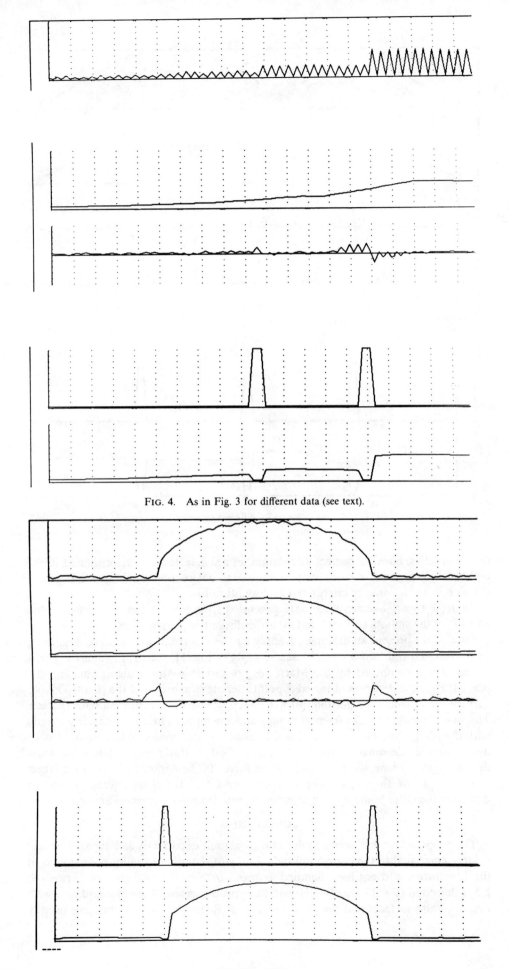

FIG. 4. As in Fig. 3 for different data (see text).

FIG. 5. As in Fig. 3 for different data (see text).

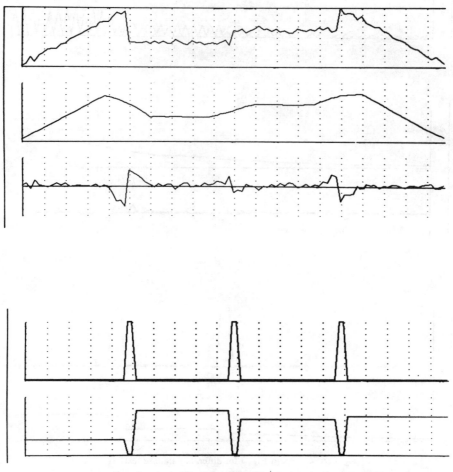

FIG. 6.   As in Fig. 3 for different data (see text).

discontinuities, once the correct discontinuities are detected and incorporated in the curve fitting process, a much more accurate reconstruction is obtained. Figure 7 shows how inflections are interpreted as discontinuities.

Figure 8 shows 2-dimensional data generated from four planes with noise added and Fig. 9 the smooth surface fitted after the discontinuity detection.

Finally, we present an example of applying the algorithm to real data. Figure 10 shows left and right eye views of a scene, while in Fig. 11, the depth values at edges in the scene, computed by the Marr–Poggio–Grimson stereo algorithm, are displayed. Here the darkness of the edge points denotes the height of the point. The old surface reconstruction algorithm [4] fits directly these data with a smooth surface. The new algorithm breaks them in groups and attempts to fit a smooth surface only within each group. Figure 12 shows the results in two views. White areas denote discontinuities detected by the method described in this paper, while dark areas denote regions where surface fitting was performed. The darker the region the larger is the height of the object. The method seems to have done a credible job in detecting the taller buildings and separating them from their surrounding areas.

CONCLUSIONS

The proposed method seems to detect discontinuities correctly as long as their size is large compared to the noise amplitude. Many of the other techniques described in the literature could not have handled at least some of the examples of Figs. 3–9. Edge detection (e.g., [8, pp. 79–86]) will have problems with the noise and also with the quadratic surfaces and the planes of Fig. 5. Region growing techniques usually

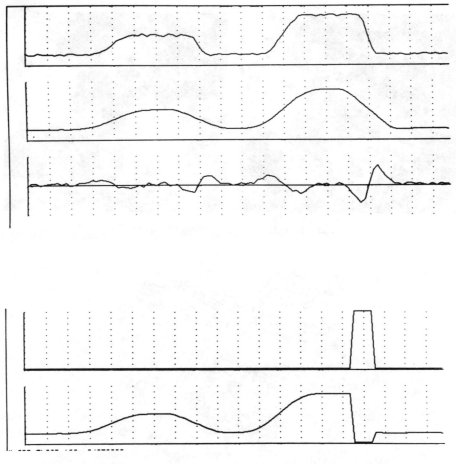

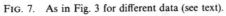

FIG. 7. As in Fig. 3 for different data (see text).

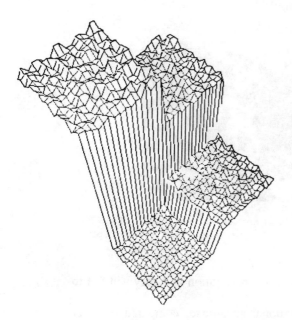

FIG. 8. Three dimensional input.

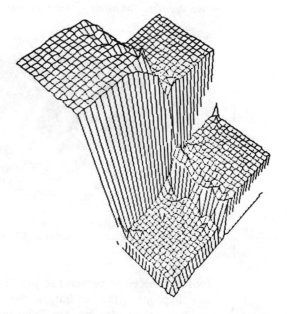

FIG. 9. Three dimensional approximation after discontinuity detection.

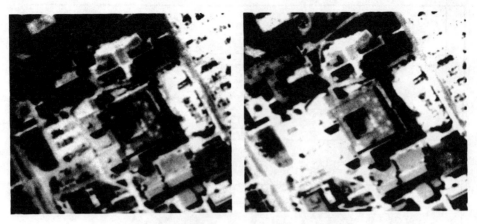

FIG. 10. Left and right eye views of a scene.

FIG. 11. Depth values of edge points in the scene of Fig. 10 detected by the Marr–Poggio–Grimson stereo algorithm. The darker a point, the greater is its height.

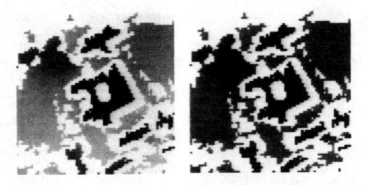

FIG. 12. Left and right eye views of the scene of Fig. 10 after processing by the new algorithm. White areas denote discontinuities and darker areas regions where surfaces were fitted. Again, the darker a point, the greater is its height.

look for piecewise constant or piecewise planar approximation and they will fail to handle properly the quadratic surfaces.

The method also has the following operational advantages compared to other techniques.

(1) There is no need to set arbitrary thresholds when deciding about discontinuities. The only threshold used is expressed in terms of the estimated variance of the noise.

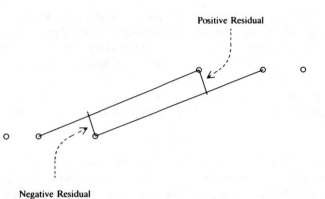

Positive Residual

Negative Residual

FIG. 13.   The sign of the residuals is independent of the distance among the data points.

(2) It can detect discontinuities regardless of spatial resolution. If the data points are very sparse, then we can obtain reliable estimates by taking the k nearest to x (see Fig. 13.) Also no false alarms are introduced because of steep quadratic curves since "steepness" does not affect the sign of the residual.

(3) The only Gibbs effects that may occur are near the noise level. Therefore we have reliable derivatives in the computed surface.

(4) There is no need to be concerned about closing contours. The final surface fitting is done by using the method of [4], which relies on a 12-point neighborhood as shown in Fig. 14.

If the sign of the residual at C and S differs (and the magnitude exceeds two standard deviations), but the sign at N, W, C, and E is the same, then the point C is treated as an edge point. If the sign at C, N, and E is the same and opposite to the sign at W and S, then C is treated as a corner point. Other configurations can be treated in a similar fashion by modifying the equation of p. 182 of [4] and deriving the correct template.

FIG. 14.   Neighborhood arrangement used for surface fitting in [4].

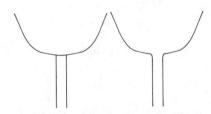

FIG. 15.   A crease (left) and an inflection (right) that appear similar.

The method is computationally expensive because of the need to compute a planar approximation at each point, but since we do need an optimal approximation the cost is not as high as it might seem. For example, in one dimension we may use the interpolant between the extreme points of an interval as the approximating line. (See [9, p. 286] for a discussion of the quality of such an approximation.) In two dimensions we may use the plane passing through three points whose projections on the plane are vertices of the triangle of maximum area (see Appendix).

Inflection points are one possible source of false alarms since they cause a change in the sign of the residual. However, they can be distinguished with some effort from discontinuities because the residual will vary linearly in their neighborhood (see Appendix). Anyway, from a perceptual viewpoint the distinction between inflection points and creases or discontinuities is not always clear. This is illustrated by Fig. 15.

APPENDIX

It is possible to give exact formulas for the residual at a point under certain simplifying assumptions. We consider the continuous 1-dimensional case and we let $f(t)$ to be a given function that plays the same role as $z(\mathbf{x})$ in the general case. If $f(t)$ is convex (or concave), then the straight line minimizing the maximum pointwise error over the interval $[-\delta, \delta]$ is the endpoint interpolant shifted halfway to the distance towards a point where the tangent to $f(t)$ is parallel to the interpolant [9]. If $f(t)$ is symmetric around $t = 0$, then a simple calculation shows that the residual will be exactly

$$e(t) = \frac{1}{2}\left[\frac{f(t-\delta) + f(t+\delta)}{2} - f(t)\right]. \qquad (A.1)$$

One could make a good case that the quantity in brackets is always close to the residual, although the factor $\frac{1}{2}$ may be too big. Certainly the sign will be valid as long as there are no inflection points. One may also decide that the interpolant is always a good approximant [9] or that Eq. (A.1) is a good definition of the residual, anyway. Clearly $e(t)$ is zero if $f(t)$ is a linear function.

There is no similar simple formula in two dimensions but the following argument can be made. Consider four points in space. They form a tetrahedron of volume, say, V. Let us select the plane formed by three of them as the approximating plane and let A be the area of the triangle formed by the three points. Then the distance of the fourth point from the plane is $6V/A$. Thus if we insist that the approximating plane be an interpolating plane, then the best selection is the one defined by the three points that form the triangle of maximum area. Shifting the plane halfway towards the fourth point reduces the error of approximation to $3V/A$. If we have more than four points, then we may select from amongst them the triplet that forms the triangle of maximum area. If the surface formed by the points is not far from the horizontal then we may select a triplet whose projections on the plane form the triangle of greatest area. With these heuristics we will find a residual which will be given by a formula similar to Eq. (A.1). However, instead of the midvalue of the interval endpoints we will have a linear combination of the three points defining the maximum area triangle.

If $f(t)$ is the parabola

$$at^2 + bt + c \qquad (A.2)$$

then a substitution of Eq. (A.2) into (A.1) yields

$$e(t) = \frac{1}{2}a\delta^2 \qquad (A.3)$$

Similarly we obtain the following values for the residual for various forms of $f(t)$.

$$\text{Cubic: } f(t) = at^3 + b^2 + ct + d \qquad (A.4a)$$

$$e(t) = \frac{\delta^2}{2}(3at + b). \qquad (A.4b)$$

We see that for a cubic the residual varies linearly.

Piecewise Linear: $f(t) = at$ for $t \le 0,$ $\qquad f(t) = bt$ for $t > 0.$ $\qquad$ (A.5)

$$e(t) = 0, \qquad t \text{ not in } [-\delta, \delta], \qquad \text{(A.6a)}$$

$$e(0) = \tfrac{1}{4}(a - b)\delta \qquad \text{varying linearly elsewhere.} \qquad \text{(A.6b)}$$

The last case represents a crease and we see that the residual at along the crease is proportional to the change in slope.

If $f(t)$ is a step function at 0 of size S, then we find

$$e(t) = 0 \, t \text{ not in } [-\delta, \delta], \qquad e(t) = \frac{S}{4} \, t \le 0, \qquad e(t) = -\frac{S}{4} \, t > 0. \qquad \text{(A.7)}$$

The difference between Eqs. (A.4b) and (A.6) can be used to distinguish steps from inflection points.

REFERENCES

1. M. Brady and B. K. P. Horn, Rotationally symmetric operators for surface interpolation, *Comput. Vision Graphics Image Process.* **22** (1983), 70–94.
2. P. C. Chen and T. Pavlidis, Image segmentation as an estimation problem, *Comput. Graphics Image Process.* **12** (1980), 153–172; *Image Modeling* (A. Rosenfeld, Ed.), pp. 9–28, Academic Press, New York, 1981.
3. S. Geman and D. Geman, Stochastic relaxation, Gibbs distributions, and the Bayesian restoration of images, *IEEE Trans. Pattern Anal. Mach. Intell.* **PAMI-6** (1984), 721–741.
4. W. E. L. Grimson, *From Images to Surfaces: A Computational Study of the Human Early Visual System*, MIT Press, Cambridge, Mass., 1981.
5. R. M. Haralick, Edge and region analysis for digital image data, *Comput. Graphics Image Process.* **12** (1980), 60–73.
6. K, Ichida, T. Kiyono, and F. Yoshimoto, Curve fitting by a one-pass method with a piecewise cubic polynomial, *ACM TOMS* **3** (1977), 164–174.
7. D. E. McClure, Computation of approximately optimal compressed representations of discretized plane curves, in *Proc. IEEE Conf. Pattern Recognition Image Process.* Troy, N.Y., 1977, pp. 175–182.
8. T. Pavlidis, *Structural Pattern Recognition*, Springer-Verlag, New York/Berlin, 1977.
9. T. Pavlidis, *Algorithms for Graphics and Image Processing*, Computer Science Press, Rockville, MD., 1982.
10. M. J. D. Powell, Curve fitting by splines in one variable, in *Numerical Approximation to Functions and Data* (J. G. Hayes, Ed.), pp. 65–83, Athlone, London, 1970.
11. D. Terzopoulos, Multilevel computational processes for visual surface reconstruction, *Computer Vision Graphics Image Process.* **24** (1983), 52–96.
12. S. W. Zucker, Region growing: Childhood and adolescence, *Computer Graphics Image Process.* **5** (1976), 382–399.

Reprinted from *IEEE Transactions on Pattern Analysis and Machine Intelligence*, Volume 10, Number 2, March 1988, pages 167-192.

Segmentation Through Variable-Order Surface Fitting

PAUL J. BESL, MEMBER, IEEE, AND RAMESH C. JAIN, SENIOR MEMBER, IEEE

Abstract—Computer vision systems attempt to recover useful information about the three-dimensional world from huge image arrays of sensed values. Since direct interpretation of large amounts of raw data by computer is difficult, it is often convenient to partition (segment) image arrays into low-level entities (groups of pixels with similar properties) that can be compared to higher-level entities derived from representations of world knowledge. Solving the segmentation problem requires a mechanism for partitioning the image array into low-level entities based on a model of the underlying image structure. Using a piecewise-smooth surface model for image data that possesses surface coherence properties, we have developed an algorithm that simultaneously segments a large class of images into regions of arbitrary shape and approximates image data with bivariate functions so that it is possible to compute a complete, noiseless image reconstruction based on the extracted functions and regions. Surface curvature sign labeling provides an initial coarse image segmentation, which is refined by an iterative region growing method based on variable-order surface fitting. Experimental results show the algorithm's performance on six range images and three intensity images.

Index Terms—Image segmentation, range images, surface fitting.

I. Introduction

COMPUTER vision systems attempt to recover useful information about the three-dimensional (3-D) world from huge image arrays of sensed values. Since direct interpretation of large amounts of raw data by computer is difficult, it is often convenient to partition (segment) image arrays into low-level entities (groups of pixels with particular properties) that can be compared to higher-level entities derived from representations of world knowledge. Solving the segmentation problem requires a mechanism for partitioning the image array into useful entities based on a model of the underlying image structure.

In most easily interpretable images, almost all pixel values are statistically and geometrically correlated with neighboring pixel values. This pixel-to-pixel correlation, or *spatial coherence*, in images arises from the spatial coherence of the physical surfaces being imaged. In range images, where each sensed value measures the distance to physical surfaces from a known reference surface, the pixel values collectively exhibit the same spatial coher-

Manuscript received January 29, 1986; revised March 12, 1987. Recommended for acceptance by W. E. L. Grimson. This work was supported by IBM Corporation, Kingston, NY.

P. J. Besl was with the Computer Vision Research Laboratory, Department of Electrical Engineering and Computer Science, University of Michigan, Ann Arbor, MI 48109. He is now with the Department of Computer Science, General Motors Research Laboratories, Warren, MI 48090.

R. C. Jain is with the Computer Vision Research Laboratory, Department of Electrical Engineering and Computer Science, the University of Michigan, Ann Arbor, MI 48109.

IEEE Log Number 8718602.

ence properties as the actual physical surfaces they represent. This has motivated us to explore the possibilities of a surface-based image segmentation algorithm that uses the spatial coherence (*surface coherence*) of the data to organize pixels into meaningful groups for later visual processes.

Many computer vision algorithms are based on inflexible, unnecessarily restricting assumptions about the world and the underlying structure of the sensed image data. The following assumptions are common: 1) all physical objects of interest are polyhedral, quadric, swept (as in generalized cylinders), convex, or combinations thereof; 2) all physical surfaces are planar, quadric, swept, or convex; 3) all image regions are rectangular or regularly shaped and are approximately constant in brightness; and 4) all image edges are linear or circular. The extensive research based on these assumptions solves many important application problems, but these assumptions are very limiting when analyzing scenes containing real-world objects with free-form, sculptured surfaces. Therefore, we have developed an image segmentation algorithm based only on the assumption that the image data exhibits *surface coherence* in the sense that the image data may be interpreted as noisy samples of a piecewise-smooth surface function. A preliminary grouping of pixels is based on the sign of mean and Gaussian surface curvature. This initial, coarse segmentation is refined by an iterative region growing procedure based on variable-order bivariate surface fitting. The order of the surface shape hypotheses is automatically controlled by *fitting surfaces* to the image data and *testing the surface fits* by 1) checking the spatial distribution of the signs of residual fitting errors (the regions test) and 2) comparing the mean square residual error of the fit to a threshold proportional to an estimate of the image noise variance. In this iterative process, images are not only segmented into regions of arbitrary shape, but the image data in those regions is also approximated with flexible bivariate functions such that it is possible to compute a complete, noiseless image reconstruction based on the extracted functions and regions. We believe that an explicit image description based on flexibly shaped approximating functions defined over arbitrary connected image regions can be useful in many computer vision applications, but will be critically important to object reconstruction and object recognition algorithms based on range imaging sensors when object volumes are bounded by free-form, smooth surfaces.

Although this segmentation algorithm may be most useful for range images, it is capable of segmenting any type of image that can be adequately represented as a noisy, sampled version of a piecewise-smooth graph surface. Therefore, we first include a brief discussion of the relationship between general computer vision and range image understanding. Since other segmentation methods in the literature involve several ideas closely related to those presented here, we also include a brief discussion of previous work in intensity image segmentation, followed by a survey of more recent work in range image analysis, in order to clarify the differences of the surface-based segmentation algorithm. Mathematical preliminaries are then presented to precisely define the problem we are attempting to solve, followed by a qualitative description of a method for general smooth surface decomposition. Several key ideas behind the algorithm philosophy are described next. Then the entire algorithm is outlined to introduce the role of the individual algorithm elements, followed by a detailed explanation of each element. Experimental results show the algorithm's excellent performance on a variety of six range and three intensity images from a database of successful test results on over forty images. We conclude with comments on future improvements and applications to other types of multidimensional image data.

A. Vision and Range

Most past computer vision research has been concerned with extracting useful information from one or more intensity images of a scene. The desired "useful" information has often been depth or range information. Indeed, the dominant images-to-surfaces vision paradigm [73], [44] dictates that various visual cues can be used to infer the distance of many scene points from sensed light intensity values as the human visual system does. Several methods for obtaining range (shape) from intensity images based on various visual cues are summarized below.

When the sampled values in an image array represent light intensity at each point, knowledge of the intensity image formation process and an appropriate set of constraints can be used to recover the shape of the physical 3-D surfaces represented by the data. Vision researchers have developed many techniques (see survey [18]) for obtaining 2.5-D descriptions (registered range images) of intensity images that indicate the sensor-to-physical-surface distance at many points in a scene: shape from shading [58], shape from texture [103], shape from contour [66], shape from binocular stereo [43], shape from photometric stereo [105], [25], shape from motion [101], [63], shape from shadows [67].

The above are predominantly *passive* approaches for obtaining range information in the sense that energy is not projected into the environment. Many *active* approaches for obtaining range images have also been developed [64] including amplitude-modulated laser radar [108]; frequency-modulated laser radar [7]; time-of-flight laser radar [71]; structured light with lines [93], grids [46], and coded binary patterns [61]; intensity ratio [21]; moire interferometry [86]; and focussing methods [68]. But once

a range image has been acquired for a given scene by any of the above methods, the extraction of useful information still requires processing a huge array of values where each value represents the distance to a physical surface from a known reference surface. Hence, the ability to obtain range at each pixel in an image does not in itself solve computer vision problems. Range images provide sampled geometric information in an *explicit form* rather than in an *implicit form* dependent on surface reflectance and illumination. The data must still be organized into a more structured form for interpretation purposes.

Witkin and Tenenbaum [104] have argued that perceptual organization mechanisms exist in the early stages of human visual processing that are independent of the high-level knowledge necessary for correct image interpretation and are independent of the image formation process. That is, people can visually segment image regions into meaningful entities even when they know nothing about the entities or the image formation process. Consider the fact that people with no knowledge of or experience with the formation of images from electron microscopes, X-ray imagers, ultrasonic sensors, and imaging radars can often partition images into important regions that are meaningful to experts in the respective fields. Therefore, it should be possible to group pixels in many types of images using only relatively low-level information. However, it is not at all clear how these general-purpose low-level grouping mechanisms operate.

We believe that perception of surfaces is a low-level grouping operation that plays a fundamental role in many image understanding tasks. Therefore, a segmentation algorithm that groups pixels based on a surface interpretation should be valuable to many applications. For example, explicit surface approximations over range image regions is directly useful for surface inspection, assembly verification, automatic shape acquisition, and autonomous navigation. If early vision processes focus on segmenting range images (however they are acquired) into surfaces defined over image regions, we believe that it will eventually be possible to achieve robust recognition of arbitrary 3-D objects by matching *perceived surface descriptions* with known object models. Although many matching approaches are based on lower dimensional features, such as points (i.e., object vertices) and edges (i.e., occluding edges and separating boundaries between surfaces), we believe that matching based on surface shape holds the most promise for general-purpose vision because surface matching would not be hindered by occlusion of individual point or edge features. Moreover, our experimental results show that surface-based segmentation is also promising for other types of images, such as intensity images, whenever the image data exhibits surface coherence properties.

B. Intensity Image Segmentation

A problem with many computer vision techniques is the assumption that there is only one physical surface or object represented in an image. When many surfaces of many objects are present, it is often necessary to organize pixels into connected groups or image regions that correspond to individual objects or surfaces, and then apply higher-level algorithms to the isolated image regions. The fundamental, complementary issues in organizing image pixels into regions are similarity (uniformity) and difference (contrast). Given the sensed values at two image pixels and their neighbors, the computer must answer the question: "does this pixel possess enough of the same properties as that pixel to say that these two pixels are similar?"

Segmentation of digital images has been an active area of research for many years (see surveys [47], [31], [37], [65], [90], [88]). Many popular segmentation techniques use histogram-based thresholding or template matching, but these methods provide little information when the image data does not conform to the restrictive image model assumptions. Edge detection techniques (see survey [29]) attempt to define regions by locating pixels that lie on the boundaries between regions using difference measures on neighboring pixels (e.g., image gradient magnitude). Region growing techniques (see survey [107]) attempt to group pixels into connected regions based on similarity measures, such as approximate equality (e.g., [20]). Edge-detection and region-growing can be data-driven operations based on generic notions of difference and similarity that make no commitment to the set of possible image interpretations, or they can be model-driven operations based on application-specific object models and domain knowledge. Model-driven techniques can reduce computational requirements by incorporating high-level knowledge about the scenes represented in images to restrict the search for valid interpretations [41].

A commonly used definition of image segmentation [57] states that if I is the set of all image pixels and $P(\ )$ is a *uniformity precidate* defined on groups of connected pixels, a segmentation of I is a partitioning set of connected subsets or image regions $\{R_1, \cdots, R_N\}$ such that

$$\bigcup_{l=1}^{N} R_l = I \quad \text{where} \quad R_l \cap R_m = \phi \quad \forall l \neq m, \quad (1)$$

the uniformity predicate $P(R_l) = $ True for all regions, and

$$P(R_l \cup R_m) = \text{False} \quad (2)$$

whenever R_l is adjacent to R_m. Different segmentation algorithms may be viewed as implementations of different uniformity predicates. Uniformity predicates may be classified according to knowledge requirements [65]: signal-level methods are based purely on the numbers in a digital image, physical-level methods include knowledge about image formation, and semantic-level methods include even more knowledge about the type of scenes being viewed. The surface-based segmentation algorithm in this paper is a signal-level method where the uniformity predicate on groups of pixels is true if almost all the pixel data in a region can be represented well by an approximating (surface) function.

Functional approximation ideas have been used on intensity images in the past to define uniformity measures for region-growing segmentation at the signal-level. Pavlidis [80] developed a region-growing segmentation approach based on a piecewise-linear scanline function approximation. Scanline intervals with similar slopes were merged to define regions. The uniformity predicate requires pixels in the same region to be approximated by straight lines with similar slopes. Haralick and Watson [48] proved the convergence of the facet iteration algorithm for flat (constant), sloped (planar), and quadratic polynomial facets (local surfaces) defined over preselected image window sizes. This algorithm was intended more for noise removal than segmentation, but may be considered as a segmentation algorithm where the image segments are the resulting small facets. A physical surface in an image is typically represented by many image facets. The uniformity predicate in this case requires pixels are well approximated by the facet surfaces. The window operator size for the surface fits, which limits the facet size, and the surface type are preselected parameters independent of the data. Pong *et al.* [82] have obtained good results with a similar algorithm based on property vectors of facets rather than the facet surface fits.

Functional approximation ideas are also used to derive window coefficients [85] for edge detection approaches to segmentation. In most edge-based techniques, pixels are simply labeled as edge or non-edge, and an edge-linking step is required to create refined region descriptions. A good example of a more complete pixel labeling scheme based on local surface function (facet) approximations is the topographic primal sketch [49]. In this approach, the output consists of 1) step edge, ridge, and valley lines, 2) peak, pit, saddle, and flat points, and 3) planar slopes, convex, concave, and saddle-shaped regions. The uniformity predicate in this case groups pixels with the same topographic label. This method is purely local however and does not prescribe the integration of global similarity information. The surface type labeling used in the surface-based segmentation algorithm also suffers from the same problem, but global information is effectively integrated by the iterative region growing algorithm.

C. Range Image Segmentation

Region growing based on function approximation ideas are used commonly in range image analysis (see survey [9]). The uniformity predicate in the work listed below requires that region pixels are well approximated by planar or quadric surfaces. Shirai and Suwa [94], Milgrim and Bjorklund [75], Henderson and Bhanu [53], Henderson [52], Bhanu [12], and Boyter [17] segment range images into fitted planar surfaces extracted via region growing. Other work has been geared toward detecting cylinders in range data [1], [77], [83], [15], [69]. Hebert and Ponce [51] segmented planes, cylinders, and cones from range data. Sethi and Jayaramamurthy [92] handled spheres and ellipsoids in addition to planes, cylinders, and cones. Oshima and Shirai [79] used planes, spheres, cylinders, and cones. Dane [27] and Faugeras *et al.* [34] at INRIA allow for region growing based on planar or general quadric surface primitives. The above do not directly address other types of surfaces except that the INRIA [33] and Henderson/Bhanu approaches have worked with arbitrary curved surfaces represented by many-faceted polyhedral approximations. Many of these methods obtain an initial segmentation of small primitive regions and then iteratively merge the small primitives until all merges (allowed by a smoothness or approximation error constraint) have taken place. The RANSAC method of Bolles and Fischler [15] has used iterative model fitting directly on the data based on randomly selected initial points (seeds). Our approach also works directly on the data, but seed regions are extracted deterministically and the model itself may change as required by the data.

Concepts and techniques from differential geometry have been useful in describing the shape of arbitrary smooth surfaces arising in range images [19], [74], [96], [62], [36], [10], [102], [32]. (This approach has also been applied to intensity image description [72], [81], [11].) For segmentation based on differential geometric quantities, such as lines of curvature or surface curvature, the uniformity predicate requires region pixels to possess similar geometric properties. As the name implies, the *differential* geometry of surfaces analyzes the *local differences* of surface points. Although *global similarities* in surface structure are also analyzed, most theorems in differential geometry address only global topological similarities, such as the one-hole equivalence of a doughnut and a coffee cup with a handle. Global shape similarity theorems do exist for the surfaces of convex objects, and they have been successfully utilized in extended Gaussian image (EGI) convex surface shape matching schemes [55]. Difficulties arise when local descriptors are used to identify the shape and global similarities of arbitrary nonconvex object surfaces from arbitrary-viewpoint range-image projections. The mathematics of differential geometry gives little guidance for an integrated global shape description or for computational matching methods in this general case. Brady *et al.* [19] extract and analyze a dense set of integrated 3-D lines of curvature across entire surface patches to describe the global surface properties. This method can take hours to describe simple objects. Our approach integrates global information into parametric surface descriptions and runs in minutes on similar objects with similar computing power.

Many researchers have favored the extraction of lower-dimensional features, such as edges, to describe range images instead of surfaces [97], [59], [60], [39], [76], [100], [95], [54], [50], [16], [13]. The uniformity predicate in these approaches requires that range and the range gradient are continuous for all pixels in region interiors where only the region boundaries are computed explicitly. By detecting and linking range and range gradient discontinuities, the space curves that bound arbitrary smooth surfaces are isolated creating an image segmentation. However, most of the above edge-based work has focussed on

straight and circular edges for matching with polyhedra and cylinders and their combinations. Although edge-based approaches offer important computational advantages for today's computer vision systems, we believe that such systems cannot provide the detailed surface information that will be required from future general-purpose range-image vision systems. Only more research experience will determine the advantages and disadvantages of these approaches for different applications, but the generality of an arbitrary surface segmentation and surface description approach is necessary today for automated free-form, sculptured surface reconstruction and shape acquisition tasks as in [84].

II. Problem Definition

In the surface-based approach to segmentation, the relevant structure of an image is viewed as a piecewise-smooth graph surface contaminated by noise as defined below. We emphasize the geometric shape of the image data in this approach, *not* the noise process as in random field image models [106], [26], [30], [24]. Several terms are introduced to give a reasonably precise description of the problem we are attempting to solve.

A 3-D *smooth graph surface* is a twice-differentiable function of two variables:

$$z = f(x, y). \tag{3}$$

A *piecewise-smooth graph surface* $g(x, y)$ can be partitioned into smooth surface primitives $f_l(x, y)$ over support regions R_l:

$$z = g(x, y) = \sum_{l=1}^{N} f_l(x, y) \, \chi(x, y, R_l) \tag{4}$$

where $\chi(x, y, R_l)$ is the characteristic function of the region R_l, which is unity if $(x, y) \in R_l$ and zero otherwise. For each piecewise-smooth surface $g(x, y)$, it is convenient to associate a *region label function* $l_g(x, y)$ defined as

$$l_g(x, y) = \sum_{l=1}^{N} l \, \chi(x, y, R_l). \tag{5}$$

If $\vec{a}_l$ is the vector of all parameters needed to precisely specify the smooth function $f_l(x, y)$, then any piecewise-smooth surface may be represented as the piecewise-constant function $l_g(x, y)$ (with minimum value 1 and maximum value N), which contains all segmentation information, and the list of N parameter vectors $\{\vec{a}_l\}$, which contains all shape information.

A *digital surface* is a noisy, quantized, discretely sampled version of piecewise-smooth graph surface:

$$z_{ij} = \tilde{g}(i, j) = \lfloor a \big(g(x(i), y(j)) \\ + n(x(i), y(j)) \big) + b \rfloor \tag{6}$$

where a and b are the quantizer's scale factor and offset respectively, the floor function indicates truncation (quantization) to an integer, and the additive noise process $n(x, y)$ is nominally zero-mean with finite variance

$\sigma^2(x, y)$ at each point. The discrete image location (i, j) need not be linearly related to the Euclidean (x, y) location allowing for the nonlinear relationships involved in some range sensors (see Appendix). A *range image* is a particular type of a digital surface where the z_{ij} values represent the distance to a physical surface from a reference surface. An *intensity image* is another type of digital surface where the z_{ij} values represent the number of visible photons incident at the (i, j) location in the focal plane of a camera. Other image types are defined based on the meaning of the sensed z_{ij} values. This underlying model is quite general and can be used to represent many types of images unless multiplicative noise or some other type of nonadditive noise is present. Many textured surfaces may also be considered as an approximating smooth surface plus random sensor noise along with structured noise to represent the given texture.

The *segmentation/reconstruction* problem that we are attempting to solve is a generalization of the segmentation problem and may be stated as follows. Given only a digital surface, denoted $\bar{g}(i, j)$ and specified by the z_{ij} values, find $\hat{N}$ approximating functions $\hat{f}_l(x, y)$ and $\hat{N}$ image regions $\hat{R}_l$ over which those functions are evaluated such that the total image representation error

$$\epsilon_{\text{tot}} = \left\| \bar{g}(i, j) - \hat{g}(x(i), y(j)) \right\|_I \quad (7)$$

between the reconstructed image function

$$\hat{g}(x, y) = \sum_{l=1}^{\hat{N}} \hat{f}_l(x, y) \chi(x, y, \hat{R}_l) \quad (8)$$

evaluated at the points $(x(i), y(j))$ and the data $\bar{g}(i, j)$ is small and the total number of functions and regions $\hat{N}$ is small. The function norm is left unspecified, but may be the max norm, the (Euclidean) root-mean-square error norm, or the mean absolute error norm. The implicit logical segmentation predicate in the above problem statement may be written as the *surface coherence* predicate:

$$P_\epsilon(R_l) = \begin{cases} \text{TRUE} & \text{if } \left\| \bar{g} - \hat{f}_l \right\|_{R_l} < \epsilon \\ \text{FALSE} & \text{otherwise} \end{cases} \quad (9)$$

where the value of ϵ depends on the mean variance of the noise process $n(x, y)$ in the image region.

The two trivial solutions may be discarded immediately. The "one pixel per region" solution minimizes the approximation error (zero error), maximizes the number of regions, and requires no work, but is of course also useless. The "one function per image" solution minimizes the number of regions (one region), maximizes the approximation error, requires work, may be useful for some purposes, but does not solve the real problem. We seek an algorithm that tends to segment images into regions that can be directly associated with meaningful high-level entities. In the case of range images, the surface functions defined over the image regions should mathe-

matically represent the 3-D shape of visible physical surfaces in the scene.

The problem statement places no constraints on the functions except that they are smooth, no constraints on the image regions except that they are connected, no constraints on the form of the additive noise term except that it is zero-mean. We want the total approximation error and the number of regions to be small, but we have not attempted to weight the relative importance of each. Without such weights, it is difficult to form an objective function and apply existing optimization methods.

It is not at all clear from the above statement that such a "chicken-and-egg" segmentation problem can be solved at the signal level. It is straightforward to fit functions to pixel data over regions if the regions have been determined, but how are the regions to be determined? Similarly, it is possible to determine the image regions if the set of functions are known, but how are the functions extracted? But even the number of functions/regions present in the data is not known. We seek a signal-level, data-driven segmentation procedure based only on knowledge of piecewise-smooth surfaces.

III. SMOOTH SURFACE DECOMPOSITION

The problem statement says that the smooth component functions $f_l(x, y)$ of the underlying model $g(x, y)$ are allowed to be arbitrary smooth surfaces, which can be arbitrarily complicated. However, arbitrary smooth surfaces can be subdivided into simpler regions of constant surface curvature sign based on the signs of the mean and Gaussian curvature at each point [10]. As shall be discussed in more detail later, there are only eight possible surface types surrounding any point on a smooth surface based on surface curvature sign: peak, pit, ridge, valley, saddle ridge, saddle valley, flat (planar), and minimal. These fundamental surface shapes, shown in Fig. 1, are very simple and do not contain inflection points (compare to codons for planar curve description as in [87]. Our hypothesis is that these simple surface types are well approximated for image segmentation (i.e., perceptual organization) purposes by bivariate polynomials of order M or less where M is small. The experimental results included here and in [8] attempt to show that this assumption is reasonable for a large class of images when $M = 4$ (biquartic surfaces). Even the range image surfaces of quadric primitives can be approximated well enough for segmentation purposes with such polynomial surfaces. This assumption is only limiting in the context of the segmentation algorithm when a large smooth surface bends much faster than x^4. If a particular application encounters a significant number of such surfaces, the limit of $M = 4$ can be raised. If a range imaging application can guarantee that only planar and quadric surfaces will appear, they can use only those types of functions for fitting purposes. In fact, any ordered set of bivariate approximating functions can be used if they satisfy the set of requirements defined below. In summary, *arbitrary smooth surfaces may be decomposed into a union of simple surface-*

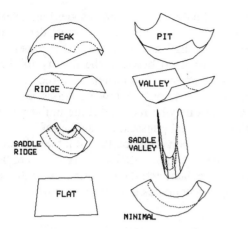

Fig. 1. Eight fundamental surface types from surface curvature sign.

curvature-sign primitives that are well approximated by low-order bivariate polynomials.

The intermediate goal of a segmentation algorithm then is to isolate all underlying *simple surfaces* (surface-curvature-sign primitives) in the image data and fit those simple surfaces with simple bivariate approximating functions. This creates an image segmentation in terms of the support regions of the simple approximating functions and an image reconstruction in terms of those simple approximating functions evaluated over the support regions. If the boundaries of the *smooth surfaces* of the underlying piecewise-smooth surface model are desired, then smoothly joining, adjacent simple surface regions can be merged to create the smooth surface support regions. This noniterative postprocessing step is covered in [8] and is not discussed here. We currently leave the function description over the smooth surface regions in the form of a collection of simple polynomial surfaces. The final collection of smooth surfaces and their support regions is the underlying piecewise-smooth image description that we wished to recover in the problem definition. In applications, it may be desirable to go back and fit the segmented smooth surface with application surfaces, such as quadrics, composite Bezier patches [35], or rational *B*-splines [99], rather than leaving it as a set of polynomial surfaces.

A. Approximating Function Requirements

Arbitrarily complicated smooth surfaces can be decomposed into a disjoint union of surface-curvature-sign surface primitives. If these surface primitives can be approximated well by a small set of approximating functions, a composite surface description for arbitrary smooth surfaces can be obtained. There are several constraints that the set of approximating functions must satisfy. Of course, the approximating functions must be able to approximate the fundamental surface-curvature-sign surface-primitives well. For *dimensionality reduction* reasons, the approximating functions should be representable by a small amount of data. For *generality*, the approximating surfaces must be well-defined over any arbitrary connected region in the image plane. The approximating functions

of the digital surface segmentation must be useful for *extrapolation* into neighboring areas of a surface in order for the region growing method to be successful. *Interpolation* capabilities are also useful for evaluating points between pixels if surface intersections are required. The approximating functions should also be easily *differentiable* so that differential geometric shape descriptors can be recomputed from them and so that other processes may compare surface normals and other differential quantities. Finally, the complete set of approximating functions should be *totally ordered* so that each approximant is capable of describing lower order approximants exactly, but cannot adequately approximate higher order functions. This provides the basis for a set of increasingly complicated hypotheses about the form of the underlying data. Note that general 3-D surface representation capability is not needed because digital surfaces are discrete representations of graph surface functions.

Low-order bivariate polynomials satisfy all of the above requirements, and the surface fitting procedure requires only a linear least-squares solver for the $p \times q$ ($p > q$) equation $[A] \vec{x} = \vec{b}$ [70], [5]. We have found that the set of planar, biquadratic, bicubic, and biquartic polynomials performed well in our experiments without significant computational requirements (a few seconds per fit on a VAX 11-780). *However, any set of approximating functions that satisfy the above constraints may be used instead.* To maintain generality in the algorithm description, it is only assumed that there is a set of approximating functions, denoted as F, that contains $|F|$ discrete types of functions that can be ordered in terms of the "shape potential" of each surface function relative to the set of fundamental surface-curvature-sign surface primitives.

In our case $|F| = 4$ and the set of approximating functions F can be written in the form of a single equation:

$$\hat{f}(m, \vec{a}; x, y)$$
$$= \sum_{i+j \le m} a_{ij} x^i y^j \qquad (10)$$
$$= a_{00} + a_{10}x + a_{01}y + a_{11}xy + a_{20}x^2$$
$$\quad + a_{02}y^2 + a_{21}x^2y + a_{12}xy^2 + a_{30}x^3$$
$$\quad + a_{03}y^3 + a_{31}x^3y + a_{22}x^2y^2$$
$$\quad + a_{13}xy^3 + a_{40}x^4 + a_{04}y^4. \qquad (m = 4) \quad (11)$$

Planar surfaces are obtained by restricting the parameter vector space $\Re^{15}$ to three-dimensional subspace where only a_{00}, a_{10}, a_{01} may be nonzero. Biquadratic surfaces are restricted to a six-dimensional subspace, and bicubic surfaces to a ten-dimensional subspace. A least-squares solver computes the parameter vector $\vec{a}$ and the RMS fit error ϵ from the digital surface data over a region quickly and efficiently. Moreover, a QR least-squares solution approach allows surface region fits to be updated recursively during the region growing process as new data points are added [42], [22] for better computational efficiency.

B. Simple to Complex Hypothesis Testing

The key idea behind the algorithm, which is independent of the set of approximating functions actually chosen, is that one should start with the simplest hypothesis about the form of the data and then gradually increase the complexity of the hypothesized form as needed. This is the *variable-order* concept, which has not been used in previous segmentation algorithms. In our case, surface type labels at each pixel allow us to find large groups of identically labeled pixels. Then, a small subset of those pixels, known as a *seed region*, is chosen using a simple shrinking method that attempts to ensure that every pixel in the seed region is correctly labeled. The simplest hypothesis for any surface fitting approach is that the data points represented in the seed region lie in a plane. The hypothesis is then tested to see if it is true. If true, the seed region is grown based on the planar surface fit. If the simple hypothesis is false, the algorithm responds by testing the next more complicated hypothesis (e.g., a biquadratic surface). If that hypothesis is true, the region is grown based on that form. If false, the next hypothesis is tested. This process continues until either 1) all preselected hypotheses have been shown to be false or 2) the region growing based on the surface fitting has converged in the sense that the same image region is obtained twice. Since all smooth surfaces can be partitioned into simple surfaces based on surface curvature sign, false hypotheses may occur only when the isolated seed region surface-type labels are incorrect (due to noise) or when the underlying surface bends faster than the highest order approximating surface. During execution of the algorithm, bad seed regions are rejected immediately when the surface fit error is poor and large quickly bending surfaces are broken into two or more surface regions.

IV. ALGORITHM PHILOSOPHY

This section includes qualitative comments about the system structure of the surface-based segmentation algorithm. The success of the algorithm is based on the effective combination of simple component algorithms, not on the capabilities of any single processing step.

A. Initial Guess Plus Iteration

Like many region growing schemes, the basic approach of this algorithm might be summarized as "make an initial guess and then iteratively refine the solution." This idea is at least as old as Newton's method for finding the zeros of a complicated function. Unlike other region growing schemes, the initial guess at the underlying surface segmentation is based on invariant differential geometric principles and is quantified in terms of surface curvature sign labels, or surface type labels [10]. The iterative refinement process is based on function approximation and region growing. Once a surface has been fitted to the kth group of connected pixels, the $(k + 1)$th group of pixels is obtained by finding all new connected pixels that are compatible with the fitted surface of the previous group. When the same group of pixels is ob-

tained twice, the iteration terminates yielding an extracted region. This process is described in more detail later.

Although we shall not prove it in this paper, there is the usual relationship between the quality of the initial guess and the number of iterations required. If the initial guess is very good, only a few iterations are required. Many iterations may be required if the initial guess is not good. For bad initial guesses, no number of iterations will yield the proper convergence to a solution. In our algorithm, the quality of the initial guess is related to the quality of the image data, and the performance of the segmentation algorithm degrades gracefully with increasing noise levels.

B. Stimulus Bound Image Analysis

The variable-order surface fitting approach may be thought of as a hypothesize and test (hypothesize and verify) algorithm where the hypotheses can be automatically changed by the input data and each surface fit is bound by (must conform to) the input data. Therefore, we suggest the use of the adjective *stimulus bound* [89] for the type of hypothesis testing done by the surface-based segmentation algorithm, where the *stimulus* is the original sensed data values. In a stimulus bound process, all interpretive processing of the data is *bound* to or constrained by the original data or stimulus in each stage of processing to reduce the probability of interpretation errors. In our case, each simple surface function hypothesis is tested against the original data via surface fitting followed by two tests: 1) an RMS fit error test (related to the chi-square test), and 2) a regions test (related to the nonparametric statistics runs test). Hence, each iteration and the final interpretation are bound by the original stimulus.

It is generally acknowledged that vision algorithms should function at several different levels using associated vision modules to process the signal and symbol information at different levels. It often occurs that each level's vision module accepts input only from the previous, lower level and provides output only to the subsequent, higher level. Fig. 2(a) shows a typical example of such a process. This assumption may be rooted in human visual models where retinal information is not directly available to the high level cerebral processes. However, human vision is a fundamentally dynamic perceptual process in which subsequent, highly correlated "video frames" are always immediately available to the visual system after any given instant in time. Therefore, it may be inappropriate to apply dynamic human visual model principles to static computational vision problems. The *stimulus bound* philosophy states that the output from all lower level vision modules should be available to high-level vision modules. In particular, the original image from the sensor must be available to every vision module in a static vision system as shown in Fig. 2(b). In the surface-based segmentation algorithm, *every pixel in every region* is constantly checked to see how close the sensed value at a given pixel is to the approximating surface function for the given region. The global grouping of pixels relies on

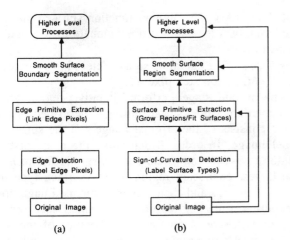

Fig. 2. Conventional edge approach versus stimulus bound approach.

simple differencing between pixel values and the interpreted surface primitives. These concepts are expressed in more detail in later sections. Without constantly checking symbolic interpretations against the original data, a vertical chain of interpretive vision modules is only as robust as the weakest module. Many edge-based intensity image vision schemes have failed in practice because precise, correctly linked edges could not be extracted from real images.

We believe that surface-based range image vision systems have an advantage over edge-based systems in that it is possible to quickly check final object or surface interpretations against the original data (via simple image differencing) because synthetic range images can be generated from models with a depth-buffer algorithm [78] using only the object or surface geometry; light and surface reflectance are not involved. The final interpretation in the form of a reconstructed range image can be subtracted from the original range image to create an *interpretation error image*, which can then be used to evaluate the quality of the image interpretation globally and locally. This is only possible when an image interpretation includes segmentation and reconstruction information as described in the problem definition.

C. Emerging Commitment

The surface-based segmentation algorithm is primarily data-driven in that only generic knowledge of surfaces, curvature, noise, and approximation are used. Of course, data-driven and model-driven elements must cooperate in any algorithm that attempts to interpret a digital image in terms of specific model information. An important feature of any image interpretation approach is the *process of commitment* to the final interpretation. A special-purpose model-driven program can make a commitment to its set of possible interpretations when the program is written or compiled [41], thus avoiding certain computations that might otherwise be required. A data-driven program may postpone making a commitment to a final interpretation in order to be more generally applicable, but it should reduce the amount of information that must be manipu-

lated by later higher-level processes that use specific world model information by generating intermediate symbolic primitives. We believe that our approach follows a *principle of emerging commitment* that is *gradual* and *locally reversible*, but not random. One must make steps toward image interpretation, yet it is impossible to always avoid errors that necessitate steps or labels being undone. An algorithm should make a series of small steps towards the goal, where each step need not produce perfect results, can easily be undone, but still produces useful information for the next step. Simulated annealing algorithms [4], [38] might also be said to follow a principle of emerging commitment, but the surface-based segmentation algorithm described here is very directed in its search process and provides a much more structured output.

V. Algorithm Description

The algorithm presented in this paper uses a general piecewise-smooth surface model to do pixel grouping assuming the image data exhibits *surface coherence* properties. If all pixel values are viewed as noisy samples of an underlying *piecewise-smooth surface* function defined over the entire image, the segmentation process should not only provide detailed definitions of the segmented regions, but should also provide the component surface functions of the underlying piecewise-smooth surface. Surface-based segmentation includes surface (image) reconstruction.

In the first stage of the segmentation algorithm described below, each pixel in an image is given a label based on its value and the values of its neighboring pixels. This label can only take on eight possible values based on two surface-curvature signs and indicates the qualitative shape of an approximating surface that best-fits the image data surrounding that point. This surface-type label image can be analyzed for connected regions using a standard connected component analysis algorithm [91], [3]. Any individual pixel label can be wrong, but it is likely to be correct if it lies in the interior of a large region of identically labeled pixels. Moreover, due to the constrained nature of the surface types represented by the eight labels, it is also likely that a simple surface function will approximate a group of correctly labeled pixels. The surface type label image is used to provide seed regions to the region-growing algorithm. A pixel's similarity with a group of other pixels is measured by comparing 1) the difference between the pixel's value and the other pixels' approximating surface value (at the given pixel location) and 2) a parameter that measures the goodness of the fit of the surface to the other pixels. This similarity measure allows for a pixel to enter and leave a group of pixels depending on the other pixels currently in that group. Hence, a mistake in grouping can be undone. Regions are grown until convergence criterion are met, and a concise, parametrically defined surface description is recorded along with a definition of the image region. It is common for images reconstructed from the segmentation description to be almost indistinguishable from the original image.

This algorithm can be viewed as a two-stage process. The first stage computes an "initial-guess" coarse segmentation in terms of regions of identical surface type labels. The second stage iteratively refines the coarse image segmentation and simultaneously reconstructs image surfaces. The entire algorithm is outlined below.

The first stage creates a surface type label image $T(i, j)$ from the original image $\tilde{g}(i, j)$ in the following manner:

- Compute partial derivative images $\tilde{g}_u(i, j)$, $\tilde{g}_v(i, j)$, $\tilde{g}_{uu}(i, j)$, $\tilde{g}_{vv}(i, j)$, $\tilde{g}_{uv}(i, j)$ from the original image $\tilde{g}(i, j)$ using local fixed-window surface fits that are accomplished via convolution operators.

- Using the partial derivative images, compute the mean curvature image $H(\tilde{g}_u, \tilde{g}_v, \tilde{g}_{uu}, \tilde{g}_{vv}, \tilde{g}_{uv})$ and the Gaussian curvature image $K(\tilde{g}_u, \tilde{g}_v, \tilde{g}_{uu}, \tilde{g}_{vv}, \tilde{g}_{uv})$.

- Compute the sign $(+, -, 0)$ of mean curvature, denoted sgn (H), and the sign of Gaussian curvature, denoted sgn (K). The signum function sgn (x) maps negative numbers to -1, positive numbers to $+1$, and zero maps to zero.

- Use surface curvature sign to determine a surface type label $T(i, j)$ for each pixel (i, j).

The second stage performs iterative region growing using variable-order surface fitting as described below. Its input consists of the original image and the surface type label image. In order to determine the next (first) seed region to use, a connected component algorithm isolates the largest connected region of any surface type in the $T(i, j)$ image, and then a 3×3 binary image erosion operator shrinks the region until a small seed region of appropriate size is obtained. The output of the second stage consists of a region label image $\hat{l}_g(i, j)$, which contains all region definitions in one image (the segmentation information), and a list of coefficient vectors $\{\vec{a}_l\}$, one for each region (the shape reconstruction information).

---

1) **Declarations:**

   Surface-Order: $m \in F = \{1 \text{ (Planar)}, 2 \text{ (Biquadratic)}, 3 \text{ (Bicubic)}, 4 \text{ (Biquartic)}\}$;

   Max-Surface-Order: $|F| = 4$ (Biquartic);

   Surface-Fit: $\{\vec{a} = \text{Coefficient Vector (3, 6, 10, or 15 numbers)}, \sigma = \text{RMS Fit Error}\}$;

   Surface-Type-Image: $T(i, j)$ where $T \in \{1, 2, 3, 5, 6, 7, 8, 9\}$;

   Region-Label-Image: $\hat{l}_g(i, j)$ where $\hat{l} \in \{1, \cdots, \hat{N}\}$;

   Surface-Fit-List: $\{\vec{a}_l\}$ where $l \in \{1, \cdots, \hat{N}\}$;

   Reconstruction-Image: $\hat{g}(i, j)$;

   Error-Image: $e(i, j) = |\hat{g}(i, j) - \tilde{g}(i, j)|$;

   Current-Region, New-Region, Seed-Region: Four-Connected Subsets of Image I

2) **Initialization:**

   Set *Error-Image* = Big Error Value;

   Set *Reconstruction-Image* = No Value;

   Set *Region-Label-Image* = No Label;

3) **Start-Iteration:**

   Set *Surface-Order* = Planar ($z = a + bx + cy$);

   Set *Seed-Region* = Next-Seed-Region (*Surface-Type-Image*);

   IF *Seed-Region* Smaller Than Threshold Size (e.g., 30 pixels),

   THEN GoTo **All-Done;**

   ELSE Set *Current-Region* = *Seed-Region*;

4) **Surface-Fitting:**

   Perform *Surface-Order* Fit to z_{ij} Values in *Current-Region* to obtain *Surface-Fit*;

5) **Surface-Fit-Testing:**

   IF *Surface-Fit* OK using RMS Error Test and Regions Test,

   THEN GoTo **Region-Growing;**

   ELSE Increment *Surface-Order*;

   (Example: Planes become Biquadratics: $z = a + bx + cy + dxy + ex^2 + fy^2$)

   IF *Surface-Order* > *Max-Surface-Order*,

   THEN GoTo **Accept-Reject;**

   ELSE GoTo **Surface-Fitting;**

6) **Region-Growing:**

   Find *New-Region* Consisting of Compatible Connected Neighboring Pixels where Compatibility means Pixel Values must be Close to Surface and Residual Error must be Smaller Than Current Value in Error Image and Derivative Estimates from Pixel Values must be Close to Surface Derivatives;

   IF *Current-Region* $\approx$ *New-Region*,

   THEN GoTo **Accept-Reject;**

   ELSE Set *Current-Region* = *New-Region*; GoTo **Surface-Fitting;**

7) **Accept-Reject:**
IF *Surface-Fit* OK using RMS Error Test,
THEN GoTo **Accept-Surface-Region;**
ELSE Zero Out *Seed-Region* Pixels in *Surface-Type-Image*; GoTo **Start-Iteration;**
8) **Accept-Surface-Region:**
Zero Out *Current-Region* Pixels in *Surface-Type-Image;*
Label *Current-Region* Pixels in *Region-Label-Image;*
Evaluate *Current-Region* Pixels in *Reconstruction-Image* using *Surface-Fit;*
Update *Current-Region* Pixels in *Error-Image* with Absolute Residual Errors;
Add *Surface-Fit* to *Surface-Fit-List;*
GoTo **Start-Iteration;**
9) **All-Done:**
Surface-Fit-List Contains All Function Definitions for Image Reconstruction
Region-Label-Image Contains All Region Definitions for Image Segmentation
Reconstruction-Image Contains Noiseless, Smooth Surface Version of Original Image;
Error-Image Contains Approximation Error at Each Pixel to Evaluate Reconstruction Quality;

It is not necessary to maintain a separate version of the reconstructed image as this can always be recomputed from the surface fit list and the region label image. However, displaying this image during program execution is an excellent way to monitor the progress of the algorithm. The error image can also be recomputed from the surface fit list, the region label image, and the original image, but it is maintained throughout the iteration process to counteract the tendency of surfaces without sharp boundaries to grow slightly beyond their actual boundaries. The error image is updated at each pixel with the absolute error between the approximating surface and the original data when a surface/region is accepted. During the region growing procedure, the error image is consulted to see if the current approximating function represents a given pixel better than it has been represented before. If so, a pixel that was labeled as a member of a previously determined region is free to be labeled with a better fitting region as long as the pixel is connected to the better fitting region. Thus, *labeling decisions are reversible.* Later surfaces in this sequential algorithm can relabel a pixel even though it was already labeled as part of another surface.

The algorithm above terminates when the next seed region extracted from the surface type label image is too small (e.g., less than 30 pixels). However, some pixels may still be unlabeled at this point. These pixels are coalesced into a binary surface type image in which all pixels that have already been labeled are turned off (black) leaving all unlabeled pixels on (white). This new "leftovers" surface type image is then processed by extracting and fitting the next seed region as usual except that the region growing constraints are relaxed (e.g., the allowable RMS fit error limit is doubled). When the next seed region from the left-overs surface type image is too small, the algorithm finally terminates.

The outline above provides a high-level description of all the main elements of the segmentation algorithm. We have omitted several details that are covered in subsequent sections. The algorithm as stated here does not always yield clean high-quality edges between regions, and

it is still possible that some pixels may be left unlabeled (ungrouped with a surface). Hence, a local region refinement operator capable of cleaning up pixel-size irregularities was used to create the final segmentations shown in the experimental results section. Also, as mentioned above, surface curvature sign primitive regions must be merged at polynomial surface primitive boundaries that lie within the boundaries of a smooth surface. The details on a region refinement operation and a one-step region merging method for smoothly joining surface primitive boundaries are available in [8], and further enhancements are currently being developed. These fine points are not at all related to the performance of the segmentation algorithm as described here since the necessary procedures are performed after the termination of the iterative region growing.

VI. Noise Estimation for Threshold Selection

Digital surfaces exhibit the property of surface coherence when sets of neighboring pixels are spatially consistent with each other in the sense that those pixels can be interpreted as noisy, quantized, sampled points of some relatively smooth surface. In order for the surface-based segmentation algorithm to group pixels based on underlying smooth surfaces, it needs to know how well the approximating functions should fit the image data. This information should be derived from the image data in a data-driven algorithm. If the noise in the image is approximately stationary ($\sigma^2(x, y) \approx \sigma^2_{img}$ = constant), we can compute a single estimate of the noise variance σ^2_{img} (that should be applicable at almost all image pixels) by averaging estimates of the noise variance at each pixel. To compute an estimate of the noise variance at each pixel, we perform a equally-weighted least-squares planar fit in the 3×3 neighborhood W_3 surrounding the pixel. If the pixel lies in the interior portion of a smooth surface region and if the radius of the mean surface curvature is larger than a few pixels, the error in the planar surface fit will be primarily due to noise. In contrast, steeply sloped image regions typically have large mean curvatures and

153

bad planar fits. To get a good estimate of the magnitude of the additive noise and the quantization noise in the image, it is necessary to exclude these pixels where the gradient magnitude is large. Therefore, we only include pixels in the mean noise variance calculation if the gradient magnitude is below a preset threshold (8 levels/pixel was used in our experiments). A more detailed discussion of this idea is given in [8]. The equation for the mean image noise variance σ_{img}^2 may be expressed as

$$\sigma_{\text{img}}^2 = E(\sigma_{W_3}^2) = \frac{1}{N_{\text{int}}} \sum_{l=1}^{N_{\text{int}}} \left(\sum_{p \in (R_l - \partial R_l)} \sigma_{W_3}^2(p) \right) \quad (12)$$

where ∂R represents the boundary of the region R, N_{int} is the total number of surface interior pixels contributing to the sum, and where $\sigma_{W_3}(p)$ is the root-mean-square-error (RMSE) of the least-squares planar surface fit (a_{00}, a_{10}, a_{01}) in the 3×3 window W_3 around the pixel p:

$$\sigma_{W_3}^2(p) = \frac{1}{9} \sum_{(i,j) \in W_3} \left(z_{ij} - (a_{00} + a_{10}i + a_{01}j) \right)^2 \quad (13)$$

where i and j are interpreted as integer row and column coordinates. Although the regions themselves are not known at the time the noise variance is estimated, we get a good approximation to σ_{img} by not averaging pixels with high slopes using the preset threshold.

The noise variance estimate allows us to automatically set the ϵ parameter of the surface coherence predicate (the maximum allowable RMS surface fit error) and two other thresholds to an appropriate value as described later. Note that we are attempting to estimate noise variance for *continuous smooth surface detection* purposes, *not for discontinuity detection* as in [45]. Although we do not claim to have solved the automatic threshold selection problem, the three relevant thresholds are directly tied to the geometric and statistical properties of the data via empirical relationships providing good performance for many images. Other noise variance estimation techniques, such as computing the mean square difference between a median filtered version of an image and the original image, are currently being evaluated.

VII. SURFACE TYPE LABELING

Differential geometry states that local surface shape is *uniquely determined* by the first and second fundamental forms. Gaussian and mean curvature combine these first and second fundamental forms in two different ways to obtain scalar surface features that are *invariant to rotations, translations, and changes in parameterization* [8]. Therefore, visible surfaces in range images have the same mean and Gaussian curvature from any viewpoint under orthographic projection. Also, *mean curvature uniquely determines the shape of graph surfaces* if a boundary curve is also specified [40] while *Gaussian curvature uniquely determines the shape of convex surfaces and convex regions of nonconvex surfaces* [23], [55]. There are eight fundamental viewpoint independent surface types that can be characterized using only the sign of the mean curvature (H) and Gaussian curvature (K) as shown in Fig.

	$K > 0$	$K = 0$	$K < 0$
$H < 0$	Peak T=1	Ridge T=2	Saddle Ridge T=3
$H = 0$	(none) T=4	Flat T=5	Minimal Surface T=6
$H > 0$	Pit T=7	Valley T=8	Saddle Valley T=9

Fig. 3. Surface type labels from surface curvature sign.

3. Gaussian and mean curvature can be computed directly from a range image using window operators that yield least squares estimates of first and second partial derivatives as in [2], [6], [48]. The key point is that every pixel in an image can be given a surface type label based on the values of the pixels in a small neighborhood about that pixel.

Surface curvature estimates are extremely sensitive to noise because they require the estimation of second derivatives, in which high frequency noise is amplified. In fact, 8-bit quantization noise alone can seriously degrade the quality of surface curvature estimates unless large window sizes are used (at least 9×9). Yet reliable estimates of surface curvature sign can still be computed in the presence of additive noise and quantization noise [10]. Since we need to compute five different derivative estimates to compute surface curvature, we could use large $N \times N$ derivative estimation window operators (N odd), or we can smooth the image with a small $L \times L$ window operator (L odd), store the smoothed values at higher precision, and operate on the smoothed image with smaller $M \times M$ derivative estimation window operators (M odd) where $L + M = N + 1$. Assuming window separability and therefore linear time requirements, the former requires time proportional to $5N$ whereas the latter requires time proportional to $N + 4M + 1$. The relative weighting factors used in determining the derivative and smoothing window coefficients have an important influence on the quality of the derivative estimates. In our experiments with 8-bit images, we obtained good consistent results using one 7×7 binomial weight (approximately Gaussian) smoother and five 7×7 equally weighted least squares derivative estimation operators with over 30 percent fewer computations than the equivalent 13×13 windows. For reference purposes, we list the specific numbers needed for this particular computation.

Since all our operators are separable, window masks can be computed as the outer product of two column vectors. The binomial smoothing window may be written as $[S] = \vec{s} \, \vec{s}^T$ where the column vector $\vec{s}$ is given by

$$\vec{s} = \frac{1}{64} [1 \ 6 \ 15 \ 20 \ 15 \ 6 \ 1]^T. \quad (14)$$

For 7×7 binomial smoothing window, it is clear that we should try to maintain an extra 12 bits ($12 = 2 \log_2 (64)$) of fractional information in the intermediate image smoothed by $[S]$. For an $L \times L$ binomial smoother, $2L - 2$ bits of fractional information should be maintained. The equally weighted least-squares derivative estimation window operators are given by

$$[D_u] = \vec{d}_0 \vec{d}_1^T \quad [D_v] = \vec{d}_1 \vec{d}_0^T \quad [D_{uu}] = \vec{d}_0 \vec{d}_2^T$$

$$[D_{vv}] = \vec{d}_2 \vec{d}_0^T \quad [D_{uv}] = \vec{d}_1 \vec{d}_1^T \qquad (15)$$

where the column vectors $\vec{d}_0$, $\vec{d}_1$, $\vec{d}_2$ for a 7×7 window are given by

$$\vec{d}_0 = \tfrac{1}{7}[1 \; 1 \; 1 \; 1 \; 1 \; 1 \; 1]^T \qquad (16)$$

$$\vec{d}_1 = \tfrac{1}{28}[-3 \; -2 \; -1 \; 0 \; 1 \; 2 \; 3]^T \qquad (17)$$

$$\vec{d}_2 = \tfrac{1}{84}[5 \; 0 \; -3 \; -4 \; -3 \; 0 \; 5]^T \qquad (18)$$

The partial derivative estimate images are computed via the appropriate 2-D image convolutions (denoted *):

$$\tilde{g}_u(i,j) = D_u * S * \tilde{g}(i,j)$$

$$\tilde{g}_v(i,j) = D_v * S * \tilde{g}(i,j) \qquad (19)$$

$$\tilde{g}_{uu}(i,j) = D_{uu} * S * \tilde{g}(i,j)$$

$$\tilde{g}_{vv}(i,j) = D_{vv} * S * \tilde{g}(i,j)$$

$$\tilde{g}_{uv}(i,j) = D_{uv} * S * \tilde{g}(i,j) \qquad (20)$$

Mean (H) and Gaussian (K) curvature images are computed using the partial derivative estimate images:

$$H(i,j) = \frac{\left(1 + \tilde{g}_v^2(i,j)\right)\tilde{g}_{uu}(i,j) + \left(1 + \tilde{g}_u^2(i,j)\right)\tilde{g}_{vv}(i,j) - 2\tilde{g}_u(i,j)\,\tilde{g}_v(i,j)\,\tilde{g}_{uv}(i,j)}{2\left(\sqrt{1 + \tilde{g}_u^2(i,j) + \tilde{g}_v^2(i,j)}\right)^3} \qquad (21)$$

$$K(i,j) = \frac{\tilde{g}_{uu}(i,j)\,\tilde{g}_{vv}(i,j) - \tilde{g}_{uv}^2(i,j)}{\left(1 + \tilde{g}_u^2(i,j) + \tilde{g}_v^2(i,j)\right)^2}. \qquad (22)$$

A toleranced signum function

$$\operatorname{sgn}_\epsilon(x) = \begin{cases} +1 & \text{if } x > \epsilon \\ 0 & \text{if } |x| \le \epsilon \\ -1 & \text{if } x < \epsilon \end{cases} \qquad (23)$$

is used to compute the individual surface curvature sign images $\operatorname{sgn}_\epsilon(H(t,j))$ and $\operatorname{sgn}_\epsilon(K(i,j))$ using a preselected zero threshold ϵ. For our experimental results, we used $\epsilon_H = 0.03$ and $\epsilon_K = 0.015$ for 7×7 windows. Ideally, these thresholds should depend on the noise variance estimate, but the algorithm performance is not very sensitive to these numbers for reasonable quality images.

The surface curvature sign images are then used to determine the surface type image:

$$T(i,j) = 1 + 3(1 + \operatorname{sgn}_{\epsilon_H}(H(i,j))$$

$$+ \left(1 - \operatorname{sgn}_{\epsilon_K}(K(i,j))\right). \qquad (24)$$

This equation is shown in table form in Fig. 3. Fig. 1 displayed the eight fundamental shapes. Depending on the number of digitized bits and the amount of noise in the original image and the window sizes used in derivative estimation, regions of a given surface type label tend to connect (in the sense of four-connectedness) with distinct, but adjacent regions with the same label. Therefore, it is not always possible, in general, to simply isolate a four-connected region of pixels of a particular surface type label and identify that region as a single surface of the appropriate type for surface fitting purposes. Hence, there is a need for a general purpose method to isolate useful interior seed regions from the larger regions of identical surface type labels extracted from the surface type label image $T(i,j)$.

VIII. Seed Region Extraction

We adopted the following strategy that breaks the unwanted connections with other adjacent regions and attempts to provide small, maximally interior regions that are good for surface fitting. The largest connected region of any fundamental surface type in the surface type label image is isolated (denoted R_T^0) and is then eroded (contracted) repetitively (using a 3×3 binary region erosion operator) until the region disappears. After the kth contraction (erosion), there exists a largest four-connected subregion R_T^k in the pixels remaining after the k contractions of the original region. If we record $|R_T^k|$, the number of pixels in the largest connected subregion, as a function of the number of contractions k, a *contraction profile* for the original region is created. Contraction profiles for five regions of a surface type label image (for the coffee cup range image) are shown in Fig. 4. A seed region size threshold t_{seed} for the minimum number of pixels required to be in a seed region (e.g., 10) is a preselected parameter. If we examine the contraction profile, there will always be an contraction number k such that $|R_T^k| \ge t_{\text{seed}}$ and $|R_T^{k+1}| < t_{\text{seed}}$. The region R_T^k is selected as the *seed region* (or kernel region) for subsequent surface fitting and region growing. The circles in Fig. 4 indicate the size of the selected seed region. The threshold t_{seed} must always be greater than or equal to the minimum number of points required for the simplest surface fit (i.e., 3 points for a plane).

The fundamental purpose of the contraction profile computation for seed region extraction is to find a small enough isolated region that 1) is not inadvertently connected to any separate, but adjacent surface regions, and 2) is far enough inside the boundaries of the actual surface primitive to provide good surface fitting. The 3×3 erosion operation (i.e., zero out pixels that have zero-valued neighbors and leave other pixels alone) is a simple, common image processing operation that can be accomplished in less than a video frame time on existing image processing hardware. Other methods for obtaining seed re-

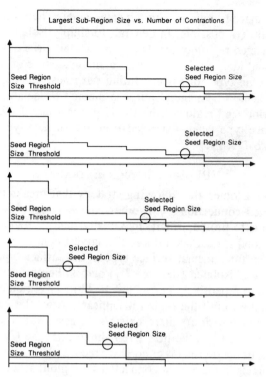

Fig. 4. Contraction profiles for five surface type regions.

gions are possible, but this method is simple and potentially very fast.

IX. ITERATIVE VARIABLE ORDER SURFACE FITTING

A plane is always fitted first to the small seed region using equally weighted least squares. If the seed region belongs to a surface that is not extremely curved, a plane will fit quite well to the digital surface defined by the original image data. If the plane fits the seed region within the maximum allowable RMS error threshold $\epsilon_{\max} = w_1 \sigma_{\text{img}}$, then the seed is allowed to grow. The value of w_1 was empirically set to 2.5 in our experiments to allow for variations in the image noise process. If not, the seed is fitted with the next higher-order surface (e.g., biquadratic), and the algorithm proceeds similarly. When the seed is allowed to grow, the functional description of the surface over the seed region is tested over the entire image to determine what pixels are compatible with the seed region as described in the next section.

This surface fitting process may be stated more precisely as follows. Let I be the rectangular image region over which a hypothetical piecewise smooth function $z = g(x, y)$ is defined. Let $\hat{R}_l^{k=0}$ denote the seed region provided by the seed extraction algorithm that is assumed to be contained in the unknown actual region R_l in the image: $\hat{R}_l^{k=0} \subseteq R_l \subseteq I$. The seed region $\hat{R}_l^{k=0}$ must be converted to a full region description $\hat{R}_l$ that approximates the desired region description R_l.

Now, let $\vec{a}_l^k$ be the parameter vector associated with the functional fit to the pixel values in the given region $\hat{R}_l^k$ of the kth iterative surface fit. Let $\mathfrak{R}^n$ denote the set of all parameter vectors for the set of approximating functions F, and let $|F|$ be the number of different types of surface

functions to be used. A particular function type (or fit order) is referred to as m^k where $1 \le m^k \le |F|$. The general fitting function of type m^k is denoted $z = \hat{f}(m^k, \vec{a}_l^k; x, y)$. The general surface fitting process, denoted $L_{\hat{f}}$, maps the original image data $\tilde{g}(x, y)$, a connected region definition $\hat{R}_l^k$, and the current fit order m^k into the range space $\mathfrak{R}^n \times \mathfrak{R}^+$ where $\mathfrak{R}^+$ is the set of possible errors (nonnegative real numbers):

$$(\vec{a}_l^k, \epsilon_l^k) = L_{\hat{f}}(m^k, \hat{R}_l^k, \tilde{g}) \quad (25)$$

and has the property that the error metric

$$\epsilon_l^k = \left\| \hat{f}(m^k, \vec{a}_l^k; x, y) - \tilde{g}(x, y) \right\|_{\hat{R}_l^k} \quad (26)$$

is the minimum value attainable for all functions of the form specified by m^k. Equally weighted least-squares surface fitting minimizes the error metric

$$(\epsilon_l^k)^2 = \frac{1}{|\hat{R}_l^k|} \sum_{(x,y)\in\hat{R}_l^k} \left(\hat{f}(m^k, \vec{a}_l^k; x, y) - \tilde{g}(x, y) \right)^2 \quad (27)$$

where $|\hat{R}_l^k|$ is the number of pixels in the region $\hat{R}_l^k$ (the area of the region). The parameter vector $\vec{a}_l^k$ and the surface fit order m^k are passed onto the region growing procedure if the RMS fit error test and the regions test are passed. Otherwise, m^k is incremented and the higher order surface is fitted. If all four fit orders were tried and the error was never less than the threshold $\epsilon_{\max}$, the seed region is rejected by marking off the pixels in the surface type label image, and then continuing by looking for the next largest connected region of any surface type.

A. RMS Fit Error Test

The RMS fit error test tests the surface fit error, which measures the variance of the error of the fit due to the noise in the data, against the maximum allowable fit error as determined from the noise variance estimate for the image: $\epsilon_l^k < \epsilon_{\max} = w_1 \sigma_{\text{img}}$. If the error is small enough, the surface fit passes the test; otherwise, it fails. The coefficient $w_1 = 2.5$ is an empirically determined parameter.

B. Regions Test

The regions test is required because it is possible for a lower order function to fit a higher order function over a finite region within the maximum allowable fit error threshold even though the lower order fit is not appropriate. It is possible to detect the presence of a higher order function in the data (without letting the fit error increase all the way up to the error threshold) by analyzing the distribution of the sign of the fit errors (residual errors) at each individual pixel of the fit. We have generalized the runs test of nonparametric statistics [28] to assist in the detection of higher order behavior. This test is discussed in detail in [8], and is summarized here.

Consider that three long residual-sign intervals occur when fitting a line to a slowly bending curve as in Fig. 5. Fitting a plane to a small portion of a sphere is very similar except that two large residual-sign regions occur as is

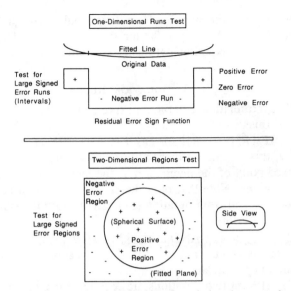

Fig. 5. Runs test and regions test ideas for noiseless data examples.

also shown in Fig. 5. The regions test is performed as follows: 1) For each original pixel value in the region $\hat{R}_l^k$ lying *above* the fitted surface $\hat{f}(m^k, a_l^k; x, y)$, turn a pixel *on* in a *positive residual error* image; for each pixel below the surface, turn a pixel on in a negative error image (all pixels initially off in both images). 2) Perform one 3×3 erosion on each error image and count the pixels left in the largest connected region in each image. 3) If either count is greater than r_t percent of the size of the current region $|R_l^k|$, then increase the fit order m^k. The experimental results used a regions test threshold of $r_t = 0.9 + 0.2\sigma_{\text{img}}$ percent, which was determined empirically.

X. REGION GROWING

After a surface of order m^k is fitted to the region $\hat{R}_l^k$ in the kth iteration, the surface description is used to grow the region into a larger region where all pixels in the larger region are connected to the original region and compatible with the approximating surface function for the original region. The parallel region growing algorithm accepts as input the original digital surface $\tilde{g}(x, y)$, the approximating function $\hat{f}(m^k, \vec{a}_l^k; x, y)$ and the surface fit error ϵ_l^k from the surface fitting algorithm. It does not use the region definition until later. To determine the zeroth-order "surface continuity" compatibility of each pixel $p \in I$ with the approximating surface description, the polynomial based prediction for the pixel value and the actual pixel value

$$\hat{z}(p) = \hat{f}(m^k, \vec{a}_l^k; x(p), y(p)) \quad \text{and}$$

$$z(p) = \tilde{g}(x(p), y(p)) \tag{28}$$

are compared to see if the pixel p is compatible with the approximating surface function. If the magnitude of the difference between the function value and the digital surface value is less than the allowed tolerance value, denoted $w_0\epsilon_l^k$, then the pixel p is added to the set of compatible pixels, denoted $C(m^k, \vec{a}_l^k, \epsilon_l^k)$, which are com-

patible with the surface fit to the region $\hat{R}_l^k$. Otherwise, the pixel is incompatible and discarded. The result of this process is the compatible pixel list:

$$C(m^k, \vec{a}_l^k, \epsilon_l^k) = \left\{ p \in I : \left| \hat{z}(p) - z(p) \right| \leq w_0\epsilon_l^k \right\}. \tag{29}$$

This set of compatible pixels $C(\cdot)$ is essentially a thresholded absolute value image of the difference between the original image data and the image created by evaluating the function $\hat{f}$ at each pixel. For our experimental results, the factor $w_0 = 2.8$ was used. This ensures that approximately 99.5 percent of all samples of a smooth surface corrupted by normally distributed measurement noise will lie within this error tolerance. This factor has been found to work well in the presence of other types of noise also.

The compatible pixel list is then post processed to remove any pixels that do not possess "surface normal continuity" compatibility with the approximating surface. Let $\tilde{g}_u(p)$ and $\tilde{g}_v(p)$ denote the first partial derivative estimates of the local surface as computed from the image data at the pixel p via convolutions as mentioned earlier. Let $\hat{g}_u(p)$ and $\hat{g}_v(p)$ denote the first partial derivatives of the approximating surface as computed from the polynomial coefficients at the pixel p. Let $\vec{n}$ be the unit normal vector as determined by the data, and let $\hat{\vec{n}}$ be the unit normal vector as determined by the approximating surface:

$$\tilde{\vec{n}} = \frac{[-\tilde{g}_u \ -\tilde{g}_v \ 1]^T}{\sqrt{1 + \tilde{g}_u^2 + \tilde{g}_v^2}} \qquad \hat{\vec{n}} = \frac{[-\hat{g}_u \ -\hat{g}_v \ 1]^T}{\sqrt{1 + \hat{g}_u^2 + \hat{g}_v^2}}. \tag{30}$$

A pixel is compatible in the sense of surface normal continuity if the angle between the two unit normals is less than some threshold angle θ_t:

$$\cos^{-1}(\hat{\vec{n}} \cdot \tilde{\vec{n}}) \leq \theta_t. \tag{31}$$

For our experimental results, the threshold angle is given by $\theta_t = 12 + 16\sigma_{\text{img}}$ degrees, where the coefficients were determined empirically. The test may be rewritten in the following form to avoid square roots and to incorporate the derivative values directly:

$$\frac{(\tilde{g}_u - \hat{g}_u)^2 + (\tilde{g}_v - \hat{g}_v)^2 + (\tilde{g}_u\hat{g}_v - \tilde{g}_v\hat{g}_u)^2}{(1 + \tilde{g}_u^2 + \tilde{g}_v^2)(1 + \hat{g}_u^2 + \hat{g}_v^2)}$$

$$\leq \sin^2(\theta_t). \tag{32}$$

Since the compatibility test for surface normal continuity involves many computations per pixel, it is only applied to those pixels that have passed the compatibility test for surface continuity. Excellent segmentation results have been obtained without the surface normal continuity test on many images that lack small orientation discontinuities. However, a data-driven smooth-surface segmentation algorithm must always perform the test to ensure that growing regions do not inadvertently grow over small or noisy orientation discontinuities.

A. Region Iteration

When the parallel region growing computation has operated on every pixel, the compatible pixel list $C(m^k, \vec{a}_l^k, \epsilon_l^k) \subseteq I$ is complete. The largest connected region in this set of pixels that overlaps the seed region $\hat{R}_l^k$ must then be extracted to create the next region $\hat{R}_l^{k+1}$. This process is denoted $\Lambda(\cdot)$. The output region $\hat{R}_l^{k+1}$ must have the property that it is the largest connected region in the list of compatible pixels satisfying

$$\hat{R}_l^k \cap \hat{R}_l^{k+1} \neq \phi = \text{Null Set} \qquad (33)$$

because it is possible to get larger connected regions in the compatible pixel list than the connected region corresponding to the seed region. The iterative process of region definition via largest, overlapping, connected region extraction may be expressed as follows:

$$\hat{R}_l^{k+1} = \Lambda(C(m^k, \vec{a}_l^k, \epsilon_l^k), \hat{R}_l^k) = \Phi(\hat{R}_l^k) \qquad (34)$$

where $\Phi(\cdot)$ represents all operations required to compute the region $\hat{R}_l^{k+1}$ from the region $\hat{R}_l^k$. It is interesting to note that since the regions of an image form a metric space [8], the desired solution region is a fixed point $R = \Phi(R)$ of the mapping $\Phi(\cdot)$.

The new region is then considered as a seed region and processed by the surface fitting algorithm

$$(\vec{a}_l^{k+1}, \epsilon_l^{k+1}) = L_f(m^{k+1}, \hat{R}_l^{k+1}, \tilde{g}) \qquad (35)$$

to obtain a new parameter vector and a new surface fit error. If this region is allowed to grow again $\epsilon_l^{k+1} < \epsilon_{\max}$, then the compatible pixel list is recomputed $C(m^{k+1}, \vec{a}_l^{k+1}, \epsilon_l^{k+1})$, the largest connected overlapping region of $C(\cdot)$ is extracted, and so on until the termination criteria are met.

B. Sequential Versus Parallel Region Growing

The region growing process is formulated above for a parallel implementation where bivariate polynomials are evaluated over images and regions. It must be noted that this simple, parallel region growing formulation is equivalent to more complicated, sequential, spiraling region growing approaches *until the last iteration*. At the last iteration, the processing of the compatible pixel list becomes an important feature of the segmentation algorithm. After the growing region has been accepted, any other sufficiently large, reasonably shaped regions in the compatible pixel list are also accepted as part of the same surface. For example, in the coffee cup range image shown in the experimental results section, the flat background visible through the handle of the cup is correctly assigned to the larger background surface without high-level knowledge, only the surface compatibility concepts. Thus, nonadjacent compatible regions can be labeled as such during the surface acceptance stage without further postprocessing operations because of the parallel region growing process during the last iteration prior to acceptance. On a sequential machine, sequential region growing methods can offer faster performance for the other it-

erations, but the parallel formulation only takes a few seconds on a VAX 11/780 for the 128×128 images shown in the experimental results section.

XI. Termination Rules

The termination criteria are expressed as the following set of rules:

1) IF $|\hat{R}_l^k| \approx |\hat{R}_l^j|$ for any $j < k$, THEN stop! Basically, this rule states the condition that we are looking for a fixed point of the mapping Φ in the metric space of image regions. Note that only the size of the region needs to be checked from iteration to iteration, not the detailed region description.

2) IF $\epsilon_l^k > \epsilon_{\max}$ AND $m^k \geq |F|$, THEN stop! The image data is varying in a way that the highest order function cannot approximate.

3) At least two iterations are required for a given surface fit order m^k before the algorithm is allowed to stop.

These rules state the essential concepts involved in terminating the surface fitting iteration. There is also a maximum limit on the number of possible iterations to prevent extremely long iterations. In all tests done to this point, the maximum limit of 30 iterations has never been reached and the average number of iterations is approximately eight.

XII. Surface Acceptance and Rejection Decisions

After the surface growing iterations have terminated, we are left with the set of compatible pixels and the connected surface region itself along with the function parameters and the fit error. For growth surface regions that exceed the error threshold $\epsilon_{\max}$, but not by much, an acceptance zone is defined above the error threshold such that surface regions within the acceptance zone are accepted. The acceptance threshold used for our experiments is 50 percent greater than $\epsilon_{\max} = w_1 \sigma_{\text{img}}$ where $w_1 = 2.5$. Surface regions with fit errors beyond the acceptance zone are rejected.

When a surface region is rejected for any reason, the seed region responsible for the surface region is marked off in the surface type label image as having been processed, which prohibits the use of the same original seed region again. When a surface region is accepted, all pixels in that region are similarly marked off in the surface type label image so that they are not considered for future seed regions. In this respect, surface rejection and surface acceptance are similar. However, the surface acceptance process also updates the region label image, the reconstruction image, and the error image. In addition, the acceptance process dilates the accepted region description and checks if there are any connected groups of pixels in that dilated region that are surface-continuity compatible with the accepted surface and connected with the accepted region. Surface-normal compatibility is not required when adding these pixels because of the difficulty in getting accurate surface normal estimates near surface region boundaries.

The surface-based segmentation algorithm has been applied successfully to more than 40 test images. In this section, the segmentation algorithm's performance on six range images and three intensity images is discussed. The following set of images is displayed for each input image:

1) original gray scale image (upper left).
2) surface type label image (lower left).
3) region label image segmentation plot (lower right).
4) reconstructed gray scale image (upper right).

The surface type label image shows the coarse "initial guess" segmentation provided by labeling each pixel with one of eight labels according to the sign of the mean and Gaussian curvature. Each region in this image is an isolated set of connected pixels that all have the same surface type label. The region label image shows the final refined segmentation obtained from the iterative region-growing algorithm. Each region in this image is the support region over which a particular polynomial surface function is evaluated. The reconstructed image is computed from the region label image and the list of surface parameters, and it shows the visual quality of the approximate surface representation. For each image, we also include the noise variance estimate computed from the orginal image and an error statistic computed from the original-reconstruction difference image.

When a user runs the program on an image, the name of the image is typically the only input required by the program. All internal parameters are either fixed or automatically varying based on the noise variance estimate. The user does have the option to change five of the fixed internal parameters and to override the three automatically set thresholds: 1) the maximum allowed RMS fit error ϵ_{max}, 2) the surface normal compatibility angle threshold θ_t, and 3) the regions test threshold r_t. Eight of the nine images shown here were obtained without any adjustments whatsoever, but more interesting results were obtained by overriding the automatically set thresholds for the computer keyboard range image, which has nonstationary noise. This was necessary because of the stationarity assumption of the current noise variance estimation algorithm, which allows us to describe the image noise with a single number.

A. Interpretation of Intensity Image Results

The entire segmentation algorithm is based only on the knowledge of piecewise-smooth surfaces and digital surfaces. Since intensity images are also digital surfaces, the algorithm can be applied to intensity images for segmentation purposes. It is important to understand that the dimensionality of a digital surface is the same regardless of the meaning of the sensed values at each pixel. And since the difference between range images and intensity images is the interpretation of the sensed values (depth versus light intensity), the difference in the algorithm output lies in how the surface segmentation is interpreted. Intensity image surface primitives are only surface function ap-

proximations to the intensity image data and nothing more. The segmentation results will be useful when intensity image surfaces correspond to physical surfaces in a scene. This is of course equivalent to an implicit assumption that edge detection approaches use: the boundaries of intensity image surfaces correspond to the boundaries of physical surfaces in a scene. However, our image description is much richer than most edge-based image descriptions because not only are guaranteed closed-curve edges of regions detected, but the *approximate value of every single image pixel* is encoded in the polynomial coefficients. If intensity image surface primitives can be reliably extracted, it is possible to apply shape from shading ideas [58] to intensity surface primitives [14].

B. Coffee Cup Range Image (ERIM)

The coffee cup range image is a 128×128 8-bit image from an ERIM phase-differencing range sensor [108]. The segmentation results are shown in Fig. 6. The measured noise variance is $\sigma_{img} = 1.02$, and the mean absolute deviation between the final reconstructed image and the original image is $E(|e(i, j)|) = 1.46$. The final segmentation clearly delineates the outside cylindrical surface of the cup, the foot of the cup, the inside cylindrical surface of the cup, the background table surface (which was recognized as a single surface with three subregions despite the nonadjacency of the region visible through the handle and the small hole in the side of the cup), and the cup handle surface (which is represented as two surfaces due to the twisting of the surface from this view). Although this image is easy to segment by many other methods, the subtle difference in surface variations between the foot and the main body of the cup is difficult to detect with an edge detector. Two small meaningless surfaces did arise on the steeply sloped sides of the cup because the laser range sensor has difficulty obtaining good results when most of the laser energy is reflected away from the sensor. Note that although this algorithm knows nothing about *cylinders*, the cylindrical surface of the cup is adequately segmented.

Fig. 7 shows discrete contour lines for the original image (left) and the reconstructed image (right). These contour lines bound regions of constant range. This presentation is needed to adequately appreciate the shape information in the noiseless reconstructed image as compared to the noisy original image. The background appears to be curved due to image parameterization distortions caused by the range sensor's two orthogonal axis mirrors and equal angle increment sampling as discussed in the Appendix. Fig. 8 shows the variations in RMS fit error, region size, and surface fit order as a function of the region growing iteration number for the background surface. Fig. 9 shows the actual polynomial coefficients used in the image reconstruction for the six primary regions: 1) background, 2) cup body, 3) cup interior, 4) top of handle, 5) bottom of handle, and 6) foot of cup. The mean absolute error (e1), the standard deviation (e2), and

Fig. 6. Segmentation results for coffee cup range image.

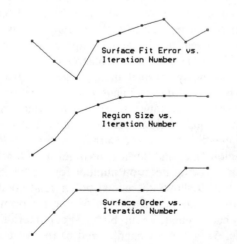

Fig. 7. Range contour lines for original and reconstructed images.

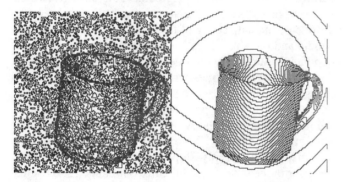

Surface Fit Error vs. Iteration Number

Region Size vs. Iteration Number

Surface Order vs. Iteration Number

Fig. 8. Fit error, region size, and surface order versus iteration number.

Polynomial Graph Surfaces for '/img/range/cofcup2' (128 x 128 Image)
            2   2   2   2   3   3   3   2 2   3   4   4
z=a+bx+cy+dxy+ex +fy +gx y+hxy +ix +jy +kx y+lx y +mxy +nx +oy

Surf# 1 Biquartic Surface
a= 41.1084853 b= 0.141577803 c= 0.2713745965
d= -0.002495014122 e= -0.0007755753671 f= -0.003601368877
g= 1.481712253e-05 h= 2.726318379e-05 i= -2.309573363e-06
j= 8.758485509e-06 k= -1.803061683e-08 l= -8.351990453e-08
m= -8.546141676e-08 n= -5.871664019e-10 o= 1.594833765e-08
0.733465 0.890638 2.81471 (e1,e2,emax) 9321 Pxls in Rgn

Surf# 2 Bicubic Surface
a= 64.72905408 b= 4.004588601 c= -0.6523437561
d= -0.008861504524 e= -0.02260194283 f= 0.008512778086
g= -4.525700906e-05 h= 4.449644712e-05 i= 7.129137939e-06
j= -5.132800061e-05
0.894967 1.12435 4.17196 (e1,e2,emax) 3301 Pxls in Rgn

Surf# 3 Biquartic Surface
a= -163.4152524 b= -5.291701634 c= 35.73599936
d= -0.822060872 e= 0.303405367 f= -0.4267766669
g= 0.000534934843 h= 0.01667119329 i= -0.002583054026
j= -0.003845895577 k= 8.273502856e-06 l= -1.84330636e-05
m= -0.0001033402269 n= 7.022812258e-06 o= 6.765861748e-05
0.862173 1.04452 2.94707 (e1,e2,emax) 846 Pxls in Rgn

Surf# 4 Bicubic Surface
a= -56553.34566 b= 1085.103359 c= 550.9673791
d= -6.935330046 e= -7.005112872 f= -1.772838004
g= 0.02117382282 h= 0.01207493125 i= 0.01546967941 j=0.001442356458
0.693086 0.870873 1.94343 (e1,e2,emax) 85 Pxls in Rgn

Surf# 5 Biquartic Surface
a= 58478.67644 b= -4177.347605 c= 5553.461039
d= -62.08406574 e= 61.15735537 f= -78.3777114
g= 0.02145723219 h= 0.980323446 i= -0.3041497425
j= 0.2363115629 k= 0.001884292974 l= -0.005593080286
m= 0.001788868803 n= 0.0003022405187 o= -0.001835806151
1.57884 1.93 5.13262 (e1,e2,emax) 107 Pxls in Rgn

Surf# 6 Biquadratic Surface
a= 16.5160474 b= 4.368161058 c= 0.9102155505
d= 0.0009597935563 e= -0.03381975184 f= -0.01009901358
1.30028 1.61381 3.97869 (e1,e2,emax) 146 Pxls in Rgn

Fig. 9. Bivariate polynomial coefficients describing coffee cup surfaces.

160

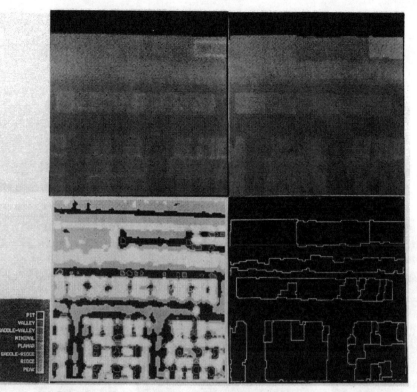

Fig. 10. Segmentation results for computer keyboard range image.

C. Computer Keyboard Range Image (ERIM)

The computer keyboard range image is a 128×128 6-bit image from the ERIM range sensor. The segmentation results are shown in Fig. 10. The measured noise variance is $\sigma_{img} = 1.68$, and the mean absolute deviation between the final reconstructed image and the original image is $E(|e(i, j)|) = 1.96$. The surface type label image shows the uneven distribution in the additive noise field. The smooth surface of the keyboard body has very little noise in comparison with the noise on the keys themselves. This results from the specularity of the key surfaces and diffuseness of the keyboard body. This nonstationarity of the noise disobeyed the stationarity assumption of the noise estimation program and the automatically set thresholds did not provide the segmentation quality of other images. Therefore, manually set thresholds were used for the results shown here. Some individual keys have been segmented whereas other keys were grouped together. However, the center of each key is available from the surface type label image if needed. Although it cannot be seen in this presentation of results, each key center is represented as a small isolated pit or valley region surrounded by ridge and peak regions representing the surrounding parts of the key.

D. Ring on Steps (ERIM)

The ring on steps range image is a noisy 128×128 8-bit image from the ERIM range sensor. The segmentation results are shown in Fig. 11. The ring has a rectangular cross section and the step lower part of the steps is cut off at an oblique angle. The measured noise variance is $\sigma_{img} = 2.05$, and the mean absolute deviation between the final reconstructed image and the original image is $E(|e(i, j)|) = 3.31$. This image is the noisiest range image in results documented here. The steeply sloped surfaces are much noisier than the other surfaces as occurred in the coffee cup image. Fig. 12 shows the contour lines for the original image (left) and the reconstructed image (right). The noiseless quality of the reconstructed image is quite apparent in this presentation.

E. Auto Part (INRIA)

The original data for the auto part was acquired from the INRIA range sensor (made available courtesy of Prof. T. Henderson of Univ. of Utah and INRIA) and was formatted as a long list of (x, y, z) points. Although the data was easily divided into scan lines, a different number of points occurred on each scan line, and the points were not regularly spaced. This data was converted to 128×128 8-bit range image by a separate processing step not documented here. The segmentation results for this auto part range image are shown in Fig. 13. The measured noise variance is $\sigma_{img} = 0.60$, and the mean absolute deviation between the final reconstructed image and the original image is $E(|e(i, j)|) = 1.48$. This 2.5-D segmentation is similar to 3-D segmentations published in [33], [12], [52].

F. Cube with Three Holes

The cube with three holes drilled through it provides an interesting nonconvex combination of flat and cylindrical

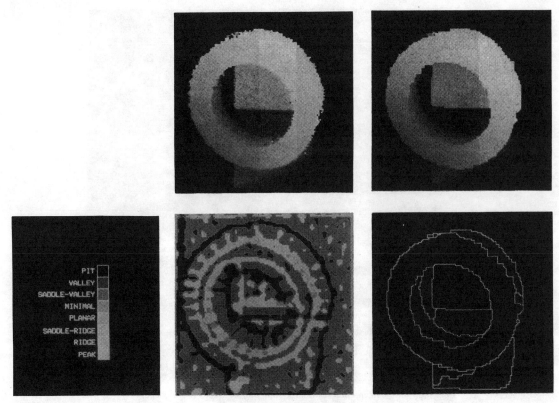

Fig. 11. Segmentation results for ring on steps range image.

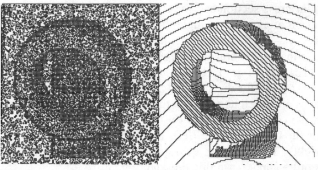

/b/img/range/ringbloc

Fig. 12. Range contour lines for original and reconstructed images.

surfaces. This range image was created using a depth-buffer algorithm on a 3-D solid model created using SDRC/GEOMOD and adding pseudo-Gaussian noise. The segmentation results are shown in Fig. 14. The measured noise variance is $\sigma_{img} = 1.89$, and the mean absolute deviation between the final reconstructed image and the original image is $E(|e(i, j)|) = 2.94$. The three linear dihedral edges of the cube have been determined to subpixel precision by intersecting the planar descriptions for the three planes. The results here show the raw segmentation in the region label image.

G. Road Scene Range Image (ERIM)

The road scene range image is a 128×128 range image from the ERIM sensor. The segmentation results are shown in Fig. 15. The measured noise variance is $\sigma_{img} =$ 1.82, and the mean absolute deviation between the final reconstructed image and the original image is $E(|e(i, j)|) = 0.96$. The edges of the road are clearly delineated in the segmentation results. The false edge crossing the road results from the limited bending capability of the biquartic polynomial within the tolerances specified by the automatic threshold setting mechanisms. This edge can be removed in several ways: 1) the error tolerances can be increased manually, 2) higher order surfaces can be used, or 3) the range data can be precorrected (resampled) to eliminate the geometric distortions produced by equal angle increment sampling in scanning laser radars that use two mirrors rotating around orthogonal axes as discussed in the Appendix.

H. Road Scene Intensity Image

A different road scene is represented in the 128×128 8-bit intensity image. The intensity image segmentation results are shown in Fig. 16. The measured noise variance is $\sigma_{img} = 2.27$, and the mean absolute deviation between the final reconstructed image and the original image is $E(|e(i, j)|) = 5.48$. The edges of the road are clearly delineated, and the quality of the image reconstruction is quite good. A faster version of the segmentation algorithm might be used for navigation by growing fixed image regions directly in front of the vehicle in both registered range and intensity images. The polynomial surface primitives will grow only over the image regions corresponding to the road. The complementary information in the range and intensity images can be combined to avoid obstacles and plan paths over smooth surfaces.

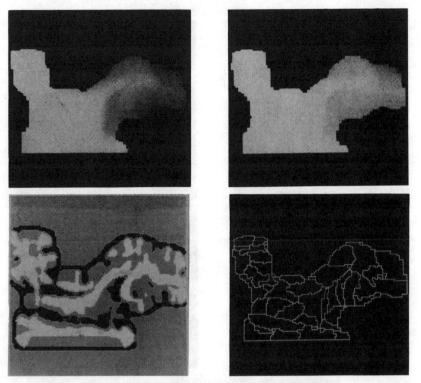

Fig. 13. Segmentation results for auto part range image.

Fig. 14. Segmentation results for cube with three holes range image.

I. Space Shuttle Intensity Image

The segmentation results for an image of a space shuttle launch are shown in Fig. 17. The measured noise variance is $\sigma_{img} = 2.71$, and the mean absolute deviation between the final reconstructed image and the original image is $E(|e(i, j)|) = 4.32$. The reconstructed image lacks detail whenever the detail in the original image consists of only a few pixels (10 or less) or is only one pixel wide. For example, a small piece of the gantry tower is missing in the reconstructed image. The surface type label image segmentation appears completely incoherent when com-

163

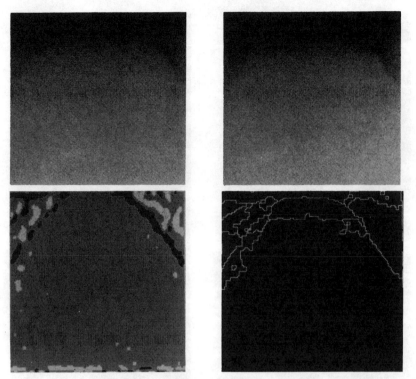

Fig. 15. Segmentation results for road scene range image.

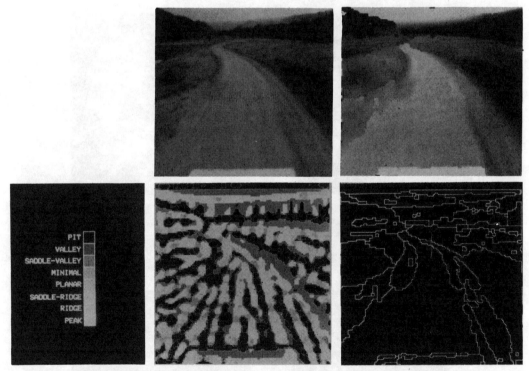

PIT
VALLEY
SADDLE-VALLEY
MINIMAL
PLANAR
SADDLE-RIDGE
RIDGE
PEAK

Fig. 16. Segmentation results for road scene intensity image.

pared to the original shuttle image. This is unlike most range images where some structure is usually perceivable. However, it still provided enough grouping information to the region growing algorithm to produce the final segmentation. The sky, the smoke clouds, the main tank, and the bright flames are isolated as intensity-image surface primitives.

J. House Scene Intensity Image (Univ. of Mass.)

A house scene, which has been segmented by many other techniques in the literature, was used to test the performance of the surface-based segmentation algorithm. The segmentation results for the 256 × 256 8-bit house scene image are shown in Fig. 18. Owing to the sequen-

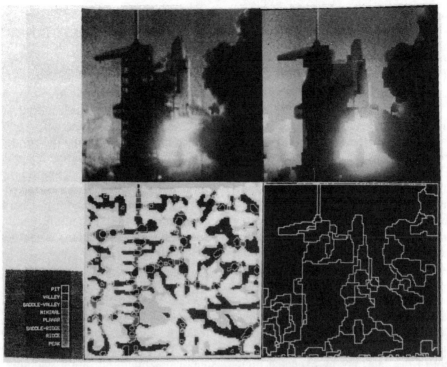

Fig. 17. Segmentation results for space shuttle intensity image.

Fig. 18. Segmentation results for house scene intensity image.

tial nature of the algorithm, segmentation processing time is related to image complexity, and several CPU hours on a VAX 11-780 were needed to compute these results consisting of 136 intensity surface primitives. The measured noise variance is $\sigma_{img} = 3.93$, and the mean absolute deviation between the final reconstructed image and the original image is $E(|e(i, j)|) = 9.44$. The sky, the roof of the house, the lawn, the garage door, the man's pants,

the shutters, the side of the house, the chimney, and the trees are all well segmented. The tree regions are very textured, but are still adequately segmented because of the final processing of coalesced unexplained pixels. Note the smoothness of the tree region in the reconstructed image. The quality of the image reconstruction and the segmentation were obtained with the exact same set of internal parameters used for five of the range images. We know

165

of no other algorithm that can claim this type of segmentation performance on such a wide variety of images.

XIV. Conclusions and Future Directions

The experimental results obtained by applying the surface-based segmentation algorithm with a fixed set of input parameters to a large test database of over 40 images, including range and intensity images, indicates that data-driven segmentation of digital surfaces based on a piecewise-smooth surface model, surface curvature sign, and polynomial surface approximations is feasible and provides excellent results. Nine sets of image results are included here to document these claims.

This surface-based approach is very general in many respects. Flat surfaces are described explicitly as being flat, and arbitrary curved surfaces are described as being curved within the context of the same variable-order surface fitting algorithm. Most techniques in the literature need to handle flat and curved (quadric) surfaces as separate special cases. No *a priori* assumptions about surface convexity, surface symmetry, or object shape are used. The final segmentation/reconstruction description is driven by the content of the data, not by expected high-level models as is done in many other approaches. Moreover, the exact same algorithm with the exact same set of parameters is shown to be capable of segmenting range images and intensity images. We believe that any image that can be represented by a piecewise-smooth surface over sufficiently large regions (more than 10–30 pixels) can be segmented well by this algorithm.

The basic sign-of-curvature/iterative variable-order fitting approach is applicable to the segmentation of signals in any number of dimensions, not just scalar functions of two variables. The method is shown to be successful for edge interval segmentation in [8]. If one-pixel wide edges are available, x and y can be parameterized as a function of arc length yielding a 2-vector function of a single variable. Only three sign-of-curvature labels are needed for each 1-D function: concave up, concave down, and flat. In the future, we hope to be able to apply the algorithm to signals representing scalar functions of three variables, such as dynamic scenes and 3-D images from CAT scanners. In that case, 27 sign-of-curvature labels are needed, and approximating functions require many coefficients (20 for a tricubic).

Perception of surfaces plays a key role in image understanding. We have shown experimentally that the segmentation of range images into scene surfaces can be data-driven and need not involve higher level knowledge of objects. The perceptual organization capabilities of the surface-based image segmentation algorithm appear to also be worthwhile capabilities for intensity image segmentation as is shown via experimental results. More research is needed to determine how higher level knowledge should be used in relating intensity-image surface primitives to the real scene surfaces.

Better methods of noise estimation are needed to improve the automatic threshold selection process. For non-stationary noise, it may be necessary to store an estimate of the noise variance for each pixel or region in the image. The noise variance estimates must then be consulted during each iteration. We are also looking into various types of adaptive smoothing, such as in [98], to improve the quality of the partial derivative estimates used to compute surface curvature and check surface normal compatibility. Also, various applications will require different types of surface models. The shape description needs for NC machining may be quite different than those for surface shape matching in 3-D object recognition, and neither application may be able to use the extracted polynomial surface primitives in the current form described here. Thus, the conversion of the shape information into more useful forms for given applications is another key issue that must be addressed.

Appendix
Equal Angle Increment Sampling

Formulas for calculating the geometric distortion introduced by equal angle increment sampling for range sensors with two orthogonal axis rotating mirrors and with spherical azimuth/elevation scanning mechanisms are included here. Let z, x, y be 3-D Cartesian coordinates with z representing depth from the x, y focal plane. Let r, θ, ϕ be 3-D orthogonal axis angular coordinates used for range sensors with two orthogonal axis mirrors. Let r, θ, ψ be 3-D spherical coordinates used for azimuth-elevation range sensors.

The transformations from orthogonal axis angular coordinates to Cartesian coordinates are given by the following:

$$x(r, \theta, \phi) = \frac{r \tan \theta}{\sqrt{1 + \tan^2 \theta + \tan^2 \phi}} \qquad (36)$$

$$y(r, \theta, \phi) = \frac{r \tan \phi}{\sqrt{1 + \tan^2 \theta + \tan^2 \phi}} \qquad (37)$$

$$z(r, \theta, \phi) = \frac{r}{\sqrt{1 + \tan^2 \theta + \tan^2 \phi}}. \qquad (38)$$

Note the symmetry between the horizontal and vertical angles. The inverse transformations are given by

$$r(x, y, z) = \sqrt{x^2 + y^2 + z^2} \qquad (39)$$

$$\theta(x, z) = \tan^{-1} \left(\frac{x}{z} \right) \qquad (40)$$

$$\phi(y, z) = \tan^{-1} \left(\frac{y}{z} \right). \qquad (41)$$

Note that horizontal angle θ is not a function of the vertical Cartesian coordinate y and that the vertical angle ϕ is not a function of the horizontal Cartesian coordinate x.

The spherical coordinate transformation from (x, y, z) to (r, θ, ϕ) coordinates is given by the following equations where ψ is the elevation angle and θ is the azimuth angle:

$$x(r, \theta, \psi) = r \cos \psi \sin \theta \qquad (42)$$

$$y(r, \psi) = r \sin \psi \qquad (43)$$

$$z(r, \theta, \psi) = r \cos \psi \cos \theta. \qquad (44)$$

The inverse transformations for r and θ are identical to the orthogonal axis case, but the expression for the elevation angle is given by

$$\psi(x, y, z) = \tan^{-1} \left(\frac{y}{\sqrt{x^2 + z^2}} \right). \qquad (45)$$

Note that ψ depends also on x in addition to y and z. Hence, the only difference between orthogonal axis angular coordinates and spherical coordinates is in the vertical angles ϕ and ψ.

The "warping" of surfaces in image coordinates by equal angle increment sampling in θ and ϕ or ψ, which was mentioned in the text, can be understood by comparing the depth expression for Cartesian coordinates to the depth expressions for orthogonal axis angular coordinates and spherical coordinates:

$$z(x, y) = \sqrt{(r(x, y))^2 - (x^2 + y^2)} \qquad (46)$$

$$z(\theta, \phi) = \frac{r(\theta, \phi)}{\sqrt{1 + \tan^2 \theta + \tan^2 \phi}} \qquad (47)$$

$$z(\theta, \psi) = r(\theta, \psi) \cos \theta \cos \psi. \qquad (48)$$

Flat surfaces in $z(x, y)$ data will appear curved in $z(\theta, \phi)$ data or $z(\theta, \psi)$ data because of the differences in surface parameterization. If given range images from an orthogonal axis coordinate $z(\theta, \phi)$ range sensor or spherical coordinate $z(\theta, \psi)$ range sensor, the Cartesian x and y coordinates can be computed for each angle pair ((θ, ϕ) for orthogonal axis angular coordinates or (θ, ψ) for spherical coordinates):

$$x_{\text{ortho}}(\theta, \phi) = z(\theta, \phi) \tan \theta$$

$$x_{\text{spher}}(\theta, \psi) = z(\theta, \psi) \tan \theta \qquad (49)$$

$$y_{\text{ortho}}(\theta, \phi) = z(\theta, \phi) \tan \phi$$

$$y_{\text{spher}}(\theta, \psi) = \sqrt{z^2(\theta, \psi) + x_{\text{spher}}^2(\theta, \psi)} \, \tan \psi. \qquad (50)$$

The "difficulty" with these x, y coordinates, from an image processing viewpoint, is that they do not lie on an equally spaced grid of image pixels. If desired, interpolation can be used to resample the surface data to obtain an equally spaced sampled Cartesian orthographic projection $z(x, y)$ range image, but this is not necessary in many cases. Since most of the range images in this paper use a relatively small field of view, the range images can be segmented and approximate surface shape can be reconstructed directly without resampling. Once the appropriate image regions have been segmented, accurate physical surface shape in Cartesian coordinates can be computed (if all range sensor parameters are known) by computing the Cartesian x, y, z coordinates from the angular coordinates at each pixel in the segmented image regions and then fitting new graph surfaces to the Cartesian data.

ACKNOWLEDGMENT

The authors would like to thank L. Watson, L. Maloney, B. Haralick, D. Chen, R. Sarraga, and the reviewers for their helpful observations and suggestions. We also thank the Environmental Research Institute of Michigan (ERIM), Structural Dynamics Research Corporation, and General Motors Research Labs.

REFERENCES

[1] G. J. Agin and T. O. Binford, "Computer description of curved objects," in *Proc. 3rd Int. Joint Conf. Artificial Intelligence*, Stanford, CA, Aug. 20–23, 1973, pp. 629–640.

[2] R. L. Anderson and E. E. Houseman, *Tables of Orthogonal Polynomial Values Extended to N = 104*, Iowa State College Agricultural and Mechanic Arts, Ames, IA, Res. Bull. 297, Apr. 1942.

[3] D. H. Ballard and C. M. Brown, *Computer Vision*. Englewood Cliffs, NJ: Prentice-Hall, 1982.

[4] S. Barnard, "A stochastic approach to stereo vision," in *Proc. 5th Nat. Conf. Artificial Intelligence*, AAAI, Philadelphia, PA, August 11–15, 1986, pp. 676–680.

[5] R. H. Bartels and J. J. Jezioranski, "Least-squares fitting using orthogonal multinomials," *ACM Trans. Math. Software*, vol. 11, no. 3, pp. 201–217, Sept. 1985.

[6] P. R. Beaudet, "Rotationally invariant image operators," in *Proc. 4th Int. Conf. Pattern Recognition*, Kyoto, Japan, Nov. 7–10, 1978, pp. 579–583.

[7] G. Beheim and K. Fritsch, "Range finding using frequency-modulated laser diode," *Appl. Opt.*, vol. 25, no. 9, pp. 1439–1442, May 1986.

[8] P. J. Besl, "Surfaces in early range image understanding," Ph.D. dissertation, Dep. Elec. Eng. Comput. Sci., Univ. Michigan, Ann Arbor, Rep. RSD-TR-10-86, Mar. 1986; see also *Surfaces in Range Image Understanding*. New York: Springer-Verlag, 1988.

[9] P. J. Besl and R. C. Jain, "Three dimensional object recognition," *ACM Comput. Surveys*, vol. 17, no. 1, pp. 75–145, Mar. 1985.

[10] ——, "Invariant surface characteristics for three dimensional object recognition in range images," *Comput. Vision, Graphics, Image Processing*, vol. 33, no. 1, pp. 33–80, Jan. 1986.

[11] P. J. Besl, E. J. Delp, and R. C. Jain, "Automatic visual solder joint inspection," *IEEE J. Robotics Automation*, vol. RA-1, no. 1, pp. 42–56, May 1985.

[12] B. Bhanu, "Representation and shape matching of 3-D objects," *IEEE Trans. Pattern Anal. Machine Intell.*, vol. PAMI-6, no. 3, pp. 340–350, May 1984.

[13] B. Bhanu, S. Lee, C. C. Ho, and T. Henderson, "Range data processing: Representation of surfaces by edges," in *Proc. Int. Pattern Recognition Conf.*, IAPR-IEEE, Oct. 1986, pp. 236–238.

[14] R. M. Bolle and D. B. Cooper, "Bayesian recognition of local 3-D shape by approximating image intensity functions with quadric polynomials," *IEEE Trans. Pattern Anal. Machine Intell.*, vol. PAMI-6, no. 4, pp. 418–429, July 1984.

[15] R. C. Bolles and M. A. Fischler, "A RANSAC-based approach to model fitting and its application to finding cylinders in range data," in *Proc. 7th Int. Joint Conf. Artificial Intelligence*, Vancouver, B.C., Canada, Aug. 24–28, 1981, pp. 637–643.

[16] R. C. Bolles and P. Horaud, "3DPO: A three-dimensional part orientation system," *Int. J. Robotics Res.*, vol. 5, no. 3, pp. 3–26, Fall 1986.

[17] B. A. Boyter, "Three-dimensional matching using range data," in *Proc. 1st Conf. Artificial Intelligence Applications*, IEEE Comput. Soc., 1984, pp. 211–216.

[18] M. Brady, "Computational approaches to image understanding," *ACM Comput. Surveys*, vol. 14, no. 1, pp. 3–71, Mar. 1982.

[19] M. Brady, J. Ponce, A. Yuille, and H. Asada, "Describing surfaces," *Comput. Vision, Graphics, Image Processing*, vol. 32, pp. 1–28, 1985.

[20] C. Brice and C. Fennema, "Scene analysis using regions," *Artificial Intell.*, vol. 1, pp. 205–226, 1970.

[21] B. Carrihill and R. Hummel, "Experiments with the intensity ratio depth sensor," *Comput. Vision, Graphics, Image Processing*, vol. 32, pp. 337–358, 1985.

[22] D. Chen, "A regression updating approach for detecting multiple curves," in *Proc. 2nd World Conf. Robotics Research*, Scottsdale,

AZ, Aug. 18–21, 1986, Paper RI/SME, MS86-764; also *IEEE Trans. Pattern Anal. Machine Intell.*, to be published.

[23] S. S. Chern, "A proof of the uniqueness of Minkowski's problem for convex surfaces," *Amer. J. Math.*, vol. 79, pp. 949–950, 1957.

[24] F. S. Cohen and D. B. Cooper, "Simple parallel hierarchical and relaxation algorithms for segmenting noncausal markovian random fields," *IEEE Trans. Pattern Anal. Machine Intell.*, vol. PAMI-9, no. 2, pp. 195–219, Mar. 1987.

[25] E. N. Coleman and R. Jain, "Obtaining shape of textured and specular surfaces using four-source photometry," *Comput. Graphics Image Processing*, vol. 18, no. 4, pp. 309–328, Apr. 1982.

[26] G. R. Cross and A. K. Jain, "Markov random field texture models," *IEEE Trans. Pattern Anal. Machine Intell.*, vol. PAMI-5, pp. 25–39, 1983.

[27] C. Dane, "An object-centered three-dimensional model builder," Ph.D. dissertation, Dep. Comput. Inform. Sci., Moore School Elec. Eng., Univ. Pennsylvania, Philadelphia, 1982.

[28] W. W. Daniel, *Applied Nonparametric Statistics*. Boston, MA: Houghton-Mifflin, 1978.

[29] L. S. Davis, "A survey of edge detection techniques," *Comput. Graphics Image Processing*, vol. 4, pp. 248–270, 1975.

[30] H. Derin and H. Elliot, "Modeling and segmentation of noisy and textured images using Gibbs random fields," *IEEE Trans. Pattern Anal. Machine Intell.*, vol. PAMI-9, no. 1, pp. 39–55, Jan. 1987.

[31] S. Dizenzo, "Advances in image segmentation," *Image and Vision Comput.*, vol. 1, no. 4, pp. 196–210, Nov. 1983.

[32] T. G. Fan, G. Medioni, and R. Nevatia, "Description of surfaces from range data using curvature properties," in *Proc. Computer Vision and Pattern Recognition Conf.*, IEEE Comput. Soc., Miami, FL, June 22–26, 1986, pp. 86–91.

[33] O. D. Faugeras and M. Hebert, "The representation, recognition, and locating of 3-D objects," *Int. J. Robotics Res.*, vol. 5, no. 3, pp. 27–52, Fall 1986.

[34] O. D. Faugeras, M. Hebert, and E. Pauchon, "Segmentation of range data into planar and quadric patches," in *Proc. 3rd Computer Vision and Pattern Recognition Conf.*, Arlington, VA, 1983, pp. 8–13.

[35] I. D. Faux and M. J. Pratt, *Computational Geometry for Design and Manufacture*. UK: Ellis Horwood, Chichester, 1979.

[36] F. P. Ferrie and M. D. Levine, "Piecing together 3D shape of moving objects: An overview," in *Proc. Computer Vision and Pattern Recognition Conf.*, IEEE Comput. Soc., San Francisco, CA, June 9–13, 1985, pp. 574–584.

[37] K. S. Fu and J. K. Mui, "A survey on image segmentation," *Pattern Recognition*, vol. 13, pp. 3–16, 1981.

[38] S. Geman and D. Geman, "Stochastic relaxation, gibbs distributions, and Bayesian restoration of images," *IEEE Trans. Pattern Anal. Machine Intell.*, vol. PAMI-6, no. 6, pp. 721–741, Nov. 1984.

[39] B. Gil, A. Mitiche, and J. K. Aggarwal, "Experiments in combining intensity and range edge maps," *Comput. Vision, Graphics, Image Processing*, vol. 21, pp. 395–411, Mar. 1983.

[40] D. Gilbarg and N. Trudinger, *Elliptic Partial Differential Equations of Second Order*. Berlin: Springer-Verlag, 1983.

[41] C. Goad, "Special purpose automatic programming for 3D model-based vision," in *Proc. Image Understanding Workshop*, DARPA, Arlington, VA, June 23, 1983, pp. 94–104.

[42] G. H. Golub and C. F. Van Loan, *Matrix Computations*. Baltimore, MD: Johns Hopkins University Press, 1983.

[43] W. E. L. Grimson, "A computer implementation of a theory of human stereo vision," M.I.T. Artificial Intelligence Lab., Cambridge, MA, Memo. 565, 1980.

[44] ——, *From Images to Surfaces*. Cambridge, MA: M.I.T. Press, 1981.

[45] W. E. L. Grimson and T. Pavlidis, "Discontinuity detection for visual surface reconstruction," *Comput. Vision, Graphics, Image Processing*, vol. 30, pp. 316–330, 1985.

[46] E. L. Hall, J. B. K. Tio, C. A. McPherson, and F. A. Sadjadi, "Measuring curved surfaces for robot vision," *Computer*, vol. 15, no. 12, pp. 42–54, Dec. 1982.

[47] R. M. Haralick and L. G. Shapiro, "Image segmentation techniques," *Comput. Vision, Graphics, Image Processing*, vol. 29, pp. 100–132, 1985.

[48] R. M. Haralick and L. Watson, "A facet model for image data," *Comput. Graphics Image Processing*, vol. 15, pp. 113–129, 1981.

[49] R. M. Haralick, L. T. Watson, and T. J. Laffey, "The topographic primal sketch," *Int. J. Robotics Res.*, vol. 2, no. 1, pp. 50–72, Spring 1983.

[50] M. Hebert and T. Kanade, "The 3-D profile method for object recognition," in *Proc. Computer Vision and Pattern Recognition Conf.*, IEEE Comput. Soc., San Francisco, CA, June 9–13, 1985, pp. 458–463.

[51] M. Hebert and J. Ponce, "A new method for segmenting 3-D scenes into primitives," in *Proc. 6th Int. Conf. Pattern Recognition*, Munich, West Germany, Oct. 19–22, 1982, pp. 836–838.

[52] T. C. Henderson, "Efficient 3-D object representations for industrial vision systems," *IEEE Trans. Pattern Anal. Machine Intell.*, vol. PAMI-5, no. 6, pp. 609–617, Nov. 1983.

[53] T. C. Henderson and B. Bhanu, "Three-port seed method for the extraction of planar faces from range data," in *Proc. Workshop Industrial Applications of Machine Vision*, Research Triangle Park, NC, May 1982, pp. 181–186.

[54] M. Herman, "Generating detailed scene descriptions from range images," in *Proc. Int. Conf. Robotics and Automation*, St. Louis, MO, Mar. 25–28, 1985, pp. 426–431.

[55] B. K. P. Horn, "Extended Gaussian images," *Proc. IEEE*, vol. 72, no. 12, pp. 1656–1678, Dec. 1984.

[56] K. Ikeuchi and B. K. P. Horn, "Numerical shape from shading and occluding boundaries," *Artificial Intell.*, vol. 17, pp. 141–184, Aug. 1981.

[57] S. L. Horowitz and T. Pavlidis, "Picture segmentation by a directed split-and-merge procedure," in *Proc. 2nd Int. Joint Conf. Pattern Recognition*, 1974, pp. 424–433.

[58] K. Ikeuchi and B. K. P. Horn, "Numerical shape from shading and occluding boundaries," *Artificial Intell.*, vol. 17, pp. 141–184, Aug. 1981.

[59] S. Inokuchi and R. Nevatia, "Boundary detection in range pictures," in *Proc. 5th Int. Conf. Pattern Recognition*, Miami, FL, Dec. 1–4, 1980, pp. 1031–1035.

[60] S. Inokuchi, T. Nita, F. Matsuday, and Y. Sakurai, "A three-dimensional edge-region operator for range pictures," in *Proc. 6th Int. Conf. Pattern Recognition*, Munich, West Germany, Oct. 19–22, 1982, pp. 918–920.

[61] S. Inokuchi, K. Sato, and F. Matsuda, "Range imaging system for 3-D object recognition," in *Proc. 7th Int. Conf. Pattern Recognition*, Montreal, P.Q., Canada, July 30–Aug. 2, 1984, pp. 806–808.

[62] R. Hoffman and A. K. Jain, "Segmentation and classification of range images," *IEEE Trans. Pattern Anal. Machine Intell.*, vol. PAMI-9, no. 5, pp. 608–620, Sept. 1987.

[63] R. Jain, "Dynamic scene analysis," in *Progress in Pattern Recognition*, vol. 2, A. Rosenfeld and L. Kanal, Eds. Amsterdam, The Netherlands: North-Holland, 1983.

[64] R. A. Jarvis, "A perspective on range finding techniques for computer vision," *IEEE Trans. Pattern Anal. Machine Intell.*, vol. PAMI-5, no. 2, pp. 122–139, Mar. 1983.

[65] T. Kanade, "Survey: Region segmentation: Signal vs. semantics," *Comput. Graphics Image Processing*, vol. 13, pp. 279–297, 1980.

[66] ——, "Recovery of the three-dimensional shape of an object from a single view," *Artificial Intell.*, vol. 17, pp. 409–460, Aug. 1981.

[67] J. R. Kender and E. M. Smith, "Shape from darkness: Deriving surface information from dynamic shadows," in *Proc. 5th Nat. Conf. Artifical Intelligence*, AAAI, Philadelphia, PA, Aug. 11–15, 1986, pp. 664–669.

[68] G. Kinoshita, M. Idesawa, and S. Naomi, "Robotic range sensor with projection of bright ring pattern," *J. Robotic Syst.*, vol. 3, no. 3, pp. 249–257, 1986.

[69] D. T. Kuan and R. J. Drazovich, "Model-based interpretation of range imagery," in *Proc. Nat. Conf. Artificial Intelligence*, Austin, TX, Aug. 6–10, 1984, pp. 210–215.

[70] C. L. Lawson and R. J. Hanson, *Solving Least Squares Problems*. Englewood Cliffs, NJ: Prentice-Hall, 1974.

[71] R. A. Lewis and A. R. Johnston, "A scanning laser rangefinder for a robotic vehicle," in *Proc. 5th Int. Joint Conf. Artificial Intelligence*, Cambridge, MA, Aug. 22–25, 1977, pp. 762–768.

[72] C. Lin and M. J. Perry, "Shape description using surface triangularization," in *Proc. Workshop Computer Vision: Representation and Control*, IEEE Comput. Soc., Rindge, NH, Aug. 23–25, 1982, pp. 38–43.

[73] D. Marr, *Vision*. New York: Freeman, 1982.

[74] G. Medioni and R. Nevatia, "Description of 3-D surfaces using curvature properties," in *Proc. Image Understanding Workshop*, DARPA, New Orleans, LA, Oct. 3–4, 1984, pp. 291–299.

[75] D. L. Milgrim and C. M. Bjorklund, "Range image processing: Planar surface extraction," in *Proc. 5th Int. Conf. Pattern Recognition*, Miami, FL, Dec. 1–4, 1980, pp. 912–919.

168

[76] B. Gil, A. Mitiche, and J. K. Aggarwal, "Experiments in combining intensity and range edge maps," *Comput. Vision, Graphics, Image Processing*, vol. 21, pp. 395–411, Mar. 1983.

[77] R. Nevatia and T. O. Binford, "Structured descriptions of complex objects," in *Proc. 3rd Int. Joint Conf. Artificial Intelligence*, Stanford, CA, Aug. 20–23, 1973, pp. 641–647.

[78] W. M. Newman and R. F. Sproull, *Principles of Interactive Computer Graphics*, 2nd ed. New York: McGraw-Hill, 1979.

[79] M. Oshima and Y. Shirai, "Object recognition using three-dimensional information," *IEEE Trans. Pattern Anal. Machine Intell.*, vol. PAMI-5, no. 4, pp. 353–361, July 1983.

[80] T. Pavlidis, "Segmentation of pictures and maps through functional approximation," *Comput. Graphics Image Processing*, vol. 1, pp. 360–372, 1972.

[81] F. G. Peet and T. S. Sahota, "Surface curvature as a measure of image texture," *IEEE Trans. Pattern Anal. Machine Intell.*, vol. PAMI-7, no. 6, pp. 734–738, Nov. 1985.

[82] T. C. Pong, L. G. Shapiro, L. T. Watson, and R. M. Haralick, "Experiments in segmentation using a facet model region grower," *Comput. Vision, Graphics, Image Processing*, vol. 25, pp. 1–23,, 1984.

[83] R. J. Popplestone, C. M. Brown, A. P. Ambler, and G. F. Crawford, "Forming models of plane-and-cylinder faceted bodies from light stripes," in *Proc. 4th Int. Joint Conf. Artificial Intelligence*, Tbilisi, Georgia, USSR, Sept. 1975, pp. 664–668.

[84] M. Potmesil, "Generating models of solid objects by matching 3D surface segments," in *Proc. 8th Int. Joint Conf. Artificial Intelligence*, Karlsruhe, West Germany, Aug. 8–12, 1983, pp. 1089–1093.

[85] J. Prewitt, "Object enhancement and extraction," in *Picture Processing and Psychopictorics*, B. Lipkin and A. Rosenfeld, Eds. New York: Academic, 1979, pp. 75–149.

[86] G. T. Reid, "Automatic fringe pattern analysis: a review," *Opt. Lasers Eng.*, vol. 7, pp. 37–68, 1986.

[87] W. Richards and D. D. Hoffman, "Codon constraints on closed 2D shapes," *Comput. Vision, Graphics, Image Processing*, vol. 31, pp. 265–281, 1985.

[88] E. M. Riseman and M. A. Arbib, "Computational techniques in the visual segmentation of static scenes," *Comput. Graphics Image Processing*, vol. 6, pp. 221–276, 1977.

[89] I. Rock, *The Logic of Perception*. Cambridge, MA: M.I.T. Press, 1983.

[90] A. Rosenfeld and L. S. Davis, "Image segmentation and image models," *Proc. IEEE*, vol. 67, no. 5, pp. 764–772, May 1979.

[91] A. Rosenfeld and A. Kak, *Digital Picture Processing*, vols. 1 and 2. New York: Academic, 1982.

[92] I. K. Sethi and S. N. Jayaramamurthy, "Surface classification using characteristic contours," in *Proc. 7th Int. Conf. Pattern Recognition*, Montreal, P.Q., Canada, July 30–Aug. 2, 1984, pp. 438–440.

[93] Y. Shirai, "Recognition of polyhedrons with a range finder," *Pattern Recognition*, vol. 4, pp. 243–250, 1972.

[94] Y. Shirai and M. Suwa, "Recognition of polyhedra with a range finder," in *Proc. 2nd Int. Joint Conf. Artificial Intelligence*, London, UK, Aug. 1971, pp. 80–87.

[95] D. R. Smith and T. Kanade, "Autonomous scene description with range imagery," *Comput. Vision, Graphics, Image Processing*, vol. 31, pp. 322–334, 1985.

[96] W. Snyder and G. Bilbro, "Segmentation of three-dimensional images," in *Proc. Int. Conf. Robotics and Automation*, IEEE Comput. Soc., St. Louis, MO, Mar. 25–28, 1985, pp. 396–403.

[97] K. Sugihara, "Range-data analysis guided by junction dictionary," *Artificial Intell.*, vol. 12, pp. 41–69, 1979.

[98] D. Terzopoulos, "Computing visible surface representations," Artificial Intell. Lab., M.I.T., Cambridge, MA, AI Memo 800, Mar. 1985.

[99] W. Tiller, "Rational B-splines for curve and surface representation," *IEEE Comput. Graphics Applications*, vol. 3, no. 6, pp. 61–69, 1983.

[100] F. Tomita and T. Kanade, "A 3D vision system: Generating and matching shape descriptions in range images," in *Proc. Int. Conf. Robotics*, IEEE Comput. Soc., Atlanta, GA, Mar. 13–15, 1984, pp. 186–191.

[101] S. Ullman, *The Interpretation of Visual Motion*. Cambridge, MA: M.I.T. Press, 1979.

[102] B. C. Vemuri, A. Mitiche, and J. K. Aggarwal, "Curvature-based representation of objects from range data," *Image and Vision Comput.*, vol. 4, no. 2, pp. 107–114, May 1986.

[103] A. P. Witkin, "Recovering surface shape and orientation from texture," *Artificial Intell.*, vol. 17, pp. 17–45, Aug. 1981.

[104] A. P. Witkin and J. Tenenbaum, "The role of structure in vision," in *Human and Machine Vision*, Beck et al., Eds. New York: Academic, 1983, pp. 481–543.

[105] R. J. Woodham, "Analysing images of curved surfaces," *Artificial Intell.*, vol. 17, pp. 117–140, Aug. 1981.

[106] J. W. Woods, "Two-dimensional discrete Markov fields," *IEEE Trans. Inform. Theory*, vol. IT-18, pp. 232–240, 1972.

[107] S. W. Zucker, "Region growing: Childhood and adolescence," *Comput. Graphics Image Processing*, vol. 5, pp. 382–399, 1976.

[108] D. M. Zuk and M. L. Delleva, "Three-dimensional vision system for the adaptive suspension vehicle," Defense Supply Service, Washington, Final Rep. 170400-3-F, ERIM, DARPA 4468, 1983.

Paul J. Besl (M'81–S'84–M'87) graduated *summa cum laude* in physics from Princeton University, Princeton, NJ, in 1978 and received the M.S. and Ph.D. degrees in electrical engineering and computer science from the University of Michigan, Ann Arbor, in 1981 and 1986, respectively. In 1987, he received a Rackham Distinguished Dissertation Award for his thesis on range image understanding from the University of Michigan.

From 1979 to 1981, he did computer simulations for Bendix Aerospace Systems in Ann Arbor, MI, and from 1981 to 1983, worked on the GEOMOD solid modeling system at Structural Dynamics Research Corp. in Cincinnati, OH. Currently, he is a Research Scientist at General Motors Research Laboratories in Warren, MI, where his primary research interest is computer vision, especially range image analysis and geometric modeling for image understanding.

Dr. Besl is a member of the Association for Computing Machinery, the American Association for Artificial Intelligence, and the Machine Vision Association of the Society of Manufacturing Engineers.

Ramesh C. Jain (M'79–SM'83) received the B.E. degree from Nagpur University in 1969 and the Ph.D. degree from the Indian Institute of Technology, Kharagpur, India, in 1975.

He is a Professor of Electrical Engineering and Computer Science, and Director of the Computer Vision Research Laboratory at the University of Michigan, Ann Arbor. Formerly he worked at General Motors Research Labs, Wayne State University, University of Texas at Austin, University of Hamburg, West Germany, and Indian Institute of Technology, Kharagpur, India. His current research interests are in computer vision, and artificial intelligence. He has been active in dynamic scene analysis, range image understanding, industrial inspection, object recognition, knowledge-based systems, and related areas. He has published research papers addressing several aspects of the above areas. He is a consultant to many companies in the areas of computer vision, artificial intelligence, and computer graphics.

Dr. Jain is a member of the Association for Computing Machinery, the American Association for Artificial Intelligence, the Pattern Recognition Society, the Cognitive Science Society, the Optical Society of America, the Society of Photo-Optical Instrumentation Engineers, and Society of Manufacturing Engineers. He has been involved in organization of several professional conferences and workshops. Currently, he is on the Editorial Boards of *IEEE Expert*, *Machine Vision and Applications*, *Computer Vision Graphics and Image Processing*, the *Bulletin of Approximate Reasoning*, and *Image and Vision Computing*.

Chapter 3: Feature Extraction and Matching

Segmented images derived using methods described in Chapter 2 are represented in a compact form to facilitate further abstraction. Often, shape and region features such as curvature and topology are extracted from the segmented images. Representation schemes are chosen to match the methods used for object recognition and description. In the following sections, schemes for representation and description that are popular in computer vision are first discussed. Then, techniques for feature extraction are described. The third section describes various matching techniques. Object recognition requires matching an object description in an image to models of known objects. The models, in turn, use certain descriptive features and their relations. Matching also plays an important role in other aspects of information recovery from images. For example, stereo and structure from motion depend upon matching selected points or features in two or more images. This problem of matching selected points is known as the "correspondence problem."

Representation and description

Symbolic representation of iconic information in a segmented image is the goal of representation schemes. Iconic information is usually very rich and redundant. Symbolic information, which is an abstraction of iconic information, contains the main features of the iconic information at the cost of minute details. While this loss may be acceptable or even desirable in some applications, it should — in general — be minimized.

Representation and description of symbolic information can be approached in many ways. One approach is to represent the object in terms of its bounding curve. Popular among several methods developed for boundary representation are chain codes, polygonalization, one-dimensional signatures, and representation using dominant points. If recognition is the only aim, then one may want to use some features, such as corners and inflection points, for representing an object. Another approach is to obtain region-based shape descriptors, such as topological or texture descriptors. Representation and shape description schemes are usually chosen such that the descriptors are invariant to rotation, translation, and scale change. In this section, we will discuss some common methods for representation of boundaries and regions, as well as characterization of two-dimensional shape.

Chain codes. One of the earliest methods for representing a boundary uses directional codes called "chain codes." The object boundary is resampled at appropriate scale, and an ordered list of points on the boundary is represented by a string of directional codes. Typical directional codes and their applications to an object boundary are illustrated in Figure 3.1.[1] Often, to retain all the information in the boundary, the resampling step is bypassed; however, resampling eliminates minor fluctuations that typically are due to noise. The use of chain codes has some attractive features. For example,

- Rotation of an object by 45° can be easily implemented.
- The derivative of the chain code, obtained by using first difference, is rotation invariant.
- Other characteristics of a region, such as area and corners, can be computed directly using the chain code.

The limitation of this representation method is attributable to the limited directions used to represent the tangent at a point. Although codes with larger number of directions[67] are occasionally used, eight-directional chain code is the most commonly used code.

Polygonalization. Polygonal approximation of boundaries of objects has been studied extensively and numerous methods have been developed. The fit is made to reduce a chosen error criterion between the approximation and the original curve. In the iterative endpoint-fit algorithm,[68] the first step is to connect a straight-line segment between the two farthest points on the boundary. The perpendicular distances from the segment to each point on the curve are measured. If any distance is greater than a chosen threshold, the segment is replaced by two segments; one each from a segment endpoint to the curve point where the distance to the segment is greatest. This process is iterated until all segments are within the threshold. In papers by Tomek,[69] Williams,[70,71] Sklansky and Gonzalez,[72] and Pavlidis,[73] a straight-line fit is constrained to pass within a radius around each data point. The line segment is grown from the first point, and when further extension of the line segment causes it to fall outside the radius of a point, a new line is started. Kurozumi and Davis[74] employed a minimax approach, in which the line segment approximations are chosen to minimize the maximum distance between the data points and the approximating line segment.

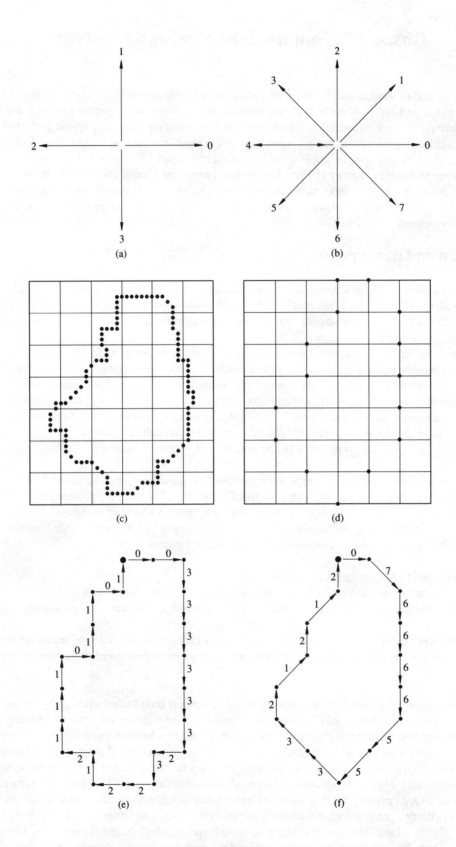

Figure 3.1: (a) Four-directional chain code; (b) eight-directional chain code; (c) digital boundary with resampling grid superimposed; (d) result of resampling; (e)-(f) corresponding four and eight directional codes. (from R.C. Gonzalez and P. Wintz, *Digital Image Processing*, © 1977 by Addison-Wesley Publishing Company. Reprinted with permission of the publisher.)[1]

In another class of techniques, area versus distance is used as a measure of "goodness" of fit. Wall and Danielsson[75] used a scan-along technique in which a new line segment is generated if the area deviation for each line segment exceeds a preset value. Wall[76] used this polygonal approximation for generating a smooth cubic curve as an approximation to the original data. Images of the coastline of Great Britain and its approximations are shown in Figure 3.2.[76]

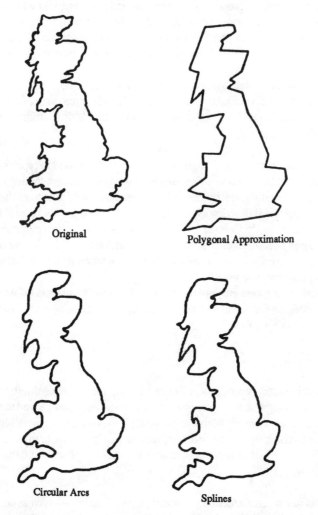

Original

Polygonal Approximation

Circular Arcs

Splines

Figure 3.2: Illustration of polygonal, circular arc, and spline approximations (from Wall)[76]

Leu and Chen[77] focus on uniqueness and accuracy of representation, two important issues of polygonal approximation. Uniqueness is achieved by starting the approximation simultaneously at places along the shape boundary where the arcs are closer to straight lines than their neighboring arcs. Polygonal approximation is performed by fitting lines to those selected arcs whose maximum arc-to-chord distance is less than a given tolerance.

Besides polygonal approximation methods, higher order curve- and spline-fitting methods are used where more precise approximations are required. These are more computationally expensive than most polygonalization methods, and they can be more difficult to apply. Some of these methods are described in Pavlidis[73,78,79] and Davis.[80]

One of the drawbacks of most of these polygonal-fit techniques is that the operations are not performed symmetrically with respect to curve features such as corners and the centers of curves. The result is that the computed breakpoints between segments may be at different locations depending on the starting and ending locations or on the direction of operation of the line fit. Extensions can be made to some of the methods to produce fewer and more consistent breakpoint locations, but these procedures are usually iterative and can be computationally expensive.

One-dimensional signatures. The slope of the tangent to the curve denoted by the angle θ as a function of position s from an arbitrary starting point is used to represent curves in many applications. Horizontal lines in s-θ curves represent straight lines, and straight lines represent circular arcs whose radii are proportional to the slope of the straight line. An s-θ curve can be treated

173

as a periodic function with a period given by the perimeter. Other functions — such as distance to the curve from an arbitrary point inside the curve plotted as a function of angle with reference to the horizontal — are also used as shape signatures.

Boundary description. Descriptors for objects represented by their boundaries may be generated using the representations described in the previous sections. Simple descriptors — such as perimeter, length and orientation of the major axis, shape number, and eccentricity — may be readily computed from boundary data. The ordered set of points on the boundary having two-dimensional coordinates (x_k, y_k), where $k = 1,...N$ and N is the total number of points on the boundary, can be treated as a one-dimensional complex function: $(x_k + iy_k)$. The coefficients of the discrete Fourier transform applied to this function can be used as a shape descriptor.

Other descriptors that use the one-dimensional signature functions may also be obtained. A major drawback of many of these descriptors is that complete data for the object boundaries are required. However, because of either problems in segmentation or occlusions in the image, complete data for object boundaries are often not available. In such instances, recognition strategies based on partial information are needed.

Region-based representation and description. Methods analogous to those used to represent object boundaries have been developed to represent regions enclosed by boundaries. Examples of such methods are medial-axis transformations, skeletons, and convex hulls and deficiencies.[1,4] Morphological operators have been developed to extract shape features and generate useful descriptions of object shape.[81-84] Topological descriptors, such as Euler number, are also useful to characterize shape. Haralick et al.[85] used a local facet model — described in Chapter 2 — to generate a topographic primal sketch of images. In their model, each pixel is uniquely described using a set of seven descriptive labels, including peak, pit, and ridge. Such a description is very useful for object matching. Shapiro[86] describes a structural model of shape based on a set of primitives and their properties; she also describes a shape-matching procedure that uses this model.

Region-based representation and description are particularly useful to describe objects for which properties within the region — for example, texture — are significant for object recognition. Many techniques have been developed to model texture using statistical,[58,59] structural,[60,61] and spectral[62] methods.

Feature extraction

Shape descriptors — such as topological descriptors or Fourier descriptors — are useful for object recognition. If the object to be recognized has unique discriminating features, special-purpose algorithms are employed to extract such features. Important for object matching and recognition are corners, high-curvature regions, or other regions along curves at which curvature discontinuities exist. In region-based matching methods, identifying groups of pixels that can be easily distinguished and identified is important. Many methods have been proposed to detect both dominant points in curves and interesting points in regions. These methods are discussed subsequently.

Detection of dominant points in curves. Detection of critical points in curves — such as corners and inflection points — is important for subsequent object matching and recognition. Most algorithms for detecting critical points follow the idea of Attneave,[87] marking the local curvature maxima points as dominant. Several feature detection algorithms using this approach were compared and evaluated by Teh and Chin.[88] Fischler and Bolles[89] analyzed the deviations of a curve from a chord to detect dominant points along a curve. In their approach, points are marked as being critical or as belonging to a smooth or a noisy interval; these markings depend on whether the curve makes a single excursion away from the chord, stays close to the chord, or makes two or more excursions away from the chord, respectively. A drawback of many such methods based on critical points of high curvature is that inflection points due to smooth changes between segments — such as transitions from a circular arc to a tangential line — are not detected.

Most of the algorithms employing critical-point detection require parameters related to the separation of minimum resolvable features. However, features of varying size and separation are usually present in a given image. Parameter values determined by the minimum-size feature may not be adequate to smooth large features; as a result, too many points may be detected as dominant points. One approach to solving this problem is to adaptively determine parameters using local feature data — with no required user parameters. Teh and Chin[88] describe an algorithm that uses such an approach. First, the region of support is adaptively determined using local properties; and local curvature is measured within this region. Then, dominant points are detected by nonmaxima suppression of local curvature. Phillips and Rosenfeld[90] discuss determination of region of support using an arc-chord distance property.

The problem of feature point detection in digital curves may also be approached as a scale-space problem.[91,92] By defining a set of primitive parameterized curvature discontinuities, Asada and Brady[91] introduced curvature primal sketch. In this approach, curvature as a function of position is computed at multiple scales; these are convolved with a Gaussian function, and the second derivative of the result is computed. Curvature primal sketch is obtained by analyzing this output.

Saint-Marc et al.[93] describe an adaptive-filtering algorithm for smoothing noisy curves. The closed curve shown in Figure 3.3(a) illustrates the performance of this algorithm. The objective is to locate all the vertices and other critical points, such as the inflection point along the curved segment, as well as points of transition from curve to straight-line segments. To obtain the curve shown in Figure 3.3(b), the curvature at each point along the line is determined using a small region of support. Because of artifacts introduced during digitization and thinning, this curve is not smooth. Smoothing is necessary to identify features such as vertices (peaks and valleys in the curvature plot), inflection points (zero-crossings in curvature), and smooth joins (points of transition from zero curvature to a significant value). A common filter used to smooth noisy signals is the Gaussian filter. However, Gaussian filtering smooths both noise and data points. Alternatively, an adaptive filter that emphasizes intraregion smoothing over interregion smoothing is useful in this situation. This filtering approach is now described.

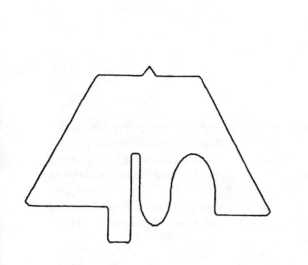

(a)

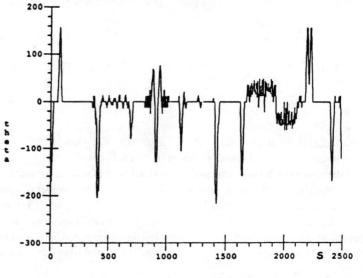

(b)

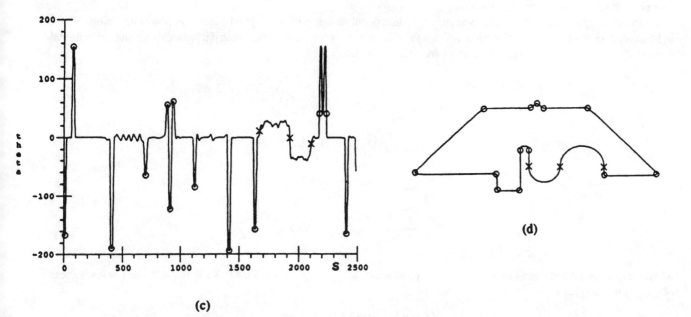

(c)

(d)

Figure 3.3: Adaptive smoothing for detection of critical points; (a) a closed curve; (b) plot of estimated curvature as a function of position; (c) curvature after adaptive smoothing; (d) critical points.

175

Let $I_0(s)$ be the signal before smoothing and $I_t(s)$ the signal at the tth iteration. The smoothed version of $I_t(s)$ is then defined at each point by

$$I_{t+1}(s) = \left(\frac{1}{\sum\limits_{i=-1}^{+1} c_t(s+i)} \right) \sum_{i=-1}^{+1} I_t(s+i)\, c_t(s+i)$$

(3.1)

where $c(s)$ is a coefficient array of the same size as $I(s)$. Values of $c(s)$ are close to zero at region boundary points and one at region interior points. Thus, two points belonging to different regions are not averaged. Because locations of the region boundary points are not known a priori, an estimate thereof, based on local curvature, is used in calculating $c(s)$, as follows:

$$c(s) = f(d(s)) = \exp\left(\frac{-d^2(s)}{2k^2} \right)$$

(3.2)

where $d(s)$ is the magnitude of the gradient at s. The value of $f(0)$ equals one and that of $f(d(s))$ approaches zero as $d(s)$ increases; hence, $c(s)$ is small at discontinuities. If k is chosen to be small, then every feature will diffuse during iteration, and the result will be the same as that obtained with Gaussian smoothing. If k is chosen to be large, then every discontinuity will stop diffusion, and no smoothing will take place. The number of iterations determines the degree of smoothing obtained. The smoothed function after 75 iterations with $k=40$ is shown in Figure 3.3(c). Some fluctuations still exist in the regions corresponding to circular arcs and the two diagonal lines. Two thresholds, one for peak detection and another for zero-crossing detection, are applied to this curve. Detected peaks are noted by $O's$ and significant zero-crossings are noted by $X's$ in Figure 3.3(c); the corresponding points in the object are noted likewise in Figure 3.3(d).

Detection of interesting points in regions. Points used in matching of points from two images must be ones that are easily identified and matched. Obviously, the points in a uniform region and on edges are not good candidates for matching. Interest operators find image areas with high variance. In applications such as stereo and structure from motion, images should have enough such interesting regions for matching.

Moravec[94] suggested that, for a window in an image, directional variances may be a good measure of how "interesting" a point is; Moravec calls this measure the "interestingness" of a point. A point is considered interesting if it has local maximum of minimal sums of directional variances. The directional variances for a window are

$$I_1 = \sum_{(x,y)\in s} \left(f(x,y) - f(x,y+1) \right)^2$$

$$I_2 = \sum_{(x,y)\in s} \left(f(x,y) - f(x+1,y) \right)^2$$

$$I_3 = \sum_{(x,y)\in s} \left(f(x,y) - f(x+1,y+1) \right)^2$$

$$I_4 = \sum_{(x,y)\in s} \left(f(x,y) - f(x+1,y-1) \right)^2$$

(3.3)

where s represents the elements in the window. Typical window size ranges from 4 x 4 to 8 x 8 pixels.[94] The interestingness of a point is then given by

$$I(x,y) = Min\,(I_1, I_2, I_3, I_4)$$

(3.4)

Choosing points as just described eliminates simple edge points since they have no variance in the direction of the edge.

Feature points are chosen where the interestingness has local maximum. A point is considered "good" as an interesting point if, in addition, local maximum is more than a preset threshold. The Moravec interest operator has found extensive use in stereo-matching applications.

Matching

Matching plays a very important role in many phases of computer vision systems. Object recognition requires matching a description of an object in an image with models of known objects. The goal of matching is to either (1) detect the presence of a known entity, object, or feature or (2) find what an unknown image component is. The difficulty in achieving these matching goals is first encountered with goal-directed matching, wherein the goal is to find a very specific entity in an image. Usually, the location of all instances of such an entity must be found. In stereo and structure-from-motion applications, entities are obtained in one image, and their locations are then determined in the second image. The second problem requires matching an unknown entity with several models to determine which model matches the best.

Depending on the application, matching may be required at different levels. Common entities involved in matching are (1) point patterns, (2) features such as corners and line segments, (3) regions, and (4) objects. Ideally, matched entities should be identical. In computer vision applications, exactly matched entities are rare; rather, matching is usually a maximization of a measure of similarity.

Commonly used matching techniques are discussed in this section.

Point pattern matching. In matching points in two slightly different images of the same scene (e.g., in a stereo pair or a motion sequence), interesting points are detected by applying an operator such as the Moravec interest operator discussed in the previous section. The correspondence process considers local structure of a selected point in one image in assigning initial matchable candidate points from the second image. For example, in stereo-matching applications, the displacement of a point from one image to the other is usually small; thus, only points within a local neighborhood are considered for matching. To obtain final correspondence, the set of initial matches is refined by computing the measure of similarity in global structure around each candidate point. For example, in dynamic-scene analysis, one may assume that motions of neighboring points do not differ significantly. To obtain final matching of points in the two images, relaxation techniques are often employed .

Template matching. In some applications, a particular pictorial or iconic structure, called a "template," should be detected in an image. Templates are usually represented by two-dimensional-intensity functions of small extent (typically, less than 64 x 64 pixels). Template matching is the process of moving the template over the entire image and detecting locations at which the template best fits the image. The commonly used measure of similarity to determine match is the normalized correlation. The arrangement for finding the correlation between the image $f(x,y)$ and the template $w(x,y)$ at a point (m,n) in the image is shown in Figure 3.4.[1] The correlation coefficient $r(m,n)$, which is independent of multiplicative changes in the image intensity function, is given by

$$r(m,n) = \frac{\sum_x \sum_y \left[f(x,y) - \overline{f}(x,y) \right] \left[w(x-m,y-n) - \overline{w} \right]}{\left[\sum_x \sum_y \left[f(x,y) - \overline{f}(x,y) \right]^2 \sum_x \sum_y \left[w(x-m,y-n) - \overline{w} \right]^2 \right]^{0.5}}$$

(3.5)

Here, $\overline{w}$ is the average intensity of the pixels in the template, $\overline{f}(x,y)$ is the average intensity of image pixels within the window, and the summations are carried out over all pixels within the window.

A major limitation of the template-matching technique is its sensitivity to scaling and rotation of objects. To match scaled and rotated objects, separate templates should be constructed. In some approaches, a template is partitioned into several subtemplates, and matching is computed for these subtemplates. The relationships among subtemplates are verified in the final matching step for the complete object.

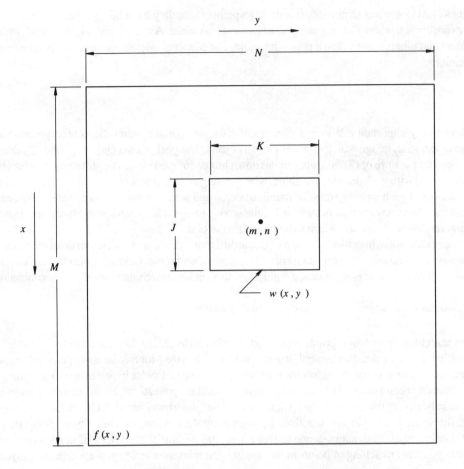

Figure 3.4: Arrangement for calculating the correlation of f(x,y) with w (x,y) at image point (m,n) (from R.C. Gonzalez and P. Wintz, *Digital Image Processing*, © 1977 by Addison-Wesley Publishing Company. Reprinted with permission of the publisher.)[1]

Hough transform. Hough transform is a useful method for recognition of straight lines and curves. For a straight line, the transformation is defined by the parametric representation of a straight line given by

$$\rho = x\cos\theta + y\sin\theta \tag{3.6}$$

where (ρ,θ) are the variables in the parameter space, represent the length and orientation, respectively, of the normal to the line from the origin. Each point (x,y) in the image plane transforms into a sinusoid in the (ρ,θ) domain, as given by the preceding equation. However, all the sinusoids corresponding to points that are collinear in the image plane intersect at a single point in the Hough domain. Thus, pixels belonging to a straight line can be easily identified in the Hough domain. Hough transform is typically implemented as a voting scheme. Each pixel in the image "votes" for several cells in the parameter space. The cell in the parameter space with the most votes characterizes the corresponding line in the spatial domain.

Hough transform can be defined to recognize other types of curves. For example, points on a circle can be detected by searching through a three-dimensional parameter space of (X_c, Y_c, R), where the first two parameters, X_c and Y_c, define the location of the center and R represents radius. The Hough transform technique has also been generalized to detect arbitrary shapes.[95] A problem with the Hough transform is the large parameter search space required to detect even simple curves. This problem can be alleviated somewhat by the use of additional information that may be available in the spatial domain. For example, in detecting circles by the brute-force method, searching must be done in three-dimensional-parameter space; however, when the direction of the curve gradient is known, the search is restricted to just one dimension.

Feature matching. An image of an object has as its components many regions. In addition, an object may appear in various orientations, locations, and scales. Identifying an object in an image requires that all of its components first be identified and then

178

that their properties or feature values and relationships be computed. Subsequently, the objective is to match these components into the corresponding components in the object model. This matching may be treated as a graph-matching problem in which nodes represent regions and arcs represent relations between regions. Nodes in such a graph are matched by considering region-based properties and the entire graph is matched by considering the structural or spatial relationships among various regions. Object recognition using this method is equivalent to the graph isomorphism problem. When the object is only partially visible in the image, subgraph isomorphism can be used.

Pattern classification. Features extracted from images may be represented in a feature space. A classifier — such as the minimum-distance classifier, which is used extensively in statistical pattern recognition — may be used to identify the object. This pattern classification method is especially useful in applications wherein the objective is to assign a label, from among many possible labels, to a region in the image. The classifier may be taught in a supervised-learning mode, by using prototypes of known object classes, or in an unsupervised mode, in which the learning is automatic. Proper selection of features is critical for the success of this approach. Several methods of pattern classification using structural relationships have also been developed.

Hierarchical decomposition and matching. Techniques such as polygonal approximation and signature analysis are useful for shape recognition only when the complete outline of the object is available. Because of occlusions or other image segmentation problems, recognizing shapes when only parts of the object are visible becomes necessary in computer vision. In some applications, the number of possible different shapes to be recognized may be large. Then, complex parts may be represented as a combination of already known simple shapes and their spatial relationships, and similar decomposition steps may be followed during object recognition.

An object recognition system that creates a library of parts by hierarchical decomposition is described by Ettinger.[96] The library organization and indexing are designed to avoid linear search of all model objects. The system has hierarchical organization for both structure (whole object-to-component subparts) and scale (gross-to-fine features). Object representation is based on the curvature primal sketch of Asada and Brady.[91] Features used are corner, end, crank, smooth-join, inflection, and bump, which are derived from discontinuities in contour orientation and curvature. Subparts consist of subsets of these features; these subsets partition the object into components. The model libraries are automatically built using the hierarchical nature of the model representations. The recognition engine is structured as an interpretation tree.[97] A constrained search scheme is used for matching scene features to model features. Early in the search process, many configurations in the search space are pruned using simple geometric constraints, such as — for pairs of features — orientation difference, direction, and distance.

Research trends

Discontinuities in detected edges and object boundaries occur frequently during low-level image analysis. Hough transform has been used extensively as an efficient method for detecting such broken edges and boundaries. Nine papers were selected for inclusion in this chapter; five are in this book and the remaining four in its companion book, *Computer Vision: Advances and Applications*. We begin this section of *Principles* with the paper entitled "Generalizing the Hough Transform to Detect Arbitrary Shapes," by Ballard. In *Advances and Applications*, "Object Recognition and Localization via Pose Clustering," by Stockman applies the Hough transform technique to cluster poses of objects in two-dimensional and three-dimensional problems. This paper demonstrates the elegance and efficiency of these clustering approaches for solving object recognition problems. Also in *Advances and Applications*, Asada and Brady in "The Curvature Primal Sketch," describe a representation scheme based on significant changes in curvature along the boundary of a planar shape. The methods introduced in this paper have been used in other applications, including the object recognition system described by Ettinger in his paper in *Advances and Applications* entitled "Large Hierarchical Object Recognition Using Libraries of Parameterized Model Sub-parts." In the final paper in *Advances and Applications*, "Scale-Based Description and Recognition of Planar Curves and Two-Dimensional Shapes," Mokhtarian and Mackworth describe a technique for finding a description of planar curves at varying levels of detail. The generalized scale-space image of a planar curve that they obtain is invariant under rotation, uniform scaling, and translation of the curve; this invariance makes matching two curves convenient. Analogous to the concept of boundary representation by curvature primal sketch is the concept for surface description that is presented in "The Topographic Primal Sketch," by Haralick et al. in *Principles*. The topographic primal sketch is derived by the classifying and grouping of underlying image intensity surface patches. The paper found in *Principles*, entitled "Image Analysis Using Mathematical Morphology," by Haralick et al., is a tutorial on morphological techniques. Also in *Principles*, "A Structural Model of Shape," by Shapiro describes a shape as consisting of a set of primitives, their properties, and their interrelationships. Her model is used in a shape-matching procedure to find mappings from a prototype shape to a candidate shape. The final paper in *Principles* by Fischler and Bolles entitled "Random Sample Consensus: A Paradigm for Model Fitting With Applications to Image Analysis and Automated Cartography" describes a technique for solving the problem of location determination. Their technique makes possible interpreting/smoothing data that contain a significant percentage of gross errors.

Clearly, features play the most important role in recognition. In the early stages of computer vision, global features — such as moments and Fourier descriptors — were used. Since these features were inadequate for occluded objects, local features — such as corners and interest points — started attracting attention. Recently, more emphasis has been placed on domain-dependent features. Now, features are being designed considering the models of objects being recognized.[98-100] Features designed using models are not dictated by their generality and mathematical representability, but by their utility in recognizing objects. The idea of object-dependent features is becoming very popular.[101] An interesting direction in feature detection is the use of robust statistics. In most applications, features are detected using a form of least squares fitting. Least squares fitting presents problems in the presence of outliers. Hough transform techniques use voting to eliminate the undesirable influence of outliers. Recently, robust statistics have been increasingly used to detect features or to estimate parameters in the presence of outliers.[102-104] Current robust techniques are computationally very demanding. The Hough transform is a fast implementation of a simple robust technique. Fast robust techniques will likely play a very important role in feature detection. Neural nets appear to offer parallel methods for fast robust detection of features,[105,106] but to date their success has been limited to very simple images. Another interesting development in early vision, especially in relation to feature detection, is the increasing attention being given to qualitative vision.[107-109] In the detection of certain features, only signs of certain variables can be used to give a gross, but robust, classification that yields qualitative feature-related information. Such detection approaches are likely to be more successful in complex vision systems than very precise, but noise-sensitive, approaches.

References Cited
Chapter 3

67. H. Freeman, "Applications of Generalized Chain Coding Scheme to Map Data Processing," *Proc. IEEE Conf. Pattern Recognition and Image Processing,* IEEE CS Press, Los Alamitos, Calif., 1978, pp. 220-226.

68. U.E. Ramer, "An Iterative Procedure for the Polygonal Approximation of Plane Curves," *Computer Graphics and Image Processing,* Vol. 1, 1972, pp. 244-256.

69. I. Tomek, "Two Algorithms for Piecewise-Linear Continuous Fit of Functions of One Variable," *IEEE Trans. on Computers,* Vol. 23, No. 4, 1974, pp. 445-448.

70. C.M. Williams, "An Efficient Algorithm for the Piecewise Linear Approximation of Planar Curves," *Computer Graphics and Image Processing,* Vol. 8, 1978, pp. 286-293.

71. C.M. Williams, "Bounded Straight-Line Approximation of Digitized Planar Curves and Lines," *Computer Graphics and Image Processing,* Vol. 16, 1981, pp. 370-381.

72. J. Sklansky and V. Gonzalez, "Fast Polygonal Approximation of Digitized Curves," *Pattern Recognition,* Vol. 12, 1980, pp. 327-331.

73. T. Pavlidis, *Algorithms for Graphics and Image Processing,* Computer Science Press, Rockville, Maryland, 1982.

74. Y. Kurozumi and W.A. Davis, "Polygonal Approximation by Minimax Method," *Computer Graphics and Image Processing,* Vol. 19, 1982, pp. 248-264.

75. K. Wall and P.E. Danielsson, "A Fast Sequential Method for Polygonal Approximation of Digitized Curves," *Computer Graphics and Image Processing,* Vol. 28, 1984, pp. 220-227.

76. K. Wall, "Curve Fitting Based on Polygonal Approximation," *Proc. Eighth Int'l Conf. Pattern Recognition,* IEEE CS Press, Los Alamitos, Calif., 1986, pp. 1273-1275.

77. J.G. Leu and L. Chen, "Polygonal Approximation of 2-D Shapes through Boundary Merging," *Pattern Recognition Letters,* Vol. 8, 1988, pp. 231-238.

78. T. Pavlidis, *Structural Pattern Recognition,* Springer-Verlag, New York, N.Y., 1977.

79. T. Pavlidis, "Survey: A Review of Algorithms for Shape Analysis," *Computer Graphics and Image Processing,* Vol. 7, 1978, pp. 243-258.

80. L.S. Davis, "Two Dimensional Shape Representation," *Handbook of Pattern Recognition and Image Processing,* eds. T.Y. Young and K.S. Fu, Academic Press, Orlando, Fla., 1986, pp. 233-245.

81. J. Serra, *Image Analysis and Mathematical Morphology,* Academic Press, New York, N.Y., 1982.

82. J. Serra, "Introduction to Mathematical Morphology," *Computer Vision, Graphics, and Image Processing,* Vol. 35, No. 3, 1986, pp. 283-325.

83. R.M. Haralick, S.R. Sternberg, and X. Zhuang, "Image Analysis Using Mathematical Morphology," *IEEE Trans. Pattern Analysis and Machine Intelligence,* Vol. 9, No. 5, 1987, pp. 532-550.

84. E.R. Dougherty and C.R. Giardina, *Morphological Methods in Image and Signal Processing,* Prentice-Hall, Englewood Cliffs, N.J., 1987.

85. R.M. Haralick, L.T. Watson, and T.J. Laffey, "The Topographic Primal Sketch," *Int'l J. Robotics Research,* Vol. 2, No. 1, 1983, pp. 50-72.

86. L.G. Shapiro, "A Structural Model of Shape," *IEEE Trans. Pattern Analysis and Machine Intelligence,* Vol. 2, No. 1, 1980, pp. 111-126.

87. F. Attneave, "Some Informational Aspects of Visual Perception," *Psycho. Review,* Vol. 61, 1954, pp. 183-193.

88. C.H. Teh and R.T. Chin, "On the Detection of Dominant Points on Digital Curves," *IEEE Trans. Pattern Analysis and Machine Intelligence,* Vol. 11, No. 8, 1989, pp. 859-872.

89. M.A. Fischler and R.C. Bolles, "Perceptual Organization and Curve Partitioning," *IEEE Trans. Pattern Analysis and Machine Intelligence,* Vol. 8, No. 1, 1986, pp. 100-105.

90. T.Y. Phillips and A. Rosenfeld, "A Method of Curve Partitioning Using Arc-Chord Distance," *Pattern Recognition Letters,* Vol. 5, 1987, pp. 245-249.

91. H. Asada and M. Brady, "The Curvature Primal Sketch," *IEEE Trans. Pattern Analysis and Machine Intelligence,* Vol. 8, No. 1, 1986, pp. 26-33.

92. K. Deguchi, "Multi-Scale Curvatures for Contour Feature Extraction," *Proc. Ninth Int'l Conf. Pattern Recognition,* IEEE CS Press, Los Alamitos, Calif., 1988, pp. 1113-1115.

93. P. Saint-Marc, J.S. Chen, and G. Medioni, "Adaptive Smoothing: A General Tool for Early Vision," *Proc. IEEE Conf. Computer Vision and Pattern Recognition,* IEEE CS Press, Los Alamitos, Calif., 1989, pp. 618-624.

94. H.P. Moravec, "Toward Automatic Visual Obstacle Avoidance," *Proc. Int'l Joint Conf. Artificial Intelligence,* Morgan Kaufmann Publishers, Inc., San Mateo, Calif., 1977, p. 584.

95. D.H. Ballard, "Generalizing the Hough Transform to Detect Arbitrary Shapes," *Pattern Recognition,* Vol. 13, No. 2, 1981, pp. 111-122.

96. G.J. Ettinger, "Large Hierarchical Object Recognition in Robot Vision," *Proc. IEEE Conf. Computer Vision and Pattern Recognition,* IEEE CS Press, Los Alamitos, Calif., 1988, pp. 32-41.

97. W.E.L. Grimson and T. Lozano-Perez, "Model-Based Recognition and Localization from Sparse Range or Tactile Data," *Int'l J. Robotics Research,* Vol. 3, No. 3, 1984, pp. 3-35.

98. R.C. Bolles and R.A. Cain, "Recognizing and Locating Partially Visible Objects: The Local-Feature-Focus Method," *Int'l J. Robotics Research,* Vol. 1, No. 3, 1982, pp. 57-82.

99. J.L. Turney, T.N. Mudge, and R.A. Volz, "Recognizing Partly Occluded Parts," *IEEE Trans. Pattern Analysis and Machine Intelligence,* Vol. 7, No. 4, 1985, pp. 410-421.

100. T. Knoll and R.C. Jain, "Recognizing Partially Visible Objects Using Feature Indexed Hypotheses," *IEEE Trans. Robotics and Automation,* Vol. 2, No. 1, 1986, pp. 3-13.

101. B. Bhanu and C. Ho, "CAD-Based 3-D Object Representation for Robot Vision," *Computer,* Vol. 20, No. 8, 1987, pp. 19-36.

102. P.J. Besl, J.B. Birch, and L.T. Watson, "Robust Window Operators," *Machine Vision and Applications,* Vol. 2, 1989, pp. 179-191.

103. R.M. Haralick et al, "Pose Estimation from Corresponding Point Data," *IEEE Trans. on Systems, Man, and Cybernetics,* Vol. 19, No. 6, 1989, pp. 1426-1446.

104. L. Liu et al, "Application of Robust Sequential Edge Detection and Linking to Boundaries of Low Contrast Lesions in Medical Images," *Proc. IEEE Conf. Computer Vision and Pattern Recognition,* IEEE CS Press, Los Alamitos, Calif., 1989, pp. 582-587.

105. K. Fukushima, "Neocognitron: A Hierarchical Neural Network Capable of Visual Pattern Recognition," *Neural Networks,* Vol. 1, 1988, pp. 119-130.

106. N. Grossberg, *Neural Networks and Natural Intelligence,* MIT Press, Cambridge, Mass., 1988.

107. S. Haynes and R.C. Jain, "A Qualitative Approach for Recovering Depths in Dynamic Scenes," *IEEE Workshop on Computer Vision,* IEEE CS Press, Los Alamitos, Calif., 1987, pp. 66-71.

108. J. Aloimonos, "Visual Shape Computation," *Proc. IEEE,* Vol. 76, No. 8, IEEE Press, New York, N.Y., 1988, pp. 899-916.

109. A. Verri and T Poggio, "Motion Field and Optical Flow: Qualitative Properties," *IEEE Trans. Pattern Analysis and Machine Intelligence,* Vol. 11, No. 5, 1989, pp. 490-498.

GENERALIZING THE HOUGH TRANSFORM TO DETECT ARBITRARY SHAPES*

D. H. BALLARD

Computer Science Department, University of Rochester, Rochester, NY 14627, U.S.A.

(*Received* 10 *October* 1979; *in revised form* 9 *September* 1980; *received for
publication* 23 *September* 1980)

Abstract—The Hough transform is a method for detecting curves by exploiting the duality between points on
a curve and parameters of that curve. The initial work showed how to detect both analytic curves[1,2] and
non-analytic curves,[3] but these methods were restricted to binary edge images. This work was generalized to
the detection of some analytic curves in grey level images, specifically lines,[4] circles[5] and parabolas.[6] The
line detection case is the best known of these and has been ingeniously exploited in several applications.[7,8,9]

We show how the boundaries of an *arbitrary* non-analytic shape can be used to construct a mapping
between image space and Hough transform space. Such a mapping can be exploited to detect instances of that
particular shape in an image. Furthermore, variations in the shape such as rotations, scale changes or figure–
ground reversals correspond to straightforward transformations of this mapping. However, the most
remarkable property is that such mappings can be composed to build mappings for complex shapes from the
mappings of simpler component shapes. This makes the generalized Hough transform a kind of universal
transform which can be used to find arbitrarily complex shapes.

Image processing	Hough transform	Shape recognition	Pattern recognition
Parallel algorithms			

1. INTRODUCTION

In an image, the pertinent information about an
object is very often contained in the shape of its
boundary. Some appreciation of the importance of
these boundary shapes in human vision can be gained
from experiments performed on the human visual
system, which have shown that crude encodings of the
boundaries are often sufficient for object recognition[10] and that the image may be initially encoded
as an 'edge image', i.e. an image of local intensity or
color gradients. Marr[11] has termed this edge image a
'primal sketch' and suggested that this ·may be a
necessary first step in image processing. We describe a
very general algorithm for detecting objects of a
specified shape from an image that has been transformed into such an edge representation. In that representation, sample points in the image no longer
contain grey level information, but instead each sample point contains a magnitude and direction representing the severity and orientation of the local grey
level change.

Operators that transform the image in such a way
are known as edge operators, and many such operators are available, all based on different models of the
local grey level changes. Two of the most used are the
gradient operator (for example, see Prewitt[12]) and the
Hueckel operator,[13] which model local grey level
changes as a ramp and a step respectively.

Our generalized Hough algorithm uses edge information to define a mapping from the orientation of an
edge point to a reference point of the shape. The
reference point may be thought of as the origin of a
local co-ordinate system for the shape. Then there is an
easy way of computing a measure which rates how well
points in the image are likely to be origins of the
specified shape. Figure 1 shows a few graphic examples
of the information used by the generalized Hough
transform. Lines indicate gradient directions. A feature
of the transform is that it will work even when the
boundary is disconnected due to noise or occlusions.
This is generally not true for other strategies which
track edge segments.

The original algorithm by Hough[2] did not use

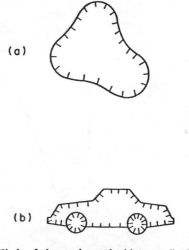

(a)

(b)

Fig. 1. Kinds of shapes detected with generalized Hough
transform. (a) Simple shape; (b) composite shape.

* The research described in this report was supported in part
by NIH Grant R23-HL-2153-01 and in part by the Alfred P.
Sloan Foundation Grant 78-4-15.

orientation information of the edge, and was considerably inferior to later work using the edge orientation for parametric curves.[5,6,14] Shapiro[15,16,17] has collected a good bibliography of previous work as well as having contributed to the error analysis of the technique.

1.1 Organization

Section 2 describes the Hough transform for analytic curves. As an example of the parametric version of the transform, we use the ellipse. This example is very important due to the pervasiveness of circles in images, and the fact that a circle becomes an ellipse when rotated about an axis perpendicular to the viewing angle. Despite the importance of ellipses, not much work has used the Hough transform. The elliptical transform is discussed in detail in Section 3. Section 4 describes the generalized algorithm and its properties. Section 5 describes special strategies for implementing the algorithm and Section 6 summarizes its advantages.

2. THE HOUGH TRANSFORM FOR ANALYTIC CURVES

We consider analytic curves of the form $f(x, a) = 0$ where x is an image point and a is a parameter vector.

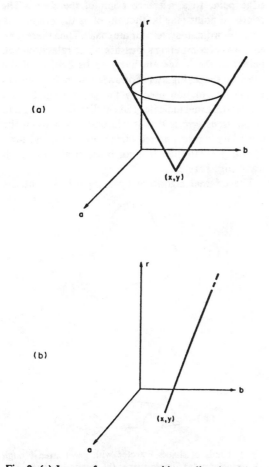

To see how the Hough transform works for such curves, let us suppose we are interested in detecting circular boundaries in an image. In Cartesian coordinates, the equation for a circle is given by

$$(x-a)^2 + (y-b)^2 = r^2. \tag{1}$$

Suppose also that the image has been transformed into an edge representation so that only the magnitude of local intensity changes is known. Pixels whose magnitude exceeds some threshold are termed *edge pixels*. For each edge pixel, we can ask the question: if this pixel is to lie on a circle, what is the locus for the parameters of that circle? The answer is a right circular cone, as shown in Fig. 2(a). This can be seen from equation (1) by treating x and y as fixed and letting, a, b, and r vary.

The interesting result about this locus in parameter space is the following. If a set of edge pixels in an image are arranged on a circle with parameters a_0, b_0, and r_0, the resultant loci of parameters for each such point will pass through the same point (a_0, b_0, r_0) in parameter space. Thus many such right circular cones will intersect at a common point.

2.1 Directional information

We see immediately that if we also use the *directional* information associated with the edge, this reduces the parameter locus to a line, as shown in Fig. 2(b). This is because the center of the circle for the point (x, y) must lie r units along the direction of the gradient. Formally, the circle involves 3 parameters. By using the equation for the circle together with its derivative, the number of free parameters is reduced to one. Formally, what happens is the equation

$$\frac{df}{dx}(x, a) = 0$$

introduces a term dy/dx which is known since

$$\frac{dy}{dx} = \tan\left[\phi(x) - \frac{\pi}{2}\right]$$

where $\phi(x)$ is the gradient direction. This suggests the following algorithm.

Hough algorithm for analytic curves in grey level images. For a specific curve $f(x, a) = 0$ with parameter vector a, form an array $A(a)$, initially set to zero. This array is termed an accumulator array. Then for each edge pixel x, compute all a such that $f(x, a) = 0$ and $df/dx(x, a) = 0$ and increment the corresponding accumulator array entries:

$$A(a) := A(a) + 1.$$

After each edge pixel x has been considered, local maxima in the array A correspond to curves of f in the image.

If only the equation $f(x, a) = 0$ is used, the cost of the computation is exponential in the number of parameters minus one, that is, where m parameters each have M values, the computation is proportional to

Fig. 2. (a) Locus of parameters with no directional information. (b) Locus of parameters with directional information.

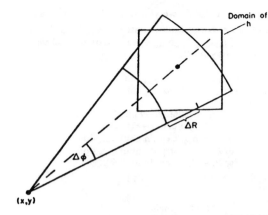

Fig. 3. Using convolution templates to compensate for errors.

M^{m-1}. This is because the equation of the curve can be used to determine the last parameter. The use of gradient directional information saves the cost of another parameter making the total effort proportional to M^{m-2}, for $m \geq 2$.

2.2 Compensating for errors

A problem arises in detecting maxima in the array $A(\mathbf{a})$. Many sources of error effect the computation of the parameter vector $\mathbf{a}$ so that in general many array locations in the vicinity of the ideal point $\mathbf{a}$ are incremented instead of the point itself. One way of handling this problem is to use a formal error model on the incrementation step. This model would specify a set of nearby points instead of a single point. Shapiro[15-18] has done extensive work on this subject. Another solution to this problem is to replace uncompensated accumulator values by a function of the values themselves and nearby points after the incrementation step. The effect of this operation is to smooth the accumulator array. We show that, under the assumption of isotropic errors, these methods are equivalent.

Returning to the initial example of detecting circles, the smoothing of the accumulator array is almost equivalent to the change in the incrementing procedure we would use to allow for uncertainties in the gradient direction ϕ and the radius r. If we recognized these uncertainties as:

$$\phi(\mathbf{x}) \pm \Delta\phi$$

$$r \pm \Delta r(r)$$

we would increment all values of $\mathbf{a}$ which fall within the shaded band of Fig. 3. We let Δr increase with r so that uncertainties are counted on a percentage basis. Figure 3 shows the two-dimensional analog of the general three-dimensional case.

Suppose we approximate this procedure by incrementing all values of $\mathbf{a}$ which fall inside the square domain centered about the nominal center shown in Fig. 3, according to some point spread function h. After the first contributing pixel which increments center $\mathbf{a}_0$ has been taken into account, the new accumulator array contents A will be given by

$$A(\mathbf{a}) = h(\mathbf{a} - \mathbf{a}_0) \qquad (2)$$

where $\mathbf{a} = (a_1, a_2, r)$ and $\mathbf{a}_0 = (a_{10}, a_{20}, r_0)$. If we include all the contributing pixels for that center, denoted by C, the accumulator is

$$A(\mathbf{a}) = C(\mathbf{a}_0)h(\mathbf{a} - \mathbf{a}_0). \qquad (3)$$

Finally for all incremented centers, we sum over $\mathbf{a}_0$:

$$A(\mathbf{a}) = \sum_{\mathbf{a}_0} C(\mathbf{a}_0)h(\mathbf{a} - \mathbf{a}_0). \qquad (4)$$

But $C(\mathbf{a}_0) = A(\mathbf{a}_0)$, so that

$$A(\mathbf{a}) = \sum_{\mathbf{a}_0} A(\mathbf{a}_0)h(\mathbf{a} - \mathbf{a}_0)$$
$$= A * h$$
$$\equiv A_s(\mathbf{a}). \qquad (5)$$

Thus within the approximation of letting the square represent the shaded band shown in Fig. 3, the smoothing procedure is equivalent to an accommodation for uncertainties in the gradient direction and radius.

3. AN EXAMPLE: ELLIPSES

The description of the algorithm in Section 2.1 is very terse and its implementation often requires considerable algebraic manipulation. We use the example of finding ellipses to show the kinds of calculation which must be done. Ellipses are an important example, as circles, which are a ubiquitous part of many everyday objects, appear as ellipses when viewed from a distant, oblique angle.

We use the center of the ellipse as a reference point and assume that it is centered at x_0, y_0 with major and minor diameters a and b. For the moment, we will assume that the ellipse is oriented with its major axis parallel to the x-axis. Later we will relax this requirement by introducing an additional parameter for arbitrary orientations. For the moment, assume a and b are fixed. Then the equation of the ellipse is:

$$\frac{(x - x_0)^2}{a^2} + \frac{(y - y_0)^2}{b^2} = 1. \qquad (6)$$

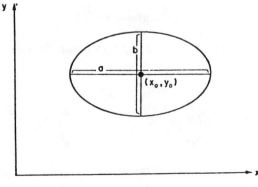

Fig. 4. Parametrization of an ellipse with major axis parallel to x-axis.

Let $X = x - x_0$, $Y = y - y_0$, then

$$\frac{X^2}{a^2} + \frac{y^2}{b^2} = 1 \qquad (7)$$

Differentiating with respect to X

$$\frac{2X}{a^2} + \frac{2Y}{b^2}\frac{dY}{dX} = 0. \qquad (8)$$

But dY/dX is known from the edge pixel information! Let $dY/dX = \xi$, then from (8)

$$X^2 = \left(\frac{a^2}{b^2}\xi\right)^2 Y^2. \qquad (9)$$

Substituting in (7)

$$\frac{Y^2}{b^2}\left(1 + \frac{a^2}{b^2}\xi^2\right) = 1 \qquad (10)$$

$$Y = \pm \frac{b^2}{\sqrt{\left(1 + \frac{a^2}{b^2}\xi^2\right)}} \qquad (11)$$

so that

$$X = \pm \frac{a^2}{\sqrt{\left(1 + \frac{b^2}{a^2\xi^2}\right)}} \qquad (12)$$

and finally, given a, b, x, y and dY/dX, we can determine x_0 and y_0 as:

$$x_0 = x \pm \frac{a^2}{\sqrt{\left(1 + \frac{b^2}{a^2\xi^2}\right)}} \qquad (13)$$

$$y_0 = y \pm \frac{b^2}{\sqrt{\left(1 + \frac{a^2\xi^2}{b^2}\right)}}. \qquad (14)$$

The four solutions correspond to the four quadrants, as shown in Fig. 5. The appropriate quadrant can be found from the gradient by testing the signed differences dY and dX.

The final step is to handle rotations by introducing a fifth parameter θ. For an arbitrary θ, we calculate (X, Y) using

$$\xi = \tan\left(\phi - \theta - \frac{\pi}{2}\right)$$

and rotate these (X, Y) by θ to obtain the correct

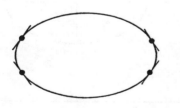

Fig. 5. Four reference point solutions resolvable with gradient quadrant information.

(x_0, y_0). In ALGOL we would implement this as:

```
procedure HoughEllipse (integer X_min X_max,
  Y_min Y_max,
  θ_min θ_max, a_min a_max, b_min b_max, x, y, x_0, y_0, dx, dy; real angle, ζ;
  integer array A, P);
  begin;
  for x: = x_min step dx to x_max do
  for y: = y_min step dy to y_max do
    begin
      dX: = P(x + delta, y) − P(x, y);
      dY: = P(x, y + delta) − P(x, y);
      for a: = a_min step da until a_max do
      for b: = b_min step db until b_max do
      for θ: = θ_min step dθ until θ_max do
        begin;
        angle: = arctan(dY/dX) − θ − π/2;
        ζ: = tan(angle);
        dx: = Sign X (dX, dY) · a²/√(1 + b²/(a²ζ²));
        dy: = Sign Y (dX, dY) · b²/√(1 + (a²/b²)²);
        Rotate-by-Theta(dx, dy);
        x_0: = x + dx;
        y_0: = y + dy;
        A(x_0, y_0, θ, a, b): = A(x_0, y_0, θ, a, b) + 1;
      end;
    end;
  end.
```

Notice that to determine the appropriate formulae for an arbitrary orientation angle θ, we need only rotate the gradient angle and the offsets dx and dy. Sign X and Sign Y are functions which return ± 1 depending on the quadrant determined by dX and dY.

3.1 Parameter space image space trade-offs

Tsuji and Matsumoto[19] recognized that a decreased computational effort in parameter space could be traded for an increased effort in edge space. It is our intent to place these ideas on a formal footing. Later we will see that the same kind of trade-off is potentially available for the case of arbitrary shapes, but is impractical to implement.

An ellipse has five parameters. Referring to the basic algorithm in Section 2.1, we use the equation for the ellipse together with its derivative to solve for two of these parameters as a function of the other three. Thus the algorithm examines every edge point and uses a three-dimensional accumulator array so that the computations are of order $O(ed^3)$. Here e is the number of edge pixels and we are assuming d distinct values for each parameters. Suppose we use pairs of edge points in the algorithm. This results in four equations, two involving the equation for an ellipse evaluated at the different points and two for the related derivatives. This leaves one free parameter. Thus the resultant computational effort is now $O(e^2d)$. The detailed derivation of this form of the Hough algorithm is presented in the Appendix.

If parameter space can be highly constrained so that the set of plausible values is small, then the former technique will be more efficient, whereas if there are

Table 1. Analytic curves described in terms of the generalized shape parameters x_r, y_r, S_x, S_y, θ

Analytic form	Parameters	Equation
Line	S, θ	$x \cos \theta + y \sin \theta = S$
Circle	x_r, y_r, S	$(x-x_r)^2 + (y-y_r)^2 = S^2$
Parabola	x_r, y_r, S_x, θ	$(y-y_r)^2 = 4S_x(x-x_r)^*$
Ellipse	$x_r, y_r, S_x, S_y, \theta$	$\dfrac{(y-y_r)^2}{S_y^2} + \dfrac{(x-x_r)^2}{S_x^2} = 1^*$

* Plus rotation by θ.

relatively few edges and large variations in parameters, the latter will be more efficient.

4. GENERALIZING THE HOUGH TRANSFORM

To generalize the Hough algorithm to non-analytic curves we define the following parameters for a generalized shape:

$$a = \{y, s, \theta\},$$

where $y = (x_r, y_r)$ is a reference origin for the shape, θ is its orientation, and $s = (s_x, s_y)$ describes two orthogonal scale factors. As before, we will provide an algorithm for computing the best set of parameters a for a given shape from edge pixel data. These parameters no longer have equal status. The reference origin location, y, is described in terms of a table of possible edge pixel orientations. The computation of the additional parameters s and θ is then accomplished by straightforward transformations to this table. [To simplify the development slightly, and because of its practical significance, we will work with the four-dimensional sunspace $a = (y, s, \theta)$, where s is a scalar.]

In a sense this choice of parameters includes the previous analytic forms to which the Hough transform has been applied. Table 1 shows these relationships.

4.1 Earlier work: arbitrary shapes in binary edge images

Merlin and Farber[3] showed how to use a Hough algorithm when the desired curves could not be described analytically. Each shape must have a specific reference point. Then we can use the following algorithm for a shape with boundary points B denoted by $\{x_B\}$ which are relative to some reference origin y.

Merlin–Farber Hough algorithm: non-analytic curves with no gradient direction information $a = y$. Form a two-dimensional accumulator array $A(a)$ initialized to zero. For each edge pixel x and each boundary point x_B, compute a such that $a = x - x_B$ and increment $A(a)$. Local maxima in $A(a)$ correspond to instances of the shape in the image.

Note that this is merely an efficient implementation of the convolution of the shape template where edge pixels are unity and others are zero with the corresponding image, i.e.,

$$A(x) = T(x)*S(x) \qquad (15)$$

where E is the binary edge image defined by

$$E(x) = \begin{cases} 1 \text{ if x is an edge pixel} \\ 0 \text{ otherwise} \end{cases}$$

and $T(x)$ is the shape template consisting of ones where x is a boundary point and zeros otherwise, i.e.,

$$T(x) = \begin{cases} 1 \text{ if x is in } B \\ 0 \text{ otherwise} . \end{cases}$$

This result is due to Sklansky.[20]

The Merlin–Farber algorithm is impractical for real image data. In an image with a multitude of edge pixels, there will be many false instances of the desired shape due to coincidental pixel arrangements. Nevertheless, it is the logical precursor to our generalized algorithm.

4.2 The generalization to arbitrary shapes

The key to generalizing the Hough algorithm to arbitrary shapes is the use of directional information. Directional information, besides making the algorithm faster, also greatly improves its accuracy. For example, if the directional information is not used in the circle detector, any significant group of edge points with quite different directions which lie on a circle will be detected. This can be appreciated by comparing Figs 2(a) and 2(b).

Consider for a moment the circular boundary detector with a fixed radius r_0. Now for each gradient point x with direction ϕ, we need only increment a single point $x+r$. For the circle:

$$|r| = r_0 \qquad (16)$$

$$\text{Angle}(r) = \phi(x) . \qquad (17)$$

Now suppose we have an arbitrary shape like the one shown in Fig. 6. Extending the idea of the circle detector with fixed radius to this case, for each point x on the boundary with gradient direction ϕ, we increment a point $a = x + r$. The difference is that now $r = a - x$ which, in general, will vary in magnitude and direction with different boundary points.

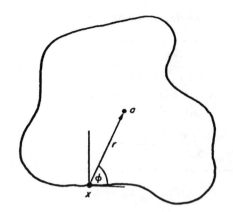

Fig. 6. Geometry for generalized Hough transform.

The fact that r varies in an arbitrary way means that the generalized Hough transform for an arbitrary shape is best represented by a table which we call the R-table.

4.3 The R-table

From the above discussion, we can see that the R-table is easily constructed by examining the boundary points of the shape. The construction of the table is accomplished as follows.

Algorithm for constructing an R-table. Choose a reference point y for the shape. For each boundary point x, compute $\phi(x)$ the gradient direction and $r = y - x$. Store r as a function of ϕ.

Notice that the mapping the table represents is vector-valued and, in general, an index ϕ may have many values of r. Table 2 shows the form of the R-table diagrammatically.

The R-table is used to detect instances of the shape S in an image in the following manner.

Generalized Hough algorithm for single shapes. For each edge pixel x in the image, increment all the corresponding points $x + r$ in the accumulator array A where r is a table entry indexed by ϕ, i.e., $r(\phi)$. Maxima in A correspond to possible instances of the shape S.

4.4 Examples

Some simple shapes are rotation-invariant, that is, the entries in the incrementation table are invariant functions of the gradient direction ϕ. Figure 7(a) shows an example for washers (or bagels). Here there are exactly two entries for each ϕ, one r units in the gradient direction and one R units in the direction opposite to the gradient direction. In another case the entries may be a simple function of ϕ. Figure 7(b)

shows such an example; hexagons. Irrespective of the orientation of the edge, the reference point locus is on a line of length l parallel to the edge pixel and $(3/2)l$ units away from it.

Another example is shown in Fig. 8. Here the points on the boundary of the shape are shown in Fig. 8(a). A reference point is selected and used to construct the R-table. Figure 8(b) shows a synthetic image of four different shapes and Fig. 8(c) shows the portion of the accumulator array for this image which has the correct values of orientation and scale. It is readily seen that edge points on the correct shape have incremented the same point in the accumulator array, whereas edge points on the other shapes have incremented disparate points.

4.5 R-table properties and the general notion of a shape

Up to this point we have considered shapes of fixed orientation and scale. Thus the accumulator array was two-dimensional in the reference point co-ordinates. To search for shapes of arbitrary orientation θ and scale s we add these two parameters to the shape description. The accumulator array now consists of four dimensions corresponding to the parameters (y, s, θ). The R-table can also be used to increment this larger dimensional space since different orientations and scales correspond to easily-computed transformations of the table. Additionally, simple transformations to the R-table can also account for figure–ground reversals and changes of reference point.

We denote a particular R-table for a shape S by $R(\phi)$. R can be viewed as a multiply-vector-valued function. It is easy to see that simple transformations to this table will allow it to detect scaled or rotated instances of the same shape. For example if the shape is scaled by s and this transformation is denoted by T_s, then

$$T_s[R(\phi)] = sR(\phi) \qquad (18)$$

i.e., all the vectors are scaled by s. Also, if the object is rotated by θ and this transformation is denoted by T_θ, then

$$T_\theta[R(\phi)] = \mathrm{Rot}\{R[(\phi - \theta)\bmod 2\pi], \theta\} \qquad (19)$$

i.e., all the indices are incremented by $-\theta$ modulo 2π, the appropriate vectors r are found, and then they are rotated by θ.

To appreciate that this is true, refer to Fig. 9. In this figure an edge pixel with orientation ϕ may be considered as corresponding to the boundary point x_A, in which case the reference point is y_A. Alternatively, the edge pixel may be considered as x_B on a rotated instance of the shape, in which case the reference point is at y_B which can be specified by translating r_A to x_B and rotating it through $+\Delta\theta$.

Figure–ground intensity reversals can also be taken into account via a simple R-table modification. The indices in the table are changed from ϕ to $(\phi + \pi)\bmod 2\pi$. Of course

$$T_{f_\theta}\{T_{f_\theta}[R(\phi)]\} = R(\phi)$$

Table 2. R-table format

i	ϕ_i	R_{ϕ_i}
0	0	$\{r \mid a - r = x,\ x \text{ in } B,\ \phi(x) = 0\}$
1	$\Delta\phi$	$\{r \mid a - r = x,\ x \text{ in } B,\ \phi(x) = \Delta\phi\}$
2	$2\Delta\phi$	$\{r \mid a - r = x,\ x \text{ in } B,\ \phi(x) = 2\Delta\phi\}$
...	...	...

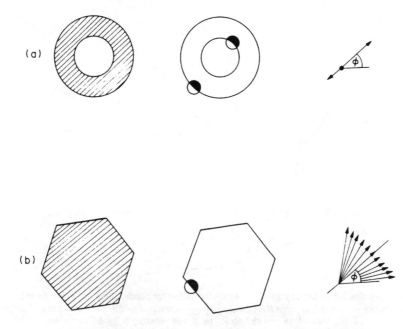

Fig. 7. Simple examples using R-tables; (a) washers; (b) hexagons.

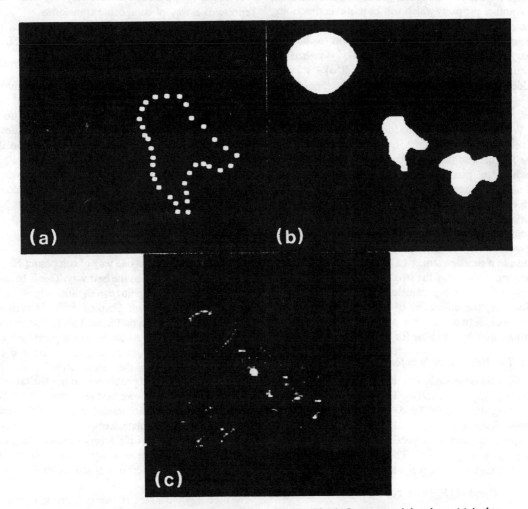

Fig. 8. An example. (a) Points on a shape used to encode R-table. (b) Image containing shape. (c) A plane through the accumulator array $A(x_r, y_r, S_0, \theta_0)$, where S_0 and θ_0 are appropriate for the shape in the image $(S_0 = 64, \theta_0 = 0)$.

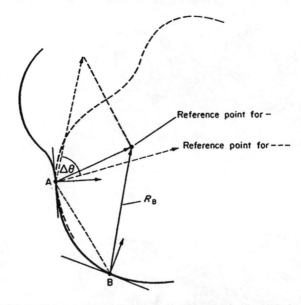

Fig. 9. Construction for visualizing the R-table transformation for a rotation by $\Delta\theta$. Point A can be viewed as: (1) on the shape (——), or (2) as point B on the shape (– – – –), rotated by $\Delta\theta$. If (2) is used then the appropriate $\mathbf{R}$ is obtained by translating $\mathbf{R}_B$ to A and rotating it by $\Delta\theta$ as shown.

where T_{f_θ} denotes the figure–ground transformations.

Another property which will be useful in describing the composition of generalized Hough transforms is the change of reference point. If we want to choose a new reference point y' such that $\mathbf{y}-\mathbf{y}' = \mathbf{r}$ then the modification to the R-table is given by $R(\phi) + \mathbf{r}$, i.e. $\mathbf{r}$ is added to each vector in the table.

4.6 Using pairs of edges

We can also entertain the idea of using pairs of edge pixels to reduce the effort in parameter space. Using the R-table and the properties of the previous section, each edge pixel defines a surface in the four-dimensional accumulator space of $\mathbf{a} = (\mathbf{y}, s, \theta)$. Two edge pixels at different orientations describe the same surface rotated by the same amount with respect to θ. Points where these two surfaces intersect (if any) correspond to possible parameters $\mathbf{a}$ for the shape. Thus in a similar manner to Section 3.1, it is theoretically possible to use the two points in image space to reduce the locus in parameter space to a single point. However, the difficulties of finding the intersection points of the two surfaces in parameter space will make this approach unfeasible for most cases.

4.7 The Hough transform for composite shapes

Now suppose we have a composite shape S which has two subparts S_1 and S_2. This shape can be detected by using the R-tables for S_1 and S_2 in a remarkably simple fashion. If y, y_1, y_2 are the reference points for shapes S, S_1 and S_2 respectively, we can compute $\mathbf{r}_1 = \mathbf{y}-\mathbf{y}_1$ and $\mathbf{r}_2 = \mathbf{y}-\mathbf{y}_2$. Then the composite generalized Hough transform $R_S(\phi)$ is given by

$$R_S(\phi) = [R_{S_1}(\phi) + \mathbf{r}_1] \cup [R_{S_2}(\phi) + \mathbf{r}_2] \quad (20)$$

which means that for each index value ϕ, $\mathbf{r}_1$ is added to $R_{S_1}(\phi)$, $\mathbf{r}_2$ is added to $R_{S_2}(\phi)$, and the union of these sets

is stored in $R_S(\phi)$. Equation 20 is very important as it represents a way of composing transforms.

In a similar manner we can define shapes as the difference between tables with common entries, i.e.,

$$R_S = R_{S_1} \dot{-} R_{S_2} \quad (21)$$

means the shape S defined by S_1 with the common entries with S_2 deleted. The intersection operation is defined similarly. The primary use of the union operation is to detect shapes which are composites of simpler shapes. However, the difference operation also serves a useful function. Using it, R-tables which explicitly differentiate between two similar kinds of shapes can be constructed. An example would be differentiating between the washers and hexagons discussed earlier.

4.8 Building convolution templates

While equation (20) is one way of composing Hough transforms, it may not be the best way. This is because the choice of reference point can significantly affect the accuracy of the transform. Shapiro[15,16,17] has shown this, emphasizing analytic forms. This is also graphically shown in Fig. 10. As the reference point becomes distant from the shape, small angular errors in ϕ can produce large errors in the vectors $R(\phi)$.

One solution to this problem is to use the table for each subshape with its own best reference point and to smooth the resultant accumulator array with a composite smoothing template. Recall that for the case of a single shape and isotropic errors (Section 2.2), convolving the accumulator array in this fashion was equivalent to taking account of the errors during the incrementation.

Where $h_i(\mathbf{y}_i)$ denotes the smoothing template for reference point $\mathbf{y}_i$ of shape S_i the composite convolution template is given by

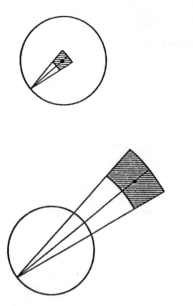

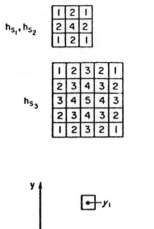

Fig. 10. Effects of changing reference point on errors.

$$H(y) = \sum_{i=1}^{N} h_i(y - y_i). \qquad (22)$$

So finally, we have the following algorithm for the detection of a shape S which is the composite of subparts $S_1 \ldots S_N$.

Generalized Hough algorithm for composite shapes. 1. For each edge point with direction ϕ and for each value of scale s and orientation θ, increment the corresponding points $x + r$ in A where r is in

$$R_s(\phi) = T_s\left\{ T_\theta\left[\bigcup_{k=1}^{N} R_{S_k}(\phi) \right] \right\}.$$

2. Maxima in $A_s = A*H$ correspond to possible instances of the shape S. Figure 11 shows a simple example of how templates are combined.

If there are n edge pixels and M points in the error point spread function template, then the number of additions in the incrementation procedure is M. Thus this method might at first seem superior to the convolution method, which requires approximately n^2M additions and multiplications where $M < n^2$, the total number of pixels. However, the following heuristic is available for the convolution since A is typicallly very sparse. Compute

$$A_s(a) \quad \text{only if} \quad A(a) > 0. \qquad (23)$$

This in practice is very effective, although it may introduce errors if the appropriate index has a zero value and is surrounded by high values.

5. INCREMENTATION STRATEGIES

If we use the strategy of incrementing the accumulator array by unity, then the contents of the accumulator array are approximately proportional to the perimeter of the shape that is detectable in the image.

Fig. 11. Example of composite smoothing template construction. (a) Convolution templates for shapes S_1, S_2, S_3. (b) Relationships between reference points y_1, y_2, and y_3 in composite shape S. (c) Combined smoothing template H as a function of h_1, h_2, and h_3 and y_1, y_2, and y_3.

This strategy is biased towards finding shapes where a large portion of the perimeter is detectable. Several different incrementation strategies are available, depending on the different quality of image data. If shorter, very prominent parts of the perimeter are detected, as might be the case in partially occluded objects, then an alternative strategy of incrementing by the gradient modulus value might be more successful, i.e.,

$$A(a): = A(a) + g(x). \qquad (24)$$

Of course the two strategies can be combined, e.g.,

$$A(a): = A(a) + g(x) + c \qquad (25)$$

where c is a constant.

Another possibility is the use of local curvature information in the incrementation function. Using this strategy, neighboring edge pixels are examined to calculate approximate curvature, K. This requires a more complicated operator than the edge operators we have considered, and complicates the table. Now along with each value of r the corresponding values of curvature must be stored. Then the incrementation

191

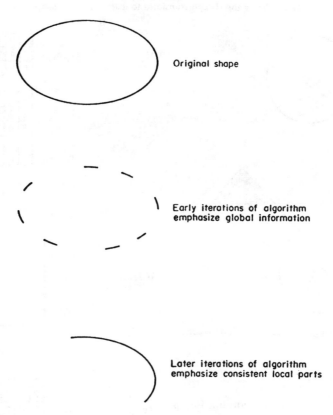

Original shape

Early iterations of algorithm
emphasize global information

Later iterations of algorithm
emphasize consistent local parts

Fig. 12. Dynamic Hough transform.

weights 'informative' high local curvature edge pixels as follows:

$$A(\mathbf{a}) := A(\mathbf{a}) + K. \qquad (26)$$

5.1 Weighting locally consistent information

Under certain circumstances we may want to weight local information that is consistent. For example, in searching for the boundary of that object, a connected set of edges conforming to the object may be more important than a set of unconnected edges. Figure 12 shows this example. Figure 12(a) might arise in situations with very noisy data. Figure 12(b) is an example where an object is occluded by another object. Wechsler and Sklansky,[6] in the analytic formulation, successfully used the related strategy of increasing the incrementation factor if there were also neighboring edge pixels with the same edge direction. However, we would like to measure local consistency in parameter space.

A simple strategy for handling this case is to explicitly record the reference points for each edge pixel during a first pass. Then on a second pass edge pixels can increment by more than unity if neighboring edge pixels are incrementing the same reference point.

A more complicated strategy is to search for connected curve segments in image space which have compatible parameters. Such an algorithm, based on dynamic programming, is described in Ballard and Sklansky.[14] The appropriate objective function for a curve segment would be

$$h(\mathbf{x}_1, \mathbf{x}_2, \ldots, \mathbf{x}_n) = \sum_{k=1}^{n} g(\mathbf{x}_k) + \sum_{k=1}^{n-1} q(\mathbf{x}_k, \mathbf{x}_{k+1}) \qquad (27)$$

where

$$g(\mathbf{x}_k) = \text{the gradient magnitude} \qquad (28)$$

and

$$q(\mathbf{x}_k, \mathbf{x}_{k+1}) = 0 \text{ if } |\phi(\mathbf{x}_\mu) - \phi(\mathbf{x}_{k-1})|_{\text{mod}\,\pi} \text{ is} \\ \text{small and } -\infty \text{ otherwise} \qquad (29)$$

In the dynamic programming algorithm, at each iteration step we can build longer compatible curves from all the edge points. Thus the incrementation function for a point x would represent the longest compatible curve from that point. (If a longer curve cannot be built at any iteration, we can easily find this out.)

In a parallel implementation of this algorithm the contents of the accumulator array could be made to vary dynamically. Initially the contents would reflect global information, but with successive iterations the contents would ·be weighted in favor of consistent, local information.

5.2 More complex strategies

When searching for a composite object, different parts may have different importance. This is readily accommodated by associating a weight w_i with each table R_{S_i} so that each entry in R_{S_i} increments by a factor w_i instead of unity.

The composite object may be searched for in a sequential manner. Applying the table sequentially could greatly improve the efficiency of the computations by limiting areas for subsequent suitable incrementations. Furthermore, standard methods[21,22] could be used to stop the process once the shape had been located to the desired confidence level.

Even more complex strategies are possible wherein the process is integrated into a larger system. Here contextual information can be used to relegate all the previous operations including (a) building composite templates, (b) choosing weights, (c) choosing application sequences, and (d) adjusting weights in new contexts.

6. CONCLUSIONS

We have described a method for detecting instances of a shape S in an image which is a generalization of the Hough transform. This transform is a mapping from edge space to accumulator space such that instances of S produce local maxima in accumulator space. This mapping is conveniently described as a table of edge-orientation reference-point correspondence termed an R-table. This method has the following properties.

1. Scale changes, rotations, figure–ground reversals, and reference point translation of S can be accounted for by straightforward modifications to the R-table.

2. Given the boundary of the shape, its R-table can be easily constructed and requires a number of operations proportional to the number of boundary points.

3. Shapes are stored as canonical forms; instances of shapes are detected by knowing the transformation from the canonical form to the instance. If this transformation is not known then all plausible transformations must be tried.

4. If a shape S is viewed as a composite of several subparts $S_1 \ldots S_n$ then the generalized Hough transform R-table for S can be simply constructed by combining the R-tables for $S_1 \ldots S_n$.

5. A composite shape S may be efficiently detected in a sequential manner by adding the R-tables for the subparts S_i incrementally to the detection algorithm until a desired confidence level is reached.

6. The accumulator table values can be weighted in terms of locally consistent information.

7. The importance of a subshape S_i may be regulated by associating a weight w_i with the R-table.

8. Last but not least, the generalized Hough transform is a parallel algorithm.

Future work will be directed towards characterizing the computational efficiency of the algorithm and exploring its feasibility as a model of biological perception.

Acknowledgements – Portions of this paper benefitted substantially from discussions with Ken Sloan and Jerry Feldman. Special thanks go to R. Peet and P. Meeker for typing this manuscript. The work herein was supported by National Institutes of Health grant R23-HL21253-02.

REFERENCES

1. R. O. Duda and P. E. Hart, Use of the Hough transform to detect lines and curves in pictures, *Communs Ass. comput. Mach.* **15**, 11–15 (1975).
2. P. V. C. Hough, Method and means for recognizing complex patterns, U.S. Patent 3069654 (1962).
3. P. M. Merlin and D. J. Farber, A parallel mechanism for detecting curves in pictures, *IEEE Trans. Comput.* **C24**, 96–98 (1975).
4. F. O'Gorman and M. B. Clowes, Finding picture edges through collinearity of feature points, Proc. 3rd Int. Joint Conf. Artificial Intelligence, pp. 543–555 (1973).
5. C. Kimme, D. H. Ballard and J. Sklansky, Finding circles by an array of accumulators, *Communs Ass. comput. Mach.* **18**, 120–122 (1975).
6. H. Wechsler and J. Sklansky, Automatic detection of ribs in chest radiographs, *Pattern Recognition* **9**, 21–30 (1977).
7. S. A. Dudani and A. L. Luk, Locating straight-line edge segments on outdoor scenes, Proc. IEEE Computer Society on Pattern Recognition and Image Processing, Rensselaer Polytechnic Institute (1977).
8. C. L. Fennema and W. B. Thompson, Velocity determination in scenes containing several moving objects, Technical Report, Central Research Laboratory, Minnesota Mining and Manufacturing Co. St. Paul (1977).
9. J. R. Kender, Shape from texture: a brief overview and a new aggregation transform, Proc., DARPA Image Understanding Workshop, pp. 79–84. Pittsburgh, November (1978).
10. F. Attneave, Some informational aspects of visual perception, *Psychol. Rev.* **61**, 183–193 (1954).
11. D. Marr, Analyzing natural images: a computational theory of texture vision, MIT-AI-Technical Report 334, June (1975).
12. J. M. S. Prewitt, Object enhancement and extraction, *Picture Processing and Psychopictorics*, B. S. Lipkin and A. Rosenfeld, eds. Academic Press, New York (1970).
13. M. Hueckel, A local visual operator which recognizes edges and lines, *J. Ass. comput. Mach.* **20**, 634–646 (1973).
14. D. H. Ballard and J. Sklansky, A ladder-structured decision tree for recognizing tumors in chest radiographs, *IEEE Trans. Comput.* **C25**, 503–513 (1976).
15. S. D. Shapiro, Properties of transforms for the detection of curves in noisy pictures, *Comput. Graphics Image Process.* **8**, 219–236 (1978).
16. S. D. Shapiro, Feature space transforms for curve detection, *Pattern Recognition* **10**, 129–143 (1978).
17. S. D. Shapiro, Generalization of the Hough transform for curve detection in noisy digital images, *Proc. 4th Int. Joint Conf. Pattern Recognition*, pp. 710–714. Kyoto, Japan, November (1978).
18. S. D. Shapiro, Transformation for the computer detection of curves in noisy pictures, *Comput. Graphics Image Process.* **4**, 328–338 (1975).
19. S. Tsuji and F. Matsumoto, Detection of elliptic and linear edges by searching two parameter spaces, Proc. 5th Int. Joint Conf. Artificial Intelligence, Vol. 2, pp. 700–705. Cambridge, MA, August (1977).
20. J. Sklansky, On the Hough technique for curve detection, *IEEE Trans. Comput.*, **C27**, 923–926 (1978).
21. K. S. Fu, *Sequential Methods in Pattern Recognition and Machine Learning*. Academic Press, New York (1968).
22. R. Bolles, Verification vision with a programmable assembly system, Stanford AI Memo, AIM-275, December (1975).

APPENDIX. ANALYTIC HOUGH FOR PAIRS OF EDGE POINTS

To develop an explicit version of the Hough algorithm for ellipses using pairs of edge points, we consider the string-tied-at-two-ends parameterization of an ellipse:

D. H. BALLARD

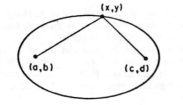

Fig. A1. String-tied-at-both-ends parameterization of an ellipse.

$$(x-a)^2 + (y-b)^2 + (x-c)^2 + (y-d)^2 = l^2$$

where (a,b) and (c,d) are the ends and l is the length of the string, as shown in Fig. A1. Now if we have two edge points (x_1, y_1) and (x_2, y_2) with gradients φ_1 and φ_2, the following equations result:

$$(x_1-a)^2 + (y_1-b)^2 + (x_1-c)^2 + (y_1-d)^2 = l^2 \quad \text{(A1)}$$

$$(x_1-a) + (y_1-b)\varphi_1 + (x_1-c) + (y_1-d)\varphi_1 = 0 \quad \text{(A2)}$$

$$(x_2-a)^2 + (y_2-b)^2 + (x_2-c)^2 + (y_2-d)^2 = l^2 \quad \text{(A3)}$$

$$(x_2-a) + (y_2-b)\varphi_2 + (x_2-c) + (y_2-d)\varphi_2 = 0 \quad \text{(A4)}$$

where in terms of the gradient direction

$$\varphi = \tan\left(\phi - \frac{\pi}{2}\right) = \frac{dy}{dx}.$$

From (A2):

$$a_1 = \varphi_1[(y_1-b) + (y_1-d)] + 2x_1 - c \cdot$$

Substituting in (4):

$$x_2 - \varphi_1[(y_1-b) + (y_1-d)] - 2x_1 + (y_2-b)\varphi_2 + (y_2-d)\varphi_2 + x_2 = 0.$$

Rearranging terms:

$$2x_2 - 2x_1 - 2\varphi_1 y_2 + (\varphi_1-\varphi_2)b + (\varphi_1-\varphi_2)d = 0.$$

Now where:

$$S = \varphi_1 - \varphi_2$$

and

$$K = 2(x_2-x_1 - \varphi_1 y_1 + \varphi_2 y_2)$$

and

$$t = \frac{K}{S}$$

we have

$$b = t - d. \quad \text{(A5)}$$

Now we substitute for b in (2)

$$x_1 - a = -(x_1-c) - \varphi_1(2y_1 - t)$$

so that we have

$$c = \eta - a \quad \text{(A6)}$$

where $n = \varphi_1(2y - t)$

$$(x_1-a)^2 + [y_1-(t-d)]^2 + [x_1 - (\eta-a)]^2 + (y_1-d)^2 = l^2 \quad \text{(A7)}$$

$$(x_2-a)^2 + [y_2-(t-d)]^2 + [x_2 - (\eta-a)]^2 + (y-d)^2 = l^2 \quad \text{(A8)}$$

Thus our strategy for using two edge points is as follows:

Step 1: choose a.
Step 2: solve equations (5) and (6), a quadratic in d, for d.
Step 3: solve equation (2) for b and equation 3 for c.
Step 4: solve equation (1) for l.

Thus the vector $\mathbf{a} = (a,b,c,d,l)$ has been determined for a pair of edge pixels and can be used to increment the accumulator array.

About the Author—DANA H. BALLARD was born in Holyoke, MA, on October 15, 1946. He received the B.Sc. degree in aeronautics and astronautics from the Massachusetts Institute of Technology, Cambridge, in 1967. He received the M.S.E. degree in information and control engineering from the University of Michigan, Ann Arbor, in 1970 and the Ph.D. degree in information engineering from the University of California, Irvine, in 1974.

From 1968 to 1971 he was a Systems Analyst for Autonetics, Anaheim, Calif. Since 1971 he has been active in computer vision research. During the academic year 1974–1975, he was a Visiting Professor at the Laboratorio Biomediche Technologie, Rome. Italy. He is presently an Assistant Professor of Computer Science and Radiology at the University of Rochester, Rochester, N.Y. His current interests are in artificial intelligence and computer vision, particularly control strategies and geometric models, and their applications to biomedical image processing.

Robert M. Haralick
Layne T. Watson
Thomas J. Laffey

Departments of Computer Science and
Electrical Engineering
Virginia Polytechnic Institute and State University
Blacksburg, VA 24061

The Topographic Primal Sketch

Reprinted from *International Journal of Robotics Research*, Volume 2, Number 1, 1983, pages 50-72, "The Topographic Primal Sketch" by R.M. Haralick, T.J. Laffey, and L.T. Watson by permission of The MIT Press, Cambridge, Massachusetts.

Abstract

A complete mathematical treatment is given for describing the topographic primal sketch of the underlying gray tone intensity surface of a digital image. Each picture element is independently classified and assigned a unique descriptive label, invariant under monotonically increasing gray tone transformations from the set (peak, pit, ridge, ravine, saddle, flat, and hillside), with hillside having subcategories (inflection point, slope, convex hill, concave hill, and saddle hill). The topographic classification is based on the first and second directional derivatives of the estimated image-intensity surface. A local, facet model, two-dimensional, cubic polynomial fit is done to estimate the image-intensity surface. Zero-crossings of the first directional derivative are identified as locations of interest in the image.

1. Introduction

Representing the fundamental structure of a digital image in a rich and robust way is a primary problem encountered in any general robotics computer-vision system that has to "understand" an image. The richness is needed so that shading, highlighting, and shadow information, which are usually present in real manufacturing assembly line situations, are encoded. Richness permits unambiguous object matching to be accomplished. Robustness is needed so that the representation is invariant with respect to monotonically increasing gray tone transformations.

This research has been supported by National Science Foundation grant MCS-8102872.

The International Journal of Robotics Research
Vol. 2, No. 1, Spring 1983
0278-3649/83/010050-23 $05.00/0

Current representations involving edges or the primal sketch as described by Marr (1976; 1980) are impoverished in the sense that they are insufficient for unambiguous matching. They also do not have the required invariance. Basic research is needed to (1) define an appropriate representation, (2) develop a theory that establishes its relationship to properties that three-dimensional objects manifest on the image, and (3) prove its utility in practice. Until this is done, computer-vision research must inevitably be more ad hoc sophistication than science.

The basis of the topographic primal sketch consists of the classification and grouping of the underlying image-intensity surface patches according to the categories defined by monotonic, gray tone, invariant functions of directional derivatives. Examples of such categories are peak, pit, ridge, ravine, saddle, flat, and hillside. From this initial classification, we can group categories to obtain a rich, hierarchical, and structurally complete representation of the fundamental image structure. We call this representation the *topographic primal sketch*.

Why do we believe that this topographic primal sketch can be the basis for computer vision? We believe it because the light-intensity variations on an image are caused by an object's surface orientation, its reflectance, and characteristics of its lighting source. If any of the three-dimensional intrinsic surface characteristics are to be detected, they will be detected owing to the nature of light-intensity variations. Thus, the first step is to discover a robust representation that can encode the nature of these light-intensity variations, a representation that does not change with strength of lighting or with gain settings on the sensing camera. The topographic classification does just that. The basic research issue is to define a set of categories sufficiently complete to form groupings and structures that have strong

The International Journal of Robotics Research

relationships to the reflectances, surface orientations, and surface positions of the three-dimensional objects viewed in the image.

1.1. THE INVARIANCE REQUIREMENT

A digital image can be obtained with a variety of sensing-camera gain settings. It can be visually enhanced by an appropriate adjustment of the camera's dynamic range. The gain setting or the enhancing, point operator changes the image by some monotonically increasing function that is not necessarily linear. For example, nonlinear, enhancing, point operators of this type include histogram normalization and equal probability quantization.

In visual perception, exactly the same visual interpretation and understanding of a pictured scene occurs whether the camera's gain setting is low or high and whether the image is enhanced or unenhanced. The only difference is that the enhanced image has more contrast, is nicer to look at, and is understood more quickly by the human visual system.

This fact is important because it suggests that many of the current-low-level computer-vision techniques, which are based on edges, cannot ever hope to have the robustness associated with human visual perception. They cannot have the robustness, because they are inherently incapable of invariance under monotonic transformations. For example, edges based on zero-crossings of second derivatives will change in position as the monotonic gray tone transformation changes because convexity of a gray tone intensity surface is not preserved under such transformations. However, the topographic categories peak, pit, ridge, valley, saddle, flat, and hillside do have the required invariance.

1.2. BACKGROUND

Marr (1976) argues that the first level of visual processing is the computation of a rich description of gray level changes present in an image, and that all subsequent computations are done in terms of this description, which he calls the *primal sketch*. Gray level changes are usually associated with edges, and

Marr's primal sketch has, for each area of gray level change, a description that includes type, position, orientation, and fuzziness of edge. Marr (1980) illustrates that from this information it is sometimes possible to reconstruct the image to a reasonable degree. Unfortunately, as mentioned earlier, edge is not invariant with respect to monotonic image transformations; besides, it is not a rich enough structure. For example, difficulty has been experienced in using edges to accomplish unambiguous stereo matching.

The topographic primal sketch we are discussing as a basis for a representation has the required richness and invariance properties and is very much in the spirit of Marr's primal sketch and the thinking behind Ehrich's relational trees (Ehrich and Foith 1978). Instead of concentrating on gray level changes as edges as Marr does, or on one-dimensional extrema as Ehrich and Foith, we concentrate on all types of two-dimensional gray level variations. We consider each area on an image to be a spatial distribution of gray levels that constitutes a surface or facet of gray tone intensities having a specific surface shape. It is likely that, if we could describe the shape of the gray tone intensity surface for each pixel, then by assembling all the shape fragments we could reconstruct, in a relative way, the entire surface of the image's gray tone intensity values. The shapes that we already know about that have the invariance property are peak, pit, ridge, ravine, saddle, flat, and hillside, with hillside having noninvariant subcategories of slope, inflection, saddle hillside, convex hillside, and concave hillside.

Knowing that a pixel's surface has the shape of a peak does not tell us precisely where in the pixel the peak occurs; nor does it tell us the height of the peak or the magnitude of the slope around the peak. The topographic labeling, however, does satisfy Marr's (1976) primal sketch requirement in that it contains a symbolic description of the gray tone intensity changes. Furthermore, upon computing and binding to each topographic label numerical descriptors such as gradient magnitude and direction, directions of the extrema of the second directional derivative along with their values, a reasonable absolute description of each surface shape can be obtained.

Haralick, Watson, and Laffey

1.3. FACET MODEL

The *facet model* states that all processing of digital image data has its final authoritative interpretation relative to what the processing does to the underlying gray tone intensity surface. The digital image's pixel values are noisy sampled observations of the underlying surface. Thus, in order to do any processing, we at least have to estimate at each pixel position what this underlying surface is. This requires a model that describes what the general form of the surface would be in the neighborhood of any pixel if there were no noise. To estimate the surface from the neighborhood around a pixel then amounts to estimating the free parameters of the general form. It is important to note that if a different general form is assumed, then a different estimate of the surface is produced. Thus the assumption of a particular general form is necessary and has consequences.

The general form we use is a bivariate cubic. We assume that the neighborhood around each pixel is suitably fit by a bivariate cubic (Haralick 1981; 1982). Having estimated this surface around each pixel, the first and second directional derivatives are easily computed by analytic means. The topographic classification of the surface facet is based totally on the first and second directional derivatives. We classify each surface point as peak, pit, ridge, ravine, saddle, flat, or hillside, with hillside being broken down further into the subcategories inflection point, convex hill, concave hill, saddle hill, and slope. Our set of topographic labels is complete in the sense that every combination of values of the first and second directional derivative is uniquely assigned to one of the classes.

1.4. PREVIOUS WORK

Detection of topographic structures in a digital image is not a new idea. There has been a wide variety of techniques described to detect pits, peaks, ridges, ravines, and the like.

Peuker and Johnston (1972) characterize the surface shape by the sequence of positive and negative differences as successive surrounding points are compared to the central point. Peuker and Douglas (1975) describe several variations of this method for detecting one of the shapes from the set (pit, peak, pass, ridge, ravine, break, slope, flat). They start with the most frequent feature (slope) and proceed to the less frequent, thus making it an order-dependent algorithm.

Johnston and Rosenfeld (1975) attempt to find peaks by finding all points P such that no points in an *n*-by-*n* neighborhood surrounding P have greater elevation than P. Pits are found in an analogous manner. To find ridges, they identify points that are either east-west or north-south elevation maxima. This is done using a "smoothed" array in which each point is given the highest elevation in a 2×2 square containing it. East-west and north-south maxima are also found on this array. Ravines are found in a similar manner.

Paton (1975) uses a six-term quadratic expansion in Legendre polynomials fitted to a small disk around each pixel. The most significant coefficients of the second-order polynomial yield a descriptive label chosen from the set (constant, ridge, valley, peak, bowl, saddle, ambiguous). He uses the continuous least-squares-fit formulation in setting up the surface-fit equations as opposed to the discrete least-squares fit used in the facet model. The continuous fit is a more expensive computation than the discrete fit and results in a steplike approximation.

Grender's (1976) algorithm compares the gray level elevation of a central point with surrounding elevations at a given distance around the perimeter of a circular window; the radius of the window may be increased in successive passes through the image. His topographic labeling set consists of slope, ridge, valley, knob, sink, saddle.

Toriwaki and Fukumara (1978) take a totally different approach from all the others. They use two local features of gray level pictures, connectivity number, and coefficient of curvature for classification of the pixel into peak, pit, ridge, ravine, hillside, pass. They then describe how to extract structural information from the image once the labelings have been made. This structural information consists of ridge-lines, ravine-lines, and the like.

Hsu, Mundy, and Beaudet (1978) use a quadratic surface approximation at every point on the image

The International Journal of Robotics Research

surface. The principal axes of the quadratic approximation are used as directions in which to segment the image. Lines emanating from the center pixel in these directions thus provide natural boundaries of patches approximating the surface. The authors then selectively generate the principal axes from some critical points distributed over an image and interconnect them into a network to get an approximation of the image data. In this network, which they call the *web representation,* the axes divide the image into regions and show important features such as edges and peaks. They are then able to extract a set of primitive features from the nodes of the network by mask matching. Global features, such as ridge-lines, are obtained by state transition rules.

Lee and Fu (1981) define a set of 3×3 templates that they convolve over the image to give each class except plain a *figure of merit.* Their set of labels includes none, plain, slope, ridge, valley, foot, shoulder. Thresholds are used to determine into which class the pixel will fall. In their scheme, a pixel may satisfy the definition of zero, one, or more than one class. Ambiguity is resolved by choosing the class with the highest figure of merit.

1.5. A MATHEMATICAL APPROACH

From the previous discussion, one can see that a wide variety of methods and labels has been proposed to describe the topographic structure in a digital image. Some of the methods require multiple passes through the image, while others may give ambiguous labels to a pixel. Many of the methods are heuristic in nature. The Hsu, Mundy, and Beudet (1978) approach is the most similar to the one discussed here.

Our classification approach is based on the estimation of the first- and second-order directional derivatives. Thus, we regard the digital-picture function as a sampling of the underlying function f, where some kind of random noise is added to the true function values. To estimate the first and second partials, we must assume some kind of parametric form for the underlying function f. The classifier must use the sampled brightness values of the digital-picture function to estimate the parameters

and then make decisions regarding the locations of relative extrema of partial derivatives based on the estimated values of the parameters.

In Section 2, we will discuss the mathematical properties of the topographic structures in terms of the directional derivatives in the continuous surface domain. Because a digital image is a sampled surface and each pixel has an area associated with it, characteristic topographic structures may occur anywhere within a pixel's area. Thus, the implementation of the mathematical topographic definitions is not entirely trivial.

In Section 3 we will discuss the implementation of the classification scheme on a digital image. To identify categories that are local one-dimensional extrema, such as peak, pit, ridge, ravine, and saddle, we search inside the pixel's area for a zero-crossing of the first directional derivative. The directions in which we seek the zero-crossing are along the lines of extreme curvature.

In Section 4, we will discuss the local cubic estimation scheme. In Section 5, we will summarize the algorithm for topographic classification using the local facet model. In Section 6, we will show the results of the classifier on several test images.

2. The Mathematical Classification of Topographic Structures

In this section, we formulate our notion of topographic structures on continuous surfaces and show their invariance under monotonically increasing gray tone transformations. In order to understand the mathematical properties used to define our topographic structures, one must understand the idea of the *directional derivative* discussed in most advanced calculus books. For completeness, we first give the definition of the directional derivative, then the defitions of the topographic labels. Finally, we show the invariance under monotonically increasing gray tone transformations.

2.1. THE DIRECTIONAL DERIVATIVE

In two dimensions, the rate of change of a function f depends on direction. We denote the directional derivative of f at the point (r, c) in the direction β by $f'_\beta(r, c)$. It is defined as

$$f'_\beta(r, c) = \lim_{h \to 0} \frac{f(r + h^* \sin \beta, c + h^* \cos \beta) - f(r, c)}{h}.$$

The direction angle β is the clockwise angle from the column axis. It follows directly from this definition that

$$f'_\beta(r, c) = \frac{\partial f}{\partial r}(r, c) * \sin \beta + \frac{\partial f}{\partial c}(r, c) * \cos \beta.$$

We denote the second derivative of f at the point (r, c) in the direction β by $f''_\beta(r, c)$, and it follows that

$$f''_\beta = \frac{\partial^2 f}{\partial r^2} * \sin^2 \beta + 2 * \frac{\partial^2 f}{\partial r \, \partial c} * \sin \beta * \cos \beta + \frac{\partial^2 f}{\partial c^2} * \cos^2 \beta.$$

The *gradient* of f is a vector whose magnitude,

$$\left(\left(\frac{\partial f}{\partial r} \right)^2 + \left(\frac{\partial f}{\partial c} \right)^2 \right)^{1/2}$$

at a given point (r, c) is the maximum rate of change of f at that point, and whose direction,

$$\tan^{-1} \left(\frac{\frac{\partial f}{\partial r}}{\frac{\partial f}{\partial c}} \right)$$

is the direction in which the surface has the greatest rate of change.

2.2. THE MATHEMATICAL PROPERTIES

We will use the following notation to describe the mathematical properties of our various topographic categories for continuous surfaces. Let

∇f = gradient vector of a function f;
$\|\nabla f\|$ = gradient magnitude;
$\omega^{(1)}$ = unit vector in direction in which second directional derivative has greatest magnitude;
$\omega^{(2)}$ = unit vector orthogonal to $\omega^{(1)}$;
λ_1 = value of second directional derivative in the direction of $\omega^{(1)}$;
λ_2 = value of second directional derivative in the direction of $\omega^{(2)}$;
$\nabla f \cdot \omega^{(1)}$ = value of first directional derivative in the direction of $\omega^{(1)}$; and
$\nabla f \cdot \omega^{(2)}$ = value of first directional derivative in the direction of $\omega^{(2)}$.

Without loss of generality, we assume $|\lambda_1| > = |\lambda_2|$.

Each type of topographic structure in our classification scheme is defined in terms of the above quantities. In order to calculate these values, the first- and second-order partials with respect to r and c need to be approximated. These five partials are as follows:

$$\partial f / \partial r, \ \partial f / \partial c, \ \partial^2 f / \partial r^2, \ \partial^2 f / \partial c^2, \ \partial^2 f / \partial r \, \partial c.$$

The gradient vector is simply $(\partial f / \partial r, \partial f / \partial c)$. The second directional derivatives may be calculated by forming the *Hessian* where the Hessian is a 2×2 matrix defined as

$$H = \begin{vmatrix} \partial^2 f / \partial r^2 & \partial^2 f / \partial r \, \partial c \\ \partial^2 f / \partial c \, \partial r & \partial^2 f / \partial c^2 \end{vmatrix}.$$

Hessian matrices are used extensively in nonlinear programming. Only three parameters are required to determine the Hessian matrix H, since the order of differentiation of the cross partials may be interchanged. That is,

$$\partial^2 f / \partial r \, \partial c = \partial^2 f / \partial c \, \partial r.$$

The eigenvalues of the Hessian are the values of the extrema of the second directional derivative, and their associated eigenvectors are the directions in which the second directional derivative is extremized. This can easily be seen by rewriting f''_β as the quadratic form

$$f''_\beta = (\sin \beta \ \cos \beta) * H * \begin{vmatrix} \sin \beta \\ \cos \beta \end{vmatrix}$$

Fig. 1. Right circular cone.

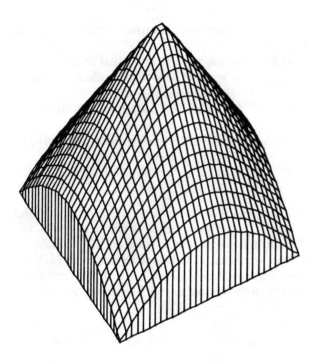

Thus

$$H\omega^{(1)} = \lambda_1\omega^{(1)}, \text{ and } H\omega^{(2)} = \lambda_2\omega^{(2)}.$$

Furthermore, the two directions represented by the eigenvectors are orthogonal to one another. Since H is a 2×2 symmetric matrix, calculation of the eigenvalues and eigenvectors can be done efficiently and accurately using the method of Rutishauser (1971). We may obtain the values of the first directional derivative by simply taking the dot product of the gradient with the appropriate eigenvector:

$$\nabla f \cdot \omega^{(1)}$$
$$\nabla f \cdot \omega^{(2)}.$$

There is a direct relationship between the eigenvalues λ_1 and λ_2 and curvature in the directions $\omega^{(1)}$ and $\omega^{(2)}$: When the first directional derivative $\nabla f \cdot \omega^{(1)} = 0$, then $\lambda_1/(1 + (\nabla f \cdot \nabla f))^{1/2}$ is the curvature in the direction $\omega^{(1)}$, $i = 1$ or 2.

Having the gradient magnitude and direction and the eigenvalues and eigenvectors of the Hessian, we can describe the topographic classification scheme.

2.2.1. *Peak*

A peak (knob) occurs where there is a local maxima in all directions. In other words, we are on a peak if, no matter what direction we look in, we see no point that is as high as the one we are on (Fig. 1). The curvature is downward in all directions. At a peak the gradient is zero, and the second directional derectional derivative is negative in all directions. To test whether the second directional derivative is negative in all directions, we just have to examine the value of the second directional derivative in the directions that make it smallest and largest. A point is therefore classified as a peak if it satisfies the following conditions:

$$\|\nabla f\| = 0, \lambda_1 < 0, \lambda_2 < 0.$$

2.2.2. *Pit*

A pit (sink, bowl) is identical to a peak except that it is a local minima in all directions rather than a local maxima. At a pit the gradient is zero, and the second directional derivative is positive in all directions. A point is classified as a pit if it satisfies the following conditions:

$$\|\nabla f\| = 0, \lambda_1 > 0, \lambda_2 > 0.$$

2.2.3. *Ridge*

A ridge occurs on a ridge-line, a curve consisting of a series of ridge points. As we walk along the ridge-line, the points to the right and left of us are lower than the ones we are on. Furthermore, the ridge-line may be flat, slope upward, slope downward, curve upward, or curve downward. A ridge occurs where there is a local maximum in one direction, as illustrated in Fig. 2. Therefore, it must have negative second-directional derivative in the direction across the ridge and also a zero first-directional derivative in that same direction. The direction in which the local maximum occurs may correspond to either of the directions in which the curvature is "extremized," since the ridge itself may be curved. For nonflat ridges, this leads to the first two cases below for ridge characterization. If the ridge is flat,

Haralick, Watson, and Laffey

Fig. 2. Saddle surface.

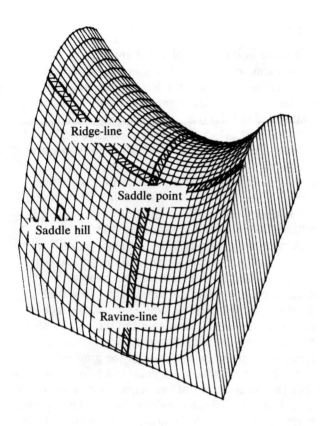

A geometric way of thinking about the definition for ridge is to realize that the condition $\nabla f \cdot \omega^{(1)} = 0$ means that the gradient direction (which is defined for nonzero gradients) is orthogonal to the direction $\omega^{(1)}$ of extremized curvature.

2.2.4. Ravine

A ravine (valley) is identical to a ridge except that it is a local minimum (rather than maximum) in one direction. As we walk along the ravine-line, the points to the right and left of us are higher than the one we are on (see Fig. 2). A point is classified as a ravine if it satisfies any one of the following three sets of conditions:

$$\|\nabla f\| \neq 0, \; \lambda_1 > 0, \; \nabla f \cdot \omega^{(1)} = 0$$

or

$$\|\nabla f\| \neq 0, \; \lambda_2 > 0, \; \nabla f \cdot \omega^{(2)} = 0$$

or

$$\|\nabla f\| = 0, \; \lambda_1 > 0, \; \lambda_2 = 0.$$

2.2.5. Saddle

A saddle occurs where there is a local maximum in one direction and a local minimum in a perpendicular direction, as illustrated in Fig. 2. A saddle must therefore have positive curvature in one direction and negative curvature in a perpendicular direction. At a saddle, the gradient magnitude must be zero and the extrema of the second directional derivative must have opposite signs. A point is classified as a saddle if it satisfies the following conditions:

$$\|\nabla f\| = 0, \; \lambda_1 * \lambda_2 < 0.$$

2.2.6. Flat

A flat (plain) is a simple, horizontal surface, as illustrated in Fig. 3. It, therefore, must have zero gradient and no curvature. A point is classified as a flat if it satisfies the following conditions:

$$\|\nabla f\| = 0, \; \lambda_1 = 0, \; \lambda_2 = 0.$$

then the ridge-line is horizontal and the gradient is zero along it. This corresponds to the third case. The defining characteristic is that the second directional derivative in the direction of the ridge-line is zero, while the second directional derivative across the ridge-line is negative. A point is therefore classified as a ridge if it satisfies any one of the following three sets of conditions:

$$\|\nabla f\| \neq 0, \; \lambda_1 < 0, \; \nabla f \cdot \omega^{(1)} = 0$$

or

$$\|\nabla f\| \neq 0, \; \lambda_2 < 0, \; \nabla f \cdot \omega^{(2)} = 0$$

or

$$\|\nabla f\| = 0, \; \lambda_1 < 0, \; \lambda_2 = 0.$$

Fig. 3. Hillside.

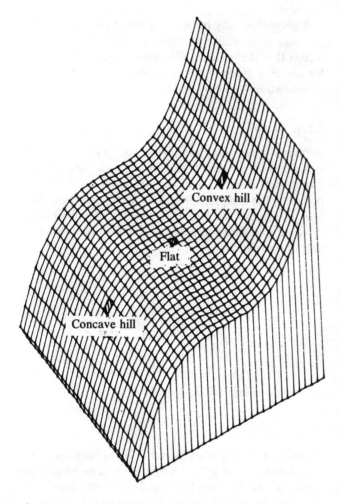

2.2.7. *Hillside*

A hillside point is anything not covered by the previous categories. It has a nonzero gradient and no strict extrema in the directions of maximum and minimum second directional derivative. If the hill is simply a tilted flat (i.e., has constant gradient), we call it a *slope*. If its curvature is positive (upward), we call it a *convex hill*. If its curvature is negative (downward), we call it a *concave hill*. If the curvature is up in one direction and down in a perpendicular direction, we call it a *saddle hill*. A saddle hill is illustrated in Fig. 2, and the slope, convex hill, and concave hill are illustrated in Fig. 3.

A point on a hillside is an *inflection point* if it has a zero-crossing of the second directional derivative taken in the direction of the gradient. The inflection-point class is the same as the *step edge* defined by Haralick (1982), who classifies a pixel as a step edge if there is some point in the pixel's area having a zero-crossing of the second directional derivative taken in the direction of the gradient.

To determine whether a point is a hillside, we just take the complement of the disjunction of the conditions given for all the previous classes. Thus if there is no curvature, then the gradient must be nonzero. If there is curvature, then the point must not be a relative extremum. Therefore, a point is classified as a hillside if all three sets of the following conditions are true ('→' represents the operation of logical implication):

$$\lambda_1 = \lambda_2 = 0 \rightarrow \|\nabla f\| \neq 0,$$

and

$$\lambda_1 \neq 0 \rightarrow \nabla f \cdot \omega^{(1)} \neq 0,$$

and

$$\lambda_2 \neq 0 \rightarrow \nabla f \cdot \omega^{(2)} \neq 0.$$

Rewritten as a disjunction of clauses rather than a conjunction of clauses, a point is classified as a hillside if any one of the following four sets of conditions are true:

$$\nabla f \cdot \omega^{(1)} \neq 0, \ \nabla f \cdot \omega^{(2)} \neq 0$$

Given that the above conditions are true, a flat may be further classified as a *foot* or *shoulder*. A foot occurs at that point where the flat just begins to turn up into a hill. At this point, the third directional derivative in the direction toward the hill will be nonzero, and the surface increases in this direction. The shoulder is an analogous case and occurs where the flat is ending and turning down into a hill. At this point, the maximum magnitude of the third directional derivative is nonzero, and the surface decreases in the direction toward the hill. If the third directional derivative is zero in all directions, then we are in a flat, not near a hill. Thus a flat may be further qualified as being a foot or shoulder, or not qualified at all.

or

$$\nabla f \cdot \omega^{(1)} \neq 0, \lambda_2 = 0$$

or

$$\nabla f \cdot \omega^{(2)} \neq 0, \lambda_1 = 0$$

or

$$\|\nabla f\| \neq 0, \lambda_1 = 0, \lambda_2 = 0.$$

We can differentiate between different classes of hillsides by the values of the second directional derivative. The distinction can be made as follows:

Slope   if $\lambda_1 = \lambda_2 = 0$
Convex   if $\lambda_1 > = \lambda_2 > = 0, \lambda_1 \neq 0$
Concave   if $\lambda_1 < = \lambda_2 < = 0, \lambda_1 \neq 0$
Saddle hill if $\lambda_1 * \lambda_2 < 0$

A slope, convex, concave, or saddle hill is classified as an inflection point if there is a zero-crossing of the second directional derivative in the direction of maximum first directional derivative (i.e., the gradient).

2.2.8. *Summary of the Topographic Categories*

A summary of the mathematical properties of our topographic structures on continuous surfaces can be found in Table 1. The table exhaustively defines the topographic classes by their gradient magnitude, second directional derivative extrema values, and the first directional derivatives taken in the directions which extremize second directional derivatives. Each entry in the table is either 0, +, −, or *. The 0 means not significantly different from zero; + means significantly different from zero on the positive side; − means significantly different from zero on the negative side, and * means it does not matter. The label "Cannot occur" means that it is impossible for the gradient to be nonzero and the first directional derivative to be zero in two orthogonal directions.

From the table, one can see that our classification scheme is complete. All possible combinations of first and second directional derivatives have a corresponding entry in the table. Each topographic category has a set of mathematical properties that uniquely determines it.

(Note: Special attention is required for the degenerate case $\lambda_1 = \lambda_2 \neq 0$, which implies that $\omega^{(1)}$ and $\omega^{(2)}$ can be *any* two orthogonal directions. In this case, there *always* exists an extreme direction ω which is orthogonal to ∇f, and thus the first directional derivative $\nabla f \cdot \omega$ is *always* zero in an extreme direction. To avoid spurious zero directional derivatives, we choose $\omega^{(1)}$ and $\omega^{(2)}$ such that $\nabla f \cdot \omega^{(1)} \neq 0$ and $\nabla f \cdot \omega^{(2)} \neq 0$, unless the gradient is zero.)

2.3. THE INVARIANCE OF THE TOPOGRAPHIC CATEGORIES

In this section, we show that the topographic labels (peak, pit, ridge, ravine, saddle, flat, and hillside), the gradient direction, and directions of second directional derivative extrema for peak, pit, ridge, ravine, and saddle are all invariant under monotoni-

Table 1. Mathematical Properties of Topographic Structures

$\|\nabla f\|$	λ_1	λ_2	$\nabla f \cdot \omega^{(1)}$	$\nabla f \cdot \omega^{(2)}$	Label
0	−	−	0	0	Peak
0	−	0	0	0	Ridge
0	−	+	0	0	Saddle
0	0	0	0	0	Flat
0	+	−	0	0	Saddle
0	+	0	0	0	Ravine
0	+	+	0	0	Pit
+	−	−	−, +	−, +	Hillside
+	−	*	0	*	Ridge
+	*	−	*	0	Ridge
+	−	0	−, +	*	Hillside
+	−	+	−, +	−, +	Hillside
+	0	0	*	*	Hillside
+	+	−	−, +	−, +	Hillside
+	+	0	−, +	*	Hillside
+	+	*	0	*	Ravine
+	*	+	*	0	Ravine
+	+	+	−, +	−, +	Hillside
+	*	*	0	0	Cannot occur

cally increasing gray tone transformations. We take *monotonically increasing* to mean positive derivative everywhere.

Let the original underlying gray tone surface be $f(r, c)$. Let w be a monotonically increasing gray tone transformation, and let $g(r, c)$ denote the transformed image: $g(r, c) = w(f(r, c))$. It is directly derivable that

$$g'_\beta(r, c) = w'(f(r, c)) * f'_\beta(r, c),$$

from which we obtain that

$$g''_\beta(r, c) = w'(f(r, c)) * f''_\beta(r, c) + w''(f_\beta(r, c)) * f'_\beta(r, c)^2.$$

Let us fix a position (r, c). Since w is a monotonically increasing function, w' is positive. In particular, w' is not zero. Hence the direction β which maximizes g'_β also maximizes f'_β, thereby showing that the gradient directions are the same. The categories peak, pit, ridge, ravine, saddle, and flat all have in common the essential property that the first directional derivative is zero when taken in a direction that extremizes the second directional derivative. To see the invariance, let β be an extremizing direction of f''_β. Then for points (r, c) having a label (peak, pit, ridge, ravine, saddle, or flat), $f'_\beta(r, c) = 0$, and $\partial f''_\beta(r, c)/\partial \beta = 0$. Notice that

$$\frac{\partial g''_\beta}{\partial \beta} = w' * \frac{\partial}{\partial \beta} f''_\beta + 2 * w' * f'_\beta \frac{\partial f'_\beta}{\partial \beta} + (f'_\beta)^2 \frac{\partial w''}{\partial \beta}.$$

Hence for these points, $g'_\beta(r, c) = 0$, and

$$\partial g''_\beta(r, c)/\partial \beta = 0,$$

thereby showing that at these points the directions that extremize f''_β are precisely the directions that extremize g''_β, and that g''_β will always have the same sign as f''_β. A similar argument shows that if β extremizes g''_β and satisfies $g'_\beta = 0$, then β must also extremize f''_β and satisfy $f'_\beta = 0$. Therefore, any points in the original image with the labels peak, pit, ridge, saddle, or flat retain the same label in the transformed image and, conversely, any points in the transformed image will have the same label in the original image.

Any pixel with a label not in the set (peak, pit, ridge, ravine, saddle, and flat) must have a hillside label. Thus, a point labeled hillside must be transformed to a hillside-labeled point. However, the subcategories (inflection point, slope, convex hill, concave hill, and saddle hill) may change under the gray tone transformation.

2.4. Ridge and Ravine Continua

Although the definitions given for ridge and ravine are intuitively pleasing, they may lead to the unexpected consequence of having entire areas of a surface classified as all ridge or all ravine. To see how this can occur, observe that the eigenvalue $\lambda = \lambda(r, c)$ satisfies

$$\lambda(r, c) = \frac{1}{2} \left| \frac{\partial^2 f}{\partial r^2}(r, c) + \frac{\partial^2 f}{\partial c^2}(r, c) \right|$$
$$\pm \left| \left| \frac{\partial^2 f}{\partial r \, \partial c}(r, c) \right|^2 \right.$$
$$\left. + \left| \frac{1}{2} \left| \frac{\partial^2 f}{\partial r^2}(r, c) - \frac{\partial^2 f}{\partial c^2}(r, c) \right| \right|^2 \right|^{1/2}.$$

For there to be a ridge or ravine at a point (r, c), the corresponding eigenvector $\omega(r, c)$ must be perpendicular to the gradient direction. Therefore, $\nabla f \cdot \omega = 0$. If this equation holds for a point (r, c) and not all points in a small neighborhood about (r, c), there is a ridge or ravine in the commonly understood sense. However, if this equation holds for all points in a neighborhood about (r, c), then we have a ridge or ravine continuum by the criteria of Sections 2.2.3 and 2.2.4.

Unfortunately, there are "nonpathologic" surfaces having ridge or ravine continuums. Simple, radially symmetric examples include the inverted right circular cone defined by

$$f(r, c) = (r^2 + c^2)^{1/2},$$

the hemisphere defined by

$$f(r, c) = (k^2 - r^2 - c^2)^{1/2},$$

or, in fact, any function of the form $h(r^2 + c^2)$. In

Haralick, Watson, and Laffey

the case of the cone, the gradient is proportional to (r, c), and the unnormalized eigenvectors corresponding to eigenvalues

$$\lambda(r, c) = (r^2 + c^2)^{-1/2} \text{ and } 0$$

are $(-c, r)$ and (r, c) respectively. The eigenvector corresponding to the nonzero eigenvalue is orthogonal to the gradient direction. The entire surface of the inverted cone, except for the apex, is a ravine. Other, nonradially symmetric examples exist as well.

The identification of points that are really ridge or ravine continuums can be made as a postprocessing step. Points that are labeled as ridge or ravine and that have neighboring points in a direction orthogonal to the gradient that are also labeled ridge or ravine are ridge or ravine continuums. These continuums can be reclassified as hillsides.

3. The Topographic Classification Algorithm

The definitions of Section 2 cannot be used directly since there is a problem of where in a pixel's area to apply the classification. If the classification were only applied to the point at the center of each pixel, then a pixel having a peak near one of its corners, for example, would get classified as a concave hill rather than as a peak. The problem is that the topographic classification we are interested in must be a sampling of the actual topographic surface classes. Most likely, the interesting categories of peak, pit, ridge, ravine, and saddle will never occur precisely at a pixel's center, and if they do occur in a pixel's area, then the pixel must carry that label rather than the class label of the pixel's center point. Thus one problem we must solve is to determine the dominant label for a pixel given the topographic class label of every point in the pixel. The next problem we must solve is to determine, in effect, the set of all topographic classes occurring within a pixel's area without having to do the impossible brute-force computation.

For the purpose of solving these problems, we divide the set of topographic labels into two subsets: (1) those that indicate that a strict, local, one-dimen-

sional extremum has occurred (peak, pit, ridge, ravine, and saddle) and (2) those that do not indicate that a strict, local, one-dimensional extremum has occurred (flat and hillside). By *one-dimensional,* we mean along a line (in a particular direction). A strict, local, one-dimensional extremum can be located by finding those points within a pixel's area where a zero-crossing of the first directional derivative occurs.

So that we do not search the pixel's entire area for the zero-crossing, we only search in the directions of extreme second directional derivative, $\omega^{(1)}$ and $\omega^{(2)}$. Since these directions are well aligned with curvature properties, the chance of overlooking an important topographic structure is minimized, and, more importantly, the computational cost is small.

When $\lambda_1 = \lambda_2 \neq 0$, the directions $\omega^{(1)}$ and $\omega^{(2)}$ are not uniquely defined. We handle this case by searching for a zero-crossing in the direction given by $\mathbf{H}^{-1} * \nabla f$. This is the *Newton direction,* and it points directly toward the extremum of a quadratic surface.

For inflection-point location (first derivative extremum), we search along the gradient direction for a zero-crossing of second directional derivative. For one-dimensional extrema, there are four cases to consider: (1) no zero-crossing, (2) one zero-crossing, (3) two zero-crossings, and (4) more than two zero-crossings. The next four sections discuss these cases.

3.1. CASE ONE: NO ZERO-CROSSING

If no zero-crossing is found along either of the two extreme directions within the pixel's area, then the pixel cannot be a local extremum and therefore must be assigned a label from the set (flat or hillside). If the gradient is zero, we have a flat. If it is nonzero, we have a hillside. If the pixel is a hillside, we classify it further into inflection point, slope, convex hill, concave hill, or saddle hill. If there is a zero-crossing of the second directional derivative in the direction of the gradient within the pixel's area, the pixel is classified as an inflection point. If no such zero-crossing occurs, the label assigned to the pixel is based on the gradient magnitude and Hessian eigenvalues calculated at the center of the pixel, local coordinates $(0, 0)$, as in Table 2.

The International Journal of Robotics Research

Table 2. Pixel Label Calculation for Case One: No Zero-Crossing

$\|\nabla f\|$	λ_1	λ_2	Label
0	0	0	Flat
+	−	−	Concave hill
+	−	0	Concave hill
+	−	+	Saddle hill
+	0	0	Slope
+	+	−	Saddle hill
+	+	0	Convex hill
+	+	+	Convex hill

Table 3. Pixel Label Calculation for Case Two: One Zero-Crossing

$\|\nabla f\|$	λ_1	λ_2	Label
0	−	−	Peak
0	−	0	Ridge
0	−	+	Saddle
0	+	−	Saddle
0	+	0	Ravine
0	+	+	Pit

Table 4. Final Pixel Classification, Case Three: Two Zero-Crossings

LABEL1	LABEL2	Resulting Label
Peak	Peak	Peak
Peak	Ridge	Peak
Pit	Pit	Pit
Pit	Ravine	Pit
Saddle	Saddle	Saddle
Ridge	Ridge	Ridge
Ridge	Ravine	Saddle
Ridge	Saddle	Saddle
Ravine	Ravine	Ravine
Ravine	Saddle	Saddle

3.2. CASE TWO: ONE ZERO-CROSSING

If a zero-crossing of the first directional derivative is found within the pixel's area, then the pixel is a strict, local, one-dimensional extremum and must be assigned a label from the set (peak, pit, ridge, ravine, or saddle). At the location of the zero-crossing, the Hessian and gradient are recomputed, and if the gradient magnitude at the zero-crossing is zero, Table 3 is used.

If the gradient magnitude is nonzero, then the choice is either ridge or ravine. If the second directional derivative in the direction of the zero-crossing is negative, we have a ridge. If it is positive, we have a ravine. If it is zero, we compare the function value at the center of the pixel, $f(0, 0)$, with the function value at the zero-crossing, $f(r, c)$. If $f(r, c)$ is greater than $f(0, 0)$, we call it a ridge, otherwise we call it a ravine.

3.3. CASE THREE: TWO ZERO-CROSSINGS

If we have two zero-crossings of the first directional derivative, one in each direction of extreme curvature, then the Hessian and gradient must be recomputed at each zero-crossing. Using the procedure described in Section 3.2, we assign a label to each zero-crossing. We call these labels LABEL1 and LABEL2. The final classification given the pixel is based on these two labels and is given in Table 4.

If both labels are identical, the pixel is given that label. In the case of both labels being ridge, the pixel

may actually be a peak, but experiments have shown that this case is rare. An anlogous argument can be made for both labels being ravine. If one label is ridge and the other ravine, this indicates we are at or very close to a saddle point, and thus the pixel is classified as a saddle. If one label is peak and the other ridge, we choose the category giving us the "most information," which in this case is peak. The peak is a local maximum in all directions, while the ridge is a local maximum in only one direction. Thus, peak conveys more information about the image surface. An analogous argument can be made if the labels are pit and ravine. Similarly, a saddle gives us more information than a ridge or valley. Thus, a pixel is assigned saddle if its zero-crossings have been labeled ridge and saddle or ravine and saddle.

It is apparent from Table 4 that not all possible label combinations are accounted for. Some combinations, such as peak and pit, are omitted because of the assumption that the underlying surface is smooth and sampled frequently enough that a peak and pit will not both occur within the same pixel's area. If such a case occurs, our convention is to choose arbitrarily one of LABEL1 or LABEL2 as the resulting label for the pixel.

3.4. CASE FOUR: MORE THAN TWO ZERO-CROSSINGS

If more than two zero-crossings occur within a pixel's area, then in at least one of the extrema directions there are two zero-crossings. If this happens, we choose the zero-crossing closest to the pixel's center and ignore the other. If we ignore the further zero-crossings, then this case is identical to case 3. This situation has yet to occur in our experiments.

4. Surface Estimation

In this section we discuss the estimation of the parameters required by the topographic classification scheme of Section 2 using the local cubic facet model (Haralick 1981). It is important to note that the classification scheme of Section 2 and the algorithm of Section 3 are independent of the method used to estimate the first- and second-order partials of the underlying digital image-intensity surface at each sampled point. Although we are currently using the cubic model and discuss it here, we expect that a spline-based estimation scheme or a discrete-cosines estimation scheme may, in fact, provide better estimates.

4.1. LOCAL CUBIC FACET MODEL

In order to estimate the required partial derivatives, we perform a least-squares fit with a two-dimensional surface, f, to a neighborhood of each pixel. It is required that the function f be continuous and have continuous first- and second-order partial derivatives

with respect to r and c in a neighborhood around each pixel in the rc plane.

We choose f to be a cubic polynomial in r and c expressed as a combination of discrete orthogonal polynomials. The function f is the best discrete least-squares polynomial approximation to the image data in each pixel's neighborhood. More details can be found in Haralick's paper (1981), in which each coefficient of the cubic polynomial is evaluated as a linear combination of the pixels in the fitting neighborhood.

To express the procedure precisely and without reference to a particular set of polynomials tied to neighborhood size, we will canonically write the fitted bicubic surface for each fitting neighborhood as

$$\begin{aligned} f(r, c) = &\ k_1 + k_2 r + k_3 c \\ &+ k_4 r^2 + k_5 rc + k_6 c^2 \\ &+ k_7 r^3 + k_8 r^2 c + k_9 rc^2 + k_{10} c^3, \end{aligned}$$

where the center of the fitting neighborhood is taken as the origin. It quickly follows that the needed partials evaluated at local coordinates (r, c) are

$$\begin{aligned} \partial f/\partial r &= k_2 + 2k_4 r + k_5 c + 3k_7 r^2 + 2k_8 rc + k_9 c^2 \\ \partial f/\partial c &= k_3 + k_5 r + 2k_6 c + k_8 r^2 + 2k_9 rc + 3k_{10} c^2 \\ \partial^2 f/\partial r^2 &= 2k_4 + 6k_7 r + 2k_8 c \\ \partial^2 f/\partial c^2 &= 2k_6 + 2k_9 r + 6k_{10} c \\ \partial^2 f/\partial r\,\partial c &= k_5 + 2k_8 r + 2k_9 c. \end{aligned}$$

It is easy to see that if the above quantities are evaluated at the center of the pixel where local coordinates $(r, c) = (0, 0)$, only the constant terms will be of significance. If the partials need to be evaluated at an arbitrary point in a pixel's area, then a linear or quadratic polynomial value must be computed.

4.2. AN OBSERVATION ABOUT CUBIC FITS

A two-dimensional cubic polynomial includes an arbitrary quadratic polynomial, and thus features like pit, peak, and saddle can be replicated exactly. For other surface features like ridges or ravines, cubics are either exact or fairly decent approximations. It is

Fig. 4. Cubic fit of step
edge that causes ravine
and ridge to occur.

Fig. 5. Cubic fit (dashed
line) of step edge (solid
line) with inflection
point outside window.

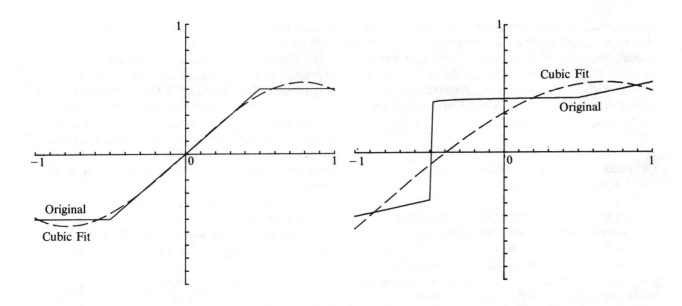

frequently possible to classify surface characteristics correctly even though the surface is not like any polynomial. For example, the center of the step edge shown in Fig. 4 can be accurately predicted by the inflection point of the cubic fit, which is quite good. However, there are smooth surfaces that (over the window being used) simply do not look like cubic polynomials, and feature classifications based on the best least-squares cubic polynomial approximation will be incorrect. For example, in Fig. 4, the cubic fit shows a prominent ravine at the foot of the slope, and the foot pixel would be (incorrectly) labeled a ravine pixel. Figure 5 shows a steplike edge whose cubic fit has an inflection point outside the entire window!

5. Summary of the Topographic Classification Scheme

The scheme is a parallel process for topographic classification of every pixel, which can be done in one pass through the image. At each pixel of the image, the following four steps need to be performed.

1. Calculate the fitting coefficients, k_1 through k_{10}, of a two-dimensional cubic polynomial

in an n-by-n neighborhood around the pixel. These coefficients are easily computed by convolving the appropriate masks over the image.

2. Use the coefficients calculated in step 1 to find the gradient, gradient magnitude, and the eigenvalues and eigenvectors of the Hessian at the center of the pixel's neighborhood, $(0, 0)$.

3. Search in the direction of the eigenvectors calculated in step 2 for a zero-crossing of the first directional derivative within the pixel's area. (If the eigenvalues of the Hessian are equal and nonzero, then search in the Newton direction.)

4. Recompute the gradient, gradient magnitude, and values of second directional derivative extrema at each zero-crossing. Then apply the labeling scheme as described in Sections 3.1–3.4.

6. Examples

In this section, we show the results of the topographic primal sketch on several test images, three of which are simply described mathematical surfaces

Fig. 6. A. Saddle surface.
B. Topographic labeling
of saddle surface.

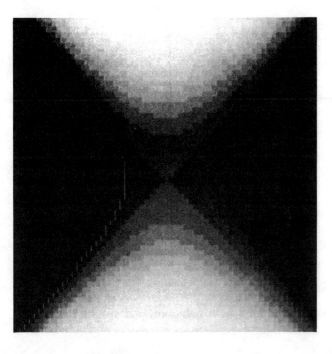

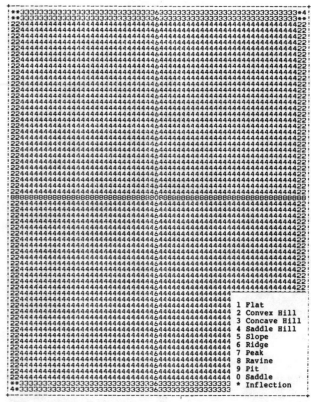

and two of which are real images. We will also examine how the size of the window affects the results of the classifier.

6.1. Saddle Surface

A perfect saddle surface of size 64×64 having no noise can be generated by the equation

$$f(r, c) = r^2 - c^2.$$

Taking the origin at image coordinates (32, 33), the surface plot is as illustrated in Fig. 2, and the gray-level image of the saddle surface is as illustrated in Fig. 6A. The results of the classifier are shown in Fig. 6B. Each number in the figure represents the label assigned the pixel by the classifier. As expected, a ridge-line one pixel in width was found running north-south, and, orthogonal to the ridge-line, a ravine-line one pixel in width was found. The center pixel of the surface was correctly classified as a saddle point. All other pixels on the surface were correctly classified as saddle hillsides.

Next, we add Gaussian noise to the saddle surface. The noise has a mean of 0.0 and standard deviation of 4.0. The results of the classifier using different sized windows (5×5, 7×7, 9×9, 11×11) on the noisy surface are shown in Fig. 7. As the window size increases, the results of the classifier improve dramatically. The classification resulting from the 11×11 window is almost identical to the classification done on the original, perfectly smooth surface. This would seem to suggest using as large a window size as possible, but in the next example we will show that this is not always a good idea.

6.2. Ridges and Valleys

A series of ridges and valleys can be generated across the column direction by the following equation:

Fig. 7. Neighborhood topographic labeling of noisy saddle surface showing ridge (black) and ravine (white). A. 5 × 5 window. B. 7 × 7 window. C. 9 × 9 window. D. 11 × 11 window.

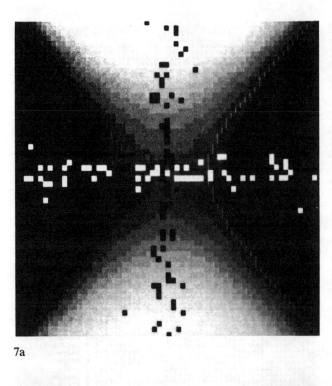

7a

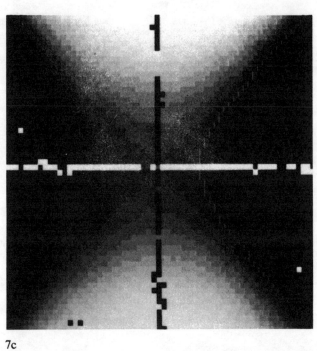

7c

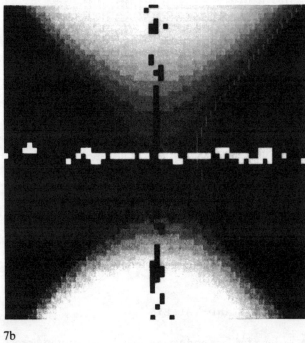

7b

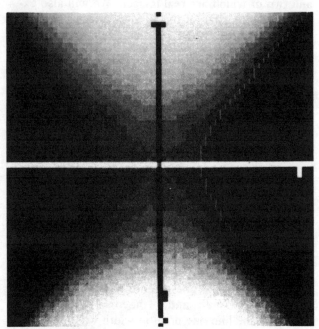

7d

Fig. 8. Image and topographic labeling of sine waves. A. Image. B. Topographic labeling with 5 × 5 window. C. Labeling with 9 × 9 window. D. Labeling with 13 × 13 window.

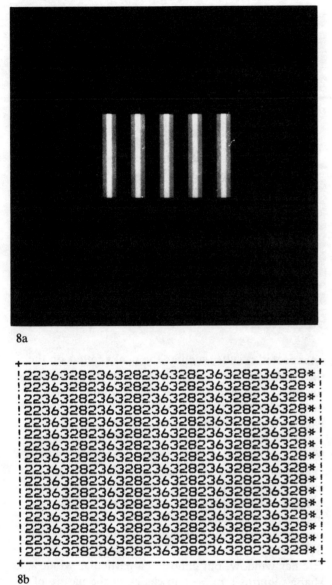

8a

```
+----------------------------------------------+
!22363282363282363282363282363282363328*!
!22363282363282363282363282363282363328*!
!22363282363282363282363282363282363328*!
!22363282363282363282363282363282363328*!
!22363282363282363282363282363282363328*!
!22363282363282363282363282363282363328*!
!22363282363282363282363282363282363328*!
!22363282363282363282363282363282363328*!
!22363282363282363282363282363282363328*!
!22363282363282363282363282363282363328*!
!22363282363282363282363282363282363328*!
!22363282363282363282363282363282363328*!
!22363282363282363282363282363282363328*!
!22363282363282363282363282363282363328*!
!22363282363282363282363282363282363328*!
!22363282363282363282363282363282363328*!
+----------------------------------------------+
```

8b

$$
f(r, c) = \begin{cases} 1 \text{ if col} = 1, 7 \\ 2 \text{ if col} = 2, 6 \\ 3 \text{ if col} = 3, 5 \\ 4 \text{ if col} = 4 \end{cases}
$$

where col = mod(c − 1, 7) + 1.

It is easy to see from the above equation that every row will be the same with a ridge occurring every sixth pixel beginning in column 4, and a ravine oc-

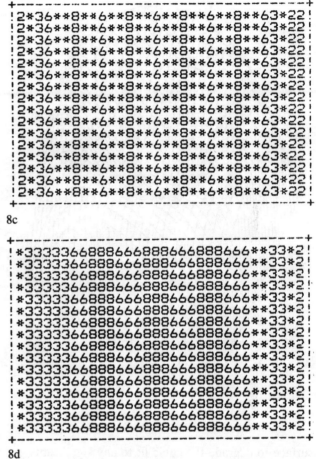

```
+------------------------------------------------+
!2*36**8**6**8**6**8**6**8**6**8**63*22!
!2*36**8**6**8**6**8**6**8**6**8**63*22!
!2*36**8**6**8**6**8**6**8**6**8**63*22!
!2*36**8**6**8**6**8**6**8**6**8**63*22!
!2*36**8**6**8**6**8**6**8**6**8**63*22!
!2*36**8**6**8**6**8**6**8**6**8**63*22!
!2*36**8**6**8**6**8**6**8**6**8**63*22!
!2*36**8**6**8**6**8**6**8**6**8**63*22!
!2*36**8**6**8**6**8**6**8**6**8**63*22!
!2*36**8**6**8**6**8**6**8**6**8**63*22!
!2*36**8**6**8**6**8**6**8**6**8**63*22!
!2*36**8**6**8**6**8**6**8**6**8**63*22!
!2*36**8**6**8**6**8**6**8**6**8**63*22!
!2*36**8**6**8**6**8**6**8**6**8**63*22!
!2*36**8**6**8**6**8**6**8**6**8**63*22!
+------------------------------------------------+
```

8c

```
+------------------------------------------------+
!*33333668886668886668886 66**33*2!
!*33333668886668886668886 66**33*2!
!*33333668886668886668886 66**33*2!
!*33333668886668886668886 66**33*2!
!*33333668886668886668886 66**33*2!
!*33333668886668886668886 66**33*2!
!*33333668886668886668886 66**33*2!
!*33333668886668886668886 66**33*2!
!*33333668886668886668886 66**33*2!
!*33333668886668886668886 66**33*2!
!*33333668886668886668886 66**33*2!
!*33333668886668886668886 66**33*2!
!*33333668886668886668886 66**33*2!
!*33333668886668886668886 66**33*2!
!*33333668886668886668886 66**33*2!
+------------------------------------------------+
```

8d

curring every sixth pixel beginning in column 7. The gray level plot of the 16 × 32 image is shown in Fig. 8A. As expected, the ridges and ravines are correctly identified. The results of the classifier using window sizes 5 × 5, 9 × 9, and 13 × 13 are found in Figs. 8B, C, and D respectively. As the window size increases, the results of the classifier become less accurate. This result is exactly the opposite of what happened on the saddle surface. The reason is that this surface is much more "busy" than the saddle surface. The larger window size on this particular surface results in too many complexities for the cubic fit to handle.

The conclusion is that the window size used should be a function of the noise and the complexity of the image surface. One should use as big a window size as possible without allowing the complexity of the

Fig. 9. Surface of revolution. A. Surface plot.
B. Ravine ridge (black)
and ravine (white) label-
ing of the surface.

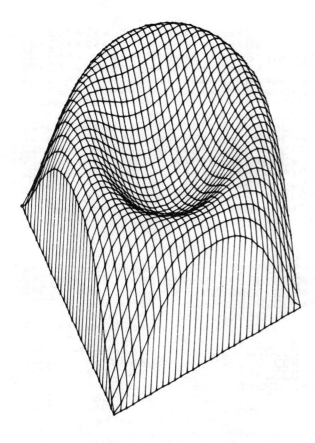

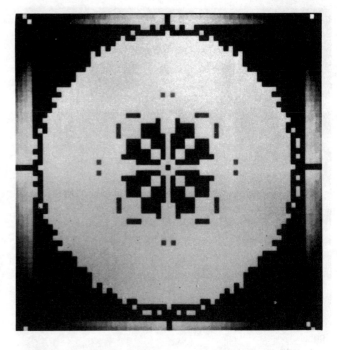

Fig. 9. Surface of revolution. A. Surface plot.
B. Ravine ridge (black)
and ravine (white) label-
ing of the surface.

surface to degrade the cubic fit to any significant
degree.

6.3. SURFACE OF REVOLUTION

A surface of revolution of size 64 × 64 with no noise
can be generated by the equation

$$f(r, c) = k * \sin (0.5 * (r^2 + c^2)),$$

with origin at image coordinates (32, 32). The surface
plot is illustrated in Fig. 9A. The topographic labeling on this surface shows some surprising results.
A continuum of ridges and a continuum of ravines
are found on the surface (see Fig. 9B). The reasons
for these ridge and ravine points were discussed in
Section 2.4. Also, the local cubic fits are very poor
on this surface of revolution. This leads to some

unexpected results, such as the peaks found on the
rim of the surface where the ridges and ravines come
together. The pixels labeled saddle on the image
occur at locations where both a ridge and ravine
were detected within the same pixel.

Notice that the labelings produced are not perfectly symmetric, as one would expect on a radially
symmetric surface. The reason for this is that the
cubic surface estimation is done with rectangular
windows, which produces different cubic approximations at the same radial distance from the axis of
revolution and hence radially unsymmetric labeling.
Symmetric labeling would be produced by using a
circular window, but choosing a particular window
shape requires a priori knowledge of the nature of
the image surface.

6.4. REAL IMAGE

In this section, we show the results of the classifier
on two real images. The results on the top left corner of a chair image are illustrated in Fig. 10B. The
results on the upper middle section of the bin of
machine parts are illustrated in Fig. 11B. The vari-

Haralick, Watson, and Laffey

212

Fig. 10. Results of the classifier on a real image. A. Chair. B. Upper left corner of chair.
C. Ridges (black) and ravines (white). D. Hillside (white).

10a

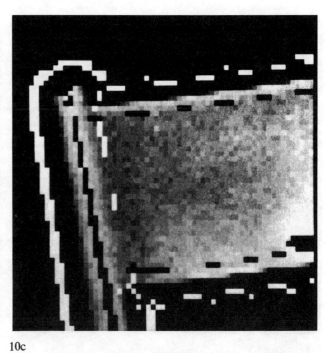

10c

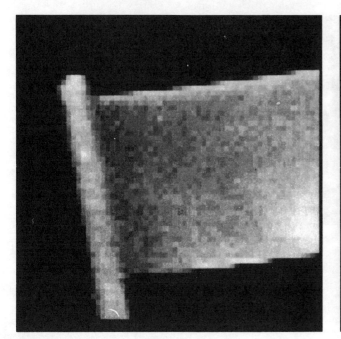

10b

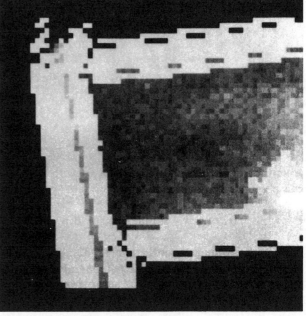

10d

Fig. 11. A. Screw. B. Ridges
(black). C. Ravines (white).
D. Convex hillside (white).
E. Concave hillside (black).

11a

11b

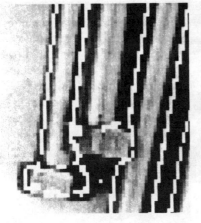

11c

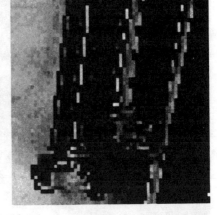

11d   11e

Fig. 12. A. Machine parts.
B. Upper left corner show-
ing subimage ridges (black)
and ravines (white). C.

Center showing subimage
ridges (black) and ravines
(white).

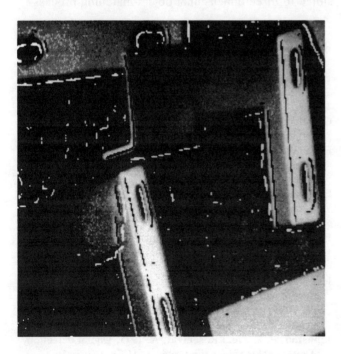

ous nonflat labels in the backgrounds of the images are caused by very slight dips and rises in the cubic surface fit. These may be cleaned up by requiring the eigenvalues to be above a certain threshold to be considered nonzero (see Fig. 10C). Figure 12 shows the labeling on an image of manufacturing parts. Notice how the highlighting can occur depending on the positioning of the parts. The ridge labels are quite useful for determining where the highlighting occurs.

7. Conclusions

In this paper, we have given a precise mathematical description of the various topographic structures that occur in a digital image and have called the classified image the topographic primal sketch. Our set of topographic categories is invariant under gray tone, monotonically increasing transformations and consists of peak, pit, ridge, ravine, saddle, flat, and hillside, with hillside being broken down further into the subcategories inflection point, slope, convex hill,

The International Journal of Robotics Research

concave hill, and saddle hill. The hillside subcategories are not invariant under the monotonic transformations.

The topographic label assigned a pixel is based on the pixel's first- and second-order directional derivatives. We use a two-dimensional cubic polynomial fit based on the local facet model to estimate the directional derivatives of the underlying gray tone intensity surface. The calculation of the extrema of the second directional derivative can be done efficiently and stably by forming the Hessian matrix and calculating its eigenvalues and their associated eigenvectors. Strict, local, one-dimensional extrema (such as pit, peak, ridge, ravine, and saddle) are found by searching for a zero-crossing of the first directional derivative in the directions of extreme second directional derivative (the eigenvectors of the Hessian). We have also identified another direction of interest, the Newton direction, which points toward the extremum of a quadratic surface. The classification scheme was found to give satisfactory results on a number of test images.

7.1. DIRECTIONS FOR FURTHER RESEARCH

Further research on the topographic primal sketch needs to be done to (1) develop better basis functions, (2) make use of fitting error, (3) find a solution for the ridge (ravine) continuum problem, and (4) develop techniques for grouping of the topographic structures. Basis functions worth considering include trigonometric polynomials, polynomials of higher order, and piecewise polynomials of lower order than cubic. The basis functions problem is to find a set of basis functions and an associated inner product for least-squares approximation that can correctly replicate all common image surface features and be simultaneously computationally efficient and numerically stable.

Fitting error needs to be used in deciding into which class a pixel falls. Noise causes the fitting error to increase, and increased fitting error increases the uncertainty of the labeling. Also, global knowledge of how the topographic structures fit together could be used to correct the misclassification error caused by noise. The way the neighborhood size affects the surface fitting error and the classification scheme needs to be investigated in detail.

The ridge (ravine) continuum problem needs to be solved. It may be that there is no way to distinguish between a true ridge and a ridge continuum using only the values of partial derivatives at a point. The solution may require complete use of the partial derivatives in a local area about the pixel.

Most important for the use of the primal sketch in a general robotics computer vision system is the development of techniques for grouping and assembling topographically labeled pixels to form the primitive structures involved in higher-level matching and correspondence processes. How well can stereo correspondence or frame-to-frame time-varying image correspondence tasks be accomplished using the primitive structures in the topographic primal sketch? How effectively can the topographic sketch be used in undoing the confounding effects of shading and shadowing? How well will the primitive structures in the topographic sketch perform in the two-dimensional to three-dimensional object-matching process?

REFERENCES

Ehrich, R. W., and Foith, J. P. 1978. Topology and semantics of intensity arrays. *Computer vision systems*, New York: Academic, pp. 111–128.

Grender, G. C. 1976. TOPO III: A Fortran program for terrain analysis. *Comput. Geosci.* 2:195–209.

Haralick, R. M. 1980. Edge and region analysis for digital image data. *Comput. Graphics Image Processing* 12(1): 60–73.

Haralick, R. M. 1981. The digital edge. *Proc. 1981 Conf. Pattern Recognition Image Processing.* New York: IEEE Computer Society, pp. 285–294.

Haralick, R. M. 1982. Zero-crossing of second directional derivative edge operator. *SPIE Proc. Robot Vision.* Bellingham, Wa.: SPIE.

Hsu, S., Mundy, J. L., and Beaudet, P. R. 1978. Web representation of image data. *4th Int. Joint Conf. Pattern Recognition.* New York: IEEE Computer Society, pp. 675–680.

Johnston, E. G., and Rosenfeld, A. 1975. Digital detection of pits, peaks, ridges, and ravines. *IEEE Trans. Syst. Man Cybern.*, July, pp. 472–480.

Haralick, Watson, and Laffey

Laffey, T. J., Haralick, R. M., and Watson, L. T. 1982. Topographic classification of digital image intensity surfaces. *Proc. IEEE Workshop Comput. Vision: Theory Contr*. New York: IEEE Computer Society, pp. 171–177.

Lee, H. C., and Fu, K. S. 1981. The GLGS image representation and its application to preliminary segmentation and pre-attentive visual search. *Proc. 1981 Conf. Pattern Recognition Image Processing*. New York: IEEE Computer Society, pp. 256–261.

Marr, D. 1976. Early processing of visual information. *Philosophical Trans. Royal Soc. London* B 275:483–524.

Marr, D. 1980. Visual information processing: The structure and creation of visual representations. *Philosophical Trans. Royal Soc. London* B 290:199–218.

Paton, K. 1975. Picture description using Legendre polynomials. *Comput. Graphics Image Processing* 4(1): 40–54.

Peuker, T. K., and Johnston, E. G. 1972 (Nov.). Detection of surface-specific points by local parallel processing of discrete terrain elevation data. Tech. Rept. 206. College Park Md.: University of Maryland Computer Science Center.

Peuker, T. K., and Douglas, D. H. 1975. Detection of surface-specific points by local parallel processing of discrete terrain elevation data. *Comput. Graphics Image Processing* 4(4):375–387.

Rutishauser, H. 1971. Jacobi method for real symmetric matrix. *Handbook for automatic computation, volume II, linear algebra, ed*. J. H. Wilkinson and C. Reinsch. New York: Springer-Verlag.

Strang, G. 1980. *Linear algebra and its applications*, 2nd ed. New York: Academic, pp. 243–249.

Toriwaki, J., and Fukumura, T. 1978. Extraction of structural information from grey pictures. *Comput. Graphics Image Processing* 7(1):30–51.

Reprinted from *IEEE Transactions on Pattern Analysis and Machine Intelligence*, Volume PAMI-9, Number 4, July 1987, pages 532-550. Copyright © 1987 by The Institute of Electrical and Electronics Engineers, Inc. All rights reserved.

Image Analysis Using Mathematical Morphology

ROBERT M. HARALICK, FELLOW, IEEE, STANLEY R. STERNBERG, AND XINHUA ZHUANG

Abstract—For the purposes of object or defect identification required in industrial vision applications, the operations of mathematical morphology are more useful than the convolution operations employed in signal processing because the morphological operators relate directly to shape. The tutorial provided in this paper reviews both binary morphology and gray scale morphology, covering the operations of dilation, erosion, opening, and closing and their relations. Examples are given for each morphological concept and explanations are given for many of their interrelationships.

Index Terms—Closing, dilation, erosion, filtering, image analysis, morphology, opening, shape analysis.

I. INTRODUCTION

MATHEMATICAL morphology provides an approach to the processing of digital images which is based on shape. Appropriately used, mathematical morphological operations tend to simplify image data preserving their essential shape characteristics and eliminating irrelevancies. As the identification of objects, object features, and assembly defects correlate directly with shape, it becomes apparent that the natural processing approach to deal with the machine vision recognition process and the visually guided robot problem is mathematical morphology.

Morphologic operations are among the first kinds of image operators used. Kirsch, Cahn, Ray, and Urban [13] discussed some binary 3 × 3 morphologic operators. Other early papers include Unger [37] and Moore [21].

Machines which perform morphologic operations are not new. They are the essence of what cellular logic machines such as the Golay logic processor [8], Diff3 [9], PICAP [15], the Leitz Texture Analysis System TAS [14], the CLIP processor arrays [3], and the Delft Image Processor DIP [6] all do. A number of companies now manufacture industrial vision machines which incorporate video rate morphological operations. These companies include Machine Vision International, Maitre, Synthetic Vision Systems, Vicom, Applied Intelligence Systems, Inc., and Leitz.

The 1985 IEEE Computer Society Workshop on Computer Architecture For Pattern Analysis and Image Database Management had an entire session devoted to computer architecture specialized to perform morphological operations. Papers included those by McCubbrey and Lougheed [19], Wilson [39], Kimmel, Jaffe, Manderville, and Lavin [12], Leonard [16], Pratt [27], and Haralick [11]. Gerritsen and Verbeek [7] show how convolution followed by a table look up operation can accomplish binary morphologic operations.

But although the techniques are being used in the industrial world, the basis and theory of mathematical morphology tend to be (with the exception of the highly mathematical books by Matheron [18] and Serra [31]) not covered in the textbooks or journals which discuss image processing or computer vision. It is the intent of this tutorial to help fill this void.

The paper is divided into three parts. Section II discusses the basic operations of dilation and erosion in an N-dimensional Euclidean space. Section III discusses the derived operations of opening and closing. Section IV gives the corresponding definition for the dilation and erosion operations for gray tone images and shows how with these definitions all the properties of dilation and erosion, opening, and closing previously derived and explained in Sections II and III hold.

II. DILATION AND EROSION

The language of mathematical morphology is that of set theory. Sets in mathematical morphology represent the shapes which are manifested on binary or gray tone images. The set of all the black pixels in a black and white image, (a binary image) consitutes a complete description of the binary image. Sets in Euclidean 2-space denote foreground regions in binary images. Sets in Euclidean 3-space may denote time varying binary imagery or static gray scale imagery as well as binary solids. Sets in higher dimensional spaces may incorporate additional image information, like color, or multiple perspective imagery. Mathematical morphological transformations apply to sets of any dimensions, those like Euclidean N-space, or those like its discrete or digitized equivalent, the set of N-tuples of integers, Z^N. For the sake of simplicity we will refer to either of these sets as E^N.

Those points in a set being morphologically transformed are considered as the selected set of points and those in the complement set are considered as not selected. Hence, morphology from this point of view is binary morphology. We begin our discussion with the binary morphological operations of dilation and erosion.

A. Dilation

Dilation is the morphological transformation which combines two sets using vector addition of set elements.

Manuscript received January 24, 1986; revised May 28, 1986. Recommended for acceptance by S. W. Zucker.

R. M. Haralick is with the Department of Electrical Engineering, University of Washington, Seattle, WA 98195.

S. R. Sternberg is with Machine Vision International, Ann Arbor, MI 48104.

X. Zhuang is with the Department of Electrical Engineering, University of Washington, Seattle, WA 98195, on leave from the Zhejiang Institute of Computing, Zhejiang, China.

IEEE Log Number 8715075.

If A and B are sets in N-space (E^N) with elements a and b, respectively, $a = (a_1, \cdots, a_N)$ and $b = (b_1, \cdots, b_N)$ being N-tuples of element coordinates, then the dilation of A by B is the set of all possible vector sums of pairs of elements, one coming from A and one coming from B.

Definition 1: Let A and B be subsets of E^N. The dilation of A by B is denoted by $A \oplus B$ and is defined by

$$A \oplus B = \{c \in E^N \mid c = a + b$$

$$\text{for some } a \in A \text{ and } b \in B\}.$$

Example: This illustrates an instance of the dilation operation. The coordinate system we use for all the examples in the next few sections is (row, column).

$$A = \{(0,1), (1,1), (2,1), (2,2), (3,0)\}$$

$$B = \{(0,0), (0,1)\}$$

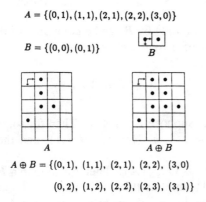

$$A \oplus B = \{(0,1), (1,1), (2,1), (2,2), (3,0)$$

$$(0,2), (1,2), (2,2), (2,3), (3,1)\}$$

Dilation as a set theoretic operation was proposed by H. Minkowski [20] to characterize integral measures of certain open (sparse) sets. Dilation as an image processing operation was employed by several early investigators in image processing as smoothing operations [13], [37], [21], [8], [28], [29]. Dilation as an image operator for shape extraction and estimation of image parameters was explored by Matheron [18] and Serra [30]. All of these early applications dealt with binary images only.

Matheron uses the term "dilatation" for dilation and both Matheron and Serra define dilation slightly differently. In essense, they define the dilation of A by B as the set $\{c \in E^N \mid c = a - b \text{ for some } a \in A \text{ and } b \in B\}$.

In morphological dilation, the roles of the sets A and B are symmetric, that is, the dilation operation is commutative because addition is commutative.

Proposition 2:

$$A \oplus B = B \oplus A.$$

Proof:

$$A \oplus B = \{c \mid c = a + b \text{ for some } a \in A, b \in B\}$$
$$= \{c \mid c = b + a \text{ for some } a \in A, b \in B\}$$
$$= B \oplus A.$$

In practice, A and B are handled quite differently. The first operand A is considered as the image undergoing analysis, while the second operand B is referred to as the structuring element, to be thought of as constituting a single shape parameter of the dilation transformation. In the

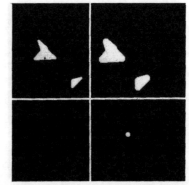

Fig. 1. The upper left shows the input image consisting of two objects. The lower right shows the octagonal structuring element. The upper right shows the input image dilated by the octagonal structuring element.

Fig. 2. The upper left shows the input image consisting of two objects. The upper right shows the input image dilated by the structuring element $\{(0, 0), (14, 0)\}$. The lower left shows the input image dilated by the structuring element $\{(0, 0), (0, 14)\}$. The lower right shows the input image dilated by the structuring element $\{(0, 0), (14, 0), (0, 14)\}$.

remainder of the paper, we will refer to A as the image and B as the structuring element.

Dilation by disk structuring elements correspond to isotropic swelling or expansion algorithms common to binary image processing. Dilation by small squares (3×3) is a neighborhood operation easily implemented by adjacency connected array architectures (grids) and is the one many image processing people know by the name "fill," "expand," or "grow." Some example dilation transformations are illustrated in Figs. 1 and 2.

Neighborhood connected image processors such as CLIP [4], Cytocomputer [32], [34], and MPP [1], [26] can implement some dilations (not all) by structuring elements larger than the neighborhood size by iteratively dilating with a sequence of neighborhood structuring elements. In particular, if image A is to be dilated by structuring element D which itself can be expressed as the dilation of B by C, then $A \oplus D$ can be computed as

$$A \oplus D = A \oplus (B \oplus C) = (A \oplus B) \oplus C$$

since addition is associative.

The form $(A \oplus B) \oplus C$ represents a considerable savings in number of operations to be performed when A is the image and $B \oplus C$ is the structuring element. The savings come about because a brute force dilation by $B \oplus C$ might take as many as N^2 operations while first dilating

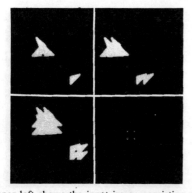

Fig. 3. The upper left shows the input image consisting of two objects. The upper right shows the input image dilated by the structuring element $\{(0, 0) (0, 14)\}$. The lower left shows the input image dilated by the structuring element $\{(0, 0), (14, 0), (0, 14) (14, 14)\}$, which is shown in the lower right. Notice that the dilated image of the lower left can be obtained by dilating the image shown in the upper right by the structuring element $\{(0, 0), (14, 0)\}$. This is a consequence of the chain rule for dilations and because $\{(0, 0), (14, 0)\} \oplus \{(0, 0), (0, 14)\} = \{(0, 0), (0, 14), (14, 0), (14, 14)\}$.

A by B and then dilating the result by C could take as few as $2N$ operations, where N is the number of elements in B and in C. This computational complexity advantage is not as strong for machines which can implement dilations only as neighborhood operations.

Proposition 3:

$$A \oplus (B \oplus C) = (A \oplus B) \oplus C.$$

Proof: $x \in A \oplus (B \oplus C)$ if and only if there exists $a \in A$, $b \in B$, and $c \in C$ such that $x = a + (b + c)$. $x \in (A \oplus B) \oplus C$ if and only if there exists $a \in A$, $b \in B$, and $c \in C$ such that $x = (a + b) + c$. But $a + (b + c) = (a + b) + c$ since addition is associative. Therefore, $A \oplus (B \oplus C) = (A \oplus B) \oplus C$.

Proposition 3 is commonly referred to as the "chain rule" for dilations. An example of performing a dilation transformation as a chain of dilations is shown in Fig. 3. Notice that this dilation transformation which can be done as a chain of dilations is not able to be done as a chain of neighborhood operations.

Since dilation is commutative, the order of application of the constituent dilations is immaterial.

Dilating an image as an iterative sequence of neighborhood operations is not necessarily the most efficient or universal approach to implementing the dilation transformation. For example, not all structuring elements can be decomposed into iterative neighborhood dilations. An example of a dilation transformation which cannot be implemented as an iterative sequence of neighborhood operations is the dilation by any of the structuring elements $\{(0, 0), (0, 14)\}$, $\{(0, 0), (14, 0)\}$ or $\{(0, 0), (0, 14), (14, 0)\}$ which are shown in Fig. 2.

Also, the implementation may not be particularly efficient in terms of processing time or computer hardware requirements. An alternative involves considering dilations in terms of image translations. So first we need the definition for translation.

Definition 4: Let A be a subset of E^N and $x \in E^N$. The

translation of A by x is denoted by $(A)_x$ and is defined by

$$(A)_x = \{c \in E^N \mid c = a + x \text{ for some } a \in A\}.$$

Example: This illustrates an instance of translation.

$$A = \{(0, 1), (1, 1), (2, 1), (2, 2), (3, 0)\}$$

$$x = (0, 1)$$

$$(A)_x = \{(0, 2), (1, 2), (2, 2), (2, 3), (3, 1)\}.$$

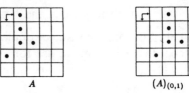

The dilation of A by B can be computed as the union of translations of A by the elements of B.

Proposition 5:

$$A \oplus B = \bigcup_{b \in B} (A)_b.$$

Proof: Suppose $x \in A \oplus B$. Then for some $a \in A$ and $b \in B$, $x = a + b$. Hence, $x \in (A)_b$ and therefore $x \in \bigcup_{b \in B} (A)_b$.

Suppose $x \in \bigcup_{b \in B} (A)_b$. Then for some $b \in B$, $x \in (A)_b$. But $x \in (A)_b$ implies there exists an $a \in A$ such that $x = a + b$. Now by definition of dilation, $a \in A$, $b \in B$, and $x = a + b$ imply $x \in A \oplus B$.

Historically, the dilation transformation was defined by Minkowski in this manner, hence the name Minkowski addition is applied to Proposition 5 in the literature (for example, see [10]). Unfortunately, Minkowksi failed to define the dual of his set addition operation, and Minkowski subtraction expressed as the intersection of translations of A by the elements of B was not formally proposed until done so by Hadwiger.

Proposition 5 emphasizes the role of image shifting to implement dilation. In pipeline digital image processors employing raster scanning, image shifting is accomplished by delay elements in the transmission path. But delay elements can only cause an image shift in a direction opposite to the row scanning direction of the raster conversion. Thus it is important to know that dilating a shifted image, which arises from previous pipeline delays, shifts the dilated result by an equivalent amount. This fact permits pipeline processors to successively operate morphologically on shifted images and to undo the total resulting shift by performing an opposite shift by the scrolling operation in the output image buffer. We call this property the translation invariance of dilation.

Translation Invariance of Dilation Proposition 6:

$$(A)_x \oplus B = (A \oplus B)_x.$$

Proof: $y \in (A)_x \oplus B$ if and only if for some $z \in (A)_x$ and $b \in B$, $y = z + b$. But $z \in (A)_x$ if and only if $z = a + x$ for some $a \in A$. Hence, $y = (a + x) + b = (a +$

b) + *x*. Now by definition of dilation and translation $y \in (A \oplus B)_x$.

A corollary to Proposition 6 applies to dilations implemented through the chain rule (Proposition 3). The corollary states that shifting any one of the structuring elements in a dilation decomposition shifts the dilated image by an equivalent amount.

Corollary 7:

$$A \oplus B_1 \oplus \cdots \oplus (B_n)_x \oplus \cdots \oplus B_N$$
$$= (A \oplus B_1 \oplus \cdots \oplus B_n \oplus \cdots \oplus B_N)_x.$$

Image shift can be compensated for in the definition of the structuring element. In particular, let the structuring element *B* be compensating for a shift in the image *A* by taking *B* to be shifted in the opposite direction. Then the shift in *B* compensates for the shift in *A*.

Proposition 8:

$$(A)_x \oplus (B)_{-x} = A \oplus B.$$

Proof:

$$(A)_x \oplus (B)_{-x} = \left(A \oplus (B)_{-x} \right)_x$$
$$= (A \oplus B)_{x-x}$$
$$= A \oplus B.$$

Similarly, compensating shifts within the sequence of decomposed structuring element dilations can balance image shifts and cause an unshifted result.

Corollary 9:

$$(A)_x \oplus B_1 \oplus \cdots \oplus (B_n)_{-x} \oplus \cdots \oplus B_N$$
$$= A \oplus B_1 \oplus \cdots \oplus B_n \oplus \cdots \oplus B_N$$

In addition to being commutative, the dilation transformation is necessarily extensive when the origin belongs to the structuring element, extensivity meaning that the dilated result contains the original.

Example: This example shows that when the origin is not in the structuring element *B*, it may happen that the dilation of *A* by *B* has nothing in common with *A*.

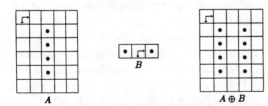

A corollary to Proposition 10 states that if the origin belongs to each of the structuring elements, in a dilation composition, each structuring element in the decomposition is necessarily contained in the original composed structuring element.

Corollary 11: If $0 \in B_1, \cdots, B_N$ then $B_m \in B_1 \oplus \cdots \oplus B_N$, $m = 1, \cdots, N$.

The dilation transformation is increasing, that is, containment relationships are maintained through dilation.

Dilation Is Increasing Proposition 12: $A \subseteq B$ implies $A \oplus D \subseteq B \oplus D$.

Proof: Suppose $A \subseteq B$. Let $x \in A \oplus D$. Then for some $a \in A$ and $d \in D$, $x = a + d$. Since $a \in A$ and $A \subseteq B$, $a \in B$. But $a \in B$ and $d \in D$ implies $x \in B \oplus D$.

Corollary 13: $A \subseteq B$ implies $D \oplus A \subseteq D \oplus B$.

The order of an image intersection operation and a dilation operation cannot be interchanged. Rather, the result of intersecting two images followed by a dilation of the intersection result is contained in the intersection of the dilation of the two images.

Proposition 14:

$$(A \cap B) \oplus C \subseteq (A \oplus C) \cap (B \oplus C)$$
$$(A \oplus (B \cap C) \subseteq (A \oplus B) \cap (A \oplus C)$$

Proof: Suppose $x \in (A \cap B) \oplus C$. Then for some $y \in A \cap B$ and $c \in C$, $x = y + c$. Now $y \in A \cap B$ implies $y \in A$ and $y \in B$. But $y \in A$, $c \in C$, and $x = y + c$ implies $x \in A \oplus C$; $y \in B$, $c \in C$, and $x = y + c$ implies $x \in B \oplus C$. Hence $x \in (A \oplus C) \cap (B \oplus C)$.

$(A \oplus (B \cap C) \subseteq (A \oplus B) \cap (A \oplus C)$ comes about immediately from the previous result since dilation is commutative.

On the other hand, the order of image union and dilation can be interchanged. The dilation of the union of two images is equal to the union of the dilations of these images.

Proposition 15:

$$(A \cup B) \oplus C = (A \oplus C) \cup (B \oplus C)$$

Proof:

$$(A \cup B) \oplus C = \bigcup_{x \in A \cup B} (C)_x$$
$$= \left[\bigcup_{x \in A} (C)_x \right] \cup \left[\bigcup_{x \in B} (C)_x \right]$$
$$= (A \oplus C) \cup (B \oplus C).$$

By the commutativity of dilation, we immediately have the following.

Corollary 16:

$$A \oplus (B \cup C) = (A \oplus B) \cup (A \oplus C).$$

This equality is significant. It permits for a further decomposition of a structuring element into a union of structuring elements. Previously we saw that the decomposition of a structuring element into the dilation of elemental structuring elements led to a chain rule for dilation. Here we see that decomposing a structuring element into the union of elemental structuring elements leads to another method of evaluating the dilation.

The distinction between structuring element decomposition by dilation and by union deserves further mention. The issue bears upon the efficiency of computing the dilations. Consider the structuring element of Fig. 4.

Structuring element *B* of Fig. 4 top consists of 16 points, hence it can be decomposed into the union of 16 structuring elements, each structuring element consisting

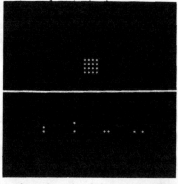

Fig. 4. This figure shows how the chain rule dilation decomposition can save operations. To dilate an image by the structuring element shown in the top half requires 15 operations. To dilate using the chain decomposition shown in the bottom half requires only 4 operations.

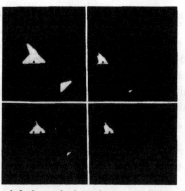

Fig. 5. The upper left shows the input image consisting of two blobs. The upper right shows the input image eroded by the structuring element $\{(0, 0), (-14, 0)\}$. The lower left shows the input image eroded by the structuring element $\{(0, 0)(0, -14)\}$. The lower right shows the input image eroded by the structuring element $\{(0, 0), (0, -14), (-14, 0)\}$.

of a single point which is suitably displaced from the origin. Dilation by a structuring element consisting of a single point is simply a shift of the original image, hence Proposition 15 becomes equivalent to the expression of Proposition 5 for the dilation, involving 15 shifts and 15 unions. By contrast, the decomposition of structuring element B into the four elemental structuring elements of Fig. 4 bottom permits dilation by B through the chain rule of Proposition 3. Here we see that only four shifts and four unions are required. Computationally, the difference involves a shift and union of the previously computed result in the case of Proposition 3's chain rule, while decomposition by union as in Proposition 15 independently accumulates the individual shifts of the original image.

B. Erosion

Erosion is the morphological dual to dilation. It is the morphological transformation which combines two sets using the vector subtraction of set elements. If A and B are sets in Euclidean N-space, then the erosion of A by B is the set of all elements x for which $x + b \in A$ for every $b \in B$. Some image processing people use the name shrink or reduce for erosion.

Definition 17: The erosion of A by B is denoted by $A \ominus B$ and is defined by

$$A \ominus B = \{x \in E^N \mid x + b \in A \text{ for every } b \in B\}$$

Example: This illustrates an instance of erosion.

$$A = \{(1, 0), (1, 1), (1, 2), (1, 3), (1, 4), (1, 5),$$
$$(2, 1), (3, 1), (4, 1), (5, 1),\}$$
$$B = \{(0, 0), (0, 1)\}$$
$$A \ominus B = \{(1, 0), (1, 1), (1, 2), (1, 3), (1, 4)\}$$

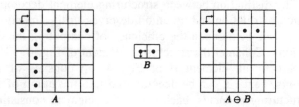

Expressed as a difference of elements a and b, Definition 17 becomes

$$A \ominus B = \{x \in E^N \mid \text{for every } b \in B, \text{ there exists an}$$
$$a \in A \text{ such that } x = a - b\}$$

This is tne definition used for erosion by [10].

The utility of the erosion transformation is better appreciated when the erosion is expressed in a different form. The erosion of an image A by a structuring element B is the set of all elements x of E^N for which B translated to x is contained in A. In fact, this was the definition used for erosion by [18]. The proof is immediate from the definition of erosion and the definition of translation.

Proposition 18:

$$A \ominus B = \{x \in E^N \mid (B)_x \subseteq A\}.$$

Thus the structuring element B may be visualized as a probe which slides across the image A, testing the spatial nature of A at every point. Where B translated to x can be contained in A (by placing the origin of B at x), then x belongs to the erosion $A \ominus B$. The erosion transformation is illustrated in Fig. 5.

The careful reader should beware that the symbol $\ominus$ used by [31] does not designate erosion. Rather it designates the Minkowski subtraction which is the intersection of all translations of A by the elements $b \in B$. Whereas the dilation transformation and the Minkowski addition of sets are identical, the erosion transformation and the Minkowski subtraction differ in a significant way. Erosion of an image A by a structuring element B is the intersection of all translations of A by the points $-b$, where $b \in B$.

Proposition 19:

$$A \ominus B = \bigcap_{b \in B} (A)_{-b}.$$

Proof: Let $x \in A \ominus B$. Then for every $b \in B$, $x + b \in A$. But $x + b \in A$ implies $x \in (A)_{-b}$. Hence for every $b \in B$, $x \in (A)_{-b}$. This implies $x \in \bigcap_{b \in B} (A)_{-b}$.

Let $x \in \bigcap_{b \in B} (A)_{-b}$. Then for every $b \in B$, $x \in (A)_{-b}$. Hence, for every $b \in B$, $x + b \in A$. Now by definition of erosion $x \in A \ominus B$.

Example: This illustrates how erosion can by computed as an intersection of translates of A.

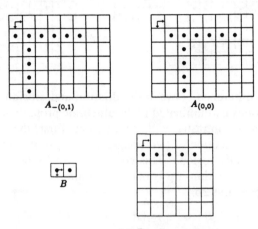

$$A \ominus B = A_{(0,0)} \cap A_{-(0,1)}$$

The erosion transformation is popularly conceived of as a shrinking of the original image. In set terms, the eroded set is often thought of as being contained in the original set. A transformation having this property is called anti-extensive. However, the erosion transformation is necessarily anti-extensive only if the origin belongs to the structuring element.

Proposition 20: If $0 \in B$, then $A \ominus B \subseteq A$.

Proof: Let $x \in A \ominus B$. Then $x + b \in A$ for every $b \in B$. Since $0 \in B$, $x + 0 \in A$. Hence $x \in A$.

Example: This illustrates how eroding with a structuring element which does not contain the origin can lead to a result which has nothing in common with the set being eroded.

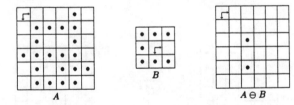

Like dilation, erosion is a translation invariant and increasing transformation.

Translation Invariance of Erosion Proposition 21:

$$A_x \ominus B = (A \ominus B)_x$$

$$A \ominus B_x = (A \ominus B)_{-x}.$$

Proof: $y \in A_x \ominus B$ if and only if for every $b \in B$, $y + b \in A_x$. But $y + b \in A_x$ if and only if $y + b - x \in A$. Now, $y + b - x = (y - x) + b$. Hence for every $b \in B$, $(y - x) + b \in A$. By definition of erosion, $y - x \in A \ominus B$ and, therefore, $y \in (A \ominus B)_x$.

$y \in A \ominus B_x$ if and only if $y + b \in A$ for every $b \in B_x$. But $y + b \in A$ for every $b \in B_x$ if and only if $y - x \in A \ominus B$. Finally $y - x \in A \ominus B$ if and only if $y \in (A \ominus B)_{-x}$.

If image A is contained in image B, then the erosion of A is contained in the erosion of B.

Erosion Is Increasing Proposition 22: $A \subseteq B$ implies $A \ominus K \subseteq B \ominus K$.

Proof: Let $x \in A \ominus K$. Then $x + k \in A$ for every $k \in K$. But $A \subseteq B$. Hence, $x + k \in B$ for every $k \in K$. By definition of erosion, $x \in B \ominus K$.

Example: This illustrates an instance showing the in-

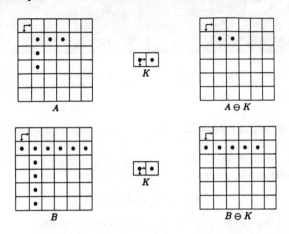

creasing property of erosion. On the other hand, if A and B are structuring elements and B is contained in A, then the erosion of an image D by A is necessarily more severe than erosion by B, that is, D eroded by A will necessarily be contained in D eroded by B.

Proposition 23: $A \supseteq B$ implies $D \ominus A \subseteq D \ominus B$.

Proof: Let $x \in D \ominus A$. Then $x + a \in D$ for every $a \in A$. But $B \subseteq A$. Hence, $x + a \in D$ for every $a \in B$. Now by definition of erosion, $x \in D \ominus B$.

Example: This illustrates an instance showing that larger structuring elements have a more severe effect than smaller ones on the erosion process.

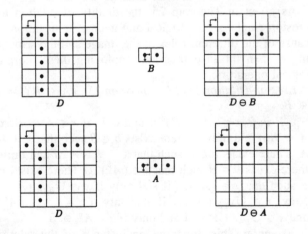

This proposition leads to a natural ordering of the erosions by structuring elements having the same shape but different sizes. It is the basis of the morphological distance transformations. Fig. 6 illustrates these distance relationships.

The dilation and erosion transformations bear a marked similarity, in that what one does to the image foreground the other does to the image background. Indeed, their similarity can be formalized as a duality relationship. Recall that two operators are dual when the negation of a

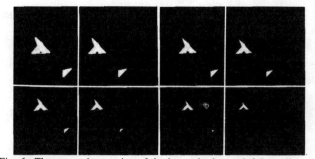

Fig. 6. The successive erosion of the image in the top left by a diamond shaped structuring element. Pixels which are white in the *i*th erosion are white pixels in the input image which have a 4-distance of greater than *i* pixels to the black background.

formulation employing the first operator is equal to that formulation employing operator on the negated variables. An example is DeMorgan's law, illustrating the duality of union and intersection,

$$(A \cup B)^c = A^c \cap B^c.$$

Here the negation of a set *A* is its complement,

$$A^c = \{x \in E^n \mid x \notin A\}.$$

In morphology, negation of a set is considered in a geometrical sense: that of reversing the orientation of the set with respect to its coordinate axes. Such reversing is called reflection.

Definition 24: Let $B \subseteq E^N$. The reflection of *B* is denoted by $\check{B}$ and is defined by

$$\check{B} = \{x \mid \text{for some } b \in B,\ x = -b\}.$$

The reflection occurs about the origin. Matheron [18] refers to $\check{B}$ as "the symmetrical set of *B* with respect to the origin." Serra [31] refers to $\check{B}$ as "*B* transpose."

As given in Theorem 25, the duality of dilation and erosion employs both logical and geometric negation because of the different roles of the image and the structuring element in an expression employing these morphological operators.

Erosion Dilation Duality Theorem 25: $(A \ominus B)^c = A^c \oplus \check{B}$.

Proof: $x \in (A \ominus B)^c$ if and only if $x \notin A \ominus B$. $x \notin A \ominus B$ if and only if there exists $b \in B$ such that $x + b \notin A$. There exists $b \in B$ such that $x + b \in A^c$ if and only if there exists $b \in B$ such that $x \in (A^c)_{-b}$. There exists $b \in B$ such that $x \in (A^c)_{-b}$ if and only if $x \in \cup_{b \in B} (A^c)_{-b}$. Now, $x \in \cup_{b \in B} (A^c)_{-b}$ if and only if $x \in \cup_{b \in \check{B}} (A^c)_b$; and $x \in \cup_{b \in \check{B}} (A^c)_b$ if and only if $x \in A^c \oplus \check{B}$.

Example: This illustrates an instance of the relationship $(A \ominus B)^c = A^c \oplus \check{B}$.

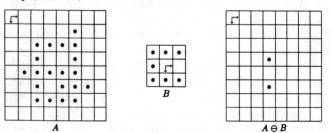

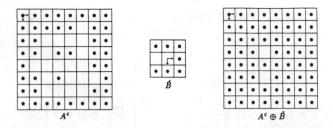

The difference between the dilation and erosion transformations is illuminated in the algebraic properties of the erosion as contrasted with the dilation. First, the erosion of the intersection of two images is equal to the intersection of their erosions. This contrasts with Proposition 14 where the relationship is one of containment.

Proposition 26:

$$(A \cap B) \ominus K = (A \ominus K) \cap (B \ominus K).$$

Proof: $x \in (A \cap B) \ominus K$ if and only if for every $k \in K$, $x + k \in A \cap B$. $x + k \in A \cap B$ if and only if $x + k \in A$ and $x + k \in B$. $x + k \in A$ for every $k \in K$ if and only if $x \in A \ominus K$. $x + k \in A$ for every $k \in K$ if and only if $x \in B \ominus K$. $x + k \in A$ for every $k \in K$ and $x + k \in B$ for every $k \in K$ if and only if $x \in (A \ominus K) \cap (B \ominus K)$.

Example: This illustrates an instance of the relationship $(A \cap B) \ominus K = (A \ominus K) \cap (B \ominus K)$.

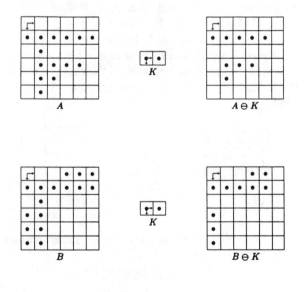

$(A \cap B) \ominus K = (A \ominus K) \cap (B \ominus K)$

On the other hand, whereas the dilation of the unions of two images is equal to the union of their dilations (Proposition 15), for the erosion transformation the relationship is one of containment.

Proposition 27: $(A \cup B) \ominus K \supseteq (A \ominus K) \cup (B \ominus K).$

Proof: Let $x \in (A \ominus K) \cup (B \ominus K)$. Then $x \in A \ominus K$ or $x \in B \ominus K$. If $x \in A \ominus K$ then since $A \cup B \supseteq A$, $x \in (A \cup B) \ominus K$. If $x \in B \ominus K$ then since $A \cup B \supseteq B$, $x \in (A \cup B) \ominus K$.

Example: This illustrates an instance in which $(A \cup B) \ominus K$ strictly contains $(A \ominus K) \cup (B \ominus K)$.

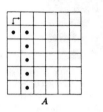

A K $A \ominus K$

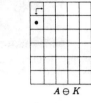

B K $B \ominus K$

$(A \cup B) \ominus K$ $(A \ominus K) \cup (B \ominus K)$

But erosion is not commutative, $A \ominus B \neq B \ominus A$. Hence the behavior of $A \ominus (B \cup C)$ indicated in the equality of Proposition 28 is different than the behavior of $(A \cup B) \ominus C$ as indicated in Proposition 27.

Proposition 28: $A \ominus (B \cup C) = (A \ominus B) \cap (A \ominus C)$

Proof: $x \in A \ominus (B \cup C)$ if and only if $x + y \in A$ for every $y \in B \cup C$. $x + y \in A$ for every $y \in B \cup C$ if and only if $x + y \in A$ for every $y \in B$ and $x + y \in A$ for every $y \in C$. $x + y \in A$ for every $y \in B$ if and only if $x \in A \ominus B$. $x + y \in A$ for every $y \in C$ if and only if $x \in A \ominus C$. $x + y \in A$ for every $y \in B$ and $x + y \in A$ for every $y \in C$ if and only if $x \in (A \ominus B) \cap (A \ominus C)$.

Example: This illustrates an instance of the relationship $A \ominus (B \cup C) = (A \ominus B) \cap (A \ominus C)$.

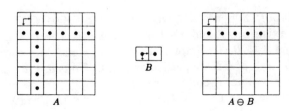

A B $A \ominus B$

A C $A \ominus C$

$B \cup C$

$A \ominus (B \cup C)$

$(A \ominus B) \cap (A \ominus C)$

The practical utility of Proposition 28 is that it indicates how to compute erosions with structuring elements which can only be decomposed as the union of individual structuring elements.

Although structuring elements can be decomposed through union into simpler structuring elements to simplify the erosion transformation, structuring elements cannot be decomposed through intersection and maintain an equality. Rather, the intersection decomposition leads to a containment relationship.

Proposition 29: $A \ominus (B \cap C) \supseteq (A \ominus B) \cup (A \ominus C)$.

Proof: Let $x \in (A \ominus B) \cup (A \ominus C)$. Then $x \in A \ominus B$ or $x \in A \ominus C$. If $x \in A \ominus B$, then $x + b \in A$ for every $b \in B$. If $x \in A \ominus C$, then $x + b \in A$ for every $b \in C$. Hence, $x + b \in A$ for every $b \in B \cap C$. Now by definition of erosion, $x \in A \ominus (B \cap C)$.

Example: This illustrates an instance in which $A \ominus (B \cap C)$ strictly contains $(A \ominus B) \cup (A \ominus C)$.

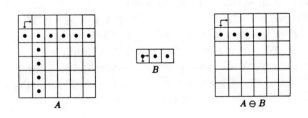

A B $A \ominus B$

225

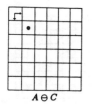

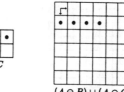

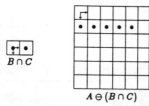

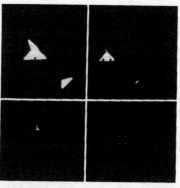

Fig. 7. The upper left shows the input image. The upper right shows the input image eroded by the structuring element $\{(0, 0), (0, -14)\}$. The lower left shows the eroded image of the upper right eroded by the structuring element $\{(0, 0), (-14, 0)\}$. This result is equivalent to eroding the input image by the structuring element $\{(0, 0), (0, -14), (-14, 0), (-14, -14)\}$ which is shown in the lower right.

Example: This illustrates an instance in which $A \oplus (B \ominus C)$ is strictly contained in $(A \oplus B) \ominus C$.

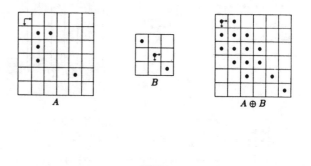

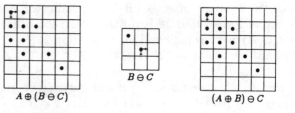

Finally, with respect to structuring element decomposition, a chain rule for erosion holds when the structuring element is decomposable through dilation,

$$A \ominus (B \oplus C) = (A \ominus B) \ominus C.$$

This relation is as important as the chain rule relation for dilation because it permits a large erosion to be computed by two successive smaller erosions.

Proposition 30: $(A \ominus B) \ominus C = A \ominus (B \oplus C)$.

Proof: Let $x \in (A \ominus B) \ominus C$. Then for every $c \in C$, $x + c \in A \ominus B$. But $x + c \in A \ominus B$ implies $x + c + b \in A$ for every $b \in B$. But $x + b + c \in A$ for every $b \in B$ and $c \in C$ implies $x + d \in A$ for every $d \in B \oplus C$.

Let $x \in A \ominus (B \oplus C)$. Then $x + d \in A$ for every $d \in B \oplus C$. Hence $x + b + c \in A$ for every $b \in B$ and $c \in C$. Now $(x + c) + b \in A$ for every $b \in B$ implies $x + c \in A \ominus B$. But $x + c \in A \ominus B$ for every $c \in C$ implies $x \in (A \ominus B) \ominus C$.

Corollary 31 extends this result to structuring elements decomposed as the dilation of K structuring elements.

Corollary 31: $A \ominus (B_1 \oplus \cdots \oplus B_K) = (\cdots (A \ominus B_1) \ominus \cdots \ominus B_K)$.

It is immediately apparent from the corollary that because dilation is commutative, the order in which successive erosions are applied is immaterial.

Fig. 7 illustrates the utility of the chain rule for erosions.

Reversing the position of dilation and erosion in Proposition 30 does not lead to an equality as in Proposition 30 but leads to a containment relation as given in Proposition 32. In some sense this indicates that when performing erosion and dilation, performing erosion first is more severe than performing dilation first.

Proposition 32: $A \oplus (B \ominus C) \subseteq (A \oplus B) \ominus C$.

Proof: Let $x \in A \oplus (B \ominus C)$. Then for some $a \in A$ and $B \ominus C$, $x = a + y$. But $y \in B \ominus C$ implies $y + c \in B$ for every $c \in C$. Now $y + c \in B$ and $a \in A$ implies $y + c + a \in A \oplus B$. Finally $y + c + a \in A \oplus B$ for every $c \in C$ implies $x = y + a \in (A \oplus B) \ominus C$.

Although dilation and erosion are dual, this does not imply that we can freely perform cancellation on morphological equalities. For example, if $A = B \ominus C$, then dilating both sides of the expression by C results in $A \oplus C = B \ominus C \oplus C \neq B$. However, a containment relationship is maintained, as indicated in Proposition 33.

Proposition 33: $A \subseteq B \ominus C$ if and only if $B \supseteq A \oplus C$.

Proof: Suppose $A \subseteq B \ominus C$. Let $x \in A \oplus C$. Then there exists $a \in A$ and $c \in C$ such that $x = a + c$. But $a \in A$ and $A \subseteq B \ominus C$ implies $a \in B \ominus C$. Hence, for every $c' \in B$, $a + c' \in B$. In particular, $c \in C$. Thus $a + c \in B$. But $x = a + c$. Therefore, $x \in B$.

Suppose $A \oplus C \subseteq B$. Let $x \in A$. Let $c \in C$. Then $x +$

$c \in A \oplus C$. But $A \oplus C \subseteq B$ so that $x + c \subseteq B$. Finally $x + c \subseteq B$ for any $c \in C$ implies $x \in B \ominus C$.

The containment is maintained for chained erosions, as follows.

Corollary 34:

$$A \subseteq (\cdots (B \ominus C_1) \ominus \cdots) \ominus C_N \text{ if and only}$$

$$\text{if } (\cdots (A \oplus C_1) \oplus \cdots) \oplus C_N \subseteq B.$$

III. Openings and Closings

In practice, dilations and erosions are usually employed in pairs, either dilation of an image followed by the erosion of the dilated result, or image erosion followed by dilation. In either case, the result of iteratively applied dilations and erosions is an elimination of specific image detail smaller than the structuring element without the global geometric distortion of unsuppressed features. For example, opening an image with a disk structuring element smooths the contour, breaks narrow isthmuses, and eliminates small islands and sharp peaks or capes. Closing an image with a disk structuring element smooths the contours, fuses narrow breaks and long thin gulfs, eliminates small holes, and fills gaps on the contours.

Of particular significance is the fact that image transformations employing iteratively applied dilations and erosions are idempotent, that is, their reapplication effects no further changes to the previously transformed result. The practical importance of idempotent transformations is that they comprise complete and closed stages of image analysis algorithms because shapes can be naturally described in terms of under what structuring elements they can be opened or can be closed and yet remain the same. Their functionality corresponds closely to the specification of a signal by its bandwidth. Morphologically filtering an image by an opening or closing operation corresponds to the ideal nonrealizable bandpass filters of conventional linear filtering. Once an image is ideal bandpassed filtered, further ideal bandpass filtering does not alter the result.

This property motivates the importance for having definitions of opening and closing, concepts first studied by Matheron [17], [18] who was interested in axiomatizing the concept of size. Both Matheron's [18] definitions and Serra's [31] definitions for opening and closing are identical to the ones given here, but their formulas appear different because they use the symbol $\ominus$ to mean Minkowski subtraction rather than erosion.

Definition 35: The opening of image B by structuring element K is denoted by $B \circ K$ and is defined as $B \circ K = (B \ominus K) \oplus K$.

Definition 36: The closing of image B by structuring element K is denoted by $B \bullet K$ and is defined by $B \bullet K = (B \oplus K) \ominus K$.

If B is unchanged by opening it with K, we say that B is open with respect to K, while if B is unchanged by closing it with K, then B is closed with respect to K.

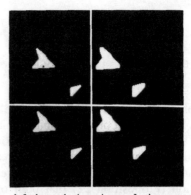

Fig. 8. The upper left shows the input image. In the upper right, the input image is dilated by a structuring element consisting of a 5×5 square. In the lower left, the dilated image is eroded by a 5×5 square structuring element. It is the closing of the input image. In the lower right, the closed image is dilated by a 5×5 square structuring element. It is the same as the initially dilated image shown in the upper right.

We approach the issue of idempotency of opening and closing by first discussing a class of sets which are unaltered by erosion followed by dilation with a given structuring element K. This class consists of all sets which can be expressed as some set dilated by K.

Proposition 37: $A \oplus K = (A \oplus K) \circ K = (A \bullet K) \oplus K$.

Proof: Let $G = A \oplus K$, $H = G \ominus K$, and $I = H \oplus K$. Now, by Proposition 33, $G = A \oplus K$ implies $A \subseteq G \ominus K = H$; $H = G \ominus K$ implies $G \supseteq H \oplus K = I$. But $A \subseteq H$ implies $A \oplus K \subseteq H \oplus K$. Since $G = A \oplus K$ and $I = H \oplus K$, $G \subseteq I$. Finally, $G \supseteq I$ and $G \subseteq I$ imply $G = I$. Hence,

$$A \oplus K = H \oplus K = (G \ominus K) \oplus K$$
$$= ((A \oplus K) \ominus K) \oplus K = (A \bullet K) \oplus K.$$

Proposition 37 is illustrated in Fig. 8. The idempotency of closing follows immediately as given by Theorem 38.

Theorem 38: $(A \bullet K) \bullet K = A \bullet K$.

Proof:

$$A \oplus K = (A \bullet K) \oplus K$$
$$(A \oplus K) \ominus K = ((A \bullet K) \oplus K) \ominus K$$
$$A \bullet K = ((A \bullet K) \bullet K).$$

Similarly, images eroded by K are unaltered by further dilation and erosion by K.

Proposition 39: $A \ominus K = (A \circ K) \ominus K = (A \ominus K) \bullet K$.

Proof: Let $G = A \ominus K$, $H = G \oplus K$, and $I = H \ominus K$. Now, $G = A \ominus K$ implies $A \supseteq G \oplus K = H$; $H = G \oplus K$ implies $G \subseteq H \ominus K = I$. But $A \supseteq H$ implies $A \ominus K \supseteq H \ominus K$ so that $G \supseteq I$. Finally $G \subseteq I$ and $G \supseteq I$ imply $G = I = H \ominus K = (G \oplus K) \ominus K$. Since $G = A \ominus K$, $A \ominus K = ((A \ominus K) \oplus K) \ominus K = (A \circ K) \ominus K$. The idempotency of opening follows immediately as given by Theorem 40.

Theorem 40: $A \circ K = (A \circ K) \circ K$.

Proof:

$$A \ominus K = (A \circ K) \ominus K$$

$$(A \ominus K) \oplus K = ((A \circ K) \ominus K) \oplus K$$

$$A \circ K = (A \circ K) \circ K.$$

As with chained dilations and erosions, we can extend these results for chained openings and closings.

Openings and closings have other properties. For example, it follows immediately from the increasing property of dilation (Proposition 12) and the increasing property of erosion (Proposition 22) that both opening and closing are increasing.

It follows immediately from the translation invariance of dilation (Proposition 6) and the translation invariance of erosion (Proposition 21) that both opening and closing are translation invariant. Unlike dilation and erosion, opening and closing are invariant to translations of the structuring elements. That is, $A \circ (B)_x = A \circ B$ and $A \bullet (B)_x = A \bullet B$. This also follows directly from Propositions 6 and 21. As stated in Proposition 41, the opening transformation is antiextensive, i.e., the opening of A by structuring element B is necessarily contained in A, regardless of whether or not the origin belongs to B.

Antiextensivity of Opening Proposition 41: $A \circ B \subseteq A$.

Proof: Let $x \in A \circ B$. Then $x \in (A \ominus B) \oplus B$. Hence there exist $u \in A \ominus B$ and $v \in B$ such that $x = u + v$. Now $u \in A \ominus B$ implies $u + b \in A$ for every $b \in B$. In particular, $v \in B$. Thus $u + v \in A$. But $x = u + v$ so that $x \in A$.

Example: Illustrates how opening can produce a result which is strictly contained in the original.

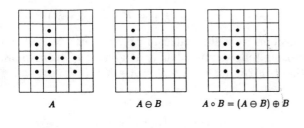

$$A \qquad A \ominus B \qquad A \circ B = (A \ominus B) \oplus B$$

$$B$$

Fig. 9 illustrates an opening by a structuring element which does not include its origin.

The closing transformation is extensive, i.e., the closing of A by structuring element B contains A regardless of whether or not B contains its origin.

Extensivity of Closing Proposition 42: $A \subseteq A \bullet B$.

Proof: Let $a \in A$. Let $b \in B$. Then $a + b \in A \oplus B$. But $a + b \in A \oplus B$ for every $b \in B$ implies $a \in (A \oplus B) \ominus B$.

Example: This illustrates an instance of the relationship $A \subseteq A \bullet B$.

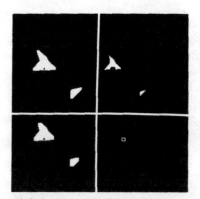

Fig. 9. The upper left shows the input image. In the upper right, the input image is eroded by the box boundary structuring element shown in the lower right. Notice that because the box is big enough to surround the hole and still be inside the blob with the hole, the eroded image has one white point whose position is in the hole. The lower left shows the image of the upper right dilated by the box boundary structuring element. This is the opening of the input image by the box boundary structuring element.

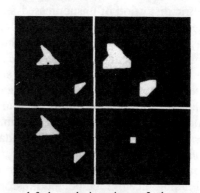

Fig. 10. The upper left shows the input image. In the upper right, the input image is dilated by a structuring element consisting of an 11 × 11 square shown in lower right. In the lower left, the dilated image is eroded by a 11 × 11 square structuring element. This results in the closing of the input image.

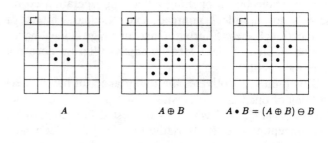

$$A \qquad A \oplus B \qquad A \bullet B = (A \oplus B) \ominus B$$

$$B$$

Fig. 10 illustrates a closing by a square structuring element.

Openings and closings, like erosion and dilations, are dual transformations. The complement of the closing of A by B is the opening of A^c by $\breve{B}$. This is illustrated in Fig. 11.

Duality of Opening and Closing Theorem 43: $(A \bullet B)^c = A^c \circ \breve{B}$.

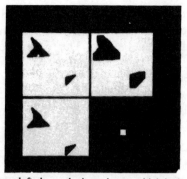

Fig. 11. The upper left shows the input image which is the complement of the input image of Fig. 10. In the upper right, the input image is eroded by a structuring consisting of an 11 × 11 square (shown in lower right). In the lower left, the eroded image is dilated by the 11 × 11 square structuring element. This results in the opening of the input image. Comparing Fig. 11 to Fig. 10, the opening of the complement is the complement of the closing for the symmetric square structuring element.

Proof:

$$(A \bullet B)^c = [(A \oplus B) \ominus B]^c$$
$$= (A \oplus B)^c \oplus \check{B}$$
$$= (A^c \ominus \check{B}) \oplus \check{B}$$
$$= A^c \circ \check{B}.$$

Proposition 44 gives a geometric characterization to the opening operation. The opening of A by B is the union of all translations of B that are contained in A.

Proposition 44:

$$A \circ B = \{x \in A \mid \text{for some } y, x \in B_y \subseteq A\}$$
$$= \bigcup_{\{y \mid B_y \subseteq A\}} B_y.$$

Proof: Suppose $x \in A \circ B$, then $x \in (A \ominus B) \oplus B$. Hence there exists a $y \in A \ominus B$ and $b \in B$ such that $x = y + b$. Since $y \in A \ominus B$, $y + b \in A$ with $b \in B$ implies $x \in B_y$.

Suppose $x \in A$ and for some y, $x \in B_y \subseteq A$, then for every $z \in B$, $z + y \in A$ and there must exist some $b \in B$ such that $x = b + y$. But $y + z \in A$ for every $z \in B$ implies by definition of erosion that $y \in A \ominus B$. And $x = b + y$ implies by definition of dilation that $x \in (A \ominus B) \oplus B = A \circ B$.

By the duality of opening and closing, it is immediate that the closing of A by B is the complement of the union of all translations of $\check{B}$ that are contained in A^c. That is, $A \bullet B = (A^c \circ \check{B}) = [\bigcup_{\{y \mid \check{B}_y \subseteq A^c\}} \check{B}_y]^c$. Proposition 45 gives another geometric characterization to the closing operation.

Proposition 45:

$$A \bullet B = \{x \in E^N \mid x \in \check{B}_y \text{ implies } \check{B}_y \cap A \neq \emptyset\}$$
$$= \bigcap_{\{y \mid \check{B}_y \cap A = \emptyset\}} \check{B}_y^c$$

Proof: By Theorem 43, $A \bullet B = (A^c \circ \check{B})^c$.
By Proposition 44, $A^c \circ \check{B} = \{x \in E^N \mid \text{for some } y, x \in \check{B}_y \subseteq A^c\}$. Hence,

$$A \bullet B = (A^c \circ \check{B})^c = \{x \in E^N \mid \text{for some } y, x \in \check{B}_y \text{ and } \check{B}_y \subseteq A^c\}^c$$
$$= \{x \in E^N \mid \text{for some } y, x \in \check{B}_y \text{ and } \check{B}_y \cap A = \emptyset\}^c$$
$$= \{x \in E^N \mid x \in \check{B}_y \text{ implies } \check{B}_y \cap A \neq \emptyset\}$$

Propositions 44 and 45 immediately imply that $A \circ B_x = A \circ B_y$ and $A \bullet B_x = A \bullet B_y$ for any x and y in E^N. Hence the origin of the structuring element makes no difference in the results of an opening or closing.

Also,

$$\left[\bigcup_{\{y \mid \check{B}_y \subseteq A^c\}} \check{B}_y\right]^c = \left[\bigcup_{\{y \mid \check{B}_y \cap A = \emptyset\}} \check{B}_y\right]^c.$$

By DeMorgan's Law,

$$\left[\bigcup_{\{y \mid \check{B}_y \cap A^c = \emptyset\}} \check{B}_y\right]^c = \bigcup_{\{y \mid \check{B}_y \cap A^c = \emptyset\}} \check{B}_y^c.$$

IV. Gray Scale Morphology

The binary morphological operations of dilation, erosion, opening, and closing are all naturally extended to gray scale imagery by the use of a min or max operation. Nakagawa and Rosenfeld [22] first discussed the use of neighborhood min and max operators. The general extensions, due to Sternberg [33], [35], keep all the relationships discussed in Sections II and III. Peleg and Rosenfeld [24] use gray scale morphology to generalize the medial axis transform to gray scale imaging. Peleg, Naor, Hartley, and Avnir [23] use gray scale morphology to measure changes in texture properties as a function of resolution. Werman and Peleg [38] use gray scale morphology for texture feature extraction. Favre, Muggli, Stucki, and Bonderet [5] use gray scale morphology for the detection of platelet thrombosis detection in cross sections of blood vessels. Coleman and Sampson [2] use gray scale morphology on range data imagery to help mate a robot gripper to an object.

We will develop the extension in the following way. First we introduce the concept of the top surface of a set and the related concept of the umbra of a surface. Then gray scale dilation will be defined as the surface of the dilation of the umbras. From this definition we will proceed to the representation which indicates that gray scale dilation can be computed in terms of a maximum operation and a set of addition operations. A similar plan is followed for erosion which can be evaluated in terms of a minimum operation and a set of subtraction operations.

Of course, having a definition and a means of evaluating the defined operations does not imply that the properties of gray scale dilation and erosion are the same as binary dilation and erosion. To establish that the relationships are identical, we explore some of the relationships between the umbra and surface operation. Our explana-

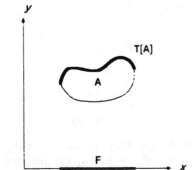

Fig. 12. The concept of top or top surface of a set.

tion shows that umbra and surface operations are essentially inverses of each other. Then we illustrate how the umbra operation is a homomorphism from the gray scale morphology to the binary morphology. Having the homomorphism in hand, all the interesting relationships follow by appropriately unwrapping and wrapping the involved sets or functions.

A. Gray Scale Dilation and Erosion

We begin with the concepts of surface of a set and the umbra of a surface. Suppose a set A in Euclidean N-space is given. We adopt the convention that the first $(N-1)$ coordinates of the N-tuples of A constitute the spatial domain of A and the Nth coordinate is for the surface. For gray scale imagery, $N = 3$. The top or top surface of A is a function defined on the projection of A onto its first $(N-1)$ coordinates. For each $(N-1)$-tuple x, the top surface of A at x is the highest value y such that the N-tuple $(x, y) \in A$. This is illustrated in Fig. 12. If the space we work in is Euclidean, we can express this using the concept of supremum. If the space is discrete, we use the more familiar concept of maximum. Since we have suppressed the underlying space in what follows, we use maximum throughout. The careful reader will want to translate maximum to supremum under the appropriate circumstances.

Definition 46: Let $A \subseteq E^N$ and $F = \{x \in E^{N-1} |$ for some $y \in E$, $(x, y) \in A\}$. The top or top surface of A, denoted by $T[A]: F \to E$, is defined by

$$T[A](x) = \max \{y | (x, y) \in A\}.$$

Definition 47: A set $A \subseteq E^{N-1} \times E$ is an umbra if and only if $(x, y) \in A$ implies that $(x, y) \in A$ for every $z \le y$.

For any function f defined on some subset F of Euclidean $(N-1)$-space the umbra of f is a set consisting of the surface f and everything below the surface.

Definition 48: Let $F \subseteq E^{N-1}$ and $f: F \to E$. The umbra of f, denoted by $U[f]$, $U[f] \subseteq F \times E$, is defined by

$$U[f] = \{(x, y) \in F \times E | y \le f(x)\}.$$

Obviously, the umbra of f is an umbra.

Example: This illustrates a discretized one-dimensional function f defined as a domain consisting of seven

successive column positions and a finite portion of its umbra which lies on or below the function f. The actual umbra has infinite extent below f. The reader should note that because the gray scale morphology so closely involves functions defined on the real line or plane, our example illustrations use the ordinary (x, y) coordinate frame instead of the row column coordinate frame employed in the examples of the binary morphology.

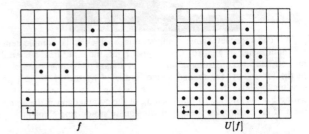

Having defined the operations of taking a top surface of a set and the umbra of a surface, we can define gray scale dilation. The gray scale dilation of two functions is defined as the surface of the dilation of their umbras.

Definition 49: Let $F, K \subseteq E^{N-1}$ and $f: F \to E$ and $k: K \to E$. The dilation of f by k is denoted by $f \oplus k$, $f \oplus k: F \oplus K \to E$, and is defined by

$$f \oplus k = T[U[f] \oplus U[k]].$$

Example: This illustrates a second discretized one-dimensional function k defined on a domain consisting of three successive column positions and a finite portion of its umbra which lies on or below the function k. The dilation of the umbras of f (from the previous example) and k are shown and the surface of the dilation of the umbras of f and k are shown.

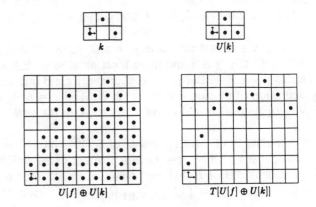

The definition of gray scale dilation tells us conceptually how to compute the gray scale dilation, but this conceptual way is not a reasonable way to compute it in hardware. The following theorem establishes that gray scale dilation can be accomplished by taking the maximum of a set of sums. Hence, gray scale dilation has the same complexity as convolution. However, instead of doing the summation of products as in convolution, a maximum of sums is performed.

Proposition 50: Let $f: F \to E$ and $k: K \to E$. Then $f \oplus$

$k: F \oplus K \to E$ can be computed by

$$(f \oplus k)(x) = \max_{\substack{z \in K \\ x-z \in F}} \{f(x - z) + k(z)\}.$$

Proof: Suppose $z = (f \oplus k)(x)$. Then $z = T[U[f] \oplus U[k]](x)$. By definition of surface,

$$z = \max \{y \,|\, (x, y) \in [U[f] \oplus U[k]]\}.$$

By definition of dilation,

$$z = \max \{a + b \,|\, \text{for some } u \in K \text{ satisfying } x - u \in F,$$
$$(x - u, a) \in U[f] \text{ and } (u, b) \in U[k]\}.$$

By definition of umbra, the largest a such that $(x - u, a) \in U[f]$ is $a = f(x - u)$. Likewise, the largest b such that $(u, b) \in U[k]$ is $b = k(u)$. Hence

$$z = \max \{f(x - u) + k(u) \,|\, u \in K, (x - u) \in F\}$$
$$= \max_{\substack{u \in K \\ (x-u) \in F}} \{f(x - u) + k(u)\}.$$

The definition for gray scale erosion proceeds in a similar way to the definition of gray scale dilation. The gray scale erosion of one function by another is the surface of the binary erosions of the umbra of one with the umbra of the other.

Definition 51: Let $F \subseteq E^{N-1}$ and $K \subseteq E^{N-1}$. Let $f: F \to E$ and $k: K \to E$. The erosion of f by k is denoted by $f \ominus k, f \ominus k: F \ominus K \to E$, and is defined by

$$f \ominus k = T[U[f] \ominus U[k]].$$

Example: Using the same function f and k of the previous example, illustrated here is the erosion of f by k by taking the surface of the erosion of the umbra of f by the umbra of k.

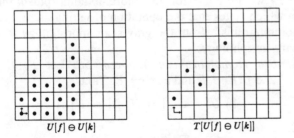

$U[f] \ominus U[k]$ $T[U[f] \ominus U[k]]$

Evaluating a gray scale erosion is accomplished by taking the minimum of a set of differences. Hence its complexity is the same as dilation. Its form is like correlation with the summation of correlation replaced by the minimum operation and the product of correlation replaced by a subtraction operation. If the underlying space is Euclidean, substitute infimum for minimum.

Proposition 52: Let $f: F \to E$ and $k: K \to E$. Then $f \ominus k: F \ominus K \to E$ can be computed by $(f \ominus k)(x) = \min_{z \in K} \{f(x + z) - k(z)\}$.

Proof: Suppose $z = (f \ominus k)(x)$. Then, $z = T[U[f] \ominus U[k]](x)$. By definition of surface, $z = \max \{y \,|\, (x, y) \in U[f] \ominus U[k]\}$. By definition of erosion

$$z = \max \{y \,|\, \text{for every } (u, v)$$
$$\in U[k], (x, y) + (u, v) \in U[f]\}.$$

By definition of umbra,

$$z = \max \{y \,|\, \text{for every } u \in K, v \leq k(u), y$$
$$+ v \leq f(x + u)\}$$
$$= \max \{y \,|\, \text{for every } u \in K, v$$
$$\leq k(u), y \leq f(x + u) - v\}.$$

But $y \leq f(x + u) - v$ for every $v \leq k(u)$ implies $y \leq f(x + u) - k(u)$. Hence,

$$z = \max \{y \,|\, \text{for every } u \in K, y \leq f(x + u) - k(u)\}.$$

But $y \leq f(x + u) - k(u)$ for every $u \in K$ implies

$$y \leq \min_{u \in K} [f(x + u) - k(u)].$$

Now,

$$z = \max \left\{ y \,\middle|\, y \leq \min_{u \in K} [f(x + u) - k(u)] \right\}$$
$$= \min_{u \in K} [f(x + u) - k(u)].$$

Fig. 13 illustrates an example of gray scale dilation and erosion.

The basic relationship between the surface and umbra operations is that they are, in a certain sense, inverses of each other. More precisely, the surface operation will always undo the umbra operation. That is, the surface operation is an inverse to the umbra operation as given in the next proposition.

Proposition 53: Let $F \subseteq E^{N-1}$ and $f: F \to E$. Then $T[U[f]] = f$.

Proof: Let $y \in T[U[f]](x)$. Then $y = \max \{z \,|\, (x, z) \in U[f]\}$. Now $(x, z) \in U[f]$ implies $z \leq f(x)$. Also, $(x, f(x)) \in U[f]$. Thus y cannot get larger than $f(x)$ and since $(x, f(x)) \in U[f]$, y can get as large as $f(x)$. Thus $y = f(x)$.

Corollary 54: $U[T[U[f]]] = U[f]$.

However the umbra operation is not an inverse to the surface operation. Without any constraints on the set A, the strongest statement which can be made is that the umbra of the surface of A contains A. This is illustrated in Fig. 14.

Proposition 55: Let $A \subseteq E^N$. Then $A \subseteq U[T[A]]$.

Proof: Let $x \in E^{N-1}$ and $y \in E$. Suppose, $(x, y) \in A$. Let $z = T[A](x) = \max \{v \,|\, (x, v) \in A\}$. Hence, $z \geq y$. But by definition of the umbra operation $z = T[A](x)$ implies $(x, w) \in U[T[A]]$ for all $w \leq z$. In particular, $y \leq z$. Hence, $(x, y) \in U[T[A]]$.

When the set A is an umbra, then the umbra of the surface of A is itself A. In this case the umbra operation is an inverse to the surface operation.

Proposition 56: If A is an umbra, then $A = U[T[A]]$.

Proof: By Proposition 54, $A \subseteq U[T[A]]$. So we just need to show that $A \supseteq U[T[A]]$. Suppose $(x, y) \in$

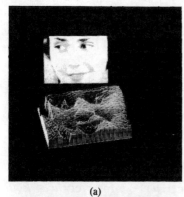

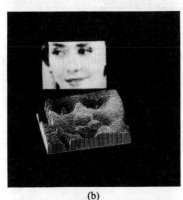

(a)

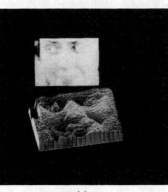

(b)

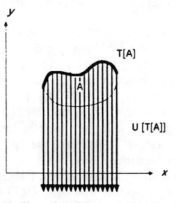

(c)

Fig. 13. A woman's face in the image form and in a perspective projection surface plot form. This image is morphologically processed with a paraboloid structuring element given by $6(8 - r^2 - c^2)$, $-2 \leq r \leq 2$, $-2 \leq c \leq 2$. (b) The erosion of the girl's face in image form and perspective projection surface plot form. (c) The dilation of the girl's face in image form and perspective projection surface plot form.

Fig. 14. The umbra of the top surface of a set.

$U[T[A]]$ and A is an umbra. By definition of the umbra operation $(x, y) \in U[T[A]]$ implies $y \leq T[A](x)$ and there exists some z such that $(x, z) \in A$. Now if there exists some z such that $(x, z) \in A$, $(x, T[A](x)) \in A$. Since A is an umbra, $(x, T[A](x)) \in A$ implies that $(x, w) \in A$ for every $w \leq T[A](x)$. In particular $y \leq T[A](x)$. Hence $(x, y) \in A$.

Having established that the surface operation is always an inverse to the umbra operation and that the umbra operation is the inverse to the surface operation when the set being operated on itself is an umbra, we are almost ready to develop the umbra homomorphism theorem. First we need to establish that the dilation of one umbra by another is an umbra and that the erosion of one umbra by another is also an umbra.

Proposition 57: Suppose A and B are umbras. Then $A \oplus B$ and $A \ominus B$ are umbras.

Proof: Suppose $(x, y) \in A \oplus B$. Let $w \leq y$. We need to demonstrate that $(x, w) \in A \oplus B$. By definition of dilation, $(x, y) \in A \oplus B$ implies that there exists $(u, v) \in B$ such that $(x - u, y - v) \in A$. Now $w \leq y$ implies $w - v \leq y - v$. And A is an umbra so that $(x - u, y - v) \in A$ and $w - v \leq y - v$ implies $(x - u, w - v) \in A$. But by definition of dilation, $(x - u, w - v) \in A$ and $(u, v) \in B$ implies $(x, w) \in A \oplus B$ which means that $A \oplus B$ is an umbra.

Suppose $(x, y) \in A \ominus B$. Let $w \leq y$. We need to demonstrate that $(x, w) \in A \ominus B$. By definition of erosion, $(x, y) \in A \ominus B$ implies that for every $(u, v) \in B$, $(x, y) + (u, v) = (x + u, y + v) \in A$. Now $w \leq y$ implies $w + v \leq y + v$. Since A is an umbra and $(x + u, y + v) \in A$ and $w + v \leq y + v$, then $(x + u, w + v) \in A$. But by definition of erosion if $(x, w) + (u, v) \in A$ for every $(u, v) \in B$ then $(x, w) \in A \ominus B$. Hence $A \ominus B$ is an umbra.

Now we are ready for the umbra homomorphism theorem which states that the operation of taking an umbra is a homomorphism from the gray scale morphology to the binary morphology.

Umbra Homomorphism Theorem 58: Let F, $K \subseteq E^{N-1}$ and $f: F \rightarrow E$ and $k: K \rightarrow E$. Then

$$1) \quad U[f \oplus k] = U[f] \oplus U[k]$$

and

$$2) \quad U[f \ominus k] = U[f] \ominus U[k]$$

Proof: 1) $f \oplus k = T[U[f] \oplus U[k]]$ so that $U[f \oplus k] = U[T[U[f] \oplus U[k]]]$. But $U[f] \oplus U[k]$ is an umbra and for sets which are umbras the umbra operation undoes the surface operation. Hence $U[f \oplus k] = U[T[U[f] \oplus U[k]]] = U[f] \oplus U[k]$.

2) $f \ominus k = T[U[f] \ominus U[k]]$ so that $U[f \ominus k] = U[T[U[f] \ominus U[k]]]$. But $U[f] \ominus U[k]$ is an umbra and for sets which are umbras, the umbra operation undoes the surface operation. Hence,

$$U[f \ominus k] = U[T[U[f] \ominus U[k]]] = U[f] \ominus U[k].$$

To illustrate how the umbra homomorphism property is

used to prove relationships by first wrapping the relationship by re-expressing it in terms of umbra and surface operations and then transforming it through the umbra homomorphism property and finally by unwrapping it using the definitions of gray scale dilation and erosion, we state and prove the commutivity and associativity of gray scale dilation and the chain rule for gray scale erosion.

Proposition 59: $f \oplus k = k \oplus f$.
Proof:

$$
\begin{aligned}
f \oplus k &= T[U[f] \oplus U[k]] \\
&= T[U[k] \oplus U[f]] \\
&= k \oplus f.
\end{aligned}
$$

Proposition 60: $k_1 \oplus (k_2 \oplus k_3) = (k_1 \oplus k_2) \oplus k_3$.
Proof:

$$
\begin{aligned}
k_1 \oplus (k_2 \oplus k_3) &= T[U[k_1] \oplus U[k_2 \oplus k_3]] \\
&= T[U[k_1] \oplus (U[k_2] \oplus U[k_3])] \\
&= T[(U[k_1] \oplus U[k_2]) \oplus U[k_3]] \\
&= T[U[k_1 \oplus k_2] \oplus U[k_3]] \\
&= (k_1 \oplus k_2) \oplus k_3.
\end{aligned}
$$

Proposition 61: $(f \ominus k_1) \ominus k_2 = f \ominus (k_1 \oplus k_2)$.
Proof:

$$
\begin{aligned}
(f \ominus k_1) \ominus k_2 &= T[U[f \ominus k_1] \ominus U[k_2]] \\
&= T[(U[f] \ominus U[k_1]) \ominus U[k_2]] \\
&= T[U[f] \ominus (U[k_1] \oplus U[k_2])] \\
&= T[U[f] \ominus U[k_1 \oplus k_2]] \\
&= f \ominus (k_1 \oplus k_2).
\end{aligned}
$$

Gray scale opening and closing are defined in an analogous way to opening and closing in the binary mopphology and they have similar properties.

Definition 62: Let $f: F \rightarrow E$ and $k: K \rightarrow E$. The gray scale opening of f by structuring element k is denoted by $f \circ k$ and is defined by $f \circ k = (f \ominus k) \oplus k$.

Definition 63: Let $f: F \rightarrow E$ and $k: K \rightarrow E$. The gray scale closing of f by structuring element k is denoted by $f \bullet k$ and is defined by $f \bullet k = (f \oplus k) \ominus k$.

Fig. 15 shows an example of gray scale opening and closing.

To prove the idempotency of gray scale opening and closing, we need the following property relating functions to their umbras.

Proposition 64: Let $f: F \rightarrow E$ and $g: G \rightarrow E$. Suppose $F \subseteq G$. Then $f \leq g$ if and only if $U[f] \subseteq U[g]$.

Proof: Suppose $f \leq g$. Let $(x, y) \in U[f]$. Then by definition of umbra, $y \leq f(x)$. But $x \in F$ and $F \subseteq G$ so that $x \in G$. By supposition, $f(x) \leq g(x)$. Hence, $y \leq g(x)$. Now by definition of umbra, $(x, y) \in U[g]$.

Suppose $U[f] \subseteq U[g]$. Let $y = f(x)$. Certainly, $(x,$

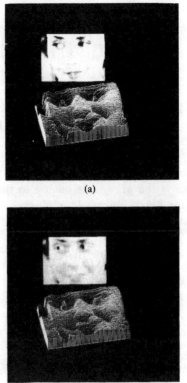

(a)

(b)

Fig. 15. The gray scale opening and closing operation. (a) The gray scale opening of the girl's face in image form and in perspective projection surface plot form. The structuring element is the paraboloid described in Fig. 13. (b) The gray scale closing of the girl's face in image form and in perspective projection surface plot form.

$y) \in U[f]$. But $U[f] \subseteq U[g]$ so that $(x, y) \in U[g]$. Now by definition of umbra, $y \leq g(x)$.

Having this property, the analog to Proposition 33 follows.

Proposition 65: $g \leq f \ominus k$ if and only if $f \geq g \oplus k$.

Proof: $g \leq f \ominus k$ if and only if $U[g] \subseteq U[f \ominus k]$. But $U[f \ominus k] = U[f] \ominus U[k]$. Now $U[g] \subseteq U[f] \ominus U[k]$ if and only if $U[f] \supseteq U[g] \oplus U[k]$. But $U[g] \oplus U[k] = U[g \oplus k]$. Finally, $U[f] \supseteq U[g \oplus k]$ if and only if $f \geq g \oplus k$.

Another property which is immediately obvious is that if one set is contained in a second, then the surface of the first will be no higher at each point than the surface of the second.

Proposition 66: Let $A \subseteq E^{N-1} \times E$ and $D \subseteq E^{N-1} \times E$. Then $A \subseteq D$ implies $T[A](x) \leq T[D](x)$.

Proof: Let $x \in E^{N-1}$ be given. Then, since $A \subseteq D$,

$$
T[A](x) = \max_{(x,z) \in A} z \leq \max_{(x,z) \in D} z = T[D](x).
$$

From this fact, it quickly follows that the gray scale opening of a function must be no larger than the function at each point in their common domain. This is the gray scale analog to the antiextensivity property of the binary morphology opening.

Proposition 67: $(f \circ k)(x) \leq f(x)$ for every $x \in F \circ K$.

233

Proof:

$$f \circ k = (f \ominus k) \oplus k = T[U(f \ominus k) \oplus U[k]]$$
$$= T[(U[f] \ominus U[k]) \oplus U[k]].$$

But $(U[f] \ominus U[k]) \oplus U[k] \subseteq U[f]$, hence by Proposition 63,

$$T[(U[f] \ominus U[k]) \oplus U[k]](x) \le T[U[f]](x)$$

for every $x \in (F \ominus K) \oplus K$. Since $T[U[f]] = f$, $T[(U[f] \ominus U[k]) \oplus U[k]](x) \le f(x)$.

Likewise, the gray scale closing of a function must be no smaller than the function at each point in their common domain. This is the gray scale analog to the extensivity property of the binary morphology closing.

Proposition 68: $f(x) \le (f \bullet k)(x)$ for every $x \in F$.

Proof:

$$f \bullet k = (f \oplus k) \ominus k = T[U[f \oplus k] \ominus U[k]]$$
$$= T[(U[f] \oplus U[k]) \ominus U[k]].$$

But $(U[f] \oplus U[k]) \ominus U[k] \supseteq U[f]$; hence $T[(U[f] \oplus U[k]) \ominus U[k]](x) \ge T[U[f]](x)$ for every $x \in F$. Since $T[U[f]] = f$, $f(x) \le T[(U[f] \oplus U[k]) \ominus U[k]](x)$.

Now the idempotency property of opening and closing can be proved by the umbra homomorphism theorem.

Proposition 69: $(f \circ k) \circ k = f \circ k$.

Proof:

$$(f \circ k) \circ k = T[(U[f \circ k] \ominus U[k]) \oplus U[k]]$$
$$= T[(((U[f] \ominus U[k]) \oplus U[k]) \ominus U[k]) \oplus U[k]]$$
$$= T[(U[f] \circ U[k]) \circ U[k]]$$
$$= T[U[f] \circ U[k]]$$
$$= T[(U[f] \ominus U[k]) \oplus U[k]]$$
$$= T[U[f \ominus k] \oplus U[k]]$$
$$= T[U[(f \ominus k) \oplus k]]$$
$$= T[U[f \circ k]]$$
$$= f \circ k.$$

Proposition 70: $(f \bullet k) \bullet k = f \bullet k$.

Proof:

$$(f \bullet k) \bullet k = T[(U[f \bullet k] \oplus U[k]) \ominus U[k]]$$
$$= T[(((U[f] \oplus U[k]) \ominus U[k]) \oplus U[k]) \ominus U[k]]$$
$$= T[(U[f] \bullet U[k]) \bullet U[k]]$$
$$= T[U[f] \bullet U[k]]$$
$$= T[(U[f] \oplus U[k]) \ominus U[k]]$$
$$= T[U[(f \oplus k) \ominus k]]$$
$$= T[U[f \bullet k]]$$
$$= f \bullet k.$$

There is a geometric interpretation to the gray scale opening and to the gray scale closing in the same manner that there is a geometric meaning to the binary morphological opening and closing (Propositions 44 and 45). To obtain the opening of f by a paraboloid structuring element, for example, take the paraboloid, apex up, and slide it under all the surface of f pushing it hard up against the surface. The apex of the paraboloid may not be able to touch all points of f. For example, if f has a spike narrower than the paraboloid, the top of the apex may only reach as far as the mouth of the spike. The opening is the surface of the highest points reached by any part of the paraboloid as it slides under all the surface of f. The formal statement of this is given in Proposition 71.

Proposition 71:

$$f \circ k = T\left[\bigcup_{\{y \mid U[k]_y \subseteq U[f]\}} U[k]_y \right].$$

Proof:

$$f \circ k = T[U[f \ominus k] \oplus U[k]]$$
$$= T[(U[f] \ominus U[k]) \oplus U[k]]$$
$$= T[U[f] \circ U[k]]$$
$$= T\left[\bigcup_{\{z \mid (U[k])_z \subseteq U[f]\}} (U[k])_z \right].$$

We have not mentioned the duality relationship between gray scale dilation and erosion. We need this in order to give the geometric interpretation to closing. The duality relationship is analogous to the relationship given in Theorem 25. Before stating and proving it, we need the definition of gray scale reflection.

Definition 72: Let $f : F \to E$. The reflection of f is denoted by $\check{f}$, $\check{f} : \check{F} \to E$, and is defined by $\check{f}(x) = f(-x)$.

Gray Scale Dilation Erosion Duality Theorem 73: Let $f : F \to E$ and $k : K \to E$. Let $x \in (F \oplus K) \cap (F \ominus \check{K})$ be given. Then $-(f \oplus k)(x) = ((-f) \ominus \check{k})(x)$.

Proof:

$$-(f \oplus k)(x) = -\max_{\substack{z \in K \\ x-z \in F}} [f(x-z) + k(z)]$$
$$= \min_{\substack{z \in K \\ x-z \in F}} [-f(x-z) - k(z)]$$
$$= \min_{\substack{z \in \check{K} \\ x+z \in F}} [-f(x+z) - \check{k}(z)]$$
$$= ((-f) \ominus \check{k})(x).$$

It follows immediately from the gray scale dilation and erosion duality that there is a gray scale opening and closing duality.

Gray Scale Opening and Closing Duality Theorem 74: $-(f \circ k) = (-f) \bullet \check{k}$.

Proof:

$$-(f \circ k) = -((f \ominus k) \oplus k)$$
$$= (-(f \ominus k)) \ominus \check{k}$$
$$= ((-f) \oplus \check{k}) \ominus \check{k}$$
$$= (-f) \bullet \check{k}.$$

Having the gray scale opening and closing duality, we immediately have $f \bullet k = -((-f) \circ \check{k})$. In essence, this means that we can think of closing like opening. To close f with a paraboloid structuring element, we take the reflection of the paraboloid in the sense of Definition 72, turn it upside down (apex down), and slide it all over the top of the surface of f. The closing is the surface of all the lowest points reached by the sliding paraboloid.

V. Summary

We have developed the basic relationships in binary morphology and have then developed the extensions of these relationships in gray scale morphology. We have shown that morphological openings are increasing, antiextensive, translation invariant, and idempotent. We have shown that morphological closings are increasing, extensive, translation invariant, and idempotent. For further algebraic depth on opening and closings, see [18] or [31].

We intend to publish two follow-on tutorials to the present one. The first will discuss a variety of topics including sieves, sampling, morphologic topography, thickenings, thinnings, boundaries, skeletons, connectivity, convexity, morphologic derivative estimation, and bounding derivatives by gray scale morphologic openings and closings. The second will be on application where we will discuss morphologic solutions to a variety of industrial vision problems.

References

[1] K. E. Batcher, "Design of a massively parallel processor," *IEEE Trans. Comput.*, vol. C-29, pp. 836–840, Sept. 1980.

[2] E. N. Coleman and R. E. Sampson, "Acquisition of randomly oriented workpieces through structure mating," in *Proc. Computer Vision Pattern Recognition Conf.*, San Francisco, CA, June 19–23, pp. 350–357.

[3] M. Duff, "Parallel processors for digital image processing," in *Advances in Digital Image Processing*, P. Stucki, Ed. New York: Plenum, 1979, pp. 265–279.

[4] M. J. B. Duff, D. M. Watson, T. M. Fountain, and G. K. Shaw, "A cellular logic array for image processing," *Pattern Recognition*, vol. 5, 1973.

[5] A. Favre, R. Muggli, A. Stucki, and P. Bonderet, "Application of morphologic filters in the assessment of platelet thrombus deposition in cross sections of blood vessels," in *Proc. 4th Scandanavian Conf. Image Analysis*, Trondheim, Norway, June 17–20, 1985, pp. 629–640.

[6] F. Gerritsen and L. G. Aardema, "Design and use of DIP-1: A fast flexible and dynamically microprogrammable image processor," *Pattern Recognition*, vol. 14, pp. 319–330, 1981.

[7] F. A. Gerritsen and P. W. Verbeek, "Implementation of cellular logic operators using 3 × 3 convolution and table lookup hardware," *Comput. Vision, Graphics, Image Processing*, vol. 27, pp. 115–123, 1984.

[8] M. J. E. Golay, "Hexagonal parallel pattern transformations," *IEEE Trans. Comput.*, vol. C-18, pp. 733–740, 1969.

[9] D. Graham and P. E. Norgren, "The Diff3 analyzer: A parallel/serial Golay image processor," in *Real Time Medical Image Processing*,

M. Onoe, K. Preston, and A. Rosenfeld, Eds. London: Plenum, 1980, pp. 163–182.

[10] H. Hadwiger, *Vorslesunger über Inhalt, Oberfläche und Isoperimetrie.* Berlin: Springer, 1957.

[11] R. M. Haralick, "A reconfigurable systolic network in computer vision," *IEEE Computer Society Workshop on Computer Architecture for Pattern Analysis and Image Database Management*, Miami Beach, FL, Nov. 18–20, 1985, pp. 507–515.

[12] M. J. Kimmel, R. S. Jaffe, J. R. Manderville, and M. A. Lavin, "MITE: Morphic image transform engine, an architecture for reconfigurable pipelines of neighborhood processors," in *Proc. IEEE Comput. Soc. Workshop Computer Architecture for Pattern Analysis and Image Database Management*, Miami Beach, FL, Nov. 18–20, 1985, pp. 493–500.

[13] R. A. Kirsch, L. Cahn, C. Ray, and G. H. Urban, "Experiments in processing pictorial information with a digital computer," in *Proc. Eastern Joint Comput. Conf.*, 1957, pp. 221–229.

[14] J. C. Klein and J. Serra, *The texture analyzer,* *J. Microscopy*, vol. 95, pp. 349–356, 1977.

[15] B. Kruse, "Design and implementation of a picture processor," Science and Technology dissertation, Univ. Linkoeping, Linkoeping, Sweden, Rep. 13, 1977.

[16] P. F. Leonard, "Pipeline architectures for real-time machine vision," *IEEE Comput. Soc. Workshop Computer Architecture for Pattern Analysis and Image Database Management*, Miami Beach, FL, Nov. 18–20, 1985, pp. 502–505.

[17] G. Matheron, *Elements Pour une Tiorre des Mulieux Poreux.* Paris: Masson, 1965.

[18] ——, *Random Sets and Integral Geometry.* New York: Wiley, 1975.

[19] D. L. McCubbery and R. M. Lougheed, "Morpholocial image analysis using a raster pipeline processor," in *IEEE Comput. Soc. Workshop Computer Architecture for Pattern Analysis and Image Database Management*, Miami Beach, FL, Nov. 18–20, 1985, pp. 444–452.

[20] H. Minkowski, "Volumen und oberfläche," *Math. Ann.*, vol. 57, pp. 447–495, 1903.

[21] G. A. Moore, "Automatic scanning and computer processes for the quantitative analysis of micrographs and equivalent subjects," in *Pictorial Pattern Recognition*, G. C. Cheng *et al.*, Eds. Washington, DC: Thompson, 1968, pp. 275–326.

[22] Y. Nakagawa and A. Rosenfeld, "A note on the use of local min and max operations in digital picture processing," *IEEE Trans. Syst., Man, Cybern.*, vol. SMC-8, pp. 632–635, Aug. 1978.

[23] S. Peleg, J. Naor, R. Hartley, and D. Avnir, "Multiple resolution texture analysis and classification," *IEEE Trans. Pattern Anal. Machine Intell.*, vol. PAMI-6, pp. 518–523, 1984.

[24] S. Peleg and A. Rosenfeld, "A min max medial axis transformation," *IEEE Trans. Pattern Anal. Machine Intell.*, vol. PAMI-3, pp. 206–210, 1981.

[25] J. L. Potter, "MPP architecture and programming," in *Multicomputers and Image Processing*, K. Preston and L. Uhr, Eds. New York: Academic, 1982, pp. 275–290.

[26] ——, "Image processing on the massively parallel processor," *Computer*, vol. 16, no. 1, pp. 62–67, Jan. 1983.

[27] W. K. Pratt, "A pipeline architecture for image processing and analysis," in *Proc. IEEE Comput. Soc. Workshop Computer Architecture for Pattern Analysis and Image Database Management*, Miami Beach, FL, Nov. 18–20, 1985, pp. 516–520.

[28] K. Preston, Jr., "Machine techniques for automatic identification of binucleate lymphocyte," in *Proc. Fourth Int. Conf. Medical Electronics*, Washington, DC, July 1961.

[29] ——, "Application of cellular automata to biomedical image processing," in *Computer Techniques in Biomedicine and Medicine.* Philadelphia, PA: Auerbach, 1973.

[30] J. Serra, "Stereology and structuring elements," *J. Microscopy*, pp. 93–103, 1972.

[31] ——, *Image Analysis and Mathematical Morphology.* London: Academic, 1982.

[32] S. R. Sternberg, "Parallel architectures for image processing," in *Proc. IEEE COMPSAC*, Chicago, IL, 1979.

[33] ——, "Cellular computers and biomedical image processing," in *Biomedical Images and Computers*, J. Sklansky and J. C. Bisconte, Eds. Berlin: Springer-Verlag, 1982, pp. 294–319 (also presented at United States–France Seminar on Biomedical Image Processing, St. Pierre de Chartreuse, France, May 27–31, 1980).

[34] ——, "Pipeline architectures for image processing," in *Multicomputers and Image Processing*, K. Preston and L. Uhr, Eds. New York: Academic, 1982, pp. 291–305.

[35] ——, "Esoteric iterative algorithms," in *Proc. Second Int. Conf. Image Analysis and Processing*, Selva di Fasano, Brindisi, Italy, Nov. 15–18, 1982.

[36] ——, "Biomedical image processing," *Computer*, vol. 16, no. 1, pp. 22–34, Jan. 1983.

[37] S. H. Unger, "A computer oriented to spatial problems," *Proc. IRE*, vol. 46, pp. 1744–1750, 1958.

[38] M. Werman and S. Peleg, "Min–max operators in texture analysis," *IEEE Trans. Pattern Anal. Machine Intell.*, vol. PAMI-7, pp. 730–733, Nov. 1985.

[39] S. Wilson, "The Pixie-5000—A systolic array processor," in *Proc. IEEE Comput. Soc. Workshop Computer Architecture for Pattern Analysis and Image Database Management*, Miami Beach, FL, Nov. 18–20, 1985, pp. 477–483.

Robert M. Haralick (S'62–M'69–SM'76–F'84) was born in Brooklyn, NY, on September 30, 1943. He received the B.A. degree in mathematics from the University of Kansas, Lawrence, in 1964, the B.S. degree in electrical engineering in 1966, the M.S. degree in electrical eiengineering in 1967, and the Ph.D. degree from the University of Kansas in 1969.

He has worked with Autonetics and IBM. In 1965 he worked for the Center for Research, University of Kansas, as a Research Engineer and in 1969 he joined the faculty of the Department of Electrical Engineering there where he last served as a Professor from 1975 to 1978. In 1979 he joined the faculty of the Department of Electrical Engineering at Virginia Polytechnic Institute and State University where he was a Professor and Director of the Spatial Data Analysis Laboratory. From 1984 to 1986 he served as Vice President of Research at Machine Vision International, Ann Arbor, MI. He now holds the Boeing Clairmont Egtvedt chaired professorship in the Department of Electrical Engineering, University of Washington, Seattle. He has done research in pattern recognition, multi-image processing, remote sensing, texture analysis, data compression, clustering, artificial intelligence, and general systems theory, and has published over 180 papers. He is responsible for the development of GIPSY (General Image Processing System), a multi-image processing package which runs on a minicomputer system.

Dr. Haralick is a member of the Association for Computing Machinery, Sigma Xi, the Pattern Recognition Society, and the Society for General Systems Research.

Stanley R. Sternberg received the Bachelor of Science degree in electrical engineering from Drexel Institute of Technology, Philadelphia, PA, in 1962, the Master of Science degree in computer sciences, and the Ph.D. degree in industrial engineering, both from the University of Michigan, Ann Arbor, in 1965 and 1971, respectively.

He is Chief Technical Officer of Machine Vision International Corporation, Ann Arbor. In 1981 he founded the corporation under the name CytoSystems Corporation to produce and market video rate processors for industrial inspection, robot vision, and biomedical image analysis. He is the holder of 20 U.S. patents for his developments of novel methods of infrared imaging, image processing and laser line-of-site data transmissions. He is the recipient of two Civil Service Outstanding Service Awards for his contributions as Manager of quality control and reliability for a major United States Air Force program. He is a founder of the Computer and Image Processing Research Network of the University of Michigan and a director of the Automated Vision Association of the Robotic Industries Association. From 1974 to 1981, he was Senior Research Scientist and head of the Department of Computer Design at the Environmental Research Institute of Michigan (ERIM) where he directed and conducted research and development of cellular computers for image processing. He designed and built a highly parallel real-time image processor, the Cytocomputer, investigated high level languages for parallel image processing, and applied these concepts to biomedical and industrial image analysis. He is Adjunct Associate Professor of Electrical and Computer Engineering at the University of Michigan where he teaches cellular computers and image processing on a part-time basis.

Dr. Sternberg is a member of Tau Beta Pi, Sigma Xi, and Eta Kappa Nu.

Xinhua Zhuang graduated from Peking University, Peking, China, in 1963, after a four-year undergraduate program and a two-year graduate program in mathematics.

Before 1983 he served as a Senior Research Engineer in the Computing Technique Institute, Hangzhou, China. He was a Visiting Scholar of Electrical Engineering at the Virginia Polytechnic Institute and State University, Blacksburg, from 1983 to 1984, a Visiting Scientist of Electrical and Computer Engineering at the University of Michigan, Ann Arbor, granted by Machine Vision International, Ann Arbor, from 1984 to 1985. He was selected as a consultant to the Advisory Group for Aerospace Research and Development, NATO, in 1985. From 1985 to 1986 he was a Visiting Research Professor with the Coordinated Science Laboratory and a Visiting Professor of Electrical and Computer Engineering at the University of Illinois at Urbana-Champaign. From 1986 to 1987 he was a Visiting Scientist in the Department of Electrical Engineering, University of Washington, Seattle. His professional interests lie in applied mathematics, image processing, computer and robotic vision, artificial intelligence, and computer architecture. He is a contributor (with E. Ostevold and R. M. Haralick) of the book *Image Recovery: Theory and Application*, edited by Henry Stark; Editor (with R. M. Haralick) of the book *Consistent Labeling Problems in Pattern Recognition*; and author (with T. S. Huang and R. M. Haralick) of the planned book titled *Image Time Sequence Motion Analysis*.

A Structural Model of Shape

LINDA G. SHAPIRO

Abstract—Shape description and recognition is an important and interesting problem in scene analysis. Our approach to shape description is a formal model of a shape consisting of a set of primitives, their properties, and their interrelationships. The primitives are the simple parts and intrusions of the shape which can be derived through the graph-theoretic clustering procedure described in [31]. The interrelationships are two ternary relations on the primitives: the intrusion relation which relates two simple parts that join to the intrusion they surround and the protrusion relation which relates two intrusions to the protrusion between them. Using this model, a shape matching procedure that uses a tree search with look-ahead to find mappings from a prototype shape to a candidate shape has been developed. An experimental Snobol4 implementation has been used to test the program on hand-printed character data with favorable results.

Index Terms—Decomposition, matching, relational description, relaxation, shape description, shape recognition, tree search.

I. Introduction

SHAPE description and characterization is an important problem in scene analysis. There have been many different analytic methods used in shape analysis including transformations and decompositions of the boundary of the shape, and partitions of the interior of the shape into simple pieces.

Manuscript received October 30, 1978; revised April 13, 1979. This work was supported by the National Science Foundation under Grant MCS77-23945.

The author is with the Department of Computer Science, Virginia Polytechnic Institute and State University, Blacksburg, VA 24061.

Shape descriptions have included numeric values, feature vectors, character strings, trees, and graphs. The major problem seems to be the lack of a mathematical model for characterizing a shape.

Our approach to shape description is to construct a topological model of a shape which consists of a set of primitives, their properties, and their interrelationships. The primitives we use are the simple parts (near-convex pieces) and intrusions of the shape which can be derived through a decomposition procedure described in a previous paper [31]. The interrelationships are two ternary relations on the primitives: the intrusion relation and the protrusion relation. The intrusion relation is a set of triples of the form (s_1, i, s_2) where the two simple parts s_1 and s_2 touch or nearly touch and form part of the boundary of intrusion i. The protrusion relation is a set of triples of the form (i_1, s, i_2) where simple part s protrudes between the two intrusions i_1 and i_2. These two relations seem to satisfactorily characterize a shape in a manner that agrees with human intuition on familiar shapes such as hand-printed characters. Our topological approach to shape matching is that one shape matches another if there is a mapping from the primitives of the first shape to the primitives of the second shape that preserves the interrelationships. In this approach, the metric and statistical properties of the shape and its parts are suppressed.

In this paper, we define a formal shape model and a shape matching procedure that uses a tree search with look-ahead to find mappings from a prototype shape to a candidate shape.

Section II discusses related work, Section III describes a general structural model for shape and defines our particular relational model, Section IV discusses shape matching, and Section V describes an experimental shape matching system.

II. RELATED WORK

There have been several different approaches to the shape recognition problem. (For a complete survey, see Pavlidis [26].) On the statistical side, shapes have been described by such features as area, perimeter, moments, and coefficients of Fourier series. Description by moments includes the work of Alt [1] and Hu [19] among others. Description using coefficients of Fourier series includes the work of Zahn and Roskies [36], Richard and Hemami [28], Persoon and Fu [27], and Granlund [13]. Agrawala and Kulkarni [2] present a sequential one-pass algorithm for extracting simple shape features such as perimeter, area, and moments. All of these approaches work with a discrete representation of the boundary of the shape.

Much of the recent work has been structural in nature. Blum [4] suggests the application of the medial axis transformation which transforms a shape into a line drawing representing its "skeleton." The skeleton can be used to derive properties of the shape and, together with information about the distance of the boundary from the skeleton, allows reconstruction of the shape. A second structural approach involves the decomposition of the boundary of the shape into a sequence of line segments. Work in this area includes the Freeman chain code [11], the analysis of convex blobs by computing dominant points [20], [23], [29], [30], and Davis' work with angles, sides, and symmetry [6]–[8].

Also in the structural domain is the work on syntactic shape recognition. This includes Pavlidis and Ali's syntactic analysis of shapes [24] using regular expressions over the terminal symbols QUAD (arcs that can be approximated by quadratic curves), TRUS (sharp protrusions or intrusions), LINE (long linear segments), and BREAK (short segments). Also using the syntactic approach are Horowitz [18] and Lozano-Perez [21], both of whom parse piecewise linear approximations of one-dimensional waveforms to determine the structure of the peaks and valleys and Fu and Lu [12] who encode line patterns as strings and use error-correcting parsers to determine the distance from an input pattern to grammars describing each of the possible pattern classes. A clustering algorithm then determines which class the input pattern belongs to.

Another recent effort in syntactic shape recognition is the work of You and Fu [35] on attributed shape grammars. In an attributed shape grammar, each curve segment (primitive or nonterminal) is described by four attributes: the vector spanning its endpoints, its length, its angular change, and a symmetry measure. Grammar rules specify the generation of curve segments from smaller curve segments connected by angle primitives and are of the context free form $N \rightarrow (XA)*X$ where N is a nonterminal, X can be a primitive curve segment or a nonterminal, and A is an angle primitive. In this case, the description of the curve segment N can be obtained directly from the descriptions of the curve segments composing N and the angles between them. Two recognition algorithms have been developed which accomplish parsing and primitive extraction simultaneously, using high-level knowledge to drive low-level processes.

Syntactic pattern recognition has the main advantage of having well-defined, often linear, parsing algorithms. The main disadvantage of this approach to shape recognition is that the shape is usually first encoded as a one-dimensional string of symbols which is the input to the parser. The You and Fu work is an exception in that the parser directs the low-level processes that extract and encode primitives. However, the parsing is still inherently a one-dimensional process due to the nature of context free grammars. While the attributed shape grammar and associated recognition algorithms seem to be more powerful than previous shape grammars, they typically handle only adjacency relationships on the boundary of the shape.

It is not clear to us that all the information in a two-dimensional shape can be preserved in a one-dimensional representation. In particular, the intrusion and protrusion relations defined in this paper cannot be expressed naturally by one-dimensional grammar rules since they capture non-linear information about the shape.

The approaches that are most related to our work are those that attempt to decompose the whole shape into two-dimensional parts. This includes the work of Pavlidis [25], Feng and Pavlidis [10], Maruyama [22], and Eden [9]. In the Feng and Pavlidis work, a shape is decomposed into convex parts, T-shaped parts, and spirals and described by a labeled graph indicating connections between pairs of parts. Maruyama suggests a decomposition of shapes into angularly simple regions where each such region has at least one interior point that can "see" its entire boundary. Eden decomposes script characters into meaningful primitive strokes.

In [31] we presented an algorithm for the decomposition of a two-dimensional shape into simple parts. The input to this algorithm is an ordered sequence of (x, y) coordinates representing the vertices of a polygonal approximation to the boundary of a shape. From these points the interior line segment relation LI is computed. LI is a binary relation consisting of all pairs of vertices such that the straight line segment joining them lies wholly within the shape. A graph-theoretic clustering algorithm on the relation LI yields a set of clusters, each consisting of a subset of the original set of vertices. These clusters are the *interior clusters* or *simple parts* of the shape.

The decomposition algorithm has three important properties.

1) The algorithm is independent of the starting point on the boundary of the shape.

2) The relation LI is invariant under linear transformations and perspective transformations; thus, a transformation of a shape yields the same decomposition as the original shape.

3) The clusters produced by the graph-theoretic clustering algorithm can be controlled by numerical parameters; they are not necessarily convex or even disjoint. Thus, the definition of simple part remains flexible.

Fig. 1(a) shows the decomposition of a hand-printed letter E by this method.

In [31] we defined the exterior line segment relation LE,

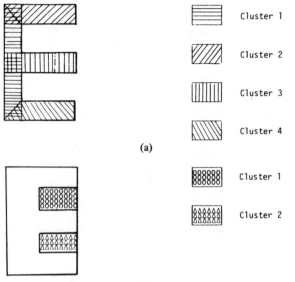

Cluster 1

Cluster 2

Cluster 3

Cluster 4

(a)

Cluster 1

Cluster 2

(b)

Fig. 1. Illustrates the decomposition of a shape into simple parts and intrusions. (a) Shows the simple parts or interior clusters of a hand-printed letter E. (b) Shows the intrusions or exterior clusters of the hand-printed letter E.

consisting of all pairs of vertices such that the straight line joining them lies exterior to the shape, and suggested that LE would be useful in obtaining a structural description of the shape. The clusters of the LE relation, obtained with the same graph-theoretic clustering algorithm, correspond to *intrusions* into the boundary of the shape. Fig. 1(b) shows these *exterior clusters* for the letter E of Fig. 1(a).

In Section III we will describe a structural model for a shape based on the simple parts, the intrusions, their properties, and their interrelationships.

III. THE MODEL

A structural description of a shape must include a set of shape primitives, their properties, and their interrelationships. In this section we will define a general, formal, structural model for the description of two-dimensional shapes. We will then define a specific structural description that we have been using in our shape matching experiments.

The General Model and Some Examples

We define a shape description D to be a 5-tuple $D = (N, T, G, P, R)$ where N is the *name* of the shape being described, T is the *type* of the shape, G is an attribute-value table containing the *global attributes* of the shape, P is a set of *shape primitives* obtained from a structural analysis of the shape, and R is a set $\{R_1, \cdots, R_k\}$ of *relations* on P. For each k, there is a positive integer N_k and a possibly singleton label set L_k such that $R_k \subseteq P^{N_k} \times L_k$, $k = 1, \cdots, K$. Thus, each R_k is a labeled N_k-ary relation. Haralick and Kartus [14] call R_k an "arrangement."

The name N and the type T are identifying information. The name might identify a region in an image being analyzed or it might be a character string that the experimenter wants to associate with a particular input file. The type identifies a class that the shape belongs to. For instance, if zip codes

are being analyzed, the type might be "numeral." The purpose of the type is to limit the number of stored prototypes that are considered for a match. (See Section V.) Of course in the worst case, where the origin of the shape is completely unknown, no type information can be input.

A structural description of a shape includes a table of attribute-value pairs pertaining to the shape as a whole, a set of primitives that the shape can be broken down into, and a set of relations showing the interrelationships among the primitives. While the primitives P and the relations R define the structure of complex shapes, we feel that it is also important to record any global attributes that are available. If the shape is associated with a region of an image, then it might be convenient to consider intensity or texture information as global attributes of the shape. The global attributes may also include statistical descriptors such as circularity, elongation, convexity, crenation (notched boundary), and so on [17]. For simpler shapes, the global attributes may be more important than the primitives and relations, which may be missing altogether. The primitives and relations will differ with each particular shape model. We will illustrate with a few examples borrowed from the literature.

Shaw [32] defined a picture description language (PDL) in which pictures could be defined hierarchically in terms of primitives. Each primitive in PDL is a two-dimensional entity having two connection points, a *head* and a *tail*. The operators $+, -, \times$, and $*$ indicate the head-to-tail, head-to-head, tail-to-tail, and head-to-head with tail-to-tail connection of two primitives. For example, the expression "A + B" indicates that the head of A is to be connected to the tail of B. The resultant entity has its tail at the tail of A and its head at the head of B and can be connected to other primitives or higher entities. PDL sentences are expressions consisting of primitives, operators, and parentheses indicating the order of applying the operators. For example, "A * (B + C)" indicates that the head of B is connected to the tail of C to form a new entity. Then the new entity is connected to A, head-to-head and tail-to-tail.

We will give an example of a simple shape description using Shaw's operators, but not using the PDL expression concept. The primitives of our example shape are rectangles one unit long and one-half unit wide of various orientations. Fig. 2 illustrates a set of such primitives. The primitives can be connected head-to-tail, head-to-head, and tail-to-tail. (Since they are not curved, the head-to-head with tail-to-tail connection is not possible.) We will assume that for each pair of primitives, the method for joining them in each of the possible connections has been specified. We can describe certain simple shapes such as block letters in terms of these primitives and their pairwise connections.

A description for a block letter would be a 5-tuple $D1 = (N, T, G, P, R)$ where N is the name of the letter, T is the type "block letter," G contains global attributes of the letter such as the number of primitives, P is the subset of the primitives of Fig. 2 that the letter is composed of, and R contains a single labeled binary connection relation $C \subseteq \{(p_1, p_2, O) | p_1, p_2 \in S, O \in \{+, -, \times\}\}$. Fig. 3 illustrates this type of description for the block letter E.

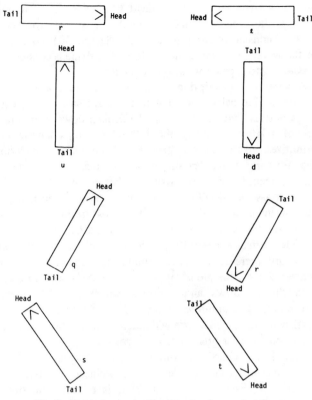

Fig. 2. Illustrates a set of rectangular shape primitives.

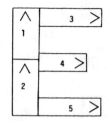

```
D1 = ('E',block letter,G,P,{C})

G = {(number-of-primitives,5)}

P = {1,2,3,4,5}

C = {(2,1,+)(1,3,+)(1,4,x)(2,4,+)(2,5,x)}

1 = u

2 = u

3 = r

4 = r

5 = r
```

Fig. 3. Illustrates a shape description for a block letter E. The primitives are directed, oriented rectangles, and the relation C consists of triples of the form (primitive 1, primitive 2, operator) where the operator determines the way in which the two primitives connect. The idea of directed primitives and the operators + (head-to-tail connection) and × (tail-to-tail) connection are from the work of Shaw [32].

```
D2 = ('E',block letter, G,P,{J})

G = {(number-of-segments,12)}

P = {(1,2,3,4,...,12)}

J = {(1,2,-90),(2,3,-90),(3,4,-90)
     (4,5,90),(5,6,90),(6,7,-90)
     (7,8,90 ),(8,9,90),(9,10,90)
     (10,11,-90),(11,12,-90),(12,1,-90)}

1 = 4 units    4 = 1 unit    7 = 1 unit    10 = 1 unit
2 = 2 units    5 = ½ unit    8 = 1 unit    11 = 1 unit
3 = 1 unit     6 = 1 unit    9 = ½ unit    12 = 2 units
```

Fig. 4. Illustrates a second shape description for a block letter E. The primitives, which are line segments, have one attribute–their relative length. The relation J consists of triples of the form (segment1, segment2, angle) where segment1 and segment2 join and angle is the angle between them. For the purpose of calculating the angles, the line segments are considered to be directed clockwise.

Another approach to shape description is in terms of an ordered sequence of line segments comprising the boundary of the shape. The relative lengths of each line segment and the relative angles between successive segments complete the model. A description for a block letter in this system would be a 5-tuple $D2 = (N, T, G, P, R)$ where N, T, and G are as above, P is a set of line segments whose attributes include length, and R contains the labeled binary relation $J = \{(\ell_1, \ell_2, a) | \ell_1, \ell_2 \in P, \ell_1$ connects to ℓ_2 and a is the angle between ℓ_1 and $\ell_2\}$. Fig. 4 illustrates this type of description for the block letter E.

Both description D1 and description D2 are size invariant since all lengths specified are also relative. In description D1, the primitives are defined according to their orientation. Thus, the structural descriptions are not rotation invariant. This sort of description can work very well in applications like character recognition where the text is assumed to be right-side up, but descriptions using orientations cannot handle a general shape recognition problem. Description D2 is rotation invariant since the only orientation information is the set of relative angles between adjacent pairs of line segments. A description like D2 which concentrates on the boundary of the shape is useful in shape matching problems where the boundary is of primary importance. Map data is an example of this class of shapes.

A Structural Model Based on Simple Parts and Intrusions

One aspect of shape is its size and orientation invariance. This is the aspect that we attempt to capture with the structural model presented here. Let $S = \{s_1, \cdots, s_n\}$ be the set of simple parts of a shape, and let $I = \{i_1, \cdots, i_m\}$ be the set of intrusions. S and I are assumed to be obtained from the shape by a decomposition procedure such as the one described in [31]. We will treat each simple part and each intrusion as a two-dimensional region having area and a closed boundary. Let $P = S \cup I$. P consists of the simple parts and intrusions. Let $\delta: P \times P \to [0, \infty)$ be a distance function which gives a relative measure of the distance between two simple parts, two intrusions, or a simple part and an intrusion with the property that if p_1 and p_2 touch or overlap, then $\delta(p_1, p_2) = 0$. Let Δ be a nonnegative real number. Define the Boolean function p: $P^3 \rightarrow$ {true, false} by

$$p(p_1, p_2, p_3) = \begin{cases} \text{true if } \delta(p_1, p_2) \leqslant \Delta, \\ \qquad \delta(p_2, p_3) \leqslant \Delta, \text{ and} \\ \text{it is possible to draw a straight line from} \\ \text{a boundary point of } p_1 \text{ through } p_2 \text{ to a} \\ \text{boundary point of } p_3 \\ \text{false otherwise.} \end{cases}$$

Thus, $p(p_1, p_2, p_3)$ is true if both p_1 and p_3 touch or almost touch p_2 and a part of p_2 lies between p_1 and p_3. A shape is characterized by a 5-tuple $M = (N, T, G, P, R)$ where N is the name of the shape, T is the type of the shape, G = {(number-of-simple-parts, #S), (number-of-intrusions, #I)}, P = S ∪ I, and R = {R_p, R_i}. R_p = {$(i_1, s, i_2) \in I \times S \times I \mid p(i_1, s, i_2) =$ true} and R_i = {$(s_1, i, s_2) \in S \times I \times S \mid p(s_1, i, s_2) =$ true and $\delta(s_1, s_2) \leqslant \Delta$}. Thus, R_p consists of triples of the form (intrusion 1, simple part, intrusion 2) where the simple part protrudes between the two intrusions, and R_i consists of triples of the form (simple part 1, intrusion, simple part 2) where the two simple parts touch or nearly touch and form part of the boundary of the intrusion. Note that although the relations R_i and R_p are currently defined using the predicate p which returns true or false, alternate definitions could be formulated where p would return a numeric value. So far no provision has been made for describing each simple part and each intrusion of a shape. The decomposition algorithm was designed to produce near-convex primitives, and it does not seem useful to decompose these primitives any further. However, a list of the properties of each primitive would add to the completeness of the description of the entire shape. Some of the properties of a primitive that might be useful are listed below:

1) circularity
2) elongation
3) convexity
4) crenation
5) relative length
6) relative width
7) relative area.

Example

Fig. 1 illustrates the decomposition of a block letter E into four simple parts and two intrusions. We will name the simple parts 1, 2, 3, and 4 corresponding to clusters 1, 2, 3, and 4 in Fig. 1(a) and the intrusions 11 and 12 corresponding to clusters 1 and 2, respectively, in Fig. 1(b). Then the structural description of the letter E for any value of Δ is

('E', letter, G, P, {R_p, R_i})
G = {(number-of-simple-parts, 4) (number-of-intrusions, 2)}
P = {1, 2, 3, 4, 11, 12}
R_p = {(11, 3, 12)}
R_i = {(1, 11, 2),
(1, 11, 3),
(1, 12, 3),
(1, 12, 4)}.

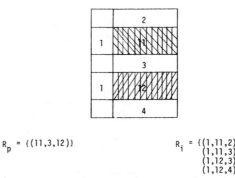

R_p = {(11, 3, 12)}

R_i = {(1, 11, 2),
(1, 11, 3),
(1, 12, 3),
(1, 12, 4)}

Fig. 5. Illustrates the protrusion relation R_p and the intrusion relation R_i of a block letter "E."

Fig. 5 illustrates this symbolically and Fig. 6 compares the decompositions of five block letters E, G, I, C, and B into simple parts and intrusions and the R_p and R_i relations for each letter. (Note that for brevity, we list only triples of the form (p_1, p_2, p_3), $p_1 < p_3$ and omit their symmetric counterparts.)

IV. Shape Matching

For our purposes, two shapes *match* if there is a function that maps the primitives of the first shape to the primitives of the second in such a way that primitives map to like primitives and the interrelationships among the primitives are preserved. Such a structure preserving function is called a homomorphism. Haralick and Kartus [14] define a *relational homomorphism* as follows.

Let A be a finite set of objects, let L be a finite set of labels, let $R \subseteq A^N \times L$ be a labeled N-ary relation, and let h: $A \rightarrow B$ be a mapping from A to a second set B. The *composition* of the relation R with the function h is the labeled N-ary relation R ∘ h defined by

R ∘ h = {$(b_1, \cdots, b_N, \ell) \in B^N \times L \mid$ there exists $(a_1, \cdots, a_N, \ell) \in R$ with $h(a_i) = b_i, i = 1, \cdots, N$}.

Suppose $R \subseteq A^N \times L$ and $R' \subseteq B^N \times L$. A *relational homomorphism* from R to R' is a function h: $A \rightarrow B$ such that R ∘ h ⊆ R'.

Thus, the composition of an N-ary relation with a function produces a second N-ary relation. The relational homomorphism is a structure preserving function that maps a labeled N-ary relation onto a subset of a second labeled N-ary relation. If shapes are represented by labeled relations, then two shapes match if there is a relational homomorphism from one relation to the other.

The structural description of a shape defined in Section III includes two ternary relations: R_p, the protrusion relation, and R_i, the intrusion relation. In order to simplify our description of the shape matching process, we will combine R_i and R_p to form a labeled ternary relation R(R_i, R_p) defined by

R(R_i, R_p) = {$(p_1, p_2, p_3, \ell) \in P^3 \mid$ either (p_1, p_2, p_3) ∈ R_i and ℓ = i or (p_1, p_2, p_3) ∈ R_p and ℓ = p}.

Each element of R(R_i, R_p) is a triple of either R_i or R_p with a label indicating whether it is from R_i or R_p.

The elements of R(R_i, R_p) contain information about the

	E	G	I	C	B

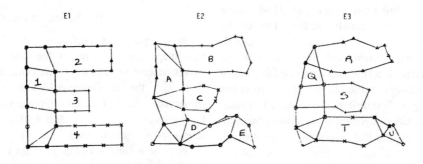

R_p	11,3,12	11,5,12	11,1,12	empty	empty
R_i	1,11,2	1,12,2	1,11,2	1,11,2	1,11,1
	1,11,3	2,11,3	1,12,2	2,11,3	
	1,12,3	3,11,4	1,11,3	3,11,4	
	1,12,4	4,11,5	1,12,3	4,11,5	
		2,12,3			

Fig. 6. Illustrates decompositions of five different block letters and the R_p and R_i relations for each letter.

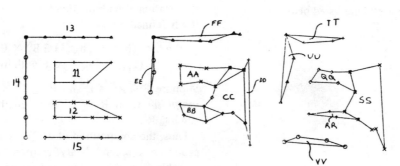

Fig. 7. Illustrates the decomposition of three shapes into simple parts and intrusions. Shape E1 was hand-printed and is considered a prototype letter "E." Shapes E2 and E3 were produced by adding noise to shape E1.

structure of the shape and indicate which primitives are simple parts and which are intrusions. One form of shape matching is to compare candidate shapes to a prototype shape and determine whether the candidate is similar enough to the prototype to be considered a match. Let $S_1 = (N_1, T_1, G_1, S_1 \cup I_1, \{R_{p1}, R_{i1}\})$ be a *prototype shape* and $S_2 = (N_2, T_2, G_2, S_2 \cup I_2, \{R_{p2}, R_{i2}\})$ be a *candidate shape*. Let $R_1 = R(R_{i1}, R_{p1})$ and $R_2 = R(R_{i2}, R_{p2})$. The candidate shape S_2 matches the prototype shape S_1 if there is a relational homomorphism h from R_1 to R_2.

For example, consider the decomposition of shapes $E_1, E_2,$

and E_3 in Fig. 7. Suppose E_1 is a prototype shape for the letter 'E' and E_2 and E_3 are candidate shapes. The relations R_1, R_2, and R_3 corresponding to E_1, E_2, and E_3 are given below. Very thin exterior clusters (13, 14, 15, EE, DD, FF, TT, UU, and VV in Fig. 7) which correspond to almost straight parts of the boundary rather than true intrusions, have been eliminated from the descriptions. These "false intrusions" will be eliminated by the program that calculates R_i and R_p. They are currently produced by the algorithm used to find the LE relation and have not been eliminated earlier because we think they may prove useful in future shape analyses.

R_1	R_2	R_3
(1, 11, 2, i)	(A, AA, B, i)	(Q, QQ, R, i)
(1, 11, 3, i)	(A, AA, C, i)	(Q, QQ, S, i)
(1, 12, 3, i)	(A, BB, C, i)	(Q, RR, S, i)
(1, 12, 4, i)	(A, BB, D, i)	(Q, RR, T, i)
(11, 3, 12, p)	(A, BB, E, i)	(T, SS, U, i)
	(D, BB, E, i)	(QQ, S, RR, p)
	(D, CC, E, i)	(RR, U, SS, p)
	(AA, C, BB, p)	(RR, T, SS, p).
	(AA, C, CC, p)	

Now for E_2 to match E_1 there must be a homomorphism $h_{12}: (S_1 \cup I_1) \rightarrow (S_2 \cup I_2)$ from R_1 to R_2. Four such homomorphisms are given below:

$p \in (S_1 \cup I_1)$	$\langle 1 \rangle$ $h_{12}(p)$	$\langle 2 \rangle$ $h_{12}(p)$	$\langle 3 \rangle$ $h_{12}(p)$	$\langle 4 \rangle$ $h_{12}(p)$
1	A	A	A	A
2	B	B	D	E
3	C	C	C	C
4	D	E	B	B
11	AA	AA	BB	BB
12	BB	BB	AA	AA

For each, i, $1 \leqslant i \leqslant 4$, it is easy to show that $R_1 \circ h_{12}^{\langle i \rangle} \subseteq R_2$. For example, $R_1 \circ h_{12}^{\langle 1 \rangle} = \{(A, AA, B, i), (A, AA, C, i), (A, BB, C, i), (A, BB, D, i), (AA, C, BB, p)\} \subseteq R_2$. Similarly, there are homomorphisms $h_{13}: (S_1 \cup I_1) \rightarrow (S_3 \cup I_3)$ from R_1 to R_3. Thus, both candidate E_2 and candidate E_3 can be said to match prototype E_1. Notice that some of the homomorphisms from a model to a candidate shape really represent the mappings from the model to the mirror image of the candidate. In the above example, $h_{12}^{\langle 3 \rangle}$ and $h_{12}^{\langle 4 \rangle}$ are the mirror image mappings.

A shape matching procedure must find a homomorphism from a prototype shape to a candidate shape. Several important considerations pertain to the design of such a procedure.

1) Some of the relationships in the prototype shape may be more important than others. Thus, it is desirable to assign weights to tuples in the description of the prototype.

2) It is possible for two similar shapes to decompose into different numbers of primitives. Thus, the mapping should be able to assign the same primitives in the candidate to several primitives in the prototype if they are physically close enough to each other. (If we choose to look for a binary relation instead of a mapping, then several primitives in the candidate could be associated with one primitive in the prototype.)

3) A homomorphism corresponds to a match, but does not necessarily indicate a good match. We need a measure of the goodness of a match. In the remainder of this section we will discuss each of these considerations in more detail.

Mappings on Weighted Relations

Suppose $R_1 \subseteq P_1^3 \times \{i, p\}$ is a prototype relation and $R_2 \subseteq P_2^3 \times \{i, p\}$ is a candidate relation. Let W be the set

[0, 1] of real numbers between 0 and 1. A *weighting function* for R_1 is a mapping w: $R_1 \rightarrow W$ that assigns a weight to each triple of R_1 such that $\Sigma_{r \in R_1} w(r) = 1$. Let h be a mapping from P_1 to P_2 and w a weighting function for R_1. A triple r of R_1 is *satisfied* by h with respect to R_2 if $h(r) \in R_2$. If h is a homomorphism from R_1 to R_2, then

$$\sum_{\substack{r \in R_1 \\ [r \ not \ satisfied \ by \ h]}} w(r) = 0 \text{ since } R_1 \circ h \subseteq R_2.$$

In order to allow imperfect matches, we define an ϵ-homomorphism to be a mapping h: $P_1 \rightarrow P_2$ such that

$$\sum_{\substack{r \in R_1 \\ [r \ not \ satisfied \ by \ h]}} w(r) \leqslant \epsilon.$$

Thus, in an ϵ-homomorphism the sum of the weights of those triples that are not satisfied is not greater than ϵ. A homomorphism, as defined earlier, is a 0-homomorphism.

Using these ideas, a human or a computer can assign weights to the triples of the prototype relation. One method of obtaining the weights would be to let a program induce them from imperfect matches ranked as to goodness of match. Then the shape matching problem is to find ϵ-homomorphisms from the prototype to the candidate.

Mappings That Can Assign Several Candidate Primitives to One Prototype Primitive

We would like to allow mappings that are not one-one, but with the restriction that only primitives that are near enough to each other can map to a single primitive. This leads to the *mergeability relation* $M \subseteq (S_1 \times S_1) \cup (I_1 \times I_1)$. If $(p_1, p_2) \in M$ then p_1 and p_2 may map to the same candidate primitive. One possible definition for M is

$$M = \{(p_1, p_2) \,|\, \delta(p_1, p_2) \leqslant \Delta\}.$$

A mapping h: $P_1 \rightarrow P_2$ is consistent with M if $h(p) = h(q)$ implies $(p, q) \in M$. Thus, we can expand the shape matching problem to find all ϵ-homomorphisms that are consistent with M.

Measuring the Goodness of a Match

The quantity

$$\sum_{\substack{r \in R_1 \\ [r \ satisfied \ by \ h]}} w(r)$$

measures the relational goodness of a mapping h. Two other measures are of interest:

1) a measure of the similarity between each primitive p of the prototype to the corresponding primitive h(p) of the candidate;

2) a measure of the size of the matched subset of the candidate primitives.

The measure 1) would take into account properties of a primitive such as those mentioned in Section III. The strictness or lenience of the enforcement of this measure in the matching criteria will determine how close to identical two shapes must be in order to match. The measure 2) might simply be the ratio of the area of the matched primitives (or just the simple parts) of the candidate to the total area of the primitives (or simple parts) of the candidate.

The Shape Matching Procedure

The problem of finding homomorphisms has been with us for some time. (See Barrow, Ambler, and Burstall [3], Ullman [33], and Corneil and Gotlieb [5].) Finding homomorphisms can be accomplished by means of a tree search incorporating a "look-ahead" or "relaxation" operator (see Haralick and Shapiro [15]). Finding ϵ-homomorphisms can be accomplished by a similar procedure. We now define a simple procedure for finding ϵ-homomorphisms that are consistent with a mergeability relation. The following high-level algorithm describes the procedure for finding all ϵ-homomorphisms that are consistent with mergeability relation M from a weighted N-ary relation R_1 on a set U of primitives of a prototype to an N-ary relation R_2 on a set L of primitives of a candidate. The primitives of U are referred to as *units* and the primitives of L as *labels*.

```
procedure MAIN ( );
comment  LABELS is a table
         LABELS (u) contains a list of those elements
         of L that u may be mapped to by the homomorphism
         to be found;
read (ε);                          comment error threshold;
read (M);                          comment mergeability relation;
read (U);                          comment primitives of the prototypes;
read (L);                          comment primitives of the candidate;
read (R₁);                         comment N-ary relation on U;
read (R₂);                         comment N-ary relation on L;
R: = R₁ × R₂;                      comment used in relaxation;
for each u ∈ U do
    read (LABELS(u));
call TREESEARCH (R1,R,LABELS);
stop
end MAIN;

procedure TREESEARCH(R1,R,LABELS);
comment Recursively perform a tree search to find mappings from the set
        U of primitives of the prototype to the set L of primitives of
        the candidate.  The mappings found will be ε-homomorphisms from
        R1 to R2 where R = R1 × R2;
THISUNIT := an element of U that has the least number of labels;
NEXTLABEL: if (there are no more labels in LABELS(THISUNIT)
           then return;
THISLABEL := next label in LABELS(THISUNIT);
R' := RESTRICTION(R,THISUNIT,THISLABEL);
LABELS' := EPSILON_ PROJECTION(R1,R',LABELS);
if (LABELS' = ∅) then goto NEXTLABEL
comment the following 4 statements are included if the treesearch is to
        use a relaxation procedure on R;
RELAXR: R' := EPSILON_ RELAX(R1,R',LABELS');
LABELS' := EPSILON_ PROJECTION(R1,R',LABELS');
if (LABELS' = ∅) then goto NEXTLABEL;
if (EPSILON_ RELAX removed any N-tuples from R')
then goto RELAXR;
comment If relaxation is not being used, the partial homomorphism defined
        by those elements of U that have only one label left in LABELS'
        must be checked to see that it meets the requirements of an ε-
        homomorphism;
if (¬ EPSILON_CONSISTENT(LABELS')) then goto NEXTLABEL;
comment Now if all the elements of U have only a single label left in LABELS',
        we have a homomorphism, otherwise continue the tree search;
if (LABELS' is single-valued)
then print ('HOMOMORPHISM',LABELS')
```

```
        else call TREESEARCH(R1,R′,LABELS′);
        comment Continue looking for more mappings;
        goto NEXTLABEL;
        end TREESEARCH

procedure EPSILON_PROJECTION(R1,R,LABELS);
comment Produce a new table containing for each unit u those labels that an
        ε-homomorphism may still map u to, given the current state of R;
for each unit UNIT that has only one label in LABELS do
    begin
        EPSILON_PROJECTION(UNIT) := LABELS(UNIT);
        PARTIAL(UNIT) := LABELS(UNIT)
    end;
for each unit UNIT that has more than one label in LABELS do
    for each label LAB in LABELS(UNIT) do
        begin
            PARTIAL(UNIT) := LAB;
            if EPSILON_CONSISTENT(PARTIAL,R1,R)
            then add LAB to EPSILON_PROJECTION(UNIT)
        end;
return;
end EPSILON_PROJECTION;

procedure EPSILON_CONSISTENT(LABELS,R1,R)
comment determine if the partial function defined by the single-valued
        entries in LABELS is an ε-homomorphism;
ERROR_SUM := 0;
for each N-tuple (u₁,...,u_N) ∈ R1 | such that each of u₁,...,u_N has just
        one label left in LABELS do
    begin
        if ((u₁,LABELS(u₁)),...,(u_N,LABELS(u_N))) is
            not in R
        then ERROR_SUM := ERRORSUM + weight (u₁,...,u_N);
        if ERROR_SUM > ε then goto FAIL
    end;
EPSILON_CONSISTENT = true;
return;
FAIL: EPSILON_CONSISTENT = false;
return
end EPSILON_CONSISTENT;
```

The algorithm described by the above procedures was used for shape matching. The relations R_i and R_p were used in place of the general relation R. R_i and R_p were stored, restricted, projected, and relaxed on separately because the program ran faster using the two smaller separate relations and combining their results than by merging them into one larger relation. The program was tested with and without a relaxation operator. Because the shape relations are relatively small, the overhead involved in setting up and carrying out the relaxation was greater than the amount of time required to perform the tree-search with the restriction and projection, but without the relaxation. The weighted discrete relaxation procedure, which *does* improve time significantly on larger relations, will be described in a future paper.

V. EXPERIMENTAL RESULTS

The shape matching procedure has been tested on character data. The data consist of a set of hand-printed characters which are considered to be prototype shapes and for each prototype shape, a set of imperfect versions of the shape. The imperfect versions were obtained by starting with a list of the boundary points of the prototype shape and calling on a uniform random number generator to produce horizontal and vertical displacements which were then added to the coordinates of the boundary points. By using different seeds for the random number generator, each prototype shape was used to generate several imperfect shapes with the same number of points, but with distorted boundaries. The amount of distortion was controlled by the range of displacements. Fig. 8 shows the prototype shapes and a set of corresponding imperfect versions.

The characters were first decomposed into simple parts and intrusions using the graph-theoretic clustering procedure described in [31]. Then the R_p and R_i relations were hand-coded for each character. In the hand-coding, we followed the definitions of R_p and R_i given in Section III as closely as

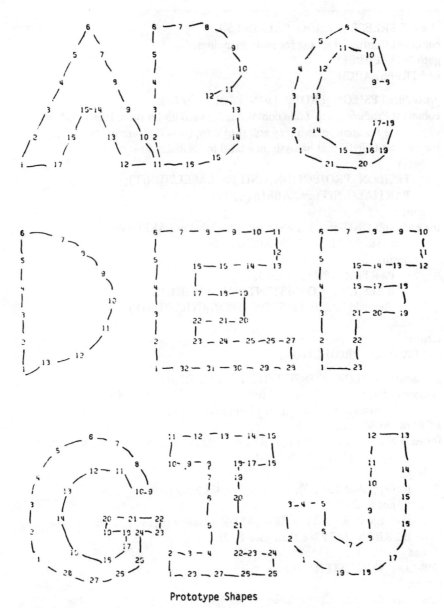

Prototype Shapes

Fig. 8. Illustrates the prototype shapes and a set of corresponding imperfect versions.

possible using a distance function δ defined by δ(p_1, p_2) = 0 if p_1 and p_2 have a point in common or if a point of p_1 is adjacent (along the boundary of the shape) to a point of p_2 and δ(p_1, p_2) = ∞ otherwise. (The software to automatically produce the relations is under current development.) Several extra test shapes were constructed totally by hand in order to have some shapes which were not just imperfect versions of the prototype shapes, but were "near-misses" as used in Winston's concept-learning experiments [34]; that is, some important property of these shapes was missing. These shapes were used to further test the inexact matching.

In each test, the matching program was given the R_p and R_i relations, a weighting function, and a mergeability relation for the prototype shape; the R_p and R_i relations for the candidate shape, and the inexact matching threshold ϵ. We will first describe some results where the weighting function assigned equal weights to each triple in the prototype relations, the mergeability relation M was empty or fixed, and ϵ was set to 0 for exact matching. We will then describe the effects of

varying ϵ, the mergeability relation, and the weights. We would like to emphasize at this point that our goals in running these experiments were not to test a new character recognition algorithm, but instead to learn about the concept of shape. Thus, for each test run, our interest was not in whether two shapes matched, but how much they matched and how much work the program had to do to decide how much they matched.

Example of Tests with Equal Weights,
Fixed Mergeability, and $\epsilon = 0$

We will illustrate this kind of test with a few characteristic examples. In one such test letter E1 of Fig. 7 was used as the prototype shape and letter E2 as the candidate shape. The program found the four legal 0-homomorphisms from E1 to E2 with a tree search in which 39 nodes were processed. Fig. 9 shows the tree search for this run. It is of interest to note that when the program used relaxation at each node of the tree search, only 16 nodes were processed, but the program

246

Imperfect Versions of
Prototype Shapes

Fig. 8. (Continued.)

performed so many more operations due to the overhead of the relaxation that it executed four times as long.

As examples of nonmatches, letter E1 was matched against letter I3, and letter I1, the prototype I, was run against letter E2. The decompositions of letter I1 and letter I3 are shown in Fig. 10. In both cases the program reported no homomorphisms found while searching only six nodes of the tree. The tree searches are illustrated in Fig. 11.

Examples of Tests Where ε Was Varied

A number of tests were performed where ϵ was varied in order to watch the behavior of the program as it went from exact matching to inexact matching and to see what kind of inexact matches occurred at higher values of ϵ. The E1-E2 experiment which processed 39 nodes for $\epsilon = 0$, processed 31 nodes for $\epsilon = 0.25$, finding the four 0-homomorphisms plus four 0.25-homomorphisms. The additional 0.25 homomorphisms are given as follows:

1	2	3	4	11	12
A	D	C	E	AA	BB
A	E	C	D	AA	BB
A	D	C	E	BB	AA
A	E	C	D	BB	AA

The E1-I3 experiment which processed 6 nodes for $\epsilon = 0$, processed 45 nodes for $\epsilon = 0.5$, again reporting no homomorphisms. The I1-E2 experiment, which processed 6 nodes and found no matches for $\epsilon = 0$, processed 69 nodes in the time it was allowed to run and had found 13 0.5-homomorphisms before it reached its time limit. One such 0.5-homomorphism was {(1, C), (2, A), (3, A), (4, B), (5, B), (11, AA), (12, BB)}. In this mapping, the triples (1, 11, 2) and (1, 12, 3) of R_i were satisfied and the triples (1, 11, 4) and (1, 12, 5) of R_i were not satisfied. Since half the triples of R_i

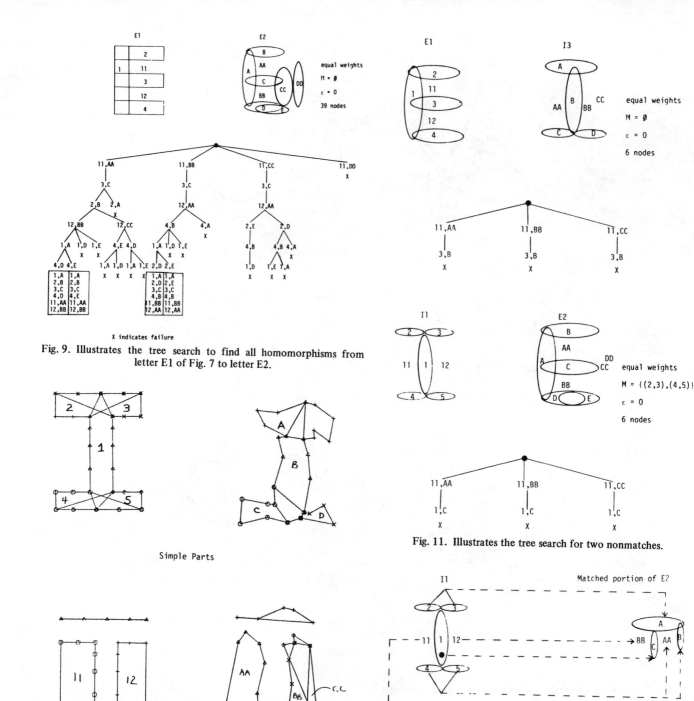

Fig. 9. Illustrates the tree search to find all homomorphisms from letter E1 of Fig. 7 to letter E2.

Simple Parts

Fig. 10. Illustrates the simple parts and intrusions for the prototype shape I1 and the imperfect shape I3.

Fig. 11. Illustrates the tree search for two nonmatches.

Fig. 12. Illustrates an inexact match of I1 to a portion of E2 at $\epsilon = 0.5$.

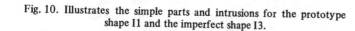

were satisfied, the mapping was a valid 0.5-homomorphism on R_i. R_p contained only the triple (11, 1, 12) which was satisfied. Fig. 12 illustrates this inexact match.

Fig. 13 shows the relations used in another inexact matching experiment. The prototype shape was letter E1 and the candidate a constructed relation NOT_E2. The program found no homomorphism for $\epsilon = 0$ processing 10 nodes, no homomorphisms for $\epsilon = 0.05$ processing 17 nodes, and no homomorphisms for $\epsilon = 0.25$ processing 31 nodes. The reason for no homomorphisms in this example is that no mapping could satisfy the R_p relation, which forces one of

the mappings {(11, AA), (3, C), (12, BB)} or {(11, BB), (3, C), (12, AA)}, and simultaneously satisfy the R_i relation.

Fig. 14 shows the relations used and the tree searches in a

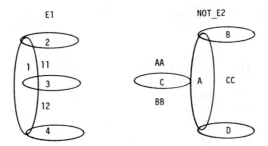

Fig. 13. Illustrates the relations used in an inexact matching experiment where no homomorphisms were found for $\epsilon = 0, 0.05,$ or 0.25.

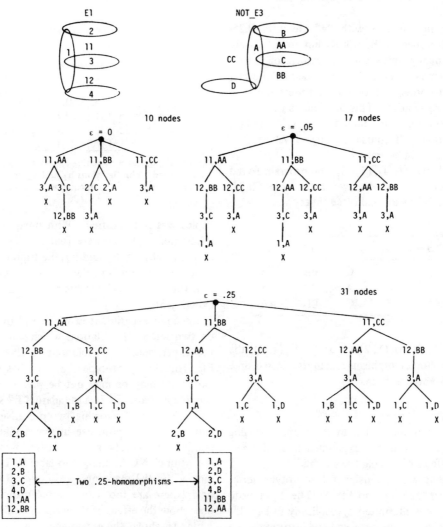

Fig. 14. Illustrates the relations and tree searches for an inexact matching experiment where two homomorphisms were found for $\epsilon = 0.25$.

similar experiment with prototypes E1 and candidate NOT_E3. This time two inexact matches were found when ϵ was set to 0.25. The program processed 10 nodes for $\epsilon = 0$, 17 nodes for $\epsilon = 0.05$, and 31 nodes for $\epsilon = 0.25$.

Examples of Tests Where M Was Varied

The mergeability relation M was the empty set for prototype E1 and was fixed at $\{(2, 3), (4, 5)\}$ for prototype I1 in the above examples. In this section we will describe some experiments using prototype I1 where M was varied.

Prototype I1 was matched against candidate I3 (both shown in Fig. 10) with M = $\emptyset$, M = $\{(2, 3)\}$, M = $\{(1, 2), (1, 3), (1, 4),$ $(1, 5)\}$, and M = $\{(2, 3) \, (4, 5), (1, 2), (1, 3), (1, 4), (1, 5)\}$. Each value of M was tested with $\epsilon = 0$ and $\epsilon = 0.25$. For M = $\emptyset$, the program found no homomorphisms either with $\epsilon = 0$ or with $\epsilon = 0.25$. For M = $\{(2, 3)\}$, the program found two homomorphisms with $\epsilon = 0$ and eight homomorphisms with $\epsilon = 0.25$. The 0-homomorphisms are listed below:

1	2	3	4	5	11	12
B	A	A	C	D	AA	BB
B	A	A	D	C	BB	AA

249

The 0.25-homomorphisms include the 0-homomorphisms and the six listed below:

1	2	3	4	5	11	12
* B	C	C	A	D	AA	BB
* B	D	D	C	A	AA	BB
B	A	A	C	D	AA	CC
* B	C	C	D	A	BB	AA
* B	D	D	A	C	BB	AA
B	A	A	D	C	CC	AA

Note that the mappings marked with "*" are valid 0.25-homomorphisms with respect to R_i and R_p but are intuitively invalid because they map primitives 4 and 5 which touch to A and C or A and D which do not. This is caused by the fact that 4 and 5 join but border no intrusion and therefore were not included in the R_i relation. This problem can be solved by defining a null intrusion i_0 and including $(4, i_0, 5)$ and $(2, i_0, 3)$ in the R_i relation. Of course, for higher values of ϵ, these extra constraints could be ignored.

For M = {(1, 2), (1, 3), (1, 4), (1, 5)}, the program found no 0-homomorphisms and had discovered the three 0.25-homomorphisms listed below in its allotted time:

1	2	3	4	5	11	12
B	B	A	D	C	BB	AA
B	B	C	D	A	BB	AA
B	D	A	B	C	BB	AA

Finally, for M = {(2, 3), (4, 5), (1, 2), (1, 3), (1, 4), (1, 5)} the program found four 0-homomorphisms and in its allotted time had found 222 0.25-homomorphisms.

Examples of Tests Where Weights Were Varied

The weighting function was added to the shape matching procedure to add flexibility to the experiments. In this section we discuss the effects of varying the weights.

A simple experiment was run using the prototype letter "C" and imperfect version shown in Fig. 8. The decomposition of the two shapes is illustrated symbolically in Fig. 15. The prototype C1 has five simple parts and one intrusion while the candidate C2 has only four simple parts and one intrusion. In the experiment the mergeability relation M was fixed at {(1, 2), (2, 3), (3, 5), (1, 4)} so that any two simple parts that touched or nearly touched could map to a single simple part. The experimental weighting function assigned high weights (0.45) to the triples (1, 11, 2) and (2, 11, 3) which represent the joining of the three main primitives of the shape and low weights (0.05) to the triples (1, 11, 4) and (3, 11, 5) which represent the joining of the two optional end primitives to the remainder of the shape. The experiment was also run with equal weights as a comparison. The error threshold ϵ was fixed at 0.2.

As expected, the program reported no 0.2-homomorphisms when the weights were equal, since at least one of the four

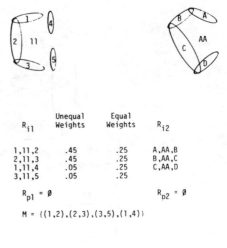

R_{i1}	Unequal Weights	Equal Weights	R_{i2}
1,11,2	.45	.25	A,AA,B
2,11,3	.45	.25	B,AA,C
1,11,4	.05	.25	C,AA,D
3,11,5	.05	.25	
R_{p1} = ∅			R_{p2} = ∅

M = {(1,2),(2,3),(3,5),(1,4)}

	1	2	3	4	5	11	Not Satisfied	Error With Unequal Weights	Error With Equal Weights
h_1	A	B	C	D	A	AA	(1,11,4) (3,11,5)	.1	.5
h_2	B	C	D	A	D	AA	(3,11,5)	.05	.25

Fig. 15. Illustrates a matching experiment on letter C's where weights were varied. The functions h_1 and h_2 are two of the 0.2-homomorphisms found when the unequal weights were used.

triples was not satisfied. With unequal weights a number of 0.2-homomorphisms were found. Fig. 15 gives two of these homomorphisms, h_1 and h_2, the triples that were not satisfied by each function, and the corresponding error for each function for the unequal weights experiment and the equal weights experiment.

A second experiment in which weights were varied was run on two letter "T" relations which were created expressly for the experiment. The relations for these shapes is shown in Fig. 16. The prototype shape T1 has several optional extra parts that may or may not be present on a letter "T." The candidate shape T2 is a standard "T" shape. In this experiment, instead of allowing two primitives in the prototype to map to a single primitive in the candidate, the mergeability relation was empty and primitives were allowed to map to the symbol NL meaning "no label." Thus, the effect was to look at partial mappings. Although the approach is impractical (there are too many partial mappings), the experiment does show the effect of the weights on the mappings found.

Fig. 16 shows the experimental weighting function and the equal weights function. The experimental weighting function assigns the highest weights to the relationships that make a shape "T"-shaped and lower weights to the optional relationships. The mapping h in Fig. 16 is one of the 0.2-homomorphisms that was found with the unequal weights, but did not exist when the equal weights were used. The two experiments show that varying the weights can be used to set up a model with many low priority optional parts and relationships.

VI. DISCUSSION AND CONCLUSIONS

We have discussed a general model for a structural description of a shape and defined a specific model based on decomposing the shape into simple parts and intrusions. In our model two relations, the intrusion relation and the protrusion

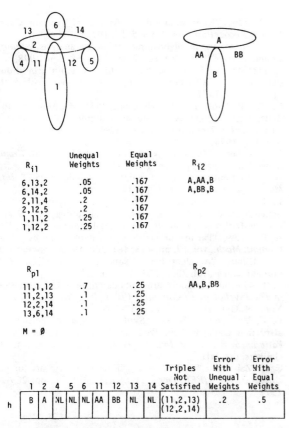

R_{i1}	Unequal Weights	Equal Weights	R_{i2}
6,13,2	.05	.167	A,AA,B
6,14,2	.05	.167	A,BB,B
2,11,4	.2	.167	
2,12,5	.2	.167	
1,11,2	.25	.167	
1,12,2	.25	.167	

R_{p1}			R_{p2}
11,1,12	.7	.25	AA,B,BB
11,2,13	.1	.25	
12,2,14	.1	.25	
13,6,14	.1	.25	

M = ∅

	1	2	4	5	6	11	12	13	14	Triples Not Satisfied	Error With Unequal Weights	Error With Equal Weights
h	B	A	NL	NL	NL	AA	BB	NL	NL	(11,2,13) (12,2,14)	.2	.5

Fig. 16. Illustrates a matching experiment on two letter T's where weights were varied. The function h is a 0.2-homomorphism found when the unequal weights were used.

relation, characterize the shape. The descriptions can be enhanced by adding properties of the simple parts and intrusions.

We have defined shape matching as the problem of finding relational homomorphisms from a prototype shape to a candidate shape. We have discussed homomorphisms on weighted relations and homomorphisms that can assign several candidate primitives to one prototype primitive. We have also discussed some measures for the goodness of a match. Finally, we have described an experimental shape matching procedure that uses a tree search to find homomorphisms from prototype shapes to candidate shapes. At this point, we would like to comment on the results so far and the work yet to be done.

The main contribution of this work is the relational shape model and specialized shape matching procedure. The intrusion and protrusion relations appear to be sufficient to characterize a shape. The model is both simple and powerful. The shape matching procedure incorporating weights, thresholds, and a mergeability relation is a highly flexible matching procedure. Because not all of the parts have to be distinct and not all of the relationships have to be satisfied, inexact matches and partial matches are possible. Thus, shapes that are distorted or obstructed can still match their prototypes. This important characteristic is needed in scene analysis systems.

The entire shape recognition system at present consists of a set of Fortran programs that perform the decomposition of a shape and a Snobol program that performs the shape match-

ing procedure. The automation of extracting the R_i and R_p relations and other information from the results of the decomposition is currently being tackled. For a shape represented by N points, the Fortran programs perform $O(N^3)$ operations for computing relations and $O(N^2)$ operations for graph-theoretic clustering. We hope to reduce the complexity of the $O(N^3)$ program by improving the algorithm used. (The current one is just brute force.) The Snobol program, in the worst case, would search the entire tree since finding homomorphisms is an NP-complete problem. However, in our experiments, the program searched a relatively small portion of the tree. As mentioned previously, the program executed faster on these simple shapes without the relaxation procedure. However, when relaxation was used, the program rarely made a mistake requiring backup. Thus, for very complex shapes with many primitives to be matched, a relaxation procedure should be used. In practice, the number of nodes searched seems to be proportional to the number of primitives of the prototype shape times the number of homomorphisms found. As the error threshold ϵ increases, the program tends to search more nodes and to find more homomorphisms. Occasionally, the program will search fewer nodes with a higher value of ϵ because the order of the search has changed.

The current Snobol shape matching procedure is very slow; approximately $2\frac{1}{4}$ nodes/s are searched. This is mostly due to the fact that the program uses character strings to represent most data objects (triples, lists, units, and labels) and character string operators such as pattern matching and concatenation for manipulating the data objects. The program was initially written in Snobol4 because the powerful data structures and facilities of the language made for a short program and an equally short debugging time. More efficient matching programs are currently being developed in Fortran and Pascal.

The results reported here are only initial experimental results. We expect to perform many more experiments using more extensive data and studying further the effects of different weighting schemes and mergeability relations. We also wish to study the effects of adding properties of the primitives to the model (putting statistical and structural descriptions together), and we will be adding symmetry to the model. Another goal is to develop a shape matching procedure that constructs a third shape from which there are homomorphisms to each of two shapes being tested for similarity. This will take care of the problem of a primitive of the prototype shape mapping to two different primitives of the candidate shape. In summary, the shape recognition procedure as a whole seems to be a promising tool in scene analysis.

REFERENCES

[1] F. L. Alt, "Digital pattern recognition by moments," *J. Ass. Comput. Mach.*, vol. 11, pp. 240–258, 1962.
[2] A. K. Agrawala and A. V. Kulkarni, "A sequential approach to the extraction of shape features," *Comput. Graphics Image Processing*, vol. 6, pp. 538–557, Dec. 1977.
[3] H. G. Barrow, A. P. Ambler, and R. M. Burstall, "Some techniques for recognizing structures in pictures," in *Frontiers of Pattern Recognition*, S. Watanabe, Ed. New York: Academic, 1972, pp. 1–29.
[4] H. Blum, "A transformation for extracting new descriptions of shape," in *Symp. on Models for the Perception of Speech and Visual Form.* Cambridge, MA: M.I.T. Press, 1964.
[5] D. G. Corneil and C. C. Gottlieb, "An efficient algorithm for

graph isomorphism," *J. Ass. Comput. Mach.*, vol. 17, pp. 51–64, Jan. 1970.

[6] L. S. Davis, "Shape matching using relaxation techniques," *IEEE Trans. Pattern Anal. Machine Intell.*, vol. PAMI-1, no. 1, pp. 60–72, 1979.

[7] ——, "Understanding shape: Angles and sides," *IEEE Trans. Comput.*, vol. C-26, pp. 236–242, Mar. 1977.

[8] ——, "Understanding shape II: Symmetry," *IEEE Trans. Syst., Man, Cybern.*, vol. SMC-7, pp. 204–212, Mar. 1977.

[9] M. Eden, "Handwriting and pattern recognition," *IRE Trans. Inform. Theory*, vol. IT-8, pp. 160–166, 1962.

[10] H. F. Feng and T. Pavlidis, "Decomposition of polygons into simpler components: Feature generation for syntactic pattern recognition," *IEEE Trans. Comput.*, vol. C-24, pp. 636–650, June 1975.

[11] H. Freeman, "Computer processing of line drawing images," *Computing Surveys*, vol. 6, pp. 57–97, Mar. 1974.

[12] K. S. Fu and S. Y. Lu, "A clustering procedure for syntactic patterns," *IEEE Trans. Syst., Man, Cybern.*, vol. SMC-7, pp. 734–742, 1977.

[13] G. H. Granlund, "Fourier preprocessing for hand print character recognition," *IEEE Trans. Comput.*, vol. C-21, pp. 195–201, Feb. 1972.

[14] R. M. Haralick and J. Kartus, "Arrangements, homomorphisms, and discrete relaxation," *IEEE Trans. Syst., Man, Cybern.*, vol. SMC-8, pp. 600–612, Aug. 1978.

[15] R. M. Haralick and L. G. Shapiro, "The consistent labeling problem," *IEEE Trans. Pattern Anal. Machine Intell.*, vol. PAMI-1, no. 2, 1979.

[16] ——, "Decomposition of polygonal shapes by clustering," in *Proc. First IEEE Conf. on Pattern Recognition and Image Processing*, June 1977, pp. 183–190.

[17] R. M. Haralick, "Statistical shape descriptors for simple shapes," unpublished work.

[18] S. L. Horowitz, "Peak recognition in waveforms," in *Syntactic Pattern Recognition Applications*, K. S. Fu, Ed. Berlin, Germany: Springer-Verlag, 1977.

[19] M. K. Hu, "Visual pattern recognition by moment invariants," *IRE Trans. Inform. Theory*, vol. IT-8, pp. 179–187, Feb. 1962.

[20] D. Langridge, "On the computation of shape," in *Frontiers of Pattern Recognition*, S. Watanabe, Ed. New York: Academic, 1962, pp. 347–365.

[21] T. Lozano-Perez, "Parsing intensity profiles," *Comput. Graphics Image Processing*, vol. 6, pp. 43–60, 1977.

[22] K. Maruyama, "A study of visual shape perception," Dep. Comput. Sci., Univ. of Illinois, Rep. VIVCDCS-R-72-533, Oct. 1972.

[23] J. F. O'Callaghan, "Recovery of perceptual shape organization from simple closed boundaries," *Comput. Graphics Image Processing*, vol. 3, pp. 300–312, Dec. 1974.

[24] T. Pavlidis and F. Ali, "A hierarchical syntactic shape analyzer," *IEEE Trans. Pattern Anal. Machine Intell.*, vol. PAMI-1, pp. 2–9, Jan. 1979.

[25] T. Pavlidis, "Representation of figures by labelled graphs," *Pattern Recognition*, vol. 4, pp. 5–17, 1972.

[26] ——, "A review of algorithms for shape analysis," *Comput. Graphics Image Processing*, vol. 7, pp. 243–258, Apr. 1978.

[27] E. Persoon and K. S. Fu, "Shape discrimination using Fourier descriptors," *IEEE Trans. Syst., Man, Cybern.*, vol. SMC-7, pp. 170–179, 1977.

[28] C. W. Richard and H. Hemami, "Identification of three-dimensional objects using Fourier descriptors of the boundary curve," *IEEE Trans. Syst., Man, Cybern.*, vol. SMC-4, pp. 371–377, July 1974.

[29] B. Rosenberg, "The analysis of convex blobs," *Comput. Graphics Image Processing*, vol. 1, pp. 183–192, 1972.

[30] ——, "Computing dominant points on simple shapes," *Int. J. Man-Machine Studies*, vol. 6, pp. 1–12, 1975.

[31] L. G. Shapiro and R. M. Haralick, "Decomposition of two-dimensional shapes by graph-theoretic clustering," *IEEE Trans. Pattern Anal. Machine Intell.*, vol. PAMI-1, pp. 10–20, Jan. 1979.

[32] A. C. Shaw, "Parsing of graph-representable pictures," *J. Ass. Comput. Mach.*, vol. 17, pp. 453–481, July 1970.

[33] J. R. Ullman, "An algorithm for subgraph isomorphism," *J. Ass. Comput. Mach.*, vol. 23, pp. 31–42, Jan. 1976.

[34] P. H. Winston, "Learning structural descriptions from examples," in *The Psychology of Computer Vision*, P. H. Winston, Ed. New York: McGraw-Hill, 1975, pp. 157–209.

[35] K. C. You and K. S. Fu, "Syntactic shape recognition using attributed grammars," in *Proc. 1978 EIA Symp. on Emerging Patterns in Automatic Imagery Pattern Recognition*, Apr. 3–4, Gaithersburg, MD.

[36] C. T. Zahn and R. Z. Roskies, "Fourier descriptors for plane closed curves," *IEEE Trans. Comput.*, vol. C-21, pp. 269–281, 1972.

Linda G. Shapiro was born in Chicago, IL, in 1949. She received the B.S. degree in mathematics from the University of Illinois at Urbana-Champaign in 1970, and the M.S. and Ph.D. degrees in computer science from the University of Iowa, Iowa City, in 1972 and 1974, respectively.

She was an Assistant Professor of Computer Science at Kansas State University, Manhattan, from 1974 to 1978. She is currently an Assistant Professor at Virginia Polytechnic Institute and State University, Blacksburg. Her research interests include scene analysis, pattern recognition, spatial information systems, computer graphics, and data structures. She has completed an undergraduate textbook on data structures with R. Baron.

Dr. Shapiro is a member of the IEEE Computer Society, the Association for Computing Machinery, and the Pattern Recognition Society.

"Random Sample Consensus: A Paradigm for Model Fitting with Applications to Image Analysis and Automated Cartography" by M.A. Fischler and R.C. Bolles from *Communications of the ACM*, Volume 24, Number 6, June 1981, pages 381-395. Copyright 1981, Association for Computing Machinery, Inc., reprinted with permission.

Graphics and
Image Processing

J. D. Foley
Editor

Random Sample Consensus: A Paradigm for Model Fitting with Applications to Image Analysis and Automated Cartography

Martin A. Fischler and Robert C. Bolles
SRI International

A new paradigm, Random Sample Consensus (RANSAC), for fitting a model to experimental data is introduced. RANSAC is capable of interpreting/smoothing data containing a significant percentage of gross errors, and is thus ideally suited for applications in automated image analysis where interpretation is based on the data provided by error-prone feature detectors. A major portion of this paper describes the application of RANSAC to the Location Determination Problem (LDP): Given an image depicting a set of landmarks with known locations, determine that point in space from which the image was obtained. In response to a RANSAC requirement, new results are derived on the minimum number of landmarks needed to obtain a solution, and algorithms are presented for computing these minimum-landmark solutions in closed form. These results provide the basis for an automatic system that can solve the LDP under difficult viewing

The work reported herein was supported by the Defense Advanced Research Projects Agency under Contract Nos. DAAG29-76-C-0057 and MDA903-79-C-0588.

Authors' Present Address: Martin A. Fischler and Robert C. Bolles, Artificial Intelligence Center, SRI International, Menlo Park CA 94025.

© 1981 ACM 0001-0782/81/0600-0381$00.75

and analysis conditions. **Implementation details and computational examples are also presented.**

Key Words and Phrases: model fitting, scene analysis, camera calibration, image matching, location determination, automated cartography.

CR Categories: 3.60, 3.61, 3.71, 5.0, 8.1, 8.2

I. Introduction

We introduce a new paradigm, Random Sample Consensus (RANSAC), for fitting a model to experimental data; and illustrate its use in scene analysis and automated cartography. The application discussed, the location determination problem (LDP), is treated at a level beyond that of a mere example of the use of the RANSAC paradigm; new basic findings concerning the conditions under which the LDP can be solved are presented and a comprehensive approach to the solution of this problem that we anticipate will have near-term practical applications is described.

To a large extent, scene analysis (and, in fact, science in general) is concerned with the interpretation of sensed data in terms of a set of predefined models. Conceptually, interpretation involves two distinct activities: First, there is the problem of finding the best match between the data and one of the available models (the classification problem); Second, there is the problem of computing the best values for the free parameters of the selected model (the parameter estimation problem). In practice, these two problems are not independent—a solution to the parameter estimation problem is often required to solve the classification problem.

Classical techniques for parameter estimation, such as least squares, optimize (according to a specified objective function) the fit of a functional description (model) to *all* of the presented data. These techniques have no internal mechanisms for detecting and rejecting gross errors. They are averaging techniques that rely on the assumption (the smoothing assumption) that the maximum expected deviation of any datum from the assumed model is a direct function of the size of the data set, and thus regardless of the size of the data set, there will always be enough good values to smooth out any gross deviations.

In many practical parameter estimation problems the smoothing assumption does not hold; i.e., the data contain uncompensated gross errors. To deal with this situation, several heuristics have been proposed. The technique usually employed is some variation of first using all the data to derive the model parameters, then locating the datum that is farthest from agreement with the instantiated model, assuming that it is a gross error, deleting it, and iterating this process until either the maximum deviation is less then some preset threshold or until there is no longer sufficient data to proceed.

It can easily be shown that a single gross error ("poisoned point"), mixed in with a set of good data, can

PROBLEM: Given the set of seven (x,y) pairs shown in the plot, find a best fit line, assuming that no valid datum deviates from this line by more than 0.8 units.

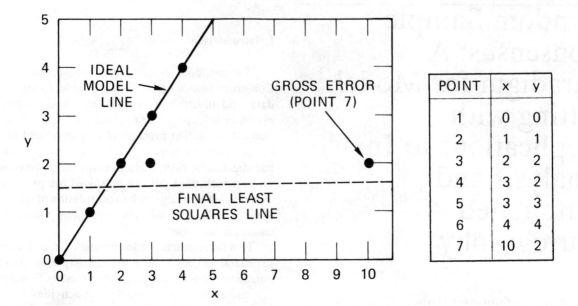

POINT	x	y
1	0	0
2	1	1
3	2	2
4	3	2
5	3	3
6	4	4
7	10	2

COMMENT: Six of the seven points are valid data and can be fit by the solid line. Using Least Squares (and the "throwing out the worst residual" heuristic), we terminate after four iterations with four remaining points, including the gross error at (10,2) fit by the dashed line.

SUCCESSIVE LEAST SQUARES APPROXIMATIONS		
ITERATION	DATA SET	FITTING LINE
1	1, 2, 3, 4, 5, 6, 7	1.48 + .16x
2	1, 2, 3, 4, 5, 7	1.25 + .13x
3	1, 2, 3, 4, 7	0.96 + .14x
4	2, 3, 4, 7	1.51 + .06x

COMPUTATION OF RESIDUALS				
POINT	ITERATION 1 RESIDUALS	ITERATION 2 RESIDUALS	ITERATION 3 RESIDUALS	ITERATION 4 RESIDUALS
1	-1.48	-1.25	-.96*	—
2	-0.64	-0.38	-.10	-.57
3	-0.20	0.49	.76	.37
4	0.05	0.36	.63	.31
5	1.05	1.36*	—	—
6	1.89*	—	—	—
7	-1.06	-0.57	-.33	-.11

cause the above heuristic to fail (for example, see Figure 1). It is our contention that averaging is not an appropriate technique to apply to an unverified data set.

In the following section we introduce the RANSAC paradigm, which is capable of smoothing data that contain a significant percentage of gross errors. This paradigm is particularly applicable to scene analysis because local feature detectors, which often make mistakes, are the source of the data provided to the interpretation algorithms. Local feature detectors make two types of errors—classification errors and measurement errors. Classification errors occur when a feature detector incorrectly identifies a portion of an image as an occurrence of a feature. Measurement errors occur when the feature detector correctly identifies the feature, but slightly miscalculates one of its parameters (e.g., its image location). Measurement errors generally follow a normal distribution, and therefore the smoothing assumption is applicable to them. Classification errors, however, are gross errors, having a significantly larger effect than measurement errors, and do not average out.

In the final sections of this paper the application of RANSAC to the location determination problem is discussed:

Given a set of "landmarks" ("control points"), whose locations are known in some coordinate frame, determine the location (relative to the coordinate frame of the landmarks) of that point in space from which an image of the landmarks was obtained.

In response to a RANSAC requirement, some new results are derived on the minimum number of landmarks needed to obtain a solution, and then algorithms are presented for computing these minimum-landmark solutions in closed form. (Conventional techniques are iterative and require a good initial guess to assure convergence.) These results form the basis for an automatic system that can solve the LDP under severe viewing and analysis conditions. In particular, the system performs properly even if a significant number of landmarks are incorrectly located due to low visibility, terrain changes, or image analysis errors. Implementation details and experimental results are presented to complete our description of the LDP application.

II. Random Sample Consensus

The RANSAC procedure is opposite to that of conventional smoothing techniques: Rather than using as much of the data as possible to obtain an initial solution and then attempting to eliminate the invalid data points, RANSAC uses as small an initial data set as feasible and enlarges this set with consistent data when possible. For example, given the task of fitting an arc of a circle to a set of two-dimensional points, the RANSAC approach would be to select a set of three points (since three points are required to determine a circle), compute the center and radius of the implied circle, and count the number of points that are close enough to that circle to suggest

their compatibility with it (i.e., their deviations are small enough to be measurement errors). If there are enough compatible points, RANSAC would employ a smoothing technique such as least squares, to compute an improved estimate for the parameters of the circle now that a set of mutually consistent points has been identified.

The RANSAC paradigm is more formally stated as follows:

Given a model that requires a minimum of n data points to instantiate its free parameters, and a set of data points P such that the number of points in P is greater than n [$\#(P) \geq n$], randomly select a subset $S1$ of n data points from P and instantiate the model. Use the instantiated model $M1$ to determine the subset $S1^*$ of points in P that are within some error tolerance of $M1$. The set $S1^*$ is called the consensus set of $S1$.

If $\#(S1^*)$ is greater than some threshold t, which is a function of the estimate of the number of gross errors in P, use $S1^*$ to compute (possibly using least squares) a new model $M1^*$.

If $\#(S1^*)$ is less than t, randomly select a new subset $S2$ and repeat the above process. If, after some predetermined number of trials, no consensus set with t or more members has been found, either solve the model with the largest consensus set found, or terminate in failure.

There are two obvious improvements to the above algorithm: First, if there is a problem related rationale for selecting points to form the S's, use a deterministic selection process instead of a random one; second, once a suitable consensus set S^* has been found and a model M^* instantiated, add any new points from P that are consistent with M^* to S^* and compute a new model on the basis of this larger set.

The RANSAC paradigm contains three unspecified parameters: (1) the error tolerance used to determine whether or not a point is compatible with a model, (2) the number of subsets to try, and (3) the threshold t, which is the number of compatible points used to imply that the correct model has been found. Methods are discussed for computing reasonable values for these parameters in the following subsections.

A. Error Tolerance For Establishing Datum/Model Compatibility

The deviation of a datum from a model is a function of the error associated with the datum and the error associated with the model (which, in part, is a function of the errors associated with the data used to instantiate the model). If the model is a simple function of the data points, it may be practical to establish reasonable bounds on error tolerance analytically. However, this straightforward approach is often unworkable; for such cases it is generally possible to estimate bounds on error tolerance experimentally. Sample deviations can be produced by perturbing the data, computing the model, and measuring the implied errors. The error tolerance could then be set at one or two standard deviations beyond the measured average error.

The expected deviation of a datum from an assumed model is generally a function of the datum, and therefore the error tolerance should be different for each datum. However, the variation in error tolerances is usually relatively small compared to the size of a gross error. Thus, a single error tolerance for all data is often sufficient.

B. The Maximum Number of Attempts to Find a Consensus Set

The decision to stop selecting new subsets of P can be based upon the expected number of trials k required to select a subset of n good data points. Let w be the probability that any selected data point is within the error tolerance of the model. Then we have:

$$E(k) = b + 2*(1 - b)*b + 3*(1 - b)^2*b$$

$$\cdots + i*(1 - b)^{i-1}*b + \cdots,$$

$$E(k) = b*[1 + 2*a + 3*a^2 \cdots + i*a^{i-1} + \cdots],$$

where $E(k)$ is the expected value of k, $b = w^n$, and $a = (1 - b)$.
An identity for the sum of a geometric series is

$$a/(1 - a) = a + a^2 + a^3 \cdots + a^i + \cdots.$$

Differentiating the above identity with respect to a, we have:

$$1/(1 - a)^2 = 1 + 2*a + 3*a^2 \cdots + i*a^{i-1} + \cdots.$$

Thus,

$$E(k) = 1/b = w^{-n}$$

The following is a tabulation of some values of $E(k)$ for corresponding values of n and w:

w	$n = 1$	2	3	4	5	6
0.9	1.1	1.2	1.4	1.5	1.7	1.9
0.8	1.3	1.6	2.0	2.4	3.0	3.8
0.7	1.4	2.0	2.9	4.2	5.9	8.5
0.6	1.7	2.8	4.6	7.7	13	21
0.5	2.0	4.0	8.0	16	32	64
0.4	2.5	6.3	16	39	98	244
0.3	3.3	11	37	123	412	—
0.2	5.0	25	125	625	—	—

In general, we would probably want to exceed $E(k)$ trials by one or two standard deviations before we give up. Note that the standard deviation of k, $SD(k)$, is given by:

$$SD(k) = sqrt [E(k^2) - E(k)^2].$$

Then

$$E(k^2) = \sum_{i=0}^{\infty} (b*i^2*a^{i-1}),$$

$$= \sum_{i=0}^{\infty} [b*i*(i - 1)*a^{i-1}] + \sum_{i=0}^{\infty} (b*i*a^{i-1}),$$

but (using the geometric series identity and two differentiations):

$$2a/(1 - a)^3 = \sum_{i=0}^{\infty} (i*(i - 1)*a^{i-1}).$$

Thus,

$$E(k^2) = (2 - b)/(b^2),$$

and

$$SD(k) = [sqrt (1 - w^n)]*(1/w^n).$$

Note that generally $SD(k)$ will be approximately equal to $E(k)$; thus, for example, if $(w = 0.5)$ and $(n = 4)$, then $E(k) = 16$ and $SD(k) = 15.5$. This means that one might want to try two or three times the expected number of random selections implied by k (as tabulated above) to obtain a consensus set of more than t members.

From a slightly different point of view, if we want to ensure with probability z that at least one of our random selections is an error-free set of n data points, then we must expect to make at least k selections (n data points per selection), where

$$(1 - b)^k = (1 - z),$$

$$k = [\log(1 - z)]/[\log(1 - b)].$$

For example, if $(w = 0.5)$ and $(n = 4)$, then $(b = 1/16)$. To obtain a 90 percent assurance of making at least one error-free selection,

$$k = \log(0.1)/\log(15/16) = 35.7.$$

Note that if $w^n \ll 1$, then $k \approx \log(1 - z)E(k)$. Thus if $z = 0.90$ and $w^n \ll 1$, then $k \approx 2.3E(k)$; if $z = 0.95$ and $w^n \ll 1$, then $k \approx 3.0E(k)$.

C. A Lower Bound On the Size of an Acceptable Consensus Set

The threshold t, an unspecified parameter in the formal statement of the RANSAC paradigm, is used as the basis for determining that an n subset of P has been found that implies a sufficiently large consensus set to permit the algorithm to terminate. Thus, t must be chosen large enough to satisfy two purposes: that the correct model has been found for the data, and that a sufficient number of mutually consistent points have been found to satisfy the needs of the final smoothing procedure (which computes improved estimates for the model parameters).

To ensure against the possibility of the final consensus set being compatible with an incorrect model, and assuming that y is the probability that any given data point is within the error tolerance of an incorrect model, we would like y^{t-n} to be very small. While there is no general way of precisely determining y, it is certainly reasonable to assume that it is less than w (w is the *a priori* probability that a given data point is within the error tolerance of the correct model). Assuming $y < 0.5$, a value of $t - n$ equal to 5 will provide a better than 95 percent probability that compatibility with an incorrect model will not occur.

To satisfy the needs of the final smoothing procedure, the particular procedure to be employed must be specified. If least-squares smoothing is to be used, there are many situations where formal methods can be invoked to determine the number of points required to produce a desired precision [10].

D. Example

Let us apply RANSAC to the example described in Figure 1. A value of w (the probability that any selected data point is within the error tolerance of the model) equal to 0.85 is consistent with the data, and a tolerance (to establish datum/model compatibility) of 0.8 units was supplied as part of the problem statement. The RANSAC-supplied model will be accepted without external smoothing of the final consensus set; thus, we would like to obtain a consensus set that contains all seven data points. Since one of these points is a gross error, it is obvious that we will not find a consensus set of the desired size, and so we will terminate with the largest set we are able to find. The theory presented earlier indicates that if we take two data points at a time, compute the line through them and measure the deviations of the remaining points from this line, we should expect to find a suitable consensus set within two or three trials; however, because of the limited amount of data, we might be willing to try all 21-combinations to find the largest consensus set. In either case, we easily find the consensus set containing the six valid data points and the line that they imply.

III. The Location Determination Problem (LDP)

A basic problem in image analysis is establishing a correspondence between the elements of two representations of a given scene. One variation of this problem, especially important in cartography, is determining the location in space from which an image or photograph was obtained by recognizing a set of landmarks (control points) appearing in the image (this is variously called the problem of determining the elements of exterior camera orientation, or the camera calibration problem, or the image-to-database correspondence problem). It is routinely solved using a least-squares technique [11, 8] with a human operator interactively establishing the association between image points and the three-dimensional coordinates of the corresponding control points. However, in a fully automated system, where the correspondences must be based on the decisions of marginally competent feature detectors, least squares is often incapable of dealing with the gross errors that may result; this consideration, discussed at length in Sec. II, is illustrated for the LDP in an example presented in Sec. IV.

In this section a new solution to the LDP is presented based on the RANSAC paradigm, which is unique in its ability to tolerate gross errors in the input data. We will first examine the conditions under which a solution to the LDP is possible and describe new results concerning this question; we then present a complete description of the RANSAC-based algorithm, and finally, describe experimental results obtained through use of the algorithm.

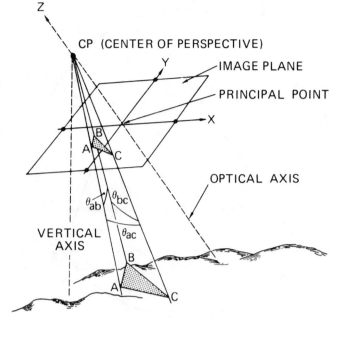

Fig. 2. Geometry of the Location Determination Problem.

The LDP is formally defined as follows:

Given a set of m control points, whose 3-dimensional coordinates are known in some coordinate frame, and given an image in which some subset of the m control points is visible, determine the location (relative to the coordinate system of the control points) from which the image was obtained.

We will initially assume that we know the correspondences between n image points and control points; later we consider the situation in which some of these correspondences are invalid. We will also assume that both the principal point in the image plane (where the optical axis of the camera pierces the image plane) and the focal length (distance from the center of perspective to the principal point in the image plane) of the imaging system are known; thus (see Figure 2) we can easily compute the angle to any pair of control points from the center of perspective (CP). Finally, we assume that the camera resides outside and above a convex hull enclosing the control points.

We will later demonstrate (Appendix A) that if we can compute the lengths of the rays from the CP to three of the control points then we can directly solve for the location of the CP (and the orientation of the image plane if desired). Thus, an equivalent but mathematically more concise statement of the LDP is

Given the relative spatial locations of n control points, and given the angle to every pair of control points from an additional point called the Center of Perspective (CP), find the lengths of the line segments ("legs") joining the CP to each of the control points. We call this the "perspective-n-point" problem (PnP).

In order to apply the RANSAC paradigm, we wish to determine the smallest value of n for which it is possible to solve the PnP problem.

Fig. 3. Geometry of the P2P Problem.

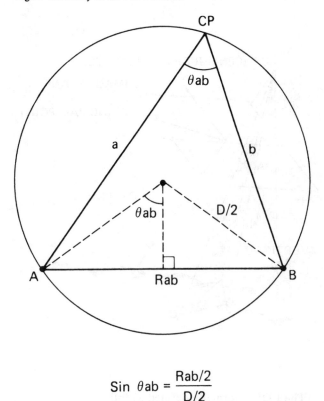

$$\text{Sin } \theta ab = \frac{Rab/2}{D/2}$$

$$D = \frac{Rab}{\text{Sin } \theta ab}$$

A. Solution of the Perspective-*n*-Point Problem

The P1P problem ($n = 1$) provides no constraining information, and thus an infinity of solutions is possible. The P2P problem ($n = 2$), illustrated in Figure 3, also admits an infinity of solutions; the CP can reside anywhere on a circle of diameter Rab/sin(θab), rotated in space about the chord (line) joining the two control points A and B.

The P3P problem ($n = 3$) requires that we determine the lengths of the three legs of a tetrahedron, given the base dimensions and the face angles of the opposing trihedral angle (see Figure 4). The solution to this problem is implied by the three equations [A^*]:

$$(Rab)^2 = a^2 + b^2 - 2*a*b*[\cos(\theta ab)]$$

$$(Rac)^2 = a^2 + c^2 - 2*a*c* [\cos(\theta ac)] \qquad [A^*]$$

$$(Rbc)^2 = b^2 + c^2 - 2*b*c* [\cos(\theta bc)]$$

It is known that n independent polynomial equations, in n unknowns, can have no more solutions than the product of their respective degrees [2]. Thus, the system A^* can have a maximum of eight solutions. However, because every term in the system A^* is either a constant or of second degree, for every real positive solution there is a geometrically isomorphic negative solution. Thus, there are at most four positive solutions to A^*, and in Figure 5 we show an example demonstrating that the upper bound of four solutions is attainable.

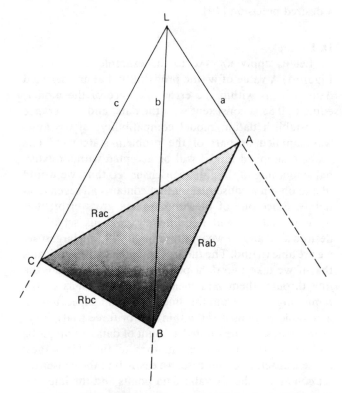

In Appendix A we derive an explicit algebraic solution for the system A^*. This is accomplished by reducing A^* to a biquadratic (quartic) polynomial in one unknown representing the ratio of two legs of the tetrahedron, and then directly solving this equation (we also present a very simple iterative method for obtaining the solutions from the given problem data).

For the case $n = 4$, when all four control points lie in a common plane (not containing the CP, and such that no more than two of the control points lie on any single line), we provide a technique in Appendix B that will always produce a unique solution. Surprisingly, when all four control points do not lie in the same plane, a unique solution cannot always be assured; for example, Figure 6 shows that at least two solutions are possible for the P4P problem with the control points in "general position."

To solve for the location of the CP in the case of four nonplanar control points, we can use the algorithm presented in Appendix A on two distinct subsets of the control points taken three at a time; the solution(s) common to both subsets locate the CP to within the ambiguity inherent in the given information.

The approach used to construct the example shown in Figure 6 can be extended to any number of additional points. It is based on the principle depicted in Figure 3: If the CP and any number of control points lie on the same circle, then the angle between any pair of control points and the CP will be independent of the location on the circle of the CP (and hence the location of the CP cannot be determined). Thus, we are able to construct the example shown in Figure 7, in which five control points in general position imply two solutions to the P5P

Fig. 5. An Example Showing Four Distinct Solutions to a P3P Problem.

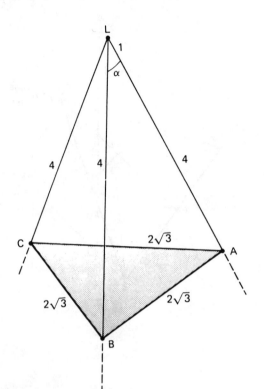

(a)

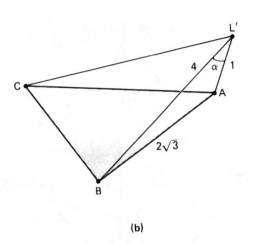

(b)

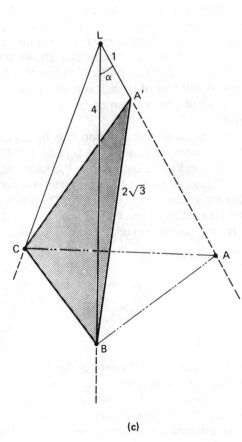

(c)

Consider the tetrahedron in Figure 5(a). The base *ABC* is an equilateral triangle and the "legs" (i.e., *LA*, *LB*, and *LC*) are all equal. Therefore, the three face angles at *L* (i.e., <*ALB*, <*ALC*, and <*BLC*) are all equal. By the law of cosines we have:

$Cos(\alpha) = 5/8.$

This tetrahedron defines one solution to a P3P problem. A second solution is shown in Figure 5(b). It is obtained from the first by rotating *L* about *BC*. It is necessary to verify that the length of *L'A* can be 1, given the rigid triangle *ABC* and the angle alpha. From the law of cosines we have:

$(2*\sqrt{3})^2 = 4^2 + (L'A)^2 - 2*4*(L'A)*(5/8)$

which reduces to:

$(L'A - 1) * (L'A - 4) = 0.$

Therefore, *L'A* can be either 1 or 4. Figure 5(a) illustrates the *L'A* = 4 case and Figure 5(b) illustrates the *L'A* = 1 case.

Notice that repositioning the base triangle so that its vertices move to different locations on the legs is equivalent to repositioning *L*. Figure 5(c) shows the position of the base triangle that corresponds to the second solution.

Since the tetrahedron in Figure 5(a) is threefold rotationally symmetric, two more solutions can be obtained by rotating the triangle about *AB* and *AC*.

259

Fig. 6. An Example of a P4P Problem with Two Solutions.

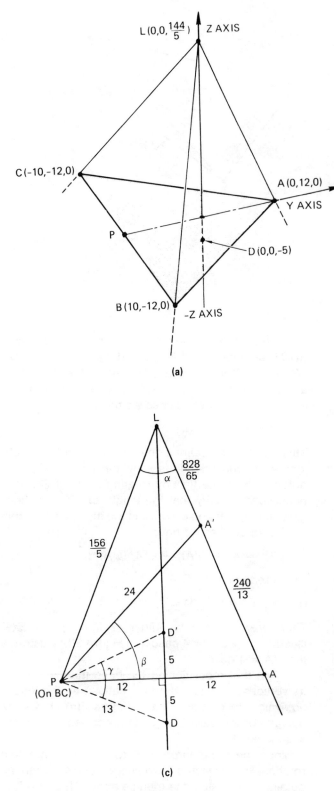

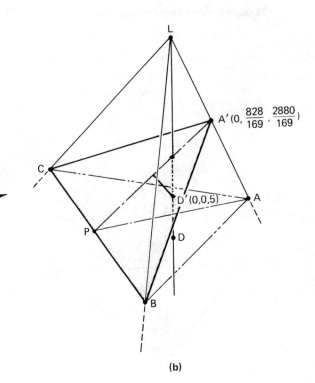

(a)

(b)

(c)

Figure 6(a) specifies a P4P problem and demonstrates one solution. A second solution can be achieved by rotating the base about BC so that A is positioned at a different point on its leg (see Figure 6(b)). To verify that this is a valid solution consider the plane X = O, which is normal to BC and contains the points, L, A, and D. Figure 6(c) shows the important features in this plane. The cosine of alpha is 119/169. A rotation of beta about BC repositions A at A'. The law of cosines can be used to verify the position of A'.

To complete this solution it is necessary to verify that the rotated position of D is on LD. Consider the point D' in Figure 6(c). It is at the same distance from P as D is and by the law of cosines we can show that gamma equals beta. Therefore, D', which is on LD, is the rotated position of D. The points A', B, C, and D' form the second solution to the problem.

problem. While the same technique will work for six or more control points, four or more of these points must now lie in the same plane and are thus no longer in general position.

To prove that six (or more) control points in general position will always produce a unique solution to the P6P problem, we note that for this case we can always solve for the 12 coefficients of the 3 × 4 matrix T that specifies the mapping (in homogeneous coordinates) from 3-space to 2-space; each of the six correspondences provides three new equations and introduces one additional unknown (the homogeneous coordinate scale factor). Thus, for six control points, we have 18 linear equations to solve for the 18 unknowns (actually, it can be shown that, at most, 17 of the unknowns are independent). Given the transformation matrix T, we can construct an additional (synthetic) control point lying in a common plane with three of the given control points and compute its location in the image plane; the technique described in Appendix B can now be used to find a unique solution.

IV. Implementation Details and Experimental Results

A. The RANSAC/LD Algorithm

The RANSAC/LD algorithm accepts as input the following data:

(1) A list L of m 6-tuples—each 6-tuple containing the 3-D spatial coordinates of a control point, its corresponding 2-D image plane coordinates, and an optional number giving the expected error (in pixels) of the given location in the image plane.

(2) The focal length of the imaging system and the image plane coordinates of the principal point.

(3) The probability $(1 - w)$ that a 6-tuple contains a gross mismatch.

(4) A "confidence" number G which is used to set the internal thresholds for acceptance of intermediate results contributing to a solution. A confidence number of one forces very conservative behavior on the algorithm; a confidence number of zero will call almost anything a valid solution.

Fig. 7. An Example of a P5P Problem with Two Solutions.

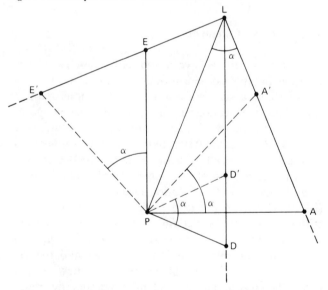

This example is the same as the P4P example described in Figure 6 except that a fifth control point, E, has been added. The initial position for E and its rotated position, E', are shown in Figure 7. The points E and E' were constructed to be the mirror images of A' and A about the line LP; therefore, a rotation of alpha about P repositions E at E'. One solution of the P5P problem is formed by points A, B, C, and D (shown in Figure 6(a)) plus point E. The second solution is formed by points A', B, C, D', and E'. Consequently there are two different positions of L such that all five points lie on their appropriate legs.

The RANSAC/LD algorithm produces as output the following information:

(1) The 3-D spatial coordinates of the lens center (i.e., the Center of Perspective), and an estimate of the corresponding error.

(2) The spatial orientation of the image plane.

The RANSAC/LD algorithm operates as follows:

(1) Three 6-tuples are selected from list L by a quasirandom method that ensures a reasonable spatial distribution for the corresponding control points. This initial selection is called S1.

(2) The CP (called CP1) corresponding to selection S1 is determined using the closed-form solution provided in Appendix A; multiple solutions are treated as if they were obtained from separate selections in the following steps.

(3) The error in the derived location of CP1 is estimated by perturbing the given image plane coordinates of the three selected control points (either by the amount specified in the 6-tuples or by a default value of one pixel), and recomputing the effect this would have on the location of the CP1.

(4) Given the error estimate for the CP1, we use the technique described in [1] to determine error ellipses (dimensions based upon the supplied confidence number) in the image plane for each of the control points specified in list L; if the associated image coordinates reside within the corresponding error ellipse, then the 6-tuple is appended to the consensus set S1/CP1.

(5) If the size of S1/CP1 equals or exceeds some threshold value t (nominally equal to a value between 7 and mw), then the consensus set S1/CP1 is supplied to a least-squares routine (see [1] or [7]) for final determination of the CP location and image plane orientation.[1] Otherwise, the above steps are repeated with a new random selection S2, S3, . . .

(6) If the number of iterations of the above steps exceeds $k = [\log (1 - G)]/[\log(1 - w^3)]$, then the largest consensus set found so far is used to compute the final solution (or we terminate in failure if this largest consensus set contains fewer than six members).

B. Experimental Results

To demonstrate the validity of our theoretical results, we performed three experiments. In the first experiment we found a specific LDP in which the common least-squares pruning heuristic failed, and showed that RANSAC successfully solved this problem. In the second experiment, we applied RANSAC to 50 synthetic problems in order to check the reliability of the approach over a wide range of parameter values. In the third experiment we used standard feature detection techniques to locate landmarks in an aerial image and then used RANSAC to determine the position and orientation of the camera.

C. A Location Determination Problem Example of a Least Squares Pruning Error

The LDP in this experiment was based upon 20 landmarks and their locations in an image. Five of the 20 correspondences were gross errors; that is, their given locations in the image were further than 10 pixels from their actual locations. The image locations for the good

---

[1] An alternative to least squares would be to average the parameters computed from random triples in the consensus set that fall within (say) the center 50 percent of the associated histogram.

correspondences were normally distributed about their actual locations with a standard deviation of one pixel.

The heuristic to prune gross errors was the following:

* Use all of the correspondences to instantiate a model.
* On the basis of that model, delete the correspondence that has the largest deviation from its predicted image location.
* Instantiate a new model without that correspondence.
* If the new model implies a normalized error for the deleted correspondence that is larger than three standard deviations, assume that it is a gross error, leave it out, and continue deleting correspondences. Otherwise, assume that it is a good correspondence and return the model that included it as the solution to the problem.

This heuristic successfully deleted two of the gross errors; but after deleting a third, it decided that the new model did not imply a significantly large error, so it returned a solution based upon 18 correspondences, three of which were gross errors. When RANSAC was applied to this problem, it located the correct solution on the second triple of selected points. The final consensus set contained all of the good correspondences and none of the gross errors.

D. 50 Synthetic Location Determination Problems

In this experiment RANSAC was applied to 50 synthetic LDPs. Each problem was based upon 30 landmark-to-image correspondences. A range of probabilities were used to determine the number of gross errors in the problems; the image location of a gross error was at least 10 pixels from its actual location. The location of a good correspondence was distributed about its actual location with a normal distribution having a standard deviation of one pixel. Two different camera positions were used—one looking straight down on the landmarks and one looking at them from an oblique angle. The RANSAC algorithm described earlier in this section was applied to these problems; however, the simple iterative technique described in Appendix A was used to locate solutions to the P3P problems in place of the closed form method also described in that appendix, and a second least-squares fit was used to extend the final consensus set (as suggested in Sec. II of this paper). Table I summarizes the results for ten typical problems (RANSAC successfully avoided including a gross error in its final consensus set in all of the problems); in five of these problems the probability of a good correspondence was 0.8, and in the other five problems, it was 0.6. The execution time for the current program is approximately 1 sec for each camera position considered.

E. A "Real" Location Determination Problem

Cross correlation was used to locate 25 landmarks in an aerial image taken from approximately 4,000 ft with a 6 in. lens. The image was digitized on a grid of 2,000 × 2,000 pixels, which implies a ground resolution of approximately 2 ft per pixel. Three gross errors were

Table I. Typical Experimental Results Using RANSAC.

No. of Good Correspondences	No. of Correspondences in Final Consensus Set	No. of Triples Considered	No. of Camera Positions Considered
	$w = 0.8$		
22	19	6	10
23	23	1	3
19	19	2	3
25	25	1	2
24	23	3	8
	$w = 0.6$		
21	20	11	21
17	17	1	1
17	16	6	8
18	16	9	21
21	18	9	15

made by the correlation feature detector. When RANSAC was applied to this problem, it located a consensus set of 17 on the first triple selected and then extended that set to include all 22 good correspondences after the initial least-squares fit. The final standard deviations about the camera parameters were as follows:

X: 0.1 ft	Heading: 0.01°
Y: 6.4 ft	Pitch: 0.10°
Z: 2.1 ft	Roll: 0.12°

V. Concluding Comments

In this paper we have introduced a new paradigm, Random Sample Consensus (RANSAC), for fitting a model to experimental data. RANSAC is capable of interpreting/ smoothing data containing a significant percentage of gross errors, and thus is ideally suited for applications in automated image analysis where interpretation is based on the data provided by error-prone feature detectors.

A major portion of this paper describes the application of RANSAC to the Location Determination Problem (LDP): Given an image depicting a set of landmarks with known locations, determine that point in space from which the image was obtained. Most of the results we presented concerning solution techniques and the geometry of the LDP problem are either new or not generally known. The current photogrammetric literature offers no analytic solution other than variants of least squares and the Church method for solving perspective-n-point problems. The Church method, which provides an iterative solution for the P3P problem [3, 11], is presented without any indication that more than one physically real solution is possible; there is certainly no indication that anyone realizes that physically real multiple solutions are possible for more than three control points in general position. (It should be noted that because the multiple solutions can be arbitrarily close together, even when an iterative technique is initialized to a value close to the correct solution there is no assurance that it will converge to the desired value.)

In the section on the LDP problem (and associated appendices) we have completely characterized the P3P problem and provided a closed-form solution. We have shown that multiple physically real solutions can exist for the P4P and P5P problems, but also demonstrated that a unique solution is assured when four of the control points reside on a common plane (solution techniques are provided for each of these cases). The issue of determining the maximum number of solutions possible for the P4P and P5P problems remains open, but we have shown that a unique solution exists for the P6P problem when the control points are in general position.

Appendix A. An Analytic Solution for the Perspective-3-Point Problem

The main body of this paper established that P3P problems can have as many as four solutions. In this appendix a closed form expression for obtaining these solutions is derived. Our approach involves three steps: (1) Find the lengths of the legs of the ("perspective") tetrahedron given the base (defined by the three control points) and the face angles of the opposing trihedral angle (the three angles to the three pairs of control points as viewed from the CP); (2) Locate the CP with respect to the 3-D reference frame in which the control points were originally specified; (3) Compute the orientation of the image plane with respect to the reference frame.

1. A Solution for the Perspective Tetrahedron (see Figure 4)

Given the lengths of the three sides of the base of a tetrahedron (Rab, Rac, Rbc), and given the corresponding face angles of the opposing trihedral angle (θab, θac, θbc), find the lengths of the three remaining sides of the tetrahedron (a, b, c).

A solution to the above problem can be obtained by simultaneously solving the system of equations:

$$(Rab)^2 = a^2 + b^2 - 2*a*b* \cos(\theta ab), \tag{A1}$$
$$(Rac)^2 = a^2 + c^2 - 2*a*c* \cos(\theta ac), \tag{A2}$$
$$(Rbc)^2 = b^2 + c^2 - 2*b*c* \cos(\theta bc). \tag{A3}$$

We now proceed as follows:

Let $b\ \ = x*a$ and $c = y*a$, \hfill (A4)
$$(Rac)^2\ = a^2 + (y^2)*(a^2) - 2*(a^2)*y* \cos(\theta ac), \tag{A5}$$
$$(Rab)^2\ = a^2 + (x^2)*(a^2) - 2*(a^2)*x* \cos(\theta ab), \tag{A6}$$
$$(Rbc)^2\ = (x^2)*(a^2) + (y^2)*(a^2) \\ \qquad - 2*(a^2)*x*y* \cos(\theta bc). \tag{A7}$$

From Eqs. (A5) and (A7)

$$[(Rbc)^2]*[1 + (y^2) - 2*y* \cos(\theta ac)] \\ = [(Rac)^2]*[(x^2) + (y^2) - 2*x*y* \cos(\theta bc)]. \tag{A8}$$

From Eqs. (A6) and (A7)

$$[(Rbc)^2]*[1 + (x^2) - 2*x* \cos(\theta ab)] \\ = [(Rab)^2]*[(x^2) + (y^2) - 2*x*y* \cos(\theta bc)], \tag{A9}$$

Let $\dfrac{(Rbc)^2}{(Rac)^2} = K1$ \qquad and \qquad $\dfrac{(Rbc)^2}{(Rab)^2} = K2.$ \hfill (A10)

From Eqs. (A8) and (A9)

$$0 = (y^2)*[1 - K1] + 2*y*[K1* \cos(\theta ac) \\ - x* \cos(\theta bc)] + [(x^2) - K1]. \tag{A11}$$

From Eqs. (A9) and (A10)

$$0 = (y^2) + 2*y*[-x* \cos(\theta bc)] \\ + [(x^2)*(1 - K2) + 2*x*K2* \cos(\theta ab) - K2]. \tag{A12}$$

Equations (A11) and (A12) have the form:

$$0 = m*(y^2) + p*y + q, \tag{A13}$$
$$0 = m'*(y^2) + p'*y + q'. \tag{A14}$$

Multiplying Eqs. (A13) and (A14) by m' and m, respectively, and subtracting,

$$0 = [p*m' - p'*m]*y + [m'*q - m*q']. \tag{A15}$$

Multiplying Eqs. (A13) and (A14) by q' and q, respectively, substracting, and dividing by y,

$$0 = [m'*q - m*q']*(y^2) + [p'*q - p*q']*y, \\ 0 = [m'*q - m*q']*y + [p'*q - p*q']. \tag{A16}$$

Assuming $m'*q \neq m*q'$,

$$[(x^2) - K1] \neq [(x^2)*(1 - K1)*(1 - K2) + \\ 2*x*K2*(1 - K1)* \cos(\theta ab) - (1 - K1)*K2],$$

then Eqs. (A15) and (A16) are equivalent to Eqs. (A13) and (A14). We now multiply Eqs. (A15) by $(m'*q - m*q')$, and Eq. (A16) by $(p*m' - p'*m)$, and subtract to obtain

$$0 = (m'*q - m*q')^2 \\ \qquad - [p*m' - p'*m]*[p'*q - p*q']. \tag{A17}$$

Expanding Eq. (A17) and grouping terms we obtain a biquadratic (quartic) polynomial in x:

$$0\ \ = G4*(x^4) + G3*(x^3) + G2*(x^2) + G1*(x) \\ \qquad + GO, \tag{A18}$$

where

$$G4\ = (K1*K2 - K1 - K2)^2 \\ \qquad - 4*K1*K2*[\cos(\theta bc)^2], \tag{A19}$$

$$G3 = 4*[K1*K2 - K1 - K2]*K2*(1 - K1)* \\ \qquad \cos(\theta ab) + 4*K1* \cos(\theta bc)*[(K1*K2 \\ \qquad + K2 - K1)* \cos(\theta ac) \\ \qquad + 2*K2* \cos(\theta ab)* \cos(\theta bc)], \tag{A20}$$

$$G2 = [2*K2*(1 - K1) \cos(\theta ab)]^2 \\ \qquad + 2*[K1*K2 + K1 - K2]*[K1*K2 - K1 \\ \qquad - K2] + 4*K1*[(K1 - K2)* (\cos(\theta bc)^2) \\ \qquad + (1 - K2)*K1* (\cos(\theta ac)^2) \\ \qquad - 2*K2*(1 + K1)* \cos(\theta ab)* \cos(\theta ac)* \\ \qquad \cos(\theta bc)], \tag{A21}$$

$$G1\ = 4*(K1*K2 + K1 - K2)*K2*(1 - K1)* \\ \qquad \cos(\theta ab) + 4*K1*[(K1*K2 - K1$$

$$+ K2)^* \cos(\theta ac)^* \cos(\theta bc) \tag{A22}$$
$$+ 2^*K1^*K2^* \cos(\theta ab)^* (\cos(\theta ac)^2)],$$

$$G0 = (K1^*K2 + K1 - K2)^2 - 4^*(K1^2)^*K2^* \tag{A23}$$
$$(\cos(\theta ac)^2).$$

Roots of Eq. (A18) can be found in closed form [5], or by iterative techniques [4]. For each positive real root of Eq. (A18), we determine a single positive real value for each of the sides a and b. From Eq. (A6) we have

$$a = \frac{Rab}{SQRT[(x^2) - 2^*x^* \cos(\theta ab) + 1]}, \tag{A24}$$

and from Eq. (A4) we obtain

$$b = a^*x. \tag{A25}$$

If $m'^*q \neq m^*q'$, then from Eq. (A16) we have

$$y = \frac{p'^*q - p^*q'}{m^*q' - m'^*q}. \tag{A26}$$

If $m'^*q = m^*q'$, then Eq. (A26) is undefined and we obtain two values of y from Eq. (A5):

$$y = \cos(\theta ac)$$
$$\pm SQRT\left[(\cos(\theta ac))^2 + \frac{(Rac)^2 - (a^2)}{(a^2)}\right]. \tag{A27}$$

For each real positive value of y, we obtain a value of c from Eq. (A4):

$$c = y^*a \tag{A28}$$

When values of y are obtained from Eq. (A5) rather than Eq. (A26), the resulting solutions can be invalid; they must be shown to satisfy Eq. (A3) before they are accepted.

It should be noted that because each root of Eq. (A18) can conceivably lead to two distinct solutions, the existence of the biquadratic does not by itself imply a maximum of four solutions to the P3P problem; some additional argument, such as the one given in the main body of this paper, is necessary to establish the upper bound of four solutions.

2. Example

For the perspective tetrahedron shown in Figure 5, we have the following parameters:

$$Rab = Rac = Rbc = 2^*SQRT(3),$$
$$\cos(\theta ab) = \cos(\theta ac) = \cos(\theta bc)$$
$$= \frac{(a^2) + (b^2) - (Rab)^2}{2^*a^*b} = \frac{20}{32}.$$

Substituting these values into Eqs. (A19) through (A23), we obtain the coefficients of the biquadratic defined in Eq. (A18):

$$[-0.5625, 3.515625, -5.90625, 3.515625, -0.5625]$$

The roots of the above equation are

$$[1, 1, 4, 0.25]$$

For each root

Root	a	b	y	c
1	4	4	1	4
1	4	4	0.25	1
4	1	4	4	4
0.25	4	1	1	4

3. An Iterative Solution for the Perspective Tetrahedron (see Figure 8)

A simple way to locate solutions to P3P problems, which is sometimes an adequate substitute for the more involved procedure described in the preceding subsection, is to slide one vertex of the control-point triangle down its leg of the tetrahedron and look for positions of the triangle in which the other two vertices lie on their respective legs. If vertex A is at a distance a from L (L is the center of perspective), the lengths of the sides Rab and Rac restrict the triangle to four possible positions. Given the angle between legs LA and LB, compute the distance of point A from the line LB and then compute points $B1$ and $B2$ on LB that are the proper distance from A to insert a line segment of length Rab. Similarly, we compute at most two locations for C on its leg. Thus, given a position for A we have found at most four positions for a triangle that has one side of length Rab and one of length Rac. The lengths of the third sides (BC) of the four triangles vary nonlinearly as point A is moved down its leg. Solutions to the problem can be obtained by iteratively repositioning A to imply a third side of the required length.

4. Computing the 3-D Location of the Center of Perspective (see Figure 9)

Given the three-dimensional locations of the three control points of a perspective tetrahedron, and the lengths of the three legs, the 3-D location of the center of perspective can be computed as follows:

(1) Construct a plane $P1$ that is normal to AB and passes through the center of perspective, L. This plane can be constructed without knowing the position of L, which is what we are trying to compute. Consider the face of the tetrahedron that contains vertices A, B, and L. Knowing the lengths of sides LA, LB and AB, we can use the law of cosines to find the angle LAB, and then the projection QA of LA on AB. (Note that angle LQA is a right angle, and the point Q is that point on line AB that is closest to L). Construct a plane normal to AB passing through Q; this plane also passes through L.

(2) Similarly construct a plane $P2$ that is normal to AC and passes through L.

(3) Construct the plane $P3$ defined by the three points A, B, and C.

(4) Intersect planes $P1$, $P2$, and $P3$. By construction, the point of intersection R is the point on $P3$ that is closest to L.

(5) Compute the length of the line AR and use that in conjunction with the length of LA to compute the length of the line RL, which is the distance of L from the plane $P3$.

(6) Compute the cross product of vectors AB and AC to form a vector perpendicular to $P3$. Then scale that vector by the length of RL and add it to R to get the 3-D location of the center of perspective L.

Fig. 8. Geometry for an Iterative Solution to the P3P Problem.

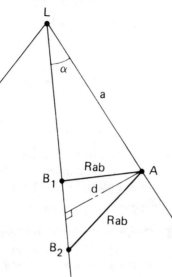

(a)

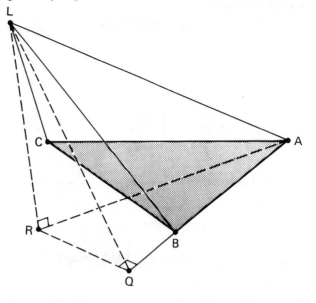

(1) Compute the 3-*D* reference frame coordinates of the center of perspective (as described above).

(2) Compute the 3-*D* coordinates of the image locations of the three control points: since we know the 3-*D* coordinates of the CP and the control points, we can compute the 3-*D* coordinates of the three rays between the CP and the control points. Knowing the focal length of the imaging system, we can compute, and subtract from each ray, the distance from the CP to the image plane along the ray.

(3) Compute the equation of the plane containing the image using the three points found in step (2). The normal to this plane, passing through the CP, gives us the origin of the image plane coordinate system (i.e., the 3-*D* location of the principal point), and the *Z* axis of this system.

(4) The orientation of the image plane about the *Z* axis can be obtained by computing the 3-*D* coordinates of a vector from the principal point to any one of the points found in step (2).

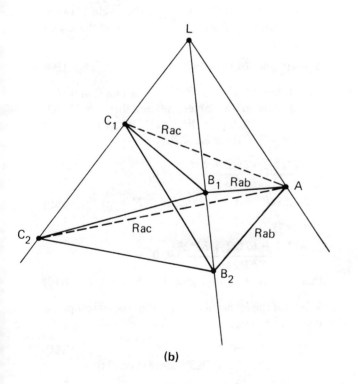

(b)

Appendix B. An Analytic Solution for the Perspective-4-Point Problem (with all control points lying in a common plane)

In this appendix an analytic technique is presented for obtaining a unique solution to the P4P problem when the four given control points all lie in a common plane.

1. Problem Statement (see Figure 10)

GIVEN: A correspondence between four points lying in a plane in 3-*D* space (called the object plane), and four points lying in a distinct plane (called the image plane); and given the distance between the center of perspective and the image plane (i.e., the focal length of the imaging system); and also given the principal point in the image plane (i.e., the location, in image plane coordinates, of the point at which the optical axis of the lense pierces the image plane).

FIND: the 3-*D* location of the center of perspective relative to the coordinate system of the object plane.

If the focal length of the camera and the principal point in the image plane are known, it is possible to compute the orientation of the image plane with respect to the world coordinate system; that is, the location of the origin and the orientation of the image plane coordinate system with respect to the 3-*D* reference frame. This can be done as follows:

Fig. 10. Geometry of the P4P Problem (With all Control Points Lying in a Common Plane).

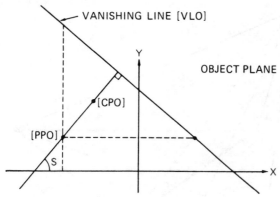

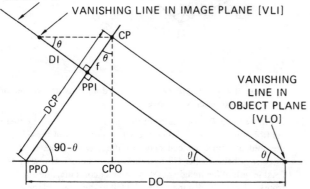

2. Notation

* Let the four given image points be labeled $\{Pi\}$, and the four corresponding object points $\{Qi\}$.
* We will assume that the 2-D image plane coordinate system has its origin at the principal point (PPI).
* We will assume that the object plane has the equation $Z = 0$ in the reference coordinate system. Standard techniques are available to transform from this coordinate system into a ground reference frame (e.g., see [6] or [9]).
* Homogeneous coordinates will be assumed [12].
* Primed symbols represent transposed structures.

3. Solution Procedure

(a) Compute the 3×3 collineation matrix T which maps points from object plane to image plane (a procedure for computing T is given later):

$[Pi] = [T]*[Qi],$

where

$[Pi] = [ki*xi, ki*yi, ki]',$
$[Qi] = [Xi, Yi, 1]'.$

(B1)

(b) The ideal line in the object plane, with coordinates $[0, 0, 1]'$ is mapped into the vanishing line in the image plane $[VLI]$ by the transformation:

$[VLI] = [\text{inv}[T]]'*[0, 0, 1]'.$ (B2)

(c) Determine the distance DI from the origin of the image plane (PPI) to the vanishing line $[VLI] =$

$[a1, a2, a3]'$:

$$DI = \left| \frac{a3}{sqrt[(a1)^2 + (a2)^2]} \right|$$ (B3)

(d) Solve for the dihedral (tilt) angle θ between the image and object planes:

$\theta = \arctan(f/DI),$ (B4)

where $f = $ focal length.

(e) The ideal line in the image plane with coordinates $[0, 0, 1]'$ is mapped into the vanishing line in the object plane $[VLO]$ by the transform

$[VLO] = [T]'*[0, 0, 1]'.$ (B5)

(f) Compute the location of point $[PPO]$ in the object plane ($[PPO]$ is the point at which the optical axis of the lense pierces the object plane):

$[PPO] = [\text{inv}[T]]'*[0, 0, 1]'$ (B6)

(g) Compute the distance DO from $[PPO] = [c1, c2, c3]'$ to the vanishing line $[VLO] = [b1, b2, b3]'$ in the object plane:

$$DO = \left| \frac{b1*c1 + b2*c2 + b3*c3}{c3*sqrt[(b1)^2 + (b2)^2]} \right| .$$ (B7)

(h) Solve for the "pan" angle \$ as the angle between the normal to $[VLO] = [b1, b2, b3]'$ and the X axis in the object plane:

$\$ = \arctan(-b2/b1).$ (B8)

(i) Determine $XSGN$ and $YSGN$: If a line (parallel to the X axis in the object plane) through $[PPO]$ intersects $[VLO]$ to the right of $[PPO]$, then $XSGN = 1$. Otherwise $XSGN = -1$. Thus,

if $\dfrac{b1*c1 + b2*c2 + b3*c3}{b1*c3} < 0,$

then $XSGN = 1$, otherwise $XSGN = -1$. (B9)

Similarly,

if $\dfrac{b1*c1 + b2*c2 + b3*c3}{b2*c3} < 0$

then $YSGN = 1$, otherwise $YSGN = -1$. (B10)

(j) Solve for the location of the CP in the object plane coordinate system:

$DCP = DO* \sin(\theta)$ (B11)
$XCP = XSGN*abs[DCP* \sin(\theta)* \cos(\$)]$
$\qquad + c1/c3$ (B12)
$YCP = YSGN*abs[DCP* \sin(\theta)* \sin(\$)]$
$\qquad + c2/c3$ (B13)
$ZCP = DCP* \cos(\theta)$ (B14)

Note: If $[VLI]$, as determined in (b), has the coordinates $[0, 0, k]$, then the image and object planes are parallel ($\theta = 0$). Rather than continuing with the above procedure, we now solve for the desired information using similar triangles and Euclidean geometry.

4. Computing the Collineation Matrix T

Let

$$[Q] = \begin{Vmatrix} X1 & Y1 & 1 \\ X2 & Y2 & 1 \\ X3 & Y3 & 1 \end{Vmatrix} = [[Q1]', [Q2]', [Q3]'],$$

$$[P] = \begin{Vmatrix} x1 & y1 & 1 \\ x2 & y2 & 1 \\ x3 & y3 & 1 \end{Vmatrix} = [[P1]', [P2]', [P3]'],$$

$$[Q4] = [X4, Y4, 1]',$$
$$[P4] = [x4, y4, 1]',$$
$$[V] = [inv[P]]'*[P4] = [v1, v2, v3]',$$
$$[R] = [inv[Q]]'*[Q4] = [r1, r2, r3]',$$
$$w1 = \frac{v1}{r1} * \frac{r3}{v3},$$
$$w2 = \frac{v2}{r2} * \frac{r3}{v3},$$
$$[w] = \begin{Vmatrix} w1 & 0 & 0 \\ 0 & w2 & 0 \\ 0 & 0 & 1 \end{Vmatrix}.$$

Then,

$$[T]' = [inv[Q]]*[W]*[P]$$

such that

$$[Pi] = ki*[xi, yi, 1] = [T]*[Qi].$$

5. Example

Given:

$f = 0.3048$ m (12 in.)

$P1 = (-0.071263, \quad 0.029665)$	$Q1 = (\ -30, \quad 80)$
$P2 = (-0.053033, -0.006379)$	$Q2 = (-100, \ -20)$
$P3 = (-0.014063, \quad 0.061579)$	$Q3 = (\ 140, \quad 50)$
$P4 = (\ 0.080120, -0.030305)$	$Q4 = (\ -40, -240)$

(a)
$$[T]' = \begin{Vmatrix} 0.000212 & 0.000236 & 0.000925 \\ -0.000368 & 0.000137 & 0.000534 \\ -0.025404 & 0.021650 & 0.843879 \end{Vmatrix}$$

(b)
$$[inv[T]]' = \begin{Vmatrix} 1117.14 & -2038.86 & 0.0 \\ 3371.56 & 2302.22 & -5.14991 \\ -51.0636 & -120.442 & 1.31713 \end{Vmatrix}$$

(c) $[VLI] = [0, -5.14991, 1.31713]'$

(d) $DI = 0.255758$

(e) $\theta = 0.872665$ rad (50°)

(f) $[VLO] = [0.000925, 0.000534, 0.843880]'$

(g) $[PPO] = [-51.0636, -120.442, 1.31713]'$

(h) $DO = 711.196$

(i) $\$ = -0.523599$ rad (−30°)

$XSGN = -1$
$YSGN = -1$

(j)
$DCP = 544.8081$
$XCP = -400.202$
$YCP = -300.117$
$ZCP = \ 350.196$

Received 4/80; revised 1/81; accepted 1/81

References
1. Bolles, R.C., Quam, L.H., Fischler, M.A., and Wolf, H.C. The SRI road expert: Image to database correspondence. In Proc. Image Understanding Workshop, Pittsburgh, Pennsylvania, Nov., 1978.
2. Chrystal, G. *Textbook of Algebra* (Vol 1). Chelsea, New York, New York 1964, p. 415.
3. Church, E. Revised geometry of the aerial photograph. *Bull. Aerial Photogrammetry.* 15, 1945, Syracuse University.
4. Conte, S.D. *Elementary Numerical Analysis.* McGraw Hill, New York, 1965.
5. Dehn, E. *Algebraic Equations.* Dover, New York, 1960.
6. Duda, R.O., and Hart, P.E. *Pattern Classification and Scene Analysis.* Wiley-Interscience, New York, 1973.
7. Gennery, D.B. Least-squares stereo-camera calibration. Stanford Artificial Intelligence Project Internal Memo, Stanford, CA 1975.
8. Keller, M. and Tewinkel, G.C. Space resection in photogrammetry. ESSA Tech. Rept C&GS 32, 1966, U.S. Coast and Geodetic Survey.
9. Rogers, D.P. and Adams, J.A. *Mathematical Elements for Computer Graphics.* McGraw Hill, New York, 1976.
10. Sorensen, H.W. Least-squares estimation: from Gauss to Kalman. *IEEE Spectrum* (July 1970), 63–68.
11. Wolf, P.R. *Elements of Photogrammetry.* McGraw Hill, New York, 1974.
12. Wylie, C.R. Jr. *Introduction to Projective Geometry.* McGraw-Hill, New York, 1970.

Chapter 4: Constraint Exploitation and Shape Recovery

Mapping from a scene to an image is a many-to-one mapping; hence, in principle, information about a scene cannot be recovered unambiguously from its image. Information recovery is possible only if some assumptions are made about the objects in the scene and the relations among these objects. These assumptions are based on several kinds of knowledge. To recover information, vision systems exploit

- Knowledge about the image formation process;
- Domain-independent knowledge about the world; and
- Knowledge about the specific application domain.

Knowledge about the image formation process, such as the projection mechanism, helps in relating artifacts in the image to physical phenomena in the scene. Domain-independent knowledge helps in early vision because it involves general processes from which information recovery can begin. This type of knowledge comes in many different forms. One common example of domain-independent knowledge is surface coherence; many other forms of domain-independent knowledge are used in shape-from-shading, shape-from-stereo, and other similar intermediate-level operations. Knowledge about the specific application domain is usually the most explicit. It may be in the form of geometric models or feature models or in some other similar form.

Major issues in recovery of information in images include the representation and utilization of different types of knowledge in a vision system. The amount and quality of knowledge available, the knowledge representation methods, and the methodologies of applying knowledge in the system strongly influence the performance of a vision system. In fact, the extensibility, flexibility, and generality of a vision system are dependent on the blending of knowledge sources in the system. A system that makes explicit the representation and utilization of knowledge generally is easier to modify and maintain than a system that uses knowledge implicitly. Computer vision operations are usually categorized as low level, intermediate level, and high level. Low-level operations are mostly image related. Knowledge is used at this level implicitly and in minimal amounts. Good examples of low-level knowledge application are the use of similar intensity values for grouping points or the use of thresholds for obtaining binary images. Intermediate-level operations use image formation knowledge and knowledge about the environment, both usually in the form of constraints. In high-level operations, knowledge about the objects is represented explicitly.

A constraint represents a relationship between two or more entities in the "world" that is always satisfied. Constraints are the result of observations or assumptions. A major problem in computer vision is identifying suitable constraints that will help in recovering information without seriously constraining the applicability of the system. Many difficult problems become solvable once suitable constraints are discovered and techniques are developed to exploit them. On the other hand, the use of constraints that are valid only in a limited "world" will restrict the applicability of the system.

In this chapter, several variations of constraint-related problems will be discussed. The emphasis will be on applying constraints, not discovering them. The labeling problem will be examined first. Component labeling plays an important role in intermediate-level processes, after some initial segmentation. Methods for assigning labels to objects using directly available relational information and knowledge about valid relations expressed as constraints will be considered. Techniques for recovering three-dimensional shape from two-dimensional images — either by exploiting image cues such as shading, texture, and blur or by matching multiple images of the same scene — are also described in this chapter.

The labeling problem

The labeling problem involves a given set of objects and a set of labels that are to be assigned to the objects. The relationships between the objects in the image are known; based on knowledge about the domain, the conditions under which a certain set of labels may or may not be applied to a set of objects is also known. The problem, then, is to assign proper labels to the objects. In a general labeling problem, the following sets are given

- A set $O = O_1, O_2,..., O_n$ of objects;
- A set $L = L_1, L_2,..., L_m$ of labels;
- A set of relations R over the objects; and
- A set of constraints C specifying valid labels for related objects.

A solution to a labeling problem is a set (O_k, L_k), where $O_k \in O$ and $L_k \in L$, which gives a label for each object. In most applications, an object should be assigned a unique label.

Although an exhaustive search for all possible object/label assignments satisfying all of the constraints would certainly result in a correct labeling of the objects, the combinatorial explosion in the search space makes this impractical. Several approaches that use computationally efficient heuristic techniques have been suggested for solving this problem.

A sequential approach. Initially, every label may be assigned to each object. The objective is to discard incorrect labels, using the relations and constraints given for the problem. Each object is considered, and any labels that are inconsistent with the labels of "related" objects are eliminated. It may be necessary to repeatedly examine the list of objects until either (1) each object has been assigned a unique label that is consistent with other objects or (2) no further elimination of labels is possible. The following example illustrates this approach.

An image has been segmented into several regions using a domain-independent method. (See Figure 4.1.[110]) The identification of these regions is now required. If it is given that the image represents an office scene, knowledge about the nature of objects in this domain may be used. To introduce this knowledge, a set of possible labels for the regions and a set of constraints on the regions will be required. The labels for objects in this domain are

$$L = \{Door, Wall, Floor, Picture, Baseboard, Doorknob\}$$

Based on observation, the following constraints should be satisfied by the objects in an image:

- Within: (Picture, Wall), (Doorknob, Door);
- Above: (Wall, Baseboard), (Baseboard, Floor), (Door, Floor);
- Beside: (Wall, Door), (Baseboard, Door); and
- Small: (Doorknob), (Picture).

The objects to be labeled are regions in the image, which have been numbered as

$$O = \{0_1, 0_2, 0_3, 0_4, 0_5, 0_6\}$$

Spatial relationships between regions are determined from the segmented image. These relationships are as follows:

- Within: $(0_2, 0_1)$, $(0_4, 0_3)$;
- Above: $(0_1, 0_5)$, $(0_5, 0_6)$, $(0_3, 0_6)$;
- Beside: $(0_1, 0_3)$, $(0_5, 0_3)$; and
- Small: (0_4), (0_2).

Initially, each region is assigned all labels. The relations obtained from the image and the known constraints are then applied sequentially to eliminate incorrect labels. The process is iterated, if necessary. In this example, that each region is eventually assigned a unique label is easily verified.

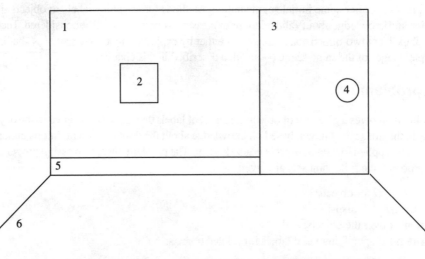

Figure 4.1: A scene with six regions (from Barrow and Tennenbaum) [110]

270

The preceding example illustrates the application of known properties and relationships in solving a labeling problem. Knowledge in the form of constraints can be used to resolve local ambiguities or uncertainties and can lead to a solution of the global problem. Although the filtering at each step uses local relationships between at most two objects, the effect is propagated to other objects.

Several problems exist with the approach just illustrated. The first is that the outcome of such a sequential process is dependent on the starting point. Second, the convergence of the approach is not well understood. A third problem is posed because determination of a unique labeling for a given set of constraints and relationships generally cannot be guaranteed. Since the process is iterative, a stopping point should be well defined. If a unique labeling can be achieved, then the stopping criterion is well defined. If not, a general rule may be to stop after going through a predetermined number of iterations over all objects; however, several objects may then not be assigned unique labels. An object may be assigned multiple labels if (1) not enough iterations were allowed, (2) the labeling problem is unsolvable based on the information, or (3) the given relations are "impossible" in the "world" that obeys the given constraints.

A parallel approach. In many cases, the labeling problem can be represented as a graph, with each node representing an object or entity that should be assigned a label. The arcs are labeled to represent different relationships between objects. Since the constraints specify relationships between only a few objects, the labeling process may be applied in parallel.

In the parallel approach, a processor is assumed at each node. Each processor "knows" the label of its node and of all nodes that are connected to it. It also knows the set of constraints C and all relationships involving its node. In the first iteration, the possible label set P_i of node i is L for all i. In other words, all nodes initially are assigned all possible labels. The labeling process will iteratively eliminate invalid labels from P_i. At any stage, labels are discarded considering only the node, its relationships, and the constraints; hence, each processor has sufficient information to refine its label set P_i. Thus, all processors can work synchronously. In each cycle, a processor uses the current information to refine its P_i by discarding invalid labels. However, each iteration propagates the effect through its neighbor or related nodes to other nodes that are not directly related; therefore, the circle of influence of a node increases with each iteration.

In the just-described formulation of the consistent-labeling problem, the assumption was that the process started with no knowledge about the objects. Under this assumption, every label in L was initially assigned to each object. In most applications, some knowledge about the objects is already available at the start of the labeling process. Segmentation, or some other process that takes place before labeling, often gives information that can be used to refine the initial set P_i for a node. A labeling process, known as "relaxation labeling," may be used to further refine these sets.

Relaxation processes

Although relaxation labeling[111] is another solution to the labeling problem, it differs from the preceding formulation in that it begins with an initial set of confidence values assigned to labels. Based on some unary relations, a label set can be assigned to an object. A confidence value is assigned to each possible label. As in subjective probability, this confidence value indicates a belief that the label is correct based on evidence in the image. Thus, for each element $L_k \in L$, a nonnegative probability p_{ik} represents the confidence that the label L_k is the correct label for object 0_i

The task of the relaxation-labeling process[111] is now to use the constraints to refine the confidence value for each label. When the confidence in one label for a node is significantly stronger than the confidence in the other labels, that label can be assigned to the node. The confidence value will be influenced by the confidence values in the labels of the connected nodes. The process may terminate when either each node has been assigned a unique label or the confidence values achieve a steady state. Relaxation labeling can be considered to be a form of constraint propagation in which nodes are processed in parallel.

In relaxation labeling, the constraints are specified in terms of compatibility functions. Suppose that objects O_i and O_j are related by R_{ij} and that, under this relationship, labels L_k for object O_i and L_l for object O_j are highly likely to occur. The knowledge about the likelihood of these labels can be expressed in terms of a function that will increase the confidence in these labels for the objects under consideration. In such a situation, the presence of L_k at O_i encourages the assignment of L_l to O_j. In addition, the incompatibility of certain labels can be used to discourage labels by decreasing their confidence values.

Discrete relaxation labeling. In discrete relaxation labeling, label confidence values are allowed only two values: zero and one. The strategy used in constraint propagation is as follows:

(1)   Keep the label $\lambda = L_k$ at node O_i only if, for every neighbor O_j, a label $\lambda' \in L$ exists that is compatible with λ.

(2)   Repeat until no label is discarded.

Because of the parallel nature of this labeling, the number of iterations required for termination is determined by the maximum distance the information should travel to disambiguate the worst node. The local perspective of relaxation labeling may not be able to disambiguate some global inconsistencies. Thus, even after a large number of iterations, the process may not terminate. The convergence properties of a relaxation-labeling process generally cannot be predicted from the formulation of the problem.

Probabilistic relaxation labeling. As just discussed, confidence values can be assigned to the possible labels for an object. In probabilistic relaxation labeling, the probabilities of the labels are updated during each iteration instead of the labels being discarded. Compatibility functions replace constraint relations for updating the probabilities of labels. Both positive and negative influences can be propagated using compatibility functions. Determining the best label at a node involves considering both competing and cooperating forces. The confidence in a label is determined based on the sum of these competing and cooperating forces.

Like constraints, compatibility functions may be obtained by analyzing a problem. One way to formulate the relaxation-labeling problem is to use probability theory. The labels assigned to an object should satisfy probabilistic axioms. Thus, the probability of the label L_k for the object O_i must satisfy the following:

$$0 \leq p_i(L_k) \leq 1$$

$$and \quad \sum_{k=1}^{m} p_i(L_k) = 1 \tag{4.1}$$

To find suitable compatibility functions, all possible situations may be analyzed to find conditional probabilities $p_{ij}(L_k / L_l)$ such that object O_i has label L_k, given that its neighboring object O_j has label L_l. The probability of a label at a node can then be updated using

$$p_i(L_k) = \sum_j c_{ij} \sum_{l=1}^{m} p_{ij}(L_k \mid L_l) \, p_j(L_l)$$

$$where \quad \sum_j c_{ij} = 1 \tag{4.2}$$

and where c_{ij} represents the compatibility of node j with node i. Once appropriate values of c_{ij} have been selected, such as assigning larger values of C_{ij} to objects which are closer to 0_i and smaller values to those which are farther, and the initial probabilities for these labels have been obtained, this probability equation can be used to update the probabilities of the labels. When the probabilities for labels converge, the process stops.

The two principal limitations to the method just discussed are now given. First, the probabilities converge to a solution that depends on the compatibility functions and the conditional probabilities obtained from an analysis of the application domain; initial labels assigned using image analysis are ignored. Second, incompatible assignment of labels is not properly propagated in updated probabilities.[111] An improved updating scheme uses compatibility functions that have a range of [-1,1]. The rule for updating the probability during the iteration step $t+1$ is then given by

$$P_i^{t+1}(L_k) = \frac{P_i^t(L_k) \cdot (1 + q_i^t(L_k))}{\sum_{l=1}^{m} P_i^t(L_l) \cdot (1 + q_i^t(L_l))}$$

$$where$$

$$q_i^t(L_k) = \sum_j c_{ij} \sum_{L_l \in L} r_{ij}(L_k, L_l) \, P_j^t(L_l) \,, \tag{4.3}$$

and where c_{ij} values are the coefficients analogous to those for the linear model and $r_{ij}(L_k, L_l)$ is the correlation between the following events: that O_i has label L_k and that O_j has label L_l. Thus, $P_i(t+1)$ is a function of both the previous estimate and the contributions from the probability distributions on the neighboring label sets. In many cases, the compatibility and the weights may be combined into one term. The updating equation just given combines the effects of all of the neighbors of an object. This relaxation method has been applied to many applications.

Although the process in the method just described is local, the sphere of influence for each node grows with the iteration number. Thus, this process allows even weak evidence to make an appropriate contribution to the final result by propagating throughout an image. The local nature is very attractive for real-time implementation using special architecture. A major problem in the implementation of relaxation labeling has been convergence characteristics. In most cases, no definite termination point exists. Heuristics stop either after there are no changes in labels or after a certain number of iterations are commonly used.

Understanding block-world scenes

A system that analyzes images of block-world scenes can demonstrate the efficacy of constraint propagation in achieving global consistency using only local information. If line segments that have been detected in a scene are given, constraint propagation can be used to determine the number and nature of the objects in the scene. By considering simple block-world scenes, the following discussion examines a few key ideas related to discovering and using constraints .

Suppose that a scene contains only polyhedral objects and, furthermore, that the scene contains only objects that have trihedral junctions. (A trihedral junction is a vertex of an object where a maximum of three planes meet.) To simplify even further, we will consider only scenes without shadows. The task of the system is to understand a block-world image; that is, to determine the number of three-dimensional objects (blocks) and the relationships between the objects in the scene. The scene-understanding problem can be posed as a labeling problem. By assigning proper labels to the lines in an image, objects can be separated from each other and relationships between objects can be determined.

For a known polyhedral object, the edges can be classified into a small number of classes. Labels can be assigned to edges depending on the nature of the edge. For trihedral objects, the labels will be one of the following:

- Boundary lines are assigned a directional label > or <. The direction depends on the direction in which the boundary should be traveled in order to keep the object always on the right.
- Convex edges are assigned a + label. These edges indicate where the surface normal is toward the viewer.
- Concave edges are assigned a - label. These edges indicate where the surface normal is away from the viewer.

Figure 4.2 shows an object to which labels have been correctly assigned. For a known object, labels can be easily assigned. For an unknown object, the nature of the object can be roughly determined by assigning labels, which may be helpful in analyzing the scene. The problem of assigning labels to lines should be approached by first analyzing the physical world to determine what types of junctions are formed by different types of lines. The first step, then, is to determine constraints of the physical world that will restrict the set of all possible junctions formed by different types of edges to only physically valid junctions. Analyzing the physical world to obtain constraints is a key idea.

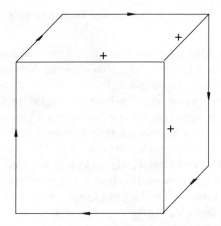

Figure 4.2: Assignment of labels to edges

For the simple case of trihedral objects, the junctions formed by the vertices must be one of the following types: ARROW, L, FORK, or T. In a more general situation, where the assumptions of trihedral objects and shadowless images are relaxed, a similar analysis will result in more applicable line labels and many more types of junctions.

Since only four labels (>, <, +, and -) can be considered for each line, only a finite number of possible ways exist to label a junction. A simple analysis shows that a FORK, an ARROW, and a T can each be labeled in 4^3 different ways and that an L can be labeled in 4^2 different ways. Thus, the total number of possible junction combinations is 208. An analysis of the physical world under the given restrictions shows that not all of these junctions actually occur. Considering all configurations of trihedral junctions shows that only 18 of the 208 possible junction combinations are really possible. Clearly, many labels for a junction can be eliminated immediately since they are impossible in the real world. The set of possible junction types in the shadowless trihedral-blocks world is given in Figure 4.3. This set represents the constraints imposed by the domain and can be used to assign proper labels to lines in a scene. An examination of the set of possible junctions provides more clues that may be helpful in scene analysis, as follows:

- The > and < labels appear only on borders.
- Only one ARROW junction exists that has > labels on its barbs; the shaft of this arrow has a + label.
- Only one FORK junction with any + label exists; all of its lines have + labels.

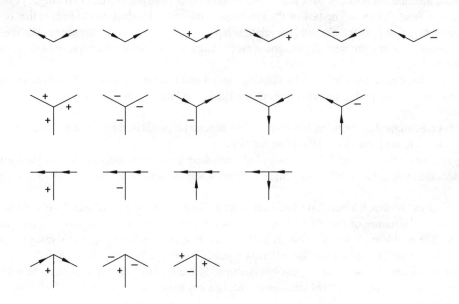

Figure 4.3: The set of possible junctions

In scene analysis, all lines must be found by using a segmentation scheme. Segmentation should give information about all of the lines in a scene and the junctions formed by these lines. The labeling process can then start by the assignment of > and < labels to all boundary lines. After the boundary lines have been labeled, arrows with > barbs are found, and + is assigned to their shafts. Then, any FORK with a + label on any of its lines can have a + assigned to all of its lines. If all of the lines in the scene are not labeled after the completion of these steps, then each junction that has at least one unlabeled line is examined. Considering the type of junction and the labels of the lines that have been assigned, all possible labels are assigned to the remaining unlabeled lines. Since a line is part of two junctions, its set of labels will be influenced from two sides. Since only one correct label exists for any line, the label eventually assigned is the one that is assigned by both junctions. This step can be iterated. In each iteration, some labels can be removed from the set of labels assigned to a line. In the case of the physically realizable trihedral-blocks world, this propagation process will eventually terminate, resulting in a labeling for a scene.

If, for some line, no unique label can be assigned, then the scene violates the assumptions about the world. Such a scene contains "impossible" objects. An impossible object, in this context, is one that cannot be realized using trihedral blocks. This labeling method demonstrates the following two important concepts:

- Local constraints can be used to derive a global interpretation of an image. The constraints are applied locally at each junction, but the effects of the constraints propagate through the image to yield a global interpretation of the scene.
- Constraints should be determined through an analysis of the physical world. Constraints may be available already in some cases; however, in many applications, suitable constraints must be discovered by an analysis of the problem domain.

Shape recovery

In Chapter 1, we discuss briefly the relationships among properties of objects (e.g., orientation and reflectance) in the three-dimensional scene and their two-dimensional image intensities. In this section, we discuss techniques for exploiting image cues — such as shading, texture, and blurring — to recover three-dimensional shape from two-dimensional images. We also describe briefly binocular- and photometric-stereo methods for recovering three-dimensional shape from multiple two-dimensional images. Shape recovery from motion is described in Chapter 6.

Shape from shading. Chapter 1 explains that the image intensity at a point is a function of the surface orientation. This dependence is captured in reflectance maps. For fixed illumination and imaging conditions and for a surface with known reflectance properties, changes in surface orientation translate into corresponding changes in image intensity. The inverse problem — recovering surface shape from changes in image intensity — is known as the "shape-from-shading problem." The following discussion summarizes the procedure for solving this problem using the surface smoothness constraint. Details can be found in Horn[3] and Ikeuchi and Horn.[112]

The relationship between image irradiance $E(x,y)$ and the orientation (p,q) of the corresponding point on the surface is given by

$$E(x,y) = R(p,q) \tag{4.4}$$

where $R(p,q)$ is the reflectance map of the surface. The goal is to recover surface shape by calculating the orientation (p,q) on the surface for each point (x,y) in the image. Note that although we have only one equation, two degrees of freedom for orientation exist. Thus, this problem cannot be solved unless additional constraints are imposed. A commonly imposed constraint is that of surface smoothness. We assume that objects are made up of piecewise smooth surfaces that depart from smoothness constraint only along edges.

Ikeuchi and Horn[112] described an iterative method to solve the shape-from-shading problem using occluding contours to supply boundary conditions. Since points along the occluding contours correspond to points at infinity in gradient space, they proposed the use of a stereographic projection coordinate system (f,g) instead of a gnomonic projection coordinate system (p,q), as shown in Figure 4.4.[3] In the stereographic projection system, points on the occluding contour correspond to points on a circle of radius 2 units in the (f,g) plane. Let $R(p,q)$, expressed in this new coordinate system, be denoted by $R_s(f,g)$. The smoothness constraint can be specified as minimizing the integral of the sum of the squares of the partial derivatives of surface orientation given by

$$e_s = \iint ((f_x^2 + f_y^2) + (g_x^2 + g_y^2))dxdy \tag{4.5}$$

where the subscripts denote the variables of partial derivatives. Strictly speaking, we must minimize this integral subject to the constraint specified in the equation $E(x,y) = R(p,q)$; however, to account for noise that causes departure from this equation, the problem is posed as that of minimizing total error e, given by

$$e = e_s + \lambda e_i \tag{4.6}$$

where λ is a parameter that weighs the error in smoothness constraint relative to the error in image irradiance equation, which is given by

$$e_i = \iint (E(x,y) - R_s(f,g))^2 dxdy \tag{4.7}$$

Minimizing total error is a problem in the calculus of variations. An iterative solution for updating the value of (f,g) during the $n+1$ iteration is given by Ikeuchi and Horn, as follows:[112]

$$f_{ij}^{n+1} = f_{ij}^{*n} + \lambda [E_{ij} - R_s(f_{ij}^{*n}, g_{ij}^{*n})]\frac{\partial R_s}{\partial f} \ ,$$

$$g_{ij}^{n+1} = g_{ij}^{*n} + \lambda [E_{ij} - R_s(f_{ij}^{*n}, g_{ij}^{*n})]\frac{\partial R_s}{\partial g} \ , \tag{4.8}$$

where * denotes the average values computed in a 2 x 2 neighborhood and the subscript *ij* denotes discrete coordinates in the image plane. Although the computations for a given iteration are local, global consistency is achieved by the propagation of constraints over many iterations.

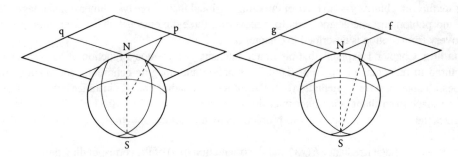

Figure 4.4: Illustration of *gnomonic* (left) and *stereographic* (right) projection (from B.K.P. Horn, *Robot Vision*, © 1986 McGraw-Hill, Inc., reprinted with permission.)[3]

In the shape-from-shading problem, we are attempting to recover the surface shape from a single image. When multiple images acquired from different illumination orientations are available, shape recovery is simplified. This technique, known as "photometric stereo," is described in the next section.

Shape from photometric stereo. In photometric stereo,[113] two or more images of the scene are captured under different orientations of illuminating sources. Both the camera and the objects in the scene are assumed to remain in the same position, which implies that a point in the scene will have the same image coordinates in all the images. The correspondence problem of finding matching points in two images is thus avoided. Under these assumptions, we have as many equations of the form given by $E(x,y) = R(p,q)$ as there are images. If these equations are linear and independent, just two images are adequate to solve for the surface orientation parameters p and q. For other cases, we may need more than two images to obtain a unique solution. For example, in the case of a Lambertian surface illuminated by two different orientations of point sources, at most two surface orientations exist that produce a particular pair of image intensity values. These surface orientations are obtained by finding the intersections of corresponding contours in the gradient space, as shown in Figure 4.5.[3] To find a unique solution, a third image is required. In principle, we are not required to impose additional constraints — such as surface smoothness — to recover shape from photometric stereo. However, applying such constraints helps in obtaining better results when the data are corrupted by noise. Having more than two images also helps to recover albedo, which characterizes the changes in reflectance properties of surfaces made up of the material. In other words, the actual reflectance map for a surface is the product of its albedo times the normalized reflectance map for the material.

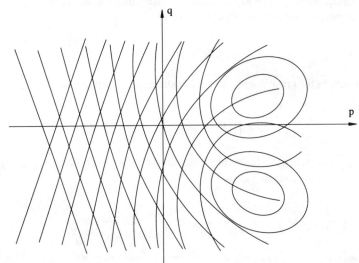

Figure 4.5: Illustration of shape recovery using photometric stereo method (from B.K.P. Horn, *Robot Vision*. Copyright © 1986 McGraw-Hill, Inc., reprinted with permission.)[3]

276

Shape from stereo. In the previous section, a method was described for recovering shape from multiple images acquired from different lighting conditions. Multiple images are much more easily captured by changing the camera position. In the literature, results of extensive research to recover three-dimensional shape from stereo pairs of images are reported. We do not even attempt to summarize these results here; we simply illustrate the principles and general methodologies involved.

A simple camera geometry for binocular-stereo imaging is shown in Figure 4.6.[3] Let the baseline connecting the two lens centers be oriented parallel to the x-axis and perpendicular to the optical axes of the imaging system. The images of a point (x,y,z) are formed at (x_l,y_l) and (x_r,y_r) in the left and right camera planes, respectively. In the imaging system shown in Figure 4.6, with identical cameras and coplanar image planes that are perpendicular to the plane containing the two optical axes, the two y-coordinates, y_l and y_r, will be equal. The relationship between the disparity $(x_l - x_r)$ and the depth z, in terms of the imaging-system parameters, baseline length b, and focal length f, is given by

$$z = \frac{bf}{(x_l - x_r)} \tag{4.9}$$

Thus, the depth can be recovered if the disparities of corresponding image points are known.

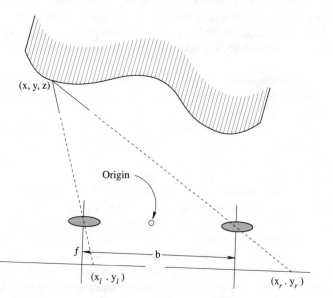

(4.6)

Figure 4.6: Simple camera geometry for stereo imaging (from B.K.P. Horn, *Robot Vision*. Copyright © 1986 McGraw-Hill, Inc., reprinted with permission.)[3]

One of the primary problems in recovering depth is finding corresponding points in the two images. One of the many methods developed for finding corresponding points is to identify "interesting points" in both images and to match these points using methods described in the previous chapter. Note that the image points corresponding to a scene point lie along the line of intersection between the image plane and the epipolar plane, which is defined as the plane containing the scene point and the two lens centers; thus, the search space is limited significantly. Such matching techniques yield sparse depth maps; additional constraints are applied to recover depth at all points. For example, iterative relaxation techniques that use the surface smoothness constraint are often employed to obtain consistent solutions.

A principal difficulty in stereo reconstruction is the selection of interesting points. This selection typically is based on high local variance in intensity, which unfortunately occurs more frequently at corners and at other surface discontinuities, where the smoothness constraint does not hold well. In some machine vision applications, the problem of selecting interesting points is solved by using structured light. Patterns of light are projected onto the surface, creating interesting points even in regions that would be otherwise smooth. Finding and matching such points are further simplified when the geometry of the projected patterns is known. Since these patterns create artificial texture on the surfaces, shape-from-texture techniques, described in the next section, can also be used to recover shape.

Shape from texture. Image plane variations in texture properties such as density, size, and orientation are the cues exploited by shape-from-texture algorithms.[114] For example, the orientation of the surface can be determined using the texture gradient,

277

defined as the magnitude and direction of maximum change in the primitive size of texture elements. Also useful in determining orientation is quantifying the changes in the shape of the texture elements (e.g., circles appearing as ellipses). Orientation can be uniquely determined by finding vanishing points in images of surfaces with textures made up of regular grids of lines that are possibly attributable to structured lighting.[115] Blostein and Ahuja[116] describe an integrated algorithm for extracting texture elements and estimating surface orientation.

Shape from focus. That imaging systems have a finite depth of field is well known. Thus, only objects at a proper distance appear focused in the image, whereas those at other depths are blurred, in proportion to their distances. Algorithms to exploit this blurring effect have been proposed recently.[117-119] The image is modeled as a convolution of focused image, with a point spread function determined by the camera parameters and the distance of the object from the camera. The depth is recovered by estimating the amount of blur in the image and using the known or estimated line spread function.

Research trends

Constraints play a very important role in all levels of vision. In the early processing of visual information, constraints are usually specified by some general laws, such as smoothness of surfaces, and then an iterative approach — using a form of optimization technique — is employed. These iterative approaches usually result in computations commonly called "relaxation processes."[111] Relaxation processes have been used extensively to propagate local constraints in computer vision algorithms in order to obtain globally consistent labels.

Seven papers were selected for inclusion in this chapter: four are in this book and the remaining three in its companion book, *Computer Vision: Advances and Applications*. We begin the collection of papers reprinted in this chapter of *Principles* with "Cooperating Processes for Low-Level Vision: A Survey," by Davis and Rosenfeld, in which various approaches to using cooperating parallel processes are reviewed. Brightness discontinuities at surface boundaries, as depicted in line drawings, convey important information about surface shape. Ullman[120] presents an approach for designing a distributed computation of constrained optimization problems by networks of locally interconnected simple processors. Such computations are essential in parallel constraint propagation for solving many vision problems. Barrow and Tenenbaum[121] present a computational model for interpreting line drawings based on constraints on local surface orientation along extremal and discontinuity boundaries. This type of computation has been used for many tasks, including determining optical flow,[122] solving correspondence problems,[123,124] and recovering shape-from-shading,[112] and is very well suited to implementations using neural network approaches.[125,126] These optimization-based approaches, including regularization and random-field approaches, are effective when no discontinuities are present in images. The presence of discontinuities poses serious problems that are now attracting the attention of researchers.

During the last decade, one of the most active research topics in computer vision was shape-from-X techniques. Many techniques were developed to recover three-dimensional information from images using a variety of available information. Shape-from-shading[127] and shape-from-texture[128] techniques have been investigated by several groups. Ikeuchi and Horn[112] describe an iterative shape-from-shading algorithm using occluding boundary information. The next set of papers describe various techniques for shape recovery from image cues. In *Principles*, "Photometric Method for Determining Surface Orientation From Multiple Images," by Woodham describes a method for recovering shape information from multiple images acquired by varying the direction of illumination. Since the position of objects relative to the camera remains unchanged, this photometric-stereo technique does not suffer from the correspondence problem. In *Advances and Applications*, Nayer et al. in "Shape From Interreflections," consider the problem of concave objects resulting in secondary illuminations.

Controlling the illumination in practical applications is often not possible, whereas obtaining stereo pairs of images of the same scene by using cameras that are spatially separated by a known distance is relatively simple. Analysis of such stereo pairs of images has received considerable attention in computer vision research. We have included "Region-Based Stereo Analysis for Robotic Applications," by Marapane and Trivedi in *Principles* that covers this topic; Ohta and Kanade[129] also discuss stereo analysis. The most popular and well-investigated shape-from-X technique is certainly stereo. Many different forms of stereo have been investigated, including trinocular stereo[130,131] and motion stereo.[132,133] For solving difficulties in correspondence problems, different features were tried. Interesting points,[94] lines,[134-136] and areas[137,138] have all been used. The current trend is to combine stereo and motion[139,140] and to use correspondenceless methods.[141,142]

Analysis of texture plays a very important role in many applications of machine vision. Papers describing texture modeling, analysis, and segmentation are discussed in earlier chapters.[39,42,59] In "Shape From Texture: Integrating Texture-Element Extraction and Surface Estimation," Blostein and Ahuja in *Principles* describe a method for identifying texture elements while simultaneously recovering the orientation of the textured surfaces. In this method, true texture elements are selected from a set of candidates by finding the planar surface that best predicts the observed texture elements.

In some applications, especially those requiring qualitative depth information, shape from focus may prove very useful.[117,119]

The finite depth-of-focus in an imaging system results in blurring of edges of out-of-focus objects. In *Advances and Applications*, "Depth Recovery From Blurred Edges," by Subbarao and Gurumoorthy describes a method that exploits this blurring effect to recover depth information. Many such inverse reconstruction problems are mathematically ill-posed. Reformulating these inverse reconstruction problems as well-posed variational principles using regularization theory has been studied. We conclude *Advances and Applications* with the paper entitled "Regularization of Inverse Visual Problems Involving Discontinuities," by Terzopoulos, which describes a method that reformulates such an inverse reconstruction problem using controlled-continuity constraints. Clearly, approaches in which information from various clues is combined or in which various sensors are used will be successful in recovering three-dimensional information. Such approaches are now receiving attention.[143,144]

High-level constraints are domain dependent. Approaches that use high-level constraints are the main focus of knowledge-based vision systems[145,146] and are also discussed in Chapter 7.

References Cited
Chapter 4

110. Barrow and Tenenbaum, "A System for Reasoning About Scences," Technical Note #121, *Technical Note #MSYS*, Artificial Intelligence Center, Stanford Research Institute, March 1976.

111. A. Rosenfeld, R.A. Hummel, and S.W. Zucker, "Scene Labeling by Relaxation Operations," *IEEE Trans. Systems, Man, and Cybernetics*, Vol. 6, 1976, pp. 420-433.

112. K. Ikeuchi and B.K.P. Horn, "Numerical Shape from Shading and Occluding Boundaries," *Artificial Intelligence*, Vol. 17, 1981, pp. 141-184.

113. R.J. Woodham, "Photometric Method for Determining Surface Orientation from Multiple Images," *Optical Engineering*, Vol. 29, No. 1, 1980, pp. 139-144.

114. J.J. Gibson, *The Perception of the Visual World*, Riverside Press, Cambridge, Mass., 1950.

115. J.R. Kender, *Shape from Texture*, PhD thesis, Carnegie-Mellon University, 1980.

116. D. Blostein and N. Ahuja, "Shape from Texture: Integrating Texture-Element Extraction and Surface Estimation," *IEEE Trans. Pattern Analysis and Machine Intelligence*, Vol. 11, No. 12, 1989, pp. 1233-1251.

117. A.P. Pentland, "A New Sense for Depth of Field," *IEEE Trans. Pattern Analysis and Machine Intelligence*, Vol. 9, No. 4, 1987, pp. 523-531.

118. P. Grossman, "Depth from Focus," *Pattern Recognition Letters*, Vol. 5, 1989, pp. 63-69.

119. M. Subbarao and N. Gurumoorthy, "Depth Recovery from Blurred Edges," *Proc. IEEE Conf. Computer Vision and Pattern Recognition*, IEEE CS Press, Los Alamitos, Calif., 1988, pp. 498-503.

120. S. Ullman, "Relaxation and Constrained Optimization by Local Processes," *Computer Graphics and Image Processing*, Vol. 10, No. 2, 1979, pp. 115-125.

121. H.G. Barrow and J.M. Tenenbaum, "Interpreting Line Drawings as Three Dimensional Surfaces," *Artificial Intelligence*, Vol. 17, 1981, pp. 75-116.

122. B.K.P. Horn and B.G. Schunck, "Determining Optical Flow," *Artificial Intelligence*, Vol. 17, 1981, pp. 185-203.

123. D. Marr and T. Poggio, "Cooperative Computation of Stereo Disparity," *Science*, Vol. 194 (4262), 1976, pp. 283-287.

124. D. Marr and T. Poggio, "A Computational Theory of Human Stereo Vision," *Proc. Royal Soc. Lond. B*, Vol. B204, 1979, pp. 301-328.

125. G.E. Hinton and T.J. Sejnowski, "Learning and Relearning in Boltzmann Machines," *Parallel Distributed Processing*, Vol. 1: Foundation, MIT Press, Cambridge, Mass., 1986.

126. Hutchinson, et al, "Computing Motion Using Analog and Binary Resistive Networks," *Computer*, Vol. 21, No. 3, 1988, pp. 52-63.

127. B.K.P. Horn and M.J. Brooks, eds., *Shape from Shading*, MIT Press, Cambridge, Mass., 1989.

128. K. Kanatani and T.C. Chou, "Shape from Texture: General Principle," *Artificial Intelligence*, Vol. 38, No. 1, 1989, pp. 1-48.

129. Y. Ohta and T. Kanade, *IEEE Trans. Pattern Analysis and Machine Intelligence*, Vol. 7, No. 2, 1985, pp. 139-154.

130. N. Ayache and F. Lustman, "Fast and Reliable Trinocular Stereovision," *Proc. First Int'l Conf. Computer Vision*, IEEE CS Press, Los Alamitos, Calif., 1987, pp. 422-427.

131. C. Hansen, N. Ayache, and F. Lustman, "Towards Real-Time Trinocular Stereo," *Proc. Second Int'l Conf. Computer Vision*, IEEE CS Press, Los Alamitos, Calif., 1988, pp. 129-133.

132. R. Nevatia, "Depth Measurement by Motion Stereo," *Computer Graphics and Image Processing*, Vol. 5, 1976, pp. 203-214.

133. R.C. Jain, S. Bartlett, and N. O'Brien, "Motion Stereo Using Ego-Motion Complex Logarithmic Mapping," *IEEE Trans. Pattern Analysis and Machine Intelligence*, Vol. 9, No. 3, 1987, pp. 356-369.

134. N. Ayache and B. Faverjon, "Efficient Registration of Stereo Images by Matching Graph Descriptions of Edge Segments," *Int'l J. Computer Vision*, 1987, pp. 107-131.

135. L.B. Wolff, "Accurate Measurement of Orientation from Stereo Using Line Correspondence," *Proc. IEEE Conf. Computer Vision and Pattern Recognition*, IEEE CS Press, Los Alamitos, Calif., 1989, pp. 410-415.

136. G. Medioni and R. Nevatia, "Segment-Based Stereo Matching," *Computer Vision, Graphics, and Image Processing*, Vol. 31, 1985, pp. 2-18.

137. L. Cohen et al, "Hierarchical Region-Based Stereo Matching," *Proc. IEEE Conf. Computer Vision and Pattern Recognition*, IEEE CS Press, Los Alamitos, Calif., 1989, pp. 416-421.

138. S.B. Marapane and M.M. Trivedi, "Region-Based Stereo Analysis for Robotic Applications," *IEEE Trans. Systems, Man, and Cybernetics*, Vol. 19, No. 6, 1989, pp. 1447-1464.

139. Z. Zhang, O.D. Faugeras, and N. Ayache, "Analysis of a Sequence of Stereo Scenes Containing Multiple Moving Objects Using Rigidity Constraints," *Proc. Second Int'l Conf. Computer Vision*, IEEE CS Press, Los Alamitos, Calif., 1988, pp. 177-186.

140. E. Grosso, G. Sandini, and M. Tistarelli, "3-D Object Reconstruction Using Stereo and Motion," *IEEE Trans. Systems, Man, and Cybernetics*, Vol. 19, No. 6, 1989, pp. 1465-1476.

141. B.D. Lucas, and T. Kanade, "Optical Navigation by the Method of Differences," *Proc. Int'l Joint Conf. Artificial Intelligence*, Morgan Kaufmann Publishers, Inc., San Mateo, Calif., 1985, pp. 981-984.

142. K. Skifstad and R.C. Jain, "Range Estimation from Intensity Gradient Analysis," *Machine Vision and Applications*, Vol. 2, 1989, pp. 81-102.

143. E.P. Krotkov, *Active Computer Vision by Cooperative Focus and Stereo*, Springer-Verlag, New York, N.Y., 1989.

144. J.Y. Aloimonos and D. Shulman, *Integration of Visual Modules: An Extension of the Marr Paradigm*, Academic Press, Boston, Mass., 1989.

145. D.M. McKeown, Jr., "Building Knowledge-Based Systems for Detecting Man-Made Structures from Remotely-Sensed Imagery," *Proc. Royal Soc. Lond. B,* Vol. A324, 1988, pp. 423-435.

146. B.A. Draper et al, "The Schema System," *Int'l J. Computer Vision,* Vol. 2, No. 3, 1989, pp. 209-250.

Cooperating Processes for Low-level Vision: A Survey

Larry S. Davis

*Department of Computer Sciences, University of Texas,
Austin, TX 78712, U.S.A.*

Azriel Rosenfeld

*Computer Science Center, University of Maryland,
College Park, MD 20742, U.S.A.*

ABSTRACT

*Cooperating local parallel processes can be used as aids in assigning numerical or symbolic labels to
image or scene parts. Various approaches to using such processes in low-level vision are reviewed, and
their advantages are discussed. Methods of designing and controlling such processes are also
considered.*

1. Introduction

The early stages of computer vision involve assigning symbolic and numerical
labels to image parts. For example, pixels can be assigned symbolic land-use
category labels based on their spectral signatures, or numerical stereo or
motion disparity labels based on local comparisons between pairs of pictures.

The enormous amount of data comprising an image demands that such
labelling processes be very fast. Sequential labelling processes, while they can
make full use of context, cannot be speeded up in general. Moreover, the
labellings which they compute are often sensitive to the order in which the
parts are considered. A more promising approach—one that is also motivated
by studies of biological visual systems—is to make the processes highly *parallel*.
This requires that each picture part be analyzed and labelled independently of
the others. When we do this, however, many errors are made, because
contextual information is not adequately used.

A solution to this problem is to assess the labelling possibilities for every part
independently and then compare each part's assessments to those of other,

Artificial Intelligence 17 (1981) 245–263

0004–3702/81/0000–0000/$02.50 © North-Holland

related parts, in order to detect and correct potential inconsistencies. Since both the assessment and the comparison can be done independently for every part, each stage of the process is parallel. On the other hand, context is now being used at the comparison stage, when related parts are able to communicate and 'cooperate'. To keep the computational cost low, the comparisons should be *local*; they should involve only parts that are directly related (e.g., neighboring pixels). This localness can be compensated for by *iterating* the comparison process, in order to allow information to propagate.

These considerations lead naturally to the design of a 'cooperative' approach to labelling picture parts which allows context to be used in the labelling process while still permitting fast parallel implementation and low computational cost. Such processes are called 'relaxation' processes, because of their resemblance to certain iterative processes used in numerical analysis. Very generally, a relaxation process is organized as follows:

(a) A list of possible labels is independently selected for each part, based on its intrinsic characteristics. A measure of confidence can also be associated with each possible label.[1]

(b) The possibilities (and confidences) for each part are compared with those for related parts, based on a model for the relationships between the possible labels of picture parts. Labels are deleted or confidences are adjusted to reduce inconsistencies.

(c) Step (b) can be iterated as many times as required.

This approach is very general: We have not specified how to formulate label relationship models, choose possibilities, estimate confidences, or adjust them; nor have we discussed when the process should be iterated, and if so, how many times. The next three sections of this paper discuss these issues, and survey applications of such processes to problems in low-level computer vision.

2. Cooperation/Competition

A relaxation process is a computational mechanism which allows a set of 'myopic' local processes associated with picture parts to interact with one another in order to achieve a globally consistent interpretation of a picture. This interaction involves the updating of each picture part's self-assessment which is represented as a discrete or fuzzy *labelling*. A discrete labelling simply associates a set of possible labels, or names, with each picture part, while a fuzzy labelling additionally associates a likelihood with each label.

Labels are usually specified extensionally by actually listing the appropriate labels for each picture part. The list is a subset of some given, finite universe of labels. For some applications the natural label set is infinite. For example, the

---

[1]It is tacitly assumed that the correct label of each part is on the initial list of labels for that part.

label for a picture part might represent the range, or distance, from the sensor to some specific point in the picture part such as its centroid. In such cases, a labelling may need to be specified intensionally; for example, an interval of numbers may be used to specify the range—i.e., we assume that the true range is between a nearest distance r_1 and a farthest distance r_2. All the applications we will consider in this paper use only finite universes of labels.

2.1. Neighborhood models

A relaxation process is determined by specifying a model for the neighborhood of a picture part and a model for the interaction between labellings of neighboring picture parts.

The neighborhood model for a relaxation process specifies which pairs of picture parts directly communicate with one another in the relaxation process, and determines the topology of the graph on which the relaxation process operates. This graph has individual picture parts as nodes. Its arcs connect those pairs of parts that communicate with one another. The neighborhood model is usually designed to establish connections only between 'nearby' parts to satisfy the locality constraint.

A neighborhood model is specified by a set of neighbor relations $r = \{r_1, r_2, \ldots, r_n\}$. Each r_i is a binary relation defined over the appropriate set of picture parts. For example, if the picture parts are pixels, then the neighborhood model might specify that a pixel is connected to every pixel in its 3×3 neighborhood. In this case, there are still several possibilities for the relations contained in the set r. For example, r might be the set {directly above, directly below, etc.} which would distinguish between pairs of points that are horizontally adjacent, vertically adjacent, etc., or it could be the singleton relation 'in the 3×3 neighborhood'. In the latter case, the connections between pairs of pixels would not be recoverable from the graph on which the relaxation process will operate. The choice of r will, in general, be determined by the isotropy of the universe of labels. For example, if we are designing a relaxation process for edge reinforcement, then the relative positions of pixels are crucial since edges generally 'line up', while if we are designing a relaxation process to enhance an image's grey levels, then the positional information may not be required.

When the picture parts are regions rather than pixels, then connections might be formed between adjacent regions only. In some situations, it might be necessary to distinguish between regions that are above, below, inside, surrounding, etc.

The neighborhood model determines which pairs of picture parts directly communicate through the relaxation process. The next section discusses the various ways in which they may communicate.

2.2. Interaction models

The interaction model defines how a picture part changes its labelling based on the labellings of its neighbors. An interaction model is composed of two parts:

(1) a *knowledge representation* for the relationships between labels, and

(2) a mechanism, or procedure, for applying the knowledge in (1) to change, or update, labellings.

For discrete labellings the simplest knowledge representation is a set of the pairs of labels that can simultaneously be associated with pairs of neighboring picture parts. It can be represented by a binary relation R defined over the universe of labels D. Intuitively, $(d,d') \in R$ if a pair of neighbors can simultaneously be labelled with d and d'. In general, there is a binary relation associated with each neighbor relation.

The most obvious updating mechanism is a label discarding process, which looks at pairs of picture parts at a time. A label, d, can be deleted from the labelling of a picture part if, for some neighboring picture part, that neighbor does not contain a label, d', in its labelling with $(d,d') \in R$. This is, essentially, Waltz's filtering algorithm [1]. Rosenfeld et al. [2] show that label discarding can, in principle, be applied in parallel at every picture part and that by iterating the process of discarding labels a unique, maximally consistent labelling is computed. The process can be generalized in a variety of ways—e.g., the knowledge representation might be in terms of n-ary relations (for example, a 3-ary relation is required to specify that a picture part is between two others). The label discarding process now considers a picture part and n-1 of its neighbors at a time, rather than one neighbor at a time. There are many other possibilities based on computing lower-order projections of n-ary relations. See Haralick et al. [3] and Haralick and Shapiro [4] for a detailed discussion.

The binary relation knowledge representation can be generalized to fuzzy labellings by specifying a real-valued compatibility function, C, whose domain is $D \times D$. As before, in general, a compatibility function is defined for each picture relation in the set r. A variety of applications have used compatibility functions whose range is $(-1, 1)$. Intuitively, if $C(d,d') = -1$, then d and d' are maximally incompatible, and the strong presence of d' at one picture part (i.e., d' has a high likelihood at that part) should depress the likelihood of d at a neighboring picture part. If $C(d,d') = 1$, then d and d' are maximally compatible, and the strong presence of d' at a picture part should increase the likelihood of d at a neighboring picture part. Finally, if $C(d,d') = 0$, then the presence of d' at a picture part should have no effect on the likelihood of d at a neighboring part. Intermediate values of C should have intermediate effects.

As an example, suppose we are designing a relaxation process to enhance the results of a local line detection algorithm. Then the set of labels may be horizontal (h), vertical (v), left-diagonal (dl), and right-diagonal (dr), and the set r might contain the relations vertically-adjacent (V), horizontally-adjacent (H), left-diagonally-adjacent (L) and right-diagonally-adjacent (R). If, in the class of images being considered, linear features are thin and have few corners (i.e., the curvature is ordinarily low), then we would expect, e.g., that $C_V(v,v)$ would be high, while $C_V(v,h)$ would be low, since an h vertically adjacent to a v would form a right angle. $C_H(v,v)$, on the other hand, would be low, since the linear features are thin.

Several mechanisms have been suggested for applying this knowledge representation to updating labellings. For example, Rosenfeld et al. [2] suggested the formula:

$$p_i'(d) = p_i(d)(1 + Q_i(d))/N$$

where

$$Q_i(d) = \sum_j m_{ij} \sum_{d'} C(d,d')p_j(d')$$

and N is a normalizing factor which guarantees that $\Sigma\, p_i(d) = 1$. The m_{ij} values can be used to give higher weight to some neighbors at part i than others. $Q_i(d)$ measures the overall support of the neighborhood of part i for label d; it takes on values in the range $[-1, 1]$ and can be interpreted similarly to C. The above operation is applied in parallel at every part and for every label. The p' values then replace the p values, and the operation can be iterated.

Variations on the above theme are possible and lead to better results in some applications. For example, one can apply a 'max–min' rule where

$$Q_i(d) = \min_j\{\max_{d'}\{C(d,d')p_j(d')\}\}$$

which reduces to the discrete algorithm described above when C and p are constrained to take on only the values 0 or 1.

There are several disadvantages to the relational knowledge representation for the interactions between labels. First, it is a single-level representation scheme. The solution to many image understanding problems requires that images be described at several levels of abstraction. Attempting to compile all interactions between conceptually higher-level pictorial entities down to interactions between only the lowest level pictorial features is almost always cumbersome and inefficient, and is sometimes impossible. Section 2.3 discusses hierarchical relaxation systems.

A second important shortcoming of the relational framework is that the algebraic combination of evidence treats all of the interactions between labels uniformly, which is often not desirable. Furthermore, there are classes of intuitively plausible constraints that can only be represented very inefficiently in a relational framework. For example, the very simple constraint

> A picture part can be a d_1 only if all adjacent picture parts
> can be d_2's

requires an n-ary relation to represent it, where n is the maximum degree of any node in the graph on which the relaxation procedures operates.

Such problems can be overcome by adopting a more powerful representation for label interactions than relations. For example, constraints between labels can be represented using logic statements [5]. This allows a much wider class of constraints to be efficiently represented and applied to the analysis of a picture. The natural mechanism for applying the constraints is, then, a general inference procedure. Such a scheme has not yet been applied to any image understanding problem; its application to linear feature detection is currently under investigation.

2.3. Hierarchy

Very often, a natural and economical solution to an image analysis problem requires that pictorial entities be described at several levels of detail. For example, to recognize an image segment as the top view of an airplane based on the shape of its boundary might require recognizing airplane pieces as engines, wings, tail sections, etc., and then grouping them into larger pieces of airplanes, and finally into a complete airplane shape. Or, as a second, more complex, example, reading a word in cursive script involves segmenting the word into primitive parts such as strokes, grouping the strokes into large letter pieces, those pieces into letters and finally the letters into a word.

As discussed above a single level relaxation system is specified by a neighborhood model and a label interaction model. To design a hierarchical relaxation system having k levels, one needs to not only define a neighborhood model and an interaction model at each level, but also a *construction* model (which, given the labelling of pieces at level m, can construct the pieces and their labellings at level $m + 1$), and an across-level neighborhood model. This last model is ordinarily based simply on constituency—i.e., a level $m + 1$ piece is linked to each of the level m pieces from which it was formed [6].

An important design criterion for such processes is that the construction models and the interaction models be *consistent*. Intuitively, the consistency constraint means that the relations between level m labels implied by the construction models for all higher levels do not contradict the explicit relations between level m labels mentioned in the level m interaction model. A simple example should help clarify this point.

Suppose that we are constructing a hierarchical relaxation system for reading cursive script, and that for the particular corpus of words that we wish to read, there are no words in which the letter 'h' precedes the letter 'u'. Now, suppose that at the large letter piece level, an h ends with a piece p_1 and a u begins with a piece p_2, and that no other letter contains either a p_1 or a p_2. Then clearly, the compatibility of p_1 and p_2 at the large letter piece level should be as low as possible. If it were not, then the construction model taking letters into words would be inconsistent with the interaction model for large letter pieces.

One possible approach to guaranteeing such consistency is to specify only the construction models, and then *compile* the interaction models from the construction models. This not only guarantees that the interaction models are consistent with the construction models, but also avoids the tedious task of specifying all the constraints contained in the interaction models.

For example, in reading cursive script from a known corpus, the letter cooccurrence probabilities can be compiled directly from the corpus, and these can be used as an interaction model at the letter level. Then, given a decomposition of letters into large letter pieces a similar process can produce cooccurrence probabilities for large letter pieces, etc. This was done by Hayes [7] in his handwriting analysis system.

As a second example, in [8] Davis and Henderson describe a hierarchical shape analysis system. Shapes are modeled by hierarchical relational networks which describe the arrangement and geometrical properties of shape pieces at several levels of detail. The representation is designed in such a way that local constraints about the appearance of the shape can be automatically compiled from the representation. Thus the representation serves as a set of construction models, and the compiled constraints are used as interaction models.

Although the compilation of interaction models from construction models is a powerful idea in the design of hierarchical relaxation systems, it does not address the issue of how one determines whether or not additional constraints, not derivable from the construction model, can be consistently added to the interaction models. This situation might arise when analysis of one part of an image yields information that can be used to guide the analysis of other parts, or if prior knowledge is available that is not ordinarily available. The following simple example illustrates the problem. Suppose that we are attempting to recognize airplanes, and that prior information is available about the angle that the wings of planes will make with the fuselage. How can we determine that this extra information is consistent with the existing airplane model? (If it is not, no shapes will be recognized as airplanes!) How does the relaxation process even make use of this information, assuming that it is consistent with its interaction models? For currently existing systems, there is no effective means for checking the consistency of externally specified information with current knowledge, or for uniformly applying such information to enhance the relaxation process. This points out another advantage of the logic representation mentioned in Section 2.2. If construction models are specified as statements in logic, then interaction models can still be compiled from the construction models. Furthermore, the consistency of added information with current knowledge can be determined, and the general inferencing capabilities associated with logic would enable such a system to make use of any additional information as well.

3. Applications

A wide variety of labelling processes can be used at various stages of computer vision. Many of these processes operate at the pixel level—i.e., the parts to be labelled are individual pixels, and the interaction is between neighboring pixels. In general, image segmentation can be regarded as pixel labelling, with the labels defining a partition of the image into subsets. Thus relaxation methods are applicable to most of the standard image segmentation techniques, including pixel classification based on gray level or color (thresholding, multispectral classification), as well as detection of local features (peaks or spots, ridges or curves, edges, corners, or matches to arbitrary templates). Many examples of such methods are given in Sections 3.1 and 3.2.

Relaxation methods can also be applied to situations involving several images (e.g., disparity measurement in motion or stereo), or several sets of labels simultaneously applied to a single image (e.g., 'intrinsic image' labels); see Section 3.3. They can also be used to label picture parts that are larger than single pixels, i.e., windows or regions, and to detect specified local configurations of such parts, as briefly discussed in Section 3.4.

3.1. Pixel classification based on gray level or color

Suppose that a scene is composed of a few objects or regions each of which is homogeneous in color. The colors of the pixels in an image of that scene should then display clustering behavior: There should be clusters in the scatter plot of color values, corresponding to the color characteristics of the regions. Under these circumstances, a natural way to segment the image is to classify the pixels as belonging to these clusters. In fact, this is the standard method of segmenting multispectral terrain images into terrain types or land use classes, based on clustering the spectral signatures of the pixels. It is also widely used to segment black-and-white images into light and dark regions by thresholding the gray levels so as to separate peaks on the histogram. Analogous methods can be used for arrays of other types of values, e.g., range data.

Conventionally, the pixels are classified independently. In order to use a cooperative approach, possible class memberships must be determined, or class membership confidences estimated, for each pixel, and the results compared with those for neighboring pixels. To define an appropriate interaction model, some assumptions must be made about the kinds of neighbors that we expect a pixel to have. Since the scene consists of a few homogeneous regions, most pixels will be in the interior of a region. The neighbors of those pixels should all be alike. Some pixels, of course, will be on interregion boundaries; in this case some of the neighbors of the pixel will belong to the same region as the pixel itself, but others will belong to a different region. Neighborhoods at which three or more regions meet will be rare, and will be ignored here.

The situation just described is characteristic of a large class of cooperative pixel labelling problems: the neighbors of a pixel belong, with rare exceptions, to at most two classes, one of which is the class containing the pixel itself. Several types of interaction models can be used in such situations:

(1) The neighborhood used can consist, for each pixel, of those neighbors that most resemble the pixel. If the neighbors cluster into two classes, this is straightforward; if not, one can use a fixed number of 'best' neighbors, on the assumption that these neighbors are the ones most likely to belong to the same region as the pixel. For the chosen neighbors, the interaction model is then quite simple: like reinforces like [9].

Alternatively, we can examine a set of one-sided neighborhoods of the pixel, and choose the one in which the gray level or color is most homogeneous. This one is presumably contained within a single region, so that we can safely use a like-reinforces-like scheme on it [10, 11].

(2) If we do not want to commit ourselves to choosing a fixed set of neighbors, we can assign weights to the neighbors, or define link strengths between the pixels and the neighbors, such that neighbors similar to the pixel get high weights (or link strengths). In the interaction model, the reinforcement contributions are then proportional to the weights. For example, the m_{ij} factors in eq. (2) can be chosen so as to give some neighbors more weight than others. If the reinforcement process is iterated, the weights can themselves be adjusted at each iteration, based on revised estimates of neighbor similarity—e.g., the m_{ij} might change from one iteration to the next [12–14].

(3) Finally, we can simply use the same neighborhood for every pixel, and let like reinforce like. For pixels in the interior of a region, this behaves as desired; but on the border of a region, the pixel labels are likely to remain ambiguous, since they are being influenced by neighbors that belong to two regions. In fact, sharp corners on the borders will be smoothed out, since a pixel at such a corner will have most of its neighbors in another region, so that the reinforcement process will make it confident that it too belongs to that region [15, 16].

It should be pointed out that, rather than reinforce label confidences, we can adjust the pixel gray level or color values themselves; in other words, we can use the methods just described to smooth an image without blurring the edges between regions. Fig. 1 illustrates one of the methods.

The preceding discussion assumed that each region is 'flat', i.e., has relatively constant gray level or color. This is a reasonable assumption about some classes of scenes (e.g., characters on a printed page, chromosomes against a uniform background), but is not correct for others. More generally, the image can be modeled as piecewise linear and the relaxation process can examine a set of one-sided neighborhoods of the pixel, and choose the one that best fits a plane. Within the chosen neighborhood, the reinforcements should depend on closeness of fit to the hypothesized plane, rather than on similarity [17].

A similar approach applies, in principle, if we want to classify pixels based on the values of local properties measured over their neighborhoods, assuming

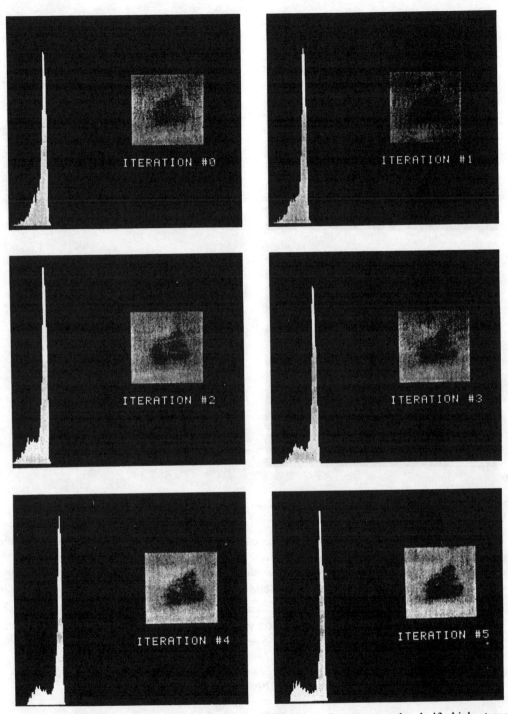

FIG. 1. Cooperative pixel classification based on gray level. (Lowest gray level: 13; highest gray level: 49.)

#0: Original (infrared image of a tank) and its histogram. The gray levels in this image were mapped into 'light' and 'dark' probabilities proportional to their distances from the ends of the grayscale.

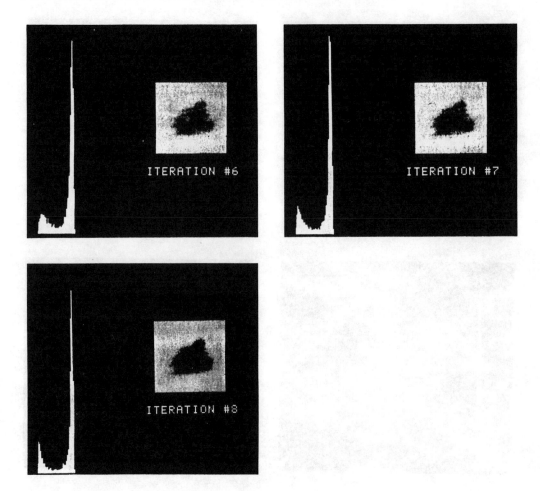

FIG. 1. Continued.

#1–#8: Eight iterations of a relaxation process (like reinforcing like) applied to the initial probabilities, with the resulting probabilities displayed as gray levels using the inverse mapping. As the histograms show, the probabilities are tending toward (0, 1) and (1, 0), resulting in good discrimination between the tank and the background.

Iteration #	Mean pixel value	Scale (pixels/dot)
0	40.20	7
1	40	7
2	40.19	6
3	40.01	7
4	39.92	7
5	39.80	7
6	39.36	8
7	39.58	8
8	39.52	10

that the image consists of regions that are homogeneously textured. Here, however, larger neighborhoods should be used, since local properties tend to be more variable than single-pixel properties. Of course, when we use large neighborhoods, the problems encountered at region borders become more severe.

3.2. Local feature detection

If the labelling task involves local feature detection or template matching, we must use neighborhood and interaction models appropriate to the type of feature or pattern being detected. In the following paragraphs we discuss the detection of spots (i.e., peaks), streaks (ridges, curves), edges, and corners, as well as matches to an arbitrary template.

To detect peaks, i.e., local maxima, the neighborhood must be large enough to contain a peak. The peak label at a pixel is then positively reinforced by the presence of lower values at its neighbors, and negatively reinforced by higher values, where the amounts of reinforcement depend on the differences in value. In other words, small reinforces large, while large competes with large. Detection of pits (local minima) is exactly analogous. The same approach can be used to detect peaks on waveforms, histograms, or scatter plots [18, 19].

To detect ridges or ravines, i.e., high-valued lines or streaks on a low-valued background or vice versa, as in linear feature detection, we use a neighborhood somewhat larger than the streak width. The reinforcement model should now depend on the orientation of the streak; high values should reinforce one another along the streak, while low values should reinforce high values across the streak. To implement this, we initially estimate a streak confidence for each orientation, or more simply, estimate a single streak confidence and an associated streak direction. For neighbors in the direction along the streak, high values reinforce one another, provided the orientations are consistent; for neighbors in the direction across the streak, low values reinforce high ones, as in the case of peak detection [20, 21]. This approach is illustrated in Fig. 2.

Detecting edges is similar to detecting streaks, since an edge is a streak-like locus of high rates of change. Note that in this case directions must be measured modulo 360° rather than modulo 180°; in other words, for a given direction, we must take into account the sign of the rate of change, so that high edge values reinforce one another only if their dark sides and light sides match, and they compete otherwise. If desired, we can associate edge values with the 'cracks' between adjacent pairs of pixels, rather than with the pixels themselves; this is more appropriate if the edges are sharp [22, 23].

For both edges and streaks, our model implicitly assumes that they are straight or smoothly curved; if they have sharp corners or angles, dissimilar directions will be present in a single neighborhood, and these will compete with one another. To detect corners, we must allow a pixel to interact with pairs of

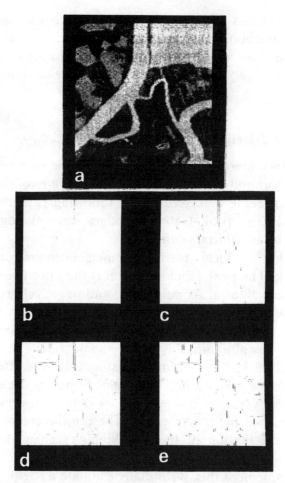

FIG. 2. Cooperative detection of smooth edges. (a): Portion of a LANDSAT image. (b): Result of applying an edge detector to (a), and scaling the results to yield a 'no edge' probability, and edge probabilities in each of 8 directions, at each point. For display purposes, if the highest probability is 'no edge', the point is displayed as white; otherwise, the highest edge probability is displayed as a gray level (1 = black). (c)–(e): Results of three iterations of a relaxation process (see text) applied to the initial probabilities, with the new probabilities displayed in the same way.

its neighbors, rather than with each neighbor separately; we can then reinforce the 'cornerity' value of the pixel if there exist pairs of neighboring edge or streak values that have sharply different directions. [Alternatively, we can detect corners in the gray level (or color) domain based on the presence of suitable combinations of high and low levels at neighbors, e.g., a high value on one side and low values on several other sides; but this requires us to work with k-tuples of neighbors for $k > 2$.] At the same time, low cornerity values at the neighbors of a pixel should reinforce a high value at the pixel, just as in the case of peak detection. Analogous methods can be used to detect corners on ideal borders or curves represented by chain codes; here again, cornerity is reinforced by the presence of neighboring slopes that differ sharply, and by low neighbor cornerity [24].

In general, we can employ a cooperative approach to detect matches of a given template with the image by considering the template as composed of pieces; detecting matches with the pieces by some conventional method; and reinforcing a match to a given piece based on the occurrence of matches to the other pieces in approximately the correct relative positions. This approach is preferable to straightforward matching of the entire template for two reasons: it has lower computational cost, and it is less sensitive to geometrical distortion. Note that in this reinforcement process, if there are matches to a given piece in several neighboring positions, we can use the best one, but we should not sum their influences, since only one of them can be correct; thus a reinforcement rule using the max, rather than the sum, is more appropriate here [25, 26].

3.3. Processes involving multiple properties or multiple images

A more complex class of cooperating processes can be used to assign two or more interrelated sets of labels to the pixels in an image. As an example, consider the gray level and edge labelling processes discussed in Sections 3.1 and 3.2. These two sets of labels are not independent; for example, the gray levels on the light side of an edge are more likely to belong to a light than to a dark class, and vice versa. Thus we can design a compound cooperating process in which both sets of labels interact; such processes should yield better results than if we use either of the individual processes alone [27, 28].

The gray level at a given pixel of an image is the resultant of several 'intrinsic' properties at the corresponding point of the scene, including illumination, reflectivity, and surface slope. It is impossible to separate the effects of these factors by examining the pixels individually; but one can attempt to separate them using a cooperative process, based on assumptions about how the factors vary from point to point. For example, let us assume that the scene is composed of regions over which the intrinsic properties are constant. It may then be possible to determine which property is changing at a given edge, by analyzing the gray level variations at the edge. If this can be done, we can try to estimate the property values cooperatively, by hypothesing initial values and letting like reinforce like except across edges [29].

Finally, we consider cooperating processes that involve more than one image. Given two images of the same scene, taken at different times or from different positions, it will not be possible in general to register the images globally, since parts of the scene may have moved, or their projections on the image may have shifted by different amounts because they are at different distances from the sensor. However, we can try to match pieces of one image with pieces of the other to determine a piecewise correspondence; from the variations in this correspondence we can then estimate the motion or distance information. The accuracy of these estimates can be enhanced using a cooperative approach, if we assume that the scene is made up of parts each having a uniform motion or distance; the approach is analogous to that used in Section 3.1 (see [30, 31]).

3.4. Region-level processes

Cooperating processes can also be used to assign labels to windows or regions of an image, or to detect configurations of regions that match given models. Such processes are briefly discussed in the following paragraphs.

As a simple example, suppose that we have broken up an image into windows, and want to classify the textures in the windows. If we use small windows, the classifications become unreliable; but if we use large ones, border effects become a major factor, since it is hard to classify windows that overlap two or more differently textured windows. One solution is to use small windows, and adjust the classifications (or the feature values) cooperatively, based on those of neighboring windows, in such a way that windows belonging to different regions (most likely) do not influence one another; this is analogous to the cooperative approach to pixel classification described in Section 3.1 (see [32]).

More generally, suppose that we have segmented an image into regions, and want to classify the regions, based on their geometrical or textural properties. If we know what pairs of classifications are possible for neighboring pairs of regions in given relative positions, we can use this knowledge to cooperatively adjust the label possibilities or confidences. For example: (1) In labelling the edges in a blocks-world scene as convex, concave, or occluding, we can use the constraints imposed when the edges meet at junction [1]. (2) In assigning regions in an indoor scene to classes such as 'door', 'doorknob', 'wall', and 'light switch', the light switch label is reinforced, and the doorknob label weakened, by the wall label on a surrounding region, and vice versa for the door label on a surrounding region [33].

Matching a configuration of regions to a given model is analogous to matching a piece of an image to a template. We can represent the regions, their properties, and their relationships by a 'scene graph' in which the nodes and arcs are labelled by property or relation names (and values). The model can be similarly represented by a labelled graph, and we can then attempt to find occurrences of the model graph as a subgraph of the scene graph. Just as in the template case, this can be done cooperatively by finding scene graph nodes that match model graph nodes, and reinforcing matches for which the proper neighboring nodes are present [34, 35].

4. Issues

Relaxation processes have proved very useful for deriving relatively unambiguous labellings of image or scene parts at a variety of levels. The design and control of such processes, however, are not as yet well understood. Given a labelling task, how do we choose appropriate neighborhood and interaction models? (In other words, how do we represent our knowledge about the given problem domain in the form of an iterative local process?) Given such a process, how many times should it be iterated, and how should its performance be evaluated? In this section we briefly review some of the approaches that have been proposed to these problems of knowledge representation and control in relaxation processes.

4.1. Knowledge representation

As mentioned in Section 2.2, for discrete relaxation processes the interaction model is defined by a set of compatible label pairs; but for fuzzy labellings, the compatibility relation must be quantitative. It can be defined, for example, by specifying a 'compatibility coefficient' for each pair of labels on each pair of neighboring parts. These coefficients can be defined in a problem-specific manner; for example, the compatibility between two given edge or line directions at a pair of neighboring pixels could be taken as inversely proportional to the bending energy required to bend a spline so that it changes direction in the given way.

Another possibility is to define compatibilities on probabilistic grounds. Consider the probability ratio $r(d,d') \equiv p(d,d')/p(d)p(d')$, where the numerator is the joint probability of the pair of labels (d,d') on the given pair of neighboring objects, and the terms in the denominator are the prior probabilities of the two labels. Intuitively, if d and d' are compatible, $p(d,d')$ should be greater than $p(d)p(d')$; if d and d' are independent, they should be equal; and if d and d' are incompatible, $p(d,d')$ should be less than $p(d)p(d')$. Thus we have $r(d,d') > 1$, $= 1$, and < 1 iff d and d' are compatible, independent, or incompatible, respectively. If we want compatibilities that lie in the range $[-1, 1]$, we can use $\log r$ rather than r; this is positive, zero, or negative according to whether d and d' are compatible, independent, or incompatible. (The log does not automatically lie in the range $[-1, 1]$; if we want it to, it must be truncated and rescaled.) Note that $\log r$ is the *mutual information* of the pair of labels d, d'. The probabilities can be estimated by counting occurrences of d and d', and joint occurrences of both. The use of mutual information to define compatibilities is suggested in [36]. If we drop the restriction that the compatibilities lie in the range $[-1, 1]$, we can use r itself, rather than $\log r$, as a compatibility function. In fact, in a Bayesian approach to relaxation developed by Peleg, the compatibility coefficients turn out to be the r's (see [37]).

4.2. Control

A second critical question concerns the control of relaxation processes: when should the iteration be stopped? How can its progress be evaluated?

For a discrete relaxation process, termination criteria are straightforward to formulate and justify. For example, when binary (or higher-order) relations are used as a knowledge representation, then the process terminates when no further labels can be discarded from any picture part. At this point, each label at each picture part (if any remain) has a consistent label at every neighboring picture part. Or, if logic statements are used as a knowledge representation, then the process terminates when no new inferences can be formed. In both cases, the destination of the process is a consistent labelling, the notion of consistency is well-defined and it is straightforward to prove that the relaxation process has as its 'fixed point' a consistent labelling.

For a probabilistic relaxation process, the situation is more complicated. One possible approach is that the relaxation process should be iterated until the probability densities for each picture part converge. There are, however, both practical and theoretical disadvantages to this approach:

(a) In practice, relaxation processes often converge to results which are quite poor, even though the first several iterations lead to significant improvements.

(b) There are very few theoretical results concerning convergence, and these simply characterize sufficient conditions for convergence, rather than necessary conditions [38]. Moreover, the limit points have not be characterized as solutions to a well-defined problem, except in some specific cases [39].

Various criteria have been proposed for evaluating the performance of relaxation processes [40], but none of them seem to be satisfactory. Convergence (i.e., decrease in rate of change) is not an acceptable criterion, since the limit point may not be a desirable labelling. Unambiguity (e.g., low entropy) is also not acceptable, since there are many unambiguous labelings, most of which are highly inconsistent with the given initial labelling. Combinations of these criteria might be used [41], but these are also subject to similar objections [42]. A more promising approach uses a composite criterion for evaluating a labelling based on its consistency with both the initial labelling and the model (i.e., the compatibilities) [43]. This area is still the subject of active research.

5. Concluding Remarks

Relaxation processes have potential speed advantages because they can be implemented in parallel (hardware permitting). They have been successfully applied to a wide variety of labelling problems by a growing number of investigators; our survey makes no claim to completeness. In spite of these successes, little is as yet known about the design and control of these processes. However, a number of promising approaches to their theoretical formulation are being pursued, and it is hoped that a deeper understanding of their nature will soon be achieved.

ACKNOWLEDGMENT

The support of the National Science Foundation under Grants MCS-76-23763 to the University of Maryland, and ENG-79-04037 to the University of Texas, is gratefully acknowledged, as is the help of Eleanor Waters in preparing this paper. The authors also wish to thank Shmuel Peleg and Michael O. Shneier for helpful discussions and comments.

REFERENCES

1. Waltz, D., Understanding line drawings of scenes with shadows, in: Winston, P.H. (Ed.), *The Psychology of Computer Vision* (McGraw-Hill, New York, 1975) 19–91.
2. Rosenfeld, A., Hummel, R. and Zucker, S.W., Scene labelling by relaxation operations, *IEEE Trans. Systems, Man, Cybernetics* **6** (1976) 420–433.
3. Haralick, R.M., Davis, L.S., Milgram, D.L. and Rosenfeld, A., Reduction operators for constraint satisfaction, *Information Sci.* **14** (1978) 199–219.
4. Haralick, R.M. and Shapiro, L.G., The consistent labelling problem: Part I, *IEEE Trans. Pattern Analysis Machine Intelligence* **1** (1979) 173–183, Part II, ibid. **2** (1980) 193–203.
5. Davis, L S., A logic model for constraint propagation, Tech. Rept. TR-137, Computer Sciences Dept., Univ. of Texas (1980).
6. Davis, L.S. and Rosenfeld, A., Hierarchical relaxation for waveform parsing, in: Hanson, A. and Riseman, E. (Eds.), *Computer Vision Systems* (Academic Press, New York, 1978) 101–109.
7. Hayes, K.C. Jr., Reading handwritten words using hierarchical relaxation, TR-783, Computer Science Center, University of Maryland, College Park, MD (July 1979) Abridged version to appear in *Computer Graphics Image Processing*.
8. Davis, L.S. and Henderson, T.C., Hierarchical constraint processes for shape analysis, TR-115, Computer Sciences Dept., University of Texas, Austin, TX (November 1979).
9. Davis, L.S. and Rosenfeld, A., Noise cleaning by iterated local averaging, *IEEE Trans. Systems, Man, Cybernetics* **8** (1978) 705–710.
10. Tomita, F. and Tsuji, S., Extraction of multiple regions by smoothing in selected neighborhoods, *IEEE Trans. Systems, Man, Cybernetics* **7** (1977) 107–109.
11. Nagao, M. and Matsuyama, T., Edge preserving smoothing, *Computer Graphics Image Processing* **9** (1979) 394–407.
12. Lev, A., Zucker, S.W. and Rosenfeld, A., Iterative enhancement of noisy images, *IEEE Trans. Systems, Man, Cybernetics* **7** (1977) 435–442.
13. Scher, A., Velasco, F.R.D. and Rosenfeld, A., Some new image smoothing techniques, *IEEE Trans. Systems, Man, Cybernetics* **10** (1980) 153–158.
14. Eklundh, J.O. and Rosenfeld, A., Image smoothing based on neighbor linking, *IEEE Trans. Pattern Analysis Machine Intelligence* **3** (1981) in press.
15. Eklundh, J.O., Yamamoto, H. and Rosenfeld, A., A relaxation method in multispectral pixel classification, *IEEE Trans. Pattern Analysis Machine Intelligence* **2** (1980) 72–75.
16. Rosenfeld, A. and Smith, R.C., Thresholding using relaxation, *IEEE Trans. Pattern Analysis Machine Intelligence* **3** (1981) in press.
17. Haralick, R.M. and Watson, L., A facet model for image data, *Proc. IEEE Conf. Pattern Recognition Image Processing* (August 1979) 489–497.
18. Davis, L.S. and Rosenfeld, A., Iterative histogram modification, *IEEE Trans. Systems, Man, Cybernetics* **8** (1978) 300–302.
19. Peleg, S., Iterative histogram modification, 2, *IEEE Trans. Systems, Man, Cybernetics* **8** (1978) 555–556.
20. Eberlein, R., An iterative gradient edge detection algorithm, *Computer Graphics Image Processing* **5** (1976) 245–253.

21. Zucker, S.W., Hummel, R.A. and Rosenfeld, A., An application of relaxation labeling to line and curve enhancement, *IEEE Trans. Computers* **26** (1977) 394–403, 922–929.

22. Schachter, B.J., Lev, A., Zucker, S.W. and Rosenfeld, A., An application of relaxation methods to edge reinforcement, *IEEE Trans. Systems, Man, Cybernetics* **7** (1977) 813–816.

23. Hanson, A.R. and Riseman, E.M., Segmentation of natural scenes, in: Hanson, A. and Riseman, E. (Eds.), *Computer Vision Systems* (Academic Press, New York, 1978) 129–163.

24. Davis, L.S. and Rosenfeld, A., Curve segmentation by relaxation labelling, *IEEE Trans. Computers* **26** (1977) 1053–1057.

25. Davis, L.S. and Rosenfeld, A., An application of relaxation labelling to spring-loaded template matching, *Proc. 3rd Int. Joint Conf. on Pattern Recognition* (November 1976) 591–597.

26. Ranade, S. and Rosenfeld, A., Point pattern matching by relaxation, *Pattern Recognition* **12** (1980) 269–275.

27. Zucker, S.W. and Hummel, R.A., Toward a low-level description of dot clusters: Labelling edge, interior, and noise points, *Computer Graphics Image Processing* **9** (1979) 213–233.

28. Danker, A. and Rosenfeld, A., Blob extraction by relaxation, *IEEE Trans. Pattern Analysis Machine Intelligence* **3** (1981) in press.

29. Barrow, H.G. and Tenenbaum, J.M., Recovering intrinsic scene characteristics from images, in: Hanson, A. and Riseman, E. (Eds.), *Computer Vision Systems* (Academic Press, New York, 1978) 3–26.

30. Marr, D. and Poggio, T., Cooperative computation of stereo disparity, *Science* **194** (1976) 283–287.

31. Barnard, S.T. and Thompson, W.B., Disparity analysis of images, *IEEE Trans. Pattern Analysis Machine Intelligence* **2** (1980) 333–346.

32. Hong, T.H., Wu, A.Y. and Rosenfeld, A., Feature value smoothing as an aid in texture analysis, *IEEE Trans. Systems, Man, Cybernetics* **10** (1980).

33. Barrow, H.G. and Tenenbaum, J.M., MSYS: A system for reasoning about scenes, TN-121, Artificial Intelligence Center, SRI, Inc., Menlo Park, CA (April 1976).

34. Kitchen, L. and Rosenfeld, A., Discrete relaxation for matching relational structures, *IEEE Trans. Systems, Man, Cybernetics* **9** (1979) 869–874.

35. Kitchen, L., Relaxation applied to matching quantitative relational structures, *IEEE Trans. Systems, Man, Cybernetics* **10** (1980) 96–101.

36. Peleg, S. and Rosenfeld, A., Determining compatibility coefficients for curve enhancement relaxation processes, *IEEE Trans. Systems, Man, Cybernetics* **8** (1978) 548–555.

37. Peleg, S., A new probabilistic relaxation scheme, *IEEE Trans. Pattern Analysis Machine Intelligence* **2** (1980) 362–369.

38. Zucker, S.W., Leclerc, Y.G. and Mohammed, J.L., Continuous relaxation and local maxima section—conditions for equivalence, *Proc. 6th Int. Joint Conf. on Artificial Intelligence* (August 1979) 1014–1016.

39. Ullman, S., Relaxation and constrained optimization by local processes, *Computer Graphics Image Processing* **10** (1979) 115–125.

40. Fekete, G., Eklundh, J.O. and Rosenfeld, A., Relaxation: evaluation and applications, *IEEE Trans. Pattern Analysis Machine Intelligence* **3** (1981) in press.

41. Faugeras, O. and Berthod, M., Scene labelling: an optimization approach, *Proc. IEEE Conf. Pattern Recognition Image Processing* (August 1979) 318–326.

42. Peleg, S. and Rosenfeld, A., A note on the evaluation of probabilistic labellings, TR-805, Computer Science Center, University of Maryland, College Park, MD (August 1979).

43. Peleg, S., Monitoring relaxation algorithms using labelling evaluation, TR-842, Computer Science Center, University of Maryland, College Park, MD (December 1979).

Received October 1980

Photometric method for determining surface orientation from multiple images

Robert J. Woodham

Department of Computer Science
University of British Columbia
2075 Wesbrook Mall
Vancouver, B.C., Canada
V6T 1W5

Abstract. A novel technique called photometric stereo is introduced. The idea of photometric stereo is to vary the direction of incident illumination between successive images, while holding the viewing direction constant. It is shown that this provides sufficient information to determine surface orientation at each image point. Since the imaging geometry is not changed, the correspondence between image points is known *a priori*. The technique is photometric because it uses the radiance values recorded at a single image location, in successive views, rather than the relative positions of displaced features.

Photometric stereo is used in computer-based image understanding. It can be applied in two ways. First, it is a general technique for determining surface orientation at each image point. Second, it is a technique for determining object points that have a particular surface orientation. These applications are illustrated using synthesized examples.

Key Words: bidirectional reflectance distribution function (BRDF), image processing, imaging geometry, incident illumination, photometric stereo, reflectance map, surface orientation.

Optical Engineering 19:1:139-144 (January/February 1980).

I. INTRODUCTION

Work on computer-based image understanding has led to a need to model the imaging process. One aspect of this concerns the geometry of image projection. Less well understood is the radiometry of image formation. Relating the radiance values recorded in an image to object shape requires a model of the way surfaces reflect light.

A reflectance map is a convenient way to incorporate a fixed scene illumination, surface reflectance and imaging geometry into a single model that allows image intensity to be written as a function of surface orientation. This function is not invertible since surface orientation has two degrees of freedom and image intensity provides only one measurement. Local surface shape cannot, in general, be determined from the intensity value recorded at a single image point. In order to determine object shape, additional information must be provided.

This observation has led to a novel technique called photometric stereo in which surface orientation is determined from two or more images. Traditional stereo techniques determine range by relating two images of an object viewed from different directions. If the correspondence between picture elements is known, then distance to the object can be calculated by triangulation. Unfortunately, it is difficult to determine this correspondence. The idea of photometric stereo is to vary the direction of the incident illumination between successive images, while holding the viewing direction constant. It is shown that this provides sufficient information to determine surface orientation at each image point. Since the imaging geometry is not changed, the correspondence between image points is known *a priori*. The technique is photometric because it uses the radiance values recorded at a single image location, in successive views, rather than the relative positions of displaced features.

Original manuscript 5015 received Feb. 20, 1979.
Revised manuscript received March 12, 1979.
Accepted for publication July 18, 1979.
This paper is a revision of a paper presented at the SPIE seminar on Image Understanding Systems & Industrial Applications, Aug. 30-31, 1978, San Diego, which appears in SPIE Proceedings Vol. 155.

II. THE REFLECTANCE MAP

The fraction of light reflected by an object surface in a given direction depends upon the optical properties of the surface material, the surface microstructure and the spatial and spectral distribution and state of polarization of the incident illumination. For many surfaces, the fraction of the incident illumination reflected in a particular direction depends only on the surface orientation. The reflectance characteristics of such a surface can be represented as a function $\phi(i,e,g)$ of the three angles i, e and g defined in Figure 1. These are called, respectively, the *incident*, *emergent* and *phase* angles. The angles i and e are defined relative to a local surface normal. $\phi(i,e,g)$ determines the ratio of surface radiance to irradiance measured per unit surface area, per unit solid angle, in the direction of the viewer. The reflectance function $\phi(i,e,g)$ defined here is related to the bidirectional reflectance distribution function (BRDF) defined by the National Bureau of Standards.[1]

Image forming systems perform a perspective transformation, as illustrated in Figure 2(a). If the size of the objects in view is small compared to the viewing distance, then the perspective projection can be approximated as an orthographic projection, as illustrated in Figure 2(b). Consider an image forming system that performs an orthographic projection. To standardize the imaging geometry, it is convenient to choose a coordinate system such that the viewing direction is aligned with the negative z-axis. Also, assume appropriate scaling of the image plane such that object point (x,y,z) maps onto image point (u,v) where u = x and v = y. With these assumptions, image coordinates (x,y) and object coordinates (x,y) can be referred to interchangeably.

If the equation of an object surface is given explicitly as:

$$z = f(x,y)$$

then a surface normal is given by the vector:

$$\left[\frac{\partial f(x,y)}{\partial x}, \frac{\partial f(x,y)}{\partial y}, -1 \right]$$

If parameters p and q are defined by:

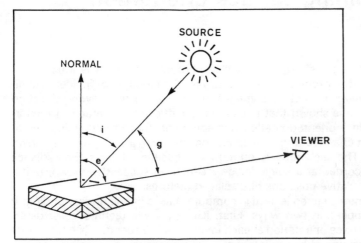

Figure 1. Defining the three angles i, e and g. The incident angle i is the angle between the incident ray and the surface normal. The emergent angle e is the angle between the emergent ray and the surface normal. The phase angle g is the angle between the incident and emergent rays.

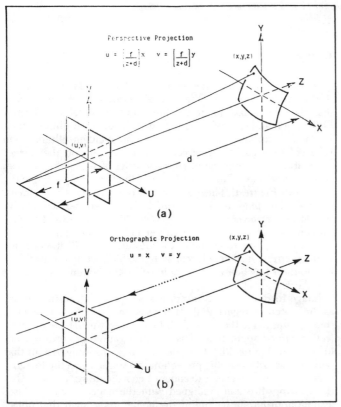

Perspective Projection

$$u = \left[\frac{f}{z+d}\right]x \quad v = \left[\frac{f}{z+d}\right]y$$

(a)

Orthographic Projection

$$u = x \quad v = y$$

(b)

Figure 2. Characterizing image projections. (a) illustrates the well-known perspective projection. [Note: to avoid image inversion, it is convenient to assume that the image plane lies in front of the lens rather than behind it.] For objects that are small relative to the viewing distance, the image projection can be modeled as the orthographic projection illustrated in (b). In an orthographic projection, the focal length f is infinite so that all rays from object to image are parallel.

$$p = \frac{\partial f(x,y)}{\partial x} \quad \text{and} \quad q = \frac{\partial f(x,y)}{\partial y}$$

then the surface normal can be written as [p,q,–1]. The quantity (p,q) is called the *gradient* of f(x,y) and *gradient space* is the two-dimensional space of all such points (p,q). Gradient space is a con-

venient way to represent surface orientation. It has been used in scene analysis.[2] In image analysis, it is used to relate the geometry of image projection to the radiometry of image formation.[3] This relation is established by showing that image intensity can be written explicitly as a function of gradient coordinates p and q.

An ideal imaging device produces image irradiances proportional to scene radiances. In an orthographic projection, the viewing direction, and hence the phase angle g, is constant for all object points. Thus, for a fixed light source and viewer geometry, the ratio of scene radiance to irradiance depends only on gradient coordinates p and q. Further, suppose each object surface element receives the same incident radiance. Then, the scene radiance, and hence image intensity, depends only on gradient coordinates p and q.

The *reflectance map* R(p,q) determines image intensity as a function of p and q. A reflectance map captures the surface reflectance of an object material for a particular light source, object surface and viewer geometry. Reflectance maps can be determined empirically, derived from phenomenological models of surface reflectivity or derived from analytic models of surface microstructure.

In this paper, it will be assumed that image projection is orthographic and that incident illumination is given by a single distant point source. Extended sources can be modeled as the superposition of single sources. The reflectance map can be extended to incorporate spatially varying irradiance and perspective. A formal analysis of the relation between the reflectance map and the bidirectional reflectance distribution function (BRDF) has been given.[4]

Expressions for cos(i), cos(e) and cos(g) can be derived using normalized dot products of the surface normal vector [p,q,–1], the vector [p_s,q_s,–1] which points in the direction of the light source and the vector [0,0,–1] which points in the direction of the viewer. One obtains:

$$\cos(i) = \frac{1 + pp_s + qq_s}{\sqrt{1 + p^2 + q^2}\sqrt{1 + p_s^2 + q_s^2}}$$

$$\cos(e) = \frac{1}{\sqrt{1 + p^2 + q^2}}$$

$$\cos(g) = \frac{1}{\sqrt{1 + p_s^2 + q_s^2}}.$$

These expressions can be used to transform an arbitrary surface reflectance function ϕ(i,e,g) into a reflectance map R(p,q).

One simple idealized model of surface reflectance is given by:

$$\phi_a(i,e,g) = \varrho\cos(i).$$

This reflectance function corresponds to the phenomenological model of a perfectly diffuse (lambertian) surface which appears equally bright from all viewing directions. Here, ϱ is a reflectance factor and the cosine of the incident angle accounts for the foreshortening of the surface as seen from the source. The corresponding reflectance map is given by:

$$R_a(p,q) = \frac{\varrho(1 + pp_s + qq_s)}{\sqrt{1 + p^2 + q^2}\sqrt{1 + p_s^2 + q_s^2}}.$$

A second reflectance function, similar to that of materials in the maria of the moon and rocky planets, is given by:

$$\phi_b(i,e,g) = \frac{\varrho\cos(i)}{\cos(e)}.$$

302

This reflectance function corresponds to the phenomenological model of a surface which reflects equal amounts of light in all directions. The cosine of the emergent angle accounts for the foreshortening of the surface as seen from the viewer. The corresponding reflectance map is given by:

$$R_b(p,q) = \frac{\varrho (1 + pp_s + qq_s)}{\sqrt{1 + p_s^2 + q_s^2}} .$$

It is convenient to represent $R(p,q)$ as a series of iso-brightness contours in gradient space. Figure 3 and Figure 4 illustrate the two simple reflectance maps $R_a(p,q)$ and $R_b(p,q)$, defined above, for the case $p_s = 0.7$, $q_s = 0.3$ and $\varrho = 1$.

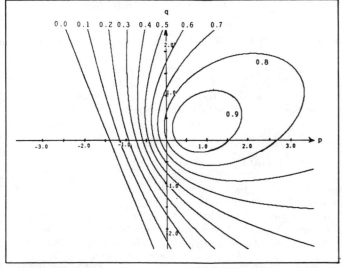

Figure 3. The reflectance map $R_a(p,q)$ for a lambertian surface illuminated from gradient point $p_s = 0.7$ and $q_s = 0.3$ (with $\varrho = 1.0$). The reflectance map is plotted as a series of contours spaced 0.1 units apart.

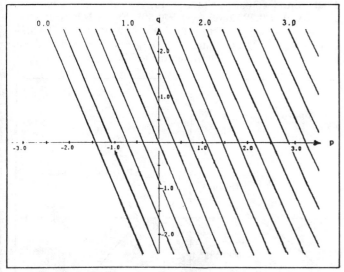

Figure 4. The reflectance map $R_b(p,q)$ for a surface illuminated from gradient point $p_s = 0.7$ and $q_s = 0.3$ (with $\varrho = 1.0$). The reflectance map is plotted as a series of contours spaced 0.2 units apart.

Reflectance map techniques

Using the reflectance map, the basic equation describing the image-forming process can be written as:

$$I(x,y) = R(p,q) . \tag{1}$$

One idea is to use Eq. (1) directly to generate shaded images of surfaces. This has obvious utility in computer graphics applications including hill-shading for automated cartography[5] and video input for a flight simulator.[6] Synthesized imagery can be registered to real imagery to align images with surface models. This technique has been used to achieve precise alignment of Landsat imagery with digital terrain models.[7]

Equation (1) can also be used in image analysis to determine object shape from image intensity. Equation (1) is a nonlinear first-order partial differential equation. Direct solution is tedious.[8] More generally, one can think of Eq. (1) as one equation in the two unknowns p and q. Determining object shape from image intensity is difficult because Eq. (1) is underdetermined. In order to calculate object shape, additional assumptions must be invoked.

Recent work has helped to make these assumptions explicit. For certain materials, such as the material of the maria of the moon, special properties of surface reflectance simplify the solution.[3,8,9] Other methods for determining object shape from image intensity embody assumptions about surface curvature.[3,10] Simple surfaces have been proposed for use in computer aided design.[11] When properties of surface curvature are known *a priori*, they can be exploited in image analysis.[12] This is useful, for example, in industrial inspection since there are often constraints on surface curvature imposed by the drafting techniques available for part design and by the fabrication processes available for part manufacture.[13]

Reflectance map techniques deepen our understanding of what can and cannot be computed directly from image intensity. Photometric stereo is a novel reflectance map technique that uses two or more images to solve Eq. (1) directly.

III. PHOTOMETRIC STEREO

The idea of photometric stereo is to vary the direction of incident illumination between successive views, while holding the viewing direction constant. Suppose two images $I_1(x,y)$ and $I_2(x,y)$ are obtained by varying the direction of incident illumination. Since there has been no change in the imaging geometry, each picture element (x,y) in the two images corresponds to the same object point and hence to the same gradient (p,q). The effect of varying the direction of incident illumination is to change the reflectance map $R(p,q)$ that characterizes the imaging situation.

Let the reflectance maps corresponding to $I_1(x,y)$ and $I_2(x,y)$ be $R_1(p,q)$ and $R_2(p,q)$ respectively. The two views are characterized by two independent equations:

$$I_1(x,y) = R_1(p,q) . \tag{2}$$

$$I_2(x,y) = R_2(p,q) . \tag{3}$$

Two reflectance maps $R_1(p,q)$ and $R_2(p,q)$ are required. But, if the phase angle g is the same in both views (i.e., the direction of illumination is rotated about the viewing direction), then the two reflectance maps are rotations of each other.

For reflectance characterized by $R_b(p,q)$ above, Eqs. (2) and (3) are linear equations in p and q. If the reflectance factor ϱ is known, then two views are sufficient to determine surface orientation at each image point, provided the directions of incident illumination are not collinear in azimuth.

In general, Eqs. (2) and (3) are nonlinear so that more than one solution is possible. One idea would be to obtain a third image:

$$I_3(x,y) = R_3(p,q) \tag{4}$$

to overdetermine the solution.

For reflectance characterized by $R_a(p,q)$ above, three views are sufficient to uniquely determine both the surface orientation and the reflectance factor ϱ at each image point, as will now be shown.[14] Let $\underset{\sim}{I} = [I_1, I_2, I_3]'$ be the column vector of intensity values recorded at a point (x,y) in each of three views (' denotes vector transpose). Further, let

$$\underset{\sim}{n_1} = [n_{11}, n_{12}, n_{13}]'$$

$$n_2 = [n_{21}, n_{22}, n_{23}]'$$
$$n_3 = [n_{31}, n_{32}, n_{33}]'$$

be unit column vectors defining the three directions of incident illumination. Construct the matrix $\underset{\sim}{N}$ where

$$\underset{\sim}{N} = \begin{bmatrix} n_{11} & n_{12} & n_{13} \\ n_{21} & n_{22} & n_{23} \\ n_{31} & n_{32} & n_{33} \end{bmatrix}$$

Let $\underset{\sim}{n} = [n_1, n_2, n_3]'$ be the column vector corresponding to a unit surface normal at (x,y). Then,

$$\underset{\sim}{I} = \varrho \underset{\sim}{N} \underset{\sim}{n}$$

so that,

$$\varrho \underset{\sim}{n} = \underset{\sim}{N}^{-1} \underset{\sim}{I}$$

provided the inverse N^{-1} exists. This inverse exists if and only if the three vectors n_1, n_2 and n_3 do not lie in a plane. In this case, the reflectance factor and unit surface normal at (x,y) are given by:

$$\varrho = |\underset{\sim}{N}^{-1} \underset{\sim}{I}|$$

and

$$\underset{\sim}{n} = (1/\varrho)\underset{\sim}{N}^{-1}\underset{\sim}{I} . \qquad (5)$$

Unfortunately, since the sun's path across the sky is very nearly planar, this simple solution does not apply to outdoor images taken at different times during the same day.

Even when the simplifications implied by $R_a(p,q)$ and $R_b(p,q)$ above do not hold, photometric stereo is easily implemented. Initial computation is required to determine the reflectance map for each experimental situation. Once calibrated, however, photometric stereo can be reduced to simple table lookup and/or search operations. Photometric stereo is a practical scheme for environments, such as industrial inspection, in which the nature and position of the incident illumination is known or can be controlled.

The multiple images required for photometric stereo can be obtained by explicitly moving a single light source, by using multiple light sources calibrated with respect to each other or by rotating the object surface and imaging hardware together to simulate the effect of moving a single light source. The equivalent of photometric stereo can also be achieved in a single view by using multiple illuminations which can be separated by color.

Applications of photometric stereo

Photometric stereo can be used in two ways. First, photometric stereo is a general technique for determining surface orientation at each image point. For a given image point (x,y), the equations characterizing each image can be combined to determine the corresponding gradient (p,q).

Second, photometric stereo is a general technique for determining object points that have a particular surface orientation. This use of photometric stereo corresponds to interpreting the basic image-forming Eq. (1) as one equation in the unknowns x and y. For a given gradient (p,q), the equations characterizing each image can be combined to determine corresponding object points (x,y). This second use of photometric stereo is appropriate for the so-called industrial "bin-of-parts" problem. The location in an image of key object points is often sufficient to determine the position and orientation of a known object on a table or conveyor belt so that the object may be grasped by an automatic manipulator.

A particularly useful special case concerns object points whose surface normal directly faces the viewer (i.e., object points with $p = 0$ and $q = 0$). Such points form a unique class of image points whose intensity value is invariant under rotation of the illumina-

tion direction about the viewing direction. Object points with surface normal directly facing the viewer can be located without explicitly determining the reflectance map $R(p,q)$. The value of $R(0,0)$ is not changed by varying the direction of illumination, provided only that the phase angle g is held constant.

These applications of photometric stereo will now be illustrated using a simple, synthesized example. Consider a sphere of radius r centered at the object space origin. The explicit representation of this object surface, corresponding to the viewing geometry of Figure 2(b), is given by:

$$z = f(x,y) = -\sqrt{r^2 - x^2 - y^2} . \qquad (6)$$

The gradient coordinates p and q are determined by differentiating Eq. (6) with respect to x and y. One finds:

$$p = \frac{-x}{z} \quad \text{and} \quad q = \frac{-y}{z}$$

Suppose that the sphere is made of a perfectly diffusing object material and is illuminated by a single distant point source at gradient point (p_s, q_s). Then, the reflectance map is given by $R_a(p,q)$ above so that the corresponding synthesized image is:

$$I(x,y) = \begin{cases} 0 & \text{if } x^2 + y^2 > r^2 \\ \max(0, R_a(-x/z, -y/z)) & \text{otherwise} \end{cases} \qquad (7)$$

Equation (7) generates image intensities in the range 0 to ϱ. In the example below, $r = 60$ and $\varrho = 1$.

Multiple images are obtained by varying the position of the light source. Consider three different positions. Let the first be $p_s = 0.7$ and $q_s = 0.3$ as in Figure 3. Let the second and third correspond to rotations of the light source about the viewing direction of $-120°$ and $+120°$ respectively (i.e., $p_s = -0.610$, $q_s = 0.456$ and $p_s = -0.090$, $q_s = -0.756$). Let the three reflectance maps be $R_1(p,q)$, $R_2(p,q)$ and $R_3(p,q)$. The phase angle g is constant in each case. Let the corresponding images generated by Eq. (6) be $I_1(x,y)$, $I_2(x,y)$ and $I_3(x,y)$.

First, consider image point $x = 15$, $y = 20$. Here, $I_1(x,y) = 0.942$, $I_2(x,y) = 0.723$ and $I_3(x,y) = 0.505$. Figure 5 illustrates the reflectance map contours $R_1(p,q) = 0.942$, $R_2(p,q) = 0.723$ and $R_3(p,q) = 0.505$. The point $p = 0.275$, $q = 0.367$ at which these three contours intersect determines the gradient corresponding to

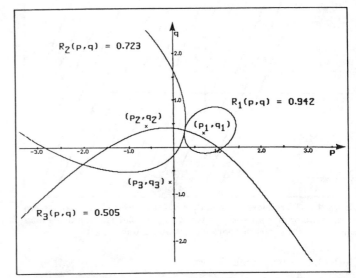

Figure 5. Determining the surface orientation (p,q) at a given image point (x,y). Three reflectance map contours are intersected where each contour corresponds to the intensity value at (x,y) obtained from three separate images. $I_1(x,y) = 0.942$, $I_2(x,y) = 0.723$ and $I_3(x,y) = 0.505$.

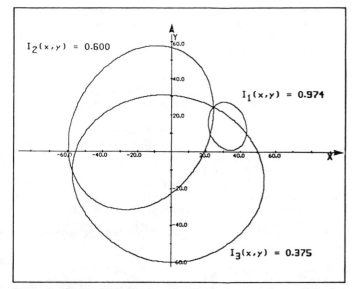

Figure 6. Determining image points (x,y) whose surface orientation is a given (p,q). Three image intensity contours are intersected where each contour corresponds to the value at (p,q) obtained from three separate reflectance maps. $R_1(p,q) = 0.974$, $R_2(p,q) = 0.600$ and $R_3(p,q) = 0.375$.

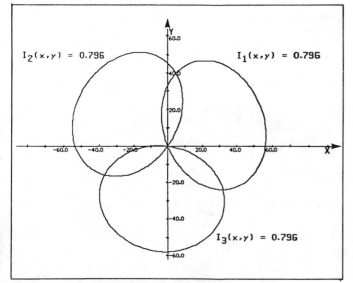

Figure 7. Determining image points (x,y) whose surface normal directly faces the viewer. Three image intensity contours are intersected where each contour corresponds to the value at (0,0) obtained from three separate reflectance maps. Note that the reflectance map value at (0,0) does not change with light source position, provided the phase angle g is held constant.

image point x = 15, y = 20.

Second, consider gradient point p = 0.5, q = 0.5. Here, $R_1(p,q) = 0.974$, $R_2(p,q) = 0.600$ and $R_3(p,q) = 0.375$. Figure 6 illustrates the image intensity contours $I_1(x,y) = 0.974$, $I_2(x,y) = 0.600$ and $I_3(x,y) = 0.375$. The point x = 24.5, y = 24.5 at which these three contours intersect determines an object point whose gradient is p = 0.5, q = 0.5.

Finally, Figure 7 repeats the example given in Figure 6 but for the case p = 0, q = 0. Here, $R_1(p,q) = R_2(p,q) = R_3(p,q) = 0.796$. Object points with surface normal directly facing the viewer form a unique class of points whose image intensity is invariant for rotations of the light source about the viewing direction. The point x = 0, y = 0 at which these three contours intersect determines an object point with surface normal directly

facing the viewer. This result would hold even if the form of R(p,q) is unknown.

Accuracy considerations

Photometric stereo is most accurate in regions of gradient space where the density of reflectance map contours is great and where the contours to be intersected are nearly perpendicular. Several factors influence the density and direction of reflectance map contours. The reflectance properties of the surface material play a role. Figures 3 and 4 illustrate the difference between two idealized materials viewed under identical conditions of illumination. In general, increasing the specular component of reflection will increase the density of contours in one region of gradient space at the expense of other regions. Using extended light sources rather than point sources will alter the shape and distribution of reflectance map contours. Imaging systems can be configured to exploit these facts.[15]

For a given surface material, the main determiner of accuracy is the choice of phase angle g. In photometric stereo, there is a trade-off to acknowledge. A large phase angle increases the density of reflectance map contours in illuminated portions of gradient space. At the same time, a large phase angle results in more of gradient space lying in shadow. A practical compromise must be arrived at for each application.

The relative positions of the light sources must also be considered. Figures 8 and 9 give some indication of the trade-off associated with light source position. In each case, reflectance is

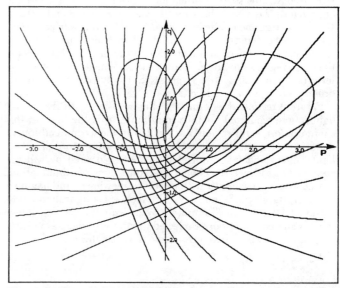

Figure 8. Superimposed reflectance maps $R_1(p,q)$ and $R_2(p,q)$ where $R_1(p,q)$ is $R_a(p,q)$ with $p_s = 0.7$, $q_s = 0.3$, $\varrho = 1$ and $R_2(p,q)$ is $R_a(p,q)$ with $p_s = -0.3$, $q_s = 0.7$, $\varrho = 1$. Each region indicates how an error in intensity measurement determines a corresponding error in the estimation of surface gradient (p,q).

assumed to be characterized by $R_a(p,q)$ above. Figure 8 considers a two-source configuration in which the light source directions are separated by 90° in azimuth with respect to the viewer. Figure 8 superimposes reflectance map contours, spaced 0.1 units apart, for $R_1(p,q)$ and $R_2(p,q)$ where $R_1(p,q)$ is $R_a(p,q)$ with $p_s = 0.7$ $q_s = 0.3$ $\varrho = 1$ and $R_2(p,q)$ is $R_a(p,q)$ with $p_s = -0.3$ $q_s = 0.7$ $\varrho = 1$. Each region of Figure 8 corresponds to a region of equal measurement error. For example, if $I_1(x,y)$ is determined to lie between 0.4 and 0.5 and $I_2(x,y)$ is determined to lie between 0.5 and 0.6 then surface orientation can be determined to ±6.8° of its true value. This corresponds to an area of gradient space in the third quadrant where the error regions are small. Here, a measurement error of 1 gray level in 10 in each of $I_1(x,y)$ and

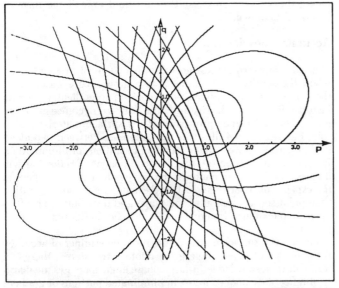

Figure 9. Superimposed reflectance maps R₁(p,q) and R₂(p,q) where R₁(p,q) is $R_a(p,q)$ with $p_s = 0.7$, $q_s = 0.3$, $\varrho = 1$ and R₂(p,q) is $R_a(p,q)$ with $p_s = -0.7$, $q_s = -0.3$, $\varrho = 1$. Each region indicates how an error in intensity measurement determines a corresponding error in the estimation of surface gradient (p,q).

$I_2(x,y)$ constrains surface orientation to within $\pm 6.8°$. On the other hand, if $I_1(x,y)$ is determined to lie between 0.9 and 1.0 and $I_2(x,y)$ is determined to lie between 0.5 and 0.6 then surface orientation can be determined to $\pm 25.8°$ of its true value. This corresponds to an area of gradient space in the first quadrant where the error regions are large. Here, a measurement error of 1 gray level in 10 in each of $I_1(x,y)$ and $I_2(x,y)$ only constrains surface orientation to within $\pm 25.8°$.

Figure 9 repeats the example of Figure 8 but with the second light source separated by 180° in azimuth from the first. In this configuration, error regions are smallest in the second and fourth quadrants of gradient space. Combinations using more than two light sources can be arranged to achieve a desired overall accuracy. One idea is to choose four directions of illumination, spaced evenly in azimuth with respect to the viewer and having a relatively large phase angle g.[13] In such a configuration, most points of interest are illuminated by at least three independent sources and contours can be selected to intersect which are nearly perpendicular and where error regions are small.

CONCLUSIONS

Surface orientation can be determined from the image intensities obtained under a fixed imaging geometry but with varying lighting conditions. Photometric methods for determining surface orientation can be considered complementary to methods based on the identification of corresponding points in two images taken from different viewpoints:

1. Traditional stereo allows the accurate determination of distances to objects. Photometric stereo is best when the surface gradient is to be found.
2. Traditional stereo works well on rough surfaces with discontinuities in surface orientation. Photometric stereo works best on smooth surfaces with few discontinuities.
3. Traditional stereo works well on textured surfaces with varying surface reflectance. Photometric stereo is best when applied to surfaces with uniform surface properties.

Photometric stereo does have some unique advantages:
1. Since the images are obtained from the same point of view, there is no difficulty identifying corresponding points in the two images. This is the major computational task in traditional stereo.
2. Under appropriate circumstances, the surface reflectance factor can be found because the effect of surface orientation on image intensity can be removed. Traditional stereo provides no such capability.
3. Describing object shape in terms of surface orientation is preferable in a number of situations to description in terms of range or altitude above a reference plane.

Photometric stereo depends on a detailed understanding of the imaging process. In addition, the imaging instrument must be of high caliber so that the gray levels produced can be dependably related to scene radiance. Fortunately, our understanding of image formation and the physics of light reflection has advanced sufficiently, and the quality of imaging devices is now high enough, to make this endeavor feasible.

ACKNOWLEDGMENTS

The author would like to thank Berthold K. P. Horn for his help and guidance. Mike Brady, Anni Bruss, Mark Lavin, Tomas Lozano-Perez, Alan Mackworth, David Marr and Patrick Winston provided useful comments and criticisms.

Work reported herein was conducted while the author was at the Artificial Intelligence Laboratory of the Massachusetts Institute of Technology. Support for the laboratory's artificial intelligence research is provided in part by the Advanced Research Projects Agency of the Department of Defence under Office of Naval Research Contract number N00014-75C-0643.

REFERENCES

1. Nicodemus, F. E., Richmond, J. C. and Hisa, J. J., "Geometrical considerations and nomenclature for reflectance," NBS Monograph 160, National Bureau of Standards, Washington, D. C., 1977.
2. Mackworth, A. K., "Interpreting pictures of polyhedral scenes," *Artificial Intelligence*, Vol. 4, pp. 121-137, 1973.
3. Horn, B. K. P., "Understanding image intensities," *Artificial Intelligence*, Vol. 8, pp. 201-231, 1977.
4. Horn, B. K. P. and Sjoberg, R. W., "Calculating the reflectance map," *Applied Optics*, Vol. 18, No. 11, pp. 1770-1779, 1979.
5. Horn, B. K. P., "Automatic hill-shading using the reflectance map," *Proc. Image Understanding Workshop*, Palo Alto, California, April 1979.
6. Strat, T. M., "Shaded perspective images of terrain," TR-463, M.I.T. A.I. Laboratory, Cambridge, Mass., 1978.
7. Horn, B. K. P. and Bachman, B. L., "Using synthetic images to register real images with surface models," *Comm. ACM*, Vol. 21, No. 11, pp. 914-924, 1978.
8. Horn, B. K. P., "Obtaining shape from shading information," *The Psychology of Computer Vision*, P. H. Winston (ed.), McGraw-Hill, pp. 115-155, 1975.
9. Rindfleisch, T., "Photometric method for lunar topography," *Photogrammetric Engineering*, Vol. 32, pp. 262-276, 1966.
10. Woodham, R. J., "A cooperative algorithm for determining surface orientation from a single view," *Proc. IJCAI-77*, pp. 635-641, Cambridge, Mass., 1977.
11. Huffman, D. A., "Curvature and creases: a primer on paper," *Proc. Conf. Computer Graphics, Pattern Recognition and Data Structures*, IEEE Pub. 75CH0981-1C, pp. 360-370, 1975.
12. Woodham, R. J., "Relating properties of surface curvature to image intensity," *Proc. IJCAI-79*, pp. 971-977, Tokyo, Japan, 1979.
13. Woodham, R. J., "Reflectance map techniques for analyzing surface defects in metal castings," TR-457, M.I.T. A.I. Laboratory, Cambridge, Mass., 1978.
14. Horn, B. K. P., "Three source photometry," (personal communication), 1978.
15. Ikeuchi, K. and Horn, B. K. P., "An application of the photometric stereo method," *Proc. IJCAI-79*, pp. 413-415, Tokyo, Japan, 1979. ∃

Region-Based Stereo Analysis
for Robotic Applications

SURESH B. MARAPANE, STUDENT MEMBER, IEEE, AND MOHAN M. TRIVEDI, SENIOR MEMBER, IEEE

Reprinted from *IEEE Transactions on Systems, Man, and Cybernetics*, Volume 19, Number 6, November/December 1989, pages 1447-1464. Copyright © 1989 by The Institute of Electrical and Electronics Engineers, Inc. All rights reserved.

Abstract —The development of a practical binocular stereo approach for the purpose of extracting depth information is considered. Accurate measurement of depth is required for many robotic tasks such as object recognition, manipulation, assembly, and obstacle avoidance. The ability to produce precise depth measurements over a wide range of distances and the passivity of the approach requiring simple and commonly available sensors, make binocular stereo an attractive approach. Yet rigid input requirements and high computational costs have prevented stereo approaches from being adopted for practical robotic applications. For effective use in this application domain, a stereo system must seek a balance between input flexibility, output sufficiency, and computational complexity. At the heart of a binocular stereo approach lies the task of stereo matching. The importance of semantic content and stability of the matching primitive is emphasized and the use of homogeneous regions as features in stereo matching is introduced. The region-based matching is more accurate than those using edge-based primitives since regions have higher discrimination capability. Also, region-based approaches are more efficient since there are fewer features to be matched. However, while the use of regions makes stereo matching more accurate, reliable, and efficient than edge-based matching, region-based matching processes typically yield coarse disparity maps. The generation of accurate and finer resolution disparity maps (and subsequently depth measurements) can be better accomplished using edge-based techniques. Both regions and edges play important, but somewhat complementary, roles in the binocular stereo process. It is, therefore, critical that an efficient and robust stereo system utilize the most appropriate set of primitives at each stage of the process. A hierarchical stereo approach that exploits and integrates the power of different primitives at appropriate stages of the stereo process is proposed. Several experiments to evaluate the performance of a region-based stereo matcher and a disparity and depth generation module are presented. It is shown that the approach is efficient, robust, and successful in generating depth measurements within ±5 percent accuracy.

I. INTRODUCTION

MOST of the robotic systems currently in use are restricted in their operations due to either the lack of or the underutilization of external sensory feedback. These systems are inflexible and require a highly structured work environment. A robotic system has to possess sophisticated sensory mechanisms to autonomously perform tasks in a complex unstructured environment. Such sensor-driven robotic systems are more flexible, versatile, reliable, dexterous, less expensive, and easier to teach [1], [2].

Advanced robotic systems will utilize many different sensory modalities such as vision, range, force, and touch in their operations. While vision is one of the most important sensory modalities used for sensing the operating environment, three-dimensional range information is also critical for the success of many robotic tasks. Range information is required for obstacle avoidance and navigation; for object recognition and pose determination; and for inspection, manipulation, and assembly of objects. Efficiency, accuracy, resolution, noise immunity, and robustness are some of the parameters that must be addressed in selecting a range-sensing approach. The specific robotic application considered in the present study is that of automatic inspection and manipulation in an "in-plant" environment. In particular, we discuss the development of a binocular stereo approach.

The ability to produce precise depth measurements over a wide range of distances and the passivity of the approach make binocular stereo an attractive tool for range sensing. At the heart of the binocular stereo approach lies the task of stereo matching. This task deals with the problem of identifying for each image feature associated with the projection of a particular surface structure in one image, the corresponding feature in the other image that is the projection of the same surface structure. The ability to solve this correspondence problem accurately, reliably, and efficiently, depends to a great extent on the types of features used in this matching. Most existing stereo approaches use edge-based primitives as features for matching. In this paper, we introduce the use of regions as the matching primitive.

Typically, in an image there are fewer regions than edge pixels (edgels) or edge segments. Regions possess a higher semantic content and, hence, higher discrimination capabilities than edge-based primitives. The reduction of the number of features to be matched, along with the region's high discrimination power, greatly decreases the number of mismatches, false targets, possible and makes the region-based matcher more accurate and reliable. Furthermore fewer features to be matched makes establishing correspondence quite efficient. The high semantic content of the regions also facilitates the use of a wide range of representational schemes to describe the structural details in images. This allows utilization of both local and global infor-

Manuscript received October 30, 1988; revised April 10, 1989. This work was supported by the DOE's University Program in Robotics for Advanced Reactors (Universities of Florida, Michigan, Tennessee, and Texas, and the Oak Ridge National Laboratory) under Grant No. DOE DE-FG02-86NE37968.

The authors are with the Electrical and Computer Engineering Dept., Ferris Hall, University of Tennessee, Knoxville, TN 37996-2100.

IEEE Log Number 8930351.

mation in matching. Thus a region-based stereo matcher will yield a robust, accurate, and more globally consistent solution efficiently.

Yet while regions exhibit many desirable properties, they typically lack the capability to generate an accurate disparity map of fine resolution. Edge pixels on the other hand are better suited for the disparity generation stage. A stereo approach that utilizes a hierarchy of primitives such as regions, edge segments, and edge pixels in stereo matching and disparity generation should be able to address the limitations of purely region-based or edge-based approaches. In such a multilevel, hierarchical stereo system, results of stereo matching at higher levels of the hierarchy can be used for guidance at the lower levels, and disparity maps generated at each level can be fused to obtain an accurate and fine resolution disparity map. Such a system would also provide the capability to selectively analyze regions with varying resolutions. This selective focusing capability would further enhance its performance.

In this paper we address two specific objectives. The first objective is to characterize a robotic application domain and to evaluate the strengths and limitations of the range-sensing approaches utilized in the robotic environment. The second objective is to present details of a region-based stereo matcher and its associated disparity-depth generation module. This efficient region-based approach should form the highest level of the hierarchical stereo system. Our final goal is to build a complete and effective hierarchical stereo system suitable for use in a robotic environment. The development of a hierarchical stereo system is a complex and challenging task. It requires selection of appropriate primitives for each level and design of various methodologies to integrate the results from these levels. Those design issues are not addressed in depth in this paper, however.

The organization of the paper is as follows. First, characteristics of the robotic environment are discussed along with a brief review of some of the well established range-sensing techniques. This discussion is followed by a detailed description of the binocular stereo approach. Finally the region-based stereo matcher and a series of experiments conducted to systematically evaluate the performance of the region-based approach are presented.

II. RANGE SENSING FOR ROBOTIC APPLICATIONS

In this section we describe important characteristics of the robotic application domain. A brief review of some of the popular range-sensing approaches is also presented.

A. Characteristics of the Application Domain

An intelligent robotic system may utilize depth information and associated 3-D cues in performing one or more of the following tasks:

1) object recognition,
2) object position and orientation determination,
3) object surface or status inspection,

4) object manipulation or assembly, and
5) obstacle avoidance and navigation.

Tasks 1)–4) can be grouped in the general category of object recognition, inspection, and manipulation, whereas item 5) can be identified as the mobility and navigation in unstructured environments. Obviously the type and nature of the range information required are task dependent. For example object recognition and inspection may require a detailed 3-D surface profile of an object whereas in obstacle avoidance and navigation tasks it may be sufficient to detect the presence or absence of an object (unrecognized). It is important to note that the overall environment in which object recognition, inspection and manipulation tasks are performed is generally quite different from that of mobility and navigation tasks. Typically for object inspection and manipulation tasks, the scene containing the work space is imaged from close distance. The work space usually consists of man-made objects having smooth and finished surfaces that lack rich, highly textured surface details. Furthermore it may not be possible or practical to utilize active illumination sources like textured light patterns [3], because this might interfere and obstruct human operators, who are generally present in the "in-plant" environments. A range-sensing system for these tasks is often required to provide, accurately and efficiently, a complete depth map of the workspace for the entire field of view of the sensor. On the other hand a range-sensing system for mobility and navigation tasks may function in outdoor environments typically characterized as having rich, textured surface details. For these tasks, only 3-D cues for resolving the volume occupancy type of decision need to be extracted [4].

In developing practical range-sensing systems for robotic applications, several, often competing, design parameters need consideration. The following is a list of these parameters:

- efficiency—primarily in speed with which depth information is generated,
- accuracy,
- resolution—spatial as well as of the depth measurements produced,
- input flexibility—should tolerate minor variations in the imaging process,
- noise immunity,
- measurement mode—to derive either the absolute or relative depths,
- reliability,
- repeatability,
- robustness—in handling variations caused by factors such as illumination variations, viewing geometry, work space composition, etc.,
- complexity, and
- cost.

An effective 3-D information extraction system must perform well under these often competing criteria and generate depth information required for a given robotic task. Thus, a balance must be sought between input flexibility, output sufficiency and computational cost [4].

B. Range-Sensing Techniques

Range-finding techniques can be loosely classified as either active or passive. Active techniques utilize artificial sources of energy to illuminate the workspace, but passive techniques do not require such energy sources. Popular active techniques include: contrived lighting approaches and direct range finders based on time-of-flight measurements. Common examples of passive techniques include: stereo, both binocular and photometric; shape from shading; shape from texture; and focusing methods. Passive methods are preferred in many application areas because they do not use an artificial energy source. These application areas include environments where active illumination is impractical or hazardous. A brief discussion of some popular active and passive techniques is given next. A comprehensive review of range sensing and sensors can be found in [5].

The contrived-lighting approach involves illuminating the scene with a controlled lighting pattern and interpreting the projection of the pattern to derive a depth profile of the scene [6], [7]. Data acquisition is slow in these types of approaches. Such active illumination can also be disadvantageous in an outdoor or hostile environment. This method may also fail because of the specular reflectivity of the objects appearing in the scene. The main advantage of this approach is its simplicity and low cost. In time-of-flight range finders, distance is estimated by the elapsed time between the transmission and the reception of an ultrasonic or laser signal. Ultrasonic range finders lack good depth resolution and are useful for detecting obstacles in navigation tasks. Range finders that use lasers have better resolution than ultrasonic range finders. The major disadvantage of laser ranging techniques is their high cost. Also using lasers in an uncontrolled environment could be hazardous to humans. The advantage of time-of-flight techniques are the following: range measurement is directly available, it produces a dense range map, no (or very little) image analysis is required, and registration of range and intensity images is simple. Another simple, active depth-sensing technique is based upon triangulation and utilizes a narrow light beam to illuminate the scene one spot at a time [5]. This approach also suffers from many of the disadvantages associated with other contrived lighting approaches.

Passive techniques for range sensing typically require simpler and less expensive setup than do active approaches. The binocular stereo approach falls into this category and will be discussed in the next section. Here we briefly discuss some of the other passive techniques. In the shape from shading approach, surface orientation is derived from the gray-level intensity values, using information about the light source and the surface reflectivity of objects [8]. One of the disadvantages of this type of approach is that it requires many photometric assumptions.

Shape has also been derived from texture gradients [5], [9]. However such methods require scenes to be highly and uniformly textured. Distance can also be derived from focusing a camera until objects appear sharp [5]. The difficulty in measuring sharpness in visually homogeneous regions prohibits these techniques from producing range measurements for such regions. Also, accuracy of this method is reduced as the range increases.

Two different classes of stereo techniques have been used for deriving range information: photometric stereo and binocular stereo. Of these, photometric stereo has been used to compute orientation of surfaces [8], [10], and it seems to work well on surfaces with uniform reflectance functions. This approach, however, has difficulty when the surface is covered with high contrast markings [3]. Binocular stereo on the other hand relies heavily on the presence of surface detail and has been found to operate flexibly under a wide range of conditions without requiring strong photometric assumptions.

III. RANGE-SENSING BY BINOCULAR STEREO

Binocular stereo can produce precise depth measurements over a wide range of distances, which makes it one of the most attractive passive range-finding methods. Yet the high computational cost of the algorithms has prevented it from being widely used in robotic environments. It is however recognized by many in the computer vision and robotics research communities to offer the most promise for the future [11].

If a 3-D object point is sensed from two different locations, the relative positions of its image differ in the two views. In the binocular stereo approach one measures this difference (disparity) in the relative positions in the images to compute depth information. Typically the binocular stereo approach is characterized by the following four steps.

Step 1)   An image feature of interest, corresponding to a surface point, is located in one image.
Step 2)   The other image of the stereo image pair, is examined to identify the unique image feature corresponding to the projection of the same surface point.
Step 3)   The disparity in the locations is measured.
Step 4)   Disparity value is converted into actual range information using geometric transformations.

Of the four steps, Step 2), which deals with the stereo matching or the correspondence problem, lies at the heart of the binocular stereo approach.

To deal with the correspondence problem, and its concomitant problem of avoiding false targets in determining the correct correspondence or match, it is vital to focus on appropriate representations or primitives, to be matched and on the matching constraints and rules matching. The success and efficiency of a binocular stereo approach is dependent on both the nature of the primitive used and the matching technique itself. The issues related to the selection of an appropriate matching primitive and a description of some of the common constraints and rules that can be utilized for making the matching process computationally tractable are discussed in the following. A brief discussion of some of the popular matching techniques is also presented.

A. Role of Matching Primitives

The comparison of image brightness (gray-level) between left and right images is a weak indication of the correspondence, because imaging geometry, camera characteristics, and noise make the image elements differ in their gray-level values. Furthermore featureless areas of nearly homogeneous brightness values in images make the matching of gray levels unsuitable for solving correspondences. Accordingly most computational stereo algorithms include some form of primitive extraction phase to derive, from the images, features or measurements that can be used for effective stereo matching.

Two important properties sought in matching primitive are its invariance to small variations in image viewpoint, (referred to as stability), and its descriptive power to resolve ambiguities. Selection of an appropriate matching primitive is influenced by the following characteristics of the primitive [12]:

- dimensionality (point like vs. edge like),
- size (spatial frequency),
- contrast,
- semantic content,
- density of occurrence (sparse vs. dense),
- ease in extracting attributes, and
- distinguishability/uniqueness.

Most stereo algorithms use low-level primitives, i.e., those that do not require sophisticated semantic analysis in their extraction. This may be partially attributed to the fact that there is a trade-off between the complexity of the monocular analysis used to extract the features to be matched and the complexity of the process utilized in matching them. Furthermore investigations into human stereopsis have suggested that stereopsis occurs very early in the visual process rather than following a detailed analysis of each monocular image separately [13]. The stereopsis experiments by Julesz on random dot stereograms, substantiates this theory [14], [15].

Popularly used matching primitives include: sign of the Laplacian of the Gaussian: i.e., $\nabla^2 G$ [3]: zero crossings of $\nabla^2 G$ [13], [16]; edges [17] and linked edge segments [18], [19]. These types of primitives are relatively sparse in images and thus require more careful and more explicit matching rules to eliminate false targets. In an efficient and accurate stereo system the matching primitive needs to be easy to extract without much image analysis, yet should possess adequate semantic information. They should not be very dense in occurrence but should be sufficient for useful interpretation. Furthermore the matching technique itself should be designed to exploit the characteristics of the primitives.

B. Constraints and Rules for Stereo Matching

Similarity is the guiding principal for solving the correspondence problem. Derivation of a matching primitive that contains adequate power to resolve ambiguities and is truly invariant with respect to the viewing geometries, is a difficult task. Hence, in general, for a particular image feature in one image, there will be many candidate matches in the corresponding image. Matching rules derived from the constraints underlying the physical environment and imaging are used to restrict this pool of candidate matches.

Some of the common constraints incorporated in stereo algorithms, as identified by Nishihara and Poggio, [4] are the following.

1) *Surface continuity constraint*: Assumes that the physical world is composed of surfaces that are almost continuous everywhere. This suggests that disparities ought to vary smoothly.

2) *Surface uniqueness constraint*: Relates to the fact that the imaged surfaces, for the most part, are opaque, allowing us to assume that the image element recorded by a camera corresponds to a unique point lying physically on the surface of an object. Thus correspondence should be unique.

3) *General position constraint*: Relates to the observation that certain events occur quite infrequently, in a statistical sense, to rule out false correspondences. Both surface continuity and surface uniqueness constraints were formulated and used by Marr and Poggio [13], while Arnold and Binford [20], [21] have utilized general position constraints.

Nishihara and Poggio have identified two broad categories of matching rules in stereo algorithms [4]. Most of the existing algorithms seem to use at least one rule from each class. These categories are as follows: spatial-domain rules and gradient-limit rules. We discuss them in detail next.

1) Spatial-domain rules: This class of rules is based on the surface continuity and the general position assumptions of the matching environment. Examples include the following.

Area statistics: Matching primitives collected over an image measurement patch are compared across images to obtain a single similarity measure. Correlation of image features is an example of this class. This rule typically implies a strong continuity assumption, because it imposes approximately constant disparity over the patch. Nishihara's Prism stereo algorithm [3] belongs to the class of algorithms that uses this type of matching rule.

Contour statistics: In this the comparison is restricted along a contour. The assumption of physical surface continuity is made weaker by assuming disparity to be smooth along contours but allowing them to change abruptly across contours. Figural continuity, as suggested by Mayhew and Frisby [22] and used in Grimson's stereo algorithm [16] is an example of this type. Similar contour based constraints have also been used by Arnold and Binford [20].

2) Gradient limit rules: This class of rules is based on the manner in which images are manifested. The following are examples of rules from this class.

Ordering constraints: Impose the restriction that along epipolar lines, the matched primitives must occur in the same order. This is equivalent to the assumption that imaged surfaces are not transparent and are continuous. This type of constraints have been used by Arnold [21] and also by Baker and Binford [17].

Disparity gradient limits: Restrict the maximum disparity gradient allowed between matched primitives. Pollard, Mayhew, and Frisby have suggested that for most natural scene surfaces the disparity gradient between correct matches is usually less than one [23]. They have proposed a stereo algorithm based upon this observation.

Coarse-to-fine analysis: In this analysis disparity information obtained at a coarser scale is used to limit the search domain for the matching of finer scale primitives. This is used with scale specific matching primitives. Many including Marr and Poggio [13], Grimson [16], and Nishihara [3] have used this strategy for stereo matching.

C. Edge-Based Stereo Approaches

Most stereo approaches use matching primitives based on gray-level discontinuities or edges. Stereo-matching algorithms that use edges are usually more efficient than those using more densely occuring primitives. However because of the sparse and irregularly distributed nature of these features the edge-based matching approaches produce a sparse depth map. Such methods must be augmented by an interpolation step if a complete depth map of the scene is desired. They also require carefully selected and more explicit matching rules to eliminate false targets. Explicit global consistency mechanisms are also incorporated in these algorithms for satisfying constraints such as surface continuity, figural continuity, and constraints due to ordering and disparity gradients. Examples of edge-based matching algorithms include those by Marr and Poggio [13], [24], Grimson [16], Arnold [20], [21], Baker and Binford [17], and Medioni and Nevatia [18]. While Nishihara's Prism system does not use edges as matching primitives, his representation, sign of the $\nabla^2 G$, is still derived based on gray-level discontinuities [3]. In this subsection we briefly review and analyze the abovementioned algorithms in the context of their utility in a robotic environment and present some enhancements recently proposed by Hoff and Ahuja [25] and Mohan *et al.* [26] to improve the performance of edge-based techniques.

Marr and Poggio use the zero crossings of the circularly symmetric Laplacian of Gaussian, $\nabla^2 G$ operator as the matching primitive and features are extracted at several different spatial frequencies, or scales (coarse-to-fine), by convolving the image with different size masks. Given a set of these zero crossing representations at different scales for each of the images, the matching process includes an iterative examination of coarse-to-fine scale features. The matches at coarse scales are used to constrain the matching of finer details. The sparse features from coarse spatial filtering reduces search space and makes matching easier. Matching is performed along horizontal epipolar lines, and the search range for matching is constrained by the size of the convolution mask in use. A match is detected if the zero crossings have the same contrast sign and roughly the same orientation. In cases where the region under consideration does not lie within the current disparity range examined by the matcher, an area statistic based on the continuity assumption is used to distinguish correct matches from random ones. Finally the sparse disparities obtained from the coarser filters are used to realign the images and bring the finer representations within the range of the matcher. This coarse-to-fine control strategy allows matching of very dense zero crossing descriptions with a greatly reduced false target problem. While the overall performance of the algorithm is demonstrated on number of natural and random dot images the computational complexity of the algorithm makes it unsuitable for use in an "in-plant" environment. The algorithm relies heavily on rich surface detail and performs poorly in the absence of such detail. Matching will also fail if repeated or uniform detail is present. And, finally the stringent epipolar matching geometry makes the method extremely sensitive to small vertical misalignments, an effect difficult to arrest in imaging in a robotic environment.

While the use of continuity constraints for eliminating unacceptable candidate matches in the zero crossings algorithm was sound, the difficulties in the implementation of it, by means of statistical measures computed over a region led to the development of Grimson's algorithm. In this rather than imposing a condition of disparity continuity over an area in the image it requires a continuity along a contour in the filtered image. This is a contour-based analogy to the regional check used by the previous algorithm and is essentially the figural continuity suggested by Mayhew and Frisby [22]. This algorithm also relaxed the assumption of epipolar-matching geometry slightly at the expense of a heavy computational burden. The computational times of order of an hour are reported for processing 512×512 images with 100-pixel disparity range on a specialized MIT Lisp machine [3]. Such long processing times prohibit this algorithm from being used in a robotic environment, because depth extraction is just one of the many functions a sensor-driven robot must perform. The algorithm will perform poorly in the absence of rich detail or in the presence of repetitive or periodic detail. Performance will also degrade rapidly for images with vertical misalignments in excess of one or two epipolar lines.

Nishihara's Prism system uses a correlation based approach to stereo matching using the sign of the $\nabla^2 G$ convolution as the matching primitive rather than the zero crossings of the $\nabla^2 G$ operator. In order to deal with visually homogeneous regions within the field of view of the camera, the scene is illuminated by projecting an unstructured texture pattern using a slide projector. The Prism was designed to be used in a robotic environment to rapidly detect obstacles and to determine their rough extents and heights. It produces a coarse surface elevation map over the entire camera field as an output. It uses a near/far matching strategy similar to the coarse-to-fine approach, where matching at a finer scale is loosely coupled with coarser results guiding the search at the next finer scale. While it performs efficiently to produce a 36×26 disparity array over the entire field of view of the camera, it utilizes specialized hardware to perform the computations. Furthermore illuminating the scene with a textured light pattern may not be possible or practical for many inspection and manipulation tasks, because this might interfere with and obstruct human operators, who are generally present in the robot's environment.

Arnold's stereo algorithm matches edges using epipolar geometry. In this implementation, edges are extracted interactively by superimposing line drawings on the gray-scale images. Rather than matching edges in isolation using only local information, he uses several constraints based upon global information to reduce ambiguity and to arrive at a globally consistent interpretation. Constraints used include the following: occlusion constraints, ordering constraints, edge angle and edge interval constraints, and constraints based on the edge continuity in the context of adjacent epipolar lines. Matching is performed by a dynamic programming algorithm developed by Viterbi [27], which is modified to incorporate these constraints. The modified Viterbi algorithm finds the best match between two given sequences of edge points of two epipolar lines from the left and right images. The cost evaluation function used for scoring utilizes the constraints on the edge angle and edge interval [20]. While the goal of the Viterbi algorithm is to find an optimal match, it is noted that a globally optimal match might, indeed, be suboptimal in the limited context of a single epipolar line. Hence the modified Viterbi algorithm is extended to avoid the premature discarding of suboptimal matches. This extended version maintains a pool of suboptimal matches, which is later filtered by an iterative process that enforces consistency across adjacent epipolar lines. This algorithm too suffers from high computational complexity to be effective in a robotic environment.

Baker and Binford also use the modified Viterbi algorithm in their edge and intensity-based stereo matcher. The matching primitives used in their algorithm are linked edges and ordering constraints are utilized to match them. Matching is restricted to epipolar lines and proceeds in a coarse-to-fine manner. However, a cooperative process discards, based upon the connectivity of edges across adjacent epipolar lines, correspondences that violate global continuity assumptions. Following edge-based matching, a further matching phase is performed on the intensity values from the intervals between paired edges, again using the modified Viterbi algorithm. The result is a complete depth map over the entire scene. Heavy dependence on linked linear edges and epipolar matching may make this approach too fragile to use in a robotic environment.

The algorithm developed by Medioni and Nevatia uses straight line segments extracted by a linear feature extractor [28] as the primitive of stereo matching. Important characteristics of their segment-based stereo approach include the following: they use line segments to make inter-line connectivity implicit in their matcher, one segment is allowed to be matched with more than one segment in the other image to deal with fragmentation that may occur during extraction of these features, and matches are sought over the total extent of epipolar lines in which a given segment appears rather than one epipolar line at a time. The matches are chosen based on an evaluation function that uses a disparity continuity constraint, but does not adhere to an ordering constraint. Their results clearly demonstrate the power of choosing primitives that are semantically richer than individual edge points. They have suggested that some higher-level monocular cues might be required, in addition to line segments, to solve correspondences in complex scenes. Computational times of several minutes are reported for their experiments.

Recently proposed enhancements of stereo approaches include attempts to detect and correct errors committed by stereo matching [26] and integration of feature matching with disparity generation [25]. While accuracy of the results has been improved, both approaches have resulted in a heavy increase in computational time. In addition to the heavy computational requirements of the edge-based approaches, there are several other major difficulties that these approaches encounter in robotic environments. These include issues related to noise immunity, accuracy, and robustness.

IV. REGION-BASED ANALYSIS FOR A HIERARCHICAL STEREO SYSTEM

A practical stereo system for robotic applications should produce a depth map of sufficient detail to accomplish the prescribed robotic task efficiently. The system must also exhibit a high-noise tolerance level for its inputs. It is critical for such a system to employ an accurate, reliable, and efficient module for stereo matching. The choice of the matching primitives will greatly influence the performance of such a matching module. In this section we will introduce the use of homogeneous regions as features in stereo matching. Region-based stereo matching is typically more accurate, reliable, and efficient than edge-based matching. Yet a region-based matcher lacks the capability to generate an accurate disparity map of fine resolution. Generation of an accurate and fine resolution disparity map (and subsequently depth) can be better accomplished using edge-based techniques. Consequently regions and edges both play important and somewhat complementary roles in the binocular stereo process. Therefore it is critical that an efficient and robust stereo system utilizes the most appropriate set of primitives at each stage of the process. It is believed that a hierarchical, multilevel stereo approach that exploits and integrates the power of different primitives at the appropriate stages of the computational process, will be most useful in building an effective stereo system. In such a hierarchical stereo system results of stereo matching from the higher levels of the hierarchy can be used for guidance at the lower level, and disparity maps

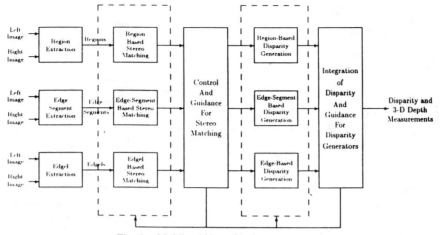

Fig. 1. Multilevel hierarchical stereo system.

generated at each level can be fused to obtain an accurate and fine resolution disparity map.

A schematic of a hierarchical stereo system is presented in Fig. 1. The proposed multilevel system incorporates hierarchical stereo matching as well as hierarchical disparity generation. A system that utilized hierarchy of primitives to solve only the matching problem was presented by Lim and Binford [19]. In our approach we have addressed both matching and disparity generation in a hierarchical framework. The system utilizes primitives from three hierarchical levels. At the highest level are region primitives, followed by edge segments, and at the lowest level are the single pixel-edge elements, edgels. Matching and disparity generation can be performed at three levels, and lower-level processes can utilize results of the higher levels for guidance. This system offers many advantages over those that use only a single primitive for stereo matching and disparity generation. The multilevel hierarchy will greatly reduce mismatches and inconsistencies and, thereby, produce an accurate, globally consistent, and reliable output. Control and guidance mechanisms provide the capability to selectively analyze regions with varying resolution. This selective focusing capability would further enhance its performance by concentrating on critical areas, eliminating the need for detailed examination of the entire image [3]. Note that the complete stereo problem is solved entirely at each level. Obviously their computational requirements differ and the results derived at different levels would differ in accuracy as well as resolution. Multilevel processing also enables the system to generate outputs of only sufficient detail, required for a particular task, and further reduces demands on resources. Such a system will exhibit a high level of adaptability to different robotic tasks, requiring depth information in varying degrees of detail and resolution.

Development of a complete hierarchical stereo system is a complex and challenging task. It requires careful and detailed conceptualization, design, and evaluation of each individual component making up the complete system. Our final objective is to develop such a system. In order to pursue this objective, we have attempted to systematically

conceptualize, design, and test each component separately. Even though development is carried out separately, the components will eventually have to be integrated.

The primary focus of this section is to present the detailed development and evaluation of region-based stereo matching module and disparity generation module associated with the highest level of a hierarchical stereo system. We begin by presenting the rationale for the use of homogeneous regions as primitives for matching and then describe the region-based stereo matcher and disparity generator. Finally with the help of a series of experiments, we evaluate the robustness, accuracy, and efficiency of these modules.

A. Use of Regions as Matching Primitives

As described in Section III-A, two of the main properties sought in an effective stereo-matching primitive are its stability and its descriptive capability to resolve ambiguities. In image analysis there are basically two complimentary approaches for extracting low-level information from images. The first is based on the property of dissimilarity, i.e., edge-based, and the second is based on the utilization of the property of similarity, i.e., region-based [29]. Primitives extracted from either of these approaches can be utilized in a stereo system. The higher semantic content of a region makes it a good candidate for a matching primitive. Also regions will be more stable than those primitives that depend on local gray-level discontinuities such as edges [29], [30]. Thus region-based primitives are more tolerant to noise than edge-based primitives. Furthermore in an image there will be typically fewer regions than edges or zero crossings of the Laplacian of a Gaussian operator. Therefore establishing image correspondences will be more efficient using regions as features, because the number of candidates to be evaluated is greatly reduced. This reduction in the number features along with the region-based primitive's high discrimination power reduces the number of mismatches (false targets) and, therefore, increases the accuracy of matching.

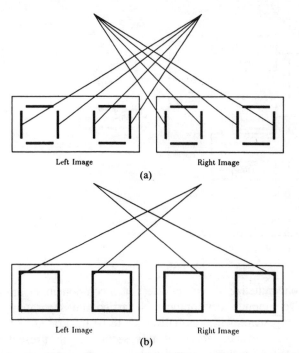

Fig. 2. Resolution of ambiguity in stereo correspondence. (a) Shows various combinations that need to be resolved if edge-segments are used as features. (b) Shows situation when regions are used as features.

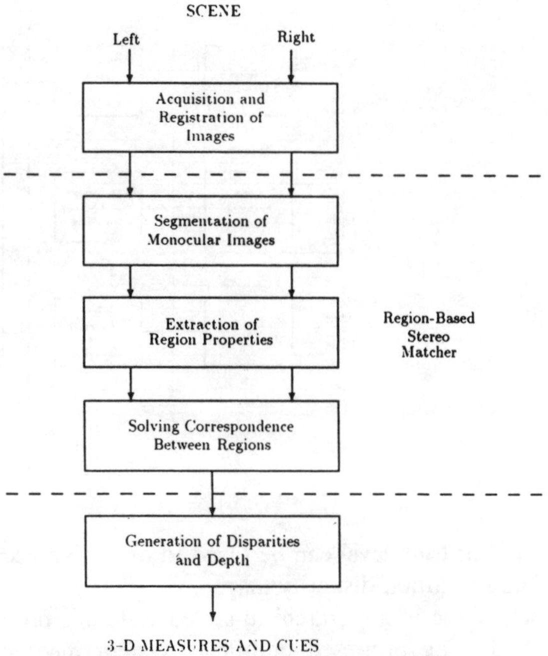

Fig. 3. Region-based analysis for stereo matching and disparity generation.

The improved efficiency and the reduction in the number of mismatches using regions as features in stereo matching can be illustrated with the help of a simple example. Fig. 2(a) shows the horizontal and vertical edges extracted in the stereo image pair of a scene containing two similar square objects. If edge segments are used as features, an attempt to match the four vertical segments in the left image with the similar four segments in the right (Fig. 2(a)) will yield 24 possible combinations. Also if one observes the epipolar constraints, an attempt to match the top two horizontal segments gives rise to two possibilities. The same can be stated for the two bottom segments as well. Thus segment-based matching between the eight segments appearing in each image will lead to a total of $24 \times 2 \times 2 = 96$ combinations, of which only one combination is correct. If individual edge pixels rather than segments are used as features, the total number of combinations will be greatly increased. On the other hand if regions are used as as features, then matching requires solving correspondence among the two square regions, as shown in Fig. 2(b). Therefore when using regions as features there will be fewer features to be matched, and the higher semantic content and reduced number of features will also decrease the number of false targets. Another advantage of using regions in stereo matching is that they make some of the matching constraints (described in Section III-B) implicit or easier to incorporate. Finally the high semantic content of the regions also makes it possible to use a wide range of region representation and description schemes that, in turn, allow the use of a variety of matching techniques. It is therefore believed that region-based stereo will yield a reliable, accurate, and more globally consistent solution efficiently satisfying the constraints of an effective stereo system for robotic applications.

B. Design of a Region-Based Stereo Matcher

The region-based component of a hierarchical stereo system consists of two modules. The region-based matching module solves the correspondence problem, and the second module generates the disparities. The processing sequence of the region-based component is shown in Fig. 3. It includes the following steps.

Step 1) Acquisition and registration of the stereo image pair.
Step 2) Segmentation of the two monocular images.
Step 3) Extraction of the region properties.
Step 4) Solving correspondence between regions.
Step 5) Generation of disparities.

The matching module includes processing Steps 2), 3), and 4), whereas Step 5) corresponds to the disparity generation module. We now present a detailed discussion of these steps.

Two types of imaging geometries have been commonly used in stereo-image acquisition. In type one, the cameras are oriented such that their optical axes converge at a point called the fixation point. The disparities between the image features in this geometry can be either positive or negative. The sign of the disparity depends on the location of the physical surface point (giving rise to the image feature) with respect to the fixation point. For a particular image feature $\mathscr{F}$ in one image, its corresponding feature in the other image, may lie to the left or right of $\mathscr{F}$. Thus search for correspondence needs to be carried out on both sides of $\mathscr{F}$. The second type of camera geometry, known as the parallel axis geometry, employs two cameras whose optical axes are parallel. This geometry can be thought of as having the fixation point at infinity. Here all disparities have the same sign and, hence, the search for correspondence is restricted to only one side. As compared to the convergent axes geometry, parallel axis geometry yields less overlap in the left and right images of the scene being imaged. It is also desirable to maintain the epipolar lines along the horizontal image scan lines in both parallel and convergent axes geometries. Thus registration of left and right images may be required to bring the images into sufficient vertical and rotational alignment in order to satisfy input requirements of the matching module.

The processing step following image acquisition and registration deals with the segmentation of each of the two monocular images separately. Image segmentation refers to the partitioning of an image into meaningful regions. It is important to note that meaningful regions may not necessarily correspond to any physical objects appearing in the scene. Formally given a definition of "uniformity" a segmentation is a partitioning of an image into connected subsets, each of which is uniform, but such that no union of adjacent subsets is uniform [31]. There are two basic approaches to segmentation: the first is based on edge or boundary formation, and the second is based on region formation [29]. Typical region-forming approaches utilize uniformity (or homogeneity) primitives based on such image properties as gray levels, multispectral or color measurements, and texture. There are numerous techniques proposed for segmentation, and a good comprehensive review can be found in reference [29]. For the proposed region-based stereo approach, the choice of a segmentation algorithm is arbitrary. However, the algorithm should be robust and capture the uniformity or homogeneity properties of the region accurately.

In Step 3), the segmented homogeneous regions are further processed to extract various properties of these regions. These properties may include spectral and spatial as well as relational properties. Typical spectral properties may include measurements derived from gray levels recorded in single or multiple channels. Both boundary and region descriptors may be used to describe the spatial properties of regions. Popular boundary descriptors include length, diameter, curvature, and chain codes. Regions may be described by area, perimeter, compactness, major and minor axes, length and width, aspect ratio, moments, texture, and topological descriptors such as Euler numbers. Relational descriptors can be used to describe the structural relationships existing between elements of interest, in this case, the regions. These relationships can be described using relational graphs. The availability of such a wide array of descriptors allows utilization of rich descriptive vocabulary when using regions as features.

Finally in Step 4) correspondence will be resolved based on the similarity between the candidate regions. Regions satisfying a variety of constraints or rules, such as those described in Section II-B, are selected as candidate regions. Solving for correspondence can be accomplished through a variety of matching techniques including, but not limited to, minimum distance classifiers based on a similarity metric, optimization methods, and graph theoretical approaches. Distance-based matching is implicit in many edge-based stereo algorithms that match individual edge pixels based on the similarity of such properties as contrast and orientation of candidates. Typical optimization methods, such as dynamic programming, relaxation techniques, and simulated annealing have been used in solving stereo correspondence [21], [32]–[34]. Recently graph-matching, using a graph isomorphism algorithm, has also been used in stereo vision [35]. The choice of a matching technique is dependent on the properties and representation schemes used in Step 3) for describing the regions, as certain representations support specific matching techniques better than others.

C. Implementation of the Region-Based Modules

In order to verify the performance of the region-based stereo approach, we implemented a region-based matching module and a disparity generation module. Our implementation uses a single camera mounted on a Cincinnati Milacron T^3-726 industrial robot. Stereo image pairs are acquired by moving the robot arm to two locations using parallel-axis geometry with horizontal epipolar lines. The use of a single robot-mounted camera provides a flexible image acquisition system with a variable baseline. Experiments performed indicate that the robot arm could be positioned accurately to guarantee that the acquired images are in sufficient vertical and rotational alignment to satisfy the input requirements of the stereo matcher. Thus no image registration is required.

Image segmentation is accomplished by a region-growing algorithm, which employs a homogeneity criterion based on the mean and the standard deviation of the gray-level values of a region. In addition to segmenting images into regions (or blobs), the segmentor also extracts various spectral and spatial domain properties for each of those segmented regions [36]. These properties include: mean gray level, size (area), minimum enclosing rectangle, centroid, perimeter length, principal axis (PA), width along the PA, height perpendicular to the PA in pixels, and width-to-height (aspect) ratio. Constraints on the size of regions are used to discard small noise regions and large uniform background regions.

Solving correspondences between blobs in the left and right images requires a metric to measure similarity (or dissimilarity). For comparing similarities/dissimilarities between blobs, we have chosen to describe each blob by six region descriptors. The six features chosen as attributes of a blob are: mean gray level, area, perimeter, width, length, and the aspect ratio. These features, except for aspect ratio, are normalized in both left and right images to facilitate matching. The current implementation uses Euclidean distance in the six-dimensional measurement space as the metric of dissimilarity between blobs. Thus the correspondence for a blob among several candidate blobs is found in the measurement space using the minimum distance rule. Candidates are chosen based on epipolar constraints similar to those used by Medioni and Nevatia in their edge-segment based stereo matcher [18], as follows. For each blob, R, in the segmented right image, only those blobs in the left image that lie between the epipolar extent of R and are within the maximum disparity range of the matcher are chosen as the candidates for matching. Of the pool of candidates, the nearest (or least dissimilar) blob, in terms of minimum distance in the measurement space, is selected, and correspondence is established if this minimum distance is less than a preset threshold. No match is reported for blob R, if no blobs in the left image lie within the epipolar extent of R, or no blobs in the left image that lie within the epipolar extent of R are within the preset distance threshold in the measurement space.

Once correspondence is established between a blob in the left image and a blob in the right image, disparity between them is computed to be the displacement (in pixels), along the epipolar line, required to produce the maximum overlap in their spatial extent. Specifically the blob in the left image is translated along the epipolar line towards the left, and the overlap area between the left and right blobs is computed. The overlap area is normalized by dividing it by the area of the larger of the two blobs. The displacement at which this normalized overlap area is a maximum is considered to be the disparity between the two blobs. If this maximum normalized overlap is greater than a preset threshold, the displacement (in pixels) that the left blob was translated is accepted to be the disparity and is assigned to the region of overlap between the two blobs. The range in which a maximum overlap is sought can be computed by using the minimum depth expected in the operating environment and the imaging parameters. Finally the disparities are converted to actual depth measurements, using the imaging and camera parameters. The equations for this conversion are described in Kim and Aggarwal [33].

D. Experimental Evaluations of the Region-Based Analysis Modules

The performance of the region-based stereo component was evaluated by conducting a series of experiments. No specialized lighting was utilized in conducting these experiments, and scenes analyzed were comparable to the types of scenes reported in current stereo literature. The experiments were designed to evaluate specifically the following.

1) Stability of the regions as matching features.
2) Discriminatory power of the measures derived from regions.
3) Accuracy of region-based matching.
4) Efficiency of region-based matching.
5) Accuracy of disparities and depth measurements derived by the region-based approach.

The first experiment consists of a simple scene containing two objects and only two depth levels. Figs. 4 (a)–(b) show a pair of 256×256 stereo images. Of the two objects, the cylindrical jar is taller than the plier. The results of segmentation of the stereo image pair are shown in Figs. 4(c)–(d). Six normalized descriptors were extracted from each blob in left and right segmented images. Of the five blobs found in the segmented left image, blob 1 corresponds to the plier and blob 4 corresponds to the jar. Similarly, in the segmented right image, blob 1 is the plier and blob 3 is the jar. None of the remaining blobs correspond to any physical object and they are not stable across the images. This demonstrates that regions manifested due to the physical composition of the scene tend to be more stable than those regions that arise due to photometric effects. Similar observations are also made in edge-based stereo systems [12].

The dissimilarities between blobs in the right and left segmented images are tabulated in Table I. Though all possible distances are listed in the table, not all entries need to be computed, because the epipolar constraint eliminates several comparisons. The relatively small dissimilarities, as opposed to other entries in the table, between the left blob 1 and the right blob 1, and the left blob 4 and the right blob 3, indicate the discriminatory capability of regions as matching primitives. The highlighted entries denote the correct match among the candidates. The computed correspondence and the disparity measures are shown in Table II. The minimum distance rule is able to correctly establish correspondences. Disparities indicate that the cylindrical object is indeed closer to the viewer than the plier. A 3-D plot of the resulting disparity map is shown in Fig. 5.

For the second experiment, we utilize a scene comprised of a number of industrial parts. They include a rectangular box, a circular jar, a valve, and a plier. The scene has four distinct depth levels. The 256×256 stereo image pair, acquired from a distance of about 1.3 feet, is shown in Figs. 6 (a)–(b). The results of segmentation are shown in Figs. 6(c)–(d). Normalized descriptors for each segmented blob in the left and right images were calculated. Pairwise dissimilarities between the blobs are shown in Table III. Dissimilarities indicate that regions possess sufficient information to identify corresponding blobs. The correspondences established, based upon the minimum distance rule and the disparity obtained using normalized overlap ratio, are shown in Table IV. Once again, the correspondence is solved correctly, and disparities agree with the actual depth levels. The disparity map generated by the region-based approach is shown in Fig. 7. These disparities are then converted to actual depth. The computed distance, measured distance, and percentage error for each of the objects is tabulated in Table V. The results are quite accurate.

The third experiment consists of a scene containing doughnut-shaped objects (rings) on a table top. A pair of 256×256 stereo images, acquired from about 1.3 feet from the table top, is shown in Figs. 8(a)–(b). The smaller ring with lighter shade is supported by two darker rings. These

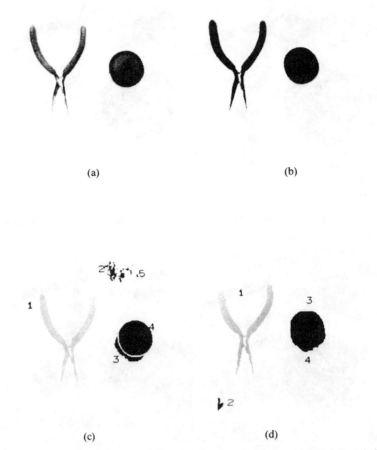

Fig. 4. Simple scene with two objects. The 256×256 stereo image pair is shown in (a) left and (b) right. Results of segmentation are shown in (c) and (d).

TABLE I
SIMPLE SCENE: SIMILARITY MEASURES BETWEEN DETECTED BLOBS

Blob ID Left Image	Blob ID Right Image			
	1	2	3	4
1	**0.07**	1.82	1.05	1.44
2	1.64	0.58	1.06	0.46
3	1.26	0.81	0.73	0.41
4	1.06	1.24	**0.03**	0.96
5	1.46	0.82	0.98	0.56

Fig. 5. 3-D disparity map for simple scene.

TABLE II
SIMPLE SCENE: CORRESPONDENCES AND DISPARITIES
BETWEEN DETECTED BLOBS

Blob ID Left Image	Blob ID Right Image	Similarity Measure	Overlap Ratio	Disparity (in pixels)
1	1	0.07	0.90	41
4	3	0.03	0.90	46

rings are of same height. The fourth ring is much taller (about three times) than the other rings. Thus this scene contains four different depth levels. The results of segmentation are shown in Figs. 8(c)–(d). The correspondences and disparities computed are shown in Table VI. The table indicates that correspondences were established accurately

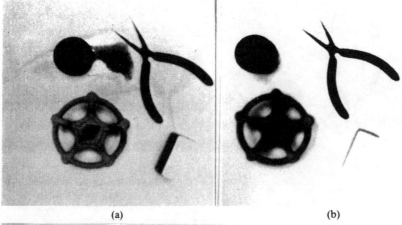

(a) (b)

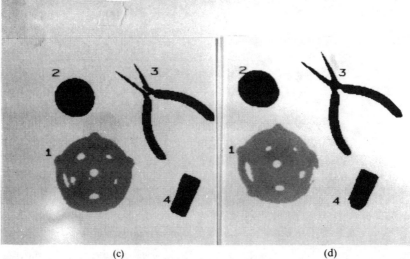

(c) (d)

Fig. 6. Scene composed of industrial parts: The 256×256 stereo image pair is shown in (a) left and (b) right. Results of segmentation are shown in (c) and (d).

TABLE III
INDUSTRIAL PARTS: SIMILARITY MEASURES BETWEEN
DETECTED BLOBS

Blob ID Left Image	Blob ID Right Image			
	1	2	3	4
1	**0.10**	1.02	0.95	1.35
2	0.97	**0.09**	1.07	0.77
3	0.84	1.10	**0.35**	1.42
4	1.37	0.87	1.32	**0.11**

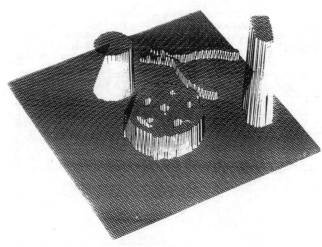

Fig. 7. 3-D disparity map for scene composed of industrial parts.

TABLE IV
INDUSTRIAL PARTS: CORRESPONDENCES AND DISPARITIES

Blob ID Left Image	Blob ID Right Image	Similarity Measure	Overlap Ratio	Disparity (in pixels)
1	1	0.10	0.91	61
2	2	0.09	0.91	64
3	3	0.35	0.77	59
4	4	0.11	0.87	69

for all of the blobs that were matched. One of the dark rings that supports the smaller ring is erroneously assigned the same disparity as the smaller ring. Disparities assigned to all other rings were consistent with their heights (Fig. 9). An analysis of depth measurements is tabulated in Table VII.

318

(a)   (b)

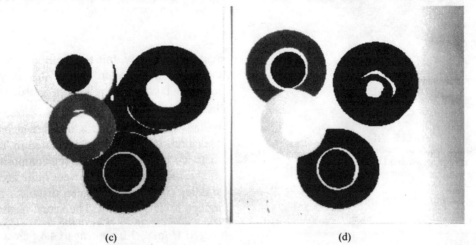

(c)   (d)

Fig. 8. Scene composed of four rings. The 256×256 stereo image pair is shown in (a) left and (b) right. Results of segmentation are shown in (c) and (d).

TABLE V
INDUSTRIAL PARTS: COMPARISON OF COMPUTED
AND MEASURED DISTANCES

Object	Actual Distance	Computed Distance	% Error
Plier	17.25"	17.80"	-3.2%
Valve	16.25"	17.22"	-5.9%
Jar	15.75"	16.41"	-4.2%
Box	15.625"	15.23"	2.5%

TABLE VI
RINGS: CORRESPONDENCES AND DISPARITIES

Blob ID Left Image	Blob ID Right Image	Similarity Measure	Overlap Ratio	Disparity (in pixels)
1	2	0.04	0.94	33
2	1	0.15	0.87	34
3	3	0.05	0.92	32
4	4	0.04	0.93	34
5	5	0.03	0.95	32
7	6	0.04	0.93	37

The fourth scene contains a test panel, used in our testbed, for robotics experiments. The panel contains typical instruments commonly found in an industrial environment (Fig. 10). These include analog meters, digital meters, valves, a slider control, push-button switches, etc. The input stereo image pair and the segmented images are shown in Fig. 11. This scene was imaged from about 2.5 feet from the panel. The panel contains many objects and several of them are quite similar in appearance. Also there are distinct depth levels associated with these objects. A total of 17 regions in the left image and 21 in the right image were extracted. Matching results indicate that correspondences were established correctly for most of the blobs associated with various objects. A total of 12 blobs

were matched, and all of them were correct. All but one object mounted on the panel were successfully matched. Two identical LCD meters at the bottom of the panel seem to confuse the matcher, as there are no ordering constraints in the current implementation. Thus only one LCD was correctly matched. This experiment clearly demonstrates the robustness of the stereo matcher. The depth map generated by the region-based approach is shown in Fig. 12. Finally the computed distances, measured distances and percentage error for selected objects are presented in Table VIII. The disparities generated provided depth measurements within about ±2.5 percent of the actual depths.

Fig. 9. 3-D disparity map for scene composed of four rings.

Fig. 10. Experimental set-up showing robot mounted camera and test panel with variety of displays, meters, valves, controls, and switches.

TABLE VII
RINGS: COMPARISON OF COMPUTED
AND MEASURED DISTANCES

Object	Actual Distance	Computed Distance	% Error
Table Top	17.50"	17.91"	-2.3%
Two Dark Rings	16.625"	17.38" & 16.86"	-4.5% & -1.4%
Small Ring	16.00"	16.86"	-5.4%
Single Ring	15.00"	15.19"	-3.3%

The fifth and the final experiment analyzes a scene of a circuit board with numerous integrated circuit chips (ICs). Figs. 13 (a)–(b) show a pair of 256×256 stereo images, which were acquired from a distance of about 2.2 feet. This experiment poses many challenges to the stereo matcher. First IC's are mounted very densely on the circuit board, which makes region extraction difficult. Second there are many similar objects that may confuse the stereo matcher. And finally while there are only a few depth levels in the scene, depth variation among them is quite small. For example the height difference between the larger IC's and the smaller IC's is only approximately 0.25 in. Thus the stereo system would be required to resolve depths to 1/4 of an inch for objects lying about 2 ft away. The result of segmentation on the stereo pair is shown in Figs. 13(c)–(d). There are 94 regions extracted from the left image and 104 regions from the right. While not all IC's are extracted as individual regions (e.g., notice that in the segmented left image the cluster of large IC's closer to the right edge of the board was extracted as one composite region), this effect appears consistently in both images. The region-based matcher found correspondences for 40 blobs and all of them were correct. While matching accuracy was perfect, slightly less than half of the extracted regions were matched. The disparity map for the scene is shown in Fig. 14. It indicates that all larger chips were

mapped correctly, but the method had difficulty mapping some of the smaller chips. This is partly due to the compact layout of the circuit board. Dense mounting of the chips makes it difficult to extract "meaningful" regions. The actual depth measurements are compared to measured depth and are tabulated in Table IX. While the distance measurements for the composite regions A and B in the segmented images were quite accurate, many of the smaller chips were assigned distances ranging from 27.02 inches to 25.57 inches. The actual measured distance however was 26.75 inches. Thus the error for smaller chips ranged from -1.0 percent to 4.4 percent.

Matching accuracies of the region-based matcher for the aforementioned experiments are summarized in Table X. In each of the experiments, segmentation performed quite well, and regions associated with the physical objects or their parts were successfully extracted. The six simple and easy-to-extract descriptors proved sufficient for measuring region similarities. Thus the minimum distance rule was able to solve correspondences satisfactorily. Table X shows that the region-based matcher performed perfectly in each experiment. The circuit board experiment shows that while the accuracy of matching remains perfect, small regions may be difficult to match. It should, however, be noted that a high degree of accuracy is more important than a high number of matches. Thus the matching results indicate a high degree of confidence. These experiments also showed that correct matches yield very high overlap ratios. The final analysis of depth measurements indicates that the disparities generated, based upon the normalized overlap ratios, were adequate to provide reasonably high accuracies (± 5 percent) in deriving the distance measures. The accuracies of depth measurements for all the experiments are summarized in Table XI.

The disparities generated and the distances computed are generally quite satisfactory; however small regions and perspective effects in viewing make the assignment of disparity to overlapping areas based upon normalized overlap ratio, limited in accuracy. Therefore, improved methods may be needed to generate finer disparity maps.

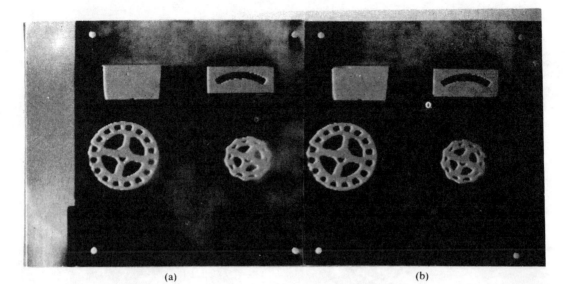

(a)   (b)

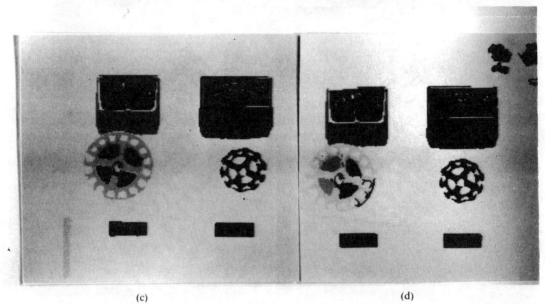

(c)   (d)

Fig. 11.   Scene composed of test panel. The 256×256 stereo image pair is shown in (a) left and (b) right. Results of segmentation are shown in (c) and (d).

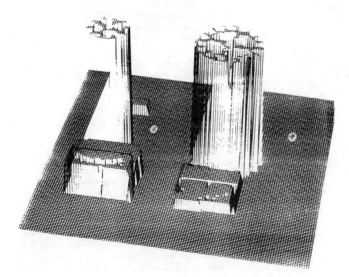

Fig. 12.   3-D disparity map for test panel scene.

TABLE VIII
PANEL: COMPARISON OF COMPUTED AND MEASURED DISTANCES

Object	Actual Distance	Computed Distance	% Error
LCD	31.25"	31.44"	-0.6%
Large Valve	27.125"	26.95"	0.6%
Small Valve	27.325"	26.95"	1.4%
Right Meter Base	30.875"	30.8"	0.2%
Left Meter Base	30.875"	31.4"	-1.7%

A multilevel, hierarchical disparity generation module, based on matching results of both edge features as well as regions, seemingly offers attractive features.

Finally a practical stereo system must also address the issue of efficiency. A multiuser VAX 11/785 computing environment was used in the aforementioned experiments. The computational times for the experiments are summarized in Table XII. Processing time of about a minute for these experiments without any optimized or specialized

321

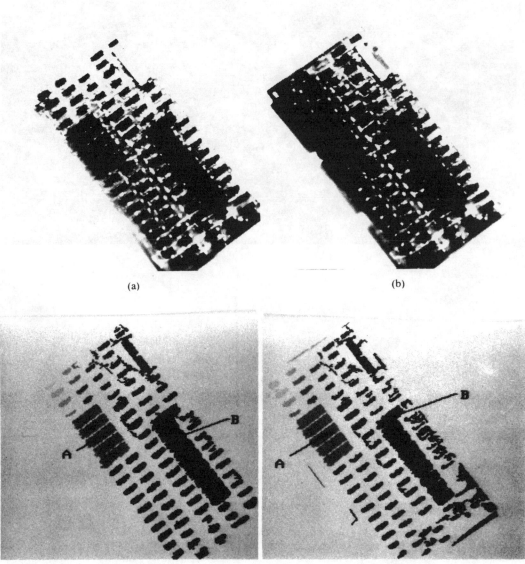

(a)   (b)

(c)   (d)

Fig. 13. Scene containing circuit board. The 256×256 stereo image pair is shown in (a) left and (b) right. Results of segmentation are shown in (c) and (d).

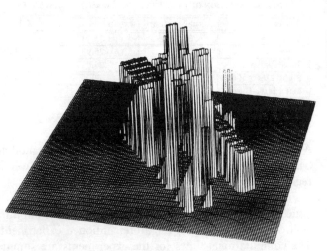

Fig. 14. 3-D disparity map for circuit board scene.

TABLE IX
CIRCUIT BOARD: COMPARISON OF COMPUTED
AND MEASURED DISTANCES

Object	Actual Distance	Computed Distance	% Error
Region A	26.50"	26.28"	0.8%
Region B	26.50"	27.02"	-1.9%
Small Chips(see text)	26.75"	27.03" ~ 25.57"	-1.0% ~ -4.4%

TABLE X
ACCURACY OF REGION-BASED
STEREO MATCHING

Experiment	No. of Blobs in Left Image	No. of Blobs in Right Image	Number of Blobs Matched	Number of Matching Errors Commited	Accuracy Of Matching (%)
Simple scene	5	4	2	None	100
Industrial parts	4	4	4	None	100
Rings	7	7	6	None	100
Panel	17	21	12	None	100
Circuit board	94	104	10	None	100

TABLE XI
Accuracy of Depth Measurements

Experiment	Approximate Imaging Distance (feet)	Absoulte %Error in Depth (Max.-Min.)
Industrial parts	1.2	6.0% ~ 2.6%
Rings	1.3	5.4% ~ 1.4%
Panel	2.5	1.8% ~ 0.3%
Circuit board	2.2	4.4% ~ 0.8%

TABLE XII
Efficiency of Region-Based Stereo Module

Experiment	No. of Blobs in Left Image	No. of Blobs in Right Image	Maximum Disparity	Processing Time (Seconds)
Simple scene	5	4	50	55.87
Industrial parts	4	4	75	71.55
Rings	7	7	40	86.8
Panel	17	21	75	84.60
Circuit board	94	104	45	85.14

modules, supports the promise of a region-based stereo approach for on-line robotic tasks. The scenes analyzed the quite comparable to the types of scenes appearing in current stereo literature, but we are unable to quantitatively analyze the accuracy of the derived measurements against others, because only a few studies have presented data on actual depth measurements. Also different imaging parameters would make such a comparison difficult. However the accuracy of about ±5 percent achieved by the region-based approach, within a fraction of the time that most existing stereo algorithms require, demonstrates the practical utility of the region-based approach.

V. Conclusion

In this paper we have discussed issues related to the design and development of a binocular stereo approach for a robot vision system. We presented the characteristics of the application domain and identified the needs and goals of a practical depth extraction system for a vision system for robotic applications. The binocular stereo approach offers an attractive, passive means for deriving detailed depth maps for a scene without using specialized illumination or energy sources. Yet high computational costs and rigid input requirements have prevented stereo approaches from being adopted for practical robotic applications. For effective use in this application domain, a stereo system must seek a balance between input flexibility, output sufficiency, and computational complexity. At the heart of a binocular stereo approach lies the task of stereo matching. In this paper we emphasized the importance of semantic content and stability of the primitive used in this matching and introduce the use of homogeneous regions as features in stereo matching. Considering the fewer number of features and the higher discrimination power of the primitive, the region-based matcher is more efficient and accurate

than those using edge-based primitives. A region-based matching technique can utilize both local and global information and thus yield a more globally consistent solution. However while the use of regions makes stereo matching more accurate, reliable, and efficient than edge-based matching, region based matching processes typically yield coarse disparity maps. The generation of accurate and finer resolution disparity maps (and subsequently depth measurements) can be better accomplished using edge-based techniques. Both regions and edges play important, but somewhat complementary, roles in the binocular stereo process. It is therefore critical that an efficient and robust stereo system utilize the most appropriate set of primitives at each stage of the process. In this paper a hierarchical stereo approach that exploits and integrates the power of different primitives at appropriate stages of the stereo process is proposed. We presented several experiments to evaluate the performance of a region-based stereo matcher and a straightforward disparity and depth generation module. It is shown that the approach is efficient, robust, and successful in generating depth measurements within ±5 percent accuracy.

An effective stereo system for robotic applications should include a component that relies on rich surface texture as well as one that relies on the uniformity of surface details. While more research is required before such a system can be engineered, the direction suggested in this research offers promise. For dealing with typical robotic scenes, a multilevel, hierarchical system, utilizing a hierarchy of primitives appears to be suitable. In such a system, results of stereo matching at higher levels of the hierarchy can be used for guidance at the lower levels, and disparity maps generated at each level can be fused to obtain an accurate and fine resolution disparity map. Such a system would also provide the capability to selectively analyze regions with varying resolutions.

Acknowledgment

The software developed by Chu Xin Chen for segmentation was useful in our studies. Final manuscript preparation was done by Mrs. Janet Smith. We also thank the reviewers for many insightful and valuable comments.

References

[1] A. C. Kak and J. S. Albus, *Handbook of Industrial Robotics*, ch. on "Sensors for intelligent robots." New York: John Wiley, 1985.
[2] K. S. Fu, R. C. Gonzalez, and C. S. G. Lee, *Robotics: Control, Sensing, Vision, and Intelligence*. New York: McGraw-Hill, 1987.
[3] H. K. Nishihara, "Practical real-time imaging stereo matcher," *Optical Engineering*, vol. 23, pp. 536–545, Sept. 1984.
[4] H. K. Nishihara and T. Poggio, "Stereo vision for robotics," in *First Int. Symp. Robotics Res.*, IEEE Press, 1983, pp. 489–505.
[5] R. A. Jarvis, "A perspective on range finding techniques for computer vision," *IEEE Trans. Pattern Anal. Machine Intell.*, vol. PAMI-5, pp. 122–139, Mar. 1983.
[6] A. C. Kak, *Handbook of Industrial Robotics*, ch. on "Depth perception for robots." New York: John Wiley, 1985.

[7] G. Stockman, S. Chen, G. Hu, and N. Shrikhande, "Recognition of rigid objects using structured light," in *Proc. 1987 IEEE Int. Conf. Syst. Man Cybern.*, Aug. 1987, pp. 877–883.

[8] B. K. P. Horn, *Robot Vision*. Cambridge, MA: MIT Press, 1986.

[9] D. H. Ballard and C. M. Brown, *Computer Vision*. Englewood Cliffs, NJ: Prentice-Hall, 1982.

[10] K. Ikeuchi, "Determining surface orientations of specular surfaces by using the photometric stereo method," *IEEE Trans. Pattern Anal. Machine Intell.*, vol. PAMI-3, pp. 661–669, Nov. 1981.

[11] R. C. Jain and A. K. Jain, "Review of the NSF range sensing workshop," in *Comput. Vision Pattern Recognition Conf.*, Ann Arbor, MI, May 1988.

[12] S. T. Barnard and M. A. Fischler, "Computational stereo," *Computing Surveys*, vol. 14, pp. 553–572, Dec. 1982.

[13] D. Marr and T. Poggio, "A computational theory of human stereo vision," *Proc. Royal Soc. London*, vol. B 204, 1979, pp. 301–328.

[14] B. Julesz, "Binocular depth perception of computer-generated patterns," *Bell System Tech. J.*, vol. 39, pp. 1125–1162, 1960.

[15] ——, *Foundation of Cyclopean Perception*. Chicago, IL: Univ. of Chicago Press, 1971.

[16] W. E. L. Grimson, "Computational experiments with a feature-based stereo algorithm," *IEEE Trans. Pattern Anal. Machine Intell.*, vol. PAMI-7, pp. 17–34, Jan. 1985.

[17] H. H. Baker and T. O. Binford, "Depth from edge and intensity-based stereo," in *Proc. 7th Int. Joint Conf. AI*, 1981, pp. 631–636.

[18] G. Medioni and R. Nevatia, "Segment-based stereo matching," *Comput. Vision, Graphics Image Processing*, vol. 31, pp. 2–18, July 1985.

[19] H. S. Lim and T. O. Binford, "Stereo correspondence: A hierarchical approach," in *DARPA Image Understanding Workshop*, Los Angeles, CA, 1987.

[20] R. D. Arnold and T. O. Binford, "Geometric constraints in stereo vision," in *Image Processing for Missile Guidance*, pp. 281–292, SPIE, 1980.

[21] R. D. Arnold, *Automated Stereo Perception*. Ph.D. dissertation, Dept. of Computer Science, Stanford University, CA, 1983.

[22] J. E. W. Mayhew and J. P. Frisby, "Psychophysical and computational studies towards a theory of human stereopsis," *Artificial Intell.*, vol. 17, pp. 349–385, 1981.

[23] S. B. Pollard, J. E. W. Mayhew, and J. P. Frisby, "PMF: A stereo correspondence algorithm using a disparity gradient limit," *Perception*, vol. 14, pp. 449–470, 1981.

[24] W. E. L. Grimson, *From Images to Surfaces: A Computational Study of the Human Early Visual System*. Cambridge, MA: MIT Press, 1981.

[25] W. Hoff and N. Ahuja, "Surface from stereo: Integrating feature matching, disparity estimation, and contour detection," *IEEE Trans. Pattern Anal. Machine Intell.*, vol. PAMI-11, pp. 121–136, Feb. 1989.

[26] R. Mohan, G. Medioni, and R. Nevatia, "Stereo error detection, correction, and evaluation," *IEEE Trans. Pattern Anal. Machine Intell.*, vol. PAMI-11, pp. 113–120, Feb. 1989.

[27] G. D. Forney Jr., "The Viterbi algorithm," *Proc. IEEE*, vol. 61, Mar. 1973, pp. 268–278.

[28] R. Nevatia and K. R. Babu, "Linear feature extraction and description," *Comput. Vision Graphics Image Processing*, vol. 13, pp. 257–269, June 1980.

[29] A. Rosenfeld and A. C. Kak, *Digital Picture Processing*, vol. 2. Orlando, FL: Academic Press, 1982.

[30] R. Nevatia, *Machine Perception*. Englewood Cliffs, NJ: Prentice-Hall, 1982.

[31] T. Pavlidis, *Structural Pattern Recognition*. New York: Springer, 1977.

[32] Y. Ohta and T. Kanade, "Stereo by intra- and inter-scanline search using dynamic programming," *IEEE Trans. Pattern Anal. Machine Intell.*, vol. PAMI-7, pp. 139–154, Mar. 1985.

[33] Y. C. Kim and J. K. Aggarwal, "Positioning three-dimensional objects using stereo images," *IEEE J. Robotics Automation*, vol. RA-3, pp. 361–373, Aug. 1987.

[34] S. T. Barnard, "A stochastic approach to stereo vision," Tech. Rep. 373, SRI International, Menlo Park, CA 94025, Apr. 1986.

[35] N. M. Nasrabadi, Y. Liu, and J. Chiang, "Stereo vision correspondence using a multichannel graph matching technique," in *Proc. 1988 IEEE Int. Conf. Robotics Automation*, Apr. 1988, pp. 1804–1809.

[36] M. M. Trivedi, C. Chen, and S. B. Marapane, "Vision system for robotic inspections," *Computer*, vol. 22, no. 6, pp. 91–97, June 1989. Special issue on Autonomous Intelligent Machines.

Suresh B. Marapane is a doctoral student in electrical and computer engineering at the University of Tennessee, Knoxville. He earned the B.S. and M.S. degrees, both in electrical and computer engineering from Louisiana State University.

His research interests include computer vision, robotics, and concurrent computing. He is a member of Phi Kappa Phi and Eta Kappa Nu, and a student member of SPIE.

Mohan M. Trivedi (S'76–M'79–SM'86) for photograph and biography please see page 1335 of this TRANSACTIONS.

Shape from Texture: Integrating Texture-Element Extraction and Surface Estimation

DOROTHEA BLOSTEIN, MEMBER, IEEE, AND NARENDRA AHUJA, SENIOR MEMBER, IEEE

Abstract—A perspective view of a slanted textured surface shows systematic changes in the density, area, and aspect-ratio of texture elements. These apparent changes in texture element properties can be analyzed to recover information about the physical layout of the scene. However, in practice it is difficult to identify texture elements, especially in images where the texture elements are partially occluded or are themselves textured at a finer scale. To solve this problem, it is necessary to integrate the extraction of texture elements with the recognition of scene layout. We present a method for identifying texture elements while simultaneously recovering the orientation of textured surfaces. A multiscale region detector, based on measurements in a $\nabla^2 G$ (Laplacian-of-Gaussian) scale-space, is used to construct a set of candidate texture elements. True texture elements are selected from the set of candidate texture elements by finding the planar surface that best predicts the observed areas of the candidate texture elements. Results are shown for a variety of natural textures, including waves, flowers, rocks, clouds, and dirt clods.

Index Terms—Integration, multiscale structure, natural textures, perspective view, region detection, shape from texture, surface orientation, texture elements, texture gradients, texture homogeneity, three-dimensional vision.

I. INTRODUCTION

TEXTURE variation due to projective distortion provides important cues for recovering the three-dimensional structure of the surfaces visible in an image [11]. A uniformly-textured surface undergoes two types of projective distortions during the imaging process. Firstly, an increase in the distance from the surface to the viewer causes a uniform compression of increasingly large areas of surface onto a fixed area of image. Secondly, foreshortening (due to the angle between the surface and the image plane) causes an anisotropic compression of the texture. These texture variations provide information about the relative distances and orientations of the textured surfaces in an image.

A primary goal of the work reported in this paper is to demonstrate the feasibility of extracting useful measures of texture gradients from images of natural scenes. A ma-

jor challenge in texture analysis is to identify texture scale consistently. Natural surfaces exhibit a rich hierarchy of textures and subtextures. All texture measurements are prone to distortion due to the presence of subtexture, since the imaging process captures more subtexture details for close texture samples than for distant ones. As discussed in Section II-A-1, existing shape-from-texture algorithms do not address the problem of scale. The algorithms presented here provide good surface-orientation estimates even in the face of significant sub- and supertexture.

A. Texels and Texture Gradients

The term *texel*, short for *texture element*, denotes the repetitive unit of which a texture is composed. "Texel" refers to the physical texture element in the real world as well as to the appearance of the texture element in the image. In cases where the distinction must be made, we use the phrases *physical texel* versus *image texel*. Distance and foreshortening changes alter the image texel, but not the physical texel.

Projective distortion affects many texture features, and hence gives rise to a variety of texture gradients. Consider first the idealized texture of Fig. 1(a): a planar surface covered with nonoverlapping circular disks of constant size. The disks project as ellipses in the image. The major axis of each ellipse is perpendicular to the tilt,[1] whereas the minor axis is parallel with the tilt. Scanning the image from bottom to top (in the direction of tilt), the apparent size of the major axes decreases linearly, due to increasing distance from the viewer (the *perspective gradient*). However, the apparent size of the minor axes decreases quadratically: in addition to the distance scaling, the minor axes are foreshortened. Thus the eccentricity of the ellipses increases in the tilt direction (the *aspect-ratio gradient*). Similarly, the area of the ellipses decreases fastest in the direction of tilt (the *area gradient*). This is accompanied by an increase in the density of the ellipses (the *density gradient*). In this idealized texture, the uniformity in the size, shape and placement of the texture elements leads to pronounced texture gradients.

Manuscript received September 15, 1988; revised January 30, 1989. Recommended for acceptance by A. K. Jain. This work was supported by the Air Force Office of Scientific Research under Grant AFOSR 86-0009 and by the Eastman Kodak Company.

D. Blostein was with the Coordinated Science Laboratory, University of Illinois, Urbana, IL 61801. She is now with the Department of Computing and Information Science, Queen's University, Kingston, Ont. K7L 3N6, Canada.

N. Ahuja is with the Coordinated Science Laboratory and the Department of Electrical and Computer Engineering, University of Illinois, Urbana, IL 61801.

IEEE Log Number 8929956.

[1]We express surface orientation in terms of two angles, *slant* and *tilt* [23]. Slant, ranging from 0° to 90°, is the angle between the surface and the image plane. Tilt, ranging from 0° to 360°, is the direction in which the surface normal projects in the image; a tilt of 0° indicates that distance to the viewed surface increases fastest toward the right side of the image. The synthetic textures shown in Fig. 1(a) illustrate the definition of slant and tilt.

Reprinted from *IEEE Transactions on Pattern Analysis and Machine Intelligence*, Volume 11, Number 12, December 1989, pages 1233-1251. Copyright © 1989 by The Institute of Electrical and Electronics Engineers, Inc. All rights reserved.

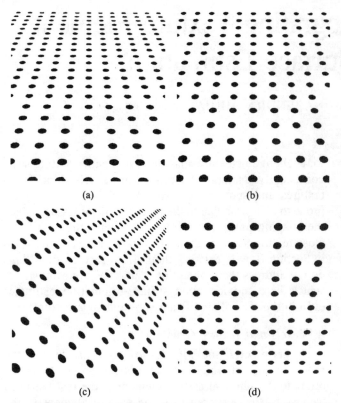

Fig. 1. Synthetic textures illustrating various slants and tilts. Slant is the angle between the textured surface and the image plane. Tilt is the direction in which the surface normal projects in the image. (a) Slant 60°, tilt 90°. (b) Slant 50°, tilt 90°. (c) Slant 60°, tilt 45°. (d) Slant 45°, tilt 270°.

Natural textures are much less regular than the idealized texture of Fig. 1(a); therefore the texture gradients are not as easily observed. Natural textures display considerable variability of texel size, shape, coloration and density. Physical texels are typically three-dimensional, unlike the disks portrayed in Fig. 1(a). Highlights, shadows, and occlusions between texels result. Also, physical texels have a complex structure. In contrast to a uniform synthetic disk, a physical texel changes in appearance as the distance to the camera decreases: more subtexture is visible for the nearby texels than for the distant texels. Supertexture regions arise when small image texels, corresponding to distant physical texels, blur into larger regions of relatively uniform gray level. These factors make it difficult to identify texture elements and extract texture gradients from real images.

The importance of various texture gradients has been studied extensively in the psychology literature (see, for example, [7], [19], [21], [22]). Vickers [24] was among the first to advocate an approach involving accumulation of evidence from multiple texture gradients. Cutting and Millard [9] attempt to quantify the relative importance of various texture gradients. They test human subjects on synthetically generated textures, which are designed to contain only a subset of the normally-occurring texture gradients. Experimental results show that for slant judgements of flat surfaces the perspective and density gradients are more important than the aspect-ratio gradient,

whereas in the perception of curved surfaces the aspect-ratio gradient is dominant, with perspective and density gradients having little impact.

II. THE INFERENCE OF SURFACE SHAPE FROM TEXTURE GRADIENTS

We now turn to a discussion of the basic requirements for a system that infers surface-shape from texture gradients. In Section II-A we argue that correct measurement of texture gradients requires explicit identification of image texels, especially when textures show three-dimensional relief, when texels exhibit significant subtexture, or when it is unknown *a priori* which texture gradients carry surface-shape information. In Section II-B we address the problem of texel identification. Texture elements cannot be identified in isolated image areas since texels are defined only by the repetitive nature of the texture as a whole. Therefore, the identification of texture elements is best done in parallel with the estimation of the shape of the textured surface.

A. The Importance of Texel Identification

The extraction of texels is an essential step in measuring texture gradients, because it permits correct analysis of textures containing subtexture. Explicit texel identification also provides the basis for a unified treatment of the various texture gradients (area gradient, density gradient, aspect-ratio gradient) that may be present in an image. Previous researchers have avoided texel identification because it is quite difficult to do in real images.[2] Instead, indirect methods are used to estimate texel features. We give below several examples of such methods, and indicate why these methods may give erroneous results.

1) Previous Work: Most previous shape-from-texture algorithms use indirect methods to estimate texel features, by making some assumptions about the nature of texture elements. For example, texel density may be estimated by measuring edge density, under the assumption that all detected edges correspond to the borders of texture elements [1],[3] [2], [14], [20]. Alternatively, texture elements may be assumed to have uniform edge direction histograms; surface orientation can then be estimated from any deviations from isotropy observed in the distribution of edge directions [10], [13], [26]. However, the directional-isotropy assumption is very restrictive; for example, it does not hold true in images containing elongated texels such as waves. Texture coarseness and directionality may be characterized using Fourier domain measurements [3], ignoring the effect of super- and subtextures. Various researchers [12], [15], [16] have developed

[2]Ohta *et al.* [18] use the observed areas of pairs of texels to obtain vanishing points. However, the method has been tested only on synthetic texture images. The problem of extracting texels from natural images is not addressed.

[3]The theoretical analysis in this paper is based on texel area. In application to real images, edge-density is used instead, under the assumption that the edge detector finds texel boundaries.

algorithms to analyze textures containing parallel and perpendicular lines. Most natural textures are too irregular to be analyzed in this way.

All of these methods may encounter problems when applied to complex natural textures seen under natural lighting conditions. Since texels are not identified and explicitly dealt with, it becomes difficult to distinguish between responses due to texels and those due to other image features, such as subtexture. It appears to be necessary to recognize the texture elements before the various measures can be computed as intended.

Consider, for example, methods based on measuring edge density. If these algorithms are applied to edges produced by an edge-detector, the measurements are made inaccurate by contributions from subtexture and supertexture edges. Fig. 2(a)–(c), which shows the response of an edge detector to several texture images,[4] illustrates that it would be incorrect to interpret all of the detected edges as boundaries of texture-elements. Additional edges result from subtexture; these edges are not artifacts of this particular edge detector, since they are clearly present in the original images. Many natural textures have a hierarchical physical structure that causes observed edge density to be nearly constant throughout the image: edges from subtexture and subsubtexture are observed to whatever detail the camera resolution permits.

In order to measure edge-density as intended by [2] and [14], it is necessary to eliminate subtexture edges. This cannot simply be done by applying a global threshold, since the contrast of texels far from the camera is comparable to the contrast of subtexture features in the foreground. Aloimonos [2] distinguishes between a ''strong segmentation'' (finding texels) and a ''weak segmentation'' (finding edges, where the edges are supposed to be texel boundaries), and states that weak segmentation is easy to obtain (apply any general-purpose edge detector). We argue that correct weak segmentation is not possible without simultaneously performing a strong segmentation: in order to eliminate all edges except those that arise from texel boundaries, one has to in effect identify the texels.

2) Multiple Texture Gradients: Explicit texel identification offers an additional advantage: texels provide a unifying framework for examination of the various texture gradients (such as gradients of apparent texel area, aspect ratio, density etc.) that may be present in an image. A given image may exhibit a combination of texture gradients. In general, the accuracy of the surface information obtainable from these gradients varies from image to image.[5] Since it is not known in advance which texture gra-

dients are useful for determining the three-dimensional orientation of surfaces, a shape-from-texture system should evaluate the information content of different types of gradients in a given image, and use an appropriate mix of these gradients for surface estimation.

B. Integration of Texel Identification and Surface-Shape Estimation

Texel identification is difficult because texels have tremendously varied shapes, sizes and gray-level characteristics. A texel cannot be identified in isolation, since texels are only defined by the repetitive nature of the texture as a whole. In order to determine if an image region is a texel, it is necessary to test if the region has properties consistent with the properties of many other image texels, i.e. whether the image region is part of a *texture field*.

We use the term *texture field* (or *field of texels*) to denote a collection of image texels that exhibit one or more consistent texture gradients. Consistency is defined with respect to a perspective view of a given surface. It is not uncommon for a single image to contain several texture fields. First, many images are composed of closely associated bright and dark texture fields which arise from lighting effects. For example, the aerial view of houses in Fig. 5(a) contains a field of bright texels composed of the houses and a field of dark texels composed of the shadows cast by the houses. Second, it is possible for physically separated textured surfaces to be spatially interleaved in an image. This is strikingly illustrated by the birds-over-water image shown in Fig. 7(a). Finally, the same physical surface may contain different texture fields: an aerial view of a residential neighborhood shows one texture field consisting of houses and another texture field consisting of trees.

Texels can only be identified in the context of a texture field, where consistent texture gradients must exist across the whole field. The consistency of a texture gradient can only be evaluated for a particular surface shape and orientation. Thus, texel identification must be combined with surface estimation.

C. Overview

Motivated by the above discussion, we now summarize the requirements for an ideal shape-from-texture algorithm, and the extent to which our work meets these requirements. Many open problems remain.

---

[4]We use an edge operator described by Nevatia and Babu [17]. Six 5-by-5 edge masks at different orientations are used; the mask giving the highest output at each pixel is recorded. The edges are thinned by suppressing non-maxima perpendicular to the edge directions.

[5]This may be illustrated by the following examples. It is common for physical texels to be fairly uniform in size and shape, but for the gaps between the texels to be much less uniform [Figs. 7(a), 19(a), 23(a), and 25(a)]. In these images, it is more accurate to infer a three-dimensional

surface from the area and aspect-ratio gradients than from the density gradient or the gradient of spacings between texels. As a second example, the potential accuracy of the aspect-ratio gradient is higher in textures where the physical texels are separated by gaps than in textures where the physical texels overlap and occlude one another [the lily pads in Fig. 25(a) show a much better aspect-ratio gradient than do the rocks in Fig. 3(a)]. Thirdly, for the water hyacinths of Fig. 29(a), the random three-dimensional arrangement of the leaves makes the aspect-ratio gradient very weak, while the area gradient is still quite significant. Finally, in images with partial occlusions [Figs. 13(a) and 15(a)], the perspective gradient (length of the unforeshortened texel dimension) is more accurate than the area gradient: if only part of a texel is occluded, the apparent texel area is decreased, whereas the complete unforeshortened dimension may remain in view.

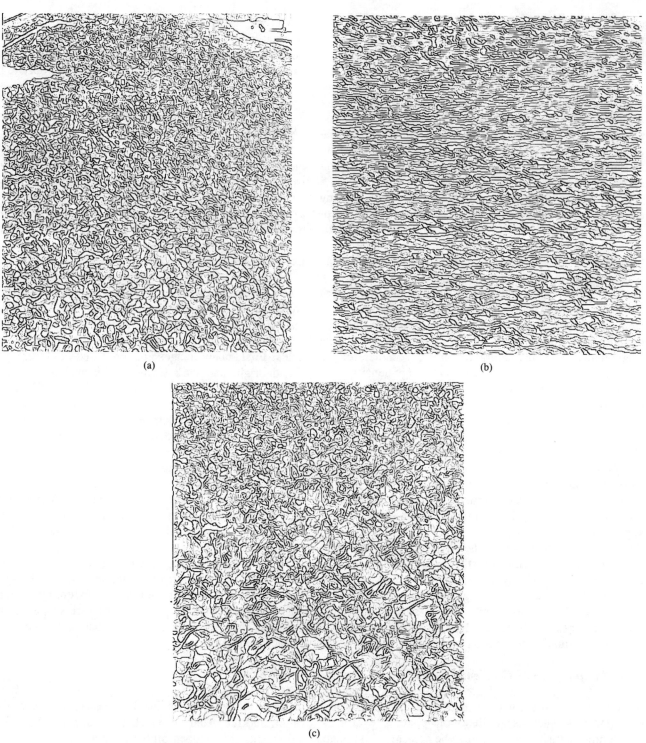

Fig. 2. Edges extracted from three texture images. Only a subset of the detected edges are boundaries of texture elements. If edge density is to be effective in capturing the texture gradient, all edges that do not correspond to texel boundaries must be removed. Such edge removal cannot be accomplished without, in effect, performing an identification of texture elements. (a) Edges from the rock-pile image shown in Fig. 3(a). (b) Edges from the image of birds flying over water, shown in Fig. 7(a). (c) Edges from the water hyacinths image shown in Fig. 29(a).

Texel Identification: As discussed in Section II-A, texel identification is important for correct shape-from-texture analysis. In general, physical texels can give rise to complex gray-level patterns. However, it is difficult to test for repetitive patterns of arbitrary gray-level configuration. In our implementation, we restrict image texels to be regions that have small gray-level variation relative to a neighborhood of their size. Under this restriction, a physical texel can give rise to several image texels: often the physical repetitive unit of a texture contains both bright and dark regions [for example, the sunflowers in Fig. 15(a)]. We treat the bright and dark image texels as two texture fields, which we analyze separately.

Texture Gradients: A shape-from-texture system should test each image for the presence of various texture gradients (area gradient, aspect-ratio gradient, density gradient), and combine these various sources of information to produce a surface estimation. In our current implementation, the only texture gradient we test for is a gradient in texel area.[6] However, we do independent analyses of the area-gradients in positive-contrast and negative-contrast image regions; these two types of regions may correspond to foreground and background, or to different portions of the physical texels. Some images contain bright texels on dark backgrounds, other images contain dark texels on bright backgrounds, and yet other images have no visible ''background'' region because texels are densely placed. Measurements of foreground regions are often more accurate than measurements of background regions, since texel area tends to be less variable than texel spacing.

Surface Estimation: Ideally, a system tests for texture gradients produced by a variety of surface shapes (planar, cylindrical, spherical etc.), and is able to locate discontinuities in depth and surface orientation. Much work remains to be done in this area. We restrict ourselves to fitting a single planar surface to the entire image. This is a common restriction in current implementations of shape-from-texture algorithms, although a theoretical treatment of the nonplanar case has been performed by [1], and has been tested on synthetic images.

Three-Dimensional Texel Effects: For accurate image analysis, it is necessary to model the effects of three-dimensional relief on observed texture gradients. We do not address this problem in our current implementation: the equations we use for expected area-gradients are derived under the assumption that texels do not have three-dimensional relief, i.e., that they are ''painted'' on the textured surface. For textures with relief, this assumption results in a redefinition of texels: ideally, only those parts of physical texels that are parallel to the underlying surface are recognized as defining a texture field. The detected consistency is reduced if the texels have parts that are not parallel to the surface. If the texel relief is regular (so that the texels are mutually parallel), the detected gradient may still be significant and nearly correct recovery of surface orientation may be possible. For example, we obtain satisfactory results on the sunflower image of Fig. 15, where the texels are not parallel to the surface.

Although some theoretical treatment of the foreshortening of textures with relief exists (e.g., [15]), no one has addressed how in-plane texels could be distinguished from out-of-plane texels in real images.

Multiple Textures: A general shape-from-texture system must be able to handle images containing multiple textures; the system must perform texture segmentation as well as shape-from-texture estimation. To solve this problem it is necessary to separate texture variations due to distance and foreshortening effects from texture variations due to a boundary between different physical textures. Our current implementation does not address this problem: each of our images contains only a single texture. Ongoing research is aimed at extending the method to apply to images containing multiple textures.

The rest of the paper describes our two-step algorithm for texel identification and surface estimation. In the first step, we use a multiscale region detector to construct a set of candidate texels (Section III). In the second step we use surface-fitting to identify the true texels from among the candidates, while simultaneously constructing an approximation to the shape of the textured surface (Section IV). The second step thus enforces perspective viewing constraints to select texels. Section V presents results for a variety of images of textured natural scenes.

III. IDENTIFYING CANDIDATE TEXELS: MULTISCALE REGION DETECTION

We now turn to a description of the multiscale region detector used to construct the set of candidate texels. The set of candidate texels includes all image regions that have small gray-level variation relative to a neighborhood of their size. These image regions may be of any shape and size, and they may be nested, since there is no *a priori* way to distinguish texture regions from subtexture and super-texture regions.

To simplify the problem of extracting regions of arbitrary shapes and sizes, we assume that each region can be represented as a union of overlapping circular disks. Large disks define the rough shape of a region, with overlapping smaller disks capturing finer shape details such as protrusions and concavities. In Section III-A we derive a method of extracting all circular image regions of relatively uniform gray level. Section III-B discusses how sets of overlapping disks are used to form candidate texels.

The region detector is based on the image response to convolution with $\nabla^2 G$ filters over a range of scales. Related work includes [27] (a scale-space representation of $\nabla^2 G$ zero-crossings) and [8] (a representation of $\nabla^2 G$ peaks and ridges over a range of scales[7]). We find circular image regions of uniform gray level by convolving the image with $\nabla^2 G$ masks over a range of scales, and comparing the convolution output to that expected for an ideal circular disk of constant gray level. Here we present a brief summary of the region detection algorithm; a more detailed discussion may be found in [6].

---

[6]Our extraction of texel shape is not accurate enough to permit useful measures of aspect-ratio. We also cannot measure texel density accurately because we do not extract all of the texels. Ongoing research into improved texel-extraction will permit the analysis of several texture gradients.

[7]Crowley and Parker use a difference-of-Gaussian operator, which is a discrete approximation to $(\partial / \partial \sigma) G$ and hence to $\nabla^2 G$. By the diffusion equation, $\nabla^2 G = (1/\sigma)(\partial / \partial \sigma) G$.

A. A Closed Form Expression for the $\nabla^2 G$ Response of a Disk

The algorithm for uniform-region extraction is based on calculations of the $\nabla^2 G$ and $(\partial/\partial\sigma)\nabla^2 G$ responses of a disk image. Given a function $I(x, y)$ which specifies the intensity of an image, the $\nabla^2 G$ response of this image at (x, y) is given by the following convolution:

$$\nabla^2 G(x, y) * I(x, y)$$

$$= \int\limits_{-\infty}^{+\infty}\int \frac{2\sigma^2 - (u^2 + v^2)}{\sigma^4} e^{-(u^2 + v^2)/2\sigma^2}$$

$$\cdot I(x - u, y - v) \, du \, dv. \qquad (1)$$

Mathematical analysis of the response of the $\nabla^2 G$ filter to most images is difficult because the convolution integrals of (1) do not have closed form solutions. However, a closed-form solution can be derived for the center point of a circular disk of constant intensity. We analyze the $\nabla^2 G$ response at the center of an ideal circular disk in the continuous domain; to generate the $\nabla^2 G$ convolution of digitized images, we sample the $\nabla^2 G$ filter values and perform a discrete convolution. The image of a disk of diameter D and contrast C is defined by

$$\text{disk image: } I(x, y) = \begin{cases} C & \text{if } x^2 + y^2 \leq D^2/4 \\ 0 & \text{elsewhere.} \end{cases} \qquad (2)$$

Using this definition of $I(x, y)$ in (1), and setting x and y to zero, we find [6] that at the disk center

$$\nabla^2 G \text{ response} = \frac{\pi C D^2}{2\sigma^2} e^{-D^2/8\sigma^2} \qquad (3)$$

$$\frac{\partial}{\partial\sigma} \nabla^2 G \text{ response} = \frac{\pi C D^2}{2} \left(\frac{D^2}{4\sigma^5} - \frac{2}{\sigma^3} \right) e^{-D^2/8\sigma^2}. \qquad (4)$$

Dividing these expressions, we solve for the diameter D and contrast C of the disk:

$$D = 2\sigma \sqrt{\sigma \left(\frac{\partial}{\partial\sigma} \nabla^2 G * I \right) \bigg/ (\nabla^2 G * I) + 2}$$

$$C = \frac{2\sigma^2}{\pi D^2} e^{D^2/8\sigma^2} (\nabla^2 G * I) \qquad (5)$$

where the convolutions are evaluated at the center of the disk.

B. Extracting Candidate Texels in Real Images

We construct an approximation of image texels by first fitting disks to uniform image regions, and then forming unions of connected disks. (An alternative approach is presented by [25]. They extract texture elements by convolving the image with a $\nabla^2 G$ filter and then selecting components of above-threshold pixels that have suitable geometrical properties, such as compactness.) For the first step, we use (5) to estimate disk diameter and disk contrast from the $\nabla^2 G * I$ and $(\partial/\partial\sigma)\nabla^2 G * I$ values at the center of a region. Disks are fit at the extrema of the $\nabla^2 G * I$ images. The disks fit to local maxima have positive contrast (regions brighter than the surround), whereas the disks fit to local minima have negative contrast (regions darker than the surround).

We use a range of filter sizes. For a region R in image I, local extrema in $\nabla^2 G * I$ occur at the center of R when the $\nabla^2 G$ filter size approximately matches the region-diameter. Thus, to fit disks as accurately as possible, we accept a disk only if the computed diameter D is close to the $\nabla^2 G$ filter size used to detect the disk.

Parts (b) of Figs. 3–30 illustrate the result of this disk-fitting for the positive-contrast and negative-contrast regions of each image. Implementation details for the disk-fitting are as follows.

1) Compute the convolutions $\nabla^2 G * I$ and $(\partial/\partial\sigma)\nabla^2 G * I$ for the following six σ values: $\sqrt{2}$, $2\sqrt{2}$, $3\sqrt{2}$, $4\sqrt{2}$, $5\sqrt{2}$, and $6\sqrt{2}$. (The center lobes of the six $\nabla^2 G$ filters have diameters of 4, 8, 12, 16, 20, and 24 pixels, respectively.) To compute $\nabla^2 G * I$ for a particular σ value, the image is convolved with a mask whose coefficients are taken from

$$\frac{2\sigma^2 - r^2}{\sigma^4} e^{-r^2/2\sigma^2}$$

To compute $(\partial/\partial\sigma)\nabla^2 G * I$ for a particular σ value, the image is convolved with a mask whose coefficients are taken from

$$\frac{6r^2\sigma^2 - r^4 - 4\sigma^4}{\sigma^7} e^{-r^2/2\sigma^2}.$$

2) Mark the locations where disks will be fit. To analyze the positive-contrast regions of the original image, mark all local maxima in the $\nabla^2 G * I$ images. To analyze the negative-contrast regions of the original image, mark all local minima in the $\nabla^2 G * I$ images. Local maxima and minima are computed relative to a 3×3 neighborhood.

3) At each marked location, use the measured $\nabla^2 G * I$ and $(\partial/\partial\sigma)\nabla^2 G * I$ values in (5) to compute a disk diameter and disk contrast. Accept the disk only if $w - 2 \leq D \leq w + 2$, where $w = 2\sqrt{2}\sigma$ is the diameter of the center lobe of the $\nabla^2 G$ filter. Form a single set of disks by taking the union of the disks detected at the various filter sizes.

After the disk-fitting is completed, we form unions of overlapping disks to construct candidate texels. Overlapping disks form concavities. There is no *a priori* way to tell whether a set of disks should be split at a concavity or not: some concavities arise at the border between two neighboring texels; at other times the concavities are part of the shape of an individual texel. Thus both possibilities are included in the list of candidate texels. The implementation details are as follows:

To form the list of candidate texels, extract all subsets of disks that are spatially connected and contain no concavities greater than 90°. If a concavity is in

330

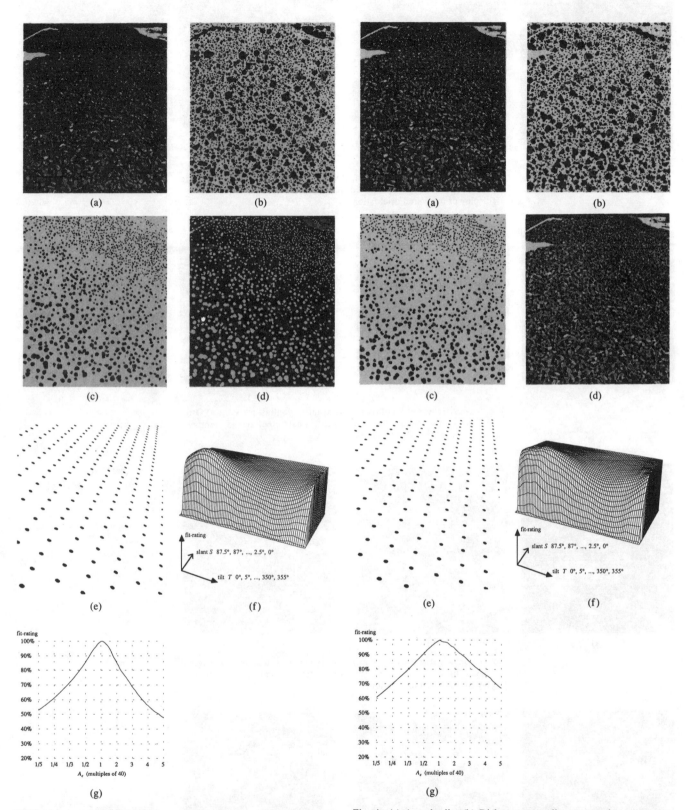

Fig. 3. (a) A rock pile. (b) Disks corresponding to positive-contrast regions of relatively uniform gray level. Disks are shown with a darkness proportional to the contrast of the region. (c) Extracted texels. These are all regions (sets of overlapping disks) having area within a factor of two of the area expected by the best planar fit ($A_c = 40$, slant 62.5°, tilt 65°). The texels that fit the plane most closely are printed darkest. (d) The texels superimposed on a dark reproduction of the original. (e) Synthetic image to illustrate the planar fit $A_c = 40$, slant 62.5°, tilt 65°. (f) and (g) Rating of various possible planar fits. In (f) slant and tilt are varied while A_c is constant at 40. In (g) A_c is varied while slant and tilt are constant at 62.5° and 65°, respectively.

Fig. 4. (a) A rock pile. (b) Disks corresponding to negative-contrast regions of relatively uniform gray level. Disks are shown with a darkness proportional to the contrast of the region. (c) Extracted texels. These are all regions (sets of overlapping disks) having area within a factor of two of the area expected by the best planar fit ($A_c = 40$, slant 60°, tilt 75°). The texels that fit the plane most closely are printed darkest. (d) The texels superimposed on a bright reproduction of the original. (e) Synthetic image to illustrate the planar fit $A_c = 40$, slant 60°, tilt 75°. (f) and (g) Rating of various possible planar fits. In (f) slant and tilt are varied while A_c is constant at 40. In (g) A_c is varied while slant and tilt are constant at 60° and 75°, respectively.

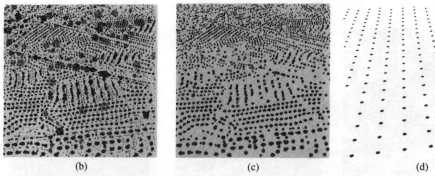

Fig. 5. Aerial view of Levittown, PA: positive contrast texture. (a) Original image, (b) regions detected, (c) texels extracted, and (d) synthetic display of recovered orientation.

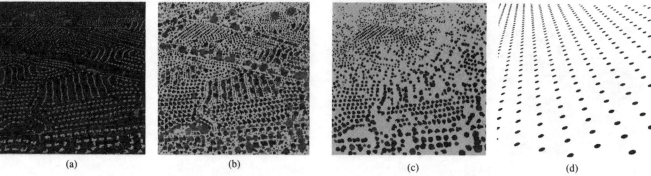

Fig. 6. Aerial view of Levittown, PA: negative contrast texture. (a) Original image, (b) regions detected, (c) texels extracted, and (d) synthetic display of recovered orientation.

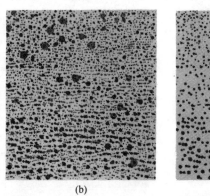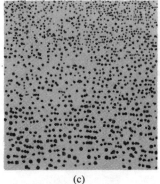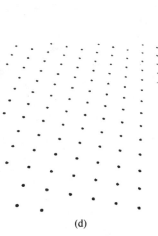

Fig. 7. Snow geese over Back Bay: positive contrast texture. (a) Original image, (b) regions detected, (c) texels extracted, and (d) synthetic display of recovered orientation.

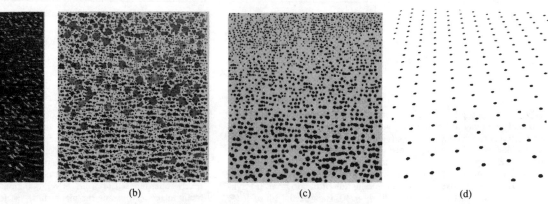

Fig. 8. Snow geese over Back Bay: negative contrast texture. (a) Original image, (b) regions detected, (c) texels extracted, and (d) synthetic display of recovered orientation.

 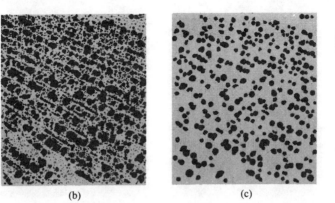

(a) (b) (c) (d)

Fig. 9. Prayer at a mosque: positive contrast texture. (a) Original image, (b) regions detected, (c) texels extracted, and (d) synthetic display of recovered orientation.

 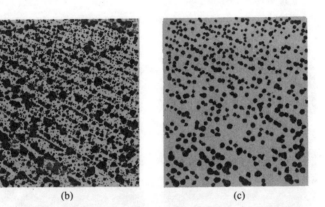 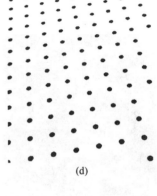 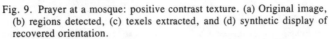

(a) (b) (c) (d)

Fig. 10. Prayer at a mosque: negative contrast texture. (a) Original image, (b) regions detected, (c) texels extracted, and (d) synthetic display of recovered orientation.

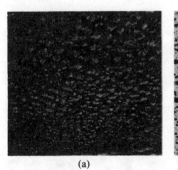 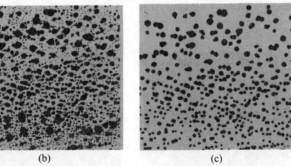 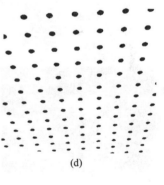

(a) (b) (c) (d)

Fig. 11. Fleecy clouds: positive contrast texture. (a) Original image, (b) regions detected, (c) texels extracted, and (d) synthetic display of recovered orientation.

 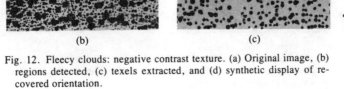

(a) (b) (c) (d)

Fig. 12. Fleecy clouds: negative contrast texture. (a) Original image, (b) regions detected, (c) texels extracted, and (d) synthetic display of recovered orientation.

333

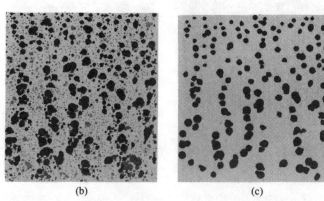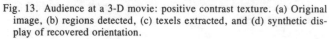

(a)   (b)   (c)   (d)

Fig. 13. Audience at a 3-D movie: positive contrast texture. (a) Original image, (b) regions detected, (c) texels extracted, and (d) synthetic display of recovered orientation.

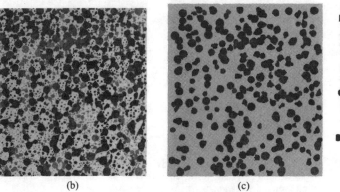

(a)   (b)   (c)   (d)

Fig. 14. Audience at a 3-D movie: negative contrast texture. (a) Original image, (b) regions detected, (c) texels extracted, and (d) synthetic display of recovered orientation.

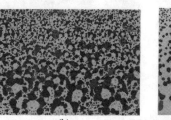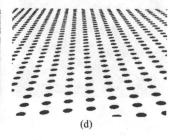

(a)   (b)   (c)   (d)

Fig. 15. Sunflowers: positive contrast texture. (a) Original image, (b) regions detected, (c) texels extracted, and (d) synthetic display of recovered orientation.

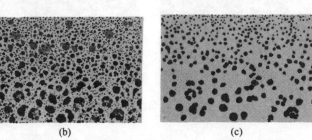

(a)   (b)   (c)   (d)

Fig. 16. Sunflowers: negative contrast texture. (a) Original image, (b) regions detected, (c) texels extracted, and (d) synthetic display of recovered orientation.

 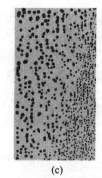 

(a) (b) (c) (d)

Fig. 17. Tree trunk: positive contrast texture. (a) Original image, (b) regions detected, (c) texels extracted, and (d) synthetic display of recovered orientation.

 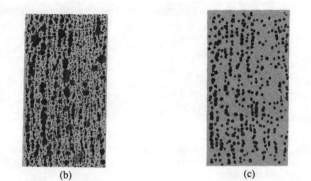

(a) (b) (c) (d)

Fig. 18. Tree trunk: negative contrast texture. (a) Original image, (b) regions detected, (c) texels extracted, and (d) synthetic display of recovered orientation.

 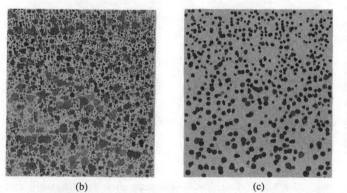 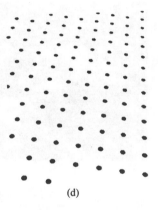

(a) (b) (c) (d)

Fig. 19. Bathers on the Ganges: positive contrast texture. (a) Original image, (b) regions detected, (c) texels extracted, and (d) synthetic display of recovered orientation.

 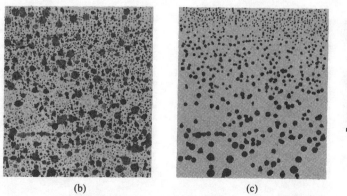

(a) (b) (c) (d)

Fig. 20. Bathers on the Ganges: negative contrast texture. (a) Original image, (b) regions detected, (c) texels extracted, and (d) synthetic display of recovered orientation.

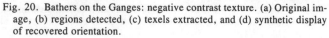

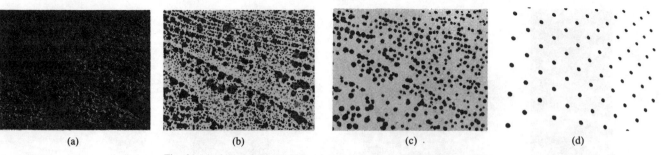

(a) (b) (c) (d)

Fig. 21. A plowed field: positive contrast texture. (a) Original image, (b) regions detected, (c) texels extracted, and (d) synthetic display of recovered orientation.

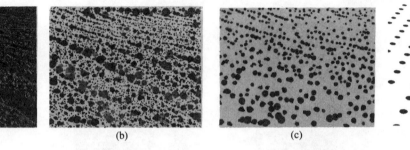

(a) (b) (c) (d)

Fig. 22. A plowed field: negative contrast texture. (a) Original image, (b) regions detected, (c) texels extracted, and (d) synthetic display of recovered orientation.

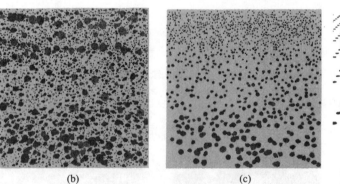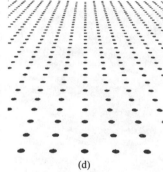

(a) (b) (c) (d)

Fig. 23. A field of flowers: positive contrast texture. (a) Original image, (b) regions detected, (c) texels extracted, and (d) synthetic display of recovered orientation.

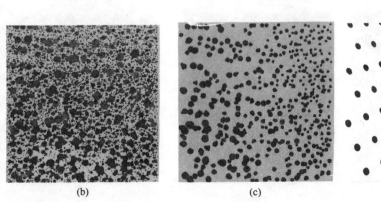

(a) (b) (c) (d)

Fig. 24. A field of flowers: negative contrast texture. (a) Original image, (b) regions detected, (c) texels extracted, and (d) synthetic display of recovered orientation.

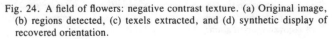

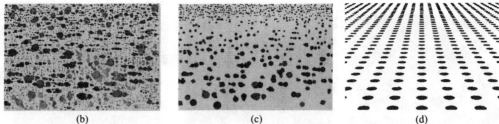

(a) (b) (c) (d)

Fig. 25. Water lilies: positive contrast texture. (a) Original image, (b) regions detected, (c) texels extracted, and (d) synthetic display of recovered orientation.

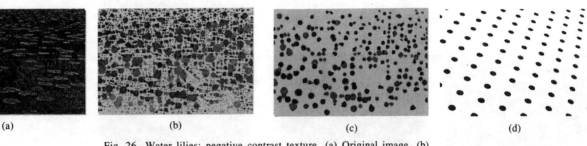

(a) (b) (c) (d)

Fig. 26. Water lilies: negative contrast texture. (a) Original image, (b) regions detected, (c) texels extracted, and (d) synthetic display of recovered orientation.

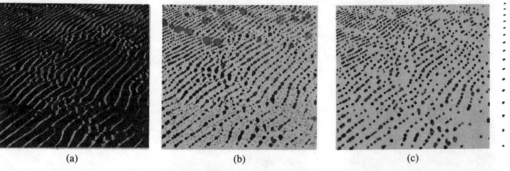

(a) (b) (c) (d)

Fig. 27. Ripple marks in a shallow sea: positive contrast texture. (a) Original image, (b) regions detected, (c) texels extracted, and (d) synthetic display of recovered orientation.

the range 50°–90°, use the disks to form three candidate texels[8]: one large region consisting of all the disks, and two smaller regions resulting from splitting the large region at the concavity.[9] Mark mutual exclusion between candidate texels that share a disk: at most one of them can contribute support to a planar fit and be chosen as a true texture element.

---

[8]The particular values 50° and 90° are not critical; we have found that the range 50°–90° is large enough to capture the regions of interest and yet small enough to prevent a combinatorial explosion in the number of candidate texels generated.

[9]Region splitting is implemented as follows. We begin with a set P of overlapping disks, which together cover an image region R. The largest concavity in R is found by computing the angles formed by every pair of neighboring disks on the border of R. Suppose that X and Y are two neighboring disks on the border of R, and that they form a concavity that causes a split into smaller, more convex regions. The concavity is split by 1) removing X from P and repeating the above process, and then 2) removing Y from P and repeating the above process.

IV. SURFACE ESTIMATION AND TEXEL IDENTIFICATION

Our goal in analyzing image texture is to find a spatial layout of homogeneously-textured surfaces that could result in the given image texture. We do this by testing many spatial layouts and choosing the one that is the most consistent with a maximal subset of the candidate texels. The surface parameters are determined at the same time that the true texels are chosen from among the candidates.

A. The Expected Distribution of Texel Areas for a Planar Surface

The current implementation is restricted to fitting a single planar surface to the image, based on the observed areas of the candidate texels. In order to find a planar fit to the candidate texels, we need to know the distribution of texel areas that occurs in an image of an idealized textured plane. To derive this relationship, we assume a

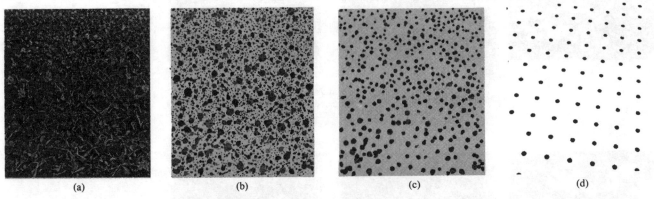

Fig. 28. Ripple marks in a shallow sea: negative contrast texture. (a) Original image, (b) regions detected, (c) texels extracted, and (d) synthetic display of recovered orientation.

Fig. 29. Water hyacinths: positive contrast texture. (a) Original image, (b) regions detected, (c) texels extracted, and (d) synthetic display of recovered orientation.

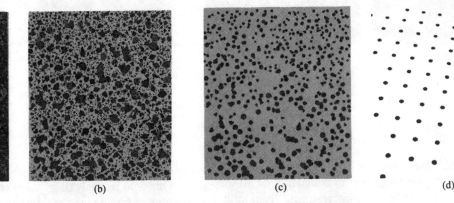

Fig. 30. Water hyacinths: negative contrast texture. (a) Original image, (b) regions detected, (c) texels extracted, and (d) synthetic display of recovered orientation.

planar textured surface covered with identical texels, where the texels show no three-dimensional relief (the texels are "painted" on the surface). Natural textures are typically more complicated: they are composed of highly variable texels that show three-dimensional relief. Our experiments show that the equations derived from consideration of idealized textures are useful for analyzing a variety of natural textures as well (Section V).

We derive two expressions to describe the size of image texels. The first expression characterizes the foreshortened image-texel dimension F_i; this is the texel dimension parallel to the tilt (Fig. 31). The second expression characterizes the unforeshortened image-texel dimension U_i; this is the texel dimension perpendicular to the tilt. Combining these we obtain an expression for A_i, the expected image-texel area.

As illustrated in Fig. 31, an image location is specified by (X, Y), in a normalized coordinate system which does not depend on the number of pixels in the image: X and Y are zero at the image center, and are -1 or 1 at the image border. (For notational simplicity, we are assuming square images.)

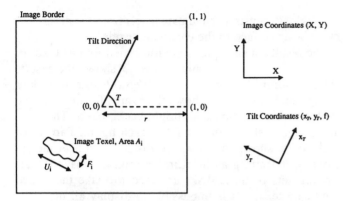

Fig. 31. Image and tilt coordinate systems.

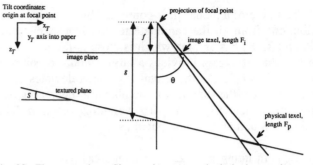

Fig. 32. The x_T–z_T plane. Since y_T is constant, both the image plane and the textured plane are perpendicular to the drawing.

The camera parameters we use are the focal length f and the physical width of the film r. The final expressions use only the ratio r/f, which is a measure of the field-of-view of the camera lens. Telephoto lenses have a low value of r/f, whereas fish-eye lenses have a high value of r/f.

The slant and tilt of the textured plane are denoted by S and T, respectively. Simple derivations may be obtained by defining a *tilt coordinate system*, (x_T, y_T, z_T), with origin at the focal point, the z_T axis perpendicular to the image plane, and the x_T axis in the tilt direction. The view direction is along the positive z axis; thus this is a left-handed coordinate system. A point (X, Y) in image coordinates is transformed to tilt coordinates by

$$x_T = X \cos T + Y \sin T$$

$$y_T = X \sin T + Y \cos T$$

$$z_T = f.$$

Shown in Fig. 32 is the x_T–z_T plane, which is perpendicular to both the image plane and the textured plane. The angle $\theta = \tan^{-1}(x_T(r/f))$ for an image location with tilt coordinates (x_T, y_T, f); given raw image coordinates (X, Y),

$$\theta = \tan^{-1}((X \cos T + Y \sin T)(r/f)). \quad (6)$$

From the geometry in Fig. 32 we derive that [4]

$$F_i = F_p \frac{f}{g} \cos S (1 - \tan \theta \tan S)^2.$$

The only approximation made is that θ does not change significantly across the texel. To eliminate the dependence on the surface-depth g, we calculate F_i in terms of F_c, the foreshortened dimension of a texel at the image center:

$$F_i = F_c (1 - \tan \theta \tan S)^2. \quad (7)$$

Similarly, we derive that U_i, the unforeshortened image-texel dimension, is related to U_c, the unforeshortened dimension of a texel at the image center by

$$U_i = U_c (1 - \tan \theta \tan S). \quad (8)$$

If the image texel has a compact shape, the area A_i of the image texel is proportional to the product of F_i and U_i.

(For example, if the physical texel is a circle, the image texel is an ellipse with $A_i = (\pi/4) F_i U_i$; if the physical texel is a rectangle, the image texel is a parallelogram with $A_i = F_i U_i$.) Thus, $A_i = k F_i U_i$, where k is a constant of proportionality which depends upon the texel shape. Therefore A_i, the area of a texel at location (X, Y) in the image[10] is related to A_c, the area of a texel at the image center by

$$A_i = A_c (1 - \tan \theta \tan S)^3. \quad (9)$$

Substituting θ from (6) into (9), we see that the following values are needed to predict the texel area anywhere in the image:

• A_c, the area that would be measured for a texel located at the center of the image.

• S and T, the slant and tilt of the textured plane.

• The ratio r/f, which is related to the field-of-view of the camera lens.

In our work we assume that the field-of-view is known. The other three quantities (A_c, S, T) form the parameter space we search to find the best planar fit for a given texture image.

B. Fitting a Planar Surface to the Candidate Texels

Having extracted candidate texels from an image of a textured surface, we find the orientation of the textured plane that best agrees with the observed areas of the candidate texels. A planar surface is characterized by the triple (A_c, S, T), where A_c is the texel area expected in the image center, S is the slant, and T is the tilt. In order to find the best planar fit for the image texture, we discretize the possible values of A_c, S, and T, and evaluate each possible planar fit. For each choice of (A_c, S, T), (9) gives the expected texel area at each image location. These expected areas are compared to the region areas actually occurring in the image, and a fit-rating is computed for the plane. The plane that receives the highest fit-rating is selected as the estimate of the textured surface. The candidate texels that support the best planar fit are interpreted as true image texels.

---

[10] As pointed out by a reviewer, this result can also be derived from equations (2-1) and (3-2) in [18]; they also use the approximation that θ is constant across the texel.

The rating of a planar fit is computed by summing contributions from all the candidate texels. If a texel at location (X, Y) has an area which is close to the ideal area in (9), then the texel provides a large amount of support for the planar fit. As the actual texel area deviates from the ideal area, the support for the planar fit decreases; we use an exponentially-decreasing weighting function. The rating of a planar fit is computed as

$$\text{fit rating} = \sum_{\text{all regions}} (\text{region area})$$
$$\cdot |\text{region contrast}| e^{-(\text{region-fit})^2/4}$$
$$\text{where region-fit} = \frac{\max (\text{expected area, actual area})}{\min (\text{expected area, actual area})}.$$

(10)

The region-fit is 2.0 for a candidate texel that is either half as big or twice as big as the size predicted by the planar fit.

We begin with a coarse fit, in which the (A_c, S, T) space is searched at sparse locations: A_c (in units of pixels) takes on the values $\{10, 20, 40, 80, 160, 320, 640\}$, S takes on the values $\{0°, 5°, 10°, \cdots, 70°, 75°, 80°\}$, and T takes on the values $\{0°, 20°, 40°, \cdots, 300°, 320°, 340°\}$. To refine the planar fit, a more detailed search of the (A_c, S, T) space is done in the neighborhood of the best plane from the coarse fit: S is changed in increments of $2.5°$, T in increments of $5°$, and A_c in increments of less than 25 percent. As illustrated in parts (e) of Figs. 3 and 4 the fit-rating values change smoothly as a function of A_c, slant, and tilt. The plane that receives the highest fit-rating is selected as the best estimate of the textured surface. True image texels are those regions that have an area close to the area expected by the best planar fit.

V. APPLICATION OF THE ALGORITHM TO REAL IMAGES

We have conducted experiments with a variety of images of natural textures, having different mixes of texel shapes, number of fields, types of gradients, tilt directions, and three-dimensional texel effects. The results of the performance of the algorithm on a large variety of textures should help in judging the strengths, weaknesses, and generality of the algorithm and its current implementation. Part (a) of Figs. 3–30 show 14 of the images we have used in our experiments. A few of the images are photographs of outdoor scenes taken by one of the authors in Urbana, Illinois. The rest are illustrations in books (see [4] for references), which we have rephotographed. All of these images are digitized off of the photographic negatives using a drum scanner. The images are 512 by 512 pixels; the image sizes in the figures vary because image borders have been trimmed. All of the images are processed the same way; the method has no parameters that need to be tuned to particular images. As was described in Sections III and IV, the processing of an image is divided into three main phases: fit disks to the uniform image regions, construct candidate texels from the disks, and fit a planar surface to the candidate texels.

The results of each phase are illustrated for one texture, a rock pile, in Figs. 3 and 4. Fig. 3 shows the results obtained for the positive contrast (bright) texture over dark background, and Fig. 4 shows the results for the negative contrast (dark) texture over bright background. The original image is shown in part (a) of each figure. Part (b) of each figure shows the extracted disks that model the regions of uniform gray level in the original image. Overlapping sets of these disks are used to make the list of candidate texels. It is impossible to display all the disks in a single image, since many disks are spatially contained in larger disks. This spatial containment typically means that either 1) the large disk is part of a texture element and the small disks are subtexture, or 2) the small disks are texels and the large disk is supertexture. In case 1) the large disk usually has higher contrast than the smaller disks, whereas in case 2) the smaller disks usually have higher contrast than the large disk. Wherever disks overlap, our figures shows the disk of higher contrast. Therefore most subtexture disks in part (b) are not visible: they are covered by a larger, higher-contrast disk corresponding to part of a texture element.

The parameters of the best planar fit are illustrated by the synthetic texture images in part (e) of the figures. The detected texels are shown in parts (c) and (d): these are all candidate texels having area within a factor of two of the area expected by the best planar fit.

Parts (f) and (g) illustrate the change of fit-rating as a function of A_c, slant, and tilt. The height fields in part (f) of each figure show fit-rating as a function of slant and tilt, with A_c fixed at the value that produces the best planar fit for the texture in question.[11] The height fields flatten out near the back because tilt becomes less important as slant decreases; tilt is irrelevant when the slant is zero. The graphs in part (g) of each figure show fit-rating as a function of A_c, with slant and tilt fixed at the values that produce the best planar fit for the texture in question.

Figs. 5–30 illustrate selected results for 13 additional images of natural textures. The results obtained for each image are illustrated in two successive figures. The first figure shows the results for the positive-contrast texture, and the second figure shows the results for the negative-contrast texture. Parts (a), (b), and (c) of Figs. 5–30 are analogous to the corresponding parts of Figs. 3 and 4, whereas part (d) of Figs. 5–30 is analogous to part (e) of Figs. 3 and 4. For brevity, the details shown in parts (d), (f), and (g) of Figs. 3 and 4 are not repeated for the textures in Figs. 5–30.

The shape of the fit-rating peak is related to the properties of the image texture. A sharp fit-rating peak indicates that the texels have small size variance. This observation is supported by the fit-rating plots for the aerial view of houses (Figs. 5 and 6) and by the field of sun-

[11] In these height fields, the fit-rating values have been squared for display purposes.

flowers (Figs. 15 and 16), although, for brevity, these plots are not shown in the figures. If the texel sizes have larger variance, as for the clouds (Figs. 11 and 12) and the rock pile (Figs. 3 and 4), then the peak is much broader. (In the rock-pile image, the nonplanarity of the original textured surface also contributes to the broadness of the fit-rating peak.) The texels shown in part (c) of the figures are those candidate texels having area within a factor of two of the area expected by the planar fit. Using this same factor of two for all images causes incomplete extraction of texels in images where texel size is highly variable. More complete texel extraction can be achieved by adjusting the criteria for choosing texels from the set of candidate texels: the criteria should vary as a function of the broadness of the fit-rating peak in (A_c, S, T) space.

The accuracy of the results may be illustrated in two ways. First, the reader can compare his perception of the textured surfaces (part (a) of Figs. 3–30) with the planar surface fitted by the program. Agreement with human perception is quite good for many of the images. Second, since the processing of the positive-contrast and negative-contrast regions is performed totally independently, the agreement between the slants and tilts obtained by the two analyses strengthens the confidence in the results. (Note that the A_c parameters are not expected to be similar for the positive-contrast and negative-contrast regions—the positive-contrast and negative-contrast regions may be of very different sizes.) However, the two analyses may not always lead to the same estimates of slant and tilt, because a texture may not be homogeneous in both texel size and texel separation. Thus, an agreement among multiple analyses (such as the two discussed here) should not be required; instead, a method of automatically assessing the accuracies of the results obtained by different analyses, and selecting and integrating the pertinent analyses must be devised. Work is underway to address this problem.

Table I summarizes the planar fits obtained for all images. These fits use slants that are multiples of 2.5° and tilts that are multiples of 5°. The slant and tilt values computed from the positive-contrast and negative-contrast regions are frequently within 15° of each other. For reference, a 30° difference in tilt is equal to the angular distance between adjacent numbers on a clock face. A 30° difference in slant, on the other hand, is a more serious error. In many of those images that have a large discrepancy between the two planar fits, attributes of the original texture lead us to expect the fits to differ in accuracy. We have identified four reasons for the observed discrepancies. In the field of flowers (Fig. 23) and the water lilies (Fig. 25), the spaces between the texels are less regular than are the areas of the texels; therefore the fit to the negative-contrast regions is not as accurate as the fit to the positive-contrast regions. A second reason the background regions produce inaccurate results is because the properties of the physical texels are more important than the properties of background regions. In images where the physical texels are separated by gaps, the intertexel spacing carries more information than does the shape or area

TABLE I

Description	Figures	Fit to positive-contrast regions			Fit to negative-contrast regions			Difference	
		A_c	slant	tilt	A_c	slant	tilt	slant	tilt
A rock pile	3, 4	40	62.5°	65°	40	60°	75°	2.5°	10°
Aerial view of houses	5, 6	35	62.5°	95°	60	67.5°	110°	5°	15°
Birds flying over water	7, 8	35	45°	80°	40	57.5°	100°	12.5°	20°
Prayer at a mosque	9, 10	160	27.5°	50°	120	42.5°	100°	15°	50°
Fleecy clouds	11, 12	100	55°	275°	160	55°	280°	0°	5°
3D movie audience	13, 14	280	45°	105°	320	7.5°	330°	large	
Sunflowers	15, 16	160	70°	95°	200	70°	90°	0°	5°
A tree trunk	17, 18	70	65°	345°	80	42.5°	0°	25.5°	15°
Bathers on the Ganges	19, 20	100	45°	80°	80	65°	85°	20°	5°
A plowed field	21, 22	80	42.5°	40°	100	65°	80°	22.5°	40°
A field of flowers	23, 24	50	70°	90°	140	52.5°	20°	large	
Water lillies	25, 26	120	75°	90°	160	52.5°	70°	22.5°	20°
Ripples	27, 28	50	52.5°	105°	120	62.5°	105°	10°	0°
Water Hyacinths	29, 30	100	37.5°	80°	100	40°	80°	2.5°	0°

of the background regions. Thus, the results for the negative-contrast regions of the movie image (Fig. 14) and the lily pad image (Fig. 26) are inaccurate because the area of the background regions poorly reflects the intertexel spacing. A third reason for discrepancies between the two slant and tilt estimates is a large variability in texel area (as occurs in Fig. 9, the image of prayer at a mosque). This causes a broad peak in the planar fit space; hence the exact peak location is not as accurate for these images as for others. A fourth reason for inaccurate results is that the current extraction of uniform regions fragments noncompact regions in an arbitrary way, increasing the variabilities of the measured areas. This effect can be seen in the background of the movie image (Fig. 14). For nearly all of the images, at least one of the two analyses produces results that are in good agreement with human perception.

VI. Summary

We have presented a general discussion of the problem of recovering scene-layout information from the texture cues present in an image. We argue that extraction of texels is useful and perhaps even necessary for correct interpretation of texture gradients in the face of subtexture and supertexture. In order to separate texture elements from other regions (such as subtexture) it is necessary to perform texel identification and surface fitting simultaneously.

We have presented an implementation that is based on these ideas; the implementation is restricted to the detection of gradients of texel area. A multiscale region detector is developed from the response of an ideal disk to convolution with a Laplacian-of-Gaussian $(\nabla^2 G)$ over a range of scales. The output of the region detector is used to form a list of candidate texels. These candidate texels then provide the evidence needed to choose a good planar fit to the image texture; at the same time, the best planar fit determines which of the candidate texels are true texels. Results are shown for a variety of natural textures.

One consequence of the integration approach presented in this paper is that all regions whose properties are not unified by the gradient of a given property are treated as noise. For any given property, the noise regions do not contribute significantly to the fit-rating quality by virtue of the exponential function in (10). Such regions could be the result of noise in the original image or in the region detection process. However, these noise regions could be valid texels if the gradient of a different property is considered, and they could quite possibly support the same surface orientation as the nonnoise regions. As long as there is some property whose gradient is supported by regions occupying a sufficiently large image area, the corresponding regions must be treated as texels. This is why the use of multiple texture gradients is necessary. A goal of our ongoing research is to estimate surface orientation from an integrated analysis of several relevant texture gradients, including area gradients, aspect-ratio gradients, and density gradients.

Because of the significant variability which is characteristic of natural textures, texture gradient as a cue of surface orientation appears to be more useful to obtain a coarse judgment of surface orientation and scene layout than as a source of obtaining accurate estimates. Stereo and other sources of scene information may be more appropriate for obtaining greater accuracy, e.g., for extracting shapes of curved, complex surfaces. In this sense, the analysis based on planar surfaces may suffice for most natural scenes containing textured surfaces, although mathematically (or for use with synthetic textures, where texture variability could be controlled), the approach presented in this paper could be extended to apply to curved surfaces. The extension required would be only in the surface fitting process. A much more important use of texture cues in real scenes is for segmentation of a scene into different textured surfaces [25]. With such segmentation available, it would be possible to identify image parts to which the approach of this paper could be applied meaningfully. As we stated earlier, we have not addressed the problem of texture segmentation in this paper.

REFERENCES

[1] J. Aloimonos and M. Swain, "Shape from texture," in *Proc 9th Int. Joint Conf. AI*, 1985, pp. 926–931.
[2] J. Aloimonos, "Detection of surface orientation from texture I: The case of planes," in *Proc. IEEE Conf. Computer Vision and Pattern Recognition*, 1986, pp. 584–593.
[3] R. Bajcsy and L. Lieberman, "Texture gradient as a depth cue," *Comput. Graphics Image Processing*, vol. 5, pp. 52–67, 1976.
[4] D. Blostein, "Recovering the orientation of textured surfaces in natural scenes," Ph.D. dissertation, Univ. Illinois, Coordinated Science Lab. Rep. UILU-ENG-87-2219, Apr. 1987.
[5] D. Blostein and N. Ahuja, "Representation and three-dimensional interpretation of image texture: An integrated approach," in *Proc. IEEE First Int. Conf. Computer Vision*, June 1987, pp. 444–449.
[6] ——, "A multi-scale region detector," *Comput. Vision, Graphics, Image Processing*, vol. 45, no. 1, pp. 22–41, Jan. 1989.
[7] M. L. Braunstein and J. W. Payne, "Perspective and form ratio as determinants of relative slant judgments," *J. Exp. Psychol.*, vol. 81, no. 3, pp. 584–590, 1969.
[8] J. Crowley and A. Parker, "A representation for shape based on peaks and ridges in the difference of low pass transform," *IEEE Trans. Pattern Anal. Machine Intell.*, vol. PAMI-6, no. 2, pp. 156–170, Mar. 1984.
[9] J. E. Cutting and R. T. Millard, "Three gradients and the perception of flat and curved surfaces," *J. Exp. Psychol.: General*, vol. 113, no. 2, pp. 198–216, 1984.

[10] L. Davis, L. Janos, and S. Dunn, "Efficient recovery of shape from texture," *IEEE Trans. Pattern Anal. Machine Intell.*, vol. PAMI-5, no. 5, pp. 485–492, Sept. 1983.
[11] J. Gibson, *The Perception of the Visual World*. Boston, MA: Houghton Mifflin, 1950.
[12] K. Ikeuchi, "Shape from regular patterns (an example of constraint propagation in vision)," MIT A.I. Memo 567, Mar. 1980.
[13] K. Kanatani, "Detection of surface orientation and motion from texture by a stereological technique," *Artificial Intell.*, vol. 23, pp. 213–237, 1984.
[14] K. Kanatani and T. Chou, "Shape from texture: General principle," in *Proc. IEEE Conf. Computer Vision and Pattern Recognition 86*, Miami, FL, June 1986, pp. 578–583.
[15] J. Kender, "Shape from texture," Ph.D. dissertation, Carnegie-Mellon Univ., Rep. CMU-CS-81-102, Nov. 1980.
[16] H. Nakatani, S. Kimura, O. Saito, and T. Kitahashi, "Extraction of vanishing point and its application to scene analysis based on image sequence," in *Proc. Int. Conf. Pattern Recognition*, 1980, pp. 370–372.
[17] R. Nevatia and K. R. Babu, "Linear feature extraction and description," *Comput. Graphics Image Processing*, vol. 13, pp. 257–269, 1980.
[18] Y. Ohta, K. Maenobu, and T. Sakai, "Obtaining surface orientation from texels under perspective projection," in *Proc. Int. Joint Conf. Artificial Intelligence*, 1981, pp. 746–751.
[19] R. J. Phillips, "Stationary visual texture and the estimation of slant angle," *Quart. J. Psychol.*, vol. 22, pp. 389–397, 1970.
[20] A. Rosenfeld, "A note on automatic detection of texture gradients," *IEEE Trans. Comput.*, vol. C-24, pp. 988–991, Oct. 1975.
[21] R. R. Rosinski, "On the ambiguity of visual stimulation: A reply to Eriksson," *Perception Psychophys.*, vol. 16, no. 2, pp. 259–263, 1974.
[22] R. Rosinski and N. Levine, "Texture gradient effectiveness in the perception of surface slant," *J. Exp. Child Psychol.*, vol. 22, pp. 261–271, 1976.
[23] K. A. Stevens, "Slant-tilt: The visual encoding of surface orientation," *Biol. Cybern.*, vol. 46, pp. 183–195, 1983.
[24] D. Vickers, "Perceptual economy and the impression of visual depth," *Perception and Psychophys.*, vol. 10, no. 1, pp. 23–27, 1971.
[25] H. Voorhees and T. Poggio, "Detecting textons and texture boundaries in natural textures," in *Proc. IEEE First Int. Conf. Computer Vision*, June 1987, pp. 25–258.
[26] A. P. Witkin, "Recovering surface shape and orientation from texture," *Artificial Intell.*, vol. 17, pp. 17–45, 1981.
[27] ——, "Scale space filtering," in *Proc. Eighth Int. Joint Conf. Artificial Intelligence*, Karlsruhe, West Germany, Aug. 1983, pp. 1019–1022.

Dorothea Blostein (S'87–M'88) received the B.S. degree in mathematics and computer science from the University of Illinois, Urbana-Champaign, in 1978, the M.S. degree in computer science from Carnegie-Mellon University, Pittsburgh, PA, in 1980, and the Ph.D. degree in computer science from the University of Illinois in 1987.

From 1980 to 1982, she worked at Intel Corporation. During 1987–1988, she worked at the University of Illinois Computer-Based Education Research Laboratory. She is currently an Assistant Professor in the Department of Computing and Information Science at Queen's University in Kingston, Ontario. Her research interests include computer vision, pattern recognition, computer music, and user-interface design.

Narendra Ahuja (S'79–M'79–SM'85) received the B.E. degree with honors in electronics engineering from the Birla Institute of Technology and Science, Pilani, India, in 1972, the M.E. degree with distinction in electrical communication engineering from the Indian Institute of Science, Bangalore, India, in 1974, and the Ph.D. degree in computer science from the University of Maryland, College Park, in 1979.

From 1974 to 1975 he was Scientific Officer in the Department of Electronics, Government of India, New Delhi. From 1975 to 1979 he was at the Computer Vision Laboratory, University of Maryland, College Park. Since 1979 he has been with the University of Illinois at Urbana-Champaign where he is currently (1988–) a Professor in the Department of Electrical and Computer Engineering, the Coordinated Science Laboratory, and the Beckman Institute. His interests are in computer vision, robotics, image processing, and parallel algorithms. He has been involved in teaching, research, consulting, and organizing conferences in these areas. His current research emphasizes integrated use of multiple image sources of scene information to construct three-dimensional descriptions of scenes, the use of the acquired three-dimensional information for object manipulation and navigation, and multiprocessor architectures for computer vision.

Dr. Ahuja received the University Scholar Award (1985), Presidential Young Investigator Award (1984), National Scholarship (1967–1972), and President's Merit Award (1966). He has coauthored the books *Pattern Models* (Wiley, 1983) with Bruce Schachter, and *Motion and Structure from Image Sequences* (Springer-Verlag, to appear) with Juyang Weng and Thomas Huang. He is Associate Editor of the journals IEEE TRANSACTIONS ON PATTERN ANALYSIS AND MACHINE INTELLIGENCE, and *Computer Vision, Graphics, and Image Processing*. He is a member of the American Association for Artificial Intelligence, the Society of Photo-Optical Instrumentation Engineers, and the Association for Computing Machinery.

Chapter 5: Three-Dimensional Object Recognition

The real world that we see and touch is primarily composed of three-dimensional solid objects. When an object is viewed for the first time, people typically gather information about that object from many different viewpoints. The process of gathering detailed object information and storing that information is referred to as "model formation." Once a person is familiar with many objects, the objects are then identified from an arbitrary viewpoint without further investigation. People are also able to identify, locate, and qualitatively describe the orientation of objects in black-and-white photographs. This basic capability is significant to computer vision because it involves the spatial variation of a single parameter within a framed rectangular region that corresponds to a fixed, single view of the world. The ability to identify, locate, and describe objects motivates the following definition of the autonomous, single arbitrary-view, three-dimensional-object recognition problem:

- Given any collection of labeled solid objects, each object can be examined and labeled models can be created using information from this examination.
- Given digitized sensor data corresponding to one particular, but arbitrary, field of view of the real world and the list of distinguishable objects, the following issues must be addressed for each object: Does the object appear in the digitized sensor data? If so, how many times and in what locations in the sensor data? For each occurrence, what are the three-dimensional location and orientation with respect to a known coordinate system?

Recognition system components

Recognition implies awareness of something already known. In modeling real-world objects for recognition purposes, many different kinds of schemes have been used. These are briefly described in the next section. To determine how recognition will take place, a method for matching model data to sensor data must be considered. A straightforward blind-search approach would entail (1) transforming all possible combinations of all possible known object models in all possible distinguishable orientations and locations into a digitized sensor data format and (2) matching based on minimization of a matching-error criterion. Clearly, this approach is impractical. On the other hand, since object models contain more object information than the sensor data, we are prohibited from transforming sensor data into complete model data and matching in the model data format. However, this does not prevent us from matching with partial model data. As a result, working with an intermediate domain that is computable from both sensor and model data is advantageous. This domain is referred to as the "symbolic scene description domain." A matching procedure is carried out on the quantities in this domain, which are referred to as "features."

Interactions between the individual components of a recognition system are illustrated in Figure 5.1.[147] The image formation process (represented on the figure by *I*) creates intensity or range data based purely on physical principles. The description process (*D*) acts on the sensor data and extracts relevant application-independent features. This process is completely data-driven and includes only the knowledge of the image formation process. The modeling process (*M*) provides object models for real-world objects. Object reconstruction from sensor data is one method for building models automatically. The understanding, or recognition, process (*U*) involves an algorithm to perform matching between models and data descriptions. This process might include data- and model-driven subprocesses, where segmented sensor data regions seek explanations in terms of models and hypothesized models seek verification from the data. The rendering process (*R*) produces synthetic sensor data from object models. Rendering provides an important feedback link by allowing an autonomous system to check on its own understanding of the sensor data by comparing synthetic images to the sensed images.

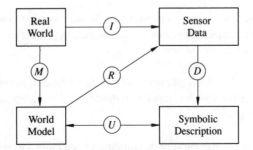

Figure 5.1: General object recognition system structure. I, image formation process; M, world-modeling process; D, description process; U, understanding process; R, model-rendering process (from P. Besl and R.C. Jain, "Three Dimensional Object Recognition," *ACM Computing Surveys*, Vol. 17, No. 1, Copyright 1985, Association for Computing Machinery, Inc., reprinted with permission). [147]

Object representation schemes

Numerous schemes have been developed for representing three-dimensional objects. The choice of a particular scheme is governed by its intended application. In computer graphics, schemes such as wire-frame representation and constructive solid-geometry representation are popular since their data structures are suitable for image-rendering operations. In computer vision systems, other methods for representing three-dimensional objects, such as generalized cones and characteristic views, are used extensively. Using characteristic views for object recognition has been an important research topic in recent years and is discussed in a separate section. In this section we present an overview of other representation schemes.

Wire-frame representation. Wire-frame representation of a three-dimensional object consists of a three-dimensional vertex point list and an edge list of vertex pairs. Although this representation is very simple, it is an ambiguous representation for determining such quantities as surface area and volume of an object. Wire-frame models can sometimes be interpreted as several different solid objects or as different orientations of the same object.

Constructive solid-geometry representation. Constructive solid-geometry (CSG) representation of an object is specified in terms of a set of three-dimensional volumetric primitives (blocks, cylinders, cones, and spheres are typical examples of volumetric primitives) and a set of Boolean operators: union, intersection, and difference. Figure 5.2(a)[148] shows an example of computational solid-geometry representation. The corresponding solid object is shown in figure 5.2(b). The storage data-structure is a binary tree, where the terminal nodes are instances of primitives and the branching nodes represent Boolean set operations and positioning information. CSG trees define object surface area and volume unambiguously and can, with very little data, represent complex objects. However, the boundary evaluation algorithms required to obtain usable surface information are very computationally intensive. Also, general sculptured surfaces are not easily represented using CSG models.

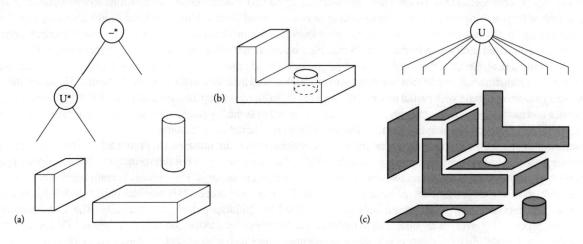

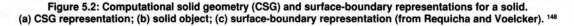

Figure 5.2: Computational solid geometry (CSG) and surface-boundary representations for a solid.
(a) CSG representation; (b) solid object; (c) surface-boundary representation (from Requicha and Voelcker). [148]

Spatial-occupancy representation. Spatial-occupancy representation uses nonoverlapping subregions of the three-dimensional space occupied by an object to define that object. This method unambiguously defines an object's volume. Commonly used single primitive representations of this type are discussed below.

Voxel representation. Voxels are small-volume elements of discretized three-dimensional space. They are usually fixed-size cubes. Objects are represented by the list of voxels occupied by the object. Voxel representation is very memory intensive, but algorithms using it tend to be very simple.

Octree representation. An octree is a hierarchical representation of spatial occupancy.[149,150] Volumes are decomposed into cubes of different sizes, where the cube size depends on the distance from the root node. Each branching node of the tree represents a cube and points to eight other nodes, each of which describes object volume occupancy in the corresponding octant subcubes of the branching node cube. Octree representation offers the advantages of the voxel description but is more compact. Because of this compactness, more complicated algorithms are required for many computations than those needed for voxel representation.

Other representations. Two other representations used are tetrahedral cell decomposition and hyperpatch representation. Tetrahedral decomposition of three-dimensional objects is similar to the lower dimensional analog of decomposing flat surfaces into triangles. Tetrahedral decomposition defines volume and surface area unambiguously and is useful for mathematical purposes. In hyperpatch representation, each volume element is a hyperpatch, or a generalization of bicubic surface patches.[151] A hyperpatch defines volume, surface area, and internal density variations of a solid element. It is more general than most solid models — which allow only uniform density within a solid primitive — but a price is paid in memory and algorithm complexity. (For example, 192 scalars are required for each volume element.)

Surface boundary representation. Surface boundary representation defines a solid object by defining the three-dimensional surfaces that bound the object. Figure 5.2(c)[148] shows an example of surface boundary representation for the object shown in figure 5.2(b). The simplest boundary representation is the triangle-faced polyhedron, which can be stored as list of three-dimensional triangles. Arbitrary surfaces are approximated to any desired degree of accuracy by utilizing many triangles. A slightly more compact representation allows the replacement of adjacent, connected, coplanar triangles with arbitrary n-sided planar polygons. This type of representation is popular because model surface area and volume are well defined and all object operations are carried out using piecewise planar algorithms. Structural relationships between bounding surfaces may also be included as part of a model; Lu and Fu[152] proposed a syntactic model that uses a context-free three-dimensional plex grammar for this purpose.

The object representation schemes relating to surface boundary representation discussed above have been used successfully to provide realistic renderings of real-world scenes. On the other hand, each real-world object shape requires, for matching, a unique description within the framework of a given representation. Most representations do not guarantee unique numerical descriptions of object shapes. Points, edges, faces, and/or primitives of a given representation can often be reordered or reorganized to obtain the same shape. If a modeling scheme suffers from a nonuniqueness problem, then model-based matching algorithms for computer vision systems must be made insensitive to this nonuniqueness. Badler and Bajcsy,[153] Bajcsy,[154] Brown,[155] Requicha,[156] and Requicha and Voelcker[148,157] present more details on the relative merits of the above representation schemes. Three-dimensional representation schemes popular in computer vision literature are now briefly described.

Generalized-cone or sweep representation. In generalized-cone (or generalized-cylinder) representation, an object is represented by: a three-dimensional space curve that acts as a spine or axis of the cone, a two-dimensional cross-sectional figure, and a sweeping rule that defines how the cross section is to be swept and possibly modified along the space curve.[158,159] Generalized cones are well suited for representing many real-world shapes; however, certain objects — such as a human face or an automobile body — are almost impossible to represent as generalized cones. Despite its limitations, generalized-cone representation is popular in computer vision.

Multiple two-dimensional projection representation. For some applications, a library of two-dimensional silhouette projections that represent three-dimensional objects can be conveniently stored. For recognition of three-dimensional objects with a small number of stable orientations on a flat light table, this representation is ideal, if object silhouettes are different enough. Silhouettes have also been used to recognize aircraft in any orientation against a well-lit sky background.[160] However, because many different three-dimensional-object shapes can possess the same set of silhouette projections, this type of representation is not a general-purpose technique. Recently, more powerful two-dimensional projection representation schemes, known as "aspect graphs" and "characteristic views," are becoming popular. Because of their current importance, these schemes are discussed in more detail in the section entitled "Aspect Graphs and Characteristic Views."

Skeleton representation. Skeleton representation uses space-curve skeleton models.[161,162] A skeleton can be considered an abstraction of the generalized cone description that consists of only the spines. Nackman[163] generalized the symmetric-axis-transform concept for arbitrary three-dimensional objects that have surface skeletons. Skeleton geometry provides useful abstract information. If a radius function is specified at each point on the skeleton, this representation is capable of general-purpose object description.

Surface representation schemes. The object recognition problem requires a representation that can model arbitrary solid objects to any desired level of detail and that can provide abstract shape properties for matching purposes. Because both range and intensity images are strongly influenced by object surface properties, surfaces must be evaluated explicitly in at least one module of a vision system — no matter what representations are used. Thus, object recognition is dependent on surface perception. To avoid unnecessary computation when explicit surface information is required, a surface boundary representation is the natural choice. For polyhedral objects, surface representation can be easily accomplished using planar polygons. In this section, we now discuss briefly methods for representing surfaces of smooth-curved objects.

A general surface in three dimensions is written as

$$S = \{(x,y,z) : F(x,y,z) = 0\}. \tag{5.1}$$

This equation is referred to as an "implicit" representation of a surface. If the gradient vector ∇F exists, is continuous, and is nonzero for every point (x,y,z), then S is a smooth surface. The implicit surface representation is useful for low-order polynomials of the spatial variables. Planar surfaces are precisely represented with only four coefficients (which describe three degrees of freedom), as follows:

$$F_{plane}(x,y,z) = Ax + By + Cz + D \tag{5.2}$$

A, B, and C specify the direction of the single normal to the surface and D specifies the distance of the plane from the origin of the coordinate system if A, B, and C are properly normalized. Quadric surfaces require 10 coefficients (which describe nine degrees of freedom), as follows:

$$F_{quadric}(x,y,z) = Ax^2 + By^2 + Cz^2 + Gxy + Hyz + Izx + Ux + Vy + Wz + D \tag{5.3}$$

Only three coefficients are needed to describe the shape of a quadric surface of a given type, whereas six parameters are needed to locate and orient the surface in space. If a quadric surface is properly translated and rotated, at least six of the 10 coefficients will be zero. All quadric surfaces can then be classified as one of the following types, using three or four nonzero coefficients in that particular coordinate system:

(1) Ellipsoid *(A > 0, B > 0, C > 0, D = -1)*;
(2) Elliptic paraboloid *(A > 0, B > 0, W = -1)*;
(3) Hyperbolic paraboloid *(A > 0, B < 0, W = -1)*;
(4) Hyperboloid of one sheet *(A > 0, B > 0, C < 0, D = -1)*;
(5) Hyperboloid of two sheets *(A > 0, B < 0, C < 0, D = -1)*; and
(6) Quadric cone *(A > 0, B > 0, C < 0)*.

Suppressing undesired undulations in polynomial surface functions becomes more difficult as the order of the polynomial increases. Therefore, implicit surface representation unfortunately is not generally useful for arbitrary surface descriptions — unless surfaces are decomposed into a collection of locally homogeneous surface patches.

The standard alternative approach is to use "explicit" parametric surface representation, as follows:

$$S = \{(x,y,z) : x = h(u,v), y = g(u,v), z = f(u,v), (u,v) \in D \subseteq R^2 \}, \tag{5.4}$$

where f, g, and h are smooth scalar functions of two variables. A less general, but still useful, parametric description of surfaces is given via the graph surface (or Monge patch) representation, as follows:

$$S = \{(x,y,z) : x = u, y = v, z = f(u,v), (u,v) \in D \subseteq R^2 \}, \tag{5.5}$$

Gray-level surfaces in intensity images and depth surfaces in range images are typically analyzed using this common representation.

A wide variety of techniques has been developed for representing objects and surfaces for digital-computing purposes. To make informed decisions, designers of object recognition systems should be aware of these techniques.

348

Aspect graphs and characteristic views

Koenderink and Van Doorn[164,165] introduced the concept of aspect graphs for representing shapes of three-dimensional objects. The space of viewpoints is partitioned into maximal regions, where every viewpoint in each region gives the same qualitative view of the object, called the "aspect" of the object. Within each region, projections of the object will have the same number and types of features, with identical spatial relationships among them. However, the quantitative properties of these features, such as lengths of edges, vary with change in viewpoint. Changes in the aspect, called "visual events," take place at the boundaries between regions. Two aspects are said to be connected by a visual event if their corresponding regions are adjacent in the viewpoint space. An aspect graph is a graph structure whose nodes represent aspects and their associated regions and whose arcs denote visual events and boundaries between adjacent regions. Figure 5.3[147] shows an aspect graph for a cube; the nodes represent various aspects, and the arcs that connect these nodes represent visual events that transform one aspect to another.

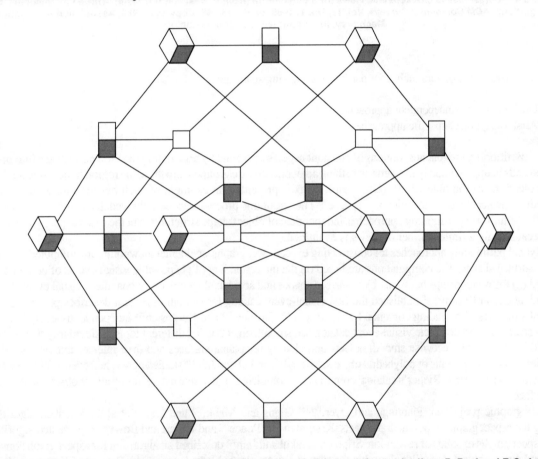

Figure 5.3: Nodes illustrating aspects and arcs respresenting visual events for a cube (from P. Besl and R.C. Jain, "Three Dimensional Object Recognition," *ACM Computing Surveys,* Vol. 17, No. 1, 1985, pp. 75-145. Copyright 1985, Association for Computing Machinery, Inc., reprinted with permission.)[147]

Using a concept similar to that of the aspect graph, Chakravarty and Freeman[166] proposed representing an object by a set of characteristic views. In Chakravarty and Freeman's system, all of the infinite two-dimensional perspective projection views of an object are grouped into a finite number of topologically equivalent classes. Different views within an equivalence class are related via linear transformations. A representative member of an equivalence class is called a "characteristic view." In this system, objects rest on a supporting plane; hence, they are restricted to appear in a number of stable positions. Characteristic views of objects are derived with certain constraints on camera configuration. Figure 5.4[147] shows representative characteristic views for a polyhedron. Because characteristic views specify the three-dimensional structure of an object, they provide a general-purpose representation of that object.

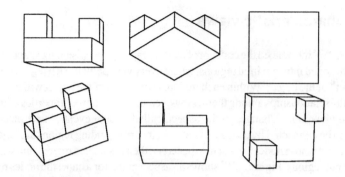

Figure 5.4: Representative characteristic views for a polyhedron (from P. Besl and R.C. Jain, "Three Dimensional Object Recognition," *ACM Computing Surveys,* Vol. 17, No. 1, 1985, pages 75-145. Copyright 1985, Association for Computing Machinery, Inc., reprinted with permission.)[147]

The two general types of approaches for partitioning viewing space are

(1)   Uniform, object-independent approaches and
(2)   Analytical, object-specific approaches.

In uniform partitioning approaches, regions of constant aspects are found by tessellating the viewpoint space into uniformly distributed cells of approximately the same size; then, adjacent cells are grouped into the same region if they give qualitatively similar projections of the object.[167-172] (Gigus and Malik[173] presented an example of such partitioning with a tessellated dodecahedron projected onto the viewing sphere.) The grouping process can be achieved by using a region-growing method.[171] The uniform partitioning approach is independent of object shape structures, but the exact aspect graph cannot be created because only a finite number of views is examined.

In analytical partitioning approaches for constructing exact aspect graphs, accidental viewpoints are computed directly from the object surface shapes. The computations are based on the understanding of (1) possible visual events of certain classes of objects and (2) the relationships between object surface shapes and accidental viewpoints where these visual events take place. Koenderink and Van Doorn[164,165] published the first visual-event catalog for smooth objects; it describes possible changes in topological structures of occluding contours. Later, Arnold,[174] Gaffney,[175] and Kergosien[176] independently compiled all of the individual catalogs into a complete visual-event catalog for smooth objects using different tools in singularity theory. Rieger[177] extended this catalog for piecewise smooth objects bounded by nonplanar surfaces and their intersection curves. Gigus and Malik[173] described visual events of polyhedral objects. Sripradisvarakul and Jain[178] studied new visual events for curved objects, which, together with those in Rieger's catalog, comprise the complete list of visual events for arbitrary objects with planar and curved surfaces.

For orthographic projection, Plantinga and Dyer,[179,180] Gigus and Malik,[173] and Gigus et al.[181] described algorithms for computing the aspect graphs of polyhedral objects. Kriegman and Ponce[182] and Eggert and Bowyer[183] presented algorithms for creating aspect graphs of solids of revolution. Sripradisvarakul and Jain[178] described an algorithm for aspect graph construction for a general curved object. A similar algorithm for curved objects was published recently by Ponce and Kriegman.[184]

For perspective projection, Castore,[185] Stewman and Bowyer,[186,187] and Watts[188] gave algorithms for creating aspect graphs of convex polyhedral objects.

Object recognition systems

ACRONYM is a model-based system for three-dimensional interpretation of two-dimensional images.[189-190] It is a complex, large-scale, domain-independent modular system that uses view-independent volumetric object models. Figure 5.5[189] shows for the ACRONYM system both the block diagram and the hierarchical geometric-reasoning process diagram. The system is based on the prediction-hypothesis-verification paradigm. The three main data structures of the system are the following:

Object graph: Nodes of the object graph are generalized-cone object models. Arcs of the object graph correspond to the spatial relationships between the nodes (e.g., relative translations and rotations) and the subpart relations (e.g., is-a-part-of).

- Restriction graph: Nodes of the restriction graph are constraints on the object models of a given object class. The directed arcs of the restriction graph represent subclass inclusions.
- Prediction graph: Nodes of the prediction graph are "invariant" and "quasi-invariant" observable-image object features. Arcs of the prediction graph specify the image relationships between the invariant features. These arcs are of the following types: must-be, should-be, and exclusive.

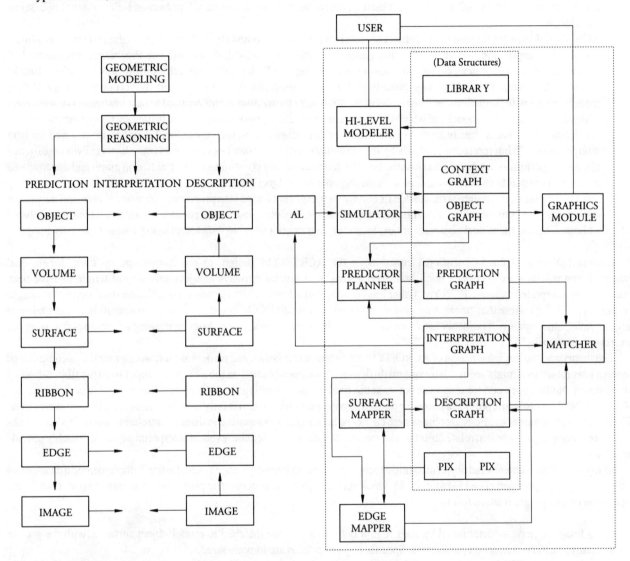

Figure 5.5: The block diagram and hierarchical geometric reasoning process diagram of the ACRONYM system (from Brooks et al., "The ACRONYM Model-Based Vision System," *Proc. 6th Int'l Conf. on Artificial Intelligence,* **Copyright Int'l Joint Conf. on Artificial Intelligence, Inc.)**[189]

Each data object of the system is referred to as a "unit." Every unit has associated slots to hold descriptive information. For example, a cylinder has a length slot and a radius slot. Slots accept numeric fillers or quantifier expressions. The ACRONYM system operates approximately as follows:

- An a priori world model is given to the system as a set of object sets and object classes. Simple objects are represented as generalized cones with specific dimensions. Each object and object class can be a hierarchy of subparts, each with its own local coordinate system. Object classes are represented as objects with constraints on subpart dimensions and configurations. An object graph, a restriction graph, and a prediction graph are formed based on the world model and a set of production rules.

- The system is given a digitized intensity image, a camera model, and the three graph data structures formed in the preceding step.
- The image is processed in two steps. First, an edge operator is applied to the image. Second, an edge linker is applied to the output of the edge operator and is directed to look for ribbons and ellipses. (Ribbons are the two-dimensional image projections of elongated bodies and ellipses are the ends of generalized-cone models.) The high level of three-dimensional geometric reasoning in ACRONYM is based entirely on the two-dimensional ribbon-and-ellipse symbolic scene description.
- ACRONYM searches for instances of object models in terms of ribbons and ellipses. The heart of the system is a nonlinear constraint manipulation system (CMS) that generalizes the linear SUP-INF methods of Presburger arithmetic.[191,192] Constraint implications are propagated "downward" during prediction and "upward" during interpretation. Brooks describes the interpretation-matching process as follows: "Matching does not proceed by comparing image feature measurements with predictions for those measurements. Rather the measurements are used to put constraints on parameters of the three-dimensional models, of which the objects in the world are hypothesized to be instances. Only if constraints are consistent with what is already known of the model in three dimensions, then these local matches are retained for later interpretation."[190] Interpretation proceeds by the combination of local matches of ribbons into clusters. Two consistency checks are performed on the ribbon clusters: Each match must satisfy constraints of the prediction graph and accumulated matching constraints must be consistent with the hypothesized object model.
- The final output of the system is the labeled ribbons of the consistent image interpretation. Since orientation and translation constraints have been propagated during matching, three-dimensional positioning parameters are available for the labeled ribbons. Three-dimensional object identities, locations, and orientations are thus found using a single intensity image.

Despite the detailed three-dimensional concerns in the ACRONYM design, to our knowledge no three-dimensional interpretation results have ever been published. Aerial images of jets on runways and jets near airport terminals have been successfully interpreted using ACRONYM. Other less complicated schemes exist that could yield similar results on aerial images of this type. Binford wrote that "there is no profound reason why ACRONYM could not recognize aircraft in images taken at ground level, although it will probably break when tested on such images because of bugs or missing capabilities that were not exercised previously."[193]

The theory and the implementation of ACRONYM are two separate issues, but readers are left wondering if this complicated system is as robust as it might seem. Many system difficulties have been blamed on the quality of output from the ribbon-finding mechanism. No feedback connections exist between the final decision-making mechanism and the original data.

ACRONYM's problems provide a reminder for us that any open-loop system is only as robust as its most limited component. Even the best possible geometric-reasoning system cannot be successful if its input is consistently unreliable and no feedback paths exist. Rendering algorithms that relate object models to sensor data at intermediate levels of interpretation could possibly provide feedback.

Many other three-dimensional object recognition schemes based on intensity images exist. Fisher[194] implemented a data-driven object recognition program called IMAGINE, in which surfaces are used as geometric primitives. The three major stages in the operation of this program are as follows:

(1)   Image regions — determined by their region boundaries — are matched to model object surfaces, with the goal of estimating surface orientation parameters. Specific object surfaces are hypothesized.
(2)   Hypothesized object surfaces are related to object models constrained by the structural relationships implied by the objects. Specific objects are hypothesized.
(3)   Hypothesized objects are verified using consistency checks against constraints due to adjacency and ordering.

The four specific goals of the IMAGINE program are

- To locate instances of three-dimensional objects in two-dimensional images;
- To locate image features corresponding to all features of the model or to explain why the image features are not present;
- To verify that all features are consistent with the geometric and topological predictions of the model; and
- To extract translation and rotation parameters associated with all objects in the scene.

The input to the IMAGINE program is presegmented surface regions that have the property that all boundaries between regions correspond to surface or shape discontinuities. The only information used by IMAGINE is the two-dimensional boundary shape of the segmented surface regions. The object models of the program are surface boundary models wherein all surfaces are planar or have only a single axis of curvature. Subcomponent hierarchies for objects determine the joint connections of subparts. Model surface-to-image region matching is performed using a set of heuristics that generate hypotheses about rotation, slant and tilt, distance, and x-y translation in a plane. These heuristics gave reasonable results in 94 of 100 test cases[194]. Given the hypothesized surfaces and their positions and orientations in space, a set of 10 rules is applied to generate object model hypotheses. Another set of occlusion-handling rules is applied for object verification. Fisher[194] provided his own list of program criticisms, which include the following:

- The heuristic parameter estimation techniques require mostly planar surfaces.
- The program's surface modeling does not account for surface shape internal to the region boundary.
- Surface segmentation is currently done by hand, with the assumption that adequate techniques will soon be available.
- The program's object models are nongeneric.

Despite these criticisms, the program did achieve its goals of recognizing and locating, in a test image, a PUMA robot and "understanding" its three-dimensional structure. Valuable ideas concerning occlusion are presented in Fisher's[194] paper.

Chakravarty and Freeman[166] developed a technique that uses characteristic views — described earlier — as a basis for three-dimensional object recognition in intensity images. Matching is performed using line junction labeling constraints on detected edges, which requires silhouette determination to guide the matching process. (This requirement is a disadvantage for occlusion handling.) In addition to identifying objects, this technique produces — as output — position and orientation information.

Some three-dimensional object recognition techniques are based purely on object silhouettes; as a result, these techniques cannot distinguish between objects having the same set of silhouettes. McKee and Aggarwal[195] worked on recognizing three-dimensional curved objects from a partial-silhouette description. However, three-dimensional object models are not used in this system. During the training process, the system learns the global silhouette boundary description for each view of an object and then stores the description in an object view library. The recognition algorithm accepts a partial-boundary description and then lists all of the compatible objects in the library. The work of McKee and Aggarwal[195] did not include view-independent processing and had problems with noisy edges. Dudani et al.[196] and Reeves et al.[197] used global moment-based silhouette shape description techniques for aircraft shape description. Sadjadi and Hall[198] discussed three-dimensional moment invariants.

Casasent et al.[199] developed a pattern recognition approach to object recognition based on synthetic-discriminant functions (SDFs), maximum-common-information filters, and decorrelation transformations. An SDF is a linear combination of matched spatial filters. It processes an entire input image without segmentation or preprocessing. Image correlations are performed instantaneously using optical means. SDFs are synthesized from training data chosen to represent various views of different objects. A type of nongeometric-model formation occurs during this training phase. Casasent et al.[199] discuss experimental results for two different objects. Thirty-six images of each object were obtained (10-degree rotation increments); for each of the two objects, six of these images were used for training. With two SDFs created from 12 images, 60 additional images taken from different views were correctly classified. A two-class mutual-orthogonal-function filter recognized the object and gave the correct orientation for 90 percent of the 72 images used.

Silberberg et al.[200] used a generalized Hough transform to match detected two-dimensional line segments with three-dimensional-model line segments and observed two-dimensional edge junctions to three-dimensional model vertices. Silberberg et al.[200] assumed that (1) all objects are polyhedra with single, stable positions, (2) the ground plane is known, and (3) camera position and parameters are known. They discussed experimental results for a synthetic image of a nonconvex polyhedron.

Goad[201] presented a technique for object recognition based on special-purpose automatic programming. In his technique, individual object descriptions are compiled into programs in which the only task is recognizing one object from any view. Time-consuming shape analysis is performed off-line prior to the recognition phase, so that actual recognition execution time is minimal (about one second). Goad[201] used a multiple-view object feature model that incorporates 218 different three-dimensional views of each object. Features are line segments stored as a pair of endpoints and a 218-bit bit-string, which describes the visibility of the feature in each of the 218 discrete views. Edges for objects are ordered by their expected utility for matching purposes. Goad[202] showed experimental results for a jumbled pile of key-caps for keyboards.

Shneier[202] proposed a combined multiple-object representation — a "graph of models" — where each graph node represents a three-dimensional surface primitive. The nodes contain a set of properties describing surface shape and a set of pointers to the object names to which the surface belongs. The arcs between the nodes describe relationships between surfaces and also contain pointers to the model names where those relationships occur. The integration of multiple objects into a single, shared-data structure provides a compact representation that is indexed quickly for fast recognition processing.

We conclude this section on a historical note. The pioneering work of Roberts,[203] published in 1965, involved an intensity-image-based three-dimensional object recognition system. In this system, objects were constrained to be blocks, wedges, prisms, or combinations thereof. A cross operator was used to detect edges, and collinear segments were merged into lines to produce a line drawing of the scene. Regions were classified as triangles, quadrilaterals, and hexagons; these regions were matched to faces of prototype objects. Possible object part model matches were rendered using a hidden-line algorithm to verify correct object matches. Recognized object parts were cut away from the image, and the same process was repeated until all detected edges and vertices were explained. After identifying an object, the system could draw the object from any view to demonstrate its understanding of the object shape. This research by Roberts was followed by the more advanced work of Guzman,[204] published in 1968, Waltz,[205] published in 1972, and others, which concentrated on line edge and edge junction labeling for detecting polygonal regions. These early systems addressed many of the fundamental problems encountered in computer vision, but were limited to processing high-quality images of block-world scenes. The algorithms were not robust enough to handle problems of real-world scenes, such as noise and curved objects.

Research trends

Automatic generation of three-dimensional-object representations from images has been the goal of many computer vision systems. Eleven papers were selected that are representative of papers dealing with the topics covered in this chapter. Six are included in this book and the other five in the companion book *Computer Vision: Advances and Applications*. In *Principles*, the paper entitled "Volumetric Descriptions of Objects From Multiple Views," by Martin and Aggarwal describe a system in which occluding contours from multiple images acquired from different — but known — viewpoints are used to construct a bounding volume. This volume approximates the three-dimensional structure of the object.

Many object recognition systems are built upon low-level vision modules that operate upon images to derive depth measurements. These measurements are often incomplete and unreliable, thereby adversely affecting the performance of higher level recognition modules. In contrast Lowe[206] describes in detail a system in which bottom-up image description is designed to generate viewpoint-invariant groupings of image features. These features are used to reduce the search space for model matching. The viewpoint consistency constraint is applied, and object level data are mapped directly onto the image to determine model parameters. The ACRONYM system,[189] as already described in an earlier section, is a domain-independent model-based interpretation system that uses generalized cylinders to describe model and scene objects. ACRONYM's interpretation of aerial images is described by Brooks in "Model-Based Three-Dimensional Interpretations of Two-Dimensional Images" found in *Principles*.

Most object recognition research has considered a small set of objects. If a very large number of objects are to be recognized, the recognition task will be dominated by hypothesize-and-test approaches. The hypothesis formation phase requires organization of models indexed by features so that, based on observed features, a small set of likely objects can be selected. Later, these selected models can be used in object recognition to verify which object from this set is present in the given image. Such hypothesize-and-test approaches are already being designed.[100,96,207,208]

In many industrial applications, detailed geometric models of objects are available. These models can be used for generating recognition strategies, including feature selection, for three-dimensional objects. CAD-based object recognition is now being studied at several places.[101,167,172,209,210] An important step in recognition of three-dimensional objects is to consider their possible two-dimensional projections to determine effective features and recognition strategy. Classification of infinite two-dimensional projection views of objects into topologically equivalent classes and the application thereof to object recognition is described in *Principles* by Chakravarty and Freeman in "Characteristic Views as a Basis for Three-Dimensional Object Recognition." In *Advances*, "Computing the Aspect Graph for Line Drawings of Polyhedral Objects," authors Gigus and Malik describe an algorithm that partitions the set of viewpoints on the Gaussian sphere around an object into regions such that the qualitative structure of the line drawing remains unchanged. Their algorithm, which assumes orthographic projection, also computes a representative view of the object for each region. Recently, algorithms have been designed for computing aspect graphs for curved objects also.[178,182,183] In *Principles*, "Fleshing Out Projections," by Wesley and Markowsky describes an algorithm that finds all solid polyhedral objects with a given set of two-dimensional orthographic projections. This problem reduces to that of a wire-frame interpretation problem if the projections are labeled. This algorithm has practical applications in the automatic conversion of engineering drawings into their corresponding volumetric representations.

In "Automatic Generation of Object Recognition Programs," Ikeuchi and Kanade in *Advances* describe a novel system in which object and sensor models are automatically compiled into a visual-recognition strategy. The system extracts from the models those features that are useful for recognition and determines the control sequence that must be applied to handle different object appearances. An alternative to this kind of approach is the neural-network approach to object recognition. Object recognition is one of the most researched areas in neural networks; however, most neural-network research has addressed only two-dimensional objects limited in the number of objects, simple shapes, binary images, and success.

In "Recognizing Three-Dimensional Objects Using Surface Descriptions," Fan et al. in *Principles* describe the system they designed that, using range image data, generates a symbolic object description in terms of visible surface patches. This segmented image, which is treated as a graph describing the patches and their interrelationships, is decomposed into subgraphs corresponding to different objects. In *Advances*, "CAD-Based Computer Vision," by Flynn and Jain presents a method for deriving features for recognition of objects from CAD models and then use them in object recognition. Also in *Advances*, "The Evolution and Testing of a Model-Based Object Recognition System," by Mundy and Heller, discusses several important aspects of an object recognition system, from an approach to selecting features using models to a performance evaluation of the system. The last paper in *Advances*, "Geometric Reasoning for Recognition of Three-Dimensional Object Features" by Marefat and Kashyap, describes a method of extracting shape features from boundary representation of polyhedral objects. The method is based on "cavity graphs," which provide a topological and geometric description of the depressions in the object boundary. Finally, in *Principles*, we have included a survey paper, "Model-Based Recognition in Robot Vision," by Chin and Dyer. Other extensive surveys on object recognition are found in a paper by Besl and Jain[147] and in the paper entitled "Survey of Model-Based Image Analysis Systems," by Binford, which is reprinted in Chapter 7 of this book.

References Cited
Chapter 5

147. P. Besl and R.C. Jain, "Three Dimensional Object Recognition," *ACM Computing Surveys*, Vol. 17, No. 1, 1985, pp. 75-145.

148. A.A. Requicha and H.B. Voelcker, "Solid Modeling: Current Status and Research Directions," *IEEE Computer Graphics and Applications*, Vol. 3, No. 7, 1983, pp. 25-37.

149. D.J. Meagher, "Geometric Modeling Using Octree Encoding," *Computer Graphics and Image Processing*, Vol. 19, 1981, pp. 129-147.

150. D.J. Meagher, "Efficient Synthetic Image Generation of Arbitrary 3-D Objects," *Proc. Pattern Recognition and Image Processing*, IEEE CS Press, Los Alamitos, Calif., 1982, pp. 473-478.

151. M.S. Casale and E.L. Stanton, "An Overview of Analytic Solid Modeling," *IEEE Computer Graphics and Applications*, Vol. 5, No. 2, 1985, pp. 45-56.

152. H.R. Lu and K.S. Fu, "A General Approach to Inference of Context-Free Programmed Grammars," *IEEE Trans. Systems, Man, and Cybernetics*, Vol. 14, 1984, pp. 191-202.

153. N. Badler and R. Bajcsy, "Three Dimensional Representation for Computer Graphics and Computer Vision," *ACM Computer Graphics*, Vol. 12, 1978, pp. 153-160.

154. R. Bajcsy, *Proc. Workshop on Representation of Three-Dimensional Objects*, University of Pennsylvania, Philadelphia, 1979.

155. C.M. Brown, "Some Mathematical and Representational Aspects of Solid Modeling," *IEEE Trans. Pattern Analysis and Machine Intelligence*, Vol. 3, No. 4, 1981, pp. 444-453.

156. A.A. Requicha, "Representations for Rigid Solids: Theory, Methods, and Systems," *ACM Computing Surveys*, Vol. 12, 1980, pp. 437-464.

157. A.A. Requicha and H.B. Voelcker, "Solid Modeling: A Historical Summary and Contemporary Assessment," *IEEE Computer Graphics and Applications*, Vol. 2, No. 2, 1982, pp. 9-24.

158. S.A. Shafer and T. Kanade, "The Theory of Straight Homogeneous Generalized Cylinders and a Taxonomy of Generalized Cylinders," *Tech. Report CMU-CS-83-105*, Carnegie-Mellon University, Dept. of Computer Science, 1983.

159. B.I. Soroka and R.K. Bajcsy, "A Program for Describing Complex Three-Dimensional Objects Using Generalized Cylinders as Primitives," *Proc. Pattern Recognition and Image Processing*, IEEE CS Press, Los Alamitos, Calif., 1978, pp. 331-339.

160. T.P. Wallace and P.A. Wintz, "An Efficient Three-Dimensional Aircraft Recognition Algorithm Using Normalized Fourier Descriptors," *Computer Graphics and Image Processing*, Vol. 13, 1980, pp. 96-126.

161. G. Garibotto and R. Tosini, "Description and Classification of 3-D Objects," *Proc. Sixth Int'l Conf. Pattern Recognition*, IEEE CS Press, Los Alamitos, Calif., 1982, pp. 833-835.

162. K.J. Udupa and I.S.N. Murthy, "New Concepts for Three-Dimensional Shape Analysis," *IEEE Trans. Computer*, Vol. 26, 1977, pp. 1043-1049.

163. L.R. Nackman, "Three-Dimensional Shape Description Using the Symmetric Axis Transform," PhD thesis, Computer Science Dept., University of North Carolina, Chapel Hill, 1982.

164. J.J. Koenderink and A.J. van Doorn, "The Singularities of the Visual Mapping," *Biological Cybernetics*, Vol. 24, 1976, pp. 51-59.

165. J.J. Koenderink and A.J. van Doorn, "The Internal Representation of Solid Shape with Respect to Vision," *Biological Cybernetics*, Vol. 32, 1979, pp. 211-216.

166. I. Chakravarty and H. Freeman, "Characteristic Views as a Basis for Three-Dimensional Object Recognition," *Proc. SPIE Conf. Robot Vision*, Vol. 336, 1982, pp.37-45.

167. C. Hansen and T. Henderson, "CAGD-Based Computer Vision," *IEEE Trans. Pattern Analysis and Machine Intelligence*, Vol. 11, No. 11, 1989, pp. 1181-1193.

168. K. Ikeuchi, "Generating an Interpretation Tree from a CAD Model for 3-D Object Recognition in Bin-Picking Tasks," *Int'l J. Computer Vision*, 1987, pp. 145-165.

169. K. Ikeuchi and T. Kanade, "Automatic Generation of Object Recognition Programs," *Proc. IEEE*, Vol. 76, No. 8, IEEE Press, New York, N.Y., 1988, pp. 1016-1035.

170. A.C. Kak et al, "Knowledge-Based Robotics," *Proc. IEEE Int'l Conf. Robotics and Automation*, IEEE CS Press, Los Alamitos, Calif., 1987, pp. 637-646.

171. M.R. Korn and C.R. Dyer, "3-D Multiview Object Representations for Model-Based Object Recognition," *Pattern Recognition*, Vol. 20, No. 1, 1987, pp. 91-103.

172. L.G. Shapiro, "A CAD-Model-Based System for Object Localization," *Proc. SPIE Digital and Optical Shape Representation and Pattern Recognition*, Vol. 938, 1988, pp. 408-418.

173. Z. Gigus and J. Malik, "Computing the Aspect Graph for Line Drawings of Polyhedral Objects," *IEEE Trans. Pattern Analysis and Machine Intelligence*, Vol. 12, No. 2, 1990, pp. 113-122.

174. V.I. Arnold, "Singularities of Systems of Rays," *Russian Mathematical Surveys*, Vol. 38, No. 2, 1983, pp. 87-176.

175. T. Gaffney, "The Structure of TA(f), Classification and an Application to Differential Geometry," *Proc. Symposia in Pure Mathematics*, Vol. 40, American Math. Society, 1983, pp. 409-427.

176. Y.L. Kergosien, "La Famille des Projections Orthogonales d'une Surface et ses Singularités," *C.R. Acad. Sc. Paris*, Vol. 292, 1981, pp. 929-932.

177. J.H. Rieger, "On the Classification of Views of Piecewise Smooth Objects," *Image and Vision Computing*, Vol. 5, No. 2, 1987, pp. 91-97.

178. T. Sripradisvarakul and R.C. Jain, "Generating Aspect Graphs for Curved Objects," *Proc. IEEE Workshop on Interpretation of 3-D Scenes*, IEEE CS Press, Los Alamitos, Calif., 1989, pp. 109-115.

179. H.W. Plantinga and C.R. Dyer, "An Algorithm for Constructing the Aspect Graph," *Proc. 27th Symp. on Foundation of Computer Science*, IEEE CS Press, Los Alamitos, Calif., 1986, pp. 123-131.

180. H.W. Plantinga and C.R. Dyer, "The Asp: A Continuous Viewer-Centered Representation for 3-D Object Recognition," *Proc. First Int'l Conf. Computer Vision*, IEEE CS Press, Los Alamitos, Calif., 1987, pp. 626-630.

181. Z. Gigus, J.F. Canny, and R. Seidel, "Efficiently Computing and Representing Aspect Graphs of Polyhedral Objects," *Proc. Second Int'l Conf. Computer Vision*, IEEE CS Press, Los Alamitos, Calif., 1988, pp. 30-39.

182. D.J. Kriegman and J. Ponce, "Computing Exact Aspect Graphs of Curved Objects: Solids of Revolution," *Proc. IEEE Workshop on Interpretation of 3-D Scenes*, IEEE CS Press, Los Alamitos, Calif., 1989, pp. 109-115.

183. D. Eggert and K. Bowyer, "Computing the Orthographic Projection Aspect Graph of Solids of Revolution," *Proc. IEEE Workshop on Interpretation of 3-D Scenes*, IEEE CS Press, Los Alamitos, Calif., 1989, pp. 102-108.

184. J. Ponce and D.J. Kriegman, "Computing Exact Aspect Graphs of Curved Objects: Parametric Surfaces," *Tech. Report UIUCDCS-R-90-1579*, Dept. of Computer Science, University of Illinois at Urbana-Champaign, 1990.

185. G. Castore, "Solid Modeling, Aspect Graphs, and Robot Vision," in *Solid Modeling by Computers: From Theory to Applications*, M.S. Picket and J.W. Boyse, eds., Plenum, New York, N.Y., 1984.

186. J. Stewman and K. Bowyer, "Aspect Graphs for Planar-Face Convex Objects," *Proc. IEEE Workshop on Computer Vision*, IEEE CS Press, Los Alamitos, Calif., 1987, pp. 123-130.

187. J. Stewman and K. Bowyer, "Creating the Perspective Projection Aspect Graph of Polyhedral Objects," *Proc. Second Int'l Conf. Computer Vision*, IEEE CS Press, Los Alamitos, Calif., 1988, pp. 494-500.

188. N.A. Watts, "Calculating the Principal Views of a Polyhedron," *Proc. Ninth Int'l Conf. Pattern Recognition*, IEEE CS Press, Los Alamitos, Calif., 1988, pp. 316-322.

189. R.A. Brooks, R. Greiner, and T.O. Binford, "The ACRONYM Model-Based Vision System," *Proc. Sixth Int'l Joint Conf. on Artificial Intelligence*, Morgan Kaufmann Publishers, Inc., San Mateo, Calif., 1979, pp. 105-113.

190. R.A. Brooks, "Symbolic Reasoning among 3-D Models and 2-D Images," *Artificial Intelligence*, Vol. 17, 1981, pp. 285-348.

191. W.W. Bledsoe, "The Sup-Inf Method in Presbuger Arithmetic", *Tech. Report ATP-18*, Dept. of Mathematics and Computer Science, University of Texas, Austin, 1974.

192. R.E. Shostak, "On the Sup-Inf Method for Proving Presbuger Formula," *J. ACM*, Vol. 24, 1977, pp. 529-543.

193. T.O. Binford, "Survey of Model-Based Image Analysis," *Int'l J. Robotics Research*, Vol. 1, No. 1, 1982, pp. 18-64.

194. R.B. Fischer, "Using Surfaces and Object Models to Recognize Partially Obscured Objects," *Proc. Int'l Joint Conf. Artificial Intelligence*, Morgan Kaufmann Publishers, Inc., San Mateo, Calif., 1983, pp. 989-995.

195. J.W. McKee and J.K. Aggarwal, "Computer Recognition of Partial Views of Three-Dimensional Curved Objects," *Tech. Report 171*, Dept. of Computer Science, University of Texas, Austin, 1975

196. S. Dudani, K.J. Breeding, and R.B. McGhee, "Aircraft Identification by Moment Invariants," *IEEE Trans. Computer*, Vol. 26, 1977, pp. 39-46.

197. A.P. Reeves, R.J. Prokop, and F.P. Kuhl, "Three-Dimensional Shape Analysis Using Fourier Descriptors," *Proc. Seventh Int'l Conf. Pattern Recognition*, IEEE CS Press, Los Alamitos, Calif., 1984, pp. 447-450.

198. F.A. Sadjadi and E.L. Hall, "Three-Dimensional Moment Invariants," *IEEE Trans. Pattern Analysis and Machine Intelligence*, Vol. 2, No. 2, 1980, pp. 127-136.

199. D. Casasent, B.V.K. Vijaya-Kumar, and V. Sharma, "Synthetic Discriminant Functions for Three-Dimensional Object Recognition," *SPIE Proc. of Conf. on Robotics and Industrial Inspection*, Vol. 360, 1982, pp. 136-142.

200. T.M. Silberberg, D.A. Harwood, and L.S. Davis, "Object Recognition Using Oriented Model Points," *Computer Vision, Graphics and Image Processing*, Vol. 35, 1986, pp. 47-71.

201. C. Goad, "Special Purpose Automatic Programming for 3-D Model-Based Vision," *Proc. DARPA Image Understanding Workshop*, 1983, pp. 94-104.

202. M.O. Shneier, "Models and Strategies for Matching in Industrial Vision," *Computer Science Tech. Report, TR-1073*, University of Maryland, College Park, Md., July, 1981.

203. L.G. Roberts, "Machine Perception of Three-Dimensional Solids," in *Symposium On Optical and Electro-Optical Information Processing Technology*, J.T. Tippett et al, eds., MIT Press, Cambridge, Mass., 1965.

204. A. Guzman, *Computer Recognition of Three-Dimensional Objects in a Visual Scene*, PhD thesis, MIT, Cambridge, Mass., 1968.

205. D.L. Waltz, "Generating Semantic Descriptions from Drawing of Scenes with Shadows", *Tech. Report AI-TR-271*, Artificial Intelligence Laboratory, MIT, Cambridge, Mass., 1972.

206. D.G. Lowe, "Three-Dimensional Object Recognition from Single Two-Dimensional Images," *Artificial Intelligence*, Vol. 31, No. 3, 1987, pp. 355-395.

207. W.E.L. Grimson, "Recognition of Object Families Using Parameterized Models," *Proc. First Int'l Conf. Computer Vision*, IEEE CS Press, Los Alamitos, Calif., 1987, pp. 93-101.

208. Y. Lamdan and H.J. Wolfson, "Geometric Hashing: A General and Efficient Model-Based Recognition Scheme," *Proc. Second Int'l Conf. Computer Vision*, IEEE CS Press, Los Alamitos, Calif., 1988, pp. 238-249.

209. T.O. Binford, "Spatial Understanding: The SUCCESSOR System," *Proc. DARPA Image Understanding Workshop*, 1989, pp. 12-20.

210. N. Narasimhamurthi and R.C. Jain, "Computer-Aided, Design-Based Object Recognition: Incorporating Metric and Topological Information," *Proc. SPIE Conf. Digital and Optical Shape Representation and Pattern Recognition*, Vol. 938, 1988, pp. 436-433.

Reprinted from *IEEE Transactions on Pattern Analysis and Machine Intelligence*, Volume PAMI-5, Number 2, March 1983, pages 150-158.

Volumetric Descriptions of Objects from Multiple Views

WORTHY N. MARTIN, MEMBER, IEEE, AND J. K. AGGARWAL, FELLOW, IEEE

Abstract—Occluding contours from an image sequence with viewpoint specifications determine a bounding volume approximating the object generating the contours. The initial creation and continual refinement of the approximation requires a volumetric representation that facilitates modification yet is descriptive of surface detail. The "volume segment" representation presented in this paper is one such representation.

Index Terms—Dynamic scene analysis, occluding boundary, surface description, volume description.

I. INTRODUCTION

VOLUMETRIC models have been the basis of numerous three-dimensional object modeling systems. In order to represent the desired volume, various types of primitives have been specified. Initially, polyhedrons were used as combinations of a small set of simple volumes [1] and later as general

Manuscript received May 17, 1982; revised August 17, 1982. This work was supported in part by the U.S. Air Force Office of Scientific Research under Grant AFOSR 82-0064.

W. N. Martin was with the Laboratory for Image and Signal Analysis, University of Texas, Austin, TX 78712. He is now with the Department of Applied Mathematics and Computer Sciences, University of Virginia, Charlottesville, VA 22901.

J. K. Aggarwal is with the Laboratory for Image and Signal Analysis, University of Texas, Austin, TX 78712.

volumes [2]. Each face of a polyhedron may be considered to be part of the bounding plane of a half-space. The interior of the polyhedron can then be described procedurally by the "addition" and "subtraction" of these half-spaces. Requicha [3] defines "general regularized set operators" and a syntax for specifying the procedural description in a constructive solid geometry scheme. The operators will always yield "valid" representations if the primitives have finite volumes. Through additional operators general sweep representations can also be specified. Generalized cylinders are a class of sweep representations that have been studied extensively [4]-[8]. Elsewhere, spheres [9] have been used in structures approximating symmetric surfaces, i.e., three-dimensional generalizations of symmetric axes [10].

Most of the systems referenced to this point are geometric modeling systems [11] primarily developed for computer aided design applications, such as BUILD [2] and PADL [12], or for image interpretation, such as MSYS [13], VISIONS [14], and ACRONYM [15]. These systems usually have interactive procedures for deriving the three-dimensional models and often have a major interest in the suitability of the model for graphical display [16]-[18]. The primary concern of this paper is the development of volumetric descriptions suitable for deriving three-dimensional object representations from two-dimensional images. Determining such representations has been the goal of many computer vision systems since Roberts' original paper [1]. Roberts demonstrated that three-dimensional information about the actual objects in a single image can be derived under two classes of constraints. The first class included overall scene domain constraints, e.g., the objects were planar faced, while the second class involved specific object constraints, e.g., the objects were combinations of a limited number of polyhedrons. These polyhedrons were the primitives instanced in various sizes and arrangements to form the actual objects in the scene.

Roberts' paper is extremely important for having established a paradigm that many researchers in scene analysis have followed. Attempts have been made to lessen the restrictions imposed by either or both classes of constraints. For example, the specific object constraints were replaced by more extensive domain constraints in the thorough work on line drawings of polyhedral scenes; see [19]-[22]. Different sorts of scene constraints have also been applied. For instance, known properties of special illumination conditions can indicate surface orientations; see [23]-[27].

The constraints can be reduced further by using multiple views of the scene, often with a time ordering resulting in an image sequence [28], [29]. For each view in the sequence feature points can be detected and a correspondence [30] formed between the features in successive views. The image positions of the corresponding feature points provide additional constraints that can be written in the form of a set of nonlinear equations [31]-[33]. Solving the set of equations yields a wire-frame model of the three-dimensional positions of the scene components underlying the image features. The multiple views presented in image sequences can result from either camera or object movement (or both) and provide an additional source of constraints through the control [34], [35] or restriction [36] of the exhibited motions. In the system we have developed the motion creating the multiple views will not be controlled but will be precisely known through viewpoint specifications.

Our work has been in the pursuit of two major goals. The first goal is the development of a system that is capable of deriving three-dimensional object description images, yet does not depend completely on feature point measurements. The second goal is the development of a scheme for representing three-dimensional objects that is descriptive of surface detail, while remaining functional in the context of a structure from multiple view system. The result of this work is a system which uses the occluding contours from multiple images with viewpoint specifications to construct a bounding volume approximating the actual three-dimensional structure of the rigid object generating the contours. The representation constructed to facilitate the creation and continual refinement of the bounding volume is referred to as a "volume segment" representation and will be discussed in Section III.

II. Volumes from Contours

By an "occluding contour" we mean the boundary in the image plane of the silhouette of an object generated by an orthogonal projection. In an intensity image the silhouette

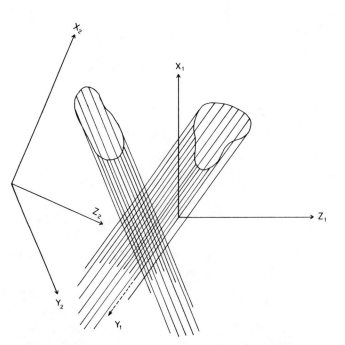

Fig. 1. Silhouettes and contour generating lines for two views.

can most often be formed by a simple thresholding of the intensity values. A connected component analysis [37] of the resulting binary valued image yields the boundary of the object silhouette.

Throughout this paper, the orientation of a view will be specified by a point and three mutually perpendicular directions that form a right-handed, three-axis coordinate system with the given point as origin. The y-axis of each coordinate system is considered to be the direction of the line of sight with the (x, z)-plane being the image plane, i.e., the silhouette is projected onto the image plane by lines parallel to the line of sight. Thus, an occluding contour is generated by the lines that are parallel to the y-axis and that intersect the object, but do so only at points which are on the object surface. For objects with smooth surfaces this means that the lines are in the tangent planes of their intersection points.

Clearly, then, the object surface must touch each contour generating line. The problem is to determine which points on the line are also object surface points. This problem is solved by using the constraints imposed by the contour generating lines from a second (and subsequent) view. The situation of two views is shown in Fig. 1. The contours are displayed in their respective image planes and some representative contour generating lines are indicated by equal length sections of lines that are parallel to the appropriate y-axis. The set of contour generating lines for a given view defines a volume which bounds the actual object, however, this volume is by itself infinite. A second view will also define an infinite volume that contains the object, and if the second view is distinct, i.e., the two lines of sight are not parallel, then the intersection of the two volumes will still encompass the object and will be of finite extent. Intersecting the volumes to define the approximation is in the spirit of the geometric modeling systems [2], [3], [12], yet is a process that can be applied to image data.

It is clear from Fig. 1 that each contour generating line for one of the views serves to constrain the extent of the possible

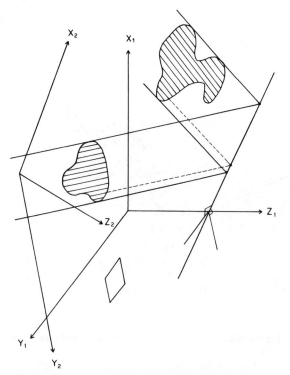

Fig. 2. Scan line derivation of parallelogram constraints.

is rasterized to scan lines in the direction perpendicular to the common line and in the appropriate image plane. That is, the scan lines are chosen parallel to the limiting projection rays and at equal intervals along the common line. The rasterized area is a set of parallel line segments, the endpoints of which specify boundary points of the area (see Newman and Sproull [38] or Martin and Aggarwal [39]). For a given scan line, e.g., the dotted line in Fig. 2, the endpoints of the associated segments determine the boundary points that specify the contour generating lines for the plane containing the scan line. The second contour has a corresponding scan line and thus a set of contour generating lines that are also in the given plane.

The mutual constraints provided by these two sets of contour generating lines are as follows. A given scan line segment in one view has two contour generating lines. These two lines form limits for each of the contour generating lines from the second view that are in the plane defined by the given scan line. The limits specify the extent over which points of the contour generating lines can also be object surface points, i.e., the portion of the contour generating line that is between the limiting lines. Of course, the limited contour generating line is also associated with a scan line segment for the second view and so is paired to another contour generating line for that view. This pair of lines, then, constrains the lines from the first view in the given plane. In particular, the latter pair combines with the original pair from the first view to form mutual constraints on the object volume. The combined constraints are in the form of a parallelogram in the plane containing the scan lines. Each pair of lines specifies a pair of opposing sides on the parallelogram. For example, the dotted scan lines in Fig. 2 form the shown parallelogram.

Each such parallelogram is a bounding figure for the cross section of the object generated by the given plane. The parallelograms circumscribe the cross sections in that a cross section must have at least one point in common with each side of the parallelogram. Of course, there may be more than one parallelogram in a given plane, but that is indicative of the cross section being disconnected with each connected subset bounded by a separate parallelogram. The locus of all the parallelograms in the planes of the various scan lines is the bounding volume which establishes the initial estimate of the object structure.

With the object structure described in this manner, the system is ready to form the volume segment representation which will be used in the subsequent refining process. The next section will define the volume segment representation and then discuss how it is derived from this initial parallelogram structure.

The process described in this section should be contrasted with computer aided tomography [40] and other cross-sectional methods [9], [41], [42] on two main points. First, the source of data is a sequence of simple binary images possibly from a television camera as opposed to the elaborate data acquisition mechanisms required for tomography and range measurement [43]. Second, neither the initial volume specification described above nor the refinement process explained in Section IV depends on predefined cross-sectional decomposition of the data.

object surface points on some of the contour generating lines for the other view. In order to establish the initial estimate of the object, the system must determine how each contour generating line constrains the volume from the other view and create a structure that satisfies the various constraints simultaneously.

To see how these constraints are specified consider Fig. 2. Again, two contours are shown in their respective image planes with the lines of sight corresponding to the y-axes. Since these directions are distinct, the image planes are not parallel and thereby must share a common line. The common line for the two image planes is shown on the right-hand side of Fig. 2. This line is in the direction of the cross-product of the two y-axes, and so is perpendicular to both axes, as indicated in the figure. Now, the upper right contour is in the $(x1, z1)$-plane and can be orthogonally projected in that plane onto the common line. The two solid lines, i.e., projection rays, that are tangent to the contour and intersect the common line delimit the projection of the contour onto the common line. In a similar manner, the second contour has two limiting projection rays, as indicated.

The fundamental property of the contours making the construction of the initial estimate possible is that each of the limiting rays for one contour projects onto the common line precisely at the point onto which a limiting ray from the other contour projects. In particular, the projection is orthogonal so that each ray is perpendicular to the common line. Thus, two rays that meet at a point on the common line are coplanar and this plane contains the contour generating lines corresponding to the points on the contour intersected by the limiting rays. It is these coplanar contour generating lines which provide the mutual constraints that determine the bounding volume.

In order to find the coplanar generating lines, each boundary

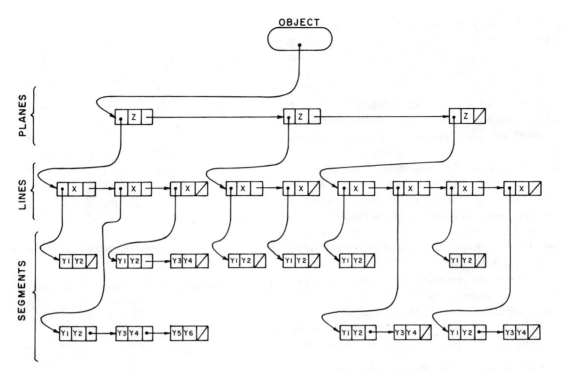

Fig. 3. Data structure schema for the volume segment representation.

III. Volume Segment Representation

The three-dimensional structure to be derived from the sequence of occluding contours is a bounding volume approximating the actual object. For this reason the representation incorporated in this system is based on volume specification through a "volume segment" data structure. The volume segment representation is a generalization to three dimensions of the rasterized area description. For the rasterized area, the segments each denote a rectangular area. The generalization to three dimensions is to have each segment represent a volume, i.e., a rectilinear parallelepiped with edges parallel to the coordinate axes. In addition to grouping collinear segments into lists, the set of segment lists is partitioned so that the subsets contain lists having coplanar segments. The primary dimension of the rectilinear parallelepiped specified by a segment is the length of the segment. The second dimension is given by the interline spacing within the plane of the segment, while the third dimension is the interplane distance. The latter two dimensions are specified to be uniform throughout the volume segment representation.

The structure then maintains an ordered pair of values for each volume segment: the values are the y-coordinates of the segment endpoints and are ordered into lists of segments having the same x-coordinate, i.e., collinear. The x-level lists are then coalesced into z-level ordered lists by common z-coordinate, i.e., coplanar. From the top down this structure is a set of "planes" parallel to the $z = 0$ plane, that are ordered by z-value. Each "plane" contains a set of "lines" parallel to the y-axis, that are ordered by x-value. Each "line" comprises a set of disjoint segments that are ordered by endpoint y-value. Fig. 3 shows a schematic of a volume segment structure using linked lists to order the various components.

In a general situation the primary advantage of this structure

is that the process of determining whether an arbitrary point is within the surface boundary consists of a simple search of three ordered lists: select a "plane" by z-coordinate; select a "line" by x-coordinate; and finally, check for inclusion of the y-coordinate in a segment. The simplicity of this process is in contrast to that required by a representation scheme such as constructive solid geometry [3] wherein the object is represented using regularized set operations on primitive solids. For a particular object represented by given solids, point inclusion is specified by determing if the point is in each primitive solid (possibly a difficult problem itself) and then performing the logical operations corresponding to the set operations from which the object representation is constructed.

The volume segment structure can also provide a fairly succinct representation, particularly for objects that are elongated in the direction of the y-axis. It becomes more verbose as the elongation extends in the z-axis direction, however, it always remains more compact than surface-ordered enumerative representations, e.g., connected sets of "voxel" faces [44]. In comparing a volume segment structure to a connected voxel face structure one should observe that each leaf in the tree of the volume segment structure represents two voxel faces and remains only two levels from the root of the structure. In addition each voxel face must maintain its three-dimensional position and connections to four edge-adjacent faces. In balance, surface connectivity is not specified directly in the volume segment structure and may require a small amount of searching to compute. As will be shown by the example in Section V, forming a surface description from the volume segments is possible and is computed as a matter of course by this system.

Before proceeding with the details of that system let us indicate a comparison with another volume oriented representation, that of oct-trees [45]. Consider a simple cube measuring 2^n units on each edge that is embedded with standard orientation in a single octant of a space extending 2^{n+1} units in each direction. For the volume segment structure to represent the cube requires 2^n z-planes each having 2^n x-lines with 2 y-endpoints per line. This yields 2^{2n} volume segments represented by a tree having a total of $(1 + 2^n + 2^{2n} + 1)$ nodes. Note the connected voxel face structure would require 2^{2n} voxel faces for each side of the cube, yielding $6(2^{2n})$ faces.

In contrast, the cube can be represented by an oct-tree of just nine nodes. Of course, this example is a best case for oct-trees. Now, translate the cube one unit in the x direction so that the cube intersects two octants of the embedding space: the volume segment structure and connected voxel face structure do not change. However, the oct-tree representation expands to require $1 + 6 + ((4^{n+2} - 10)/3)$ nodes. Unit translations of the cube in the remaining two principle directions will yield further expansion of the oct-tree. Rotation of the cube can cause expansion in both the volume segment and connected voxel face structures, but these expansions would not be of the magnitude described for the oct-tree structure.

IV. CONSTRUCTION AND REFINEMENT FOR THE VOLUME REPRESENTATION

This section describes both the process by which the volume segment representation is initially constructed from the parallelogram structure detailed in Section II and the process that refines the representation using subsequent views. The first step in the initial construction process is to define a new coordinate system, relative to which the volume segment representation will be specified. Consider, now Fig. 4, in which the contours from two views are displayed in their image planes. Also shown are the lines common to both image planes and a few appropriate scan line segments for the contours. For the bottom scan line of each contour the limiting contour generating lines, i.e., the dotted lines parallel to the respective y-axes, are shown forming the parallelogram for that plane. Also shown are the parallelograms for the planes specified by the remaining scan line segments. Note that the top scan line of the triangular contour is a single point, resulting in a degenerate parallelogram. Again, each parallelogram is in a plane that is perpendicular to the comon line. This observation suggests that the common line could be used as the z-axis of the volume segment representation's coordinate system. Making that choice, the y-axis of the new system is defined to be in the direction of the line of sight for the first view, while the x-axis is selected to complete the right-handed coordinate system, e.g., the (x', y', z')-axes in Fig. 4. Of course, either line of sight could be used for the y-axis as it is known that both are perpendicular to the common line. The choice of one of these two directions is made to simplify the next step: parallelogram rasterization.

Each parallelogram is taken as an area in the appropriate (x', y')-plane and rasterized along scan lines parallel to the y'-axis. For the plane of a parallelogram, the rasterization results in a set of line segments parallel to the y'-axis for each x'-value. Thus there is a set of planes each having various lines that are broken into segments. With this information all

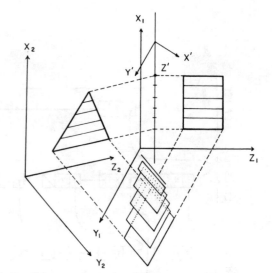

Fig. 4. Parallelogram structure yielding the initial volume segment representation.

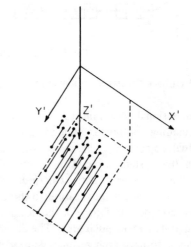

Fig. 5. Volume segment representation in its own coordinate axis system.

that is needed is to add the linking structure and the volume segment representation will be complete. Fig. 5 displays the representation formed for the parallelogram structure of Fig. 4. In Fig. 5 the segments are drawn relative to the representation's coordinate axis system. The dotted line from the z-axis indicates the plane containing the segments derived from what was the bottom parallelogram in Fig. 4. The other segments are in planes nearer the origin. Fig. 6 displays a summary of the algorithm to create the initial volume segment representation that was just explained, while Fig. 7 exhibits a summary of the volume segment representation refinement process that is described in the remainder of this section.

The refinement process is applied as each new frame (after the first two) of the dynamic image is obtained. As was stated earlier, this process makes extensive use of the clipping procedure that is based on rasterized area descriptions. To see how this is done consider Fig. 8. The volume segment representation of Fig. 5 is again shown, however, the contour, image plane and line of sight for a new frame are included in the figure. The overall process is to clip the volume segments

1. obtain image and viewpoint specification for first frame.

2. form silhouette and extract boundary coordinate list for first frame.

3. obtain image and viewpoint specification for second frame.

4. form silhouette and extract boundary coordinate list for second frame.

5. determine line common to the image planes from the first and second frames.

6. rasterize the boundaries along scan line direction perpendicular to the common line.

7. merge mutual constraints from corresponding scan line segments to form the parallelogram description of the object.

8. define the coordinate axis system for the volume segment representation having the z-axis in direction of the common line and the y-axis in the direction of the line of sight for the first frame.

9. rasterize the parallelograms in each z-plane of the new axis system to define the segments of the volume representation.

10. add the linkage structure to complete the volume segment representation.

Fig. 6. Initial representation creation.

Algorithm summary:

1. obtain image and viewpoint specification for new frame.

2. form silhouette and extract boundary coordinate list for new frame.

3. project the y-axis of the volume segment representation's coordinate system along the line of sight and onto the image plane of the new frame.

4. rasterize the new boundary along scan lines that are parallel to the projection of the y-axis in the image plane.

5. for each segment in the volume segment representation do the following:

    5a. project the segment along the line of sight and onto the image plane of the new frame.

    5b. clip the projected segment to the rasterized boundary.

    5c. update the actual segment with respect to the clipped projection.

6. create surface description if desired.

7. continue at step 1 if there are more frames, else stop.

Fig. 7. Continuing representation refinement.

by the new contour. For this to be done, the contour must be rasterized properly. The required direction for the scan lines is the direction in the image plane of the projection, along the new line of sight, of the y-axis for the volume segment representation. The dotted lines in Fig. 8 from the y-axis into the (x',z')-plane indicate this projection. Note that the resulting direction will not normally be parallel to the original y-axis. The contour in Fig. 8 is shown to be rasterized along scan lines parallel to this projected direction.

Given the properly rasterized area description of the new contour the refinement procedure is as follows. Each segment of the volume representation is projected onto the new image plane, again according to the direction of the new line of sight. The projected segment, then, is in the image plane and

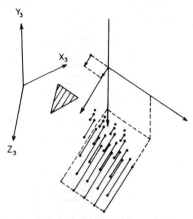

Fig. 8. Refining the volume segment representation by subsequent views.

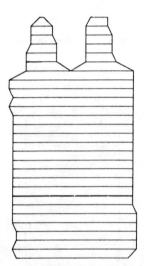

Fig. 9. Contour from first view with "raster" lines inserted.

can be clipped as described previously for the two-dimensional case. The original volume segment can then be updated by modifying its length in a proportion equivalent to that by which the projected segment was clipped. In geometric terms, the clipped segment could be inversely projected onto the line of the original volume segment, with the resulting segment replacing the original segment. A special case occurs when the line of sight happens to be parallel to the y-axis of the coordinate system of the volume segment representation. However, in this case each volume segment projects onto a single point in the image plane and a simple point inclusion test on the area description (rasterized to an arbitrary direction) determines whether the entire volume segment is to be retained in or deleted from the representation.

V. AN EXAMPLE DYNAMIC SCENE

To illustrate the volume segment representation and the process which constructs it, an example is presented in this section. The various stages of the example are shown in Figs. 9–17. The four frames, with raster lines inserted, of the input dynamic scene are presented in Figs. 9–12. In these frames the object rotates about a vertical axis so that it traverses 90° between the first and last views. The combination of the first

Fig. 10. Contour from second view.

Fig. 11. Contour from third view.

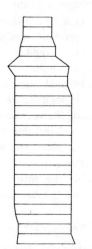

Fig. 12. Contour from the fourth and last view.

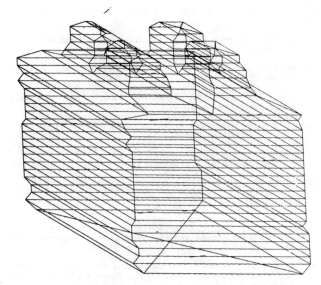

Fig. 13. "Parallelogram cross section" surface description derived from the views displayed in Figs. 9 and 10.

Fig. 14. The volume segment representation of the surface in Fig. 13.

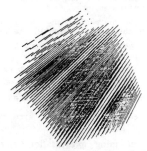

Fig. 15. The volume segment representation derived by constraining the representation shown in Fig. 14 by the contour displayed in Fig. 11.

two views, i.e., Figs. 9 and 10 results in the surface shown in Fig. 13. Each pair of "raster" lines (one from each view) generates a parallelogram which lies in a plane parallel to the global (x, y)-plane. The parallelograms have been connected along corresponding corners with the top and bottom faces marked by crossing lines. The volume segment representation resulting from this surface is exhibited in Fig. 14. As stated earlier, each segment is parallel to the global y-axis. In Fig. 14 perspective cues have been added to provide the proper sense of depth. The third and fourth frames are then processed to constrain the volume segment representation to be as it is displayed in Figs. 15 and 16, respectively. Finally, the volume segment representation of Fig. 16 is transformed into a surface description, as illustrated in Fig. 17. It should be noted that the surface representation of Fig. 17 is derived directly from the volume segment representation and is much more general than the surface description shown in Fig. 13.

Fig. 16. The final volume segment representation for the dynamic scene.

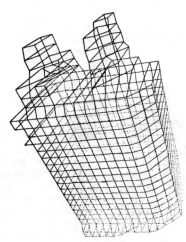

Fig. 17. The general surface description derived from the volume segment representation illustrated in Fig. 16.

VI. CONCLUSION

The two major goals pursued in this work are, first, to lessen the dependence on feature point measurements in a structure from multiple views system, and second, to develop a descriptive three-dimensional object representation that was suitable for a dynamic process of volume refinement. The results are twofold: 1) a system has been developed which constructs a volumetric structure for an object from a sequence of occluding contours and 2) an algorithm has been formulated for the representation and refinement of this structure.

The occluding contours with viewpoint specifications from a dynamic image are analyzed to initially form and continually update a description of the three-dimensional object generating the contours. The description is a bounding volume for the object and is successively refined to yield finer approximations to the actual object. Of course, from the silhouettes that form the occluding contours it is not possible to resolve certain kinds of concavities. In particular, object surface points for which every tangent line (in the tangent plane, any line that contains the given surface point) also intersects the object at some nonsurface point cannot be resolved using silhouettes. However, the class of objects that can be described exactly is large, and in fact, the object surface may have saddle points and holes.

Clearly, to analyze the structure of objects a system must provide a representation scheme. For three-dimensional objects many different schemes have been proposed and used.

The details of the representations usually are determined either by the data acquisition techniques or by the ultimate application of the system, with an important problem being the development of methods for transforming between structures of the first type and structures of the second type; see Aggarwal *et al.* [46]. The volume segment representation described in this paper has been developed to facilitate the acquisition of three-dimensional information from dynamic images. The main attributes of the volume segment representation are that it is easy to update (as required by the continual refinement), maintains fine surface detail, simplifies the point inclusion test, and can be readily transformed into a surface representation.

For these reasons the work presented in this paper provides an excellent basis for further research. In particular, the work is appropriate to industrial automation applications. For example, selecting one of several parts on a conveyer using the views taken from several cameras fixed along the line of travel, or in conjunction with a manipulator arm that could successively reposition a part until an adequate approximation was derived. In such applications there are usually fixed sets of possible objects from which an unknown object must be recognized, implying the need for a representation scheme suitable for creating a library of possible objects, describing the unknown sample and matching it to the library entries. Future research should be directed toward exploiting the methods developed here in those applications.

REFERENCES

[1] L. G. Roberts, "Machine perception of three-dimensional solids," in *Computer Methods in Image Analysis*, J. K. Aggarwal, R. O. Duda, and A. Rosenfeld, Eds. New York: IEEE Press, 1977, pp. 285–323.

[2] I. C. Braid, "The synthesis of solids bounded by many faces," *Commun. Ass. Comput. Mach.*, vol. 18, pp. 209–216, Apr. 1975.

[3] A. A. G. Requicha, "Representations for rigid solids: Theory, method and systems," *Comput. Surveys*, vol. 12, no. 4, pp. 437–464, 1980.

[4] G. J. Agin and T. O. Binford, "Computer description of curved objects," *IEEE Trans. Comput.*, vol. C-25, pp. 439–449, Apr. 1976.

[5] J. Hollerbach, "Hierarchical shape description of objects by selection and modification of prototypes," MIT AI-TR-346, Nov. 1975.

[6] B. I. Soroka and R. K. Bajcsy, "A program for describing complex three-dimensional objects using generalized cylinders as primitives," presented at the IEEE Conf. Pattern Recognition and Image Processing, Chicago, IL, 1978.

[7] R. Nevatia and T. O. Binford, "Description and recognition of curved objects," *Artificial Intell.*, vol. 8, pp. 77–98, 1977.

[8] D. Marr, "Visual information processing: The structure and creation of visual representations," in *Proc. IJCAI-6*, Tokyo, Aug. 1979, pp. 1108–1126.

[9] J. O'Rourke and N. Badler, "Decomposition of three-dimensional objects into spheres," *IEEE Trans. Pattern Anal. Machine Intell.*, vol. PAMI-1, pp. 295–305, July 1979.

[10] H. Blum, "A transformation for extracting new descriptors of shape," in *Models for the Perception of Speech and Visual Form*, W. Dunn, Ed. Cambridge, MA: MIT Press, 1964, pp. 362–380.

[11] B. G. Baumgart, "Geometric modeling for computer vision," Stanford AI Lab. Memo. AIM-249, Oct. 1974.

[12] H. B. Voelcker, A. A. G. Requicha, E. E. Hartquist, W. B. Fisher, J. E. Shapiro, and N. K. Birrell, "An introduction to PADL:

Characteristics, status, and rationale," Univ. Rochester, Prod. Automat. Project Tech. Memo. TM-22, Dec. 1974.

[13] H. G. Barrow and J. M. Tenenbaum, "MSYS: A system for reasoning about scenes," SRI AI Center, Tech. Note 121, Mar. 1976.

[14] A. Hansen and E. Riseman, "VISIONS: A computer system for interpreting, scenes," in *Computer Vision Systems*, A. Hansen and E. Riseman, Eds. New York: Academic, 1978, pp. 303-333.

[15] R. A. Brooks, "Symbolic reasoning among 3-D models and 2-D images," Dep. Comput. Sci., Stanford Univ., Rep. STAN-CS-81-861, June 1981.

[16] E. Miyamoto and T. O. Binford, "Display generated by a generalized cone representation," presented at the IEEE Conf. Comput. Graphics and Image Processing, May 1975.

[17] J. H. Clark, "Hierarchical geometric models for visible surface algorithms," *Commun. Ass. Comput. Mach.*, vol. 19, pp. 547-554, Oct. 1976.

[18] N. Badler and R. K. Bajcsy, "Three-dimensional representations for computer graphics and computer vision," *Comput. Graphics*, vol. 12, pp. 153-160, Aug. 1978.

[19] D. Huffman, "Impossible objects as nonsense sentences," in *Machine Intelligence 6*, B. Meltzer and D. Michie, Eds. Edinburgh, Scotland: Edinburgh Univ. Press, 1971.

[20] M. Clowes, "On seeing things," *Artificial Intell. J.*, vol. 2, no. 1, pp. 79-116, 1971.

[21] D. Waltz, "Understanding line drawings of scenes with shadows," in *Psychology of Computer Vision*, P. H. Winston, Ed. New York: McGraw-Hill, 1975, pp. 19-92.

[22] A. Mackworth, "Interpreting pictures of polyhedral scenes," *Artificial Intell. J.*, vol. 4, pp. 121-137, 1973.

[23] P. M. Will and K. S. Pennington, "Grid coding: A preprocessing technique for robot and machine vision," in *Proc. 2nd IJCAI*, London, 1971, pp. 66-70.

[24] B. K. P. Horn, "Understanding image intensities," *Artificial Intell. J.*, vol. 8, pp. 201, 231, 1977.

[25] R. J. Woodham, "A cooperative algorithm for determining surface orientation from a single view," in *Proc. 5th Int. Joint Conf. Artificial Intell.*, Cambridge, MA, 1977, pp. 635-641.

[26] Y. Shirai and M. Suiva, "Recognition of polyhedrons with a range finder," in *Proc. 2nd Int. Joint Conf. Artificial Intell.*, London, 1971, pp. 71-79.

[27] H. Freeman and M. Potmesil, "Curved surface representation utilizing data extracted from multiple photographic images," in *Proc. Workshop on the Representation of Three-Dimensional Objects*, Philadelphia, PA, 1979.

[28] W. N. Martin and J. K. Aggarwal, "Survey: Dynamic scene analysis," *Comput. Graphics Image Processing*, vol. 7, pp. 356-374, June 1978.

[29] H.-H. Nagel, "Image sequence analysis: What can we learn from applications?," in *Image Sequence Analysis*, T. S. Huang, Ed. Heidelberg, Germany: Springer-Verlag, 1981, pp. 19-228.

[30] J. K. Aggarwal, L. S. Davis, and W. N. Martin, "Correspondence processes in dynamic scene analysis," *Proc. IEEE*, vol. 69, no. 5, pp. 562-572, May 1981.

[31] S. Ullman, *The Interpretation of Visual Motion*. Cambridge, MA: MIT Press, 1979.

[32] J. W. Roach and J. K. Aggarwal, "Determining the movement of objects from a sequence of images," *IEEE Trans. Pattern Anal. Machine Intell.*, vol. PAMI-2, pp. 554-562, Nov. 1980.

[33] H.-H. Nagel, "Representation of moving rigid objects based on visual observations," *IEEE Computer*, vol. 14, no. 8, pp. 29-39, Aug. 1981.

[34] R. Nevatia, "Depth measurement by motion stereo," *Comput. Graphics Image Processing*, vol. 15, pp. 203-214, 1976.

[35] H. H. Baker, "Three-dimensional modelling," in *Proc. 2nd IJCAI*, London, 1977, pp. 649-655.

[36] J. A. Webb and J. K. Aggarwal, "Visually interpreting the motion of objects in space," *IEEE Computer*, vol. 14, pp. 40-46, Aug. 1981.

[37] A. Rosenfeld and A. C. Kak, *Digital Picture Processing*. New York: Academic, 1976, pp. 336-347.

[38] W. E. Newman and R. F. Sproull, *Principles of Interactive Computer Graphics*, 2nd ed. New York: McGraw-Hill, 1979, pp. 229-245.

[39] W. N. Martin and J. K. Aggarwal, "Analyzing dynamic scenes," Lab. for Image and Signal Anal., Univ. Texas, Austin, Rep. TR-81-5, pp. 51-56, Dec. 1981.

[40] G. T. Herman, *Image Reconstruction from Projections: The Fundamentals of Computerized Tomography*. New York: Academic, 1980.

[41] C. Levinthal and R. Ware, "Three-dimensional reconstruction from serial sections," *Nature*, vol. 236, pp. 207-210, Mar. 1972.

[42] H. Fuchs, Z. M. Kedem, and S. P. Uselton, "Optimal surface reconstruction from planar contours," *Commun. Ass. Comput. Mach.*, vol. 20, pp. 693-702, Oct. 1977.

[43] D. Nitzan, A. E. Brain, and R. O. Duda, "The measurement and use of registered reflectance and range data in scene analysis," *Proc. IEEE*, vol. 65, pp. 206-220, Feb. 1977.

[44] G. T. Herman and H. K. Liu, "Dynamic boundary surface detection," *Comput. Graphics Image Processing*, vol. 7, pp. 130-138, 1978.

[45] C. L. Jackins and S. L. Tanimoto, "Oct-trees and their use in representing three-dimensional objects," *Comput. Graphics Image Processing*, vol. 14, pp. 249-270, 1980.

[46] J. K. Aggarwal, L. S. Davis, W. N. Martin, and J. W. Roach, "Survey: Representation methods for three-dimensional objects," in *Progress in Pattern Recognition*, vol. 1, L. Kanal and A. Rosenfeld, Eds. Amsterdam, The Netherlands: North-Holland, 1981, pp. 337-391.

Worthy N. Martin (S'78-M'79-S'80-M'81) was born on November 24, 1951. He received the B.A. degree in mathematics, the M.A. degree in computer science, and the Ph.D. degree in computer science in 1981, all from the University of Texas, Austin.

He is currently an Assistant Professor of Computer Science at the Department of Applied Mathematics and Computer Sciences, University of Virginia, Charlottesville. From 1980 to 1982, he was associated with the Laboratory for Image and Signal Analysis and during the 1981-1982 academic year was on the faculty of the Department of Computer Sciences at the University of Texas, Austin.

Dr. Martin is a member of the IEEE Computer Society and the Association for Computing Machinery.

J. K. Aggarwal (S'62-M'65-SM'74-F'76) received the B.S. degree in mathematics and physics from the University of Bombay in 1956, the B.Eng. degree from the University of Liverpool, Liverpool, England, in 1960, and the M.S. and Ph.D. degrees from the University of Illinois, Urbana, in 1961 and 1964, respectively.

He joined the University of Texas in 1964 as an Assistant Professor and has since held positions as Associate Professor (1968) and Professor (1972). Currently, he is the John J. McKetta Energy Professor of Electrical Engineering and of Computer Sciences at the University of Texas, Austin. Further, he was a visiting Assistant Professor to Brown University, Providence, RI (1968), and a visiting Associate Professor to the University of California, Berkeley, during 1969-1970. He has published numerous technical papers and several books, *Notes on Nonlinear Systems* (1972), *Nonlinear Systems: Stability Analysis* (1977), *Computer Methods in Image Analysis* (1977), *Digital Signal Processing* (1979), and *Deconvolution of Seismic Data* (1982). His current research interests are image processing and digital filters.

Dr. Aggarwal is an active member of the IEEE, Pattern Recognition Society, and Eta Kappa Nu. He was an ADCOM member of the Circuits and Systems Society (1972-1975), Chairman of the Technical Committee on Signal Processing (1974-1975), and Co-Editor of the Special Issues on Digital Filtering and Image Processing (CAS TRANSACTIONS, March 1975) and on Motion and Time Varying Imagery (PAMI TRANSACTIONS, November 1980). Currently he is an Associate Editor of the journal *Pattern Recognition*, and Guest Editor for a Special Issue of *Computer Graphics and Image Processing*.

Model-Based Three-Dimensional Interpretations
of Two-Dimensional Images

RODNEY A. BROOKS

Abstract—ACRONYM is a comprehensive domain independent model-based system for vision and manipulation related tasks. Many of its submodules and representations have been described elsewhere. Here the derivation and use of invariants for image feature prediction is described. Predictions of image features and their relations are made from three-dimensional geometric models. Instructions are generated which tell the interpretation algorithms how to make use of image feature measurements to derive three-dimensional size, structural, and spatial constraints on the original three-dimensional models. Some preliminary examples of ACRONYM's interpretations of aerial images are shown.

Index Terms—Algebraic vision, computer vision, constraint systems, geometric models, model-based vision, spatial reasoning.

I. INTRODUCTION

THE ACRONYM system has always relied on detailed three-dimensional geometric models to direct image understanding. Originally, it used models of specific objects to direct a qualitative geometric reasoning system in labeling images [8].

The scope of ACRONYM has now been increased to include object class recognition and extraction of three-dimensional information from images (including monocular images), reasoning about how to grasp objects [3], and real-time simulation of multiple manipulator work stations for purposes of off-line programming and the design and analysis of new manipulators [11]. ACRONYM has moved from using a purely geometric representation and qualitative geometric reasoning system to a system with a combined algebraic and geometric representation and a geometric reasoning system which can make precise deductions about partially specified situations. The geometric and algebraic aspects of the representation complement each other during image interpretation.

To support these extended capabilities a large number of new techniques had to be developed. They include the addition of a class and subclass relation representation scheme to the geometric modeling system. This is based on the use of symbolic algebraic constraints. In support of this a con-

Manuscript received December 12, 1981; revised September 8, 1982. This work was supported in part by the Defense Advanced Research Projects Agency under Contract MDA903-80-C-0102, in part by the National Science Foundation under Contract DAR78-15914, and in part by a grant from the ALCOA Corporation. An earlier version of this paper was presented at the International Joint Conference on Artificial Intelligence, Vancouver, Canada, August 1981.

The author was with the Stanford Artificial Intelligence Laboratory, Stanford University, Stanford, CA 94305. He is now with the Artificial Intelligence Laboratory, Massachusetts Institute of Technology, Cambridge, MA 02139.

straint manipulation system which includes a partial decision procedure on consistency of sets of nonlinear inequalities was formulated and implemented. A geometric reasoning system which can deal with underconstrained spatial relations was developed. These are all detailed in [7].

This paper deals with techniques developed for image feature and feature-relation prediction, and a matching process which is directed by both geometric relations and algebraic constraints during image interpretation. Some first examples of the performance of the re-built ACRONYM system on some real images are presented. The low-level bottom-up processes used in these experiments (for reasons of expedience) provide either little or noisy data. Nevertheless, ACRONYM makes strong and accurate deductions about the objects appearing in the images. Even better performance is expected when more accurate low-level descriptive processes become available.

A. Model Domain

The reader is referred to Brooks [7] for a complete description of the ACRONYM modeling system. A short overview is given here to make the paper reasonably self-contained.

An *a priori* model of the world is given to ACRONYM. The world is modeled as a coordinate system. Objects are modeled as subpart hierarchies of generalized cones, each with a local coordinate system related to an object coordinate system. Cameras are modeled as coordinate systems (with viewing direction along the $-z$ axis) and a focal ratio. Objects and cameras are placed in the world by constraining the transforms between their local coordinate systems and the world coordinate system.

The particular domain considered in this paper is aerial views of airfields. However, ACRONYM has no particular knowledge of airfields and is applicable to other domains, and camera geometries other than aerial cameras—an example of such is given in Section II.

Generalized cones, introduced by Binford [2], describe a three-dimensional volume. A generalized cone is represented by a curve through space, called the spine, along which a two-dimensional shape, called the cross section, is swept. The cross section is kept at a constant angle to the tangent of the spine, and is deformed according to a deformation function called the sweeping rule.

In ACRONYM generalized cones are restricted to having straight line segments or circular arcs as spines, cross sections bounded by straight lines and circular arcs, and sweeping rules which are linear magnification functions about the spine, or

Reprinted from *IEEE Transactions on Pattern Analysis and Machine Intelligence*, Volume PAMI-5, Number 2, March 1983, pages 140-150. Copyright © 1983 by The Institute of Electrical and Electronics Engineers, Inc. All rights reserved.

linear in two orthogonal directions about the spine. By convention in ACRONYM the coordinate systems of generalized cones have their origins at one end of the spine, with the cross section laying in the y-z plane at that point, and the spine extending into the positive x half-space. For cross sections which are to be kept normal to the spine this implies that the tangent of the spine at the origin lies along the x-axis.

In ACRONYM, generalized cones, the subpart hierarchy of objects, and the affixment tree representing spatial relationships of objects are all represented as *units* with *slots* and *fillers* (e.g., Bobrow and Winograd [5]). Thus, a generalized cone is represented by a unit with slots called *SPINE*, *CROSS-SECTION*, and *SWEEPING-RULE*, each of which is filled with a unit of the appropriate type. Eventually, the units hierarchy bottoms out in units with slots filled with numbers. For instance, a spine unit for a straight spine has a slot called *LENGTH* which can be filled with a number representing the length of the spine.

The above describes a representation scheme sufficiently rich to model a large class of specific objects where all parameters are completely specified. However, for image interpretation tasks it is often the case that not all details of objects in the world are known *a priori*. Thus, it is desirable to be able to represent classes of objects. More particularly, it is often desirable to be able to talk about classes of objects classified according to their function. For instance, an image interpretation task might involve identification of automobiles, buildings, or oil refineries.

Fortunately, the functionality of many man-made objects is reflected in the geometric structure. For instance, automobiles have four cylindrical sections (wheels) in contact with the ground and with their axes parallel to the ground plane. The cylindrical sections are paired with colinear axes, and the centroids of the cylinders form a rectangle (or perhaps an isosceles trapezium). An essentially box-like structure is above the ground with base parallel to the ground and below the rectangle formed by the wheelbase. In addition there may be a section of the box-like structure which extends higher than the rest which is as wide as the main body but not as long. Such general geometric descriptions of functional classes will be referred to as *generic* descriptions throughout the rest of the paper. ACRONYM includes mechanisms for representing such generic object classes.

Representation of geometric classes is achieved by representing commonality of class members by shared structure, and variations across class members by generalizing the fillers of slots which ordinarily might contain a number. Generalizing the slots of the generalized cones allows representation of variations in size and shape, the slots in the subpart hierarchy allow representation of variations in structure, and those in the affixment tree allow variations in spatial relationships. The generalization is to allow numbers to be replaced by formal variables (referred to below as *quantifiers*) and algebraic expressions over formal variables. Additionally, constraints are placed on the formal variables (generally as inequalities, not necessarily linear). The constraints and the geometric unit slot representations together represent the class of all objects which have the given geometric structure and whose parameters satisfy the constraints. The reader is referred to Brooks [7] for details of this modeling scheme.

As an example of a use of quantifiers consider the problem of representing the fact that airplanes on the ground are usually upright with their wings and fuselage parallel to the ground, but be headed in arbitrary directions. Also they can be found at many places at ground level within the confines of an airfield. Suppose the world coordinate system has $z = 0$ as the ground plane, with positive z above the ground. Then the coordinate transform relating the coordinate system of the airplane to the ground would consist of a translation and a rotation. The translation would have its x and y component slots filled by quantifiers bounded only to lie within the confines of the airfield (for a polygonal shaped airfield this would simply be a conjunction of linear inequalities over the two quantifiers), and its z slot filled by some constant dependent on the airplane (the height of the airplane origin above the ground). The rotation would be about the z axis with its magnitude slot filled by a quantifier bound only to lie in the range 0 to 2π.

B. Image Domain

ACRONYM is given images which have been preprocessed by a line finder due to Nevatia and Babu [9]. Figs. 3(b), 4(b), and 5(b) show examples of this processing.

From the edges, a rather poor performance module extracts descriptions of the images as ribbons and ellipses. A ribbon is a two-dimensional analog of a generalized cone. In the ACRONYM implementation they are restricted to having straight spines and linear sweeping rules. Ellipses are described by the lengths of their major and minor axes.

In addition to the ribbons and ellipses ACRONYM is told the resolution in pixels of the original digitization. It uses this to estimate pixel error magnitudes.

In the examples of this paper ACRONYM is given preprocessed images of airfields with a number of airplanes in view on the ground.

C. The Image Interpretation Task

This paper is concerned with the image interpretation tasks performed by ACRONYM. It is given some classes of generic geometric models. The world is described in terms of the typical coordinate transforms of those objects to the world coordinate system (as in the example of the airplane on the ground, above). A camera is also modeled by the relationship of its coordinate system to the world coordinate system.

ACRONYM is given a preprocessed image as above. Its task is to identify instances of the object model classes in the image, along with their location and orientation in world coordinates, to make any subclass identification which is possible, to determine constraints implied by the image on the quantifiers in the models (i.e., determine three-dimensional parameters of the objects from the image) and finally to determine the location and orientation of the camera if that was not completely determined *a priori*.

In the examples of Section III the task which ACRONYM must carry out is to locate airplanes and identify their type. In addition it determines parameters of the camera.

II. Prediction

In the ACRONYM system generic object classes and specific objects are represented by volumetric models based on generalized cones along with a partial order on sets of nonlinear algebraic inequalities relating model parameters. Image features and relations between them which are invariant over variations in the models and camera parameters are identified by a geometric reasoning system. Such predictions are combined first to give guidance to low-level image description processes, then to provide coarse filters on image features which are to be matched to local predictions. Predictions also contain instructions on how to use noisy measurements from identified image features to construct algebraic constraints on the original three-dimensional models. Local matches are combined subject both to consistently meeting predicted image feature relations, and the formation of consistent sets of algebraic constraints derived from the image. The result is a three-dimensional interpretation of the image.

This section describes some of the invariants that are identified by the reasoning system, and gives examples of how the back constraints are set up giving three-dimensional information about the instances of the models which appear in images.

A. Constraints

To illuminate the discussion in succeeding subsections the uses and capabilities of ACRONYM's constraint mechanism are briefly discribed along with the allowed structure of constraints themselves.

ACRONYM's three-dimensional models are represented by *units* and *slots* (e.g., Bobrow and Winograd [5]). Any slot which admits numeric *fillers* also admits *quantifiers* (predeclared variable names) and expressions over quantifiers using the operators $+$, $-$, $\times$, $/$, and $\sqrt{\ }$.

Constraints can be put on quantifiers. They take the form of inequalities between expressions as defined above, along with the possibility of including max and min (on the left and right of $\leqslant$, respectively). Equality can be encoded as two inequalities. For instance suppose a cylinder is represented as a generalized cone whose straight spine has its length defined by the quantifier CYL-LENGTH and whose cross section is a circle with radius CYL-RADIUS. Then the class of all cylinders of volume 5 (in some units) can be represented by the two constraints:

$$5 \geqslant \text{CYL-LENGTH} \times \text{CYL-RADIUS} \times \text{CYL-RADIUS} \times \pi$$

$$5 \leqslant \text{CYL-LENGTH} \times \text{CYL-RADIUS} \times \text{CYL-RADIUS} \times \pi$$

The ACRONYM constraint manipulation system (CMS), described in detail in [7], operates on sets of constraints. A set of constraints (implicitly conjunctive) defines a subset of n-dimensional space for which all constraints are true (where n is the number of quantifiers mentioned in the constraint set). This is called the satisfying set, and is empty if the constraints are inconsistent. The CMS is used for three tasks related to this constraint set.

1) Given a set of constraints partially decide whether their satisfying set is empty. The outcomes are *"empty"* or *"I don't know."*

2) Find numeric (or $\pm\infty$) upper and lower bounds on an ex-

pression in quantifiers over the satisfying set of a constraint set. This uses procedures called SUP and INF.

3) (A generalization of task 2.) For an expression E and a set of quantifiers V find expressions L and H in V such that $L \leqslant E \leqslant H$ identically over the satisfying set of the constraint set.

In tasks 2 and 3 the expressions being bounded can include trigonometric functions such as sin, cos, and arcsin.

The CMS implemented in ACRONYM is a nonlinear generalization [7] of the linear SUP-INF method described by Bledsoe [4] and Shostak [10]. In [7] it was shown that ACRONYM's CMS behaves identically to that described by Shostak for purely linear sets of constraints and linear expressions, and determines least upper and greatest lower bounds.

For nonlinear expressions and constraints there is not such a well delineated characterization of the behavior of the CMS. The proofs of [7] can be extended to cases of sums of independent terms, each of which is a product or quotient of terms whose sign can be determined purely from the subset of constraints which are linear, i.e., in those cases the CMS produces the best bounds possible.

Informal empirical evidence suggests that there are other cases where the CMS produces good bounds. No good characterization of these cases exists. It is also possible to demonstrate cases where the bounds found by the CMS are not good. If all terms have signs determinable from the subset of constraints which are linear then the bounds are no worse than considering all terms to be independent. If some terms have indeterminate signs then the bounds may be quite poor.

Much of the expertise in the ACRONYM system lies in being able to reduce sets of constraints by projection into subspaces where better bounds can be found on expressions. Sometimes, of course, it is not possible to find such a projection, and then poor bounds must suffice. The rules used for prediction and interpretation were written with these limitations in mind.

B. The Prediction Process

The prediction module of ACRONYM is implemented as a set of approximately 280 product-type rules.

The major control paradigm is backward chaining, i.e., rules set up subgoals and recursively invoke the rule mechanism to satisfy those subgoals. Both subgoals and rule capabilities are represented as Lisp s-expressions. Rules are invoked if they unify with a stated subgoal. The unification process allows passing of multiple parameters to rules, and receiving multiple results from them. In addition, the pattern matching aspect of unification provides rule selection criteria.

A global assertional database, and additional local databases provide the means for recording the state of the prediction computation. The data structures embodying the predictions are built as side effects of the rules firing.

During a typical prediction phase, e.g., in the example of Section III of this paper, there are on the order of 6000 rule firings.

The order of rule firings, and flow of control can not be characterized at a local level as it is completely dependent on the models given to the system. At a global level the order of computations can be roughly described as follows.

A breadth first walk down the subpart hierarchy of the

models is made. At each level prediction is carried out, followed by partial interpretations of the images. Then refined predictions are made at the next level of the hierarchy. (In the examples of Section III only the first level of interpretations are carried out).

At each level the coordinate transforms of the generalized cones, relative to the camera are computed and examined. Visibility conditions and implications of visibility are computed. Individual shape predictions are made for the generalized cones. Relationships between the generalized cones are examined for invariant characterizations. These four steps are summarized in more detail in the following paragraphs.

The affixment tree is transversed to get a symbolic expression for the coordinate transform relating a generalized cone's local coordinate system to that of the camera. The transform is represented as a product of rotations and translations. Typically, these products are long (i.e., over ten terms) and contain many quantifiers. The reader is referred to [7] for the details of some rules which make such expressions manageable. During later phases of prediction these rules are applied in a goal directed manner to find a simplication of the products in the form most suitable for the task at hand. (Again examples are given in [7].)

One can associate with a camera a volume of space (an infinite pyramid with rectangular cross section and apex at the focal point of the camera) in which objects can be visible. Outside of that volume an object is definitely invisible to a camera. Thus, for the purposes of predicting the appearance of a generalized cone it can be assumed that it lies within the sight of the camera, since otherwise it will not be seen anyway. Therefore, constraints are added to the object model which confine its coordinates so that it lies within the visible volume. If these constraints are inconsistent with those that already exist then the object is definitely invisible and no further prediction need be made. Otherwise it provides possibly tighter constraints on the possible range of positions and orientations possible for the object. Once the visibility conditions for individual generalized cones are established, pairwise comparisons are made to see if it can definitely be established that one cone always occludes another. This process is carried out by tentatively adding constraints that imply the converse (i.e., one cone never occludes the other). If these constraints are inconsistent then the obscuration must always occur. If they cannot be shown to be inconsistent (recall that the decision procedure is only partial) then it can be concluded that perhaps the obscuration will not always occur, so both cones may be visible.

Actual predictions of shapes proceeds in five phases. These are described in detail in Section II-C.

. An exhaustive pairwise examination of shapes produced by different generalized cones is carried out. The geometric reasoning system tries to find invariant characterizations of the relationships between the shapes in terms of the relationships detailed in Section II-D.

C. Shape Prediction

Shapes are predicted as *ribbons* (the two-dimensional analog of three-dimensional generalized cones) and *ellipses*. These are also the features which are found by the low-level descriptive process which are temporarily being used in ACRONYM.

Ribbons are a good way of describing the images generated by generalized cones. Consider a ribbon which corresponds to the image of the swept surface of a generalized cone. For straight spines, the projection of the cone spine into the image would closely correspond to the spine of the ribbon. Thus, a good approximation to the observed angle between the spines of two generalized cones is the angle between the spines of the two ribbons in the image corresponding to their swept surfaces. A quantitative theory of these correspondences is not used. Ellipses are a good way of describing the shapes generated by the ends of generalized cones. The perspective projections of ends of cones with circular cross-sections are exactly ellipses.

Shape prediction involves deciding what shapes will be visible, predicting ranges for shape parameters (to be used as a coarse filter during interpretation and also to guide the low level descriptive processes) and deriving instructions about how to locally invert the perspective transform and hence use image measurements to generate constraints on the original three-dimensional models.

To predict the shapes generated by a single generalized cone, ACRONYM does not explicitly predict all possible quantitatively different viewpoints. Rather, it predicts what shapes may appear in the image, and associates with them methods to compute constraints on the model that are implied by their individual appearance in an image. For example, identification of the image of the swept surface of a right circular cone constrains the relative orientation of the cylinder to the camera (these are called back constraints). Identification of an end face of the cylinder provides a different set of constraints. If both the swept surface and an end face are identified then both sets of constraints apply. Also predicted are specific relations between shapes that will be true if they are both observed correctly. For more complex cones, the payoff is even greater for predicting individual shapes rather than exhaustive analysis of which shapes can appear together.

At other times during prediction invariant cases of obscuration are noticed. For instance, it may be noticed that one cone abuts another so that its end face will never be visible. The consequences of such realizations are propagated through the predictions.

Prediction of shapes proceeds in five phases. First, all the contours of a generalized cone which could give rise to image shapes are indentified by a set of special purpose rules. These include occluding contours and contours due purely to internal cone faces. Thus, for instance, a right square cylinder will generate contours for the end faces, the swept faces, and contours generated by the swept edges at diagonally vertices of the square cross section. The contours are generated independently of camera orientation, and in terms of object dimensions rather than image quantities.

Second, the orientation of the generalized cone relative to the camera (this is done by the geometric reasoning system; see [7]) is then examined to decide which contours will be visible and how their image shapes will be distorted over the range of variations in the model parameters which appear in the orientation expressions.

The third phase predicts relations between contours of a single generalized cone (see Section II-D).

Fourth, the actual shapes are then predicted. The expected

values for shape parameters in the image are estimated as closed intervals (see below).

Finally, the back constraints which will be instantiated during interpretation are constructed.

1) *Back Constraints:* Consider the following simple camera geometry. Suppose that it is desired to predict the length of an observable feature which is generated by something of length l lying in a plane parallel to the camera image plane, at distance d from the camera. Furthermore, suppose the camera has a focal ratio of f. Then the measured length of the observed feature is given by $p = (l \times f)/d$. Any or all of l, f, and d may be expressions in quantifiers, rather than numbers. Using the CMS bounds can be obtained on the above expression for image feature length, giving that it will lie in some range $P = [p_l, p_h]$ where p_l and p_h are either numbers or $\pm\infty$. For more complex geometries the expression for p will be more complex, but the method is the same (trigonometric functions are usually involved).

Now, given an image feature, which is hypothesized to correspond to the prediction it must be decided whether it is acceptable on the basis of its parameters. The low-level descriptive processes are noisy and provide an error interval, rather than an exact measurement for image parameters. Suppose the interval is $M = [m_l, m_h]$ for a feature parameter predicted with expression p. Then the parameter is acceptable if $P \cap M$ is nonempty. This is the coarse filtering used during initial hypothesis of image feature to feature prediction matches.

But note also that it must be true that the true value of p for the particular instance of the model which is being imaged must lie in the range M. Thus the constraints

$$m_l \leqslant (l \times f)/d$$

$$m_h \geqslant (l \times f)/d$$

can be added to the instance of the model being hypothesized, where l, f, and d are numbers or expressions in quantifiers.

The above is the analysis for the simplest possible camera geometry. In general the predicted geometry is much more complex and requires stronger symbolic analysis methods. ACRONYM has individual rules which are capable of handling all cases of up to three orthogonal degrees of freedom in orientation of objects relative to the camera.

2) *Trigonometric Back Constraints:* When the expression p involves trigonometric functions the above method of generating back constraints will not work. It would generate constraints involving trogonmetric functions, which ACRONYM's CMS cannot handle.

One approach to this problem is to bound expression p above and below by expressions involving no quantifiers contained in arguments to trigonometric functions, and then use these expressions in setting up the back constraints. This has the unfortunate side effect of losing all information implied by the image feature about the quantifiers eliminated from the bounds.

A second approach is sometimes applicable. If a trigonometric function has as its argument e, an expression, and if the CMS determines that e is bounded to lie within a region of the function's domain where it is strictly monotonic and

hence invertible, then specific back constraints on e can be computed at interpretation time (as distinct from during prediction). An example illustrates this. A cylinder with length CYL-LENGTH is sitting upright on a table. A camera with unknown but constrained pan and tilt (the latter is constrained to lie in the interval $[\pi/12, \pi/6]$) is looking across from the side of the table, and it is elevated above table top height. The geometric details and numeric constants are not important here. Suffice it to say that the geometric reasoning system deduces that the pan of the camera is irrelevant to the prediction of the length of the ribbon corresponding to the swept surface of the cylinder. It predicts that the length of the ribbon in the image will in fact be

$$\frac{-2.42 \times \text{CYL-LENGTH} \times \cos{(-\text{TILT})}}{\text{CYLINDER.CAMZ}}$$

where 2.42 is the focal ratio of the camera and CYLINDER.CAMZ is an internal quantifier generated by the prediction module. Since cosine is invertible over the range $[\pi/12, \pi/6]$ the expression can be solved for TILT.

Both of the above approaches are used to generate back constraints to ensure coverage of all the relevant quantifiers. They are

$$m_h \geqslant -2.096 \times \text{CYL-LENGTH} \times (1/\text{CYLINDER.CAMZ})$$

$$m_l \leqslant -2.338 \times \text{CYL-LENGTH} \times (1/\text{CYLINDER.CAMZ})$$

$$-\text{TILT} \leqslant -\arccos{(\sup{(-0.413 \times m_h} }$$
$$\times \text{CYLINDER.CAMZ} \times (1/\text{CYL-LENGTH})))$$

$$-\text{TILT} \geqslant -\arccos{(\inf{(-0.413 \times m_l} }$$
$$\times \text{CYLINDER.CAMZ} \times (1/\text{CYL-LENGTH})))$$

The first two are nontrigonometric back constraints and at interpretation time a simple substitution of the measured numeric quantities for m_l and m_h is done. The latter two require further computation at interpretation time. After the substitution, expressions must be bounded over the satisfying set of all the known constraints, and the function arccos applied to give numeric upper and lower bounds on the quantifier TILT.

The technique described here work for a more general class of functions than trigonometric functions (in the current implementation of ACRONYM it is used for functions sin, cos, and arcsin). The requirement is that the domain of the function (e.g., the interval $[-\pi, \pi]$ for sin and cos), can be subdivided into a finite number of intervals over which the function is strictly monotonic, and hence locally invertible.

D. Feature Relation Prediction

Image feature (shape) predictions are organized as the nodes of the *prediction graph*. The arcs of the graph predict image-domain relations between the features. During interpretation correspondences are constructed which match image features and prediction nodes. More global interpretations are derived by taking pairs of such correspondences and trying to instantiate any prediction arcs linking the two prediction nodes. The semantics of the arc types used are now described in detail.

As with shape predictions (Sections II-C1 and 2) many relation predictions involve measurable parameters. For each parameter associated with a relation prediction, both a range of acceptable values and a set of back constraints are computed. When instantiating the prediction of measured parameters can be quickly checked against the value range prediction as a coarse filter to eliminate grossly inconsistent instantiations. The back constraints are then used both to check for more global consistency and to compute what the particular instantiation of the prediction arc implies about the model.

Prediction arcs are generated between pairs of shapes arising in two ways.

1) Prediction arcs are generated to relate multiple shapes predicted for a single cone. For instance a right circular cylinder prediction includes shapes for the swept surface and perhaps each of the end faces (depending on whether the camera geometry is known well enough to determine *a priori* exactly which faces will be visible). It can be predicted that a visible end face will be coincident at least one point in the image with a visible swept surface. (In fact, a stronger prediction can be made: the straight spine of the swept surface image ribbon can be extended through the center of mass of the elliptical image of the end face.)

2) Prediction arcs are also generated between shapes associated with predictions for different generalized cones. These are actually of more importance in arriving at a consistent global interpretation of collections of image features as complex objects.

The semantics of the arc types currently used are as follows.

1) *Exclusive:* If a generalized cone has a straight spine, and during sweeping, the cross section is kept at a constant angle to the spine, then at most one of the cone's end faces can be visible in a single image. *Exclusive* arcs relate image features which are mutually exclusive for this or other reasons. (Note that in this case, instantiations of the two end faces would probably result in inconsistent back constraints being applied to the spatial orientation of the original model, so that eventually the CMS would detect an inconsistency. However, checking for the existence of a simple arc at an early stage is computationally much cheaper than waiting to invoke the decision procedure.)

2) *Collinear:* If two straight line segments in three-space are *collinear* then any two-space image of them will either be a single degenerate point or two collinear line segments. As was pointed out earlier, the spine of the image shape corresponding to the swept surface of a cone is usually a good approximation to the projection of the spine of the cone into the image. Thus, if two cones are known to have collinear spines in three dimensions, a collinear spine arc between the prediction of their swept surfaces can be included.

3) *Coincident:* If two cones are physically *coincident* at some point(s) in three-space, then for any camera geometry, if they are both visible then their projections will be coincident at some point(s) (except for some cases of obscuration). Failure to match predicted coincident arcs turns out to be the strongest pruning process during image interpretation.

4) *Angle:* If the *angle* between the spines of two generalized cones as viewed from the modeled camera is invariant over all the rotational variations in the model, or if an expression for the observed angle can be symbolically computed and is sufficiently simple, then a prediction of the observed angle can be made. For example, wing–wing and wing–fuselage angles are invariant when an aircraft is viewed from above—that is because the only rotational freedom of an aircraft on the ground is about an axis parallel to the direction of view of an overhead camera. Again the fact that the projections of model spines correspond to image spines is used here. This arc type includes (trigonometric) back constraints which make use of the observed angle. Some such constraints constrain relative spatial orientations of generalized cones. Others provide constraints on the orientation of the plane of rotation, which generated the angle, relative to the camera, and hence constraints on an object's orientation relative to the camera.

5) *Approach-Ratio:* Suppose a cone B is affixed at one end of its spine to another cone A, with a straight spine, somewhere along its length. The spines need not be coincident, but the cones must be. Suppose the spine of cone A has endpoints a_1 and a_2, and let a_3 be the point on the spine of A closest to the end of the spine of B. Then the *approach-ratio* is the ratio of the length of the spine segment from a_1 to a_3 and the length of the complete spine from a_1 to a_2. If the spines of A and B are both observable, then the approach-ratio is invariant under a normal projection for all camera geometries. Thus it is a quasi-invariant for a perspective projection for a camera sufficiently far from the object. For example, the ratio of the distance from the rear of the fuselage to the point of wing attachment, to the length of the fuselage, is almost invariant over all viewing angles for objects sufficiently far from the camera. Again this relies on the correspondences between the projection of a cone spine and the spine of the ribbon generated by the image of its swept surface. Approach-ratios arcs are only generated for pairs of image features which have a coincident arc. They provide back constraints on the model via the symbolic expression which describes the modeled spine approach ratio.

6) *Distance:* Sometimes symbolic expressions for the image distance between two image features can be computed. *Distance* arcs are only generated for pairs of image features which also have an angle arc, but no coincident arc. Distance arcs generate back constraints on the original model.

7) *Ribbon-Contains:* This is a directed arc type which two dimensionally relates two predicted ribbons, one of which will contain the other in the image. For instance, *ribbon-contains* arcs are built between the ribbon predicted from the occluding contour of a generalized cone with rectangular cross section, and each of the ribbons generated by the two visible swept faces.

III. Some Image Interpretations

The image interpretations reported here are of a rather preliminary nature. They are based on a low-level descriptive module [6] chosen for its availability rather than its performance and an environment where experimentation has been hampered by address space limitations—the current system occupies two 256K address spaces on a DEC-10. The system

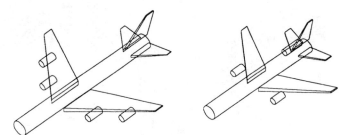

Fig. 1. Instances drawn by ACRONYM of 747's and L-1011's, which are themselves both subclasses of the generic class of wide-bodied passenger jet aircraft.

has been transported to a **VAX**. Further experimentation is planned on that version by a number of people.

In the examples to be described here ACRONYM was given a generic model of wide-bodied passenger jet aircraft, along with class specializations to L-1011's and Boeing-747's. The Boeing-747 class had further subclass specializations to Boeing-747B and Boeing-747SP. The subclasses do not completely partition their parent classes. The classes are described by sets of constraints on some 30 quantifiers. Fig. 1 shows instances of the two major modeled classes of jet aircraft. These diagrams were draw by ACRONYM from the models given it to carry out the image interpretations. The constraints for the generic class of wide bodied jets are given in Fig. 2. Units are in meters. The diagrams of Fig. 1 demonstrate the range of variations represented in the generic model. The geometric structure consists of a cylindrical fuselage, two symmetrically placed wings perhaps with rudder, and perhaps a centrally mounted cylindrical rear engine.

The camera was modeled as being between 1000 and 12 000 m above the ground. Thus there is little *a priori* knowledge of the scale of the images. A specific focal ratio was given: 20. (Similar interpretations have been carried out with a variable focal ratio, but then the final constraints on camera height and focal ratio are coupled, and not as clear for illustrative purposes—no accuracy is lost due to the nonlinearities that are introduced into the constraints, although both computation time and garbage collection time are increased.)

The aircraft models, the camera model and the number of pixels in each dimension of the image (512×512 in these examples) were the only pieces of world knowledge input to ACRONYM. It has no special knowledge of aerial scenes: all its rules are about geometry and algebraic manipulation. These were applied to the particular generic models it was given, to make predictions and then to carry out interpretations.

Figs. 3–5 show three examples of interpretations carried out by ACRONYM. In each case part (a) is a half-tone of the original gray level image. The (b) version is the result of applying the line finder of Nevatia and Babu [9]. That line finder was designed to find linear features such as roads and rivers in aerial photos. Close examination of results on these images indicate many errors, and undue enlargement in width of narrow linear features. It also produces many noise edges in smooth brightness gradients (not visible at the resolution of the reproductions of these figures). These edges are the lowest level input to ACRONYM.

An edge linker [6] is directed by the predictions to look

$$\text{ENG-DISP-GAP} \in [6, 10]$$
$$\text{ENG-DISP} \in [0, 4]$$
$$\text{ENG-GAP} \in [7, 10]$$
$$\text{STAB-ATTACH} \in [3, 5]$$
$$\text{R-ENG-ATTACHMENT} \in [3, 5]$$
$$\text{ENG-OUT} \in [5, 12]$$
$$\text{WING-ATTACHMENT} \in [20, 40]$$
$$\text{WING-ATTACHMENT} \geq 0.4*\text{FUSELAGE-LENGTH}$$
$$\text{WING-ATTACHMENT} \leq 0.6*\text{FUSELAGE-LENGTH}$$
$$\text{STAB-RATIO} \in [0.2, 0.55]$$
$$\text{STAB-SWEEP-BACK} \in [3, 7]$$
$$\text{STAB-LENGTH} \in [7.6, 13]$$
$$\text{STAB-THICK} \in [0.7, 1.1]$$
$$\text{STAB-WIDTH} \in [5, 11]$$
$$\text{RUDDER-RATIO} \in [0.3, 0.4]$$
$$\text{RUDDER-SWEEP-BACK} \in [3, 9]$$
$$\text{RUDDER-LENGTH} \in [8.5, 14.2]$$
$$\text{RUDDER-X-HEIGHT} \in [7, 13]$$
$$\text{RUDDER-X-WIDTH} \in [0.7, 1.1]$$
$$\text{WING-RATIO} \in [0.35, 0.45]$$
$$\text{WING-THICK} \in [1.5, 2.5]$$
$$\text{WING-WIDTH} \in [7, 12]$$
$$\text{WING-WIDTH} \leq 0.5*\text{WING-LENGTH}$$
$$\text{WING-LIFT} \in [1, 2]$$
$$\text{WING-SWEEP-BACK} \in [13, 18]$$
$$\text{WING-LENGTH} \in [22, 33.5]$$
$$\text{WING-LENGTH} \geq 2*\text{WING-WIDTH}$$
$$\text{WING-LENGTH} \geq 0.43*\text{FUSELAGE-LENGTH}$$
$$\text{WING-LENGTH} \leq 0.65*\text{FUSELAGE-LENGTH}$$
$$\text{REAR-ENGINE-LENGTH} \in [6, 10]$$
$$\text{ENGINE-LENGTH} \in [4, 7]$$
$$\text{ENGINE-RADIUS} \in [1, 1.8]$$
$$\text{FUSELAGE-RADIUS} \in [2.5, 4]$$
$$\text{FUSELAGE-LENGTH} \in [40, 70]$$
$$\text{FUSELAGE-LENGTH} \geq 1.66666666*\text{WING-ATTACHMENT}$$
$$\text{FUSELAGE-LENGTH} \geq 1.53846154*\text{WING-LENGTH}$$
$$\text{FUSELAGE-LENGTH} \leq 2.5*\text{WING-ATTACHMENT}$$
$$\text{FUSELAGE-LENGTH} \leq 2.3255814*\text{WING-LENGTH}$$
$$\text{R-ENG-QUANT} \in [0, 1]$$
$$\text{R-ENG-QUANT} \leq 2 + -1*\text{F-ENG-QUANT}$$
$$\text{F-ENG-QUANT} \in [1, 2]$$
$$\text{F-ENG-QUANT} \leq 2 + -1*\text{R-ENG-QUANT}$$

Fig. 2. The constraints implied by the model given to ACRONYM for the generic class of wide-bodied passenger aircraft.

for ribbons and ellipses. In this case there is very little *a priori* information about the scale of the images. The (c) versions of each figure show the ribbons fitted to the linked edges when it is searching for candidate matches for the fuselage and wings of aircraft. There is even further degradation of image information at this stage. These are the only data which the ACRONYM reasoning system is given to interpret. Notice that in the Fig. 5 almost all the shapes corresponding to aircraft are lost. Quite a few aircraft in Fig. 4 are lost also. Besides losing many shapes, the combination of the edge finder and edge linker conspire to give very inaccurate image measurements. It is assumed that all image measurements have a ±30 percent error, except that for very small measurements, it is assumed that pixel noise swamps even those error estimates. Then the error is estimated to be inversely proportional to the measurement with a 2 pixel measurement admitting a 100 percent error. Thus the data which ACRONYM really gets to work with are considerably more fuzzy than indicated by the (c) series of Figs. 3–5.

It is intended to make use of new and better low-level de-

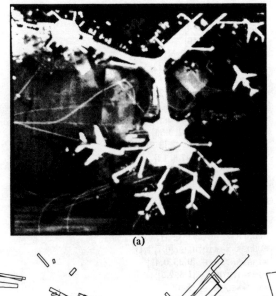

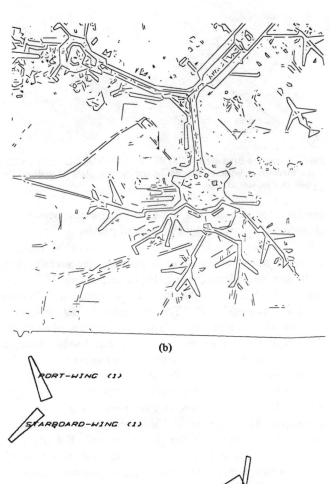

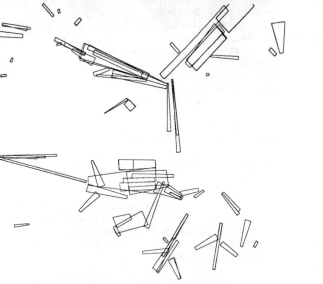

Fig. 3. Illustrations of some of the computations performed by ACRONYM in interpreting an image. The text contains the details.

scriptive processes being developed by other researchers as soon as they become robust enough for every day use (e.g., Baker [1] whose descriptions from stereo will also include surface and depth information).

Despite this very noisy descriptive data ACRONYM makes good interpretations of the images. Figs. 3(d), 4(d), and 5(d) show their interpretations with the ribbons labeled by what part of the model they were matched to. (The numbers which may be unreadable in Fig. 3(d) show the groupings into individual aircraft.)

ACRONYM first uses the most general set of constraints, those associated with the generic class of wide-bodied jets, when carrying out initial prediction and interpretation. Interpretation adds additional constraints for each hypothesized aircraft instance. For example, in finding the correspondences in Fig. 4(d) constraints were added which eventually constrained the WING-WIDTH (the width of the wings where they attach to fuselage) to lie in the range [7, 10.5677531] compared to the modeled bounds of [7, 12]. The height of the camera, modeled to lie in the range [1000, 12 000] is constrained by the interpretation to the range [2199, 3322].

Once a consistent match or partial match to a geometric model has been found in the context of some set of constraints (model class), it is easy to check whether it might also be an instance of a subclass. Only the extra constraints associated with the subclass need be added and checked for consistency with those already implied by the interpretation using the CMS as described in Section II-A. The aircraft located in Fig. 4(d) is consistent with the constraints for an L-1011, but not for a Boeing-747. Examination of the images by the author had previously indicated that the aircraft was an L-1011. The additional symbolic constraints implied by accepting that the aircraft is in fact an L-1011 propagate through the entire constraint set. Although the constraints describing an L-1011 do not include constraints on camera height, the back constraints deduced during interpretation relate quantifiers representing such quantities as length of the wings to the height (and focal ratio in the more general case). Thus the height of the camera is further constrained in Fig. 4(d) to lie in the range [2356, 2489]. Recall that all image measurements were subject to ±30 percent errors, and that this estimate has taken all such errors into account.

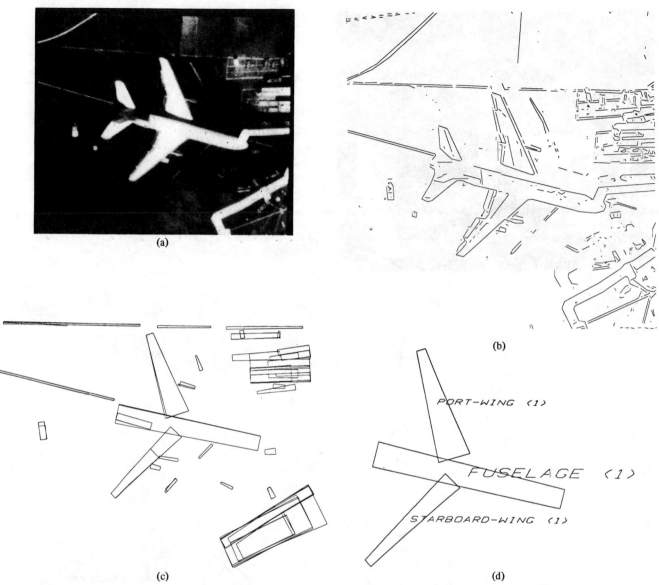

Fig. 4. Illustrations of some of the computations performed by ACRONYM in interpreting an image. The text contains the details.

Fig. 3(d) indicates matches were found for three airplanes. Examination of the data in Fig. 3(c) indicates that this is the best that could be expected. Note, however, that only partial matches were found in all three cases. For such small ribbons errors were apparently larger than the generous estimate used. The fuselage ribbon in the leftmost aircraft (number 1), for instance, fails to pass the coarse filtering stage. Despite the partial match, this particular aircraft is found to be consistent with the constraints for an L-1011, but not consistent with those of a Boeing-747. Again this is correct.

The other two aircraft identified are even more interesting. The author had thought from casual inspection of the grey level image that they were instances of Boeing-747's. They both gave matches consistent with the class of wide-bodied jets. As expected neither was consistent with the extra constraints of an L-1011. However, although each indi-

vidual parameter range from the interpretation constraint sets was consistent with the individual parameter value or range for the class of Boeing-747's, neither set of constraints was consistent with that subclass (the constraints contain much finer information than just the parameter ranges–in the same manner as in the example above where constraints on wing length propagate to constrain the camera height). On close examination of the gray level image it was determined that the aircraft were not in fact Boeing-747's. The author used the fact that they were much smaller than the L-1011 to make that deduction, but ACRONYM made the deduction at the local level before considering comparisons between aircraft.

It also found the inconsistency at a more global level. The aircraft (probably Boeing-707's) are in fact too small to be wide-bodied jets of any type. Since the scale of the image is unknown *a priori* this cannot be deduced locally. However, it

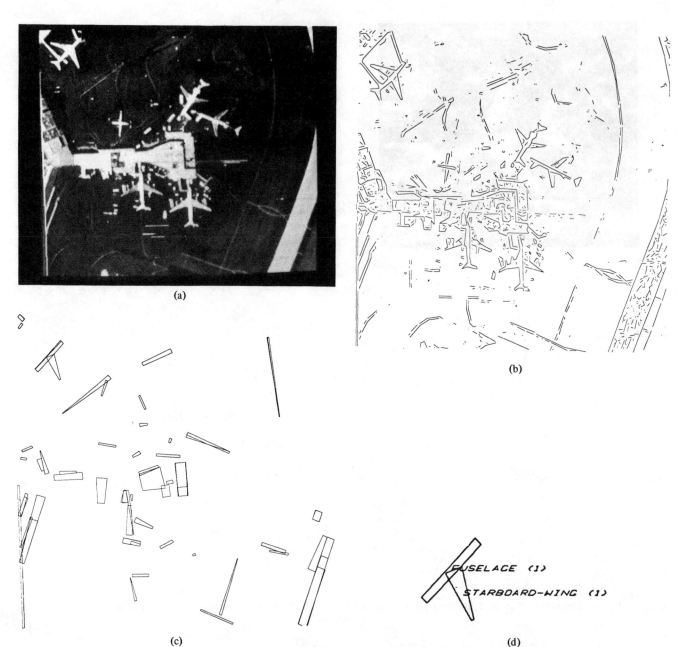

(a)

(b)

FUSELAGE (1)

STARBOARD-WING (1)

(c)   (d)

Fig. 5. Illustrations of some of the computations performed by ACRONYM in interpreting an image. The text contains the details.

is reflected in the height estimates derived at the local level—[5400, 8226] interpreting the L-1011 just as a generic wide-body, ([5786, 6170] as an L-1011), and [9007, 11846] for the rightmost aircraft. Thus ACRONYM deduces that either the left aircraft is a wide-body and the others are not, or the right two are wide-bodies and the left one is not (it is too big).

Finally, note that geometrically there were other candidates for aircraft in the ribbons of Fig. 3(c). For instance, the wing of the aircraft just to the right of those identified and a ribbon found for its passenger ramp could be the two wings of an aircraft with a fuselage missing between them. In fact, these two ribbons were instantiated as an aircraft on the basis of the coarse filters on the nodes and arcs. However, the set of back constraints they generated were mutually inconsistent.

Thus, it can be seen from the examples that even with very poor and noisy data the combined use of geometry and symbolic algebraic constraints can lead to accurate image interpretations. They system should be tested on more accurate low-level data to fully evaluate the power of this approach.

REFERENCES

[1] H. H. Baker and T. O. Binford, "Edge based stereo correlation," in *Proc. 7th Joint Int. Conf. Artificial Intell.*, Vancouver, Canada, Aug. 1981, pp. 631–636.
[2] T. O. Binford, "Visual perception by computer," presented at the IEEE Syst., Sci., Cybern. Conf., Miami, FL, invited paper, Dec. 1971.
[3] —, "Computer integrated assembly systems," in *Proc. NSF Grantees Conf. Industrial Automation*, Cornell Univ., Sept. 1979.

[4] W. W. Bledsoe, "The sup-inf method in Presburger arithmetic," Dep. Math. and Comput. Sci., Univ. Texas, Austin, Memo. ATP-18, Dec. 1974.

[5] D. G. Bobrow and T. Winograd, "An overview of KRL: A knowledge representation language," *Cognitive Sci.*, vol. 1, pp. 3–46, 1977.

[6] R. A. Brooks, "Goal-directed edge linking and ribbon finding," in *Proc. ARPA Image Understanding Workshop*, Menlo Park, Apr. 1979, pp. 72–76.

[7] —, "Symbolic reasoning among 3-D models and 2-D images," *Artificial Intell. J.*, vol. 17, pp. 285–348, 1981; a longer version is available as Stanford AIM-343, Dep. Comput. Sci., Stanford, CA.

[8] R. A. Brooks, R. Greiner, and T. O. Binford, "The ACRONYM model-based vision system," in *Proc. IJCAI-6*, Tokyo, Japan, Aug. 1979, pp. 105–113.

[9] R. Nevatia and K. R. Babu, "Linear feature extraction and description," *Comput. Graphics and Image Processing*, vol. 13, pp. 257–269, 1980.

[10] R. E. Shostak, "On the sup-inf method for proving Presburger formulas," *J. Ass. Comput. Mach.*, vol. 24, pp. 529–543, 1977.

[11] B. I. Soroka, "Debugging manipulator programs with a simulator," presented at the Autofact West Conf., Soc. Manuf. Eng., Anaheim, CA, Nov. 1980.

Rodney A. Brooks was born in Adelaide, South Australia, on December 30, 1954. He received the B.Sc. and M.Sc. degrees in mathematics from Flinders University, Adelaide, Australia, in 1974 and 1977, respectively, and the Ph.D. degree in computer science from Stanford University, Stanford, CA, in 1981.

He was a Visiting Scientist in the Department of Computer Science, Carnegie-Mellon University, Pittsburgh, PA, from June through September 1981. Since then he has been a Research Associate in the Artificial Intelligence Laboratory, Massachusetts Institute of Technology, Cambridge. His research interests span computer vision, robotics, spatial reasoning and planning, and issues in Lisp language and system development.

Characteristic views as a basis for three-dimensional object recognition

Indranil Chakravarty,* Herbert Freeman
Rensselaer Polytechnic Institute, Troy, New York 12181

Abstract

This paper describes a new technique for modeling 3D objects that is applicable to recognition tasks in advanced automation. Objects are represented in terms of canonic 2D models which can be used to determine the identity, location and orientation of an unknown object. The reduction in dimensionality is achieved by factoring the space of all possible perspective projections of an object into a set of characteristic views, where each such view defines a characteristic-view domain within which all projections are topologically identical and related by a linear transformation. The characteristic views of an object can then be hierarchically structured for efficient classification. The line-junction labelling constraints are used to match a characteristic view to a given unknown-object projection, and determination of the unknown-object projection-to-characteristic view transformation then provides information about the identity as well as the location and orientation of the object.

Introduction

A problem of current interest is the development of efficient procedures for the computer recognition of three-dimensional objects. This paper describes a modeling scheme which facilitates the recognition of arbitrarily positioned objects on a platform so that a mechanical arm can pick up and hold the object in a known manner. The environment consists of a fixed set of different objects with which the vision system must cope during a task period. For all objects in the set, a computer model is presumed to exist. There are no restrictions on the shape of the objects.

There are three facets to the recognition problem: to establish the identity of the object(s) currently in the field of view, to determine their location, and to determine their orientation. It is instructive to divide the recognition problem into two subproblems- that of object modeling and that of object recognition. The purpose of the research described here was to develop an efficient scheme for solving both these subproblems for objects of general shape. We shall assume that we are dealing with objects for which a pure silhouette-based recognition scheme would be inadequate. Instead moderate-resolution, gray-level images will be required from which the object-describing line structure can be derived. The objects will be assumed to be in a stable position; however, the camera-to-object attitude will be allowed to vary. Furthermore, we will assume that the scene illumination is arranged to be as favorable as possible for the recognition task.

A variety of different schemes have been used in the past for representing the computer model of an object. Although any recognition procedure necessarily requires the existence of a modeling scheme, the converse is not true. As a result many innovative modeling schemes have not been suitable for recognition. Computer models of an object can be classified as belonging to one of the following three classes: (1) volumetric representations based either on the use of generalized cones and cylinders [1,2] or an ordered subdivision of 3D space into homogenous cubes [3], (2) surface descriptions utilizing bicubic patches [4], quadric-surface patches [5,6] or polygonal approximations [7,8], and (3) multiple-view representations [9,10].

In a multiple-view representation a set of two-dimensional projections is used to describe a three-dimensional object. The object's line structure is then characterized in terms of a variety of two-dimensional features. Shape and feature matching techniques, invariant to rotation, translation and scaling are used for identification. This approach is characterized by the work of Chen et al. [11], Holland et al [10], and Perkins [9] and requires stringent positioning of the object with respect to the camera. Other efforts have been directed towards extracting spatial relationships and 3D features from an object's line-drawing projections. In this case the scene interpretation is attempted at a more global level using constraints based on object-level knowledge. This approach has been characterized by Brooks [13], Marr [2], Shapiro et al. [14] and Barrow and Tennenbaum [12].

*Current address: Schlumberger-Doll Research, Old Quarry Road, Ridgefield, CT 06877.

378

The approach developed in this paper utilizes low-level image operations that are guided by object-level knowledge. This knowledge is embodied in the form of function and line semantics and an hierarchical representation of a 3D object by a class of visible-line projections.

The Characteristic-View Model of an Object

The modeling scheme described here consists of representing a 3D object by means of a relatively large set of visible-line projections. Each projection, called a <u>characteristic-view</u> (CV), is a representation member of one of a finite set of equivalence classes called <u>characteristic-view partitions</u> (CVPs) into which the possible perspective projections of the object can be partitioned. The set of characteristic views is used as a basis for hierarchical object representation. The primary advantage this has over a 3D model is that the line-structure bears a more direct relationship to what is observed by a TV camera. By this we mean that the visibility of the lines and junctions is already predetermined for a given vantage-point domain.

In the following sections we develop (1) the necessary criteria for partitioning the projection set of a 3D object, (2) the geometric relationships that must exist among members of a CVP, and (3) the transformations with which one can determine the identity, orientation and location of a given projection with respect to the stored CV.

Characteristic view partitions

When we examine a projection of a body, such as a picture of a 3D object obtained with a camera, we find that only a portion of the body's edges and vertices are visible. The edges not seen are the so-called "hidden lines" of the object relative to the observer (vantage point). Now if we slowly change the vantage point, we observe that the projected-edge structure will not exhibit any change in topology until we come to a position at which some edges and vertices are no longer visible in the projection, or some new edges and vertices come into view. This leads to the conclusion that for every 3D object the universe of all vantage point locations can be divided into a finite set of <u>vantage-point domains</u> such that for each domain the projected edge structure will exhibit a <u>junction-line identity</u>. We shall use the term <u>junction</u> to refer to the projection of a vertex, and the term <u>line</u> to refer to the projection of an edge. By a junction-line identity we thus mean that for every vantage point in a domain, precisely the same junctions and lines are displayed with the same connectivity relationships, though, the lengths of the lines may differ. An example is given in Figure 1, where a cube with a hole is shown, observed from six different vantage points. Views (a) through (d) belong to the same vantage-point domain and, therefore, exhibit junction-line identity; views (e) and (f) each belong to different vantage-point domains and do not share junction-line identity with any of the other views. Alternately stated, if C_0 and C_1 are two distinct vantage points in the same domain, then there must exist a continuous path from C_0 to C_1 such that all points along this path project the object into the same characteristic-view partition. It may be possible to generate identical projections from two different vantage-point domains. These, however, according to our definitions would belong to distinct CVPs.

Let us define Q to the set of all perspective projections of a body on a plane. The set of projections Q can be partitioned into subsets P_i, i=1,2,---,k, where each subset is associated with a particular vantage-point domain. We shall call these subsets the

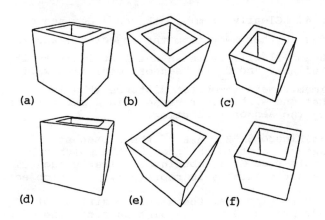

(a) (b) (c)

(d) (e) (f)

Figure 1. Six views of a cube with a hole.

characteristic-view partitions (CVPs) of Q. Note that junction-line identity is a necessary but not a sufficient condition for two projections to belong to the same CVP.

The approach taken in solving the recognition problem will be to determine whether a given arbitrary projection belongs to one of the characteristic-view partitions of the known set of bodies. Thus we need to show that there exists a characteristic view, among the characteristic-view sets for all bodies, into which the given projection can be transformed.

The stable positions of an object

Although the characterization of bodies in terms of their CVs is useful, the resulting set of visible-line projections may be large even for a simple object. We will, therefore, develop a more restrictive partitioning scheme for the projection set Q. This will permit not only a reduction of CVs required for representation but will also allow us to compute a linear transformation for determining the orientation and location of the body in 3-space. For two projections to belong to the same partition, they must be junction-line identical and it must be possible to compute this linear transformation.

To reduce the number of vantage-point domains we impose the following restrictions:

1. Objects will be assumed to appear only in <u>stable positions</u>. These are the positions in which the object would come to rest if thrown on a flat, horizontal surface. The surface is called the <u>supporting plane</u>.

2. The camera-to-supporting-plane geometry remains fixed during the recognition process.

3. The camera-to-object distance is limited to a fixed range.

Let us examine the relationship among the camera-to-object distance, the resolution of the sensor, and the number of CVs that need to be represented. Consider the object shown in Figure 2(a) and its plan view shown in Figure 2(b). C_0 and C_1 are two vantage points

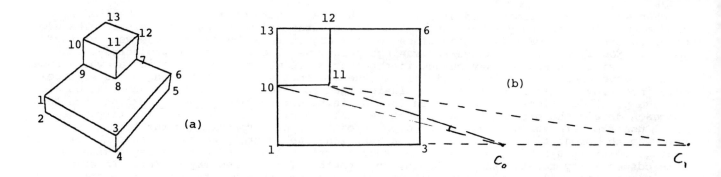

Figure 2. Illustration of maximum camera-to-object distance limitation.

lying in the plane defined by vertices 1, 3, and 4. Clearly from C_0, the edge defined by vertices 10 and 11 will be visible. As C_0 recedes further away from the object the angular separation between the projection of vertices 10 and 11 will decrease until at infinity it vanishes completely. At some distance between infinity and C_0 the sensor resolution will prevent the edge from being discerned. The maximum camera-to-object distance thus is governed by two factors - the level of detail that one wishes to represent in distinguishing one CV from another and the limitation imposed by the sensor resolution.

One must also consider the case illustrated in Figure 3. Because of the closeness of the vantage point to the face of the polyhedron, a single-face CV is obtained. Clearly such CVs are not desirable in representing a 3D object.

Note also that the stable positions of a body provide a non-disjoint partitioning of Q; that is, different stable positions of an object may yield perspective projections that are members of the same CVP. This is illustrated using the polyhedron with 14 vertices and 9 faces shown in Figure 2(a). The first CV is generated where the polyhedron is in a stable position with the face specified by vertices 2, 4, 5, 14 on the supporting plane as shown in Figure 4(a). The same CV, however can be generated with the polyhedron in another stable position with the face specified by vertices 1, 2, 14, 13, 10, 9 on the supporting plane as illustrated in Figure 4(b).

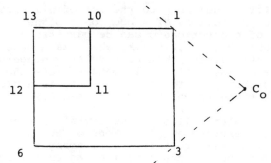

Figure 3. Minimum camera-to-object distance limitation.

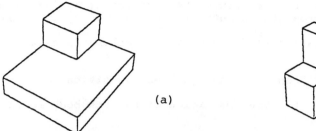
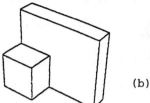

(a)
(b)

Figure 4. Identical CVs generated from two different stable positions.

Projection-to-CV transformation

Four coordinate systems are used to compute the projection-to-CV transformation, as shown in Figure 5:

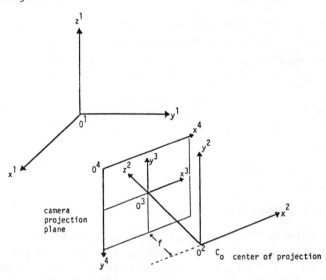

camera projection plane

Figure 5. Camera geometry

1. The homogeneous global coordinate system $0^1(x^1, y^1, z^1, 1)$, in which all bodies are defined.

2. The homogeneous camera coordinate system $0^2(x^2, y^2, z^2, 1)$ with origin at the center of the projection, C_0.

3. The homogeneous projection plane coordinate system $0^3(x^3, y^3, 1)$ with origin along z^2 at a distance equal to the focal length of the camera.

4. The homogeneous image plane coordinate system, $0^4(x^4, y^4, 1)$, coplanar with 0^3, but translated and rotated so that x^4 coincides with the first scan line of the image and y^4 passes through the first pixel of each scan line.

A scene is defined in 0^1. In the 2D projection of the scene, (i.e., the image), edges are projected as <u>lines</u>, and vertices as <u>junctions</u>. A face is a portion of a surface bounded by edges or closed on itself. A <u>region</u> is the projection of a connected visible part of a face. We define the picture-taking process as a projective mapping of coordinate vectors from 0^1 to 0^4. The use of homogeneous coordinates makes this a linear transformation. The projection transformation is a function of the camera parameters, that is, the pan, tilt and swing angles, the location of the camera lens in 0^1, and focal length of the lens. The transformation can be expressed as a single 4x3 matrix. Our objective is to determine a procedure for calculating the coefficients of this matrix. Once this transformation is known, the camera is calibrated with respect to the global coordinate system. This transformation is then used to generate the CVs from the 3D model. Notice that projection of the 3D model using the camera transformation matrix is the same as imaging the object except that the hidden lines/surfaces are not removed.

The projection transformation can be expressed as follows:

$$k_i \begin{bmatrix} x_i^4 \\ y_i^4 \\ 1 \end{bmatrix} = [T_c] \begin{bmatrix} x_i^1 \\ y_i^1 \\ z_i^1 \\ 1 \end{bmatrix} \qquad i = 1, 2, 3, ---, n$$

where $(x^4, y^4, 1)$ and $(x^1, y^1, z^1, 1)$ are homogeneous coordinate vectors in 0^4 and 0^1, respectively, and $[T_C]$ is the transformation matrix. The coefficient k_i indicates that the homogeneous coordinates of the projected points are unique only up to a scale factor.

We will use the following notation to describe the relationship between 3D objects and corresponding CVs:

1. B_{ij} is the ith body in the scene, in the jth stable position.

2. CV_{ijk} is the kth characteristic-view partition of the ith body in the jth stable position.

3. Any perspective projection (view) of a body B_{ij} is denoted by V_{ij}. Since V_{ij} must be a member of some characteristic-view partition, we write the equivalence as $V_{ij} \epsilon CV_{ijk}$.

Let us assume that we obtain an image of an object and, based upon the describing line-structure, conclude that $V_{ij} \epsilon CV_{ijk}$. Since the camera transformation matrix is known, we also know that

$$CV_{ijk}(x_p^4, y_p^4, 1) = [T_C] B_{ij}(x_p^1, y_p^1, z_p^1, 1) \qquad p=1,2,--,n$$

This transformation maps the visible points on B_{ij} into the projected line structure described by CV_{ijk}. Since $V_{ij} \epsilon CV_{ijk}$ implies that B_{ij} could only have been displaced and rotated on the supporting plane (since we have constrained it to be in a stable position) with respect to the camera, the total transformation from B_{ij} to V_{ij} can be written as follows:

$$\underline{V}_{ij}(x_p^4 \ y_p^4 \ 1) = [T_C] [T_R] [T_D] \underline{B}_{ij}(x_p^1 \ y_p^1 \ z_p^1 \ 1)$$

where

$[T_C]$ is the camera transformation matrix

$[T_R]$ is the rotation matrix about the z^1-axis

$[T_D]$ is the displacement matrix on the x^1-y^1 (supporting) plane

Since $[T_C]$, B_{ij} and V_{ij} are all known, we can determine the displacement and rotation operator. This requires that we be able to match at least two points between the given projection and the stored CV whose 3D coordinates are known. The CV model must, therefore contain not only the 2D image coordinates of junctions (or some selected critical points) but must, as a minimum, contain the 3D coordinates of at least two such points.

We summarize briefly what the above transformation accomplishes for us in the context of recognition. Each CV is a mapping of the visible lines and junctions of a 3D body. The junctions are specified in image coordinates (2D) and the visible vertices in global co-ordinates (3D). The mapping is given by the calibration matrix $[T_C]$. Let us assume that we are given an arbitrary projection of the body and wish to test whether it is a member of a particular CVP. If we can match two points between the projection and the CV and, assuming that the 3D coordinates of these points are known, then we can determine a transformation which maps the 3D coordinates of the model (from which the CV was obtained) into this arbitrary projection.

Classification and generation of CVs

We shall develop in this section a scheme for classifying the CVs of an object. The classification is used both for storing the CVs of an object in an hierarchical manner and for narrowing down the possible choices for matching. It is evident that some CVs in certain specified stable positions convey more information than others. It is desirable that this be reflected in the classification hierarchy.

Since one criterion used for partitioning the projection set Q is the junction-line identity property, it is natural to develop a classification scheme based on the number and type of label associated with each junction. The labels used are the generalized line and junction labels which are applicable to both planar and curved surface objects [15]. A hierarchy of junctions can be established by noting that non-occluding lines forming a junction convey more information about the object than occluding lines. The eight generalized junction types developed in [15] can be ordered as follows:

Junction Type	Number of Regions per Line		
	Line 1	Line 2	Line 3
Y	2	2	2
W,S	1	2	1
V,C	1	2	
V,A	1	1	
T	{1 1	2 1	1} 1

Note that junction types S,C and A are associated only with curved objects. We now define an ordered label set $L = (M_Y, M_{WS}, M_{VC}, M_{VA}, M_T)$ where M_X refers to the number of occurrences of junction type X in a CV. Characteristic views are now classified in terms of the ordered set L. Two CVs are placed in the same class if they have the same number for the most significant junction type. Thus L = {3,2,2,1,1} is in the same class as L = {3,2,1,1,1} even though the total number of junctions and lines in the CVs are different.

This type of classification permits a hierarchical, canonic representation of a 3D object in terms of a set of 2D perspective projections [16]. We illustrate this with the poly-hedron of Figure 2a. This object has 10 CV classes. Of these, only the first one does not contain any T junctions. Listed in order of increasing degeneracy, the classes are as follows:

$$(3,-,-,-,-)$$
$$(2,-,-,-,-)$$
$$(1,-,-,-,-)$$
$$(0,5,-,-,-)$$
$$(0,4,-,-,-)$$
$$(0,3,-,-,-)$$
$$(0,2,-,-,-)$$
$$(0,0,0,7,-)$$
$$(0,0,0,6,-)$$
$$(0,0,0,4,-)$$

The CVs corresponding to the first class are illustrated in Figure 6. One member from each

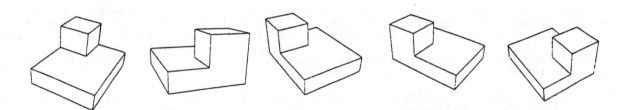

Figure 6. CVs of ordered label set L=(3,-,-,-,-)

of the remaining nine classes is shown in Figure 7 (a-i). For the purpose of representation, it is necessary to use only the non-degenerate CVs corresponding to each stable position. Although we have not placed any importance on the hierarchy of stable positions, this can be incorporated into the above structure if an object is known to appear more often in one stable position than another. Lastly, one must state that the exact number of CVs of an object that needs to be used for representation depends not only upon the object itself but also on the other 3D objects from which it must be distinguished.

Experimental results

An overall summary of the recognition scheme used is shown in Figure 8. We shall illus-trate the intermediate processing steps used in the recognition scheme by a sequence of images which depict the processing of an actual object.

The digitized image of a bracket on a table top is shown in Figure 9(a). The object was digitized under normal room lighting at a 256x256 pixel resolution. The 3D model of this object was obtained by measurements made on the object and the surfaces were approximated by planes. An image of the resulting model with the vertices labeled is shown in Figure 9(b). The binary image resulting from applying an edge operator is shown in Figure 9(c). The bi-nary image is then chain-encoded into a representation where the lines and junctions can be explicitly accessed for further processing [17]. The encoded image is shown in Figure 9(d).

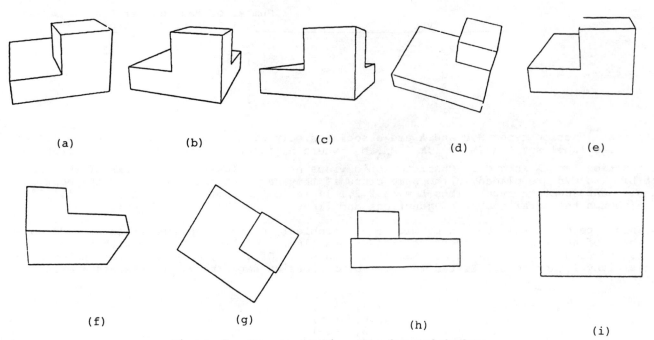

Figure 7. Representative CVs for polyhedron.

The next image, Figure 9(e) shows the line structure obtained after deleting dangling lines from junctions and isolated segments. The silhouette obtained after labeling is shown in Figure 9(f). The junctions used for correlating the line structure to the stored CV is shown in Figure 9(g). The ∇ marks the W junctions used for determining the projection-to-CV transformation. The CV matched is shown in Figure 9(h). The computed projection from the 3D model that corresponds to the unknown object projection is shown in Figure 9(i).

Summary

This paper has described a new technique for modeling 3D objects based on partitioning the projection set. We have illustrated the usefulness of the method for representation as well as for matching. We summarize briefly the three key ideas that have been developed:

1. The notion of CVs which provide a systematic way to partition the projection set of a body based on associated label sets.

2. The development of a uniform approach in handling objects of general shape; that is, no distinction is made either in partitioning or labeling between curved and polyhedral objects.

3. The development of a projection-to-CV transformation which is used both for recognition and for verifying the reliability of the match.

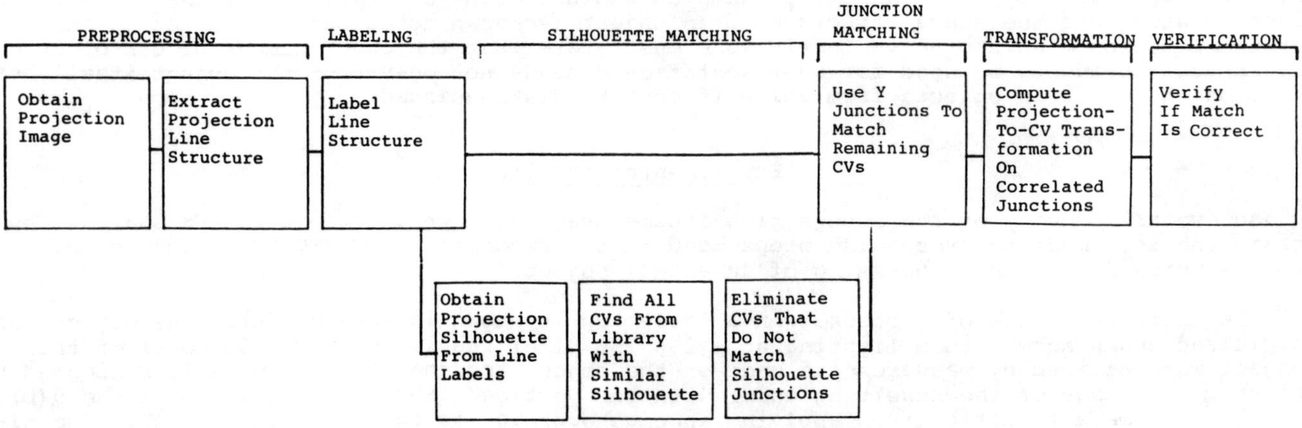

PREPROCESSING		LABELING	SILHOUETTE MATCHING	JUNCTION MATCHING	TRANSFORMATION	VERIFICATION
Obtain Projection Image	Extract Projection Line Structure	Label Line Structure		Use Y Junctions To Match Remaining CVs	Compute Projection-To-CV Transformation On Correlated Junctions	Verify If Match Is Correct
			Obtain Projection Silhouette From Line Labels	Find All CVs From Library With Similar Silhouette	Eliminate CVs That Do Not Match Silhouette Junctions	

Figure 8. The recognition scheme.

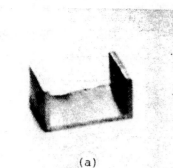 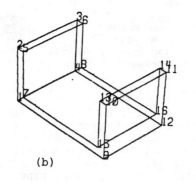 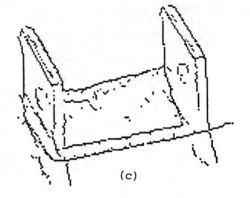

(a)

(b)

(c)

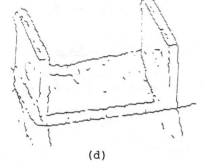 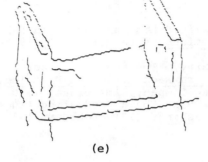 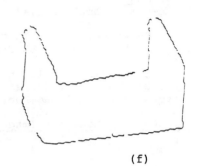

(d)

(e)

(f)

 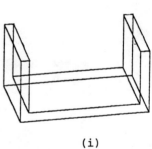

(g)

(h)

(i)

Figure 9.   Steps in the processing of the image of a simple bracket.

Acknowledgment

The research reported here was supported by the National Science Foundation, Automation, Bioengineering and Sensing Systems Program, under grant ENG-7904821. This support is gratefully acknowledged.

References

1. Agin, G. J., "Hierarchical Representations of 3D Objects", Final Report SRI, SRI Project 1187, Stanford Research Institute, Stanford, CA , March 1977.
2. Marr, D. and Nishihara, H. K., "Representation and Recognition of the Spatial Organization of Three-Dimensional Shapes", MIT A.I. Laboratory Memo 377, August 1976.
3. Srihari, S. N., "Representation of Three-Dimensional Digital Images", ACM Computing Surveys, Vol. 13, (4), December 1981.
4. Potmesil, M., "Generation of 3D Surfaces from Images of Pattern Illuminated Images", IEEE Computer Society Conference on PRIP, Chicago, Ill, July 1979.
5. Dane, C. and Bajcsy, R., "Three-Dimensional Segmentation Using the Gaussian Image and Spatial Information", IEEE Computer Society Conference on PRIP, Dallas, TX , August 1981.

6. Levin, J. Z., "Mathematical Models for Determining the Intersections of Quadric Surfaces", <u>Computer Graphics and Image Processing</u>, Vol. 11, 1979, pp. 73-87.

7. Baker, H., "Three-Dimensional Modeling", <u>Proceedings of the 5th International Joint Conference on A. I.</u>, Cambridge, MA, August 1977, pp. 649-655.

8. Wesley, M. A., "Construction and Use of Geometric Models", <u>Computer Aided Design Modeling, Systems Engineering, CAD Systems</u>, edited by J. Encarnacao, Springer Verlag, New York, 1980.

9. Perkins, W. A., "A Model-Based Vision System for Industrial Parts", <u>IEEE Trans. on Computers</u>, C-27, (2), February 1978, pp. 126-143.

10. Holland, S. W., Rossol, L. and Ward, W. R., "CONSIGHT-1: A Vision Controlled Robot System for Transferring Parts from Belt Conveyors", <u>Computer Vision and Sensor Based Robots</u>, edited by G. C. Dodd and L. Rossol, Plenum Press, New York, 1979.

11. Chen, N., Birk, J. and Kelly, R., "Estimating Workpiece Pose Using the Feature Point Method", <u>IEEE Trans. on Automatic Control</u>, AC-25, (6), December 1980.

12. Barrow, H. G. and Tennenbaum, J. M., "Interpreting Line Drawings as Three-Dimensional Surfaces", <u>Artificial Intelligence</u>, Vol. 17, August 1981, pp. 75-116.

13. Brooks, R. A., "Symbolic Reasoning Among 3-D Models", <u>Artificial Intelligence</u>, Vol. 17, August 1981, pp. 285-348.

14. Shapiro, L. G., Haralick, R. M., Moriarty, J. D. and Mulgaonkar, P. G., "Matching Three-Dimensional Models", <u>IEEE Computer Society Conference on PRIP</u>, Dallas, TX, August 1981, pp. 534-541.

15. Chakravarty, I., "A Generalized Line and Junction Labelling Scheme with Application to Scene Analysis", <u>IEEE Transactions on Pattern Analysis and Machine Intelligence</u>, PAMI-1, (2), April 1979.

16. H. Freeman and I. Chakravarty, "The Use of Characteristic Views in the Recognition of Three-Dimensional Objects", <u>Pattern Recognition in Practice</u>, E. Gelsema and L. Kanal, editors, North-Holland Publishing Company, Amsterdam, 1980.

17. Chakravarty, I., "A Single Pass Chain Generating Algorithm for Region Boundaries", <u>Computer Graphics and Image Processing</u>, (15), February 1981.

M. A. Wesley
G. Markowsky*

"Fleshing Out Projections" by M.A. Wesley and G. Markowsky
from *IBM Journal of Research and Development*, Volume 25,
Number 6, November 1981, pages 934-954. Copyright 1981 by
International Business Machines Corporation; reprinted with
permission.

Fleshing Out Projections

In an earlier paper, the authors presented an algorithm for finding all polyhedral solid objects with a given set of vertices and straight line edges (its wire frame*). This paper extends the Wire Frame algorithm to find all solid polyhedral objects with a given set of two dimensional projections. These projections may contain depth information in the form of dashed and solid lines, may represent cross sections, and may be overall or detail views. The choice of labeling conventions in the projections determines the difficulty of the problem. It is shown that with certain conventions and projections the problem of fleshing out projections essentially reduces to the problem of fleshing out wire frames. Even if no labeling is used, the Projections algorithm presented here finds all solutions even though it is possible to construct simple examples with a very large number of solutions. Such examples have a large amount of symmetry and various accidental coincidences which typically do not occur in objects of practical interest. Because of its generality, the algorithm can handle pathological cases if they arise. This Projections algorithm, which has applications in the conversion of engineering drawings in a Computer Aided Design, Computer Aided Manufacturing (CADCAM) system, has been implemented. The algorithm has successfully found solutions to problems that are rather complex in terms of either the number of possible solutions or the inherent complexity of projections of objects of engineering interest.*

1. Introduction

In an earlier paper [1] the authors presented an algorithm for finding all polyhedral solid objects with a given set of vertices and straight line edges (its wire frame). The Wire Frame algorithm was based on the concepts of algebraic topology and rigorous definitions of the geometric entities involved. It recognized that many solid objects may have the same wire frame and was able to find all possible solutions efficiently.

In this paper we extend the Wire Frame algorithm to polyhedral objects described by a set of two dimensional projections such as might be seen on an engineering drawing. The projection process may introduce another level of ambiguity into reconstruction problems and increases the possibility of there being many objects with the same set of projections. The Projections algorithm presented here can work with very little information, for

example, only two projections, and find all possible objects matching the data. However, it is seen that the number of solutions may be very large and that it may be reasonable to provide more information in the form of three or more projections, by labeling corresponding features in divers views, and by providing depth information. The Projections algorithm is able to make use of this extra information and can also accept other forms of advice, such as whether given points are inside material.

Quite apart from its mathematical interest, the algorithm has practical applications in the automatic conversion of digitized engineering drawings into solid volumetric representations of the geometry of objects. These solid volumetric representations become the basis for the simulation and synthesis of large parts of the design validation, analysis, manufacture, inspection, and documentation process [2, 3].

The subject of reconstruction of solid polyhedral objects from their projections has been studied over a period

---

*Consistent use of alphabetical ordering of authors' names tends to slight people whose names begin with letters towards the end of the alphabet. Thus, the order of names on this paper is not meant to pass judgement on the relative contributions of the authors, but rather to illustrate the fact that names appearing in alphabetical order is not a "natural law."

Copyright 1981 by International Business Machines Corporation. Copying is permitted without payment of royalty provided that (1) each reproduction is done without alteration and (2) the *Journal* reference and IBM copyright notice are included on the first page. The title and abstract may be used without further permission in computer-based and other information-service systems. Permission to *republish* other excerpts should be obtained from the Editor.

of years. Early work [4–6] was largely based on labeling corresponding information in different views and requiring the user to conform to constraints on the manner of description of features such as faces. The historical trend has been to free the user of as many constraints as possible [7]. However, the relaxation of constraints has led to the possibility of multiple solutions to a given problem, and workers have tended to concentrate on heuristic approaches to find a probable solution. A recent paper [8] reports such a heuristic approach that allows complete freedom of input and has been implemented; another paper [9] outlines an approach that would allow certain views of cylindrical surfaces but does not include an implementation. None of this work appears to be based on formal geometric definitions and the concepts of algebraic topology. A closely related development path has been followed by workers in the fields of Computer Vision and Scene Analysis. This path has been based on vertex and edge configurations in a single view [10–12] and has generally been restricted to objects with trihedral vertices and views with no chance alignments; this approach has led to the Origami World [13] and a linear programming approach [14].

This paper presents a very general and complete approach based on the authors' previously published Wire Frame algorithm. In addressing the problem of constructing a solid object from a number of two dimensional views, it is shown that, on the one hand, complete labeling of edges and vertices leads to the previously published Wire Frame algorithm. On the other hand, the Projections algorithm described here is capable of working with no further information than the lines and points of the two dimensional projections and is able to enumerate all possible solutions to a given set of projections, with a cost commensurate with the number of solutions. The techniques presented are applicable when two or more projections are available. Of course, the one projection case has, in general, infinitely many solutions and is not discussed further in this paper. The chief advantage gained from providing more projections is quite naturally to reduce the number of possible ambiguities.

The Projections algorithm constructs polyhedral objects from projections containing only straight lines. The logical component of this algorithm is topological in nature and is, in principle, independent of whether the components are linear or nonlinear. While extension to objects with curved surfaces and projections with curved lines appears to be feasible, the ease of actually carrying out such an extension would depend greatly on the family of allowable curves and surfaces, as well as the projection conventions used.

The paper is organized as follows: Section 2 reviews the definitions of objects, faces, edges, and vertices used in the paper describing the Wire Frame algorithm [1] and then develops the basic results dealing with back projections and labeled projections. Section 3 outlines the original Wire Frame algorithm and describes the Basic Projections algorithm which handles the general case of unlabeled projections of wire frames of objects. Section 4 presents some extensions to the Basic Projections algorithm which enable it to make use of more general forms of input data. For example, various types of views (overall, detail, and cross section) and depth information distinguishing between visible and occulted lines are considered. In Section 5, some examples are given to clarify this discussion. These examples illustrate the execution of the algorithm in both the stylized world of geometric puzzles with multiple solutions and the practical world of engineering drawings. The engineering objects successfully constructed from their projections are sufficiently complicated that a human unfamiliar with the solid object generally has some difficulty envisioning it. Thus, the algorithm appears capable of handling real world problems.

2. Basic concepts and results

The basic concepts defined in this section are based on some fundamental topological ideas which are described in detail in [15]. Throughout the paper the standard topology in $\mathbb{R}^3$ and the induced topology on subsets of $\mathbb{R}^3$ are assumed. Vertices refer to points in $\mathbb{R}^3$ and edges refer to line segments defined by two points in $\mathbb{R}^3$. The approach used in this section is to define faces, objects, wire frames, and projections, and then describe the consequences of these definitions.

Definition 1
A *face*, f, is the closure of a nonempty, bounded, connected, coplanar, open (in the relative topology) subset of $\mathbb{R}^3$ whose boundary (denoted by ∂f) is the union of a finite number of line segments. P_f is used to denote the unique plane which contains f. $\square$

Definition 2
An *object*, $\mathcal{O}$, is the closure of a nonempty, bounded, open subset of $\mathbb{R}^3$ whose boundary (denoted by $\partial\mathcal{O}$) is the union of a finite number of faces. $\square$

From the definitions above it is easy to see that the "cube," $\{x, y, z \in \mathbb{R}^3 \mid 0 \le x \le 1, 0 \le y \le 1, 0 \le z \le 1\}$ is an object and that $\{(1, y, z) \in \mathbb{R}^3 \mid 0 \le y \le 1, 0 \le z \le 1\}$ is one of its "square" faces. Starting off with open sets means that faces and objects have nontrivial interiors. Notice that it is not assumed that an object is the closure of a connected set. This allows objects that consist of disjoint "solids" or even objects which intersect only in

M. A. WESLEY AND G. MARKOWSK

388

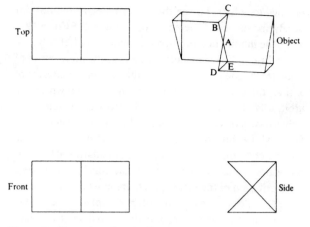

Figure 1 Examples of projections.

1. The endpoints of e belong to V(𝒪);
2. No interior point of e belongs to V(𝒪);
3. For every point p of e, two noncoplanar faces can be found, f_1, $f_2 \subseteq \partial\mathcal{O}$ such that $p \in f_1 \cap f_2$.

(e) Let 𝒪 be an object. The *wire frame* of 𝒪, WF(𝒪), is defined to be the ordered pair (V(𝒪), E(𝒪)). □

It can be shown that the edges of an object can intersect only at vertices of the object, *i.e.*, at their endpoints.

The Wire Frame algorithm detailed in [1] allows one to construct all possible objects which have a given wire frame. It happens to be true, but not immediately obvious from the definitions, that V(f), E(f), V(𝒪), and E(𝒪) are all finite and well-defined. These facts and others are discussed in greater detail in [1].

The Wire Frame algorithm described in [1] runs on any collection of points and line segments in $\mathbb{R}^3$ and either returns all objects having the given collection as their wire frame or shows that the given collection could not be a valid wire frame. In presenting the Projections algorithm the first things to consider are the projections of the wire frame of a valid object. At this point it is necessary to make clear exactly what is meant by a projection.

Definition 4
Let 𝒪 be an object, $\mathbf{P} \subset \mathbb{R}^3$ a plane, and $\pi_p : \mathbb{R}^3 \to \mathbf{P}$ the perpendicular projection. By the *P-projection* of 𝒪, denoted by 𝒪 | **P**, is meant the ordered pair, (V(𝒪|**P**), E(𝒪|**P**)), of **P**-*vertices* and **P**-*edges* of 𝒪 defined by the following process. Let E* be the set of images under π_p of all edges of 𝒪 which are not perpendicular to **P**. Then the **P**-vertices of 𝒪 are those points of **P** which lie on at least two noncolinear line segments in E*. The **P**-edges of 𝒪 are those line segments of **P** which have elements of V(𝒪|**P**) as endpoints, have no points of V(𝒪|**P**) as interior points, and are subsets of unions of elements of E*.

XY, YZ, and ZX are used to denote the planes Z = 0, X = 0, and Y = 0, respectively. □

Figure 1 shows some of the things that can happen as a result of projection. The vertex A disappears in the front and top views. Furthermore, the edges AB, AC, AD, and AE do not appear as such in these views. Rather a single edge appears which is the union of the projections of the four aforementioned line segments. However, in the side view the vertex A projects into a vertex, and the projections of AB, AC, AD, and AE form distinct line segments.

At this point it seems appropriate to discuss the situations in which vertices of an object project into vertices in

edges, etc. One can argue that this last case does not represent a "real" object, but in practice all sorts of strange objects can appear. Thus, we decided to handle the most general case possible. Furthermore, this generality does not exact any penalty other than creating a large number of solutions.

Another point worth noticing is that Definitions 1 and 2 allow many different representations of the boundaries of faces and objects by line segments and faces (respectively). However, there are canonical representations of the boundaries which correspond to one's intuitive notions about such things. To get to these representations it is necessary to introduce several additional concepts.

Definition 3
(a) Let f be a face. The *vertices* of f, V(f), are defined to be the set of all points for which two noncolinear line segments, contained in ∂f, can be found whose intersection is the given point.

(b) Let f be a face. The *edges* of f, E(f), are defined to be the set of all line segments e, contained in ∂f, satisfying the following conditions:

1. The endpoints of e belong to V(f);
2. No interior point of e belongs to V(f).

(c) Let 𝒪 be an object. The *vertices* of 𝒪, V(𝒪), are defined to be the set of all points p for which faces f_1, f_2, f_3 $\subseteq \partial\mathcal{O}$ can be found such that $\{p\} = f_1 \cap f_2 \cap f_3 = P_{f_1} \cap P_{f_2} \cap P_{f_3}$.

(d) Let 𝒪 be an object. The *edges* of 𝒪, E(𝒪), are defined to be the set of all line segments e, contained in $\partial\mathcal{O}$, satisfying the following conditions:

a given projection. Note that if a vertex of a polyhedral object is the intersection of at least three noncoplanar line segments, the image of that vertex under any projection is the intersection of at least two noncolinear line segments and is thus a vertex in that projection. For convenience, vertices which are the intersections of at least three noncoplanar line segments are called *Class I vertices*. Thus, if two different projections of an object are given, the Class I vertices are a subset of the set of all intersections of all the perpendiculars erected at the vertices in each projection.

All vertices of an object which are not Class I are to be called *Class II vertices*. In Fig. 1, vertex Λ is Class II; all other vertices are Class I. In general, one cannot expect to recover Class II vertices simply by erecting perpendiculars and computing their intersections.

There are a number of properties of Class I and Class II vertices which are useful in recovering an object from its projections. The key observation, which is formalized below, is that the wire frame of $\mathcal{O}$ can be recovered from the Class I vertices of $\mathcal{O}$ and certain line segments joining these vertices.

Definition 5
The *skeleton*, $S(\mathcal{O})$, of an object $\mathcal{O}$ is the ordered pair $(SV(\mathcal{O}), SE(\mathcal{O}))$ of *skeletal vertices* and *skeletal edges* where $SV(\mathcal{O})$ is the set of the Class I vertices of $\mathcal{O}$ and $SE(\mathcal{O})$ is a set of line segments joining the elements of $SV(\mathcal{O})$. For $v_1, v_2 \in SV(\mathcal{O})$, there exists $w \in SE(\mathcal{O})$, joining v_1, v_2 iff there exists an edge or colinear sequence of edges of $\mathcal{O}$ joining v_1 and v_2 and not containing any other Class I vertex. $\square$

Theorem 6
Let $\mathcal{O}$ be an object. Then the wire frame of $\mathcal{O}$, $(V(\mathcal{O}), E(\mathcal{O}))$, can be recovered from the skeleton of $\mathcal{O}$, $(SV(\mathcal{O}), SE(\mathcal{O}))$, as follows. First, $V(\mathcal{O}) = V^*(\mathcal{O})$ where

$$V^*(\mathcal{O}) = SV(\mathcal{O}) \cup \{v | \{v\} = e_1 \cap e_2, e_1, e_2 \in SE(\mathcal{O})\}.$$

Thus, to get all vertices of $\mathcal{O}$ it is enough to add all intersection points of skeletal edges to the skeletal vertices. Second, $E(\mathcal{O})$ is simply the set of line segments which result from partitioning the skeletal edges using their points of intersection.

Proof   Observe that from Definition 5 it follows that every skeletal edge is the union of edges of $\mathcal{O}$. Thus, the intersection of two skeletal edges is a point of intersection of two edges. However, edges of $\mathcal{O}$ intersect only in vertices of $\mathcal{O}$. Thus, $V^*(\mathcal{O}) \subseteq V(\mathcal{O})$.

It remains to show that $V(\mathcal{O}) \subseteq V^*(\mathcal{O})$. In particular it must only be demonstrated that every Class II vertex of $\mathcal{O}$

belongs to $V^*(\mathcal{O})$. To see this it is necessary to consider briefly the nature of the edges of $\mathcal{O}$. Let $e \in E(\mathcal{O})$, $p \in e$, and ℓ the infinite line through p containing e. Let X be the set of disjoint line segments formed by the intersection of ℓ and the boundary of $\mathcal{O}$. Now either p is in the interior of X (*i.e.*, there are points of X on both sides of p which are arbitrarily close to p) or p has arbitrarily close neighbors only to one side of it. Let f_1 and f_2 be the two noncoplanar faces whose intersection contains e. If p is not in the interior of X, then, since p is on the boundaries of f_1 and f_2 but is not in the interior of any of the edges, it must be a vertex of each of the faces, *i.e.*, there must be edges, $e_1 \in f_1$, $e_2 \in f_2$, not colinear with e such that $\{p\} = e \cap e_1 = e \cap e_2$. But in this case there are three noncoplanar edges through p, namely, e, e_1, and e_2. Thus, p is a Class I vertex.

The point of the preceding paragraph is to show that either a point, p, of an edge, e, is a Class I vertex or the line through p containing e has boundary points of $\mathcal{O}$ arbitrarily close to p, *i.e.*, there exists a line segment $s \supseteq e$ contained in $\partial\mathcal{O}$ for which p is an interior point. In particular, an edge, e, containing a Class II vertex p can be extended to a line segment s lying in $\partial\mathcal{O}$ containing e whose endpoints are Class I vertices, *i.e.*, every edge of $\mathcal{O}$ is contained in some skeletal edge. Since every vertex of $\mathcal{O}$ must lie on at least three edges, every Class II vertex of $\mathcal{O}$ must lie on at least two skeletal edges and hence $V(\mathcal{O}) = V^*(\mathcal{O})$.

Since every edge of $\mathcal{O}$ lies in some skeletal edge and $V(\mathcal{O}) = V^*(\mathcal{O})$, it follows that the edges of $\mathcal{O}$ are exactly the pieces into which the skeletal edges are partitioned by the vertices of $\mathcal{O}$. $\square$

Theorem 6 gives some insight into the working of the Projections algorithm. Back projection yields a *pseudo skeleton* consisting of a set of vertices which includes the Class I vertices and a set of edges. This pseudo skeleton is processed to produce a *pseudo wire frame*. In general, the pseudo skeleton and pseudo wire frame contain vertices and edges not in the skeleton and wire frame of the original object. However, they do contain all the vertices and a partition of the edges of the skeleton and wire frame of the original object. In fact, the additional complexity of the Projections algorithm is based on the fact that back projection generally yields many vertices and edges not in the original object. The Projections algorithm thus proceeds along the lines laid down by the Wire Frame algorithm, but with suitable modifications made to deal with surplus information.

The discussion of Class II vertices in the proof of Theorem 6 shows that they have various properties, one of which appears as Theorem 7. Theorem 7 is very useful in showing that certain points which arise from back projection cannot be vertices of $\mathcal{O}$. Example 4 later in the paper illustrates the power of this observation.

Theorem 7

Let $\mathcal{O}$ be an object and v a Class II vertex of $\mathcal{O}$. Any plane, **P**, through v separates $\mathbb{R}^3$ into two components each of which contains interior points of $\mathcal{O}$ which are arbitrarily close to v.

Proof From the proof of Theorem 6 it follows that v is the intersection of two noncolinear line segments, e_1 and e_2, which are unions of line segments of $\mathcal{O}$, are contained in the boundary of $\mathcal{O}$, and contain v as an interior point. Any plane through v not containing e_1 or e_2 is clearly going to contain interior points of $\mathcal{O}$ near v, and in this case this theorem is true. Also, there is only one plane, P, containing e_1 and e_2. If all of $\mathcal{O}$ were to one side of P, there would be a contradiction, since at least four noncoplanar faces would go through v, but all the edges containing v would be coplanar. $\square$

The remainder of this section shows how much simpler things are when items are labeled or when special projections are used. The discussion of the unlabeled case is resumed in Section 3.

In mechanical drawing practice, one generally starts with $\mathcal{O}|XY$, $\mathcal{O}|YZ$, and $\mathcal{O}|ZX$, although it is always possible to use other planes. In fact, as will now be shown, for each object $\mathcal{O}$ it is always possible to find a plane **P** such that π_p distinguishes all the elements of WF($\mathcal{O}$).

Proposition 8

Let $\mathcal{O}$ be an object. Then there exists a plane **P** containing the origin for which π_p projects each element of V($\mathcal{O}$) into a distinct vertex of $\mathcal{O}|P$, elements of E($\mathcal{O}$) project into distinct line segments which can intersect in at most one point, and no point in V($\mathcal{O}$) projects into a projection of an element of E($\mathcal{O}$) unless it is a member of it.

Proof The set of all planes in $\mathbb{R}^3$ containing the origin can be identified with the unit sphere, S^2, in $\mathbb{R}^3$, where each unit vector corresponds to the plane for which it is a unit normal. Clearly, in this manner exactly two points of S^2 correspond to each plane through the origin. In order for a projection π_p to map each vertex of $\mathcal{O}$ to a distinct member of V($\mathcal{O}|P$), **P** cannot be perpendicular to any line which goes through at least two of the points of V($\mathcal{O}$) and cannot be perpendicular to any plane containing all edges incident with a Class II vertex. Each of these restrictions rules out exactly one plane, *i.e.*, two points on S^2. Thus, in order to get an injection on V($\mathcal{O}$), at most

$$2\left[\binom{|V(\mathcal{O})|}{2} + |V(\mathcal{O})|\right]$$

points on S^2 must be avoided.

Two elements of E($\mathcal{O}$) can have an intersection of more than one point in some projection if and only if they are coplanar. Furthermore, they can project with a nontrivial overlap only into planes which are perpendicular to the plane containing both of the elements of E($\mathcal{O}$). The set of all planes through the origin perpendicular to a given plane corresponds to a great circle of S^2. Thus, to get the desired behavior at most

$$\binom{|E(\mathcal{O})|}{2}$$

great circles on S^2 must be avoided.

To keep a point from projecting onto a line segment not containing it there are two cases to consider. First, the point and line segment might be colinear. In this case, one must avoid the plane perpendicular to the given line. Again this means avoiding two points. Thus, at most $2|V(\mathcal{O})|\,|E(\mathcal{O})|$ points must be avoided. Second, the point and line segment are not colinear. In this case it is enough to avoid all planes perpendicular to a given plane as before. Thus, at most $|V(\mathcal{O})|\,|E(\mathcal{O})|$ great circles on S^2 must be avoided.

Since points and great circles are nowhere dense in S^2 and the number of sets which must be avoided is finite, it follows from the Baire Category Theorem (see [15]) that there must be points of S^2 which do not lie in any of the forbidden sets. Using any such point yields a plane with the desired properties. $\square$

Definition 9

Let $\mathcal{O}$ be an object, **P** a plane in 3-space, and π_p the projection of 3-space onto **P**. Projection π_p is said to be a *distinguishing projection* for $\mathcal{O}$ if it has all the properties of Proposition 8. $\square$

Note that the proof of Proposition 8 shows that for a given object "most" projections are distinguishing projections since the nondistinguishing ones have a two dimensional measure of 0. The probability of picking a nondistinguishing projection at random is thus zero in an ideal model. However, in most practical situations there are only a finite number of choices for coordinates, and there is a nonzero probability of picking a nondistinguishing projection. Many objects of engineering interest have planar features aligned with the "natural" axes of the object, and the set of three standard views contains a maximum degree of concealment and self alignment.

At this point it is worthwhile to consider two cases. In the first case, the image of each vertex in each projection carries the labels of all the vertices of $\mathcal{O}$ that project into it, *i.e.*, the P-projections are labeled. In the second case, there are no labels on the vertices of the P-projection.

In the first case there is, quite naturally, significantly less ambiguity than in the second case. The following theorem shows exactly how much information can be recovered from labeled P-projections.

Theorem 10
Let P_1 and P_2 be two nonparallel planes in $\mathbb{R}^3$, and let $\mathcal{O}$ be an object. Assume that the P_1 and P_2 projections of $\mathcal{O}$ are labeled. Then there is a unique set of points in $\mathbb{R}^3$ which can be $V(\mathcal{O})$. Furthermore, if either of the projections is distinguishing or if all the edges in at least one P-projection are labeled with the pairs of vertices they connect, then $WF(\mathcal{O})$ can be reconstructed uniquely. In this case, reconstructing objects from projections reduces to the problem of reconstructing objects from wire frames.

Proof If P_1-vertices and P_2-vertices are labeled, to reconstruct a point $x \in SV(\mathcal{O})$, the images of x under the two projections are found and perpendiculars erected at those points. Since P_1 and P_2 are not parallel, these perpendiculars can meet in at most one point. Since they both go through x, x can be recovered as their unique intersection point. In this way $SV(\mathcal{O})$ can be reconstructed uniquely, which, by Theorem 6, means that $V(\mathcal{O})$ can also be reconstructed uniquely.

Clearly, if the edges of at least one P-projection are labeled as described above, $E(\mathcal{O})$ can be uniquely reconstructed. If one of the projections is distinguishing, $E(\mathcal{O})$ can be reconstructed by joining together two points of $V(\mathcal{O})$ if and only if they are joined together in the distinguishing projection (or in both projections). □

Thus, given a fairly small amount of information on projections, one can quickly and easily reconstruct a unique wire frame. In many practical situations, where the emphasis is on getting things done and not on creating puzzles, it seems quite likely that there will be ample information for constructing the correct wire frame easily. Unfortunately, there will also be many situations with inadequate information. The techniques developed for handling the unlabeled case are of great importance in such situations.

To complete the development of the labeled case, the situation in which there are no distinguishing projections must be discussed. Since this problem is a subset of the unlabeled case, the unlabeled case is considered next.

In the unlabeled case, there can be a number of distinguishing projections and it may not be possible to recover a wire frame uniquely. The following example illustrates this in the case of three distinguishing projections.

Example 11
Let $\mathcal{O}_1$ be the tetrahedron with vertices $\{(1, 1, 1), (1, 2, 2), (2, 1, 2), (2, 2, 1)\}$ and $\mathcal{O}_2$ the tetrahedron with vertices $\{(1, 1, 2), (1, 2, 1), (2, 1, 1), (2, 2, 2)\}$. The projections of $\mathcal{O}_1$ and $\mathcal{O}_2$ into the XY, XZ, and YZ planes are all distinguishing and are identical in each plane, but do not allow construction of a unique wire frame. Actually, the projections into the various planes are all essentially the same, *i.e.*, by ignoring the coordinate which is fixed at 0 in each case, one gets the points $\{(1, 1), (1, 2), (2, 1), (2, 2)\}$ and the six possible lines between them, *i.e.*, each projection looks like a square with both of its diagonals drawn in. In Section 5, the problem of reconstructing all objects for which all three standard projections look like a square with its diagonals is discussed in more detail. As shall be seen, there are surprisingly many solutions to this problem. □

The above discussion shows that labeling projections can be very useful in reducing the difficulty of reconstructing objects from projections. The truth of the preceding sentence becomes even more apparent after the discussion of the algorithm for reconstructing objects from unlabeled projections in Section 3 and the discussion of the examples in Section 5.

3. Fleshing out unlabeled projections
In order to aid in the comprehension of this rather complex algorithm, a basic form of the algorithm, which accepts only limited data, is presented here (Section 3). The basic algorithm constructs all polyhedral solid objects whose wire frames have a given set of projections (or *views*). The extension of the algorithm to a more general set of projection forms (*i.e.*, overall, detail, and cross section), and to the use of depth information to distinguish between visible and occulted edges, is deferred until Section 4. Since the Projections algorithm is an extension to the Wire Frame algorithm, the basic concepts of the Wire Frame algorithm and its terminology are reviewed first.

In the Wire Frame algorithm the input data [a wire frame, Fig. 2(a)] are processed to find all graphs containing more than two noncolinear edges. For each such graph, minimum enclosed areas are found and nested in a tree hierarchy. From this hierarchy candidate faces with an exterior boundary and possibly interior boundaries (*i.e.*, a face may have holes) are constructed—these are

M. A. WESLEY AND G. MARKOWSKI

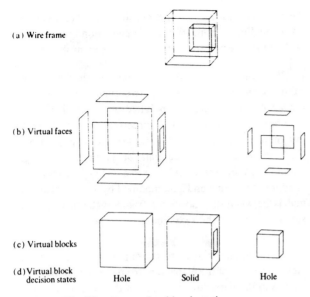

(a) Wire frame

(b) Virtual faces

(c) Virtual blocks

(d) Virtual block decision states

Hole   Solid   Hole

Figure 2 The Wire Frame algorithm in action.

called *virtual faces* [Fig. 2(b)]. For each edge, a list of virtual faces is formed and ordered radially around the edge. Minimum enclosed volumes are found and nested, again in a tree hierarchy. From this hierarchy, candidate volume regions called *virtual blocks* are found [Fig. 2(c)]. A final decision process assigns state solid or hole to each virtual block [Fig. 2(d)], glues the solid blocks together, and finds all possible solid objects with the input wire frame. Note that one virtual block is always an infinite envelope block (*i.e.*, it is inside out) and is always a hole.

The ability to handle all possible cases is embedded in the parts of the algorithm for finding enclosed regions (for example, bridges are ignored), for the handling of illegal intersections between virtual faces (Type I and Type II intersections, see below), and in the final decision process. The correctness of objects is derived from the use of directed edges and faces and from rules governing the number of times and directions with which edges and faces are used.

The several stages of the Projections algorithm are now described. Since many of these stages are quite similar to the corresponding stages of the Wire Frame algorithm, details are given about only those points which are different. The presentation is given in two parts: first, a brief outline of the stages, and second, a more detailed description of each stage.

The early stages (1, 2, and 3) of the Projections algorithm are concerned with converting, by means of a

back projection process, a set of projections of an object to a pseudo skeleton and thence to a pseudo wire frame for the object. This pseudo wire frame contains supersets of the vertices of all objects with the given projections. Furthermore, the edges of this pseudo wire frame partition the edges of all objects with the given projections. The existence of various edges and vertices in objects may be known for certain or may be uncertain. All components of the pseudo wire frame are consistent with all the views.

The later stages (*i.e.*, 4–7) apply an extended form of the Wire Frame algorithm to a pseudo wire frame to find all polyhedral solid objects with the given projections.

● *Outline of the Basic Projections algorithm*

1. Check input data   The input data to the basic algorithm are assumed to be a set of at least two distinct parallel projections of the wire frame of a polyhedral object. Extensions to handle more general forms of input data are presented in Section 4. The data are checked for validity and reduced to canonical form with edges and vertices distinct and with edges intersecting only in vertices.

2. Construct pseudo vertex skeleton   The vertices in each view are back projected to find all Class I vertices (*i.e.*, vertices formed by the intersection of noncoplanar edges) and some Class II vertices (*i.e.*, vertices formed by the intersection of only coplanar edges); at this point it is not possible to distinguish between vertex classes. The vertices discovered here, and the remainder of any Class II vertices missed in this stage and found in Stage 3, are called *candidate vertices*. While not all vertices of $\mathbb{O}$ may be recovered at this stage, enough are recovered to enable the recovery of all vertices after passing through the next stage. Note also that candidate vertices may not be vertices or even points of $\mathbb{O}$.

3. Construct pseudo wire frame   The vertices constructed in Stage 2 form a skeleton for the pseudo wire frame in the same sense that WF($\mathbb{O}$) derives from S($\mathbb{O}$). Edges are introduced based on the edges in the projections. These edges are checked for mutual internal intersections. Intersections are introduced as additional vertices and used to partition the edges. The remaining Class II vertices are constructed in this manner. The vertices constructed here and in Stage 2 are the set of candidate vertices (denoted CV($\mathbb{O}$)), and the final set of edges constructed in this stage is the set of candidate edges (denoted CE($\mathbb{O}$)). Together the candidate edges and vertices form the *pseudo wire frame*. The candidate vertices are a superset of V($\mathbb{O}$), and the candidate edges partition the elements of E($\mathbb{O}$). The edge connectivity of all vertices is examined and the candidate edge and vertex lists edited. The editing process may remove impossible items, simplify colinear edges, and update the classification of vertices as Class I or II. Candidate edges and vertices which are the only possible candidates for some edges and vertices appearing in one of the projections are labeled as certain and must appear in a solution object; all others are labeled uncertain and may or may not appear in solution objects. For both candidate edges and vertices, cross reference lists are maintained between view edges and vertices and pseudo wire frame edges and vertices, and *vice versa*.

4. Construct virtual faces Beginning with the pseudo wire frame generated in Stage 3, all virtual faces are found in a manner analogous to that used in the Wire Frame algorithm. All uncertain edges are checked for containment in at least two noncoplanar virtual faces. Any edges not meeting this criterion are deleted and the virtual faces updated. Any impossible virtual faces (*e.g.*, a certain edge piercing the interior of a virtual face) are deleted. The consequences of deletions are propagated until a stable condition is reached.

5. Introduce cutting edges Illegal intersections between two virtual faces such that both faces cannot exist in an object are handled by the introduction of a temporary *cutting edge* along their line of intersection. The cutting edge partitions the virtual face into smaller independent virtual faces and will be removed in the final stages. All the partitioning processes in the algorithm, be they of edges or faces, generate lists of siblings with common parent edge or face, and also lists of correlations between edges or faces which cannot co-exist in an object; these data structures are used in the final stages of the algorithm.

6. Construct virtual blocks Virtual faces are pieced together to form *virtual blocks* in exactly the same manner as in the Wire Frame algorithm.

7. Make decisions A depth first decision process is used to assign solid or hole state to the virtual blocks and to find all objects with the given projections. The process ensures that all cutting edges disappear in solution objects (*i.e.*, that they are either totally surrounded by space or by material or they separate coplanar surfaces). Efficiency in the search process is obtained by careful pruning of the decision tree, for example, by recognizing that decisions involving partitioned edges and virtual faces may be propagated to the whole original edge or virtual face.

● *Detailed description of the Basic Projections algorithm*
To make the description of the algorithm more comprehensible, the example based on Fig. 1 is used to illustrate the various stages, *i.e.*, the problem is to recover the object in Fig. 1 from its three views. For brevity, this problem is referred to as the Two Wedges problem.

1. Check input data The input data to the basic algorithm are assumed to be a set of two dimensional views of the whole wire frame of a polyhedral object. The views may be at arbitrary projection directions, but must meet a minimum requirement of at least two distinct projections. Each view is an ordered pair of vertices and edges (Definition 4) expressed relative to a local two dimensional coordinate frame and accompanied by a transformation matrix between the coordinate frame of the three dimensional object and the two dimensional view.

In this and later stages, tests are performed on the data input to a stage of the algorithm, for detection of inconsistencies in the data, for reduction of the data to canonical form for the stage, and to obtain information to be used in later stages. The exact choice of which tests to include depends on the characteristics of the input data and performance trade-offs between the cost of performing a test first, the usefulness of information generated for later stages, and the desirability of reporting errors before incurring the cost of executing the algorithm. These issues are not considered further here. However, it will be seen that the combinatorial problems of the projections algorithm may be very severe, and there is therefore a need to minimize the quantity of surplus information generated in the early stages of the algorithm.

2. Construct pseudo vertex skeleton As stated earlier, in this stage perpendiculars are erected at each vertex of each view. Then, only those vertices lying on at least two noncolinear perpendiculars and which are consistent with all other projections, *i.e.*, their images are either vertices or interior points of edges, are selected. As noted after Definition 4, all Class I vertices and possibly some Class II vertices are recovered. In order for the projections to be consistent, it is necessary that every P-vertex have at least one element of CV($\mathcal{O}$) in its inverse image. This check may be performed as part of this stage. In addition, if some P-vertex has a unique element of CV($\mathcal{O}$) in its inverse image, then that element of CV($\mathcal{O}$) must actually be an element of V($\mathcal{O}$). Such a vertex is assigned type certain, and all other vertices are assigned type uncertain.

Each intersection is tested to see if it coincides with a previously found vertex and, if not, is introduced as a new vertex. Each vertex found is accompanied by a list of cross references to the view-vertex pairs from which it has been generated. Conversely, for each view vertex, a list is formed of the wire frame vertices into which it projects.

M. A. WESLEY AND G. MARKOWSK

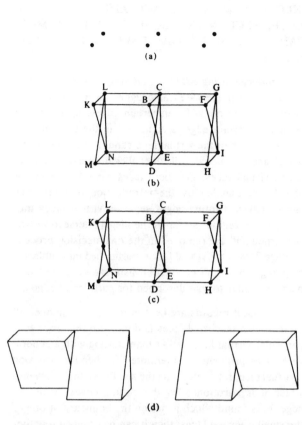

Figure 3 (a) The vertex pseudo skeleton of the Two Wedges problem. Edge recovery in the Two Wedges problem: (b) the pseudo skeleton and (c) the pseudo wire frame. (d) The two solutions to the Two Wedges problem.

The pseudo vertex skeleton of the Two Wedges problem consists of 12 points: the 8 points corresponding to the vertices of a cuboid and 4 points corresponding to the mid-points of the 4 horizontal edges [see Fig. 3(a)].

3. Construct pseudo wire frame In this stage all pseudo skeletal edges are constructed as a prelude to constructing the pseudo wire frame. To do this, simply join two vertices in the pseudo vertex skeleton by an edge iff in every projection the images of these two vertices coincide or are joined by an edge or colinear set of edges and no other vertex of the pseudo vertex skeleton would be an interior point of the edge.

In general, these pseudo skeletal edges may intersect in mutually interior points. To obtain the pseudo wire frame from this skeleton it is only necessary to duplicate the techniques of Theorem 6, *i.e.*, to introduce edges in the obvious way so that all edges have vertices as endpoints, that two edges intersect only in a vertex, and that no vertex be an interior point of an edge.

Note that the proof of Theorem 6 shows that $V(\mathcal{O}) \subseteq CV(\mathcal{O})$ and that every edge of $\mathcal{O}$ can be written as the union of candidate edges.

Many of the checks of Stage 2 are used on the vertices produced in this stage. With modification these checks are used on candidate edges. Thus, it should be verified that every P-edge has some element of CE($\mathcal{O}$) in its inverse image. In particular, if some P-edge has a unique inverse image, then that element of CE($\mathcal{O}$) must be real, *i.e.*, it must actually be an element of E($\mathcal{O}$) and, like the rule for vertices above, is classified as type certain. At the end of this stage pruning operations are performed. All vertices with edge connectivity of degree ≤ 1 are removed, together with any incident edges. If the vertex has degree 2, the incident edges are checked for colinearity. If they are colinear, the vertex is removed and the two edges are merged into a single edge. If they are not colinear, they are removed together with the vertex. If a vertex of degree ≥ 3 has only coplanar edges, then any edges not having a colinear extension, and possibly also the vertex, are removed. Whenever edges are removed, the effects of the change are propagated until a stable configuration is achieved. In a similar manner to the vertices, cross reference lists are maintained from pseudo wire frame edges to view-edge pairs, and conversely, for each view edge, a cross reference list to the pseudo wire frame edges is formed.

Figures 3(b) and (c) show the results obtained during this stage in the case of the Two Wedges problem. Note that vertex A of the original figure appears in the pseudo wire frame exhibited in Fig. 3(c) but does not appear in the skeleton [Fig. 3(b)]. Note also that by Theorem 7 vertices J and O are clearly spurious since all solid material lies to one side of the planes KLN and FGI. However, these conditions cannot be derived until a later stage of the algorithm. □

The stages described above are fairly straightforward. Before describing the later stages of the Projections algorithm it will be helpful to understand exactly what has been produced so far. The pseudo wire frame (CV$\mathcal{O}$, CE($\mathcal{O}$)) looks like a wire frame. Indeed, in many cases (CV($\mathcal{O}$), CE($\mathcal{O}$)) is exactly the wire frame of $\mathcal{O}$ and feeding (CV($\mathcal{O}$), CE($\mathcal{O}$)) to the Wire Frame algorithm will yield the correct solutions directly. The important thing is to understand the way in which simply applying the Wire Frame algorithm to (CV($\mathcal{O}$), CE($\mathcal{O}$)) can fail to find all solutions. The chief problem is that the original Wire Frame algorithm treats vertices and edges as real entities, whereas the pseudo wire frame contains uncertain edges and vertices, any of which may or may not exist in a solution. Any solid object having a *subset* of (CV($\mathcal{O}$),

CE($\mathcal{O}$)) as its wire frame and producing the correct projections is a solution of the projections problem. Thus, the Wire Frame algorithm approach may fail to find all solutions of the projections problem (it may in fact fail to find any). The assumption of reality of edges and vertices is crucial to two places in the Wire Frame algorithm:

• Dealing with illegal intersections between virtual faces, and
• Making decisions.

Whenever an edge pierces a virtual face (a Type I intersection) in a legitimate wire frame problem, it is safe to drop the virtual face since it is known that the edge is "real" and that "real" edges cannot pierce faces which separate solid material from space (these are the only important faces). In the present situation, it might very well be that the edge is not real and should itself be dropped instead. Of course, if it is known that a particular edge is real (*i.e.*, certain), the algorithm can proceed as before.

In the Wire Frame algorithm the decision process was concerned with finding those combinations of virtual blocks which made every edge (except the cutting edges) an edge of a real object. In the case of the Projections algorithm it is necessary only to find combinations of virtual blocks with projections agreeing with the given projections. In general, this means that not every uncertain element of (CV($\mathcal{O}$), CE($\mathcal{O}$)) is actually a member of (V($\mathcal{O}$), E($\mathcal{O}$)). Thus, the decision procedure must be modified to check that every edge in each projection comes from a candidate edge which becomes a real edge in the corresponding solution.

Cutting edges were introduced in [1] to handle illegal intersections between virtual faces when no internal point of an edge from one face was contained in the interior of another face, but there were points common to the interior of both faces (a Type II intersection). This situation was interpreted as one where the two faces could not co-exist in the solution, and temporary edges—cutting edges—were introduced along the line of intersection of the two faces. The cutting edges partitioned the faces into nonintersecting sub-faces, which could be used to build more, smaller, virtual blocks. The decision process ensured that cutting edges did not remain in the final solutions. Although introduced originally for Type II intersections, cutting edges are applicable also to Type I intersections, and are particularly relevant to the case of uncertain edges.

4. Construct virtual faces This stage is essentially identical with Stage 4 of the Wire Frame algorithm. As noted earlier, each candidate edge is checked to see whether it lies in at least two noncoplanar virtual faces. Thus, in the Two Wedges problem, 19 virtual faces [KLO, LON, MON, ABC, ACE, ADE, FGJ, GIJ, HIJ, KLCB, NLCE, MNED, BCGF, ECGI, DEIH, MOLCAD, KONEAB, DACGJH, BAEIJF in Fig. 3(c)] are discovered.

5. Introduce cutting edges This stage is very similar to its equivalent in the wire frame algorithm but has a minor modification to allow for uncertain edges. If an interior point of a certain edge is contained in the interior of a virtual face, then the virtual face cannot be a face of the object and is deleted. All other illegal intersections between virtual faces, *i.e.*, both faces cannot exist in the object, are handled by the introduction of temporary cutting edges. Cutting edges separate virtual faces into independent regions so far as the illegal intersection was concerned and are removed in the final decision process in Stage 7. When a virtual face is partitioned into subfaces, mapping tables and correlation lists are generated in a manner similar to that described for partitioned edges.

Note that if records are kept in the correct manner all reprocessing of virtual faces is done with reference to a particular virtual face, rather than starting with a general wire frame problem. Furthermore, if, when reprocessing a virtual face, f, to determine the smaller virtual faces into which it is partitioned by the cutting edges, a cutting edge, e, is found which is not on the boundary of one of the smaller virtual faces, then it can be dropped together with any virtual face, g, whose intersection with f is e. Face g can be dropped since it is impossible for g to be a member of a virtual block. As usual, dropping a virtual face will in general have other repercussions which are exploited until a stable situation results. For brevity, virtual faces found in Stage 4 will be called *original virtual faces*. Those arising because of cutting edges will be called *new virtual faces*.

In the Two Wedges problem, two cutting edges [OA and AJ in Fig. 3(c)] are introduced. These two edges partition four virtual faces (CADHJG, BAEIJF, MOLCAD, KONEAB) into eight virtual faces (CAJG, ADHJ, BAJF, AEIJ, KOAB, ONEA, MOAD, OLCA).

6. Construct virtual blocks This stage is identical with the corresponding stage in the Wire Frame algorithm. In the Two Wedges problem, six finite virtual blocks are uncovered:

B_1:(MONEAD),
B_2:(NOLCAE),
B_3:(LOKBAC),
B_4:(DAEIJH),
B_5:(EACGJI),
B_6:(BACGJF),

where the description of virtual blocks is in terms of the labeling of Fig. 3(c). The seventh virtual block, B_0, is the unique infinite empty block.

7. Make decisions The set of virtual blocks is fed to a decision procedure, which is an extension of the decision procedure used in the Wire Frame algorithm. The differences between the two procedures revolve around the fact that the Projections algorithm is aware that not every vertex and edge must be real.

The chief difference consists of the fact that whenever the nature of a new virtual face is determined (*i.e.*, whether or not it separates solid material and space), the same determination can be made for all other new virtual faces which are subdivisions of the same original virtual face. Furthermore, as soon as it is determined (or assumed) that an original virtual face, f, does separate solid material and space, all original virtual faces sharing a cutting edge with f are forced to be spurious. This means that any pair of virtual blocks using any part of any virtual face "cutting" f as a common boundary must both be assigned the same state. Similarly, if a virtual face is known to be spurious, all virtual blocks using any part of it as a boundary must have the same state.

These facts speed up the decision procedure considerably and offset the greater number of virtual blocks that have been introduced. Similar arguments apply to entire edges which have been partitioned in Stage 3. In the final solution, no cutting edge can be a real edge. Of course, all decisions respect the fact that the final outcome must be consistent with the original projections.

In this stage virtual blocks are fitted together to generate all objects with the given projections. Basically, each virtual block may have solid or hole state and, when a state assignment has been made to each virtual block, an object is obtained. However, not all assignments of solid and hole yield the desired projections. An assignment of solid or hole to the virtual blocks yields an object with the correct wire frame iff

1. *Every* certain edge element $e \in E(\mathbb{O})$ belongs to two noncoplanar virtual faces f_1 and f_2 each of which belongs to one virtual block assigned solid state and one assigned hole state;
2. *No* cutting edge belongs to two noncoplanar virtual faces f_1 and f_2 each of which belongs to one virtual block assigned solid state and one assigned hole state.
3. *Every* uncertain edge element $e \in E(\mathbb{O})$ may be assigned either to state certain and obeys the rule for certain edges (1) above or to state not-visible and obeys the rule for cutting edges (2) above, in a manner consistent with the input projections.

The decision process is performed by assigning states in a virtual block state vector, whose elements are ordered *a priori*. The first element of the state vector is the unique infinite virtual block, which is assigned the empty state. For each edge, a list is formed of the faces containing the edge and the blocks they bound; this list is sorted around the edge and allows the angular sequence of block state transitions to be discovered.

The decision process proceeds as a depth first search in the virtual block decision space tree. At any node in the tree, the current state vector is checked for consistency and consequential states are assigned. Thus, although the state vector may have dimension of many hundreds, the consistency check may be expected to prune large sections of the tree, while the propagation of consequential states may be expected to reduce substantially the number of decisions to be made.

The checks for consistency are essentially those listed above. The consequential state assignments are performed to meet the following criteria:

- A certain edge with all except one containing block assigned the same state forces the remaining block to be assigned the opposite state.
- An uncertain edge totally surrounded by either all material or by all space becomes nonvisible; an uncertain edge contained in blocks producing exactly two coplanar state transitions around the edge becomes nonvisible; an uncertain edge contained by blocks of both hole and solid states and with at least two noncoplanar state transitions around the edge becomes certain.
- An uncertain edge that is the only edge remaining to create a view edge becomes certain.
- A cutting edge whose surrounding blocks have the same state, *i.e.*, both solid or both hole, spanning regions 180 degrees apart, allows the same state to be assigned to *all* blocks around the edge.
- A cutting edge whose surrounding blocks have the same state <180 degrees apart around the edge allows any intermediate blocks to be assigned to the same state.
- A new virtual face which is a real face, *i.e.*, it separates blocks of different states, and which is a subdivision of an original virtual face formed by cutting edges allows the same solid-hole relationship to be given to all blocks containing sibling faces from the original virtual face. Similar rules apply when the face is not real.
- An uncertain edge which becomes a certain edge and which is a subdivision of an original wire frame edge allows its sibling edges to be upgraded to certain state.

In some cases, particularly those where there are high degrees of symmetry and a limited number of views, giving rise to many highly correlated uncertain edges, there may be a very large number of objects producing the given projections. Thus, although the depth first search and also heuristic search approaches to this problem [8] allow a solution to be found efficiently, an exhaustive search must ultimately be used, and efficient pruning of the decision tree is very important. It is evident that, in the case of problems with multiple solutions, the provision of rather small amounts of extra information by the user, for example, labeling of some uncertain edges, and assigning states to points in 3-space, can resolve the ambiguities completely. Thus, in a practical system, the user may be requested to assist with extra information when requested. The basis for the system requesting extra information in the early stages of the algorithm is the preponderance of uncertain edges, discovered in Stage 3, and self intersection of uncertain edges, dicovered in Stages 4 and 5.

At this point it can be appreciated that the use of cutting edges has allowed construction of a set of virtual blocks having the property that every solution of the projection problem can be built out of the virtual blocks in this set.

Stage 7 feeds into an output module which puts the output together in forms which can be understood by the user of the system. In our implementation of the algorithm, the output is in the form of a polyhedron for the Geometric Design Processor system [2].

In the case of the Two Wedges problem, this stage produces the two solutions shown in Fig. 3(d). The decision procedure works as follows in this case. Suppose that the search in this case deals with the virtual blocks $B_0, \cdots, B_6$ in that order. B_0 is known to be empty. Thus, the first branch of the decision tree corresponds to determining the state of B_1.

If B_1 is assumed to be solid, MOAD is seen to separate solid from space. This means that the entire virtual face MOLCAD must separate solid from space. In particular, B_2 must be solid and B_3 empty. Thus, the next step is to decide whether B_4 is solid or empty. Assuming that B_4 is solid forces B_5 to be solid and B_6 to be empty. However, the object resulting from making B_1, B_2, B_4, B_5 solid and B_0, B_3, B_6 empty clearly fails to have the right projections. Thus, the decision procedure backs up to the B_4 decisions and assigns hole to B_4. This means that the new virtual face DAJH is spurious and that the original virtual face DACGJH is spurious. Thus, B_5 and B_6 must have the same state. If they are both assumed to be empty, the

object that results is just a simple wedge, which clearly has the wrong projections. Thus, B_5 and B_6 must both be assumed to be solid. The object that results is a left-right transform of the original object in Fig. 3 and clearly has the correct projections.

On the other hand, if B_1 is assigned hole, B_2 and B_3 must both be assigned the same state. Clearly, if B_2 and B_3 are also empty, it is impossible to obtain the correct front and top views. Thus, B_2 and B_3 must be solid in this case. Furthermore, assuming B_4 to be solid forces B_5 to be solid and B_6 to be empty. This yields the original object. Assuming B_4 to be empty forces B_5 and B_6 to have the same state. The objects that result are both wedges of differing width and are clearly not solutions.

It is clear that keeping track of the number of objects remaining in the inverse image of a projected artifact can be helpful in the decision procedure, *i.e.*, if assigning a particular state to a given virtual block removes the last vertex or edge in the back projection of some vertex or edge, then that assignment can be rejected and its consequences need not be explored further. □

The following section describes ways in which additional information can be extracted from various drawing conventions. The final section contains examples which should clarify the discussion in this and the next section.

4. Additional information from drawing conventions

Designers and draftsmen use a number of conventions and aids to clarify and help reduce ambiguity in engineering drawings. Extensions to the Basic Projections algorithm are presented in this section. These extensions cover two concepts: the generalization of the set of types of views to include overall, detail, and cross sectional, and the use of depth and detail information expressed by line types. The presentation is made within the context of the various stages of the algorithm presented previously.

● *Stages of the algorithm reconsidered*

1. Check input data

In extending the basic algorithm to handle several different types of view (*i.e.*, overall, detail, and cross sectional), the central problem is to be able to relate information from the different types of views. This is achieved here by classification of the edges of the object into two types: gross and detail. The gross edges describe the main structure of the object; the detail edges add more information in regions where there is fine structure in the object.

The edges of the views are labeled with edge types according to an agreed drawing standard. For example,

M. A. WESLEY AND G. MARKOWSK

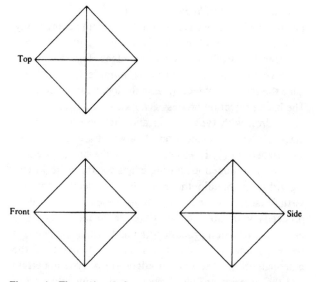

Figure 4 Three views of an object related to an octahedron.

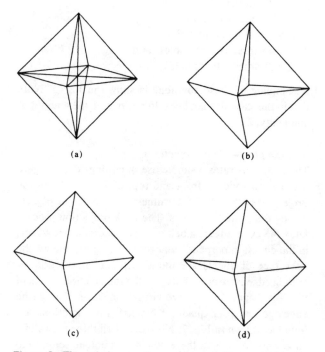

Figure 5 The solution to the problem of Figure 4: (a) the pseudo wire frame; all external edges are of type certain, internal edges are of type uncertain; (b, c, d) some of the 35 solid objects with the views of Fig. 4.

visible edges are generally drawn with line type *solid* and occulted edges with type *dashed*, which provides depth information. Another possibility, namely the omission of occulted edges, is not permitted; the Projections algorithm is based on geometric concepts and the premise that all edges are shown in all projections. An algorithm that attempts to fill in missing information would have to be based on heuristic ideas of what a most likely object would be as well as on the concepts of geometry.

An overall view is a projection of the major features of the whole object onto a plane outside the object. The set of overall views of the object contain projections of only the gross edges. Thus, every gross edge of the object is represented as an edge or a vertex in every overall view. Similarly, every object vertex that is the intersection of gross edges appears as a vertex or a point in an edge in every overall view.

A detail view is a projection of a portion of the object. The view has a defined polyhedral boundary and two extents along the projection direction. The boundary and extents define a right prismatic region in 3-space. The detail view is a projection of all edges and vertices of the object contained in the region. A detail view contains projections of both the gross and detail edges, without distinction, contained within its defined region.

A cross sectional view may be either overall or detail. The view is a planar cross section normal to the projection direction. In this case the view transformation contains the location of the section plane in the coordinate frame of the object. Note that edges are shown at the cross section plane that may not be present in the object (they lie in surfaces of the object), and may not be shown in other views of the object.

2. Construct pseudo vertex skeleton

This stage proceeds in a manner similar to before. However, somewhat greater care must be taken to treat the various projections consistently. Intersections between back projections of vertices from appropriate pairs of different views are considered candidate vertices. Appropriate means noncolinear projection directions and the same type of view, *i.e.*, both overall or both detail. In the case of pairs of detail views, the intersection point must lie within the intersection of their respective prismatic regions. In the case of a cross sectional view, the intersection point must lie in the halfspace defined by the section plane and projection direction. Also, a cross sectional view generates a set of vertices and edges in the plane of the view.

3. Construct pseudo wire frame

This stage is essentially unchanged from Stage 3 in Section 3. However, the following is a very useful observation: whenever a view shows two noncolinear solid (*i.e.*, visible) lines intersecting internally in a point, p, then there must be some vertex of O visible in the appropriate direction which projects onto p and which has only visible edges incident with it corresponding to the solid lines incident with p. In particular, if in moving along the perpendicular from p one first encounters candidate vertices which are clearly not vertices of O (see discussion of Stage 3 in Section 3), then these vertices and all incident edges may be discarded. To appreciate the power of this observation see Example 4.

4. Construct virtual faces
This stage is essentially the same as Stage 4 in Section 3. However, it is possible at this point to use line type depth information to edit out some type II vertices and uncertain candidate edges, as well as to extract additional information for use at a later time.

The cross reference lists from view edges to edges in the wire frame are concatenated with the list of original (*i.e.*, before any partitioning) virtual faces and sorted by distance along the projection direction from the mid-point of the view edge. For any edge that is visible, *i.e.*, not dashed, the nearest pseudo wire frame edge is identified. Any interposing virtual faces cannot exist and are deleted. For an edge to be dashed, there must be at least one occulting virtual face in the projection direction. If there is only one such face, then it must be a real face separating solid material from space, and since the projection is from outside, the directedness of the face is known. This information is fed forward to the decision process as initial certain states of blocks and faces. As before, the consequences must be fully propagated.

5 and 6. Introduce cutting edges and form virtual blocks
These stages are the same as in Section 3.

7. Make decisions
This stage again is very similar to the corresponding stages described in Section 3. Clearly, however, the decision procedure must accommodate the drawing conventions in the correct manner. It is fairly apparent how this is to be done. Thus, for example, in the case that occulted edges are represented explicitly in views, each view edge must contain a visible edge in the view projection direction, and each nonvisible view edge must be occulted by an interposed face in the view projection direction. □

The examples in the next section illustrate the points made above. As shall be seen, pathological features do not appear to be common in objects of practical interest.

5. Examples
To clarify the discussion in Sections 3 and 4, several examples are presented in this section. The examples are chosen to illustrate particular features of the algorithm and some of the performance trade-offs involved in providing extra information.

• Example 1—octahedron projections
The octahedron illustrates a simple problem having many solutions, but for which the Projections algorithm does not need to introduce any cutting edges. Figure 4 shows three views of an octahedron. It is interesting to determine the set of all objects having the identical projections. The back projection process generates the 12 edges of the octahedron with type certain and the three intersecting diagonals with type uncertain. In a wire frame example of an octahedron [1] it was shown that the diagonal edges must be introduced as cutting edges for the Wire Frame algorithm to handle the mutually intersecting interior virtual faces. In the Projections case, the algorithm proceeds with no need to generate further edges and enters the decision process with eight virtual blocks, one for each octant around the intersection point of the diagonals. Since the interior edges are of type uncertain and the exterior are all of type certain, any selection of octants such that no two hole octants share a face is a solution. The decision process finds 35 solutions:

  1 with all octants solid,
  8 with one octant a hole,
 16 with two octants holes,
  8 with three octants holes, and
  2 with four octants holes.

A sampling of these solutions is shown in Fig. 5. Note that in this case dashed lines do not reduce the amount of ambiguity. □

• Example 2—cube projections
The cube illustrates a simple use of cutting edges. Figure 6 shows two views, front and top, of a cube. Again the Projections algorithm determines the number of objects having the same two views. The back projection process finds the cube edges, albeit as type uncertain. However, in the direction perpendicular to the two given views, the cube face diagonals are found without intersection. A cutting edge is inserted between the intersection points of the face diagonals, and five virtual blocks are found (the envelope and four quadrant blocks). Five solutions are found as shown in Fig. 7. Note that if all three views of a cube were furnished, there would be a unique solution to this projections problem. □

• Example 3—Two Y's problem
Figure 8 shows a well known mechanical drawing puzzle: find all objects having the top and front views shown. Because of the way edges line up in the two views, the back projection process finds the pseudo skeleton with 29 edges and 12 vertices shown in Fig 9. Intersections of the edges yield three additional vertices where the diagonals intersect, and intersections of virtual faces yield eight cutting edges. The final pseudo wire frame is shown in

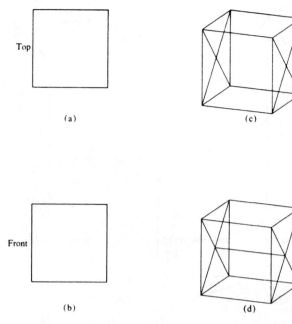

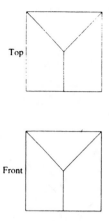

Figure 8 The Two Y's, a well known mechanical drawing puzzle: front and top views of an object.

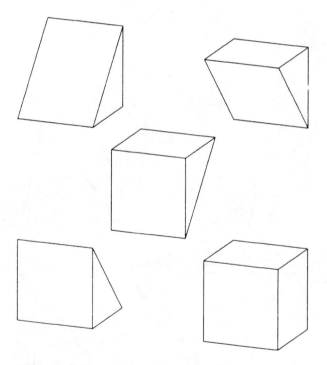

Figure 6 (a, b) Two views of an object related to a cube; (c) the pseudo wire frame; (d) the pseudo wire frame with a cutting edge inserted.

Figure 7 Objects with the views shown in Fig. 6 (a, b).

Fig. 10. The 16 internal virtual blocks found in Stage 7 are shown in Fig. 11. Under the assumptions of Section 3 there are 55 solutions to this problem. Under the assump-

tions of Section 4 (*i.e.*, all lines in the views are assumed to be solid, that is, visible) there are seven solutions. These are shown in Fig. 12.

The Two Y's problem is very sensitive to numerical considerations. If the branch point of one of the Y's is moved from the center of its view, there are no solutions to the corresponding projections problem. □

● *Example 4—Three X's problem*

The Three X's problem illustrates vividly the savings that can result from the use of depth information. Figure 13 shows an apparently minor modification to the problem of Fig. 4; the object is now clearly contained within a cube. However, further investigation shows that the solution process becomes surprisingly complex. The back projection process produces nine vertices—the cube vertices (uncertain) and its midpoint (certain) and thirty-two edges, all uncertain—the twelve cube edges, twelve face diagonal edges (initially with type II intersections, but later changed to mutually exclusive intersections), and eight cube diagonals from the midpoint. Note that, in contrast to the situation with Fig. 4, none of the edges found are of type certain and that ambiguities can be expected to stem from this lack of definite information. The pseudo skeleton that is obtained by back projection is shown in Fig. 14.

In the case without depth information, *i.e.*, all edges drawn regardless of occultation, the partitioning process, of intersecting edges to generate sub-edges and virtual faces to generate sub-virtual faces with cutting edges, divides space into many small regions. A total of 96 internal virtual blocks are found and the decision process uncovers 38 065 solutions. Clearly, searching a 96-level decision tree for 38 065 solutions is a complex process.

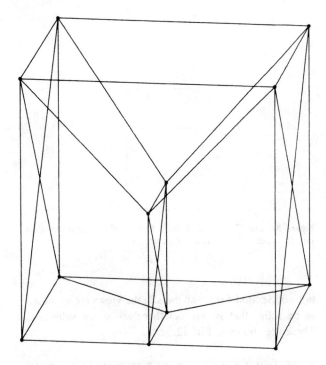

Figure 9 The pseudo skeleton of the Two Y's problem.

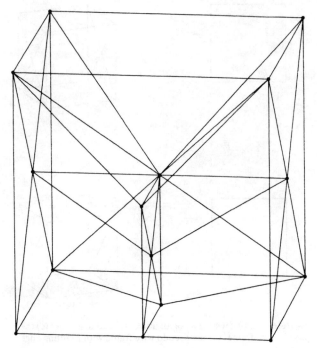

Figure 10 The pseudo wire frame with cutting edges added.

Figure 11 Sixteen virtual blocks found from the two views of Fig. 8.

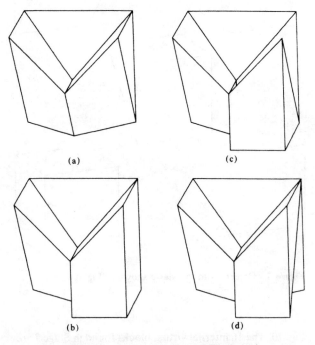

(a)

(c)

(b)

(d)

Figure 12 Objects with the two views of Fig. 8: (a) is symmetric; (b, c, d) are asymmetric and each is typical of a pair of objects.

M. A. WESLEY AND G. MARKOWSK

Top

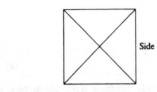

Front

Side

Figure 13 The Three X's problem: three views of an object whose extent is bounded by a cube.

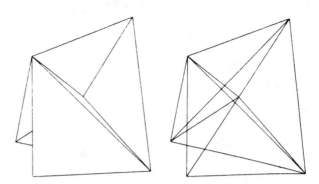

Figure 15 One of 38,065 objects found with the views of Fig. 13 and assuming that all edges are shown in each projection. The object is based on three tetrahedra.

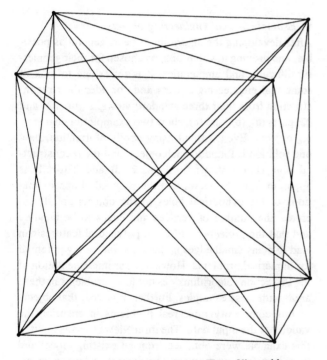

Figure 14 The pseudo skeleton for the Three X's problem.

The solution is made practicable by making heavy use of the mappings and correlations between original faces and edges and their partitioned forms. One solution, picked at random, is shown in Fig. 15. The object is hard to

understand, even with a model in one's hand. It is a set of three tetrahedra, a pair with a common face and a third with edge contact only, *i.e.*, it is decomposable into two disjoint objects. The solutions found could be filtered to reject unstable objects of this form, but this test has not been executed.

The analysis of the case with depth information shows the power of Theorem 7 when used in Stage 3. Each of the three views shows solid lines intersecting in the center point. Following a perpendicular from any of the center points of any view leads first to a point in the center of a face of the cube containing the pseudo wire frame. This vertex cannot be a Class I vertex since all candidate edges incident with it are coplanar. It also cannot be a Class II vertex since all solid material lies to one side of the plane containing the face in question. Thus, the center points and all diagonal edges may be discarded from the front, top, and appropriate side faces of the cube. Furthermore, in Stage 4 corresponding faces of the cube are also discarded since they would obscure a vertex and lines in the interior. With these faces discarded, three of the leading edges of the cube must be discarded also since they no longer contain at least two noncoplanar virtual faces.

After these reductions, the algorithm goes on to find the ten solutions shown in Fig. 16. The solutions may be considered as being based on the union of three pyramids, as shown in Fig. 16(a). In all solutions, the view of the objects in the projection directions are the four triangular faces of the union of the three pyramids. The distinguishing features between the solutions are cavities in the "rear"; the viewpoint for the solutions in Figs. 16(b)–(g) is chosen to illustrate these cavities. The solutions are grouped as follows:

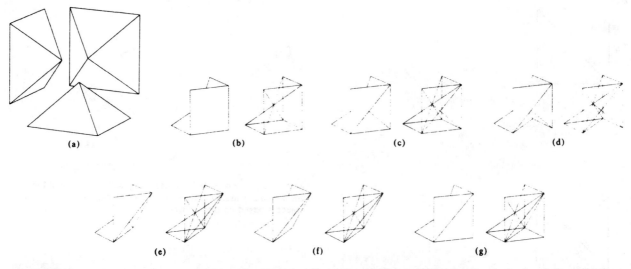

Figure 16 All ten solutions to the Three X's problem in dashed line mode: (a) three pyramids forming the basic solutions; (b) three pyramid solution; (c) one pyramid bisected; (d) two pyramids bisected; (e) all three pyramids bisected; (f) solution (b) cut by plane containing the diagonals of the square faces; (g) solution (b) with an internal tetrahedral cavity.

- Figure 16(b) shows all three pyramids complete,
- Figure16(c) shows one pyramid bisected and is one of a set of three solutions,
- Figure 16(d) shows two pyramids bisected and is one of a set of three solutions,
- Figure 16(e) shows all three pyramids bisected,
- Figure 16(f) shows the object (b) above cut by the plane containing the diagonals of the three square faces,
- Figure 16(g) shows the object (b) with an internal tetrahedral cavity just visible as diagonal edges of the square faces.

- *Example 5—Two Ramps problem*

The Two Ramps problem illustrates the effectiveness of the pruning operations of Stage 3. Figure 17 shows this well known two view puzzle problem reputed to have twelve solutions. The back projection process produces an array of three by four, *i.e.*, twelve, vertices on the left-hand face and an array of two by four for the right-hand face. Twelve edges are found linking the left and right sides. However, the number of possible edges in the end faces, *i.e.*, in the direction normal to the two given views, is large; see Fig. 18. Fortunately many of those in the left-hand face are rejected by the edge and virtual face connectivity test at the end of Stage 3 (Fig. 19). Some 108 internal virtual blocks are found and 107 distinct solutions. Only 12 of the solutions, however, pass the stable object criterion. Some of the solutions are shown in Fig. 20. ☐

- *Example 6—real engineering objects*

After developing the algorithm to be as general as possible, and proving it with problems chosen for their geometric difficulty and ambiguities, it is refreshing to look at some real engineering objects and consider their reconstruction from their three standard views. Figures 21 and 22, parts (a), (b), and (c), show two examples of engineering objects. Even without using depth information, only one solution is found to each object, and the reconstructed objects are shown in Figs. 21(d) and 22(d). It is apparent from the views that the polyhedral approximations of the cylindrical holes in the objects greatly increase the number of vertices and edges to be handled and that the projections of these polyhedral features can lead to many small edges in the view, indicating potential for numerical problems. However, our implementation of the Projections algorithm does not have problems in these areas with these examples. Further, it is clear that objects of this complexity raise real problems in ensuring the validity of the input data. The three views used as input in this example were obtained from an existing model and were therefore guaranteed to be correct. A human generating these views directly would have some difficulty ensuring their correctness and self consistency. The Projections algorithm in its present form does not attempt to handle incorrect (or incomplete) data. ☐

6. Summary

The Projections algorithm presented in this paper finds all polyhedral objects *O* with a given set of projections. It has

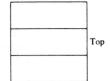

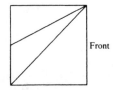

Figure 17 The Two Ramps problem: two views of an object.

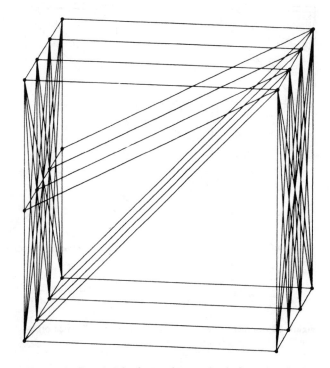

Figure 19 Pseudo wire frame after pruning in Stage 3; note the reduction of edges in the left-hand face.

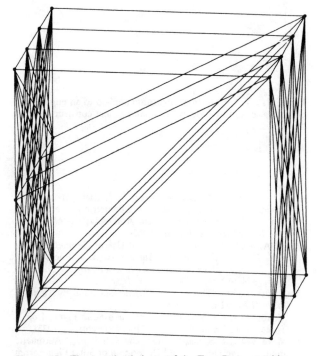

Figure 18 The pseudo skeleton of the Two Ramps problem.

been shown that, if the projections are labeled, the problem may be solved by the Wire Frame algorithm [1]; in the unlabeled case an extended form of the Wire Frame algorithm, the Projections algorithm, is needed.

It has been shown that an inverse projection process may be used to construct a superset of Class I vertices of $\mathcal{O}$ (vertices contained in at least three noncoplanar edges) together with a superset of unions of edges of $\mathcal{O}$. These edges and vertices constitute the skeleton of $\mathcal{O}$.

It has also been shown that a superset of the Class II vertices of $\mathcal{O}$ (vertices contained only in a set of coplanar edges) may be found as intersections of skeleton edges. These updated vertices and edges constitute a pseudo wire frame.

A pseudo wire frame differs from a wire frame in that it contains supersets of the edges and vertices of the wire frame. Some of these elements have been identified uniquely and have type certain; the rest are of type uncertain. Any object whose wire frame is composed of the certain elements of the pseudo wire frame and any subset of the uncertain elements and produces the correct projections is a solution.

The pseudo wire frame is processed to find candidate faces (virtual faces). Virtual faces are connected to enclose volume regions (virtual blocks). A depth first decision process with heavy pruning is used to find all state assignments of hole or solid to virtual blocks that produce solid objects with the correct projections.

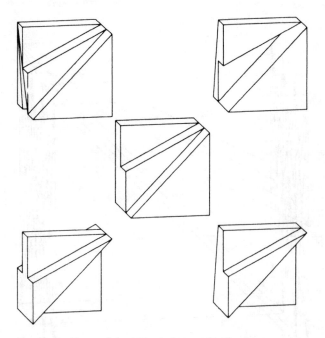

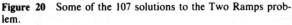

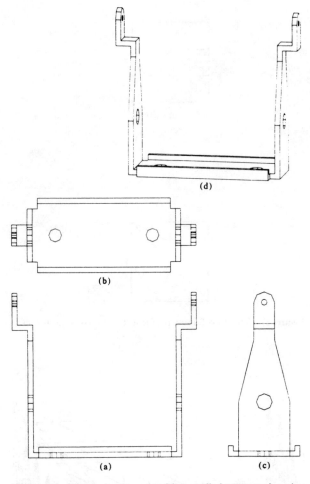

Figure 20 Some of the 107 solutions to the Two Ramps problem.

The Basic Projections algorithm accepts projections of the wire frame of Ô; extensions handle a more general set of projection types (detail, overall, and cross sectional) and projection conventions such as depth information obtained from occulted edges in a projection being shown as dashed.

The Projections algorithm has been implemented and its operation has been illustrated by a set of examples. These examples have shown that problems of a mechanical drawing puzzle nature, which typically have high degrees of symmetry leading to large numbers of uncertain elements in the pseudo wire frame, can have very large numbers of solutions. On the other hand, engineering objects, with projections sufficiently complex to require careful thought from a human, have been run and have produced unique solutions.

Figure 21 The Projections algorithm applied to an engineering object: (a, b, c) three views; (d) unique object constructed from the views.

Acknowledgments
Our thanks are due to D. D. Grossman for encouraging us to tackle the projection reconstruction problem. A. F. Nightingale suggested the Two Ramps problem, and V. J. Milenkovic implemented the stable object test.

References
1. George Markowsky and Michael A. Wesley, "Fleshing Out Wire Frames," *IBM J. Res. Develop.* **24**, 582–597 (September 1980).
2. M. A. Wesley, T. Lozano-Pérez, L. I. Lieberman, M. A. Lavin, and D. D. Grossman, "A Geometric Modeling System for Automated Mechanical Assembly," *IBM J. Res. Develop.* **24**, 64–74 (January 1980).
3. M. A. Wesley, "Construction and Use of Geometric Models," Chapter 2, *Computer Aided Design,* J. Encarnacao, Ed., *Lecture Notes in Computer Science No. 89,* Springer-Verlag, New York, 1980.
4. I. Sutherland, "Three Dimensional Data Input by Tablet," *Proc. IEEE* **62** (April 1974).
5. M. Idesawa, "A System to Generate a Solid Figure from a Three View," *Bull. JSME* **16**, 216–225 (February 1973).
6. M. Idesawa, T. Soma, E. Goto, and S. Shibata, "Automatic Input of Line Drawing and Generation of Solid Figure from Three-View Data," *Proceedings of the International Joint Computer Symposium 1975,* pp. 304–311.
7. G. Lafue, "Recognition of Three-Dimensional Objects from Orthographic Views," *Proceedings 3rd Annual Conference on Computer Graphics, Interactive Techniques, and Image Processing,* ACM/SIGGRAPH, July 1976, pp. 103–108.
8. K. Preiss, "Constructing the 3-D Representation of a Plane-Faced Object from a Digitized Engineering Drawing," *Proceedings of International Artificial Intelligence Conference,* Brighton, England, April 1980.

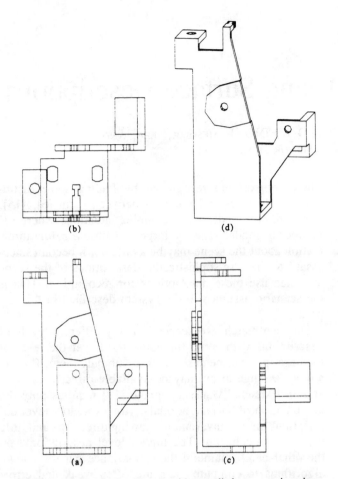

Figure 22 The Projections algorithm applied to an engineering object: (a, b, c) three views; (d) unique object constructed from the views.

9. T. C. Woo and J. M. Hammer, "Reconstruction of Three-Dimensional Designs from Orthographic Projections," *Proceedings of 9th CIRP Conference*, Cranfield Institute of Technology, Cranfield, England, 1977.
10. D. A. Huffman, "Impossible Objects as Nonsense Sentences," *Machine Intelligence* **6**, B. Meltzer and D. Michie, Eds., Edinburgh University Press, Edinburgh, Scotland, 1971, pp. 295–324.
11. M. B. Clowes, "On Seeing Things," *Artificial Intelligence* **2**, 79–116 (1971).
12. D. Waltz, "Understanding Line Drawings of Scenes with Shadows," *The Psychology of Computer Vision*, P. H. Winston, Ed., McGraw-Hill Book Co., Inc., New York, 1975, pp. 19–91.
13. T. Kanade, "A Theory of Origami World," *Report No. CMU-CS-78-144*, Department of Computer Science, Carnegie-Mellon University, Pittsburgh, September 1978.
14. K. Sugihara, "Mathematical Structures of Line Drawings of Polyhedra—Towards Man-Machine Communication by Means of Line Drawings," Third Laboratory of the Department of Information Science, Faculty of Engineering, Nagoya University, Nagoya, Japan, May 1981.
15. J. G. Hocking and G. S. Young, *Topology*, Addison-Wesley Publishing Co., Reading, MA, 1961.

Received April 27, 1981; revised June 2, 1981

The authors are located at the IBM Thomas J. Watson Research Center, Yorktown Heights, New York 10598.

Reprinted from *IEEE Transactions on Pattern Analysis and Machine Intelligence*, Volume 11, Number 11, November 1989, pages 1140-1157. Copyright © 1989 by The Institute of Electrical and Electronics Engineers, Inc. All rights reserved.

Recognizing 3-D Objects Using Surface Descriptions

TING-JUN FAN, MEMBER, IEEE, GERARD MEDIONI, MEMBER, IEEE, AND
RAMAKANT NEVATIA, SENIOR MEMBER, IEEE

Abstract—Object recognition is a key problem in machine vision. The issues to be addressed relate to the representation of the data and the method used to establish correspondences. We present a system which takes as input dense range data and automatically produces a symbolic description of the objects in the scene in terms of their visible surface patches. This segmented representation may be viewed as a graph whose nodes capture information about the individual surface patches and whose links represent the relationships between them, such as occlusion and connectivity. Based on these relations, a graph for a given scene is decomposed into subgraphs corresponding to different objects.

For the purpose of matching, a model is represented by a set of such descriptions from multiple viewing angles, typically 4–6. Models can therefore be acquired and represented automatically.

Matching between the objects in a scene and the models is performed by three modules: the *screener*, in which we find the most likely candidate views for each object, the *graph matcher*, which performs a detailed comparison between the potential matching graphs and computes the 3-D transformation between them, and the *analyzer*, which takes a critical look at the results and proposes to split and merge object graphs. We present results on a variety of scenes containing multiple complex objects with occlusion.

Index Terms—Object description, object recognition, range image analysis.

I. INTRODUCTION

RECOGNIZING objects in a scene is a primary goal of computer vision. The difficulty of this task depends on several factors such as: the number and complexity of objects in the scene, the number of objects in the model database, and the amount of *a priori* information about the scene. The appropriate techniques for object recognition depend on the difficulty of the task. In our case, we attempt to recognize rather complex objects in range images.

The simplest tasks assume that objects are unoccluded and occur in one or more of standard viewing positions. This essentially reduces to a 2-D recognition task. In another set of tasks, model-based techniques are used.

Manuscript received July 22, 1988; revised May 1, 1989. Recommended for acceptance by O. D. Faugeras. This work was supported by the Defense Advanced Research Projects Agency under Contract F33615-87-C-1436, monitored by the Air Force Wright Aeronautical Laboratories, DARPA Order No. 3119.

T.-J. Fan was with the Institute for Robotics and Intelligent Systems, School of Engineering, University of Southern California, Los Angeles, CA 90089. He is now with the IBM Thomas J. Watson Research Center, Yorktown Heights, NY 10598.

G. Medioni and R. Nevatia are with the Institute for Robotics and Intelligent Systems, School of Engineering, University of Southern California, Los Angeles, CA 90089.

IEEE Log Number 8929959.

There, objects are recognized by finding some distinguishing features and relations between them [6], [15]. However, to handle more complex situations where the number of models may be large and little *a priori* information about the scene may be available, it becomes necessary to first use sophisticated descriptions of the scene and then use these descriptions for recognition. This is the scenario assumed in the system described in this paper.

One can match two scenes at many different levels of descriptions with some tradeoffs: the lower the level of the descriptions, the easier it is to compute them. For example, a range array may be available directly as input and an Extended Gaussian Image [19] requires only the computation of surface normals. However, low level descriptions are not invariant to viewing directions and little tolerant to occlusion. The higher level descriptions, on the other hand, maintain their invariance but the known algorithms to compute them are often weak and error-prone. The appropriate level of description to be used for matching thus depends on the expected variations in the scenes and on the state-of-art in computing descriptions of the scene.

We have decided, in this paper, to use object descriptions in terms of their surfaces. The surface of an object is described by segmenting it into *surface patches* and the complete description consists of the description of each patch separately, and their interrelationships. Such a description can be viewed as an *attributed graph* with the patches as the *nodes* and relations between them as the *links*. The segmentation and description of the surface is based on measured curvature properties of the surface. We describe this process briefly in Section III, complete details are given in [12], [13].

We believe that our chosen representation has many advantages for scene and object matching. The description is *rich*, so that similar objects can be identified, *stable*, so that local changes do not radically alter it, and has *local support* so that partially visible objects can be identified. It also enables us to recreate, from its features, a shape reasonably close to the original one. The surface descriptions are much higher level than pointwise or edge descriptions, but not as high as volumetric descriptions. The surface descriptions are invariant for smaller changes in viewing angle than would be the case for volume descriptions. However, techniques for volume descriptions are not yet fully developed, whereas our previous work allows us to have high-quality surface descriptions.

In general, there are two steps involved in object recognition: *building models* and *recognizing scene objects*. We think that a good recognition system should provide the following.

- It should automatically build object models from range images.
- The descriptions used for models and for scenes of unknown objects should be compatible, or at least it should be easy to go from one to the other.
- The search should be efficient in finding correspondences between models and scene objects.

We have decided to use the same description format for both model and scene objects. As a result, the computation of the model descriptions can be achieved automatically, and there is no need to *translate* one description into another. We have tested our system on a number of scenes containing multiple complex objects with occlusion, and obtained very good recognition results. Some examples are given later in Section V.

In the next section, we review existing object recognition systems. Section III provides a brief summary of how we go from a dense range map to a set of surface patches, and how these patches are further organized into partial objects. Section IV presents the details of our recognition system, which uses the descriptions given above. Section V shows results of our recognition system on real range images. Finally, Section VI summarizes our contribution.

II. Survey of Recognition Systems

In this section, we review the most successful object recognition systems to date, and point out how they address the issues of model representation, choice of scene features, and matching methods. We also discuss their limitations.

A. Extended Gaussian Image (EGI)

Horn *et al.* use multiview EGI models to recognize 3-D objects [19]–[21]. Each model object is represented by its mapping on the Gaussian sphere, and each scene object is also represented by an EGI. The EGI's of scene objects and model views are compared. To constrain the search space, the two EGI's are first aligned along the directions of minimum EGI mass inertia, then a match measure is specified by comparing the similarity in their mass distributions. The model that maximizes this measure is chosen as the matched model. This method has the advantage that EGI can be computed directly; no complicated description stage is needed. The main disadvantage is that EGI is sensitive to occlusion and is unique for convex objects only. Furthermore, when multiple objects are present in a single scene, it would be necessary to segment the EGI into regions corresponding to separate objects, and it is not clear how to achieve this, except for simple-shaped objects.

B. 3DPO

Horaud and Bolles [18] and Bolles *et al.* [6] developed the 3DPO system for recognizing and locating 3-D parts in range data. The model consists of two parts: an augmented CAD model and a feature classification network. The CAD model describes edges, surfaces, vertices, and their relations. The feature-classification network classifies observable features by type and size. The system recognizes unknown objects by searching for features that match features for some model, for example, a cylindrical curve with a given radius. Then objects are hypothesized by determining whether a pair of observed segments are consistent with a given model's feature. This system has been shown to recognize objects in highly complex scenes, but with very few models. Since the models are represented in 3-D, it is very difficult to compute them automatically, therefore a CAD model is required that usually needs help from a user, it also needs a very complex network. Furthermore, this system relies heavily on detecting circular arcs and straight dihedral edges, so the shape of the objects it can recognize is restricted.

C. Grimson and Lozano-Pérez

Grimson and Lozano-Pérez [15], [16] discussed how local measurements of 3-D positions and surface normals can be used to identify and locate objects from among a set of unknown objects. Models consist of polyhedral objects represented by their planar faces. The information about these faces (such as their equations) and the relations between faces (such as distance) are also computed. Sparse range or tactile data of 3-D objects are used as scene features. The matching process contains two steps: in the first step, a set of feasible interpretations of the sensory data is constructed. Interpretations consist of pairings of each sensed point with some object surface of one of the models. Interpretations inconsistent with local constraints are discarded. In the second step, the feasible interpretations are verified by a transformation test. An interpretation is accepted if it can be used to solve for a transformation that would place each sensed point on an object surface. Only polyhedral objects or objects with a sufficient number of planar surfaces can be used in this system.

D. Ikeuchi

Ikeuchi [22] developed a method for object recognition in bin-picking tasks. Object models are generated under various viewer directions, apparent shapes are then classified into groups. Since this system is mainly designed for tasks for bin-picking, only *one* type of object, which is the same one as in the model, appears in the scene. The same surface features used in models are extracted and classified by the help of the model. In the recognition process, an *interpretation tree* is generated according to various model views. The orientation and location of the scene object are then decided by comparing their surface features and classified by the interpretation tree. Strictly speaking, this is not a recognition system, but a system which identifies a given 3-D object to be picked up.

409

E. Faugeras and Hebert

Faugeras and Hebert [14] developed a system to recognize and locate rigid objects in 3-D space. Model objects are represented in terms of linear features such as points, lines, and planes. The same features such as significant points, lines, and planes are used to describe scene objects. The system uses *rigidity constraints* to guide the matching process. At first, possible pairings between model and scene features are established, the transformation is estimated using quaternions. Then, further matches are predicted and verified by the rigidity constraints. This system has been shown to recognize fairly complex objects, but in scenes without occlusion from other objects. As the segmentation of objects in this system results in a large number of surface patches, and since the segmentation is not guided, we believe it is going to be highly sensitive to small changes in the surfaces.

F. Oshima and Shirai

Oshima and Shirai [25], [26] developed a model-based recognition system for objects with planar and curved surfaces. Each model is represented by a *relational-feature graph* whose nodes represent planar or smoothly curved surfaces, and links represent relations between adjacent surfaces. Matching is achieved by a combination of data-driven and model-driven searching processes. At first, *kernel nodes* which consist of large, planar surfaces with no occlusion are extracted. Next, an exhaustive search of all model graphs is performed and those containing regions which match the kernel nodes are selected as candidates. Finally, a *depth-first search* is applied to build the correspondences for remaining surfaces. Since only one view is used for each model object, if objects may be viewed from multiple directions, then a separate relational graph must be constructed for each view, and these models must be treated independently by the matching process. Furthermore, no occlusion is allowed for curved surfaces.

G. Nevatia and Binford

Nevatia and Binford [24] developed a system in mid-1970's that used generalized cones as the basic representation. This system uses range data as input. Model acquisition and scene description follow the same procedure, hence the models can be acquired automatically. This system also handles articulation of parts of objects. It is tested on objects of the complexity of a doll and a horse. This system also uses an *indexing* scheme based on gross features so that recognition does not require a search through all models in the database. The main limitation of this system would come from the ability to generate appropriate generalized cone descriptions for complex objects. This is a difficult problem as we discuss later.

A. ACRONYM

Brooks [9], [10] developed an image understanding system called ACRONYM which uses generalized cylinders for descriptions of model and scene objects. The model objects are represented by hierarchical graphs of primitive volumes described by generalized cylinders (GC). The user constructs a tree for each object, where nodes contain parts of objects represented by GC, and links represent their subpart relation. The user is also required to construct a model class hierarchy called a *restriction graph*. This graph contains sets of constraints for different classes of objects and is used later to guide the match between model and scene objects. *Ribbons* and *ellipses* are used to describe scene objects. The descriptions are finally represented by an *observation graph* whose nodes contain ribbon and ellipse descriptions and links specify spatial relations between nodes. Matching is performed at two levels: first, predicted ribbons must match image ribbons, and second, these local matches must be globally consistent. The main restriction of ACRONYM is that models and restriction graphs are constructed by the user, which is very expensive and restricts the possibility of automatic model building. Furthermore, since both models and scenes are represented by GC's that consist of ribbons and ellipses, the shape of model and scene objects is restricted; in addition, the viewing direction is assumed to be approximately known.

Other contributions in object recognition are due to Bolles and Cain [5], Bhanu [4], Ayache [1]. A more detailed survey can be found in [2], [7], [11].

III. Computing Symbolic Scene Descriptions

As discussed in Section I, we have chosen segmented surface descriptions for representing objects in this work. Discontinuities such as *jump boundaries*, *limbs*, and *creases* are chosen to segment surfaces as they are explicit features of the surfaces of 3-D objects. Our method consists of two stages. In the first stage, surfaces objects are segmented at discontinuities which can be detected by examining the *zero-crossings* and *extremal* values of surface curvature measures. Then these detected discontinuities are used to segment a complex surface into simpler meaningful components called *surface patches* or *patches*. These patches can then be approximated by simple surface models. Finally, these surface patches are grouped into meaningful 3-D objects, and *attributed graphs* are generated to describe these objects.

A. Extracting and Describing Surface Patches

Given a complex surface, we wish to decompose it into simple surface patches. Our approach is to determine the boundaries of the surfaces by computing *local* properties and then inferring the patches from them. Similar ideas for segmentation have been used in [3], [8]. In particular, we seek to find the following kinds of boundaries.

1) *Jump boundaries*—where the surface undergoes a discontinuity.

2) *Creases*—which correspond to surface orientation discontinuities.

We infer these boundaries from curvature properties of the surface. In particular, we use curvature *zero-crossings* and *extrema* [12]. A *jump boundary* creates a zero-crossing of the curvature in a direction normal to that of the boundary; a *crease* causes a local extremum of the curvature at that point. Crease boundaries may also create zero-crossings away from the location of the boundary itself.

These features, when connected using contiguity, give us *partial* boundaries for patches in which the surface should be segmented but not necessarily a *complete* segmentation. These partial boundaries are then completed by simple extension [12]; we have found this process to be satisfactory for the large number of examples we have tested it on. The resulting *regions* are assumed to correspond to elementary surface patches. These regions could be segmented further, either based on the region shape or on the results of surface fitting; we have not found it necessary to do so for the examples we have tried.

The surface patches are approximated by a second-order polynomial in (x, y, z), whose coefficients are computed by a least-squares method. The details are given in [12]. Figs. 1 and 2 illustrate this early processing on a synthetic and a real range scene, respectively.[1] In both figures, (a) shows the shaded image, (b) shows the curves obtained by our feature detection process, and (c) shows the regions bounded by the previous curves.

B. Object Inference

At the end of the above process, we have a symbolic representation of a scene as a *graph* whose nodes represent the patches and whose links express geometric relationships between patches, making it an appropriate level to use in a matching process. We can further group these patches into *objects*, or rather visible faces of objects, by reasoning on the type of connections between adjacent patches. This higher level of description facilitates the matching process. The procedure used to obtain these *objects* is described in detail in [12], we only provide the outline below.

Up until now, we have classified the boundaries into two classes only: jump boundaries and creases. Once each patch is approximated by an analytic function, it becomes possible to distinguish true jump boundaries from *limbs* (also called axial contour generators [28]), for which the normal to the surface becomes perpendicular to the viewing direction. This distinction is important for matching, as limbs are *not* intrinsic properties of an object, but depend on the viewing direction. We therefore end up with the following set of four labels: *convex creases* (+), *concave creases* (−), *limbs* (L), and *jumps* (J).

---

[1]Most researchers display range images by encoding depth by grey level, but this produces images with very poor dynamic range; in the rest of the paper, we present range images by borrowing a technique from computer graphics: we assume that the object is Lambertian, compute the normal to the surface in a small (3 × 3) neighborhood, and generate a *reflectance* image in which the intensity is inversely proportional to the angle between the light source and the surface normal. (The brightness of a point on the surface is proportional to the cosine of the angle between the light source and the surface normal under the Lambertian assumption.)

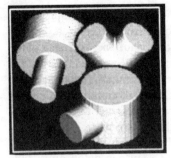
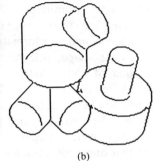

(a)　　　　　　　　　　　(b)

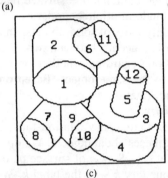

(c)

Fig. 1. Segmentation of a synthetic range image: (a) original scene, (b) detected discontinuities, (c) result of segmentation.

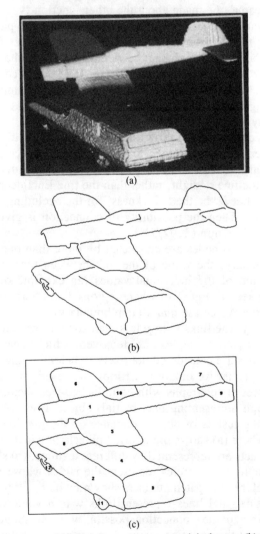

(a)

(b)

(c)

Fig. 2. Segmentation of a real range image: (a) original scene, (b) detected discontinuities, (c) result of segmentation.

The match primitives are composed of graphs and subgraphs. We create a *node* for each surface patch, which contains the *unary* information about the surface patch such as the shape, orientation, and location. Then, for each pair of nodes that share a common boundary, we create a *link* between them. This link contains the *binary* information between these two nodes such as the boundaries and the *possibility* that these two nodes (which represent two surface patches) belong to the same object. Note that one node contains one surface patch only, but one link may include multiple boundaries.

Surfaces are only parts of solid objects. In a segmented scene, the type of adjacency between two patches conveys strong information regarding whether or not these two patches belong to the same object. Based on our labels, the adjacency information we can derive is that of *occlusion* or *connectivity*.

From the type of adjacency relationships, it is possible to generate hypotheses about objects. We do this by looking at each triplet (S_i, S_j, b_k) of surface patches S_i and S_j connected by boundary b with the label k. Whenever k is a convex crease, we directly conclude that S_i and S_j belong to the same object. Such a strong conclusion, however, cannot be made about the other junction types. We have chosen to compute the possibility p that two patches belong to the same object. This number p, between 0 and 1, encodes our belief that two patches belong to the same object. p is 1 for a convex crease, 0.75 for a concave crease, and between 0 and 0.5 for a limb or jump, depending on the distance between the two patches in the vicinity of this boundary. The precise value in the last case is computed as follows: let D be the smallest distance between the two patches S_i and S_j, along the common boundary b_k (for simplicity, we compute the distance along the line of sight, rather than the true Euclidean distance). Let D' be the "thickness" of the occluding patch along b_k. Then the possibility of connection is given by $0.5 \times (1 - \min(1, D/D'))$.

When two nodes are connected by more than one type of boundary, the value of the link between them is the maximum of the individual values (an example of this can be seen in Fig. 1(c) where regions 3 and 5 are linked by a concave crease *and* a jump boundary).

Finally, the links with p less than some threshold (0.3 for all of our examples) are removed, which means the two nodes are considered not likely to belong to the same object. Thus, we obtain a partition of the original graph into a set of subgraphs with no links between them, each subgraph representing one (partial) object. Figs. 3 and 4 show the results of object inference on the previous images where (a) shows the inferred objects in which different objects are represented by different textures, (b) shows the graph where circles represent the nodes whose numbers refer to the patch numbers shown in the result of segmentation, and lines represent links with a value corresponding to the connection possibility p. It should be noted that the grouping may not be perfect, as is the case in Fig. 4 where the right wing of the plane is inferred as

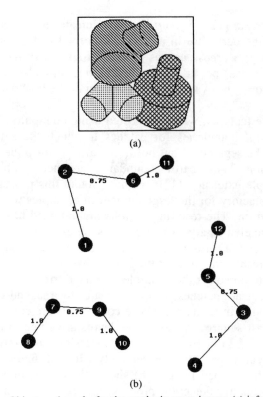

(a)

(b)

Fig. 3. Objects and graphs for the synthetic range image: (a) inferred objects, (b) graphs.

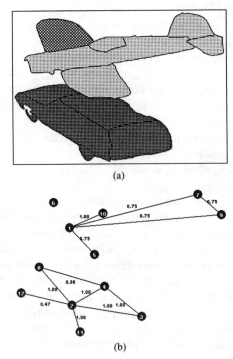

(a)

(b)

Fig. 4. Objects and graphs for the real range image: (a) inferred objects, (b) graphs.

a separate object because of occlusion. Our matching system needs to handle such errors in description.

C. Representing Objects by Attributed Graphs

Each object is represented by an *attributed* graph in which a node n_i contains the geometric information about

412

the corresponding surface patch, and a link I_{ij} between *connected* nodes n_i and n_j represents the relationships between them. The choice of these attributes is largely intuitive. However, their descriptive power and robustness has been demonstrated by testing on a large number of examples with no changes to the parameter values. Some of the attributes (such as the averages of the principal curvatures, given below) are global and could change with varying amounts of occlusion. However, as explained later, these attributes are used only to select a subset of likely models in the matching process; recognition itself involves evaluating a geometrical transformation between the data and the model and is not directly dependent on these gross measures. The attributes we use are described below.

1) Node Attributes: For each visible surface patch n_i, we compute the following:

• *Visible area $A(i)$:* This is the 3-D area of the visible surface patch. It is computed from the image of the patch in 2-D and the knowledge of surface normal at each point of the patch, by making a piece-wise planar approximation of each pixel. The 3-D area is given by $\Sigma_j \, 1/\cos(\alpha_j)$, where α_j is the angle between the surface normal and the line of sight at the jth pixel and the sum is over all pixels in the image region corresponding to the surface.

• *Orientation $\vec{n}(i)$:*
—For planar surfaces: the direction of the normal.
—For cylindrical or conic surfaces: the direction of the axis.
—For other surfaces: the direction of least curvature, which is defined as follows: let $\kappa_\theta(p)$ denote the curvature at point p in direction θ, and let $\kappa_\theta = \Sigma_{p \in n_i} |\kappa_\theta(p)|$. Then the orientation is chosen as the direction θ for which κ_θ is the smallest, the direction along which the patch is the least curved.

• *Average of Principal Curvatures $K_1(i)$ and $K_2(i)$:* $K_1(i)$ is the average of the maximum curvature at each point of the patch n_i; similarly $K_2(i)$ is the average of the minimum curvature at each point. Note that these are not the same as the "mean" curvatures commonly used in differential geometry.
—For planar surfaces: $K_1(i) = K_2(i) = 0$.
—For other surfaces: let $\vec{n}(i)$ represent the orientation of the surface, and V_1 the projection of $\vec{n}(i)$ on the x-y-plane. Let V_2 be the vector on the x-y-plane perpendicular to V_1. Then $K_1(i)$ is the average curvature at every point of the surface patch along the direction of V_1 and $K_2(i)$ that of V_2.

Hence $K_1(i)$ and $K_2(i)$ reflect the *flatness* of the patch.

• *Estimated Ratio of Occlusion $R(i)$:* A surface patch n_i is said to be occluded by another surface patch n_j if there exists a limb or jump contour c_{ij} between n_i and n_j where the depth value of n_i in the vicinity of c_{ij} is less that of n_j (note that depth is encoded such that the higher the value, the closer the point is to the viewer). Let $L_{\text{occ}}(i)$ denote the total length of set of boundaries of n_i that are occluded by other patches, and $L_{\text{tot}}(i)$ be the total length

of the boundaries of n_i, then the estimated ratio of occlusion R of n_i is equal to $L_{\text{occ}}(i)/L_{\text{tot}}(i)$.

• *Centroid $\vec{C}(i)$:* The centroid of n_i is given by the average of the (3-D) coordinates of the visible surface points belonging to n_i.

2) Link Attributes: For each pair of nodes n_i and n_j connected by at least one boundary, the link l_{ij} expresses the following.

• *The Type of Adjacency $t(i, j)$:* The adjacency between n_i and n_j can be any combination or none of the following:
—n_i is occluded by n_j at a jump or a limb,
—n_j is occluded by n_i at a jump or a limb,
—n_i and n_j are connected by a convex crease,
—n_i and n_j are connected by a concave crease.

• *The Connection Possibility $p(i, j)$ as Given Earlier:*
—$p = 1$ if n_i and n_j are connected by a convex crease, otherwise,
—$p = 0.75$ if n_i and n_j are connected by a concave crease, otherwise,
—$0.3 \le p \le 0.5$ if n_i occludes (is occluded by) n_j.

These attributes that we associate to nodes and links are the ones which we found most appropriate for establishing correspondences.

IV. Object Recognition

Matching between the objects in a scene and the database of the models is performed by three modules: the *screener*, in which we find the most likely candidate views for each object, the *graph matcher*, which performs a detailed comparison between the potential matching graphs and computes the 3-D transformation between them, and the *analyzer*, which takes a critical look at the results and proposes to split and merge object graphs. Since the matching program is rather intricate, we start by giving an overview of the core ideas, then describe each module in detail. Finally, we present a detailed case study on one of our test scenes in Section V.

A. Overview of the Matching Process

We have decided to use multiview surface models in our recognition system. Each model consists of several views (2–6, chosen by us based on the complexity of the object). These views are taken so that most of the significant surfaces of the model objects are contained in at least one of these views.

We want to recognize *objects* in occluded *scenes*. Each scene S_j may contain multiple (unknown) objects S_j^1, S_j^2, $\cdots$, $S_j^{N_j}$ with self and mutual occlusion. The scene is processed and described using the method presented in the previous section. Each scene object S_j^k is represented by an attributed graph.

We have access to a database of several known objects, called *models*, $M_1, M_2, \cdots, M_N$. Each model M_i consists of several *views* $M_i^1, M_i^2, \cdots, M_i^{N_i}$, and each view is represented by an attributed graph computed as before.

The goal of the matching process is to find, for each object in the scene, the most similar model view. The object is then recognized as the model which contains that view.

The matching process contains three major blocks: the *screener*, the *graph matcher*, and the *analyzer*. The top-level block diagrams of these three modules are shown in Figs. 5, 6, and 7, respectively.

• *Screener:* This module serves to find the likely model view candidates for each object in the scene. It is a fast search involving the computation of coarse differences in properties of the nodes of the graphs. The output is an ordered list (with at most 5 elements) of candidates. The details are given in Section IV-B.

• *Graph Matcher:* Once this list of candidates has been computed for each scene object, we perform an extensive comparison between the graphs representing the model view and the object, until one match is found to be "good enough" (defined later), or there are no candidates left.

The strongest constraint imposed by the matching process involves the geometric transform (rotation and translation) of a rigid object. However, this constraint cannot be applied until *after* a candidate match has been computed! As a result, we rely on weaker, partial constraints, and on an incremental estimate of the true transform.

The graph matching procedure consists of finding the pairs (*model node, object node*) forming the largest set consistent with a single rigid 3-D transform. We begin by finding all the possible pairs $\langle m, s \rangle$ where m and s are the model and object nodes, respectively. Then we compare the attributes of these nodes. For instance, a planar patch in the model cannot correspond to a cylindrical patch in the object. Once we have these pairs, we incrementally group them into sets consistent with a 3-D transform. This is done by tree search, updating the transformation as we go. The details of this process are given in Section IV-C.

• *Analyzer:* The previous steps can be improved with critical feedback. Two possible deficiencies of previous steps are:

—The segmentation of the scene graph may not be perfect, especially if objects are close together.
—The heuristic arguments invoked during matching may have led to wrong pairings or discarded valid ones.

There is a module in our system, called the *analyzer*, which tries to detect and correct such errors by merging unmatched objects with existing matches, or by splitting objects with many unmatched nodes into smaller objects. The details are given in Section IV-D.

B. Module 1: Screener

In principle, the number of model views and scene objects may be large, and evaluating each pair to find possible correspondences would be prohibitively expensive. Instead, we use a heuristic method to order the model views for every scene object S, according to coarse differences between S and these views, and use only the highly ranked views for detailed matching. This process significantly reduces searching time.

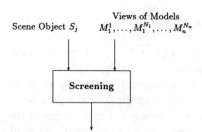

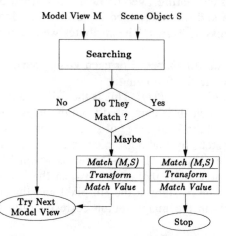

Fig. 5. Block diagram for the screener.

Fig. 6. Block diagram for the graph matcher.

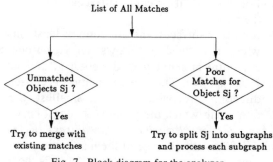

Fig. 7. Block diagram for the analyzer.

To measure the difference between two graphs, we first introduce a normalized measure between 0 and 1 as follows:

$$d(a, b) = \frac{|a - b|}{\max (a, b)}. \tag{1}$$

The following *differences* are computed between each model view $\mathfrak{M}$ and scene object $\mathcal{S}$:

• *Number of Nodes:* Let $N(\mathfrak{M}, \mathcal{S}) = d(N_\mathfrak{M}, N_\mathcal{S})$ where $N_\mathfrak{M}$ and $N_\mathcal{S}$ denote the number of nodes in $\mathfrak{M}$ and $\mathcal{S}$, respectively.

• *Number of Planar Nodes (Surface Patches):* Let $R(\mathfrak{M}, \mathcal{S}) = d(R_\mathfrak{M}, R_\mathcal{S})$ where $R_\mathfrak{M}$ and $R_\mathcal{S}$ denote the number of planar nodes in $\mathfrak{M}$ and $\mathcal{S}$, respectively.

• *The Visible 3-D Area of the Largest Node:* Let $A(\mathfrak{M}, \mathcal{S}) = d(A_\mathfrak{M}, A_\mathcal{S})$ where $A_\mathfrak{M}$ and $A_\mathcal{S}$ denote the visible 3-D area of the largest nodes in $\mathfrak{M}$ and $\mathcal{S}$, respectively.

If any of the following conditions occurs, $\mathfrak{M}$ and $\mathcal{S}$ are considered not similar enough and the model view $\mathfrak{M}$ is discarded:

- $N(\mathfrak{M}, \mathcal{S}) > 40$ percent
- $R(\mathfrak{M}, \mathcal{S}) > 30$ percent
- $A(\mathfrak{M}, \mathcal{S}) > 30$ percent.

If they pass the above test, the *difference* between $\mathfrak{M}$ and $\mathcal{S}$ is measured by

$$\alpha(\mathfrak{M}, \mathcal{S}) = N(\mathfrak{M}, \mathcal{S}) + R(\mathfrak{M}, \mathcal{S}) + A(\mathfrak{M}, \mathcal{S}). \quad (2)$$

A model view $\mathfrak{M}_1$ is said to be more similar to scene object $\mathcal{S}$ than model view $\mathfrak{M}_2$ if $\alpha(\mathfrak{M}_1, \mathcal{S})$ is smaller than $\alpha(\mathfrak{M}_2, \mathcal{S})$.

The output of the screening module is an ordered list $P(\mathcal{S}) = \{M_1, M_2, \cdots, M_N\}$ of model views such that $\alpha(\mathfrak{M}_i, \mathcal{S}) \leq \alpha(\mathfrak{M}_j, \mathcal{S})$ for all $i < j$. In addition, we impose the restriction that $N \leq 5$.

C. Module 2: Graph Matcher

The purpose of this module is to find, from a small list of candidate model views produced by the screening module, the most likely view, if any, to correspond to a given scene object. The problem is therefore to find the largest subgraph in the model view for which every node maps onto a node of the object graph according to the geometric operations which transform the view onto the object.

Exhaustive search on all possible sets of pairs is an exponential process, so we perform a two-stage depth-first exploration on this tree, whose block diagram is shown in Fig. 8.

a) Computing All The Possible Pairs: For each pair $\langle m, s \rangle$, where m and s are model and scene nodes, respectively, we check whether or not they are compatible (according to relation ξ_0 defined later), and if they are, we assign a measure of goodness to this pair.

b) Search Stage 1: We try to incrementally build a set with 4 pairs. This is done by depth-first tree search: we expand, that is, we try to add a pair to, the (ordered) pairs of this tree in a depth-first manner until a "good enough" set of pairs is found. Since we cannot enforce the compatibility relation based on the true 3-D transform, we rely instead on weaker constraints (ξ_1–ξ_6 as defined later) and on the current estimate of the true transform (ξ_7). We associate a measure of goodness with each set; if a set of size 4 has a high enough measure, the search terminates, otherwise it continues. This restriction to four pairs is imposed in order to focus the search on the most promising paths only.

c) Search Stage 2: We now look for the largest set containing the *best* set found in the previous step. The search tree is expanded from that set only, in depth-first fashion, using the same compatibility constraints as before. It may appear that the search is too focused, and that we may miss promising nodes at earlier stages, but one should remember that we are interested in all the pairs in the path from the root to a leaf, regardless of their order. Therefore, if an unexpanded pair at an earlier level of the tree

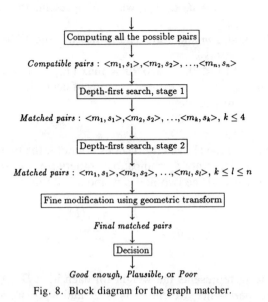

Fig. 8. Block diagram for the graph matcher.

is compatible with the expanded path, it will eventually be appended to it.

In both stage 1 and stage 2, the search terminates if one of the following conditions occurs.

    i) The current path is "good enough" (defined precisely in Section IV-C-5).
    ii) There is no more possible expansion.
    iii) The number of expanded nodes is large enough.

d) Fine Modification: We now have a good estimate of the actual transform, and can therefore enforce a strong compatibility constraint between pairs in a set of matches. As a result, we may include pairs that were rejected by the approximate constraints, or reject pairs that were included. We update the transform and the measure of goodness after such modifications.

e) Decision: We have two thresholds, $\mathcal{K}_1$ and $\mathcal{K}_2$, with $\mathcal{K}_1 < \mathcal{K}_2$, on the measure of goodness $\mathcal{K}$ of the maximal set of matches.

- If $\mathcal{K} < \mathcal{K}_1$, the object is considered not to correspond to the model.
- If $\mathcal{K} \geq \mathcal{K}_2$, the match is considered good, the object matches the model, and the search stops.
- If $\mathcal{K} \leq \mathcal{K} < \mathcal{K}_2$, the match is considered plausible, but the next candidate model views are also evaluated. Finally, the match with the highest $\mathcal{K}$ is selected.

We now give in detail the definition of our compatibility relationships, our similarity measures, and the fine modification procedure.

1) Compatibility Between Nodes of Model View and Scene Graph (ξ_0): In measuring the similarity between two nodes m of the model view and s of the scene object, we first compute the normalized measure (1) of the *difference* for each of the following properties:

a) $d_{m,s}(1) = d(A_m, A_s)$, where A_m and A_s represent the 3-D visible area of m and s, respectively.

b) $d_{m,s}(2) = d(K_m, K_s)$, where K represents the average curvature K_1.

c) $d_{m,s}(3) = d(k_m, k_s)$, where k represents the average curvature K_2.

The nodes m and s are said to be ξ_0-compatible if and only if:

• $d_{m,s}(1) < 0.30 + 0.70 \times \max(R_m, R_s)$, where R_m and R_s represent the estimated ratios of occlusion of nodes m and s, respectively.

• $d_{m,s}(2) < 0.30$.

• $d_{m,s}(3) < 0.30$.

If any of the above criteria does not hold, the two nodes are considered not ξ_0-compatible, otherwise, the *similarity measure* of the two nodes m and s is defined by

$$d_{m,s} = \frac{\sum_{i=1}^{3} w_i d_{m,s}(i)}{\sum_{i=1}^{3} w_i} \quad (3)$$

where w_i represents the weight for each item $D_{m,s}(i)$. In our experiments, we chose $w_2 = 2$, and $w_1 = w_3 = 1$.

At the end of the above process, all the ξ_0-compatible pairs are ordered according to their similarity measure. Then, in the graph matching module, the pairs are examined according to this order.

2) Compatibility Between Two Pairs of Matching Nodes: Everytime a pair of nodes $\langle m_i, s_i \rangle$ is selected, it is compared to all the already matched pairs $\langle m_j, s_j \rangle$ using a compatibility constraint. If this constraint is not satisfied, the chosen pair $\langle m_i, s_i \rangle$ is discarded. The constraint contains the following *consistency* checks.

a) Uniqueness Consistency (ξ_1): $\langle m_i, s_i \rangle$ and $\langle m_j, s_j \rangle$ are said to be ξ_1-compatible if and only if $m_i \neq m_j$ and $s_i \neq s_j$.

b) Connection Consistency (ξ_2): Let l_1 and l_2 represent the links between m_i and m_j and between s_i and s_j, respectively. Then the types (i.e., limb, jump, convex, or concave) of l_1 and l_2, denoted as t_1 and t_2, respectively, are said to be ξ_2-compatible if and only if one of the following satisfies:

• t_1 is equal to t_2, or

• one of them is a jump and the other one is a convex crease (a change of view point may transform one into the other)

• either one or both of them is NULL (the nodes are not adjacent, this is possible especially when shadows occur).

Note that l_1 and l_2 may have multiple types, as explained in Section III-B earlier. In this case, we require that *any* of the multiple types match.

c) Direction Consistency (ξ_3): Let θ_1 and θ_2 denote the angles between the orientation of $\langle m_i, m_j \rangle$ and $\langle s_i, s_j \rangle$, and let $\theta = |\theta_1 - \theta_2|$, then the pairs $\langle m_i, s_i \rangle$ and $\langle m_j, s_j \rangle$ are said to be ξ_3-compatible if and only if θ is less than a fixed threshold θ_{tol}. Here we choose $\theta_{\text{tol}} = 25°$.

d) Distance Consistency (ξ_4): Let L_1 and L_2 denote the distance between the centroid of inertia of m_i and m_j, and s_i and s_j, respectively. Let

$$L = \frac{|L_1 - L_2|}{\max(L_1, L_2)}, \quad (4)$$

then, the pairs $\langle m_i, s_i \rangle$ and $\langle m_j, s_j \rangle$ are said to be ξ_4-compatible if and only if L is less than a threshold. Here we choose the threshold as 0.30.

e) 3-D Geometry Consistency (ξ_5): For all the matched pairs $\langle m_k, s_k \rangle$ other than $\langle m_i, s_i \rangle$ and $\langle m_j, s_j \rangle$, let $\vec{U}_{ij}$, $\vec{V}_{ij}$, $\vec{U}_{ik}$, and $\vec{V}_{ik}$ represent the vector connecting the centroid of m_i to that of m_j, s_i to s_j, m_i to m_k, and s_i to s_k, respectively. Let θ_1 and θ_2 denote the *directed angle* from $\vec{U}_{ij}$ to $\vec{U}_{ik}$, and from $\vec{V}_{ij}$ to $\vec{V}_{ik}$, respectively. And let

$$\theta = |\theta_1 - \theta_2|. \quad (5)$$

Then the three pairs $\langle m_i, s_i \rangle$, $\langle m_j, s_j \rangle$, and $\langle m_k, s_k \rangle$ are said to be ξ_5 compatible if and only if θ is less than a threshold. Here we choose the threshold to be 25°. This consistency check is mainly used to remove a match between two objects which are geometrically similar by mirror effect, as shown in Fig. 9.

If these four consistency conditions are fulfilled, we say that $\langle m_i, s_i \rangle$ and $\langle m_j, s_j \rangle$ are mutually consistent. This only happens, however, when no abrupt changes occur as a result of a difference in viewing angle. To take into account such changes, we define an additional condition as follows.

• *Enclosure* (ξ_6): To determine whether a surface patch m is (*partially*) enclosed in 2-D by another surface patch s, we start from the center point $C = (x, y)$ of m, where x and y are the first two coordinates of the centroid of m, and search outward in 8 directions, each 45° apart, if 6 or more out of the 8 searches encounter any point in surface s, we say m is enclosed by s. With this definition, we accept two pairs even if they fail all of the consistency conditions above except for condition 1, as long as m_i encloses (is enclosed by) m_j *and* s_i encloses (is enclosed by) s_j.

The motivation for this constraint is to allow looser matching of smaller regions contained inside larger and already matched regions (such as pushbuttons on the telephone in one of the examples shown later). The constraints ξ_2–ξ_5 tend to be not reliable in such cases. Note that the matches accepted at this stage must still agree with the geometric transformation computed later.

It should be noted that the above criteria are not perfect, especially when parts of the objects are occluded, and mostly serve to prune the search tree. The true compatibility between nodes is established by the computation of the geometric transform.

3) Computing the Geometric Transform: Computing the geometric transform between matched objects not only indicates how to bring matched objects in correspondence, but also helps to verify the matching process. If the error in the transform for the current partial match is too large, the match should be abandoned.

The matching process gives the correspondences between surfaces of model view $\mathfrak{M}$ and scene object $\mathfrak{S}$. By extracting the orientation and location of the corresponding surfaces, we can compute the (geometric) transform which brings $\mathfrak{M}$ in registration with $\mathfrak{S}$. Here we introduce a noniterative method in which the axis of the rotation is first computed using the orientation of the matched nodes,

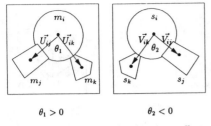

$$\theta_1 > 0 \qquad \theta_2 < 0$$

Fig. 9. Geometric similarity by mirror effect.

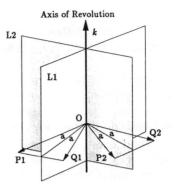

Fig. 10. Computing transforms.

then the angle of the rotation is obtained using a two-level search. Finally, the translation is computed from the centroids of the matched nodes, using a least-square method. Since this method is noniterative, we believe it is faster than iterative methods which are used by many researchers [14], [17]. The details of the geometric transform computation are given below.

The rigid transform between objects can be represented in homogeneous coordinates by a 4 × 4 matrix as follows:

$$\begin{pmatrix} R_{(3\times3)} & T_{(3\times1)} \\ 0_{(1\times3)} & 1 \end{pmatrix} \qquad (6)$$

where R represents the rotation and T the translation, respectively. A rotation can be represented by a rotation of angle θ about a unit vector k (axis of revolution) located at the origin. Let k_x, k_y, and k_z represent the three components of the axis k, then the relation between the coefficients of R and θ, k_x, k_y, k_z can be expressed as follows [27]:

$$R(k, \theta) = \begin{pmatrix} k_x k_x v + c & k_y k_x v - k_z s & k_z k_x v + k_y s \\ k_x k_y v + k_z s & k_y k_y v + c & k_z k_y v - k_x s \\ k_x k_z v - k_y s & k_y k_z v + k_x s & k_z k_z v + c \end{pmatrix} \qquad (7)$$

where $s = \sin \theta$, $c = \cos \theta$, and $v = 1 - c$.

To find the axis k, the orientation vectors for each matched node pairs are first retrieved. Let $\langle m_i, s_i \rangle$, $i = 1, \cdots, N$ be the matched node pairs between two objects $\mathfrak{M}$ and $\mathfrak{S}$ where $m_i \in \mathfrak{M}$, $s_i \in \mathfrak{S}$, and N is the number of matched node pairs, respectively. Let $\langle P_i, Q_i \rangle$ denote the orientation vectors of the matched node pair $\langle m_i, s_i \rangle$, as shown in Fig. 10 for $i = 1, 2$, where both orientation vectors have been brought to the origin O. Assuming the rotated angle is $\theta = 2a$ as indicated in Fig. 10, it is easy to show that the axis of revolution k for P_1 and Q_1 must lie on the plane $L1$ that bisects the angle $P_1 O Q_1$. In other words, the angle between P_1 and its projection on L_1 is equal to that between Q_1 and L_1, and this angle is equal to a (unless P_1 and Q_1 coincide at k, in this case, however, L_1 is an arbitrary plane that contains k). The same reasoning can be applied to all the other $\langle P_i, Q_i \rangle$ pairs. Thus to find the axis k, we only have to find all the planes L_i, then k is at their intersections. In our implementation, we find all the intersections k_{ij} of each two pairs L_i and L_j, then for each k_{ij} we compute the sum of the angle be-

tween all other k_{ij}, the one with the least sum is our choice of axis k.

The angle θ is found as follows. Let $\Theta(a, b)$ denote the angle between vector a and b. Given a rotation θ, for each matched pair $\langle m_i, s_i \rangle$, $\Theta(R(\theta) P_i, Q_i)$ is computed where $R(\theta) P_i$ represent the vector of P_i after rotating it by an angle θ. Then the best θ is found by minimizing the following equation:

$$E_\theta = \sum_i \Theta(R(\theta) P_i, Q_i). \qquad (8)$$

After the rotation matrix R is computed, the translation T can be obtained easily. Let $\langle E_i, C_i \rangle$ denote the centroids of each matched pair $\langle m_i, s_i \rangle$ and $C_i' = R(\theta) E_i$. Then the translation T is as follows:

$$\frac{1}{N} \sum_i C_i - C_i'. \qquad (9)$$

In our experiments, we have found that this computation gives highly accurate results; an example is shown later (in Section V-B).

4) Modifications Based on the Geometric Transform: Since the compatibility constraints presented previously are not perfect, some corresponding nodes may not have fulfilled the conditions imposed and may therefore have been rejected. Using the transform for the match allows us to rectify this situation. To achieve this, the transform between the model view and the scene object is computed first, using the current match L, then the model object is transformed and *superimposed* on the scene. Each surface s of the scene object is then checked by the following constraint ξ_7:

• If s is not yet matched and there exists an unmatched model surface m whose transformed surface m' is close enough to s, then include $\langle m, s \rangle$ into the match L. Surfaces m' and s are said to be close enough if and only if the distance between the centroids of m' and s are less than twice the smaller *average width* of m and s, where the average width W of a surface m is computed as follows:

$$W = \frac{w_1 + 3w_2}{4} \qquad (10)$$

where w_1 and w_2 indicate the distance from the 2-D center of the surface m to its farthest and closest boundaries, respectively.

• If s is a matched node and the corresponding transformed model node m' is not close enough, then $\langle m, s \rangle$ is removed from the match L.

After the modification, the transform is recomputed.

5) Measuring the Goodness of a Match: Throughout the graph matching procedure, a *match value* $\mathcal{K}$ is attached to the current match which is computed as follows:

$$\mathcal{K} = \frac{\max(N_m, N_s) + \max(A_m, A_s)}{2} \quad (11)$$

where N_m, N_s, A_m, and A_s represent the ratio between the number of matched model nodes and the number of total model nodes, the number of matched scene nodes and the number of total scene nodes, the 3-D area of matched model nodes and that of all the model nodes, and the 3-D area of matched scene nodes and that of all the scene nodes, respectively. The highest value of $\mathcal{K}$ is 1, which represents a complete match, and the lowest value of $\mathcal{K}$ is 0, which means that nothing is matched. A match is considered "good enough" when $\mathcal{K}$ reaches $\mathcal{K}_2 = 0.80$, and the graph matching step is immediately terminated. Otherwise, the search continues until the search tree can no longer be expanded. Finally, if the match value $\mathcal{K}$ of the resulting match is less than $\mathcal{K}_1 = 0.60$, the match is discarded.

D. Module 3: Analyzer

Input scenes may contain multiple objects, and, as we have mentioned before, the object inference step may not produce perfect results. For example, when two objects touch, it is possible that we would consider them as one object instead of two, i.e., the result of object inference may produce just one *object shell* (i.e., a single graph) for these two touching objects. On the other hand, due to occlusions, shadows, or a special view point, real objects may appear as separate pieces in range image. In this case, more than one *object shell* is generated for different parts of the same object. In both cases, the match between model views and such objects will not be satisfactory. To correct this, a refining process which *splits* and/or *merges* objects according to current matches and their geometric relationships is applied next; we call this module the *analyzer*.

1) Splitting Objects: Suppose that our scene contains two objects A and B which are inferred as one object shell (represented by graph $\mathcal{S}$). Since we allow only one model view being matched for one object shell, let us assume that the model view $\mathcal{Q}$ matches $\mathcal{S}$ (as the result after step 2) where $\mathcal{Q}$ is the view of the model object which is similar to scene object A. We also assume that there is another model view $\mathcal{B}$ whose model is similar to scene object B. At this time, the match between $\mathcal{B}$ and B has not yet been found. Fig. 11(a) illustrates this situation, where all surface patches are numbered for convenience. From the figure, we see that patch 3 of the scene is touching

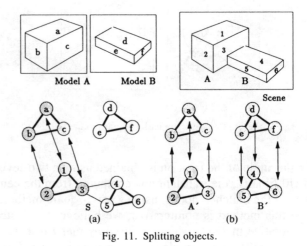

Fig. 11. Splitting objects.

patches 4 and 5. The scene graph $\mathcal{S}$ and the model graphs $\mathcal{Q}$ and $\mathcal{B}$ are also shown. The shaded nodes represent the currently matched nodes (the correspondences between two matched nodes are indicated by bidirectional arrows). After matching, we find that half of the nodes in $\mathcal{S}$ are not matched (surfaces 4, 5, and 6); however, by examining $\mathcal{S}$, it is possible to *split* the two objects in the scene.

The following two rules are followed in splitting objects.

a) $\mathcal{R}_1$: Splitting can only be achieved by removing links for which p is strictly less than 1.

b) $\mathcal{R}_2$: The set of already matched patches should not be split into subsets.

By looking at the scene and the graph $\mathcal{S}$, we know that surfaces 1-2, 2-3, 1-3, 4-5, 4-6, and 5-6 are connected by convex creases ($p = 1$) and from Rule 1 they can not be split (displayed by thick lines); however, surfaces 3-4 and 3-5 are connected by concave creases ($p = 0.75$) and may be split (displayed by thin lines). By removing the links 3-4 and 3-5 from $\mathcal{S}$, we obtain two separate graphs $\mathcal{Q}'$ (which contains surfaces 1, 2, and 3) and $\mathcal{B}'$ (which contains surfaces 4, 5, and 6). Furthermore, by looking at the match we notice that the *matched surfaces* (surfaces 1, 2, and 3) are contained only in $\mathcal{Q}'$, thus the result of splitting does not break Rule 2.

After splitting, we now can match scene object $\mathcal{B}'$ to model view $\mathcal{B}$ and the result is shown in Fig. 11(b).

From the above reasoning, we have derived the following procedure to split objects:

a) After graph searching, if there exists a *matched* scene object $\mathcal{S}$ such that more than 40 percent of its nodes are not matched, try to split it.

b) Split $\mathcal{S}$ according to the two rules $\mathcal{R}_1$ and $\mathcal{R}_2$ stated above. Let $\mathcal{S}_1$ represent the split object which contains all the already matched nodes, and $\mathcal{S}_2, \mathcal{S}_3, \cdots, \mathcal{S}_N$ represent the remaining split objects sorted in the descending order of number of containing nodes.

c) *Reconnect* $\mathcal{S}_2, \mathcal{S}_3, \cdots, \mathcal{S}_N$ into one object $\mathcal{S}'$, try to match it with model views, if no model views can be matched, remove $\mathcal{S}_N$ (which contains the least number of nodes) and retry the match. The idea is that we want to match from the largest possible objects.

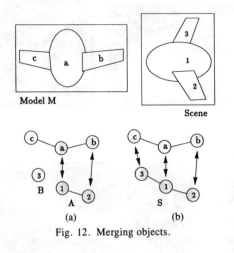
Fig. 12. Merging objects.

d) Repeat steps a)–c) until no more splitting is achievable.

2) Merging Objects: Suppose that our scene contains only one object $\mathcal{S}$; however, due to self occlusion, it is inferred as two object shells (represented by graphs $\mathcal{A}$ and $\mathcal{B}$, respectively). Also assume that after graph searching, $\mathcal{A}$ is matched to a model view $\mathfrak{M}$ (which is supposed to match the entire object $\mathcal{S}$) and $\mathcal{B}$ is not matched (usually because it contains too few nodes). This is illustrated in Fig. 12(a) where $\mathcal{A}$ contains two *matched* surfaces 1 and 2, $\mathcal{B}$ contains one *unmatched* surface 3, and model view $\mathfrak{M}$ contains three surfaces a, b, and c. In the current match, surfaces a and b match surfaces 1 and 2, respectively, while surface c is not matched (which is supposed to match surface 3 of $\mathcal{B}$).

To refine the match, merging can be used to bring separate pieces that actually belong to the same object. The idea is that by merging two objects $\mathcal{A}$ and $\mathcal{B}$ into one object $\mathcal{S}$ (which matches $\mathfrak{M}$), not only the similarity constraints between corresponding *matching* nodes ($\langle c, 3 \rangle$ in this example) should be satisfied, but the binary constraints and the transform constraints between each pair of matching nodes ($\langle a, 1 \rangle$, $\langle b, 2 \rangle$, and $\langle c, 3 \rangle$ in this example) should also be satisfied.

In the example we show here, $\mathcal{A}$ and $\mathcal{B}$ are merged into $\mathcal{S}$ and the new match result is shown in Fig. 12(b).

From the above reasoning, we have derived a general procedure to merge objects as follows:

a) After graph searching, try to merge any *unmatched* scene object $\mathcal{B}$.

b) Select among matched objects the one which is geometrically closest to $\mathcal{B}$. Let $\mathcal{A}$, $\mathfrak{M}$, and L denote the selected object, its matched model view, and the match between $\mathcal{A}$ and $\mathfrak{M}$, respectively.

c) Use the graph searching process presented in the previous section to find the correspondences between the nodes in $\mathcal{B}$ and the *unmatched* nodes in $\mathfrak{M}$, assuming that the match L has already been established. More matches can be added to L only if the resulting match meets the constraints of node similarity, binary constraints between each pair of matching pixels, and the transformation constraint.

d) Repeat steps a)–c) until either no more unmatched scene objects exist or no more merging is achievable.

V. Experimental Results

In this section, we show the results and an evaluation of our recognition process, using a database of 10 objects, resulting in 32 views. We first show a detailed case study, then show results on a few more scenes.

A. The Models

In this work, we have selected 10 objects to build models. Then scenes which consist of these objects are acquired and recognized using these models. The model objects include a car, a chair, a telephone, a table, a mask, a hatchback car, a wagon, two boats, and an airplane. In order to save space, we only show *one* view for each of these objects in Fig. 13, but it is important to remember that the database consists of *all* the views for all the objects, 32 in all.

Our data comes from an active range finder using a light-stripe and triangulation technique, it is described in detail in [23]. The system consists of a laser, a video camera, a video monitor, a terminal, and a computer-driven rotary table.

Our composite scenes were obtained by first scanning each object in an arbitrary position and orientation, then combining these objects (synthetically) to generate the scene as it would have appeared if we had scanned it. This is necessary because of the technical difficulty in actually scanning the scene using a rotary table, which would create too many shadow regions.

B. A Detailed Case Study

In order to better understand how the system works, we take one of our test scenes, shown in Fig. 2(a), and follow each step of the system as it processes this scene. Table I shows the computation times for the various steps of processing on a Symbolics 3645 computer (with a floating point accelerator and 1 Megaword of memory). Note that the recognition takes only a small fraction of the total time. This is consistent with our design philosophy that good representations vastly simplify recognition. Also note that most of the time is spent on relatively simple, local computations that can be performed in parallel in a straightforward way.

1) Search Nodes Expanded in Recognition: As mentioned before, the object inference cannot be expected to always generate perfect results. In the scene, the right wing of the airplane is segmented into a separate object as the result of object inference, shown in Fig. 14, where different textures represent different objects. Thus, at the beginning of the recognition process, the scene consists of three "objects": the airplane without the right wing, the wagon, and the wing.

The first step of the recognition process is to screen the model views for each of the three objects. The single wing, which consists of only one surface patch, does not find any candidate model views, thus is ignored tempo-

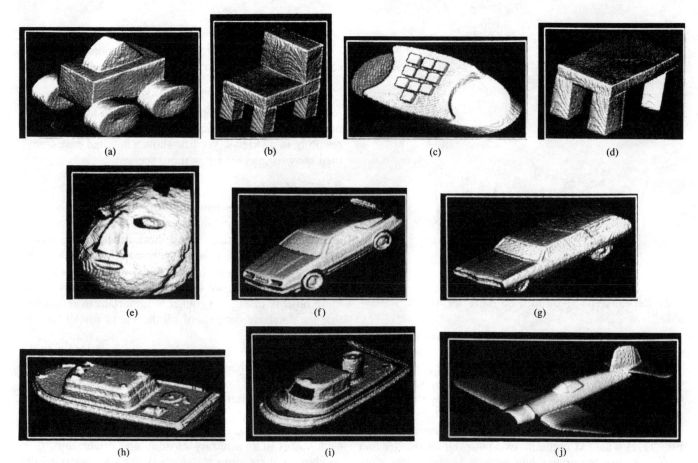

Fig. 13. Model views: (a) model car (4 views), (b) model chair (4 views), (c) model phone (4 views), (d) model table (4 views), (e) model mask (6 views), (f) model hatchback (2 views), (g) model wagon (2 views), (h) model Boat 1 (2 views), (i) model Boat 2 (2 views), (j) model plane (2 views).

TABLE I
DETAILED TIMING INFORMATION FOR THE FIRST SCENE

	Step		Overall
CV	Time: 693 seconds		17%
	Gaussian convolution	50%	
	$L \circ G$ convolution	50%	
SG	Time: 433 seconds		10%
	Zero-crossing detection	18%	
	Extrema detection	22%	
	Space grouping	17%	
	Surface segmentation	43%	
AP	Time: 2851 seconds		68%
	Planar surface approximation	7%	
	Quadric surface approximation	41%	
	Approximation error computation	52%	
GR	Time: 37 seconds		1%
	Computation of graph	50%	
	Object inference	50%	
RC	Time: 147 seconds		4%
	Screener (Module 1)	1%	
	Graph Matcher (Module 2)	92%	
	Analyzer (Module 3)	7%	

CV : Time for Gaussian and LoG convolution
SG : Time for feature detection and segmentation
AP : Time for surface approximation
GR : Time for computation of graph and object inference
RC : Time for recognition

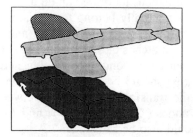

Fig. 14. Result of object inference for the first scene.

• The plane: 1) plane, view 1, 2) plane, view 2, 3) chair, view 1.

The second step examines each of the selected candidates in the order shown above. As the result of graph matching, the first four candidates for the wagon are discarded. In this case study, we show the search trees expanded by matching between the scene object "wagon" and the second view of the model "wagon," and between the scene object "airplane" and the first view of the model "plane," where both models are selected as the final match.

Fig. 15 shows the surface patches of the first view of the model plane, the second view of the model wagon, and the scene, respectively, with each surface patch (node) having a unique number. Figs. 16 and 17 show the search trees in matching the wagon and the airplane, respec-

rarily. The screening results for the other two objects are as follows:

• The wagon: 1) plane, view 1, 2) hatchback, view 2, 3) wagon, view 1, 4) chair, view 2, 5) wagon, view 2.

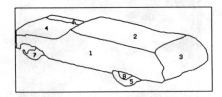

"Wagon" view 2

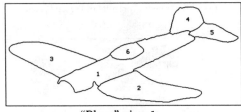

"Plane" view 1

(a)

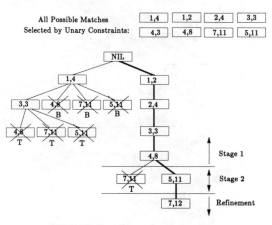

(b)

Fig. 15. Node numbers of the models and the first scene: (a) matched model views, (b) matched objects}.

All Possible Matches Selected by Unary Constraints:

1,4	1,2	2,4	3,3
4,3	4,8	7,11	5,11

Fig. 16. Search tree for the wagon.

All Possible Matches Selected by Unary Constraints:

1,1	2,5	4,9
5,7	4,7	5,9

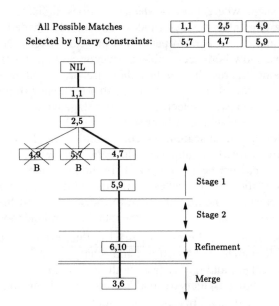

Fig. 17. Search tree for the airplane.

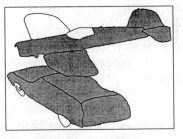

Fig. 18. Nodes expanded in stage 1.

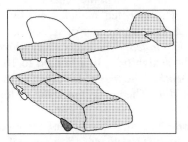

Fig. 19. Nodes expanded in stage 2.

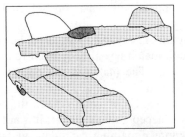

Fig. 20. Nodes expanded after refinement.

tively. In these figures, each tree node, represented by a pair of numbers inside a box $\boxed{a, b}$, indicates a possible match between model node a and scene node b. The order of expansion is from left to right, then top to bottom. In Fig. 16, for example, the order of expansion is $\boxed{1, 4}$, $\boxed{3, 3}$, $\boxed{4, 8}$ at level 2, $\boxed{7, 11}$ at level 2, $\boxed{5, 11}$ at level 2, $\boxed{4, 8}$ at level 3, $\boxed{7, 11}$ at level 3, $\boxed{5, 11}$ at level 3, $\boxed{1, 2}$, and so on. A cross over a tree node indicates that this match is rejected, either by binary constraints (marked ''B'') or by transform constraints (marked ''T''). Note that the unary constraints are applied to select all the possible match pairs *before* the search begins. The final selected matches are indicated by thicker links. Figs. 18, 19, and 20 show the scene nodes expanded in each stage where heavily shaded regions indicate currently expanded patches (nodes) and lightly shaded regions indicate expanded patches at previous stages. Note that we show both scene objects (wagon and airplane) in the same figures, but in fact they are processed in sequence. From these figures we see that the major (larger) surfaces are always selected in the first stage while smaller surfaces are matched in later stages.

After the graph search, the correspondences of the wagon are correctly established while the right wing of the airplane has not been recognized. In the next step, merging is applied to the scenes. Since the wing (scene node 6) is closer to the airplane than to the wagon, and there is only one unmatched node in the matched airplane model (model node 3), the match $\boxed{3, 6}$ is thus selected as a possible match. The transform and binary constraints are then checked, and in this case, both of them are satisfied, thus the wing is merged to the airplane and the match $\boxed{3, 6}$ is included. It should be noted that to verify the transform constraint, we simply transform the model views of the airplane and *superimpose* it on the scene, which is shown in Fig. 21, and then find that the two nodes $\boxed{3, 6}$ are close enough. Fig. 22 shows the expanded node in the merging step.

Fig. 23 shows the recognition results where Fig. 23(a) shows the matched model views and Fig. 23(b) shows the matched scene objects. In this figure, corresponding textures are used to represent corresponding objects, and corresponding numbers are used for matched nodes. Table II summarizes the recognition results. The entries are to be interpreted as follows.

- *Object:* The object in the scene.
- *Model:* The selected model view by the screener. The views are sorted by order of selection.
- *Nodes Expanded:* The number of *search nodes* expanded in the search tree. It is limited to 100.
- *Max. Depth:* The maximum depth of the search tree.
- *Max. Width:* The maximum width of the search tree, it is limited to 5.
- *Decision:* The final decision of the recognition:
  1) *Matched:* The object and the model view are considered matched (good enough in Module 2 (Graph matcher), i.e., match value $\mathcal{H} \geq 0.8$). If this happens, the remaining selected model views are ignored.
  2) *Ignored:* The view is ignored because a good-enough match has already been found.
  3) *Rejected:* The match is too poor to be accepted ($\mathcal{H} < 0.6$).
  4) *Plausible:* The match between the object and the view is acceptable; however, it is not good enough to ignore remaining candidate views ($0.6 \leq \mathcal{H} < 0.8$). In this case, the match and its match value $\mathcal{H}$ are kept for further comparison. If a good-enough match is found during the subsequent exploration, this plausible match is discarded, otherwise, the plausible match with the largest $\mathcal{H}$ is selected as the final match.

Fig. 21. Transform results of the first scene.

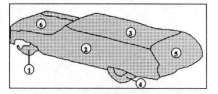

Fig. 22. Nodes expanded after merging.

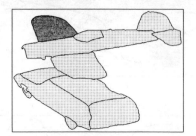

"Wagon" view 2

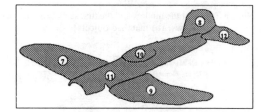

"Plane" view 1

(a)

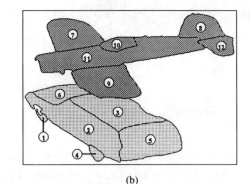

(b)

Fig. 23. Result of recognition on the first scene: (a) matched model views, (b) matched objects}.

C. Results for Other Scenes

We have performed succesful experiments on several such composite scenes. The complete set can be found in [13]; here, we only present results for two other scenes in order to save space. They are shown in Figs. 24 and 25,

TABLE II
Summary for the First Scene

Object	Model	Expanded Nodes	Max. Depth	Max. Width	Decision
The wagon	plane, view 1	8	2	3	Rejected
	hatchback, view 2	3	2	2	Rejected
	wagon, view 1	4	1	2	Rejected
	chair, view 2	5	2	2	Rejected
	wagon, view 2	15	6	4	*Matched*
The plane	plane, view 1	7	5	3	*Matched*
	plane, view 2	-	-	-	Ignored
	chair, view 1	-	-	-	Ignored

Fig. 24. The second scene.

Fig. 25. The third scene.

Phone, view 1   Car, view 1

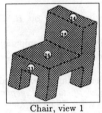   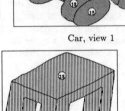

Chair, view 1   Table, view 1

(a)

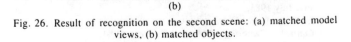

(b)

Fig. 26. Result of recognition on the second scene: (a) matched model views, (b) matched objects.

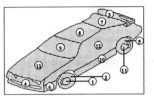

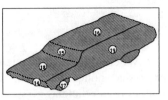

"Hatchback" view 1   "Wagon" view 1

(a)

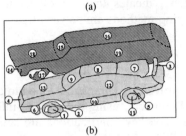

(b)

Fig. 27. Result of recognition on the third scene: (a) matched model views, (b) matched objects.

TABLE III
Summary for the Second Scene

Object	Model	Expanded Nodes	Max. Depth	Max. Width	Decision
The phone	phone, view 1	20	10	4	*Matched*
	phone, view 2	-	-	-	Ignored
	chair, view 3	-	-	-	Ignored
	hatchback, view 1	-	-	-	Ignored
The car	hatchback, view 2	5	2	2	Plausible
	plane, view 2	3	2	2	Rejected
	chair, view 1	17	3	3	Plausible
	car, view 1	18	4	5	*Matched*
	plane, view 1	-	-	-	Ignored
The chair	chair, view 1	7	4	3	*Matched*
The table	table, view 1	2	2	1	*Matched*
	mask, view 6	-	-	-	Ignored

TABLE IV
Summary for the Third Scene

Object	Model	Expanded Nodes	Max. Depth	Max. Width	Decision
The hatch-back	table, view 2	2	1	2	Rejected
	chair, view 3	14	3	5	Rejected
	hatchback, view 1	15	8	3	*Matched*
The wagon	wagon, view 1	7	4	2	*Matched*
	wagon, view 2	-	-	-	Ignored
	chair, view 2	-	-	-	Ignored
	hatchback, view 2	-	-	-	Ignored
	chair, view 1	-	-	-	Ignored

together with the recognition results shown in Figs. 26 and 27. Tables III and IV summarize the recognition process.

It should be noted that if a good-enough match cannot be found after graph matching, further analysis may be necessary to find the best match from the plausible matches. Several possibilities include increasing the resolution, focusing on one part, or changing viewing angles.

Several conclusions can be drawn from the following results.

• Most of the correct matches are found at the first or second selected views, this proves that our screening is powerful.

- Whenever a correct view is selected, the number of expanded nodes is small. This proves that our graph matching is efficient.
- The inferred objects do correspond to the physical objects, which indicates that our object inference and splitting/merging methods are powerful.

VI. Conclusion

This paper provides a complete method to describe and recognize 3-D objects, using the surface information of these objects. The key contributions are summarized as follows.

- *It provides a complete system to describe and recognize 3-D objects.* We present a set of techniques to retrieve significant features of 3-D objects, describe them, match the descriptions, build the models in multi-views, and finally recognize them.

- *It is data-driven in that no a priori scene knowledge is required.* The descriptions of the objects are computed without any knowledge about existing models, which is important when the environment is unknown, or the number of interesting objects is large.

- *Moderately complex objects can be well described and matched.* A large number of different objects were tested and good results were obtained. These objects vary in sizes, shape, and complexity. Some of them are highly symmetric while others are different from every view point. This shows the generality and robustness of our method.

- *Partially occluded objects can be well described and matched.* Occlusion is one of the major problems in computer vision. The method presented here tackles this problem in a very effective way. More than two thirds of the surfaces can be heavily occluded or completely missing and a plausible match is still achievable.

Our system can be improved in several ways:

- Better segmentation methods will help. Specifically, additional methods for segmenting "smooth" surfaces are needed.

- Under heavy occlusion, it may be necessary to further group fragmented surfaces before matching is attempted.

- It would be nice to have a single, 3-D volumetric representation of the models, rather than the multiple views. The multiple views could then be computed from the single model. Alternately, volume descriptions may be computed from the data. The latter is a difficult problem, but we believe that our surface descriptions are a key step for this process also.

References

[1] N. Ayache, "A model-based vision system to identify and locate partially visible industrial parts," in *Proc. Conf. IEEE Computer Vision and Pattern Recognition*, Washington, DC, 1983, pp. 492–494.

[2] P. J. Besl and R. C. Jain, "Three-dimensional object recognition," *ACM Comput. Surveys*, vol. 17, no. 1, pp. 75–145, Mar. 1985.

[3] P. J. Besl and R. C. Jain, "Segmentation through variable-order surface fitting," *IEEE Trans. Pattern Anal. Machine Intell.*, vol. 10, no. 2, pp. 167–192, Mar. 1988.

[4] B. Bhanu, "Representation and shape matching of 3-D objects," *IEEE Trans. Pattern Anal. Machine Intell.*, vol. PAMI-6, no. 3, pp. 340–350, May 1984.

[5] R. C. Bolles and R. A. Cain, "Recognizing and locating partially visible objects: The local feature-focus method," *Int. J. Robotics Res.*, vol. 1, no. 3, pp. 637–643, 1982.

[6] R. C. Bolles and P. Horaud, "3DPO: A three-dimensional part orientation system," *Int. J. Robotics Res.*, vol. 5, no. 3, pp. 3–26, Fall 1986.

[7] M. Brady, "Computational approaches to image understanding," *ACM Comput. Surveys*, vol. 14, no. 1, pp. 3–71, Mar. 1982.

[8] M. Brady, J. Ponce, A. Yuille, and H. Asada, "Describing surfaces," In H. Hanafusa and H. Inoue, editors, *Proc. 2nd Int. Symp. Robotics Research*, H. Hanafusa and H. Inoe, Eds. Cambridge, MA: M.I.T. Press, 1985.

[9] R. A. Brooks, "Symbolic reasoning among 3-D models and 2-D images," *Artificial Intell.*, vol. 17, pp. 285–348, 1981.

[10] ——, "Model-based three-dimensional interpretations of two-dimensional images," *IEEE Trans. Pattern Anal. Machine Intell.*, vol. PAMI-5, no. 2, pp. 140–150, Mar. 1983.

[11] R. T. Chin and C. R. Dyer, "Model-based recognition in robot vision," *ACM Comput. Surveys*, vol. 18, no. 1, pp. 67–108, Mar. 1986.

[12] T. J. Fan, G. Medioni, and R. Nevatia, "Segmented descriptions of 3-D surfaces," *IEEE J. Robotics Automation*, pp. 527–538, Dec. 1987.

[13] T. J. Fan, "Describing and recognizing 3-D objects using surface properties," Ph.D. dissertation, Dep. Comput. Sci., Univ. Southern California, Los Angeles, Aug. 1988.

[14] O. D. Faugeras and M. Hebert, "The representation recognition and locating of 3-D objects," *Int. J. Robotics Res.*, vol. 5, no. 3, pp. 27–52, Fall 1986.

[15] W. E. L. Grimson and T. Lozano-Pérez, "Model-based recognition and localization from sparse range or tactile data," *Int. J. Robotics Res.*, vol. 3, no. 3, pp. 3–35, Fall 1984.

[16] ——, "Localizing overlapping parts by searching the interpretation tree," *IEEE Trans. Pattern Anal. Machine Intell.*, vol. PAMI-9, no. 4, July 1987.

[17] K. T. Gunnarsson, "Optimal part localization by data base matching with sparse data and dense data," Ph.D. dissertation, Dep. Mech. Eng., Carnegie-Mellon Univ., Pittsburgh, PA, Apr. 27, 1987.

[18] P. Horaud and R. C. Bolles, "3DPO's strategy for matching three-dimensional objects in range data," in *Proc. Int. Conf. Robotics*, Atlanta, GA, Mar. 13–15, 1984, pp. 78–85.

[19] B. K. P. Horn, "Extended Gaussian images," *Proc. IEEE*, vol. 72, pp. 1656–1678, Dec. 1984.

[20] B. K. P. Horn and K. Ikeuchi, "The mechanical manipulation of randomly oriented parts," *Science America*, vol. 251, no. 2, pp. 100–111, Aug. 1984.

[21] K. Ikeuchi, "Recognition of 3-D objects using the extended Gaussian image," in *Proc. 7th Int. Joint Conf. Artificial Intelligence*, Vancouver, B.C., Canada, Aug. 24–28, 1981, pp. 595–600.

[22] ——, "Precompiling a geometrical model into an interpretation tree for object recognition in bin-picking tasks," in *Proc. DARPA Image Understanding Workshop*, Feb. 1987, pp. 321–339.

[23] J. L. Jezouin, P. Saint-Marc, and G. Medioni, "Building an accurate range finder with off the shelf components," in *Proc. IEEE Conf. Computer Vision and Pattern Recognition*, Ann Arbor, MI, June 5–9, 1988.

[24] R. Nevatia and T. O. Binford, "Description and recognition of complex-curved objects," *Artificial Intell.*, vol. 8, pp. 77–98, 1977.

[25] M. Oshima and Y. Shirai, "A scene description method using three-dimensional information," *Pattern Recognition*, vol. 11, pp. 9–17, 1979.

[26] ——, "Object recognition using three-dimensional information," *IEEE Trans. Pattern Anal. Machine Intell.*, vol. 3, no. 4, pp. 353–361, July 1983.

[27] R. P. Paul, *Robot Manipulators: Mathematics, Programming, and Control.* Cambridge, MA: M.I.T. Press, 1984.

[28] K. Rao and R. Nevatia, "Generalized cone descriptions from sparse 3-D data," in *Proc. IEEE Conf. Computer Vision and Pattern Recognition*, Miami Beach, FL, June 22–26, 1986, pp. 256–263.

Ting-Jun Fan (M'88) received the B.S. degree in electrical engineering from the National Taiwan University, Taipei, in 1980, the M.S. degree in computer engineering from the National Chiao-Tung University, Hsinchu, Taiwan, in 1982, and the M.S. and Ph.D. degrees in computer science from the University of Southern California, Los Angeles, in 1986 and 1988, respectively.

He is currently a Research Staff Member at IBM Thomas J. Watson Research Center, Yorktown Heights, NY. His research interests include computer graphics, user interface design, computer animation, and computer vision.

Dr. Fan is a member of the Association for Computing Machinery.

Gerard Medioni (S'82–M'83) received the Diplome d'Ingenieur Civil from the Ecole Nationale Superieure des Telecommunications, Paris, France, in 1977, and the M.S. and Ph.D. degrees in computer science from the University of Southern California, Los Angeles, in 1980 and 1983, respectively.

He is currently an Assistant Professor in the Departments of Electrical Engineering and Computer Science, University of Southern California. His research interests include computer vision, artificial intelligence, and robotics.

Dr. Medioni is a member of the Association for Computing Machinery and the American Association for the Advancement of Science.

Ramakant Nevatia (S'71–M'74–SM'86), for a photograph and biography, see this issue, p. 1139.

Model-Based Recognition in Robot Vision

ROLAND T. CHIN

Electrical and Computer Engineering Department, University of Wisconsin, Madison, Wisconsin 53706

CHARLES R. DYER

Computer Sciences Department, University of Wisconsin, Madison, Wisconsin 53706

This paper presents a comparative study and survey of model-based object-recognition
algorithms for robot vision. The goal of these algorithms is to recognize the identity,
position, and orientation of randomly oriented industrial parts. In one form this is
commonly referred to as the "bin-picking" problem, in which the parts to be recognized
are presented in a jumbled bin. The paper is organized according to 2-D, $2\frac{1}{2}$-D, and 3-D
object representations, which are used as the basis for the recognition algorithms. Three
central issues common to each category, namely, feature extraction, modeling, and
matching, are examined in detail. An evaluation and comparison of existing industrial
part-recognition systems and algorithms is given, providing insights for progress toward
future robot vision systems.

Categories and Subject Descriptors: I.2.9 [**Artificial Intelligence**]: Robotics—*sensors*;
I.2.10 [**Artificial Intelligence**]: Vision and Scene Understanding—*modeling and
recovery of physical attributes*; I.4.6 [**Image Processing**]: Segmentation; I.4.7 [**Image
Processing**]: Feature Measurement—*invariants*; *size and shape*; *texture*; I.4.8 [**Image
Processing**]: Scene Analysis; I.5.4 [**Pattern Recognition**]: Applications—*computer
vision*

General Terms: Algorithms

Additional Key Words and Phrases: Bin picking, computer vision, 2-D, $2\frac{1}{2}$-D, and 3-D
representations, feature extraction, industrial part recognition, matching, model-based
image understanding, modeling, robot vision

INTRODUCTION

Research and development in computer
vision has increased dramatically over the
last thirty years. Application areas that
have been extensively studied include character recognition, medical diagnosis, target
detection, and remote sensing. Recently,
machine vision for automating the manufacturing process has received considerable
attention with the growing interest in robotics. Although some commercial vision
systems for robotics and industrial auto-

mation do exist, their capabilities are still
very primitive. One reason for this slow
progress is that many manufacturing tasks
require sophisticated visual interpretation,
yet demand low cost and high speed, accuracy, and flexibility. The following deline-
ates some of these requirements:

- *Speed.* The processing speed of acquiring
  and analyzing an image must be comparable to the speed of execution of the
  specific task. Often, this "real-time" rate
  is less than fractions of a second per part.

CONTENTS

- *Accuracy.* The recognition rate of objects in the scene and the accuracy in determining parts' locations and orientations must be high. Although there are instances where engineering solutions can be applied to improve accuracy (e.g., by controlling lighting and positional uncertainty), these solutions may not be realistic in terms of the actual environment in which these tasks must be performed.

- *Flexibility.* The vision system must be flexible enough to accommodate variations in the physical dimensions of multiple copies of a given part, as well as uncertainties in part placement due to individual workstation configurations. Furthermore, many robot vision tasks are distinguished by their performance in dirty and uncontrolled environments.

To be fully effective, future robot vision systems must be able to handle complex industrial parts. This includes recognizing various types of parts and determining their position and orientation in industrial environments. In addition, vision systems must be able to extract and locate salient features of parts in order to establish spatial references for assembly and handling operations and be able to verify the success of these operations.

The performance requirements indicated above are not the only factors distinguishing robot vision from other application areas and general computer vision research. The nature of the domain of objects must also be recognized. Most industrial parts-recognition systems are *model-based systems* in which recognition involves matching the input image with a set of predefined models of parts. The goal of such systems is to precompile a description of each of a known set of industrial parts, then to use these object models to recognize in an image each instance of an object and to specify its position and orientation relative to the viewer. In an industrial environment the following types of constraints and properties that distinguish this problem domain are usually found:

- The number of parts in a given domain is usually small (1–50).

- Parts may be exactly specified, with known tolerances on particular dimensions and features.

- Parts often have distinctive features (e.g., holes and corners), which are commonly found on many different types of parts.

- In scenes containing multiple parts, there are a number of possible configurations (e.g., touching parts, overlapping parts, and parts at arbitrary orientations with respect to one another and the camera).

A growing number of studies have been conducted investigating various approaches to machine recognition of industrial parts. The body of literature generated from this developing field is both vast and scattered. Numerous journal publications have discussed issues involved in industrial vision system design and requirements. A significant number of research activities have been reported on the development of prototype systems for certain specific industrial applications. These studies are concerned with providing pragmatic solutions to current problems in industrial vision. Some of them show the adequacy of image-processing techniques and the availability of technology needs for practical automation systems. Others are concerned with the development of more general parts-recognition algorithms that work in less controlled environments.

While several related survey papers have been published on the topic of robot vision and industrial-parts recognition (see Section 6), this paper presents a broader and more comprehensive approach to this subject. We concentrate on a comparative survey of techniques for model-based recognition of industrial parts. Related topics that are largely or entirely omitted from this paper are (a) industrial visual inspection applications, methodologies, and systems; (b) machine vision applications and research activities in private industry that have not been published; (c) the role of software and hardware implementation and the use of special-purpose optical and digital imaging devices; (d) the use of other sensory data (e.g., tactile data) as additional aids for recognition; and (e) the examination of the economic, social, and strategic issues that justify the use of robot vision.

1. MODEL-BASED OBJECT RECOGNITION

A number of factors limit the competence of current recognition systems for complex industrial parts. One of the major limitations is the low dimensionality in spatial representation and description of parts. Simple objects presented against a high-contrast background with no occlusion are recognized by extracting simple 2-D features, which are matched against 2-D object models. The lack of higher dimensional spatial descriptions (e.g., 3-D volumetric representations) and their associated matching and feature extraction algorithms restrict the system's capabilities to a limited class of objects observed from a few fixed viewpoints. The ability to recognize a wide variety of rigid parts independent of viewpoint demands the ability to extract view-invariant 3-D features and match them with features of 3-D object models. Another problem is the lack of descriptions of surface characteristics of industrial

parts. Without using properties of the surface, many recognition tasks cannot be accomplished by machine vision. It can be concluded that the dimensionality of spatial description and representation is highly dependent on both the particular application and its intended level of accomplishment. Many levels of spatial description (2-D, 3-D, and intermediate levels that fill the gap that exists between images and physical objects) are needed to fulfill various tasks. See, for example, Binford [1982], Brady [1982b], and Tenenbaum et al. [1979] for more discussion of the limitations of current robot vision systems.

Three central issues arise as a consequence of the problems mentioned above: (1) What *features* should be extracted from an image in order to describe physical properties and their spatial relations in a scene adequately? (2) What constitutes an adequate representation of these features and their relationships for characterizing a semantically meaningful class of objects; that is, in what form should features be combined into object *models* such that this description is appropriate for recognizing all objects in the given class? (3) How should the correspondence or *matching* be done between image features and object models in order to recognize the parts in a complex scene?

In this paper we discuss a variety of solutions to these issues. It is convenient to categorize all industrial parts-recognition systems into several classes before focusing on their problems, requirements, limitations, and achievements. The selected cases fall into three categories on the basis of their dimensionality of spatial description. To be more specific, we have grouped the reported studies into three classes: 2-D, $2\frac{1}{2}$-D, and 3-D representations, presented in Sections 3, 4, and 5, respectively. It is natural to organize the studies in this fashion since systems within each class usually make similar assumptions. The grouping is also intended to provide the readers with an easy understanding of the state-of-the-art technology related to industrial parts recognition. Associated with each category are issues related to feature extraction, modeling, and matching, and these are discussed in detail.

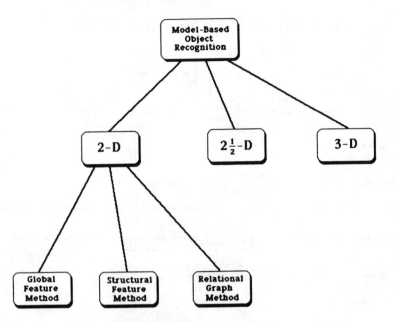

Figure 1. Organization of the survey.

Section 2 discusses the goals of each of these three components. Figure 1 provides a graphical summary of our organization.

3-D spatial descriptions define exact representations in "object space" using an object-centered coordinate system. 3-D representations are viewpoint-independent, volumetric representations that permit computations at an arbitrary viewpoint and to an arbitrary precision of detail.

2-D spatial descriptions are viewer-centered representations in "image space." Each distinct view is represented using, for the most part, shape features derived from a gray-scale or binary image of a prototype object. This class of representation is appropriate when the viewpoint is fixed and only a small number of stable object positions are possible. The 2-D representations are further subdivided into three classes according to their method of object modeling. They are (a) the global feature method, (b) the structural feature method, and (c) the relational graph method. This categorization is discussed in more detail in Section 3.

$2\frac{1}{2}$-D representations have attributes of both 2-D and 3-D representations, using features defined in "surface space." These spatial descriptions are viewer-centered

representations, but depend on local surface properties of the object in each view, for example, range (i.e., depth) and surface orientation.

Many reported studies using the above image representations are worth mentioning, but it is impossible to discuss all of them in detail. These studies are included in the sections under "Other Studies." They are included to provide a more complete annotated bibliography on industrial parts-recognition algorithms.

2. MODELS, FEATURES, AND MATCHING

A parts-recognition system can be broken down into a training phase and a classification phase, as illustrated in Figure 2. The three major components of the system are *feature extraction*, *object modeling*, and *matching*. The sensor and feature extraction components in training are not necessarily the same as those in classification. In this section we specify the general goals of each of these three segments.

Models. The use of models for image understanding has been studied extensively (e.g., see Binford [1982] and Rosenfeld and Davis [1979]). However, most of the models

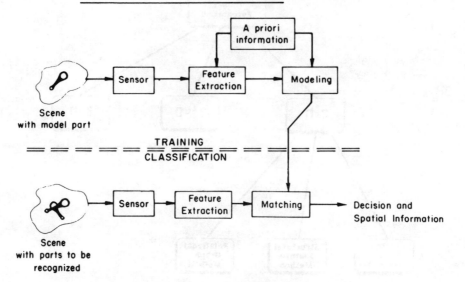

Figure 2. Components of a model-based recognition system.

that have been investigated are relatively simple and do not provide adequate descriptions for recognizing industrial parts in complex scenes. Although many models of regions and images have been developed on the basis of the homogeneity of gray-level properties (e.g., texture and color), they have not been widely used for industrial applications. For this reason, this type of model is not discussed further here.

Models based on geometric properties of an object's visible surfaces or silhouette are commonly used because they describe objects in terms of their constituent shape features. Throughout this paper we focus on alternative methods for representing object models using 2-D, $2\frac{1}{2}$-D, and 3-D shape features.

2-D models have the advantage that they can be automatically constructed from a set of prototype objects, one from each possible viewpoint. (In general, it is nontrivial to automatically construct 3-D representations from a set of 2-D views.) They have the disadvantage that they do not make the full 3-D description of an object explicit—their completeness depends on the complexity of the object and the number and positions of the viewpoints used. In industrial parts-recognition applications, however, it is frequently the case that limited

allowable viewpoints, limited possible stable configurations, and object symmetries substantially reduce the number of distinct views that must be considered.

$2\frac{1}{2}$-D models use viewer-centered descriptions of surfaces instead of boundaries and therefore have the advantage of more accurately representing the complete object and hence improving chances for reliable recognition. Their disadvantages include the additional step of accurately deriving the surface description and the need, as with 2-D methods, for separate viewpoint-specific representations.

3-D models allow the most general and complete descriptions of objects from an unconstrained viewpoint. They can be derived directly from a CAD-like representation and describe the physical volume filled by objects. Of course, this compact description is not directly comparable with 2-D or $2\frac{1}{2}$-D features, which are extracted from an image. Therefore the principle disadvantage is that a more sophisticated 2-D to 3-D correspondence procedure must be defined.

Features. The problem of selecting the geometric features that are the components of the model is integrally related to the problem of model definition. Image features such as edge, corner, line, curve, hole, and boundary curvature define individual feature components of an image. These features and their spatial relations are then combined to generate object descriptions. Because they represent specific higher level primitives that correspond to physically meaningful properties of the scene, features are less sensitive to variations than the original noisy gray-level values. Usually, the decision of what features to use is rather subjective and application specific.

The features important for industrial-image analysis are most often boundaries and geometric measurements derived from boundaries. These features can be roughly categorized into three types: global, local, and relational features. Examples of *global features* are perimeter, centroid, distance of contour points from the centroid, curvature, area, and moments of inertia. Examples of *local features* include line segment, arc segment with constant curvature, and corner, defining pieces of an object's boundary. Examples of *relational features* include a variety of distance and relative orientation measurements interrelating substructures and regions of an object.

Most existing industrial-vision systems and algorithms extract features from industrial objects against a high-contrast background with controlled lighting to eliminate shadows, highlights, and noisy backgrounds. The process of feature extraction usually begins by generating a binary image from the original gray-scale image by choosing an appropriate threshold, or simply by using a sensor that produces binary images. The use of a binary representation reduces the complexity of data that must be handled, but it places a serious limitation on the flexibility and capabilities of the system. After thresholding, 2-D features are extracted from the binary image. Thus, in these systems features are simple functions of a part's silhouette. A tutorial on binary image processing for robot-vision applications is given in Kitchin and Pugh [1983].

Most feature-extraction algorithms used in these binary imaging systems are simple outline-tracing algorithms. They detect boundaries of simple planar objects but usually fail to detect low-contrast surface boundaries. Another limitation is that they attempt to deal with 3-D physical objects in terms of 2-D features. This simplification might meet the cost requirement of many industrial applications, but it lacks the capability and flexibility required by many other industrial-vision tasks. Finally, current systems seldom have representations of physical surface properties such as surface reflectance and surface orientation (i.e., $2\frac{1}{2}$-D representations). Such information is lost in reducing the gray-scale image to a binary image or to a piecewise constant image. Without using these properties of the object's surface, many important industrial-vision tasks that are easy for people to perform will remain beyond the competence of computer-vision systems.

A few current vision systems are capable of extracting useful information from images of complex industrial parts with considerable noise caused by dirt and unfavorable lighting conditions. These systems process gray-scale images with reasonable dynamic range. The most important drawback of gray-scale image processing is the slow processing rate in extracting features. Most of these systems employ sophisticated feature-extraction methods, but their matching procedures are still based on 2-D models.

Matching. Given a set of models that describes all aspects of all parts to be recognized, the process of model-based recognition consists of matching features extracted from a given input image with those of the models. The general problem of matching may be regarded as finding a set of features in the given image that approximately matches one model's features. Some methods rely on total image matching using cross-correlation types of measures applied to image intensities or coefficients of some mathematical expansion (e.g., orthogonal expansion). They can be formulated as global optimization problems to achieve great reliability, but are computationally too expensive. Moreover, the image is generally noisy, and parts within the image will be occluded and located at random positions and orientations.

Consequently, matching algorithms of this type has little value in industrial parts-recognition systems.

Matching techniques using 2-D global, local, or relational features, or a combination of these features, provide a way to recognize and locate a part on the basis of a few key features. Matching using features becomes a model-driven process in which model features control the matching process. Several model-driven matching techniques have been developed. Most are invariant to translation and rotation, and are not too sensitive to noise and image distortion. The choice of matching process is highly dependent on the type of model used for object representation. Models using global features are usually associated with statistical pattern-recognition schemes. Models based on local features are usually associated with syntactic matching methods, and models using a combination of local and relational features are usually associated with graph-matching techniques.

Matching using $2\frac{1}{2}$-D models requires procedures that must compare sets of planar or curved surface patches. This can be done either directly by finding best-fitting regions between the image and models, or indirectly by comparing features derived from these surfaces. Matching with 3-D models requires the most extensive processing in order to make explicit the 2-D projection of the model that best matches the image features.

3. 2-D IMAGE REPRESENTATIONS

In this section we review recognition algorithms that are based on 2-D image representations. Each 3-D part is modeled by a set of one or more distinct views. This set of 2-D views can be determined either by training the system with the part in each of its possible stable positions or by computing these positions directly from a CAD description. Figure 3 shows a set of stable orientations of a part and their corresponding models [Lieberman 1979]. These viewer-centered representations treat each view independently, reducing the problem to 2-D by using 2-D image features and

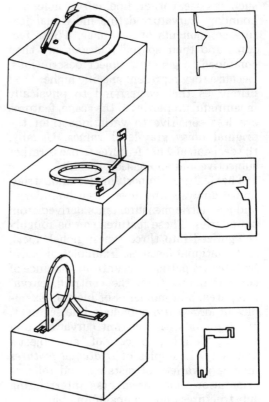

Figure 3. A set of stable orientations for a part and the corresponding silhouettes calculated for each of the orientations when viewed from directly overhead. (From Lieberman [1979].)

their relations as primitives. For each viewpoint, a sufficient set of image-space-derived features and relations are combined for modeling the object.

We classify 2-D object-recognition methods into three classes based on the kinds of models and matching algorithms they employ. The first type of method uses global features of an object's size and shape (e.g., perimeter and area) organized in geometric property lists. This class of method is referred to as the *global feature method*.

The second type of method uses local features that describe more complex properties of the object, usually in terms of line and curve segments defining the object's boundary. Typically, the features are organized as a highly structured and abstracted representation. This class of

Table 1. The Three Methods Based on 2-D Image Representations

Method	Feature	Model	Matching
Global feature	Global scalar	Feature vector (unordered)	Statistical pattern recognition
Structural feature	Local	Ordered string of features or abstract description of feature strings	Syntactical or verification of string descriptions
Relational graph	Local and relational	Relational graph	Graph searching

method is referred to as the *structural feature method*.

The third type uses local and relational features which are organized in a graph. Nodes describe local features and arcs have associated properties that describe the relationship between the pairs of features that they connect. This type is referred to as the *relational graph method*.

The three types of object-recognition methods are summarized in Table 1. All three components (feature, models, and matching) of each type have distinctly different characteristics. Their strengths and weaknesses are discussed in detail in the following.

Global Feature Method. Global features such as area and perimeter are relatively easy to extract from a single image. In some systems the feature set also includes position and orientation descriptors, such as center of gravity, and moments of inertia, which provide useful information for part manipulation. Models using global features are feature lists, and the order of features in the feature list is unimportant. This type of method is usually associated with the classical feature-space classification scheme. The features of a part may be thought of as points in n-dimensional feature space, where n is the number of global feature measurements. The recognition of an unknown part with an n-dimensional feature vector involves statistical pattern-recognition methods where the feature vector is compared with each of the model feature vectors. Both parallel (e.g., the Bayes classifier) and hierarchical/sequential decision rules (e.g., the decision-tree classifier) can be used. The computational expense associated with the parallel classification increases steeply with dimension, but optimal results are achievable. There are numerous advantages to hierarchical

classification. Most important, the decision procedure can be designed to be both inexpensive and effective, but the overall accuracy is not so great as with the parallel decision rules.

Structural Feature Method. Models can be constructed using abstracted and precise geometric representations such as arcs, lines, and corners. These features are local in nature, each describing a portion of the object. They are organized in a highly structured manner, such as an ordered list or a sequence of equations. The ordering of features in this type of method is usually related to the object's boundary in such a way that following the entire feature list sequentially is equivalent to tracing the boundary of the object. Recognition (matching) uses a hypothesis-verification procedure. The structured local features of the model are used to predict where objects are located in the scene. Then, features of the hypothesized object are measured, on the basis of the prediction hypothesized by the model, in order to verify and fine-tune the match. In addition, this type of method allows the use of syntactic pattern-recognition approaches, in which local features are transformed into primitives which are organized into strings (sentences) by some highly structured grammatical rules. Matching is performed by parsing.

Relational Graph Method. Objects can be represented structurally by graphs. In this method, geometrical relations between local features (e.g., corner and line) are of particular interest. The relational structure can be represented by a graph in which each node represents a local feature and is labeled with a list of properties (e.g., size) for that feature. Arcs represent relational features linking pairs of nodes and are labeled with lists of relation values (e.g., distance and adjacency). Recognition of the object becomes a graph-matching process. This type of method can be used to handle overlapping parts where a partially visible part corresponds to a subgraph. The matching reduces to one of finding the subgraph.

The remainder of this section covers examples of each of these three methods in detail.

3.1 Examples of Global Feature Methods

The predominant method to date, especially in commercial systems, uses a set of 2-D, global shape features describing each possible stable object view. Recognition is achieved by directly comparing features of an object with those of the model. This type of model is compact and facilitates fast matching operations because of the limited number and size of the feature vectors extracted from a given image.

The major limitations of this type of model are (1) each possible 2-D view of an object must be described by a separate model; (2) all objects in an image must be extracted by a single predefined threshold (hence lighting, shadows, and highlights must be controlled); and (3) objects may not touch or overlap one another, nor may objects have significant defects. (A defective object that is not sufficiently similar to any model can be recognized as a reject, but this may not be adequate in many applications.)

3.1.1 Example 1: A System Based on Connected Components

Model. The SRI Vision Module [Gleason and Agin 1979] is the prototypical system of the global feature method. The user interactively selects a set of global features which are used to construct an object model as a feature vector. This process is an example of the "training by showing" method of modeling. For each distinct viewpoint of each object modeled, a sample prototype is used to compute the values of each feature selected. The selection of which features are sufficient to discriminate adequately among objects is determined by trial and error. Thus, if a new object is introduced

later into the system, the complete process of feature selection must be repeated in order to discriminate properly among all of the possible objects in a scene.

Features. Each connected component in the input binary image is extracted so that each of these regions can be analyzed independently. For each connected component a number of gross scalar shape descriptors are computed (such as number of holes, area, perimeter, boundary chain code, compactness, number of corners, and moments of inertia). All of these features can be computed in a single pass through the image, either from the binary image representation or from the image's run-length encoded representation (which is more compact).

Matching. Matching uses a decision-tree method based on the list of global features associated with each model [Agin and Duda 1975]. The tree is automatically constructed from the models as follows. (1) The feature values with the largest separation for a given feature and pair of object models are found, and this feature is used to define the root node of the tree. That is, a threshold is selected for this feature that distinguishes between these two models. (2) Two children of the root node are constructed such that all models that have a feature value less than or equal to the threshold are associated with the left child; the right child is assigned all models with a feature value greater than the threshold. (3) This procedure is repeated recursively, dividing a set of model candidates associated with a node into two disjoint subsets associated with its two children. A terminal node in the tree is one that contains a single model. Figure 4 illustrates such a decision tree.

The decision-tree method has the primary advantage of speed, but it also has the disadvantage of not allowing similar models to be explicitly compared with a given list of image features.

Alternatively, the best matching model to a given list of global features extracted from an object in an image is computed using statistical pattern-recognition schemes (e.g., a nearest-neighbor classifier)

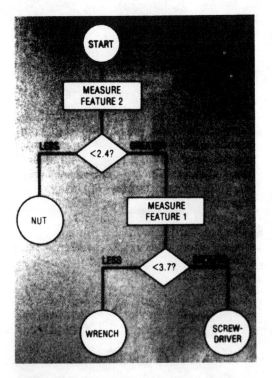

Figure 4. A decision tree classifier. (From Agin [1980]; © IEEE 1980.)

in feature space, as illustrated in Figure 5. That is, if n features are used to describe all models, then each model is represented by a point in n-dimensional feature space. Given a new feature list extracted from an image, the component is recognized as being an instance of the model that is closest in feature space.

3.1.2 Example 2: Using Global Features to Identify Grasp Points

Kelley et al. [1982] have developed a simple system for rapidly determining grasp points for a robot arm which must remove randomly oriented cylindrical workpieces piled in a bin. Thus all parts are known to be of the same type, and only their positions and orientations are unknown. In this case several simplifications of the SRI Vision Module approach are possible. First, a shrinking operator is applied to reduce the regions in the original binary image into small, connected components of pixels. These components are then sorted in order by size

(i.e., number of pixels), and the largest component is selected as the grasp-point location for the gripper. Position and orientation features of the selected region (e.g., the centroid and axes of minimum and maximum moments of inertia through the centroid) are computed to determine the location and orientation of the gripper relative to the image. An additional feature, the ratio of eigenvalues of axes of minimum and maximum moments of inertia, is also computed to determine the inclination of the cylinder with respect to the image plane, so as to determine the appropriate opening of the gripper's fingers. The "i-bot" system is based on this technique [Zuech and Ray 1983]. This system computes the locations and orientations of a maximum of three workpieces in a bin in 2 seconds.

3.1.3 Other Studies

Several systems based on the SRI Vision Module have been developed commercially, including Machine Intelligence Corporation's VS-100 system, Automatix's Autovision system, Unimation's Univision I, Control Automation's V-1000, Intelledex V-100 Robot Vision System, and Octek's Robot Vision Module. The VS-100 system (and the related system for Puma robots, Univision I) accepts images up to 256 × 256 and thresholds them at a user-specified gray level. Up to 12 objects can be in an image and up to 13 features can be used to model each part. Recognition times of from 250 milliseconds (ms) (1 feature) to 850 ms (11 features) per object are typical [Rosen and Gleason 1981]. The Autovision 4 system processes images up to 512 × 256, and recognition performance is listed at over 10 parts per second for simple parts [Villers 1983].

Birk et al. [1981] model objects by a set of coarse shape features for each possible viewpoint. For a given viewing position, the thresholded object is overlaid with a 3 × 3 grid (each grid square's size is selected by the user), centered at the object's centroid and oriented with respect to the minimum moment of inertia. A count of the number of above threshold pixels in each grid square is used to describe the object.

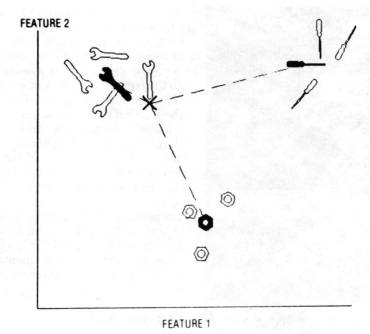

FEATURE 1

Figure 5. A nearest neighbor classifier. (From Agin [1980]; © IEEE 1980.)

CONSIGHT-I [Holland et al. 1979] avoids the problem of threshold selection for object detection by employing a pair of line light sources and a line camera focused at the same place across a moving conveyor belt of parts. Part boundaries are detected as discontinuities in the light line, as shown in Figure 6. Features, such as centroid and area, are computed for each object as it passes through the line of light.

Fourier descriptors [Zahn and Roskiew 1972] have been suggested as shape descriptors for industrial-parts recognition by Persoon and Fu [1977]. A finite number of harmonics of the Fourier descriptors are computed from the part boundary and compared with a set of reference Fourier descriptors. A minimum-distance classification rule is used for the recognition of various classes of parts.

In gray-scale image processing the first step is usually to segment the image to find regions of fairly uniform intensity. This greatly increases the degree of organization for generating higher level descriptions such as shape and size. Perkins [1980] has developed a region-segmentation method for industrial parts using edges. This

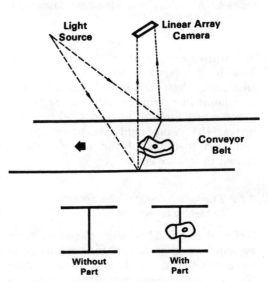

Figure 6. Basic lighting principle of the CONSIGHT-1 system and the computer's view of a part. (From Holland et al. [1979].)

method uses an expansion–contraction technique in which the edge regions are first expanded (to close gaps) and then contracted after the separate uniform regions have been identified. The process

436

is performed iteratively to preserve small segments.

An industrial-vision system, S.A.M., has been developed by Tropf et al. [1982], using binary image processing to extract global scalar features for inspection and parts recognition. The system is now commercially available for flexible manufacturing assembly systems [Brune and Bitter 1983]. A development system for machine vision based on the Machine Intelligence Corp. VS-100 has been developed and marketed [Chen and Milgram 1982]. The performance of the above vision system has also been evaluated by Rosen and Gleason [1981].

An experimental system has been developed by Page and Pugh [1981] to manipulate engineering parts from random orientation. Simple global scalar features are used to identify gripper locations. Typical recognition times are in the range 0.5–3 seconds.

3.2 Examples of Structural Feature Methods

The system described in the previous section included global shape and size features, which consisted, for the most part, of simple integral or real-valued descriptors. In this section we describe methods that use more complex features, for the most part structural descriptions of object boundaries.

3.2.1 Example 1: Line and Arc Boundary Segment Descriptions

Model. Perkins [1978] constructs 2-D models from boundary segments, called concurves, constructed from line segments and arcs that are extracted from training images of each stable view of each part. The list of concurves comprises a structural approach to describing objects that is not as sensitive to noise as most global features.

The model uses an object-centered coordinate system in which the origin is defined by either (a) the center of area of the largest closed concurve or (b) the center of a small closed concurve if it is sufficiently close to the center of the largest closed concurve. The axes are defined in terms of the direction of the least moment of inertia of the largest concurve.

For each concurve in the model a property list is computed, including type (circle, arc, line segment, complex curve, etc.), total length or radius of arcs, magnitude of total angular change, number of straight lines, number of arcs, bending energy, and compactness. In addition, rotational symmetries of the concurve and the complete object are computed as additional descriptors. Rotational symmetry is computed using a correlation-like technique which determines whether a sufficient percentage of concurve "multisectors" intersects the rotated concurve. Multisectors are short line segments that are placed at equal intervals along the concurve and at orientations perpendicular to the tangent directions at these points.

Features. Concurve features are used in order to represent the 2-D shape of a part as a line drawing of its boundary. This representation is compact and, because the boundary is smoothed before the concurves are computed, relatively insensitive to noise in the imaging system and environment. First, a gray-scale image is transformed into an edge map using the Hueckel edge operator [Hueckel 1971]. Next, edge points are thinned and connected together into long chains by using knowledge of proximity, directional continuity, and gray-scale continuity.

Finally, the chains are transformed into a group of concurves. A concurve is defined as an ordered list of shape descriptions which are generated by fitting a segment of the chain data to straight lines, or circular arcs, or a combination of both. This curve-fitting step is quite similar to the one used by Shirai [1975] in his feature-extraction algorithm. The fitting procedure first examines the curvature of the chain data (i.e., connected edge points). Next, it looks for abrupt changes in curvature and picks out end points (critical points) to set the bounds of each grouping. The chain of edge points in each group is fitted with a circular arc or straight line using Newton's method. An additional step that verifies and corrects for a poor fit is included. Figure 7 shows

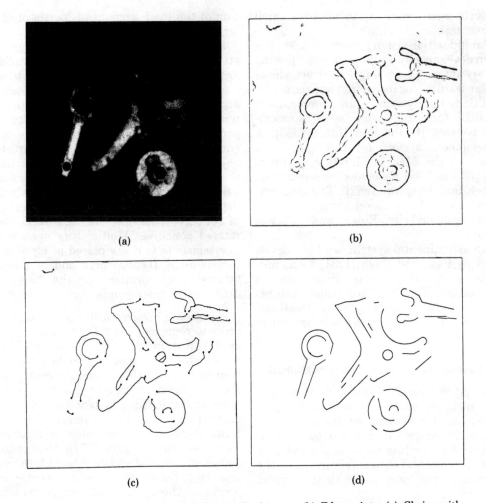

Figure 7. Concurve representation. (a) Digitized image. (b) Edge points. (c) Chains with critical points at the ends of open chains. (d) Concurves. (From Perkins [1978]; © IEEE 1978.)

the various stages of extracting concurves from a sample image.

Matching. The matching process is performed in three steps. First, scalar measurements (length, area, etc.) extracted from the model and image concurves are compared. The comparison is an exhaustive matching procedure applied to all possible pairings between the model concurves and the image concurves, and the results, given in terms of likelihood measures, are arranged in an ordered list. Second, one model concurve is matched against one image concurve to determine a tentative transformation (x, y, θ) from model to image coordinates. The pair with the highest likelihood is used first; successive pairs are compared until a tentative transformation is found. In cases in which the model concurve is symmetric, two matching pairs are required to determine the transformation. Third, a global check of the tentative transformation is performed by matching the complete model with the image. In this step a set of model multisectors is first transformed using the tentative transformation determined in the previous step. The transformed multisectors of the model are then superimposed on the image for a final comparison by intersecting each multisector with the image concurves. This matching process is shown to be successful with closed concurves and has been tested with images containing partially overlapping parts.

3.2.2 Example 2: Hierarchical Boundary Segment Models

Model. In the system developed by Shirai [1978], object models are organized as a hierarchy of features consisting of main and secondary features. These features are edges represented by a description of their curvature in terms of an equation and endpoints. The main feature is the most obvious one found in an object, and it is used to imply the presence of the object during the initial stage of the search. Successful detection of the main feature generates clues for verifying the recognition. Secondary features are details of the object. These are chosen on the basis of the ease with which they may be found in a scene. For recognizing a cup, for example, the main feature can be a pair of vertical edges corresponding to the sides of a cup, and the secondary features can be other detail contours connected to the sides.

Features. The features used by Shirai are similar to those used by Perkins, consisting of long, connected edge segments that describe pieces of an object's boundary. The system first extracts edges using a conventional gradient operator. The extracted edges are classified into three types according to their intensity profiles. Next, an edge kernel is located by searching for a set of edge points of the same type which have similar gradient directions. A tracking algorithm is applied in both directions of the kernel to find a smoothly curved edge and its endpoints. Several passes are applied to locate all sets of smoothly connected edges in the scene. Finally, straight lines and elliptic curves are fit to each segment, and segments are merged together, if possible.

Matching. Recognition involves three steps. First, the main feature is located to get clues for the object. Next, a secondary feature is searched for to verify the main feature and to determine the region occu-

pied by the object. Finally, the other lines of the object are located to confirm the recognition.

3.2.3 Example 3: Accumulating Local Evidence by Clustering Pairs of Image and Model Boundary Segments

Model. Stockman et al. [1982] have proposed a method in which models of 2-D objects are defined by organizing (1) real vectors describing boundary segments and (2) abstract vectors linking primitive features (e.g., a vector connecting two holes) into a set. The set is in an object-centered coordinate system and is defined by modeling rules (e.g., size of the object, known a priori) to permit only certain combinations of features to be linked. The resulting model is a line-drawing version of the object, plus additional abstract vectors to allow increased precision and control over the matching process.

Features. Directed edge elements (vectors) are used as one type of primary feature containing directional, positional, and size information. First, point features (i.e., the tip and tail of a vector) are extracted, and then vectors are formed from suitable point pairs. Straight edge detectors, curved edge detectors, circle detectors, and intersection detectors are employed to define vectors between point pairs. Holes are detected by a set of circular masks, and curves and intersections are detected by linking edges together. Details of the feature-extraction procedure are presented in Stockman [1980].

Matching. Matching is done using a clustering procedure. The procedure matches all possible pairs of image and model features on the basis of local evidence. The matching in cluster space consists of points, each representing a match of an image feature to a model feature. A cluster of match points in this space is a good indication that many image features are matched to corresponding model features. In order to handle randomly placed objects, a rotation, scaling, and translation transformation is derived to extract parameters from all possible pairs of features.

Clustering is then performed in the space of all possible transformation parameter sets. This method is believed to be more robust because the clustering procedure integrates all local information before any recognition decision is made. A set of simulated carburetor covers and T-hinges are used to demonstrate the method. The reported results indicate that this method works well with isolated objects, but the success rate for recognizing overlapping parts is low.

3.2.4 Other Studies

Hattich [1982] uses contour elements, described in terms of straight-line segments, as the global structural features. Matching is done by iteratively constructing the model contour from image data.

Experiments on occluded part recognition have been performed by Turney et al. [1985] using edges as the features. Recognition is based on template matching between the model edge template and the edge image in the generalized Hough transform space [Ballard 1981a]. This algorithm is shown to be more efficient than direct template matching. Dessimoz [1978a, 1978b] recognizes overlapping parts by first mapping the objects' boundaries into a set of curves and then matching the curves with those in the model. Tropf [1980, 1981] has developed a recognition system for overlapping workpieces using corner and line primitives and semantic labeling. Structural knowledge of workpieces is used to construct models. Recognition uses heuristic search to find the best match based on a similarity measure. Ayache [1983] uses binary images and polygonal approximations to each connected component. Models are automatically constructed by analyzing a prototype part in its different stable positions. The matching is done first by generating a hypothesis of the object location and then by matching model segments to scene segments. The model location is sequentially adjusted by evaluating each match until the best match is found.

Bhanu has developed a hierarchical relaxation labeling technique for shape matching and has performed experiments using 2-D occluded industrial parts [Bhanu 1983; Bhanu and Faugeras 1984]. Two-dimensional shapes are used as the global structural features, and they are represented by a polygonal approximation. The technique involves the maximization of an evaluation function which is based on the ambiguity and inconsistency of classification. Umetani and Taguchi [1979] use "general shapes," defined as artificial and nonartificial shapes, to study the properties and procedures for complex shape discrimination. Feature properties based on vertices, symmetry, complexity, compactness, and concavity have been investigated. These features are chosen on the basis of some psychological experiments, and a procedure to discriminate random shapes has been proposed [Umetani and Taguchi 1982].

Vamos [1977] has proposed the use of syntactic pattern recognition for modeling machine parts from picture primitives: namely, straight line, arc, node, and undefined. A set of syntax rules is used to characterize the structural relationships of these strings of primitives describing the part. The matching process is a syntax analysis or parsing procedure involving the use of similarity measures between two grammar strings or two graphs. Jakubowski has conducted a similar study using straight lines or curves as primitives to model machine part shapes and to generate part contours [Jakubowski 1982; Jakubowski and Kasprzak 1977].

Takeyasu et al. [1977] and Kashioka et al. [1977] have developed an assembly system for vacuum cleaners using integrated visual and tactile sensory feedback. First, global scalar features of various parts of the vacuum cleaner are used to locate the cleaner. Then, structural features, such as circles and arcs, are used in a template-matching step for the assembly operation.

Foith et al. [1981] describe an object boundary with respect to the centroid of the "dominant blob" defining the 2-D binary object. Circles of prespecified radii are centered on the centroid, their intersections with the object boundary are marked, and line segments are then drawn between these intersections and the centroid. The sequence of angles between successive line segments is used as a rotation-invariant model of the object boundary.

3.3 Examples of Relational Graph Methods

This class of methods is based on a graph representation of a part. The graph is constructed in terms of locally detectable primitive features and the geometric relations between pairs of these features. This class of method is thus based on local rather than global features and has the following advantages: (a) local features may be cheaper to compute because they are simpler and can be selectively (sequentially) detected; (b) models are less sensitive to minor differences in instances of a given object type; (c) if a few local features are missing (owing to noise or occlusion), it may still be possible to recognize the object on the basis of the remaining features associated with the model; and (d) since a few types of local features are often sufficient to describe a large number of complex objects, it is possible to specify only a few types of local feature detectors which are applied to the image.

A disadvantage with this type of method is the fact that a large number of features must be detected and grouped together to recognize an object. Thus the matching algorithm used with these models must be more complex and may be somewhat slower than the matching algorithms used with the previous methods.

3.3.1 Example 1: A Two-Level Model of Coarse and Fine Features

Model. Yachida and Tsuji [1977] use a simple kind of feature graph representation plus a two-level model (for coarse-to-fine processing) to speed the search process. Each object is described by a set of models, one for each possible viewpoint. Each model contains a coarse representation of the object using global features, such as area and elongatedness, plus a description of the outer boundary (in polar coordinates). Each component extracted from an image is compared with each coarse model to determine whether it is sufficiently similar to warrant further comparison. Object boundaries are compared by using cross-correlation as the measure of shape match.

The fine level of representation of each model is based on a higher resolution image and consists of a list of features such as outer boundary, holes, edges, and texture. Associated with each feature is an attribute list, location (relative to the object's centroid), and the expected likelihood that the feature can be extracted reliably. Features are ordered in the model by their reliability value.

Features. The feature-extraction process in this system is divided into several stages by using the idea of "planning"; that is, knowledge of the structure of an object guides the feature-extraction module in a top-down manner. Simple features are detected first in a coarse resolution image, and then more complex features are sought on the basis of the locations of the coarse features. Industrial parts used for demonstration are parts of a gasoline engine. In the preprocessing stage, a low-resolution version of the image is analyzed and outlines of objects are detected by thresholding. Each outline is then analyzed separately, using a high-resolution image of the region of interest to extract a finer outline of the object. By employing the method in Chow and Kaneko [1972], local histogramming and dynamic thresholding based on 11×11 windows are used in this step. Next, the object's gross properties, such as size, thinness ratio, and shape, are computed. This coarse description of the object is used to select candidate models for matching and to guide the extraction of finer features for final recognition. There are four features extracted in the fine-resolution processing stage, and they include circle, line, texture, and small hole. Each feature is extracted from a search region around the expected location in the gray-scale image. The circle detector uses thresholding as in the preprocessing step; the line finder, using dynamic programming, searches for the optimum sequence of edge points in the region that maximizes a measure of goodness; the texture detector measures edge strength per unit area and average edge direction; the small-hole detector uses neighbor merging to locate circular objects.

Matching. The matching process examines the current information obtained from the scene and the model graphs of objects to propose the next matching step. The model relates features at a coarse resolution with more detailed features at a fine resolution, enabling the matching to be performed using simple features as cues. Given a tentative match between an image component and an object model based on the coarse model features, the fine model features are then successively compared. The object boundary matched at the coarse level determines a tentative match angle of rotation. For a given feature extracted from the image, a measure of the dissimilarity between it and each of the model features is computed. A cumulative dissimilarity measure is kept for each active model. When a model's dissimilarity exceeds a threshold, the model is rejected as a possible match. After the current feature has been compared with each of the remaining candidate models, a next-feature proposer analyzes the features described in these candidate models and proposes the most promising feature among them as the one to be examined next for recognizing the input object.

3.3.2 Example 2: Corner and Hole Relational Models

Model. Chen et al. [1980] estimate the position and orientation of workpieces using the 3-D locations of at least three noncollinear feature points. The location of features is computed using trigonometric relations between corresponding features from two stereo views of the workpiece. The model is in the form of a local feature graph. Each node is a (feature-type, position) pair, and arcs connect pairs of nodes when an edge connects the pair of features on the part. Feature types are corners and small holes. Feature position is specified using an object-centered coordinate system.

Features. Local image features include small holes and corners. Corner and small hole detection is based on diameter-limited

gradient direction histograms [Birk et al. 1979] in which intensity variations in several directions and various heuristic thresholds are examined. Detected features from the image are evaluated to eliminate redundant features. The resultant corner points are fine-tuned for accuracy by fitting a pair of lines in an 11 × 11 window. The intersection of the two lines yields the final corner location. Finally, the interfeature distances between every pair of features are computed. Workpiece examples used in the experiments include simple planar industrial parts and 3-D block objects.

Matching. The matching is carried out by a sequential pairwise comparison algorithm in which a feature point is matched in turn to all model feature points of the same type. The matching process starts with the selection of the feature point that has the highest confidence. The remaining feature points are then matched with all model points. In this step feature type, interfeature distance, and edge information are used as matching criteria, and redundant matched points are deleted. If enough feature points are successfully matched with the model points, and a transformation test, used to eliminate problems due to symmetry, is passed, a match is considered to be found. Finally, the position and orientation of the workpiece are computed from the correspondence between workpiece and model features.

3.3.3 Example 3: Combining Model Graphs Based on Distinctive Focus Features

Model. Bolles and Cain [1982] have developed a sophisticated modeling system for 2-D objects called the local-feature-focus method. Two types of local features are used: corners and regions. An object model consists of three parts. The first is a polygonal approximation of the object's borders. The second is a list of local features, where each is specified by a unique name, its type, position, and orientation relative to the object's centroid, and rotational symmetries about the centroid. Position and orientation values also have associated allowable tolerances. Third, for each distinct feature type, an unambiguous detector uses neighbor merging to locate circular objects.

Matching. The matching process examines the current information obtained from the scene and the model graphs of objects to propose the next matching step. The model relates features at a coarse resolution with more detailed features at a fine resolution, enabling the matching to be performed using simple features as cues. Given a tentative match between an image component and an object model based on the coarse model features, the fine model features are then successively compared. The object boundary matched at the coarse level determines a tentative match angle of rotation. For a given feature extracted from the image, a measure of the dissimilarity between it and each of the model features is computed. A cumulative dissimilarity measure is kept for each active model. When a model's dissimilarity exceeds a threshold, the model is rejected as a possible match. After the current feature has been compared with each of the remaining candidate models, a next-feature proposer analyzes the features described in these candidate models and proposes the most promising feature among them as the one to be examined next for recognizing the input object.

3.3.2 Example 2: Corner and Hole Relational Models

Model. Chen et al. [1980] estimate the position and orientation of workpieces using the 3-D locations of at least three noncollinear feature points. The location of features is computed using trigonometric relations between corresponding features from two stereo views of the workpiece. The model is in the form of a local feature graph. Each node is a (feature-type, position) pair, and arcs connect pairs of nodes when an edge connects the pair of features on the part. Feature types are corners and small holes. Feature position is specified using an object-centered coordinate system.

Features. Local image features include small holes and corners. Corner and small hole detection is based on diameter-limited gradient direction histograms [Birk et al. 1979] in which intensity variations in several directions and various heuristic thresholds are examined. Detected features from the image are evaluated to eliminate redundant features. The resultant corner points are fine-tuned for accuracy by fitting a pair of lines in an 11×11 window. The intersection of the two lines yields the final corner location. Finally, the interfeature distances between every pair of features are computed. Workpiece examples used in the experiments include simple planar industrial parts and 3-D block objects.

Matching. The matching is carried out by a sequential pairwise comparison algorithm in which a feature point is matched in turn to all model feature points of the same type. The matching process starts with the selection of the feature point that has the highest confidence. The remaining feature points are then matched with all model points. In this step feature type, interfeature distance, and edge information are used as matching criteria, and redundant matched points are deleted. If enough feature points are successfully matched with the model points, and a transformation test, used to eliminate problems due to symmetry, is passed, a match is considered to be found. Finally, the position and orientation of the workpiece are computed from the correspondence between workpiece and model features.

3.3.3 Example 3: Combining Model Graphs Based on Distinctive Focus Features

Model. Bolles and Cain [1982] have developed a sophisticated modeling system for 2-D objects called the local-feature-focus method. Two types of local features are used: corners and regions. An object model consists of three parts. The first is a polygonal approximation of the object's borders. The second is a list of local features, where each is specified by a unique name, its type, position, and orientation relative to the object's centroid, and rotational symmetries about the centroid. Position and orientation values also have associated allowable tolerances. Third, for each distinct feature type, an unambiguous

443

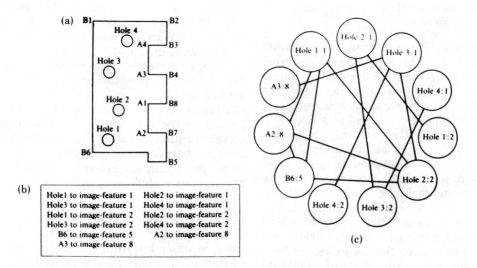

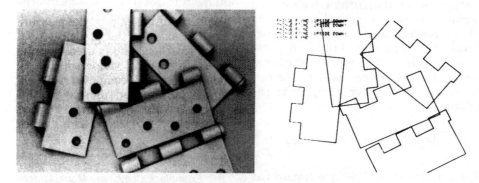

Figure 9. (a) Definitions of the model features of the hinge. (b) List of model-feature-to-image-feature assignments. (c) Graph of pairwise-consistent assignments. Each node represents a possible assignment of a model feature to an image feature. Two nodes are connected if the two assignments they represent are mutually consistent. (From Bolles and Cain [1982].)

Figure 10. Image of five hinges and the recognition result. (From Bolles and Cain [1982].)

forms clusters of them to hypothesize part occurrences, and finally performs template matches to verify these hypotheses.

After locating all the features found in the image, the system selects one feature (the focus feature) around which it tries to find a cluster of consistent secondary features. If this attempt fails to lead to a hypothesis, the system seeks another potential focus feature for a new attempt. As it finds matching features, it builds a list of possible model-feature-to-image-feature assignments. This list is transformed into a graph by creating a node for each assignment pair and adding an arc between pairs

of nodes referencing the same model; Figure 9 shows the possible assignments and the resulting graph. The result from the first stage of the matching algorithm is used to hypothesize an object. At the final stage, two tests are used to verify the hypotheses by looking at other object features and checking the boundary of the hypothesized object. Figure 10 shows an example.

3.3.4 Example 4: Template Feature Relations

Models. An automatic system for transistor wire bonding has been implemented by Kashioka et al. [1976]. The model

444

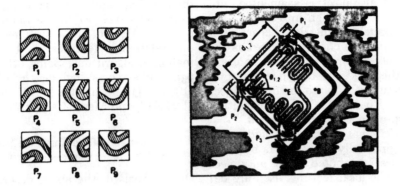

Figure 11. Nine corner templates and the recognition of the circuit position by evaluating relations between pairs of matched templates. (From Kashioka et al. [1976]; © IEEE 1976.)

consists of three sets of three 12 × 12 binary templates, which are selected by the user from three different orientations of a given prototype chip. For each triple of patterns in a set, an associated distance and direction (relative to the image's x axis) pair is computed from the same binary image of the chip used to define the templates. Chips are assumed to be of a fixed size (camera position above the table is fixed); orientation of a chip is fixed with a tolerance of up to 15 degrees in either direction. It was empirically determined that a triple of templates is a reasonable model for rotations of up to 7 degrees from the normal orientation. Therefore, in order to meet system-orientation specifications, three sets of templates are selected by the user with the prototype chip positioned at orientations −10, 0, and 10 degrees from the normal orientation.

Features. In most of the recognition systems for IC alignment and bonding, multiple template-matching procedures are used. Features used for template matching are distinct patterns such as corners and bonding pads. Relational features, such as the distance and angle between pairs of successfully matched templates, are also used. In most cases these features are extracted by thresholding. The Hitachi transistor wire-bonding system is a typical example of such systems.

Matching. In the multiple template matching of Kashioka et al. [1976], a set of characteristic 12 × 12 binary templates is used. The process searches a 160 × 120 image for the local region which best matches the first template. It then searches for the best match to a second template. From these positions, a distance and a direction angle are computed and compared with the values predetermined from the geometry of the chip. If the measurements are not close to the predefined values, a third local template is used, and measurements are again computed. Locations of bonding pads are computed using the measurements obtained from the multiple local template-matching. Figure 11 shows a set of templates and the matching process.

3.3.5 Other Studies

The SIGHT-I system locates integrated circuit chips by using a set of local templates [Baird 1978]. This model consists of the specification of the possible relative positions of the four corners of a chip. A set of four 4 × 4 templates is used to evaluate the probability that a corner is present at a given position. A coarse processing stage is applied to the gray-scale image before the relational template-matching step. In this step the approximate orientation of the chip is determined by analyzing the edge-orientation histogram to find the most prominent edge orientation. This enables the matching stage to search for corners in known orientations.

Cheng and Huang [1982] have developed a method for recognizing curvilinear objects by matching relational structures. The boundary of an object is segmented into curve segments and then into chords. Attributes (parallel, symmetric, adjacent, etc.) associated with the chords are used as the nodes in the relational structure representation of the object. Matching is based on a star structure representation of the object [Cheng and Huang 1981]. The recognition of overlapping tools has been shown.

Segen [1983] has developed a method for recognizing partially visible parts by using local features computed from an object boundary. The local features used are defined at points of local maximum and minimum of contour curvature. A local feature from the image is matched with a feature from the model, and they determine a transformation (rotation and translation). All features are used in the matching, and a set of transformations is generated. The algorithm then clusters together features that imply similar transformations. The center of each cluster is used to define a candidate transformation that may possibly give a partial match. Finally, these candidate transformations are tested with a point-by-point matching of the image contour and the transformed model contour.

Westinghouse's gray-level robot vision system uses a simple form of the relational feature graph approach. In one of the reported studies [Schachter 1983], edges are used to form corners where a corner is defined as two intersecting edge vectors. The matching algorithm searches for four edge vectors forming two opposing corners such that the center of the line segment joining the corner pair coincides with the part center. The assumption that the object center and the two opposing corners are collinear restricts the applicability of the algorithm to limited types of industrial parts.

In semiconductor chip manufacturing, each die is visually inspected for the bonding of the die onto the package substrate and the bonding of wires from the die pads to the physically larger package leads. The process involves the recognition of the chip boundary, the determination of the chip position and orientation, and the recognition of bonding pads. Conventionally, human operators have to perform all of these functions. Recently, a number of automatic die-bonding and wire-bonding systems have been developed for the manufacturing of chips. Most of these systems are based on relational features and associated matching algorithms. Some other IC recognition systems include those of Horn [1975a], Hsieh and Fu [1979], Igarashi et al. [1979], and Mese et al. [1977].

3.4 Comparison of the Three Methods for 2-D Object Representation

On the basis of the above descriptions of 2-D object-recognition algorithms, the following general conclusions can be made about global feature, structural feature, and relational graph methods. A summary of this comparison is shown in Table 2.

Features used in the global feature method are easy to compute from binary images, and their ordering in the model is unimportant. This makes the training process a relatively simple task. Features can be computed in real-time from, for example, a run-length encoding of the image. This method also has the advantage that the features can often be simply defined to be shift and rotation invariant. That is, objects may be placed at any position and orientation, and the camera geometry does not have to be fixed. In addition, optimal matching accuracy can be achieved by using standard statistical pattern-recognition techniques. The main disadvantage of global feature methods is the assumption that almost all of the objects must be visible in order to measure these features accurately. Thus, objects are not allowed to touch or overlap one another or contain defects. Unless the environment can be sufficiently controlled to eliminate these conditions, we are not likely to find global features because they are so large (e.g., due to occlusion).

The structural feature method is an improvement over the global feature method in terms of capability and robustness, but its complexity requires more sophisticated training and matching processes. This makes it computationally more expensive. Local and extended boundary features are used to represent smoothed, intermediate-level symbolic descriptions. Since gray-level images are generally used, the

Table 2. Comparison of the (a) Global Feature, (b) Structural Feature, and (c) Relational Graph Methods

Global feature method	Structural feature method	Relational graph method
Features are functions of the entire silhouette; controlled environment for binary image processing is required	Features describe local properties; binary image processing is not required	Features describe local properties; binary image processing is not required
Unable to handle noisy images	Able to handle noisy images by gray-level processing	Able to handle noisy images by gray-level processing
Global features are relatively easy and inexpensive to extract	Feature extraction is expensive when compared with the other two methods; it involves the transformation of local features into abstracted representations	Feature extraction is less expensive than in the structural feature method; local features are used directly in the model
Extracted features are invariant to rotation, shift, and size	Extracted features do not have the invariance properties	Local and relational features are not invariant to rotation, shift, or size
The training (modeling) process is simple, involving the generation of an unordered feature list	Modeling involves the generation of a structured feature list which describes the object's outline; it is relatively straightforward	Modeling involves the generation of a graph which relates all chosen local features; it requires carefully thought-out strategies
Matching involves statistical pattern-recognition schemes; optimal matching accuracy is achievable	Matching involves trial-and-error (hypothesize-verification) procedures	Matching involves graph-searching procedures
Matching is fast if a small number of features is used	Matching is a sequential process; slow if a large number of hypotheses is needed	Matching is slow if the model graph is complex
Unable to handle occlusion	Able to handle occlusion if a significant portion of the outline is apparent	Able to handle occlusion if key features of the object are apparent

resulting features are more reliable than the features extracted from a thresholded image. Methods using image enhancement and feature smoothing and abstraction (e.g., using the best fitting line or curve to represent a boundary segment) lead to systems that are much more flexible and less sensitive to noise than the methods using simple global image features. Of course, because many local features are used to model an object, the search procedure used for matching image features with model features must avoid testing all possible correspondences. Another difficulty is that boundary features are not usually invariant under translation and rotation. Consequently, matching usually consists of a sequential procedure that tentatively locates a few local features and then uses them to constrain the search for other features. This hypothesis-verification procedure will become very time consuming if the model is not appropriately designed. Unlike the global feature method, partial occlusion of

objects can be handled. However, a significant portion of an object's boundary has to be unobscured for successful recognition because most features are derived from the boundary.

The relational graph method further relaxes the requirements of how an object has to be presented for successful recognition. Since the model contains both local and relational features in the form of a graph, matching does not depend only on the presence of certain boundary features, but also on other features and properties of their interrelations (e.g., distance). Each local feature provides a local cue for the recognition of objects that overlap each other. The only requirement for successful recognition is that a sufficient set of key local features has to be visible and in the correct relative positions. When this method is compared with the global feature and structural feature methods, the design of the model and the matching procedure are more complex and of increasing importance. The matching procedure involves graph-searching techniques that are computationally intensive and too slow without special-purpose hardware for many industrial applications. Hierarchical graph-searching techniques (e.g., Barrow and Tenenbaum [1981]) can reduce the time complexity of the matching process by decomposing the model into independent components.

4. $2\frac{1}{2}$-D SURFACE REPRESENTATIONS

The previous section presented methods based on image intensities, deriving features from gray-level or binary images to represent the projection of an object in two dimensions. In this section we present another class of methods, which is also viewer centered, but which is based on physical-scene characteristics of a single view of an object. This representation maintains information in register with the original gray-scale image and includes *intrinsic images* [Barrow and Tenenbaum 1978], $2\frac{1}{2}$-D *sketch* [Marr 1978], *needle map* [Horn 1979], *parameter images* [Ballard 1981b], and *surface-orientation map* [Brady 1982a]. Intrinsic scene parameters include surface range, orientation, discontinuities, reflectance, illumination, color, and velocity. Since this local information is obtained over a whole region within some boundaries, it is more robust than the edge-based techniques used with many of the 2-D representations discussed in the previous section.

All of the methods in this section use scene surface properties derived from a single viewpoint to define features and construct models. If multiple views of an object are required, each is modeled independently. We have included range maps as part of this class of representation despite the fact that 3-D data are used. This is because the models that use these data are viewer centered and emphasize the description of observable surface features from a single viewpoint. Models that describe a complete (viewpoint-insensitive) 3-D object are included in the next section as 3-D representations.

Most current research is focusing on the problem of how to compute these intrinsic surface maps. See, for example, Ballard and Brown [1982], Barrow and Tenenbaum [1978], Brady [1982a], Jarvis [1983a], and Marr [1982], for surveys of many applicable techniques. The present survey does not consider this "measurement" stage.

Of particular interest for applications in industrial-parts recognition is the computation and use of range maps and local surface-orientation (needle) maps. Jarvis [1983a] and Poje and Delp [1982] give recent overviews of range-finding techniques using both active and passive methods. Active methods include ultrasonic and light time-of-flight measurement, and structured light projection using a plane or grid of light. Although early methods of these types have been slow, expensive, and of low accuracy, many recent improvements have been made [Agin and Highnam 1982; Altschuler et al. 1981; Jarvis 1983b; Kanade and Asada 1981; Pipitone and Marshall 1983; Popplestone et al. 1975].

Instead of extracting a range map, other researchers are focusing on obtaining local surface orientation as a descriptor of surface shape. This includes such direct methods as shape from shading [Horn 1975b], shape from texture [Bajcsy 1973; Bajcsy and Lieberman 1976; Kender 1980; Stevens 1981; Witkin 1981], and shape from photometric stereo [Woodham 1978].

One method of computing surface orientation that shows considerable promise for industrial-parts recognition is called photometric stereo [Woodham 1978]. Local surface orientation is computed using a reflectance map for each of three different incident illumination directions, but from a single viewing direction. Since an object point corresponds to the same pixel in each of these three gray-level images, the surface orientation at this point can be obtained from the intersection of isobrightness contours in the reflectance maps associated with each light source. The method has been implemented very efficiently by inverting the reflectance maps into a lookup table which gives surface orientation from a triple of gray levels [Silver 1980]. So far

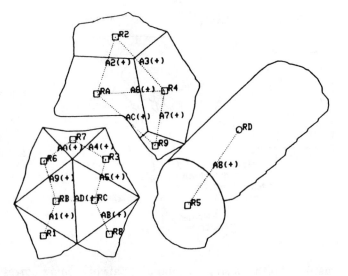

Figure 12. Relational graph description of planar and curve surfaces derived from a range map. (From Oshima and Shirai [1983]; © IEEE 1983.)

the technique has been defined for objects containing Lambertian and specular surfaces [Ikeuchi 1981a; Woodham 1978], and error analysis has been performed [Ray et al. 1983].

To date, researchers have developed only a few model-based recognition systems predicated on features derived from one or more surface maps. Hence application to industrial parts-recognition has yet to be extensively investigated. In the remainder of this section we present some of the techniques that have been studied. All of these methods are based on features derived from either a range map or a needle map. We expect that considerable future work will be devoted to expanding this class of techniques.

4.1 Example 1: A Relational Surface Patch Model

Model. Oshima and Shirai [1983] construct a relational-feature graph in which nodes represent planar or smoothly curved surfaces extracted from a range map, and arcs represent relations between adjacent surfaces. Surface types include planar, ellipsoid, hyperboloid, cone, paraboloid, cylinder, and others. For each pair of adjacent regions, the type of intersection (convex, concave, mixed, or no intersection), angle between the regions, and relative positions of the centroids are stored. Figure 12 illustrates this relational-graph description for

a scene containing three objects. If objects may be viewed from multiple viewing positions, then a separate relational graph must be constructed for each view, and these models must be treated independently by the matcher. Partial occlusion of certain secondary planar surfaces is allowed, although the extent is dependent on the predefined thresholds used by the matcher. Currently, curved surfaces may not be occluded in the scene.

Features. A range map is used as the basis for segmenting an image into regions. First, connected points with similar range values are grouped into small surface elements. Next, the equation of the best plane surface through each of these elements is computed, and then these surface elements are merged into maximal planar and curved regions. For each region, a set of global features is computed, including surface type (planar, ellipsoid, cone, cylinder, etc.), number of adjacent regions, area, perimeter, compactness, occlusion, minimum and maximum extent, and mean and standard deviation of radius.

Matching. Matching is performed by comparing an observed relational graph of surface descriptions with a set of graphs for each viewpoint of each object modeled. First, regions corresponding to maximal smooth surfaces are extracted from the range map of a given scene. A *kernel* con-

449

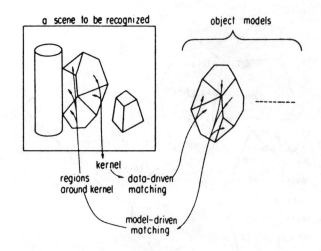

sisting of either a single region or a pair of adjacent regions is then selected from the surface descriptors of the given scene in order to guide the search for matching model graphs. The kernel represents regions with high confidence of being found; criteria include no occlusion, planar surfaces, and large region area. Next, an exhaustive search of all model graphs is performed, selecting as candidate models all those that contain regions which match the kernel. Finally, the system performs a depth-first search which attempts to determine the correspondence between each remaining region in the current candidate model and the regions extracted from the scene. A model region and a scene region match if their region properties are similar, all adjacencies to previously matched regions are consistent, and the properties of all new relations between regions are similar. This process is repeated for other kernel regions in the scene until a globally consistent interpretation, in which each scene region is found to correspond to exactly one model region, is achieved. If multiple consistent interpretations are possible, then the system returns each one. Figure 13 illustrates this matching process.

4.2 Example 2: A Relational Surface Boundary Model

Model. Nevatia and Binford [1977] construct a relational graph description of each view of an object using a set of *generalized* *cones* corresponding to elongated subparts of the object. In particular, cones are represented as *ribbonlike* descriptors containing 2-D cross-sections of range discontinuity points [Brooks 1979]. Given a set of these ribbons defining an object, a set of *joints* is constructed indicating which ribbons are adjacent to each other. A joint description includes an ordered list of ribbons connected to it and a designated dominant ribbon having the largest width. A relational graph is constructed; in this graph joints are represented by nodes and ribbons by arcs. Figure 14 shows the spines of the ribbons detected in a scene containing a reclining doll and the resulting relational graph description. In addition, a set of coarse descriptors is associated with this object graph, including number of ribbons, number of elongated ribbons, number of joints, bilateral symmetries, and a set of *distinguished* ribbons having the largest widths. For each distinguished piece of an object a three-bit description code is used to permit efficient organization and search of the set of models. The three descriptors encoded are the part's connectivity, type (long or wide part), and conicity, that is, whether or not it is conical. Models are sorted by their description code and secondarily by the maximum number of parts attached at either end of the distinguished piece.

Features. As an alternative to extracting planar and curved surfaces from range maps, some researchers have developed

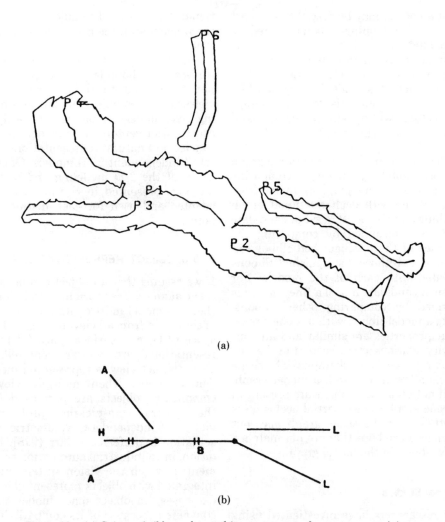

Figure 14. (a) Spines of ribbons detected in a range map for a scene containing a reclining doll. Range discontinuities are used to define the boundary of the object. (b) The relational graph constructed from (a). (From Nevatia and Binford [1977].)

techniques for detecting surface boundaries by detecting and linking points at which range discontinuities occur. Nevatia and Binford use a range map to derive a boundary description of a given view of an object. Rather than directly use this global structural feature to describe an object, they immediately construct a relational graph using ribbonlike primitives to describe subparts in terms of the 2-D projections of the boundaries [Brooks 1979]. A ribbon is the 2-D specialization of a 3-D generalized cylinder [Binford 1971]. Ribbons are specified by three components: spine, cross-section, and sweeping rule. By sweeping a planar cross-section at a constant angle along a spine according to the sweeping rule, a planar shape is generated. Nevatia and Binford first construct a set of local ribbons restricted to having straight axes in eight predefined directions and smoothly varying cross-sections. This is done by linking midpoints of cross-sections (runs of object points perpendicular to the axis direction) that are adjacent and have similar cross-sections. These local ribbons are then extended by extrapolating the axes of the local ribbons and constructing new cross-sections. This process allows the resulting axis to curve smoothly. In general, a single part of an object may be described by (part of) several overlapping ribbons. To reduce this redundancy, ribbons that are not so elongated or rectangular as other ribbons overlapping them are deleted. Each ribbon is associated with a crude description of its shape given by its axis length, average cross-section width, elongatedness, and type (conical or cylindrical).

Matching. As in the 2-D relational graph methods, matching involves comparing parts of the relational graph extracted from a given scene with each relational graph describing a model. First, a set of candidate models is determined by comparing the properties of the distinguished ribbons in the scene with those distinguished ribbons associated with each of the models. For each such candidate model a finer match is performed by comparing other ribbons, pairing a model ribbon with a scene ribbon if their properties are similar and all connectivity relations are consistent in the current pair of matched subgraphs. The scene graph is allowed to match a model graph, even if not all model ribbons are present in the scene graph (hence partial occlusion is permitted), but the scene graph may not contain extra ribbons that are not matched by any ribbon in the model graph.

4.3 Other Studies

Many researchers have investigated using range maps as the basis for segmenting an image into regions by grouping (merging) points into planar surfaces, cylindrical surfaces, surfaces on generalized cylinders, and other smoothly curved surface patches [Agin and Binford 1976; Bolles 1981; Bolles and Fischler 1981; Duda et al. 1979; Henderson 1982; Henderson and Bhanu 1982; Milgram and Bjorklund 1980; Oshima and Shirai 1979; Popplestone et al. 1975; Shirai 1972]. Alternatively, range maps can be segmented by locating discontinuities in depth. For example, Sugihara [1979] segments a range map by finding such edges. To aid this process, a *junction dictionary* is precomputed listing all possible ways junctions can occur in range maps for scenes containing only trihedral objects. The dic-

tionary is then used to guide the search in the range map for edges of the appropriate types.

For the most part, however, the resulting surface and boundary descriptions have not been used to define corresponding viewer-centered object models and matching techniques. This is primarily because object-centered 3-D models are more concise and natural representations than a set of independent $2\frac{1}{2}$-D models. Of course, many of the 3-D modeling and matching methods presented in Section 5 could be adapted and used for each distinct viewpoint.

5. 3-D OBJECT REPRESENTATIONS

If we assume that an object can occur in a scene at an arbitrary orientation in 3-space, then the model must contain a description of the object from all viewing angles. Image-space (2-D) and surface-space ($2\frac{1}{2}$-D) representations are viewer centered, and each distinct view is represented independently. Thus, when multiple views of complicated objects are permitted (as in the general bin-picking problem), a viewpoint-independent, volumetric representation is preferred [Marr 1978]. In addition, in an industrial automation environment in which the vision system must be integrated with objects represented in CAD databases, an object-space model may be convenient because of its compatibility. In contrast to the previous representations, a single model is used to represent an object, implicitly describing all possible views of the object.

Researchers have investigated two main types of 3-D representations. These are (1) *exact representations* using surface, sweep, and volume descriptions; (2) *multiview feature representations* in which a set of 2-D or $2\frac{1}{2}$-D descriptions are combined into a single composite model. This includes the specification of a set of topologically distinct views or a uniformly sampled set of 2-D viewpoints around an object. The first representation method completely describes an object's spatial occupancy properties, whereas the second only represents selected visible 2-D or $2\frac{1}{2}$-D surface features (and sometimes their 3-D spatial relationships).

Exact representations include the class of complete, volumetric methods based on the exact specification of a 3-D object using either surface patches, spines and sweeping rules, or volume primitives. Object-centered coordinate systems are used in each case. See, for example, Badler and Bajcsy [1978], Ballard and Brown [1982], and Requicha [1980] for a general introduction to this class of representations. Surface model descriptions specify an object by its boundaries or enclosing surfaces using primitives such as edge and face. Baumgart's [1972] "winged edge" representation for planar polyhedral objects is an elegant example of this type of model. Volume representations describe an object in terms of solids such as generalized cylinders, cubes, spheres, and rectangular blocks. The main advantage of this class of representations is that it provides an exact description that is object centered. The main disadvantage is that it is difficult to use in a real-time object-recognition system since the processing necessary to perform either 2-D to 3-D or 3-D to 2-D projections (for matching 2-D observed image features with a 3-D model) is very costly. For example, in the ACRONYM system [Brooks and Binford 1981] camera constraints are built in so as to limit the number of 3-D to 2-D projections that must be hypothesized and computed at run time.

Multiview feature representation can include the work on storing 2-D descriptions for each stable configuration of an object. We restrict our discussion here to coordinated representations of multiple views that permit the specification of efficient matching procedures that take advantage of intraview and interview feature similarities.

One class of multiview representations is based on the description of the *characteristic views* of an object. This requires the specification of all topologically distinct views. Koenderink and vanDoorn [1976a, 1976b, 1979] are studying the properties of the set of viewing positions around an object, and the qualitative nature of the stability of most viewing positions. That is,

small changes in viewing position do not affect the topological structure of the set of visible object features (i.e., point and line singularities). On the basis of the topological equivalence of neighboring viewpoints, they define an "aspect graph" of feature-distinct viewpoints (see Figure 15).

Fuchs et al. [1980] have also used this idea to perform a recursive partitioning of a 3-D scene using the polygons that describe the surfaces of the constituent 3-D objects. That is, a *binary space-partitioning* tree, in which each node contains a single polygon, is constructed. Polygons associated with a node's left subtree are those contained in one half-space defined by the plane in which the current polygon lies; the polygons in the right subtree are the ones in the other half-space. Using this structure they perform hidden surface elimination from a given viewpoint by a simple in-order tree traversal, in which subtrees are ordered by their "visibility" from the given viewpoint. In this representation each leaf defines a characteristic view volume; hence the set of leaf nodes defines a partition of 3-space into distinct viewing positions.

Another type of multiview representation, the *discrete view-sphere representation*, is the "viewing sphere" of all possible viewpoints (at a fixed distance) around an object, storing a viewer-centered description for each sample viewpoint. This can be precomputed from a complete 3-D volumetric description and provide a description that is compatible with the features extracted from a test image at run time. Thus it is a more convenient representation, and yet it provides sufficient accuracy of description, except at pathological viewing positions.

5.1 Example 1: A Surface Patch Graph Model

Model. Shneier [1979, 1981] constructs 3-D *surface* models from a set of light-stripe images of the object to be modeled. Each distinctly different plane surface that is extracted is represented by a unique node in a *graph of models*, which describes all models to be recognized. Associated with each node is a set of properties that describes the surface's shape and a set of

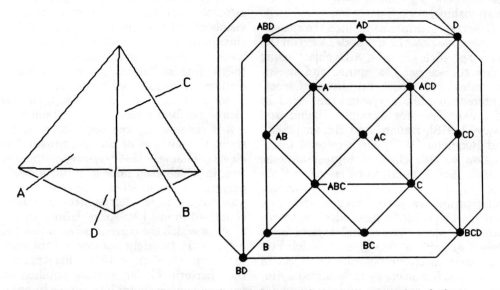

Figure 15. The aspect graph for a tetrahedron. Nodes are of three types representing whether one, two, or three faces are visible. Arcs connect a pair of nodes when some arbitrarily small change in viewing direction suffices to change the set of visible faces from the faces visible at one node to those visible at the other node without going through any intermediate set of visible faces.

pointers to the names of the models of which this primitive shape is a part. Thus, if two surface shape descriptions are similar with regard to the same or different objects, they are represented by a single node in the graph. Arcs connect pairs of nodes using a set of predefined relation schemata (e.g., the "is adjacent to" relation). Arguments to relation schemata are surface descriptions, not actual surfaces. Relation schemata also index the models in which they occur and the primitives that form their arguments. Thus nodes and arcs in the graph of models may be shared within models and across models. This integration of multiple object models into a single graph has the advantages of being very compact and enabling a rapid indexing scheme to be used.

Features. Planar surfaces are determined from a set of light-stripe images using techniques described in Section 4.

Matching. The set of observed planar surfaces extracted from a given scene are matched with the graph of models for all possible objects using a two-step procedure. First, for each observed surface that is sufficiently similar to a node in the graph of models, a node is created in the *scene graph*

indicating this match. Since each node in the graph of models corresponds to one or more surfaces in one or more objects, each possibility is tested using a predefined set of procedures. These procedures decide whether an interpretation is possible for the observed surface and assign confidences to these interpretations. A subgraph of the scene graph is created for each possible interpretation, and each surface/model-node pair is assigned to one or more such subgraphs. Next, the scene graph is traversed, deleting surfaces that are insufficiently substantiated and propagating constraints in order to remove multiple interpretations for a single surface.

5.2 Example 2: Hierarchical Generalized Cylinders

Model. Brooks' ACRONYM system constructs *sweep* models using part/whole hierarchical graphs of primitive volume elements described by generalized cylinders [Binford 1971; Brooks 1983a, 1983b; Brooks and Binford 1981]. A *generalized cylinder* (GC) describes a 3-D volume by sweeping a planar cross-section along a space-curve spine; the cross-section is held

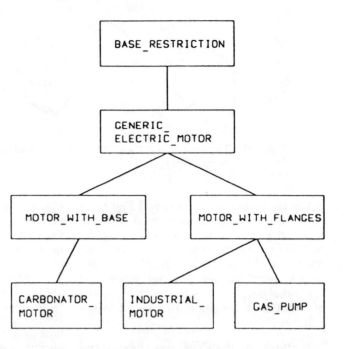

Figure 16. The restriction graph for the classes of electric motors used in ACRONYM. (From Brooks [1983a].)

at a constant angle to the spine, and its shape is tranformed according to some sweeping rule. The user constructs a tree for each object, where nodes include GC descriptions and arcs indicate the subpart relation. The tree is designed to provide a hierarchical description of an object, where nodes higher in the tree correspond to more significant parts in the description. For example, the root of an "electric motor" tree describes the cylinder for the large cylindrical body of the motor. Arcs from this node point to nodes describing cylinders for the small flanges and spindle, which are part of a lower priority level of description of the motor.

Each GC has its own local coordinate system, and additional affixment arcs between nodes specify the relations between coordinate systems. If multiple parts of the same type are associated with a single object, they are represented by a single node in the tree with a quantity value and a set of coordinate transformations specifying the location of each part. Furthermore, in order to allow variations in size, structure, and spatial relationships in GC descriptions, any numeric slot in a node's description may be filled by an algebraic expression ranging over numeric constants and variables. Classes of objects are speci-

fied by constraints (i.e., inequalities on algebraic expressions that define the set of values that can be taken by quantifiers).

A scene is modeled by defining objects and affixing them to a world-coordinate system. A camera node is also included, specifying bounds on its position and orientation relative to the world-coordinate system.

To aid the matching of models with image features, the user constructs from the static object graph a model class hierarchy called the restriction graph. That is, the sets of constraints on quantifiers in the object graph are used to build a specialization hierarchy of different classes of models. The root node represents the empty set of constraints for all restriction graphs. A node is added as the child of another node by constructing its constraint list from the union of its parent's constraints and the additional constraints needed to define the new node's more specialized model class. The volumetric structure associated with a node is retrieved indirectly by a pointer from the node to the object graph. An arc in the graph always points from a less restrictive model class (larger satisfying set of constraints) to a more restrictive one (smaller satisfying set). Figure 16 illustrates a restriction

Figure 17. Three instances of the model classes associated with the three leaf nodes in Figure 16 (From Brooks [1983a].)

graph for classes of motors, and Figure 17 shows three instances associated with the leaf nodes' sets of constraints. During the matching process, other nodes are also added to the restriction graph in order to specialize further a given model for case analysis, or to specify an instance of a match of the model to a set of image features.

Features. ACRONYM uses ribbons and ellipses as low-level features describing a given image. A *ribbon* is the 2-D analog of a 3-D generalized cylinder. In particular, Brooks considers the special case in which a ribbon is defined by sweeping a symmetric width line segment normally along another straight-line segment while changing the width of the first segment linearly with distance swept. Ellipses are used to describe the shapes generated by the ends of GCs. For example, ellipses describe ends of a cylinder and ribbons describe the projection of the cylinder body.

The extraction of these features is performed by the descriptive module of the ACRONYM system [Brooks 1979]. First, an edge-linking algorithm creates sets of linked edges (contours) from the image data. Linking edges into a contour is formulated as a tree-searching problem searching for the best edge direction at a given point. A contour is retained only if it satisfies certain global shape criteria. Next, an algorithm fits ribbons and ellipses to the sets of contours by extracting potential boundary points of a ribbon from a histogram of the angles of the edge elements making up the contour. Finally, redundant ribbons in a single area of the image are removed. A graph structure, the *observation graph*, is the output of the descriptive mod-

ule. The nodes of the graph are ribbon and ellipse descriptions, and the arcs linking the nodes together specify spatial relations between ribbons.

Matching. ACRONYM predicts appearances of models in terms of ribbons and ellipses that can be observed in an image. Rather than make exhaustive predictions based on all possible viewing positions, viewpoint-insensitive symbolic constraints are used. These indicate features that are invariant or quasi-invariant over a large range of viewing positions. To generate predictions, a rule-based module is used to identify contours of model faces that may be visible. Case analysis is used to restrict predictions further and produce predicted contours in the viewer's coordinate system.

As a result of this constraint-manipulation process, a *prediction graph* is built. In this graph nodes either represent specific image features or join prediction subgraphs containing lower level features. Arcs of the graph denote image relations between features, relating multiple feature shapes predicted for a single GC. Arcs are labeled either "must be," "should be," or "exclusive." Associated with a prediction graph is a node in the restriction graph that specifies the object class being predicted.

Matching is performed at two levels. First, predicted ribbons must match image ribbons, and second, these "local" matches must be globally consistent. That is, relations between matched ribbons must satisfy the constraints specified in the arcs of the prediction graph, and the accumulated constraints for each maximal subgraph matched in the observation graph must be consistent with the 3-D model constraints in the associated restriction node. Local

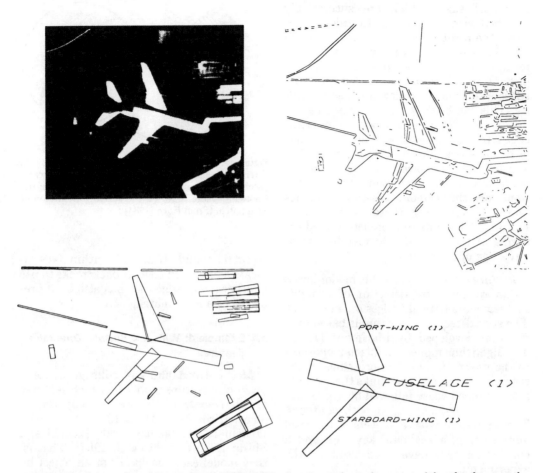

Figure 18. Results of Brooks' matching procedure. The first figure shows the output of the edge detector, the second figure shows the output of the ribbon finder. The final figure is the output of the matcher. (From Brooks [1983b]; © IEEE 1983.)

matches of predicted ribbons with image ribbons also provide additional "back constraints" which are used to further restrict model parameters. Finally, matching is first done for GCs of highest priority in each model's object-graph hierarchy in order to limit the search initially to include only the most important parts. Figure 18 illustrates the results of this method.

5.3 Example 3: Multiview Feature Vectors

Model. Goad [1983] builds a *multiview* feature model of an object by constructing a list of object features and the conditions under which each is visible. The single object feature used is a straight-line segment representing a portion of the object's surface at which either a surface normal or a reflectivity discontinuity occurs.

The set of possible viewing positions is represented by partitioning the surface of a unit viewing sphere into small, relatively uniform-size, patches. The current implementation uses 218 patches. To represent the set of positions from which a given edge feature is visible, a bit-map representation of the viewing sphere is used to encode whether or not the feature is wholly visible from each patch on the sphere (i.e., a line's projection is longer than a threshold). Thus each feature is stored as a pair of endpoint coordinates plus 218 bits to describe its visibility range.

The matching procedure used with this model requires a sequential enumeration of model edges which are successively matched with image edges. In order to improve the run-time efficiency of the search for a consistent set of matches (which determines a unique view position), it is important to select an order that presents edges in decreasing order of expected utility. This can be done by preprocessing the list of features in the model using each edge's (a) likelihood of visibility, (b) range of possible positions of the projected edge, and (c) focusing power (i.e., if a match is made, how much information about restrictions on the camera position becomes known). Combining these factors for a given model results in a predetermined ordering of the best edge to match next at any stage of the search.

Features. Goad restricts his model-based vision system to the detection of straight-line segments (straight edges on an object). The edge detection algorithm is based on a program developed by Marimont [1982]. The algorithm applies a Laplacian operator to the image, detects zero crossings in the resulting image, and then links these points into extended edges followed by segmentation into a sequence of smooth contours. Three different types of objects, a universal joint casting, a keyboard key cap, and a connecting rod, have been used in the experiments.

Matching. A sequential matching procedure with backtracking is implemented in Goad's system. The matching involves a search for a match between image and model edges. At any given time in the search, a hypothesis about the position and orientation of the object relative to the camera is used to restrict the search area to some reasonable bounds. The hypothesis is refined sequentially during the matching process.

The procedure starts with predicting the position and orientation of the image projection based on the current hypothesis. Then, a model edge is selected to match with image edges. If a match is found, the measured location and orientation of the new edge are used to update the hypothesis. The algorithm repeats the searching and updating until a satisfactory match of an

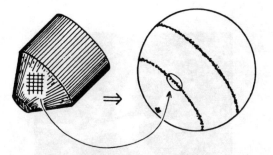

Figure 19. Representation of an object (left) by its extended Gaussian image (right) in which discrete patches of the object are mapped onto points on the Gaussian sphere based on the surface orientation of each patch. (From Horn [1984].)

object is found. If the algorithm fails to locate a predicted edge, it backtracks to use another image edge that has also been predicted as a good match.

5.4 Example 4: Multiview Surface Orientation Features

Model. Horn and his colleagues use a *multiview* feature model in which features are derived from the needle map for an object [Brou 1984; Horn 1979; Horn 1984; Ikeuchi 1981b; Ikeuchi 1983; Ikeuchi and Shirai 1982; Ikeuchi et al. 1984]. That is, they model each viewpoint of an object by the distribution of its surface-orientation normals on the Gaussian sphere, ignoring positional information by moving all surface normals to the origin. By associating a unit of mass with each point on the unit sphere, we obtain a distribution of mass called the "extended Gaussian image" (EGI) [Horn 1984; Smith 1979]. Segments of developable surfaces (such as planes and cylinders) map into high concentrations of points in known configurations. Figure 19 illustrates this representation for a simple object. A 3-D object is then modeled using a set of (normalized) EGIs, one for each possible viewing direction on a uniformly sampled viewing sphere [Ikeuchi 1981b, 1983; Ikeuchi and Shirai 1982; Ikeuchi et al. 1984]. More specifically, a two-dimensional table is constructed for each possible (viewpoint, mass-distribution) pair. An element in this table stores the mass (surface area) corresponding to the total surface description for the given viewpoint. If multiple objects are to be recognized, then a table is constructed for each object.

Features. The complete surface-orientation map in the form of the normalized EGI is used as a global-feature descriptor.

Matching. Matching is performed by comparing an observed EGI with each model EGI. To constrain the set of match tests that must be made for each pair, the observed EGI and model EGI mass centers are aligned, constraining the line of sight. Next, the observed and model spheres are rotated about the candidate line of sight so as to align their directions of minimum EGI mass inertia. These two constraints completely specify the alignment of the observed EGI with a model EGI. A match measure for a given pair of normalized EGIs is specified by comparing the similarity in their mass distributions; the model that maximizes this measure is the estimate of the observed line of sight. When multiple objects are present in a single scene, it is first necessary to segment the surface-orientation map into regions corresponding to separate objects.

5.5 Other Studies

The principle features used in most 3-D recognition systems are based on surface properties such as faces, edges, and corners. The references given in Section 4.3 for grouping range data into planar, cylindrical, and other smoothly curved surfaces are also used for 3-D surface description and modeling. Potmesil [1983] constructs 3-D surface models from a series of partially overlapping range images by an iterative merging algorithm which first groups local surface patches into locally smooth surface sheets (using a quadtree representation) and then merges partially overlapping surface representations using a heuristic search procedure.

Bolles et al. [1984] use a *surface* model as the primary structure for generalizing their local-feature-focus method (see Section 3.3.3) to 3-D using a system called

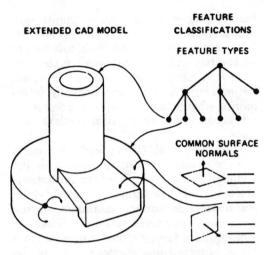

Figure 20. 3DPOs-augmented CAD model and feature classification network. (From Bolles, R. C., Horaud, P., and Hannah, M. J. 1984. 3 DPO: A three-dimensional part orientation system. In *Robotics Research: The 1st International Symposium*, M. Brady and R. Paul, Eds. MIT Press, Cambridge, Mass., © MIT Press 1984.)

3DPO. A model consists of two parts: an augmented CAD model and a set of feature-classification networks. The augmented CAD model is similar to Baumgart's [1972], describing edges, surfaces, and vertices and their relations with one another. The feature-classification network classifies observable features by type and size, for example, surface elements that have the same normal direction and cylinders that have a common axis. Each feature contains a pointer to each instance in all of the augmented CAD models. Figure 20 illustrates this modeling method.

Bolles uses range data to detect surface discontinuities in an image. Two methods are used: detecting discontinuities occurring in 1-D slices of the range finder and finding zero crossings in the output of a second-difference operator applied to the complete range map.

Bolles' matching scheme is similar to that used for the 2-D local-feature-focus method [Bolles and Cain 1982]. First, the system searches for features that match some model's feature (e.g., a cylinder with a given radius). This is accomplished by grouping edges that lie in the same plane, partitioning each such set of points into line segments and arcs of circles, and associating properties with each line or arc on the basis of relations between the surfaces that meet to form the given segment. Second, objects are hypothesized by determining whether a pair of observed segments are consistent with a given model's features.

Silberberg et al. [1984] model an object using a *multiview* representation to define a Hough space of possible transformations of a set of 3-D line segments (edges), which are observable surface markings on the given object in a given viewpoint. They use a generalized Hough transform to match a set of observed line segments with model lines for each viewpoint. A 3-D Hough space is used to represent a viewpoint (two dimensions for position on the view-sphere, one dimension for orientation at a viewpoint). For each viewpoint and pair of line segments, one from a model and one from the image, the model line is projected onto the image plane, incrementing the corresponding bin in Hough space if the pair of lines match. This procedure is first used with a coarsely quantized Hough space to select a few, approximate, candidate viewpoint regions. Next, each of these viewpoint regions is successively refined to provide a finer resolution estimate of the exact viewing position.

Chakravarty and Freeman [1982] define a *multiview* model using characteristic views for recognizing curved and polyhedral objects. For a given object, they define a finite set of equivalence classes called *characteristic view partitions*, which define a set of *vantage-point domains* on the sphere of possible viewpoints. Each topologically distinct patch is described by a list of the visible lines and junctions in the given object. In order to reduce the number of patches in the partition of the view-sphere, they assume objects will occur in a fixed number of stable positions. The set of possible camera positions is also limited. With these restrictions, two viewpoints are part of the same patch if they contain the same image junctions and lines with the same connectivity relationships, although the lengths of the lines may differ. A linear transformation describes features within a patch. An object is now modeled as a list of patch descriptors, where each list specifies the number of visible junctions of each of the five possible distinct types for this class of objects [Chakravarty 1979].

Features are combined into a list containing the number of occurrences of each of eight generalized junction types possible for planar and curved-surface objects. Lists are ordered by decreasing significance for recognition and organized into a hierarchical decision tree.

A multistage matching procedure is used for a given observed set of lines and junctions. First, all viewing patches that have similar boundaries to the given observed image boundary are selected; second, patches that do not contain matching junction types are removed; finally, a projection is computed on the basis of the correlated junctions, and this transformation is verified with the original image data.

Faugeras and his colleagues [Faugeras and Hebert 1983; Faugeras et al. 1983, 1984] have developed a system using a surface model computed from a range map. Each object is approximated by a set of planar faces, resulting in a relational graph model in which nodes correspond to faces and arcs connect adjacent faces. Matching is performed using a best-first search for a consistent pairing between observed faces and model faces.

Bhanu [1982] uses a relaxation-labeling technique for identifying which model face is associated with each observed image face. Range data are first merged into planar faces [Henderson and Bhanu 1982]. A two-stage relaxation procedure is then used. In the first stage compatibilities between pairs of adjacent faces are used; in the second stage compatibilities between a face and two of its neighboring faces are used. The compatibility of a face in an unknown view with a face in a model is computed by finding transformations (scale, rotation, translation), applying them, and computing feature value mismatches. The initial probabilities for a face are computed as a function of global features of the face, including area, perimeter, number of vertices, and radius.

Grimson and Lozano-Perez [1984] define a hypothesize-and-test search procedure for matching a set of observed surface points (specified by their 3-D position and surface orientation) with a set of polyhedral models (specified by their planar faces). All feasible interpretations of the observed point data are constructed by determining consistent pairings of points to model faces (a point may be mapped into any location on the associated face). Interpretations that are locally inconsistent are rejected. That is, they exploit local constraints on nearby points involving properties such as distance, angle, and direction to rapidly reduce the candidate pairings between a given point and the model faces. For each feasible interpretation of the point data, a final consistency check is made to verify the match.

6. RELATED SURVEYS

There have been published recently a number of survey papers and tutorials that provide selected information on computer vision for industrial automation and robotics. Most of these papers have been organized as summaries of the latest robot vision systems and techniques. In contrast, this paper has attempted to present a more complete listing of results and uses a common descriptive format to clarify similarities and differences in the approaches.

Rosen [1979] examined the desired functions and industrial requirements for machine vision that are applicable to sensor-controlled manipulation. Industrial implementations, as well as selected research problems, are described. Examples are grouped into bin picking, the manipulation of isolated parts on conveyors, the manipulation in manufacturing and assembly, and visual inspection. He also comments that present machine vision techniques are sufficiently advanced to be used in factories in a cost-effective way.

Myers [1980] presents a survey of existing systems, including operational systems in manufacturing and feasibility demonstrations. He describes work done at General Motors Research Laboratories (one of the first to apply computer vision technology to a production line), as well as other inspection systems. Yachida and Tsuji [1980] survey industrial machine vision activities in Japan and present a number of successful vision systems that are now operational in Japanese manufacturing. Chin [1982] presents a bibliography on industrial vision for discrete parts.

Kruger and Thompson [1981] present a summary and survey of techniques and applications relevant to the field. They look at generic examples in the areas of inspection, part recognition, and discrete component assembly, and discuss sample systems that exemplify the current state of the art. The authors also make economic projections and given recommendations to guide future investigations. The survey concludes with some comments on the fact that the efficacy of the techniques in any application of machine vision depends on both technical factors and economic considerations.

Foith et al. [1981] discuss selected methods in image processing and analysis related to industrial applications and point out why practical systems perform binary image processing. A brief survey and some specific approaches used in several state-of-the-art systems are presented.

Bolles [1981] reviews some possible applications of image-understanding research to industrial automation, and compares the characteristics of current image-understanding systems with that of industrial automation systems. He points out a few ways in which current image-understanding techniques may be used in the future to enhance the capabilities of industrial systems.

Binford [1982] presents a survey of several general-purpose, model-based image-analysis systems and points out many of the weaknesses of current systems. Besl and Jain [1985] survey general methods for three-dimensional object recognition. Brady [1982a] presents a general survey of image-understanding research.

Kinnucan [1983] briefly looks at the development of machine vision in the United States in the past twenty years and surveys the current activities of several major research laboratories and industries. He also examines current market activities of existing commercial machine vision systems.

On automated visual inspection, Jarvis [1980] uses three practical examples to illustrate the nature of the techniques and problems. Chin and Harlow [1982] present an extensive survey and discuss the inspection of printed circuit boards, photomasks, and IC chips. Porter and Mundy [1980] provide a comprehensive list of the types of visual-inspection techniques currently in use.

Other related surveys and overviews include Agin [1980], Aleksander et al. [1983], Casler [1983], Fu [1983], Kelly [1983], Kelly et al. [1983], Pot et al. [1983], Pugh [1983], Rossol [1983], Trombly [1982], Tropf et al. [1982], and West [1982].

7. SUMMARY

An extensive review of robot vision techniques for industrial parts recognition has been presented. The major motivation for using industrial machine vision is to increase flexibility and reduce cost of these tasks. Up to the present, primarily very simple techniques based on 2-D global scalar features have been applied in real-time manufacturing processes. More sophisticated techniques will have to be developed in order to deal with less structured industrial environments and permit more task versatility. These techniques will incorporate higher level modeling (e.g., highly organized graph models containing $2\frac{1}{2}$-D and 3-D descriptions), more powerful feature-extraction methods (e.g., global structural features of object boundaries, surfaces, and volumes), and more robust matching procedures for efficiently comparing large sets of complex models with observed image features.

Recent trends indicate that multiple, disparate sensor types, including vision, range, and tactile sensors, will significantly improve the quality of the features that can be determined about a scene. The use of 3-D models is essential for reliably recognizing parts in the presence of significant uncertainty about their identities and positions in a robot's workspace. The choice of a 3-D representation that can be efficiently used with a matching procedure is still an important research question, however. As more experience is gained, significant speed improvements can be expected with special-purpose hardware for performing this costly search task.

ACKNOWLEDGMENTS

This work was supported in part by the National Science Foundation under grants ECS-8352356 and ECS-8301521, and in part by the General Motors Foundation, Inc., Dearborn, Michigan.

REFERENCES

AGIN, G. J. 1980. Computer vision systems for industrial inspection and assembly. *Computer 13*, 5 (May), 11–20.

AGIN, G. J., AND BINFORD, T. O. 1976. Computer description of curved objects. *IEEE Trans. Comput. 25*, 4 (Apr.), 439–449.

AGIN, G. J., AND DUDA, R. O. 1975. SRI vision research for advanced automation. In *Proceedings of the 2nd U.S.A.–Japan Computer Conference* (Tokyo, Japan, Aug.), pp. 113–117.

AGIN, G. J., AND HIGHNAM, P. T. 1982. A movable light-stripe sensor for obtaining three-dimensional coordinate measurements. In *Proceedings of the Society of Photo-Optical Instrumentation Engineers Conference on Robotics and Industrial Inspection* (San Diego, Calif., Aug.), vol. 360. SPIE, Bellingham, Wash.

ALEKSANDER, I., STONHAM, T. J., AND WILKIE, B. A. 1983. Computer vision systems for industry: Comparisons. In *Artificial Vision for Robots*, I. Aleksander, Ed. Chapman and Hall, New York, pp. 179–196.

ALTSCHULER, M. D., POSDAMER, J. L., FRIEDER, G., ALTSCHULER, B. R., AND TABOADA, J. 1981. The numerical stereo camera. In *Proceedings of the Society of Photo-Optical Instrumentation Engineers Conference on 3-D Machine Perception* (Washington, D.C., Apr.), vol. 283. SPIE, Bellingham, Wash., pp. 15–24.

AYACHE, N. J. 1983. A model-based vision system to identify and locate partially visible industrial parts. In *Proceedings of the IEEE Computer Society Conference on Computer Vision and Pattern Recognition* (Washington, D.C., June). IEEE, New York, pp. 492–494.

BADLER, N., AND BAJCSY, R. 1978. Three-dimensional representations for computer graphics and computer vision. *ACM Comput. Gr. 12*, 3 (Aug.), 153–160.

BAIRD, M. L. 1978. Sight I: A computer vision system for automated IC chip manufacture. *IEEE Trans. Syst. Man Cybern. 8*, 2 (Feb.), 133–139.

BAJCSY, R. 1973. Computer identification of visual surface. *Comput. Gr. Image Process. 2*, 2 (Oct.), 118–130.

BAJCSY, R., AND LIEBERMAN, L. 1976. Texture gradient as a depth cue. *Comput. Gr. Image Process. 5*, 1 (Mar.), 52–67.

BALLARD, D. H. 1981a. Generalizing the Hough transform to detect arbitrary shapes. *Pattern Recogn. 13*, 2, 111–122.

BALLARD, D. H. 1981b. Parameter networks: Towards a theory of low level vision. In *Proceedings of the 7th International Joint Conference on Artificial Intelligence* (Vancouver, Canada, Aug.). Kaufmann, Los Altos, Calif., pp. 1068–1078.

BALLARD, D. H., AND BROWN, C. M. 1982. *Computer Vision*. Prentice-Hall, Englewood Cliffs, N.J.

BARROW, H. G., AND TENENBAUM, J. M. 1978. Recovering intrinsic scene characteristics from images. In *Computer Vision Systems*, A. R. Hanson and E. M. Riseman, Eds. Academic Press, Orlando, Fla., pp. 3–26.

BARROW, H. G., AND TENENBAUM, J. M. 1981. Computational vision. *Proc. IEEE 69*, 5 (May), 572–595.

BAUMGART, B. G. 1972. Winged edge polyhedron representation. Tech. Rep. AIM-179, Computer Science Dept., Stanford Univ., Stanford, Calif.

BESL, P. J., AND JAIN, R. C. 1985. Three-dimensional object recognition. *ACM Comput. Surv. 17*, 1 (Mar.), 75–145.

BHANU, B. 1982. Surface representation and shape matching of 3-D objects. In *Proceedings of the IEEE Computer Society Conference on Pattern Recognition and Image Processing* (Las Vegas, Nev., June). IEEE, New York, pp. 349–354.

BHANU, B. 1983. Recognition of occluded objects. In *Proceedings of the 8th International Joint Conference on Artificial Intelligence* (Karlsruhe, West Germany, Aug.). Kaufmann, Los Altos, Calif., pp. 1136–1138.

BHANU, B., AND FAUGERAS, O. D. 1984. Shape matching of two-dimensional objects. *IEEE Trans. Pattern Anal. Mach. Intell. 6*, 2 (Mar.), 137–156.

BINFORD, T. O. 1971. Visual perception by computer. In the *IEEE Systems Science and Cybernetics Conference* (Miami, Fla., Dec.). IEEE, New York.

BINFORD, T. O. 1982. Survey of model-based image analysis systems. *Int. J. Robotics Res. 1*, 1 (Spring), 18–63.

BIRK, J. R., KELLEY, R. B. CHEN, N.-Y., AND WILSON, L. 1979. Image feature extraction using diameter-limited gradient direction histograms. *IEEE Trans. Pattern Anal. Mach. Intell. 1*, 2 (Apr.), 228–235.

BIRK, J. R., KELLEY, R. B., AND MARTINS, H. 1981. An orienting robot for feeding workpieces stored in bins. *IEEE Trans. Syst. Man Cybern. 11*, 2 (Feb.), 151–160.

BOLLES, R. C. 1979a. Symmetry analysis of two-dimensional patterns for computer vision. In *Proceedings of the 6th International Joint Conference on Artificial Intelligence* (Tokyo, Japan, Aug.). Kaufmann, Los Altos, Calif., pp. 70–72.

BOLLES, R. C. 1979b. Robust feature matching through maximal cliques. In *Proceedings of the Society of Photo-Optical Instrumentation Engineers Conference on Imaging Applications for Automated Industrial Inspection and Assembly* (Washington, D.C., Apr.), vol. 182. SPIE, Bellingham, Wash., pp. 140–149.

BOLLES, R. C. 1981. Overview of applications of image understanding to industrial automation. In *Proceedings of the Society of Photo-Optical Instrumentation Engineers Conference on Techniques and Applications of Image Understanding* (Washington, D.C., Apr.), vol. 281. SPIE, Bellingham, Wash., pp. 134–140.

BOLLES, R. C., AND CAIN, R. A. 1982. Recognizing and locating partially visible objects: The local-feature-focus method. *Int. J. Robotics Res. 1*, 3, 57–82.

BOLLES, R. C., AND FISCHLER, M. A. 1981. A RANSAC-based approach to model fitting and its application to finding cylinders in range data. In *Proceedings of the 7th International Joint Conference on Artificial Intelligence* (Vancouver, Canada, Aug.). Kaufmann, Los Altos, Calif., pp. 637–643.

BOLLES, R. C., HORAUD, P., AND HANNAH, M. J. 1984. 3DPO: A three-dimensional part orientation system. In *Robotics Research: The 1st International Symposium*, M. Brady and R. Paul, Eds. MIT Press, Cambridge, Mass., pp. 413–424.

BRADY, M. 1982a. Computational approaches to image understanding. *ACM Comput. Surv. 14*, 1 (Mar.), 3–71.

BRADY, M. 1982b. Parts description and acquisition using vision. In *Proceedings of the Society of Photo-Optical Instrumentation Engineers Conference on Robot Vision* (Arlington, Va., May), vol. 336. SPIE, Bellingham, Wash., pp. 20–28.

BROOKS, R. A. 1979. Goal-directed edge linking and ribbon finding. In *Proceedings of the Image Understanding Workshop* (Menlo Park, Calif., Apr.). Science Applications, Arlington, Va., pp. 72–76.

BROOKS, R. A. 1983a. Symbolic reasoning among 3-D models and 2-D images, *Artif. Intell. 17*, 1 (Aug.), 285–348.

BROOKS, R. A. 1983b. Model-based three-dimensional interpretations of two-dimensional images. *IEEE Trans. Pattern Anal. Mach. Intell. 5*, 2 (Mar.), 140–150.

BROOKS, R. A., AND BINFORD, T. O. 1981. Geometric modeling in vision for manufacturing. In *Proceedings of the Society of Photo-Optical Instrumentation Engineers Conference on Robot Vision* (Washington, D.C., Apr.), vol. 281. SPIE, Bellingham, Wash., pp. 141–159.

BROU, P. 1984. Using the Gaussian image to find the orientation of objects. *Int. J. Robotics Res. 3*, 4 (Winter), 89–125.

BRUNE, W., AND BITTER, K. H. 1983. S.A.M. Opto-electronic picture sensor in a flexible manufacturing system. In *Robot Vision*, A. Pugh, Ed. Springer-Verlag, New York, pp. 325–337.

CASLER, R. J. 1983. Vision-guided robot part acquisition for assembly packaging applications. Tech. Paper MS83-219, Society of Manufacturing Engineers, Dearborn, Mich.

CHAKRAVARTY, I. 1979. A generalized line and junction labeling scheme with applications to scene analysis. *IEEE Trans. Pattern Anal. Mach. Intell. 1*, 2 (Apr.), 202–205.

CHAKRAVARTY, I., AND FREEMAN, H. 1982. Characteristic views as a basis for three-dimensional object recognition. In *Proceedings of the Society of Photo-Optical Instrumentation Engineers Conference on Robot Vision* (Arlington, Va., May), vol. 336. SPIE, Bellingham, Wash., pp. 37–45.

CHEN, M. J., AND MILGRAM, D. L. 1982. A development system for machine vision. In *Proceedings of the IEEE Computer Society Conference on Pattern Recognition and Image Processing* (Las Vegas, Nev., June). IEEE, New York, pp. 512–517.

CHEN, N.-Y., BIRK, J. R., AND KELLEY, R. B. 1980. Estimating workpiece pose using the feature points method. *IEEE Trans. Auto. Control 25*, 6 (Dec.), 1027–1041.

CHENG, J. K., AND HUANG, T. S. 1981. Image recognition by matching relational structure. In *Proceedings of the IEEE Computer Society Conference on Pattern Recognition and Image Processing* (Dallas, Tex., Aug.). IEEE, New York, pp. 542–547.

CHENG, J. K., AND HUANG, T. S. 1982. Recognition of curvilinear objects by matching relational structure. In *Proceedings of the IEEE Computer Society Conference on Pattern Recognition and Image Processing* (Las Vegas, Nev., June). IEEE, New York, pp. 343–348.

CHIN, R. T. 1982. Machine vision for discrete part handling in industry: A survey. In *Conference Record of the Workshop on Industrial Applications of Machine Vision* (Research Triangle Park, N.C., May). IEEE, New York, pp. 26–32.

CHIN, R. T., AND HARLOW, C. A. 1982. Automated visual inspection: A survey. *IEEE Trans. Pattern Anal. Mach. Intell. 4*, 6 (Nov.), 557–573.

CHOW, C. K., AND KANEKO, T. 1972. Automatic boundary detection of the left ventricle from cineangiograms. *Comput. Biomed. Res. 5*, 4 (Aug.), 388–410.

DESSIMOZ, J.-D. 1978a. Visual identification and location in a multiobject environment by contour tracking and curvature description. In *Proceedings of the 8th International Symposium on Industrial Robots* (Stuttgart, West Germany, May), pp. 746–776.

DESSIMOZ, J.-D. 1978b. Recognition and handling of overlapping industrial parts. In *Proceedings of the International Symposium on Computer Vision and Sensor-Based Robots* (Warren, Mich., Sept.). General Motors Research Symposium, Warren, Mich.

DUDA, R. O., NITZAN, D., AND BARRET, P. 1979. Use of range and reflectance data to find planar surface regions. *IEEE Trans. Pattern Anal. Mach. Intell. 1*, 3 (July), 259–271.

FAUGERAS, O. D., AND HEBERT, M. 1983. A 3-D recognition and positioning algorithm using geometrical matching between primitive surfaces. In *Proceedings of the 8th International Joint Conference on Artificial Intelligence* (Karlsruhe, West Germany, Aug.). Kaufmann, Los Altos, Calif., pp. 996–1002.

FAUGERAS, O. D., GERMAIN, F., KRYZE, G., BOISSONNAT, J., HEBERT, M., PONCE, J., PAUCHON, E., AND AYACHE, N. 1983. Towards a flexible vision system. In *Robot Vision*, A. Pugh, Ed. Springer-Verlag, New York, pp. 129–142.

FAUGERAS, O. D., HEBERT, M., PAUCHON, E., AND PONCE, J. 1984. Object representation, identification, and positioning from range data. In *Robotics Research: The First International Symposium*, M. Brady and R. Paul, Eds. MIT Press, Cambridge, Mass., pp. 425–446.

FOITH, J. P., EISENBARTH, C., ENDERLS, E., GEISSELMANN, H., RINGSHAUSER, H., AND ZIMMERMANN, G. 1981. Real-time processing of binary images for industrial applications. In *Digital Image Processing Systems*, L. Bolc and Z. Kulpa, Eds. Springer-Verlag, Berlin, pp. 61–168.

FU, K. S. 1983. Robot vision for machine part recognition. In *Proceedings of the Society of Photo-Optical Instrumentation Engineers Conference on Robotics and Robot Sensing Systems* (San Diego, Calif., Aug.), vol. 442. SPIE, Bellingham, Wash.

FUCHS, H., KEDEM, Z. M., AND NAYLOR, B. F. 1980. On visible surface generation by a priori tree structures. In *Proceedings of SIGGRAPH '80* (Seattle, Wash., July). ACM, New York, pp. 124–133.

GLEASON, G. J., AND AGIN, G. J. 1979. A modular system for sensor-controlled manipulation and inspection. In *Proceedings of the 9th International Symposium on Industrial Robots* (Washington, D.C., Mar.). Society of Manufacturing Engineers, Dearborn, Mich., pp. 57–70.

GOAD, C. 1983. Special-purpose automatic programming for 3D model-based vision. In *Proceedings of the Image Understanding Workshop* (Arlington, Va., June). Science Applications, Arlington, Va., pp. 94–104.

GRIMSON, W. E. L., AND LOZANO-PEREZ, T. 1984. Model-based recognition and localization from sparse range or tactile data. *Int. J. Robotics Res. 3*, 3 (Fall), 3–35.

HATTICH, W. 1982. Recognition of overlapping workpieces by model directed construction of object contours. *Digital Syst. Ind. Autom. 1*, 223–239.

HENDERSON, T. C. 1982. Efficient segmentation method for range data. In *Proceedings of the Society of Photo-Optical Instrumentation Engineers Conference on Robot Vision* (Arlington, Va., May), vol. 336. SPIE, Bellingham, Wash., pp. 46–47.

HENDERSON, T. C., AND BHANU, B. 1982. Three-point seed method for the extraction of planar faces from range data. In *Conference Record of the Workshop on Industrial Applications of Machine Vision* (Research Triangle Park, N.C., May). IEEE, New York, pp. 181–186.

HOLLAND, S. W., ROSSOL, L., AND WARD, M. R. 1979. CONSIGHT-I: A vision-controlled robot system for transferring parts from belt conveyors. In *Computer Vision and Sensor-Based Robots*, G. G. Dodd and L. Rossol, Eds. Plenum, New York, pp. 81–97.

HORN, B. K. P. 1975a. A problem in computer vision: Orienting silicon integrated circuit chips for lead bonding. *Comput. Gr. Image Process. 4*, 3 (Sept.) 294–303.

HORN, B. K. P. 1975b. Obtaining shape from shading information. In *The Psychology of Computer Vision*, P. H. Winston, Ed. McGraw-Hill, New York, pp. 115–155.

HORN, B. K. P. 1979. SEQUINS and QUILLS—Representations for surface topography. Artificial Intelligence Laboratory Memo 536, MIT, Cambridge, Mass., May.

HORN, B. K. P. 1984. Extended Gaussian images. *Proc. IEEE 72*, 12 (Dec.), 1671–1686.

HSIEH, Y. Y., AND FU, K. S. 1979. A method for automatic IC chip alignment and wire bonding. In *Proceedings of the IEEE Computer Society Conference on Pattern Recognition and Image Processing* (Chicago, Ill., Aug.). IEEE, New York, pp. 101–108.

HUECKEL, M. F. 1971. An operator which locates edges in digitized pictures. *J. ACM 18*, 1 (Jan.), 113–125.

IGARASHI, K., NARUSE, M., MIYAZAKI, S., AND YAMADA, T. 1979. Fully automated integrated circuit wire bonding system. In *Proceedings of the 9th International Symposium on Industrial Robots* (Washington, D.C., Mar.). Society of Manufacturing Engineers, Dearborn, Mich., pp. 87–97.

IKEUCHI, K. 1981a. Determining surface orientations of specular surfaces by using the photometric stereo method. *IEEE Trans. Pattern Anal. Mach. Intell. 3*, 6 (Nov.), 661–669.

IKEUCHI, K. 1981b. Recognition of 3-D objects using the extended Gaussian image. In *Proceedings of the 7th International Joint Conference on Artificial Intelligence* (Vancouver, Canada, Aug.). Kaufmann, Los Altos, Calif., pp. 595–600.

IKEUCHI, K. 1983. Determining the attitude of an object from a needle map using the extended Gaussian image. Artificial Intelligence Laboratory Memo 714, M.I.T., Cambridge, Mass., Apr.

IKEUCHI, K., AND SHIRAI, Y. 1982. A model-based vision system for recognition of machine parts. In *Proceedings of the National Conference on Artificial Intelligence* (Pittsburgh, Pa., Aug.). Kaufmann, Los Altos, Calif., pp. 18–21.

IKEUCHI, K., HORN, B. K. P., NAGATA, S., CALLAHAN, T., AND FEINGOLD, O. 1984. Picking up an object from a pile of objects. In *Robotics Research: The First International Symposium*, M. Brady and R. Paul, Eds. MIT Press, Cambridge, Mass., pp. 139–162.

JAKUBOWSKI, R. 1982. Syntactic characterization of machine parts shapes, *Cybern. Syst. 13*, 1 (Jan.–Mar.), 1–24.

JAKUBOWSKI, R., AND KASPRZAK, A. 1977. A syntactic description and recognition of rotary machine elements. *IEEE Trans. Comput. 26*, 10 (Oct.), 1039–1042.

JARVIS, J. F. 1980. Visual inspection automation. *Computer 13*, 5 (May), 32–39.

JARVIS, R. A. 1983a. A perspective on range finding techniques. *IEEE Trans. Pattern Anal. Mach. Intell. 5*, 2 (Mar.), 122–139.

JARVIS, R. A. 1983b. A laser time-of-flight range scanner for robotic vision. *IEEE Trans. Pattern Anal. Mach. Intell. 5*, 5 (Sept.), 505–512.

KANADE, T., AND ASADA, H. 1981. Noncontact visual three-dimensional ranging devices. In *Proceedings of the Society of Photo-Optical Instrumentation Engineers Conference on 3-D Machine Perception* (Washington, D.C., Apr.), vol. 283. SPIE, Bellingham, Wash., pp. 48–53.

KASHIOKA, S., EJIRI, M., AND SAKAMOTO, Y. 1976. A transistor wire-bonding system utilizing multiple local pattern matching techniques. *IEEE Trans. Syst. Man Cybern. 6*, 8 (Aug.), 562–569.

KASHIOKA, S., TAKEDA, S., SHIMA, Y., UNO, T., AND HAMADA, T. 1977. An approach to the integrated intelligent robot with multiple sensory feedback: Visual recognition techniques. In *Proceedings of the 7th International Symposium on Industrial Robots* (Tokyo, Japan, Oct.). Japan Industrial Robot Association, pp. 531–538.

KELLEY, R. B. 1983. Binary and gray-scale robot vision. In *Proceedings of the Society of Photo-Optical Instrumentation Engineers Conference on Robotics and Robot Sensing Systems* (San Diego, Calif., Aug.), vol. 442. SPIE, Bellingham, Wash.

KELLEY, R. B., BIRK, J. R., MARTINS, H. A. S., AND TELLA, R. 1982. A robot system which acquires cylindrical workpieces from bins. *IEEE Trans. Syst. Man Cybern. 12*, 2 (Mar./Apr.), 204–213.

KELLEY, R. B., MARTINS, H. A. S., BIRK, J. R., AND DESSIMOZ, J.-D. 1983. Three vision algorithms for acquiring workpieces from bins. *Proc. IEEE 71*, 7 (July), 803–820.

KENDER, J. R. 1980. Shape from texture. Ph.D. dissertation, Computer Science Dept., Carnegie-Mellon Univ., Pittsburgh, Pa.

KINNUCAN, P. 1983. Machines that see. *High Technol. 3*, 4 (Apr.), 30–36.

KITCHIN, P. W., AND PUGH, A. 1983. Processing of binary images. In *Robot Vision*, A. Pugh, Ed. Springer-Verlag, New York, pp. 21–42.

KOENDERINK, J. J., AND VANDOORN A. J. 1976a. The singularities of the visual mapping. *Biol. Cybern. 24*, 51–59.

KOENDERINK, J. J., AND VANDOORN A. J. 1976b. Visual perception of rigidity of solid shape. *J. Math. Biol. 3*, 79–85.

KOENDERINK, J. J., AND VANDOORN, A. J. 1979. The internal representation of solid shape with respect to vision. *Biol. Cybern. 32*, 211–216.

KRUGER, R. P., AND THOMPSON, W. B. 1981. A technical and economic assessment of computer vision for industrial inspection and robotic assembly. *Proc. IEEE 69*, 12 (Dec.), 1524–1538.

LIEBERMAN, L. 1979. Model-driven vision for industrial automation. In *Advances in Digital Image Processing*, P. Stucki, Ed. Plenum, New York, pp. 235–246.

MARIMONT, D. H. 1982. Segmentation in Acronym. In *Proceedings of the Image Understanding Workshop* (Palo Alto, Calif., Sept.). Science Applications, Arlington, Va., pp. 223–229.

MARR, D. 1978. Representing visual information. In *Computer Vision Systems*, A. R. Hanson and E. M. Riseman, Eds. Academic Press, Orlando, Fla., pp. 61–80.

MARR, D. 1982. *Vision.* Freeman, San Francisco.

MESE, M., YAMAZAKI, I., AND HAMADA, T. 1977. An automatic position recognition technique for LSI assembly. In *Proceedings of the 5th International Joint Conference on Artificial Intelligence* (Cambridge, Mass., Aug.). Kaufmann, Los Altos, Calif., pp. 685–693.

MILGRAM, D. L., AND BJORKLUND, C. M. 1980. Range image processing: Planar surface extraction. In *Proceedings of the 5th International Conference on Pattern Recognition* (Miami Beach, Fla., Dec.). IEEE, New York, pp. 912–919.

MYERS, W. 1980. Industry begins to use visual pattern recognition. *Computer 13*, 5 (May), 21–31.

NEVATIA, R., AND BINFORD, T. O. 1977. Description and recognition of curved objects. *Artif. Intell. 8*, 1 (Jan.), 77–98.

OSHIMA, M., AND SHIRAI, Y. 1979. A scene description method using three-dimensional information. *Pattern Recogn. 11*, 1, 9–17.

OSHIMA, M., AND SHIRAI, Y. 1983. Object recognition using three-dimensional information. *IEEE Trans. Pattern Anal. Mach. Intell. 5*, 4 (July), 353–361.

PAGE, C. J., AND PUGH, A. 1981. Visually interactive gripping of engineering parts from random orientation. *Digital Syst. Ind. Autom. 1*, 1, 11–44.

PERKINS, W. A. 1978. A model-based vision system for industrial parts. *IEEE Trans. Comput 27*, 2 (Feb.), 126–143.

PERKINS, W. A. 1980. Area segmentation of images using edge points. *IEEE Trans. Pattern Anal. Mach. Intell. 2*, 1 (Jan.), 8–15.

PERSOON, E., AND FU., K. S. 1977. Shape discrimination using Fourier descriptors. *IEEE Trans. Syst. Man Cybern. 7*, 3 (Mar.), 170–179.

PIPITONE, F. J., AND MARSHALL, T. G. 1983. A wide-field scanning triangulation rangefinder for machine vision. *Int. J. Robotics Res. 2*, 1 (Spring), 39–49.

POJE, J. F., AND DELP, E. J. 1982. A review of techniques for obtaining depth information with applications to machine vision. Tech. Rep. RSD-TR-2-82, Center for Robotics and Integrated Manufacturing, Univ. of Michigan, Ann Arbor.

POPPLESTONE, R. J., BROWN, C. M., AMBLER, A. P., AND CRAWFORD, G. F. 1975. Forming models of plane-and-cylinder faceted bodies from light stripes. In *Proceedings of the 4th International Joint Conference on Artificial Intelligence* (Tbilisi, USSR, Sept.). Kaufmann, Los Altos, Calif., pp. 664–668.

PORTER, G. B., AND MUNDY, J. L. 1980. Visual inspection system design. *Computer 13*, 5 (May), 40–49.

POT, J., COIFFET, P., AND RIVES, P. 1983. Comparison of five methods for the recognition of industrial parts. In *Developments in Robotics*, B. Rooks, Ed. Springer-Verlag, New York.

POTMESIL, M. 1983. Generating models of solid objects by matching 3D surface segments. In *Proceedings of the 8th International Joint Conference on Artificial Intelligence* (Karlsruhe, West Germany, Aug.). Kaufmann, Los Altos, Calif., pp. 1089–1093.

PUGH, A., ED. 1983. *Robot Vision.* Springer-Verlag, New York.

RAY, R. BIRK, J., AND KELLEY, R. B. 1983. Error analysis of surface normals determined by radiometry. *IEEE Trans. Pattern Anal. Mach. Intell. 5*, 6 (Nov.), 631–645.

REQUICHA, A. A. G. 1980. Representations for rigid solids: Theory, methods, and systems. *ACM Comput. Surv. 12*, 4 (Dec.), 437–464.

ROSEN, C. A. 1979. Machine vision and robotics: Industrial requirements. In *Computer Vision and Sensor-Based Robots*, G. G. Dodd and L. Rossol, Eds. Plenum, New York, pp. 3–20.

ROSEN C. A., AND GLEASON, G. J. 1981. Evaluating vision system performance. *Robotics Today* (Fall).

ROSENFELD, A., AND DAVIS L. S. 1979. Image segmentation and image models. *Proc. IEEE 67*, 5 (May), 764–772.

ROSSOL, L. 1983. Computer vision in industry. In *Robot Vision*, A. Pugh, Ed. Springer-Verlag, New York, pp. 11–18.

SCHACHTER, B. J. 1983. A matching algorithm for robot vision. In *Proceedings of the IEEE Computer Society Conference on Computer Vision and Pattern Recognition* (Washington, D.C., June). IEEE, New York, pp. 490–491.

SEGEN, J. 1983. Locating randomly oriented objects from partial views. In *Proceedings of the Society of Photo-Optical Instrumentation Engineers Conference on Robot Vision and Sensory Controls*, (Cambridge, Mass., Nov.), vol. 449. SPIE, Bellingham, Wash.

SHIRAI, Y. 1972. Recognition of polyhedrons with a range finder. *Pattern Recogn. 4*, 3 (Oct.), 243–250.

SHIRAI, Y. 1975. Edge finding, segmentation of edges and recognition of complex objects. In *Proceedings of the 4th International Joint Conference on Artificial Intelligence* (Tbilisi, USSR, Sept.). Kaufmann, Los Altos, Calif., pp. 674–681.

SHIRAI, Y. 1978. Recognition of real-world objects using edge cues. In *Computer Vision Systems*, A. R. Hanson and E. M. Riseman, Eds. Academic Press, New York, pp. 353–362.

SHNEIER, M. 1979. A compact relational structure representation. In *Proceedings of the 6th International Joint Conference on Artificial Intelligence* (Tokyo, Japan, Aug.). Kaufmann, Los Altos, Calif., pp. 818–826.

SHNEIER, M. 1981. Models and strategies for matching in industrial vision. Tech. Rep. TR-1073, Computer Science Dept., Univ. of Maryland, College Park, July.

SILBERBERG, T. M., DAVIS, L. S., AND HARWOOD, D. 1984. An iterative Hough procedure for three-dimensional object recognition. *Pattern Recogn.* 17 6, 621–629.

SILVER, W. M. 1980. Determining shape and reflectance using multiple images. M.Sc. thesis, M.I.T., Cambridge, Mass.

SMITH, D. A. 1979. Using enhanced spherical images for object representation. Artificial Intelligence Laboratory Memo 530, M.I.T., Cambridge, Mass., May.

STEVENS, K. A. 1981. The information content of texture gradients. *Biol. Cybern.* 42, 95–105.

STOCKMAN, G. C. 1980. Recognition of parts and their orientation for automatic machining, handling and inspection. Rep. NSF-SIBR-Phase I, NTIS Order PB 80-178817.

STOCKMAN, G. C., KOPSTEIN, K., AND BENETT, S. 1982. Matching images to models for registration and object detection via clustering. *IEEE Trans. Pattern Anal. Mach. Intell.* 4, 3 (May), 229–241.

SUGIHARA, K. 1979. Range-data analysis guided by a junction dictionary. *Artif. Intell.* 12, 1 (May), 41–69.

TAKEYASU, K., KASAI, M., SHIMOMURA, R., GOTO, T., AND MATSUMOTO, Y. 1977. An approach to the integrated intelligent robot with multiple sensory feedback. In *Proceedings of the 7th International Symposium on Industrial Robots* (Tokyo, Japan, Oct.), pp. 523–530.

TENENBAUM, J. M., BARROW, H. G., AND BOLLES, R. C. 1979. Prospects for industrial vision. In *Computer Vision and Sensor-Based Robots*, G. G. Dodd and L. Rossol, Eds. Plenum, New York, pp. 239–256.

TROMBLY, J. E. 1982. Recent applications of computer aided vision in inspection and part sorting. In *Proceedings of the Robot VI Conference* (Detroit, Mich., Mar.). Society of Manufacturing Engineers, Dearborn, Mich.

TROPF, H. 1980. Analysis-by-synthesis search for semantic segmentation applied to workpiece recognition. In *Proceedings of the 5th International Conference on Pattern Recognition* (Miami Beach, Fla., Dec.). IEEE, New York, pp. 241–244.

TROPF, H. 1981. Analysis-by-synthesis search to interpret degraded image data. In *Proceedings of the 1st International Conference on Robot Vision and Sensory Controls* (Stratford-upon-Avon, England, Apr.). IFS, Kempston, England, pp. 25–33.

TROPF, H., GEISSELMANN, H., AND FOITH, J. P. 1982. Some applications of the fast industrial vision system S.A.M. In *Conference Record of the Workshop on Industrial Applications of Machine Vision* (Research Triangle Park, N.C., May). IEEE, New York, pp. 73–79.

TURNEY, J. L., MUDGE, T. N., AND VOLZ, R. A. 1985. Recognizing partially occluded parts. *IEEE Trans. Pattern Anal. Mach. Intell.* 7, 4 (July), 410–421.

UMETANI, Y., AND TAGUCHI, K. 1979. Feature properties to discriminate complex shapes. In *Proceedings of the 9th International Symposium on Industrial Robots* (Washington, D.C., Mar.). Society of Manufacturing Engineers, Dearborn, Mich., pp. 367–378.

UMETANI, Y., AND TAGUCHI, K. 1982. Discrimination of general shapes by psychological feature properties. *Digital Syst. Ind. Autom.* 1, 2–3, 179–196.

VAMOS, T. 1977. Industrial objects and machine parts recognition. In *Applications of Syntactic Pattern Recognition*, K. S. Fu, Ed. Springer-Verlag, New York.

VILLERS, P. 1983. Present industrial use of vision sensors for robot guidance. In *Robot Vision*, A. Pugh, Ed. Springer-Verlag, New York, pp. 157–168.

WEST, P. C. 1982. Overview of machine vision. Tech. Paper MS82-184, Society of Manufacturing Engineers, Dearborn, Mich.

WITKIN, A. P. 1981. Recovering surface shape and orientation from texture. *Artif. Intell.* 17, 1 (Aug.), 17–47.

WOODHAM, R. J. 1978. Photometric stereo: A reflectance map technique for determining surface orientation from image intensity. In *Proceedings of the Society of Photo-Optical Instrumentation Engineers Conference on Image Understanding Systems and Industrial Applications* (San Diego, Calif., Aug.), vol. 155. SPIE, Bellingham, Wash., pp. 136–143.

YACHIDA, M., AND TSUJI, S. 1977. A versatile machine vision system for complex industrial parts. *IEEE Trans. Comput. 26*, 9 (Sept.), 882–894.

YACHIDA, M., AND TSUJI, S. 1980. Industrial computer vision in Japan. *Computer 13*, 5 (May), 50–63.

ZAHN, C. T., AND ROSKIEW, R. Z. 1972. Fourier descriptors for plane closed curves. *IEEE Trans. Comput. 21*, 3 (Mar.), 269–281.

ZUECH, N., AND RAY, R. 1983. Vision guided robotic arm control for part acquisition. In *Proceedings of the Control Engineering Conference* (West Lafayette, Ind.). Purdue Univ., West Lafayette, Ind.

Received January 1984; final revision accepted February 1986

Chapter 6: Dynamic Vision

Early computer vision systems were concerned primarily with static scenes. However, the world is dynamic. Designing computer vision systems capable of analyzing dynamic scenes has received increasing attention in the last few years. For a computer vision system engaged in the performance of nontrivial real-world operations and tasks, the ability to cope with moving and changing objects and viewpoints is vital. Most biological vision systems have evolved to cope with the changing world.

The input to a dynamic-scene analysis system is a sequence of image frames taken from a changing world. The camera used to acquire the image sequence may also be in motion. Each frame represents an image of the scene at a particular instant in time. The changes in a scene may be due to camera motion, object motion, illumination changes, or changes in object structure, size, or shape. Changes in a scene are usually assumed to be due to camera and/or object motion. Objects are usually assumed to be either rigid or quasi-rigid. Other changes are not allowed. The tasks of a dynamic-scene analysis system are to

- Detect changes;
- Determine the motion characteristics of the observer and the objects;
- Characterize the motion using high-level abstraction;
- Recover the structure of the objects; and
- Recognize moving objects.

Future systems will possibly be required to first observe a scene and then describe in natural language the events taking place.

A scene usually contains several objects. An image of the scene at a given time represents a projection of part of the scene; the part of the scene projected depends on the position of the camera. The following cases represent the four possibilities for the dynamic-camera/world setup:

(1) Stationary camera, stationary objects (*SCSO*);
(2) Stationary camera, moving objects (*SCMO*);
(3) Moving camera, stationary objects (*MCSO*); and
(4) Moving camera, moving objects (*MCMO*).

The first case is simply static-scene analysis. In many applications, processing a single image to obtain the required information may be necessary and/or possible. However, many more applications exist that require information to be extracted from a dynamic environment. Some applications require a vision system to understand a dynamic process, such as cell motion.

Clearly, a sequence of image frames offers much more information to aid in understanding a scene, but significantly increases the amount of data to be processed by the system. Applying static-scene analysis techniques to each frame of a sequence requires an enormous amount of computation, while still suffering from all of the problems of static-scene analysis. Fortunately, research in dynamic-scene analysis has shown that information recovery may be easier in dynamic scenes than in static scenes; in some cases, total computational effort may be significantly less and performance better (e.g., segmenting a scene).

SCMO scenes have received the most attention in dynamic-scene analysis. The objectives of such scene analysis usually are to detect motion, to extract masks of moving objects with the aim of recognizing them, and to compute their motion characteristics. *MCSO* scenes have recently received some attention, but *MCMO* scenes have been virtually ignored. *MCMO* is the most generalized case and possibly presents the most difficult situation in dynamic-scene analysis. Many techniques that have been developed assuming a stationary camera are not applicable if the camera is allowed to move. Likewise, techniques that have been developed for a moving camera have generally assumed a stationary scene and are usually not applicable if the objects are allowed to move. *SCMO* and *MCSO* have found many applications and have been studied by researchers in various contexts under various assumptions.

Dynamic-scene analysis can be considered to be composed of three phases: peripheral, attentive, and cognitive. The peripheral phase is concerned with extraction of approximate information, which is very helpful in the later phases. This information indicates the activity in a scene; it is used to decide the parts of the scene that need careful analysis. The attentive phase concentrates its analysis on the active parts of the scene and extracts information that can be used for object recognition, analysis of object motion, preparation of a history of events taking place in the scene, or other related phenomena. The cognitive phase applies knowledge about objects, motion verbs, and other application-dependent concepts to analyze the scene in terms of the objects present and the events taking place.

The input to a dynamic-scene analysis system is a frame sequence, represented by $F(x,y,t)$, where x and y are the spatial coordinates in the frame representing the scene at time t. The value of the function represents the intensity of the pixel. The image is assumed to be obtained using a camera located at the origin of a three-dimensional coordinate system. The projection used in this observer-centered system may be either perspective or orthographic. The three-dimensional coordinates of a point are (X,Y,Z) and the projection of the point onto the image plane is denoted by (x,y). The line of sight, or the optical axis, of the camera is assumed to be along the Z-axis. Since the frames are usually taken at regular intervals, we will assume that t represents the tth frame of the sequence, rather than the frame taken at absolute time t.

Change detection

Any perceptible motion in a scene results in some change in the sequence of frames of the scene. If such changes are detected, motion characteristics can be analyzed. A good quantitative estimate of the motion components of an object can be obtained if the motion is restricted to a plane that is parallel to the image plane; for three-dimensional motion, only qualitative estimates are possible. Historically, dynamic-scene analysis is based on the detection of change in a frame sequence. By analyzing frame-to-frame changes, a global analysis of the sequence can be performed. Changes can be detected at different levels: pixel, edge, or region. Changes detected at the pixel level can be aggregated to obtain useful information with which the computational requirements of later phases can be constrained.

Pixel-level change detection. The most obvious method of detecting change between two frames is to directly compare the corresponding pixels of the frames to determine whether or not they are the same. In the simplest form, a binary difference picture $DP_{jk}(x,y)$ between frames $F(x,y,j)$ and $F(x,y,k)$ is obtained by

$$DP_{jk}(x,y) = 1 \quad if \, | \, F(x,y,j) - F(x,y,k) \, | \, > \tau$$
$$= 0 \quad otherwise$$

$$(6.1)$$

where τ is a threshold.

In the difference picture, pixels that have value 1 may be considered to be the result of object motion, assuming that the frames have been properly registered and that the illumination in the image has remained constant. Because of noise, such a simple test on real scenes usually results in unsatisfactory results. A simple size filter may be used to ignore pixels not forming a connected cluster of a minimum size. Then only those pixels in a difference picture with a value of 1 that belong to a four-connected (or eight-connected) component larger than some threshold size will be attributed to motion. The fact that noise entries are usually isolated and that changes due to the motion of surfaces form connected clusters in difference pictures comprise the motivations behind the use of this filter. The filter is very effective in reducing noise, but it also unfortunately filters some desirable signals, such as those from slow or small moving objects.

To make change detection more robust, regions or groups of pixels at the same location in two frames may be considered and their intensity characteristics may be compared more rigorously. A method that illustrates making change detection more robust is based on comparing the frames using the likelihood ratio.[211] Thus, we can compute

$$\lambda = \frac{\left[\dfrac{\sigma_1^2 + \sigma_2^2}{2} + \left(\dfrac{\mu_1 - \mu_2}{2} \right)^2 \right]^2}{\sigma_1^2 \, \sigma_2^2}$$

$$(6.2)$$

where μ denotes the mean gray value and σ denotes the square root of the variance from the frames for the sample areas. Then we use

$$DP_{jk}(x,y) = 1 \quad if \, \lambda > \tau$$
$$= 0 \quad otherwise$$

$$(6.3)$$

where τ is a threshold.

The likelihood ratio can be applied to areas only and not to single pixels. This limitation presents a minor problem, which can be solved by considering corresponding areas of the frames. The likelihood ratio test, combined with the use of a size filter, work quite well for noise removal. The likelihood ratio test can be applied to every point in each frame by considering overlapping areas centered on each pixel of the image.

Superpixels effectively raise the size threshold for the detection of slow and small moving objects; thus, the problem of missing detection of such objects is exacerbated. However, this problem can be solved by analyzing change over a sequence of frames, instead of between just two frames, and using an accumulative-difference picture (ADP) to detect the motion of slow and small moving objects. An accumulative-difference picture is formed by comparing every frame of an image sequence to a reference frame and increasing the entry in the accumulative-difference picture by one whenever the likelihood ratio for the area exceeds the threshold. Thus, an accumulative-difference picture ADP_k is acquired over k frames by

$$ADP_0 \ (x,y) = 0$$
$$ADP_k \ (x,y) = ADP_{k-1} \ (x,y) + DP_{1k} \ (x,y) \tag{6.4}$$

The first frame of a sequence is usually the reference frame, and the accumulative-difference picture ADP_0 is initialized to zero, as illustrated in Figure 6.1.[212]

```
        9
        10   00000000
        11   00000000
        12   00000000
(a)     13   00000000
        14   00000000
        15   00000000
        16
        9                        9
        10   00000000           10   1              1
        11   00000000           11   1              1
        12   00000000           12   1              1
(b)     13   00000000           13   1              1           (f)
        14   00000000           14   1              1
        15   00000000           15   1              1
        16                       16
        9                        9
        10   00000000           10   21             21
        11   00000000           11   21             21
        12   00000000           12   21             21
(c)     13   00000000           13   21             21          (g)
        14   00000000           14   21             21
        15   00000000           15   21             21
        16                       16
        9                        9
        10   00000000           10   321            321
        11   00000000           11   321            321
        12   00000000           12   321            321
(d)     13   00000000           13   321            321         (h)
        14   00000000           14   321            321
        15   00000000           15   321            321
        16                       16
        9                        9
        10       00000000       10   A98765438887654321
        11       00000000       11   A98765438887654321
        12       00000000       12   A98765438887654321
(e)     13       00000000       13   A98765438887654321         (i)
        14       00000000       14   A98765438887654321
        15       00000000       15   A98765438887654321
        16                       16
```

Figure 6.1: Calculation of Accumulative Difference Picture (ADP); (a-e) Frames 1,2,3,4, and 11; (f-i) corresponding ADP's (from Jain).[212]

471

The likelihood test just discussed is based on the assumption of uniform second-order statistics over a region. The performance of the likelihood ratio test can be improved significantly by using facets and quadratic surfaces to approximate the intensity values of pixels belonging to superpixels. These higher order approximations allow for better characterization of intensity values and result in more robust change detection.

The most attractive aspect of the difference picture is its simplicity. In its simplest form, the difference picture appears to be noise-prone. Electronic noise of the camera and changes in illumination and registration of the camera can result in many false alarms. A likelihood ratio, in conjunction with a size filter, can eliminate most of the camera noise. Changes in illumination will create problems for any intensity-based approach and can only be handled at a symbolic level. Misregistration of frames results in the assignment of false motion components. If the misregistration is not severe, accumulative-difference pictures can eliminate its effects.

Emphasis should be placed on the fact that measuring dissimilarities at the pixel level can detect only intensity changes. In dynamic-scene analysis, this is the lowest level of analysis. After such intensity changes have been detected, other processes are required to interpret these changes. Experience has shown that the most efficient use of the difference picture is to have peripheral processes direct the attention of interpretation processes to areas of the scene where some activity is taking place. Approximate information about events in a scene can be extracted using some features of difference pictures.

Static segmentation and matching. Segmentation is the task of identifying meaningful components in the context of an application of an image and grouping the pixels belonging to such components. Segmentation need not necessarily be performed in terms of objects; it may also be performed in terms of features — or predicates based on intensity characteristics. If an object or feature appears in two or more images, segmentation may be necessary in order to identify the object in the images. The process of identifying the same object or feature in two or more frames is called the "correspondence process."

Static-scene analysis techniques can be used to segment, or at least to partially segment, each frame of a dynamic sequence. Matching can then be used to determine correspondences and to detect changes in the location of corresponding segments. Cross-correlation and Fourier domain features have been used as a form of matching to detect cloud motion. Several systems have been developed that segment each frame of a sequence to find regions, corners, edges, or other features in the frames. Features in consecutive frames are then matched to detect any displacement. Some restriction on the possible matches for a feature can be achieved by predicting the new location of the feature based on the displacements in previous frames.

In the approaches just described, segmentation presents the major difficulty: Segmentation of an image in a static scene has been a difficult problem. Even after Herculean efforts, most attempts to segment complex real-world scenes give only good segmentations. However, better segmentation is widely believed to be producible using motion detection, in contrast to using segmentation and matching.

Using motion for segmentation

The goal of many dynamic-scene analysis systems is to recognize moving objects and to find their motion characteristics. If the system uses a stationary camera, the segmentation task generally involves separating moving components from stationary components in the scene. Then, the individual moving objects are identified based on either their velocity or on other characteristics. For systems using a moving camera, the segmentation task may be the same as above, or it may include further segmentation of the scene's stationary components by exploiting the camera's motion. Most research efforts for the segmentation of dynamic scenes have assumed a stationary camera.

Researchers in perception have argued that motion cues are helpful in segmentation. Computer vision techniques for segmenting SCMO scenes perform well compared to those for segmenting stationary scenes. In a system using a moving camera, segmentation into stationary and nonstationary components has only recently received any attention. One problem in segmenting moving-camera scenes is the fact that every surface in the scene has image plane motion. For segmenting moving-camera scenes, the motion assigned to components in the images that is due to the motion of the camera should be removed. The fact that the image motion of a surface depends on both the surface's distance from the camera and the structure of the surface complicates the situation.

Segmentation can be performed using either region-based or edge-based approaches. In this section, some approaches for segmenting of dynamic scenes are discussed.

A moving edge in a frame is (1) moving and (2) an edge. Moving edges can be detected by combining spatial and temporal gradients using an AND operator. This AND can be implemented through multiplication. Thus, the time-varying edgeness of a point in a frame $E_t(x,y,t)$ is given by

$$E_t(x,y,t) = \frac{dF(x,y,t)}{dS} \bullet \frac{dF(x,y,t)}{dt}$$
$$= E(x,y,t) \bullet D(x,y) \tag{6.5}$$

Various conventional edge detectors can be used to compute the spatial gradient, and a simple difference can be used to compute the temporal gradient. In most cases, this edge detector works effectively. By applying a threshold to the product, rather than first differencing and then applying an edge detector or first detecting edges and then computing their temporal gradient, this method overcomes the problem of slow-moving or weak edges being missed.

Using difference pictures. Difference and accumulative-difference pictures find the areas in a scene that are changing. (An area is usually changing because of object movement.) Although change detection results based on difference pictures are sensitive to noise, the areas produced by a difference picture are good places from which to start segmentation. In fact, as discussed by Jain,[213] segmentation of a scene can be performed with very little computation by using accumulative-difference pictures.

Using velocities. The relationship between the spatial (F_x and F_y) and temporal (F_t) gradients of intensities can be exploited for segmenting images. These gradients are related to the velocity components (u,v) by the following equation:

$$F_t = \frac{\partial F(x,y,t)}{\partial t} = -(F_x \bullet u + F_y \bullet v) \tag{6.6}$$

Assuming the same velocity component for points coming from the same object in an image, a Hough transform approach can be used to segment a scene into different moving objects.[214]

Optical flow

Optical flow is the distribution of velocity, relative to the observer, over the points of an image. Optical flow carries information that is valuable in dynamic-scene analysis. Several methods of dynamic-scene analysis have been proposed; these methods assume that optical-flow information is available. Although optical flow has received significant attention from researchers, the techniques developed for computing optical flow unfortunately produce results whose quality will not allow the valuable information to be recovered. Currently used methods of computing optical flow and information that is intrinsic to optical flow are discussed in this section.

Computation of the optical flow. Optical flow is determined by the velocity vector of each pixel in an image. Several methods have been devised for calculating optical flow based on two or more frames of a sequence. These methods can be classified into two general categories: feature-based and gradient-based. If a stationary camera is used, most of the points in an image frame will have zero velocity. This is assuming that a very small subset of the scene is in motion, which is usually true. Thus, most applications for optical flow involve a moving camera.

Feature-based methods. Feature-based methods for computing optical flow first select some features in the image frames, then match these features and calculate the disparities between frames. As discussed in an earlier section, the correspondence can be solved on a stereo-image pair using relaxation. The same approach can be used to solve the correspondence problem in dynamic scenes.[215] However, the problem of selecting features and establishing correspondence is not easy. Moreover, this method produces velocity vectors only at sparse points.

Gradient-based methods. Gradient-based methods exploit the relationship between the spatial and temporal gradients of intensity. As discussed earlier, this relationship can be used to segment images based on the velocity of points. The relationship between the spatial and temporal gradients and the velocity components is

$$F_x u + F_y v + F_t = 0 \tag{6.7}$$

In this equation, F_x, F_y, and F_t can be computed directly from the image. Then, at every point in an image, there are two unknowns, u and v, yet there is only one equation. Thus, the velocity components at a point cannot be obtained without making further assumptions.

The velocity field can be assumed to vary smoothly over an image. Under this assumption, an iterative approach for computing optical flow using two or more frames can be developed. The following iterative equations are used for the computation of optical flow:

$$u = u_{av} - F_x \frac{P}{D}$$
$$v = v_{av} - F_y \frac{P}{D}$$
$$where \qquad P = F_x u_{av} + F_y v_{av} + F_t$$
$$D = \lambda^2 + F_x^2 + F_y^2$$

(6.8)

In these equations, F_x, F_y, F_t, and λ represent the spatial gradients in the x- and y-directions, the temporal gradient, and a multiplier, respectively. When only two frames are used, the computation is iterated over the same frames many times. For more than two frames, each iteration uses a new frame. Because object surfaces may be at different depths, the smoothness constraint is not satisfied at the boundaries of objects. When overlapping objects are moving in different directions, this constraint will also be violated. These abrupt changes in the velocity field at the boundaries cause problems. Figure 6.2[5,122] illustrates the results of applying the above method of optical-flow calculation to synthetic data for a rotating checkered sphere.

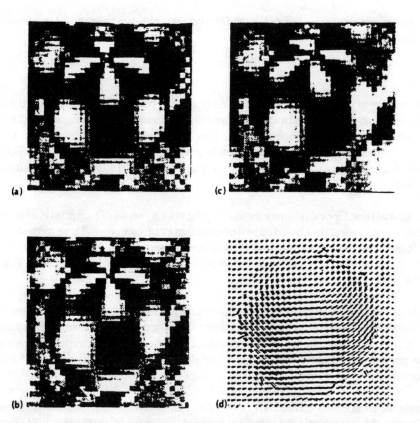

Figure 6.2: Calculation of Optical Flow; (a-c) three frames of a rotating checkered sphere; (d) calculated flow using 32 frames (from Ballard and Brown [5]; originally from Horn and Schunck [122])

An important fact to remember about gradient-based methods is that they assume a linear variation of intensities and compute the pointwise velocities under this assumption. This assumption is typically expected to be satisfied at edge points in images; hence, the velocity can be computed at these points.

Information in optical flow. Many researchers have studied what kind of information can be extracted from an optical-flow field, assuming that high-quality optical flow has been computed. Assume the following: (1) an environment that contains rigid, stationary surfaces at known depths and (2) an observer—i.e., the camera—that locomotes through this environment. The optical flow can be derived from the known three-dimensional structure of the environment. Thus, the structure of the environment can be obtained, in principle, from the optical-flow field that is computed.

Areas with smooth velocity gradients correspond to single surfaces in the image and contain information about the structure of the surface. Areas with large gradients contain information about occlusion and boundaries, since only different objects at different depths can move at different speeds relative to the camera. Using an observer-based coordinate system, a relationship between smooth velocity gradients and surface orientation can be derived. The orientation is specified with respect to the direction of motion of the observer.

The translational component of object motion is directed toward a point in the image called the "focus of expansion" (FOE), when the observer is approaching, or the "focus of contraction" (FOC), when the observer is receding. (Figure 6.3[5] illustrates the FOE due to observer motion.) This point is the intersection of the direction of object motion in the image plane. Surface structure can be recovered from the first and second spatial derivatives of the translational component. The angular velocity is fully determined by the rotational component.

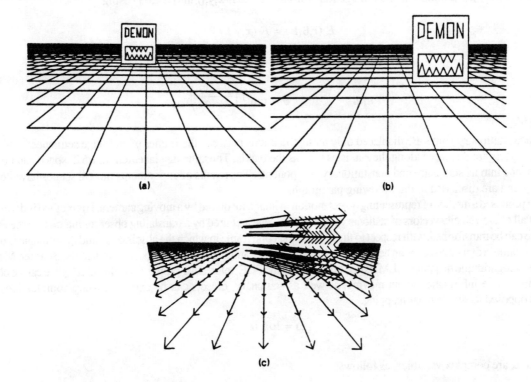

Figure 6.3: Illustration of focus of expansion (FOE) due to observer motion. (a-b) two time frames; (c) different FOEs for static floor and moving object (from D.H. Ballard and C.M. Brown, *Computer Vision*, © 1982 by Prentice-Hall. Reprinted with permission). [5]

If the FOE is correctly determined, it can be used for computing the translational components of optical flow. Since all flow vectors meet at the FOE, their direction is already known and only their magnitudes remain to be computed. Thus, the two-dimensional problem of optical-flow computation is reduced to a one-dimensional problem. Although this fact has been noted by many researchers, it has not been applied, possibly because of the uncertainty in the proposed approaches for locating the FOE in real scenes.

Segmentation using a moving camera

If the camera is moving, then every point in the image has nonzero velocity relative to the camera. (Note that an exception would be the pathological case in which object points are moving with the same velocity as that of the camera.) The velocity relative to the camera depends on both the velocity of the point itself and the distance of the point from the camera. Approaches based on difference pictures may be extended for segmenting moving-camera scenes. However, if the aim is to extract images of moving objects, then additional information will be required to decide whether the motion at a point is due solely to its depth or is due to a combination of its depth and its motion. Gradient-based approaches also will require additional information.

If the camera's direction of motion is known, then the FOE with respect to the stationary components in a scene can easily be computed. The FOE will have coordinates

$$x_f = \frac{dx}{dz}$$

$$and \qquad y_f = \frac{dy}{dz} \qquad (6.9)$$

in the image plane. The velocity vectors of all of the stationary points in a scene project onto the image plane so that they intersect at the FOE. A transformation with respect to the FOE can be used to simplify the task of segmentation. The ego-motion polar (EMP) transformation of an image transforms a frame $F(x,y,t)$ into $E(r,\theta,t)$ using

$$E(r,\theta,t) = F(x,y,t)$$

$$where \qquad r = \sqrt{(x - x_f)^2 + (y - y_f)^2}$$

$$and \qquad \theta = \tan^{-1}\left(\frac{y - y_f}{x - x_f}\right). \qquad (6.10)$$

In EMP space, stationary points are displaced only along the θ-axis between the frames of an image sequence, while points on moving objects are displaced along the r-axis as well as the θ axis. Thus, the displacement in EMP space can be used to segment a scene into its stationary and nonstationary components. The results of experiments on real scenes have been very encouraging and are discussed in the following paragraphs.

Jain[216,217] proposed a method of representing object motion in images acquired by a moving camera. His method is derived from the fact that all of the velocity vectors of stationary objects in a scene acquired by a translating observer intersect at the FOE. An image frame can be transformed, with respect to the FOE, to a second frame in which the abscissa is r and the ordinate is θ. Under this transformation, a dynamic scene can be segmented into its moving and stationary components, as discussed earlier. Moreover, when complex logarithmic mapping (CLM) is performed about the FOE, interesting properties in the EMP space can be obtained.

Apparently, more information about moving, as well as stationary, objects can be extracted using complex logarithmic mapping as opposed to simple polar mapping.

$$\omega = \log \alpha \qquad (6.11)$$

where ω and α are complex variables, as follows:

$$\alpha = x + iy$$
$$= r(\cos\theta + i\sin\theta)$$
$$= re^{i\theta}$$
$$and \qquad \omega = u(z) + iv(z) \qquad (6.12)$$

Under this transformation, it can be shown that

$$u(r,\theta) = \log r$$
$$v(r,\theta) = \theta. \qquad (6.13)$$

These results state the following fact: If the observer is moving, the horizontal displacement of a stationary point in CLM-space depends only on the depth of the point and, furthermore, the vertical displacement is zero. This fact is apparently very useful, not only in segmenting dynamic scenes into moving and stationary components, but also in determining the depth of stationary points. Schwartz[218-221] and Cavanaugh[222,223] studied this complex logarithmic mapping in the context of biological vision systems. Schwartz found that retino-striate mapping can be approximated by a complex log function. Complex logarithmic mapping appears to be responsible for size, rotation, and projection invariances in biological systems. Cavanaugh[222] argues that such mapping is justified only in limited cases. Jain[217] showed that some of the limitations with respect to the projection invariance may be removed if the mapping is obtained with respect to the FOE. The complex EMP-space produces an observer-centered representation of an image sequence through the use of the ego-motion of the observer. This representation may play an important role in MCMO dynamic scenes.

Recovering three-dimensional information

The interpretation of two-dimensional displacements in terms of three-dimensional motion is complicated. During the picture formation process, information loss occurs, which results in a two-dimensional projection of three-dimensional events. Recovery of three-dimensional-motion parameters and three-dimensional object structure has been an active research area. An assumption about the rigidity of objects may be helpful in recovering the structure of objects. The rigidity assumption states that any set of elements undergoing a two-dimensional transformation that has a unique interpretation as a rigid body moving in space should be so interpreted. Research in human perception suggests that the human visual system exploits this assumption.

Approaches to recovering three-dimensional structure from image sequences can be divided into two general classes, as follows:

(1) Recovering structure using tokens and
(2) Recovering structure using the trajectories.

Recovering structure using tokens. Suppose that an interest operator is applied to consecutive frames of a sequence and that some interesting points (or "tokens") — such as corners — have been extracted. Also suppose that the correspondence problem between interesting points has been solved, using any method discussed earlier. If token correspondence has been established, then the three-dimensional location of four noncoplanar points can be recovered from their orthogonal projections, giving an implicit three-dimensional structure for an object. If the points are noncoplanar, then a unique structure can be recovered; if the points are coplanar, then the structure can be recovered to a reflection.

Feature-based methods for the recovery of three-dimensional structure or for the estimation of motion parameters require two difficult steps, as follows:

(1) Determining the precise location of points (or tokens) in an image and
(2) Determining the correspondence between points (or tokens) in an image pair.

If interest operators are applied based on small neighborhoods, then the number of tokens extracted in a real image is very large, making correspondence a difficult problem. If interest operators are applied based on large neighborhoods and higher order gray-level characteristics, then the number of tokens extracted is more reasonable for determining correspondences; however, the locations of tokens may not be precise. Apparently, results obtained using the methods just discussed may not be reliable, even if the location is obtained to pixel resolution.

Recovering structure using trajectories. All of the methods just discussed depend on a set of points in two or three frames. If a token is traced over several frames by solving correspondences, a two-dimensional trajectory of the token is obtained. Methods for recovering three-dimensional structure and motion from trajectories apparently may be more reliable than methods based on sets of features in a few frames. Curve-fitting techniques can be used to interpolate a trajectory in order to obtain better resolution of the two-dimensional path. Moreover, the correspondence problem may be simplified by considering more than two frames and extending relaxation across the frames.

Motion understanding

Dynamic-scene analysis may result in the extraction of

- Images of moving objects;
- Three-dimensional object structures; and
- Frame-to-frame object displacements.

In many applications, the aim may be to name the moving objects and to describe the events taking place in the scene. Object recognition may be performed based on an image or on the three-dimensional structure of the object. Apparently, motion characteristics of objects may also help in recognition. Different objects have different kinds of motion: cars run and airplanes fly. The motion characteristics of objects are difficult to obtain directly from frame-to-frame displacements. Much human recognition and object analysis require neither fine detail nor precise analysis of small details or parts. Details are only brought into play when the object is the focus of attention.

An object that has complex motion in each of its several parts can initially be abstracted to a simple moving block undergoing rigid motion. The abstracted motion will be a simple translation or rotation, whereas the real motion is very complex. At the next level of analysis, the motion of the separate parts of the object can be analyzed; knowledge about the abstract motion of the object may be helpful in analyzing the motion of the individual components of the object. Apparently, a correct approach to determining the more detailed motion of lower level parts is to compensate somehow for the known motion of the higher level abstraction of the object.

Research trends

One of the first tasks in dynamic-scene analysis is detection of moving objects. Thompson and Pong[224] conclude that detection using visual information alone is quite difficult, especially when the camera is moving. They develop detection algorithms to use when information about camera motion and/or scene structure is also available. Jain[225] and Liou and Jain[226] present approaches to motion detection based on the transformation of image sequences using knowledge of camera motion.

Fourteen papers were selected that are representative of papers dealing with the topics covered in this chapter. Six are included in this book and the other eight in the companion book *Computer Vision: Advances and Applications*. We begin the first chapter in *Principles* with the paper by Horn and Schunck entitled "Determining Optical Flow" which describes a robust method for finding optical-flow patterns that is based on a constraint on intensity gradients. Since flow velocity has two components, an additional constraint is needed. Smoothness of the displacement vector field is used in their iterative algorithm as the second constraint. However, a difficulty is presented because such smoothness constraints are violated along occluding contours. In the paper entitled "An Investigation of Smoothness Constraints for the Estimation of Displacement Vector Fields From Image Sequences," Nagel and Enkelmann in *Principles* overcome this difficulty by formulating and evaluating an oriented-smoothness constraint. In *Advances*, Meygret and Thonnat in "Segmentation of Optical Flow and Three-Dimensional Data for the Interpretation of Mobile Objects" describe an approach for the detection of three-dimensional moving objects using stereo and motion information. In their approach, the scene is detected and then it is interpreted in terms of isolated rigid or deformable objects.

Determination of optical flow has been a very active research area; Aisbett,[227] Heeger,[228] Mitiche et al.,[229] and Nagel[230] present some recent approaches. In *Principles*, Barnard and Thompson in "Disparity Analysis of Images," introduce a feature-based matching algorithm to estimate geometric disparity between two images. Small, distinct features are detected in both images, and initial estimates of the probability of a match between candidate pairs of features in the two images are obtained. A relaxation algorithm that uses local continuity of disparity is applied to improve these estimates. Clocksin[231] and Longuet-Higgins and Prazdny[232] describe the significance of optical flow and its potential in extracting information about surface orientation and structure.

The nonlinear system of equations relating optical flow and its first- and second-order derivatives to object structure and motion parameters are derived, and solutions for planar and curved surface patches are obtained, by Waxman et al. in the paper entitled "Closed-Form Solutions to Image Flow Equations for Three-Dimensional Structure and Motion" found in *Advances*. Optical flow (which is a measure of changes in image brightness) and the underlying motion field (which is the perspective projection of the true three-dimensional velocity field of moving surfaces in space) are in general different. For example, a smooth Lambertian sphere rotating in space has a motion field, although it has no corresponding optical-flow field. In "Motion Field and Optical Flow: Qualitative Properties," Verri and Poggio in *Advances* show that stable qualitative properties of the motion field, which contain useful information about the three-dimensional motion and structure of objects, can be obtained from the optical flow. In "Determining Three-Dimensional Motion and Structure From Optical Flow Generated by Several Moving Objects," Adiv describes in *Advances* an approach for interpreting sparse, noisy, and partially incorrect flow fields. In this approach, connected segments of flow vectors subject to the rigid motion of a roughly planar surface constraint are first obtained; then they are grouped under the hypothesis of a single rigid moving object. The hypotheses are tested for compatibility with all segments in the group in order to recover three-dimensional motion parameters. Ullman[233] proposed structure-from-motion approaches using N points in M frames. This research direction has been very popular in the last few years. In "Uniqueness and Estimation of Three-Dimensional Motion Parameters of Rigid Objects With Curved Surfaces," Tsai and Huang in *Advances* show that seven point correspondences in two perspective views are sufficient to determine the three-dimensional motion parameters of a curved surface.

However, finding solutions to nonlinear equations is required. They show that, by obtaining eight point correspondences, motion parameters can be determined by solving eight linear equations and a singular value decomposition. Also in *Advances*, the paper entitled "Motion and Structure From Two Perspective Views: Algorithm, Error Analysis, and Error Estimation," by Weng et al., presents a method for estimating motion parameters and scene structure. Weng et al. discuss the performance of Tsai and Huang's algorithm in the presence of errors. Faugeras and Maybank,[234] Mitiche et al.,[235] and Jerian and Jain[236] present more recent structure-from-motion approaches. Jerian and Jain[237] give a classification of several approaches, with their convergence properties and noise sensitivities.

In the papers just discussed, the techniques described attempt to derive motion parameters using two images. In *Principles*, Sethi and Jain in "Finding Trajectories of Feature Points in a Monocular Image Sequence," consider a sequence of images to determine trajectories of feature points. By applying the smoothness-of-motion constraint on the image sequences, they formulate the correspondence problem as an optimization problem, and they describe an iterative algorithm to solve this problem. The presence of noise in the image coordinates of the object match points results in inaccuracies in the estimation of motion parameters. These inaccuracies can be alleviated by using a larger number of match points to obtain an overdetermined set of estimation equations. An alternative technique to alleviate these inaccuracies is to use a larger number of image frames. Broida and Chellappa describe such a technique (which is based on an iterated extended Kalman filter) in *Advances* in the paper entitled "Estimation of Object Motion Parameters From Noisy Images."

The use of a large number of image frames taken at short intervals also helps in minimizing the correspondence problem, since the amount of change in successive images is expected to be very small. This concept has led to so-called "epipolar-plane image analysis," in which images are acquired using a moving camera. Explicit representation of both the spatial and temporal structures of such image sequences is captured in a spatio-temporal surface. A tracking mechanism that operates locally on these evolving surfaces to obtain three-dimensional scene reconstruction is described by Baker and Bolles in *Principles* in the paper entitled "Generalizing Epipolar-Plane Image Analysis on the Spatio-Temporal Surface." Several other approaches based on the spatio-temporal image solid are discussed by Heeger,[228] Watson and Ahumada, Jr.,[238] and Liou and Jain.[226]

Determining optical flow and solving the correspondence problem have been two difficult problems in dynamic vision. In the last few years, several approaches that bypass optical flow and correspondence for direct computation of motion properties have been proposed by Jain,[213] Aloimonos and Rigoutsos,[239, 240] and Negahdaripour and Horn.[241] These approaches appear promising.

In "Analysis of a Sequence of Stereo Scenes Containing Multiple Moving Objects Using Rigidity Constraints," Zhang et al. in *Principles* approach the motion determination problem as a stereo-matching and motion-estimation problem. Rigidity constraints are used to register two stereo frames. First, ego-motion is determined; then, it is taken into account in computing the motion of objects. The stereo-and-motion approach is also used by Grosso et al. in their system, which is described in "Three-Dimensional Object Reconstruction Using Stereo and Motion" in *Advances*. However, in their system, the objects remain stationary, and multiple views are obtained by moving the cameras around the objects while maintaining the direction of gaze fixed toward a point in space. A survey of many dynamic-scene analysis methods is given by Aggarwal and Nandhakumar.[242] Tsotsos et al.[243] describe a framework for the abstraction of motion concepts from image sequences. Included in the framework are semantic nets for knowledge representation and associated algorithms operating in a competing and cooperating feedback mode.

References Cited
Chapter 6

211. H.H. Nagel, "Formation of an Object Concept by Analysis of Systematic Time Variation in the Optically Perceptible Environment," *Computer Graphics and Image Processing,* Vol. 7, 1978, pp. 149-194.

212. R.C. Jain, "Dynamic Scene Analysis Using Pixel-Based Processes," *Computer,* Vol. 12, No. 1, 1981, pp. 12-18.

213. R.C. Jain, "Segmentation of Frame Sequence Obtained by a Moving Observer," *IEEE Trans. Pattern Analysis and Machine Intelligence,* Vol. 6, No. 5, 1984, pp. 624-629.

214. C.L. Fennema and W.B. Thompson, "Velocity Determination in Scenes Containing Several Moving Objects," *Computer Graphics and Image Processing,* Vol. 9, No. 4, 1979, pp. 301-315.

215. S.T. Barnard and W.B. Thompson, "Disparity Analysis of Images," *IEEE Trans. Pattern Analysis and Machine Intelligence,* Vol. 2, No. 4, 1980, pp. 822-825.

216. R.C. Jain, "Directed Computation of the Focus of Expansion," *IEEE Trans. Pattern Analysis and Machine Intelligence,* Vol. 5, No. 1, 1983, pp. 58-64.

217. R.C. Jain, "Complex Logarithmic Mapping and the Focus of Expansion," *SIGGRAPH/SIGART Workshop on Motion: Representation and Control,* 1983, pp. 42-49.

218. E.L. Schwartz, "A Quantitative Model of the Functional Architecture of Human Striate Cortex with Application to Vision Illusion and Cortical Texture Analysis," *Biological Cybernetics,* Vol. 37, 1980, pp. 63-76.

219. Schwartz, E.L., "Computational Anatomy and Functional Architecture of Striate Cortex: A Spatial Mapping Approach to Perceptual Coding," *Vision Research,* Vol. 20, 1980, pp. 645-669.

220. E.L. Schwartz, "Cortical Anatomy, Size Invariance, and Spatial Frequency Analysis," *Perception,* Vol. 10, 1981, pp. 455-468.

221. E.L. Schwartz, "Columnar Architecture and Computational Anatomy in Primate Visual Cortex: Segmentation and Feature Extraction via Spatial Frequency Coded Difference Mapping," *Biological Cybernetics,* Vol. 42, 1982, pp. 157-168.

222. P. Cavanaugh, "Size and Position Invariance in the Vision System," *Perception,* Vol. 7, 1978, pp. 167-177.

223. P. Cavanaugh, "Size Invariance: Reply to Schwartz," *Perception,* Vol. 10, 1981, pp. 469-474.

224. W.B. Thompson and T.C. Pong, "Detecting Moving Objects," *Int'l J. Computer Vision,* Vol. 4, 1990, pp. 39-57.

225. R.C. Jain, "Difference and Accumulative Difference Pictures in Dynamic Scene Analysis," *Image and Vision Computing,* Vol. 2, No. 2, 1984, pp. 99-108.

226. S.P. Liou and R.C. Jain, "Motion Detection in Spatio-Temporal Space," *Computer Vision, Graphics, and Image Processing,* Vol. 45, 1989, pp. 227-250.

227. J. Aisbett, "Optical Flow with an Intensity-Weighted Smoothing," *IEEE Trans. Pattern Analysis and Machine Intelligence,* Vol. 11, No. 5, 1989, pp. 512-522.

228. D.J. Heeger, "Optical Flow from Spatiotemporal Filters," *Int'l J. Computer Vision,* 1988, pp. 279-301.

229. A. Mitiche, Y.F. Wang, and J.K. Aggarwal, "Experiments in Computing Optical Flow with the Gradient-Based, Multiconstraint Method," *Pattern Recognition,* Vol. 20, No. 2, 1987, pp. 173-179.

230. H.H. Nagel, "On the Estimation of Optical Flow: Relations between Different Approaches and Some New Results," *Artificial Intelligence,* Vol. 33, 1987, pp. 299-324.

231. W.F. Clocksin, "Perception of Surface Slant and Edge Labels from Optical Flow: A Computational Approach," *Perception,* Vol. 9, No. 3, 1980, pp. 253-269.

232. H.C. Longuet-Higgens and K. Prazdny, "The Interpretation of a Moving Retinal Image," *Proc. Royal Society of London, B,* 1980, Vol. 208, pp. 385-397.

233. S. Ullman, *The Interpretation of Visual Motion,* MIT Press, Cambridge, Mass., 1979.

234. O.D. Faugeras and S. Maybank, "Motion from Point Matches: Multiplicity of Solutions," *Int'l J. Computer Vision,* Vol. 4, No. 3, 1990, pp. 225-246.

235. A. Mitiche, O. Faugeras, and J.K. Aggarwal, "Counting Straight Lines," *Computer Vision, Graphics, and Image Processing,* Vol. 47, 1989, pp. 353-360.

236. C. Jerian and R.C. Jain, "Structure from Motion: A Critical Analysis of Methods," *IEEE Trans. Systems, Man, and Cybernetics,* 1991.

237. C. Jerian and R.C. Jain, "Polynomial Methods for Structure from Motion," *IEEE Trans. Pattern Analysis and Machine Intelligence,* Vol. 12, No. 12, 1990, pp. 1150-1166.

238. A.B. Watson and A.J. Ahumada, Jr., "Model of Human Visual-Motion Sensing," *J. Opt. Soc. Am. A.,* Vol. 2, No. 2, 1985, pp. 322-342.

239. J.Y. Aloimonos and I. Rigoutsos, "Determining the 3-D Motion of a Rigid Surface Patch Without Correspondence Under Perspective Projection. I. Planar Surfaces; II Curved Surfaces," *Proc. Nat'l Conf. on Artificial Intelligence,* 1986, pp. 681-688.

240. J.Y. Aloimonos and I. Rigoutsos, "Determining the 3-D Motion of a Rigid Planar Patch Without Correspondence, Under Perspective Projection," *Proc. Workshop on Motion,* 1986, pp. 167-174.

241. S. Negahdaripour and B.K.P. Horn, "Direct Passive Navigation," *IEEE Trans. Pattern Analysis and Machine Intelligence,* Vol. 9, No. 1, 1987, pp. 168-176.

242. J.K. Aggarwal and N. Nandhakumar, "On the Computation of Motion from Sequences of Images: A Review," *Proc. IEEE,* Vol. 76, No. 8, IEEE Press, New York, N.Y., 1988, pp. 917-935.

243. J.K. Tsotsos, et al., "A Framework for Visual Motion Understanding," *IEEE Trans. Pattern Analysis and Machine Intelligence,* Vol. 2, No. 6, 1980, pp. 5653-573.

ARTIFICIAL INTELLIGENCE

Determining Optical Flow

Berthold K.P. Horn and Brian G. Schunck

Artificial Intelligence Laboratory, Massachusetts Institute of Technology, Cambridge, MA 02139, U.S.A.

ABSTRACT

Optical flow cannot be computed locally, since only one independent measurement is available from the image sequence at a point, while the flow velocity has two components. A second constraint is needed. A method for finding the optical flow pattern is presented which assumes that the apparent velocity of the brightness pattern varies smoothly almost everywhere in the image. An iterative implementation is shown which successfully computes the optical flow for a number of synthetic image sequences. The algorithm is robust in that it can handle image sequences that are quantized rather coarsely in space and time. It is also insensitive to quantization of brightness levels and additive noise. Examples are included where the assumption of smoothness is violated at singular points or along lines in the image.

1. Introduction

Optical flow is the distribution of apparent velocities of movement of brightness patterns in an image. Optical flow can arise from relative motion of objects and the viewer [6, 7]. Consequently, optical flow can give important information about the spatial arrangement of the objects viewed and the rate of change of this arrangement [8]. Discontinuities in the optical flow can help in segmenting images into regions that correspond to different objects [27]. Attempts have been made to perform such segmentation using differences between successive image frames [15, 16, 17, 20, 25]. Several papers address the problem of recovering the motions of objects relative to the viewer from the optical flow [10, 18, 19, 21, 29]. Some recent papers provide a clear exposition of this enterprise [30, 31]. The mathematics can be made rather difficult, by the way, by choosing an inconvenient coordinate system. In some cases information about the shape of an object may also be recovered [3, 18, 19].

These papers begin by assuming that the optical flow has already been determined. Although some reference has been made to schemes for comput-

Artificial Intelligence 17 (1981) 185–203

ing the flow from successive views of a scene [5, 10], the specifics of a scheme for determining the flow from the image have not been described. Related work has been done in an attempt to formulate a model for the short range motion detection processes in human vision [2, 22]. The pixel recursive equations of Netravali and Robbins [28], designed for coding motion in television signals, bear some similarity to the iterative equations developed in this paper. A recent review [26] of computational techniques for the analysis of image sequences contains over 150 references.

The optical flow cannot be computed at a point in the image independently of neighboring points without introducing additional constraints, because the velocity field at each image point has two components while the change in image brightness at a point in the image plane due to motion yields only one constraint. Consider, for example, a patch of a pattern where brightness[1] varies as a function of one image coordinate but not the other. Movement of the pattern in one direction alters the brightness at a particular point, but motion in the other direction yields no change. Thus components of movement in the latter direction cannot be determined locally.

2. Relationship to Object Motion

The relationship between the optical flow in the image plane and the velocities of objects in the three dimensional world is not necessarily obvious. We perceive motion when a changing picture is projected onto a stationary screen, for example. Conversely, a moving object may give rise to a constant brightness pattern. Consider, for example, a uniform sphere which exhibits shading because its surface elements are oriented in many different directions. Yet, when it is rotated, the optical flow is zero at all points in the image, since the shading does not move with the surface. Also, specular reflections move with a velocity characteristic of the virtual image, not the surface in which light is reflected.

For convenience, we tackle a particularly simple world where the apparent velocity of brightness patterns can be directly identified with the movement of surfaces in the scene.

3. The Restricted Problem Domain

To avoid variations in brightness due to shading effects we initially assume that the surface being imaged is flat. We further assume that the incident illumination is uniform across the surface. The brightness at a point in the image is then proportional to the reflectance of the surface at the corresponding point on the object. Also, we assume at first that reflectance varies smoothly and has no spatial discontinuities. This latter condition assures us that the image brightness is differentiable. We exclude situations where objects occlude one another, in part, because discontinuities in reflectance are found at object boundaries. In two of the experiments discussed later, some of the problems occasioned by occluding edges are exposed.

In the simple situation described, the motion of the brightness patterns in the image is determined directly by the motions of corresponding points on the surface of the object. Computing the velocities of points on the object is a matter of simple geometry once the optical flow is known.

---

[1]In this paper, the term brightness means image irradiance. The brightness pattern is the distribution of irradiance in the image.

4. Constraints

We will derive an equation that relates the change in image brightness at a point to the motion of the brightness pattern. Let the image brightness at the point (x, y) in the image plane at time t be denoted by $E(x, y, t)$. Now consider what happens when the pattern moves. The brightness of a particular point in the pattern is constant, so that

$$\frac{dE}{dt} = 0.$$

Using the chain rule for differentiation we see that,

$$\frac{\partial E}{\partial x}\frac{dx}{dt} + \frac{\partial E}{\partial y}\frac{dy}{dt} + \frac{\partial E}{\partial t} = 0.$$

(See Appendix A for a more detailed derivation.) If we let

$$u = \frac{dx}{dt} \quad \text{and} \quad v = \frac{dy}{dt},$$

then it is easy to see that we have a single linear equation in the two unknowns u and v,

$$E_x u + E_y v + E_t = 0,$$

where we have also introduced the additional abbreviations E_x, E_y, and E_t for the partial derivatives of image brightness with respect to x, y and t, respectively. The constraint on the local flow velocity expressed by this equation is illustrated in Fig. 1. Writing the equation in still another way,

$$(E_x, E_y) \cdot (u, v) = -E_t.$$

Thus the component of the movement in the direction of the brightness gradient (E_x, E_y) equals

$$-\frac{E_t}{\sqrt{E_x^2 + E_y^2}}.$$

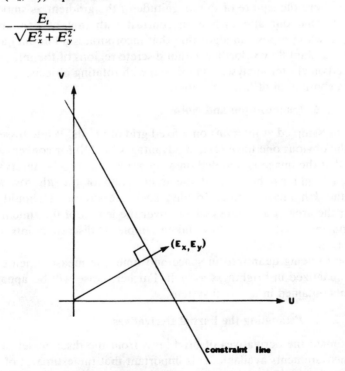

FIG. 1. The basic rate of change of image brightness equation constrains the optical flow velocity. The velocity (u, v) has to lie along a line perpendicular to the brightness gradient vector (E_x, E_y). The distance of this line from the origin equals E_t divided by the magnitude of (E_x, E_y).

We cannot, however, determine the component of the movement in the direction of the iso-brightness contours, at right angles to the brightness gradient. As a consequence, the flow velocity (u, v) cannot be computed locally without introducing additional constraints.

5. The Smoothness Constraint

If every point of the brightness pattern can move independently, there is little hope of recovering the velocities. More commonly we view opaque objects of finite size undergoing rigid motion or deformation. In this case neighboring points on the objects have similar velocities and the velocity field of the brightness patterns in the image varies smoothly almost everywhere. Discontinuities in flow can be expected where one object occludes another. An algorithm based on a smoothness constraint is likely to have difficulties with occluding edges as a result.

One way to express the additional constraint is to minimize the square of the magnitude of the gradient of the optical flow velocity:

$$\left(\frac{\partial u}{\partial x}\right)^2 + \left(\frac{\partial u}{\partial y}\right)^2 \quad \text{and} \quad \left(\frac{\partial v}{\partial x}\right)^2 + \left(\frac{\partial v}{\partial y}\right)^2.$$

Another measure of the smoothness of the optical flow field is the sum of the squares of the Laplacians of the x- and y-components of the flow. The Laplacians of u and v are defined as

$$\nabla^2 u = \frac{\partial^2 u}{\partial x^2} + \frac{\partial^2 u}{\partial y^2} \quad \text{and} \quad \nabla^2 v = \frac{\partial^2 v}{\partial x^2} + \frac{\partial^2 v}{\partial y^2}.$$

In simple situations, both Laplacians are zero. If the viewer translates parallel to a flat object, rotates about a line perpendicular to the surface or travels orthogonally to the surface, then the second partial derivatives of both u and v vanish (assuming perspective projection in the image formation).

We will use here the square of the magnitude of the gradient as smoothness measure. Note that our approach is in contrast with that of Fennema and Thompson [5], who propose an algorithm that incorporates additional assumptions such as constant flow velocities within discrete regions of the image. Their method, based on cluster analysis, cannot deal with rotating objects, since these give rise to a continuum of flow velocities.

6. Quantization and Noise

Images may be sampled at intervals on a fixed grid of points. While tesselations other than the obvious one have certain advantages [9, 23], for convenience we will assume that the image is sampled on a square grid at regular intervals. Let the measured brightness be $E_{i,j,k}$ at the intersection of the ith row and jth column in the kth image frame. Ideally, each measurement should be an average over the area of a picture cell and over the length of the time interval. In the experiments cited here we have taken samples at discrete points in space and time instead.

In addition to being quantized in space and time, the measurements will in practice be quantized in brightness as well. Further, noise will be apparent in measurements obtained in any real system.

7. Estimating the Partial Derivatives

We must estimate the derivatives of brightness from the discrete set of image brightness measurements available. It is important that the estimates of E_x, E_y, and E_t be consistent. That is, they should all refer to the same point in the image at the same time. While there are many formulas for approximate differentiation [4, 11] we will use a set which gives us an estimate of E_x, E_y, E_t at a point in the center of a cube formed by eight measurements. The relationship in space and time between these measurements is shown in Fig. 2. Each of the estimates is the average of four first differences taken over adjacent measurements in the cube.

$$E_x \approx \tfrac{1}{4}\{E_{i,j+1,k} - E_{i,j,k} + E_{i+1,j+1,k} - E_{i+1,j,k}$$
$$+ E_{i,j+1,k+1} - E_{i,j,k+1} + E_{i+1,j+1,k+1} - E_{i+1,j,k+1}\},$$
$$E_y \approx \tfrac{1}{4}\{E_{i+1,j,k} - E_{i,j,k} + E_{i+1,j+1,k} - E_{i,j+1,k}$$
$$+ E_{i+1,j,k+1} - E_{i,j,k+1}| + E_{i+1,j+1,k+1} - E_{i,j+1,k+1}\},$$
$$E_t \approx \tfrac{1}{4}\{E_{i,j,k+1} - E_{i,j,k} + E_{i+1,j,k+1} - E_{i+1,j,k}$$
$$+ E_{i,j+1,k+1} - E_{i,j+1,k} + E_{i+1,j+1,k+1} - E_{i+1,j+1,k}\}.$$

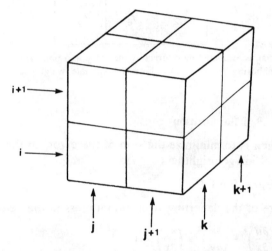

FIG. 2. The three partial derivatives of images brightness at the center of the cube are each estimated from the average of first differences along four parallel edges of the cube. Here the column index j corresponds to the x direction in the image, the row index i to the y direction, while k lies in the time direction.

Here the unit of length is the grid spacing interval in each image frame and the unit of time is the image frame sampling period. We avoid estimation formulae with larger support, since these typically are equivalent to formulae of small support applied to smoothed images [14].

8. Estimating the Laplacian of the Flow Velocities

We also need to approximate the Laplacians of u and v. One convenient approximation takes the following form

$$\nabla^2 u \approx \kappa(\bar{u}_{i,j,k} - u_{i,j,k}) \quad \text{and} \quad \nabla^2 v \approx \kappa(\bar{v}_{i,j,k} - v_{i,j,k}),$$

where the local averages $\bar{u}$ and $\bar{v}$ are defined as follows

$$\bar{u}_{i,j,k} = \tfrac{1}{6}\{u_{i-1,j,k} + u_{i,j+1,k} + u_{i+1,j,k} + u_{i,j-1,k}\}$$
$$+ \tfrac{1}{12}\{u_{i-1,j-1,k} + u_{i-1,j+1,k} + u_{i+1,j+1,k} + u_{i+1,j-1,k}\},$$

$$\bar{v}_{i,j,k} = \tfrac{1}{6}\{v_{i-1,j,k} + v_{i,j+1,k} + v_{i+1,j,k} + v_{i,j-1,k}\}$$
$$+ \tfrac{1}{12}\{v_{i-1,j-1,k} + v_{i-1,j+1,k} + v_{i+1,j+1,k} + v_{i+1,j-1,k}\}.$$

The proportionality factor κ equals 3 if the average is computed as shown and we again assume that the unit of length equals the grid spacing interval. Fig. 3 illustrates the assignment of weights to neighboring points.

$1/12$	$1/6$	$1/12$
$1/6$	-1	$1/6$
$1/12$	$1/6$	$1/12$

FIG. 3. The Laplacian is estimated by subtracting the value at a point from a weighted average of the values at neighboring points. Shown here are suitable weights by which values can be multiplied.

9. Minimization

The problem then is to minimize the sum of the errors in the equation for the rate of change of image brightness,

$$\mathscr{E}_b = E_x u + E_y v + E_t,$$

and the measure of the departure from smoothness in the velocity flow,

$$\mathscr{E}_c^2 = \left(\frac{\partial u}{\partial x}\right)^2 + \left(\frac{\partial u}{\partial y}\right)^2 + \left(\frac{\partial v}{\partial x}\right)^2 + \left(\frac{\partial v}{\partial y}\right)^2.$$

What should be the relative weight of these two factors? In practice the image brightness measurements will be corrupted by quantization error and noise so that we cannot expect $\mathscr{E}_b$ to be identically zero. This quantity will tend to have an error magnitude that is proportional to the noise in the measurement. This fact guides us in choosing a suitable weighting factor, denoted by α^2, as will be seen later.

Let the total error to be minimized be

$$\mathscr{E}^2 = \int \int (\alpha^2 \mathscr{E}_c^2 + \mathscr{E}_b^2) \, dx \, dy.$$

The minimization is to be accomplished by finding suitable values for the optical flow velocity (u, v). Using the calculus of variation we obtain

$$E_x^2 u + E_x E_y v = \alpha^2 \nabla^2 u - E_x E_t,$$
$$E_x E_y u + E_y^2 v = \alpha^2 \nabla^2 v - E_y E_t.$$

Using the approximation to the Laplacian introduced in the previous section,

$$(\alpha^2 + E_x^2)u + E_x E_y v = (\alpha^2 \bar{u} - E_x E_t),$$
$$E_x E_y u + (\alpha^2 + E_y^2)v = (\alpha^2 \bar{v} - E_y E_t).$$

The determinant of the coefficient matrix equals $\alpha^2(\alpha^2 + E_x^2 + E_y^2)$. Solving for u and v we find that

$$(\alpha^2 + E_x^2 + E_y^2)u = +(\alpha^2 + E_y^2)\bar{u} - E_x E_y \bar{v} - E_x E_t,$$
$$(\alpha^2 + E_x^2 + E_y^2)v = -E_x E_y \bar{u} + (\alpha^2 + E_x^2)\bar{v} - E_y E_t.$$

10. Difference of Flow at a Point from Local Average

These equations can be written in the alternate form

$$(\alpha^2 + E_x^2 + E_y^2)(u - \bar{u}) = -E_x[E_x\bar{u} + E_y\bar{v} + E_t],$$
$$(\alpha^2 + E_x^2 + E_y^2)(v - \bar{v}) = -E_y[E_x\bar{u} + E_y\bar{v} + E_t].$$

This shows that the value of the flow velocity (u, v) which minimizes the error $\mathscr{E}^2$ lies in the direction towards the constraint line along a line that intersects the constraint line at right angles. This relationship is illustrated geometrically in Fig. 4. The distance from the local average is proportional to the error in the basic formula for rate of change of brightness when $\bar{u}$, $\bar{v}$ are substituted for u and v. Finally we can see that α^2 plays a significant role only for areas where the brightness gradient is small, preventing haphazard adjustments to the estimated flow velocity occasioned by noise in the estimated derivatives. This parameter should be roughly equal to the expected noise in the estimate of $E_x^2 + E_y^2$.

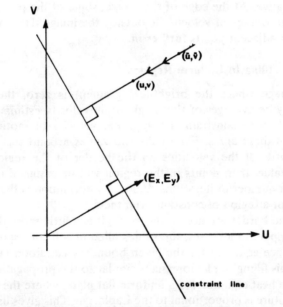

FIG. 4. The value of the flow velocity which minimizes the error lies on a line drawn from the local average of the flow velocity perpendicular to the constraint line.

11. Constrained Minimization

When we allow α^2 to tend to zero we obtain the solution to a constrained minimization problem. Applying the method of Lagrange multipliers [33, 34] to the problem of minimizing $\mathscr{E}_c^2$ while maintaining $\mathscr{E}_b = 0$ leads to

$$E_y\nabla^2 u = E_x\nabla^2 v, \qquad E_x u + E_y v + E_t = 0$$

Approximating the Laplacian by the difference of the velocity at a point and the average of its neighbors then gives us

$$(E_x^2 + E_y^2)(u - \bar{u}) = -E_x[E_x\bar{u} + E_y\bar{v} + E_t],$$
$$(E_x^2 + E_y^2)(v - \bar{v}) = -E_y[E_x\bar{u} + E_y\bar{v} + E_t].$$

Referring again to Fig. 4, we note that the point computed here lies at the intersection of the constraint line and the line at right angles through the point $(\bar{u}, \bar{v})$. We will not use these equations since we do expect errors in the estimation of the partial derivatives.

12. Iterative Solution

We now have a pair of equations for each point in the image. It would be very costly to solve these equations simultaneously by one of the standard methods, such as Gauss–Jordan elimination [11, 13]. The corresponding matrix is sparse and very large since the number of rows and columns equals twice the number of picture cells in the image. Iterative methods, such as the Gauss–Seidel method [11, 13], suggest themselves. We can compute a new set of velocity estimates (u^{n+1}, v^{n+1}) from the estimated derivatives and the average of the previous velocity estimates (u^n, v^n) by

$$u^{n+1} = \bar{u}^n - E_x[E_x\bar{u}^n + E_y\bar{v}^n + E_t]/(\alpha^2 + E_x^2 + E_y^2),$$
$$v^{n+1} = \bar{v}^n - E_y[E_x\bar{u}^n + E_y\bar{v}^n + E_t]/(\alpha^2 + E_x^2 + E_y^2).$$

(It is interesting to note that the new estimates at a particular point do not depend directly on the previous estimates at the same point.)

The natural boundary conditions for the variational problem turns out to be a zero normal derivative. At the edge of the image, some of the points needed to compute the local average of velocity lie outside the image. Here we simply copy velocities from adjacent points further in.

13. Filling In Uniform Regions

In parts of the image where the brightness gradient is zero, the velocity estimates will simply be averages of the neighboring velocity estimates. There is no local information to constrain the apparent velocity of motion of the brightness pattern in these areas. Eventually the values around such a region will propagate inwards. If the velocities on the border of the region are all equal to the same value, then points in the region will be assigned that value too, after a sufficient number of iterations. Velocity information is thus filled in from the boundary of a region of constant brightness.

If the values on the border are not all the same, it is a little more difficult to predict what will happen. In all cases, the values filled in will correspond to the solution of the Laplace equation for the given boundary condition [1, 24, 32].

The progress of this filling-in phenomena is similar to the propagation effects in the solution of the heat equation for a uniform flat plate, where the time rate of change of temperature is proportional to the Laplacian. This gives us a means of understanding the iterative method in physical terms and of estimating the number of steps required. The number of iterations should be larger than the number of picture cells across the largest region that must be filled in. If the size of such regions is not known in advance one may use the cross-section of the whole image as a conservative estimate.

14. Tightness of Constraint

When brightness in a region is a linear function of the image coordinates we can only obtain the component of optical flow in the direction of the gradient. The component at right angles is filled in from the boundary of the region as described before. In general the solution is most accurately determined in regions where the brightness gradient is not too small and varies in direction from point to point. Information which constrains both components of the optical flow velocity is then available in a relatively small neighborhood. Too violent fluctuations in brightness on the other hand are not desirable since the estimates of the derivatives will be corrupted as the result of undersampling and aliasing.

15. Choice of Iterative Scheme

As a practical matter one has a choice of how to interlace the iterations with the time steps. On the one hand, one could iterate until the solution has stabilized before advancing to the next image frame. On the other hand, given a good initial guess one may need only one iteration per time-step. A good initial guess for the optical flow velocities is usually available from the previous time-step.

The advantages of the latter approach include an ability to deal with more images per unit time and better estimates of optical flow velocities in certain regions. Areas in which the brightness gradient is small lead to uncertain, noisy estimates obtained partly by filling in from the surround. These estimates are improved by considering further images. The noise in measurements of the images will be independent and tend to cancel out. Perhaps more importantly, different parts of the pattern will drift by a given point in the image. The direction of the brightness gradient will vary with time, providing information about both components of the optical flow velocity.

A practical implementation would most likely employ one iteration per time step for these reasons. We illustrate both approaches in the experiments.

16. Experiments

The iterative scheme has been implemented and applied to image sequences corresponding to a number of simple flow patterns. The results shown here are for a relatively low resolution image of 32 by 32 picture cells. The brightness measurements were intentionally corrupted by approximately 1% noise and then quantized into 256 levels to simulate a real imaging situation. The underlying surface reflectance pattern was a linear combination of spatially orthogonal sinusoids. Their wavelength was chosen to give reasonably strong brightness gradients without leading to undersampling problems. Discontinuities were avoided to ensure that the required derivatives exist everywhere.

Shown in Fig. 5, for example, are four frames of a sequence of images depicting a sphere rotating about an axis inclined towards the viewer. A smoothly varying reflectance pattern is painted on the surface of the sphere. The sphere is illuminated uniformly from all directions so that there is no shading. We chose to work with synthetic image sequences so that we can compare the results of the optical flow computation with the exact values calculated using the transformation equations relating image coordinates to coordinates on the underlying surface reflectance pattern.

17. Results

The first flow to be investigated was a simple linear translation of the entire brightness pattern. The resulting computed flow is shown as a needle diagram in Fig. 6 for 1, 4, 16, and 64 iterations. The estimated flow velocities are depicted as short lines, showing the apparent displacement during one time step. In this example a single time step was taken so that the computations are based on just two images. Initially the estimates of flow velocity are zero. Consequently the first iteration shows vectors in the direction of the brightness gradient. Later, the estimates approach the correct values in all parts of the image. Few changes occur after 32 iterations when the velocity vectors have errors of about 10%. The estimates tend to be two small, rather than too large, perhaps because of a tendency to underestimate the derivatives. The worst errors occur, as one might expect, where the brightness gradient is small.

In the second experiment one iteration was used per time step on the same

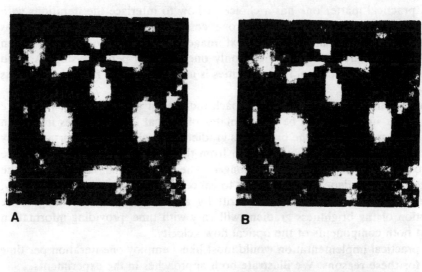

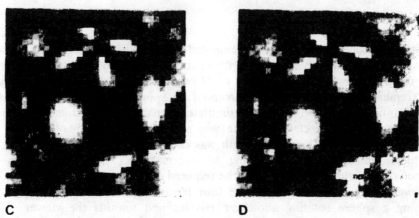

FIG. 5. Four frames out of a sequence of images of a sphere rotating about an axis inclined towards the viewer. The sphere is covered with a pattern which varies smoothly from place to place. The sphere is portrayed against a fixed, lightly textured background. Image sequences like these are processed by the optical flow algorithm.

linear translation image sequence. The resulting computed flow is shown in Fig. 7 for 1, 4, 16, and 64 time steps. The estimates approach the correct values more rapidly and do not have a tendency to be too small, as in the previous experiment. Few changes occur after 16 iterations when the velocity vectors have errors of about 7%. The worst errors occur, as one might expect, where the noise in recent measurements of brightness was worst. While individual estimates of velocity may not be very accurate, the average over the whole image was within 1% of the correct value.

Next, the method was applied to simple rotation and simple contraction of the brightness pattern. The results after 32 time steps are shown in Fig. 8. Note that the magnitude of the velocity is proportional to the distance from the origin of the flow in both of these cases. (By origin we mean the point in the image where the velocity is zero.)

In the examples so far the Laplacian of both flow velocity components is zero everywhere. We also studied more difficult cases where this was not the case.

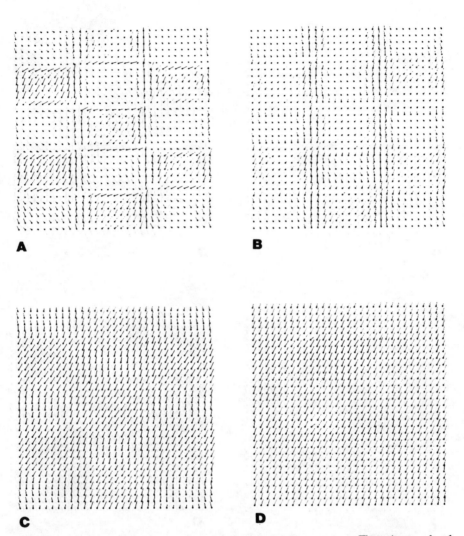

FIG. 6. Flow pattern computed for simple translation of a brightness pattern. The estimates after 1, 4, 16, and 64 iterations are shown. The velocity is 0.5 picture cells in the x direction and 1.0 picture cells in the y direction per time interval. Two images are used as input, depicting the situation at two times separated by one time interval.

In particular, if we let the magnitude of the velocity vary as the inverse of the distance from the origin we generate flow around a line vertex and two dimensional flow into a sink. The computed flow patterns are shown in Fig. 9. In these examples, the computation involved many iterations based on a single time step. The worst errors occur near the singularity at the origin of the flow pattern, where velocities are found which are much larger than one picture cell per time step.

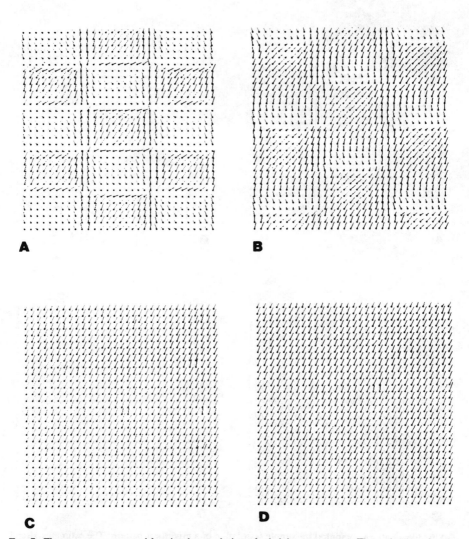

FIG. 7. Flow pattern computed for simple translation of a brightness pattern. The estimates after 1, 4, 16, and 64 time steps are shown. Here one iteration is used per time step. Convergence is more rapid and the velocities are estimated more accurately.

Finally we considered rigid body motions. Shown in Fig. 10 are the flows computed for a cylinder rotating about its axis and for a rotating sphere. In both cases the Laplacian of the flow is not zero and in fact the Laplacian for one of the velocity components becomes infinite on the occluding bound. Since the velocities themselves remain finite, resonable solutions are still obtained. The correct flow patterns are shown in Fig. 11. Comparing the computed and exact values shows that the worst errors occur on the occluding boundary. These

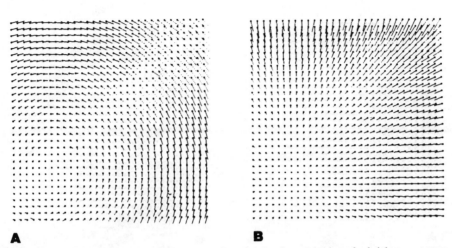

FIG. 8. Flow patterns computed for simple rotation and simple contraction of a brightness pattern. In the first case, the pattern is rotated about 2.8 degrees per time step, while it is contracted about 5% per time step in the second case. The estimates after 32 times steps are shown.

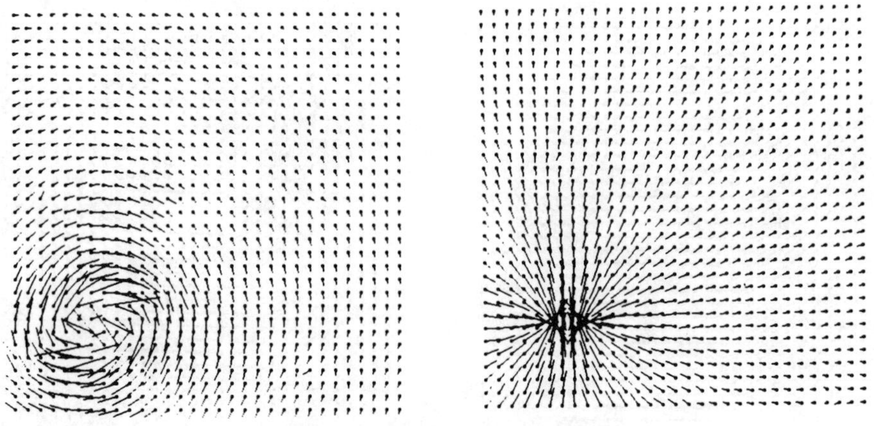

FIG. 9. Flow patterns computed for flow around a line vortex and two dimensional flow into a sink. In each case the estimates after 32 iterations are shown.

boundaries constitute a one dimensional subset of the plane and so one can expect that the relative number of points at which the estimated flow is seriously in error will decrease as the resolution of the image is made finer.

In Appendix B it is shown that there is a direct relationship between the Laplacian of the flow velocity components and the Laplacian of the surface height. This can be used to see how our smoothemess constraint will fare for different objects. For example, a rotating polyhedron will give rise to flow

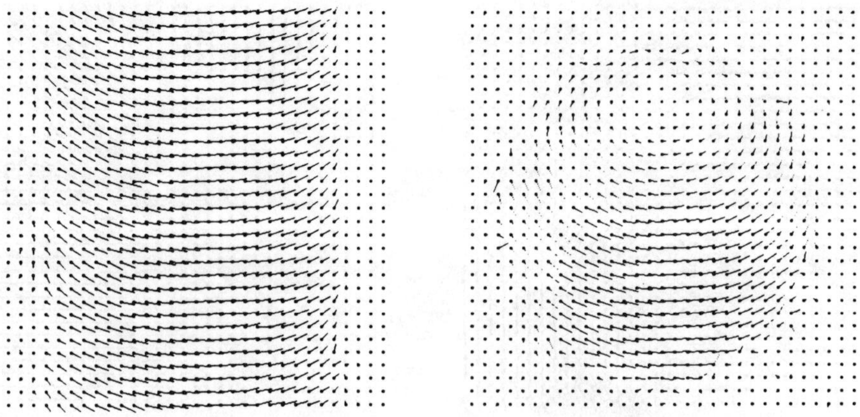

A   **B**

FIG. 10. Flow patterns computed for a cylinder rotating about its axis and for a rotating sphere. The axis of the cylinder is inclined 30 degrees towards the viewer and that of the sphere 45 degrees. Both are rotating at about 5 degrees per time step. The estimates shown are obtained after 32 time steps.

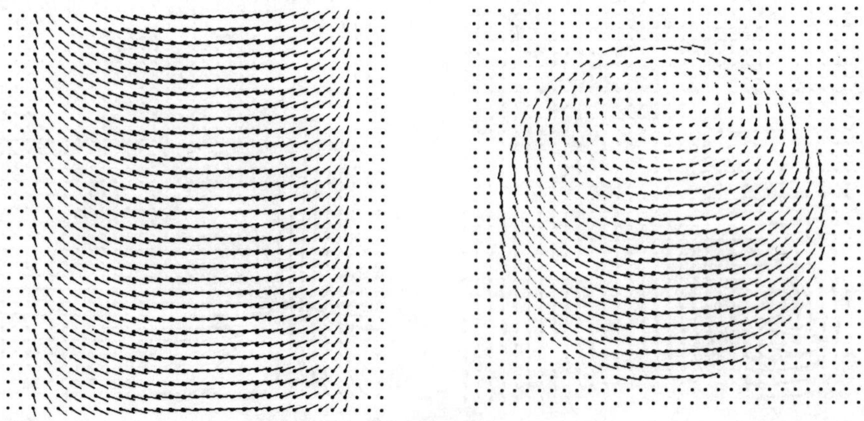

A   **B**

FIG. 11. Exact flow patterns for the cylinder and the sphere.

which has zero Laplacian except on the image lines which are the projections of the edges of the body.

18. Summary

A method has been developed for computing optical flow from a sequence of images. It is based on the observation that the flow velocity has two components and that the basic equation for the rate of change of image brightness provides only one constraint. Smoothness of the flow was introduced as a second constraint. An iterative method for solving the resulting equation was then developed. A simple implementation provided visual confirmation of convergence of the solution in the form of needle diagrams. Examples of several different types of optical flow patterns were studied. These included cases where the Laplacian of the flow was zero as well as cases where it became infinite at singular points or along bounding curves.

The computed optical flow is somewhat inaccurate since it is based on noisy, quantized measurements. Proposed methods for obtaining information about the shapes of objects using derivatives (divergence and curl) of the optical flow field may turn out to be impractical since the inaccuracies will be amplified.

ACKNOWLEDGMENT

This research was conducted at the Artificial Intelligence Laboratory of the Massachusetts Institute of Technology. Support for the laboratory's research is provided in part by the Advanced Research Projects Agency of the Department of Defense under Office of Naval Research contract number N00014-75-C0643. One of the authors (Horn) would like to thank Professor H.-H. Nagel for his hospitality. The basic equations were conceived during a visit to the University of Hamburg, stimulated by Professor Nagel's long-standing interest in motion vision. The other author (Schunck) would like to thank W.E.L. Grimson and E. Hildreth for many interesting discussions and much knowledgable criticism. W.E.L. Grimson and Katsushi Ikeuchi helped to illuminate a conceptual bug in an earlier version of this paper. We should also like to thank J. Jones for preparing the drawings.

Appendix A. Rate of Change of Image Brightness

Consider a patch of the brightness pattern that is displaced a distance δx in the x-direction and δy in the y-direction in time δt. The brightness of the patch is assumed to remain constant so that

$$E(x, y, t) = E(x + \delta x, y + \delta y, t + \delta t).$$

Expanding the right-hand side about the point (x, y, t) we get,

$$E(x, y, t) = E(x, y, t) + \delta x \frac{\partial E}{\partial x} + \delta y \frac{\partial E}{\partial y} + \delta t \frac{\partial E}{\partial t} + \epsilon.$$

Where ϵ contains second and higher order terms in δx, δy, and δt. After subtracting $E(x, y, t)$ from both sides and dividing through by δt we have

$$\frac{\delta x}{\delta t} \frac{\partial E}{\partial x} + \frac{\delta y}{\delta t} \frac{\partial E}{\partial y} + \frac{\partial E}{\partial t} + \mathcal{O}(\delta t) = 0,$$

where $\mathcal{O}(\delta t)$ is a term of order δt (we assume that δx and δy vary as δt). In the limit as $\delta t \to 0$ this becomes

$$\frac{\partial E}{\partial x} \frac{dx}{dt} + \frac{\partial E}{\partial y} \frac{dy}{dt} + \frac{\partial E}{\partial t} = 0.$$

Appendix B. Smoothness of Flow for Rigid Body Motions

Let a rigid body rotate about an axis $(\omega_x, \omega_y, \omega_z)$, where the magnitude of the vector equals the angular velocity of the motion. If this axis passes through the origin, then the velocity of a point (x, y, z) equals the cross product of $(\omega_x, \omega_y, \omega_z)$, and (x, y, z). There is a direct relationship between the image coordinates and the x and y coordinates here if we assume that the image is generated by orthographic projection. The x and y components of the velocity can be written,

$$u = \omega_y z - \omega_z y, \qquad v = \omega_z x - \omega_x z.$$

Consequently,

$$\nabla^2 u = +\omega_y \nabla^2 z, \qquad \nabla^2 v = -\omega_x \nabla^2 z.$$

This illustrates that the smoothness of the optical flow is related directly to the smoothness of the rotating body and that the Laplacian of the flow velocity will become infinite on the occluding bound, since the partial derivatives of z with respect to x and y become infinite there.

REFERENCES

1. Ames, W.F., *Numerical Methods for Partial Differential Equations* (Academic Press, New York, 1977).
2. Batali, J. and Ullman, S., Motion detection and analysis, *Proc. of the ARPA Image Understanding Workshop*, 7–8 November 1979 (Science Applications Inc., Arlington, VA 1979) pp. 69–75.
3. Clocksin, W., Determining the orientation of surfaces from optical flow, *Proc. of the Third AISB Conference*, Hamburg (1978) pp. 93–102.
4. Conte, S.D. and de Boor, C., *Elementary Numerical Analysis* (McGraw-Hill, New York, 1965, 1972).
5. Fennema, C.L. and Thompson, W.B., Velocity determination in scenes containing several moving objects, *Computer Graphics and Image Processing* **9** (4) (1979) 301–315.
6. Gibson, J.J., *The Perception of the Visual World* (Riverside Press, Cambridge, 1950).
7. Gibson, J.J., *The Senses Considered as Perceptual Systems* (Houghton-Mifflin, Boston, MA, 1966).
8. Gibson, J.J., On the analysis of change in the optic array, *Scandinavian J. Psychol.* **18** (1977) 161–163.
9. Gray, S.B., Local properties of binary images in two dimensions, *IEEE Trans. on Computers* **20** (5) (1971) 551–561.
10. Hadani, I., Ishai, G. and Gur, M., Visual stability and space perception in monocular vision: Mathematical model, *J. Optical Soc. Am.* **70** (1) (1980) 60–65.
11. Hamming, R.W., *Numerical Methods for Scientists and Engineers* (McGraw-Hill, New York, 1962).
12. Hildebrand, F.B., *Methods of Applied Mathematics* (Prentice-Hall, Englewood Cliffs, NJ, 1952, 1965).
13. Hildebrand, F.B., *Introduction to Numerical Analysis* (McGraw-Hill, New York, 1956, 1974).
14. Horn, B.K.P., (1979) Hill shading and the reflectance map, *Proc. IEEE* **69** (1) (1981) 14–47.
15. Jain, R., Martin, W.N. and Aggarwal, J.K., Segmentation through the detection of changes due to motion, *Computer Graphics and Image Processing* **11** (1) (1979) 13–34.
16. Jain, R. Militzer, D. and Nagel, H.-H., Separating non-stationary from stationary scene components in a sequence of real world TV-images, *Proc. of the 5th Int. Joint Conf. on Artificial Intelligence*, August 1977, Cambridge, MA, 612–618.
17. Jain, R. and Nagel, H.-H., On the analysis of accumulative difference pictures from image sequences of real world scenes, *IEEE Trans. on Pattern Analysis and Machine Intelligence* **1** (2) (1979) 206–214.
18. Koenderink, J.J. and van Doorn, A.J., Invariant properties of the motion parallax field due to the movement of rigid bodies relative to an observer, *Optica Acta* **22** (9) 773–791.
19. Koenderink, J.J. and van Doorn, A.J., Visual perception of rigidity of solid shape, *J. Math. Biol.* **3** (79) (1976) 79–85.
20. Limb, J.O. and Murphy, J.A., Estimating the velocity of moving images in television signals, *Computer Graphics and Image Processing* **4** (4) (1975) 311–327.
21. Longuet-Higgins, H.C. and Prazdny, K., The interpretation of moving retinal image, *Proc. of the Royal Soc. B* **208** (1980) 385–387.

22. Marr, D. and Ullman, S., Directional selectivity and its use in early visual processing, Artificial Intelligence Laboratory Memo No. 524, Massachusetts Institute of Technology (June 1979), to appear in *Proc. Roy. Soc. B.*

23. Mersereau, R.M., The processing of hexagonally sampled two-dimensional signals, *Proc. of the IEEE* **67** (6) (1979) 930–949.

24. Milne, W.E., *Numerical Solution of Differential Equations* (Dover, New York, 1953, 1979).

25. Nagel, H.-H., Analyzing sequences of TV-frames, *Proc. of the 5th Int. Joint Conf. on Artificial Intelligence*, August 1977, Cambridge, MA, 626.

26. Nagel, H.-H., Analysis techniques for image sequences, *Proc. of the 4th Int. Joint Conf. on Pattern Recognition*, 4–10 November 1978, Kyoto, Japan.

27. Nakayama, K. and Loomis, J.M., Optical velocity patterns, velocity-sensitive neurons and space perception, *Perception* **3** (1974) 63–80.

28. Netravali, A.N. and Robbins, J.D., Motion-compensated television coding: Part I, *The Bell System Tech. J.* **58** (3) (1979) 631–670.

29. Prazdny, K., Computing egomotion and surface slant from optical flow. Ph.D. Thesis, Computer Science Department, University of Essex, Colchester (1979).

30. Prazdny, K., Egomotion and relative depth map from optical flow, *Biol. Cybernet.* **36** (1980) 87–102.

31. Prazdny, K., The information in optical flows. Computer Science Department, University of Essex, Colchester (1980) mimeographed.

32. Richtmyer, R.D. and Mortin, K.W, *Difference Methods for Initial-Value Problems* (Interscience, John Wiley & Sons, New York, 1957, 1967).

33. Russell, D.L., *Calculus of Variations and Control Theory* (Academic Press, New York, 1976).

34. Yourgau, W. and Mandelstam, S., *Variational Principles in Dynamics and Quantum Theory* (Dover, New York, 1968, 1979).

Received March 1980

Reprinted from *IEEE Transactions on Pattern Analysis and Machine Intelligence*, Volume PAMI-8, Number 5, September 1986, pages 565-593.

An Investigation of Smoothness Constraints for the Estimation of Displacement Vector Fields from Image Sequences

HANS-HELLMUT NAGEL, MEMBER, IEEE, AND WILFRIED ENKELMANN

Abstract—A mapping between one frame from an image sequence and the preceding or following frame can be represented as a displacement vector field. In most situations, the mere gray value variations do not provide sufficient information in order to estimate such a displacement vector field. Supplementary constraints are necessary, for example the postulate that a displacement vector field varies smoothly as a function of the image position. Taken as a general requirement, this creates difficulties at gray value transitions which correspond to occluding contours. Nagel therefore introduced the "oriented smoothness" requirement which restricts variations of the displacement vector field only in directions with small or no variation of gray values. This contribution reports results of an investigation about how such an "oriented smoothness" constraint may be formulated and evaluated.

Index Terms—Displacement vector fields, image registration, image sequences, optical flow, smoothness constraints, stereo matching.

I. INTRODUCTION

THE planar displacement vector field $u(x) = (u(x), v(x))^T$ links the pixel at image location $x = (x, y)^T$ in one frame to the corresponding pixel position in another frame. The reliable estimation of displacement vector fields is of great importance for the extraction of spatial information from stereo-pairs as well as for the interpretation of image sequences about scenes with temporal variations—see, e.g., [18].

In most situations the mere gray value variations do not provide sufficient information to completely determine $u(x)$. Horn and Schunck [11], therefore, postulated that displacement vector fields should vary smoothly as a function of the image coordinate vector x. This postulate enabled them to estimate both components u and v of $u(x)$. Such a general smoothness requirement, however, forces the estimated displacement vector field to vary smoothly even across the image of occluding edges. Several approaches have been investigated in order to cope with this difficulty.

Manuscript received October 11, 1984; revised February 11, 1986. Recommended for acceptance by S. L. Tanimoto. This work was supported in part by the Deutsche Forschungsgemeinschaft.

H.-H. Nagel is with the Fraunhofer-Institut für Informations- und Datenverarbeitung, Sebastian-Kneipp-Str. 12-14, 7500 Karlsruhe 1, West Germany, and the Fakultät für Informatik, Universität Karlsruhe, West Germany.

W. Enkelmann was with the Fachbereich Informatik, Universität Hamburg, Schlüterstr. 70, 2000 Hamburg 13, West Germany. He is now with the Fraunhofer-Institut für Informations- und Datenverarbeitung, Sebastian-Kneipp-Str. 12-14, 7500 Karlsruhe 1, West Germany.

IEEE Log Number 8609321.

Yachida [25] assumed that a displacement vector can be estimated at prominent points. He propagated such estimates into neighboring areas with large gray value gradients, based on the method of Horn and Schunck [11]. His iterative improvement scheme employed the inverse variance of displacement estimates from a 5×5 window as a weight in order to suppress the propagation of displacement estimates with large local variations.

Cornelius and Kanade [2] deactivated the smoothness requirement in the neighborhood of zero-crossing contours in order to avoid that estimates spill across potential discontinuities of the displacement vector field.

Wu *et al.* [24] (see also [3]) propagated a displacement estimate only along a contour line between corner points. At each new contour point, they combined the estimated displacement vector from the previous contour point with new estimates of the contour direction and of the displacement component perpendicular to the contour in order to update the tangential component of the displacement vector.

Hildreth [8] minimized the sum of two terms, integrated along a zero-crossing contour. The first term is the squared difference between the "measured" and the estimated displacement component perpendicular to the contour. The second term represents the squared derivative of the displacement vector field with respect to the arclength along the zero-crossing contour, expressing the smoothness requirement (see also [7], [9], [10]).

Nagel [16], [17] suggested an approach which does not require the explicit determination of gray value transition fronts such as edge lines or zero-crossing contours. Whereas Yachida [25] employed some indirect evidence—namely the inverse variance of the estimated displacement vector field—as a weight, the approach of Nagel relied upon the gray value variation directly in order to constrain the variation of the displacement vector field.

The idea to let the gray value variations themselves influence the smoothness constraints originally occurred to Nagel [15] in a slightly different context. Since then, a continuous interaction between theoretical and experimental investigations has resulted in a gradual development of how this idea might be formulated mathematically and how such a formulation might be evaluated.

The introduction of a supplementary constraint evidently contains some arbitrariness. It appears useful, there-

498

fore, to delineate the gradual development of a constraint formulation: potential alternatives are exposed as well as their advantages and disadvantages. In this manner, it is hoped to contribute to a better understanding of the entire problem area.

The next section quickly recapitulates the development up to the formulation presented in [17]. A first solution approach for the resulting system of partial differential equations is outlined in Section III. Difficulties encountered during the implementation of this solution approach resulted in a series of modifications to both the solution approaches as well as the mathematical formulation of the "oriented smoothness" constraint. These steps are discussed in subsequent sections. The final section presents encouraging results from the currently pursued constraint formulation applied to examples taken from a real-world image sequence.

II. Initial Steps Towards an "Oriented Smoothness" Constraint

Based on an analysis of experimental attempts to characterize "corners" by Kitchen and Rosenfeld [12], [13] as well as independent ones by Dreschler and Nagel [4], [5], Nagel [15] found both approaches to be compatible with the following definition:

Identify a "gray value corner" with the position of maximum planar curvature in the locus line of steepest gray value slope.

Dreschler and Nagel [6] compared the locations obtained from this definition with locations of maximum planar curvature in zero-crossing contours in the Laplacian applied to real world images with and without Gaussian smoothing. More recently, Zuniga and Haralick [26] compared their results for slight variations of the approach as defined above to those of the original attempts by Kitchen and Rosenfeld [12], [13] and those by Dreschler and Nagel [4], [5]. All these results support the hypothesis that the definition given above captures essential aspects of visually prominent corners in gray value images.

Since the position of a gray value corner is well defined, it should be possible to estimate both components of its displacement vector. This could indeed be shown by Nagel [15] based on the following approach.

The gray value $g(x)$ is taken to be a twice continuously differentiable function of the image position vector x. A local coordinate system can be chosen such that a gray value corner is characterized by

$$g_x = \frac{\partial g}{\partial x} = \text{maximum} \neq 0$$

$$g_{xx} = \frac{\partial^2 g}{\partial x^2} = 0 \tag{1a}$$

$$g_y = \frac{\partial g}{\partial y} = 0$$

$$g_{yy} = \frac{\partial^2 g}{\partial y^2} = \text{maximum} \neq 0 \tag{1b}$$

The observed gray values in an image window are approximated by a bivariate polynomial of second order. Nagel [15] derived a closed form solution for both components u and v of the displacement vector u at the center position of a symmetric window provided the approximating polynomial conforms to the requirements of (1).

A. Iterative Refinement for Corner Displacement Estimates

Since the conditions (1) will be rarely satisfied exactly at a pixel position, Nagel [15] developed an iterative approach to refine the displacement estimate whenever (1) would be satisfied only approximately. This iterative approach provided the starting point for the development to be presented in this contribution. It will be outlined, therefore, to serve as a reference for later discussions.

Assume that all pixels within the image window under consideration have been provided with a serial index i. All pixels within this window are assumed to be displaced by the unknown displacement vector u for which an estimate u_0 may be available such that

$$u = u_0 + Du. \tag{2}$$

Let $g1(x) = g(x, t_1)$ represent the gray value at location x in frame 1 and analogously $g2(x) = g(x, t_2)$ for frame 2. The displacement correction Du and thereby u itself should be estimated by minimizing a weighted sum of squared gray value differences within the image window. These differences are denoted by

$$dg = g2(x) - g1(x - u) \tag{3a}$$

$$= g2(x) - g1(x - u_0 - Du) \tag{3b}$$

where the column vector dg has the components

$$dg_i = g2(x_i) - g1(x_i - u_0 - Du) \tag{3c}$$

for $i = 1, \cdots N$ with N indicating the number of pixels in the window.

The expression to be minimized is given as

$$(dg)^T W_G(dg) \Rightarrow \text{minimum}. \tag{4}$$

The symmetric weight matrix W_G depends on the variance σ^2 of the gray value measurements and on the window size, but does not depend on the gray values themselves. W_G has been given in [15]. The dependence of dg and thus the expression (4) on $Du = (Du, Dv)^T$ may be made explicit by substituting a bivariate approximation polynomial for $g1(x - u_0 - Du)$. Since Du is assumed to be small, higher than linear terms in the components of Du may be neglected.

$$g1(x - u_0 - Du)$$
$$\simeq g1(x - u_0) - (\nabla g1)^T Du + u_0^T(\nabla\nabla g1)Du \tag{5}$$

where the following notational abbreviations have been used

$$\nabla g1 = \begin{pmatrix} g1_x(x) \\ g1_y(x) \end{pmatrix} \tag{6a}$$

499

$$\nabla\nabla g1 = \begin{pmatrix} g1_{xx}(x) & g1_{xy}(x) \\ g1_{xy}(x) & g1_{yy}(x) \end{pmatrix}. \tag{6b}$$

The first and second partial derivatives in (6) are taken to be the coefficients of the second-order bivariate polynomial which is obtained by a least squares approximation to $g1(x)$ within the window under consideration:

$$\sum_{\text{window}} [g1(x) - g1 - (\nabla g1)^T x$$

$$- \tfrac{1}{2} x^T (\nabla\nabla g1) x]^2 \Rightarrow \text{minimum}. \tag{7}$$

The vector $\nabla g1 - u_0^T(\nabla\nabla g1)$ which enters into the scalar product with Du in (5) is nothing but the approximation to the gradient of $g1(x)$ at location $x - u_0$.

If the matrix of partial derivatives of dg with respect to the components Du and Dv of Du is denoted by B^T, i.e.

$$B^T = \frac{\partial dg}{\partial Du} \tag{8}$$

we may write (4) in the form

$$(g2(x) - g1(x - u_0) + BDu)^T W_G$$

$$\cdot (g2(x) - g1(x - u_0) + BDu) \tag{4a}$$

from which we obtain—provided $\det(B^T W_G B) \neq 0$—

$$Du = -(B^T W_G B)^{-1} B^T W_G(g2(x) - g1(x - u_0)). \tag{9}$$

Nagel [15] has shown that this solution for the correction vector Du yields immediately a closed form solution for gray value corners, i.e., if the coefficients of the approximation polynomial satisfy (1). An implementation of this iterative improvement gave results supporting our expectations [20].

Although the approach based on (9) should improve the displacement estimate in the immediate vicinity of a gray value corner, it appeared attractive to employ it for the propagation of this displacement estimate into the surrounding environment. This was expected to work as long as $\det(B^T W_G B)$ would remain significantly different from zero. An experimental investigation in this direction encountered convergence problems even if the determinant of $B^T W_G B$ yielded values exceeding 10^4.

Upon closer inspection, the cause turned out to be a gross imbalance between the two eigenvalues of $B^T W_G B$. Using the abbreviation

$$h1_x = g1_x - g1_{xx} u_0 - g1_{xy} v_0 \tag{10a}$$

$$h1_y = g1_y - g1_{xy} u_0 - g1_{yy} v_0 \tag{10b}$$

and assuming a square window, i.e.,

$$\overline{x^2} = \overline{y^2}$$

the 2×2 matrix $B^T W_G B$ may be written

This matrix contains remarkable information about the local gray value variation within the window—see [19]. This becomes even more obvious if the local coordinate system is aligned with the principal curvature directions of $g(x)$ at the window center: in this case the mixed second derivative g_{xy} vanishes, yielding

$$B^T W_G B = \frac{N}{2\sigma^2} \begin{pmatrix} h1_x^2 + \overline{x^2} g1_{xx}^2 & h1_x h1_y \\ h1_x h1_y & h1_y^2 + \overline{x^2} g1_{yy}^2 \end{pmatrix}. \tag{11b}$$

If both second partial derivatives vanish, i.e., if the gray value function $g(x)$ is locally planar such as along a straight line zero-crossing section, $\det(B^T W_G B)$ becomes zero. It does not vanish, however, if only one principal curvature becomes zero, for example in the situation specified by (1) with $u_0 = 0$. In this case one obtains

$$B^T W_G B = \frac{N}{2\sigma^2} \begin{pmatrix} g1_x^2 & 0 \\ 0 & \overline{x^2} g1_{yy}^2 \end{pmatrix}. \tag{11c}$$

This demonstrates that both the gray value slope and the change in the direction of the gray value slope explicitly influence this matrix.

For the following discussion it is assumed that the local coordinate system is aligned with the eigenvectors of $B^T W_G B$. Then we may write

$$B^T W_G B = \begin{pmatrix} \kappa & 0 \\ 0 & \lambda \end{pmatrix}. \tag{12}$$

If one of the eigenvalues, say λ, is much smaller than the other, the determinant given by

$$\det(B^T W_G B) = \kappa\lambda \tag{13}$$

may still yield a sizable numerical value. Such a situation, however, implies that both the gradient and the curvature along the direction corresponding to the eigenvector associated with λ are small. Locally, the gray value variation $g(x)$ can be approximated by a cylinder with an axis parallel to the eigenvector direction associated with λ. In this case, the gray value variation does not provide enough information to reliably estimate the displacement vector component along this direction.

Since (13) as well as the following one

$$\text{trace}(B^T W_G B) = \kappa + \lambda \tag{14}$$

are invariant against rotation of the x-coordinate system, one can write

$$\frac{\det(B^T W_G B)}{[\tfrac{1}{2}\text{trace}(B^T W_G B)]^2} = \left(\frac{\sqrt{\kappa\lambda}}{\tfrac{1}{2}(\kappa + \lambda)} \right)^2. \tag{15}$$

This is the squared ratio of the geometric and arithmetic mean of the eigenvalues. If $\lambda \ll \kappa$, one may write

$$\frac{\det(B^T W_B B)}{[\tfrac{1}{2}\text{trace}(B^T W_G B)]^2} = 4 \frac{\kappa\lambda}{(\kappa + \lambda)^2} \simeq 4 \frac{\lambda}{\kappa}. \tag{16}$$

$$B^T W_G B = \frac{N}{2\sigma^2} \begin{pmatrix} h1_x^2 + \overline{x^2}(g1_{xx}^2 + g1_{xy}^2) & h1_x h1_y + \overline{x^2} g1_{xy}(g1_{xx} + g1_{yy}) \\ h1_x h1_y + \overline{x^2} g1_{xy}(g1_{xx} + g1_{yy}) & h1_y^2 + \overline{x^2}(g1_{xy}^2 + g1_{yy}^2) \end{pmatrix}. \tag{11a}$$

(a)

(d)

(b)

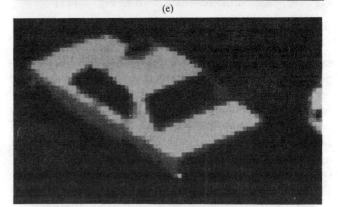

(e)

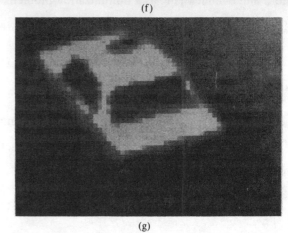

(f)

(c)

(g)

Fig. 1. Several frames from the real-world image sequence used to study
the approach described in this contribution: (a) frame 11; (b) frame 12;
(3) frame 20; (d) frame 30. A window around the bright taxicab in the
center of the image (e) from frame 11, (f) from frame 20, and (g) from
frame 30.

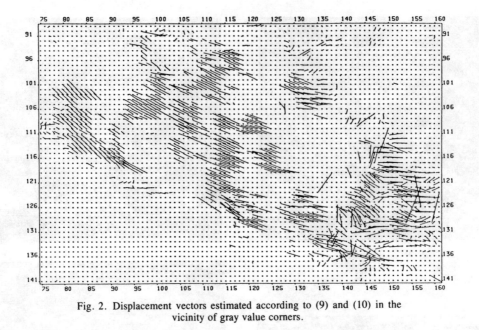

Fig. 2. Displacement vectors estimated according to (9) and (10) in the vicinity of gray value corners.

Comparing the ratio (16) to a threshold is, therefore, a straightforward test to suppress those windows where the gray value variation is insufficient for a reliable estimation of both displacement vector components. An implementation of this approach applied to the image sequence of Fig. 1(e) yielded the results shown in Fig. 2 [21].

B. Heuristic Introduction of "Oriented Smoothness"

The idea to let the gray value variation directly influence the smoothness requirement had already been suggested by Nagel [15]. The investigation described in the preceding section shed new light on how $B^T W_G B$ incorporates essential information about both slope and curvature of the gray value variation. This insight induced Nagel [16] to suggest that $(B^T W_G B)^{-1}$ might be explored as a suitable weight matrix for an "oriented smoothness" constraint.

A general smoothness constraint has been introduced by Horn and Schunck [11] as a minimization problem

$$\iint dxdy \ \{(\nabla g^T u + g_t)^2 + \alpha^2(u_x^2 + u_y^2 + v_x^2 + v_y^2)\} \Rightarrow \min. \quad (17)$$

This has been rewritten by Nagel in the form

$$\iint dxdy \ \{(\nabla g^T u + g_t)^2 + \alpha^2 \ \text{trace} \ [(\nabla u)^T (\nabla u)]\} \Rightarrow \min. \quad (18)$$

where

$$\nabla u = \begin{pmatrix} u_x & v_x \\ u_y & v_y \end{pmatrix} \quad (19)$$

represents the matrix of partial derivatives of the displacement vector components with respect to the image coordinates. The second term in (18) represents the smoothness requirement introduced by Horn and Schunck [11].

The factor α^2 denotes the strength of the smoothness requirement relative to the first term.

The idea of Nagel [16] has been to introduce the inverse of $B^T W_G B$ as a weight matrix into the smoothness term:

$$\iint dxdy \ \{(\nabla g^T u + g_t)^2 + \alpha^2 \ \text{trace} \ ((\nabla u)^T (B^T W_G B)^{-1} (\nabla u))\} \Rightarrow \min. \quad (20)$$

$B^T W_G B$ has been shown in [16] to be positive semidefinite. Since the second order terms in the polynomial approximation of $g(x)$ are sometimes important, the first term in (20) has been replaced by the squared "displaced gray value difference":

$$\iint dxdy \ \{(g2(x) - g1(x - u))^2 + \alpha^2 \ \text{trace} \ ((\nabla u)^T (B^T W_G B)^{-1} (\nabla u))\} \Rightarrow \min. \quad (21)$$

The idea behind this approach becomes more evident if it is assumed that the coordinate system happens to be aligned with the eigenvector directions of $B^T W_G B$ at the location under discussion.

Using (12), the integrand may then be written as

$$(g2(x) - g1(x - u))^2 + \alpha^2 \ \text{trace} \ \left((\nabla u)^T \begin{pmatrix} \kappa & 0 \\ 0 & \lambda \end{pmatrix}^{-1} (\nabla u) \right) \quad (22a)$$

or

$$(g2(x) - g1(x - u))^2 + \alpha^2 \left(\frac{u_x^2}{\kappa} + \frac{u_y^2}{\lambda} + \frac{v_x^2}{\kappa} + \frac{v_y^2}{\lambda} \right). \quad (22b)$$

502

If both κ and λ are large, the gray value variation contains sufficient information to estimate both u and v based on the interframe displaced gray value difference $(g2(x) - g1(x - u))$. In this situation, the smoothness contribution to the estimation of both u and v would be suppressed by a factor $1/\kappa$ or $1/\lambda$, respectively.

If the gray value variation $g1(x)$ corresponds locally to a cylinder parallel to the x, y-plane, one of the eigenvalues, say λ, will be much smaller than the other as discussed in the preceding section. In this case, the smoothness contribution would be suppressed only in the direction with strong gray value variation, i.e., the eigenvector direction associated with κ.

If both eigenvalues are small then the smoothness term would constrain the variation of both displacement vector components: large variations of u or v would contribute sizable terms to the integrand. Therefore, the minimization of the integral would tend to diminish variations of u and v in image areas with more or less constant gray values.

C. Derivation of the "Oriented Smoothness" Constraint

The heuristic modification of (17) appeared plausible enough to search for some rationalization. Nagel [17] could show that a weight matrix with essentially the structure of $B^T W_G B$ could be obtained by the following line of argumentation:

1) The variation of the displacement vector u in the direction perpendicular to the gradient should become as small as possible. This variation is captured by the two-component row vector

$$\begin{pmatrix} g_y \\ -g_x \end{pmatrix}^T \nabla u. \tag{23}$$

The norm of this vector can be written in the form:

$$\left(\begin{pmatrix} g_y \\ -g_x \end{pmatrix}^T \nabla u \right) \left(\begin{pmatrix} g_y \\ -g_x \end{pmatrix}^T \nabla u \right)^T$$

$$= \text{trace} \left((\nabla u)^T \begin{pmatrix} g_y \\ -g_x \end{pmatrix} \begin{pmatrix} g_y \\ -g_x \end{pmatrix}^T (\nabla u) \right). \tag{24}$$

2) The variation of the displacement vector u should be as small as possible in the direction perpendicular to the principal curvature direction associated with a large curvature. The variation of u in the direction perpendicular to the principal curvature orientations can be expressed in a manner not depending on a particular choice of the coordinate system by the matrix

$$\begin{pmatrix} g_{yy} & -g_{xy} \\ -g_{xy} & g_{xx} \end{pmatrix}^T (\nabla u)$$

$$= \begin{pmatrix} g_{yy} u_x - g_{xy} u_y & g_{yy} v_x - g_{xy} v_y \\ -g_{xy} u_x + g_{xx} u_y & -g_{xy} v_x + g_{xx} v_y \end{pmatrix}. \tag{25}$$

The sum of the scalar products for each of the two column vectors with themselves can be written in the form

$$\text{trace} \left\{ \left[\begin{pmatrix} g_{yy} & -g_{xy} \\ -g_{xy} & g_{xx} \end{pmatrix}^T (\nabla u) \right]^T \left[\begin{pmatrix} g_{yy} & -g_{xy} \\ -g_{xy} & g_{xx} \end{pmatrix}^T (\nabla u) \right] \right\} \tag{26a}$$

$$= \text{trace} \left\{ (\nabla u)^T \left[\begin{pmatrix} g_{yy} & -g_{xy} \\ -g_{xy} & g_{xx} \end{pmatrix} \begin{pmatrix} g_{yy} & -g_{xy} \\ -g_{xy} & g_{xx} \end{pmatrix}^T \right] (\nabla u) \right\}. \tag{26b}$$

3) The "oriented smoothness" constraint demands that the variation of u in the direction perpendicular to significant gray value variations is minimized. This can be achieved by minimizing a weighted sum of the expressions in (24) and (26).

$$F = \left\{ \begin{pmatrix} g_y \\ -g_x \end{pmatrix} \begin{pmatrix} g_y \\ -g_x \end{pmatrix}^T + b^2 \begin{pmatrix} g_{yy} & -g_{xy} \\ -g_{xy} & g_{xx} \end{pmatrix} \begin{pmatrix} g_{yy} & -g_{xy} \\ -g_{xy} & g_{xx} \end{pmatrix}^T \right\} \tag{27}$$

where the factor b^2 denotes the relative weight of the two contributions. One possible way to express the oriented smoothness constraint consists in minimizing

$$(\nabla u)^T F (\nabla u). \tag{28}$$

4) In order to obtain an expression analogous to (21), Nagel [17] argued that the expression (28) should be normalized. The determinant of F appeared as a suitable scalar norm of this matrix. If (28) is divided by $\det (F)$, one obtains the weight matrix

$$C^{-1} = \frac{F}{\det F} \tag{29}$$

with C given by

$$C = \begin{pmatrix} g_x^2 + b^2(g_{xx}^2 + g_{xy}^2) & g_x g_y + b^2 g_{xy}(g_{xx} + g_{yy}) \\ g_x g_y + b^2 g_{xy}(g_{xx} + g_{yy}) & g_y^2 + b^2(g_{xy}^2 + g_{yy}^2) \end{pmatrix} \tag{30a}$$

$$= ((\nabla g)(\nabla g)^T + b^2(\nabla \nabla g)(\nabla \nabla g)^T) \tag{30b}$$

Comparison of (30a) to equation (11a) shows the structural analogy between C and $B^T W_G B$.

III. First Attempts at a Solution

The estimation of a displacement vector field describing the displacement between gray value images $g1(x)$ and $g2(x)$ requires the minimization of the following integral—see (21):

$$\iint dx\,dy \left\{ (g2(x) - g1(x - u))^2 + \alpha^2 \text{trace} ((\nabla u)^T C^{-1}(\nabla u)) \right\} \Rightarrow \min. \tag{31}$$

503

As has been pointed out in [17], this integral can be specialized to the one introduced by Horn and Schunck [11] if the following simplifications are applied:

1) The influence of the smoothness constraint related to principal curvature directions is suppressed, i.e., the factor b^2 in (30) is set to zero.

2) The directional sensitivity of the smoothness requirement is suppressed, i.e., the outer product matrix $(\nabla g)(\nabla g)^T$ in (30) is replaced by the unit matrix.

3) The "displaced interframe gray value difference" between the outer pair of parentheses of (31) is replaced by a first order Taylor approximation.

The following derivation assumes that only the gray value distribution in frame 1 enters into the derivatives appearing in the matrix C of (31).

The Euler–Lagrange equations for the minimization problem (31) yield

$$-(g2(x) - g1(x - u)) \frac{\partial g1(x - u)}{\partial u}$$

$$- \alpha^2 \begin{pmatrix} \dfrac{d}{dx} \\ \dfrac{d}{dy} \end{pmatrix}^T C^{-1} \begin{pmatrix} u_x \\ u_y \end{pmatrix} = 0 \qquad (32a)$$

$$-(g2(x) - g1(x - u)) \frac{\partial g1(x - u)}{\partial v}$$

$$- \alpha^2 \begin{pmatrix} \dfrac{d}{dx} \\ \dfrac{d}{dy} \end{pmatrix}^T C^{-1} \begin{pmatrix} v_x \\ v_y \end{pmatrix} = 0. \qquad (32b)$$

In order to visualize the effect of the oriented smoothness term, assume that the coordinate system is aligned with the eigenvector directions of C at the image location of interest. This results in

$$C = \begin{pmatrix} c_1 & 0 \\ 0 & c_2 \end{pmatrix}. \qquad (33)$$

The second term in (32a) may then be written as

$$\begin{pmatrix} \dfrac{d}{dx} \\ \dfrac{d}{dy} \end{pmatrix}^T \begin{pmatrix} c_1^{-1} & 0 \\ 0 & c_2^{-1} \end{pmatrix} \begin{pmatrix} u_x \\ u_y \end{pmatrix}$$

$$= \begin{pmatrix} -\dfrac{1}{c_1^2} \dfrac{dc_1}{dx} \\ -\dfrac{1}{c_2^2} \dfrac{dc_2}{dy} \end{pmatrix}^T \begin{pmatrix} u_x \\ u_y \end{pmatrix} + \frac{u_{xx}}{c_1} + \frac{u_{yy}}{c_2}. \qquad (34)$$

If both eigenvalues are large, they suppress the contribution of the smoothness term compared to the first term in (32). In order to simplify the subsequent attempts to solve (32), the components of C are considered to vary

slowly from pixel to pixel so that the derivatives of C can be neglected. This assumption enables us to simplify (32) into

$$-(g2(x) - g1(x - u)) \frac{\partial g1(x - u)}{\partial u} -$$

$$\alpha^2 \text{ trace} \left(C^{-1} \begin{pmatrix} u_{xx} & u_{xy} \\ u_{xy} & u_{yy} \end{pmatrix} \right) = 0 \qquad (35a)$$

$$-(g2(x) - g1(x - u)) \frac{\partial g1(x - u)}{\partial v} -$$

$$\alpha^2 \text{ trace} \left(C^{-1} \begin{pmatrix} v_{xx} & v_{xy} \\ v_{xy} & v_{yy} \end{pmatrix} \right) = 0. \qquad (35b)$$

These equations (35) provide the starting point for the first two solution approaches.

A. Iterative Approach Based on the Gray Value Difference

This approach, originally suggested in [17], assumes that an approximate solution $u_0(x)$ for the displacement vector field is known. Substitution of $u_0(x)$ for u will in general not satisfy (35). The problem then consists in the determination of a correction vector field $Du(x)$ such that (35) become satisfied. The initial approach along this line neglected the influence of the correction term $Du(x)$ in the determination of $\nabla\nabla u$ and $\nabla\nabla v$, respectively. It only investigated the effect of $Du(x)$ on the first term in (35).

Since Du is considered to be small, we retain only first order terms in components of Du and average over the environment which is used to estimate the first and second partial derivatives of the gray values as well as of the displacement vector field u. This approach—see Appendix 1 for the detailed derivation of (A1-7)—yielded:

$$CDu = -\overline{[g2(x) - g1(x - u_0)]\nabla g1}$$

$$+ \alpha^2 \overline{\begin{bmatrix} \text{trace } (C^{-1}\nabla\nabla u_0) \\ \text{trace } (C^{-1}\nabla\nabla v_0) \end{bmatrix}}. \qquad (36)$$

Here, the overbar indicates the result of the averaging process. The solution approach envisaged in [17] consisted of the following steps:

1) Initialize $u_0(x) \equiv 0$.

2) Select those image areas where $\det (C) \neq 0$ and, in analogy to (16),

$$\frac{\det C}{(\frac{1}{2} \text{ trace } C)^2} > \text{threshold}, \qquad (37)$$

i.e., where there is sufficient gray value variation to estimate both components of the displacement vector without recourse to a smoothness requirement. This should essentially cover the image areas around gray value corners as shown in [21]—see Fig. 2.

3) Set $\alpha^2 = 0$, estimate the displacement vector at image locations selected according to step 2) and improve these estimates by an iterative procedure analogous to the one described in Section II-A.

4) Switch on the "oriented smoothness" constraint by letting α^2 become nonzero and spread the estimates obtained in step 3) into other image areas hitherto spared.

The implementation of this approach made obvious that the following problem could not be handled as anticipated. Image areas excluded in step 2) are characterized by an ill-conditioned matrix C. Originally, it has been anticipated to substitute minimal values for the elements of C. These minimal values should have been chosen based on the error estimates for first and second partial derivatives of $g1$ as given in the Appendix of [15]. It turned out, however, that these estimates appeared to be too small to prevent numerical difficulties. Therefore, the inversion of C to obtain the solution of equation (36) resulted in severe numerical difficulties.

Once this explanation had been corroborated, it appeared sensible to drop the simplification of relying only on the first term in (35) in order to estimate an initial correction vector field Du.

B. Extended Iterative Approach

Following the analysis discussed at the end of the preceding section, the effect of a correction Du on the terms containing $\nabla\nabla u$ and $\nabla\nabla v$ has been investigated as well—see Appendix 2 for details. It resulted in the following equation:

$$[(\nabla g1)(\nabla g1)^T + b^2(\nabla\nabla g1)(\nabla\nabla g1)^T$$
$$+ \alpha^2 m \text{ trace } C^{-1}I] \, Du$$
$$= -\overline{[g2(x) - g1(x - u_0)]\nabla g1}$$
$$+ \alpha^2 \begin{bmatrix} \text{trace } (C^{-1}\nabla\nabla u_0) \\ \text{trace } (C^{-1}\nabla\nabla v_0) \end{bmatrix}. \tag{38}$$

Here, I denotes a 2×2 unit matrix and m stands for the magnitude value of the weight factor at the center pixel position in the operator mask for $\partial^2/\partial x^2$. In the case of a 5×5 Beaudet operator mask [1], this results in the value $m = \frac{2}{35}$.

The important difference between (36) and (38) consists of the addition of the term $\alpha^2 m \cdot \text{trace } (C^{-1})$ in both diagonal elements of the coefficient matrix for the unknown correction vector Du.

Its influence may be visualized by the following qualitative argument. Assume that the same solution steps as outlined in Section III-A are performed on the basis of (38). Since α^2 will be zero throughout the first three steps, the difference between (36) and (38) will become relevant only in step 4). Extension of solutions obtained around gray value corners into areas with ill-conditioned C-matrices will result in large values for trace (C^{-1}). The addition of such large values to the diagonal elements of the coefficient matrix for Du should prevent the coefficient matrix for Du from becoming singular. It is expected, therefore, that one may be able to invert this coefficient matrix and hence get a solution for Du.

Implementation of this approach did not yield results

commensurate with our expectations. The trouble could be diagnosed to be related to the constant α^2 which indicates the relative weight between the smoothness term and the gray value difference term in (31).

In order to achieve a noticeable effect by the term $\alpha^2 m \cdot \text{trace } (C^{-1})$, α^2 had to be given values between 500 and 1000 which appeared to be unreasonably high. Such values had the consequence that the smoothness contribution on the right-hand side of (38) would dominate the other term on the right hand side which is based on the gray value difference. Since for low iteration indexes in step 4) the values of $u_0(x)$ would differ from zero only around gray value corners, the estimates of $\nabla\nabla u_0$ and $\nabla\nabla v_0$ turned out to be somewhat erratic initially. Large values for α^2 would exacerbate this behavior.

It is illuminating to discuss equation (38) at the beginning of step 4) in a situation where $u_0(x)$ is still zero throughout the image window under consideration. We may assume that the local coordinate system is aligned with the principal curvature directions of the gray value distribution within this window, i.e., $g1_{xy} = 0$. Using these conventions, (38) reduces to

$$[C + I\alpha^2 m \text{ trace } C^{-1}]Du$$
$$= -\overline{[g2(x) - g1(x - u_0)]\nabla g1} \tag{39}$$

because $u_0(x) \equiv 0$ implies $\nabla\nabla u_0 = \nabla\nabla v_0 = 0$. This vector equation for the components Du and Dv of the correction vector Du can be solved explicitly—see Appendix 3:

$$Du = -\frac{\overline{g2(x) - g1(x - u_0)}}{g1_x} \cdot \frac{1}{1 + \alpha^2 m \dfrac{1 + b^2 g1_{yy}^2/g1_x^2}{b^2 g1_x^2 g1_{yy}^2}} \tag{40a}$$

$$Dv = -\frac{g2_y}{g1_{yy}} \cdot \frac{1}{1 + \alpha^2 m \dfrac{1 + g1_x^2/(b^2 g1_{yy}^2)}{b^2 g1_x^2 g1_{yy}^2}}. \tag{40b}$$

The expressions (40) facilitate a quantitative discussion of the influence exerted during the initial iterations by an oriented smoothness constraint in the form given by (29) and (31).

If the smoothness constraint is omitted, i.e., $\alpha^2 = 0$, the results can be related to previously known entities:
• Du is equal to minus the gray value difference divided by the gradient.
• Dv is equal to the closed form solution obtained by Nagel [15] at gray value corners.

Since all terms in the correction factor are positive, the contributions with $\alpha^2 \neq 0$ reduce these estimates.

For 192×256 pixel 8-bit gray value images like those in Fig. 1, a 5×5 operator mask will yield numerical values well exceeding 10 for both $g1_x$ and $g1_{yy}$ at gray value corners. The value of b^2 has been set equal to

$$\overline{\xi^2} = 2$$

for this mask size. Since $m = \frac{2}{35}$, even values of 10^3 for α^2 do not result in noticeable corrections. This does not matter at gray value corners since there the uncorrected estimates are known to be acceptable.

The smoothness constraint should influence the estimate along straight line gray value transitions because there only one component of the displacement vector will be determined by the gray value distribution. We may study the behavior of Du according to (40) by "unbending" the corner, that is by reducing the curvature $g1_{yy}$ of a locus line with strong gray value slope $g1_x$. In the limit of vanishing $g1_{yy}$ both components of Du as given by (40) will tend to zero.

If we study the origin of this factor, we see that it is related to trace (C^{-1}) and there to the fact that our smoothness weight matrix F has been normalized by its determinant—see (29).

As a consequence of this analysis, it has been attempted to use some other convention than division by det (F) in order to normalize F.

IV. Different Normalizations of the Weight Matrix

Another way to formulate the insight provided by the discussion of (40) consists in the following consideration. If the locus line of maximum gray value slope—i.e., large $g1_x$—exhibits only a small curvature $g1_{yy}$, then the term $b^2 g1_{yy}^2$ in the numerator of trace (C^{-1})—see (A3-6b)—may be dropped compared to $g1_x^2$. As a result, trace (C^{-1}) becomes approximately equal to $1/(b \cdot g1_{yy})^2$ which assumes values between 0.1 and 1. Even with $\alpha^2 = 100$, the term $\alpha^2 m/(b^2 g1_{yy}^2)$ added to the diagonal elements of C in (39) does not significantly reduce the imbalance between the eigenvalues of the coefficient matrix on the left hand side of this equation. The consequence is to raise the weight of the smoothness term by looking for another normalization factor in (29).

A. Normalization by Trace (F) Instead of by Det (F)

One possibility which springs to the mind consists of taking trace (F) rather than det (F) (see also [23]). Instead of (31) we therefore investigate the minimization of:

$$\iint dx\, dy \left\{ [g2(x) - g1(x - u)]^2 + \alpha^2 \text{ trace} \left[(\nabla u)^T \frac{F}{\text{trace } F} (\nabla u) \right] \right\} \Rightarrow \min. \quad (41)$$

If we take into account the contribution of the smoothness term in (41), we obtain the following result for a gray value corner:

$$Du = -\frac{\overline{g2(x)} - \overline{g1(x - u_0)}}{g1_x} \cdot \frac{1}{1 + \frac{\alpha^2 m}{g1_x^2}}$$

$$+ \alpha^2 \frac{b^2 g1_{yy}^2 u_{0xx} + g1_x^2 u_{0yy}}{(g1_x^2 + b^2 g1_{yy}^2)(g1_x^2 + \alpha^2 m)} \quad (42a)$$

$$Dv = -\frac{g2_y}{g1_{yy}} \cdot \frac{1}{1 + \frac{\alpha^2 m}{b^2 g1_{yy}^2}}$$

$$+ \alpha^2 \frac{b^2 g1_{yy}^2 v_{0xx} + g1_x^2 v_{0yy}}{(g1_x^2 + b^2 g1_{yy}^2)(b^2 g1_{yy}^2 + \alpha^2 m)}. \quad (42b)$$

If we completely "unbend" the gray value corner, i.e., if we set $g1_{yy} = 0$, we obtain instead of (42):

$$Du = -\frac{\overline{g2(x)} - \overline{g1(x - u_0)}}{g1_x} \cdot \frac{1}{1 + \frac{\alpha^2 m}{g1_x^2}}$$

$$+ \alpha^2 \frac{u_{0yy}}{(g1_x^2 + \alpha^2 m)} \quad (43a)$$

$$Dv = \frac{1}{m} v_{0yy}. \quad (43b)$$

Equation (43) shows the influence of the "oriented smoothness" constraint in an especially clear manner. At maximum slope of a strong straight line gray value transition, i.e., large values for $g1_x$ and small values for all other first and second order partial derivatives, the component perpendicular to the edge will essentially correspond to $(-g1_t/g1_x)$. The correction for the displacement vector component parallel to the edge will only vanish if the second partial derivative of the displacement vector field in this direction vanishes.

B. Using F without Normalization

In addition to the choice of both det (F) as well as trace (F) as a normalization factor for the weight matrix in an "oriented smoothness" constraint, we have explored the alternative of using F given by (27) without normalization [22]. Instead of (31) we minimize

$$\iint dx\, dy \left\{ [g2(x) - g1(x - u)]^2 + \alpha^2 \text{ trace} \left[(\nabla u)^T F(\nabla u) \right] \right\} \Rightarrow \min. \quad (44)$$

In analogy to (40), the first correction vector Du at a location of maximum gray value slope after starting with $u_0(x) \equiv 0$ will be

$$Du = -\frac{\overline{g2(x)} - \overline{g1(x - u_0)}}{g1_x}$$

$$\cdot \frac{1}{1 + \alpha^2 m(1 + b^2 g1_{yy}^2/g1_x^2)} \quad (45a)$$

$$Dv = -\frac{g2_y}{g1_{yy}} \cdot \frac{1}{1 + \alpha^2 m(1 + g1_x^2/(b^2 g1_{yy}^2))}. \quad (45b)$$

The factor α^2 can be chosen to be smaller than in the case of (40). One would expect that α^2 should be of the order of the variance of gray value differences $[g2(x) - g1(x - u)]$ although this consideration does not take into account the "orientation" aspect of the smoothness constraint. Nevertheless, a value of α^2 in the range of $2\sigma^2$ appears to be more attractive *a priori* than 10 or 100 times this value.

V. Heuristic Modifications

Although the preceding sections have shown how it is possible to derive closed form expressions for the correction terms and thereby how to study the influence of certain parameters analytically, we feel that we still have some way to go towards a solution of the nonlinear system of partial differential equations resulting from the various formulations for the "oriented smoothness" constraint. Unless we can study such solutions, however, it is difficult to judge the relative merits of these and other possible formulations.

In addition to the approach outlined in the preceding section we have studied in our current implementation several heuristic modifications. These have been motivated by attempts to counterbalance certain effects observed during an extended range of experiments. We did not hesitate to make some effects more visible or to suppress them by heuristic modifications. Our experience has shown us that once an effect could be clearly identified, it has been possible to study it not only experimentally but also through specific modifications to the theoretical approach. It appears useful, therefore, to present these more or less heuristic modifications and to demonstrate their effect.

A. Enhancement of the Smoothness Term in the Coefficient Matrix for Du

Larger values of α^2 result in greater contributions to the diagonal terms of the coefficient matrix on the left-hand side of (38) and the analogous equations for the other choices of the weight matrix discussed in Section IV. This facilitates obtaining estimates for both components of the displacement vector along almost straight line gray value transitions. The disadvantage is that the terms multiplied by α^2 on the right-hand side of these equations may achieve a weight which does not appear to be necessarily beneficial during early iterations. We therefore introduced a heuristic correction factor c such that, for example, the term $c \cdot \alpha^2 m \cdot \text{trace}(F)$ is added to the diagonal elements of C in order to obtain the coefficient matrix for Du. This factor c has been set to 8 in the case where the weight matrix $W = F$ has been used.

B. Lower Limit for Eigenvalues of the Coefficient Matrix

In order to prevent a singularity of the coefficient matrix for Du in areas with practically homogeneous gray values, the eigenvalues of C are replaced by a lower limit $\gamma = 2\sigma^2 (\sim 5-12)$ whenever they drop below this threshold. If both eigenvalues are smaller than γ the first term on the right hand side of (38)—and analogously for the other choices of normalization—will be suppressed.

C. Averaging u_0

The second partial derivatives of u_0 and v_0 are computed by applying Beaudet's operators [1] to the components u_0 and v_0 of the displacement vector field estimate u_0 obtained in the course of the iterative solution approach. These operators are based on the assumption that the variation of $u_0(x)$ and $v_0(x)$ can be approximated within the operator window by a bivariate polynomial. As a consequence of this approach the value of $u_0(x)$ as well as $v_0(x)$ averaged over the window is not identical to the value of u_0 or v_0, respectively, at the window center. Since the correction Du will eventually become smaller than the difference between the average and the center value, the center value at each pixel location is replaced by the average value obtained by application of Beaudet's averaging operator to the field u_0 within the operator window.

D. Interframe Average for Derivatives

Nagel [14] has shown that one may use the interframe average for the computation of first and second partial derivatives rather than using the derivatives obtained from frame 1 alone. Although this ensues a slightly greater number of iterations, it extends the range wherein the approach catches on. This can be understood, for example, in the case of the edge line between the rear cab window and the car top. Between frame 1 and frame 2 in Fig. 1, the rear window area moves across the fairly constant bright area of the car top. Since the gradient in this area of frame 1 is small, one initially obtains large displacement estimates. They are a consequence of the attempt to explain the large gray value difference between bright car top and dark rear window on the basis of too small a gray value slope. The gray value slope averaged between the areas to be compared gives a better displacement estimate. Of course, the opposite effect happens for example at the transition between rear window and trunk. There the estimate resulting from this approach will be somewhat larger than in the case where only the gradient from frame 1 had been used. The overall effect of this modification, however, appears to be positive. Once the iteration converges, the two windows to be compared will exhibit essentially the same gray value variation and hence the averaging process does not bias the final result.

E. The Strength of the Smoothness Constraint as a Function of the Iteration Count

During experiments with the weight matrix $W = F$, the value of α^2 has been handadjusted during the iteration in order to keep the maximum contribution from the smoothness correction below a heuristic limit.

Deviating from the steps outlined towards the end of Section III-A, we start immediately with $u_0(x) \equiv 0$ and omit steps 1)–3). In order to prevent the coefficient matrix of Du to become ill-conditioned in image areas with almost constant gray values, α^2 is not set to zero but to a small nonzero value. Fig. 3 presents our current choice of α^2 as a function of the iteration count.

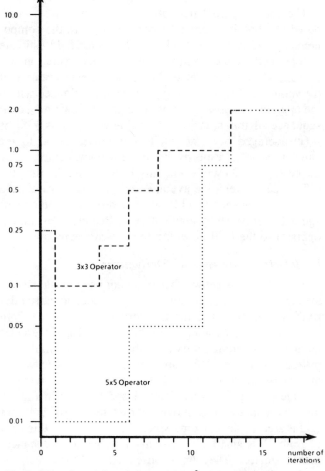

Fig. 3. The value of the relative weight α^2 of the smoothness constraint as a function of the iteration count in case where the weight matrix $W = F$ has been used.

displaced gray value differences. The following formula is employed to estimate the correction Du:

$$Du = -\frac{\overline{(g2(x) - \overline{g1(x - u_0)})}}{g1(x - u_0)_x^2 + g1(x - u_0)_y^2 + \alpha^2}$$

$$\begin{pmatrix} g1(x - u_0)_x \\ g1(x - u_0)_y \end{pmatrix} \qquad (46)$$

It can be seen that this alone provides a considerable improvement compared to the method described by Horn and Schunck [11]. Fig. 4(c) demonstrates to what extend the use of interframe averages for the first derivatives as explained in Section V-D modifies the results in comparison with Fig. 4(b). The correction term has been computed in this case according to the following formula:

$$Du = -\frac{\overline{(g2(x) - \overline{g1(x - u_0)})}}{g_x^2 + g_y^2 + \alpha^2}\begin{pmatrix} g_x \\ g_y \end{pmatrix} \qquad (47a)$$

with

$$g_x = \frac{g2_x(x) + g1_x(x - u_0)}{2} \qquad (47b)$$

and

$$g_y = \frac{g2_y(x) + g1_y(x - u_0)}{2} \qquad (47c)$$

3×3 Beaudet operators have been used to compute the derivatives. The data for $g1(x - u_0)$ has been obtained by bilinear interpolation according to the current value of u_0. A value of $\alpha^2 = 50$ has been used in these experiments. Figs. 5–7 present analogous results after 3, 10, and 30 iterations.

B. "Oriented Smoothness" with Weight Matrix $W = F$

Fig. 8(a) presents the result of the "oriented smoothness" approach outlined in Section IV-B, i.e., with just F as the weight matrix, after the first iteration for a 3×3 pixel operator window. This result may be compared directly to the smoothness approach. One can see that the estimates are different from zero in image areas where significant gray value variations have been displaced between frame 11 and frame 12. Fig. 8(b) shows analogous results for a 5×5 pixel operator window. It can be seen that the 3×3 window is somewhat more susceptible to digitization noise because only nine measurements are available to estimate the six unknowns required to describe the Taylor expansion up to the second order. A 5×5 window provides 25 measurements to estimate the same coefficients. Within a 3×3 operator window, moreover, the curvature estimate of the gray value distribution is somewhat larger. This has to be taken into account by an appropriate choice of the parameters. Fig. 9 shows how these estimates have improved after the third iteration. The iteration process has been stopped manually after the maximal magnitude of the correction term

During experiments with $W = F/\text{trace}(F)$, the value of α^2 has been doubled as soon as the maximum correction dropped below 0.1 pixels per frame.

VI. RESULTS

In order to facilitate a comparison of the approaches investigated here with earlier ones, the approach of Horn and Schunck [11] has been reimplemented and applied to our data. Since our approach incorporates various modifications in addition to the "oriented smoothness" constraint, we include a series of experimental results which demonstrate the gradual transition from the Horn and Schunck approach to the ones discussed in previous sections.

A. The Approach of Horn and Schunck with Modifications

Fig. 4(a) presents the result of applying the approach of Horn and Schunck [11] to the window shown in Fig. 1(e) and the corresponding window from the subsequent frame. Fig. 4(b) presents the result of applying to the same data a general smoothness approach according to Horn and Schunck—modified, however, by using interframe

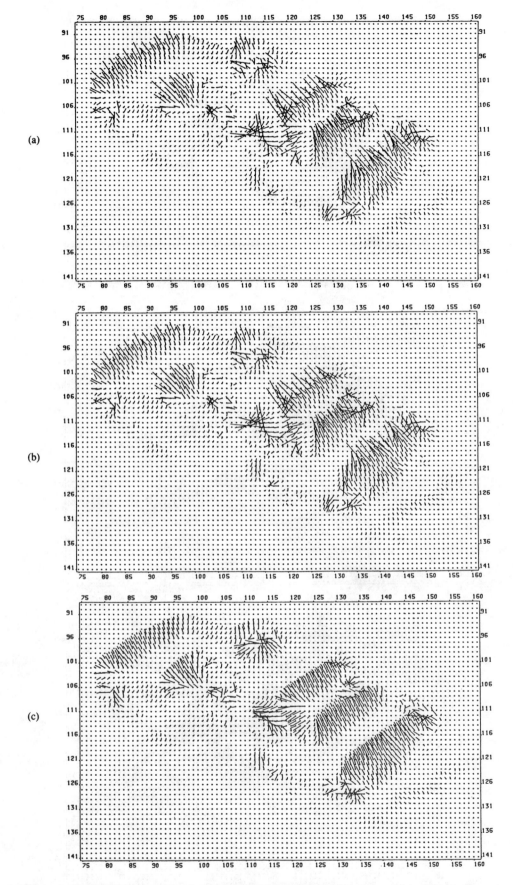

Fig. 4. Result after iteration 1 for the approach of Horn and Schunck [11], applied to the window shown in Figure 1e and the corresponding window from the subsequent frame: (a) as described by Horn and Schunck [11]; (b) analogous to (a), but using the displaced frame difference according to (46) in order to compute the correction term; (c) analogous to (b), but including in addition the interframe average of gradients according to (47).

509

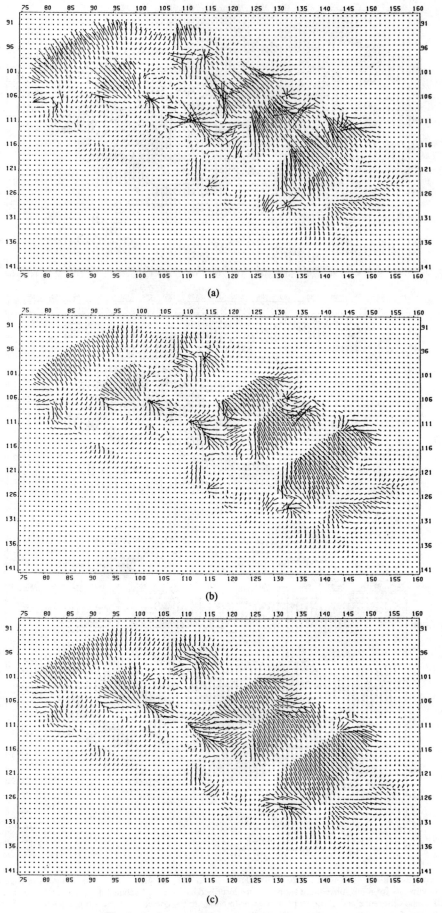

(a)

(b)

(c)

Fig. 5. Analogous to Fig. 4, but after iteration 3.

510

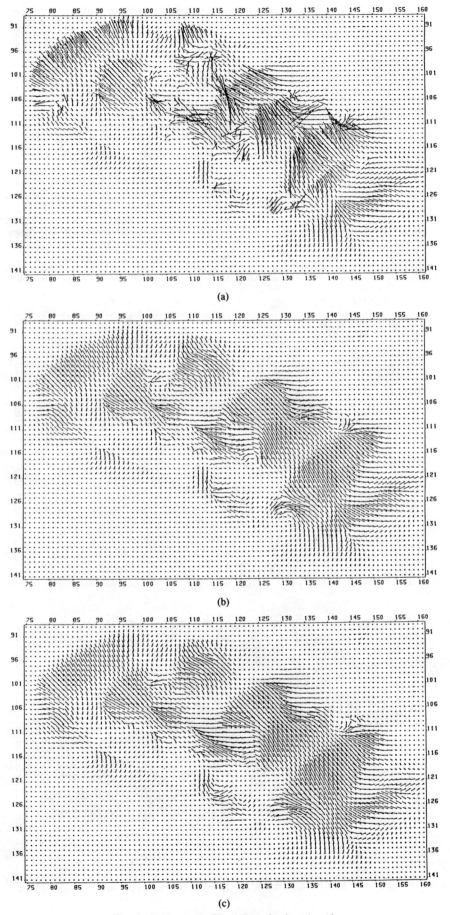

(a)

(b)

(c)

Fig. 6. Analogous to Fig. 4, but after iteration 10.

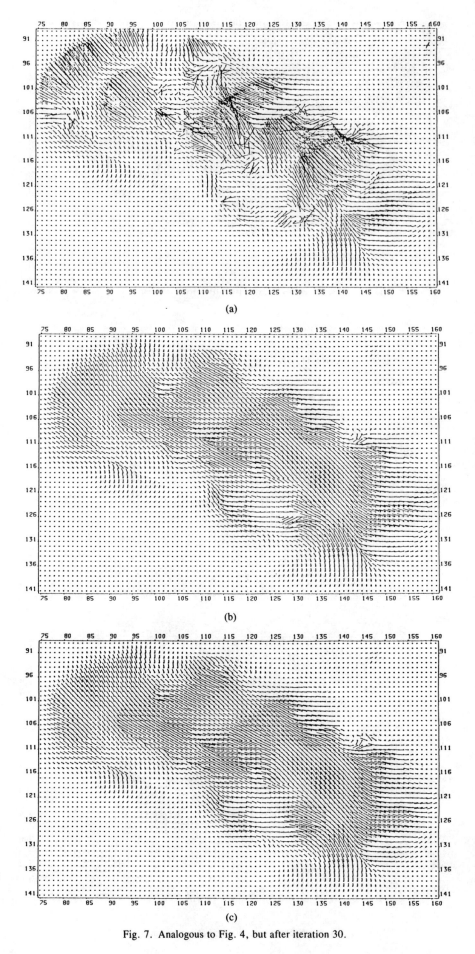

Fig. 7. Analogous to Fig. 4, but after iteration 30.

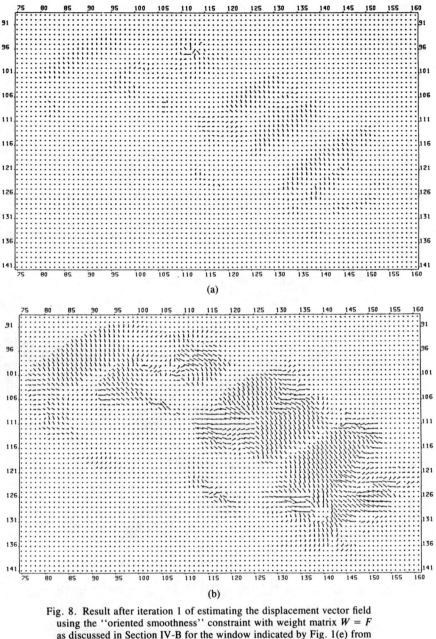

(a)

(b)

Fig. 8. Result after iteration 1 of estimating the displacement vector field
using the "oriented smoothness" constraint with weight matrix $W = F$
as discussed in Section IV-B for the window indicated by Fig. 1(e) from
frames 11 and 12. The initial value has been $u_0(x) \equiv 0$: (a) for 3×3
pixel operator window with $\alpha^2 = 0.25$; $c = 8$; $\gamma = 12.5$; (b) for 5×5
pixel operator window with $\alpha^2 = 0.25$; $c = 8$; $\gamma = 5$.

dropped below $\frac{1}{5}$ of a pixel per frame in the 13th and 17th iteration, respectively. The final result is shown in Fig. 10.

Attention is drawn to the following aspects:

1) Apart from the moving shadow area behind the taxicab—which is, moreover, partially occluded by branches of the tree in the foreground—the displacement vector field is fairly smooth inside the area covered by the image of the moving taxicab. This displacement vector field is plausible.

2) The displacement vector field exhibits the expected (near) discontinuities, both along contours parallel to the displacement as well as along contours perpendicular to the displacement.

3) The displacement vector field does not exhibit sizable discontinuities across strong gray value transitions within the image area of the moving car.

One problem observed in these experiments is connected with the choice for the relative weight of the smoothness term, i.e., α^2. Small values for α^2 will yield reasonable results around gray value corners where F takes on large values. In rather homogeneous image areas like those for the roof or the trunk of the taxicab, a large number of iterations is required in order to spread the displacement vector estimates from areas with greater gray value variations where both components of the displacement vector field can be estimated. If one gets impatient and increases the weight of the smoothness term in order to

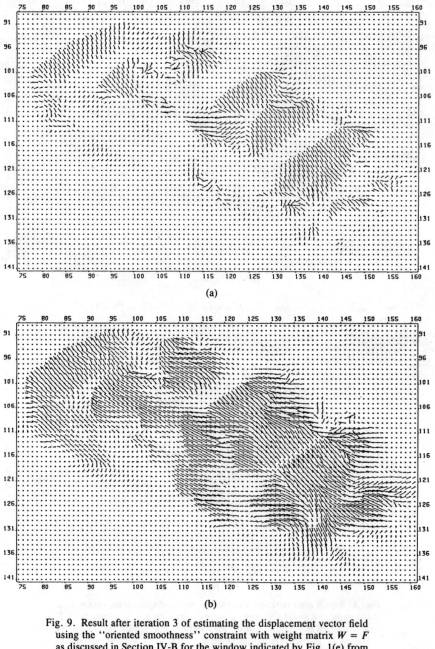

Fig. 9. Result after iteration 3 of estimating the displacement vector field using the "oriented smoothness" constraint with weight matrix $W = F$ as discussed in Section IV-B for the window indicated by Fig. 1(e) from frames 11 and 12: (a) for 3 × 3 pixel operator window with $\alpha^2 = 0.1$; $c = 8$; $\gamma = 12.5$; (b) for 5 × 5 pixel operator window with $\alpha^2 = 0.01$; $c = 8$; $\gamma = 5$.

spread displacement estimates faster into such areas, then the second partial derivatives $\nabla\nabla u_0$ and $\nabla\nabla v_0$ must already be sufficiently small around gray value corners or along strong edges in order to avoid too large correction terms.

C. "Oriented Smoothness" with Weight Matrix $W = F/$ trace (F)

Fig. 11(a) presents the result for the first iteration starting from $u_0 \equiv 0$ and using the weight matrix $W = F/$ (trace F) as discussed in Section IV-A. A 3 × 3 pixel operator window has been used. The analogous result for a 5 × 5 pixel operator window is shown in Fig. 11(b).

The result for iterations 3, 10, and 30 are given in Figs. 12–14.

D. Using Previous Results to Predict Starting Values

Such a large number of iterations appears to be only necessary if no knowledge about the displacement vector field is available. In most cases, the displacement vector field has to be calculated for an image sequence where the results from preceding frames can be used as a starting value rather than the uniformly vanishing starting field employed for the first frame pair. Fig. 15(a) shows the result obtained after 12 iterations for a window around the bright taxicab in the center of Fig. 1(c) as given in Fig.

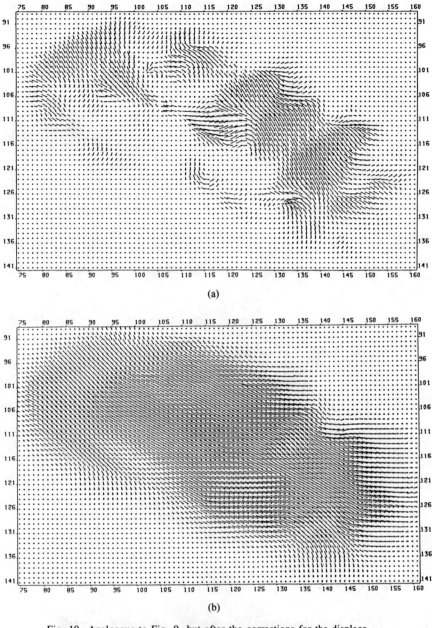

Fig. 10. Analogous to Fig. 9, but after the corrections for the displacement vector have been everywhere smaller than $\frac{1}{5}$ of a pixel per frame: (a) for 3×3 pixel operator window with $\alpha^2 = 1$; $c = 8$; $\gamma = 12.5$; iteration 13; (b) for 5×5 pixel operator window with $\alpha^2 = 2$; $c = 8$; $\gamma = 5$; iteration 17.

1(f) and the corresponding window from the subsequent frame, i.e., frames 20 and 21, again with the uniformly vanishing starting field $u_0 \equiv 0$. Fig. 15(b) presents the result after four additional iterations for windows from the subsequent frame pair 21 and 22, initialized with the results shown in Fig. 15(a). Similarly, Fig. 15(c) presents the analogous results for frame pair 22 and 23 after two further iterations.

This approach has been pursued for each frame pair between frames 21 and 30. The window from the last frame of this series, frame 30, is shown in Fig. 1(g). The result for the displacement vector field in this window obtained

after two iterations starting from the result of the preceding frame pair (28 and 29) as initialization is shown in Fig. 16(a). For comparison, the result for the same windows, but obtained with $u_0 \equiv 0$ as the starting value is shown in Fig. 16(b). The difference between these two results, i.e., the dependency upon the initialization, is shown in Fig. 16(c). The differences in Fig. 16(c) are partially due to the fact that the fairly homogeneous gray value area behind the moving taxicab can be matched with either starting value. In one case this area is assumed to be stationary, whereas in the other case this area is assumed to move with the car. This latter hypothesis is ac-

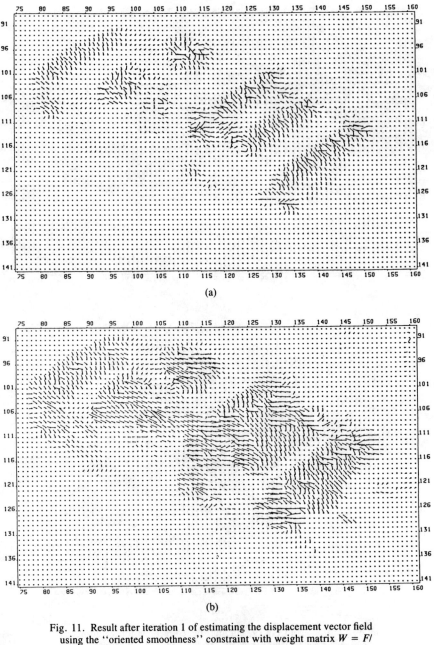

Fig. 11. Result after iteration 1 of estimating the displacement vector field using the "oriented smoothness" constraint with weight matrix $W = F/$ trace (F) as discussed in Section IV-A for the window indicated by Fig. 1(e) from frames 11 and 12. The initial value has been $u_0(x) \equiv 0$: (a) for 3×3 pixel operator window with $\alpha^2 = 50$; $c = 2$; $\gamma = 12.5$; (b) for 5×5 pixel operator window with $\alpha^2 = 10$; $c = 1$; $\gamma = 12.5$.

ceptable to the extent that the gray values are due to the shadow moving together with the car. Discrimination between these two hypotheses requires additional assumptions about what caused the observed gray values. It will have to be studied to which extend conceptually inappropriate starting values can be balanced by more iterations in image areas with fairly homogeneous gray values and gradual gray value transitions.

It can be seen that a few iterations will be sufficient for image areas with sizable gray value variations if appropriate starting values are available as in the case of an image sequence.

It should be noticed that another object with different displacement intrudes into the window. The estimates seem to be reliable enough to warrant segmentation approaches based on such displacement vector fields.

In conclusion, these observations are taken to be evidence that the concept of an "oriented smoothness" constraint as implemented appears to be a good step towards the solution of the problem to estimate displacement vector fields from image sequences. The analysis has been pushed to the point where closed form solutions for the correction term can be discussed, based on fairly general assumptions about the operators employed to compute the

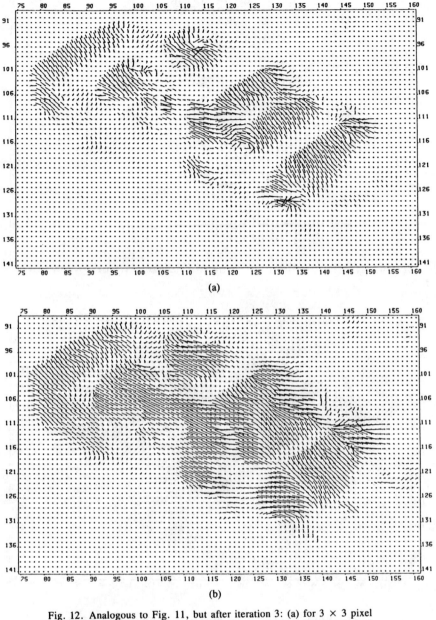

(a)

(b)

Fig. 12. Analogous to Fig. 11, but after iteration 3: (a) for 3×3 pixel operator window with $\alpha^2 = 50$; $c = 2$; $\gamma = 12.5$; (b) for 5×5 pixel operator window with $\alpha^2 = 10$; $c = 1$; $\gamma = 12.5$.

partial derivatives. It has been possible to study the dependency on the window size for 3×3 and 5×5 operator windows without any modification to the formulas.

As has been mentioned in previous sections, there remain a number of problems which we currently investigate. We have drawn attention to these problems which we have identified so far in order to enable the reader to form his own judgement about the merits of this approach.

APPENDIX 1
DERIVATION OF (36)

We start from (35). In order to simplify the notation, the argument x for the approximate displacement vector field $u_0(x)$ as well as for the correction vector field $Du(x)$ will be omitted henceforth.

Since Du is considered to be small, we retain only first order terms in components of Du:

$$g1(x - u) = g1(x - u_0 - Du)$$
$$\simeq g1(x - u_0) - (\nabla g1(x - u_0))^T Du$$

$$(A1-1)$$

and

$$\frac{\partial g1(x - u)}{\partial u} \simeq \frac{\partial g1(x - u_0)}{\partial u} = -\frac{\partial g1(x - u_0)}{\partial x}$$

$$(A1-2a)$$

$$\frac{\partial g1(x - u)}{\partial v} \simeq \frac{\partial g1(x - u_0)}{\partial} = -\frac{\partial g1(x - u_0)}{\partial y}.$$

$$(A1-2b)$$

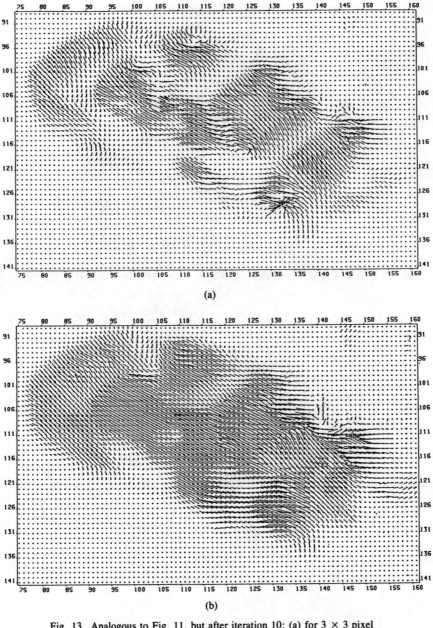

Fig. 13. Analogous to Fig. 11, but after iteration 10: (a) for 3×3 pixel operator window with $\alpha^2 = 50$; $c = 2$; $\gamma = 12.5$; (b) for 5×5 pixel operator window with $\alpha^2 = 10$; $c = 1$; $\gamma = 12.5$.

Introduction of these approximations into (35) yields

$$-[g2(x) - g1(x - u_0) + (\nabla g1(x - u_0))^T Du]$$

$$\cdot \frac{\partial g1(x - u_0)}{\partial x} + \alpha^2 \text{ trace} \left(C^{-1} \begin{pmatrix} u_{0_{xx}} & u_{0_{xy}} \\ u_{0_{xy}} & u_{0_{yy}} \end{pmatrix} \right) = 0$$

(A1-3a)

$$-[g2(x) - g1(x - u_0) + (\nabla g1(x - u_0))^T Du]$$

$$\cdot \frac{\partial g1(x - u_0)}{\partial y} + \alpha^2 \text{ trace} \left(C^{-1} \begin{pmatrix} v_{0_{xx}} & v_{0_{xy}} \\ v_{0_{xy}} & v_{0_{yy}} \end{pmatrix} \right) = 0.$$

(A1-3b)

This system of equations can be rewritten as a matrix equation where for simplicity of notation the argument $x - u_0$ is suppressed for all derivatives $g1(x - u_0)$:

$$(\nabla g1)(\nabla g1)^T Du = -[g2(x) - g1(x - u_0)]\nabla g1$$

$$+ \alpha^2 \begin{bmatrix} \text{trace} \left(C^{-1} \begin{pmatrix} u_{0_{xx}} & u_{0_{xy}} \\ u_{0_{xy}} & u_{0_{yy}} \end{pmatrix} \right) \\ \text{trace} \left(C^{-1} \begin{pmatrix} v_{0_{xx}} & v_{0_{xy}} \\ v_{0_{xy}} & v_{0_{yy}} \end{pmatrix} \right) \end{bmatrix}$$

(A1-4)

It is not possible to solve (A1-4) immediately for Du, because the coefficient matrix of Du consists of the outer

518

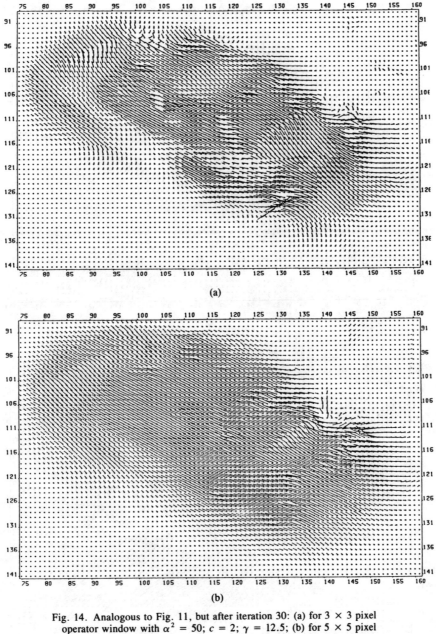

Fig. 14. Analogous to Fig. 11, but after iteration 30: (a) for 3×3 pixel
operator window with $\alpha^2 = 50$; $c = 2$; $\gamma = 12.5$; (b) for 5×5 pixel
operator window with $\alpha^2 = 40$; $c = 1$; $\gamma = 12.5$.

product of a vector $\nabla g1$ with itself and, therefore, has only rank one. At this point, the discussion of the matrix $B^T W_G B$ in Section II-A can be of help. It essentially represents a weighted product of gradients averaged over the image window under consideration. Since the derivatives of $g1$ as well as of u or v have eventually to be determined by applying some digital derivative operator to an environment around the position $x - u_0$, it appears plausible to average the coefficient matrix $(\nabla g1)(\nabla g1)^T$ over this environment. Assuming that this environment is small enough so that the variation of the gradient may be taken into account by its first order Taylor expansion, we obtain:

$$\nabla g1(x - u_0 + \xi) = \nabla g1(x - u_0) + (\nabla \nabla g1(x - u_0))\xi \tag{A1-5}$$

$$\overline{(\nabla g1(x - u_0 + \xi))(\nabla g1(x - u_0 + \xi))}^T$$
$$= (\nabla g1)(\nabla g1)^T + \overline{\xi^2}(\nabla \nabla g1)(\nabla \nabla g1)^T \tag{A1-6}$$

where the overbar indicates the averaging over all positions ξ in the environment around $x - u_0$. If we equate the weight factor b^2 in the matrix C of (30) with the average value of ξ^2, the averaging process transforms the outer product matrix $(\nabla g1)(\nabla g1)^T$ into the matrix C. Equation (A1-4) could thus be written as

$$CDu = -\overline{[g2(x) - g1(x - u_0)]\nabla g1}$$
$$+ \alpha^2 \begin{bmatrix} \text{trace } (C^{-1}\nabla\nabla u_0) \\ \text{trace } (C^{-1}\nabla\nabla v_0) \end{bmatrix}. \tag{A1-7}$$

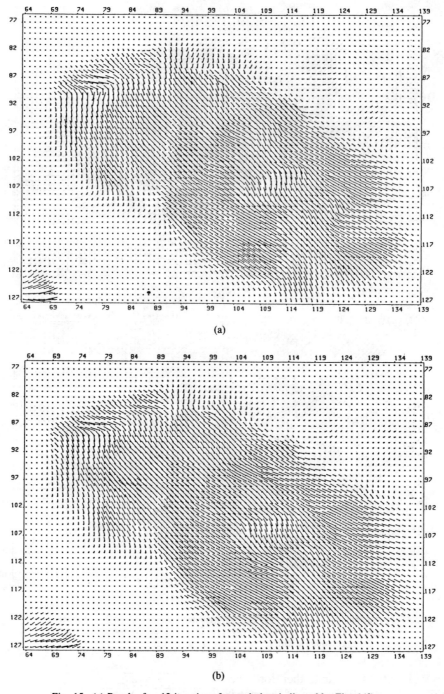

Fig. 15. (a) Result after 12 iterations for a window indicated by Fig. 1(f) from frames 20 and 21 with a uniformly vanishing starting value $u_0(x) \equiv 0$; (b) result after four additional iterations for the corresponding windows from frames 21 and 22 with the result from (a) as a starting value; (c) analogously for frames 22 and 23 after two additional iterations with the result from (b) as starting value.

The calculation of $\nabla\nabla u$ and $\nabla\nabla v$ is accomplished by application of the operators described by Beaudet [1] to the digital representation of u and v. This implies some averaging across the operator window. The overbar has been omitted, therefore, atop the second term on the right-hand side of (A1-7) because the averaging process is essentially implied by the calculation of this term. The matrix C is supposed to be essentially constant across the

window needed to determine the partial derivatives of $g1$ and u as well as v at location $x - u_0$. ∎

APPENDIX 2
DERIVATION OF (38)

In order to study the influence of Du on the estimation of partial derivatives of the displacement vector field $u(x)$, the following example shows the operators employed for

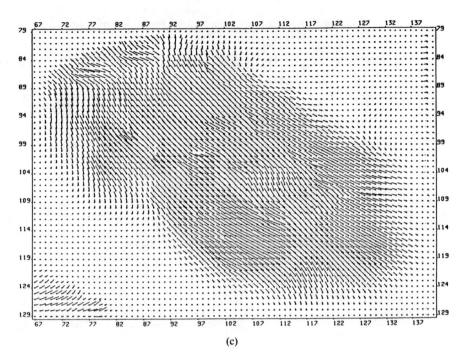

(c)

Fig. 15. (*Continued.*)

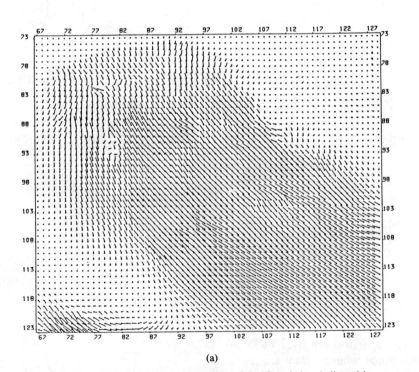

(a)

Fig. 16. (a) The result after two iterations for the window indicated by Fig. 1(g) from frame 30 and the preceding one, frame 29, taking the result of a propagation of starting values from frame 22 and 23 as given in Fig. 15(c) through frames 28 and 29 as initial values for the displacement vector field; (b) result after 30 iterations for the same window as in (a), but using $u_0(x) \equiv 0$ as the starting value; (c) difference between the results shown in (a) and (b) in order to illustrate the dependency on the initial displacement vector field. Since the shadowy area behind the car is of fairly homogeneous gray value, both the vanishing displacement estimate as well as the displacement estimate of the moving car are solutions which are acceptable in principle. A gradual fading of the displacement estimate with diminishing contributions from the moving shadow seems to offer the intuitively most plausible solution.

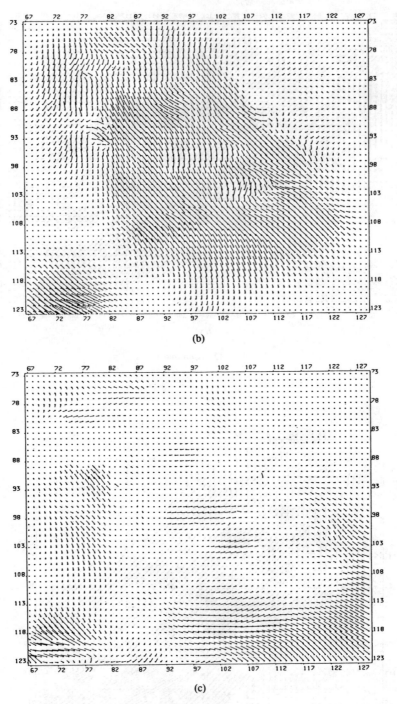

(b)

(c)

Fig. 16. (*Continued.*)

a 5 × 5 pixel window. These operators are given by Beaudet [1] in (row, column)-format whereas they are represented here in a regular (x, y)-format:

$$\left(\frac{\partial^2}{\partial x^2}\right) = \left(\frac{\partial^2}{\partial y^2}\right)^T = \frac{1}{35} = \begin{pmatrix} 2 & -1 & -2 & -1 & 2 \\ 2 & -1 & -2 & -1 & 2 \\ 2 & -1 & -2 & -1 & 2 \\ 2 & -1 & -2 & -1 & 2 \\ 2 & -1 & -2 & -1 & 2 \end{pmatrix}$$

(A2-1a)

$$\left(\frac{\partial^2}{\partial x \partial y}\right) = \frac{1}{100} = \begin{pmatrix} -4 & -2 & 0 & 2 & 4 \\ -2 & -1 & 0 & 1 & 2 \\ 0 & 0 & 0 & 0 & 0 \\ 2 & 1 & 0 & -1 & -2 \\ 4 & 2 & 0 & -2 & -4 \end{pmatrix}$$

(A2-1b)

It is seen that the central pixel contributes to the second partial derivatives with respect to x as well as to y with a weight factor $-2/35$. The central pixel does not contribute to the mixed second partial derivative. As can be seen, for example, from the Appendix of [15], this latter aspect is a general property for all odd mask sizes of operators derived based on the following assumption: the functional variation within the operator mask can be approximated by a bivariate second-order polynomial in the image plane coordinates.

Exploiting these properties of operators for the computation of second order partial derivatives, the substitution of $u_0 + Du$ for u at the center pixel has the following effect:

$$\text{trace}\left(C^{-1}\begin{pmatrix} u_{xx} & u_{xy} \\ u_{xy} & u_{yy} \end{pmatrix}\right) \simeq \text{trace}\left(C^{-1}\begin{pmatrix} u_{0xx} & u_{0xy} \\ u_{0xy} & u_{0yy} \end{pmatrix}\right)$$
$$- mDu \ \text{trace} \ C^{-1} \quad \text{(A2-2a)}$$

$$\text{trace}\left(C^{-1}\begin{pmatrix} v_{xx} & v_{xy} \\ v_{xy} & v_{yy} \end{pmatrix}\right) \simeq \text{trace}\left(C^{-1}\begin{pmatrix} v_{0xx} & v_{0xy} \\ v_{0xy} & v_{0yy} \end{pmatrix}\right)$$
$$- mDv \ \text{trace} \ C^{-1} \quad \text{(A2-2b)}$$

where m stands for the magnitude value of the weight factor at the center pixel position in the operator mask for $\partial^2/\partial x^2$. In the case of a 5×5 operator mask, this results in the value $m = 2/35$.

Taking into account these effects of the approximation implied by the substitution of $u_0 + Du$ for u into (35), the derivation follows closely the one discussed in Appendix 1. In analogy to (A1-3) we obtain

$$-[g2(x) - g1(x - u_0) + (\nabla g1)^T Du] \frac{\partial g1}{\partial x}$$
$$+ \alpha^2[\text{trace} (C^{-1}\nabla\nabla u_0) - mDu \ \text{trace} \ C^{-1}] = 0$$
$$\text{(A2-3a)}$$

$$-[g2(x) - g1(x - u_0) + (\nabla g1)^T Du] \frac{\partial g1}{\partial y}$$
$$+ \alpha^2[\text{trace} (C^{-1}\nabla\nabla v_0) - mDv \ \text{trace} \ C^{-1}] = 0.$$
$$\text{(A2-3b)}$$

This can be transformed into the following matrix equation:

$$\left[(\nabla g1)(\nabla g1)^T + \alpha^2 m \ \text{trace} \ C^{-1}\begin{pmatrix} 1 & 0 \\ 0 & 1 \end{pmatrix}\right] Du$$
$$= -[g2(x) - g1(x - u_0)] \nabla g1$$
$$+ \alpha^2 \begin{bmatrix} \text{trace} (C^{-1}\nabla\nabla u_0) \\ \text{trace} (C^{-1}\nabla\nabla v_0) \end{bmatrix} \quad \text{(A2-4)}$$

The averaging process will then yield—using the derivation expressed by (A1-5)–(A1-6)—with I denoting a 2 $\times$ 2 unit matrix:

$$[(\nabla g1)(\nabla g1)^T + b^2(\nabla\nabla g1)(\nabla\nabla g1)^T$$
$$+ \alpha^2 m \ \text{trace} \ C^{-1} I] \ Du$$
$$= -\overline{[g2(x) - g1(x - u_0)]} \ \nabla g1$$
$$+ \alpha^2 \begin{bmatrix} \text{trace} (C^{-1}\nabla\nabla u_0) \\ \text{trace} (C^{-1}\nabla\nabla v_0) \end{bmatrix} \quad \text{(A2-5)}$$

■

APPENDIX 3
DERIVATION OF (40)

We may assume that the local coordinate system is aligned with the principal curvature directions of the gray value distribution within this window, i.e., $g1_{xy} = 0$. We further assume that $u_0(x)$ is still zero throughout the image window under consideration. Using these conventions, (38) reduces to

$$[C + I\alpha^2 m \ \text{trace} \ C^{-1}] \ Du$$
$$= -\overline{[g2(x) - g1(x - u_0)]} \ \nabla g1 \quad \text{(39)}$$

because $u_0(x) \equiv 0$ implies $\nabla\nabla u_0 = \nabla\nabla v_0 = 0$.

The explicit solution of this system of two equations with the two unknowns Du and Dv can be written in a more compact form if the following identity is used which can be easily verified:

$$[C + I\alpha^2 m \ \text{trace} \ C^{-1}]^{-1}$$
$$= \frac{C^{-1} \det C + I\alpha^2 m \ \text{trace} \ C^{-1}}{\det (C + I\alpha^2 m \ \text{trace} \ C^{-1})}. \quad \text{(A3-1)}$$

In order to evaluate the right-hand side of (39) we proceed in analogy to the transition between (A1-5) and (A1-6) (see also [15]). The image window is assumed to be square with sides parallel to the axes of the local coordinate system ξ centered in the window. We use (A1-5) to make explicit how the gradient $\nabla g1(x - u_0 + \xi)$ depends on ξ. We thus obtain

$$[g2(x + \xi) - g1(x - u_0 + \xi)] \nabla g1(x - u_0 + \xi)$$
$$\simeq [g2(x + \xi) - g1(x - u_0 + \xi)] \nabla g1(x - u_0)$$
$$+ [g2(x + \xi) - g1(x - u_0 + \xi)]$$
$$\cdot (\nabla\nabla g1(x - u_0))\xi. \quad \text{(A3-2)}$$

If this equation is averaged over the image window, the first term on the right-hand side will simply result in

$$\overline{[g2(x) - g1(x - u_0 + \xi)]} \ \nabla g1.$$

The second term has to be treated in more detail. We develop the square bracket of the second term up to first order in components of ξ:

$$[g2(x + \xi) - g1(x - u_0 + \xi)] (\nabla\nabla g1)\xi = [g2(x)$$
$$+ (\nabla g2)^T \xi - g1(x - u_0) - (\nabla g1)^T \xi] (\nabla\nabla g1)\xi.$$
$$\text{(A3-3)}$$

Since the window is symmetric with respect to the components of ξ over which we have to average, all terms containing odd powers of components of ξ vanish in this process. We retain

$$\overline{[g2(x) - g1(x - u_0)] \nabla g1(x - u_0)}$$

$$= [\overline{g2(x)} - \overline{g1(x - u_0)}] \nabla g1 + \overline{\xi^2}\begin{pmatrix} (g2_x - g1_x) g1_{xx} \\ (g2_y - g1_y) g1_{yy} \end{pmatrix}$$

$$(A3-4)$$

where the derivatives of $g2$ have been taken at location x and those of $g1$ at location $x - u_0$. Combining (39), (A3-1), and (A3-4) yields

$$Du = \frac{-1}{\det (C + I\alpha^2 m \text{ trace } C^{-1})} \cdot (C^{-1} \det C + I\alpha^2 m \text{ trace } C^{-1})$$

$$\cdot \begin{pmatrix} [\overline{g2(x)} - \overline{g1(x - u_0)}] g1_x + \overline{\xi^2}(g2_x - g1_x) g1_{xx} \\ [\overline{g2(x)} - \overline{g1(x - u_0)}] g1_y + \overline{\xi^2}(g2_y - g1_y) g1_{yy} \end{pmatrix}.$$

$$(A3-5)$$

It should be remembered that due to the alignment of the local coordinate system with the prinicpal curvature directions of $g1$, the mixed second partial derivative $g1_{xy}$ vanishes.

We may now specialize (A3-5) to the case of a gray value corner in frame 1 at location $x - u_0$. Then, according to (1) we have:

$$g1_x = \text{maximum} \neq 0 \qquad g1_{xx} = 0$$

$$g1_y = 0 \qquad g1_{yy} = \text{maximum} \neq 0.$$

Insertion of these values into equation (A3-5) yields:

$$C^{-1} = \frac{1}{b^2 g1_x^2 g1_{yy}^2}\begin{pmatrix} b^2 g1_{yy}^2 & 0 \\ 0 & g1_x^2 \end{pmatrix} \tag{A3-6a}$$

$$\text{trace } C^{-1} = \frac{g1_x^2 + b^2 g1_{yy}^2}{b^2 g1_x^2 g1_{yy}^2} \tag{A3-6b}$$

$$[C^{-1} \det C + I\alpha^2 m \text{ trace } C^{-1}] = \begin{pmatrix} b^2 g1_{yy}^2 + \alpha^2 m \dfrac{g1_x^2 + b^2 g1_{yy}^2}{b^2 g1_x^2 g1_{yy}^2} & 0 \\ 0 & g1_x^2 + \alpha^2 m \dfrac{g1_x^2 + b^2 g1_{yy}^2}{b^2 g1_x^2 g1_{yy}^2} \end{pmatrix} \tag{A3-6c}$$

$$\det (C + I\alpha^2 m \text{ trace } C^{-1}) = \det (C^{-1} \det C + I\alpha^2 m \text{ trace } C^{-1}) \tag{A3-6d}$$

We thus obtain by setting

$$b^2 = \overline{\xi^2}$$

[see discussion following (A1-6)]:

$$Du = -\frac{\overline{g2(x)} - \overline{g1(x - u_0)}}{g1_x} \cdot \frac{1}{1 + \alpha^2 m \dfrac{1 + b^2 g1_{yy}^1/g1_x^2}{b^2 g1_x^2 g1_{yy}^2}} \tag{A3-7a}$$

$$Dv = -\frac{g2_y}{g1_{yy}} \cdot \frac{1}{1 + \alpha^2 m \dfrac{1 + g1_x^2/(b^2 g1_{yy}^2)}{b^2 g1_x^2 g1_{yy}^2}}. \tag{A3-7b}$$

∎

APPENDIX 4
EVALUATION OF THE WEIGHT MATRIX NORMALIZED BY TRACE (F)

Instead of (31) we investigate the minimization of

$$\iint dxdy \left\{ [g2(x) - g1(x - u)]^2 + \alpha^2 \text{ trace} \left[(\nabla u)^T \frac{F}{\text{trace } F} (\nabla u) \right] \right\} \Rightarrow \min. \tag{41}$$

The analogy to the derivation resulting in (A2-2a) now yields

$$\text{trace} \left[\frac{F}{\text{trace } F} (\nabla \nabla u) \right] \simeq \text{trace} \left[\frac{F}{\text{trace } F} (\nabla \nabla u_0) \right] - mDu \frac{\text{trace } F}{\text{trace } F} \tag{A4-1}$$

and analogously for (A2-2b). We thus obtain instead of (A2-4):

$$[(\nabla g1)(\nabla g1)^T + \alpha^2 m\mathbf{I}]Du$$

$$= -[g2(x) - g1(x - u_0)]\nabla g1$$

$$+ \frac{\alpha^2}{\text{trace } F}\begin{bmatrix}\text{trace } (F\nabla\nabla u_0)\\\text{trace } (F\nabla\nabla v_0)\end{bmatrix}. \quad \text{(A4-2)}$$

In analogy to (A2-5) or (38) we obtain

$$[C + \alpha^2 m\mathbf{I}]Du = -\overline{[g2(x) - g1(x - u_0)]\nabla g1}$$

$$+ \frac{\alpha^2}{\text{trace } F}\begin{bmatrix}\text{trace } (F\nabla\nabla u_0)\\\text{trace } (F\nabla\nabla v_0)\end{bmatrix} \quad \text{(A4-3)}$$

and in analogy to (A3-7) or (40):

$$Du = -\frac{\overline{g2(x)} - \overline{g1(x - u_0)}}{g1_x} \cdot \frac{1}{1 + \dfrac{\alpha^2 m}{g1_x^2}} \quad \text{(A4-4a)}$$

$$Dv = -\frac{g2_y}{g1_{yy}} \cdot \frac{1}{1 + \dfrac{\alpha^2 m}{b^2 g1_{yy}^2}}. \quad \text{(A4-4b)}$$

In analogy to the discussion following (40) we "unbend" the gray value corner. With typical values along an almost straight line gray value transition—$g1_x$ around 30 and $b \cdot g1_{yy}$ around 1—(A4-4) yields a correction factor of $1/(1 + \alpha^2 m/900)$ for Du and $1/(1 + \alpha^2 m)$ for Dv.

With such values for the correction factors, the estimate for Du in (A4-4a) essentially reflects the contribution of the first term on the right hand side of equation (A4-3), namely the well known displacement estimate parallel to the gradient, usually written in the form $-g_t/g_x$. The estimate for Dv in (A4-4b) depends under these conditions more strongly on the value of α^2. Since this value of α^2 also influences the contribution due to nonzero second derivatives of u_0 and v_0 for other than the initial iteration where $u_0 \equiv 0$ and thus $\nabla\nabla u_0 = \nabla\nabla v_0 = 0$, the choice of α^2 has to be studied with great care.

If we take into account the second term on the right-hand side of (A4-3), we obtain instead of (A4-4) the following result for a gray value corner:

$$Du = -\frac{\overline{g2(x)} - \overline{g1(x - u_0)}}{g2_x} \cdot \frac{1}{1 + \dfrac{\alpha^2 m}{g1_x^2}}$$

$$+ \alpha^2 \frac{b^2 g1_{yy}^2 u_{0xx} + g1_x^2 u_{0yy}}{(g1_x^2 + b^2 g1_{yy}^2)(g1_x^2 + \alpha^2 m)} \quad \text{(A4-5a)}$$

$$Dv = -\frac{g2_y}{g1_{yy}} \cdot \frac{1}{1 + \dfrac{\alpha^2 m}{b^2 g1_{yy}^2}}$$

$$+ \alpha^2 \frac{b^2 g1_{yy}^2 v_{0xx} + g1_x^2 v_{0yy}}{(g1_x^2 + b^2 g1_{yy}^2)(b^2 g1_{yy}^2 + \alpha^2 m)} \quad \text{(A4-5b)}$$

ACKNOWLEDGMENT

We thank B. Radig for his help in sustaining our long-distance cooperation and the Deutsche Forschungsgemeinschaft for partial support of these investigations. The idea to compare the results from different initializations as presented in Figs. 16(b) and (c) was suggested by S. Ullman during a discussion about the "oriented smoothness" constraint. We are grateful to R. Kories, T. Krämer, and the referees for suggestions to improve the style of this paper.

REFERENCES

[1] P. R. Beaudet, "Rotationally invariant image operators," in *Proc. Int. Joint Conf. Pattern Recognition*, Kyoto, Japan, 1978, pp. 579-583.

[2] N. Cornelius and T. Kanade, "Adapting optical flow to measure object motion in reflectance and X-ray image sequences," in *Proc. ACM Siggraph/Sigart Interdisciplinary Workshop on Motion: Representation and Perception*, Toronto, Ont., Canada, Apr. 4-6, 1983, pp. 50-58.

[3] L. S. Davis, Z. Wu, and H. Sun, "Contour-based motion estimation," *Comput. Vision, Graphics, Image Processing*, vol. 23, pp. 313-326, 1983.

[4] L. Dreschler and H.-H. Nagel, "Volumetric model and 3D trajectory of a moving car derived from monocular TV frame sequences of a street scene," in *Proc. Int. Joint Conf. Artificial Intell.*, Vancouver, B.C., Canada, Aug. 1981, pp. 692-697.

[5] ——, "Volumetric model and 3D trajectory of a moving car derived from monocular TV frame sequences of a street scene," *Comput. Graphics Image Processing*, vol. 20, pp. 199-228, 1982 (complemented and extended version of the contribution to IJCAI-81).

[6] ——, "On the selection of critical points and local curvature extrema of region boundaries for interframe matching," in *Proc. Int. Conf. Pattern Recognition*, Munich, 1982, pp. 542-544; also in T. S. Huang, Ed., *Image Sequence Processing and Dynamic Scene Analysis, NATO ASI Series F2*. Berlin: Springer-Verlag, 1983, pp. 457-470.

[7] E. C. Hildreth, "The integration of motion information along contours," in *Proc. Workshop Comput. Vision: Representation and Control*, Rindge, NH, Aug. 23-25, 1982, pp. 83-91.

[8] ——, "Computing the velocity field along contours," in *Proc. ACM Siggraph/Sigart Interdisciplinary Workshop on Motion: Representation and Perception*, Toronto, Ont., Canada, Apr. 4-6, 1983, pp. 26-32.

[9] ——, "The measurement of visual motion," Ph.D. dissertation, Dep. Elec. Eng. Comput. Sci., Massachusetts Inst. Technol., Cambridge, MA, Aug. 1983.

[10] ——, "Computations underlying the measurement of visual motion," *Artificial Intell.*, vol. 23, pp. 309-354, 1984.

[11] B. K. P. Horn and B. G. Schunck, "Determining optical flow," *Artificial Intell.*, vol. 17, pp. 185-203, 1981.

[12] L. Kitchen and A. Rosenfeld, "Gray-level corner detection," Comput. Sci. Center, Univ. Maryland, College Park, Tech. Rep. 887, Apr. 1980.

[13] ——, "Gray-level corner detection," *Pattern Recognition Lett.*, vol. 1, pp. 95-102, 1982.

[14] H.-H. Nagel, "On change detection and displacement vector estimation in image sequences," *Pattern Recognition Lett.*, vol. 1, pp. 55-59, 1982.

[15] ——, "Displacement vectors derived from second order intensity variations in image sequences," *Comput. Vision, Graphics, Image Processing*, vol. 21, pp. 85-117, 1983.

[16] ——, "On the estimation of dense displacement vector fields from image sequences," in *Proc. ACM SIGGRAPH/SIGART Interdisciplinary Workshop on Motion: Representation and Perception*, Toronto, Ont., Canada, Apr. 4-6, 1983, pp. 59-65.

[17] ——, "Constraints for the estimation of displacement vector fields from image sequences," in *Proc. Int. Joint Conf. Artificial Intell.*, Karlsruhe, West Germany, 1983, pp. 945-951.

[18] ——, "Spatio-temporal modeling based on image sequences," in *Proc. Int. Symp. Image Processing and Its Applications*, Univ. Tokyo, Inst. Industrial Sci., Jan. 18-21, 1984; also in *Progress in Image Processing*, M. Onoe, Ed. Tokyo: Univ. Tokyo, pp. 222-252.

[19] ——, "Recent advances in image sequence analysis," in *Proc. Pre-

mier Colloque Image—Traitement, Synthèse, Technologie et Applications, Biarritz, France, May 21–25, 1984, pp. 545–558.

[20] H.-H. Nagel and W. Enkelmann, "Investigations of second order gray value variations to estimate corner point displacements," in *Proc. Int. Conf. Pattern Recognition*, Munich, West Germany, Oct. 19–22, 1982, pp. 768–773.

[21] ——, "Iterative estimation of displacement vector fields from TV-frame sequences," in *Proc. Second European Signal Processing Conf. (EUSIPCO-83)*, H. W. Schüssler, Ed., Erlangen, West Germany, Sept. 12–16, 1983, pp. 299–302.

[22] ——, "Towards the estimation of displacement vector fields by 'oriented smoothness' constraints," in *Proc. Int. Conf. Pattern Recognition*, Montreal, P.Q., Canada, July 30–Aug. 2, 1984, pp. 6–8.

[23] ——, "Berechnung von Verschiebungsvektorfeldern in Bildbereichen mit linienhaften oder partiell homogenen Grauwertverteilungen," in *Proc. Deutsche Arbeitsgemeinschaft für Mustererkennung*, W. Kropatsch, Ed., Graz, Austria, Oct. 2–4, 1984; also *Informatik-Fachberichte 87*. Berlin: Springer-Verlag, 1984, pp. 154–160.

[24] Z. Wu, H. Sun, and L. S. Davis, "Determining velocities by propagation," in *Proc. Int. Conf. Pattern Recognition*, Munich, West Germany, Oct. 19–22, 1982, pp. 1147–1149.

[25] M. Yachida, "Determining velocity by spatio-temporal neighborhoods from image sequences," *Comput. Vision, Graphics, Image Processing*, vol. 21, pp. 262–279, 1983; also in *Proc. IJCAI-81*, pp. 716–718.

[26] O. A. Zuniga and R. M. Haralick, "Corner detection using the facet model," in *Proc. IEEE Conf. Comput. Vision and Pattern Recognition*, 1983, pp. 30–37.

Hans-Hellmut Nagel (M'77) received the Doctor degree in physics from the Universität Bonn, Bonn, West Germany, in 1964.

Subsequently, he spent 18 months at M.I.T. working on the automatic analysis of bubble chamber film, continuing this work at the Deutsche Elektronen-Synchrotron at Hamburg as well as at the Physikalische Institut der Universität Bonn from 1966 through 1971. In Fall 1971 he became Full Professor of Informatik (computer science) at the Universität Hamburg. Since 1983 he has been Director of the Fraunhofer-Institut für Informations- und Datenverarbeitung at Karlsruhe in a joint appointment as Full Professor (pattern recognition and digital image processing) at the Fakultät für Informatik der Universität Karlsruhe (TH). Since 1971, he has been interested in the evaluation of image sequences, especially TV-frame sequences. In addition, his interests include the implementation and use of higher level programming languages for the realization of image analysis systems.

Dr. Nagel is Associate Editor of *Computer Vision, Graphics, and Image Processing*, and a member of the Editorial Board of *Artificial Intelligence Journal*, as well as of *Pattern Recognition Letters*. He currently serves on the Advisory Board of IEEE TRANSACTIONS ON PATTERN ANALYSIS AND MACHINE INTELLIGENCE and *Future Generation Computer Systems*.

Wilfried Enkelmann received the Dipl.Inform. degree and the Ph.D. degree in informatik (computer science) from the University of Hamburg, Hamburg, West Germany, in 1982 and 1985, respectively.

Since mid-1985 he has been with the Fraunhofer-Institut für Informations- und Datenverarbeitung in Karlsruhe, West Germany. His field of interest is computer vision and image sequence analysis.

Reprinted from *IEEE Transactions on Pattern Analysis and Machine Intelligence*, Volume PAMI-2, Number 4, July 1980, pages 333-340.

Disparity Analysis of Images

STEPHEN T. BARNARD, MEMBER, IEEE, AND WILLIAM B. THOMPSON, MEMBER, IEEE

Abstract—An algorithm for matching images of real world scenes is presented. The matching is a specification of the geometrical disparity between the images and may be used to partially reconstruct the three-dimensional structure of the scene. Sets of candidate matching points are selected independently in each image. These points are the locations of small, distinct features which are likely to be detectable in both images. An initial network of possible matches between the two sets of candidates is constructed. Each possible match specifies a possible disparity of a candidate point in a selected reference image. An initial estimate of the probability of each possible disparity is made, based on the similarity of subimages surrounding the points. These estimates are iteratively improved by a relaxation labeling technique making use of the local continuity property of disparity that is a consequence of the continuity of real world surfaces. The algorithm is effective for binocular parallax, motion parallax, and object motion. It quickly converges to good estimates of disparity, which reflect the spatial organization of the scene.

Index Terms—Disparity, matching, motion, relaxation labeling, scene analysis, stereo.

I. INTRODUCTION

DIFFERENCES in images of real world scenes may be induced by the relative motion of the camera and the scene, by the relative displacement of two cameras, or by the motion of objects in the scene. The differences are important because they encode information that often allows a partial reconstruction of the three-dimensional structure of the scene from two-dimensional projections. When such differences occur between two images we say that there is a *disparity* between the two images, which we represent as a vector field mapping one image into the other. The determination of disparity has been called the *correspondence* problem [1], [2]. A contingent problem is the *interpretation* of disparity into meaningful statements about the scene, such as specifications of depth, velocity, and shape.

There is much evidence that disparity is important in human vision. Gibson discussed the nature of visual perception in a dynamic environment [3]. He argued that the visual stimulus is inherently dynamic and that the patterns of change in the stimulus are important sources for the perception of the spatial environment. Gibson described the patterns of optical flow that occur when the observer moves. He argued that binocular disparity and retinal motion are highly informative stimulus variables for spatial perception, and that along with other important visual phenomena, such as texture gradient and linear perspective, they interact with the kinesthetic "body senses" in the perception of a stable, upright, three-dimensional world.

Julesz's experiments with random dot stereograms [4] support the contention that the human visual system is able to process differences between images. A stereogram is a pair of images that are recorded simultaneously by laterally separated sensors. A random dot stereogram is artificially constructed by shifting parts of an image of random dots to the left or right to form a second image. Both images consist of uncorrelated random dots, but there is a disparity relationship between the two which specifies the apparent relative depth of the shifted parts. People with normal stereo vision can easily achieve a binocular fusion of the two images and perceive the apparent relative depth of the various "surfaces." Even though each separate image of a random dot stereogram contains no depth information, people are able to perceive depth in the pair of images by measuring the disparity between the shifted areas.

Disparity analysis may be broadly defined as the determination of the geometric differences between two or more images of the same or similar scenes. The differences may be the result of binocular parallax, motion parallax, object motion, or some combination of these modes. The goal of the analysis is to assign disparities, which are represented as two-dimensional vectors in the image plane, to a collection of points in one of the images. Disparity analysis is useful for image understanding in several ways. There is information in a disparate pair of images that is difficult to find or even absent in any single image. This point is convincingly made by Julesz's random dot stereogram experiments. Disparity provides a way, independent of high-level knowledge, of determining the spatial relationships between points and surfaces in a scene. The objects in the scene may be completely unfamiliar, but their observed disparities will conform to precise rules that depend only on the location and velocity of objects in three-dimensional space. Disparity is therefore a very general property of images which may be used in a variety of situations. The measurement of depth and velocity will certainly be useful in many applications, but there is a more fundamental requirement in image understanding. A system for understanding dynamic scenes can use observed disparity to establish conceptual relationships between images that are invariant over several observations. Visual invariants can be used to predict future observations, to eliminate noise in any one observation, and in general to link several observations into one perceptually coherent whole.

II. MATCHING

Matching is a natural way to approach disparity analysis. Assigning disparity classifications to points in a sequence of images is equivalent to finding a matching between sets of

Manuscript received March 5, 1979; revised September 14, 1979. This work was supported in part by the National Science Foundation under Grant MCS-78-20780.

S. T. Barnard was with the Department of Computer Science, University of Minnesota, Minneapolis, MN 55455. He is now with SRI International, Menlo Park, CA 94025.

W. B. Thompson is with the Department of Computer Science, University of Minnesota, Minneapolis, MN 55455.

points from each image. Let $S_1 = \langle s_1^x, s_1^y \rangle$ and $S_2 = \langle s_2^x, s_2^y \rangle$ be points in images 1 and 2, respectively. These two points should be matched if and only if they are image plane projections of the same real world surface point. Matching S_1 with S_2 is the same as assigning to S_1 a disparity with respect to image 2 of $D_1^2 = \langle s_1^x - s_2^x, s_1^y - s_2^y \rangle$, where $D_j^k(S)$ is a vector function defined on points of image j, which specifies the disparity of point S in image j with respect to image k.

A matching approach to disparity analysis must solve two problems. First, how are points selected for matching? It is clear that not all points can be matched with equal confidence because some are located in regions which lack identifying detail. Some points may not be matched at all because they may be visible in one image but not in another. To avoid ambiguous matches, it is advantageous to attempt to match only points which are easily distinguished from their neighbors. It is important to select only those points which are projections of distinct, precisely positioned local features on real world surfaces, such as spots, corners, and other small local forms. Interest operators sensitive to local variance, edges, and other properties of subimages can be used to choose potentially matchable points [5]-[9]. An alternative to this strategy is to partially segment each static image independently and then use properties of the segments, such as shape and color, as similarity variables [10], [11]. This is an attempt to match entire surfaces, not points.

The second problem in matching is to determine the basis for deciding which matches are correct. The matched points should have similar properties, of course, because they are both projections of the same surface point, but in many cases there will be ambiguity. Many studies have used cross correlation or mean-square difference as a measure of similarity. Typically, a small region in image 1 surrounding an interesting point is used as a template, and a search is made for the region of maximum similarity in image 2. Two problems with this approach are that the correct match may not be the one of maximum similarity due to noise or distortion (there are ambiguous matches), and the cost of searching a two-dimensional image is high. One way to avoid ambiguity is to increase the sensitivity of the similarity measurement. Levine, O'Handley, and Yagi [7] use an adaptive correlation window, the size of which varies inversely with the variance of the region surrounding the point. Mori, Kidode, and Asada [12] use a Gaussian-weighted correlation window to minimize the errors due to distortion of the extremities. They also vary the window size with ambiguity of the match and use a prediction/correction algorithm, modifying one image to fit the other according to a predicted matching and iteratively using the error of fit to improve the prediction. Stochastic matched filtering can reduce ambiguity by improving similarity detection in the presence of noise [13].

Several strategies have been used to limit search in a cross correlation approach. Studies of stereopsis use a fixed camera model to constrain the search to one dimension [5], [7], [8], [12]. Nevatia uses a series of progressive views to constrain disparity to small values [8]. This also reduces the chance of ambiguous matches and increases the sensitivity of the similarity measurement by minimizing distortion. Another strategy is to use a coarse search to approximately locate the matching points, followed by a fine search to more accurately locate them [7], [14], [15]. Sequential similarity detection can be used for more efficient matching [16].

Many studies have used heuristics based on real world models to limit search and to resolve or avoid ambiguity. Julesz [4] and Gibson [3] observed that disparity varies continuously across unoccluded surfaces and discontinuously only at occluding edges. Marr and Poggio [17] used this property, which they call the adjacency constraint, in an iterative cooperative matching algorithm which fuses random dot stereograms. Levine et al. [7] use it to limit the range of search of proximate points, and Mori et al. [12] use it to avoid ambiguity by matching "well-contrasting" regions with high confidence and favoring these disparities for nearby points.

In the studies discussed above we can identify three properties of image pairs which can strongly influence disparity classification. The first, which we call discreteness, is a property of individual points. Discreteness is a measurement of the individual distinctness of a point, and is important for selecting good candidates for matching. The interest operators described above are good examples of discreteness measures. The second property, similarity, is a measurement of how closely two points resemble one another. Such measures are usually simple functions of small areas surrounding the points. The third property, consistency, is a measurement of how well a particular match (that is, a particular disparity classification) conforms to nearby matches. The three-dimensional spatial continuity of real world surfaces constrains the two-dimensional spatial distribution of disparity in the image plane. Disparity is discontinuous only at occluding edges. The continuity of disparity over most of the image can be used to avoid false matches based on similarity alone, by suppressing matches in the absence of supporting local evidence.

III. A LOCALLY PARALLEL MODEL FOR MATCHING

This section describes a computational model for analyzing disparity in a variety of real world situations. Object motion, stereo, and motion parallax modes of disparity are treated uniformly. Because the model has the locally parallel, globally sequential structure of a relaxation labeling algorithm, the notation in this section follows Rosenfeld, Hummel, and Zucker [18]. The general approach is similar to matching models proposed by Julesz [4] and Marr and Poggio [17] for the fusion of random dot stereograms and to a matching model proposed by Ullman [2] for retinal motion.

The theory behind the locally parallel model is that the discreteness, similarity, and consistency properties can interact to enhance the overall performance and rigor of a matching algorithm. The use of multiple properties reduces the chance of error by minimizing the dependence on any one property. The consistency property allows the most obvious classifications to improve the analysis of the more difficult ones. The discreteness property is used to minimize expensive searching. Sets of candidate matching points are selected from each image, and searching is done between these two relatively sparse sets instead of between the two gray-valued images. The emphasis throughout the formulation of the model has been on simplicity. We will demonstrate the effectiveness of this matching approach in even a minimal system.

The first step is to find the points in the two images which will be candidates for matching. Matchable points should locate small discrete local features such as spots and corners which are likely to be detectable in both images. They should be the centers of highly variable areas, and furthermore the variance should be high in all directions. (If the variance is high in general but low along one direction, as would be the case with a straight line, for example, the point will not be easily distinguishable from its neighbors along that direction). A very simple interest operator described by Moravec [19] is effective in selecting these matchable points. The sums of the squares of the differences of pixels in four directions (horizontal, vertical, and the two diagonals) are computed over a small area (5 × 5 areas are used in all examples presented here). The initial value of the interest operator for the center point is the minimum of these variances. A point will have a high initial value only if there is a high variance in all four directions. The final values of the interest operator are obtained by suppressing (i.e., setting to zero) the initial values of all but the local maxima. Any point with a nonzero final interest value must be located in an area with a high variance in all four directions, and the initial value of the point must be greater than that of any of the point's neighbors.

The interest operator is applied independently to each image. Points with locally maximal but very small interest values are rejected by thresholding. The selection of the threshold is not critical. In the examples shown in this paper it was set to give a reasonable number of points, expressed as a percentage of the total number of pixels in each image.

After the two sets of candidate points are found the next step is to construct a set of possible matches. Ideally, we would like to match each candidate point from image 1 with exactly one candidate from image 2 such that the two points are image plane projections of the same real world point. However, we can realistically expect to find valid matches for only some of the points of image 1 because the interest operator does not perform perfectly, and because some points may be occluded, shadowed, or not visible in image 2 for some reason. An initial set of possible matches is constructed by pairing each candidate point from image 1 with every candidate from image 2 within some maximum distance of the (x, y) location of the point in image 1. This distance r is the maximum detectable disparity in the x or y direction. The set of possible matches is organized as a collection of "nodes" $\{a_i\}$, one node for each candidate point from image 1. Associated with each node a_i is a tuple (x_i, y_i) which is the location of the point in image 1, and a set of labels L_i which represents possible disparities that may be assigned to the point. Each label in L_i is either a disparity vector (l_x, l_y), where l_x and l_y are integers in $[-r, r]$, or it is a distinguished label l^* denoting "undefined disparity." A node a_i has undefined disparity if point (x_i, y_i) in image 1 does not correspond to any candidate point in image 2. Every label set L_i must initially contain the element l^*. The point (x_i, y_i) in image 1 is tentatively matched to a point at (x', y') in image 2 by entering a label $l = (x_i - x', y_i - y')$ into L_i. Note that not every vector with integral coor-

dinates in the square of side $2r + 1$ need be represented in the label set of all possible matches for a node, but that the undefined disparity is always represented.

For every node a_i we want to associate with every label $l = (l_x, l_y)$ in L_i a number $p_i(l)$ which we can interpret as an estimate of the probability that point (x_i, y_i) in image 1 has disparity l. This requires that $p_i(l)$ be in $[0, 1]$ and $\Sigma_l p_i(l) = 1$. These probability estimates will be successively improved by applying the consistency property. If relatively many nearby points have a high probability of having disparity l, then $p_i(l)$ will increase. Otherwise, $p_i(l)$ will decrease.

The initial probabilities $p_i^0(l)$ are based on the sum of the squares of the differences between a small window from image 1 centered on (x_i, y_i) and a window from image 2 centered on $(x_i + l_x, y_i + l_y)$. (The window sizes in all examples presented here are 5 × 5.) Let this sum be $s_i(l)$ for $l \neq l^*$. When $s_i(l)$ is small $p_i^0(l)$ should be large, and *vice versa*.

Let

$$w_i(l) = \frac{1}{1 + c * s_i(l)}, \qquad l \neq l^* \tag{1}$$

be the "weight" associated with the label l of node a_i for some positive constant c. ($c = 10$ for all examples presented in this paper.) A disparity label which associates highly similar pairs of regions will have a large weight value. Note that $w_i(l)$ is in the interval $[0, 1]$ and is inversely related to $s_i(l)$, but in general the sum of the weights is not 1 and $w_i(l^*)$ is undefined, so we cannot use these weights as our probability estimates. Nevertheless, $w_i(l)$ has the proper qualitative behavior for probability estimates.

We first estimate the initial probability of the undefined disparity, $p_i^0(l^*)$, by observing that in many cases the label of maximum weight is the correct one. If no label has a high weight then there is probably no valid match. It may often be the case that the correct label is not the one of maximum weight, but if there is a significant correlation between maximum weight and ground truth the relationship will prove an adequate initial estimate of the probability that each node is matchable.

Using this relationship, let

$$p_i^0(l^*) = 1 - \max_{l \neq l^*} (w_i(l)) \tag{2}$$

be the initial estimate of the probability that the point (x_i, y_i) in image 1 corresponds to no point in image 2.

We can apply Bayes' rule to obtain an initial estimate of the probability that a_i should be label l for labels other than l^*. Let

$$p_i^0(l) = p_i(l|i) * (1 - p_i^0(l^*)), \qquad l \neq l^* \tag{3}$$

where $p_i(l|i)$ is the conditional probability that a_i has label l given that a_i is matchable, and $(1 - p_i^0(l^*))$ is the probability that a_i is matchable. We can estimate $p_i(l|i)$ with

$$p_i(l|i) = \frac{w_i(l)}{\sum_{l' \neq l^*} w_i(l')}. \tag{4}$$

529

Equations (2), (3), and (4) can be used to calculate the initial probabilities for every label of every node.

The initial probabilities, which depend only on the similarity of neighborhoods of candidate matching points, can be improved by using the consistency property. We want a rule for updating $p_i^k(l)$ which has the following property. The new probability $p_i^{k+1}(l)$ should tend to increase when nodes with highly probable labels consistent with l are found near node a_i. Labels are considered consistent if they represent nearly the same disparities,

$$\|l - l'\| \leqslant \Theta$$

for an appropriate threshold. For the examples used in this paper the condition for consistency is

$$\|l - l'\| = \max(|l_x - l'_x|, |l_y - l'_y|) \leqslant 1.$$

A node a_j may be considered near a_i if

$$\max(|x_i - x_j|, |y_i - y_j|) \leqslant R.$$

That is, the points corresponding to a_i and a_j in image 1 are no more than R rows or columns apart. ($R = 15$ in all examples presented here.)

The degree to which the label l' of a_j reinforces $p_i(l)$ should be related to the estimated likelihood that l' is correct. To compute the new probabilities $p_i^{k+1}(l)$ for all l in L_i we examine each node in an area surrounding a_i, but not including a_i. Let

$$q_i^k(l) = \sum_{\substack{j \ni a_j \\ \text{near } a_i \\ j \neq i}} \left[\sum_{\substack{l' \ni \\ \|l - l'\| \leqslant \Theta}} p_j^k(l') \right], \quad l \neq l^*. \tag{5}$$

In all cases $q_i^k(l) \geqslant 0$. This quantity is zero if and only if no nodes surrounding a_i have possible matches with disparity labels similar to l. It will be large when there are several nodes with highly probable matches surrounding a_i which have disparity labels similar to l. In general, $q_i(l)$ varies according to the consistency of l with the current estimate of the disparities in the local neighborhood of a_i. All nodes surrounding a_i are treated uniformly.

We can use the following rule to update the label probabilities of node a_i using q_i. Let

$$\hat{p}_i^{k+1}(l) = p_i^k(l) * (A + B * q_i^k(l)), \quad l \neq l^* \tag{6}$$

and

$$\hat{p}_i^{k+1}(l^*) = p_i^k(l^*). \tag{7}$$

We must normalize the $\hat{p}$'s to obtain the new probabilities,

$$p_i^{k+1}(l) = \frac{\hat{p}_i^{k+1}(l)}{\sum_{l' \text{ in } L_i} \hat{p}_i^{k+1}(l')}. \tag{8}$$

Parameters A and B are positive constants which influence the convergence characteristics of the model ($A = 0.3$ and $B = 3$ in all examples presented here). The role of A is to delay the total suppression of unlikely labels. Even if $q_i(l)$ is zero, the positive A ensures that the new probability does not become zero. This is desirable because information may propagate to a_i from other nodes which will eventually cause

$p_i(l)$ to increase. The role of B is to determine the rate of convergence. The larger B is relative to A the faster will be the convergence of the disparity assignments. A and B may be interpreted as damping and gain parameters. There is an effective constant correlation for label pairs which are similar, and a negative correlation for all others. (For a more general discussion of updating rules in relaxation labeling algorithms see [18].)

The probability of the label l^* (undefined disparity) is affected only by the normalization step (8). If the net contribution to $\hat{p}_i(l), l \neq l^*$, is such that

$$\sum_{l \neq l^*} \hat{p}_i^{k+1}(l) < \sum_{l \neq l^*} p_i^k(l), \tag{9}$$

then the probability that a_i has disparity l^* increases, but if this is not the case the probability decreases or perhaps remains the same.

The complete procedure to estimate the most likely disparities for each potentially matchable point in image 1 can be summarized as follows. First, a network of nodes corresponding to possible matches is constructed. Each possible match is assigned an initial likelihood using (1), (2), (3), and (4). These likelihood estimates are iteratively refined using (5), (6), (7), and (8). We have observed that after a few iterations most of the possible matches have very low probability. To increase the efficiency of the algorithm it is effective to purge these from the set of possible matches after each iteration. (In the examples presented here we purge a tentative match when its probability falls below 0.01.) If a node a_i loses all its possible matches, then (x_i, y_i) is classified as "unmatchable." That is, $p_i(l^*) = 1$. This procedure may be repeated until the network reaches a steady state, but in practice we arbitrarily stop it at ten iterations. Those nodes having a disparity with an estimated likelihood of 0.7 or greater are considered to be matched. Some nodes may remain ambiguous, with several potential matches retaining nonzero probabilities.

IV. RESULTS

An interesting and important property of this matching algorithm is that it works for any mode of disparity and does not require precise information about camera orientation, position, and distortion. Disparity in multiple images of the same scene may be due to translation or rotation of the sensor or due to motion of objects in the scene. At least three specific cases are commonly found in real world situations. The disparity is strictly temporal when a single, stationary camera records a sequence of images. Temporal disparity specifies the motion of objects in the image plane. The disparity is stereoptic when two horizontally displaced cameras simultaneously record the same scene. Often the focal axes are also rotated about a fixation point which has an arbitrary disparity of $\langle 0, 0 \rangle$. (If the focal axes are parallel the fixation point is at infinity.) Another salient mode is forward sensor motion. While the motion is commonly along the focal axis, camera rotations and/or off-axis motion may also occur. The computational model described in the previous section was tested on examples of each of these cases. A precise photogrammetric model could translate these results into quantitative

(a)   (b)

Fig. 1. Stereogram.

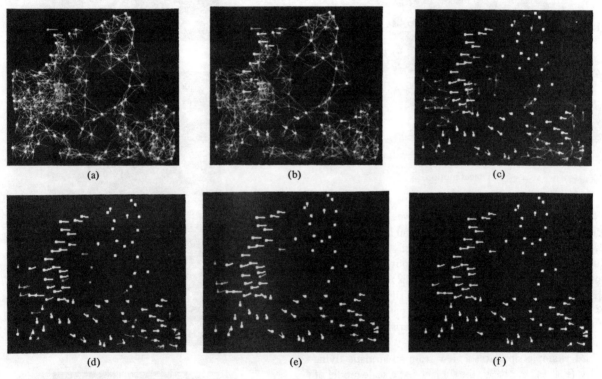

(a)   (b)   (c)

(d)   (e)   (f)

Fig. 2. (a) Initial probability assignments for Fig. 1. (b)–(f) Iterations
2, 4, 6, 8, and 10.

measurements of velocity and depth, but we shall only discuss their qualitative significance.

The first case is a stereogram (Fig. 1). The candidate matching points selected by the interest operator are superimposed on the images. Fig. 2 shows the performance of the model over ten iterations, displaying every second iteration in addition to the initial state. Each point represents a node and each line a possible match. Each line is in the direction of the corresponding disparity vector, and the length is proportional to the length of the vector. A match of small disparity appears only as a point because the line is too small to be visible. The brightness of each point is proportional to the probability that the point is matchable, $(1 - p_i^k(l^*))$, and the brightness of each line is proportional to the probability of the disparity assignment, $p_i^k(l)$. Initially, there are many possible matches with relatively low probability, but by iteration 4 [Fig. 2(c)] almost

all of them have been discarded. On iteration 10 [Fig. 2(f)] only those classifications with probability greater than 0.7 are shown. The cameras are fixated on the person's head, which has a disparity of $\langle 0, 0 \rangle$. More distant points have disparities with positive x components and nearer points have disparities with negative x components. Observe that from the person's head to his left knee and then to his left foot disparity varies smoothly, following the smooth transition from far to near and back to far [Fig. 2(f)]. Between the person and the background, however, there is a step change in depth at the occluding edge, and here the assigned disparities exhibit an abrupt transition from near to far. The nonzero y components of some of the closer points is due to motion of the subject between exposures (only one camera was used to record this stereogram).

The next example illustrates temporal disparity. Fig. 3

(a)

(b)

Fig. 3. Object motion.

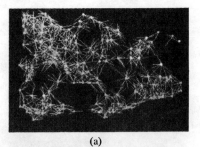

(a)

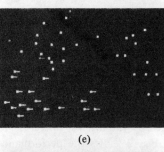

(b)

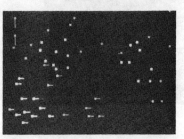

(c)

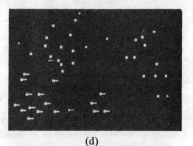

(d)

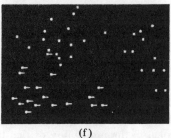

(e)

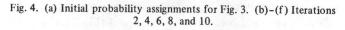

(f)

Fig. 4. (a) Initial probability assignments for Fig. 3. (b)–(f) Iterations 2, 4, 6, 8, and 10.

shows a sequence in which the truck moves approximately seven pixels to the right while the camera, and hence the background, remains stationary. The truck is easily distinguishable as a cluster of points with disparity of about $\langle 7, 0 \rangle$ and the background as a cluster of points with disparity of about $\langle 0, 0 \rangle$ [Fig. 4(f)]. An error occurs at a point slightly above the roof of the truck. The point is actually part of the background but its estimated disparity is characteristic of the truck surface.

The third example simulates a view from an airplane flying over a city (Fig. 5). Actually, the subject was a scale model of downtown Minneapolis which was photographed with an ordinary camera and tripod. As the camera "flies" over the "city" it rotates downward in the frontal plane to fixate on a point near the center of the image (Fig. 6). The final disparity vectors diverge from the fixation point which has disparity $\langle 0, 0 \rangle$ [Fig. 7(f)]. Two distinctive features in Fig. 7(f) are the cluster of points on the large building in the near foreground, which has a large disparity because it is very close, and the cluster of points in the far background (upper left corner), which has mainly vertical disparity because of the rotation of the camera. The algorithm is susceptible to an aliasing effect when it encounters a dense cluster of similar points, such as would occur in a high frequency periodic subimage. An example of this may be seen at the middle of the right border of Fig. 7(f), where a number of points have been misclassified. One way to avoid this problem would be to enlarge the area in which interest values must be locally maximal to produce feature points, thereby constraining the density of feature points to a relatively small value.

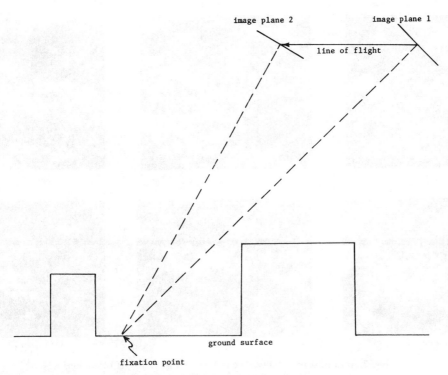

Fig. 5. Schematic of third example.

Fig. 6. Motion parallax.

V. Summary and Conclusions

Disparity relationships between images convey important information for spatial perception. The conventional cross correlation approach to matching for disparity analysis is prone to errors caused by distortion in the imaging process and the unavoidable occurrence of ambiguous matches. Increasing the sophistication of similarity detection can reduce the problem of ambiguity, but the necessary adaptive windowing or extensive preprocessing can also reduce the efficiency and reliability of the matching process. Geometric distortion may prevent accurate similarity measurement by cross correlation. Constraining the search with a precisely known camera geometry restricts the process to special cases.

Another way to attack the ambiguity problem is to use information other than similarity to resolve ambiguous matches. The continuity of real world surfaces, a very general property which is independent of camera geometry, constrains disparity to values which are consistent with the local matching context. The consistency property can be used to iteratively refine a probabilistic estimate of disparity classification which allows ambiguous matches. The initial estimate may be obtained from a simple measure of similarity. Expensive searching is minimized by applying a simple interest operator to both images to find two sets of discrete feature points, resulting in a greatly reduced search space.

In practice the procedure is effective in a wide variety of cases, converging quickly to an unambiguous disparity classification which accurately reflects the large-scale spatial characteristics of real world scenes. It is robust in that it is not very sensitive to noise and distortion and does not require careful registration of images. It does not require complicated, carefully tuned updating functions, nor very precise initial probability estimates. The success of the method comes in large part from its ability to integrate effectively different sources of information into a simple procedure.

Acknowledgment

We would like to thank R. Hummel, C. Lemche, H. Nagel, S. Sahni, and A. Yonas for useful suggestions and criticism. We would also like to thank W. Franta and the staff of the

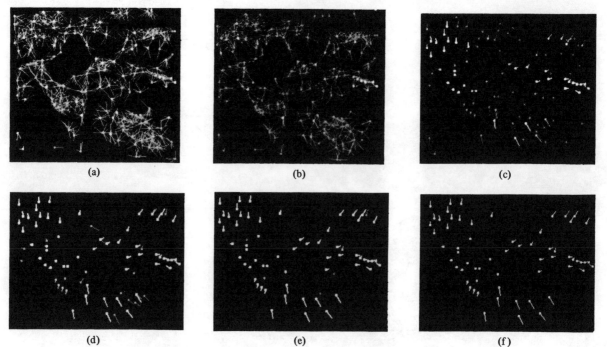

(a)   (b)   (c)

(d)   (e)   (f)

Fig. 7. (a) Initial probability assignments for Fig. 6. (b)–(f) Iterations 2, 4, 6, 8, and 10.

Special Interactive Computing Laboratory, University of Minnesota, for their helpful assistance and for the use of their excellent facilities.

REFERENCES

[1] R. O. Duda and P. E. Hart, *Pattern Recognition and Scene Analysis.* New York: Wiley, 1973.
[2] S. Ullman, "The interpretation of visual motion," Ph.D. dissertation, Mass. Inst. Technol., Cambridge, MA, May 1977.
[3] J. J. Gibson, *The Perception of the Visual World.* Cambridge, MA: Riverside, 1950.
[4] B. Julesz, *Foundations of Cyclopean Perception.* Chicago, IL: Univ. Chicago Press, 1971.
[5] M. J. Hannah, "Computer matching of areas in stereo images," Stanford A.I. Memo. 239, July 1974.
[6] L. H. Quam, "Computer comparison of pictures," Stanford A.I. Memo, AIM-144, May 1971.
[7] M. D. Levine, D. A. O'Handley, and G. M. Yagi, "Computer determination of depth maps," *Comput. Graphics Image Processing*, vol. 2, pp. 131–150, 1973.
[8] R. Nevatia, "Depth measurement by motion stereo," *Comput. Graphics Image Processing*, vol. 5, pp. 203–214, 1976.
[9] D. J. Kahl, A. Rosenfeld, and A. Danker, "Some experiments in point pattern matching," Univ. Maryland, Tech. Rep. TR-690, Sept. 1978.
[10] K. Price and D. R. Reddy, "Change detection and analysis in multispectral images," in *Proc. Int. Joint Conf. Artificial Intell.*, pp. 619–625, 1977.
[11] H. Nagel, "Formation of an object concept by analysis of systematic time variations in the optically perceptible environment," *Comput. Graphics Image Processing*, vol. 7, pp. 149–194, 1978.
[12] K. Mori, M. Kidode, and H. Asada, "An iterative prediction and correction method for automatic stereocomparison," *Comput. Graphics Image Processing*, vol. 2, pp. 393–401, 1973.
[13] W. K. Pratt, *Digital Image Processing.* New York: Wiley, 1978.
[14] D. B. Gennery, "A stereo vision system for an autonomous vehicle," in *Proc. 5th Int. Joint Conf. Artificial Intell.*, Cambridge, MA, Aug. 1977, pp. 576–582.
[15] S. L. Tanimoto, "A comparison of some image searching methods," in *Proc. IEEE Comput. Soc Conf. Pattern Recognition Image Processing*, Chicago, IL, June 1978, pp. 280–286.
[16] D. I. Barnea and H. F. Silverman, "A class of algorithms for fast image registration," *IEEE Trans. Comput.*, vol. C-21, pp. 179–186, Feb. 1972.
[17] D. Marr and T. Poggio, "Cooperative computation of stereo disparity," *Science*, vol. 194, pp. 283–287, Oct. 15, 1976.
[18] A. Rosenfeld, R. A. Hummel, and S. W. Zucker, "Scene labeling by relaxation operations," *IEEE Trans. Syst., Man, Cybern.*, vol. SMC-6, June 1976.
[19] H. P. Moravec, "Towards automatic visual obstacle avoidance," in *Proc. 5th Int. Joint Conf. Artificial Intell.*, Cambridge, MA, Aug. 1977, p. 584.

Stephen T. Barnard (S'78–M'79) received the B.S. degree in mechanical engineering from Case Western Reserve University, Cleveland, OH, and the M.S. and Ph.D. degrees in computer science from the University of Minnesota, Minneapolis.

He has worked for Sperry Univac, the 3M Corporation, and Honeywell, Inc. He is currently with the Artificial Intelligence Center, SRI International, Menlo Park, CA, where he is working on image understanding and automated visual inspection.

William B. Thompson (S'72–M'75) was born in Santa Monica, CA, in August 1948. He received the Sc.B. degree in physics from Brown University, Providence, RI in 1970, and the M.S. and Ph.D. degrees in computer science from the University of Southern California, Los Angeles, in 1972 and 1975, respectively.

From 1972 to 1975 he was a member of the Image Processing Institute at the University of Southern California. Since September 1975, he has been an Assistant Professor in the Department of Computer Science, University of Minnesota, Minneapolis. His interests are in artificial intelligence and scene analysis.

Dr. Thompson is a member of Sigma Xi, Eta Kappa Nu, and the Association for Computing Machinery.

Reprinted from *IEEE Transactions on Pattern Analysis and Machine Intelligence*, Volume PAMI-9, Number 1, January 1987, pages 56-73. Copyright © 1987 by The Institute of Electrical and Electronics Engineers, Inc. All rights reserved.

Finding Trajectories of Feature Points in a Monocular Image Sequence

ISHWAR K. SETHI, MEMBER, IEEE, AND RAMESH JAIN, SENIOR MEMBER, IEEE

Abstract—Identifying the same physical point in more than one image, the correspondence problem, is vital in motion analysis. Most research for establishing correspondence uses only two frames of a sequence to solve this problem. By using a sequence of frames, it is possible to exploit the fact that due to inertia the motion of an object cannot change instantaneously. By using *smoothness of motion*, it is possible to solve the correspondence problem for arbitrary motion of several nonrigid objects in a scene. We formulate the correspondence problem as an optimization problem and propose an iterative algorithm to find trajectories of points in a monocular image sequence. A modified form of this algorithm is useful in case of occlusion also. We demonstrate the efficacy of this approach considering synthetic, laboratory, and real scenes.

Index Terms—Correspondence, motion object tracking, path coherence, smoothness of motion, structure from motion.

I. INTRODUCTION

THE last few years have seen increasing interest in dynamic scene analysis. The input to a dynamic scene analysis system is a sequence of images. As is well known, an image represents a 2-D projection of a 3-D scene at a time instant. A major problem in a computer vision system is to recover the information about objects in a scene from images. This problem cannot be solved without some assumptions about the world. A sequence of frames allows one additional dimension to recover the information about the 3-D world that is lost in the projection process. Multiple views of a moving object acquired using a stationary camera may allow recovery of the structure of the object [4], [36], [32]–[34], [31], [24]. A mobile camera may be used to acquire information about the structure of the stationary objects in a scene using optical flow [6], [22], axial motion stereo [20], and other methods [16], [14].

Many researchers in psychology of vision support the recovery of information from image sequences, rather than an image, representing a scene [19], [6], [16]. Gibson [16] argued in support of active information pickup by the observer in an environment. Johansson [16] demonstrated the efficacy of only motion information in recognition of

Manuscript received April 18, 1985; revised February 6, 1986. Recommended for acceptance by W. B. Thompson. This work was supported in part by the NSF under Grant DCR-8500717.

I. K. Sethi is with the Department of Computer Science, Wayne State University, Detroit, MI 48202.

R. Jain is with the Department of Electrical Engineering and Computer Science, The University of Michigan, Ann Arbor, MI 48109.

IEEE Log Number 8609395.

objects using moving light displays. Neisser [19] proposed a model according to which the perceptual processes continually interact with the incoming information to verify anticipations formed on the basis of available information until a given time instant. In computer vision systems, the efficacy of even noise-sensitive approaches, such as difference and accumulative difference pictures, was demonstrated by using hypothesize-and-test mechanisms to analyze complex real-world scenes [13]. Although many researchers are addressing the problem of recovering information in dynamic scenes, it appears that due to the legacy of static scenes most researchers are approaching the recovery problem using just two or three frames of a sequence. This self-imposed restriction results in approaches suitable for *quasi-dynamic* scene analysis, rather than dynamic scene analysis. Since the information recovery process requires constraints about the scene, the analysis based on a minimal number of frames rests on assumptions that ignore the most important information in dynamic scenes—the motion of objects.

Structure from motion has attracted significant research efforts recently from researchers working in the field of dynamic scene analysis [27], [31], [32], [34], [36], [38]. Ullman popularized the *rigidity assumption* in computer vision. This assumption states that any set of elements undergoing a 2-D transformation which has a unique interpretation as a rigid body moving in space should be so interpreted. The rigidity assumption allows recovery of the structure of objects, under certain conditions, in three frames.

Another popular approach for the recovery of the structure and motion is to use optical flow fields [16], [22], [14], [18], [26], while others try to recover the same information using points in frames. The optical flow is the field of retinal velocities. In computer vision, it is considered the velocity field for all image points. It has been shown that the optical flow contains information about the motion of the observer and the environment. Approaches for the computation [10] and for the recovery of structure [37] have been proposed. Considering the difficulties in computing optical flow of acceptable quality, some efforts are being made to recover the structure using the characteristics of optical flow, but without computing it [11], [20].

Recently, the trajectory-based recovery has attracted some attention [31], [28], [38], [24], [15]. It has been shown that the human visual system requires an extended frame sequence to recover the structure of moving patterns [31], [24] and that the noise sensitivity of the system improves with an increase in the number of frames [3]. We believe that the trajectory-based approach to the recovery of structure is more suitable for complex scenes. This approach will allow successive refinement of the structure of objects as more frames are observed. Using the first few frames, an initial, although tentative, structure of an object might be hypothesized, and then this structure could be refined based on later observations. A major advantage of such an approach would be to free ourselves from assumptions of rigidity and rely more on natural assumptions of motion characteristics.

A major step in the recovery using a token-based approach, both in quasi-dynamic and dynamic approaches, is identifying images of a physical point in several frames, usually called the correspondence problem. This paper addresses the problem of establishing correspondence for tokens in a sequence of images. Contrary to most other approaches, we do not try to solve the correspondence problem using just two frames. In two frames, one can use only the location of the tokens and has to make assumptions about the nature of the objects or about the maximum velocity of objects. A longer sequence of frames allows the use of velocity information in solving the problem [35]. Jenkin [15] proposed an approach for establishing correspondence in a binocular image sequence. He suggested the use of the smoothness of velocity, and his approach is influenced by the Gestalt rules. We also believe that the smoothness of velocity is more general and more powerful compared to the rigidity assumption. As shown in a latter section, our approach is similar to Jenkin's in using smoothness, but is very different from his approach in many other respects.

The smoothness constraint has been used by some other researchers, also in dynamic scenes [10], [8]. The smoothness used by them, however, is different from the smoothness we are using. Horn and Schunck use the smoothness of velocity of neighboring points on a surface to propagate velocity vectors computed at some points of the surface to the other points of the surface in the same frame. Hildreth also uses the smoothness of the velocity field to compute the optical flow for rigid objects. We use the smoothness of motion of a point over several frames.

We propose an optimization approach to the correspondence problem and propose an iterative optimization algorithm to find optimal trajectories. This computational approach allows solution of the correspondence problem incrementally. As new frames are acquired, our iterative optimization approach establishes the correspondence. Thus, solution of the correspondence problem also gives us trajectories of points, which, in turn, may be used to obtain structure. Our approach is able to handle limited occlusion and disocclusion also. A limitation of the proposed approach, similar to Jenkin's, is that it assumes uniform motion. If for some reason there is a sudden change in motion, this approach will not be able to detect it and may result in wrong correspondence.

Section II discusses approaches used for correspondence, with emphasis on Jenkin's approach because of its similarity to our approach. Section III gives possible applications of the proposed approach. Path coherence and smoothness of motion, as used in our approach, are discussed in Section IV, and the optimization approach to the correspondence is presented in Section V. Section VI gives the greedy exchange algorithm for establishing correspondence. The issues related to the formulation of the path coherence function are discussed in Section VII, and results of the application of the algorithm are given in Section VIII. The basic algorithm has some problems. These problems and modifications to handle occlusion are discussed in Section IX. Results for laboratory sequences and a real movie (*Superman*) sequence are presented to show the efficacy of the algorithm.

II. Correspondence Problem

In the recovery of structure from motion, the establishment of the token correspondence has been a major hurdle. Ullman [36] proposed a minimal mapping approach to this problem. His approach was based on the 2-D features of the tokens and the 2-D distance between tokens. His elegant approach is computationally very attractive because of the possibility of implementation using a network of processors. The major problem with the approach is, however, that it fails to consider the fact that most realistic motion analysis must be performed by considering an extended region of space–time. Correspondence based on 2-D distances alone may lead to erroneous results in scenes containing several objects moving in assorted directions and in case of nonrigid motion. In fact, psychological experiments conducted to study the feasibility of this approach consider only a few points in artificial motion situations; Todd [31] shows that most human observers require several frames to infer the structure of moving objects, even in simple experimental situations.

Barnard and Thompson [1] and Prager and Arbib [23] proposed relaxation-based approaches to the solution of this problem. In relaxation-based methods, all tokens in frame 2 that are within a spatial neighborhood of a token in frame 1 are assigned a weight indicating the match strength between the token in frame 1 and the tokens in frame 2. It is assumed that only one of these matches is correct. The correct match is obtained by using relaxation. The relaxation process tries to find the most consistent matches based on the disparities. The most consistent match implies uniform motion and hence *rigid* objects. These approaches also use 2-D displacements in two frames as a major factor in establishing the correspondence.

These approaches to the solution of the correspondence problem try to solve the problem using tokens in two frames only. In fact, most reasearch in dynamic scene analysis, or time-varying image analysis, has been concerned with only two or three frames, *not with dynamic scenes*. It is not clear why most researchers in this field have been concerned with the recovery of information considering a minimal number of points in a minimal number of frames, rather than with the recovery of reliable information (see Brady's comment on Todd's paper in [2]). It appears that for real-world problems, like many other problems in dynamic scene analysis, the correspondence problem may be solved more reliably using more than two frames. Due to the self-imposed limitation of working with only two frames, some form of the rigidity assumption is essential for solving the problem. In two frames, the most powerful constraint is the spatial uniformity of displacements. The rigidity assumption, with orthographic projections, is very appealing because it guarantees the uniformity of displacements and is domain independent. If we consider more than two frames in establishing correspondence, however, we may admit nonrigid objects in our analysis. Thus, assumptions about the nature of motion can be used to relax those about the nature of objects. In its simplest form, the smoothness of motion is used to relax the rigidity of objects.

This can be done using *path coherence* and assuming *smoothness of motion*. In this paper, we introduce the notion of *path coherence* and use it for solving the correspondence problem as an optimization problem.

Jenkin [15] proposed a novel approach for combining the solution of correspondence problems for stereo and motion. He argues in support of the smoothness assumption. He is interested, like us, in an approach that is based not on assumptions like rigidity [36], planarity [9], and rotation and translation [38], but on the smoothness of motion. His notion of smoothness is related to 3-D motion. It is based on the following.

1) The location of a given point would be relatively unchanged from one frame to the next.

2) The scalar velocity, or speed of a given point, would be relatively unchanged from one frame to the next.

3) The direction of motion of a given point would be relatively unchanged from one frame to the next.

To solve the correspondence problem, he assumed that at all instants all points were visible in both images of the binocular frame sequence and that the 3-D position and velocity of the points were known at some initial time. As will be shown in the next section, our approach uses smoothness of image motion and uses a monocular sequence. Moreover, we have extended the algorithm to cope with limited occlusion; severe occlusion requires characteristics of objects. Since we are concerned only with points, our domain in this paper may be considered to be similar to that of Rashid [25], O'Rourke and Badler [21], and Jenkin [15]. In this paper, we do not address the problem of occlusion analysis in general cases using other than simple motion characteristics.

III. Applications of the Tracking

The tracking approach proposed here will play an important role in many different applications. A complete object may be assumed to be a point, and then the proposed algorithms may be applied to those points. This approach will be useful in the analysis of scenes containing several moving objects. Some possible applications are traffic analysis, cell motion analysis, and others. A more important application of the proposed algorithm may be in the segmentation of dynamic scenes by grouping points with similar motion in one object [5]. A nonrigid or jointed object can be segmented by tracking individual points and then grouping these points based on common motion characteristics, as is done by humans as demonstrated by Johansson [16]. This segmentation will give an idea of the general structure of an object. For rigid objects, by tracking several points on the object, one may use the structure from motion approaches using trajectories [28], [31].

IV. Path Coherence and Smoothness of Motion

We exploit the fact that, due to inertia, the motion of a physical entity cannot change instantaneously. If a frame sequence is acquired at a rate such that no dramatic changes take place between two consecutive frames, then for most physical objects no abrupt change in the motion can be observed. Thus, a very reasonable assumption for the analysis of real-world dynamic scenes is: *the motion of an object at any time instant cannot change arbruptly.* This is *path coherence.*

Note that this assumption will be valid for all moving objects, rigid and nonrigid. If the objects collide, then some high-level process may be required to analyze the motion after the collision. In most other cases, if the sampling rate is high enough, then the changes in the motion will be gradual.

The projection of a smooth 3-D trajectory will be a smooth 2-D trajectory in both orthographic and perspective projections. This can be easily verified by considering the projection equations and analyzing first and second derivatives of the projected points. It can be shown that for any continuous variations in the velocity of a point in space, the velocity of the projected point will also be continuous. This fact allows us to study the correspondence problem using path coherence in images, rather than in 3-D space as in [15].

Let us consider a trajectory T_i for a point P_i in an image sequence. The coordinates of the point are given by a vector X_i in a frame. The coordinates in the kth frame for this point are denoted by X_{i_k}. Let us represent a trajectory T_i as

$$T_i = \langle X_{i_1}, X_{i_2}, \cdots, X_{i_n} \rangle \tag{1}$$

where X_{i_k} is the point in the kth frame participating in the ith trajectory. A set of points in the kth frame will be denoted by X^k.

Now let us consider the deviation d_i^k in the path of the point in the kth frame. We denote a measure of deviation in the path, and hence a measure of path coherence, as

$$d_i^k = \Psi(\overline{X_{i_{k-1}} X_{i_k}}, \overline{X_{i_k} X_{i_{k+1}}}) \tag{2}$$

where Ψ is a path coherence function. This function may consider the direction or magnitude, or both, of the displacements of the point in an image sequence.

We may define the deviation for the trajectory as

$$D_i = \sum_{k=2}^{n-1} d_i^k. \tag{3}$$

Note that for translational motion, the difference in the direction will be a suitable measure of deviation; in more complex cases, one may need more rigorous measures. For uniform translational motion in an image plane, D_i will be zero for a correct trajectory. For an arbitrary trajectory, if the motion is smooth, the value of D_i will be very small.

Let us consider the projection of two points in frames of a sequence, as shown in Fig. 1. The points are moving in different directions. The three frames under consideration are at the crossover of the trajectories of the points. The rigidity assumption cannot be used in this situation. Moreover, if distances between points in two frames are the basis for finding the trajectory of the points, then one will obtain an abrupt change in the direction of motion from the second frame to the third frame. The path coherence will allow determination of the correct correspondences over three frames and will result in the correct trajectories, as shown in Fig. 2. If we are considering a trajectory, then the instantaneous change in the motion of a physical entity may be obtained by comparing the motion vectors from the previous frame and the current frame. Path coherence requires that there not be abrupt changes in the motion vectors obtained from consecutive frames.

In a scene, several objects may be undergoing random motions. The objects may be rigid, jointed, or arbitrary; the motion of each object, however, will be smooth. Thus, if a dynamic scene is sampled at a rate fast enough to capture all significant events in the scene, then the observed motion of all objects will be smooth trajectories. As suggested by Todd [31], more reliable motion perception may be achieved by considering the primitive units of motion perception to be the global trajectories in an optic array defined over an extended region of space–time.

Now, if there are m points in a sequence of n frames, resulting in m trajectories, then the deviation for all the trajectories should be considered. This deviation is given by

$$D(T_1, T_2, \cdots, T_m) = \sum_{i=1}^{m} \sum_{k=2}^{n-1} d_i^k. \tag{4}$$

The problem we are facing is to determine these trajectories. Thus, our problem, in its simplest form, may be stated as: *given m points in each of the n frames of a sequence, determine m trajectories.* Since there are m^n total possible trajectories, only m of which are to be selected, we need a method to judiciously select these m trajectories. We know that each trajectory is smooth, and hence a reasonable approach is to try to maximize the smoothness of the set of trajectories that are selected as the correct set. This approach is consistent with those pro-

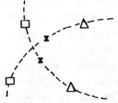

Fig. 1. In this figure, we show the trajectories of two points. We are concerned with the three points on the crossover of the trajectories. The points in the first, second, and third frames are, □, x, and △, respectively.

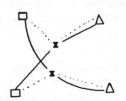

Fig. 2. The correspondence established using 2-D distance and the smoothness of motion are shown using broken and full lines, respectively.

posed by [15], [24], [31]. This approach of maximizing smoothness of motion may be stated as: *if a set of points undergoing a 2-D tranformation has a unique interpretation as a set of points following smooth 3-D trajectories, then it should be so interpreted.*

Note that the above smoothness of motion conjecture is an extension of the path coherence assumption. The path coherence assumption for a point in a frame considers its motion from the previous frame to the current frame and from the current frame to the next frame; the smoothness of motion hypothesis extends this notion of *smooth velocity changes* to a longer sequence. It should be emphasized here that this hypothesis gives more importance to the continuity of motion, rather than displacements in just two frames, and considers individual point characteristics for establishing correspondence in a dynamic scene. Clearly, two frames are not enough to apply smoothness of motion, not even to use path coherence. We require at least three frames to compute the change in the motion. For verifying smoothness of motion, more frames will be required.

V. Finding Trajectories

In a general but noise-free case, elements may be moving in assorted directions. Suppose that a feature detector, such as a moving corner detector [29], gives points in each frame. In the problem formulation, let us assume that the number of moving points in each frame is m. The problem now is to find trajectories of m points in n frames. We can make general assumptions based only on motion characteristics, not on the nature of objects. These assumptions are the following.

1) An element in a frame can only belong to one trajectory.

2) There should be m trajectories, each containing n points.

3) For each trajectory, the deviation should be minimal.

4) The sum of the deviations for trajectories should be minimal.

The first two assumptions above are to assign each point to only one unique trajectory. The path coherence assumption requires that the deviation in the path be minimal at every time instant for a point. Path coherence alone may lead to wrong trajectories near the points of intersection of trajectories. The smoothness of motion, which is presented in the form of the fourth assumption above, comes to the rescue in such situations.

In order to represent the correct correspondence of points on a trajectory, we define an n-dimensional array C to represent m valid trajectories. This array will have

$$C(i_1, i_2, \cdots, i_n) = 1 \qquad (5)$$

for a valid ith trajectory. All other entries will be zero. Thus, for a set of trajectories under consideration, m out of m^n entries in the array C will be 1, while the rest will be 0. In Fig. 3 we show points on four trajectories in five frames. For the trajectories shown in the figure, only the following elements of the C array will have nonzero values:

$$C(1, 2, 3, 4, 4) = 1$$
$$C(2, 1, 1, 2, 3) = 1$$
$$C(3, 4, 4, 3, 1) = 1$$
$$C(4, 3, 2, 1, 2) = 1.$$

Now we can formulate the trajectory-finding method as an optimization problem. The total number of all possible trajectories is m^n; however, only m of those are valid. One may consider exhaustively all possible combinations of trajectories to find the correct solution. The exhaustive approach will be computationally very expensive, however. Before we consider the computational approach, let us consider the solution of the problem. According to the hypothesis of the smoothness of motion, we want to select those trajectories from the set of all possible trajectories that maximize the smoothness of the trajectories. Thus, we want to select that set which minimizes the function $D(T_1, T_2, \cdots, T_m)$, given by

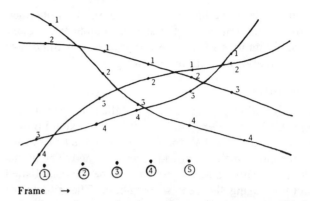

Fig. 3. The points on four trajectories are shown in five frames. This figure is a composite frame showing locations of points in different frames. The points are numbered, and the trajectories are shown by lines. The frame number is assumed increasing from left to right. The number shown next to a point indicates that in its frame it is the kth point.

and

$$C(i_1, i_2, \cdots, i_n) \geq 0 \qquad \text{for} \quad X_{i_1} \in X^1, \cdots, X_{i_n} \in X^n. \qquad (8)$$

The set of trajectories $T_1, T_2, \cdots, T_m$ that minimizes this function should be interpreted as the correct set describing the motion of m points in n frames.

VI. OPTIMIZATION ALGORITHM

As pointed out in an earlier section, an exhaustive solution of the optimization problem to establish the correspondence is computationally a difficult problem. Although established optimization methods like branch and bound and dynamic programming can be applied to solve our problem, they are inadequate for two reasons. First, the computational requirements of these optimization methods are still quite high, and they do not exploit the redundancy of information available in dynamic scenes. Moreover, in our problem, it will be desirable to have an incremental algorithm that assigns points in the $(k + 1)$th frame to trajectories that have already been obtained up to the kth frame.

We use an iterative optimization algorithm to assign points to proper trajectories. Suppose that initial trajectories are obtained using some criterion, such as closeness alone. Points from a new frame may be tentatively as-

$$D(T_1, T_2, \cdots, T_m) = \sum_{X_{i_1} \in X^1} \cdots \sum_{X_{i_n} \in X^n} \left(\sum_{k=2}^{n-1} \Psi(\overline{X_{i_{k-1}} X_{i_k}}, \overline{X_{i_k} X_{i_{k+1}}}) \right) * C(i_1, i_2, \cdots, i_n), \qquad (6)$$

subject to the conditions

$$\sum_{X_{i_1} \in X^1} C(i_1, i_2, \cdots, i_n) = 1$$

$$\vdots$$

$$\sum_{X_{i_n} \in X^n} C(i_1, i_2, \cdots, i_n) = 1 \qquad (7)$$

signed to trajectories using a weak criterion, and then the resulting trajectories can be refined using a stepwise optimization procedure to minimize the overall deviation of the trajectories while establishing correspondence. Like hill-climbing procedures in general, stepwise optimization procedures guarantee only local optimization. Also, in these procedures, the initial correspondence plays an important role in the final solution. The solution obtained is strongly influenced by the starting point. With these general limitations of stepwise approaches in mind, we propose an algorithm in the following.

A. Algorithm

The algorithm proposed here is called the *greedy exchange (GE) algorithm*. This algorithm will extend trajectories up to the $(k + 1)$th frame, assuming the trajectories up to the kth frame have already been obtained. The points of the $(k + 1)$th frame are assigned to be the established trajectories using the nearest neighbors. These tentative trajectories are then iteratively refined using the following method. The value of the criterion D for the tentative trajectories for the $(k + 1)$th frame is

$$D = \sum_{p=1}^{m} D_p = \sum_{p=1}^{m} \sum_{q=2}^{k} d_p^q. \tag{9}$$

Now let us consider two trajectories, the ith and the jth, and rewrite the above equation as

$$D = \sum_{p=1;p \neq i,j}^{m} D_p + \sum_{q=2}^{k} d_i^q + \sum_{q=2}^{k} d_j^q$$

$$= \sum_{p=1;p \neq i,j}^{m} D_p + \sum_{q=2}^{k-1} d_i^q + \sum_{q=2}^{k-1} d_j^q + d_i^k + d_j^k. \tag{10}$$

Suppose now we exchange the points from the $(k + 1)$th frame on the ith and jth trajectories. Clearly, such an exchange would not affect the first three terms in the above equation. Now let d_i^k and d_j^k be the new path coherence measures for the ith and jth trajectories after the exchange. Then, for the above exchange to be profitable, we must have

$$\boldsymbol{d}_i^k + \boldsymbol{d}_j^k < d_i^k + d_j^k, \tag{11}$$

or

$$g_{ij}^k \equiv d_i^k + d_j^k - (\boldsymbol{d}_i^k + \boldsymbol{d}_j^k) \tag{12}$$

should be positive.

If we are to select only one such exchange from all possible exchanges, then we should make a decision in favor of the exchange maximizing the gain, i.e., exchange i and j if

$$g_{ij}^k \geq g_{rs}^k \tag{13}$$

for all possible values of i, j, r, and s. This idea leads to the following GE algorithm.

1. *Initialization:* For each point in X^k, $k = 1, 2, \cdots, n - 1$, determine the nearest neighbor in X^{k+1}. Using these nearest neighbors, initialize m trajectories, such that the point $X_{i_{k+1}}$. In case of multiple nearest neighbors, the decisions are arbitrary, and a point in any frame is assigned to only one trajectory.

2. *Exchange Loop:* For each frame value $k = 2$ to $n - 1$:
   a. Compute the gain g_{ij}^k for $i = 1$ to $m - 1$ and $j = i + 1$ to m.
   b. Pick the i–j pair providing the maximum gain.
   c. Exchange the points in the $(k + 1)$th frame on the T_i and T_j trajectories, and set the exchange flag on.

3. *Termination:* Check the exchange flag at the end of exchange loop. If an exchange was made during a frame, go back to exchange loop; otherwise, stop.

Clearly, the complexity of the algorithm is of $O(nm^2)$. If we choose our path coherence measure such that the D cannot become negative, then the above procedure will terminate after a finite number of iterations.

VII. PATH COHERENCE FUNCTION

In selecting a function for path coherence, we used four guiding principles.

1) The function should not be negative.

2) The function should consider the amount of deviation in the direction of motion, not the sense (left or right) of the deviation. Thus, the sign of the angle of deviation should not factor in the computation of the function.

3) The function should respond equally to increases and decreases in speed.

4) If there is no change in the motion characteristics, then the function should be zero.

These four conditions help us in selecting a suitable function to represent path coherence at a point. We used the following function in our experiments:

$$\Psi(X_{i_{k-1}}, X_{i_k}, X_{i_{k+1}}) = w_1 \left(1 - \frac{\overline{X_{i_{k-1}} X_{i_k}} \cdot \overline{X_{i_k} X_{i_{k+1}}}}{\|\overline{X_{i_{k-1}} X_{i_k}}\| \cdot \|\overline{X_{i_k} X_{i_{k+1}}}\|} \right)$$
$$+ w_2 \left[1 - \frac{2[\|\overline{X_{i_{k-1}} X_{i_k}}\| \cdot \|\overline{X_{i_k} X_{i_{k+1}}}\|]^{1/2}}{[\|\overline{X_{i_{k-1}} X_{i_k}}\| + \|\overline{X_{i_k} X_{i_{k+1}}}\|]} \right] \tag{14}$$

where w_1 and w_2 are weights.

As can be easily verified, this function satisfies the above four conditions and takes into account both the direction and the magnitude of changes in the motion. In fact, the first term in the above expression can be considered *directional coherence* and the second term can be considered *speed coherence*. Note that the first term is the dot product of the displacement vectors, and the second considers the geometric and arithmetic mean of the magnitude of these vectors. The weights w_1, w_2 are experimentally selected to be 0.1 and 0.9, respectively. It should be pointed out here that one may also consider acceleration in the path coherence. This will require extending the notion of the path coherence to more than three frames so that acceleration may be computed. In our current study, no effort was made to account for acceleration.

VIII. EXPERIMENTS

We studied the efficacy of the proposed approach considering several synthetic and real scenes. In the synthetic data, we considered assorted motions of points in several frames and added random noise to the position of points. In all cases, excellent results were obtained. Here we present results of two synthetic sequences to show how our algorithm works.

In the first experiment, we generated four points in space. These points were undergoing different rotational motions. The proposed algorithm tracked the images of the points and found the trajectories shown in Fig. 4.

In the next experiment with the synthetic data, we considered four points in ten frames. A composite frame showing the location of points in all frames is shown in Fig. 5. All points are moving left to right. As can be seen from the figure, the trajectories of points cross between the fourth and sixth frames. During this period, the location of points is such that a correspondence scheme based only on the location of points is likely to give wrong results. We applied our iterative algorithm to these data, using the path coherence function discussed above. The initialization phase resulted in the trajectories shown in Fig. 6(a). Note that the initialization phase considers only the location of points from frame to frame, and hence it is not surprising that the resulting trajectories are wrong. In fact, these trajectories are completely counterintuitive, when one considers the data. In the first iteration, four corrections are made. The trajectories after the first correction and after the first iteration are shown in Fig. 6(b) and (c), respectively. Note that the first correction removes the abrupt change in direction due to a wrong correspondence of the fifth frame points on the second and fourth trajectories (trajectories are numbered from top to bottom). After the first iteration, the trajectories are improved, but are far from being correct. In fact, not even one trajectory is correct. The trajectories after two, three, and four iterations are shown in Fig. 6(d)-(f), respectively. As can be seen, after each iteration the trajectories are refined. The fourth iteration results in correct trajectories, and the algorithm terminates.

We generated a real sequence in our laboratory to study the efficacy of our algorithm in real scenes. In the scene shown in Fig. 7, three blocks are moving such that their trajectories intersect. We manually obtained interesting points on these blocks. We selected several points on each block and applied our algorithm. In order to show the behavior of our algorithm, without unnecessary complications, we show results for the four points on three blocks.

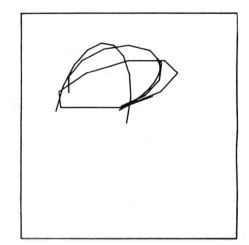

Fig. 4. The trajectories obtained by the algorithm for rotation of points in a sequence.

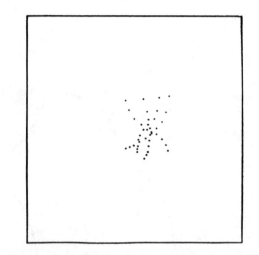

Fig. 5. A composite frame shows four points in ten frames. The points move from left to right in this figure.

The initial trajectories are shown in Fig. 8(a). The first iteration requires four corrections; the trajectories after each correction are shown in Fig. 8(b)-(e), respectively. The second iteration was enough to give the correct results, resulting in the trajectories shown in Fig. 8(f). The trajectories for all interesting points were successfully determined by our algorithm and are shown, for six frames, in Fig. 9. It required eight iterations for the convergence to final trajectories.

We applied this algorithm to a real sequence from a movie (*Superman*). The frames of the movie are shown in Fig. 10. We tracked manually selected points on the belt and head of three soldiers. These points are shown in Table I. Our algorithm converged after four iterations, giving the trajectories shown in Fig. 11. Although soldiers are moving in different directions, the motion is not really very complex, and this allowed the algorithm to converge very quickly for this case.

IX. MODIFIED GE ALGORITHM

A close look at the GE algorithm reveals that the correspondence for the first two frames is never altered as the

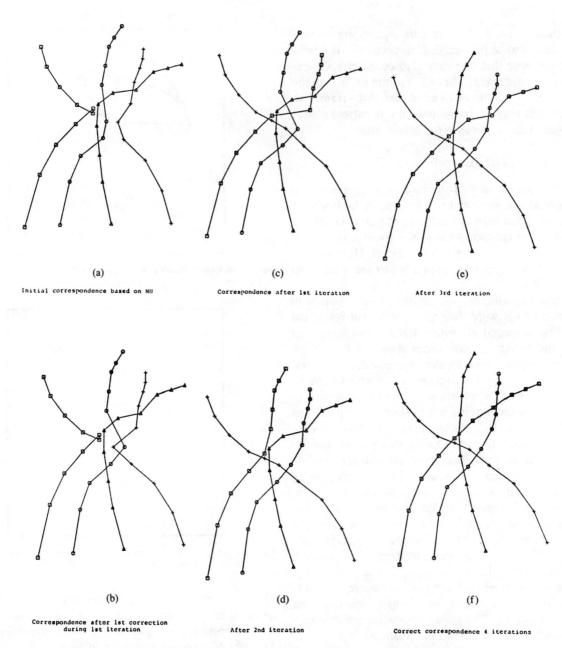

(a)

Initial correspondence based on NN

(c)

Correspondence after 1st iteration

(e)

After 3rd iteration

(b)

Correspondence after 1st correction
during 1st iteration

(d)

After 2nd iteration

(f)

Correct correspondence 4 iterations

Fig. 6. The trajectories of the points after several iterations and corrections are shown in this figure.

exchange loop operates from the second frame onward. Thus, for the above algorithm to provide correct correspondence, it is essential that the correspondence for the first two frames be correct to start with. Since the initial correspondence is based purely on the closeness of feature points in successive frames, the GE algorithm was found to give poor results for the case where the displacement of the objects was comparable to the object size. Fig. 12 shows a sequence generated in our laboratory to study the efficacy of this approach. The objects and their motion were selected to confuse the algorithm. Fig. 13(a) shows the trajectories obtained by the GE algorithm for one such laboratory-generated sequence. Clearly, the source of error in this case is the initial correspondence between the first two frames, which is never altered. In order to remove this kind of error source, we modified the GE al-

gorithm. The modified greedy exchange algorithm (MGE) essentially allows the exchange loop to operate in both directions, i.e., forward and backward. By changing the termination criterion to have a cascade of exchange free loops in either direction, it becomes possible to alter the correspondence in any frame. The steps of the MGE algorithm are given below.

A. MGE Algorithm

1. *Initialization:* Set the forward and backward iteration flags on. For each point in X^k, $k = 1, 2, \cdots$, $n - 1$, determine the nearest neighbor in X^{k+1} using these nearest neighbors, and initialize m trajectories.

2. *Forward Exchange Loop:* For each frame value $k = 2$ to $n - 1$:

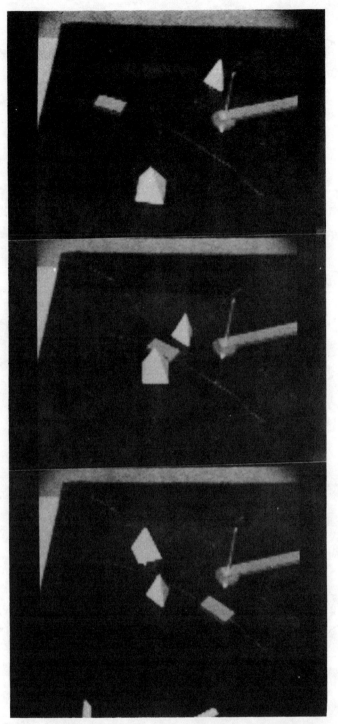

Fig. 7. Three frames of a block scene. The blocks were manually moved, and the interesting points were also manually obtained.

    a. Compute the gain g_{ij}^k for $i = 1$ to $m - 1$ and $j = i + 1$ to m.

    b. Pick the i–j pair providing the maximum gain.

    c. Exchange the points in the $(k + 1)$th frame on the T_i and T_j trajectories, and set the exchange flag on.

    d. Check the exchange flag at the end of the loop. If any exchange was made during the entire pass, set the backward iteration flag on and go back to the beginning of the forward exchange loop.

Otherwise, clear the forward iteration flag and go to the termination check step.

3. *Backward Exchange Loop:* For each frame value $k = n - 1$ to 2:

    a. Go through the exchange loop similarly to above, with exchanges now being made in the $(k - 1)$th frame.

    b. Check the exchange flag at the end of the loop. If any exchange was made, then set the forward iteration flat on and go back to the beginning of

(a)

Initial correspondence (::)

(b)

After First correction in 1st iteration

(c)

After 2nd correction in 1st iteration

(d)

After 3rd correction, 1st iteration

(e)

After 1st iteration

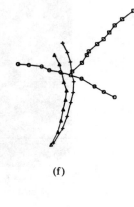

(f)

After 2nd iteration

Fig. 8. The trajectories of four points in the block scene. We considered ten frames.

the loop. Otherwise, clear the backward iteration flag and go to the termination check step.

4. *Termination Check:* Check the forward and backward iteration flags. If both are off, then stop; otherwise, go to the (forward/backward exchange) loop for which the corresponding flag is on.

Fig. 13(a) shows the trajectories which were obtained after the iterations ended in the forward exchange loop. Fig. 13(b) shows the trajectories which were available at the end of iterations in the backward exchange loop. The annoying correspondence of the first two frames has clearly been changed. The final and correct trajectories

544

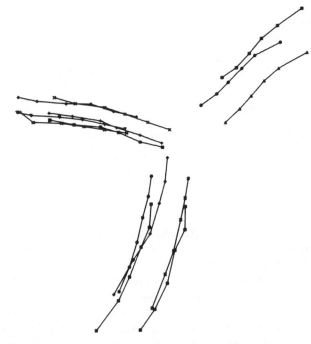

Fig. 9. Trajectories for all interesting points in six frames for the block scene.

are shown in Fig. 13(c), which required 22 iterations in the forward direction, 10 iterations in the backward direction, 8 iterations in the forward direction again, and 1 exchange-free iteration in the backward direction.

X. Occlusion

When working with a large sequence of frames, it is possible that some objects may disappear totally or partially. Similarly, some new objects may appear in the frame sequence from some intermediate frame onward. In order to handle the problem of occlusion in an effective way, it is necessary that the system have much more information than just the number and location of feature points. For example, consider the case of two rectangles moving linearly in different planes parallel to the optical axis of the camera. Suppose the positions of these two rectangles are as shown in Fig. 14(a) in one frame and in the next frame some of the different possibilities are as shown in Fig. 14(b)–(d).

For all the cases of the next frame shown above, a corner detector will detect eight feature points, and there is no way of telling whether an occlusion has occurred or not by simply looking at the number of feature points. In fact, until and unless some assumptions about the rigidity of the feature point configurations are made or the object structural information is available, it is difficult to say that an occlusion has occurred. Thus, it is our contention that for any method of correspondence analysis to be successful with respect to occlusion, much more information than just the number and location of feature points is needed.

Does this imply that the problem of occlusion cannot be taken care of when the only information available is the set of moving points? The answer is "no," as is evident from some psychological studies [30], [24]. It has

Fig. 10. Three frames from the *Superman* sequence. The points tracked by the algorithm are on the belt and head of the three soldiers that are running towards the camera.

TABLE I
POINTS FROM THE SUPERMAN SEQUENCE

Frame	Head-1; Belt-1	Head-2; Belt-2	Head-3; Belt-3
1	(73, 306); (72, 261)	(147, 305); (140, 240)	(295, 300); (290, 256)
2	(79, 302); (78, 261)	(154, 302); (147, 239)	(291, 296); (288, 254)
3	(86, 305); (83, 259)	(171, 301); (166, 234)	(278, 296); (276, 249)
4	(95, 312); (93, 261)	(189, 303); (185, 236)	(275, 304); (273, 253)
5	(95, 309); (95, 258)	(200, 303); (196, 238)	(266, 303); (263, 250)
6	(108, 307); (106, 256)	(229, 292); (222, 222)	(254, 303); (249, 244)
7	(120, 310); (119, 254)	(249, 300); (242, 228)	(251, 307); (243, 240)
8	(129, 313); (130, 252)	(256, 298); (257, 222)	(243, 307); (240, 236)
9	(138, 313); (137, 254)	(262, 301); (262, 222)	(250, 307); (242, 233)
10	(149, 307); (147, 245)	(268, 303); (271, 223)	(256, 305); (245, 229)

Fig. 11. The trajectories obtained by the algorithm after four iterations.

been shown that the human visual system is capable of filling in the missing points by relying on the integration of information over several frames. Shaw and Ramachandran [30] have determined that for the filling in to take place, it is necessary that at least two frames on either side of the frame with missing points be available. The availability of at least two frames on either side possibly allows the hypothesize-and-test situation where the missing point position is interpolated using the previous two frames and the interpolated value is tested against the subsequent two frames.

With respect to the concepts of path coherence and smoothness of motion, the findings of Shaw and Ramachandran are not surprising in the sense that with five frames the interpolated value of the feature point appears in all three local path coherence measures, which are integrated to verify the filling in by checking the overall smoothness of the motion. Thus, within the framework of feature point location alone, it is possible to hypothesize and test the occurrence of occlusion with the constraint that any change in the number of feature points signifies occlusion. We have found the following hypothesize-and-test occlusion algorithm useful in several experiments. The algorithm is discussed with respect to occlusion, but can be modified easily to take care of disocclusion.

A. Hypothesize-and-Test Occlusion Algorithm

Assumption: If the number of feature points is the same, then it implies no occlusion. There is only one frame in which some points disappear. For simplicity, we assume that, at least on one side of the frame with missing points, there are three frames available.

1) Determine the frame with some missing points. Let it be the pth frame, and let the number of points in this frame be $m_p (< m)$. Let A represent this set of points with individual points, denoted as A_j, $j = 1, 2, \cdots, m_p$.

2) Establish the correspondence using the MGE algorithm up to $(p - 1)$ frames and from the $(p + 1)$th frame to the nth frame. As per the stated assumption, it should be possible to obtain correspondence at least on one side, say, up to $(p - 1)$th frame.

3) For each of the m trajectories up to the $(p - 1)$th frame obtained through correspondence, predict the trajectory points for the pth frame using forward interpolation. Let this set of predicted points be denoted by P, and let P_i represent the predicted point for the ith trajectory.

4) For each A_j, $j = 1$ to m_p, determine the ordered list of nearest neighbors from the set P of predicted points.

5) From the ordered list of nearest neighbors for every A_j, construct the sets $N_1, N_2, \cdots, N_m$, respectively, as the set of the first nearest neighbors, the set of up to the second nearest neighbor, and through the set of up to the $(m - 1)$th nearest neighbors. Thus, if $P_i \in N_j$, then P_i is at least the jth nearest neighbor of one of the points from set A.

6) Count the number of distinct points from the sets N_j's for $j = 1$ to m. Stop at the set when the count value is the same as m_p, say, at the jth set. The remaining $(m - m_p)$ predicted points not in the jth set are then selected as candidate points for filling in. However, if no N_j with count value is m_p, then determine the set N_j with count values such that $count(N_j) < m_p < count(N_{j+1})$ predicted points as candidate points for filling in.

7) Complete the correspondence for n frames by using in the pth frame the given m_p points A and the candidate points from step 6).

8) For the case of multiple candidate sets for filling in, retain that candidate set which yields the best filling in measured in terms of D.

We applied the above algorithm to the frame sequence of Fig. 12. Points on the third and fourth trajectories from the fifth frame were suppressed, thus creating occlusion. The correspondence up to the fourth frame was then determined, and the points for the fifth frame were then predicted. Table II shows the location of 10 actual points from frames and 12 predicted points for frame 5. Table III gives the ordered set of nearest neighbors, while the set N_1, N_2, and N_3 is shown in Table IV.

The candidate points for filling in are then any two points from P_4, P_{11}, and P_{12}. Fig. 15(a)–(c) shows the

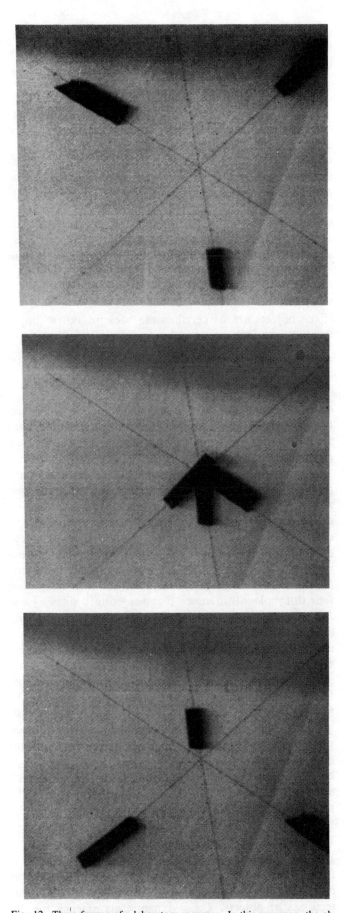

Fig. 12. Three frames of a laboratory sequence. In this sequence, the objects are of uniform color, and their shapes are also similar. At a point in the sequence, points of one object are not visible due to occlusion.

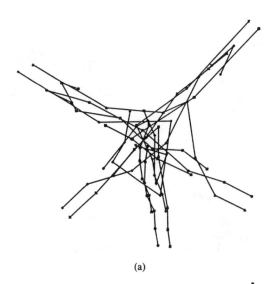

(a)

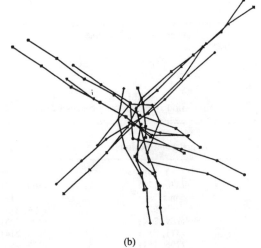

(b)

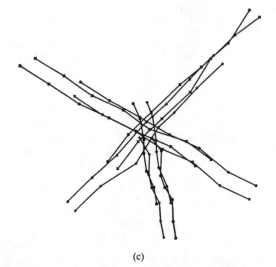

(c)

Fig. 13. The trajectories obtained by the modified algorithm. (a) The trajectory obtained after the first forward pass. (b) After the forward and backward pass. (c) After the forward, backward, and, again, forward passes.

trajectories obtained by using P_4-P_{12}, P_4-P_{11}, and $P_{11}-P_{12}$ as filling-in points, respectively.

Comparing these trajectories to the actual trajectory of Fig. 15(d), one important observation can be made, and

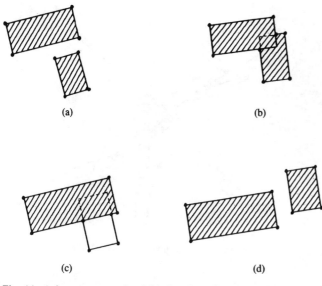

(a) (b)

(c) (d)

Fig. 14. A frame sequence in which there is occlusion, but the number of vertices remains same.

TABLE II
ACTUAL AND PREDICTED POSITION FOR FRAME

Trajectory Number	Actual Point Position	Predicted Point Position
1	(389, 195)	(386, 184)
2	(376, 171)	(360, 159)
3	missing	(313, 249)
4	missing	(276, 239)
5	(289, 214)	(292, 225)
6	(311, 212)	(318, 214)
7	(296, 151)	(275, 150)
8	(317, 149)	(298, 133)
9	(237, 189)	(256, 225)
10	(273, 173)	(299, 227)
11	(304, 262)	(329, 288)
12	(323, 250)	(342, 221)

TABLE III
ORDERED SETS OF NEAREST NEIGHBORS FOR A'S FROM P'S

A_1	$\{P_1, P_2, P_{12}, P_6, P_3, P_{10}, P_5, P_8, P_{11}, P_4, P_7, P_9\}$
A_2	$\{P_1, P_2, P_{12}, P_6, P_8, P_{10}, P_5, P_3, P_7, P_4, P_{11}, P_9\}$
A_5	$\{P_5, P_{10}, P_4, P_6, P_9, P_3, P_{12}, P_7, P_8, P_{11}, P_2, P_1\}$
A_6	$\{P_6, P_{10}, P_5, P_{12}, P_3, P_4, P_9, P_7, P_2, P_{11}, P_1, P_8\}$
A_7	$\{P_8, P_7, P_2, P_6, P_5, P_{10}, P_{12}, P_9, P_4, P_1, P_3, P_{11}\}$
A_8	$\{P_8, P_7, P_2, P_6, P_{12}, P_1, P_5, P_{10}, P_9, P_4, P_3, P_{11}\}$
A_9	$\{P_9, P_7, P_4, P_5, P_{10}, P_8, P_6, P_3, P_{12}, P_2, P_{11}, P_1\}$
A_{10}	$\{P_7, P_8, P_9, P_5, P_{10}, P_6, P_4, P_{12}, P_3, P_2, P_1, P_{11}\}$
A_{11}	$\{P_3, P_{10}, P_{11}, P_4, P_5, P_6, P_{12}, P_9, P_1, P_7, P_2, P_3\}$
A_{12}	$\{P_3, P_{10}, P_{12}, P_6, P_{11}, P_5, P_4, P_9, P_1, P_2, P_7, P_8\}$

TABLE IV

N_1	$\{P_1, P_3, P_5, P_6, P_7, P_8, P_9\}$	Count = 7
N_2	$\{P_1, P_2, P_3, P_5, P_6, P_7, P_8, P_9, P_{10}\}$	Count = 9
N_3	$\{P_1, P_2, P_3, P_4, P_5, P_6, P_7, P_8, P_9, P_{10}, P_{11}, P_{12}\}$	Count = 12

that is, irrespective of the candidate points for filling in, that the overall perception of the trajectories in limited occlusion is correct.

XI. OBJECT TRACKING VIA CENTROIDS

We mentioned earlier that the present approach for correspondence can be used to track objects by representing each moving object as a point, possibly the centroid. Since this object representation is very coarse, it is not necessary to perform a precise segmentation. It should be enough if every moving object can be located approximately in a frame. Difference pictures offer one such convenient way of roughly locating moving objects [13], [40]. Let the image sequence be represented as $F_1(x, y)$, $F_2(x, y)$, $\cdots$, $F_N(x, y)$. A difference picture $D_{ik}(x, y)$ is then obtained as

$$D_{ik}(x, y) = F_{i+k}(x, y) - F_i(x, y).$$

If the objects are darker than the background, a simple thresholding such as

$$D_{ik}(x, y) = 1 \qquad \text{if } D_{ik}(x, y) \geq T$$
$$= 0 \qquad \text{otherwise}$$

can then detect most of the moving object region in the frame F_i, provided k is suitably chosen. The threshold value T can be determined by looking at the difference picture histogram.

This difference picture computation scheme was applied to the image sequence of Fig. 7, which contains three moving objects with partial occlusion taking place in one of the frames. Since there was sufficient displacement of objects in successive frames, the value for k was taken to be 1. A threshold value of 20 for T was found to yield satisfactorily portions of moving object regions from differeint frames. Fig. 16 shows portions of interest from four thresholded difference pictures using frames F_3 and F_7. After performing the connectivity analysis and discarding regions with an area smaller than 20 pixels, moving object regions from each frame were extracted. Except for one difference picture, all others yielded three moving regions. Centroid values of these regions in different thresholded difference pictures were then used as the input data to the hypothesize-and-test occlusion algorithm. The trajectories obtained by this algorithm are shown in Fig. 17 where a big circle around one point indicates that the circled point was predicted. Thus, even by doing a crude segmentation, it is possible to track moving objects based solely on the location of one representative point per object.

XII. CONCLUSION

In this paper, we show that by considering an extended frame sequence, one can use coherence in spatio-temporal properties for establishing correspondence to obtain trajectories of objects. Quasi-dynamic approaches for the analysis of motion try to solve all problems in a *minimum* number of frames. Obviously, the limited amount of data

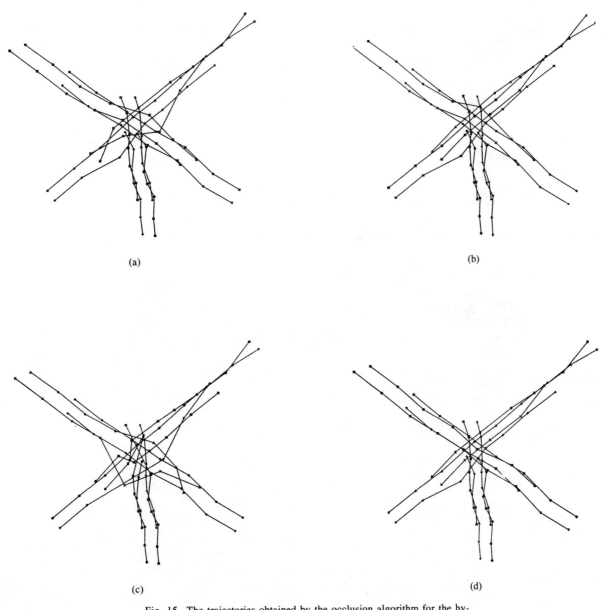

Fig. 15. The trajectories obtained by the occlusion algorithm for the hypothesized candidate pairs. (a) P_4–P_{12}. (b) P_4–P_{11}. (c) P_{11}–P_{12}. (d) The actual trajectories.

in the temporal domain necessitates some assumptions on the nature of objects. More importantly, such approaches require methods that are complex and sensitive to noise. By considering *dynamic scenes*, we can use techniques that can successively refine the information recovered from the sequence. Such methods are much less sensitive to noise and can usually be performed very fast. The smoothness of motion allows us to establish correspondence in case of occlusion of points also, in a limited situation. This is very encouraging because in most approaches to occlusion analysis one requires information about features also.

In this paper, we considered only the correspondence problem. After the trajectories are established, one may try to recover the structure of objects. As shown in [31], [28], one may use parameters of curves representing trajectories to obtain the motion characteristics and structure

of objects. It seems that one may use successive refinement in the recovery of the structure also.

The proposed approach assumes that the motion is smooth. Indeed, in many applications, one is required to detect points of discontinuities in motion. The discontinuities in motion play an important role in the analysis and verbalization of the motion of objects. We are studying techniques for detecting discontinuities in motion characteristics and their use in describing the motion of objects [7].

It should be mentioned here that in our algorithm we did not use any characteristics of points. The trajectories were determined using only locations of points in frames. The robustness and computations can be improved by considering pictorial characteristics of points in frames. This additional information may play a very important role in the initialization phase of the algorithm by eliminating

Fig. 16. The difference pictures for the sequence of Fig. 7. (a) D_{34}. (b) D_{45}. (c) D_{56}. (d) D_{67}. Note that due to occlusion D_{56} has only two regions.

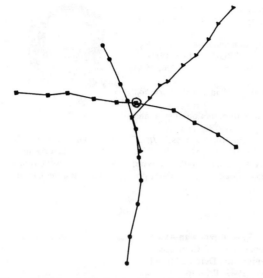

Fig. 17. The trajectories obtained using the centroids of regions in difference pictures. The predicted point is circled.

unlikely groupings of points, even if they are close to each other.

ACKNOWLEDGMENT

We are thankful to P. Besl and S. Haynes for many useful discussions and criticisms during the course of this work and to M. Shah, C. Born, V. Salari, and S. Vemuri for helping us in performing experiments.

REFERENCES

[1] S. T. Barnard and W. B. Thompson, "Disparity analysis of images," *IEEE Trans. Pattern Anal. Mach. Intell.*, vol. PAMI-2, pp. 333–340, 1980.

[2] M. Brady, "Parallelism in vision," *Artif. Intell.*, vol. 21, pp. 271–283, 1983.

[3] J. Donner, J. S. Lappin, and G. Perfetto, "Detection of three-dimensional structure in moving optical patterns," *J. Exper. Psychol.: Human Perception Performance*, vol. 10. no. 1, pp. 1, 1984.

[4] L. S. Dreschler and H.-H. Nagel, "Volumetric model and 3-D trajectory of a moving car derived from monocular TV-frame sequences of a street scene," *Comput. Graphics Image Processing*, vol. 20, pp. 199–228, 1982.

[5] B. E. Flinchbaugh and B. Chandrasekaran, "A theory of spatio-temporal aggregation for vision," *Artif. Intell.*, vol. 17, pp. 387–408, 1981.

[6] J. J. Gibson, *The Ecological Approach to Visual Perception.* Boston, MA: Houghton Mifflen, 1979.

[7] S. M. Haynes and R. Jain, "Low level motion event: Trajectory discontinuities," in *Proc. First Conf. AI Appl.*, pp. 251–256.

[8] E. C. Hildreth, "Computations underlying the measurement of visual motion," *Artif. Intell.*, vol. 23, pp. 309–354, 1984.

[9] D. D. Hoffman and B. E. Flinchbaugh, "The interpretation of biological motion," M.I.T., Cambridge, MA, AI Memo. 608, 1980.

[10] B. K. P. Horn and B. G. Schunck, "Determining optical flow," *Artif. Intell.*, vol. 17, pp. 185–203, 1981.

[11] R. Jain, "Direct computation of the focus of expansion," *IEEE Trans. Pattern Anal. Mach. Intell.*, vol. PAMI-5, pp. 58–64, 1983.

[12] R. Jain and S. Haynes, "Imprecision in computer vision," *IEEE Comput.*, Aug. 1982.

[13] R. Jain and H.-H. Nagel, "On the analysis of difference and accumulative difference pictures in dynamic scene analysis," *IEEE Trans. Pattern Anal. Mach. Intell.*, vol. PAMI-1, pp. 206–214, 1979.

[14] C. P. Jerian and R. Jain, "Determining motion parameters for scenes with translation and rotation," in *Proc. Workshop Motion: Representation Contr.*, Toronto, Ont., Canada, Apr. 4–6, 1983.

[15] M. Jenkin, "Tracking three dimensional moving light displays," in *Proc. Workshop Motion: Representation Contr.*, Toronto, Ont., Canada, 1983, pp. 66–70.

[16] G. Johansson, "Spatio-temporal differentiation and integration in visual motion perception," *Psych. Res.*, vol. 38, pp. 379–383, 1976.

[17] D. Marr, "Early processing of visual information," *Phil. Trans. Roy. Soc. London B*, vol. 275, pp. 483–524, 1976.

[18] K. M. Mutch and W. B. Thompson, "Analysis of accretion and deletion at boundaries in dynamic scenes," *IEEE Trans. Pattern Anal. Mach. Intell.*, vol. PAMI-7, pp. 133–138, Mar. 1985.

[19] U. Neisser, *Cognition and Reality.* San Francisco, CA: Freeman, 1976.

[20] N. G. O'Brien and R. Jain, "Axial motion stereo," in *Proc. Workshop Comput. Vision*, Annapolis, MD, 1984.

[21] J. O'Rourke and N. I. Badler, "Model-based image analysis of human motion using constraint propagation," *IEEE Trans. Pattern Anal. Mach. Intell.*, vol. PAMI-2, pp. 522–536, 1980.

[22] K. Prazdny, "Egomotion and relative depth map from optical flow," *Biol. Cybernet.*, vol. 36, pp. 87–102, 1980.

[23] J. M. Prager and M. A. Arbib, "Computing the optic flow: The MATCH algorithm and prediction," *Comput. Vision, Graphics, Image Processing*, vol. 24, pp. 271–304, 1983.

[24] V. S. Ramachandran and S. M. Anstis, "Extrapolation of motion path in human visual perception," *Vision Res.*, vol. 23, pp. 83–85, 1984.

[25] R. F. Rashid, "Towards a system for the interpretation of moving light displays," *IEEE Trans. Pattern Anal. Mach. Intell.*, vol. PAMI-2, pp. 574–581, 1980.

[26] J. H. Rieger and D. T. Lawton, "Determining the instantaneous axis of translation from optic flow generated by arbitrary sensor motion," in *Proc. Workshop Motion*, Toronto, Ont., Canada, 1983, pp. 33–41.

[27] J. W. Roach and J. K. Aggarwal, "Determining the movement of objects from a sequence of images," *IEEE Trans. Pattern Anal. Mach. Intell.*, vol. PAMI-2, pp. 554–562, Nov. 1980.

[28] I. K. Sethi and R. Jain, "Determining three dimensional structure of rotating objects using a sequence of monocular views," Dep. Comput. Sci., Wayne State Univ., Detroit, MI, Tech. Rep., 1983.

[29] M. A. Shah and R. Jain, "Detecting time varying corners," *Comput. Vision, Graphics, Image Processing*, vol. 28, pp. 345–355, 1984.

[30] G. L. Shaw and V. S. Ramachandran, "Interpolation during apparent motion," *Perception*, vol. 11, pp. 491–494, 1982.

[31] J. T. Todd, "Visual information about rigid and nonrigid motion: A geometric analysis," *J. Exper. Psychol. Human Perception Performance*, vol. 8, pp. 238–252, 1982.

[32] R. Y. Tsai and T. S. Huang, "Estimating three-dimensional motion parameters of a rigid planar patch," in *Proc. PRIP*, 1981, pp. 94–97.

[33] ——, "Uniqueness and estimation of three-dimensional motion parameters or rigid objects with curved surfaces," in *Proc. IEEE Conf. Pattern Recognition Image Processing*, 1982, pp. 112–118.

[34] R. Y. Tsai, T. S. Huang, and W. L. Zhu, "Estimating three-dimen-

sional motion parameters of a rigid planar patch, II: Singular value decomposition," *IEEE Trans. Acoust., Speech, Signal Processing*, vol. ASSP-30, pp. 525–534.

[35] J. K. Tsotsos, "A framework for visual motion understanding," Dep. Comput. Sci., Univ. Toronto, Tech. Rep. CSRG-114, June 1980.

[36] S. Ullman, *The Interpretation of Visual Motion*. Cambridge, MA: M.I.T. Press, 1979.

[37] A. M. Waxman, "An image flow paradigm," in *Proc. Workshop Comput. Vision*, Annapolis, MD, 1984.

[38] J. A. Webb and J. K. Aggarwal, "Structure from motion of rigid and jointed objects," *Artif. Intell.*, vol. 19, pp. 107–130, 1982.

[39] T. D. William, "Depth from motion in real world scenes," *IEEE Trans. Pattern Anal. Mach. Intell.*, vol. PAMI-2, pp. 511–516, 1980.

[40] M. Yachida, M. Asada, and S. Tsuji, "Automatic analysis of moving images," *IEEE Trans. Pattern Anal. Mach. Intell.*, vol. PAMI-3, pp. 12–19, Jan. 1981.

Ramesh Jain (M'79–SM'83) received the B.E. degree from Nagpur University, India, in 1969, and the Ph.D. degree from the Indian Institute of Technology, Kharagpur, India, in 1975.

He is an Associate Professor of Electrical Engineering and Computer Science at the University of Michigan, Ann Arbor. His current research interest is in computer vision and artificial intelligence. Formerly he worked at Wayne State University, Detroit, MI, the University of Texas, Austin, the University of Hamburg, West Germany, and the Indian Institute of Technology.

Dr. Jain is a member of the Association for Computing Machinery, the American Association for Artificial Intelligence, the Pattern Recognition Society, and the Cognitive Science Society.

Ishwar K. Sethi (M'78) is currently an Associate Professor in the Department of Computer Science, Wayne State University, Detroit, MI, which he joined in September 1982. Prior to that he was on the faculty at the Indian Institute of Technology, Kharagpur, India, for eleven years. His research interests include computer vision, image processing, and pattern recognition.

Dr. Sethi is a member of the Association for Computing Machinery.

International Journal of Computer Vision, 3, 33–49 (1989)
© 1989 Kluwer Academic Publishers, Boston. Manufactured in The Netherlands

Generalizing Epipolar-Plane Image Analysis on the Spatiotemporal Surface

H. HARLYN BAKER
ROBERT C. BOLLES
Artificial Intelligence Center, SRI International, 333 Ravenswood Avenue Menlo Park, CA 94025

Abstract

The previous implementations of our *Epipolar-Plane Image Analysis* mapping technique demonstrated the feasibility and benefits of the approach, but were carried out for restricted camera geometries. The question of more general geometries made the technique's utility for autonomous navigation uncertain. We have developed a generalization of our analysis that (a) enables varying view direction, including variation over time (b) provides three-dimensional connectivity information for building coherent spatial descriptions of observed objects; and (c) operates sequentially, allowing initiation and refinement of scene feature estimates while the sensor is in motion. To implement this generalization it was necessary to develop an explicit description of the evolution of images over time. We have achieved this by building a process that creates a set of two-dimensional manifolds defined at the zeros of a three-dimensional spatiotemporal Laplacian. These manifolds represent explicitly both the spatial and temporal structure of the temporally evolving imagery, and we term them *spatiotemporal surfaces.* The surfaces are constructed incrementally, as the images are acquired. We describe a tracking mechanism that operates locally on these evolving surfaces in carrying out three-dimensional scene reconstruction.

Introduction

1.1 Epipolar-Plan Image Analysis

In an earlier publication in this journal [1], we described a sequence analysis technique developed for use in obtaining depth estimates for points in a static scene. The approach bridged the usual dichotomy of passive depth sensing in that its large number of images led to a large baseline and thus high accuracy, while rapid image sampling gave minimal change from frame to frame, eliminating the correspondence problem. Rather than choosing quite disparate views and putting features into correspondence by stereo matching, with this technique we chose to process massive amounts of similar data, but with much simpler and more robust techniques. The technique capitalized on several constraints we could impose on the image acquisition process, namely:

1. The camera moved along a linear path.

2. It acquired images at equal spacing as it moved.
3. The camera's view was orthogonal to its direction of travel.

With these constraints, we could guarantee that

1. Individual scene features would be observed in single epipolar planes over the period of scanning.
2. Images of these planes could be constructed by collecting corresponding image scan lines in successive frames.
3. The motion of scene features in these images would appear as linear tracks.

We termed these image planes *epipolar-plane images,* or EPIs, and the process *Epipolar-Plane Image Analysis.*

1.2 Problems with the Previous Approach

In that earlier paper we commented on our previous dissatisfactions with the approach, and the limitations that would restrict its usefulness. Summarizing, the limitations were

L_1 Orthogonal viewing would preclude many of the camera attitudes one would expect to be necessary for an autonomous vehicle—notably that attitude in which the vehicle is looking along its direction of motion, or when it is to track some particular feature and follow it while moving across the scene.

L_2 A constant rate of image acquisition would be difficult to guarantee, and probably not be desirable in a general context. Sampling rates will be affected heavily by computational demands on the system, and vehicle velocities may be dictated by higher-level concerns.

L_3 A linear path would be an unacceptable or highly improbable trajectory in most every situation except extended flight.

L_4 Static scenes are the *least* likely—winds blow, clouds move; often a moving object in a scene is the one of most interest.

The dissatisfactions were

D_1 The analysis should proceed sequentially as the imagery is acquired. To insist that all data be available before scene measurement can begin would eliminate one of the principal goals of the process—to provide timely information for a vehicle in motion.

D_2 The EPI partitioning, through its selection of the temporal over the spatial analysis of images, could not provide spatially coherent results. It produced point sets. We attempted clustering operations on these, but were never satisfied with such a post hoc approach. The proper approach to obtaining spatial coherence in our results would begin with not losing it in the first place.

2 New Approach to EPI Analysis

2.1 Generalizations

We have developed generalizations to our earlier approach that enable us to resolve L_1, L_2, D_1, and

D_2. Arbitrary and varying camera attitudes and velocities are permissible in our new formulation, and we process the data sequentially as acquired, forming estimates, of increasing precision, descriptive of spatial contours rather than points. The generalizations also suggest a mechanism for dealing with the nonlinear path issue of L_3. Although we have not pursued this as yet, in section 3.4 we outline an approach consistent with our EPI analysis.

L_4 rises as an incompatibility between our performance desires for a vision system and our definition of the task we choose to address. We wish to build three-dimensional descriptions of scenes, and it is inappropriate to expect this to be possible if our view of the scene is undergoing change unrelated to our active pursuit of observations. In our previous publication we discussed this motion issue, and suggested means to recognize its presence in a scene. Once distinguished from the static elements, it would be possible to invoke higher-order models and filters to estimate these objects' dynamics (as done by Broida and Chellappa [2] and Gennery [3], but our current interest is in modeling static structure.

It is worth repeating this to clarify our goals in the current work. We are not working with changing scenes, nor is our aim to build descriptions of moving or deforming objects. Our camera is all that moves, and any changes in the imagery arise strictly from this movement. Our goal is to model the geometry of a real static scene through which the camera is moving. This distinguishes us from most of the current efforts in spatiotemporal analysis that use image-plane velocities for measuring arbitrary flows (for example Heeger [7]), or that combine the measured flow with assumptions of constant 3D motion and rigidity for estimating known-order analytic surfaces (i.e., Waxman and Wohn [4], Waxman et al. [5], and Subbarao [6]).

In common with our earlier work, our new approach involves the processing of a very large number of images acquired by a moving camera. The analysis is based on three constraints:

1. The camera's movement is restricted to lie along a linear path.
2. The camera's position and attitude at each imaging site are known.

3. Image capture is rapid enough with respect to camera movement and scene scale to ensure that the data is, in general, temporally continuous.

Within this framework, we generalize from the traditional notion of epipolar *lines* to that of epipolar *planes*—a set of epipolar lines sharing a property of transitivity (which we discuss in section 2.2). We formulate a tracking process that exploits this property for determining the position of features in the scene. This tracking occurs on

what we term the *spatiotemporal surface*—a surface defining the evolution of a set of scene features over time. Critical to visualizing this space-time approach is obtaining an understanding of the geometry of the sensing situation, and this is described in the next section.

2.2 Geometric Considerations of Camera Path and Attitude

Figure 1 shows the geometry pertaining to our analysis, indicating several imaging positions

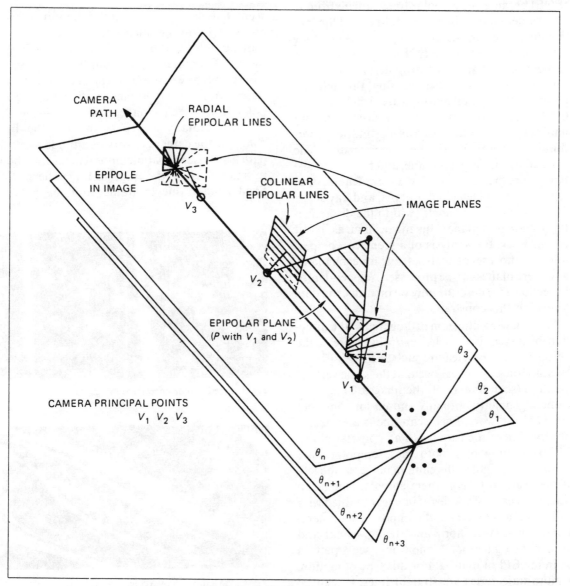

Fig. 1. General epipolar configuration.

and attitudes along a straight path. The camera is modeled as a pin-hole with image plane in front of the lens. For each feature P in the scene and two viewing positions such as V_1 and V_2, there is an *epipolar plane* that passes through P and the line joining the two lens centers. This plane intersects the two image planes along corresponding *epipolar lines* (note that, here, intersection and projection are, in a sense, equivalent). An *epipole* is the intersection of an image plane with the line joining the lens centers. In motion analysis, an epipole is often referred to as the *focus of expansion* (FOE) because the epipolar lines radiate from it. The camera moves in a straight line, and the lens centers at the various viewing positions lie along this line. Notice that the FOE is the image of the camera path. This structuring divides the scene into a pencil of planes passing through the camera path, several of which are sketched (θ_1, θ_2, θ_3, θ_n, ..., θ_{n+3}). This pencil is crucial to our analysis. We view the space as a cylindrical coordinate system with axis the camera path, angle defined by the epipolar plane, and radius the distance from the axis. Note that a scene feature is restricted to a single epipolar plane, and any scene features at the same angle (within the discretization) share that plane. This means that, as in our earlier work, the analysis of a scene can be partitioned into a set of analyses, one for each plane, and these planes can be processed independently. In section 3 we describe how we organize the data to exploit this constraint.

With viewing direction orthogonal to the direction of travel, as depicted at V_2 in figure 1, the epipolar lines for a feature such as P are horizontal scan lines, and these occur at the same vertical position (scan line) in all the images. This is the camera geometry normally chosen for computer stereo vision work. Each scan line is a projected observation of the features in an epipolar plane. The projection of P onto these epipolar lines moves to the right as the camera moves to the left. If one were to take a single epipolar line (scan line) from each of a series of images obtained with this camera geometry and compose a spatiotemporal image, with horizontal being spatial and vertical being temporal, one would see a pattern as in the EPI of figure 2. For this type of motion, feature trajectories are straight lines, as can be

Fig. 2. Orthogonal viewing.

seen. This is the case handled by our previous analysis. If, on the other hand, the camera were moving with an attitude as shown at V_3 in figure 1, the set of epipolar lines would form a pattern as shown in figure 3. For this type of motion, feature trajectories are hyperbolas. Notice that the epipolar lines are no longer scan lines—they are oriented radially and pass through the FOE. Allowing the camera to vary its attitude along the path gives rise to spatiotemporal images as shown in figure 4. Here, the epipolar line pattern is not fixed from frame to frame, and the paths of

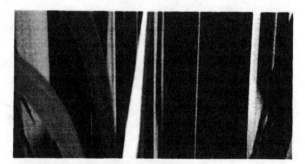

Fig. 3. Fixed, nonorthogonal viewing.

Fig. 4. View direction varying.

features in the EPI are neither linear nor hyperbolic—in fact they are arbitrary curves.

The transitivity property mentioned in section 2.1 arises from the fact that any pair of lines selected from the set form a corresponding pair. That is, for the set of epipolar lines $E^\theta = (e_0^\theta, e_1^\theta, \ldots, e_n^\theta)$ from epipolar plane θ over images I_0 through I_n, any two members comprise a pair of corresponding epipolar lines—e_0^θ with e_1^θ, e_3^θ with e_7^θ, et cetera. This occurs because the camera's linear path guarantees that a single pencil of planes defines the epipolar mapping over the entire sequence. Thus, any mapping done on the basis of e_0^θ with e_1^θ and then e_1^θ with e_2^θ implies the mapping of e_0^θ with e_2^θ. A similar argument holds for all pairs of mappings in E^θ, and the transitivity follows. If the camera path were nonlinear, no single pencil of planes could be defined, and no such set E^θ could be formed. The only complicating detail with the varying-attitude case (as indicated in figure 4) is that the pattern of epipolar lines changes from image to image: For a fixed camera attitude the pattern is the same for all images in the sequence.

2.3 Keeping the Problem Linear

Recall that our goal is to determine the position of stationary features in the scene: We do this by tracking their appearance over time as they project onto these epipolar planes. Obviously in the case of orthogonal viewing (e.g., as in figure 2 and at V_2 in figure 1), the tracking is linear. For general camera attitudes, including varying, it is nonlinear. Computational considerations make it extremely advantageous for the tracking to be posed as a linear problem. To maintain the linearity regardless of viewing direction, we find not linear feature paths in the EPIs (figures 2 through 4), but linear paths in a *dual space*. The insight here (introduced by Marimont [8]) is that no matter where a camera roams about a scene, for any particular feature, the *lines of sight* from the camera's principle point through that feature in space all intersect at the feature (modulo the measurement error). A line of sight is determined by the line from the principal point through the point in the image plane where the projected feature is ob-

served. From mathematical duality, the duals of these lines of sight lie along a line whose dual is the scene point (see figure 5); fitting a point to the lines of sight is a linear problem. This, then, gives us a metric for linear tracking of features: We map feature image coordinates to lines of sight, and use an optimal estimator to determine the point that minimizes the variance from those lines of sight.

Our estimation is done in the scene Cartesian space, not the dual space, because the error metric, nonlinear in the dual space, has more intuitive meaning and better behavior in scene space. The estimated error in each observation is a function of the size of the Gaussian filter employed and the distance of the feature from the camera. We currently model only these uncertainties in image-plane observations, and not others related to the strength of the feature signal or uncertainty in the position of the camera. These others will have to be modeled in a complete solution.

2.4 Transformations Required

Having decided on a representation that restores the linearity of our estimator, we must now demonstrate a mechanism for extracting the feature observations from the individual images in which they occur and grouping them by epipolar plane. Only in the case of viewing angle orthogonal to the motion is this grouping simple (figure 2), and this was the case our earlier work addressed. To obtain this structuring in the general cases, we could take one of two approaches. The first is to *transform the images* from the Cartesian space in which they are sampled to an epipolar representation (as has been done by Baker et al. [9] and by Jain et al. [10]). Because of aliasing effects (particularly on the observation variances) and nonlinearities in the mapping (it is singular when the FOE is in the image, and could require an infinite imaging surface for the reprojection), we prefer to avoid this transformation. Probably the best solution would be to use a sensor that delivers the data directly in the epipolar form—a spherical sensor having meridian scanning would accomplish this (the flow geometry that is the basis for such a sensor was discussed by Gib-

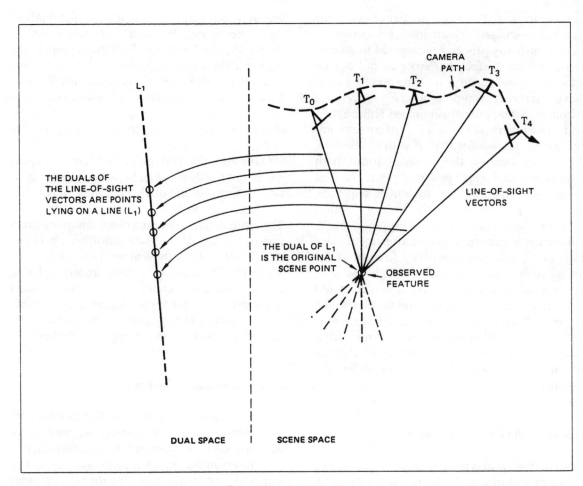

Fig. 5. Line-of-sight duality.

son [11] nearly forty years ago). Because such a sensor is not yet available, we choose an alternate approach: to *transform the features* we detect in image space to the desired epipolar space, the cylindrical coordinate system of figure 1. Here the singularity at the FOE presents no problem, and the observation variances are uniform. The structure we have developed for implementing this transformation brings us several other advantages, as the next section describes.

3 The Spatiotemporal Surface

3.1 Structuring the Data— Spatiotemporal Connectivity

We collect the data as a sequence of images, in fact stacking them up as they are acquired into a spatiotemporal volume, as shown in figure 6. As each new image is obtained, we construct its *spatial* and *temporal* edge contours. These contours are three-dimensional zeros of the Laplacian of a chosen three-dimensional Gaussian (Buxton and Buxton [12] and Heeger [7] also use spatiotemporal convolution over an image sequence), and the construction produces a spatiotemporal *surface* enveloping the signed *volumes* (note that, in two dimensions, edge contours envelop signed *regions*). The *spatial* connectivity in this structure lets us explicitly maintain object coherence between features observed on separate epipolar planes; the *temporal* connectivity gives us, as before, the tracking of features over time. See the companion paper in this issue [13] for a description of how these surfaces are constructed.

The need for maintaining this spatial connec-

Fig. 6. Spatiotemporal volume.

tivity can be observed by viewing our earlier results [1], one set of which is shown in figure 7. There, in processing the EPIs independently, we obtained separate planes of isolated scene feature estimates. Wishing to exploit the fact that there should be some spatial coherence between these sets of points, we used proximity of the resulting estimates on adjacent planes to filter outliers. Features not within the error (covariance) ellipses of those above or below them (i.e., those which could not be joined into a 3-space contour) were discarded. The remaining point field (figure 7) was sparse and fragmented, and not really representative of the continuous solid surfaces visible in the scene. The problem, however, did not lie with this post hoc filtering but with the loss of spa-

tial connectivity in the first place. Our separation of the data into EPIs, and then subsequent independent processing of these, lost the spatial connectivity apparent in the original images. We maintained instead the temporal connectivity that was critical to the feature tracking. For spatial connectivity in the scene reconstruction, spatial connectivity in the imagery must be preserved. The next two figures present a simplified example of this spatial and temporal connectivity. Figure 8 shows a sequence of simulated images depicting a camera zooming in on a set of rectangles; figure 9 shows a rendered view of the spatiotemporal surfaces arising from this motion. The spatial and temporal interpretation of these surfaces should be quite apparent.

Fig. 7. Orthogonally viewed scene: Results (displayed for crossed-eye viewing).

In our spatiotemporal-surface representation, feature observations bear (u, v, t) coordinates, and are spatiotemporal *voxel facets*. Figure 12 shows a mesh description of the facets for the spatiotemporal surfaces associated with the forward-viewing sequence whose first and last images are depicted in figure 10. These images are much more complex than those of figure 8. Let us reemphasize that the surface is defined at the zeros of a Laplacian of a 3D Gaussian applied over the sequence: There is no thresholding, and the features are simply zero crossings. In the interest of clarity, the surface representations we

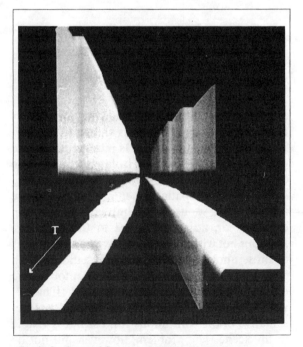

Fig. 9. Surfaces of figure 8 rendered for display.

Fig. 8. Simulation: Linear path, motion toward center.

Fig. 10. Sequence 1st and 128th images.

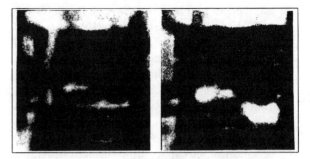

Fig. 11. 1st and 128th images at 1/8 resolution.

will show in the remaining figures are based on a simplified version of this imagery—one-eighth the linear resolution of the originals. Figure 11 shows these two frames at the reduced resolution.

Others have addressed this problem of combining spatial and temporal information, although no one has either built surfaces such as these or attempted to maintain explicit track of the temporal change. Perhaps the closest is Waxman [14], who discusses the use of *evolving contours*—isolated 2D contours whose projections over time can be used in deriving the shape of a restricted class of analytic surfaces. He provides no method for tracking the contours

through time, however, or for extracting them from real images—nor does he develop a methodology for utilizing the temporal evolution of individual components of the contours over multiple frames. Later work by Waxman and colleagues [15], presenting *convected activation profiles*, involves spatiotemporal convolution of Gaussian gradients applied at features detected in the individual spatial images by a DOG operator. In this, estimates of image-plane velocities are formed from quotients of the spatiotemporal gradients. There is, however, no estimate of scene motion, and no notion of motion associated with specific objects in the field of view—motion

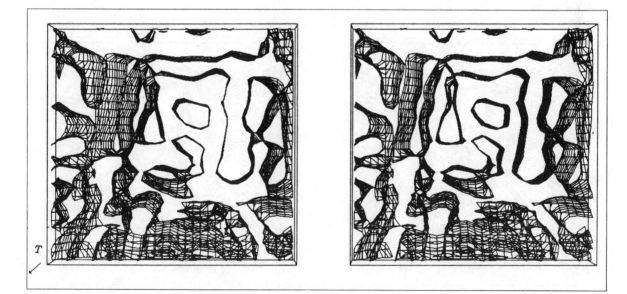

Fig. 12. Spatiotemporal-surface representation, first 10 frames.

is ascribed to pixels in the plane. Others, for example Hildreth and Grzywacz [16], who work with velocity point sets, and Negahdaripour and Horn [17], who determine relative motion of a plane from image gradients, also do not address these issues of local shape, establishing correspondence over time, associating movement with objects, or extracting the measures from real images. Although we have directed our efforts only at ego motion, our space-time surfaces provide a complete representation of these other projective velocity measures, and maintain a continuous track relating them to their underlying scene features. Our work in the future will include looking into using the surface representation for this more general form of motion analysis.

3.2 Structuring the Data— Epipolar-Plane Representation

As mentioned in the previous section, for nonorthogonal viewing directions, epipolar lines are not distinguished by the spatial v scan-line coordinate. To obtain this necessary structuring we develop within the spatiotemporal-surface representation an *embedded* representation that makes the epipolar organization explicit. Over each of the sequential images, we transform the (u, v, t) coordinates of our spatiotemporal zeros to (r, h, θ) *cylindrical coordinates* (θ indicates the epipolar-plane angle ($\theta \, \varepsilon \, [0,2\pi]$); the quantized resolution in θ is a supplied parameter; and the transform for each image is determined by the particular camera parameters). In this new coordinate system, we build a structure similar to our earlier EPI edge contours, but dynamically organized by epipolar plane. This is done by *intersecting* the spatiotemporal surfaces with the pencil of appropriate epipolar planes (as figure 1). We weave the epipolar connectivity through the spatiotemporal volume, following the known camera viewing direction changes. Figure 13 shows a sampling of the spatiotemporal surfaces as they intersect the pencil of epipolar planes (every fifth plane is depicted). You will notice the obvious radial flow pattern away from the epipole (FOE). Figure 14 shows seven of these surface/ plane intersections, along with the associated bounding planes (refer to figure 1). The edge that all share is the camera path (the epipole). These seven planes show exactly the contours one would detect in spatiotemporal intensity images such as depicted in figure 3.

In figure 15 we isolate a single surface from the top left of figure 12, and shows its spatiotemporal structure. Figure 16 shows the same surface structured by its epipolar-plane components. The

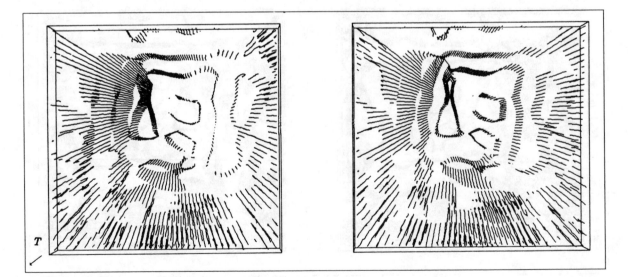

Fig. 13. Epipolar-plane surface representation.

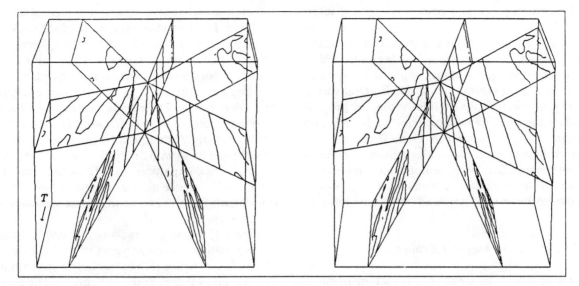

Fig. 14. Intersection: 7 epipolar planes, spatiotemporal surfaces.

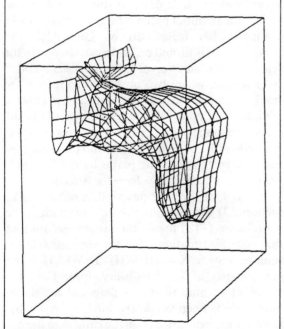

Fig. 15. Spatiotemporal surface.

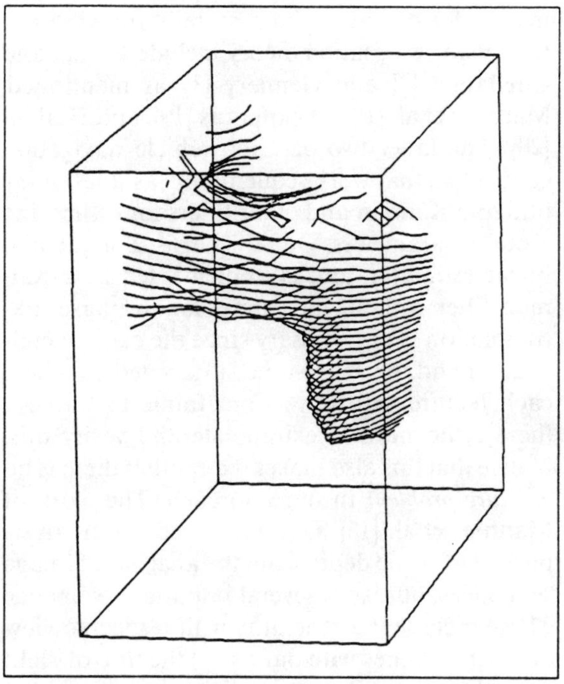

Fig. 16. Epipolar planes.

companion paper [13] gives details of the intersection operation on the spatiotemporal surface. Recall that the displays are in space-time image coordinates. If the camera had been allowed to vary its attitude, the planes depicted in figure 14 would appear skewed, perhaps helical, mirroring the migration of epipolar lines as they are projected on the imaging surface. They might vary in a manner similar to that in which figure 4 varies from figure 2, and for similar reasons. To facilitate presentation, we have not demonstrated this more general camera movement; it is, however, covered by our analysis and implementation.

3.3 Feature Tracking and Estimation

Our approach to scene reconstruction involves tracking scene features as they move in space-time, and to use techniques from estimation theory in approximating and maintaining estimates of their position. This is in distinction with, for example, the work of Hildreth and Grzywacz [16], Waxman and Wohn [4], and others who do not utilize this particular mathematics. Researchers who have built tracking systems using estimation theory include Broida and Chellappa [2] and Gennery [3], as mentioned, Matthies et al. [18], Dickmanns [19], and Hallam [20]. The latter two describe vehicle navigation controllers that work sequentially (as does ours), utilizing Kalman and other filters for estimating motion parameters. Our tracker is a sequential linear estimator, and is implemented as a Kalman filter without the extrapolation phase. Extrapolation is unnecessary since the camera constraints and the space-time surface tell us where each feature will move from frame to frame—there is no need to extrapolate and verify this. Notice that this also makes it clear that there is no *aperture problem* in our approach. The work of Matthies et al. [18] has similarities to ours in its pursuit of scene depth from the analysis of image sequences, but lacks several important elements. These include the generality with respect to view angle that comes with our use of the line-of-sight formulation, and the explicit use of spatial connectivity—they obtain only scene point estimates (as we had with our earlier approach),

rather than higher-level descriptors such as scene contours. Furthermore, they must establish feature correspondence via correlation between frames, and this is not necessary with the spatiotemporal surface. On the other hand, we do not aim currently at producing the dense depth maps that they do. Their depth maps are obtained through a combination of tracking and regularization: When we attempt full-surface reconstruction, we will do so with analysis over scale (as discussed in the companion paper [13]), and through the use of inference on the computed free space (the determination of scene free space was shown in our earlier paper [1]).

Figure 17 shows the tracking of scene features on the spatiotemporal surfaces in the vicinity of the surface of figure 15. The tracking occurs along paths such as those shown in figure 16. The final pair shows, in crossed-eye stereo form, the result of the tracking after 10 frames. The coding is as follows: initiation of a feature tracking is marked by a circle; the leading observation of a feature (active front) is shown as an $\times$; lines join feature observations; 5 observations (an arbitrary number, 2 may be sufficient) must be acquired before an estimate is made of the feature's position—at that point an initial batch estimate is made, and a Kalman filter (discussed by Gelb [21] and Mikhail [22]) is turned on and associated with the feature—this initiation of a Kalman filter is coded by a square; where two observations merge, the tracking is stopped and the features are entered into the data base—this is coded by a diamond.

As mentioned earlier, observations are expressed as line-of-sight vectors, and these are represented in the epipolar plane by the homogeneous line equation $ax + by - c = 0$ (its dual is the point (a, b, c)—see the description of duality in section 2.3). For the initial batch estimation, the coordinates (X) of the feature are the solution of the normal equations for the weighted least-squares system: $\mathbf{X} = (\mathbf{H}^T\mathbf{W}\mathbf{H})^{-1}\mathbf{H}^T\mathbf{W}\mathbf{C}$. $\mathbf{H}$ is the $m \times 2$ matrix of (a_i, b_i) observations; $\mathbf{C}$ is the vector of c_i; and $\mathbf{W}$ is the diagonal matrix of observation weights, determined by σ of the Gaussian, the distance from the camera to the observed feature at observation position i, and the focal distance. We estimate $\mathbf{X}$ first without weights, then compute the weighted solution and

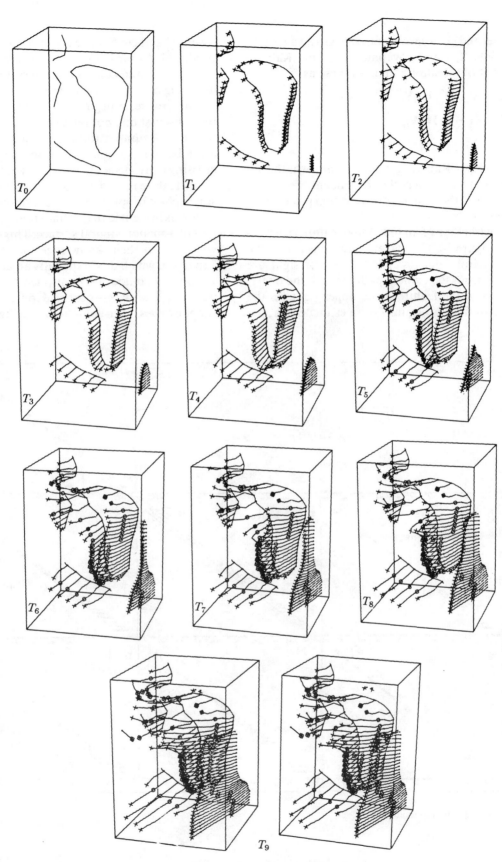

Fig. 17. Sequential feature tracking on the spatiotemporal surface.

the desired covariance matrix, $\mathbf{V}$. Given a current estimate $\mathbf{X}_{i-1}$ and covariance $\mathbf{V}_{i-1}$, the Kalman filter at observation i updates these as

$$\mathbf{K}_i = \mathbf{V}_{i-1}\mathbf{H}_i^T/[\mathbf{H}_i\mathbf{V}_{i-1}\mathbf{H}_i^T + \mathbf{w}_i]$$

$$\mathbf{V}_i = [\mathbf{I} - \mathbf{K}_i\mathbf{H}_i]\mathbf{V}_{i-1}$$

$$\mathbf{X}_i = \mathbf{X}_{i-1} + \mathbf{K}_i[\mathbf{c}_i - \mathbf{H}_i\mathbf{X}_{i-1}]$$

$\mathbf{K}_i$ is the 2×1 Kalman gain matrix, and $\mathbf{w}_i$ is the observation weight, a scalar, dependent on the distance from the camera at observation position i to the estimate $\mathbf{X}_{i-1}$.

The tracking of an individual feature is depicted in figure 18. The camera path runs across the figures from the lower left. Lines of sight are shown from the camera path through the observations of the feature at the upper right. As the Kalman filter is begun (T_4), an estimate (marked by an $\times$) and confidence interval (the ellipse) are produced. As further observations are acquired, the estimate and confidence interval are refined. Tracking continues until either the feature is lost, or the error term begins to increase—suggesting that observations not related to the tracked feature are beginning to be included. This could arise because, among other reasons, the zero crossing is erroneous, the feature is not stationary, or the feature is on a contour rather than being a single point in space. Note that although a single feature is presented in this tracking depiction, it is part of a spatiotemporal surface. This means that we have explicit knowledge of those other features to which this is spatially adjacent. Figure 19 shows a contour—a connected set of features on such a surface—observed over time as its shape evolves. Such contours are being construct-

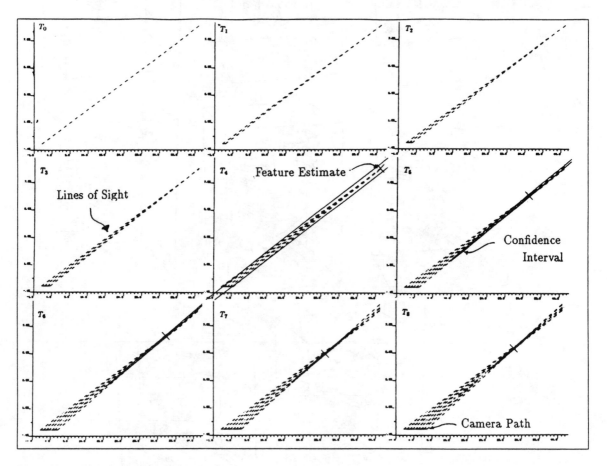

Fig. 18. Sequential estimation.

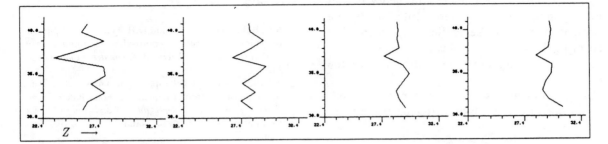

Fig. 19. Contour evolving over time.

ed and refined over the entire image as the analysis progresses. Our current representation of scene structure is based on these evolving contours.

3.4 Generality from the Spatiotemporal Surface

A crucial constraint of the current epipolar-plane image analysis is that having a camera moving along a linear path enables us to divide the analysis into planes, in fact, the pencil of planes of figure 1 passing through the camera path. With this, we are assured that a feature will be viewed in just a single one of these planes, and its motion over time will be confined to that plane. Another crucial constraint is the one we generalized from the orthogonal viewing case—we know that the set of line-of-sight vectors from camera to feature over time will all intersect at that feature, and determining that feature's position is a linear problem. The linearity of the estimator does not depend upon the linearity of the camera path. In fact, the problem would remain linear even if the camera meandered in three dimensions all over the scene.

This knowledge gives us a possibility of removing the restriction that limits us to a linear camera path. All that the linear path guarantees is that the problem is divisible into epipolar planes. If we lose this constraint, then we cannot restrict our feature tracking to separate planes. The observations will, however, still form linear paths in the space of line-of-sight vectors (not to be confused with the (u, v, t) observation space): This is because the lines of sight will all pass through the single feature point. The motion of these obser-

vations will give us *ruled* surfaces in this space—visualize pick-up-sticks jammed in a box, with the sticks being the rules. The rules can be used in the same way they have been with the linear path constraint, to determine the positions of features in the scene. The difference is that the linearities must be located—and the spatiotemporal surface is just the place for doing this. It would also be possible to track using the epipolar constraints that apply pairwise between images—that the constraints are limited to pairwise use arises because, for a nonlinear path, the images will not have the transitivity property we cited earlier.

It is equally worth noting that, when the camera attitude and position parameters are not provided, the spatiotemporal surface contains everything that is necessary for determining them. This is, of course, another problem, but one that must be addressed for a realistic vision system. Our initial work in this involves locating distinctive projective features on the spatiotemporal surface—dihedrals selected using Förstner's measure [23]—and tracking them. Depending upon knowledge of the features chosen, these can enable estimation of both relative and absolute camera parameters [24].

This generality suggests there is even broader application for the technique than we had initially thought—it seems quite adaptable to nonlinear camera paths; and should be usable equally in refining the camera model or solving for its unknown parameters.

4 Conclusions

We showed, in our earlier work, the feasibility of extracting scene depth information through

Epipolar-Plane Image Analysis. Our theory applies for any motion where the lens center moves in a straight line, with the earlier implementation covering the special case of camera sites equidistant and viewing direction orthogonal to the camera path.

The generalizations obtained through spatio-temporal-surface analysis bring us the advantages of

- Incremental analysis
- Unrestricted viewing direction (including direction varying along the path)
- Spatial coherence in our results, providing connected surface information for scene objects rather than point estimates structured by epipolar plane
- The possibility of removing the restrictions that fix us to a known linear path

The current implementation, running on a Symbolics 3600, processes the spatiotemporal surfaces at a 1-KHz voxel rate. The associated intersecting, tracking, and estimation procedures bring this rate down to about 150 Hz, 75 percent of which is consumed in the surface intersection (the surface intersection would not be required if we had a sensor of the appropriate geometry). Both the feature tracking and the surface-construction computations are well suited to MIMD (perhaps SIMD) parallel implementations. With these considerations, and the process's inherent precision and robustness, spatiotemporal-surface-based epipolar-plane image analysis shows great promise for tasks in real-time autonomous navigation and mapping.

Acknowledgements

This research has been supported by DARPA Contracts MDA 903-86-C-0084 and DACA 76-85-C-0004. David Marimont, currently with Xerox PARC, was crucial in the development of this work, providing insights for both the geometry and mathematics of the tracking process and the design of the surface builder. Lynn Quam has provided excellent image manipulation and graphics tools, and, whenever required, thoughtful assistance.

References

1. R.C. Bolles, H.H. Baker, and D.H. Marimont, "Epipolar-plane image analysis: An approach to determining structure from motion," *Intern. J. Computer Vision* 1:7–55, June 1987.
2. T.J. Broida and R. Chellappa, "Kinematics and structure of a rigid object from a sequence of noisy images," *Proc. Workshop on Motion: Representation and Analysis*, IEEE Computer Society, Kiawah Island, SC, pp. 95–100, May 1986.
3. D.B. Gennery, "Tracking known three-dimensional objects," *Proc. Nat. Conf. Artif. Intell.*, Pittsburgh, pp. 13–17, August 1982.
4. A.M. Waxman and K. Wohn, "Contour evolution, neighborhood deformation, and global image flow: Planar surfaces in motion," *Intern. J. Robotics Research* 4:95–108, Fall 1985.
5. A.M. Waxman, B. Kamgar-Parsi, and M. Subbarao, "Closed-form solutions to image flow equations for 3D structure and motion," *Intern. J. Computer Vision*, 1:239–258, October 1987.
6. M. Subbarao, "Interpretation of image motion fields: A spatio-temporal approach," *Proc. Workshop on Motion: Representation and Analysis*, IEEE Computer Society, Kiawah Island, SC, pp. 157–165, May 1986.
7. D.J. Heeger, "Depth and flow from motion energy," *Proc. 5th Nat. Conf. Artif. Intell.*, Philadelphia, pp. 657–663, August 1986.
8. D.H. Marimont, "Projective duality and the analysis of image sequences," *Proc. Workshop on Motion: Representation and Analysis*, IEEE Computer Society, Kiawah Island, SC, pp. 7–14, May 1986.
9. H.H. Baker, T.O. Binford, J. Malik, and J.F. Meller, "Progress in stereo mapping," *Proc. DARPA Image Understanding Workshop*, Arlington, VA, pp. 327–335, June 1983.
10. R. Jain, S.L. Bartlett, and N. O'Brien, "Motion stereo using ego-motion complex logarithmic maping," *IEEE. PAMI* 9:356–369, May 1987.
11. J.J. Gibson, *The Perception of the Visual World.* Houghton Mifflin: Boston, 1950.
12. B.F. Buxton and H. Buxton, "Monocular depth perception from optical flow by space time signal processing," *Proc. Roy. Soc. London,* Ser. B, 218:27–47, 1983.
13. H.H. Baker, "Building surfaces of evolution: The weaving wall," *Intern. J. Computer Vision* (this issue).
14. A.M. Waxman, "An image flow paradigm," *Proc. Workshop on Computer Vision: Representation and Control,* IEEE Computer Society, Annapolis, MD, pp. 49–57, April 1984.
15. A.M. Waxman, J. Wu, and F. Bergholm, "Convected activation profiles and the measurement of visual motion, *Proc. IEEE Conf. Computer Vision and Pattern Recognition,* Ann Arbor, MI, pp. 717–723, June 1988.
16. E.C. Hildreth and N.M. Grzywacz, "The incremental recovery of structure from motion: Position vs. velocity based formulations," *Proc. Workshop on Motion: Representation and Analysis,* IEEE Computer Society, Kiawah Island, SC, pp. 137–143, May 1986.

17. S. Negahdaripour and B.K.P. Horn, "Direct passive navigation," *IEEE Trans.* PAMI 9:168–176, January 1987.

18. L. Matthies, R. Szeliski, and T. Kanade, "Incremental estimation of dense depth maps from image sequences," *Proc. IEEE Conf. Computer Vision and Pattern Recognition,* Ann Arbor, MI, pp. 366–374, June 1988.

19. E.D. Dickmanns, "An integrated approach to feature based dynamic vision," *Proc. IEEE Conf. Computer Vision and Pattern Recognition,* Ann Arbor, MI, pp. 820–825, June 1988.

20. J. Hallam, "Resolving observer motion by object tracking," *Proc. 8th Intern. Joint Conf. Artif. Intell.,* Karlsruhe, West Germany, pp. 792–798, August 1983.

21. A. Gelb (ed.), *Applied Optimal Estimation.* Written by the Technical Staff, The Analytic Sciences Corporation, MIT Press, Cambridge, MA, 1974.

22. E.M. Mikhail, with F. Ackerman, *Observations and Least Squares.* University Press of America, Lanham, MD, 1976.

23. W. Förstner, "A feature based correspondence algorithm for image matching," *Proc. Symp. "From Analytical to Digital,"* Intern. Archives of Photogrammetry and Remote Sensing, vol. 26-III, Rovaniemi, Finland, August 1986.

24. W. Förstner, "Reliability analysis of parameter estimation in linear models with applications to mensuration problems in computer vision," *Computer Vision, Graphics, and Image Processing* 40:273–310, December 1987.

Analysis of a Sequence of Stereo Scenes Containing Multiple Moving Objects Using Rigidity Constraints*

Zhengyou Zhang   Olivier D. Faugeras   Nicholas Ayache

INRIA
Domaine de Voluceau
Rocquencourt, BP 105
78153 Le Chesnay FRANCE

Abstract

In this paper, we describe a method for computing the movement of objects as well as that of a mobile robot from a sequence of stereo frames. Stereo frames are obtained at different instants by a stereo rig, when the mobile robot navigates in an unknown environment possibly containing some moving rigid objects. An approach based on rigidity constraints is presented for registering two stereo frames. We demonstrate how the uncertainty of measurements can be integrated with the formalism of the rigidity constraints. A new technique is described to match very noisy segments. The influence of egomotion on observed movements of objects is discussed in detail. Egomotion is first determined and then eliminated before determination of the motion of objects. The proposed algorithm is completely automatic. Experimental results are provided. Some remarks conclude this paper.

Keywords: Motion from Stereo, Egomotion, Multiple Object Motions, Mobile Robot, 3D Matching, Rigidity Constraints, Uncertainty of Measurements.

1   Introduction

Instead of the interpretation and analysis of general 3D motion from two-dimensional images, our research focuses on motion from stereo. There is a broad range of applications of motion from stereo such as mobile robot navigation, target tracking and dynamic surveillance. In this article, we restrict the domain to that of mobile robot navigation in an unknown indoor environment where possibly other objects, such as other mobile robots, may also be moving.

Given a sequence of stereo frames, two operating modes are available. The first, called *Bootstrapping* mode, refers

*This work was supported in part by ESPRIT project *P*940.

to the case where nothing about the kinematics of 3D tokens is known. In order to determine ego- and object motion, we have to bring into correspondence some 3D tokens in successive frames using available constraints. When we start a session for analyzing the scene, we begin with the bootstrapping mode, because the only *a priori* information available is a partial estimation of the movement of robot from odometry. After the first few frames, however, the problem becomes simpler. We can use some *a priori* information about the kinematics of tokens extracted from previous frames to help in the estimation of the motion of 3D tokens. This is the second mode, called *Steady-state* mode. Some investigations have already been conducted in this direction [BC86a,BC86b,WHA87,Dic87].

Notice that even in the steady-state mode, there is always a little bit of the bootstrapping mode in the scene where new 3D tokens appear in the field of view about which no *a priori* information is available.

Due to the lack of *a priori* information, the bootstrapping problem is more difficult than the steady-state one. But to deal with the steady-state problem, we must take several (five, for instance) stereo frames a second, and the hardware requirements are more stringent. This article deals only with the bootstrapping problem.

Figures 1 and 2 show two 3D frames at two different instants which are reconstructed by our passive trinocular stereo system [AL87a,AL87b]. Two remarks should be made:

- Line segments are oriented due to the intensity contrast.

- Segments are noisy. Uncertainty is partially manipulated. Each segment is characterized by its orientation vector D and its midpoint M, and also by the covariance matrices W_D and W_M, corresponding to the uncertainty in its orientation and its midpoint, respectively.

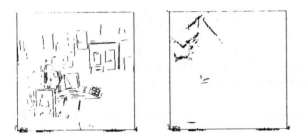

Figure 1: Stereo frame 1

Figure 2: Stereo frame 2

In [FAZ88], we have proposed an algorithm based on the hypothesize-verify paradigm to match two stereo frames. In this paper, we develop the generation of hypotheses phase and give some new results. Section 2 describes the matching process. The use of the rigidity constraint is explained in detail and a new technique is presented to match very noisy line segments. Section 3 discusses the influence of egomotion on the observed object motions. Section 4 presents some experimental results and Section 5 concludes this paper with some remarks.

2 Matching Process and Motion Estimation

2.1 General Presentation

To determine 3D continuous (small) motion from two-dimensional images, we can compute the apparent velocity field of the objects from the intensity variations in the images and relate it to the motions of objects, which in general does not require *a priori* information about feature correspondences [Hil83,Horn86]. In other cases, such as the interpretation and analysis of discrete motion from

2D or 3D frames, feature correspondences of objects between frames should be established before the computation of motion [Ull79,Hua86,AW86,CH87]. Even in the steady-state case, feature correspondences are needed to update the motion parameters. Of course, the size of the search space is drastically reduced compared with that in the bootstrapping one.

The rigidity assumption about the environment and objects is used in most matching algorithms. Our matching process is divided into two stages. In the first stage called *Generation of Hypotheses*, the rigidity constraint is heavily used to generate some hypotheses of segment correspondences between two successive frames. An estimate of motion can be computed from each hypothesis using an Iterative Extended Kalman Filter. In the second stage called *Verification*, we propagate this estimate in the whole frame to try to match more segments. Finally, the best hypothesis is retained.

In [CH87], a rigidity constraint is used in a different way, but the matching algorithm is also divided into two stages. An angular constraint on pairwise line segments is used in the first stage. Pairings whose orientations can be registered by using a tree search procedure are regarded as potential matches. A rotation is then available for each potential match. In the second stage, a Hough-like procedure is used to find translations that would bring segments into correspondence. As a result, line segments which undergo the same motion in space are grouped together.

2.2 Rigidity Constraint

The rigidity constraint implies the conservation of local structure of objects, such as angle and distance between two line segments, during their motions. However, the 3D segments which we have are very noisy (see Figures 1 and 2) and we cannot recover local structure exactly, especially the distance between two lines. Indeed, a significant change in the distance between two segments may result from a slight disturbance on the orientation of a segment. So, instead of the distance between two segments, we use in our algorithm the distance between the midpoints of two segments.

More precisely, if two pairings of segments can form one potential match, they must satisfy the following four conditions. Let AB, CD be two segments in scene 1, $A'B'$, $C'D'$ in scene 2 and M_1, M_2, M_1', M_2' be midpoints of AB, CD, $A'B'$, $C'D'$, respectively, the four conditions are then:

$$|AB| \approx |A'B'| \text{ and } |CD| \approx |C'D'|$$
$$\widehat{AB\,CD} \approx \widehat{A'B'\,C'D'}$$
$$|M_1M_2| \approx |M_1'M_2'|$$
$$\widehat{AB\,M_1M_2} \approx \widehat{A'B'\,M_1'M_2'}$$

In the following sections, we formalize the length and angle constraints explicitly taking into account the uncertainty of measurements. We approximately model the squared length of a segment and the cosine of the angle between two segments as gaussian random variables.

2.2.1 Length Constraint

Given a segment AB in the first scene with the covariance matrix W_D of its orientation, we can compute the variance of its squared length.

Let δ be the uncertainty in the orientation, with

$$E[\delta] = 0 \quad \text{and} \quad E[\delta\delta^t] = W_D$$

then, the squared length l^2 of segment AB can be represented as following:

$$
\begin{aligned}
l^2 &= [AB + \delta]^t [AB + \delta] \\
&= AB^t AB + 2AB^t \delta + \delta^t \delta
\end{aligned}
$$

If we neglect the second order terms, we have the variance of l^2

$$
\begin{aligned}
Var[l^2] &= E[(l^2 - E(l^2))^2] \\
&= 4AB^t W_D AB
\end{aligned}
$$

So, we can impose that two segments which can be matched (AB in scene 1, $A'B'$ in scene 2) must satisfy:

$$\big| \, |AB|^2 - |A'B'|^2 \, \big| < 2\kappa\sqrt{AB^t W_D AB} \tag{1}$$

where κ is a coefficient. Looking at the table of the *erf* function, we can choose an appropriate κ. For example, we can take $\kappa = 1.5$ for a probability of 87% when we consider the lengths of segments, and $\kappa = 1$ for a probability of 68% when we consider the distance between the midpoints of the two segments. That is, we impose a stricter constraint on the distance between midpoints than on the lengths of segments.

2.2.2 Angle Constraint

Given two segments AB and CD in the first scene, let δ_1 and δ_2 be the uncertainties in their orientations, $W_{\delta_1} = E[\delta_1\delta_1^t]$ and $W_{\delta_2} = E[\delta_2\delta_2^t]$ are known, and suppose that $E[\delta_1] = E[\delta_2] = 0$.

The cosine of the angle between these two segments is:

$$\cos\theta = \frac{(AB + \delta_1) \cdot (CD + \delta_2)}{|AB + \delta_1| \cdot |CD + \delta_2|}$$

Notice that

$$\frac{1}{\sqrt{x + \epsilon}} \approx \frac{1}{\sqrt{x}} - \frac{\epsilon}{2x^{3/2}} \quad \text{if } \epsilon \ll x,$$

and that

$$|AB + \delta| = \sqrt{|AB|^2 + 2AB \cdot \delta + |\delta|^2}$$

we have

$$\cos\theta = \frac{AB \cdot CD + AB \cdot \delta_2 + \delta_1 \cdot CD}{|AB| \cdot |CD|}$$

Here, we have neglected terms of orders higher than 2.

Suppose that AB and CD are independent, we can now easily compute the variance of $\cos\theta$:

$$Var[\cos\theta] = \frac{1}{|AB|^2 |CD|^2}(AB^t W_{\delta_2} AB + CD^t W_{\delta_1} CD)$$

Let $A'B'$, $C'D'$ be 2 segments in scene 2 to be matched with AB and CD, they should satisfy the following constraint:

$$
\begin{aligned}
&\big| \cos(\widehat{AB\ CD}) - \cos(\widehat{A'B'\ C'D'}) \big| < \\
&\qquad \frac{\kappa}{|AB| \, |CD|}\sqrt{AB^t W_{\delta_2} AB + CD^t W_{\delta_1} CD} \tag{2}
\end{aligned}
$$

where κ is a coefficient. We can choose $\kappa = 0.8$ for a probability of 57% or $\kappa = 1$ which corresponds to a probability of 68% for the four segments to match. Here, we choose κ smaller than for the length constraint (see Formula 1), due to the fact that the angle is more robust to segmentattion errors than the length.

2.3 Deriving Additional Constraint and Solving Local Similarity

To make full use of 3-D information obtained by our passive stereo system and to reduce the number of incorrect hypotheses, we can derive an additional constraint on the orientation of segments.

2.3.1 Orientation Congruency

Proposition : *Suppose an oriented segment undergoes a rigid displacement between two successive frames with a rotation angle between 0 and π, then the change of orientation of the segment is less than or equal to the rotation angle between the two frames.*

Proof : Let $l = (p, q, r)^t$ be the unit orientation vector of the segment in the first frame, and l' be that in the second frame, then we have $l' = Rl$ where R is the rotation matrix.

If we choose the exponential representation of rotation matrix (cf. [FAF86,Fau88]), that is

$$R = e^H$$

where

$$H = \begin{bmatrix} 0 & -c & b \\ c & 0 & -a \\ -b & a & 0 \end{bmatrix}$$

The vector $r = [a\ b\ c]^t$ gives the direction of axis of rotation and its norm is the rotation angle around this axis. The

572

relationship between R and r is the following:

$$R \begin{bmatrix} \cos\theta + a^2 g(\theta) & abg(\theta) - cf(\theta) & acg(\theta) + bf(\theta) \\ abg(\theta) + cf(\theta) & \cos\theta + b^2 g(\theta) & bcg(\theta) - af(\theta) \\ acg(\theta) - bf(\theta) & bcg(\theta) + af(\theta) & \cos\theta + c^2 g(\theta) \end{bmatrix}$$

where $\theta = \sqrt{a^2 + b^2 + c^2}$ is the rotation angle, $f(\theta) = \frac{\sin\theta}{\theta}$ and $g(\theta) = \frac{1-\cos\theta}{\theta^2}$.

Now it is easy to compute the angle between l and l' :

$$\begin{aligned} \cos(\widehat{l \ l'}) &= \cos(l \ \widehat{R}l) \\ &= \frac{1 - \cos\theta}{\theta^2}(ap + bq + cr)^2 + \cos\theta \end{aligned}$$

Because $\frac{1-\cos\theta}{\theta^2}(ap + bq + cr)^2 \geq 0$, $\cos(\widehat{l \ l'}) \geq \cos\theta$, i.e. $\widehat{l \ l'} |<| \theta |$ for $0 \leq \theta < \pi$.

Note that when $\theta \neq 0$ (not pure translation), $\widehat{l \ l'} = \theta$ if and only if $ap + bq + cr = 0$, that is, if a segment undergoes a movement whose rotation axis is perpendicular to the segment, then the angle of the change of segment orientation is equal to the rotation angle. If not, it is less than the rotation angle. **Q.E.D.**

In general, the rotation angle between two successive frames does not go beyond 60 degrees, so we can impose that the orientation difference of a pairing of segments to be matched must be less than 60 degrees.

2.3.2 Solving Local Similarity

In an indoor environment, we encounter many things which are similar such as: two windows, two tables, one window and one table, two sides of a cube block. While this phenomenon (so-called *local similarity*) can be partly solved by the above constraint (*orientation congruency*), several cases remain unsolved such as illustrated in Figure 3.

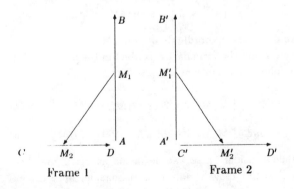

Figure 3: Local similarity

The two pairings in Figure 3 satisfy all the previous constraints, but this is evidently a wrong hypothesis. The problem is that we use "cosine" in the formulation of angle constraint. To solve it, we can use some "sine-like" information. We can, for instance, examine the congruency of

orientation between the normal to AB and M_1M_2, and that to $A'B'$ and $M_1'M_2'$. As described in Section 2.3.1, we can impose that orientation difference of normals must be less than 60 degrees. In Figure 3, the normal points "in" the paper in the first scene, and that in the second scene points "out" of the paper, so the angle between the two normals is 180 degrees, which is greater than 60 degrees. Thus, we can eliminate this improper match.

2.4 Reducing the Complexity of the Algorithm

Now, we can use the constraints described above to generate hypotheses of matches between two successive frames. If we explore all possibilities of pairs of segments, the complexity is $o(p^2 q^2)$ where p is the number of segments in the first frame and q is that in the second one. The algorithm is given in Figure 4.

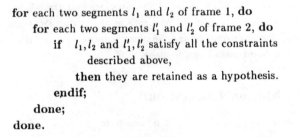
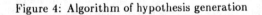

for each two segments l_1 and l_2 of frame 1, **do**
    for each two segments l_1' and l_2' of frame 2, **do**
        if l_1, l_2 and l_1', l_2' satisfy all the constraints
            described above,
            then they are retained as a hypothesis.
        endif;
    done;
done.

Figure 4: Algorithm of hypothesis generation

In order to obtain more reliable hypotheses, we use triplets of segments. Let l_1, l_2 and l_1', l_2' be two compatible pairings (in the sense that they satisfy the above constraints), if another pairing l_3 and l_3' is also compatible with l_1 and l_1', then we verify if this pairing is compatible with l_2 and l_2'. If so, l_1, l_2, l_3 and l_1', l_2', l_3' can form an hypothesis. This means that each hypothesis has propagated at least one segments, and therefore we have a more reliable hypothesis, on one hand; on the other hand, we increase the complexity of the algorithm.

Notice that we do not want to recover all matches between two frames, but to recover all potential motions between two frames, so we need not to explore the search tree exhaustively. There are a number of methods for reducing the complexity:

Sort the segments Sort all segments in each frame in decreasing length order, so that we can easily find, by binary search, the segments in the second frame which are compatible in length with the segments in the first one.

Control search depth Rather than find all possible matches compatible with a certain estimation of displacement, we can stop if we have found a sufficient number of compatible pairings (5, for instance).

Avoid redundant hypotheses If a pairing is already retained as a potential match in some early hypothesis, it is not necessary to continue our search, because it does not give us new information about the motion between two frames.

Reduce search width Consider segments of the first frame only in the central part of the frame, because segments on the sides are likely to move out of the view field in the next frame.

Reduce the number of segments Choose only the longest segments in the first scene, for instance, the p/n longest ($n = 1, 2$ or 3).

Other constraints can be easily integrated in the algorithm to speed the generation process. For example, the assumption that objects and robot only move horizontally (in the ground plane) can be used.

2.5 Motion Estimation

For each hypothesis, we can compute a preliminary estimate of motion using an Extended Kalman Filter [FAF86,AF87,FAZ88,Jaz70]. We apply this estimate to the first frame and compare the transformed frame with the second one. If a transformed segment from the first frame is near enough to some segment in the second frame (cf. Section 2.6), then this pairing is considered as matched, and again, the Extended Kalman Filter is used to update the motion estimate. In the end, the optimal motion estimate of the *best* hypothesis is retained as the motion between these two frames. *Best* is quantified as the hypothesis which can bring the largest number of segments into correspondence and yield a minimal error for these matches [FAZ88].

2.6 New Technique to Match Noisy Segments

In our earlier version of the algorithm, we measured the generalized Mahalanobis distance between endpoints of segments. A number of segments can not be matched using this technique, because a segment of an object can be differently segmented in successive images. In this section, we present a new technique which can match very noisy segments.

Let l_1 be a segment in the first frame transformed in the second frame, and l_2 a segment in the second frame.

Step 1: Examine the similarity of orientation. Using Formula 2 described in Section 2.2.2, if the following condition:

$$1 - \cos\theta < \frac{\kappa_a}{|l_1||l_2|}\sqrt{l_1^t W_{l_2} l_1 + l_2^t W_{l_1} l_2} \qquad (3)$$

is satisfied, we proceed to the next step. The above condition is reasonable (cf. Formula 2), because $E[\theta] = 0$, i.e. $E[\cos\theta] = 1$.

Step 2: Examine the distance between two segments. Two segments which can be matched must be in one of the following configurations (Figure 5):

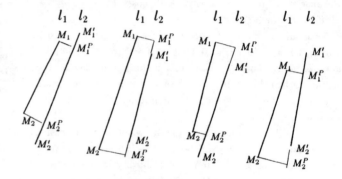

Figure 5: Configurations of matched segments

In order to know whether the configuration of two segments to be matched is among the above four configurations, we can project the two endpoints M_1 and M_2 of segment l_1 on segment l_2 (M_1^P, M_2^P are these projections, respectively), and examine the following condition:

$$(M_{1x}^P \geq M_{2x}' \quad \text{and} \quad M_{2x}^P \leq M_{1x}')$$
$$\text{or} \quad (M_{1x}^P \leq M_{2x}' \quad \text{and} \quad M_{2x}^P \geq M_{1x}')$$

where M_x is the x coordinate of point M.

Using again the formula 1 described in the Section 2.2.1, if the following conditions are satisfied:

$$|\overline{M_1 M_1^P}|^2 < 2\kappa_l \sqrt{\overline{M_1 M_1^P}^t W_{\delta 1} \overline{M_1 M_1^P}} \qquad (4)$$

$$\text{and} \quad |\overline{M_2 M_2^P}|^2 < 2\kappa_l \sqrt{\overline{M_2 M_2^P}^t W_{\delta 2} \overline{M_2 M_2^P}} \qquad (5)$$

we then consider these two segments as being matched. Note that the above condition is reasonable, since the expected distance between M_i and M_i^P is zero. In the Formulae 4 and 5, $W_{\delta i} = W_{M_i} + W_{M_i^P}$. The covariance matrix $W_{M_i^P}$ of point M_i^P can be approximated as follows:

$$W_{M_i^P} = \frac{1}{(M_{2x}' - M_{1x}')^2}[(M_{2x}' - M_{ix}^P)^2 W_{M_1'} + (M_{ix}^P - M_{1x}')^2 W_{M_2'}].$$

Using this new technique and choosing appropriate κ_a and κ_l, we can recover almost all possible matches between

574

successive frames, even if the segments are very noisy. Note that the condition 3 is not needed theoretically since we have the conditions 4 and 5. In practice, we can use the condition 3 to reject a large portion of the candidates before we enter the second step, whose computation is more expensive. Furthermore, we can replace the right hand side of Equation 3 by a constant. If Θ (for instance, 30 degrees) is the given tolerance in orientation, we can replace Equation 3 by the following:

$$\cos \theta > \cos \Theta.$$

3 Influence of Egomotion on Observed Object Motion

If there are some moving objects in the environment, we can find multiple possible motions when we register two successive frames: egomotion and motions corresponding to objects.

Suppose now there is only one moving object (the following results can be easily extended to the case of multiple objects). Using the matching process described above, we can recover two different motions: $R_E, \vec{t_E}$, the inverse of robot motion and $R_O', \vec{t_O'}$, the object motion as observed by the robot (in the coordinate system of the second frame). But notice that $R_O', \vec{t_O'}$ is not the real motion of the object. Indeed, it is influenced by the egomotion and we have following relations:

$$\begin{cases} R_O &= R_O' R_E^t \\ \vec{t_O} &= \vec{t_O'} - R_O \vec{t_E} \end{cases} \quad (6)$$

where $R_O, \vec{t_O}$ is the real object motion.

Equation 6 can be easily verified (cf. Figure 6). If the object is static, it should be observed by the robot at O_{b2}' in the second frame. $O_{b2}' = R_E O_{b1} + \vec{t_E}$, where O_{b1} is the object position in the first frame. In reality, the object is observed in O_{b2} in the second frame, so the difference between O_{b2}' and O_{b2} is the real motion of the object (still in the coordinate system of second frame), that is:

$$O_{b2} = R_O O_{b2}' + \vec{t_O}$$

But

$$O_{b2} = R_O' O_{b1} + \vec{t_O'}$$

and

$$O_{b2}' = R_E O_{b1} + \vec{t_E}$$

After a simple calculation, we obtain Equation 6.

So we have at least two approaches to correctly recover the object motions. (1) Recover all possible motions between two frames, then determine the egomotion and use the above equation to compute the real motions of objects.

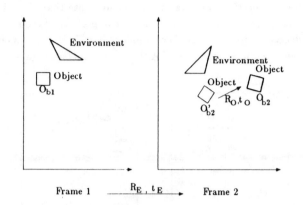

Figure 6: Influence of egomotion on observed object motion

(2) If the segments corresponding to the environment are much more numerous than those of objects, we need not explore all possible matches. We can choose only half of the segments in the first frame and take as the egomotion the motion which can bring into correspondence the largest number of segments. It is reasonable to choose only half of the segments, because we only need to match 3 segments belonging to the environment to compute the egomotion. Once the egomotion is recovered, we can apply it to the first frame. Applying again the above matching process on the transformed frame and on the second one, we now recover the real motions of objects, since we work in the same coordinate system (that of the second frame).

There remains a problem, however. How to select the egomotion among all possible motions ? As stated above, if we know that the environment has more segments than objects, we can than select the motion estimate that matches the largest number of segments. If we know an *a priori* estimate of the robot motion (for example, an estimate given by the odometric system of robot), we can select the one which is nearest to the *a priori* estimate and yields the smallest matching error.

4 Experimental Results

In this section, two experimental examples are provided to demonstrate the matching process and the multiple object motion determination. In each figure given, the left hand is the front view and the right hand is the top view.

4.1 Example for Matching Process

Figures 1 and 2 are two stereo frames constructed by our mobile robot in two different positions. The triangle in each frame represents the optical centers of the cameras of our trinocular stereo system. We have 261 segments in the first frame and 250 segments in the second. Note that there is a large displacement between these two positions (about 10 degrees of rotation and 75 centimeters of translation) which can be noticed by superposing the two frames (see Figure 7).

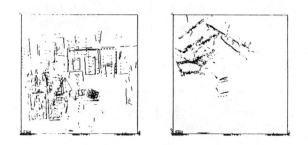

Figure 7: Superposition of the two original frames : Segments of frame 1 are in dashed lines and those of frame 2 are in solid lines

Applying our hypothesis generation procedure on these two frames, we obtain 11 hypotheses. All these hypotheses are propagated in the whole frame to match more segments and update the motion estimate. In the end, 7 hypotheses correctly give the estimate of displacement (with a slight difference). The one which matches the largest number of segments and gives the minimal matching error is kept as the best one. To determine how good this estimate is, we apply it to the first frame and superpose the transformed one on the second, *i.e.* in the coordinate system of the second frame (see Figure 8). One can observe the very good accuracy of this estimate.

Figure 8: Superposition of the transformed frame of the first one (in dashed lines) on the second (in solid lines) in the coordinate system of frame 2

In the propagation phase, we also recover matched segments. If we use the criterion of the generalized Mahalanobis distance between endpoints of segments as in our early version of algorithm, we recover only 76 matches (see Figures 9 and 10). If we use the new technique described in Section 2.6, we recover 156 matched segments (60% of the total segments) (see Figures 11 and 12). A remarkable improvement can be observed.

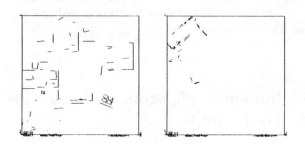

Figure 9: Matched segments of frame 1 based on distance of endpoints

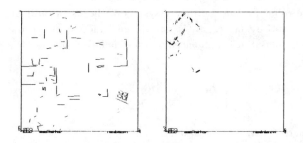

Figure 10: Matched segments of frame 2 based on distance of endpoints

In order to improve the accuracy of the segment measurements, we can fuse each pairing of matched segments. Figure 13 shows the superposition of matched segments of two frames (in the coordinate system of frame 2) and Figure 14 is the result after fusion. The improvement in accuracy is obvious.

The error of the estimate with respect to that given by the odometer of the robot is 0.66 degrees in rotation and 0.3 centimeters in translation. This error is due to the cumulation of errors in all different phases of our navigation loop, especially the error of the mechanical system of the mobile robot.

Figure 11: Matched segments of frame 1 using the new technique described in the paper

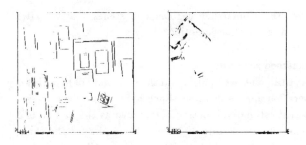

Figure 12: Matched segments of frame 2 using the new technique described in the paper

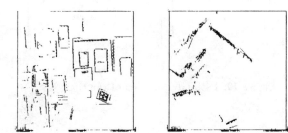

Figure 13: Superposition of the matched segments after computation of motion

Figure 14: Fusion of all matched segments

4.2 Example of the Determination of Multiple Objects Motions

We adopt the second approach described in Section 3 to determine the multiple objects motions. We demonstrate the procedure on an experimental example: Figures 15 and 16 are the horizontal and vertical projections of the reconstructed segments of an indoor scene observed by the mobile vehicle in two different positions. The two positions differed only by a rotation of the cameras by an angle of 5 degrees with respect to an almost vertical axis. We have added to the scene two synthetic objects, a small house and a chair, which have two different motions and whose segments are corrupted by noise. The simulated motion of the house is a rotation of 30 degrees with respect to a vertical axis and a translation of about 80 cms while the chair has been rotated by -40 degrees with respect to a vertical axis and translated also by about 80 cms. In a near future, we shall give examples with real moving objects.

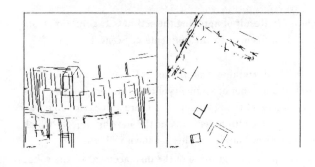

Figure 15: First 3D snapshot

In order to speed up the process of hypotheses generation, we choose only the $p/2$ longest segments in the first scene. Eight hypotheses are generated among which, five are correctly corresponding to the static environment, one is correctly corresponding to a moving object, and two are wrong

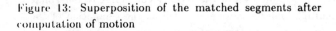

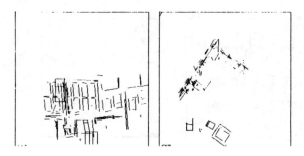

Figure 16: Second 3D snapshot

hypotheses (after verification, we find that these correspond to very few (0 to 3) segments matched). If we consider that the number of segments of the environment is larger than that of segments on the objects, we can choose the hypothesis that matches the largest number of segments as the best one. Figure 17 shows the result obtained when applying the estimated egomotion to the segments in scene 1 and displaying them in dotted lines overlaying scene 2 where segments are drawn in continuous lines. Clearly, most of the background has been matched.

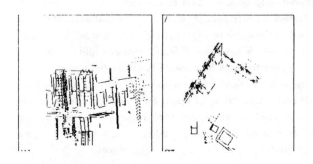

Figure 17: Result of applying the estimated egomotion from Scene 1 to Scene 2 to the segments of Scene 1

After determining the motion of the robot, we have matched a number of segments of the static environment between the two 3D snapshots. But there still exist some segments of the environment and of the moving objects which have not been matched. This is shown in Figure 18.

If we apply the estimate of the displacement of the robot that we have obtained to the first scene, and remove the segments matched (including those segments matched by the above technique) from both scenes, we get two 3D snapshots which contain only moving objects (and also some segments of the environment which have not been matched). The influence of the egomotion on the motions of these objects has been cancelled. This is shown in Figure 18 which shows the first scene after applying the estimated egomotion to its

Figure 18: Unmatched segments in scenes 1 and 2 after cancellation of the egomotion

unmatched segments.

At this point, we apply again the procedure of hypotheses generation and verification. Each hypothesis which gives a different estimate of motion is regarded as the motion of a moving object. Figure 19 shows the results for the chair, and Figure 20 shows them for the house. Clearly, the two motions have been well recovered.

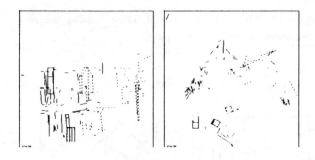

Figure 19: Estimated motion of the chair

5 Conclusion

In this paper, we have presented an algorithm based mainly on the exploitation of the rigidity constraint to determine multiple objects motions as well as the egomotion of the robot. The uncertainty of measurements is partially taken into account in the formalism of the rigidity constraint. The

Figure 20: Estimated motion of the house

constraint of segment orientation similarity is derived. A new technique is proposed to match noisy segments and uncertainty is again taken into account. The influence of egomotion on observed object motion is discussed in detail and two approaches are proposed to recover object motions correctly. The proposed algorithm is completely automatic. Two experimental examples are provided and excellent results are observed. The algorithm can be easily implemented in parallel.

References

[AW86] J.K. Aggarwal and Y.F. Wang, "Analysis of a sequence of images using point and line correspondences", In *Proc. Conference on Robotics and Automation*, pages 1275-1280, IEEE, 1986.

[AF87] N. Ayache and O.D. Faugeras, "Maintaining representations of the environment of a mobile robot", In *International Symposium on Robotics Research*, August 1987. Santa-Cruz, California.

[AL87a] N. Ayache and F. Lustman, "Fast and reliable passive trinocular stereovision", In *Proc. First International Conference on Computer Vision*, pages 422-427, IEEE, June 1987. London, U.K.

[AL87b] N. Ayache and F. Lustman, "Trinocular stereovision, recent results", In *Proc. International Joint Conference on Artificial Intelligence*, August 1987. Milano, Italy.

[BC86a] T.J. Broida and R. Chellappa, "Kinematics and structure of a rigid object from a sequence of noisy images", In *Proc. IEEE Workshop on Motion: Representation and Analysis*, pages 95-100, Charleston, SC, May 1986.

[BC86b] T.J. Broida and R. Chellappa, "Kinematics and structure of a rigid object from a sequence of noisy images: A batch approach", In *Proc. IEEE Conf. Computer Vision and Pattern Recognition*, pages 176-182, Miami Beach, FL, June 1986.

[CH87] H.H. Chen and T. Huang, "An algorithm for matching 3-D line segments with application to multiple-object motion estimation", In *Proc. of the IEEE Computer Society, Workshop on Computer Vision*, pages 151-156, November 30–December 2, 1987.

[Dic87] E.D. Dickmanns, "4D-dynamic scene analysis with integral spatio-temporal models", In *Proc. ISSR'87*, pages 73-80, Santa-Cruz, 1987.

[FAF86] O.D. Faugeras, N. Ayache, and B. Faverjon, "Building visual maps by combining noisy stereo measurements", In *Proc. International Conference on Robotics and Automation*, pages 1433-1438, April 1986. San Francisco, CA, USA.

[Fau88] O.D. Faugeras, *A Few Steps Toward Artificial 3D Vision*, Technical Report N° 790, INRIA, B.P. 105, 78153 LE CHESNAY CEDEX, 1988.

[FAZ88] O.D. Faugeras, N. Ayache, and Z. Zhang, "A preliminary investigation of the problem of determining ego- ang object motions from Stereo", In *Proc. International Conference on Pattern Recognition*, 1988, 9th, Rome, Italy.

[Hil83] E.C. Hildreth, *The Measurement of Visual Motion*, MIT Press, Cambridge, 1983.

[Horn86] B.K.P. Horn, *Robot Vision*, MIT Press and McGraw-Hill Book Company, 1986.

[Hua86] T.S. Huang, "Motion Analysis", In *AI Encyclopedia*, Wiley, 1986.

[Jaz70] A.M. Jazwinsky, *Stochastic Processes and Filtering Theory*, Academic Press, 1970.

[Ull79] S. Ullman, *The Interpretation of Visual Motion*, MIT Press, Cambridge 1979.

[WHA87] J. Weng, T.S. Huang, and N. Ahuja, "3-D Motion Estimation, Understanding, and Prediction from Noisy Image Sequences", *IEEE Trans. Pattern Anal. Machine Intell.*, Vol. PAMI-9, No. 3, pages 370-389, 1987.

Chapter 7: Knowledge-Based Vision

Computer vision systems recover useful information about a scene using knowledge of both image formation and the application domain. Image-understanding tasks have proven to be exceedingly difficult in general domains. Consequently, knowledge-engineering techniques have become popular in computer vision systems. We will briefly discuss these techniques and their impact on computer vision research in this chapter.

Knowledge representation

The central issue in the higher levels of a vision system is the representation and use of knowledge. The term, "knowledge representation" is nebulous. "Knowledge" is a collection of descriptions, assimilation procedures, and problem-solving methods that serves to organize and summarize observations and to support a useful degree of problem-solving ability.[244] A "representation" is a particular kind of symbol; the symbol's structure is perceived to correspond in some way to the structure of the thing for which the symbol stands. (A symbol stands for something else by reason of association or convention.) "Knowledge representation" combines data structures and interpretive procedures that, if used correctly in a program, will lead to knowledgeable behavior of a computer vision system. Researchers interested in knowledge representation have designed several data structure classes for storing information in computer programs, and they have developed procedures that enable intelligent manipulation of these data structures to make inferences. Many of these representations can be used in computer vision systems.

In knowledge-based vision systems, good solutions often depend on good representations. The choice of representation is crucial for the characterization of visual data, since representational primitives effectively limit what a system can perceive, know, or understand. ("Representational primitives" are the primitive elements and operators from which an open-ended range of learned concepts can be constructed.) However the choice of representation is difficult, since many possibilities exist and criteria for comparing different representations are unclear.

We must encode different kinds of knowledge for image understanding. Object representation must include individual instances, object classes, object descriptions, object relationships, and constraints. Also, performance knowledge — the knowledge of how to perform different tasks — must be encoded. This encoding can involve such tasks as finding a particular object's edges, linking edge points, and finding all points that belong to a region. Measuring performance is important in providing a feedback path by which a system can modify its strategy during processing. However, defining the necessary performance criteria is difficult, especially in low-level tasks such as segmentation. We also use metaknowledge, which is knowledge about what we know — that is, knowledge about the extent and reliability of our knowledge, in our problem solving activities.

Barr and Feigenbaum[245] and Rich[246] provided good descriptions of popular knowledge representation techniques that fall into four categories: formal logic, semantic nets, production systems, and frames.

In a computer vision system, the computer is fed information via sensing devices and then must use knowledge about the object to arrive at a decision. Various knowledge representation techniques used to tackle the decision-making problem are discussed in this section.

Semantic networks. A semantic net represents information as a set of nodes interconnected by labeled arcs that represent relationships among the nodes. Originally, Quillian[247] and Shapiro and Woodmansee[248] proposed semantic nets as a knowledge representation technique. While many kinds of networks exist, they all share the following features:

- All contain a data structure of nodes representing concepts — generally, a hierarchy of nodes connected by ISA and other property links.
- All contain specialized inferential procedures operating on the data structure of nodes. This involves the inheritance of information from the top levels of the hierarchy downward along ISA links.

Production systems. Production system architecture is the knowledge representation method that has become popular in expert systems. Newell[249] advocated this representation scheme as a model of human reasoning. Representing knowledge in this form is a natural way to extract and encode rule-based knowledge in many applications. Also, schema-based systems can be implemented using production system architecture.

A rule-based system contains antecedent-consequent pairs, called "rules." Rule antecedents usually examine data; rule consequents are responsible for data modification. Production systems are rule-based; that is, control structures can be mapped into relatively simple recognize-act paradigms. Production systems typically have the following three parts: (1) a database, (2) a set of production rules, and (3) an interpreter. The database (working memory) contains all currently true facts. Production rules are of the form antecedent = consequent. The interpreter matches antecedents with the database, selecting the appropriate rule to fire. We can define the execution of such a production system as a series of recognize-act cycles.

Production systems can represent knowledge in several independent modules, allowing greater modularity in the knowledge base than that allowed by any other scheme. In production systems, we can add or delete rules without changing other rules. Since, in most applications, the knowledge base is changed very frequently by adding and deleting rules, the system can be maintained with minimal effort. Furthermore, imprecise rules can be used, with some measure of belief or reliability associated with each rule. The inference mechanism then uses this measure to reach appropriate conclusions. A probabilistic rule-based system, in which a probability is associated with each rule, provides such a mechanism. Such a system can represent heuristic information as a set of probabilistic production rules.

The disadvantage of production systems is that certain rule modules may interfere with other modules. Antecedent parts of several rules may be satisfied simultaneously, and the interpreter must choose the most appropriate rule to be fired. In such cases, programming would be difficult.

Nazif and Levine[51] describe an expert system for low-level image segmentation — a system whose creation was motivated by the desire to provide an explicit scheme for representing knowledge embodied by numerous segmentation heuristics available in the literature. A rule-based approach provides users with an expressive coding mechanism that accommodates diverse knowledge sources. Such a representational mechanism can capture general-purpose knowledge about image formation and perceptual grouping laws. Production systems in general include condition-action rules that capture general knowledge about an image's independent low-level properties.

Frames (or schemata). Representation for vision applications should be able to capture more structured production systems information and should allow representation of some common knowledge about objects. Minsky[250] proposed that a useful knowledge base should be composed of highly modular chunks, called "frames" or "schemata." (The term "schemata" refers to "frames" used in a visual context; however, the literature uses these two terms interchangeably.) A frame is a data structure representing a stereotyped situation or class of objects. Attached to each frame are several kinds of information, such as how to use a frame and what can be expected to happen next. Frames have become popular in applications such as computer vision and natural-language understanding.

A frame can be considered a slot-and-filler structure formed by the following network of nodes and relationships:

- The frame's top levels are fixed and represent things that are always true.
- The frame's lower levels have many slots or terminals that must be filled by specific instances or data (describing aspects of objects). Associated with each slot may be a set of conditions that must be met by any filler for that slot.

Knowledge representation schemes occupy a continuum from totally declarative to totally procedural. In declarative schemes, knowledge is explicit and available for modification. In procedural schemes, the execution flow can be more easily traced; consequently, the control strategy being employed is more readily apparent. Schema-based approaches combine positive aspects of each representation scheme to overcome the limitations of any single method.

Besides knowledge representation, another reason for the interest vision researchers have evinced in schemata is the viewpoint that cognitive structures useful for vision are anticipatory schemata. The schema is perception's central cognitive structure. Neisser[251] defines schemata as those portions of the perceptual cycle that are internal to the perceiver and modifiable by experience. Schemata accept information as it becomes available at sensory surfaces and are changed by that information; they direct movements and exploratory activities that make more information available, by which information they are further modified.

Perceptual schemata are plans for learning about objects and events and for obtaining more information to fill in the format, or the slot into which a particular value goes. We can regard plans as attached procedures. During the course of perception, the schema's nature evolves from general to precise; we call this evolution "instantiation," since the schema is filled with particular instances of the more general concepts it represents. This process occurs gradually — an important point — as inferences made during one perception cycle dictate the next cycle's course of action.

Schemata are a means by which related facts can be arranged in a manner that eliminates redundancy. Furthermore, schemata can contain directives for using information present within them. Explicit relationships among schemata in a semantic network allow inferences to be drawn based on the interconnection of different nodes (for instance, the direct descendants of a node). Since schemata contain both a declarative part (facts and network links) and a procedural part (methods for manipulating facts), they can exploit the strengths of each part. Many schemata have been developed. We can judge their merits by how well they encode the knowledge required to carry out the tasks for which they have been designed.

Research trends

Interpretation of an image, in fact of any perceptual process, uses knowledge and reasoning at every stage. This knowledge could be about entities in an image and the domain of application. Early processing conventionally uses very general models — for example, edges modeled as intensity steps; later processing uses explicit object models. Image interpretation requires knowledge about the following items:

- The environment, including illumination;
- Objects: their geometry and other properties;
- Relationships among different representations;
- The sensing process (image formation); and
- The behavior of operators for different processing tasks.

All systems either explicitly or implicitly use models to represent knowledge about all of these items. Clearly, both the efficacy and the flexibility of a system depend on the models used. The more general the models are, the more flexible the system is. We have selected a set of 4 papers that are representative of papers dealing with topics covered in this chapter. Two are included in this book and the remaining two can be found in the companion book *Computer Vision: Advances and Applications*. We begin this chapter of *Principles* with the paper "Survey of Model-Based Image Analysis Systems," in which Binford discusses many important issues related to the role of knowledge in vision systems, including the strengths and limitations of several systems. In "Perceptual Organization and the Representation of Natural Form," Pentland discusses in *Advances* several issues related to representation of geometric information with the aim of object recognition. Superquadrics were popularized by Pentland in computer vision for representation and recognition of three-dimensional objects.

The major problem with general models is the computational power required to implement and use them. Compared to general models, specialized models result in relatively rigid systems that are computationally more efficient. Early in the game, vision researchers were aware of the issue of computational efficiency, and all debates about top-down versus bottom-up control structures were related to this issue. Of course, in addition to computational efficiency, many other issues should be considered in determining what models to use in a system and how to use them. Considering only the computational aspects first, we can draw a parallel here between general and specific models, and how to use them, on the one hand, and search and knowledge, on the other. Search is very important; however, without adequate use of knowledge, it is computationally impractical. This issue is basic to artificial intelligence. In fact, the best explanation of why complex systems have to abandon the goal of perfection is well advocated by Simon[252] in his principle of "satisficing." In vision, the use of general models may provide flexibility, but at the cost of Herculean computation. General models require more computation to use them while specific models require very little computation. Clearly, we need to select models that provide maximum flexibility at a reasonable computational cost.

In "Low-Level Image Segmentation: An Expert System" in *Principles*, Nazif and Levine provide a good example of how shallow, general knowledge can be used for image segmentation. Interestingly, general rules can be used, even at very early stages, in solving complex problems. Irvin and McKeown[253] show how domain-dependent knowledge can be used to solve some complex problems in the interpretation of scenes containing disparate objects. In "The Schema System," Draper et al. in *Advances* describe in detail a knowledge-based vision system that uses many different types of knowledge at different levels to analyze natural scenes.

One purpose of perception is to represent past experiences compactly and retrieve them efficiently when needed. To allow compact and flexible representation, object models should be structured. Structured models may use parametric representation of components. Moreover, at any given instant, the knowledge of the world as constructed by the system is incomplete, inexact, and uncertain. The representation should allow this incompleteness and uncertainty.[254] Although the last few years have seen increasing use of knowledge in vision systems, techniques for reasoning about geometric information are still in their infancy.

References Cited
Chapter 7

244. R.J. Brachman and B.C. Smith, eds., *SIGART Newsletter, Special Issue on Knowledge Representation,* 1980.

245. A. Barr and E.A. Feigenbaum, *The Handbook of Artificial Intelligence,* William Kaufmann Publishers, Inc., San Mateo, Calif., 1982.

246. E. Rich, *Artificial Intelligence,* McGraw-Hill, New York, N.Y., 1983.

247. M.R. Quillian, "Semantic Memory," in *Semantic Information Processing,* M. Minsky, ed., MIT Press, Cambridge, Mass., 1968.

248. S.C. Shapiro and G.H. Woodmansee, "A Net-Structure-Based Relational Question Answerer," *Proc. Int'l Joint Conf. Artificial Intelligence,* William Kaufmann Publishers, Inc., San Mateo, Calif., 1971, pp. 325-346.

249. A. Newell, "Production Systems: Models of Control Structures," in *Visual Information Processing,* W.G. Chase, ed., Academic Press, New York, N.Y., 1973.

250. M. Minsky, "A Framework for Representing Knowledge," in *The Psychology of Computer Vision,* P.H. Winston, ed., McGraw-Hill, New York, N.Y., 1975.

251. U. Neisser, *Cognition and Reality: Principles and Implications of Cognitive Psychology,* W.H. Freeman, San Francisco, Calif., 1976.

252. H.A. Simon, *The Sciences of the Artificial,* 2nd edition, MIT Press, Cambridge, Mass., 1981.

253. R.B. Irvin and D.M. McKeown, Jr., "Methods for Exploiting the Relationship Between Buildings and their Shadows in Aerial Imagery," *IEEE Trans. Systems, Man, and Cybernetics,* Vol. 19, No. 6, 1989, pp. 1564-1575.

254. A.R. Rao and R.C. Jain, "Knowledge Representation and Control in Computer Vision Systems," *IEEE Expert,* Vol. 3, No. 1, 1988, pp. 64-79.

Thomas O. Binford

Artificial Intelligence Laboratory
Computer Science Department
Stanford University

Survey of Model-Based Image Analysis Systems

Reprinted from *International Journal of Robotics Research*,
Volume 1, Number 1, 1982, pages 18-64, "Survey of Model-Based
Image Analysis Systems" by T.O. Binford by permission of The
MIT Press, Cambridge, Massachusetts.

Abstract

*A survey and critique of the state of the art in
model-based image analysis systems is presented. The
paper includes summaries of a selection of systems and
evaluates them from the viewpoint of progress toward
general vision systems. The paper also describes principles
of design of general vision systems.*

1. Introduction

Human beings pursue many goals in an unconstrained, constantly changing world with many objects; they work within a *general vision system.*
Robots work in manufacturing performing a single,
repeated task with few objects, all known, in constrained environments engineered to simplify those
tasks. In vision systems for manufacturing, many
special-case tricks are used that do not generally
apply to worlds with many objects and many goals.
However, those systems must eventually come to resemble general vision systems more than is generally
acknowledged.

Consider what is required to make improvements
in current industrial vision systems to make them
saleable in a large market. A single system must (1)
be easily programmed to accomplish many tasks of
visual control or inspection, (2) not need extensive
special-case engineering, and (3) be insensitive to
variations in lighting. A single system must be instructed effectively to determine many classes of defects, including rare defects and those not encountered in training, and to distinguish cosmetic from
real defects. While a single industrial task is very
constrained, the range of tasks and objects in a

The International Journal of Robotics Research
Vol. 1, No. 1, Spring 1982,
0278-3649/82/010018-47 $05.00/0
© 1982 Massachusetts Institute of Technology

major company, industry, or industries is not. It is
not cost-effective to build a separate system for each
task; thus, an adequate system must have modules
specialized for a particular task. Other applications
now being pursued impose even more severe requirements for high-speed object classification in
complex environments.

We work to make machines see as people do, to
understand how people see, to implement performance systems for visual applications, and to incorporate current capabilities in an experimental system to
support further research. Those activities all depend
on common visual operations and common representations.

In this paper, *prediction* refers to mappings from
object models to their predicted appearances in
images (i.e., top-down mappings in the direction
from symbol to signal). *Description* and *observation*
refer to mappings from sensed images to perceived
surfaces and objects (i.e., bottom-up mappings from
signal to symbol). *Interpretation* refers to mappings
between predictions and descriptions. *Generic* means
defined over a class (e.g., generic with respect to
viewpoint meaning defined over a range of viewpoints). One example of interpretation is *template
matching*, that is, finding the best embedding of a
template subimage to an observed image, over all
translations and rotations. One example of prediction
is the mapping of a specific object model to a specific image from a particular viewpoint by techniques
of computer graphics. Neither example is interesting
for general vision systems.

In the "bad old days," work on vision systems
was commonly justified by statements that general
segmentation and description were impossible, a
dead end. Description modules might be improved a
bit, but not much. It was not necessary to improve
them. With that doctrine, powerful vision systems
could be made by combining existing modules into
systems that used extensive world knowledge. Not
only was this the way to successful applications pro-

grams, but it was a basis for human visual performance.

A minority held the contrary view that low-level vision modules were weak, fulfilling less than 1% of their potential. This minority felt that although the problems are fundamental, segmentation and description are powerful in humans and will eventually be powerful in machines. Combining ineffective procedures, they thought, would produce little of interest. (Three pieces of junk are usually worth less than one; there are more to get rid of.) Vision systems would be inherently limited by performance of segmentation modules. Further, ad hoc building of systems would be frustrated because without effective representation and description, knowledge cannot be used effectively. There are deep problems in encoding and using world knowledge in a general way in a wide range of situations, that is, in relating world knowledge to image structures where world knowledge is typically about object classes in *three space*. This view held that combination of existing modules to build vision systems would not lead to powerful vision systems. Useful systems might be made for limited applications, however, and building systems is a useful exercise for looking at the full problem. Yet this group believed that careful theoretical analysis and implementation of individual vision operations was an essential basis for building vision systems and especially for effective applications.

The minority opinion is now held by the majority, and studies of fundamental vision science are under way. System building is no longer an end in itself, but is used for applications and demonstrations. It is now time to look at both applications and the total problem.

2. Observations About Systems Surveyed

Except for the first four, the systems surveyed will be discussed in alphabetical order. One vision system has succeeded in labeling large regions in aerial photographs (Nagao, Matsuyama, and Ikeda 1978); another has labeled large regions in a few outdoor scenes from ground-level views (Ohta 1980). ACRONYM has identified aircraft in aerial pho-

tographs (Brooks 1981). Another system has labeled objects in typical scenes of a desk (Shirai 1978). The results of these and other efforts are encouraging as first demonstrations. As general vision systems, they have a long way to go.

With several of the summaries of systems are comments about their limitations as general-purpose vision systems. The lists of limitations are only reminders with examples, not complete descriptions of the ways in which these systems would not have general applications. Complete descriptions of problems follow summaries of systems.

What works in the best of these systems? What makes them go? They succeed with quasi–two-dimensional scenes; for example, aerial photographs, industrial scenes from a fixed viewpoint, x-ray images, and ground-level photos from a fixed viewpoint. Even ACRONYM, which incorporates viewpoint-insensitive mechanisms, has been demonstrated only on aerial images, although there is reason to believe that ACRONYM will succeed with ground-level photographs also. Ohta (1980) demonstrated some success with a set of similar scenes from several viewpoints. Still, the system uses relations that are manifestly viewpoint-dependent.

The systems "use" image models. In Ohta's system (1980), the model includes the following relations: the sky touches the upper edge of the picture; the road touches the lower edge of the picture; trees are in the middle of the picture; and buildings have a linear upper boundary with the sky. One type of image model includes maps and symbolic sketches. Several systems use maps in registration of images with symbolic databases. An exception, ACRONYM (Brooks 1981), generates viewpoint-insensitive image models from object models in three space.

The systems "know" few objects. Ohta's (1980) has four objects with subobjects. Nagao (1978) mentions about nine classes of areas, but the system described apparently distinguishes only four: fields (with vegetation or bare); buildings; wooded areas; and linear features (roads, rivers, rail). ACRONYM has models of generic wide-bodied passenger aircraft, Lockheed's L-1011, and Boeing's 747-B and 747-SP. Shirai's (1978) includes a few objects found on desks: a lamp, a book stand, a cup, a telephone, and some small objects such as a pen. These four systems take advantage of the limited set of objects by using predominantly top-down interpretation of images, and relying heavily on prediction. The systems use models of specific objects. For example, Ohta's (1980) uses a model in which a car is darker than the road against which it appears.

Depth information is powerful. With depth data, input and models are at the same level. Depth data directly describes surfaces, which are natural for object interpretation. Images are two-dimensional, while objects are three-dimensional. Image-level invariants are weak, while three-dimensional invariants are strong and valuable for object-level interpretations. The projection process destroys information. The remark is often made that vision is the inverse of graphics, as if to imply that vision is thus somehow simpler than we find it to be. The inverse of projection is indeed simple, but it is useless. There is no unique inverse, only very high orders of continuous infinities of projectively equivalent surfaces. Depth can be inferred from sequences of images (stereo, observer motion, object motion, photometric stereo). A primary problem is determining corresponding elements in the sequence. Direct depth measurement avoids the correspondence problems of reconstructing depth data from image sequences. There are much greater problems in inferring surface structure and depth relations from single images.

One key to performance of systems is in their use of measurements that are simply related to characteristic properties of surfaces and to three-space relations of surfaces. Surface reflectivity and surface material are often characteristic (e.g., concrete and asphalt roads, or vegetation). Surface material can be partially inferred from color and texture. Intrinsic properties such as color, texture, and shape thus provide powerful and simple clues to interpretation. In Rubin's system (1978), 44% identification of pixels was achieved with the intensity of the blue channel alone. Remote sensing has depended on pixel classification based on spectral properties. Nagao, Matsuyama, and Ikeda (1978) use spectral properties of vegetation; shape descriptors, including elongation and straight boundary; and a simple texture descriptor. Ohta (1980) uses color, simple texture, straight boundary, and hole, in addition to nonintrinsic relations that are viewpoint-dependent.

ACRONYM (Brooks 1981) utilizes shape descriptors that are ribbons and ellipses and describes a larger class of quasi-invariant observables of shape. The use of simple intrinsic properties can be pushed much further than has been done thus far.

2.1. LIMITATIONS

What are the limitations of these systems in the restricted domains for which they were designed? How do they limit attempts to extend them to general vision systems?

In my opinion, most systems have not attempted to be general vision systems. The performance they achieve is based on a severely limited context and reveals low ambitions for the quality of scene description they generate. ACRONYM does demonstrate some progress toward the goal of a general vision system, a goal that is still distant. The fundamentalist view of systems appears to have been accurate: first, performance of vision systems is strongly limited by performance of segmentation modules; second, systems make weak use of world knowledge. Existing systems have weak description, with little use of shape. Systems, like description operations, have achieved less than 1% of their potential, even allowing for weak description. They use little information in weak ways. Systems primarily relate image relations to image observables; they lack most the ability to relate three-space models to images. Systems are being built, but there is relatively little emphasis on basic vision problems in system building. Until recently, systems efforts have been small and short-lived—a few years' effort. Focused and continuous efforts are necessary but not sufficient for system building. Just the system programming task in building a vision system is enormous.

With the exception of ACRONYM, the systems surveyed do not appear to have the capability of viewpoint-insensitive interpretation. Since the systems depend on image models and relations, they are strongly viewpoint-dependent. To generalize would require three-dimensional modeling and interpretation, as in ACRONYM.

The systems do not appear to be effective in environments with many objects. They jump to conclusions based on flimsy evidence and would probably not distinguish many objects in a complex visual environment. Humans may occasionally hallucinate in the same way, but usually they have strong evidence for interpretation.

The primary limitation in seeking stronger evidence for interpretation is weak segmentation capability and weak implementation of observation primitives. For example, in Ohta's system (1980), shadows are identified as having low intensity; black objects would be confused with shadows in typical scenes. In indoor scenes, contrast across shadow boundaries can be low. Most systems surveyed segmented images based on *pointwise properties*, that is, connected components of points that independently fall in some spectral band. Few systems used shape in segmentation of regions, that is, used continuity of edges that form ribbons. In other words, most systems segment regions then describe their shape, while a few segment well-formed regions. Simple texture measures are used; however, segmentation of extended edges is a major void, especially segmentation of textured regions. Correspondingly, shape description is primitive. Interpretation systems do not appear yet to make full use of even these limited capabilities. No system surveyed has effective texture segmentation and description such that surface texture is an intrinsic property in identification. Where range measurements are available, surfaces can be segmented directly at occlusions, that is position discontinuities. This is not the same as segmenting objects as humans do, because an object resting on a plane will not be segmented from the plane; the object and the plane are coincident. Even with range data, systems make poor symbolic, segmented descriptions of surfaces because of the fundamental weakness in segmentation.

None of the systems duplicates the human capability of color constancy, that is, the systems are incapable of sensitivity to source spectrum. Brightness constancy is related, inferring which surfaces are white and black in black-and-white images. Color constancy and brightness constancy are obtained by estimating surface reflectivity by a global partial ordering of local relations (Land and McCann 1971). It is no accident that multispectral data are useful,

since surface reflectivity is characteristic in many cases (but not unique). It is also no accident that color constancy and brightness constancy have not been integrated in the systems surveyed, since constancy requires a global computation that is much more complex than pointwise, multispectral calculation and that requires effective segmentation. Horn (1973) has demonstrated partial success with color constancy; however, that capability is not integrated in any system. To my knowledge, no use has been made of surface reflectivity in black-and-white images for those same reasons. In the case of an active ranging sensor, reflectivity can be computed directly at points from reflected intensity and range.

Systems typically use the hypothesis-verification paradigm. Hypothesis generation is the crucial part. Hypothesis generation is trivialized in the top-down case. For example, ACRONYM now searches only for aircraft. Another approach to hypothesis generation is evident in the systems surveyed. If an object class has a stable property, they assign the object class as an interpretation for any image region that has that property. For example, they assign vegetation as an interpretation for any image region that has the right color: green. That assignment has utility in restricted scene domains. But in typical cases, assignment must be generalized. For example, a house has straight lines, but to assign a house interpretation to image regions with straight lines would have little usefulness. The appropriate interpretation is not necessarily the union of all objects with straight edges, since that class is very large and the simple prescription does not tell how to break down the class. Rather, systems should relate straight lines to structural elements with straight edges. That requires powerful capabilities for inference of shape such as those being developed in ACRONYM (Binford 1981). Thus, that method of hypothesis generation is successful in restricted scene domains with a few object classes that are easily separated by local operations.

2.2. NAGAO, MATSUYAMA, AND IKEDA

In the systems described by Nagao, Matsuyama, and Ikeda (1978; 1980), an aerial photograph is first segmented into regions by several processes. Judging from the dominant features of each extracted region, specialized feature extraction and recognition programs are applied to that region only. Properties of objects are summarized and are fed back in order to reanalyze ambiguous regions.

To extract major regions, the following operations are used: (1) edge-preserving smoothing; (2) segmentation into regions that are continuous in spectral properties; (3) extraction of five kinds of regions, called *cue regions;* (4) analysis of each cue region by an object-detection program specific to region type; and (5) summary of properties of regions fed back to subsystems.

Cue regions include large homogeneous regions, elongated regions, shadow and shadow-making regions, vegetation regions, water regions, and high-contrast-texture regions. Each kind of cue region is extracted independently of the others. Some regions may appear in several types of cue regions.

Nagao and Matsuyama's book shows data from several pictures with four spectral bands taken at low altitude from an airplane. The pictures are 256×256 with 8 bits per pixel, corresponding to 50×50 cm on the ground. Spectral bands are red, green, blue, and infrared.

Pictures are first processed by an edge-preserving smoothing operator. It is intended to remove "noise" and to remove the blurring at edges of regions for pixels that overlap two regions. It is somewhat successful; however, it erodes thin lines and small regions (smaller than 3×3). It presumably rounds corners.

After smoothing, each picture in the four bands is divided into small patches with constant gray level. Patches with similar spectral properties are grouped together: if the differences in four bands are less than a threshold between a labeled pixel and its neighbor, the neighbor is merged. This is a gradient operation that allows shading. The threshold value in each spectral band is adaptively determined as follows. The differentiated picture is divided into 16 64×64 blocks and a histogram made of nearest-neighbor differences for each block. A valley is found for each histogram where the valley has a value lower than the succeeding nine values. The minimum value is chosen for valleys among the 16

blocks. This follows the reasoning that noise will have a large peak, and edges will have a smaller peak.

Small regions with less than 4 pixels are merged with neighboring large regions with the most similar spectral properties. This is done because boundaries of homogeneous regions sometimes are ragged as a result of separate smoothing in each spectral band.

One shape descriptor is the best *minimum bounding rectangle* (MBR), defined as the MBR with maximum ratio of region area/area of MBR over angles $10°$ apart. Elongation and direction are taken from the best MBR.

Large homogeneous regions are defined by making a histogram of homogeneous region size and applying a valley-detection algorithm. Small regions are assumed to result from noise. Regions larger than the threshold are processed further. They may be fields, grasslands, lakes, and sea.

Some regions are flat (e.g., fields and the sea); however, houses, buildings, and trees have height. Shadows give information about height. Shadows are usually available because aerial pictures are usually taken in good weather. Shadows are obtained in the following way. A histogram is made of brightness of smoothed pictures. The average brightness in the whole picture is calculated. The brightness is calculated that makes the interclass scatter minimum when divided into two classes. If the gradient at this value is small, it is chosen as the threshold brightness, I1. Otherwise a search is made for a valley near that value (I1). Homogeneous regions whose average brightness is less than the value I1 are chosen as shadows. Shadow-making regions are chosen to be those adjacent to shadows with a long common boundary in the direction away from the sun. Shadows are used to discriminate between flat objects and those with height.

Elongated objects include roads, rivers, and railroad lines. No analysis is made of railroad lines. Elongated regions may be broken by cars, trains, or shadows, and they may be curved. For curved regions, the MBR does not give a good estimate of elongation; the system determines an elongation effective for curved regions by taking the longest path on the skeleton of a region. If length/width >3, regions are considered to be elongated.

Vegetation areas have a small ratio of red to infrared intensity, a property that is quite stable. However, blue roofs have the same property. Thus, the system was made to exclude regions with large intensity in the blue band. Adjacent vegetation regions are merged into a large vegetation region. Water regions are identified by spectral properties, with the additional condition that water regions are darker than adjacent regions. Problems were found for water in shadow and where there were weeds. Extraction of vegetation and water are two examples of segmentation according to intrinsic properties of materials.

High-contrast texture regions are treated as follows. After smoothing, only coarse texture remains from objects 1.5 m on a side. Woods and residential areas contain small objects such as trees, houses, roads, and shadows. The authors found it almost impossible to recognize these small objects using only individual properties such as shape. Thus, the system extracts a set of small regions as a whole and recognizes each constituent region based on properties of the group of small regions. The system extracts homogeneous regions, then moves a $N \times N$ window over the image; if the window contains more than $2N$ boundary points, the system considers the central point of the window as part of a high-contrast texture region. The system removes small holes and peninsulas by growing regions two steps, shrinking four steps, then growing two steps. The system merges any homogeneous region that has more than half its area in high contrast but that is not a large homogeneous region. The common area between the high-contrast regions and the large vegetation regions is registered as a high-contrast vegetation region.

A large homogeneous region may be a crop field, bare soil, or a grassy area. Boundaries of large homogeneous regions composed of straight lines are designated *crop field* unless they are elongated regions. Boundaries are called *straight* if more than 60% of pairs of forward and backward boundary chords have angles of less than 22.5° (for point i, the forward chord is the pair of points indexed by i, i + 5, the backward chord is the pair indexed by i, i − 5). Crop fields so designated are put into two classes, one with vegetation, the other without. A region adjacent to a crop field or bare crop field is a *candidate* for either if its area is greater than half the threshold for large homogeneous regions.

Elongated regions include rivers and roads, which are used to register images. Elongated regions may be broken by bridges, cars, and shadows. They are not vegetation regions, shadows, or shadow-making regions. Road candidates are elongated, not vegetation, and not water regions. The system examines all pairs of candidate regions and connects those that have nearly the same intensity and color, adjacent ends, the same width, and the same direction. The conditions are difference of average gray scale in the four spectral bands less than a threshold (separate for each band); ratio of widths near 1 (between $^2/_3$ and $^3/_2$); smallest separation between ends less than $3W$, where W is the smaller of the two widths; and direction difference less than 45°. Roads are candidates with elongation >8 from length/width along the *skeleton* and for which the variance of widths along the skeleton is small. Intervening gaps may not be vegetation or water regions. The system traces any such road and picks up nearby side roads connected to it, with small difference in hue, with ratio of widths between $^1/_2$ and $^2/_1$, and with one end point within $3W$ of the first road found. The system recurses on side roads to find their side roads. Cars are recognized as rectangular regions on roads.

River candidate regions are water regions, not necessarily elongated. Analysis of rivers is similar to that of roads. Multispectral properties of water in shadow are greatly affected. Thus, shadow regions are merged with water if they are adjacent to a water region, if they are not a vegetation region, and if merged regions have increased elongation.

Each high-contrast vegetation area is assumed to be a wooded area. Small elements should have irregular shape (from the straightness condition above). A high-contrast vegetation region contains shadows and shadow-making regions; this distinguishes woods from grass.

The approach for finding houses is to identify candidates for residential areas first and then find houses. High-contrast regions that are not large homogeneous regions and not large vegetation areas are candidates for residential areas. Residential areas are identified as areas in which gradients are strong

Binford

Fig. 1. An aerial photograph, basis for system identifications shown in Figs. 2–17. (From Nagao and Matsuyama 1980.)

Fig. 2. Shadow regions. (From Nagao and Matsuyama 1980.)

in two orthogonal directions. Houses typically have walls at right angles. The method would be valid where houses are laid out on an orthogonal grid. HOUSE1, a recognition routine for houses, uses these properties: in a residential area; not a vegetation region, not a shadow region, not a water region, but a shadow-making region; rectangular shape. HOUSE2 extracts regions whose average gray levels in the four spectral bands are similar to those of any houses recognized by HOUSE1. HOUSE2 requires a weaker condition on rectangularity, and waives the condition that the region be a shadow-making region if it is in a residential area. Houses also appear as two rectangular elements, where two inclined surfaces are segmented as separate, adjacent regions. HOUSE3 tries to recognize parts of a roof that are not recognized and that are adjacent to roofs already recognized. HOUSE4 looks for missing houses in regular arrays. It looks for regions that fall on sites determined by "regularity vectors" of the pattern of houses. Candidates must not be vegetation region, water region, shadow region, or elongated region and must satisfy rectangular fit. Buildings are designated as regions that are not vegetation or water

regions, that are shadow-making regions, that have area greater than an ad hoc value, and a predominantly straight boundary.

System control tries to resolve conflict labels and to deal with unlabeled regions. If a region has more than one label, the most reliable label is chosen and other interpretations are rejected. Interpretations that are dependent on rejected interpretations (e.g., car identified from road) are also rejected. If regions are unlabeled because their shapes do not satisfy conditions of object classes, the system activates a split-and-merge process to attempt to split the region into two regions or to merge the region with adjacent regions. This sometimes corrects faulty segmentations. Splitting takes place at bottlenecks in width along the longest path on the skeleton of the region.

Results are shown for several images in the book (Nagao and Matsuyama 1980). The system does well for roads, fields, and forest. Figures 1–17 show steps in an example of analysis. Some areas are falsely labeled as houses by HOUSE2 (seven in one picture). About 3% of the scene is shadow that is unlabeled. Small shadows on roads and rivers can be correctly labeled; shadowed vegetation areas can

The International Journal of Robotics Research

Fig. 3. Shadow-making regions. Regions enclosed by black lines show the shadow-making regions;

gray shading denotes shadow regions. (From Nagao and Matsuyama 1980.)

Fig. 4. Vegetation regions. (From Nagao and Matsuyama 1980.)

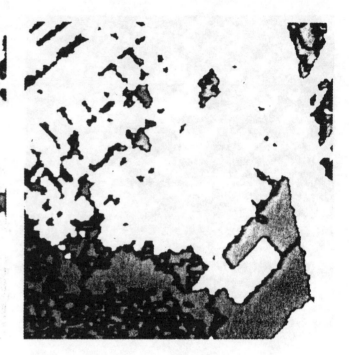

also be labeled. Otherwise, there is difficulty with large shadowed areas. A large area around houses is left unlabeled. The system has difficulties with urban scenes. For five scenes, unlabeled shadow and unrecognized areas are 3%, 19%; 1.6%, 16%; 10%, 31%; 22%, 30%; and 4%, 16% respectively. Thus, 20–52% of the area is unlabeled. This is a pessimistic evaluation, since significance of many details is not related to size. The interpretation process requires about 200 s per multispectral picture on a machine with 90 ns average instruction time, plus about 240 s of smoothing.

This is a fine and well-crafted system. It performs interesting interpretations on these examples. Its approach is to use special subsystems to recognize specific objects. Thus, it is not intended as a general vision system. The following limitations appear when it is considered as a general vision system.

Description and segmentation are limited. The system makes weak use of texture, a problem throughout the computer vision community. Its only texture descriptor is textured versus nontextured, based on boundary density. The system's shadow identification is not general and not reliable. It is

unlikely that in general scenes a valley will show up in the histogram, and unlikely that any intensity threshold will separate shadow from nonshadow. Reflectivities vary by about 0.05 to 0.90, a factor of 16, while shadow to full illumination typically has a ratio of 0.1/1.0. Their ranges overlap. Segmentation appears highly dependent on color input. The smoothing operation degrades the picture considerably.

Interpretation depends on assumptions that are not broadly useful. Shadows provide the only three-dimensional interpretation. No use is made of shadows to determine shape of objects other than as non-flat. Shadows are assumed to be adjacent to shadow-casting regions. This is not generally true and, even when true, makes assumptions about surface marking and performance of edge operators. Interpretation is appropriate for large areas, not for human-scale objects for which shape is important. There are models for only a few objects. Weak use is made of shape. Even for the domain of aerial photos, interpretations are made on weak assumptions. Grass pastures can have straight boundaries. Water can appear brighter or darker than surrounding land; the condition that water appears dark

Binford

Fig. 5. Large vegetation
areas. Each area consists
of many elementary
regions. (From Nagao and
Matsuyama 1980.)

Fig. 5. Large vegetation areas. Each area consists of many elementary regions. (From Nagao and Matsuyama 1980.)

the author's choice of color parameters is intensity-dependent. Matching searches for a many-to-one correspondence between regions and images of surfaces. Each region is evaluated for each surface interpretation rule.

Ohta determines the best set of parameters for segmentation of color regions. Ohta proposes as color parameters the three eigenvectors of the covariance matrix (Karhunen-Loeve transformation). He starts out to find eigenvectors dynamically, but finds it about as satisfactory to determine eigenvectors once and for all. The eigenvectors turn out to be: $x1 = (r + g + b)/3$; $x2 = (r - b)/2$ or $(-r + b)/2$; $x3 = (-r + 2b - b)/4$. Eight scenes were used in an experimental analysis. Ohta used 109 selected regions, large regions that split into "not-small" regions. In the wr, wb plane, eigenvector $x1$ is in the first quadrant (83 regions), $x2$ is in second and fourth quadrants (22 regions), and $x3$ is in the third quadrant (4 regions). Thus, $x1$ is by far the most important, $x2$ next, and $x3$ almost negligible. If images are synthesized based on only $x1$, $x2$, with a constant value for $x3$, the results are reasonably good except for several small regions. That is, color is roughly two-dimensional. $x1$, $x2$, and $x3$ are intensity-dependent, which may not be acceptable to everyone. Regions tend not to have constant intensity; thus, regions are broken into bands using this set of color parameters.

The system processes images 256 × 256, with 5 bits or 6 bits. Region segmentation fails with texture, so the author segments off textured regions, obtained as follows. In a 9 × 9 window, if the Laplacian of 8 out of 9 subwindows (3 × 3) exceeds threshold, it is considered a texture window. In a building scene, this process obtained the outer portions of a tree. The remainder (not strongly textured) is segmented by recursively applying thresholds determined from peaks of histograms of color parameters. A score is calculated for each peak, including the relative depth of the valleys and the sharpness of the peak. Regions thus obtained are evaluated by a *looseness criterion* related to the fraction of border cells to total cells. The segmentation with minimum looseness is chosen. Regions with size greater than a threshold are scanned with a 32 × 32 window. The data structure includes regions, boundaries, and ver-

relative to adjacent land is not general. Interpretation is image-oriented. In a view from ground level, fields would not be as prominent and models for fields would not be adequate. Houses would not appear as rectangular or L-shaped roofs.

2.3. OHTA

Ohta (1980) describes a system that assigns semantic labels to regions in color images of outdoor scenes. Ohta presents a new set of color parameters used in an Ohlander-like region analysis system (Ohlander 1975) that forms regions by splitting, using thresholds selected from histograms of the new color parameters. A plan is generated by an initial bottom-up coarse region segmentation. A symbolic description of the scene is made by top-down analysis using a production system, with knowledge of the world represented as a set of rules.

Region analysis tends to "oversegment"; that is, to split semantic regions (images of surfaces or objects) into several regions. In part, this is because

Fig. 6. A. Boundaries of elementary regions. B. Areas with high density of boundary points. C. Result of removing small holes and thin peninsulas. D. High-contrast texture area consisting of elementary regions. (From Nagao and Matsuyama 1980.)

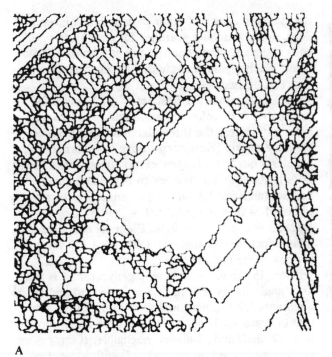

A

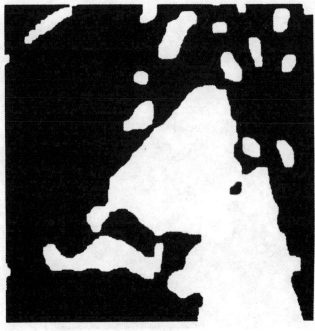

C

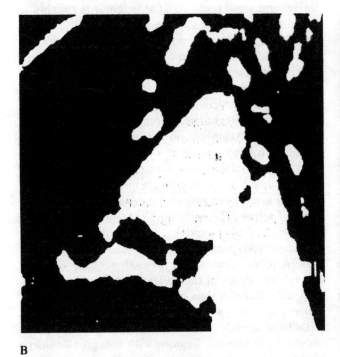

B

D

Binford

Fig. 7. **A**. Recognized crop fields. **B**. Recognized bare soil fields. (From Nagao and Matsuyama 1980.)

A

B

tices. Boundaries are four-neighbor connected and segmented into straight lines with iterative end-point fits.

Only primary features are in the data structure. Regions are represented by area; mean intensity of red, green, blue; degree of texture; contour length; center of mass; number of holes; scatter matrix of pixel positions; and MBR. The degree of texture is the mean value of the Laplacian for texture, described above. The scattering matrix is the covariance matrix of pixel positions, equivalent to an ellipse fit. Boundary segments include chain code, length, and contrast. Vertices include position and number of boundary segments. Holes have contour length. Line segments have distance from origin (rho), orientation, length, and positions of end points. Topological relations have pointers among regions and boundary curves and vertices, together with subset/superset relations for holes. In order to retrieve regions with similar color, a history of the tree of segmentations is maintained.

Calculation of properties of merged regions is described. Various secondary features can be computed easily from primary features. Only primary features are in the database. There are three functions for retrieving regions: ALL-FETCH, THERE-IS, and T-FETCH, corresponding to all regions from a set with specified properties, the first region of a set with specified properties, and all regions adjacent to a region respectively. In two results of segmentation, there are 339 and 391 regions, occupying about 90 KB for data structures.

There are four object classes: sky, trees, buildings with subobjects (windows), and roads with subobjects (cars). A plan image is generated by taking regions with large areas, called *keypatches*. The system tentatively merges all small patches to adjacent keypatches by choosing the highest score based on similarity of color and compactness of merged region. No semantic information is used in the merge.

The plan formulated by the bottom-up process is a set of object labels for keypatches and estimates of their correctness. The top-down process examines these interpretations and analyzes small, detailed structures in the context of large patches that have already been interpreted. When the top-down process makes a significant decision, the bottom-up process is activated to reevaluate the plan.

Fig. 8. A. Candidate areas for forests. B. Result of extracting large connected areas. Each area consists of a set of elementary regions. C. Result of extending shadow-making regions in candidate areas. D. Recognized forest areas. (From Nagao and Matsuyama 1980.)

A

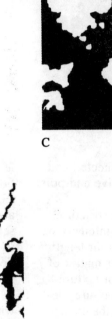

C

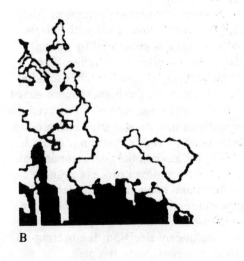

B

D

Fig. 9. *Recognized grass-lands. Some regions are recognized as crop field and forest area as well as* grassland. These conflicts are resolved by the system. (From Nagao and Mat-suyama 1980.)

Fig. 10. *Major roads iso-lated by program. (From Nagao and Matsuyama 1980.)*

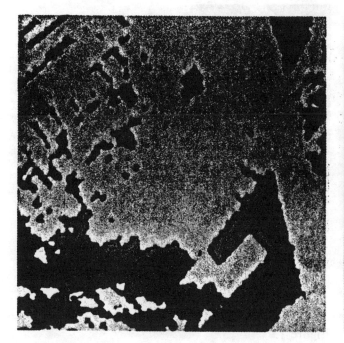

Rules for the plan are unary properties of objects and binary relations between objects. The plan manager computes a correctness value for every applicable rule applied to applicable regions in the plan image. Evaluation of relations takes place only after labels of regions are assigned.

In the top-down phase, each rule applied to each applicable region produces a score and an action to be registered on the agenda. At each step of analysis, the action with the highest score is executed and the database is changed. The agenda controls activation of production rules according to changes in the database. The agenda is updated whenever the database is changed. Each time, the number of tests is (the number of regions) times (the number of surfaces), that is, several hundreds times several tens, a total of thousands. In order to decrease computation, a coarse-to-fine analysis is made in a scene phase and an object phase. When a keypatch is labeled, the agenda activates the scene phase to reexamine keypatches that have not been interpreted. When a patch of an object is labeled, the agenda activates the object phase for that object to examine

patches touching the patch just labeled. As a result, the number of tests at each stage is several tens.

Each rule has a condition and an action. The condition is a fuzzy predicate. There are TO-DO and IF-DONE rules, corresponding to antecedent and consequent theorems of PLANNER (Hewitt 1968). Since only one region at a time is examined, there is a problem with global shape involving multiple regions. The system uses three mechanisms: the plan image; sets of patches retrieved from the database; and special rules (e.g., extracting the shape of a building).

The world model is a network of knowledge blocks that define objects, materials, and concepts. Production rules are divided into subsets stored in particular knowledge blocks; the subset for scene-level analysis is stored in the block SCENE, the subset to analyze objects is stored with the object.

Results are shown for several scenes. Patches with area greater than 300 pixels are keypatches. There were 57 rules in total. Figures 18–23 show examples of three scenes processed. A region of the building is initially assigned a high correctness value for SKY

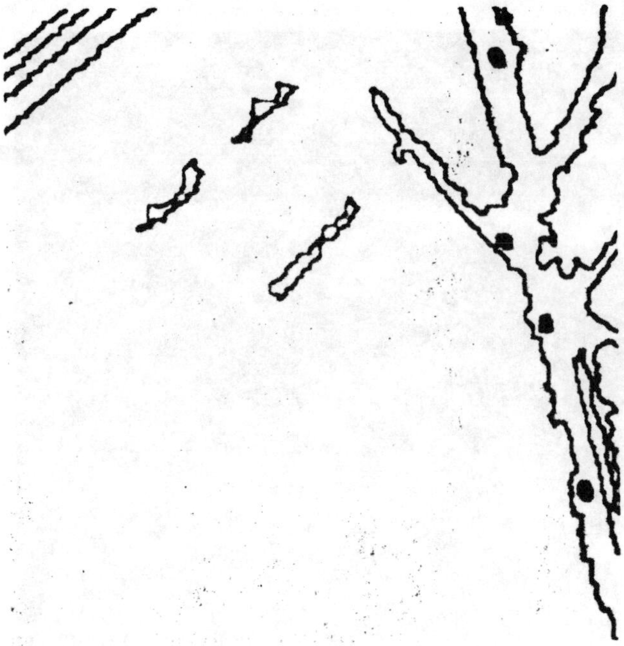

Figure 11

Figure 13

Figure 12

Figure 14

Binford

Fig. 15. Houses newly recognized by the HOUSE2 subsystem, using the multispectral properties of the already recognized houses (see Fig. 14). (From Nagao and Matsuyama 1980.)

Fig. 16. Houses newly recognized by the HOUSE3 subsystem. Two adjacent roofs of a house are merged into one region. (From Nagao and Matsuyama 1980.)

Fig. 17. Houses newly recognized by the HOUSE4 subsystem. "Missing houses" in the large residential area are recognized. (From Nagao and Matsuyama 1980.)

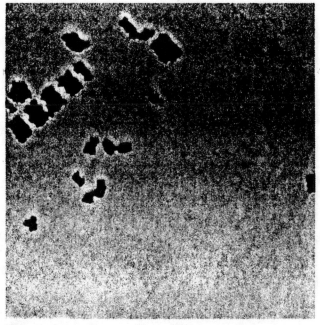

Figure 15

Figure 17

Figure 16

because it is bright and gray. In the revised plan, it has a high correctness value for BUILDING because of the relation between building and sky. Horizon is detected by a production rule. The horizon appears to be found as the lower bound of the sky by distinguishing SKY from ROAD.

The system does well overall. It demonstrates one of a few examples of reasonable performance on scenes of moderate complexity for a handful of rather different images. Ohta's thesis does not describe the rules themselves, except by a listing, or help very much in analyzing the system's performance and expected limitations. There are only a few objects in the model.

Models for analysis follow. The ROAD model has subobjects: car, shadow. It is made of asphalt, concrete. It has properties: horizontally long, touching lower edge of picture. It has relations: below horizon. The CAR in the ROAD model is horizontally long, dark, and above the ROAD. The SKY model has properties: not touching lower edge, shining, blue or gray, not texture, and touching upper edge. It has relations: linear boundary on the lower side. TREE is made of leaves. It has properties: in the

*Fig. 18. Result of the rule-
based analysis: example 1.
A. Digitized input scene,
basis for identifications*

*shown in Fig. 19. **B**. Result
of preliminary segmenta-
tion. **C**. Plan image. **D**. Result of meaningful segmen-*

*tation. S = sky; T = tree;
R = road; B = building;
U = unknown. (From Ohta
1980.)*

A

C

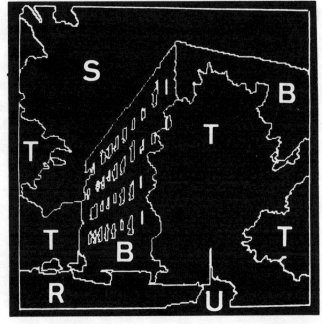

B

D

Fig. 19. Plans generated for the scene in Fig. 18. A. First plan, obtained by using only the property rules. B. Plan obtained

after using the relation rules. C. Plan obtained after extracting the horizon by the top-down analysis. D. Outlines of the building

extracted by the top-down analysis. (From Ohta 1980.)

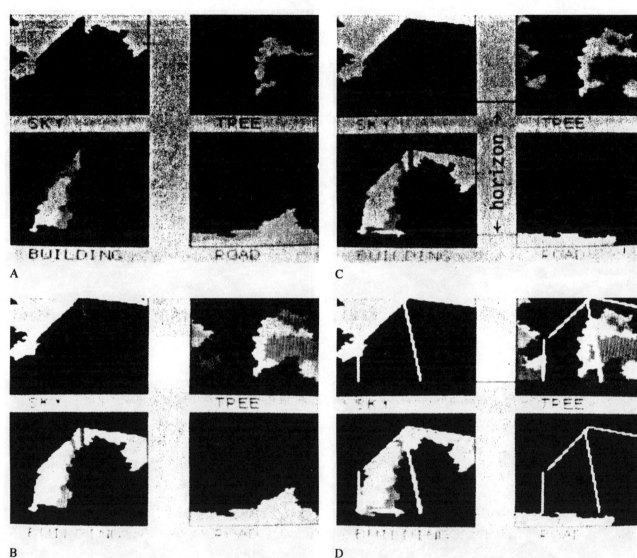

middle of the picture, heavy texture. The BUILD-ING is made of concrete, tile, or brick. It has subobjects: WINDOW. Its properties are in the middle of the picture, many holes, many straight lines, hole straight lines. It has a relation of linear upper boundary with the sky.

Some limitations of Ohta's system follow. The quality of segmentation is weak. Thin linear features that do not show up in histograms are important (e.g., in identification of cars). The description of texture is weak. The organization of relations among patches is weak. For example, colinearity of window

boundaries is not determined. Interpretation is image-dependent. Models are image-dependent. The model for road (touching the bottom edge of the picture) is too specific to be useful. Models are weak. The model for car depends on a car being on the road. It has the relation that the car appears dark relative to the road, which is not adequate even for this domain. It makes weak use of shape. A human would identify the car's make in many cases; the system's performance is inferior. There are models for few objects. The assumption that a single region contains only one object is not realistic. The ap-

Fig. 20. Result of the rule-based analysis: example 2. A. Digitized input scene. B. Result of preliminary seg-mentation. C. Plan image. D. Result of meaningful segmentation. S = sky; T = tree; B = building; R = road; C = car; CS = car shadow. (From Ohta 1980.)

A

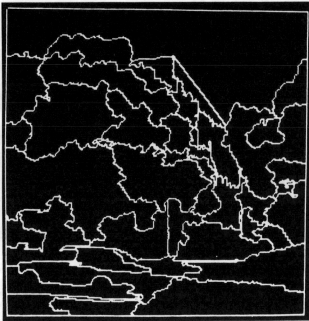

C

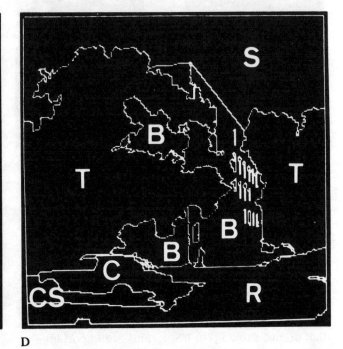

B

D

Binford

Fig. 21. Plans generated for the scene in Fig. 20. A. First plan, obtained using only the property rules. B. *plan obtained using the relation rules. C. Plan obtained after extracting the horizon from the top-down* *analysis. D. Outlines of the building extracted by the top-down analysis. (From Ohta 1980.)*

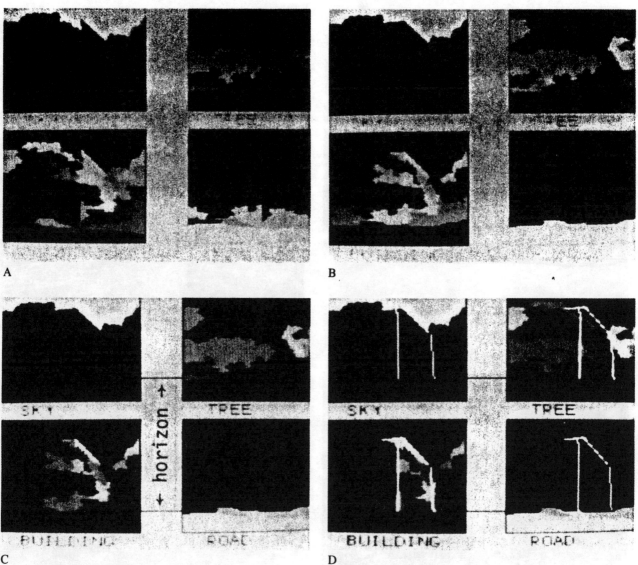

proach is ineffective in many situations in which fine details determine object labels.

2.4. ACRONYM·BROOKS

ACRONYM (Brooks 1981) is an implemented interpretation system containing a substantial core of fundamental mechanisms that are powerful and general.

Its performance demonstrated thus far depends on domain-independent capabilities, not on special domain-dependent tricks. ACRONYM as it stands is a large system that is part of a larger scheme for a general vision system. I am biased by my enthusiasm for ACRONYM, which is meant to be a general vision system. This objective requires an enormous effort involving all levels of a vision system—an effort beyond the state of the art. Substantial progress

Fig. 22. Result of the rule-based analysis: example 3. A. Digitized input scene. B. result of preliminary seg-mentation. C. Plan image. D. Result of meaningful segmentation. S = sky; T = tree; B = building; R = road; C = car; U = unknown; CS = car shadow. (From Ohta 1980.)

A

B

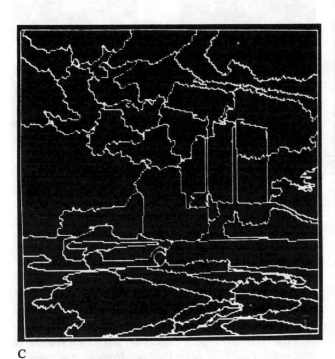

C

D

Fig. 23. Plans generated
for the scene in Fig. 22.
A. First plan, obtained using
only the property rules. B.
Plan obtained after using
the relation rules. C. Plan
obtained after extracting
the horizon by the top-
down analysis. D. Outlines
of the building extracted by
the top-down analysis.
(From Ohta 1980.)

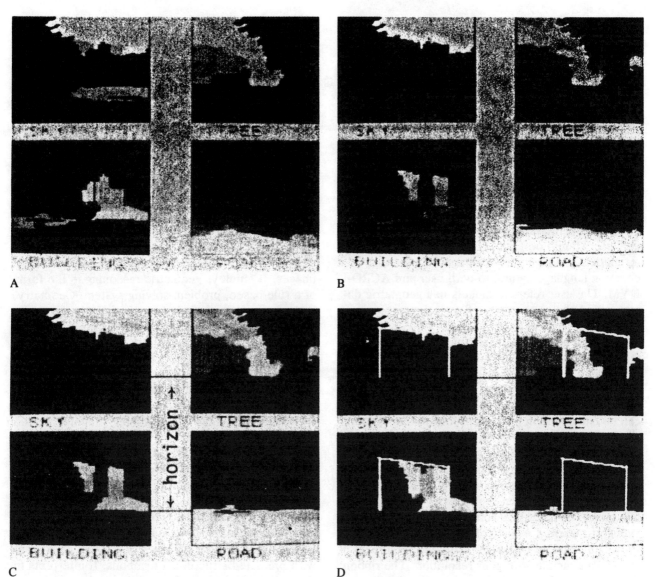

Fig. 23. Plans generated for the scene in Fig. 22. A. First plan, obtained using only the property rules. B. Plan obtained after using the relation rules. C. Plan obtained after extracting the horizon by the top-down analysis. D. Outlines of the building extracted by the top-down analysis. (From Ohta 1980.)

has been achieved. Immediate plans call for mechanisms that will greatly increase ACRONYM's power and breadth.

Objectives for ACRONYM include the attainment of three-dimensional interpretation, a rigorous scientific basis, and high performance. Important applications are typically difficult. Carefully built high-performance modules enable generality. It is intended to provide an option for a standard system, with a user base providing technology transfer. It has a large general core of powerful capabilities on which to base applications. Interpretation is generic with respect to object class, providing commonality of programs for similar applications and providing a means for inspection to distinguish essential from cosmetic flaws. Interpretation is generic with respect to observation, that is, ACRONYM is insensitive to viewpoint and flexible with varied sensor inputs.

The International Journal of Robotics Research

Mechanisms use special-case information and data. ACRONYM is complete. In the sense that interpretation makes use of total information, data, and knowledge, including multisensor data, knowledge of experts, geometric models of objects, and prediction of expectations. It incorporates powerful use of shape in modules for edges, texture and image organization, depth, shape from shading, and shape from shape. It incorporates mathematics and physics. The system is a critical mass effort over a continuing period, during which collaboration and applications are sought. It is engineered for easy use, facilitating input in the form of geometric models and rule bases, automatic programming, and user aids.

A user should program ACRONYM using geometric models and geometric task specifications, a common language natural to both user and ACRONYM. The user refers to models in a geometric database and shows examples of typical members of the object class. ACRONYM should infer specific and generic properties of the object class and contexts, especially causal relations. ACRONYM constructs perceptual programs to carry out the assigned task. ACRONYM should be general and generalizable in the sense that problem-specific information can be embedded in general, problem-independent mechanisms that provide for a natural decomposition of problems into physically meaningful elements. A core built up from a few problem domains should cover most capabilities required for other domains.

ACRONYM has been shown to be successful on a few images of aircraft in aerial images but not enough to warrant a claim of generality. Figure 24 shows an example with high resolution. Figure 25 shows an example with poor resolution. The ribbon finder has problems with the poor-resolution image, but ACRONYM recognizes the three aircraft for which ribbons are reasonable. In another image like Fig. 25, the ribbon finder did not turn up any adequate ribbon descriptions.

In a real sense, ACRONYM reasons from first principles. ACRONYM has a general core in that its rules implement algebra and projective geometry. There are no special rules for aerial images or aircraft. There is no profound reason why ACRONYM could not recognize aircraft in images taken at ground level, although it will probably break when tested on such images because of bugs or missing capabilities that were not exercised previously. For example, at ground level the fuselage appears more or less the same as from above. Wings are less observable, but engine pods and tail are more prominent. The rule base will need to be extended considerably in dealing with varied object classes, (e.g., manufactured parts, vehicles, and buildings).

ACRONYM has viewpoint-independent, three-dimensional object models in the form of part/whole graphs, in terms of generalized cylinder primitives. ACRONYM represents object classes, for which subclasses and specific objects are represented as restrictions, by constraints in the form of symbolic expressions with numeric type.

ACRONYM searches for instances of models in images. It employs geometric reasoning in the form of a rule-based, problem-solving system. Geometry is the key, while the rule-based system is simply a way of implementing geometry. A formal representation of geometry is probably necessary to make a compact and coherent set of rules in order to get additivity and consistency in a rule base. Despite claims to the contrary, it seems clear that a rule-based system in itself does not aid in making additivity and consistency of reasoning. Building a vision system is 1% a system effort of the sort familiar in computer science and 99% basic science.

ACRONYM predicts appearances of models in terms of ribbons and ellipses. It uses an edge finder to make observations of ribbons and ellipses in images. ACRONYM finds observed ribbons consistent with predicted ribbons and restricts interpretations to those which are parts of clusters consistent with predicted structures of ribbons. It interprets in three dimensions by enforcing constraints of the three-dimensional model. Thus, to identify aircraft it matches observed ribbons to predicted ribbons for wings and fuselage, then finds clusters of ribbons that are consistent with the combined wings and fuselage of a three-dimensional aircraft model.

ACRONYM makes predictions that are viewpoint-insensitive in the form of symbolic constraint expressions with variables. One mechanism of viewpoint-insensitive prediction is the use of observables that are invariant and quasi-invariant over large ranges of viewing angle. ACRONYM does not generate all

Binford

Fig. 24. Illustration of
ACRONYM's performance
on a high-resolution image.
(From Brooks 1981.)

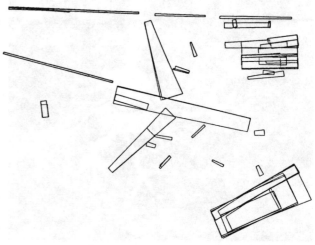

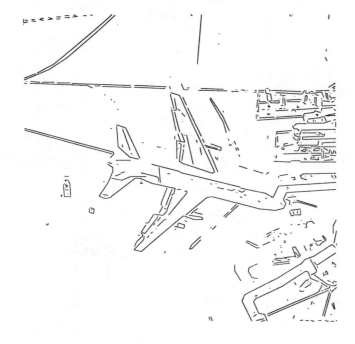

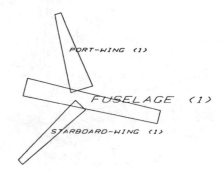

Fig. 25. ACRONYM's per-
formance on a low-
resolution image. (From
Brooks 1981.)

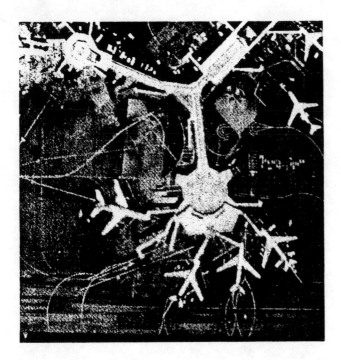

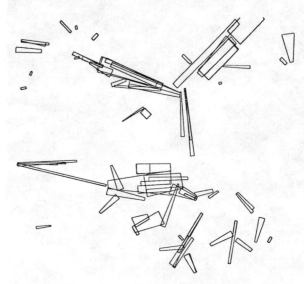

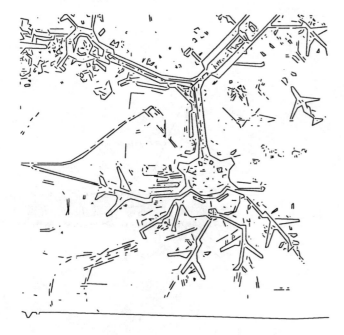

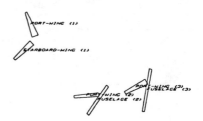

Binford

possible views of an object. Total prediction has combinatorial complexity. For a polyhedron with n distinct faces, there are $2n$ views. Instead, ACRONYM predicts partial views for individual faces of which there are of order n. Coherence of several features comes from merging constraints. The image-shape descriptors are invariant under image rotation. To generate predictions, ACRONYM starts with models in their coordinate frames. All contours of faces that might be visible are identified. They are transformed into the camera's coordinate frame, with symbolic translations and rotations represented by variables. The system simplifies the corresponding expressions and makes a projective transformation. Visible contours are identified. Relations between these contours are predicted, and the shape of the contour is predicted. Back constraints that relate image observables to model parameters are generated. Relations between ribbons are generated. Each ribbon provides a number of back constraints that combine to constrain model parameters. ACRONYM automatically determines ribbons and ellipses for parts of the object that it determines are most observable. Predictions of feature shapes are nodes of the prediction graph; arcs of the graph are image relations between features. Arcs relate multiple feature shapes predicted for a single cone. The swept surface and end surface of a cone are predicted separately. A prediction is made that they are coincident.

Interpretation proceeds by the combination of local matches of ribbons into clusters. Global interpretations must be consistent in two ways. First, they must satisfy constraints specified by the arcs of the prediction graph. Second, accumulated constraints that each local match imposes on the three-dimensional model must be satisfiable. The interpreter searches for maximum subgraphs of the observation graph that are consistent with constraints of subgraphs of the prediction graph. Each such match is an interpretation graph. The interpreter matches ribbons against predictions of ribbons. It then tries to instantiate arcs of the prediction graph by checking pairs of regions to see whether they satisfy relations predicted. For pairs that satisfy image relations, it merges constraints on the underlying three-dimensional model.

ACRONYM has been used as the basis for a simulator for robot systems and for automated grasping of objects, with a rule base for determining which surfaces are accessible in the initial position, which surfaces are accessible in the final position, and ways to grasp with maximum stability.

The top-down paradigm is only one part of the ACRONYM design. A top-down system is far from general. It is believed that this paradigm can provide only a small part of human performance, even though prediction has been made relatively powerful in ACRONYM by use of predictions that are generic with respect to object class and that are viewpoint-insensitive. The way to a general vision system lies in spatial understanding, as opposed to image understanding. That is, prediction of images and matching at the level of images is inherently limited (a convenient expedient reflecting the weakness of our descriptive mechanisms) but it is not a fundamental approach. Instead, the major part of interpretation is not at the image level but at the level of volumes. Descriptive mechanisms that generate volume descriptions are essential combined with prediction and interpretation at the level of volumes. Certainly stereo, motion parallax, and object motion are important observation capabilities, together with shading. Recent theoretical work on monocular interpretation of surfaces from images (Binford 1981; Lowe and Binford 1981) appear to promise that general mechanisms for generating spatial observations from images will be developed soon to support general vision systems.

Limitations of ACRONYM as a general system follow. ACRONYM has weak segmentation. The ribbon finder determines spurious ribbons. It misses small ribbons. Grouping of ribbons is not done in segmentation, only in interpretation. The line finder and ribbon finder perform badly with texture.

Interpretation is limited. Image prediction and matching are not sufficiently general for scenes with many objects. Interpretation has been tried with only a few objects, and the system models for very few. It tests all pairs of ribbons in establishing relations, ignoring proximity. It has been tried on only a single viewpoint. The top-down paradigm is inadequate for complex scenes.

2.5. Shirai

In Shirai's system (1978), obvious edges are found in the entire scene. They are described by straight lines or ellipses. Edge points are found, using one-dimensional profiles; edge points are classified into three types. Averaging is done over small areas, typically 3×3. The direction of the edge is determined from the gradient. An *edge kernel* is determined by a set of edge points of the same type with similar gradient directions. Continuations of edge kernels must have the same edge type. The tracking phase predicts an edge element and verifies it. Tracking may insert a fictitious edge point at the predicted position. Tracking proceeds in both directions until both ends terminate by connecting to another end. Some edges are extended to fill small gaps.

Curve description has two phases, segmentation and curve fitting. *Segmentation* uses curvature versus arc length along the curve, while *curvature* is defined as the angle difference at a center point between chords a fixed distance on either side (approximately the difference of tangents). The routine finds sequences of high curvature to place knots. It tries to classify curves: if sagitta is large, it is a curve; if angle change is small, it is a line. It tries to merge adjacent undefined or curved segments. A method symmetric in x and y is used to fit curves. Curves are fit with ellipses. If the search does not converge, the number of parameters is decreased, successively fitting a circle and straight line.

Analysis of the scene starts from the most obvious object and proceeds to the next most obvious. For object recognition, it finds the most obvious feature, then finds a secondary feature to verify identity and determine object range. It then finds other lines on the object. For recognition of a lamp, the program locates the lamp shade, then looks for the trunk of the lamp, which supports the shade, then the lamp base.

The objects in Fig. 26 include a lamp, a book stand, a cup, a telephone, and small objects. For the lamp, the primary feature is a bright elongated strip for the shade. Secondary features are a pair of vertical edges corresponding to the trunk and the contour of the lamp base. The primary feature for the book stand is a cluster of long vertical lines in a rec-tangular region. Secondary features are lines connected to the verticals. The cup has a pair of vertical edges; secondary features include the ends of the cup connected to the verticals. The telephone has an ellipse for the dial and one outside the numerals; secondary features include features surrounding the ellipses. Small objects have shape and size of contour as primary features; secondary features are shape details and light intensity of the surface.

Small objects such as pens or erasers are tried after large objects are found or many edges are obtained. Otherwise, a small object might be confused with part of a large object. The system finds more edges by decreasing the reliability level and looking in delimited areas. The system may take a close-up image where necessary.

Experiments have been conducted successfully with a range of positions and orientations of objects and varied lighting conditions.

As with previous systems, this system has substantial limitations as a general vision system. The edge finder is adequate for this task, but it would not perform well in complex scenes; the system cannot deal effectively with texture; and the system has no organization of related edges. Interpretation is likewise limited. There are only image models, not object models; there are only few objects; and the analysis is top-down, which is reasonable for few objects.

2.6. Ballard, Brown, and Feldman

Ballard, Brown, and Feldman (1978) use image models in locating ships at docks and in locating ribs in chest x-rays. Geometric constraints are used. The system is oriented to answering queries; the level of detail is determined by the query. Only a portion of the image is interpreted. The system is structured in three levels: (1) the model; (2) the sketchmap synthesized during image analysis (it relates the model and the image); and (3) image data structures, including images at different resolutions and spectral components, texture images, and edge images.

The structure is similar to that of VISIONS (see below). Perhaps the main difference is that in VISIONS, segmentation is made to a level determined by the model so that the image will be understood as

Binford

Fig. 26. An example of the recognition process. A. Original scene. B. Edges found in cycle 1. C. Description. D. Recognition. E. Description in cycle 2. F. Edges found in cycle 4. G. Recognition. 0 = lamp; 1 = book stand; 2 = telephone; 3 = cup; 4 = pipe; 5 = pen, pencil, ball-point pen, felt-tip pen. H. Description of edges found without feedback from the recognition process. (From Shirai 1978.)

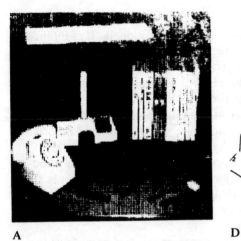

A

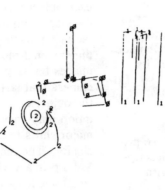

D

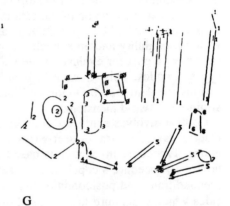

G

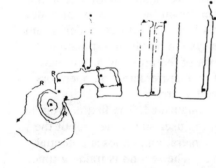

B

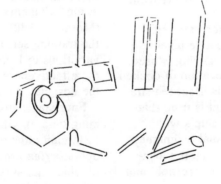

E

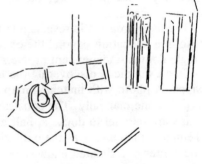

H

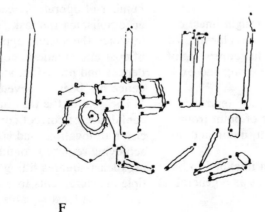

C

F

fully as possible. Here, the query determines the level of detail.

Links encode constraint relations. They include the probability that the relationship holds and include the expected value of the relationship. For example, SHIP ADJACENT DOCK is a constraint with a probability and an expected distance. A node may have a cost for evaluation, depending on its operand nodes. This allows cost-benefit analysis. Locations are delimited by union and intersection. Constraints are two-dimensional.

Control involves synthesis of a sketchmap. Queries take the form of user-written executive programs. Procedure invocation is based on a description of a procedure's capabilities, together with preconditions and postconditions. The executive decides which procedure to run based on cost-benefit, that is, the lowest cost procedure that meets preconditions. Procedure descriptions include slots that must be filled, slots the procedure can fill, cost and accuracy of the procedure, and the a priori reliability of the procedure.

The user program is responsible for "strategic" resource allocation beyond the executive level. No single domain-independent problem solving is used.

One example is discovering the location of docked ships. A photo with matching map is used; registration is done manually. The constraint is used that ships are parallel to docks at half a ship's width. Template matching was the only visual technique; the center is estimated midway between the locations at which correlation goes above threshold and goes below threshold.

In finding ribs in chest x-rays, only lower edges of ribs are found. There are procedures to locate parabolic rib segments, to translate and verify adjacent ribs, and to translate without verifying.

The representations used are (1) straight lines: ordered list of points, list of segments, circular lists of points, and (2) region boundaries: y list consisting of a y value followed by x values for entering and exiting region.

The operators included are correlation template matching, Hough, Hueckel, distance of point from segment, segment parallel to segment, union and intersection of regions.

The system is special-case and not intended to be a general vision system. Its limitations as a general vision system are many.

2.7. THE VERIFICATION VISION SYSTEM·BOLLES

The verification vision (VV) system (Bolles 1976) uses object models and image models. It is intended for inspection and visual control in repetitive manufacturing tasks. The VV system makes use of three-dimensional models, but it requires that sensed images be very similar to image models. Thus, for a camera that is 1 m from an object, the position of the object may vary by about ± 1 cm, and its orientation may vary by ± 15°, but there may not be major shifts in appearance or major changes in occlusion. The major reason for that restriction is that VV's primary visual operator is area correlation of small windows of an image with reference windows (Moravec 1980).

An object model contains a set of point features and their locations in three space. The image model includes a set of training images and features in those images. Features are small windows centered around elements determined by an interest operator (Moravec 1980). This is a weak object model. From the training set, the system builds an estimate of the variations of locations of features and an estimate of the effectiveness of its feature detection operators on the designated image features.

Four stages are distinguished. The first is programming time, in which the user states the goal of the task, calibrates the camera, and chooses potential operator/feature pairs. The second is training time, in which the system applies the operators to several sample pictures and gathers statistical information about their effectiveness. The third is planning time, in which the system ranks operators according to their expected contribution, determines the expected number of operators needed, and predicts the cost of accomplishing the task. The fourth is execution time, in which the system applies operators in their order of cost-effectiveness, combines the results into confidences and precision, and stops when desired confidence has been achieved or cost limit exceeded.

The goal of the task includes achieving sufficient confidence of correct correspondence, adequate precision of location, and sufficiently low cost of achieving required confidence and precision. VV uses least-squares fitting to combine results of multiple measurements to estimate position and precision. Since least-squares fitting is sensitive to assign-

Binford

ment errors, a Bayesian estimation scheme is used to choose assignments with few errors. Two sorts of information are used in making correct matches of image features to reference features: (1) confidences obtained from values returned by operators, and (2) relative image position of subsets of features. Because of combinatorics, the second method must be used with small subsets of features. Later, a search for maximal cliques consistent in three-space separations was used. The latter approach is much more satisfying conceptually, since relative image distances are not invariant, and their errors are not predictable without use of a three-dimensional model. Two types of features were studied: (1) cornerlike features obtained by an interest operator and matched by a binary-search correlator (Moravec 1980) and (2) curve features predicted by a geometric model of the object (Miyamoto and Binford 1975) and determined by a curve-verification procedure based on the Hueckel edge operator (Hueckel 1973). The latter were not integrated into the VV system.

The programming of VV problems was automated considerably. The program produces a set of features. The programmer filters out suggested features that are judged unreliable. In gathering statistics, VV displays a reference picture side by side with a training picture, with matching features marked. The system makes its best assignments according to consistent subsets. It asks the user for confirmation. It ranks operators according to an ad hoc quality measure. In execution, it applies operators in order of the measure.

The system is limited in that it primarily depends on small correlation windows as features. Thus, it is restricted in viewpoint. It was intended for a few objects. It uses three-dimensional models of objects, but they are point models and without shape relations.

2.8. FAUGERAS AND PRICE

In the system described by Faugeras and Price (1980), the input is a network of segments from procedures for region-based image segmentation and linear feature extraction. There are about 100–200 total segments of both types. Properties of segments include average color, simple texture measures, position, orientation, and simple shape measures. Relations between image segments include adjacency, proximity, and relative position. The model description is identical to the network of image segments. If a relation occurs in the model, it is expected to occur in the image description. The model is not a complete description of the scene, but apparently an image model.

Matching is a graph endomorphism. It is solved by stochastic matching (relaxation). Initial compatibilities are computed without relations because labels are not known; they combine weighted differences, taking up to 30 possible labels, or those with compatibility greater than $1/10$ of the best, whichever is fewer. The compatibility measure with relations is computed only with the most likely assignments for the second object (usually only one assignment). Compatibilities are computed as needed. The compatibility measure is the dot product $\mathbf{p} \cdot \mathbf{q}$, where $\mathbf{p}$ is the probability vector $(p(11), p(12) \ldots)$ and $\mathbf{q}$ is the prediction vector $(q(11), q(12), \ldots)$ for labels li.

It becomes a constrained optimization approached by steepest descent. Macro-iterations of steps are composed in order to make decisions to assign names to units with high probability (above 80%).

It is hard to tell what its performance is for the two images shown by the authors. The system has image-dependent models and is strongly restricted in viewpoint. Segmentation is relatively weak.

2.9. GARVEY

The function of the system described by Garvey (1976) is to locate objects in an office environment in which it is assumed that all objects are known. The system has as input measurements of range, reflectivity at one wavelength, and three color images. The system's strategy is to acquire image samples that might belong to the object, to validate the hypothesis, and to bound the image of the object. The system uses simple, local features rather than structured shape descriptions. It uses contextual relations, for example, a telephone is on a desk, to decrease search and to minimize the set of possibly

The International Journal of Robotics Research

ambiguous objects. The approach follows a belief that in a sufficiently restricted environment, a set of local distinguishing features can be found that are effective in initial screening for candidate matches. This depends on having models for all objects and not having many objects.

The system searches for cost-effective strategies of sequences of operators. In acquisition, it chooses an appropriate limited-search window of the image, sampling the image at a density determined by the object's size, maximum range, and least favorable orientation. Estimates are made of the cost of search with various operators and of the likelihood that the operator will be successful and correct. Which operators are effective depends on all objects in the image.

The system is programmed interactively. Objects are shown to the system by outlining them in an image. Objects are automatically characterized by conjunctions of histograms of local surface attributes such as hue, orientation, range and height, and relationships between surfaces. These characterizations provide ingredients for strategies for object finding.

In experiments, this system's performance rests strongly on having depth data and surface orientation derived from depth. To be found, a desk must have a desktop 2.5 ft high and horizontal orientation. For a door, height, orientation, and hue are not enough. Its size and location, together with a vertical rectangle characterization, are essential.

Regions are represented as lists of samples, as a list of vertices of a closed polygon boundary, by a bounding rectangle, and by vertical and horizontal bounding rectangles in space. Objects are represented by distributions of attributes of surfaces, with shape of surfaces and relations between surfaces.

Some limitations of the system follow from the approach of distinguishing features. In choosing simple features that distinguish regions corresponding to objects of interest, it is assumed that there are few objects and that all are known. The interpretation is strongly dependent on depth data and probably would not achieve similar performance without depth data. Shape, other than that obtained from depth, is used in a weak way. Also, the top-down approach does not go far in a world of many objects.

2.10. Levine

Levine (1978) describes a three-level system, of which the first two levels have been implemented. The first level segments pictures into regions without scene context. The second level has a local phase and a global phase. The local phase matches image templates with observed image regions, using A^* graph search. It performs global optimization using dynamic programming to merge regions and assign labels to them. The highest-level design includes a standard relational database and a system similar to production rules.

The system is implemented using MIPS, an interactive image processing system. Two data types are used uniformly throughout: image arrays and feature vectors. Low-level region analysis obtains about 200 regions from a 256×256 image, a reduction of about 300 to 1 in items, not necessarily in storage.

The intermediate level deals with standard views. The output of the intermediate level is an ordered list of interpretations for each region. The local intermediate-level process is a form of template matching of object descriptions. It is model-driven and uses heuristic graph search to match shape, color, and texture. The second process is global, also model-driven. It incorporates spatial relations as a global optimization problem solved by dynamic programming. Model input for this level comes from interactive designation of regions and objects, computing features, and updating the database. Symbolic information in the form of text is also a form of input.

The high-level system design includes a vision-production system with relational database.

Low-level segmentation is based on regions found by a shared, nearest-neighbor clustering modified by connectivity. Processing is approximately in order of decreasing size, using a pyramidal data structure. The edge pyramid has edges from a gradient operator. The pyramid thickens edges until, at the top level, all regions have been extinguished. Areas of the picture that are farthest from edges tend to be extinguished high in the pyramid. From a starting region, projecting down to the next level involves expanding 1 pixel into 4 pixels. Those marked as

Binford

edges are not examined at this level but are looked at in the next level down. At this level, those not marked as edges are marked for clustering, using the nearest-neighbor algorithm.

Local template matching is used to match collections of adjacent regions against all stored object prototypes. Features are stored in three classes, according to decreasing importance in reducing search time. The first class includes the MBR and its area. "Intrinsic" features make up the second category: intensity, hue, saturation, and texture. The third category includes six moment invariants as a rough measure of shape and detailed shape from a set of Fourier coefficients for the outline, used only in final template evaluation.

The A* algorithm is used for graph search with an evaluation function. Nodes are regions, while arcs are region adjacency. The estimate of the cost to node n is the number of nodes expanded from the start.

Relational information is used in the optimal search stage, done with dynamic programming. Regions may be ordered either according to region area or decreasing maximal confidence value among interpretations. The orderings of model and data do not necessarily correspond; no mention is made of whether the algorithm accounts for the difference in order. The transition function is a linear weighting of differences between structural relations in the image model and observed relations. Relations include LEFT-OF, RIGHT-OF, ABOVE, BELOW, ADJACENT-TO, CONTAINS, and CONTAINED-BY.

The knowledge database or long-term memory (LTM) in the high-level system design is a management-type relational database with accessing operations that constitute a relational algebra. Operations such as JOIN, PROJECT, INTERSECT, UNION, and RESTRICT are available. The high-level system will be a data-driven production system. Thus far, it only deals with images, not three-dimensional scenes. The LTM has subworlds for outdoor scenes, office scenes, and so on. Objects in LTM have associated actions to be taken under conditions of the short-term memory (STM). A STM contains a list of regions and their interpretations. It resembles the "blackboard" of HEARSAY. Regions are interpreted sequentially, unless an action is involved that alters the sequence. For each region, there is a list ordered by decreasing confidence. Implicit actions are invoked by the system when a region matches an object in the LTM with a confidence above threshold. Explicit actions are invoked if there is only one interpretation for a region.

Limitations of this system are found throughout. Some come from the segmentation process, which relies on a gradient operator, with all its weaknesses. The intermediate level is viewpoint-dependent. Apparently, the top level will be built upon the intermediate level, and will also be viewpoint-dependent.

2.11. PARMA, HANSON, AND RISEMAN

Parma, Hanson, and Riseman (1980) take a color image of an outdoor scene and an image model with three-dimensional relations and build a symbolic model of the three-dimensional world shown in the image, in the form of names of objects and weak relations in three space.

The model contains image locations of objects, uncertainty radii, and size radii. They emphasize representation of knowledge structures and control of knowledge sources (KSs). Their knowledge structures are schema for a scene concept, (e.g., road scene or house scene), with control for invoking a subset of KSs. They believe that schemas provide a bridge between general-purpose and special-purpose systems. They raise two issues of control: (1) the basis for invoking KSs; and (2) the use of alternative hypotheses provided by KSs. The basis for invoking KSs is top-down control driven by schema. They identify a set of six experiments with varying generality. The first is a specific scene schema from a known viewpoint. Specific two-dimensional schema can be obtained; the example in this report was a particular house from a known viewpoint. The second is a general scene schema with known viewpoint. This is confusing. How can viewpoint be known for nonspecific scenes? The third is a specific scene schema with unknown viewpoint. The fourth is a general scene schema that is known, with an unknown viewpoint. In the fifth experiment, the general scene schema is unknown. The fifth has no scene schema. A partial three-dimensional surface/volume description is constructed. This is a subset of the general vision problem, since it does not use familiar information.

Two forms of segmentation were described: edge relaxation and region relaxation using histograms. Both were implemented in a simulation of "processing cones." Both use two complementary relaxation labeling processes: boundary formation, local differences; region formation, and global similarities. Edge relaxation finds local discontinuities in a feature (intensity or color) along horizontal and vertical edges between pixels. Iterative relaxation on small neighborhoods forms boundary segments. Region analysis proceeds by cluster detection of peaks in the histogram of one feature or in the joint density function of pairs of features. Connected sets of pixels are determined as regions.

Eleven modular KSs are included, implemented in a graph processing language built in ALISP. They include inference net KS; two-dimensional curve-fitting KS; two-dimensional shape KS; occlusion KS; spectral attribute matcher KS; three-dimensional shape KS; perspective KS; horizon KS; object size KS.

The authors use a database that includes a LTM of world knowledge that is not image-specific and that is organized into schemas, objects, volumes, surfaces, regions, line segments, and vertices (RSV: regions, segments, vertices). Nodes are those levels; arcs are relations, primarily AND/OR. Interlevel arcs exist. Interpretation is viewed as a set of instantiations of nodes in LTM put into STM. Short-term memory is image-specific; it is used for constructing an interpretation. Initially, it contains only the RSV levels.

Two-dimensional curve fitting uses splines with knots determined by places of high curvature measured as angle from a point to k-neighbors on either side. If straight line segments fit, they are used, else quadratic, else cubic.

In the system, two-dimensional shape classification is hierarchical. For straight line segments, quadrilaterals include trapezoids and parallelograms, which include rectangle and rhombus. Quadratics are used for ellipses and circles. Other types of curves are labeled as *blobs*.

Occlusion depends on continuous curve generalization of T junctions. It is not clear that it is used in the experiment described later.

Some natural objects have relatively invariant color and texture. Many objects, such as manufactured objects, vary in spectral characteristics. It will sometimes be right to guess which among the class of target objects have invariant spectra. In the example, below, of 21 regions assigned on the basis of color, 11 were correct. Of the remaining, 5 were wall assigned as sky, and 2 were roof assigned as grass (Table 1).

The authors describe problems with inference nets. Probabilities are assigned to nodes and conditional probabilities to arcs, providing weighted paths by which implications of local hypotheses may be propagated up and down through the layered network. They point out problems in consistency and loops when generalizing.

The three-dimensional shape KS uses blending functions of cubic splines, defining "quilted solids." It is stated that three-dimensional shape has not been integrated into the system used in the experiment described by Parma, Hanson, and Riseman. A specific three-dimensional schema can be transformed into a specific point of view and projected onto the corresponding image plane, with hidden lines removed. Those facilities were not available at the time of the experiment, but were available when the experiment was completed. Specific two-dimensional schema were used.

Two-dimensional schema and three-dimensional schema have for each region a centroid of the expected location of its center and a radius representing decreased likelihood of the region center appearing at that location.

The perspective KS assumes a horizontal ground plane, with surfaces either vertical or horizontal. The camera model includes angle of inclination, image distance, and height above the ground. It deals with elevation, height, width, and range. The assumption is sometimes made that an object stands on the ground. If the ground is planar, objects are on the ground, and if objects are identical, the horizon line can be determined. It is in the ground plane. Tilt is given by the angle of the horizon from the center of the image. If tilt of the observer were zero, the

Binford

Table 1.

Object	Spectral Character	Texture	Location	Shape	Size
Tree	Green	?irregular*	Above horizon Above bush	Tall	
Bush	Green	?irregular	Below horizon Above grass	Low	
Grass	Green	?irregular	Below horizon Below bush	Flat	
Sky	Light blue	?uniform	Above all		Large
House walls		?uniform	Above and below horizon ?adjacent roof ?adjacent grass	?vertical trapezoid	Large
Roof		?regular	Above horizon ?adjacent walls	Trapezoid Straight lines	Large
Shutter		?uniform	Above and below horizon In walls	Trapezoid	Small Known

* Question marks indicate properties and relations that Parma, Hanson, and Riseman (1980) do not use. They apparently do not use house walls adjacent to roof, house walls vertical, shutters symmetric, shutters inside house. They do not use occlusion or texture analysis.

horizon would fall in the center of the image. Range of objects is determined by projected distance to their feet. If other objects are the same height as the camera (e.g., eyes of other people) a third plane is defined by a least–root-mean-square fit; the plane goes through the horizon. It is not clear from the report whether those capabilities were implemented. Sky regions cannot be below the horizon line; grass regions cannot be above the horizon line. The ground is assumed to be planar, the horizon a level line in the horizon KS.

If the perspective KS gives an estimate of object size in three space, the object-size KS generates a list of object hypotheses ordered by confidence based on the region size. Perspective KS returns computed size and range of size. Default range is 5%.

There are sometimes boundaries with known characteristics (e.g., long and straight, bounding roof). Top-down control of KSs directs matching of schema regions to image regions and some schema line segments to image line segments. A heuristic weighted evaluation function is left unspecified.

Experiment one matches color and texture attributes to improve a fragmented segmentation, by the rule of merging adjacent regions with the same object labels. A spectral attribute matcher is used to get a list of object types for a region. The experiment uses only regions obtained from the region segmenter. The system uses local schema regions to direct semantic merging, including adjacent regions. That is, it uses spectral properties and location. The result is to merge tree regions together, bush regions together, and grass regions together.

The system uses long straight lines in two-dimensional schema, placing a rectangular mask around the selected schema edge. The system selects lines within the mask within tolerance of slope of schema line as candidates. It merges all colinear segments within the mask and matches all resulting segments to the schema line. It matches on slope, length, distance between center, and rms error. In the example, the procedure matches three sides of the roof. The roof region now matches a parallelogram.

Symbolic region shapes are matched via two-dimensional schemata. Some schema regions have distinctive two-dimensional shapes, including trapezoid, rectangle, and ellipse. Properties for matching include size, aspect ratio, and color (Table 1).

The International Journal of Robotics Research

The system does reasonably well in making a crude segmentation of the image. Tree, roof, grass, bush, shutter, and sky are labeled appropriately. Major regions not labeled include much of the house and trees in the background.

The perspective KS uses the knowledge that bushes are vertical and stand on the ground plane to estimate the range of the bush and its size. Bush adjacent to grass implies that bush is probably not occluded. Computed size partially validates identification as bush.

The system has several interesting capabilities that belong in a general system. Its segmentation is limited. The quality of edges and regions holds back interpretation. Texture description is weak. Because it uses locations in an image, the system described is not only viewpoint-dependent but dependent on the specific scene. This system's capabilities seem better than that. The authors imply that general vision can be achieved by having many special schemata and selecting among them. I disagree.

2.12. Rubin

ARGOS uses color, texture, adjacency, occlusion, location, size, and shape factors. It generates two-dimensional models of the scene from various views. It attempts to generalize parts of the network.

Search is a form of dynamic programming with restricted transitions. Its first task is to find the view angle. Then it should name objects from known view. Without segmentation, its images were 75 × 100 pixels, with 7,500-level-deep search. Experiments shown are with hand-drawn segments. The system also uses Shafer's version of Ohlander's segmentation (Ohlander 1975; Shafer and Kanade 1980). View angle is determined to 51°.

ARGOS uses "adjacency first-order" Markov evaluation, which relates all surrounding nodes to the node under consideration. ARGOS has units called *primitive picture elements* (PPEs) that may be segments from Shafer and Kanade's system (1980) or that may be individual pixels. A PPE may be thought of as the largest region that is homogeneous in both signal and symbol. Both image models and test images are in the form of PPEs.

ARGOS mostly relies on adjacency relations. For example, images of Pittsburgh will have mountains between sky and buildings. There may be vertical or horizontal adjacency nodes between PPEs. PPEs may have within relations, but without a containment hierarchy. All relations are single-level and explicit. Networks tend to be large.

Much depends on spectral labeling. Median of blue gives 44% correct labeling. Rubin ends up choosing median red, median blue, median green, contrast red, contrast green, and contrast blue, where contrast is from Tamura, Mori, and Yamawaki 1977). ARGOS uses a weighted-Euclidean distance, weighted by an adjusted standard deviation. Statistics are obtained by computing mean and standard deviation for pixels in regions segmented by humans.

ARGOS uses locus search. It has a forward pass, keeping paths with values near the maximum value. Pruning heuristics are important. Since there is no unique order (two-dimensional), paths are recombined, using maximum over neighbors. The pruning threshold is dynamic, relative to the best value at a given depth. Transition likelihoods are the network knowledge constraints. They have only three values, 0.0, 0.1, 0.9. Likelihoods at a PPE (pixel) are normalized once computed.

In the backtrace, multiple beam pointers from the forward pass may disagree because the problem is two-dimensional. Some heuristics for conflict resolution were tried: throw a pixel away; carry along pointers when a pixel is left out; reject some possibilities based on adjacency rules; select by voting.

The internal model is a three-dimensional model of the city that is used to generate all possible views. A network of relations (predominantly adjacency relations) is constructed by multiple views. A region that appears in different views may be merged into one PPE, depending on adjacencies.

ARGOS does not segment; it labels. It works with pixels or regions. It can use absolute image location (i.e., mountains are usually found in the top of images). Each region has an MBR along horizontal and vertical axes. Proximity of MBRs is used to decide on merging two regions. Image location is used. Shape knowledge is difficult to incorporate, since segments may combine along self-transitions in the

Binford

network. Four shape measures were used: fractional fill, compactness, orientation, and elongation.

ARGOS was found to work better without size knowledge (image size) than with size. No advantage was found in making a hierarchy of knowledge sources.

Rubin discusses some extensions to other city scenes and to noncity scenes. None of these has been implemented. Image knowledge should be divided into the scene level or schema level, viewpoint level, and object level. ARGOS does not address automatic model generation. It is assumed that all models are built by hand. Rubin discusses a knowledge hierarchy for use of more general schema, starting at the most general end of the hierarchy. He observes that lower levels of the knowledge hierarchy look alike.

Fifteen pictures taken from five different vantage points around Pittsburgh were segmented and labeled by untrained workers. Human labeling was done to define ground truth. Seven pictures were chosen as a training set and the remainder as a test set.

The networks were reduced to 10%. Weights for terms were determined on the training set. The beam size was 25 entries. Data were smoothed in three ways: (1) simple smoothing (i.e., clustering, changing labels of surrounded pixels); (2) throwing out any region with less than 8 pixels; and (3) filling unlabeled holes in regions.

The system was correct in 71% of labeled cells for the test set. The author does not say what fraction are labeled. Hand-segmented data were used to determine view angle; root means square error was 41°. Accuracy of labels was 67%. Automatically segmented data gave view angle error of 60° and accuracy of labeling of 59%.

A priori, the system would not generalize for both close-up and distant pictures. Since it depends on horizontal and vertical dimensions, these are inversely proportional to distance. To include both, a very large range of dimensions would be necessary, which would make very weak dimension constraints. Adjacencies also change, for example, buildings obscure mountains. Image location is not at all general. In summary, the system uses these types of information: spectral; adjacency; horizontal and vertical image dimensions; and absolute image location. Only spectral information is viewpoint-independent. The system has little potential as a general vision system.

3. Applications

A few projections for applications of vision systems for the short term, for the mid term (2–3 years), and for the long term (3–5 years) follow.

Industrial vision systems for the short term have a small market. Whether there is a profitable evolutionary niche or not remains to be seen. I believe that the major obstacle is not the lack of knowledge of users, although that is a factor, but the lack of capability of current industrial vision systems, which use a technology that is at least 15 years old. They use thresholding to obtain binary images, two-dimensional models, and trivial global descriptors such as moments of the boundary. Now, researchers are beginning to use local descriptors such as holes and corners to deal with obscuration. Adaptive thresholding is being developed to increase the flexibility of such systems, but that is greatly inadequate. As a consequence of thresholding, few features can be obtained, lighting must be carefully engineered, and the system is not rugged at all. In most cases, industrial vision systems do not work at all. If they do work, their applicability is limited and special-case engineering is required, raising costs and risks for users.

In the mid term, attaining larger markets is an important objective that involves going from an evolutionary niche to a major impact at the 10% level in automation. To achieve the objective, systems must be much more capable, lessening the extent of custom engineering needed. They must distinguish many kinds of flaws in inspection, especially cosmetic from essential flaws. Systems can accomplish those objectives by incorporating several mechanisms, including structured light, which begins to lead to three-dimensional vision systems. Gray-scale segmentation allows more internal detail and less sensitivity to lighting. Greater speed and better shape discrimination will improve two-dimensional systems to a useful level.

In the long term, three-dimensional systems for warehousing, handling unoriented parts, and inspection of nonlaminar parts will be important. The programming of vision problems will be a major issue; thus, a single system for many applications will be essential. While a system may deal with only one object at a time, over a large company and over many companies a system will require the generality to deal with many parts. Teaching and part programming will be difficult, requiring the ability to work from data bases of geometric models. Learning may also become important.

In cartography, current applications use automated stereo for terrain. These systems work only partially for terrain. Stereo mapping is very labor-intensive. As resolution requirements are increased by a factor x, the volume of effort increases by a factor of x^2.

For the mid term in cartography, automated stereo mapping for complex cultural sites is expected in research situations and subsequently in production prototypes. Limited feature classification of linear features may be demonstrated. Aids for measurement of dimensions and data entry are expected to be important.

For the long term, automated feature classification is expected to make a major impact in mapping.

In photointerpretation in the mid term, monitoring of selected objects in restricted situations such as aircraft, vehicles on roads, and rail traffic is expected to be demonstrated to be feasible for classification, identification, counting, and measurement.

In the long term, classification of a greater variety of objects with broader context and much greater detail is expected to be demonstrated.

Many other applications appear, some bordering on science fiction. They include guidance, medical image analysis for diagnosis, laboratory analysis, and aids to handicapped. There are a number of hazardous tasks and environments in which robots with vision are expected to be used, including (1) space craft servicing; (2) communications equipment servicing in space; (3) undersea oil exploration, mineral exploitation, and naval operations; (4) firefighting; (5) servicing nuclear reactors and other power generators; (6) servicing electric lines; (7) carrying TV cameras into hazardous environments for news; and (8) the battlefield.

My own favorite is the home robot for cooking and cleaning. The home environment is complex. I do not expect to see home robots for decades.

There are important applications in psychology in determining perceptual mechanisms. Perceptual mechanisms are important in epistemology—in determining what people can know and the limits of human perception. They also have potential applications in education—in determining how to teach people in ways that make greatest use of their natural perceptual mechanisms.

4. Objectives

The summary of applications leads to six objectives for a vision system: that it demonstrate high performance; that it be general, complete, intelligent, and easy to use; and that there be system support.

High performance relates to complex scenes with many objects and applications requirements for detail, accuracy, resolution, and speed.

Generality implies that the system should be generic with respect to object class. (i.e., it should easily handle similar applications such as a mix of models of small electric motors). Generality also implies that it be generic with respect to observation (i.e., viewpoint-insensitive and sensor-insensitive). A three-dimensional system is a primary means of achieving this objective. Generality also implies a standard system for research and applications, with a large, general core plus mechanisms for special-case implementations.

Completeness means spanning all applications tasks. Completeness can be achieved by integration of all data, knowledge, and information, including multisensor data, expert knowledge, geometric models, prediction mechanisms, mathematics, and physics. It also implies powerful perceptual mechanisms for observation, including strong use of shape, edge segmentation, texture and image organization, depth and stereo, shape from shading, and shape from shape.

Intelligent implies reasoning in the domains of images and surfaces (i.e., geometric reasoning), like a human observer or analyst. Mechanisms that make a system easy to use include standard user aids from

Binford

computer science, an intelligent editor, automatic program synthesis, geometric models as a natural mode of communication common to human and machine, natural system structure to make the system intuitively clear to users at the system level, and bridges to natural language.

System support requires the existence of a large, critical mass effort with continuing development and a user base with collaborations.

5. System Design

Vision systems should integrate results of many image operators: region and edge segmentation; texture segmentation; surfaces from stereo, from motion parallax, and from object motion; shape from shape; surface interpolation; and shape from shading. Vision systems should combine such descriptions with general and domain-specific knowledge. Knowledge and observations relate geometric entities, including image, edges, structures of edges, surfaces, structures of surfaces, and objects. Thus, vision systems integrate inputs from many sources, relating several geometric types. In computer systems terms, integration requires matching input/output formats of procedures, which becomes clearer conceptually when defined in terms of data types. But vision involves geometric types with well-defined transformation properties, not just data types. Representations for geometric structures provide the basis for integrating these different data and knowledge included in images, image structures, surfaces, and objects. The fundamental scientific basis of vision systems is representation.

In building a vision system, whether through evolution or by design of a computer system, attempts are made to eliminate duplication, choose clean structures of data and control to eliminate inefficiencies of storage and computation, share data structures, and merge and streamline data types. These efforts go to decrease the size of the system (biological or computer), to increase its speed, and usually to simplify its conceptual and physical structure. The primary concern is with achieving adequate perceptual performance within limits of computational structure and power. In the human, these limits are imposed by wiring limitations, size, and power consumption. There are corresponding limits for computers. Adequate performance can be related to completeness of representation and completeness of perceptual maps, within complexity limits. These concerns for adequacy, simplicity, and efficiency are similar to those of the mathematician, who is concerned with completeness and equivalence of mathematical types or their simplest axiomatization, or who generalizes mathematical structures to treat many types uniformly; or to the worker in analysis of algorithms, who determines worst-case computational complexity. Not only is adequate representation a means of making efficient and manageable systems, but adequate representation allows the solving of hard problems by compact restatement with constructs that expose inherent complexity rather than apparent complexity. Any program or biological system is a formal system. The concepts are defined; they may not be general or well organized. The point is that analysis of generality and organization makes an important practical difference.

6. Representation

It is often useful to assume that in biological evolution there has been time for considerable optimization of the sort just described, for well-structured representations. A good starting place for exploring biological perception is from the standpoint of representation.

Representation means different things to different people. Much work deals with domain-independent representation, largely concerned with properties relevant to typed set theory, such as inheritance. Set theory is inadequate for vision and probably inadequate for most domains of artificial intelligence. Set theory or logic is general, but weak. Logic is valuable as a framework for embedding systems, but very little can actually be accomplished with such a weak theory. For vision, strong theories with limited domain are valid, for example, topology and geometry. If geometric proofs and calculations are formulated in logic or in informal reasoning systems based on set theory (e.g., production rules), their statement becomes clumsy and proofs are very long unless intermediate levels of mathematical theories are built up. Proofs are long and difficult because the language is weak. Mathematics is a compact and powerful language for expressing geometric concepts. It is important to represent these mathematical structures by building up an appropriate hierarchy of mathematical types.

In representation, we must concentrate on the problem domain and the task at hand. That does not mean that there is a separate representation for each domain and for each task. In physics, a small set of mathematical types and mathematical operations for solutions (a few hundred) is sufficient. Vector spaces, for example, are useful in many physics domains. Representation depends on the purpose, but a single representation may serve many purposes, and a few hundred representations serve all. There are few independent (inequivalent) mathematical structures and few independent (inequivalent) mathematical problems. Representations are open-ended and hierarchical, built from a few primitives and a few composition rules. Primitives at one level are compounded to become primitives one level higher. Applications tasks are built from a few fundamental mathematical tasks by composition. This promises a countable set of constructs, but not many have been constructed, and there are generalizing and compacting forces at work. Mathematics is concerned with equivalence of systems, an antidote to the process of inventing representations and names that turn out to be equivalent to other representations. Most representations are minor variations of others. A neat hierarchy has largely been defined by mathematicians.

In artificial intelligence, representation is a central concern. If representations are compounds, what are the fundamental representations that ultimately form their basis in a reductionist schema? I believe that the bases are fundamental mathematical, physical, and perceptual primitives. This does not mean mathematics and physics as taught in schools, but intuitive models that everyone apparently possesses to varying extent. Education does provide better models for some people but, on the whole, formal mathematics and physics depend on primitive, intuitive concepts. It is my belief that other domains are described by analogy with mathematics and physics.

A current view is that language determines perception, a view largely discredited by experiment. The counter view is more tenable: that the representations of language are determined by perception.

Mathematicians use *representation* to mean a map from a codomain A of some mathematical structure onto a domain of type B, a map that preserves the structure of A. Frequently, the map is from an abstract to a more concrete type; for example, representation of the rotation group by the group of orthogonal matrices as transformations in Cartesian three space. This example is a homomorphism of a group onto the group of linear transformations of a vector space, hence matrices. More generally, a representation may map a group onto the transformation group of a vector space preserving composition. In artificial intelligence, the term *representation* refers to a map of any kind, regardless of structure of codomain and domain and regardless of whether the map preserves structure (even when there is obvious structure and when standard mathematical terminology might be used).

The central theme here is *structural isomorphism*. One important representation is the shape of structural elements of objects relevant to a task. At a crude level, an artist structures a human figure as torso, arms, legs, and head and represents these parts as ellipsoids or with slightly better approximations for parts. At this level, the artist focuses on describing gross body shape with regard to part/ whole structure and articulation. For a more lifelike rendering of individual parts, the artist focuses on muscles and bones and their structural elements. Muscles are laminae that flex and extend. Since there are only a dozen or so muscles per limb, the representation at this level of detail is only slightly more complex than at the coarser level; that is, total complexity is only a small multiple of the complexity of the coarser level of detail. Representation of muscles is an obvious structure for the heart. At a tissue level, muscle fibers are natural structural elements. For biological objects, structure may be related to development. For manufactured objects, structural representations may be closely connected with fabrication and mechanical construction operations, which include milling: translation and turning; screw; extrusion; translation; and assembly

Binford

operations, including insertion and screwing. Generalized cylinders are determined by the principle of generalized translational invariance related to many such fabrication operations.

In structural representations, it is important that form equal function. Generalized cylinders were intended to provide suitable abstractions of shape to make compact, well-defined representations of function. It is a tenet that object classes are defined in two ways: by function and by abstractions from perception. Both definitions of object class are typified by abstract shape; that is, generic shape elements and relations. Structural representations thus cover a very large part of relevant representation.

7. Criteria for Shape Representation

Criteria for three-dimensional shape representation were formulated in developing generalized cylinders and were described by Thomas and Binford 1974. Generalized cylinders were initially intended for use in visual interpretation of complex objects as a means for a natural semantics for part/whole segmentation. The idea of a segmentation is not new, but the choice of primitive element determines whether the resulting segmentation into parts is useful. Also, they were intended for a compact representation of complex shapes from which symbolic relations between surfaces could be computed easily. The criteria for three-dimensional shape representation apply, with appropriate changes, to the representation of surface and image elements. The design criteria that led to the formulation of generalized cones are described in the paragraphs that follow.

A representation of shape should aid in describing a very large possible class of objects, including many we have never seen. The representation should be locally generated, like splines from local primitives. It is not reasonable to enumerate rigid primitives like cube, sphere, cylinder. Part/whole segmentation describes one form of generation, but the primitives that go into the part/whole description must be locally generated. Volumes and surfaces should be determined from samples or boundary conditions, with interpolation and extrapolation constrained by general principles.

Defining senses of similarity is a central issue of perception. Each representation introduces a sense of similarity that is natural in the representation. Generalized cylinders were introduced in order to represent locally generated constructions from fundamental geometrical operations, for example, sweeping (Binford 1971). Generalized cylinders were to be augmented by spheres, which characterize constructions based on rotations. One interpretation of the phrase *natural semantic interpretation* is in terms of these fundamental operations. A representation of shape should aid in describing similarities of classes of similar objects, that is, it should be a generic representation. Each representation introduces a sense of similarity that is natural in the representation. Generalized cylinders were based on generalized translational invariance, which defines similarity in terms of a hierarchy of congruence transformations mapping one slice of a generalized cylinder into another (Binford 1971). Congruence transformations determine the set of similarities of parts, while part/whole relations define global similarity. Thus, in this framework, a stick is similar to a snake or a ring and, in another sense, to a screw.

A representation of shape should aid in symbolic, generic prediction of appearances—generic with respect to object class and generic with respect to observation (i.e., valid over a broad range of viewpoints, illumination, and so on). A representation of shape should aid in inferring volume description from image information. More generally, it should aid in symbolic, generic description—generic with respect to object class and with respect to observation.

A representation of shape should define levels of detail, coarse to fine, by defining a natural semantic segmentation, a part/whole decomposition intuitively natural to human beings. Parts should be part/whole structures themselves. This condition helps the system "communicate" with humans, which can help them debug programs and create understandable systems. Parts should be defined by continuity. A surface is not a part in "natural semantics" (e.g., a cube has six surfaces, yet a cube is thought of by most people as a single part). If we define parts by surface continuity, then only separate objects are parts, and a man standing on a floor is not

The International Journal of Robotics Research

separate from the floor. If, on the other hand, we define parts by surface tangent plane continuity, then a cube has six "parts." Parts are volumes. Primitive parts should be generated from elements that are disjoint and for which a small, finite set gives a good approximation. This adds intuitive clarity in description and in model building. Generalized cylinders correspond to stacking volume elements like slices of bread. Ribbon surfaces correspond to stacking surface elements. A representation should be local. If we want to describe an arm of a volume, we want to limit our attention to that part of the shape. Some splines have that property. The covering by a finite set implies that the elements are volumes. In the Blum transform (Blum 1967), which is a covering by a minimal set of maximal interior disks, the elements are overlapping circles, that is, not disjoint. In the Fourier representation, components or eigenfunctions form an overlapping set. Eigenfunctions for aircraft are roughly overlapping aircraft-shaped elements additively combined. It is much more natural to make disjoint combination of parts like fuselage, wings, and tail. The Fourier transform of a shape is global. Local changes have global consequences.

Parts should be locally realizable; that is, they should be closed and nonintersecting. Surfaces must be investigated totally before closure and intersection can be tested.

At the Stanford University Artificial Intelligence Laboratory, we aim to represent elements by mathematical entities and to relate these entities by maps within and between levels. Several of the levels correspond to entities of three dimensions (volumes), two dimensions (surfaces), one dimension (curves), and zero dimensions (points) embedded in spaces of three dimensions, two dimensions, and one dimension. We have maps that decrease dimension (projections) and maps that raise dimension (sweeping operations).

Our work has been based on the following paradigm. Descriptions are made of geometric entities formed by two processes. The first is grouping by a few geometric relational operations that are more or less independent of the geometric entity and that are common to all levels. These grouping operations correspond to neighborhoods of approximately uniform shape, elongated narrow neighborhoods in all direc-

tions corresponding to longitudinal projection, and transverse projection (Nevatia and Binford 1977). The second process is segmentation by tight constraints that are specific to the geometric entity.

8. Interpretation

One paradigm for interpretation is template matching of images. This assumes image invariance and has little place in three-dimensional image analysis. Template matching requires enormous computation for three-space scenes. Even that computational inefficiency is a minor fault compared to the fatal flaw: it produces a very weak sense of identity of objects. Another interpretation paradigm is graph endomorphism, or finding an embedding of a model element in a description of an image, where both are expressed as a graph of nodes and relations.

A distinction is made between total and local representations and between total and local matching. A further distinction is made between arbitrary and semantic segmentations. Key issues are (1) generic interpretation in terms of object classes, insensitive to viewpoint; (2) semantic interpretation, that is, an evaluation function that accounts for details of the scene and observation process; and (3) semantic search in matching, using semantic segmentations and indexing.

8.1. TOTAL IMAGE MATCHING

Most recognition schemes rely on total image matching and complete image congruence. The problem posed is to match one image with another, invariant to translation and rotation. This assumes image invariance; there must be no systematic differences between images. Any systematic differences between images will result in large, unpredictable biases in location of best match. The limitations of total image matching schemes do not depend on whether they match intensities or Fourier transforms or coefficients of other orthogonal expansions or eigenvalues of such expansions. These schemes sound more relevant than they are in reality, since they refer to plane figures as "objects," which im-

Binford

plies three-space elements. The usual approach is to store a dense set of possible views (or coefficients describing them) so that any sensed image is "near enough" to one of the dense set of views. That rapidly becomes unmanageable. Consider three-space, articulated objects in arbitrary positions, orientations, and articulations. Assume that we do not know their shape exactly (the next person we see will be unlike any other). Objects are painted with irregular patterns that we do not know exactly either (people wear different clothes; different dogs have different spots). They will be in uneven illumination that we do not know exactly (this depends on atmospheric conditions and reflections from nearby objects), with shadows and obscurations. Images depend on many things, even on position within the retina, because of photometric and geometric non-uniformity (distortions and design). Sensors may have unusual response (SAR, infrared). One approach is to store a dense set of views of all possible combinations of objects in all positions, orientations, and articulations, with all possible illumination for all possible sensors. Any of these systematic effects can cause large, systematic errors in position of best match and interfere with estimation of accuracy. The complexity for three-dimensional objects with articulation and obscuration may be related to the power set of the plane with a certain granularity. We know a great deal about familiar objects and familiar scenes, but this is not the way to use that knowledge. Humans perceive scenes on postcards with ease without knowing surface pigmentation, illumination, or sensor characteristics. In a sense, humans are always seeing objects they have never seen before.

Even if total image matching could be made to work, it has little value, even for two-dimensional scenes, because it gives a trivial sense of object. Distinct views of an object in three space are separate and unrelated in such a scheme, linked only by their object name. This is not a useful sense of object. In two dimensions, any plane figure is a separate figure unrelated to any other. These schemes cannot identify shared image elements (i.e., partial image congruence), which they must do to perceive family relations.

8.2. Local Image Matching

Some concepts are defined here:

1. *Total representations* of an image depend on the full image, for example, Fourier transforms of an image are defined on the whole image. Total representations over a domain are defined on the total domain.
2. *Local or partial representations* are defined on proper subsets of the domain represented, for example, B splines are defined on a few adjacent nodes of a surface mesh. Locally generative representations like splines can be parameterized locally and composed globally to satisfy criteria such as continuity.
3. *Semantically segmented representations* of an image are local representations defined on image domains that are specific to image content. An example is a set of extended edges in an image. Semantically segmented representations of a domain (e.g., curve, surface) are local representations specific to the content of the domain. Another example is an approximation of curves by a B spline basis where nodes are chosen for optimal fit, corresponding to cusps. Local representations defined on an arbitrary tesselation of the domain are arbitrary segmented representations.
4. *Part/whole representations* are structured, semantically segmented representations with disjoint elements.
5. *Matching* is a map from two descriptions to a third description. The third description is usually a real number (distance or probability). In our work, we emphasize matches whose results are structured descriptions.
6. *Local matching* is a map from two local descriptions to a third local description.

One important generalization of interpretation is local image matching of semantically segmented descriptions that identify shared semantic image components, especially those which are locally generative like curves and ribbons in images. Local representations may be used for total matches, for example, least-squares matching of all observed curves to all model curves. There is little gain. Local or partial matching allows for identification in the presence of obscuration or physical differences between model and image. Some requirements of local matching include (1) sufficient support of local matching to generate adequate constraints and (2) semantic segmentations to limit combinatorics of matching.

For physical reasons, curves are a useful structural element in images. Many image curves and groupings of curves correspond to surface edges and inherent surface markings. Some correspond to illumination discontinuities that are also interesting. Curves are also useful for describing many strictly two-dimensional forms, for example, characters and drawings.

I suggest this principle for interpretation: incorporate models with explicit representation isomorphic to the domain of variation. In pattern recognition, this approach reduces cluster size by explicitly accounting for effects of "nuisance" variables. If the actual domain of variation is a subset of a larger domain, then representations of the larger domain can be restricted (e.g., we can find simplified special cases such as when objects are viewed in a few stable states from restricted viewpoints). Partial image matching can relate common image structure of distinctly different figures, but interprets different poses of a three-space object as different objects. If the principle just set forth is followed, three things will be represented explicitly in our models: three-space objects; the observation process; and illumination. Of course, if objects or viewpoint are restricted, then the representation is simplified. Use of image curves in image matching directly reduces some image variation caused by photometric effects (i.e., illumination, sensor differences, and sensor inhomogeneities). It is surprising how little we can do with image curves and structures of curves without three-space interpretation. Obscurations, surface markings, and edges of surfaces are three-space concepts. Image curve descriptions are compact and provide substantial reduction of combinatorics, however.

8.3. THREE-SPACE MATCHING

In total three-space matching schemes, different articulations of a doll are separate objects, related only by their object name. Structured, partial matches do relate different articulations of an object as different aspects of the same object. While they seem gloriously general, partial three-space matches are not adequate either. Our usual sense of object is not determined by a three-dimensional shape but by a class of three-dimensional shapes. While this may seem a hopelessly general paradigm for perception, it is the usual perceptual problem, and mechanisms for generic interpretation are feasible. Interpretation by partial three-space matching would recognize different configurations of a Boeing 747 as distinct, unrelated objects; also different configurations of an F4 with different radar, fuel tanks, or armament; or a truck with different loads. It would have no idea that a 747B resembled a 747SP more than a truck. Without generic perception, there would be no cognitive basis for concepts of truck, vehicle, or passenger aircraft. Coffee cups vary from conical styrofoam throwaways to ceramic handcrafted treasures, from minimum forms to the extravagant. Chairs have great variety. We have not seen all such possible forms, we cannot enumerate all possible prototypes, and if we see another that is distinctly different, we probably will interpret it correctly. Similarity, not spatial congruence, is the paradigm of interpretation in nature. As stated above, humans are always seeing objects they have never seen before. No one has ever seen me before as I am now (in the sense of spatial congruence). They may have seen me as I was on one occasion yesterday or two years ago. That is the central perceptual problem. The paradigm is recognizing a friend after 10 years' aging, a 10-lb weight loss, in different clothes, and with less hair, or recognizing a tiger from verbal descriptions and warnings about them without having seen one before, even though no two tigers are identical. We have similar motivation for incorporating generic mechanisms for applications in manufacturing or photointerpretation to deal with the problem of programming a class of related tasks. Here, object classes may be generated by a variation of a design

Binford

or manufacturing process, for example, a small motor product mix. Variation may be small within one task, but among a class of tasks the objects form a class with considerable variability yet strong similarity.

One usual approach is to characterize a class as a prototype with a distance measure or as the union of such classes or as some membership function on such sets, but that approach induces a weak sense of object class. Given fixed metrics based on three-dimensional distance for typical object classes, we conjecture that we can choose elements of these object classes that are very far apart in the metric, such that if the class diameter is relaxed to include usual members of the class, then it fails to discriminate against nonmembers.

The essential definition of object class is functional. Manufactured objects are designed for a function and living things have a teleology. Object classes have an associated three-dimensional form: form equals function. That is, an object's function is to be its form. Which aspect of its form? An object's function is often a geometric function. The function of a room is to be an enclosing volume. The function of a chair, desk, or table is to be a flat surface at a comfortable height for sitting, writing, eating. An object's function may constrain the choice of materials for its fabrication (e.g., a mattress versus a desk). Cost and available fabrication processes may constrain otherwise free choices. For example, a runway has its minimum length constrained by its function in the takeoff and landing of a class of aircraft and its maximum length constrained by cost. An important issue for interpretation is to identify which geometric parameters are causally determined such that their distributions are not just biases of the sample population (e.g., runway length). These essential characteristics enable tight discrimination, which is not possible if properties are treated only as statistical distributions. Causal relations come from function. Such reasoning allows classifying elements into natural subgroups. For example, runways can be classified according to the types of aircraft they serve, even when insufficient statistical information or none is available. This capability is important, since cases in which all distributions can be determined are probably few.

There is no great mystery about generic capability. The relevant geometric description may be at an abstract level. We must differentiate object form from function in suitable abstractions, extract descriptions of form in abstractions, and find a set of equivalences. Because there are only a few descriptors of generalized cones and thus only a few levels of abstractions, this scheme is feasible.

With statistical approaches, it is assumed that the choice of features and class definitions may be given externally; they concentrate on the manipulation of a priori and observed probabilities. I am passionately concerned about just what defines specific classes and which specific features should be used. In the light of our paradigm, general vision requires strong description and weak classification, since a central problem is defining object classes dynamically in a complex visual environment, that is, creating new object classes while living.

Because of computational limits and information limits we have limits on perception. Because of computational limits, we compute only the simplest few of the enormously many possible functions on an image. Because of information limits, we can consider only relatively simple underlying object interpretations for observations. These models represent a commitment or preconception to perceive what we can within those limits. Observations are represented as instantiations of these models.

A purely statistical approach, as opposed to a causal, structural approach, has limits that follow from those information limits. The number of possible scenes far exceeds the number of measurements: The number of possible parameter combinations also far exceeds the number of possible measurements. Some simplifications are essential. Locality and decomposability into primitives are central in structural approaches. In a sense, generalized cylinders are singly curved, hence separable in internal coordinates. By contrast, the Fourier transform is separable in external coordinates.

8.4. An Approach to Interpretation

One approach to the formalization of interpretation—to finding the "best match" between

The International Journal of Robotics Research

an observation and models—is graph embedding. In graph embedding, an isomorphism of one or more models with a subset of the observation is found (Barrow et al. 1977). This implies that models and observations have equivalent representations; for example, image models are compared with image observations (the most usual) or volume models are compared with volume observations. The chief problem lies in defining criteria for inexact matching, for which the usual approach is syntactic. For example, the best match has the fewest differences. This increases complexity of search greatly, but it also is a very unsatisfying match. In some cases we expect differences, for example, when limbs are obscured or not observable by the sensor used. Interpretation of significance of these differences is specific to the scene, to the observation process, to object class, and to articulation of the object.

Once a hypothesis has been made, predictions and measurements provide new information for the decision. Thus, the decision is not necessarily made on a fixed database; interpretation becomes a problem of knowledge acquisition. This raises the concept of "perceptual overkill." It does not seem a useful heuristic to determine the minimum information for classification as an approximation to the maximum-utility problem. In biological systems, many of the perceptual mechanisms are parallel, and there is nothing to be gained in ignoring them. In machine perception, overwhelming verification of a correct hypothesis is typically inexpensive compared to the computation required to get to the right hypothesis. These factors shift the utility balance toward getting data needed for a highly constrained decision. Very strong, relevant data are available if descriptive mechanisms can abstract them and interpretation mechanisms can use them.-Object classes likewise have strong functional characterizations. A few structural relations characterize the class. Each relation can be tested.

The interpretation process is usually defined as statistical. Here, the definition is structural, detailed verification of criteria descriptions of class characteristics. All of this falls within the scope of decision theory, but usual applications of decision theory to interpretation trivialize the models from which conditional probabilities follow. The approach can be regarded as making explicit dependencies that might be glossed over in a statistical analysis. Noise is only one issue; systematic differences are primary.

The match of an observation to a model is the set of transformations necessary to map an abstract model to make it congruent to an abstracted, observed, and semantically segmented description, both specified at the level of essential volume or surface elements. Multiple interpretations are resolved when possible by new observations as required. Essential and optional characteristics are confirmed by new observations so that all criterial structures are verified. The mapping of a structured match to a real number (probability) can often be postponed; at a final decision, a real number is usually convenient to characterize an acceptable subspace, but there are many other ways to characterize a subspace. The distance of the class of transformations can be evaluated in the semantic evaluation sense described above.

This approach is closely related to the one Evans (1968) uses in solving analogy problems. It also follows directly the fundamental definition of generalized cylinders by generalized translational invariance. Generalized cylinders are not defined by a distance function but rather by a congruence map. This approach of a metric on transformations was pursued (Nevatia 1974). The outline of a simple distance measure can be specified based on some obvious semantics that are not complete or satisfactory. The distance measure is applied to the congruence transformation, which includes articulation, scaling, rotation, obscuration, observation errors, and object variations (growth, aging, missing parts). The cost assigned to variations is highly context-dependent. For example, articulations corresponding to usual postures and gaits have low cost. Articulations outside comfortable ranges have high cost. An obscuration interpretation must be consistent with observations of obscuring objects.

In summary, a key paradigm is similarity (not spatial congruence) and the matching of objects that are similar but not identical. There are several important mechanisms: (1) description of three-space form in terms of generic shared structural elements and their abstractions; (2) inference of causally determined parameters; (3) characterization of object classes; (4)

Binford

indexing of subclasses of similar forms; and (5) distance functions evaluated in context from congruence maps.

8.5. The Search Process

The search process in matching is important because potential for complexity is high. Search for graph endomorphism has high complexity for graphs of moderate size. There must be semantic simplifications. It is not reasonable in general vision to match against all models in visual memory. At Stanford, we introduced some concepts for indexing into subsets of objects similar to observed objects (Nevatia 1974). Those techniques were aimed at perception with a relatively large visual memory, even though we worked with only six objects. These indexing techniques relied on imposing a size (attachment) hierarchy on stick figures (i.e., on the part/whole graph). The reasoning for this was that small parts are attached to large parts. This led to comparisons with similar structures (e.g., comparison of a description of a doll with models of the class of objects that have two limbs at one end and three at the opposite end). Object classes were indexed by hash coding. We have considered a similar scheme in which object structures are arranged in a graph (based on topological and metric properties of stick figures) to be referenced by traversing the graph. These are mechanisms for generating hypotheses for subsequent verification. We focus on hypothesis generation because in vision it is a crucial step. In earlier work (Nevatia 1974), an attachment hierarchy allowed the structuring of model graphs and description graphs to facilitate indexing into a subset of similar shapes. Comparison of individual graphs was much abbreviated. This approach provides some capability for identification within a large visual memory.

It is my belief that general vision systems depend on the building of three-dimensional descriptions and that prediction, description, and interpretation take place largely in three dimensions. A recent article describes constraints that lead in the direction of incorporating these capabilities in ACRONYM (Binford 1981).

One paradigm for intelligent systems is *prediction–hypothesis–verification*. The paradigm can be useful or ineffectual, depending on how adequately prediction, hypotheses generation, and verification are conceived. We refer to hypotheses as descriptive maps, cueing, or bottom-up maps. Mapping occurs upward among structures in a geometric hierarchy, from image curves to surface edges, from structures of curves to surfaces, and from structures of surfaces to objects. We use the same terms to refer to prediction maps or top-down maps. We normally think of vision hypotheses as great leaps from images to objects and predictions as great leaps from object models to images. Those are not useful starting points. Vision systems have primarily been built on this basis, with only two levels of representation, name level and image level. *Image level* includes observations extracted from images and appearances of objects. This is too shallow a geometric structure. Instead, we have long thought of hypothesis–prediction–verification loops as steps between any two levels in a well-defined geometric hierarchy—a hierarchy that is deep, with small steps between levels. Hypothesis–prediction–verification relate nearby levels, especially, from image curve elements, to extended curves, to structures of curves (image organization, one level of Gestalt organization), to surfaces, through levels of surface organization. Each loop of prediction–hypothesis–verification is at once bottom-up and top-down. We claim an essential unity of bottom-up and top-down operations. If strong context and weak visual data are available in a situation, a system appears top-down; if the system has strong visual data and weak contextual information, it appears bottom-up. Usually, both context and visual data are available. Prediction is as effective at low levels of the geometric hierarchy as at the high level. Prediction is as general as description. If we have weak contextual information, if we do not know what objects are in the scene and we do not know our viewing conditions, we still know that we can represent objects by locally generative shape primitives (e.g., part/whole graphs of generalized cylinders), and we know that we can make generic predictions of the appearances of generalized cylinders, predictions that are insensitive to viewpoint, illumination, and sensor, general conditions on

The International Journal of Robotics Research

image areas and image curves corresponding to surfaces, limbs, and edges of surfaces. I remarked above that prediction–hypothesis–verification loops link primarily nearby levels in the geometric hierarchy. The nearer the levels, the more plausible the hypothesis. In ACRONYM, cueing (i.e., hypothesis generation) is based on powerful shape descriptions, image ribbons, surface ribbons, and generalized cylinders. We originally devised generalized cylinders as a natural way to use image cues about surfaces.

References

Ballard, D., Brown, C., and Feldman, J. 1978. An approach to knowledge-directed image analysis. *Computer vision systems,* ed. A. Hanson and E. Riseman. New York: Academic.

Barrow, H. G., et al. 1977. Interactive aids for cartography and photointerpretation: Progress report. *Proc. ARPA Image Understanding Workshop,* ed. L. Baumann. McLean, Va.: Science Applications, pp. 111–127.

Binford, T. O. 1971. Visual perception by computer. *Proc. IEEE Conf. Syst. Contr.*

Binford, T. O. 1981. Inferring surfaces from images. *Artificial Intell.* 17:205–245.

Blum, H. 1967. A transformation for extracting new descriptors of shape. *Models for the perception of speech and visual form,* ed. W. Dunn. Cambridge, Mass.: MIT Press, pp. 362–380.

Bolles, R. C. 1976. Verification vision within a programmable assembly system. AIM-295. Stanford, Calif.: Stanford University Artificial Intelligence Laboratory.

Brooks, R. 1981. Symbolic reasoning among 3-dimensional models and 2-dimensional images. *Artificial Intell.* 17:285–349.

Evans, T. A. 1968. A heuristic program to solve geometric analogy problems. *Semantic information processing,* ed. M. Minsky. Cambridge, Mass.: MIT Press.

Faugeras, O., and Price, K. 1980. Semantic description of aerial images using stochastic labeling. *Proc. ARPA Image Understanding Workshop.* McLean, Va.: Science Applications, pp. 89–94.

Garvey, T. D. 1976. Perceptual strategies for purposive vision. Tech. Note 117. Menlo Park, Calif.: SRI International, SRI Artificial Intelligence Center.

Hewitt, C. 1968. Planner. Memo 168. Cambridge, Mass.: Massachusetts Institute of Technology Artificial Intelligence Laboratory.

Horn, B. K. P. 1973. On lightness. Memo 295. Cambridge, Mass.: Massachusetts Institute of Technology Artificial Intelligence Laboratory.

Hueckel, M. 1973. A local visual operator which recognizes edges and lines. *J. Assoc. Comput. Mach.* 20:634.

Kanade, T., and Reddy, R. 1981. Image understanding at CMU. *Proc. ARPA Image Understanding Workshop.* McLean, Va.: Science Applications, pp. 199–207.

Land, E. H., and McCann, J. J. 1971. Lightness and retinex theory. *J. Optical Soc. Am.* 61:1–11.

Levine, M. 1978. A knowledge-based computer vision system. *Computer vision systems,* ed. A. Hanson and E. Riseman. New York: Academic.

Lowe, D. G., and Binford, T. O. 1981. The interpretation of geometric structure from image boundaries. *Proc. ARPA Image Understanding Workshop,* ed. L. Baumann. McLean, Va.: Science Applications, pp. 39–46.

Miyamoto, E., and Binford, T. O. 1975 (May). Display generated by a generalized cone representation. Paper delivered at Conf. Comput. Graphics Image Processing, Anaheim, Calif.

Moravec, H. P. 1980. Obstacle avoidance and navigation in the real world by a seeing robot rover. Ph.D. thesis, Stanford University. AIM 304-A. Stanford, Calif.: Stanford University Artificial Intelligence Laboratory.

Nagao, M., Matsuyama, T., and Ikeda, Y. 1978. Region extraction and shape analysis of aerial photographs. *Proc. 4th Int. Conf. Pattern Recognition,* p. 620.

Nagao, M., and Matsuyama, T. 1980. *A structural analysis of complex aerial photographs.* New York: Plenum.

Nevatia, R. 1974. Structured descriptors of complex curved objects for recognition and visual memory. Ph.D. thesis, Stanford University. AIM 250. Stanford, Calif.: Stanford University Artificial Intelligence Laboratory.

Nevatia, R., and Binford, T. O. 1977. Description and recognition of curved objects. *Artificial Intell.* 8:77–98.

Ohlander, R. B. 1975. Analysis of natural scenes. Pittsburgh: Carnegie-Mellon University Department of Computer Science.

Ohta, Y. 1980. A region-oriented image-analysis system by computer. Ph.D. thesis, Kyoto University Department of Information Science.

Parma, C. C., Hanson, A. M., and Riseman, E. M. 1980. Experiments in schema-driven interpretation of a natural scene. COINS Tech. Rept. 80-10. Amherst, Mass.: University of Massachusetts.

Rubin, S. 1978. The ARGOS image understanding system. *Proc. ARPA Image Understanding Workshop.* McLean, Va.: Science Applications, pp. 159–162. Ph.D. thesis, Carnegie-Mellon University.

Binford

Shafer, S., and Kanade, T. 1980. KIWI, a flexible system for region segmentation. Tech. Rept. (in preparation). Pittsburgh: Carnegie-Mellon University.

Shirai, Y. 1978. Recognition of man-made objects using edge cues. *Computer vision systems,* ed. A. Hanson and E. Riseman. New York: Academic.

Tamura, H., Mori, S., and Yamawaki, T. 1977. Psycholog-ical and computational measurements of basic textural features and their comparison. Tech. Rept. Electrotech-nical Laboratory and Waseda University.

Thomas, A. J., and Binford, T. O. 1974. Information pro-cessing analysis of visual perception: A review. AIM-227; CS-408. Stanford, Calif.: Stanford University Artificial Intelligence Laboratory.

Several figures are reprinted from *A Structural Analysis of Complex Aerial Photographs* by Makoto Nagao and Takashi Matsuyama: Plenum Publishing Corporation 1980 with the permission of the authors and publisher; and from *Computer Vision Systems* edited by Allen R. Hanson and Edward M. Riseman: Academic Press, 1978 with the permission of the editors and publisher.

Low Level Image Segmentation: An Expert System

AHMED M. NAZIF AND MARTIN D. LEVINE, SENIOR MEMBER, IEEE

Reprinted from *IEEE Transactions on Pattern Analysis and Machine Intelligence*, Volume PAMI-6, Number 5, September 1984, pages 555-577. Copyright © 1984 by The Institute of Electrical and Electronics Engineers, Inc.

Abstract—A major problem in robotic vision is the segmentation of images of natural scenes in order to understand their content. This paper presents a new solution to the image segmentation problem that is based on the design of a rule-based expert system. General knowledge about low level properties of processes employ the rules to segment the image into uniform regions and connected lines. In addition to the knowledge rules, a set of control rules are also employed. These include metarules that embody inferences about the order in which the knowledge rules are matched. They also incorporate focus of attention rules that determine the path of processing within the image. Furthermore, an additional set of higher level rules dynamically alters the processing strategy. This paper discusses the structure and content of the knowledge and control rules for image segmentation.

Index Terms—Artificial intelligence, computer vision, expert systems, image segmentation, rule-based systems.

I. INTRODUCTION

A PRIMARY objective in contemporary computer vision research is the ability to analyze images originating from three-dimensional scenes in order to understand their content. This may be done by assigning appropriate interpretations to objects within the scene. Accordingly, an image must first be segmented into regions that roughly correspond to objects, surfaces, or parts of objects in the scene represented by that image. Two steps are thus apparent, the low level processing stage mainly concerned with segmentation, and the high level stage devoted to the interpretation of the segmented result.

The hierarchy suggested here assumes that a low level process that has no *a priori* knowledge about the objects in a scene, would be able to deliver a "plausible" output to the high level process. However, the option of receiving feedback from the latter for further processing in order to resolve high level ambiguities is left open. This research is concerned with the low level stage of an image understanding system, and is closely related to previous work on high level image interpretation [7]. It should be noted that the distinction between the two levels of analysis is primarily in terms of the knowledge available to each. Whereas the interpretation system uses domain specific knowledge about the contents of a scene, the low level segmentation stage employs general purpose models [25] that contain knowledge about images and grouping

Manuscript received June 21, 1983; revised January 4, 1984. This work was supported in part by the Natural Sciences and Engineering Research Council of Canada under Grant A4156, and by an FCAC Grant awarded by the Department of Education, Province of Quebec, under Grant EQ-633.

A. M. Nazif is with the Department of Electrical Engineering, University of Cairo, Cairo, Egypt.

M. D. Levine is with the Computer Vision and Robotics Laboratory, Department of Electrical Engineering, McGill University, Montreal, P.Q., Canada.

criteria that are independent of the class of scenes under analysis.

This paper presents a new paradigm for image segmentation, namely, the use of an expert rule-based system. Such a solution was motivated by a number of issues that needed to be addressed and studied. They can be classified under the following headings.

1) The presence of a large number of segmentation heuristics in the literature. A method is required for evaluating and organizing these to function together.

2) The absence of an explicit scheme for representing the knowledge embodied by these segmentation heuristics.

3) The lack of quantitative evaluations of a segmentation.

4) The need for a better understanding of the methods by which the segmentation heuristics should be applied to an image.

Following is a discussion of these issues and how the proposed solution affects each.

1) Integration of Knowledge Sources: Approaches to image segmentation in the past have relied on procedural algorithms for boundary detection and region growing [19]. These processes used different heuristics in their analysis, with varying degrees of success in obtaining output partitions that are compatible with human expectations. The diversity in the data structures, knowledge sources, and control mechanisms presents difficulties in finding a general framework that can integrate these efforts. A primary goal of this research was to design a complex system that not only is flexible enough to accommodate the wide variety of segmentation heuristics, but would also be capable of evaluating and selecting the best heuristics for different data situations. For example, both region analysis for grouping pixels based on the similarity of their features, and boundary analysis for partitioning the image based on discontinuities in the features, have been suggested as valid methods for segmenting an image. The proposed system is capable of doing both, with the additional potential of allowing interactions between these knowledge sources. Such an exchange of information between the various segmentation heuristics leads to a substantial improvement in the output delivered to the high level interpretation processes.

2) Explicit Knowledge Representation: The design of an expert segmentation system that blends knowledge from a wide variety of sources faces the problem of finding a suitable knowledge representation scheme. In vision systems developed so far, "explicit representations of knowledge have been reserved mainly for application domain knowledge, while general visual knowledge has been buried away in procedures" [22]. What is needed is a flexible mechanism capable of experimenting with different processing methodologies, and an expressive coding scheme that can accommodate all possible knowledge sources. The rule-based approach to control, which is proposed here, satisfies both requirements. Knowledge is detached from the application processes and coded into rules, which are modular entities that can be modified without affecting the structure of a system. An additional goal of this research was to investigate the use of the rule-based approach in general purpose image segmentation. This includes addressing control issues such as conflict resolution and focus of attention, as well as structural issues like the symbolic coding of segmentation heuristics into production rules.

3) Output Evaluation: Another aspect of the image segmentation problem is the nonuniqueness of the solution. Ideally, a complete segmentation should correspond to the objects to be interpreted. However, low level processes can only produce partitions on a nonsemantic basis, and these may not necessarily correspond to describable objects. Such partial segmentations are not unique even for humans examining a scene. This problem may not be of particular importance if the ultimate goal is to perform high level analysis with top-down feedback. Nevertheless, a method for evaluating the output is required. It provides the means for designing a system that produces the most appropriate partition, and hence minimizes the need for intervention by the high level stage. Therefore, another goal of this research was to establish design measures that indicate the distance from a known reference. The latter is taken to be a manually generated segmentation that corresponds to the objects in the image. These measures can then be used within the context of the rule-based system to "tune" the model by evaluating the rules and the control mechanisms.

The development of design measures has prompted us to search for other measures that estimate the quality of the output without the need for a reference partition. Consequently, these new measures can be used during actual processing and will be referred to as "real-time measures." Low level segmentation can now be posed as an optimization problem in which the goal is to maximize a set of performance parameters. By comparing an output partition to the input image, the real-time measures are used to modify the processing methodology in order to incrementally improve that output.

4) The Definition of a Control Strategy: For a system that employs a large number of heuristics to segment an image, two control issues must be addressed: the order in which different heuristics are applied, and the path within the image along which they are tested. Thus, a control strategy for image segmentation consists of rule-ordering and path selection components. Different strategies are available, and the best strategy to apply varies during processing. It depends on the state of the output segmentation at any given time. Consequently, a dynamic selection mechanism is used to execute the best strategy based on the data.

One of the early attempts at addressing these issues was not actually in image understanding, but rather studied the symbolic representation of visual images by humans [14]. In a system called VIS, Moran compiled a set of rules that simulated the behavior of a human describing a sequence of simple visual events. The first effort at using production systems in image

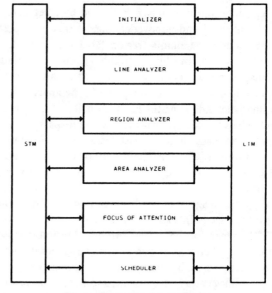
Fig. 1. The system block diagram.

understanding was reported in Sloan's [20]. The rule-based structure was limited to the interpretation stage and was clearly separated from the low level region analysis. Other interesting systems are reported in [1], [2], [10]. All the approaches have concentrated on the high level aspects of the vision problem. The rules represent specific domain knowledge that is application-dependent. What is also needed is a representational mechanism that can encompass general purpose knowledge about image formation and the laws of preceptual grouping. These information sources are independent of the specific application and the semantic content of the images. Such a formulation fills the gap between the procedural operators that measure and detect features in the image and the high level expert systems that interpret the results. This paper discusses the structure and type of low level knowledge implemented by such a rule-based system for image segmentation.

II. SYSTEM OVERVIEW

The system is designed in the form of a modular set of processes and two associative memories, as shown in Fig. 1. The input image, the segmentation data, and at the end of processing, the output, are stored in a short term memory (STM). A long term memory (LTM) embodies the model representing the system knowledge about low level segmentation, as well as control strategies. Each of the system processes has access to the information stored in the LTM, and can also read and modify the data stored in the STM. In fact, this is the only way it can communicate with the other system processes. Thus any change in the data stored in the STM, brought about by one of the system processes, will be instantaneously available to the other system processes.

The basic control structure is that of a production system, in which general knowledge about independent low level properties of an image is formulated into condition-action rules. A system process matches rules in the LTM against the data stored in the STM, and when a match occurs, the rule fires. This triggers an action that is performed by that process, and usually involves modification of the data.

The segmentation of an image is defined by a set of regions that are connected and nonoverlapping, so that each pixel in the image acquires a unique region label that indicates the region it belongs to. In addition to the regions, discontinuities in the image array are defined by lines that are also connected and nonoverlapping. In this case, pixels in the image can either have a line label indicating the line they belong to, or they can have null labels to indicate that there is no line passing through them. This approach simultaneously uses both region information, based primarily on uniformity criteria in the image array, as well as line information, that represents discontinuity criteria in that array.

Initially, the image gradient is computed and thresholded. The resulting edge points are then grouped into lines to produce an initial line map for that image. An initial region map is also computed by either selecting an arbitrary segmentation of the image into regions, or by executing a fast region growing algorithm. The image array, its gradient, and the initial region and line maps are all stored in the STM. Low level features are then extracted and stored in the STM. These include the average color features for regions and lines, position features, and spatial relationships. The latter include ADJACENCY among regions, and relationships of IN FRONT OF, BEHIND, and PARALLEL TO involving lines. Regions to the LEFT and RIGHT OF a line, and lines TOUCHING or INTERSECTING a region, describe spatial relationships between lines and regions.

Other important data entries maintained and stored in the STM are the focus of attention areas. These are areas in the image defined primarily by their position and size. An area may correspond to a region, a line, or groups of regions and/or lines in the image segmentation. These areas are used for the purpose of directing the attention of the system to the more interesting and worthwhile parts of the image, in terms of processing need and richness of segmentation information. Three types of areas are defined: smooth, textured, and areas created by long lines that close, or almost close, forming loops. The latter are referred to as bounded areas. Initially, the process responsible for generating areas computes them on the basis of the segmentation data stored in the STM. Because the resulting areas would usually not cover the entire image, a subset of the regions and lines will not belong to a specific area. These are assigned to a default area which encompasses the balance of the image less the detected areas.

The information stored in the STM is continuously updated during processing, so that it reflects the state of the segmentation of the image at any point in time. The regions, lines, areas, plus their features at the end of processing, represent the output of the low level stage to be delivered to the high level interpretation system. The higher the correspondence between regions in the output segmentation and objects in the scene, the easier the task of the high level process. Lines corresponding to major discontinuities in the image, as well as smooth and textured areas, can also be used to guide the interpretation process.

Six processes are involved in producing actions, as shown in Fig. 1. The INITIALIZER generates the initial region and line maps, and uses them to produce initial focus of attention areas. It also computes and stores the features of these initial

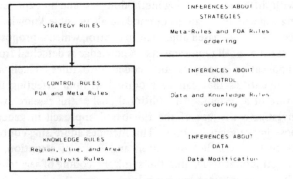

Fig. 2. Three levels of rules.

data elements in the STM. The REGION, LINE, and AREA ANALYZERS are the three main processing modules of the system. They are responsible for rule matching and data modification on their respective entities. The LINE ANALYZER, for example, matches the line analysis rules in the LTM to the data in the STM. If a rule fires, it will execute the action specified by that rule on the current line under analysis. The same applies to the REGION and AREA ANALYZERS. The FOCUS OF ATTENTION module matches its own rules to execute a defined path strategy that brings various data items to the attention of the system, in a particular order. Thus, when a focus of attention action is executed, this means that the current region, line, or area will be replaced by a new region, line, or area whose identity depends on the action specified by that rule. Finally, the SUPERVISOR acts as a monitor for system control purposes. It matches the strategy rules to select the appropriate control strategy. Consequently, a set of metarules is used to determine which set of knowledge rules, if any, is to be tested next.

III. THE RULE-BASED MODEL

The model stored in the LTM is composed of three levels of production rules, as shown in Fig. 2. At the first level, the knowledge rules encode the information about properties of regions, lines, and areas in the form of sets of situation-action pairs. Each situation is coded into a number of logical predicates that compose the conditions of a rule. The latter are either logical comparisons or evaluations on the features of regions, lines, and areas in the segmented image. The conditions are ANDed together, so that when a specific situation occurs within the image, all the conditions will be met. In this case, a match is said to have occurred, and the rule fires. The rule action is then executed. This might be splitting of a region or merging of two regions, an addition, deletion, or extension of a line, a merging of two lines, or a creation or modification of a focus of attention area. Knowledge rules are classified by their actions, so that there are region analysis rules, line analysis rules, and area analysis rules. A region rule, for example, will contain conditions that match on features of regions, lines, and areas, but will always execute its action on the current region under analysis.

The second level of rules in the LTM contains the control rules, which can be further classified into two categories. First the focus of attention rules, which are responsible for finding the next data entry to be considered. They have actions that bring to the attention of the system a next region, next line, or an entire area. Using these rules, a strategy for visiting regions and lines within a focus of attention area, and for alternating from one area to another, can be defined and executed. This strategy will be data-driven since the conditions of these rules are also logical predicates evaluated on the STM data.

The second type of control rules are actually inferences about sets of knowledge rules, or in the spirit of a production system, they are termed metarules [3]. They differ from other rules, in that their actions do not modify the data in the STM. Instead, the metarules alter the matching order of different knowledge rule sets. Each process in the system is associated with a specific set of rules. The conditions of the metarules examine the data in the STM, and their actions specify the next process to be activated (and hence the next knowledge rule set). The metarules are also responsible for evaluating the stopping criteria of the system, and consequently terminating the processing. This approach renders the whole control process to be data-driven.

Control rules execute the system control strategy: focus of attention rules define the method by which data are selected for processing; the metarules specify the order in which the rule sets are matched. The system's control strategy is comprised of six basic elements, each of which can assume more than one specific state. The first three elements are the region path strategy, the line path strategy, and the region and line updating strategy. They determine the order in which the respective data items are tested and updated by the rules. Different path strategies are implemented by employing the appropriate set of focus of attention rules. The next three elements define strategies for determining process priority, region rule priority, and line rule priority. The first specifies the order in which the different rule sets are matched. The last two order the rules within the two processes. Each strategy state is achieved by invoking a specific set of control rules. Thus, one can effectively "program" the system into executing a desired strategy by putting together the appropriate combination of focus of attention rules and metarules.

The third and highest rule level in Fig. 2 contains the strategy rules. Their function is to select, based on the data, the set of control rules (focus of attention rules and metarules) that executes the most appropriate control strategy. Strategy determination is formulated as a dynamic decision-making process which results in the assignment of a specific state to each of the strategy elements.[1] In order to make this selection, a set of performance measurements is computed for each focus of attention area in the image [9]. These include values for the average uniformity of the regions within the area, the average contrast across these regions, the connectivity of the lines, and the average contrast across time. For example, if an area had regions of low average uniformity, the region rule priorities would be set so that rules which split regions were given priority over merging rules. Other constraints define the relation between the performance measurements and all the elements of

strategy. The latter will therefore change with time, as well as spatially from one area to another.

To summarize, the system control strategy is defined by the strategy rules and executed by the control rules. Focus of attention rules specify the next data item to be tested, and metarules select the next rule set to be matched. Strategy rules, on the other hand, have actions that dynamically adjust the priorities of the metarules and the focus of attention rules.

The remaining sections of this paper describe the knowledge and control rules in more detail. The strategy rules and the dynamic strategy determination process are addressed separately in [9]. A more detailed account of the three rule levels is given in [16]. Before discussing the rules in detail, we will first define their basic structure in the next section.

IV. THE STRUCTURE OF THE RULES

Knowledge representation will largely depend on the composition of the rules constituting the model. A rule has the following format:

$$\text{CONDITION.AND.CONDITION......AND.CONDITION ACTIONS}$$

$$(1)$$

The left-hand side is composed of a set of CONDITIONS evaluated on the data. The ACTIONS on the right-hand side specify particular modifications to the data. The logical AND's indicate that the action of the rule will only be performed if *ALL* its conditions are satisfied. Note that there is no provision for a logical OR within a rule. This is because the latter can be accounted for by including another rule that encompasses the alternative situation.

Each rule depicts a certain situation that might be present in the data. A process will match a rule on the features of the regions, lines, or areas, or on some other data item stored in the STM. This is accomplished by a search conducted in the STM for the data configuration portrayed by the rule. If the search is successful, the rule will fire, and its actions will be executed. For this reason, rules have been termed situation-response tuples, or condition-action sets.

A RULE INTERPRETER interfaces the LTM rules to the processing modules, as well as to the experimenter. This two-way communication channel allows a designer to modify the rules, and provides the means for the rules to control the processing modules. As an input channel of the LTM, the INTERPRETER receives commands from a user to edit the rule-based model, adding, deleting, changing, and examining the rules. It monitors the formulation of the model, and signals any illegal syntactic combinations to ensure an error-free rule set. The output channel then translates the rules for the processing modules. The conditions are analyzed in order to specify the type of evaluations to be performed and identify the data items and features to be tested. The processing module then performs the matching operation accordingly. If a match occurs, the INTERPRETER provides pointers to the specific procedures that implement the rule actions. Fig. 3 is a schematic of the signal flow in and out of the model. The conditions and actions will now be discussed in more detail.

---

[1] Actually, the rule priorities associated with each of the possible states for each strategy element are adjusted.

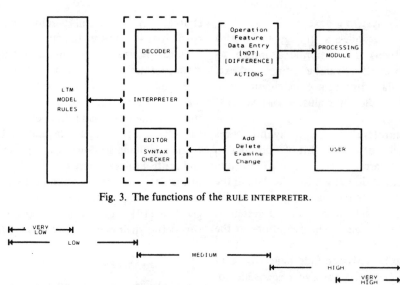

Fig. 3. The functions of the RULE INTERPRETER.

Fig. 4. Relative ranges of symbolic qualifiers.

A. The Rule Conditions

The conditions of a rule are logical entities, or equivalently, binary valued variables that can be instantiated to be either TRUE or FALSE. They correspond to logical evaluations or comparisons on the data. Each condition is composed of a logical predicate that may be preceded by the qualifier NOT, a reference to the logical complement of that predicate. The STM contains mostly numerical variables representing features of regions, lines, and areas in the image segmentation. The size of a region and the length of a line are typical examples. Some nonnumerical data are also stored. Examples of these include labels that indicate the presence or absence of a certain feature, and those that qualitatively describe a data entry (a line as being a loop, or an area as smooth).

In [16] the four classes of logical predicates that can exist in a rule condition were defined. These were classified according to the nature of the logical operation performed, as well as the type of variable that is tested. They are summarized as follows:

1) Logical comparisons on numerical variables.

    LOWER LINE GRADIENT
    EQUAL LINE DIRECTIONS
    HIGHER REGION SIZE

2) Logical comparisons on nonnumerical variables.

    SAME REGION LEFT

3) Logical evaluations on numerical variables.

    VERY LOW REGION VARIANCE
    MEDIUM REGION ADJACENCY
    HIGH LINE LENGTH

Five symbols define different ranges over the scale of each feature. If the value of a feature lies in a given range, the corresponding logical evaluation will be TRUE. The relative position of the different ranges of symbols is represented schematically in Fig. 4. Note that the ranges for LOW and HIGH include the ranges for VERY LOW and VERY HIGH, respectively. This seems to conform with the linguistic definition of these qualifiers. Other ranges using the scale of Fig. 4 are

accessible through combinations of qualifiers and the addition of the NOT qualifier (e.g., NOT LOW; HIGH.AND.NOT VERY HIGH). The choice of these symbolic qualifiers, their number, and their ranges are discussed in detail in [16].

4) Logical evaluations on non-numerical variables.

    LINE IS LOOP
    AREA IS NOT SMOOTH
    PREVIOUS PROCESS WAS REGIONS

IS (ARE) and WAS in the examples above represent the keywords that distinguish this condition type.

Note that the employment of the qualifier NOT increases the flexibility of the four operations described above. Examples include NOT LOWER, NOT SAME, NOT VERY HIGH, and WAS NOT.

One aspect that relates to the numerical variables in type 1 and 3 conditions is the addition of a DIFFERENCE qualifier. This enables the system to perform all the logical operations cited above on differences in the values of two variables, instead of on the values themselves. Thus "LOW DIFFERENCE IN REGION FEATURE 1" indicates that the difference in the values of the first color feature (average red intensity level) of two regions must be in the LOW range for the condition to be satisfied (the predicate to be TRUE). Each numerical feature must thus have an additional scale as per Fig. 4, in order to specify the range of the symbolic qualifiers on the differences in that feature. For example, a line length of less than 50 pixels might be considered LOW. On the other hand, the limit for a LOW DIFFERENCE in the length of two lines will necessarily be less than that, maybe 10 pixels. The selection of these ranges is also discussed in [16].

We can now summarize the conditions of our rules and show that they include the following basic items.

1) A symbolic qualifier that depicts the type of logical operation to be performed on the data. The type of qualifier will depend on the type of feature to be examined, according to the classification given above.

2) A symbol denoting the data entry on which the condition is to be matched. By default, it refers to the current

TABLE I
Possible Data Entries

DATA ENTRY	SYMBOL
Current Region	REG
Current Line	LINE
Current Area	AREA
Region ADJACENT to current region	REGA
Region to the LEFT OF current line	REGL
Region to the RIGHT OF current line	REGR
Line NEAR current line	LINEN
Line IN FRONT OF current line	LINEF
Line BEHIND current line	LINEB
Line PARALLEL TO current line	LINEP
Line INTERSECTING current region	LINEI

TABLE II
The Features in a Condition

NUMERICAL DESCRIPTIVE FEATURES

Feature 1	Feature 2	Feature 3
Variance 1	Variance 2	Variance 3
Intensity	Intensity Variance	Gradient
Gradient Variance	X-Centroid	Y-Centroid
Minimum X	Minimum Y	Maximum X
Maximum Y	Starting X	Starting Y
Ending X	Ending Y	Starting Direction
Ending Direction	Average Direction	Length
Start-End Distance	Size	Perimeter
Histogram Bimodality	Circularity	Aspect Ratio
Uniformity 1	Uniformity 2	Uniformity 3
Region Contrast 1	Region Contrast 2	Region Contrast 3
Line Contrast 1	Line Contrast 2	Line Contrast 3
Line Connectivity	Number of Regions	Number of Lines
Number of Areas		

NUMERICAL SPATIAL FEATURES

Number of ADJACENT Regions	Adjacency Values
Number of INTERSECTING Lines	Line Content between Regions
Distance to Line IN FRONT	Nearest Point on Line IN FRONT
Distance to Line BEHIND	Nearest Point on Line BEHIND
Distance to PARALLEL Line	Number of PARALLEL Points
Ajacency of LEFT Region	Adjacency of RIGHT Region
Number of Lines IN FRONT	Number of Lines BEHIND
Number of PARALLEL Lines	Number of Regions to the LEFT
Number of Regions to the RIGHT	

LOGICAL FEATURES

Histogram is bimodal	Region is bisected by line
Line is open	Line is closed
Line is loop	Line end is open
Line start is open	Line is clockwise
Area is smooth	Area is textured
Area is bounded	Area is new
One region to the LEFT	One region to the RIGHT

Same region to the LEFT and RIGHT OF line
Same region LEFT OF line 1 and line 2
Same region RIGHT OF line 1 and line 2
Same region to the LEFT OF line 1 and RIGHT OF line 2
Same region to the RIGHT OF line 1 and LEFT OF line 2
Two lines are touching (8 connected)

Areas are absent	Regions are absent
Lines are absent	System is starting
Process was Regions	Process was Lines
Process was Areas	Process was Focus
Process was Generate Areas	Process was active

region, line, or area considered by the system, as specified by the FOCUS OF ATTENTION module. This symbol can be omitted provided that no ambiguities result.[2] Other entries that are spatially related to the current ones may also be tested; for example, the features of an ADJACENT region or a PARALLEL line. Table I lists all such possible entries, together with the symbols that are used to express them.

[2]The tested operand can only belong to a region, a line, or an area; e.g., line length.

3) A pointer to the feature pertaining to the data entry discussed above (e.g., size, length, and gradient). The value of that feature (a number or a label) is the operand of the logical operation. All possible features are listed in Table II. A detailed description of these is given in [16].

4) An optional NOT qualifier that negates the effect of the condition.

5) An optional DIFFERENCE qualifier that applies the operation to differences in feature values.

Fig. 5 summarizes the structure of a condition. Values in

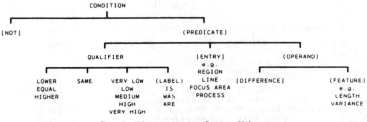

Fig. 5. The structure of a condition.

TABLE III
THE RULE ACTIONS

AREA ANALYZER ACTIONS

Create Smooth Area	Add to Smooth Area	Save Smooth Area
Create Texture Area	Add to Texture Area	Save Texture Area
Create Bounded Area	Add to Bounded Area	Save Bounded Area

Relabel Area to Smooth	Relabel Area to Texture
Relabel Area to Bounded	Delete Area

REGION ANALYZER ACTIONS

Split a Region by Histogram	Merge Two Regions
Split Region at Lines	

LINE ANALYZER ACTIONS

Extend Line Forward	Extend Line Backward
Join Lines Forward	Join Lines Backward
Insert Line Forward	Insert Line Backward
Merge Lines Forward	Merge Lines Backward
Delete Line	

FOCUS OF ATTENTION ACTIONS

Region with Highest Adjacency	Largest ADJACENT Region
Region with Lowest Adjacency	Smallest ADJACENT Region
Region with Higher Label	Next Scanned Region
Region to the LEFT OF Line	Region to the RIGHT OF Line

Closest Line IN FRONT	Closest Line BEHIND
Closest PARALLEL Line	Shortest Line that is near
Longest Line that is Near	Strongest Line that is near
Weakest Line that is Near	Line with Higher Label
Next Scanned Line	Line INTERSECTING Region

Defocus (Focus on Whole Image)	Focus on Areas
Clear Region List	Clear Line List
Freeze Area	Next Area (any)
Next Smooth Area	Next Texture Area
Next Bounded Area	

SUPERVISOR ACTIONS

Initialize Regions	Initialize Lines	Generate Areas
Match Region Rules	Match Line Rules	Match Area Rules
Match Focus Rules	Start	Stop

square brackets are optional, while those in parentheses are (variables) to be instantiated. Certain combinations of symbols are illegal, and these are flagged by the RULE INTERPRETER.

B. The Rule Actions

Each rule specifies to a processing module the action to be executed when all its conditions are met. Actions are selected from a finite list that represents the union of the capabilities of the processing modules in modifying the data in the STM. They provide the means for classifying the rules into sets according to the data entry on which each action is performed. A detailed description of how each action is accomplished is given in [16]. Table III provides a complete list of the actions

sorted into classes. Following are brief definitions of the actions within each class.

1) Actions on Areas: Some actions create new areas, add regions to existing areas, and compute and store the features of the created areas. Three such actions are defined for each area type. Other actions performed by the AREA ANALYZER include changing the type of an area when its characteristics alter during processing, and deleting areas that are of no further use to the focus of attention mechanism.

2) Actions on Regions: The REGION ANALYZER can either merge two regions into one, or split a region into several. Two different methods for splitting a region are given. The first selects a threshold from the histogram of a feature, and finds the connected pixels that are above and below that value. The second bisects a region spatially along the lines that intersect it.

3) Actions on Lines: Actions on lines are more diverse. A line can be extended forward from its last point along the highest local gradient. The same can be done backwards from the line's starting point. Alternatively, a line could be extended forward (or backward) by joining it to another line that is IN FRONT OF (or BEHIND) it. A third method for extending lines forward (or backward) is by inserting the label of the line at pixels that are at the boundary of two regions. Two lines can be merged into one line with the same label in two ways: a forward merge will combine the current line with another IN FRONT OF it, and a backward merge will do the same for the current line and one that is BEHIND it. The two lines must be touching each other. The final action deletes a line completely from the segmentation.

4) Focus of Attention Actions: The focus of attention module possesses different methods for replacing the current region and line by others. The actions listed in Table III are self-explanatory. They should be interpreted as obtaining the next region (or line) that exhibits the particular feature with respect to a current region (or line). This includes, for example, fetching the region that is to the left of the current line, or the line that intersects the current region. Actions that focus on the next area execute a selection strategy that is discussed in detail in [9], [16]. These can be limited to a specific area type, or they can be selected from any of the available areas.

5) Supervisor Actions: The actions of the metarules are different from all of the others in that they do not modify the segmentation data in the STM. They specify which set of rules is to be matched next on the data, and thus indirectly activate the different processing modules. Other commands include those that trigger the initialization, commence processing, and halt the analysis.

Having described the structure of the rules and reviewed the available conditions and actions, we will now discuss the different types of rules that constitute the model for low level image segmentation.

V. THE KNOWLEDGE RULES

The criteria that specify how an image should be segmented are at the heart of our rule-based model. Information about image intensities, region properties, and the existence of lines guide the analysis into creating an output that is in accordance with the model. By coding these knowledge sources into rules, and applying them to the data, a structured and uniform methodology will result. Other approaches to segmentation use a small number of heuristics in the analysis, as is evident by the abundance of efforts in the field, but rather because of the limitations imposed by the extremely rigid format in which the knowledge has been cast. A line detection program, for example, that is built on locating the discontinuities of features in the image array, will hardly produce a perfect (or even acceptable) line drawing. Clearly other heuristics are needed in order to account for deficiencies in the procedure. Methods for improving on the output of the above have been

investigated, but they require the execution of other programs that apply new transformations to the image. One may imagine the application of several cascaded procedures to an image, with each one accounting for some knowledge heuristic that was found to enhance the output. This is not an efficient method of analysis. In the course of improving the result, previous accomplishments may be destroyed. Even if this does not happen, we still have to contend with a large number of image transformations that yield incremental results which are usually highly localized.

The answer to this problem is to combine all useful processing heuristics into a model, and use it to guide the analysis. This is what a rule-based system accomplishes. The appropriate piece of information can be brought into the analysis when it is most needed. Thus, a specific heuristic will only be used to update that part of the image to which it is applicable. Any number of knowledge sources can be used. The model can easily be tuned by testing, modifying, deleting, and adding information. In fact, the main question becomes which heuristics to encode into the rules? Guidelines are needed for selecting the knowledge. Almost half a century ago, psychologists described a set of principles for human visual perception. What has become known as the Gestalt principles amounts to a set of general rules for perceptual grouping [5]. Although intended for high level cognitive events, these premises also have their consequences in low level context-free applications. One of the factors that has so far limited the use of Gestalt psychology in computer vision is the lack of a framework to represent these logical assertions. The rule-based vision system provides the required mechanism. By modeling the rules after the Gestalt laws, we define guidelines for creating the former and a mechanism for testing the latter. The five basic principles for grouping visual entities are: similarity, proximity, uniform destiny, good continuity, and closure. Other related, although less general factors, include simplicity, symmetry, equilibrium, and good shape. For details on each, the reader is referred to [5], [6], [24]. Our main concern is to encode these logical grouping assertions into the low level model. Each of the segmentation rules may represent some or more of the above principles. In this section, we will present typical examples of each of the three types of knowledge rules, and discuss how the Gestalt criteria are incorporated into the model.

A. Region Analysis Rules

Rules belonging to this set are concerned with modifying the regions in a segmentation in order to conform with certain criteria. The REGION ANALYZER module applies these rules to the regions stored in the STM. When a match occurs, the process is instructed to either split a region, or merge it with an ADJACENT one. Thus, the function of this rule set is to specify the merging and splitting criteria to be applied to the present region configuration in order to produce a better partition of the image.

The dominant principles in region analysis are those of proximity and similarity. Pixels that are adjacent and have similar intensity (or color) features are grouped into regions. This is the basic principle behind most region growing programs [13]. A general rule merges two ADJACENT regions (each of which can be a single pixel) as follows [15]:

RULE (801):

IF: (1) There is a LOW DIFFERENCE in REGION FEATURE 1
   (2) There is a LOW DIFFERENCE in REGION FEATURE 2
   (3) There is a LOW DIFFERENCE in REGION FEATURE 3

THEN: (1) MERGE the two REGIONS

This implies that a low difference in the average values of all three color features between the two regions must exist. This region growing rule is responsible for most of the merging that takes place. Alone however, it cannot account for all the data situations that require region merging. Analyzing an image using only this rule as the merging criterion produces many incorrect data configurations. These result when nonuniform scene characteristics such as boundaries, shadows, and highlights are subjected to noise, as well as sampling and quantization errors during the image formation process. Based on our understanding of these phenomena, new rules can be added to deal with them on a case-by-case basis. Consider the following rule:

RULE (802):

IF: (1) The REGION SIZE is VERY LOW
   (2) The ADJACENCY with another REGION is HIGH
   (3) The DIFFERENCE in REGION FEATURE 1 is NOT HIGH
   (4) The DIFFERENCE in REGION FEATURE 2 is NOT HIGH
   (5) The DIFFERENCE in REGION FEATURE 3 is NOT HIGH

THEN: (1) MERGE the two REGIONS

The first two conditions describe the situation when a region is of very small size and is mostly surrounded (or totally contained) by an ADJACENT region. This is an indication that the first region resulted from some noise source. Therefore a relaxation of the merging criteria in Rule (801) is called for. The last three conditions provide the loosened version that restricts the differences in features to be of low or medium value.

Another aspect to be accounted for is the formation of "hybrid" regions at the boundary between two regions that have high differences in their average intensities (or colors). Due to the graded quantized transition, pixels in the middle acquire a range of intensities that does not allow them to merge with either of their neighbors. Because they are at a boundary, these intermediate regions exhibit a high average gradient, and therefore will be split longitudinally in a direction parallel to the border. This will result in very thin regions along some of the boundaries. Such regions are characterized by low size, a very high (or very low) aspect ratio, and a high average gradient. The merging criteria are again relaxed to

eliminate these residual regions, as shown by the following rules.

RULE (803):

IF: (1) The REGION SIZE is LOW
   (2) The REGION AVERAGE GRADIENT is HIGH
   (3) The DIFFERENCE in REGION FEATURE 1 is NOT HIGH
   (4) The DIFFERENCE in REGION FEATURE 2 is NOT HIGH
   (5) The DIFFERENCE in REGION FEATURE 3 is NOT HIGH

THEN: (1) MERGE the two REGIONS

RULE (804):

IF: (1) The REGION SIZE is LOW
   (2) The REGION ASPECT RATIO is VERY HIGH
   (3) The DIFFERENCE in REGION FEATURE 1 is NOT HIGH
   (4) The DIFFERENCE in REGION FEATURE 2 is NOT HIGH
   (5) The DIFFERENCE in REGION FEATURE 3 is NOT HIGH

THEN: (1) MERGE the two REGIONS

A similar rule, Rule (805), exists for very low aspect ratio.

Because of the limited resolution of the image, faulty regions may also occur if a large number of regions intersect at the same spot. Rule (806) will abolish such errors allowing a merge with the most similar larger region.

RULE (806):

IF: (1) The REGION SIZE is LOW
   (2) The NUMBER of ADJACENT regions is HIGH
   (3) The DIFFERENCE in REGION FEATURE 1 is NOT HIGH
   (4) The DIFFERENCE in REGION FEATURE 2 is NOT HIGH
   (5) The DIFFERENCE in REGION FEATURE 3 is NOT HIGH
   (6) The ADJACENT REGION SIZE is NOT LOW

THEN: (1) MERGE the two REGIONS

Two ADJACENT regions of very small size are also allowed to merge more easily because of diminished contrast sensitivity. The following rule portrays this concept.

RULE (807):

IF: (1) The REGION SIZE is VERY LOW
   (2) The ADJACENT REGION SIZE is VERY LOW
   (3) The DIFFERENCE in REGION FEATURE 1 is NOT HIGH
   (4) The DIFFERENCE in REGION FEATURE 2 is NOT HIGH
   (5) The DIFFERENCE in REGION FEATURE 3 is NOT HIGH

THEN: (1) MERGE the two REGIONS

The Gestalt principle of similarity is the main factor that motivates the splitting of a region. Then, the resulting regions must consist of pixels that are more similar to each other than the pixels belonging to the original region. Histograms of features are strong indicators of the presence of subgroups of pixels. A multimodal histogram signals the need for splitting to achieve a uniform unimodal distribution of the features in the resulting partition [23]. In [16], a method was introduced for determining whether a histogram is (at least) bimodal, and to what degree. The corresponding action to split the region was also described. The following pair of rules combine the measurement with the action.

RULE (901):

    IF: (1) The REGION HISTOGRAM is BIMODAL

    THEN: (1) SPLIT the REGION according to the HISTOGRAM

RULE (902):

    IF: (1) The REGION HISTOGRAM BIMODALITY is NOT LOW

    THEN: (1) SPLIT the REGION according to the HISTOGRAM

The second rule is seen to be more restrictive since it establishes a lower limit on the degree of bimodality below which splitting will not be allowed. The following rules take into account the size of a region in addition to its histogram:

RULE (903):

    IF: (1) The REGION SIZE is HIGH
        (2) The REGION HISTOGRAM BIMODALITY is HIGH

    THEN: (1) SPLIT the REGION according to the HISTOGRAM

RULE (904):

    IF: (1) The REGION SIZE is MEDIUM
        (2) The REGION HISTOGRAM BIMODALITY is NOT LOW

    THEN: (1) SPLIT the REGION according to the HISTOGRAM

The two rules are examples of how the different ranges of symbolic features can be utilized in knowledge representation. Rule (903) demands a highly bimodal histogram for large regions, while the restriction is eased in Rule (904) for medium size regions. Histogram splitting is unreliable (and therefore not allowed) for regions with small (LOW) size because of the increasing effect of the region boundary.

There are other indicators that a region should be split. Rule (905) depicts the case when the variance of the color features is large, indicating a large spread in the feature values from the average.

RULE (905):

    IF: (1) The REGION VARIANCE 1 is HIGH
        (2) The REGION VARIANCE 2 is HIGH
        (3) The REGION VARIANCE 3 is HIGH
        (4) The REGION HISTOGRAM is BIMODAL

    THEN: (1) SPLIT the REGION according to the HISTOGRAM

The histogram must still be bimodal, although no restriction is made on the degree of bimodality. This implies that a small dip in the histogram will be sufficient. In fact, the dip is required by the rule action, since a threshold must be determined for histogram splitting. The next two rules are seen to use the average gradient over a region as the guide for splitting. A large gradient may be due to a large variance of the features, which is the case already covered by Rule (905). On the other hand, it may be caused by a local discontinuity in the feature values that might not reflect itself in the variances.

RULE (906):

    IF: (1) The REGION SIZE is HIGH
        (2) The REGION AVERAGE GRADIENT is NOT LOW
        (3) The REGION HISTOGRAM is BIMODAL

    THEN: (1) SPLIT the REGION according to the HISTOGRAM

RULE (907):

    IF: (1) The REGION SIZE is NOT LOW
        (2) The REGION AVERAGE GRADIENT is HIGH
        (3) The REGION HISTOGRAM is BIMODAL

    THEN: (1) SPLIT the REGION according to the HISTOGRAM

Lines may provide evidence for region splitting. Pixels bearing the same region label, but falling on opposite sides of a line passing through, may in fact belong to different regions. The REGION ANALYZER provides an action that splits a region along the lines that intersect it. Rule (908) illustrates how line information is used in processing regions.

RULE (908):

    IF: (1) The REGION SIZE is NOT LOW
        (2) REGION is BISECTED BY LINE
        (3) The LINE LENGTH is NOT LOW
        (4) The LINE AVERAGE GRADIENT is HIGH

    THEN: (1) SPLIT the REGION at LINES

The use of line information in region analysis is again exemplified in Rule (809). Merging two regions can be inhibited by the presence of a line at their common boundary, even if they have identical average features. This is accomplished by adding another condition to Rule (801) to produce the following:

RULE (809):

IF: (1) There is a LOW DIFFERENCE in
REGION FEATURE 1
(2) There is a LOW DIFFERENCE in
REGION FEATURE 2
(3) There is a LOW DIFFERENCE in
REGION FEATURE 3
(4) The value of LINES BETWEEN REGIONS is LOW

THEN: (1) MERGE the two REGIONS

Condition 4) above refers to the fraction of common boundary between the two regions that is covered by lines. The same condition can be added to other region merging rules. The next section introduces the rules used by the LINE ANALYZER.

B. Line Analysis Rules

Lines by their nature, provide a wider variety of data situations. They are also subject to a larger number of actions. In this section, we present examples of various line analysis rules. Unlike regions, similarity is not the main issue here. Instead, other Gestalt principles take on a more prominent role; namely, continuity and good closure. Proximity is of equal importance for lines as it was for regions.

These rules are attempting to enhance the initial line configuration that results from detecting the discontinuities in the image intensities. The latter usually produces incomplete lines, as well as faulty lines that are possibly due to noise and therefore must be eliminated. The task is then to discard illegitimate lines and to improve genuine ones. An important clue to both is the presence of a line with one (or both) ends open. Factors of both continuity and closure dictate the necessity to either expand the open end of a line until it encounters another line, or if this is not possible, delete the line.

A credible way to complete lines is by joining an open line to another that is closely IN FRONT of or BEHIND it. The situation is depicted by the following two rules.

RULE (1501):

IF: (1) The LINE END point is OPEN
(2) The DISTANCE to the LINE IN FRONT is LOW

THEN: (1) JOIN the LINES by FORWARD expansion

RULE (1601):

IF: (1) The LINE START point is OPEN
(2) The DISTANCE to the LINE BEHIND is LOW

THEN: (1) JOIN the LINES by BACKWARD expansion

The distance constraint is relaxed if the average gradient of the line is not low, or if both lines are colinear (have the same average direction). The corresponding rules are:

RULE (1502):

IF: (1) The LINE END point is OPEN
(2) The DISTANCE to the LINE IN FRONT is
NOT HIGH
(3) The LINE AVERAGE GRADIENT is NOT LOW

THEN: (1) JOIN the LINES by FORWARD expansion

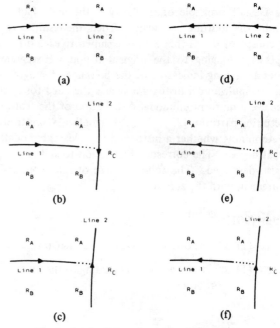

Fig. 6. Joining lines using region information.

RULE (1503):

IF: (1) The LINE END point is OPEN
(2) The DISTANCE to the LINE IN FRONT is
NOT HIGH
(3) The LINES have EQUAL AVERAGE DIRECTION

THEN: (1) JOIN the LINES by FORWARD expansion

Similar rules exist for joining a line by backward expansion to a line that is BEHIND it.

Region information is also used to aid the joining of two lines. Other constraints can be relaxed if the lines share the same regions to their left and right. This is a strong indication that both lines are part of the same boundary. The following three rules correspond to the data configurations shown in Fig. 6.

RULE (1504): [Fig. 6(a)]

IF: (1) The LINE END point is OPEN
(2) The LINE GRADIENT is NOT VERY LOW
(3) The DISTANCE to the LINE IN FRONT is
NOT VERY HIGH
(4) The two LINES have the SAME REGION
to the LEFT
(5) The two LINES have the SAME REGION
to the RIGHT

THEN: (1) JOIN the LINES by FORWARD expansion

RULE (1505): [Fig. 6(b)]

IF: (1) The LINE END point is OPEN
(2) The LINE GRADIENT is NOT VERY LOW
(3) The DISTANCE to the LINE IN FRONT is
NOT VERY HIGH
(4) SAME REGION LEFT of LINE 1 and RIGHT
of LINE 2

(5) The two LINES have the SAME REGION
to the RIGHT

THEN: (1) JOIN the LINES by FORWARD expansion

RULE (1506): [Fig. 6(c)]

IF: (1) The LINE END point is OPEN
(2) The LINE GRADIENT is NOT VERY LOW
(3) The DISTANCE to the LINE IN FRONT is
NOT VERY HIGH
(4) The two LINES have the SAME REGION
to the LEFT
(5) SAME REGION RIGHT of LINE 1 and LEFT
of LINE 2

THEN: (1) JOIN the LINES by FORWARD expansion

Joining by backward expansion produces three analogous rules
for the cases in Fig. 6(d)–(f).

In the absence of a close neighbor, an open line can still be
extended forward or backward by expanding the appropriate
end point along the maximum local gradient at that position
in the image. For this to happen, however, a single open line
must exhibit strong survival characteristics, both in length and
in strength (average gradient). The following rules represent
the above situation.

RULE (1507):

IF: (1) The LINE END point is OPEN
(2) The LINE AVERAGE GRADIENT is HIGH

THEN: (1) EXTEND the LINE FORWARD

RULE (1508):

IF: (1) The LINE END point is OPEN
(2) The LINE AVERAGE GRADIENT is NOT LOW
(3) The LINE LENGTH is NOT LOW

THEN: (1) EXTEND the LINE FORWARD

Rules for extending a line backward from its starting point
follow easily from the above.

The local gradient is also used to expand an open line that
has a large number of regions on both sides, as shown in Fig. 7.
The line is considered to be at the boundary of two textured
areas, and the maximum local gradient is used to define the
border. The rule that detects this situation is given by:

RULE (1509):

IF: (1) The LINE END point is OPEN
(2) The LINE GRADIENT is NOT LOW
(3) The NUMBER of REGIONS to the LEFT is
NOT LOW
(4) The NUMBER of REGIONS to the RIGHT is
NOT LOW

THEN: (1) EXTEND the LINE FORWARD

Rule (1609) will provide for the backward extension in a similar manner.

ADJACENT region information is also used to expand a line

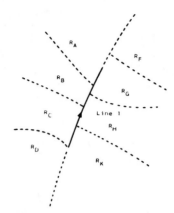

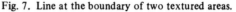

Fig. 7. Line at the boundary of two textured areas.

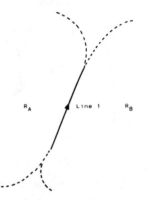

Fig. 8. Line at the boundary of two large regions.

by inserting additional points between two bordering regions.
The configuration portrayed in Fig. 8 illustrates how the
presence of two different regions, one on each side of an
incomplete line, is a strong indication that the line is indeed
part of a larger boundary. The following rule is based on this
hypothesis.

RULE (1510):

IF: (1) The LINE END point is OPEN
(2) The LINE LENGTH is NOT LOW
(3) There is ONE REGION to the LEFT of the LINE
(4) There is ONE REGION to the RIGHT of the LINE
(5) REGIONS to the LEFT and RIGHT are NOT
the SAME

THEN: (1) Expand the LINE by INSERTING FORWARD

Points are inserted at the starting point of an open line if similar conditions exist.

As a result of applying the previous rules, incomplete lines
will be extended, and will meet other lines. The resulting junctions may suggest the merging of two lines into one. This
happens when both represent different parts of the same
boundary, as shown in Fig. 9(a). In other cases, merging
produces two new lines that form a more appropriate configuration in terms of the good continuity principle. This
situation is depicted in Fig. 9(b). Rules may be constructed
to perform forward and backward line merging, examples of
which are:

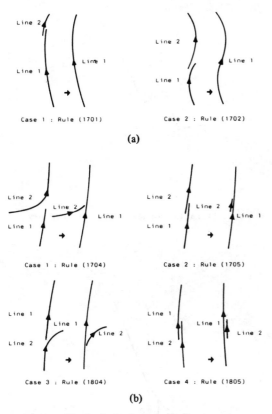

Fig. 9. Rules for merging lines.

(a) shows Case 1 : Rule (1701) and Case 2 : Rule (1702).

(b) shows Case 1 : Rule (1704), Case 2 : Rule (1705), Case 3 : Rule (1804), and Case 4 : Rule (1805).

RULE (1701): [Fig. 9(a), case 1]

IF: (1) The LINE LENGTH is NOT LOW
    (2) The LENGTH of the LINE IN FRONT is LOW
    (3) The LINES are TOUCHING
    (4) The closest POINT IN FRONT is LOW

THEN: (1) MERGE the LINES FORWARD

RULE (1702): [Fig. 9(a), case 2]

IF: (1) The LINE LENGTH is NOT LOW
    (2) The LENGTH of the LINE IN FRONT is
        NOT LOW
    (3) The LINES are TOUCHING
    (4) The closest POINT IN FRONT is VERY LOW

THEN: (1) MERGE the LINES FORWARD

The previous two rules represent the situation in Fig. 9(a) where the closest point on the second line (the line IN FRONT) is near (or at) its starting point. The two rules account for different second line lengths, so that the constraint on the position of the closest point is more stringent if the line length is high.[3] A line can also be merged with one that is BEHIND it according to the following rules.

RULE (1801):

IF: (1) The LINE LENGTH is NOT LOW
    (2) The LENGTH of the LINE BEHIND is LOW

---

[3]Note that the position of a point on the line is given as a fraction of the line length.

    (3) The LINES are TOUCHING
    (4) The closest POINT BEHIND is HIGH

THEN: (1) MERGE the LINES BACKWARD

RULE (1802):

IF: (1) The LINE LENGTH is NOT LOW
    (2) The LENGTH of the LINE BEHIND is NOT LOW
    (3) The LINES are TOUCHING
    (4) The closest POINT BEHIND is VERY HIGH

THEN: (1) MERGE the LINES BACKWARD

Merging based on similarity of lines is made possible by the following rule.

RULE (1703):

IF: (1) The LINES are TOUCHING
    (2) The closest POINT IN FRONT is NOT HIGH
    (3) The LINE IN FRONT has a HIGH GRADIENT
        VARIANCE
    (4) There is a LOW DIFFERENCE in LINE
        FEATURE 1
    (5) There is a LOW DIFFERENCE in LINE
        FEATURE 2
    (6) There is a LOW DIFFERENCE in LINE
        FEATURE 3

THEN: (1) MERGE the LINES FORWARD

An analogous rule exists for merging a line with another that is BEHIND it. Note that condition 3) above justifies the splitting of the second line in order to merge part (or all) of it with the first.

Merging to improve the continuity of lines, as in Fig. 9(b), is achieved through the following rules.

RULE (1704): [Fig. 9(b), case 1]

IF: (1) The LINES are TOUCHING
    (2) The closest POINT IN FRONT is MEDIUM
    (3) The LINES END DIRECTIONS are EQUAL
    (4) START and END DIR. of LINE IN FRONT are
        NOT EQUAL

THEN: (1) MERGE the LINES FORWARD

RULE (1705): [Fig. 9(b), case 2]

IF: (1) The LINES are TOUCHING
    (2) The LENGTH of the LINE IN FRONT is
        NOT LOW
    (3) The LINE START and END DIRECTIONS are
        EQUAL
    (4) LINE IN FRONT START and END DIRECTIONS
        are EQUAL
    (5) The closest POINT IN FRONT is LOW
    (6) The DIFFERENCE in AVERAGE DIRECTION is
        VERY LOW

THEN: (1) MERGE the LINES FORWARD

RULE (1804): [Fig. 9(b), case 3]

IF: (1) The LINES are TOUCHING
    (2) The closest POINT BEHIND is MEDIUM
    (3) The LINES START DIRECTIONS are EQUAL
    (4) START and END DIR. of LINE BEHIND are NOT EQUAL

THEN: (1) MERGE the LINES BACKWARD

RULE (1805): [Fig. 9(b), case 4]

IF: (1) The LINES are TOUCHING
    (2) The LENGTH of the LINE BEHIND is NOT LOW
    (3) The LINE START and END DIRECTIONS are EQUAL
    (4) The LINE BEHIND START and END DIRECTIONS are EQUAL
    (5) The closest POINT BEHIND is HIGH
    (6) The DIFFERENCE in AVERAGE DIRECTION is VERY LOW

THEN: (1) MERGE the LINES BACKWARD

There are a number of cases in which a line should be deleted from the segmentation. The simplest case is when the properties of the line do not justify its existence. Very short line segments that are not connected to any other lines and that exhibit a weak gradient value are considered to be due to noise factors and are consequently removed. This represents an indirect application of the principle of closure since lines are rarely assumed to end abruptly in an open space. In other words, if a line is not supported by others, and if it does not behave as a plausible independent entity, it will be deleted, as seen from the following rules.

RULE (1401):

IF: (1) The LINE LENGTH is VERY LOW
    (2) The LINE AVERAGE GRADIENT is LOW

THEN: (1) DELETE the LINE

RULE (1402):

IF: (1) The LINE LENGTH is LOW
    (2) The LINE AVERAGE GRADIENT is VERY LOW

THEN: (1) DELETE the LINE

RULE (1403):

IF: (1) The LINE is OPEN
    (2) The LINE LENGTH is LOW
    (3) The LINE AVERAGE GRADIENT is LOW

THEN: (1) DELETE the LINE

A line is also deleted if there is evidence of a multiple representation of a boundary. This commonly occurs in images of natural scenes where the edge between two regions can be several pixels wide. As a result, the process of edge location and boundary tracking will produce a number of PARALLEL lines at the position of the graded boundary. The following rule will eliminate such multiple line occurrences.

RULE (1404):

IF: (1) The LINE has LOWER LENGTH
    (2) There is a LOW DIFFERENCE in the LINES GRADIENT
    (3) The PARALLEL DISTANCE is VERY LOW

THEN: (1) DELETE the LINE

Thus, the shorter of two PARALLEL lines that are very close to each other will be deleted. Note that this rule does not apply to skewed lines (lines that are physically parallel, but have opposite directions). These lines result from the existence of a thin object on a darker or lighter background, and therefore, should not be eliminated.

The configuration of regions in the neighborhood of a line may dictate its removal. This is particularly true when the line falls within a large uniform region, and has a low local gradient as well. A rule that embodies this situation is given by:

RULE (1405):

IF: (1) The LINE is OPEN
    (2) The LINE GRADIENT is LOW
    (3) The SAME REGION to the LEFT and RIGHT

THEN: (1) DELETE the LINE

The third class of knowledge rules, those that analyze areas, is discussed in the next section.

C. Area Analysis Rules

These include rules that generate areas of attention, and others that update them during processing. The following three rules detect, add to, and save smooth areas in an image segmentation.

RULE (401):

IF: (1) The REGION SIZE is HIGH
    (2) The REGION has a LOW VARIANCE 1
    (3) The REGION has a LOW VARIANCE 2
    (4) The REGION has a LOW VARIANCE 3

THEN: (1) CREATE SMOOTH AREA

RULE (402):

IF: (1) The AREA IS SMOOTH
    (2) The REGION ADJACENCY is NOT VERY LOW
    (3) The REGION SIZE is NOT LOW
    (4) The REGION has a LOW VARIANCE 1
    (5) The REGION has a LOW VARIANCE 2
    (6) The REGION has a LOW VARIANCE 3

THEN: (1) ADD REGION TO SMOOTH AREA

RULE (403):

IF: (1) The AREA IS SMOOTH
    (2) The AREA SIZE is NOT LOW

THEN: SAVE SMOOTH AREA

Rule (401) will create the nucleus of a new smooth area from the first large smooth region encountered. Subsequent smooth ADJACENT regions (if any) are added to the area by Rule

(402). Finally, Rule (403) will save the area for further reference during processing, if its size is large enough.

Textured areas are detected in a similar fashion using the following set of rules.

RULE (501):

IF: (1) The REGION SIZE is LOW

THEN: (1) CREATE a TEXTURE AREA

RULE (502):

IF: (1) The AREA IS TEXTURE
(2) The REGION ADJACENCY is NOT VERY LOW
(3) The REGION SIZE is LOW

THEN: (1) ADD REGION TO TEXTURE AREA

RULE (503):

IF: (1) The AREA is TEXTURE
(2) The AREA SIZE is NOT LOW
(3) The NUMBER of REGIONS is NOT LOW
(4) The AREA VARIANCE 1 is NOT LOW
(5) The AREA VARIANCE 2 is NOT LOW
(6) The AREA VARIANCE 3 is NOT LOW

THEN: (1) SAVE TEXTURE AREA

The first two rules create a search for clusters of small ADJACENT regions. If the size of a cluster is large enough, and if it exhibits sufficient feature variance, it is saved as a texture area.

Bounded areas are generated by testing the lines in a segmentation. Long lines that close (or almost close) on themselves are sought in order to examine the encircled areas. Following are three criteria for detecting such occurrences.

RULE (601):

IF: (1) The LINE IS LOOP
(2) The LINE LENGTH is NOT LOW

THEN: (1) SAVE BOUNDED AREA

RULE (602):

IF: (1) The LINE LENGTH is HIGH
(2) The START-END DISTANCE is LOW

THEN: (1) SAVE BOUNDED AREA

RULE (603):

IF: (1) The LINE LENGTH is MEDIUM
(2) The START-END DISTANCE is VERY LOW

THEN: (1) SAVE BOUNDED AREA

Other area analysis rules monitor existing areas in order to modify their classification according to variations in their properties. Changes are brought about by the merging and splitting of regions, and the addition and deletion of lines. Since the boundaries of an area can be altered during processing, its physical properties may also change. It is the function of these rules to ensure that areas are consistently categorized according to their features. Examples of rules that change an area's type are:

RULE 701:

IF: (1) The AREA is SMOOTH
(2) The AREA VARIANCE 1 is NOT LOW
(3) The AREA VARIANCE 2 is NOT LOW
(4) The AREA VARIANCE 3 is NOT LOW

THEN: (1) RELABEL AREA TEXTURE

RULE (702):

IF: (1) The AREA IS TEXTURE
(2) The AREA VARIANCE 1 is LOW
(3) The AREA VARIANCE 2 is LOW
(4) The AREA VARIANCE 3 is LOW

THEN: (1) RELABEL AREA SMOOTH

Areas are locked out of processing if they are found to be stable enough, in terms of their performance characteristics [9]. This allows the system to concentrate on those areas that require further processing. Examples of rules that "freeze" areas are:

RULE (703):

IF: (1) The AREA is SMOOTH
(2) The NUMBER of REGIONS is VERY LOW
(3) LINES are ABSENT
(4) REGION UNIFORMITY 1 is HIGH
(5) REGION UNIFORMITY 2 is HIGH
(6) REGION UNIFORMITY 3 is HIGH

THEN: (1) FREEZE AREA

RULE (704):

IF: (1) The AREA is TEXTURE
(2) REGION CONTRAST 1 is HIGH
(3) REGION CONTRAST 2 is HIGH
(4) REGION CONTRAST 3 is HIGH
(5) LINE CONNECTIVITY is HIGH

THEN: (1) FREEZE AREA

RULE (705):

IF: (1) The AREA is BOUNDED
(2) LINE IS CLOCKWISE
(3) ONE REGION RIGHT OF LINE
(4) REGION UNIFORMITY 1 is HIGH
(5) REGION UNIFORMITY 2 is HIGH
(6) REGION UNIFORMITY 3 is HIGH

THEN: (1) FREEZE AREA

An analogous rule to Rule (705) exists for a counterclockwise line that has one region to its left. Note that a frozen area is still available to provide information about the part of image it represents (e.g., smooth or textured). An area is deleted from the STM only if it no longer carries useful segmentation information. The following rules will eliminate such areas.

RULE (707):

IF: (1) The AREA is SMOOTH
    (2) The NUMBER of REGIONS is HIGH
    (3) The AREA SIZE is NOT HIGH
    (4) REGION CONTRAST 1 is HIGH
    (5) REGION CONTRAST 2 is HIGH
    (6) REGION CONTRAST 3 is HIGH

THEN: (1) DELETE AREA

RULE (708):

IF: (1) The AREA is TEXTURE
    (2) The NUMBER OF REGIONS is LOW
    (3) The AREA SIZE is NOT HIGH
    (4) The REGION UNIFORMITY 1 is HIGH
    (5) The REGION UNIFORMITY 2 is HIGH
    (6) The REGION UNIFORMITY 3 is HIGH

THEN: (1) DELETE AREA

RULE (709):

IF: (1) The AREA is BOUNDED
    (2) The NUMBER OF LINES is HIGH
    (3) The LINE CONTRAST 1 is HIGH
    (4) The LINE CONTRAST 2 is HIGH
    (5) The LINE CONTRAST 3 is HIGH

THEN: (1) DELETE AREA

Regions and lines within an area are reassigned if that area is deleted. They are considered as belonging to a single area which does not include any of the specific focus of attention areas.

This concludes our discussion of the knowledge rules for low level image segmentation. From the analysis, we can conclude that the Gestalt principle of similarity plays an important role in region processing. On the other hand, closure and continuity are more prominent in line processing. Proximity is an essential factor in grouping both regions and lines. The knowledge rules presented in this section are typical examples of those used by the system. A complete listing of the knowledge rules is given in [16].

VI. THE CONTROL RULES

The focus of attention and the metarules differ from the knowledge rules in that they do not directly modify the segmentation data. Yet, their presence is essential to the functioning of the system. These control rules specify both the order in which the different sets of knowledge rules are matched, as well as the specific data entries to be tested. There exist numerous ways in which to execute any of these tasks. Each method corresponds to a particular control strategy. Elsewhere, we discuss a data-driven method for dynamically selecting the appropriate control strategy [9]. In this section, we describe how the focus of attention rules and the metarules are used to implement various strategies.

A. The FOCUS OF ATTENTION Rules

The FOCUS OF ATTENTION process performs two levels of data selection, as shown in Fig. 10. An area is selected, and

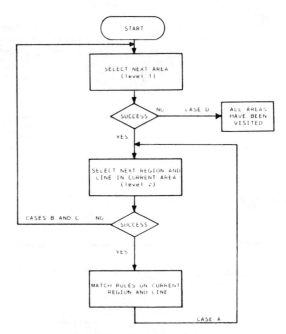

Fig. 10. Levels of data selection.

then the regions and lines within the area are chosen. When all have been visited, the process will move to a new area. The whole procedure is repreated until all the areas generated by the AREA ANALYZER are selected. When these are exhausted, the regions and lines in the image that do not belong to specific focus of attention areas are visited. This data selection method corresponds to a single pass over all the regions and lines in the image.

The transition from one area to the next is accomplished when the FOCUS OF ATTENTION process fails to select a new region or line in the current area. This failure is recorded by the system as part of the history stored in the STM. This particular cycle is then marked as INACTIVE. When this happens, the FOCUS OF ATTENTION process must be invoked again to obtain a new area. If a failure is repeated, this will signal that all the areas have been visited. An option is provided to either stop the processing, or revisit the areas.

By examining the history of processing in the previous two cycles (stored in the STM), different conclusions can be arrived at. Table IV lists the different cases and their interpretations (N/A correspond to don't care conditions). These are also indicated in Fig. 10.

In case A, the FOCUS OF ATTENTION process is invoked after a knowledge module has matched its rules on the current region or line. Therefore, a new region or line must now be fetched. This is accomplished by matching the following rule.

RULE ("1XX"):

IF: (1) The PREVIOUS PROCESS was NOT FOCUS

THEN: (1) "GET THE NEXT REGION"
    (2) "GET THE NEXT LINE"

The quotations in the rule number and in the actions indicate that they are variables to be instantiated. Actions that correspond to different methods of obtaining the next region and the next line are listed in Table III. A specific strategy

TABLE IV
INTERPRETATION OF PROCESSING HISTORY

Case	Cycle	Process	State	Interpretation
A	Previous	NOT FOCUS	N/A	A knowledge module was invoked.
B	Next Previous	NOT FOCUS	N/A	A knowledge module was invoked.
	Previous	FOCUS	INACTIVE	Could not fetch a new region or line in current area.
C	Next Previous	FOCUS	ACTIVE	A new area was fetched.
	Previous	FOCUS	INACTIVE	None of the lines or regions in new area is selected.
D	Next Previous	FOCUS	INACTIVE	No more region or lines in current area.
	Previous	FOCUS	INACTIVE	No new area.

must select the method that is most suitable for the properties of the current area [9].

Cases *B* and *C* in Table IV correspond to the situation where the current area cannot contribute any new regions or lines, and therefore a new area is now called for. The following two rules are seen to be in accordance with the two cases

RULE (101): (Case *B*)

    IF: (1) The PREVIOUS PROCESS was FOCUS
        (2) The PREVIOUS PROCESS was NOT ACTIVE
        (3) The NEXT PREVIOUS PROCESS was NOT FOCUS

THEN: (1) GET THE NEXT AREA

RULE (102): (Case *C*)

    IF: (1) The PREVIOUS PROCESS was FOCUS
        (2) The PREVIOUS PROCESS was NOT ACTIVE
        (3) The NEXT PREVIOUS PROCESS was FOCUS
        (4) The NEXT PREVIOUS PROCESS was ACTIVE

THEN: (1) GET THE NEXT AREA

The selection of the next area is also based on a data-driven decision-making methodology [9].

Case *D* in Table IV occurs when all the areas in the image have been visited. The next rule allows for an additional pass over the areas by erasing the history lists that record the regions and lines visited in the first path.

RULE (103): (Case *D*)

    IF: (1) The PREVIOUS PROCESS was FOCUS
        (2) The PREVIOUS PROCESS was NOT ACTIVE
        (3) The NEXT PREVIOUS PROCESS was FOCUS
        (4) The PREVIOUS PROCESS was NOT ACTIVE

THEN: (1) CLEAR REGION LIST
         (2) CLEAR LINE LIST

In the next section, we will describe a metarule that uses the same conditions to terminate processing.

The previous rules permit the execution of a specific strategy for visiting the areas, regions, and lines in the image. In addition, other rules can override these and fetch a region or line other than those specified by the existing strategy. This is particularly useful when an interesting data configuration is detected that requires immediate investigation. The following is an example of such a rule.

RULE (201):

    IF: (1) The LINE GRADIENT is HIGH
        (2) The LINE LENGTH is HIGH
        (3) SAME REGION LEFT and RIGHT of the LINE

THEN: (1) GET the REGION to the LEFT of the LINE

In this rule, a line that has a high gradient and length intersects a region. Thus, the latter should be examined to determine whether it should be split. Another interesting case occurs when a line encircles a region, as given by the following two rules.

RULE (202):

    IF: (1) The LINE is LOOP
        (2) The LINE is CLOCKWISE
        (3) The RIGHT REGION ADJACENCY is HIGH

THEN: (1) GET the REGION to the RIGHT of the LINE

RULE (203):

    IF: (1) The LINE is LOOP
        (2) The LINE is NOT CLOCKWISE
        (3) The LEFT REGION ADJACENCY is HIGH

THEN: (1) GET the REGION to the LEFT of the LINE

If the average gradient of a large region is high, this may be due to a line passing through it. The following rule brings any such line to the attention of the system.

RULE (204):

    IF: (1) The REGION SIZE is HIGH
        (2) The REGION AVERAGE GRADIENT is HIGH

THEN: (1) GET the LINE that INTERSECTS the REGION

PARALLEL lines also provide a configuration worth investigating, as is evident from the next rule.

RULE (205):

    IF: (1) The PARALLEL DISTANCE is NOT VERY LOW

THEN: (1) GET the PARALLEL LINE

PARALLEL lines that are very close are subject to deletion according to Rule (1404) (see Section V-B).

Rules (201)–(205) are given higher priority than Rule ("1XX") in fetching the next region or line. If none of them matches, the strategy specified by Rule ("1XX") is executed.

B. The Metarules

In addition to specifying the method for data selection, the SUPERVISOR in Fig. 1 uses the metarules to coordinate the activities of all the other processing modules. The conditions of these meta-rules are matched against the processing history stored in the STM. Their actions establish the flow of control by specifying the next process to be activated. Because each process is associated with a particular rule set, the metarules effectively select the set of rules to match against the data. The simplest examples of metarules are those that ensure proper initialization, as follows:

METARULE (1):

    IF: (1) REGIONS ARE ABSENT

THEN: (1) INITIALIZE REGIONS

METARULE (2):

    IF: (1) LINES ARE ABSENT

THEN: (1) INITIALIZE LINES

METARULE (3):

    IF: (1) AREAS ARE ABSENT

THEN: (1) GENERATE AREAS

METARULE (4):

    IF: (1) The previous PROCESS was GENERATE AREAS
        (2) The previous PROCESS was ACTIVE

THEN: (1) GENERATE AREAS

METARULE (5):

    IF: (1) The previous PROCESS was GENERATE AREAS
        (2) The previous PROCESS was NOT ACTIVE

THEN: (1) Match the FOCUS OF ATTENTION rules.

The first two rules will initialize the region and line maps according to specific procedures [16]. Areas of attention are generated when Metarule (3) matches. Metarule (4) will allow for the creation of all possible areas in the image, based on the

initial region and line configurations, and the rules discussed in Section V. Metarule (5) specifies the action to be taken when all possible areas have been generated.

A complete set of control strategies are defined by the user and stored in the STM.[4] For example, the following sequence of three metarules alternatively invoke region analysis and the focus of attention

METARULE (9):

    IF: (1) Previous PROCESS was FOCUS
        (2) Previous PROCESS was ACTIVE

THEN: (1) Match the REGION analysis rules.

METARULE (10):

    IF: (1) Previous PROCESS was REGIONS
        (2) Previous PROCESS was ACTIVE

THEN: (1) Match the REGION analysis rules.

METARULE (11):

    IF: (1) Previous PROCESS was REGIONS
        (2) Previous PROCESS was NOT ACTIVE

THEN: (1) Match the FOCUS OF ATTENTION rules.

The effect of these is to successively match the region rules on all the regions in the current area of attention. A different strategy can be created by interchanging the processes in Metarules (9)–(11).

During processing, different metarules will invoke the FOCUS OF ATTENTION process whenever a new data entry is sought for examination. Because of the two levels of data selection (see Fig. 10), the FOCUS OF ATTENTION process must fail twice before the system can conclude that all data entries have been exhausted. This corresponds to case D in Table IV. Accordingly, Metarule (6) provides a default stopping criterion for the system.

METARULE (6):

    IF: (1) Previous PROCESS was FOCUS
        (2) Previous PROCESS was NOT ACTIVE
        (3) Next previous PROCESS was FOCUS
        (4) Next previous PROCESS was NOT ACTIVE

THEN: (1) STOP

Otherwise, a single failure of the FOCUS OF ATTENTION process to obtain a new entry signals the exhaustion of the regions and lines within the current area. The following rules are used to reinvoke the focus of attention rules in order to obtain a new area.

METARULE (7):

    IF: (1) Previous PROCESS was FOCUS
        (2) Previous PROCESS was NOT ACTIVE

---

[4] For automatic strategy determination, the system selects specific states for each strategy element. This results in the implementation of one of the stored control strategies. Dynamic strategy selection is based on measuring system performance at any point in time [9].

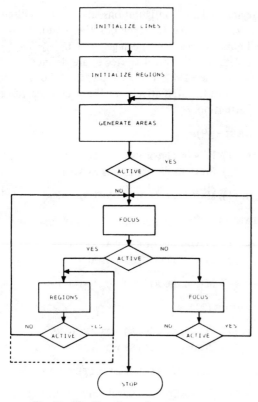

Fig. 11. The flowchart of a system strategy.

(3) Next previous PROCESS was NOT FOCUS

THEN: (1) Match the FOCUS OF ATTENTION rules.

METARULE (8):

    IF: (1) Previous PROCESS was FOCUS
        (2) Previous PROCESS was NOT ACTIVE
        (3) Next previous PROCESS was FOCUS
        (4) Next previous PROCESS was ACTIVE

THEN: (1) Match the FOCUS OF ATTENTION rules.

The previous three metarules are essential for the proper functioning of the system, irrespective of the processing strategy.

A specific control strategy can be represented by a flowchart, as shown in Fig. 11. Metarules (1)–(11) implement the particular strategy described in Fig. 11. Each region is successively modified by all the rules before moving to other regions. Replacing the crossed line by the dotted line in Fig. 11 results in an alternative strategy. In this case, the system moves to another region after a single modification of the current region by the first rule to fire. This is accomplished by replacing Metarule (10) by:

METARULE (12):

    IF: (1) Previous PROCESS was REGIONS
        (2) Previous PROCESS was ACTIVE

THEN: (1) Match the FOCUS OF ATTENTION rules.

As illustrated in the example of Fig. 11, strategy alteration is achieved by the substitution of metarules. This is an essential factor in implementing a dynamic strategy. The elements that constitute the system processing strategy and the choice of a particular strategy are discussed in detail in [16]. The same reference contains examples of other combinations of metarules that execute different strategies.

VII. EXPERIMENTAL RESULTS

To demonstrate the advantages of using the rule-based system, it was compared to earlier approaches to segmentation. The segmentation outputs of the rule-based system were computed using an optimal set of rules [10] and dynamic strategy selection [11]. Two algorithms were chosen: Ohlander's histogram splitting method [18] and the split-and-merge algorithm [21]. The first method was chosen to represent the class of region splitting algorithms that is based on histogram analysis. The second method was selected because it employs both region merging and splitting, albeit in a very restricted data structure. Whereas cluster analysis in feature space is the basis for the first method, the second method uses a structural approach based on similarity grouping.

A number of parameters must be selected to employ these methods. For histogram segmentation, a fixed set of numerical criteria is used to define the peaks within the histogram. The split-and-merge algorithm requires the instantiation of two variables. The starting level of the "initial cutset" refers to the resolution of the square grid that forms the initial region partition. The second parameter is a tolerance level that defines the allowable range of grey level features within one region.

The region partitions that resulted from applying the three methods to an outdoor scene is shown in Fig. 12 and to a "blocks world" scene, in Fig. 13. Quantitatively, the latter is seen to exhibit a superior partition that corresponds more closely to the original objects. A quantitative analysis of the results using the segmentation error measures discussed in [9] confirms this.

The histogram splitting method is seen to produce high overmerging errors that correspond to the large regions of the image which are not segmented. This is because although these regions satisfy other criteria for splitting (such as high gradient or variance), their histograms fail to meet the necessary conditions for peak selection defined in [18]. This method is clearly more suitable for extracting contrasting objects from their background than it is for general purpose segmentation.

On the other hand, the split-and-merge algorithm produces low over-merging errors, but at the expense of high under-merging components. For example, in order to detect the top face of the upper block in Fig. 11(d) the tolerance level within regions had to be lowered. This produced too much detail in the foreground. This parameter dependency became evident when other images were segmented and the values used to obtain best results varied widely. The second parameter for the split-and-merge algorithm was the starting level within the pyramid data structure. The best partitions were obtained when processing started at the highest resolution level, so that no splitting took place. In addition to being more time consuming, this contradicted the original purpose of the algorithm, because it was now reduced to a simple region grower.

(a)

(b)

(c)

(d)

Fig. 12. Segmentation of a natural scene. (a) Digitized color image of
the scene. (b) Rule-based segmentation. (c) Histogram splitting.
(d) Split-and-merge.

The split-and-merge algorithm was consistently faster than the others with an average cpu time of 370 s (Digital VAX 11/780). This is compared to 840 s for histogram segmentation and 1824 s for rule-based segmentation (an approximate ratio of 1:2.25:5). The rigidity of the data structure, the ease of applying the merging and splitting criteria, and the simplicity of the two basic actions were all factors that contributed to the speed of the split-and-merge process.

As the data structure becomes more flexible, more time is needed to compute and analyze the histograms of arbitrarily shaped regions and then split them accordingly. The rule-based system combined histogram analysis with other region and line analysis techniques in a formulation that maintained flexibility of data and control. In addition, its output conforms more closely to the human expectations of low level segmentation, with almost no over-merging errors and few undermerged regions. However, a price was paid in terms of the increased computation time required for its test and modify cycles.

VIII. DISCUSSION AND CONCLUSIONS

This section highlights the major accomplishments of the rule-based system.

1) Overall System Structure: The basic system structure follows closely that of the high level interpretation system of [7] in that it is composed of a modular set of independent processes that communicate and interact through a common database. What was presented as a single low level process in [7] is expanded to include the set of processes shown in Fig. 1. Whereas the high level model consisted mainly of a set of constraints that drive a relaxation labeling process, the basic control paradigm for the low level segmenter is that of a production system. In fact, the system presented here introduces the rule-based approach to the image segmentation problem. Previous vision systems limited the use of explicit knowledge to the semantic interpretation level. Consequently, the heuristics used for low level image segmentation were always implemented in procedural form. The approach discussed in this paper is the first to employ domain independent

(a)

(b)

(c)

(d)

Fig. 13. Segmentation of a "blocks world" image. (a) The original image. (b) Rule-based segmentation. (c) Histogram splitting. (d) Split-and-merge.

knowledge in an explicit form. Knowledge is separated from processing modules by coding it into production rules which are stored in the LTM. In addition, system control is made more accessible by introducing a set of control rules into the model. This allows a user (or the system SUPERVISOR in Fig. 1 to interactively (or automatically) program different processing strategies. The separability of knowledge and control represents a unique approach to solving the segmentation problem.

2) Data Structure: Two new aspects are introduced into the data structure. First, regions and lines are combined and are simultaneously used in the analysis. Although other systems have employed both [4], each was processed separately, and

the results combined only at the end. In this system, regions and lines share the same data structure and have common spatial features. The model includes rules that manipulate combinations of regions and lines. This allows uniformity and discontinuity information to blend together and cooperate in producing a better output. Experiments with the system prove that this type of interaction is beneficial.

The second aspect is the introduction of focus of attention areas as groupings of regions and lines that represent interesting parts of an image. In addition to providing valuable information such as texture to a high level process, these areas play an important role in the analysis by providing spatial boundaries across which the processing strategy is adjusted. This allows the system to execute the best strategy based on the individual properties of each area.

3) The Rule-Based Model: A multitude of segmentation criteria are coded in the rules. Heuristics that formed the basis of earlier segmentation techniques in the literature were extracted and organized within a uniform representation. In addition, new general purpose knowledge sources were employed, such as those driving from Gestalt principles for perceptual grouping.

The system also introduces a general symbolic coding scheme for the rules. The conditions are logical predicates evaluated on the STM data by using an automatic scaling mechanism [16], [17]. Low level symbolic processing is a step towards reducing the dependency of previous segmentation methods on numerical parameters. Thus, model learning through rule modification replaces the more ad hoc process of interactive parameter tuning.

The actions of the rules are independent entities that are carried out by the processing modules. They are designed to modify the regions, lines, and areas in finite ways, yet they have the flexibility to permit changes in different directions (e.g., merging and splitting of regions).

The conditions and actions create a "segmentation language" that provides for a wide range of data manipulation and modification. The ability to modify and expand the knowledge base is an important contribution that is a result of the symbolic coding scheme and the rule-based structure. The testing and tuning of the model [16] was only possible because of this powerful experimental feature. Furthermore, future additions and testing of new segmentation heuristics require minimum user interaction.

4) Measures of Segmentation: A primary concern of this research is the ability to evaluate intermediate and final output partitions. A set of error measures was devised that dynamically computes the distance between a test partition and a reference segmentation [8]. These are used to build the model by testing different rule combinations and selecting those that are the most effective in reducing the errors.

A second set of measures are unlike any developed so far in that they do not require a reference segmentation [9]. Performance is judged by comparing the segmentation to the original image. This enables the system to maintain "real-time" estimates of the segmentation as the processing evolves. These performance measures behaved consistently with the segmentation error measures throughout a wide variety of experiments with the system.

5) The Control Mechanism: Using the rule-based expert system discussed in this paper, a strategy determination process that varies with time and with image area has been introduced elsewhere [9], [11], [16]. The elements of control strategy were defined and their dependence on the real-time performance measures was experimentally verified. The experiments tested the effect of using different control strategies on the performance of the system, in terms of output quality and efficiency of computation. Analysis of the results led to conclusions about the best strategies to apply for different ranges of performance measures [16]. Such constraints are used in executing the dynamic strategy selection process.

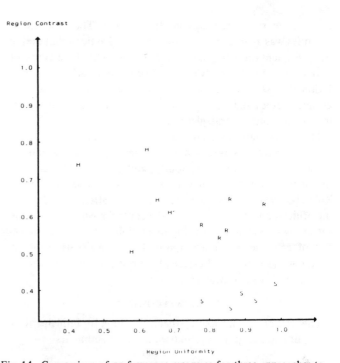

Fig. 14. Comparison of performance measures for three approaches to segmentation. *S*: Split-and-merge. *H*: Histogram splitting. *R*: Rule-based segmentation.

This dynamic strategy mechanism presents solutions to two control issues. First, for rule-based processing, conflict resolution is achieved by implementing a dynamic data-driven rule reordering process. Second, a focus of attention mechanism is created that is capable of adjusting its path of processing within the image according to the data. These factors result in a system that can select the most suitable segmentation heuristics and apply them to the parts of the image where they are most needed.

6) Experimental Results: The ability to quantitatively measure performance allowed us to conduct experiments with various knowledge rule combinations A ranking of the rules was then established based on their effectiveness in maximizing the performance measures and their frequency of firing. The contribution of these experiments is the selection of an optimal set of rules over a large collection of segmentation heuristics [10], [16].

The performance of the system operating with dynamic strategy setting and the optimal set of rules was compared to other segmentation methods in the literature. The results show a considerable improvement in the quality of the output, in the segmentation error measures, and in the performance measures. The graph in Fig. 14 summarizes these results. It indicates the range of performance parameters measured on the final output partitions of several images for three different segmentation approaches. Algorithms that employ grouping based on similarity result in partitions that are highly uniform. Histogram-based partitions exhibit high contrast between the regions. Each sacrifices one measure to enhance the other. On the other hand, rule-based segmentation produces partitions that simultaneously maximize uniformity and contrast. The details of these results are presented in [16].

In this paper, we have described the knowledge and control

rules of our rule-based segmentation system. The structure of the rules was analyzed. The conditions and actions that define our "segmentation language" were listed. The three types of knowledge rules were reviewed, showing how various segmentation heuristics are coded. Finally, the role of the focus of attention rules and the metarules in designing and implementing system control strategies was described.

This segmentation system is seen to be both knowledge-based and data-driven. The production system approach to control allows for knowledge separability, and thus provides an easy means for "tuning" the model used for low level segmentation. Rule classification, and the use of focus of attention rules and metarules permit easy access to the control mechanisms of the system, without compromising its modularity. A main objective of using such a design approach, is to assist us in understanding the nature and effect of various low level knowledge sources and control strategies.

ACKNOWLEDGMENT

The authors would like to thank W. Hong for implementing the split-and-merge algorithm used in the experiments.

REFERENCES

[1] R. A. Brooks, R. Greiner, and T. O. Binford, "The ACRONYM model-based vision system," in *Proc. 4th IJCAI*, Kyoto, Japan, Nov. 1978, pp. 105-113.
[2] B. L. Bullock, "Unstructured control and communication processes in real world scene analysis," Hughes Res. Lab., Malibu, CA, Comput. Sci. Rep. CS-1, Aug. 1977.
[3] R. Davis, "Meta-rules: Reasoning about control," *Artificial Intelligence*, vol. 15, pp. 179-222, 1980.
[4] A. R. Hanson and E. M. Riseman, "Segmenting natural scenes," in *Computer Vision Systems*, A. Hanson and E. Riseman, Eds. New York: Academic, 1978.
[5] K. Koffka, *Principles of Gestalt Psychology*. New York: Harcourt, Brace & World, 1963.
[6] W. Kohler, "The task of Gestalt psychology," Princeton, NJ: Princeton Univ., 1969.
[7] M. D. Levine and S. I. Shaheen, "A modular computer vision system for picture segmentation and interpretation," *IEEE Trans. Pattern Anal. Machine Intell.*, vol. PAMI-3, pp. 540-556, Sept. 1981.
[8] M. D. Levine and A. Nazif, "An experimental rule-based system for testing low level segmentation strategies," in *Multicomputers and Image Processing: Algorithms and Programs*, K. Preston and L. Uhr, Eds. New York: Academic, pp. 149-160, 1982.
[9] M. D. Levine and A. Nazif, "Performance measurement and strategy evaluation for rule-based image segmentation," Computer Vision and Robotics Lab., Dep. Elec. Eng., McGill University, Montreal, P.Q., Canada, TR-82-1, Mar. 1982.
[10] ——, "An optimal set of image segmentation rules," Computer Vision and Robotics Lab., Dep. Elec. Eng., McGill University, Montreal, P.Q., Canada, TR-83-6, Apr. 1983.
[11] ——, "Rule-based image segmentation: A dynamic control strategy appraoch," Computer Vision and Robotics Lab., Dep. Elec. Eng., McGill University, Montreal, P.Q., Canada, TR-83-9, June 1983.
[12] M. D. Levine, P. B. Noble, and Y. M. Youssef, "A rule-based system for characterizing blood cell motion," in *Image Sequence Processing and Dynamic Scene Analysis*, NATO ASI Series, Vol. F2, T. S. Huang, Ed. Berlin, Germany: Springer-Verlag, 1983, pp. 663-709.
[13] M. D. Levine, *Vision in Man and Machine*. New York: McGraw-Hill, to be published.
[14] T. P. Moran, "The symbolic nature of visual imagery," in *Proc. 3rd IJCAI*, Stanford, CA, Aug. 1973, pp. 472-477.
[15] J. L. Muerle and D. C. Allen, "Experimental evaluation of techniques for automatic segmentation of objects in a complex scene," in *Pictorial Pattern Recognition*, G. C. Cheng et al., Eds. Washington, DC: Thompson, 1968, pp. 3-13.
[16] A. Nazif, "A rule-based expert system for image segmentation," Ph.D. dissertation, Dep. Elec. Eng., McGill University, Montreal, P.Q., Canada, Mar. 1983.
[17] A. Nazif and M. D. Levine, "Mapping numbers into symbols," Computer Vision and Robotics Lab., Elec. Eng., McGill University, Montreal, P.Q., Canada, TR-83-5, Apr. 1983.
[18] R. Ohlander, "Analysis of natural scenes," Ph.D. dissertation, Carnegie-Mellon Univ., Pittsburgh, PA, Apr. 1975.
[19] E. M. Riseman and M. A. Arbib, "Survey: Computational techniques in the visual segmentation of static scenes," *Computer Graphics and Image Processing*, vol. 6, pp. 221-276, 1977.
[20] K. R. Sloan, "World model driven recognition of natural scenes," Ph.D. dissertation, The Moore School of Electrical Engineering, Univ. Pennsylvania, Philadelphia, PA, June 1977.
[21] S. Tanimoto and T. Pavlidis, "A hierarchical data structure for picture processing," *Computer Graphics and Image Processing*, vol. 4, pp. 104-199, 1975.
[22] J. K. Tsotsos, "Knowledge of the visual process: Content, form, and use," in *Proc. 6th IJCPR*, Munich, Germany, Oct. 19-22, 1982, pp. 654-669.
[23] S. Tsuji and F. Tomita, "A structural analyzer for a class of textures," *Computer Graphics and Image Processing*, vol. 2, pp. 216-231, 1973.
[24] M. Wertheimer, "Laws of organization in perceptual forms," in *A Source Book of Gestalt Psychology*, W. Ellis, Ed. London, England: Kegan Paul, Trench, Trubner and Co, 1938.
[25] S. W. Zucker, A. Rosenfeld, and L. S. Davis, "General purpose models: Expectations about the unexpected," in *Proc. 4th IJCAI*, Tbilisi, Georgia, USSR, Sept. 1975, pp. 716-721.

Ahmed M. Nazif was born in Cairo, Egypt, on July 1952. He received the B.Sc. and M.Sc. degrees in electrical engineering from Cairo University in 1973 and 1975, respectively, and the Ph.D. degree from McGill University, Montreal, P.Q., Canada, in 1983.

From 1973 to 1976 he was a Demonstrator at Cairo University. From 1976 to 1983 he was a Research Assistant at the Computer Vision and Robotics Laboratory of McGill University. Since July 1983, he has been an Assistant Professor at the Department of Electrical Engineering, Cairo University.

Martin D. Levine (S'59-M'66-SM'74) was born in Montreal, P.Q., Canada, on March 30, 1938. He received the B.Eng. and M.Eng. degrees in electrical engineering in 1960 and 1963, respectively, from McGill University, Montreal, and the Ph.D. degree in electrical engineering in 1965 from the Imperial College of Science and Technology, University of London, London, England.

He is currently a Professor of Electrical Engineering in the Department of Electrical Engineering, McGill University. Recently, he was appointed a Senior Fellow in the Canadian Institute of Advanced Research. During 1972-1973 he was a member of Technical Staff at the Image Processing Laboratory of the Jet Propulsion Laboratory, Pasadena, CA. During the 1979-1980 academic session, he was a Visiting Professor in the Department of Computer Science, Hebrew University, Jerusalem, Israel. His research interests are computer vision, biomedical image processing, and robotics. He has authored the book *Vision in Man and Machine* to be published (New York: McGraw-Hill), and co-authored with P. Noble, the book *Computer Assisted Analyses of Cell Locomotion and Chemotaxis* to be published (CRC Press).

Dr. Levine is an Associate Editor of *Computer Vision, Graphics and Image Processing*, and the General Chairman of the Seventh International Conference on Pattern Recognition to be held in Montreal during the summer of 1983.

Chapter 8: Applications

Many of the computer vision techniques described in Chapters 1 through 7 were developed primarily to meet the needs of specific applications. The large variety of applications in which computer vision techniques have been used prevents us from mentioning all of these applications here. Instead, we identify in this chapter a representative set of papers in which applications of computer vision techniques are emphasized. These papers are not reprinted here, but are reprinted, by topic, in Chapter 8 of the companion book, *Computer Vision: Advances and Applications*. The five major topics are

(1) Aerial image analysis;
(2) Document image analysis;
(3) Medical image analysis;
(4) Industrial inspection and robotics; and
(5) Autonomous navigation.

Additional references covering these applications can be found in the Bibliography, which is also organized into these five topics. We would like to emphasize again that even the Bibliography for this chapter is far from being comprehensive. Readers still wanting additional references are advised to consult application-oriented journals (such as *Machine Vision and Applications*); the proceedings of several machine-vision-related conferences organized by SPIE (The Optical Engineering Society) and IAPR (International Association for Pattern Recognition); and application-oriented special issues of journals (such as *IEEE Transactions on Pattern Analysis and Machine Intelligence*, January and May 1988).

A list, by topic, of the papers that are reprinted in Chapter 8 of the companion book, *Computer Vision: Advances and Applications*, appears below.

Aerial image analysis

Harlow, C.A., M.M. Trivedi, R.W. Conners, and D. Philips, "Scene Analysis of High Resolution Aerial Scenes," *Optical Engineering*, Vol. 25, No. 3, 1986, pp. 347-355

Matsuyama, T., "Knowledge-based Aerial Image Understanding Systems and Expert Systems for Image Processing," *IEEE Trans. Geoscience and Remote Sensing*, Vol. 25, No. 3, 1987, pp. 305-316

McKeown, D.M., "Toward Automatic Cartographic Feature Extraction," in *Mapping and Spatial Modelling for Navigation*, L.F. Pau, ed., NATO ASI Series, Vol. F 65, Springer-Verlag, Berlin, Heidelberg, 1990

Document image analysis

Baird, H.S., and K. Thompson, "Reading Chess," *IEEE Trans. Pattern Analysis and Machine Intelligence*, Vol. 12, No. 6, 1990, pp. 552-559

Kasturi, R., S.T. Bow, W. El-Masri, J. Shah, J.R. Gattiker, and U.B. Mokate, "An Intelligent System for Interpretation of Line Drawings," *IEEE Trans. Pattern Analysis and Machine Intelligence*, Vol. 12, No. 10, 1990, pp. 978-992

Okazaki, A., T. Kondo, K. Mori, S. Tsunekawa, and E. Kawamoto, "An Automatic Circuit Diagram Reader with Loop-Structure-Based Symbol Recognition," *IEEE Trans. Pattern Analysis and Machine Intelligence*, Vol. 10, No. 3, 1988, pp. 331-341

Wang, C.H., and S.N. Srihari, "A Framework for Object Recognition in a Visually Complex Environment and its Application to Locating Address Blocks on Mail Pieces," *Int'l J. Computer Vision*, Vol. 2, 1988, pp. 125-151

Medical image analysis

Gordon, D., and J.K. Udupa, "Fast Surface Tracking in Three-Dimensional Binary Images," *Computer Vision, Graphics, and Image Processing*, Vol. 45, 1989, pp. 196-214

Hibbard, L.S., J.S. McGlone, D.W. Davis, and R.A. Hawkins, "Three-Dimensional Representation and Analysis of Brain Energy Metabolism," *Science,* Vol. 236, 1987, pp. 1641-1646

Lifshitz, L.M., and S.M. Pizer, "A Multiresolution Hierarchical Approach to Image Segmentation Based on Intensity Extrema," *IEEE Trans. Pattern Analysis and Machine Intelligence,* Vol. 12, No. 6, 1990, pp. 529-540

Industrial inspection and robotics

Darwish, A.M., and A.K. Jain, "A Rule-Based Approach for Visual Pattern Inspection," *IEEE Trans. Pattern Analysis and Machine Intelligence,* Vol. 10, No. 1, 1988, pp. 56-68

Lougheed, R.M., and R.E. Sampson, "Three-Dimensional Imaging Systems and High-Speed Processing for Robot Control," *Machine Vision and Applications,* Vol. 1, 1988, pp. 41-57

Yoda, H., Y. Ohuchi, Y. Taniguchi, and M. Ejiri, "An Automatic Wafer Inspection System Using Pipelined Image Processing Techniques," *IEEE Trans. Pattern Analysis and Machine Intelligence,* Vol. 10, No. 1, 1988, pp. 4-16

Autonomous navigation

Dickmanns, E.D., and V. Graefe, "Applications of Dynamic Monocular Machine Vision," *Machine Vision and Applications,* Vol. 1, No. 4, 1988, pp. 241-261

Ishiguro, H., M. Yamamoto, and S. Tsuji, "Omni-Directional Stereo for Making Global Map," *Proc. Third Int'l Conf. Computer Vision,* 1990, pp. 540-547

Thorpe, C., M.H. Hebert, T. Kanade, and S.A. Shafer, "Vision and Navigation for the Carnegie-Mellon Navlab," *IEEE Trans. Pattern Analysis and Machine Intelligence,* Vol. 10, No. 3, 1988, pp. 362-373

Epilogue

Computer vision has been a very active research field in the last two decades. Because of both a better understanding of the important issues in the field and the tremendous growth in the availability of sensors and computing power, significant advances in this field have been made. Many new applications have been successful and many new application areas are emerging. The last few years have shown some new trends in computer vision research. In this section, we discuss some of these trends and the direction of research in computer vision.

The availability of range cameras encouraged many researchers to start addressing problems in surface characterization using explicit depth information. Though many early approaches were direct extensions of work in other areas, today researchers are studying differential-geometry-based approaches to better understand surface characteristics and to use them in segmentation. In many industries, these approaches will be increasingly applied to inspection and metrology of surfaces. In the near future, surface characterization techniques will be applied to data acquired using many different types of sensors. An encouraging trend in this direction is the increasing attention being given to the use of geometric models in computer vision. In the last few years, many new research projects have started to emphasize the role of geometric models in object recognition and inspection, although explicit three-dimensional reasoning using geometric models is still not very common.

Although the role of indexing in recognizing objects from a large set has been clear to researchers for at least two decades, it has not been given much attention. The problem of feature-based indexing will receive more attention in the near future. This indexing will be useful not only for recognizing objects, but also for organizing large image databases, such as those encountered in Earth Observation Systems (EOS).

The idea of integrating information from multiple sensors or multiple operators seems to be slowly maturing. After struggling with simple-minded approaches that try to combine information in image space, researchers are now starting to build incremental models in three dimensions. Volumetric approaches that represent voxel properties have become quite common in medical imaging and visualization. These techniques will become very common in computer vision. Techniques that try to combine information from multiple sources and sensors in three dimensions are likely to be very common soon. Some intrinsic surface characteristics are finally getting careful attention. Some activity in understanding color has occurred in the last few years; activity in understanding other images is also increasing. The near future will see increasing activity in these areas.

In the first few years of research in dynamic vision, papers addressed problems related to many aspects of dynamic vision. Later, for almost one complete decade, most effort was on myopic problems, such as recovering structure using a minimum number of frames or determining optical flow using two frames. Many other techniques in this area were based on first and second derivatives of optical flow and thus required a third derivative of intensity values; these techniques led to ineffective methods for real images. Some recent work on image sequence processing shows that many seemingly complex problems can be solved by using appropriate techniques — borrowed from systems engineering — that do not appear powerful when considered locally. Generally, more attention is being given to the analysis of long sequences of images to solve problems in dynamic vision. Techniques based on surface characterization and differential geometry in spatio-temporal space may facilitate motion detection, characterization of object and observer motion, and even determination of three-dimensional structure of objects in a sequence of images acquired by either a stationary or a moving camera.

Systems are now being considered that acquire images based on what needs to be done next. Although these systems do not do much reasoning yet, they represent a step in the right direction. Reasoning-based approaches are likely to pervade all aspects of computer vision systems in the next decade. A major hurdle in this direction is the explicit representation of knowledge about the operators used in different stages. Such knowledge will become increasingly available as researchers start more rigorous characterization of their operators by experimenting with images of disparate scenes acquired under different, but possibly controlled, conditions.

Increasing attention has been given to qualitative vision in the last few years. Approaches based on qualitative reasoning are a step towards analyzing phenomena that can only be captured at a qualitative level. Many current approaches try to recover very precise quantitative information; such approaches are very sensitive to noise. Many of these approaches are capable of giving good qualitative information about the scene. The effectiveness of these approaches in object recognition and navigation will result in their increasing acceptance and popularity.

Chapter 1: Image Formation
Selected Bibliography

Allen, P.K. and P. Michelman, "Acquisition and Interpretation of 3-D Sensor Data from Touch," *Proc. IEEE Workshop on Interpretation of 3D Scenes,* IEEE CS Press, Los Alamitos, Calif., 1989, pp. 33-40.

Alvertos, N., D. Brzakovic, and R.C. Gonzalez, "Camera Geometries for Image Matching in 3-D Machine Vision," *IEEE Trans. Pattern Analysis and Machine Intelligence,* Vol. 11, No. 9, 1989, pp. 897-915.

Arend, L. and A. Reeves, "Simultaneous Color Constancy," *J. Opt. Soc. Am. A,* Vol. 3, No. 10, 1986, pp. 1743-1751.

Asada, M., H. Ichikawa, and S. Tsuji, "Determining Surface Orientation by Projecting a Stripe Pattern," *IEEE Trans. Pattern Analysis and Machine Intelligence,* Vol. 10, No. 5, 1988, pp. 749-754.

Bajcsy, R., "Active Perception," *Proc. IEEE,* Vol. 76, No. 8, IEEE Press, New York, N.Y., 1988, pp. 996-1005.

Ballard, D.H., "Eye Movements and Visual Cognition," *Proc. Workshop on Spatial Reasoning and Multi-Sensor Fusion,* Morgan Kaufmann Publishers, Inc., San Mateo, Calif., 1987, pp. 188-200.

Ballard, D.H. and A. Ozcandarli, "Eye Fixation and Early Vision: Kinetic Depth," *Proc. Second Int'l Conf. Computer Vision,* IEEE CS Press, Los Alamitos, Calif., 1988, pp. 524-531.

Bastucheck, C.M., "Techniques for Real-Time Generation of Range Images," *Proc. IEEE Conf. Computer Vision and Pattern Recognition,* IEEE CS Press, Los Alamitos, Calif., 1989, pp. 262-268.

Bergstrom, S.S., "Illumination, Color, and Three-Dimensional Form," in *Organization and Representation in Perception,* J. Beck, ed., Lawrence Erlbaum Assoc., Hillsdale, N.J., 1982.

Brelstaff, G. and A. Blake, "Detecting Specular Reflections Using Lambertian Constraints," *Proc. Second Int'l Conf. Computer Vision,* IEEE CS Press, Los Alamitos, Calif., 1988, pp. 297-302.

Brown, C., "Gaze Controls with Interactions and Delays," *IEEE Trans. on Systems, Man, and Cybernetics,* Vol. 20, No. 2, 1990, pp. 518-527.

Buchanan, T., "The Twisted Cubic and Camera Calibration," *Computer Vision, Graphics and Image Processing,* No. 42, 1988, pp. 130-132.

Chelberg, D.M., "Uncertainty in Interpretation of Range Imagery," *Proc. Third Int'l Conf. Computer Vision,* IEEE CS Press, Los Alamitos, Calif., 1990, pp. 654-657.

Clark, J.J. and N.J. Ferrier, "Modal Control of an Attentive Vision System," *Proc. Second Int'l Conf. Computer Vision,* IEEE CS Press, Los Alamitos, Calif, 1988, pp. 514-523.

Collins, R.T. and R.S. Weiss, "Vanishing Point Calculation as a Statistical Inference on the Unit Sphere," *Proc. Third Int'l Conf. Computer Vision,* IEEE CS Press, Los Alamitos, Calif., 1990, pp. 400-405.

Drew, M.S. and B.V. Funt, "Calculating Surface Reflectance Using a Single-Bounce Model of Mutual Reflection," *Proc. Third Int'l Conf. Computer Vision,* IEEE CS Press, Los Alamitos, Calif., 1990, pp. 394-399.

Echigo, T., "A Camera Calibration Technique Using Three Sets of Parallel Lines," *Machine Vision and Applications,* Vol. 3, No. 3, 1990, pp. 159-167.

Forsyth, D.A., "A Novel Algorithm for Color Constancy," *Int'l J. Computer Vision,* Vol. 5, No. 1, 1990, pp. 5-36.

Forsyth, D.A. and A. Zisserman, "Mutual Illumination," *Proc. IEEE Conf. Computer Vision and Pattern Recognition,* IEEE CS Press, Los Alamitos, Calif., 1989, pp. 466-473.

Gershon, R., "Aspects of Perception and Computation in Color Vision," *Computer Vision, Graphics and Image Processing,* No. 32, 1985, pp. 244-277.

Gershon, R., A.D. Jepson, and J.K. Tsotsos, "Ambient Illumination and the Determination of Material Changes," *J. Opt. Soc. Am. A,* Vol. 3, No. 10, 1986, pp. 1700-1707.

Healey, G., "A Color Reflectance Model and its Use For Segmentation," *Proc. Second Int'l Conf. Computer Vision,* IEEE CS Press, Los Alamitos, Calif., 1988, pp. 460-466.

Healey, G., "Color Discrimination by Computer," *IEEE Trans. Systems, Man, and Cybernetics,* Vol. 19, No. 6, 1989, pp. 1613-1617.

Ho, J., B.V. Funt, and M.S. Drew, "Separating a Color Signal into Illumination and Surface Reflectance Components: Theory and Applications," *IEEE Trans. Pattern Analysis and Machine Intelligence,* Vol. 12, No. 10, 1990, pp. 966-977.

Horn, B.K.P., "Understanding Image Intensities," *Artificial Intelligence,* Vol. 8, No. 2, 1977, pp. 201-231.

Hugli, H. and W. Frei, "Understanding Anisotropic Reflectance in Mountainous Terrain," *Photogrammetric Eng. and Remote Sensing,* No. 49, 1983, pp. 671-683.

Ikeuchi, K. and K. Sato, "Determining Reflectance Parameters Using Range and Brightness Images," *Proc. Third Int'l Conf. Computer Vision,* IEEE CS Press, Los Alamitos, Calif., 1990, pp. 400-405.

Izaguirre, A., P. Pu, and J. Summers, "A New Development in Camera Calibration: Calibrating a Pair of Mobile Cameras," *Int'l J. Robotics Research,* Vol. 6, No. 3, 1987, pp. 104-116.

Kamgar-Parsi, B. and Kamgar-Parsi B., "Evaluation of Quantization Error in Computer Vision," *IEEE Trans. Pattern Analysis and Machine Intelligence,* Vol. 11, No. 9, 1989, pp. 929-940.

Kanade, T. and M. Fuhrman, "A Noncontact Optical Proximity Sensor for Measuring Surface Shape," T. Kanade, ed., *Three Dimensional Machine Vision,* Kluwer, Boston, Mass., 1987., pp. 151-192.

Klinker, G.J., S.A. Shafer, and T. Kanade, "Using a Color Reflection Model to Separate Highlights from Object Color," *Proc. First Int'l Conf. Computer Vision,* IEEE CS Press, Los Alamitos, Calif., 1987, pp. 145-150.

Klinker, G.J., S.A. Shafer, and T. Kanade, "The Measurement of Highlights in Color Images," *Int'l J. Computer Vision,* Vol. 2, No. 1, 1988, pp. 7-32.

Koenderink, J.J., "Color Atlas Theory," *J. Opt. Soc. Am. A,* Vol. 4, No. 7, 1987, pp. 1314-1321.

659

Kumar, R. and A.R. Hanson, "Sensitivity of the Pose Refinement Problem to Accurate Estimation of Camera Parameters," *Proc. Third Int'l Conf. Computer Vision,* IEEE CS Press, Los Alamitos, Calif, 1990, pp. 365-369.

Lenz, R.K. and R.Y. Tsai, "Calibrating a Cartesian Robot with Eye-on-Hand Configuration Independent of Eye-to-Hand Relationship," *Proc. IEEE Conf. Computer Vision and Pattern Recognition,* IEEE CS Press, Los Alamitos, Calif., 1988, pp. 67-75.

Maloney, L.T., "Evaluation of Linear Models of Surface Spectral Reflectance with Small Numbers of Parameters," *J. Opt. Soc. Am. A,* Vol. 3, No. 10, 1986, pp. 1673-1683.

Matsuki, M. and T. Ueda, "A Real-Time Sectional Image Measuring System Using Time Sequentially Coded Grating Method," *IEEE Trans. Pattern Analysis and Machine Intelligence,* Vol. 11, No. 11, 1989, pp. 1225-1228.

Mori, T. and M. Yamamoto, "A Dynamic Depth Extraction Method," *Proc. Third Int'l Conf. Computer Vision,* IEEE CS Press, Los Alamitos, Calif., 1990, pp. 672-676.

Mundy, J. and G.B. Porter III, "A Three-Dimensional Sensor Based on Structured Light," in *Three Dimensional Machine Vision,* T. Kanade, ed., Kluwer, Boston, Mass., 1987, pp. 3-61.

Olsen, S.I., "Stereo Correspondence by Surface Reconstruction," *IEEE Trans. Pattern Analysis and Machine Intelligence,* Vol. 12, No. 3, 1990, pp. 309-314.

Park, J.-S. and J.T. Tou, "Highlight Separation and Surface Orientations for 3-D Specular Objects," *Proc. Tenth Int'l Conf. Pattern Recognition,* IEEE CS Press, Los Alamitos, Calif., 1990, pp. 331-335.

Pentland, A., et al., "A Simple Real-Time Range Camera," *Proc. IEEE Conf. Computer Vision and Pattern Recognition,* IEEE CS Press, Los Alamitos, Calif., 1989, pp. 256-261.

Rioux, M. and F. Blais, "Compact Three-Dimensional Camera for Robotic Applications," *J. Opt. Soc. Am. A,* Vol. 3, No. 9, 1986, pp. 1518-1521.

Rioux, M., et al., "Range Imaging Sensors Development at NRC Laboratories," *Proc. IEEE Workshop on Interpretation of 3D Scenes,* IEEE CS Press, Los Alamitos, Calif., 1989, pp. 154-160.

Rubin, J.M. and W.A. Richards, "Color Vision and Image Intensities: When are Changes Material?," *Biological Cybernetics,* No. 45, 1982, pp. 215-226.

Shafer, S. and T. Kanade, "A Physical Approach to Color Image Understanding," *Int'l J. Computer Vision,* Vol. 4, No. 1, 1990, pp. 7-38.

Shmuel, A. and M. Werman, "Active Vision: 3D From an Image Sequence," *Proc. Tenth Int'l Conf. Pattern Recognition,* IEEE CS Press, Los Alamitos, Calif., 1990, pp. 48-54.

Srinivasan, V. and R. Lumia, "A Pseudo-Interferometric Laser Range Finder for Robot Applications," *IEEE Trans. Robotics and Automation,* Vol. 5, No. 1, 1989, pp. 98-105.

Suenaga, Y. and Y. Watanabe, "A Method for the Synchronized Acquisition of Cylindrical Range and Color Data," *IAPR Workshop on Machine Vision Applications,* 1990, pp. 137-142.

Swain, M.J. and D.H. Ballard, "Indexing Via Color Histograms," *Proc. Third Int'l Conf. Computer Vision,* IEEE CS Press, Los Alamitos, Calif., 1990, pp. 390-393.

Tajima, J. and M. Iwakawa, "3D Data Acquisition by Rainbow Range Finder," *Proc. Int'l Conf. Pattern Recognition,* IEEE CS Press, Los Alamitos, Calif., 1990, pp. 309-313.

Tsukada, M. and Y. Ohta, "An Approach to Color Constancy Using Multiple Images," *Proc. Third Int'l Conf. Computer Vision,* IEEE CS Press, Los Alamitos, Calif., 1990, pp. 385-390.

Vuylsteke, P. and A. Oosterlinck, "Range Image Acquisition with a Single Binary-Encoded Light Pattern," *IEEE Trans. Pattern Analysis and Machine Intelligence,* Vol. 12, No. 2, 1990, pp. 148-164.

Wandell, B.A., "The Synthesis and Analysis of Color Images," *IEEE Trans. Pattern Analysis and Machine Intelligence,* Vol. 9, No. 1, 1987, pp. 2-13.

Wang, L.-L. and W.-H. Tsai, "Computing Camera Parameters Using Vanishing-Line Information from a Rectangular Parallelpiped," *Machine Vision and Applications,* Vol. 3, No. 3, 1990, pp. 129-141.

Wang, Y.F. and J.K. Aggarwal, "Integration of Active and Passive Sensing Techniques for Representing Three-Dimensional Objects," *IEEE Trans. Robotics and Automation,* Vol. 5, No. 5, 1989, pp. 701-710.

Will, P.M. and K.S. Pennington, "Grid Coding: A Preprocessing Technique for Robot and Machine Vision," *Artificial Intelligence,* Vol. 2, 1971, pp. 319-329.

Wolff, L.B., "Using Polarization to Separate Reflection Components," *Proc. IEEE Conf. Computer Vision and Pattern Recognition,* IEEE CS Press, Los Alamitos, Calif., 1989, pp. 363-369.

Wolff, L.B. and T.E. Boult, "Polarization/Radiometric Based Material Classification," *Proc. IEEE Conf. Computer Vision and Pattern Recognition,* IEEE CS Press, Los Alamitos, Calif., 1989, pp. 387-396.

Woodham, R. and M.H. Gray, "An Analytic Method for Radiometric Correction of Satellite Multispectral Scanner Data," *IEEE Trans. Geoscience and Remote Sensing,* Vol. 25, 1987, pp. 258-271.

Yi, S., R.M. Haralick, and L.G. Shapiro, "Automatic Sensor and Light Source Positioning for Machine Vision," *Proc. Tenth Int'l Conf. Pattern Recognition,* IEEE CS Press, Los Alamitos, Calif., 1990, pp. 55-59.

Chapter 2: Segmentation
Selected Bibliography

Ahuja, N., "Dot Pattern Processing Using Voronoi Neighborhoods," *IEEE Trans. Pattern Analysis and Machine Intelligence*, Vol. 4, No. 3, 1982, pp. 336-343.

Ahuja, N. and A. Rosenfeld, "Mosaic Models for Textures," *IEEE Trans. Pattern Analysis and Machine Intelligence*, Vol. 3, No. 1, 1981, pp. 1-11.

Al-Hujazi, E. and A.K. Sood, "Range Image Segmentation with Applications to Robot Bin-Picking Using Vaccume Gripper," *IEEE Trans. on Systems, Man and Cybernetics*, Vol. 20, No. 6, 1990, pp. 1313-1325.

Babaud, J., et al., "Uniqueness of the Gaussian Kernel for Scale-Space Filtering," *IEEE Trans. Pattern Analysis and Machine Intelligence*, Vol. 8, No. 1, pp. 1986, 26-33.

Bajcsy, R. and L. Lieberman, "Texture Gradient as a Depth Cue," *Computer Graphics and Image Processing*, Vol. 5, No. 1, 1977, pp. 52-67.

Beaulieu, J.-M. and M. Goldberg, "Hierarchy in Picture Segmentation: A Stepwise Optimization Approach," *IEEE Trans. Pattern Analysis and Machine Intelligence*, Vol. 11, No. 2, 1989, pp. 150-163.

Bell, Z.W., "A Bayesian/Monte Carlo Segmentation Method for Images Dominated by Gaussian Noise," *IEEE Trans. Pattern Analysis and Machine Intelligence*, Vol. 11, No. 9, 1989, pp. 985-990.

Berzins, V., "Accuracy of Laplacian Edge Detectors," *Computer Vision, Graphics and Image Processing*, Vol. 27, 1984, pp. 195-210.

Bischof, W.F. and T. Caelli, "Parsing Scale-Space and Spatial Stability Analysis," *Computer Vision, Graphics and Image Processing*, Vol. 42, 1988, pp. 192-205.

Blostein, D. and N. Ahuja, "A Multiscale Region Detector," *Computer Vision, Graphics and Image Processing*, Vol. 45, No. 1, 1989, pp. 22-41.

Brooks, R.A., "Model-Based Three-Dimensional Interpretations of Two-Dimensional Images," *IEEE Trans. Pattern Analysis and Machine Intelligence*, Vol. 5, No. 2, 1983, pp. 140-150.

Cannon, R.L., et al., "Segmentation of a Thematic Mapper Image Using Fuzzy C-means Clustering Algorithms," *IEEE Trans. on Geoscience and Remote Sensing*, Vol. 24, No. 3, 1986, pp. 400-408.

Carlotto, M.J., "Histogram Analysis Using a Scale-Space Approach," *Proc. IEEE Conf. Computer Vision and Pattern Recognition*, IEEE CS Press, Los Alamitos, Calif., 1985, pp. 334-340.

Celenk, M., "A Recursive Clustering Technique for Color Picture Segmentation," *Proc. IEEE Conf. Computer Vision and Pattern Recognition*, IEEE CS Press, Los Alamitos, Calif., 1988, pp. 437-444.

Cheevasuvit, F., H. Maitre, and D. Vidal-Madjar, "A Robust Method for Picture Segmentation Based on a Split-and-Merge Procedure," *Computer Vision, Graphics and Image Processing*, Vol. 34, 1986, pp. 268-281.

Chen, C.-C. and R.C. Dubes, "Experiments in Fitting Discrete Markov Random Fields to Textures," *Proc. IEEE Conf. Computer Vision and Pattern Recognition*, IEEE CS Press, Los Alamitos, Calif., 1989, pp. 298-303.

Chen, J.S. and G. Medioni, "Detection, Location, and Estimation of Edges," *IEEE Trans. Pattern Analysis and Machine Intelligence*, Vol. 11, No. 2, 1989, pp. 191-198.

Chen, P.C. and T. Pavlidis, "Segmentation by Texture Using a Co-Occurrence Matrix and a Split-and-Merge Algorithm," *Computer Graphics and Image Processing*, Vol. 10, 1979, pp. 172-182.

Chu, C.-C. and J.K. Aggarwal, "The Integration of Region and Edge-Based Segmentation," *Proc. Third Int'l Conf. Computer Vision*, IEEE CS Press, Los Alamitos, Calif., 1990, pp. 117-120.

Clark, J.J., "Singularities of Contrast Functions in Scale Space," *IEEE Trans. Pattern Analysis and Machine Intelligence*, Vol. 10, 1988, pp. 491-495.

Clark, J.J., "Authenticating Edges Produced by Zero-Crossing Algorithms," *IEEE Trans. Pattern Analysis and Machine Intelligence*, Vol. 11, No. 1, 1989, pp. 43-57.

Coggins, J.M. and A.K. Jain, "A Spatial Filtering Approach to Texture Analysis," *Pattern Recognition*, Vol. 3, 1985, pp. 195-203.

Cohen, F.S. and D.B. Cooper, "Simple Parallel Hierarchical and Relaxation Algorithms for Segmenting Non-Causal Markovian Random Fields," *IEEE Trans. Pattern Analysis and Machine Intelligence*, Vol. 9, No. 2, 1987, pp. 195-219.

Cohen, P. and H.H. Nguyen, "Unsupervised Bayesian Estimation for Segmenting Textured Images," *Proc. Second Int'l Conf. Computer Vision*, IEEE CS Press, Los Alamitos, Calif., 1988, pp. 303-309.

Cooper, D.H., "An Object Location Strategy Using Shape and Grey-Level Models," *Image and Vision Computing*, Vol. 7, 1989, pp. 50-56.

Daily, M.J., "Color Image Segmentation Using Markov Fields," *Proc. IEEE Conf. Computer Vision and Pattern Recognition*, IEEE CS Press, Los Alamitos, Calif, 1989, pp. 304-312.

Darrell, T., S. Sclaroff, and A. Pentland, "Segmentation by Minimal Description," *Proc. Third Int'l Conf. Computer Vision*, IEEE CS Press, Los Alamitos, Calif., 1990, pp. 112-115.

Davis, L.S. and A. Mitiche, "Edge Detection in Textures-Maxima Selection," *Computer Graphics and Image Processing*, Vol. 16, 1981, pp. 158-165.

De Micheli, E., B. Caprile, P. Ottonello, and V. Torre, "Localization and Noise in Edge Detection," *IEEE Trans. Pattern Analysis and Machine Intelligence*, Vol. 11, No. 10, 1989, pp. 1006-1117.

De Souza, P., "Edge Detection Using Sliding Statistical Tests," *Computer Vision, Graphics and Image Processing*, Vol. 23, No. 1, 1983, pp. 1-14.

Derin, H. and H. Elliott, "Modeling and Segmentation of Noisy and Textured Images Using Gibbs Random Fields," *IEEE Trans. Pattern Analysis and Machine Intelligence*, Vol. 9, No. 1, 1987, pp. 39-55.

Duncan, J.S. and T. Birkholzer, "Edge Reinforcement Using Parameterized Relaxation Labeling," *Proc. IEEE Conf. Computer Vision and Pattern Recognition,* IEEE CS Press, Los Alamitos, Calif., 1989, pp. 19-27.

Eichel, P.H. and E.J. Delp, "Quantitative Analysis of a Moment-Based Edge Operator," *IEEE Trans. on Systems, Man, and Cybernetics,* Vol. 20, No. 1, 1990, pp. 59-66.

Eichel, P.H., et al., "A Method for a Fully Automatic Definition of Coronary Arterial Edges from Cineangiograms," *IEEE Trans. Medical Imaging,* Vol. 7, No. 4, 1988, pp. 313-320.

Eklundh, J.O., H. Yamamoto, and A. Rosenfeld, "A Relaxation Method for Multispectral Pixel Classification," *IEEE Trans. Pattern Analysis and Machine Intelligence,* Vol. 2, No. 1, 1980, pp. 72-75.

Eom, K.B. and R.L. Kashyap, "Composite Edge Detection with Random Field Models," *IEEE Trans. on Systems, Man, and Cybernetics,* Vol. 20, No. 1, 1990, pp. 81-93.

Fletcher, L.A. and R. Kasturi, "Segmentation of Binary Images into Text Strings and Graphics," *Applications of Artificial Intelligence, Proc. SPIE,* Vol. 786, 1987, pp. 533-540.

Fletcher, L.A. and R. Kasturi, "A Robust Algorithm for Text String Separation from Mixed Text/Graphics Images," *IEEE Trans. Pattern Analysis and Machine Intelligence,* Vol. 10, No. 6, 1988, pp. 910-918.

Fogel, I. and D. Sagi, "Gabor Filters as Texture Discriminator," *Biological Cybernetics,* Vol. 61, 1989, pp. 103-113.

Geiger, D. and T. Poggio, "An Optimal Scale for Edge Detection," *Int'l Joint Conf. Artificial Intelligence,* Morgan Kaufman Publishers, Inc., San Mateo, Calif., 1987, pp. 745-748.

Geman, D., et al., "Boundary Detection by Constrained Optimization," *IEEE Trans. Pattern Analysis and Machine Intelligence,* Vol. 12, No. 6, 1990, pp. 609-620.

Geman, S. and D. Geman, "Stochastic Relaxation, Gibbs Distributions, and Bayesian Restoration of Images," *IEEE Trans. Pattern Analysis and Machine Intelligence,* Vol. 6, No. 6, 1984, pp. 721-741.

Godin, G.D. and M.D. Levine, "Structured Edge Map of Curved Objects in a Range Image," *Proc. IEEE Conf. Computer Vision and Pattern Recognition,* IEEE CS Press, Los Alamitos, Calif., 1989, pp. 276-281.

Grosky, W.I. and R.C. Jain, "A Pyramid-Based Approach to Segmentation Applied to Region Matching," *IEEE Trans. Pattern Analysis and Machine Intelligence,* Vol. 8, No. 5, 1986, pp. 639-650.

Haddon, J.F. and J.F. Boyce, "Image Segmentation by Unified Region and Boundary Information," *IEEE Trans. Pattern Analysis and Machine Intelligence,* Vol. 12, No. 10, 1990, pp. 929-948.

Haralick, R.M., "Ridges and Valleys on Digital Images," *Computer Vision, Graphics and Image Processing,* Vol. 22, No. 1, 1983, pp. 28-38.

Haralick, R.M. and J.S.J. Lee, "Context Dependent Edge Detection," *Proc. IEEE Conf. Computer Vision and Pattern Recognition,* IEEE CS Press, Los Alamitos, Calif., 1988, pp. 223-228.

Harlow, C.A., M.M. Trivedi, and R.W. Conners, "Use of Texture Operators in Scene Analysis," *Optical Eng.,* Vol. 25, No. 11, 1986, pp. 1200-1206.

Hsiao, J.Y. and A.A. Sawchuk, "Supervised Textured Image Segmentation Using Feature Smoothing and Probabilistic Relaxation Techniques," *IEEE Trans. Pattern Analysis and Machine Intelligence,* Vol. 11, No. 12, 1989, pp. 1279-1292.

Hu, G. and G. Stockman, "Representation and Segmentation of a Cluttered Scene Using Fusing Edge and Surface Data," *Proc. IEEE Conf. Computer Vision and Pattern Recognition,* IEEE CS Press, Los Alamitos, Calif, 1989, pp. 313-318.

Huertas, A. and G. Medioni, "Detection of Intensity Changes with Subpixel Accuracy Using Laplacian-Gaussian Masks," *IEEE Trans. Pattern Analysis and Machine Intelligence,* Vol. 8, No. 5, 1986, pp. 651-664.

Hummel, R.A., B. Kimia, and S.W. Zucker, "Deblurring Gaussian Blur," *Computer Vision, Graphics and Image Processing,* Vol. 38, No. 1, 1987, pp. 66-80.

Hwang, V.S.S., L.S. Davis, and T. Matsuyama, "Hypothesis Integration in Image Understanding Systems," *Computer Vision, Graphics and Image Processing,* Vol. 36, 1986, pp. 321-371.

Hwang, T.-L. and J.J. Clark, "A Spatio-Temporal Generalization of Canny's Edge Detector," *Proc. Tenth Int'l Conf. Pattern Recognition,* IEEE CS Press, Los Alamitos, Calif, 1990, pp. 314-318.

Jain, A.K. and S.G. Nadabar, "Mrf Model-Based Segmentation of Range Images," *Proc. Third Int'l Conf. Computer Vision,* IEEE CS Press, Los Alamitos, Calif., 1990, pp. 667-671.

Julesz, B. and J.R. Bergen, "Textons, the Fundamental Elements in Preattentive Vision and the Perception of Textures," *Bell System Technical Journal,* Vol. 62, No. 6, 1983, pp. 1619-1644.

Kartikeyan, B. and A. Sarkar, "A Unified Approach for Image Segmentation Using Exact Statistics," *Computer Vision, Graphics and Image Processing,* Vol. 48, 1989, pp. 217-229.

Kass, M. and A. Witkin, "On Edge Detection," *IEEE Trans. Pattern Analysis and Machine Intelligence,* Vol. 8, No. 2, 1987, pp. 147-163.

Kass, M., A. Witkin, and D. Terzopoulos, "Snakes: Active Contour Models," *Int'l J. Computer Vision,* Vol. 1, No. 4, 1988, pp. 321-331.

Klinker, G.J., S.A. Shafer, and T. Kanade, "Image Segmentation and Reflection Analysis Through Color," *Proc. DARPA Image Understanding Workshop,* 1988, pp. 838-853.

Kocher, M. and R. Leonardi, "Adaptive Region Growing Technique Using Polynomial Functions for Image Approximation," *Signal Processing,* Vol. 11, No. 1, 1986, pp. 47-60.

Koenderink, J.J., "A Hitherto Unnoticed Singularity of Scale-Space," *IEEE Trans. Pattern Analysis and Machine Intelligence,* Vol. 11, No. 11, 1989, pp. 1222-1224.

Kohler, R., "A Segmentation System Based on Thresholding," *Comp. Graph. and Image Processing,* Vol. 15, No. 4, 1981, pp. 319-338.

Krumm, J. and S.A. Shafer, "Local Spatial Frequency Analysis of Image Texture," *Proc. Third Int'l Conf. Computer Vision,* IEEE CS Press, Los Alamitos, Calif., 1990, pp. 354-359.

Kube, P., "Polynomial Shift-Invariant Operators for Texture Segmentation," *Proc. IEEE Conf. Computer Vision and Pattern Recognition,* IEEE CS Press, Los Alamitos, Calif., 1988, pp. 100-104.

Kundu, A., "Robust Edge Detection," *Proc. IEEE Conf. Computer Vision and Pattern Recognition,* IEEE CS Press, Los Alamitos, Calif., 1989, pp. 11-18.

Lakshmanan, S. and H. Derin, "Simultaneous Parameter Estimation and Segmentation of Gibbs Random Fields Using Simulated Annealing," *IEEE Trans. Pattern Analysis and Machine Intelligence,* Vol. 11, No. 8, 1989, pp. 799-822.

Langridge, D.J., "Detection of Discontinuities in the First Derivatives of Surfaces," *Computer Vision, Graphics and Image Processing,* Vol. 27, 1984, pp. 291-308.

Laprade, R.H., "Split-and-Merge Segmentation of Aerial Photographs," *Computer Vision, Graphics and Image Processing,* Vol. 44, No. 1, 1988, pp. 77-86.

Le, Y.G., Image Segmentation Using Dynamic Programming, in *Advances in Computer Vision and Image Processing,* T.S. Huang, ed., Vol. 3, JAI Press Inc., 1988, pp. 39-62.

Leclerc, Y., "Capturing the Local Structure of Image Discontinuities in Two Dimensions," *Proc. IEEE Conf. Computer Vision and Pattern Recognition,* IEEE CS Press, Los Alamitos, Calif., 1985, pp. 34-38.

Leclerc, Y.G., "Constructing Simple Stable Description for Image Partitioning," *Int'l J. Computer Vision,* Vol. 3, 1989, pp. 73-102.

Leclerc, Y.G. and S.W. Zucker, "The Local Structure of Image Discontinuities in One Dimension," *IEEE Trans. Pattern Analysis and Machine Intelligence,* Vol. 9, No. 3, 1987, pp. 341-355.

Lee, C., R.M. Haralick, and T.I. Phillips, "Image Segmentation Using Morphological Pyramid," *Proc. SPIE/IEEE Applications of Artificial Intelligence Conference,* VII, 1095, 1989, pp. 208-221.

Lee, C.H. and A. Rosenfeld, "Albedo Estimation for Scene Segmentation," *Pattern Recognition,* Vol. 1, No. 3, 1983, pp. 155-160.

Lee, D., "Edge Detection, Classification, and Measurement," *Proc. IEEE Conf. Computer Vision and Pattern Recognition,* IEEE CS Press, Los Alamitos, Calif., 1989, pp. 2-10.

Lee, D., "Coping with Discontinuities in Computer Vision: Their Detection, Classification, and Measurement," *IEEE Trans. Pattern Analysis and Machine Intelligence,* Vol. 12, No. 4, 1990, pp. 321-344.

Lee, D. and T. Pavlidis, "One-Dimensional Regularization with Discontinuities," *IEEE Trans. Pattern Analysis and Machine Intelligence,* Vol. 10, No. 6, 1988, pp. 822-829.

Lee, J.S.J., R.M. Haralick, and L.G. Shapiro, "Morphologic Edge Detection," *IEEE Trans. Robotics and Automation,* Vol. 3, No. 2, 1987, pp. 142-156

Leonardis, A., A. Gupta, and R. Bajcsy, "Segmentation as the Search for the Best Description of the Image in Terms of Primitives," *Proc. Third Int'l Conf. Computer Vision,* IEEE CS Press, Los Alamitos, Calif., 1990, pp. 121-125.

Levine, M.D. and A.M. Nazif, "Dynamic Measurement of Computer Generated Image Segmentations," *IEEE Trans. Pattern Analysis and Machine Intelligence,* Vol. 7, No. 2, 1985, pp. 155-164.

Li, S.Z., "Invariant Surface Segmentation through Energy Minimization with Discontinuties," *Int'l J. Computer Vision,* Vol. 5, No. 2, 1990, pp. 161-194.

Lindeberg T., "Scale-Space for Discrete Signals," *IEEE Trans. Pattern Analysis and Machine Intelligence,* Vol. 12, No. 3, 1990, pp. 234-254.

Lindeberg, T. and J.-O. Eklundh, "Scale Detection and Region Extraction from a Scale-Space Primal Sketch," *Proc. Third Int'l Conf. Computer Vision,* IEEE CS Press, Los Alamitos, Calif., 1990, pp. 416-426.

Lunscher, W.H.H.J. and M.P. Beddoes, "Optimal Edge Detector Design," *IEEE Trans. Pattern Analysis and Machine Intelligence,* Vol. 8, No. 2, 1986, pp. 164-187.

Lyvers, E.P. and O.R. Mitchell, "Precision Edge Contrast and Orientation Estimation," *IEEE Trans. Pattern Analysis and Machine Intelligence,* Vol. 10, No. 6, 1988, pp. 927-937.

Malik, J. and P. Perona, "A Computational Model of Texture Segmentation," *Proc. IEEE Conf. Computer Vision and Pattern Recognition,* IEEE CS Press, Los Alamitos, Calif., 1989, pp. 326-332.

Malik, J. and P. Perona, "Preattentive Texture Discrimination with Early Vision Mechanisms," *J. Opt. Soc. Am. A,* Vol. 7, No. 5, May 1990, pp. 923-932.

Mallat, S.G., "Scale Change Versus Scale Space Representation," *Proc. First Int'l Conf. Computer Vision,* IEEE CS Press, Los Alamitos, Calif., 1987, pp. 592-596.

Matsuyama, T., "Expert Systems for Image Processing: Knowledge-Based Composition of Image Analysis Processes," *Computer Vision, Graphics and Image Processing,* Vol. 48, No. 1, 1989, pp. 22-49.

Mitiche, A. and J.K. Aggarwal, "Detection of Edges Using Range Information," *IEEE Trans. Pattern Analysis and Machine Intelligence,* Vol. 5, No. 2, 1983, pp. 174-178.

Mohan, R. and R. Nevatia, "Segmentation and Description Based on Perceptual Organization," *Proc. IEEE Conf. Computer Vision and Pattern Recognition,* IEEE CS Press, Los Alamitos, Calif., 1989, pp. 333-341.

Mohan, R. and R. Nevatia, "Using Perceptual Organization to Extract 3-D Structures," *IEEE Trans. Pattern Analysis and Machine Intelligence,* Vol. 11, No. 11, 1989, pp. 1121-1139.

Monga, O., "An Optimal Region Growing Algorithm for Image Segmentation," *Int'l J. Pattern Recognition and Artificial Intelligence,* Vol. 1, 1987, pp. 351-375.

Monga, O., "3D edge Detection Using Recursive Filtering: Application to Scanner Images," *Proc. IEEE Conf. Computer Vision and Pattern Recognition,* IEEE CS Press, Los Alamitos, Calif., 1989, pp. 28-37.

Morgenthaler, D.G. and A. Rosenfeld, "Multidimensional Edge Detection by Hypersurface Fitting," *IEEE Trans. Pattern Analysis and Machine Intelligence,* Vol. 3, No. 4, 1981, pp. 482-486.

Nalwa, V.S., "Edge-Detector Resolution Improvement by Image Interpolation," *IEEE Trans. Pattern Analysis and Machine Intelligence,* Vol. 9, No. 3, 1987, pp. 446-451.

Nalwa, V.S. and E. Pauchon, "Edge Aggregation and Edge Description," *Computer Vision, Graphics and Image Processing,* Vol. 40, No. 1, 1987, pp. 79-94.

Nitzberg, M. and D. Mumford, "The 2.1-D Sketch," *Proc. Third Int'l Conf. Computer Vision,* IEEE CS Press, Los Alamitos, Calif.,1990, pp. 138-145.

Pal, N.R. and S.K. Pal, "Entropic Thresholding," *Signal Processing,* Vol. 16, 1989, pp. 97-108.

Pappas, T.N. and N.S. Jayant, "An Adaptive Clustering Algorithm for Image Segmentation," *Proc. Second Int'l Conf. Computer Vision,* IEEE CS Press, Los Alamitos, Calif., 1988, pp. 310-315.

Perona, P. and J. Malik, "Scale-Space and Edge Detection Using Anisotropic Diffusion," *IEEE Trans. Pattern Analysis and Machine Intelligence,* Vol. 12, No. 7, 1990, pp. 629-639.

Perona, P. and J. Malik, "Detecting and Localizing Edges Composed of Steps, Peaks, and Roofs," *Proc. Third Int'l Conf. Computer Vision,* IEEE CS Press, Los Alamitos, Calif., 1990, pp. 52-57.

Perry, A. and D.G. Lowe, "Segmentation of Textured Images," *Proc. IEEE Conf. Computer Vision and Pattern Recognition,* IEEE CS Press, Los Alamitos, Calif., 1989, pp. 319-325.

Pong, T.-C., et al., "Experiments in Segmentation Using a Facet Model Region Grower," *Computer Vision, Graphics and Image Processing,* Vol. 25, No. 1, 1984, pp. 1-23.

Raafat, H.M. and A.K.C. Wong, "A Texture Information-Directed Region Growing Algorithm for Image Segmentation and Region Classification," *Computer Vision, Graphics and Image Processing,* Vol. 43, No. 1, 1988, pp. 1-21.

Rao, A.R., *Taxonomy for Texture Description and Identification,* Springer-Verlag, New York, N.Y., 1990.

Rao, A.R. and R.C. Jain, "Analyzing Oriented Textures Through Phase Portraits," *Proc. Tenth Int'l Conf. Pattern Recognition,* IEEE CS Press, Los Alamitos, Calif., 1990, pp. 336-340.

Rao, A.R. and B.G. Schunck, "Computing Oriented Texture Fields," *Proc. IEEE Conf. Computer Vision and Pattern Recognition,* IEEE CS Press, Los Alamitos, Calif., 1989, pp. 61-69.

Rao, K. and R. Nevatia, "Computing Volume Descriptions from Sparse 3-D Data," *Int'l J. Computer Vision,* Vol. 2, No. 1, 1988, pp. 33-50.

Reed, T.R. and H. Wechsler, "Tracking of Nonstationarities of Texture Fields," *Signal Processing,* Vol. 14, 1988, pp. 95-102.

Reed, T.R. and H. Wechsler, "Segmentation of Textured Images and Gestalt Organization Using Spatial/Spatial-Frequency Representations," *IEEE Trans. Pattern Analysis and Machine Intelligence,* Vol. 12, No. 1, 1990, pp. 1-12.

Reichenbach, S.E., S.K. Park, and R. Alter-Gartenberg, "Optimal Small Kernels for Edge Detection," *Proc. Tenth Int'l Conf. Pattern Recognition,* IEEE CS Press, Los Alamitos, Calif., 1990, pp. 57-63.

Rimey, R.D. and F.S. Cohen, "A Maximum-Likelihood Approach to Segmenting Range Data," *IEEE J. Robotics and Automation,* Vol. 4, No. 3, 1988, pp. 277-286.

Rosenfeld, A., "Image Analysis: Problems, Progress, and Prospects," *Pattern Recognition,* Vol. 17, No. 1, 1984, pp. 3-12.

Rosenfeld, A. and L.S. Davis, "Image Segmentation and Image Models," *Proc. IEEE,* Vol. 67, No. 5, IEEE Press, New York, N.Y., 1979, pp. 764-772.

Sahoo, P.K., et al., "A Survey of Thresholding Techniques," *Computer Vision, Graphics and Image Processing,* Vol. 41, 1988, pp. 233-260.

Shemlon, S., S.M. Dunn, and T. Liang, "Progressive Knowledge Use in Incremental Segmentation," *Proc. SPIE/IEEE Applications of Artificial Intelligence Conference,* VII, 1095, 1989, pp. 239-250.

Sotak. Jr., G.E. and K.L. Boyer, "The Laplacian-of-Gaussian Kernel: A Formal Analysis and Design Procedure for Fast, Accurate Convolution and Full-Frame Output," *Computer Vision, Graphics and Image Processing,* Vol. 48, 1989, pp. 147-189.

Straub, B.J. and W.E. Blanz, "Combined Decision Theoretic and Syntactic Approach to Image Segmentation," *Machine Vision and Applications,* Vol. 2, No. 1, 1989, pp. 17-30.

Tan, H.L., S.B. Gelfand, and E.J. Delp, "A Cost Minimization Approach to Edge Detection Using Simulated Annealing," *Proc. IEEE Conf. Computer Vision and Pattern Recognition,* IEEE CS Press, Los Alamitos, Calif., 1989, pp. 86-91.

Tanaka, M. and T. Katayama, "Edge Detection and Restoration of Noisy Images by the Expectation-Maximization Algorithm," *Signal Processing,* Vol. 17, 1989, pp. 213-226.

Taxt, T., P.J. Flynn, and A.K. Jain, "Segmentation of Document Images as Statistical Classification task," *IEEE Trans. Pattern Analysis and Machine Intelligence,* Vol. 11, No. 12, 1989, pp. 1322-1329.

Tenenbaum, J.M. and H.G. Barrow, "IGS: A Paradigm for Integrating Image Segmentation and Interpretation," *Proc. Third Int'l Conf. Pattern Recognition,* IEEE CS Press, Los Alamitos, Calif., 1976, pp. 435-444.

Toh, P.-S. and A.K. Forrest, "Occlusion Detection in Early Vision," *Proc. Third Int'l Conf. Computer Vision,* IEEE CS Press, Los Alamitos, Calif., 1990, pp. 126-132.

Tuceryan, M., A.K. Jain, and Y. Lee, "Texture Segmentation Using Voronoi Polygons," *Proc. IEEE Conf. Computer Vision and Pattern Recognition,* IEEE CS Press, Los Alamitos, Calif., 1988, pp. 94-99.

Van Vilet, L.J., I.T. Young, and G.L. Beckers, "A Nonlinear Laplace Operator as Edge Detector in Noisy Images," *Computer Vision, Graphics and Image Processing,* Vol. 45, 1989, pp. 167-195.

Vehel, J.L., "About Lacunarity, Some Links Between Fractal and Integral Geometry, and an Application to Texture Segmentation," *Proc. Third Int'l Conf. Computer Vision,* IEEE CS Press, Los Alamitos, Calif., 1990, pp. 380-384.

Vilnrotter, F.M., R. Nevatia, and K.E. Price, "Structural Analysis of Natural Textures," *IEEE Trans. Pattern Analysis and Machine Intelligence,* Vol. 8, No. 1, 1986, pp. 76-89.

Vistnes, R., "Texture Models and Image Measures for Segmentation," *Int'l J. Computer Vision,* Vol. 3, No. 4, 1989, pp. 313-336.

Voorhees, H. and T. Poggio, "Detecting Blobs as Textons in Natural Images," *Proc. DARPA Image Understanding Workshop,* 1987, pp. 892-899.

Williams, D.J. and M.A. Shah, "Multiple Scale Edge Linking," *Proc. SPIE/IEEE Applications of Artificial Intelligence Conference VII,* Vol. 1095, 1989, pp. 13-24.

Williams, L.R., "Perceptual Organization of Occluding Contours," *Proc. Third Int'l Conf. Computer Vision,* IEEE CS Press, Los Alamitos, Calif., 1990, pp. 133-137.

Wilson, R. and M. Spann, "Finite Prolate Spheroidal Sequences and Their Applications II: Image Feature Description and Segmentation,"

IEEE Trans. Pattern Analysis and Machine Intelligence, Vol. 10, No. 2, 1988, pp. 193-203.

Wong, A.K.C. and P.K. Sahoo, "A Gray-Level Threshold Selection Method Based on Maximum Entropy Principle," *IEEE Trans. Systems, Man, and Cybernetics,* Vol. 19, No. 4, 1989, pp. 866-871.

Yokoya, N. and M.D. Levine, "Range Image Segmentation Based on Differential Geometry: A Hybrid Approach," *IEEE Trans. Pattern Analysis and Machine Intelligence,* Vol. 11, No. 6, 1989, pp. 643-649.

Yonawitz, S.D. and A.M. Bruckstein, "A New Method for Image Segmentation," *Computer Vision, Graphics and Image Processing,* Vol. 46, No. 1, 1989, pp. 82-95.

Zhou, Y.T., V. Venkataswar, and R. Chellappa, "Edge Detection and Linear Feature Extraction Using a 2-D Random Field Model," *IEEE Trans. Pattern Analysis and Machine Intelligence,* Vol. 11, No. 1, 1989, pp. 84-95.

Zucker, S.W., "Early Orientation Selection: Tangent Fields and the Dimensionality of their Support," *Computer Vision, Graphics and Image Processing,* Vol. 32, No. 1, 1985, pp. 74-103.

Zucker, S.W., A. Dobbins, and L. Iverson, "Two Stages of Curve Detection Suggest Two Styles of Visual Computation," *Neural Computation,* Vol. 1, No. 1, 1989, pp. 68-81.

Chapter 3: Feature Extraction and Matching
Selected Bibliography

Aloimonos, J., "Visual Shape Computation," *Proc. IEEE,* Vol. 76, No. 8, IEEE Press, New York, N.Y., 1988, pp. 899-916.

Alvertos, N., D. Brzakovic, and R.C. Gonzalez, "Camera Geometries for Image Matching in 3-D Machine Vision," *IEEE Trans. Pattern Analysis and Machine Intelligence,* Vol. 11, No. 9, 1989, pp. 897-915.

Amini, A.A., T.E. Weymouth, and D.J. Anderson, "A Parallel Algorithm for Determining Two-Dimensional Object Positions Using Incomplete Information About Their Boundaries," *Pattern Recognition,* Vol. 22, No. 1, 1989, pp. 21-28.

Arcelli, C. and G.S. di Baja, "A Width-Independent Fast Thinning Algorithm," *IEEE Trans. Pattern Analysis and Machine Intelligence,* Vol. 7, No. 4, 1985, pp. 463-474.

Asada, M., "Map Building for a Mobile Robot from Sensory Data," *IEEE Trans. on Systems, Man, and Cybernetics,* Vol. 20, No. 6, 1990, pp. 1326-1336.

Bajcsy, R. and S. Kovacic, "Multiresolution Elastic Matching," *Computer Vision, Graphics and Image Processing,* Vol. 46, No. 1, 1989, pp. 1-21.

Ballard, D.H., "Strip Trees: A Hierarchical Representation for Curves," *Communications of the ACM,* Vol. 24, No. 5, 1981, pp. 310-321.

Bell, B. and L.F. Pau, "Contour Tracking and Corner Detection in a Logic Programming Environment," *IEEE Trans. Pattern Analysis and Machine Intelligence,* Vol. 12, No. 9, 1990, pp. 913-917.

Besl, P. and- R.C. Jain, "Invariant Surface Characteristics for 3-D Object Recognition in Range Images," *Computer Vision, Graphics and Image Processing,* Vol. 33, No. 1, 1986, pp. 33-79.

Beveridge, J.R., R. Weiss, and E.M. Riseman, "Optimization of 2-D Model Matching," *Proc. DARPA Image Understanding Workshop,* 1989, pp. 815-830.

Beveridge, J.R., R. Weiss, and E.M. Riseman, "Combinatorial Optimization Applied to Variable Scale 2-D Model Matching," *Proc. Tenth Int'l Conf. Pattern Recognition,* IEEE CS Press, Los Alamitos, Calif., 1990, pp. 18-23.

Boldt, M., R. Weiss, and E. Riseman, "Token-Based Extraction of Straight Lines," *IEEE Trans. Systems, Man, and Cybernetics,* Vol. 19, No. 6, 1989, pp. 1581-1594.

Bolle, R.M., A. Califano, and R. Kjeldsen, "Data and Model Driven Focus of Foveation," *Proc. Tenth Int'l Conf. Pattern Recognition,* IEEE CS Press, Los Alamitos, Calif., 1990, pp. 1-7.

Bolles, R.C. and R.A. Cain, "Recognizing and Locating Partially Visible Objects: The Local-Feature-Focus Method," *Int'l J. Robotics Research,* Vol. 1, No. 3, 1982, pp. 57-82.

Borgefors, G., "Hierarchical Chamfer Matching: A Parametric Edge Matching Algorithm," *IEEE Trans. Pattern Analysis and Machine Intelligence,* Vol. 10, No. 6, 1988, pp. 849-865.

Brady, M., et al., "Describing Surfaces," *Computer Vision, Graphics and Image Processing,* Vol. 32, No. 1, 1985, pp. 1-28.

Brown, C.M., "Inherent Bias and Noise in the Hough Transform," *IEEE Trans. Pattern Analysis and Machine Intelligence,* Vol. 5, No. 5, 1983, pp. 493-505.

Brown, M.K., "The Extraction of Curved Surface Features with Generic Range Sensors," *Int'l J. Robotics Research,* Vol. 5, No. 1, 1986, pp. 3-18.

Burns, J.B., A.R. Hanson, and E.M. Riseman, "Extracting Straight Lines," *Proc. Seventh Int'l Conf. Pattern Recognition,* IEEE CS Press, Los Alamitos, Calif., 1984, pp. 482-485.

Burt, P.J. and E.H. Adelson, "A Multiresolution Spline with Applications to Image Mosaics," *ACM Trans. on Graphics,* Vol. 2, No. 4, 1983, pp. 217-236.

Califano, A., R.M. Bolles, and R.W. Taylor, "Generalized Neighborhood: A New Approach to Complex Feature Extraction," *Proc. IEEE Conf. Computer Vision and Pattern Recognition,* IEEE CS Press, Los Alamitos, Calif., 1989, pp. 192-199.

Canning, J., et al., "Symbolic Pixel Labeling for Curvilinear Feature Detection," *Pattern Recognition Letters,* Vol. 8, No. 5, 1988, pp. 299-310.

Cao, X. and F. Deravi, "An Efficient Method for Multiple-Circle Detection," *Proc. Third Int'l Conf. Computer Vision,* IEEE CS Press, Los Alamitos, Calif., 1990, pp. 744-747.

Casasent, D. and R. Krishnapuram, "Curved Object Location by Hough Transformations and Inversions," *Pattern Recognition,* Vol. 20, No. 2, 1987, pp. 181-188.

Cass, T.A., "Feature Matching for Object Localization in the Presence of Uncertainty," *Proc. Third Int'l Conf. Computer Vision,* IEEE CS Press, Los Alamitos, Calif., 1990, pp. 360-364.

Chakravarthy, C. and R. Kasturi, "Pose Clustering on Constraints for Object Recognition," *Proc. IEEE Conf. Computer Vision and Pattern Recognition,* IEEE CS Press, Los Alamitos, Calif, 1991, pp. 16-21.

Chen, D.S., "A Data-Driven Intermediate Level Feature Extraction Algorithm," *IEEE Trans. Pattern Analysis and Machine Intelligence,* Vol. 11, No. 7, 1989, pp. 749-758.

Chen, H.H., "Pose Determination from Line-to-Plane Correspondences: Existence Condition and Closed-Form Solutions," *Proc. Third Int'l Conf. Computer Vision,* IEEE CS Press, Los Alamitos, Calif., 1990, pp. 374-379.

Chen, M.H. and P.F. Yan, "A Multiscaling Approach Based on Morphological Filtering," *IEEE Trans. Pattern Analysis and Machine Intelligence,* Vol. 11, No. 7, 1989, pp. 694-700.

Cipolla, R. and A. Blake, "The Dynamic Analysis of Apparent Contours," *Proc. Third Int'l Conf. Computer Vision,* IEEE CS Press, Los Alamitos, Calif., 1990, pp. 616-625.

Coggins, J.M. and A.K. Jain, "A Spatial Filtering Approach to Texture Analysis," *Pattern Recognition,* Vol. 3, 1985, pp. 195-203.

Coleman, E.N., Jr. and R.C. Jain, "Obtaining 3-Dimensional Shape of Textured and Specular Surface Using Four Source Photometry," *Computer Graphics and Image Processing,* Vol. 18, No. 4, 1982, pp. 309-328.

Connelly, S. and A. Rosenfeld, "A Pyramid Algorithm for Fast Curve Extraction," *Computer Vision, Graphics and Image Processing,* Vol. 49, 1990, pp. 332-345.

Costa, M., et al., "Optimal Affine-Invariant Point Matching," *Proc. SPIE/IEEE Applications of Artificial Intelligence Conf. VII,* Vol. 1095, 1989, pp. 515-530.

Cross, G.R. and A.K. Jain, "Markov Random Field Texture Models," *IEEE Trans. Pattern Analysis and Machine Intelligence,* Vol. 5, No. 1, 1983, pp. 25-39.

Deriche, R. and G. Giraudon, "Accurate Corner Cetection: An Analytical Study," *Proc. Third Int'l Conf. Computer Vision,* IEEE CS Press, Los Alamitos, Calif., 1990, pp. 66-70.

Dom, B., W. Niblack, and J. Sheinvald, "Feature Selection with Stochastic Complexity," *Proc. IEEE Conf. Computer Vision and Pattern Recognition,* IEEE CS Press, Los Alamitos, Calif., 1989, pp. 241-249.

Dougherty, E.R., "The Dual Representation of Gray-Scale Morphological Filters," *Proc. IEEE Conf. Computer Vision and Pattern Recognition,* IEEE CS Press, Los Alamitos, Calif., 1989, pp. 172-177.

Dougherty, E.R. and C.R. Giardina, "Closed-Form Representation of Convolution, Dilation, and Erosion in the Context of Image Algebra," *Proc. IEEE Conf. Computer Vision and Pattern Recognition,* IEEE CS Press, Los Alamitos, Calif., 1988, pp. 754-759.

Dougherty, E.R. and C.R. Giardina, "Morphology in Umbra Matrices," *Int'l J. Pattern Recognition and Artificial Intelligence,* Vol. 2, 1988, pp. 367-385.

Dougherty, E.R. and P. Sehdev, "A Robust Image Processing Language in the Context of Image Algebra," *Proc. IEEE Conf. Computer Vision and Pattern Recognition,* IEEE CS Press, Los Alamitos, Calif., 1988, pp. 748-753.

Dudani, S., K.J. Breeding, and R.B. McGhee, "Aircraft Identification by Moment Invariants," *IEEE Trans. Computers,* Vol. C-26, No. 1, 1977, pp. 39-46.

Dudek, G. and J. Tsotsos, "Recognizing Planar Curves Using Curvature-Tuned Smoothing," *Proc. Tenth Int'l Conf. Pattern Recognition,* IEEE CS Press, Los Alamitos, Calif., 1990, pp. 130-135.

Fahn, C.S., J.F. Wang, and J.Y. Lee, "An Adaptive Reduction Procedure for the Piecewise Linear Approximation of Digitized Curves," *IEEE Trans. Pattern Analysis and Machine Intelligence,* Vol. 11, No. 9, 1989, pp. 967-973.

Ferrie, F.P. and J. Lagarde, "Curvature Consistency Improves Local Shading Analysis," *Proc. Tenth Int'l Conf. Pattern Recognition,* IEEE CS Press, Los Alamitos, Calif., 1990, pp. 70-76.

Fischler, M.A. and P. Barrett, "An Iconic Transform for Sketch and Shape Abstraction," *Computer Graphics and Image Processing,* Vol. 13, No. 3, 1980, pp. 334-360.

Fischler, M.A. and R.C. Bolles, "Random Sample Consensus: A Paradigm for Model Fitting with Application to Image Analysis and Automated Cartography," *Communications ACM,* Vol. 24, No. 6, 1981, pp. 381-395.

Fleck, M.M., "Multiple Widths Yield Reliable Finite Differences," *Proc. Third Int'l Conf. Computer Vision,* IEEE CS Press, Los Alamitos, Calif., 1990, pp. 58-61.

Freeman, W.T. and E.H. Adelson, "Steerable Filters for Early Vision, Image Analysis, and Wavelet Decomposition," *Proc. Third Int'l Conf. Computer Vision,* IEEE CS Press, Los Alamitos, Calif., 1990, pp. 406-415.

Friedberg, S.A., "Finding Axes of Skewed Symmetry," *Computer Vision, Graphics and Image Processing,* Vol. 34, No. 2, 1986, pp. 138-155.

Fua, P. and A.J. Hanson, "Objective Functions for Feature Discrimination," *Proc. Int'l Joint Conf. Artificial Intelligence,* Morgan Kaufman Publishers, Inc., San Mateo, Calif., 1989, pp. 1596-1602.

Goldgof, D.B., T.S. Huang, and H. Lee, "A Curvature-Based Approach to Terrain Recognition," *IEEE Trans. Pattern Analysis and Machine Intelligence,* Vol. 11, No. 11, 1989, pp. 1213-1217.

Grimson, W.E.L., "On the Recognition of Curved Objects," *IEEE Trans. Pattern Analysis and Machine Intelligence,* Vol. 11, No. 6, 1989, pp. 632-643.

Grimson, W.E.L., "On the Recognition of Parameterized 2-D Objects," *Int'l J. Computer Vision,* Vol. 2, No. 2, 1989, pp. 353-371.

Grimson, W.E.L., "The Effect of Indexing on the Complexity of Object Recognition," *Proc. Third Int'l Conf. Computer Vision,* IEEE CS Press, Los Alamitos, Calif., 1990, pp. 644-653.

Grimson, W.E.L. and D.P. Huttenlocher, "On the Sensitivity of Geometric Hashing," *Proc. Third Int'l Conf. Computer Vision,* IEEE CS Press, Los Alamitos, Calif., 1990, pp. 334-339.

Grimson, W.E.L. and D.P. Huttenlocher, "On the Sensitivity of the Hough Transform for Object Recognition," *IEEE Trans. Pattern Analysis and Machine Intelligence,* Vol. 12, No. 3, 1990, pp. 255-274.

Grimson, W.E.L. and T. Lozano-Perez, "Localizing Overlapping Parts by Searching the Interpretation Tree," *IEEE Trans. Pattern Analysis and Machine Intelligence,* Vol. 9, No. 4, 1987, pp. 469-482.

Grossmann, P., "From 3-D Line Segments to Objects and Spaces," *Proc. IEEE Conf. Computer Vision and Pattern Recognition,* IEEE CS Press, Los Alamitos, Calif., 1989, pp. 216-221.

Gutfinger, D., et al., "Robust Curve Detection by Temporal Geodesics," *Proc. Third Int'l Conf. Computer Vision,* IEEE CS Press, Los Alamitos, Calif., 1990, pp. 752-756.

Han, J.H., "Detection of Convex and Concave Discontinuous Points in a Plane Curve," *Proc. Third Int'l Conf. Computer Vision,* IEEE CS Press, Los Alamitos, Calif., 1990, pp. 71-74.

Haralick, R.M., "Statistical and Structural Approaches to Texture," *Proc. IEEE,* IEEE Press, New York, N.Y., Vol. 67, No. 5, 1979, pp. 786-804.

Haralick, R.M., L.T. Watson, and T.J. Laffey, "The Topographic Primal Sketch," *Int'l J. Robotics Research,* Vol. 2, No. 1, 1983, pp. 50-72.

Harlow, C.A., M.M. Trivedi, and R.W. Conners, "Use of Texture Operators in Scene Analysis," *Optical Eng.,* Vol. 25, No. 11, 1986, pp. 1200-1206.

Henderson, T.C. and W.S. Fai, "The 3-D Hough Shape Transform," *Pattern Recognition,* 1984, pp. 235-238.

Henikoff, J. and L.G. Shapiro, "Interesting Patterns for Model-Based Machine Vision," *Proc. Third Int'l Conf. Computer Vision,* IEEE CS Press, Los Alamitos, Calif., 1990, pp. 535-539.

Horn, B.K.P. and E.J. Weldon Jr, "Filtering Closed Curves," *IEEE Trans. Pattern Analysis and Machine Intelligence,* Vol. 8, No. 5, 1986, pp. 665-668.

Hu, G., "Symmetry Detection of 2-D Figures," *Proc. SPIE/IEEE Applications of Artificial Intelligence Conf. VIII,* Vol. 1293, 1990, pp. 516-523.

Hwang, V.S.S., "Recognizing and Locating Partially Occluded 2-D Objects: Symbolic Clustering Method," *IEEE Trans. Systems, Man, and Cybernetics,* Vol. 19, No. 6, 1989, pp. 1644-1656.

Illingworth, J. and J. Kittler, "A Survey on Hough Transform," *Computer Vision, Graphics and Image Processing,* Vol. 44, No. 1, 1988, pp. 87-116.

Imai, H. and M. Iri, "Computational-Geometric Methods for Polygonal Approximations of a Curve," *Computer Vision, Graphics and Image Processing,* Vol. 36, No. 1, 1986, pp. 31-41.

Joo, H., R.M. Haralick, and L.G. Shapiro, "Toward the Automatic Generation of Mathematical Morphology Procedures Using Predicate Logic," *Proc. Third Int'l Conf. Computer Vision,* IEEE CS Press, Los Alamitos, Calif., 1990, pp. 156-167.

Kalvin, A., et al., "Two-Dimensional, Model-Based, Boundary Matching Using Footprints," *Int'l J. Robotics Research,* Vol. 5, No. 4, 1986, pp. 38-55.

Kanatani, K., "Hypothesizing and Testing Geometric Attributes of Image Data," *Proc. Third Int'l Conf. Computer Vision,* IEEE CS Press, Los Alamitos, Calif., 1990, pp. 370-373.

Kass, M., A. Witkin, and D. Terzopoulos, "Snakes: Active Contour Models," *Int'l J. Computer Vision,* Vol. 1, No. 4, 1988, pp. 321-331.

Koenderink, J.J. and A.J. van Doorn, "Representation of Local Geometry in the Visual System," *Biological Cybernetics,* Vol. 55, 1987, pp. 367-375.

Korn, A.F., "Toward a Symbolic Representation of Intensity Changes in Images," *IEEE Trans. Pattern Analysis and Machine Intelligence,* Vol. 10, No. 5, 1988, pp. 610-625.

Koshimizu, H. and M. Numada, "On the Extensive Reconstruction of Hough Transform," *Proc. Third Int'l Conf. Computer Vision,* IEEE CS Press, Los Alamitos, Calif., 1990, pp. 740-743.

Kovalevsky, V.A., "New Definition and Fast Recognition of Digital Straight Segments and Arcs," *Proc. Tenth Int'l Conf. Pattern Recognition,* IEEE CS Press, Los Alamitos, Calif., 1990, pp. 31-34.

Lee, J.C. and E.E. Milios, "Matching Range Images of Human Faces," *Proc. Third Int'l Conf. Computer Vision,* IEEE CS Press, Los Alamitos, Calif., 1990, pp. 722-726.

Li, Z.C., et al., "Harmonic Models of Shape Transformations in Digital Images and Patterns," *Proc. Tenth Int'l Conf. Pattern Recognition,* IEEE CS Press, Los Alamitos, Calif., 1990, pp. 1-7.

Liang, P., "A New Transform for Curve Detection," *Proc. Third Int'l Conf. Computer Vision,* IEEE CS Press, Los Alamitos, Calif., 1990, pp. 748-751.

Link, N.K. and S.W. Zucker, "Corner Detection in Curvilinear Dot Grouping," *Biological Cybernetics,* Vol. 59, 1988, pp. 247-256.

Lipari, C., M. Trivedi, and C. Harlow, "Geometric Modeling and Recognition of Elongated Regions in Aerial Images," *IEEE Trans. Systems, Man, and Cybernetics,* Vol. 19, No. 6, 1989, pp. 1600-1612.

Liu, H.-C. and M.D. Srinath, "Partial Shape Classification Using Contour Matching in Distance Transformation," *IEEE Trans. Pattern Analysis and Machine Intelligence,* Vol. 12, No. 11, 1990, pp. 1072-1079.

Lowe, D.G., "Organization of Smooth Image Curves at Multiple Scales," *Int'l J. Computer Vision,* Vol. 3, No. 2, 1989, pp. 119-130.

Lu, S.Y. and K.S. Fu, "A Syntactic Approach to Texture Analysis," *Computer Graphics and Image Processing,* Vol. 7, 1978, pp. 303-330.

Mackworth, A.K. and F. Mokhtarian, "The Renormalized Curvature Scale Space and the Evolution Properties of Planar Curves," *Proc. IEEE Conf. Computer Vision and Pattern Recognition,* IEEE CS Press, Los Alamitos, Calif., 1988, pp. 318-327.

Mandler, E., and M.F. Oberlander, "One-Pass Encoding of Connected Components in Multi-Valued Images," *Proc. Tenth Int'l Conf. Pattern Recognition,* IEEE CS Press, Los Alamitos, Calif., 1990, pp. 64-69.

Maragos, P., "Morphology-Based Symbolic Image Modeling, Multi-Scale Nonlinear Smoothing, and Pattern Spectrum," *Proc. IEEE Conf. Computer Vision and Pattern Recognition,* IEEE CS Press, Los Alamitos, Calif., 1988, pp. 766-773.

Maragos, P., "Optimal Morphological Approaches to Image Matching and Object Detection," *Proc. Second Int'l Conf. Computer Vision,* IEEE CS Press, Los Alamitos, Calif., 1988, pp. 695-699.

Maragos, P., "A Representation Theory for Morphological Image and Signal Processing," *IEEE Trans. Pattern Analysis and Machine Intelligence,* Vol. 11, No. 6, 1989, pp. 586-599.

Maragos, P., "Pattern Spectrum and Multiscale Shape Representation," *IEEE Trans. Pattern Analysis and Machine Intelligence,* Vol. 11, No. 7, 1989, pp. 701-716.

Marimont, D.H., "A Representation for Image Curves," *Proc. Nat'l Conf. on Artificial Intelligence,* MIT Press, Cambridge, Mass., 1984, pp. 237-242.

Marshall, S., "Review of Shape Coding Techniques," *Image and Vision Computing,* Vol. 7, No. 4, 1989, pp. 281-294.

Medioni, G. and Y. Yasumoto, "Corner Detection and Curve Representation Using Cubic B-Splines," *Computer Vision, Graphics and Image Processing,* Vol. 39, 1987, pp. 267-278.

Mehrotra, R. and W.I. Grosky, "Shape Matching Utilizing Indexed Hypothesis Generation and Testing," *IEEE Trans. Systems, Man, and Cybernetics,* Vol. 19, No. 1, 1989, pp. 70-77.

Milios, E.E., "Shape Matching Using Curvature Processes," *Computer Vision, Graphics and Image Processing,* Vol. 47, 1989, pp. 203-226.

Mitchell, O.R. and T.A. Grogan, "Global and Partial Shape Discrimination for Computer Vision," *Optical Eng.,* Vol. 23, No. 5, 1984, pp. 484-491.

Mitiche, A. and J.K. Aggarwal, "Contour Registration by Shape-Specific Points for Shape Matching," *Computer Vision, Graphics and Image Processing,* Vol. 22, 1983, pp. 396-408.

Mohan, R. and R. Nevatia, "Using Perceptual Organization to Extract 3-D Structures," *IEEE Trans. Pattern Analysis and Machine Intelligence,* Vol. 11, No. 11, 1989, pp. 1121-1139.

Mokhtarian, F., "Fingerprint Theorems for Curvature and Torsion Zero-Crossings," *Proc. IEEE Conf. Computer Vision and Pattern Recognition,* IEEE CS Press, Los Alamitos, Calif., 1989, pp. 269-275.

Mokhtarian, F. and A. Mackworth, "Scale-Based Description and Recognition of Planar Curves and Two-Dimensional Shapes," *IEEE Trans. Pattern Analysis and Machine Intelligence,* Vol. 8, No. 1, 1986, pp. 34-43.

Moravec, H.P., "Toward Automatic Visual Obstacle Avoidance," *Proc. Int'l Joint Conf. Artificial Intelligence,* Morgan Kaufmann Publishers, Inc., San Mateo, Calif., 1977, p. 584.

Mulgaonkar, P.G., L.G. Shapiro, and R.M. Haralick, "Matching 'Sticks, Plates, and Blobs' Objects Using Geometric and Relational Constraints," *Image and Vision Computing,* Vol. 2, 1984, pp. 85-98.

Nevatia, R. and R. Babu, "Linear Feature Extraction and Description," *Computer Graphics and Image Processing,* Vol. 13, No. 3, 1980, pp. 257-269.

Nevatia, R. and K.E. Price, "Locating Structures in Aerial Images," *IEEE Trans. Pattern Analysis and Machine Intelligence,* Vol. 4, No. 5, 1982, pp. 476-484.

Neveu, C.F., C.R. Dyer, and R.T. Chin, "Two-Dimensional Object Recognition Using Multiresolution Models," *Computer Vision, Graphics and Image Processing,* Vol. 34, No. 1, 1986, pp. 52-65.

Noble, J.A., "Finding Corners," *Image and Vision Computing,* Vol. 6, 1988, pp. 121-128.

Noble, J.A., "Morphological Feature Detection," *Proc. Second Int'l Conf. Computer Vision,* IEEE CS Press, Los Alamitos, Calif., 1988, pp. 112-116.

O'Gorman, L., "An Analysis of Feature Detectability from Curvature Estimation," *Proc. IEEE Conf. Computer Vision and Pattern Recognition,* IEEE CS Press, Los Alamitos, Calif., 1988, pp. 235-240.

O'Gorman, L., "K x K Thinning," *Computer Vision, Graphics, and Image Processing,* Vol. 51, 1990, pp. 195-215.

Okutomi, M. and T. Kanade, "A Locally Adaptive Window for Signal Matching," *Proc. Third Int'l Conf. Computer Vision,* IEEE CS Press, Los Alamitos, Calif., 1990, pp. 190-199.

Parent, P. and S.W. Zucker, "Trace Inference, Curvature Consistency, and Curve Detection," *IEEE Trans. Pattern Analysis and Machine Intelligence,* Vol. 11, No. 8, 1989, pp. 823-839.

Parvin, B. and G. Medioni, "Adaptive Multiscale Feature Extraction from Range Data," *Computer Vision, Graphics and Image Processing,* Vol. 45, 1989, pp. 346-356.

Pentland, A.P., "Fractal-Based Description of Natural Scenes," *IEEE Trans. Pattern Analysis and Machine Intelligence,* Vol. 6, No. 6, 1984, pp. 661-374.

Perlant, F.P. and D.M. McKeown, "Scene Registration in Aerial Image Analysis," *Proc. DARPA Image Understanding Workshop,* 1989, pp. 309-331.

Pham, S., "Digital Straight Segments," *Computer Vision, Graphics and Image Processing,* Vol. 36, No. 1, 1986, pp. 10-30.

Porrill, J., "Fitting Ellipses and Predicting Confidence Envelopes Using a Bias Corrected Kalman Filter," *Image and Vision Computing,* Vol. 8, No. 1, 1990, pp. 37-41.

Princen, J., J. Illingworth, and J. Kittler, "A Hierarchical Approach to Line Extraction," *Proc. IEEE Conf. Computer Vision and Pattern Recognition,* IEEE CS Press, Los Alamitos, Calif., 1989, pp. 92-97.

Princen, J., J. Illingworth, and J. Kittler, "Hypothesis Testing: A Framework for Analysing and Optimising Hough Transform Performance," *Proc. Third Int'l Conf. Computer Vision,* IEEE CS Press, Los Alamitos, Calif., 1990, pp. 427-435.

Qian, J. and R.W. Ehrich, "A Framework for Uncertainty Reasoning in Hierarchical Visual Evidence Space," *Proc. Tenth Int'l Conf. Pattern Recognition,* IEEE CS Press, Los Alamitos, Calif., 1990, pp. 119-124.

Rangarajan, K., M. Shah, and D. Van Brackle, "Optimal Corner Detector," *Computer Vision, Graphics and Image Processing,* Vol. 48, 1989, pp. 230-245.

Rao, K. and R. Nevatia, "From Sparse 3-D Data Directly to Volumetric Shape Descriptions," *Proc. DARPA Image Understanding Workshop,* 1987, pp. 360-369.

Rao, K. and R. Nevatia, "Shape Description from Imperfect and Incomplete Data," *Proc. Tenth Int'l Conf. Pattern Recognition,* IEEE CS Press, Los Alamitos, Calif., 1990, pp. 125-129.

Reisfeld, D., H. Wolfson, and Y. Yeshurun, "Detection of Interest Points Using Symmetry," *Proc. Third Int'l Conf. Computer Vision,* IEEE CS Press, Los Alamitos, Calif., 1990, pp. 62-65.

Rhodes, M.F., et al., "A Monolithic Hough Transform Processor Based on Restructurable VLSI," *IEEE Trans. Pattern Analysis and Machine Intelligence,* Vol. 10, No. 1, 1988, pp. 106-110.

Risse, T., "Hough Transform for Line Recognition: Complexity of Evidence Accumulation and Cluster Detection," *Computer Vision, Graphics and Image Processing,* Vol. 46, 1989, pp. 327-345.

Ritter, G.X., J.N. Wilson, and J.L. Davidson, "Image Algebra: An Overview," *Computer Vision, Graphics and Image Processing,* Vol. 49, No. 3, 1990, 297-331.

Rodriguez, J.J. and J.K. Aggarwal, "Matching Aerial Images to 3-D Terrain Maps," *IEEE Trans. Pattern Analysis and Machine Intelligence,* Vol. 12, No. 12, 1990, pp. 1138-1149.

Rodriguez, J.J. and J.K. Aggarwal, "Terrain Matching by Analysis of Aerial Images," *Proc. Third Int'l Conf. Computer Vision,* IEEE CS Press, Los Alamitos, Calif., 1990, pp. 677-683.

Rosin, P.L. and G.A.W. West, "Segmenting Curves Into Elliptic Arcs and Straight Lines," *Proc. Third Int'l Conf. Computer Vision,* IEEE CS Press, Los Alamitos, Calif., 1990, pp. 75-79.

Safaee-Rad, R., K.C. Smith, and B. Benhabib, "Accurate Estimation of Elliptical Shape Parameters from a Grey-Level Image," *Proc. Tenth Int'l Conf. Pattern Recognition,* IEEE CS Press, Los Alamitos, Calif., 1990, pp. 20-26.

Sander, P.T., "Generic Curvature Features from 3-D Images," *IEEE Trans. Systems, Man, and Cybernetics,* Vol. 19, No. 6, 1989, pp. 1623-1636.

Sander, P.T. and S.W. Zucker, "Singularities of Principle Directions Fields from 3-D Images," *Proc. Second Int'l Conf. Computer Vision,* IEEE CS Press, Los Alamitos, Calif., 1988, pp. 666-670.

Sanz, J.L.C. and T.T. Huang, "Image Representation by Sign Information," *IEEE Trans. Pattern Analysis and Machine Intelligence,* Vol. 11, No. 7, 1989, pp. 729-738.

Serra, J., ed., *Image Analysis and Mathematical Morphology 2: Technical Advances,* Academic Press, New York, N.Y., 1988.

Shahraray, B. and D.J. Anderson, "Optimal Estimation of Contour Properties by Cross-Validated Regularization," *IEEE Trans. Pattern Analysis and Machine Intelligence,* Vol. 11, No. 6, 1989, pp. 600-610.

Shapiro, L.G. and R.M. Haralick, "A Metric for Comparing Relational Descriptions," *IEEE Trans. Pattern Analysis and Machine Intelligence,* Vol. 7, No. 1, 1985, pp. 90-94.

Shapiro, L.G. and H. Lu, "Accumulator-Based Inexact Matching Using Relational Summaries," *Machine Vision and Applications,* Vol. 3, No. 3, 1990, pp. 143-158.

Shashua, A. and S. Ullman, "Structural Saliency: The Detection of Globally Salient Structures Using a Locally Connected Network," *Proc. Second Int'l Conf. Computer Vision,* IEEE CS Press, Los Alamitos, Calif., 1988, pp. 321-327.

Sherman, D. and S. Peleg, "Stereo by Incremental Matching of Contours," *IEEE Trans. Pattern Analysis and Machine Intelligence,* Vol. 12, No. 11, 1990, pp. 1102-1106.

Shih, C-C. and R. Kasturi, "Extraction of Graphic Primitives from Images of Paper-based Drawings," *Machine Vision and Applications,* Vol. 2, 1989, pp. 103-113.

Shih, F.Y. and O.R. Mitchell, "Automated Fast Recognition and Location of Arbitrarily Shaped Objects by Image Morphology," *Proc. IEEE Conf. Computer Vision and Pattern Recognition,* IEEE CS Press, Los Alamitos, Calif., 1988, pp. 774-789.

Sinha, D. and C.R. Giardina, "Discrete Black and White Object Recognition via Morphological Functions," *IEEE Trans. Pattern Analysis and Machine Intelligence,* Vol. 12, No. 2, 1990, pp. 275-293.

Sinha, S.S. and B.G. Schunck, "Discontinuity Preserving Surface Reconstruction," *Proc. IEEE Conf. Computer Vision and Pattern Recognition,* IEEE CS Press, Los Alamitos, Calif., 1989, pp. 229-234.

Sitaraman, R. and A. Rosenfeld, "Probabilistic Analysis of Two Stage Matching," *Pattern Recognition,* Vol. 22, 1989, pp. 331-343.

Skolnick, M.M., S. Kim, and R. O'Bara, "Morphological Algorithms for Computing Non-Planar Point Neighborhoods on Cellular Automata," *Proc. Second Int'l Conf. Computer Vision,* IEEE CS Press, Los Alamitos, Calif., 1988, pp. 106-111.

Staib, L.H. and J.S. Duncan, "Parametrically Deformable Contour Models," *Proc. IEEE Conf. Computer Vision and Pattern Recognition,* IEEE CS Press, Los Alamitos, Calif., 1989, pp. 98-103.

Stark, L. and K.W. Bowyer, "Using Functional Features for 3-D Object Recognition," *Proc. SPIE/IEEE Applications of Artificial Intelligence Conf. VIII,* Vol. 1293, 1990, 212-223.

Stein, F. and G. Medioni, "Efficient Fast Two-Dimensional Object Recognition," *Proc. Tenth Int'l Conf. Pattern Recognition,* IEEE CS Press, Los Alamitos, Calif., 1990, pp. 13-17.

Stevens, K.A. and A. Brookes, "Detecting Structure by Symbolic Constructions on Tokens," *Computer Vision, Graphics and Image Processing,* Vol. 37, 1983, pp. 238-260.

Stockman, G., "Object Recognition and Localization via Pose Clustering," *Computer Vision, Graphics, and Image Processing,* Vol. 40, 1987, pp. 361-387.

Stockman, G., G. Lee, and S.-W. Chen, "Reconstruction Line Drawings from Wings: The Polygonal Case," *Proc. Third Int'l Conf. Computer Vision,* IEEE CS Press, Los Alamitos, Calif., 1990, pp. 526-529.

Svalbe, I.D., "Natural Representation for Straight Lines and the Hough Transform on Discrete Arrays," *IEEE Trans. Pattern Analysis and Machine Intelligence,* Vol. 11, No. 9, 1989, pp. 941-950.

Tanaka, H.T. and D.T.L. Lee, "Representing Surface Curvature Discontinuities on Curved Surfaces," *Proc. Third Int'l Conf. Computer Vision,* IEEE CS Press, Los Alamitos, Calif., 1990, pp. 304-308.

Tanaka, H.T., O. Kling, and D.T.L. Lee, "On Surface Curvature Computation from Level Set," *Proc. Tenth Int'l Conf. Pattern Recognition,* IEEE CS Press, Los Alamitos, Calif., 1990, pp. 155-160.

Tang, Y.Y. and C.Y. Suen, "Nonlinear Shape Restoration by Transformation Models," *Proc. Tenth Int'l Conf. Pattern Recognition,* IEEE CS Press, Los Alamitos, Calif., 1990, pp. 14-19.

Taubin, G., R.M. Bolle, and D.B. Cooper, "Representing and Comparing Shapes Using Shape Polynomials," *Proc. IEEE Conf. Computer Vision and Pattern Recognition,* IEEE CS Press, Los Alamitos, Calif., 1989, pp. 510-516.

Tehrani, S., T.E. Weymouth, and B.G. Schunck, "Interpolating Cubic Spline Contours by Minimizing Second Derivative Discontinuity," *Proc. Third Int'l Conf. Computer Vision,* IEEE CS Press, Los Alamitos, Calif., 1990, pp. 713-717.

Tenenbaum, J.M., M.A. Fischler, and H.G. Barrow, "Scene Modeling: A Structural Basis for Image Description," in *Image Modeling,* A. Rosenfeld, ed., Academic Press, New York, N.Y., 1980, pp. 371-389.

Tomita, F., Y. Shirai, and S. Tsuji, "Description of Texture by Structural Analysis," *IEEE Trans. Pattern Analysis and Machine Intelligence,* Vol. 4, No. 2, 1982, pp. 183-191.

Trivedi, M.M., et al., "Object Detection Based on Gray Level Cooccurrence," *Computer Vision, Graphics and Image Processing,* Vol. 28, 1984, pp. 199-219.

Truve, S., "Image Interpretation Using Multi-relational Grammars," *Proc. Third Int'l Conf. Computer Vision,* IEEE CS Press, Los Alamitos, Calif., 1990, pp. 146-155.

Tsotsos, J.K., "The Complexity of Perceptual Search Tasks," *Proc. Int'l Joint Conf. Artificial Intelligence,* Morgan Kaufmann Publishers, Inc., San Mateo, Calif., 1989, pp. 1571-1577.

Van Gool, L., J. Wagemans, and A.J. Oosterlinck, "Regularity Detection as a Strategy in Object Modeling and Recognition," *Proc. SPIE/IEEE Applications of Artificial Intelligence Conf. VII,* Vol. 1095, 1989, 138-149.

Van Gool, L., et al., "Similarity Extraction and Modelling," *Proc. Third Int'l Conf. Computer Vision,* IEEE CS Press, Los Alamitos, Calif., 1990, pp. 530-534.

Vermuri, B.C., A. Mitiche,, and J.K. Aggarwal, "Curvature-Based Representations of Objects from Range Data," *Image and Vision Computing,* Vol. 4, No. 2, 1986, pp. 107-114.

Verri, A. and T. Poggio, "Motion Field and Optical Flow: Qualitative Properties," *IEEE Trans. Pattern Analysis and Machine Intelligence,* Vol. 11, No. 5, 1989, pp. 490-498.

Vincent, L., "Graphs and Mathematical Morphology," *Signal Processing,* Vol. 16, 1989, pp. 365-388.

Vossepoel, A.M., J.P. Buys, and G. Koelewijn, "Skeletons from Chain-Coded Contours," *Proc. Tenth Int'l Conf. Pattern Recognition,* IEEE CS Press, Los Alamitos, Calif., 1990. pp. 70-73.

Walters, D., "Selection of Image Primitives for General-Purpose Visual Processing," *Computer Vision, Graphics and Image Processing,* Vol. 37, 1987, pp. 261-298.

Wang, Y.F., "Computation of Intrinsic Surface Properties with Structured Lighting," *Proc. SPIE/IEEE Applications of Artificial Intelligence Conf. VII,* Vol. 1095, 1989, 321-332.

Wang, Y.F. and P. Liang, "A New Method for Computing Intrinsic Surface Properties," *Proc. IEEE Conf. Computer Vision and Pattern Recognition,* IEEE CS Press, Los Alamitos, Calif., 1989, pp. 235-240.

Watson, L.T., T.J. Laffey, and R.M. Haralick, "Topographic Classification of Digital Intensity Surfaces Using Generalized Splines and the Discrete Cosine Transformation," *Computer Vision, Graphics and Image Processing,* Vol. 29, 1985, pp. 143-167.

Weiss, I., "Line Fitting in a Noisy Image," *IEEE Trans. Pattern Analysis and Machine Intelligence,* Vol. 11, No. 3, 1989, pp. 325-328.

Weng, J., "A Theory of Image Matching," *Proc. Third Int'l Conf. Computer Vision,* IEEE CS Press, Los Alamitos, Calif., 1990, pp. 200-209.

Whitten, G., "A Framework for Adaptive Scale Space Tracking Solutions to Problems in Computational Vision," *Proc. Third Int'l Conf. Computer Vision,* IEEE CS Press, Los Alamitos, Calif., 1990, pp. 210-221.

Williams, D.J. and M. Shah, "A Fast Algorithm for Active Contours," *Proc. Third Int'l Conf. Computer Vision,* IEEE CS Press, Los Alamitos, Calif., 1990, pp. 592-597.

Wilson, H.R. and W.A. Richards, "Mechanisms of Contour Curvature Discrimination," *J. Opt. Soc. Am. A,* Vol. 6, No. 1, 1989, pp. 106-115.

Wilson, R. and M. Spann, "Finite Prolate Spheroidal Sequences and their Applications II: Image Feature Description and Segmentation," *IEEE Trans. Pattern Analysis and Machine Intelligence,* Vol. 10, No. 2, 1988, pp. 193-203.

Yuen, H.K., J. Illingworth, and J. Kittler, "Detecting Partially Occluded Ellipses Using the Hough Transform," *Image and Vision Computing,* Vol. 7, 1989, pp. 31-37.

Yuen, H.K., et al., "Comparative Study of Hough Transform Methods for Circle Finding," *Image and Vision Computing,* Vol. 8, No. 1, 1990, pp. 71-77.

Yuille, A.L., D.S. Cohen, and P.W. Hallinan, "Feature Extraction from Faces Using Deformable Templates," *Proc. IEEE Conf. Computer Vision and Pattern Recognition,* IEEE CS Press, Los Alamitos, Calif., 1989, pp. 104-109.

Zhong, S. and S. Mallat, "Compact Image Representation from Multiscale Edges," *Proc. Third Int'l Conf. Computer Vision,* IEEE CS Press, Los Alamitos, Calif., 1990, pp. 522-525.

Zucker, S.W., A. Dobbins, and L. Iverson, "Two Stages of Curve Detection Suggest Two Styles of Visual Computation," *Neural Computation,* Vol. 1, No. 1, 1989, pp. 68-81.

Chapter 4: Constraint Exploitation and Shape Recovery
Selected Bibliography

Abbott, L.A. and N. Ahuja, "Surface Reconstruction by Dynamic Integration of Focus, Camera Vergence, and Stereo," *Proc. Second Int'l Conf. Computer Vision,* IEEE CS Press, Los Alamitos, Calif., 1988, pp. 532-543.

Abbott, L.A. and N. Ahuja, "Active Surface Reconstruction by Integrating Focus, Vergence, Stereo, and Camera Calibration," *Proc. Third Int'l Conf. Computer Vision,* IEEE CS Press, Los Alamitos, Calif., 1990, pp. 489-493.

Adorni, G., et al., "From Early Processing to Conceptual Reasoning: An Attempt to Fill the Gap," *Proc. Int'l Joint Conf. Artificial Intelligence,* Morgan Kaufmann Publishers, Inc., San Mateo, Calif., 1987, pp. 775-778.

Ahuja, N. and M. Tuceryan, "Extraction of Early Perceptual Structure in Dot Patterns: Integrating Regions, Boundary, and Component Gestalt," *Computer Vision, Graphics and Image Processing,* Vol. 48, 1989, pp. 304-356.

Aloimonos, J., "Shape from Texture," *Biological Cybernetics,* Vol. 58, No. 5, 1988, pp. 345-360.

Aloimonos, J., "Unifying Shading and Texture Through an Active Observer," *Proc. Royal Soc. Lond. B,* Vol. 238, 1989, pp. 25-37.

Aloimonos, J.Y. and A. Basu, "Combining Information in Low-Level Vision," *Proc. DARPA Image Understanding Workshop,* 1988, pp. 862-906.

Aloimonos, J.Y. and C. Brown, "Robust Computations of Intrinsic Images from Multiple Cues," *Advances in Computer Vision,* Erlbaum, Hillsdale, N.J., 1988, pp. 115-163.

Aloimonos, J.Y. and D. Shulman, *Integration of Visual Modules: An Extension of the Marr Paradigm,* Academic Press, Boston, Mass., 1989.

Aloimonos, J. and M. Swain, "Shape from Patterns: Regularization," *Int'l J. Computer Vision,* Vol. 2, 1988, pp. 171-187.

Amadasun, M. and R. King, "Textural Features Corresponding to Textural Properties," *IEEE Trans. Systems, Man, and Cybernetics,* Vol. 19, No. 12, 1989, pp. 1264-1274.

Amini, A.A., S. Tehrani, and T.E. Weymouth, "Using Dynamic Programming for Minimizing the Energy of Active Contours in the Presence of Hard Constraints," *Proc. Second Int'l Conf. Computer Vision,* IEEE CS Press, Los Alamitos, Calif., 1988, pp. 95-99.

Ayache, N. and O.D. Faugeras, "Building, Registering, and Fusing Noisy Visual Maps," *Proc. First Int'l Conf. Computer Vision,* IEEE CS Press, Los Alamitos, Calif., 1987, pp. 73-82.

Bajcsy, R. and L. Lieberman, "Texture Gradient as a Depth Cue," *Computer Graphics and Image Processing,* Vol. 5, No. 1, 1977, pp. 52-67.

Baldwin, R., et al., "Stereo Reconstruction Through Disparity Space," *IAPR Workshop on Machine Vision Applications,* 1990, pp. 143-146.

Barnard, S.T., "Interpreting Perspective Images," *Artificial Intelligence,* Vol. 21, 1983, pp. 435-462.

Barnard, S.T., "Choosing a Basis for Perceptual Space," *Computer Vision, Graphics and Image Processing,* Vol. 29, 1985, pp. 87-99.

Barnard, S.T., "Stochastic Stereo Matching Over Scale," *Int'l J. Computer Vision,* Vol. 3, No. 1, 1989, pp. 17-32.

Barnard, S.T. and M.A. Fischler, "Computational Stereo," *ACM Computing Surveys,* Vol. 14, No. 4, 1982, pp. 553-572.

Barrow, H.G. and J.M. Tenenbaum, "Computational Vision," *Proc. IEEE,* Vol. 69, No. 5, IEEE Press, New York, N.Y., 1981, pp. 572-595.

Bertero, M., T.A. Poggio, and V. Torre, "Ill-Posed Problems in Early Vision," *Proc. IEEE,* Vol. 76, No. 8, IEEE Press, New York, N.Y., 1988, pp. 869-889.

Binford, T.O., "Inferring Surfaces from Images," *Artificial Intelligence,* Vol. 17, 1981, pp. 205-244.

Blake, A., "Specular Stereo," *Proc. Int'l Joint Conf. Artificial Intelligence,* Morgan Kaufmann Publishers, Inc., San Mateo, Calif., 1985, pp. 973-976.

Blake, A., "Comparison of the Efficiency of Deterministic and Stochastic Algorithms for Visual Reconstruction," *IEEE Trans. Pattern Analysis and Machine Intelligence,* Vol. 11, No. 1, 1989, pp. 2-12.

Blake, A. and G. Brelstaff, "Geometry from Specularities," *Proc. Second Int'l Conf. Computer Vision,* IEEE CS Press, Los Alamitos, Calif., 1988, pp. 394-403.

Blostein, S.D. and T.S. Huang, "Quantization Errors in Stereo Triangulation," *Proc First Int'l Conf. Computer Vision,* IEEE CS Press, Los Alamitos, Calif., 1987, pp. 325-334.

Bodington, R., G.D. Sullivan, and K.D. Baker, "Consistent Labeling of Image Features Using an Assumption-Based Truth Maintenance System," *Image and Vision Computing,* Vol. 7, 1989, pp. 43-49.

Boult, T.E. and L.-H. Chen, "Synergistic Smooth Surface Stereo," *Proc. Second Int'l Conf. Computer Vision,* IEEE CS Press, Los Alamitos, Calif., 1988, pp. 118-122.

Boyer, K.L., D.M. Wuescher, and S. Sarkar, "Dynamic Edge Warping: Experiments in Disparity Estimation Under Weak Constraints," *Proc. Third Int'l Conf. Computer Vision,* IEEE CS Press, Los Alamitos, Calif., 1990, pp. 471-475.

Bozma, H.I. and J.S. Duncan, "Admissibility of Constraint Functions in Relaxation Labeling," *Proc. Second Int'l Conf. Computer Vision,* IEEE CS Press, Los Alamitos, Calif., 1988, pp. 328-332.

Brady, J.M., "Computational Approaches to Image Understanding," *ACM Computing Surveys,* Vol. 14, No. 1, 1982, pp. 3-71.

Brady, J.M. and B.K.P. Horn, "Rotationally Symmetric Operators for Surface Interpolation," *Computer Vision, Graphics and Image Processing,* Vol. 22, No. 3, 1983, pp. 36-61.

Brady, M. and A. Yuille, "An Extremum Principle for Shape from Contour," in *Vision, Brain, and Cooperative Computation,* M.A. Arbib and A.R. Hanson, eds., MIT Press, Cambridge, Mass., 1987.

Brint, A.T. and M. Brady, "Stereo Matching of Curves," *Image and Vision Computing,* Vol. 8, No.1, 1990, pp. 50-56.

Brockelbank, D.C. and Y.H. Yang, "An Experimental Investigation in the Use of Color in Computational Stereopsis," *IEEE Trans. Systems, Man, and Cybernetics,* Vol. 19, No. 6, 1989, pp. 1365-1383.

Brown, L.G. and H. Shvaytser, "Surface Orientation from Projective Foreshortening of Isotropic Texture Autocorrelation," *Proc. IEEE Conf. Computer Vision and Pattern Recognition,* IEEE CS Press, Los Alamitos, Calif., 1988, pp. 510-514.

Bruckstein, A.M., "On Shape from Shading," *Computer Vision, Graphics and Image Processing,* Vol. 44, 1988, pp. 139-154.

Bulthoff, H.H. and H.A. Mallot, "Integration of Depth Modules: Stereo and Shading," *J. Opt. Soc. Am. A,* Vol. 5, No. 10, 1988, pp. 1749-1758.

Cavanagh, P., "Reconstructing the Third Dimension: Interactions Between Color, Texture, Motion, Binocular Disparity, and Shape," *Computer Vision, Graphics and Image Processing,* Vol. 37, 1987, pp. 171-195.

Chou, P.B. and C.M. Brown, "The Theory and Practice of Bayesian Image Labeling," *Int'l J. Computer Vision,* Vol. 4, No. 3, 1990, pp. 185-210.

Clark, J.J. and A.L. Yuille, "Shape from Shading via the Fusion of Specular and Lambertian Image Components," *Proc. Tenth Int'l Conf. Pattern Recognition,* IEEE CS Press, Los Alamitos, Calif., 1990, pp. 88-92.

Cochran, S.D. and G. Medioni, "Accurate Surface Description from Binocular Stereo," *Proc. IEEE Workshop on Interpretation of 3-D Scenes,* IEEE CS Press, Los Alamitos, Calif., 1989, pp. 16-23.

Coleman Jr., E. North and R.C. Jain, "Obtaining 3-Dimensional Shape of Textured and Specular Surfaces Using Four-Source Photometry," *Computer Graphics and Image Processing,* Vol. 18, No. 4, 1982, pp. 309-328.

Cooper, D.B., Y.-P. Hung, and G. Taubin, "A New Model-Based Stereo Approach for 3-D Surface Reconstruction," *Proc. Second Int'l Conf. Computer Vision,* IEEE CS Press, Los Alamitos, Calif., 1988, pp. 74-83.

Cross, G.R. and A.K. Jain, "Markov Random Field Texture Models," *IEEE Trans. Pattern Analysis and Machine Intelligence,* Vol. 5, No. 1, 1983, pp. 25-39.

Darrell, T. and K. Wohn, "Pyramid Based Depth from Focus," *Proc. IEEE Conf. Computer Vision and Pattern Recognition,* IEEE CS Press, Los Alamitos, Calif., 1988, pp. 504-509.

Das, S. and N. Ahuja, "Integrating Multiresolution Image Acquisition and Coarse-to-Fine Surface Reconstruction from Stereo," *Proc. IEEE Workshop on Interpretation of 3-D Scenes,* IEEE CS Press, Los Alamitos, Calif., 1989, pp. 9-15.

Das, S. and N. Ahuja, "Multiresolution Image Acquisition and Surface Reconstruction," *Proc. Third Int'l Conf. Computer Vision,* IEEE CS Press, Los Alamitos, Calif., 1990, pp. 485-488.

Davis, L.S. and T.C. Henderson, "Hierarchical Constraint Processes for Shape Analysis," *IEEE Trans. Pattern Analysis and Machine Intelligence,* Vol. 3, No. 3, 1981, pp. 265-277.

Davis, L.S. and A. Rosenfeld, "Cooperating Processes for Low-Level Vision: A Survey," *Artificial Intelligence,* Vol. 17, 1981, pp. 245-264.

Dhond, U.R. and J.K. Aggarwal, "Structure from Stereo - A Review," *IEEE Trans. Systems, Man, and Cybernetics,* Vol. 19, No. 6, 1989, pp. 1489-1510.

Draper, S.W., "The Use of Gradient and Dual Space in Line-Drawing Interpretation," *Artificial Intelligence,* Vol. 17, 1981, pp. 461-508.

Draper, B.A., et al., "The Schema System," *Int'l J. Computer Vision,* Vol. 2, No. 3, 1989, pp. 209-250.

Duncan, J.S. and W. Frei, "Relaxation Labeling Using Continuous Label Sets," *Pattern Recognition Letters,* Vol. 9, No. 1, 1989, pp. 7-37.

Durrant-Whyte, H.F., "Consistent Integration and Propagation of Disparate Sensor Observations," *Int'l J. Robotics Research,* Vol. 6, No. 3, 1987, pp. 3-24.

Eastman, R.D. and A.M. Waxman, "Using Disparity Functionals for Stereo Correspondence and Surface Reconstruction," *Computer Vision, Graphics and Image Processing,* Vol. 39, No. 1, 1987, pp. 73-101.

Eklundh, J.O., H. Yamamoto, and A. Rosenfeld, "A Relaxation Method for Multispectral Pixel Classification," *IEEE Trans. Pattern Analysis and Machine Intelligence,* Vol. 2, No. 1, 1980, pp. 72-75.

Ferrie, F.P. and M.D. Levine, "Where and Why Local Shading Analysis Works," *IEEE Trans. Pattern Analysis and Machine Intelligence,* Vol. 11, No. 2, 1989, pp. 198-206.

Forsyth, D. and A. Zisserman, "Shape from Shading in the Light of Mutual Illumination," *Image and Vision Computing,* Vol. 8, No. 1, 1990, pp. 42-49.

Frankot, R.T. and R. Chellappa, "A Method for Enforcing Integrability in Shape from Shading Algorithms," *IEEE Trans. Pattern Analysis and Machine Intelligence,* Vol. 10, No. 4, 1988, pp. 439-451.

Gagalowicz, A., "Collaboration Between Computer Graphics and Computer Vision," *Proc. Third Int'l Conf. Computer Vision,* IEEE CS Press, Los Alamitos, Calif., 1990, pp. 733-739.

Gamble, E., et al., "Integration of Vision Modules and Labeling of Surface Discontinuities," *IEEE Trans. Systems, Man, and Cybernetics,* Vol. 19, No. 6, 1989, pp. 1576-1580.

Garding, J., "Shape from Texture and Contour by Weak Isotropy," *Proc. Tenth Int'l Conf. Pattern Recognition,* IEEE CS Press, Los Alamitos, Calif., 1990, pp. 324-330.

Gennert, M.A., "Brightness-Based Stereo Matching," *Proc. Second Int'l Conf. Computer Vision,* IEEE CS Press, Los Alamitos, Calif., 1988, pp. 139-143.

Giblin, P. and R. Weiss, "Reconstruction of Surfaces from Profiles," *Proc. First Int'l Conf. Computer Vision,* IEEE CS Press, Los Alamitos, Calif., 1987, pp. 136-144.

Gibson, J.J., *The Perception of the Visual World,* Riverside Press, Cambridge, Mass., 1950.

Govindaraju, V., S.N. Srihari, and D.B. Sher, "A Computational Model for Face Location," *Proc. Third Int'l Conf. Computer Vision,* IEEE CS Press, Los Alamitos, Calif., 1990, pp. 718-721.

Granlund, G.H. and H. Knutsson, "Contrast of Structured and Homogeneous Representations," in *Physical and Biological Processing of Images,* O.J. Braddick and A.C. Sleigh, eds., Springer-Verlag, Berlin, 1983, pp. 1-24.

Grimson, W.E.L., "An Implementation of a Computational Theory of Visual Surface Interpolation," *Computer Graphics and Image Processing,* Vol. 22, No. 1, 1983, pp. 39-69.

Grimson, W.E.L., "Surface Consistency Constraints in Vision," *Computer Vision, Graphics and Image Processing,* Vol. 24, No. 1, 1983, pp. 28-51.

Grimson, W.E.L., "Computational Experiments with a Feature Based Stereo Algorithm," *IEEE Trans. Pattern Analysis and Machine Intelligence,* Vol. 7, No. 1, 1985, pp. 17-34.

Grimson, W.E.L., "The Combinatorics of Local Constraints in Model-Based Recognition and Localization from Sparse Data," *J. Assoc. Computing Machinery,* Vol. 33, No. 4, 1986, pp. 658-686.

Grimson, W.E.L., "The Combinatorics of Object Recognition in Clustered Environments Using Constrained Search," *Proc. Second Int'l Conf. Computer Vision*, IEEE CS Press, Los Alamitos, Calif., 1988, pp. 218-227.

Griswold, N.C. and C.P. Yeh, "A New Stereo Vision Model Based Upon the Binocular Fusion Concept," *Computer Vision, Graphics and Image Processing*, Vol. 41, 1988, pp. 153-171.

Grossberg, S. and E. Mingolla, "Neural Dynamics of Surface Perception: Boundary Webs, Illuminants, and Shape-from-Shading," *Computer Vision, Graphics and Image Processing*, Vol. 37, 1987, pp. 116-165.

Grosso, E., G. Sandini, and M. Tistarelli, "3-D Object Reconstruction Using Stereo and Motion," *IEEE Trans. Systems, Man, and Cybernetics*, Vol. 19, No. 6, 1989, pp. 1465-1476.

Gusgen, H.W. and J. Hertzberg, "Some Fundamental Properties of Local Constraint Propagation," *Artificial Intelligence*, Vol. 36, 1988, pp. 237-247.

Haralick, R., "Monocular Vision Using Inverse Perspective Projection Geometry: Analytic Relations," *Proc. IEEE Conf. Computer Vision and Pattern Recognition*, IEEE CS Press, Los Alamitos, Calif., 1989, pp. 370-378.

Haralick, R.M. and L.G. Shapiro, "The Consistent Labeling Problem: Part I," *IEEE Trans. Pattern Analysis and Machine Intelligence*, Vol. 1, No. 2, 1979, pp. 173-184.

Haralick, R.M. and L.G. Shapiro, "The Consistent Labeling Problem: Part II," *IEEE Trans. Pattern Analysis and Machine Intelligence*, Vol. 2, No. 3, 1980, pp. 193-203.

Harmon, S.Y., G.L. Bianchini, and B.E. Pinz, "Sensor Fusion Through a Distributed Blackboard," *Proc. IEEE Int'l Conf. Robotics and Automation*, IEEE CS Press, Los Alamitos, Calif., 1986, pp. 2002-2011.

Hartt, K. and M. Carlotto, "A Method for Shape-from-Shading Using Multiple Images Acquired Under Different Viewing and Lighting Conditions," *Proc. IEEE Conf. Computer Vision and Pattern Recognition*, IEEE CS Press, Los Alamitos, Calif., 1989, pp. 53-60.

Healey, G. and T.O. Binford, "Local Shape from Specularity," *Computer Vision, Graphics and Image Processing*, Vol. 42, No. 1, 1988, pp. 62-86.

Hoff, W. and N. Ahuja, "Surfaces from Stereo: Integrating Feature Matching, Disparity Estimation, and Contour Detection," *IEEE Trans. Pattern Analysis and Machine Intelligence*, Vol. 11, No. 2, 1989, pp. 121-136.

Horaud, R., "Spatial Object Perception from an Image," *Proc. Int'l Joint Conf. Artificial Intelligence*, Morgan Kaufmann Publishers, Inc, San Mateo, Calif., 1985, pp. 1116-1119.

Horaud, R. and T. Skordas, "Stereo Correspondence Through Feature Grouping and Maximal Cliques," *IEEE Trans. Pattern Analysis and Machine Intelligence*, Vol. 11, No. 11, 1989, pp. 1168-1180.

Horn, B.K.P., "Hill Shading and the Reflectance Map," *Proc. IEEE*, Vol. 69, No. 1, IEEE Press, New York, N.Y., 1981, pp. 14-47.

Horn, B.K.P., "Closed-Form Solution of Absolute Orientation Using Unit Quaternions," *J. Opt. Soc. Am. A*, Vol. 4, No. 4, 1987, pp. 629-642.

Horn, B.K.P., "Relative Orientation," *Int'l J. Computer Vision*, Vol. 4, no. 1, 1989, pp. 59-77.

Horn, B.K.P., "Height and Gradient from Shading," *Int'l J. Computer Vision*, Vol. 5, No. 1, 1990, pp. 37-75.

Horn, B.K.P. and M.J. Brooks, "The Variational Approach to Shape from Shading," *Computer Vision, Graphics and Image Processing*, Vol. 33, 1986, pp. 174-208.

Hu, G. and G. Stockman, "3-D Surface Solution Using Structured Light and Constraint Propagation," *IEEE Trans. Pattern Analysis and Machine Intelligence*, Vol. 11, No. 4, 1989, pp. 390-402.

Huffman, D.A., "Impossible Interpreting Pictures of Polyhedral Scenes," *Artificial Intelligence*, Vol. 4, 1973, pp. 121-137.

Hummel, R.A. and S.W. Zucker, "On the Foundations of Relaxation Labeling Processes," *IEEE Trans. Pattern Analysis and Machine Intelligence*, Vol. 5, No. 3, 1983, pp. 267-287.

Hutchinson, J., et al., "Computing Motion Using Analog and Binary Resistive Networks," *Computer*, Vol. 21, No. 3, 1988, pp. 52-63.

Ikeuchi, K., "Shape from Regular Patterns," *Artificial Intelligence*, Vol. 22, No. 1, 1984, pp. 49-75.

Ikeuchi, K., "Determining a Depth Map Using a Dual Photometric Stereo," *Int'l J. Robotics Research*, Vol. 6, No. 1, 1987, pp. 15-31.

Ikeuchi, K., "Determining Surface Orientation of Specular Surfaces by Using the Photometric Stereo Method," *IEEE Trans. Pattern Analysis and Machine Intelligence*, Vol. 3, No. 6, 1981, pp. 661-669.

Ikeuchi, K., et al., "Determining Grasp Configurations Using Photometric Stereo and the PRISM Binocular Stereo System," *Int'l J. Robotics Research*, Vol. 5, 1986, pp. 46-65.

Ishiguro, H., M. Yamamoto, and S. Tsuji, "Omni-directional Stereo for Making Global Map," *Proc. Third Int'l Conf. Computer Vision*, IEEE CS Press, Los Alamitos, Calif., 1990, pp. 540-547.

Iwahori, Y., H. Sugie, and N. Ishii, "Reconstructing Shape From Shading Images Under Point Light Source Illumination," *Proc. Tenth Int'l Conf. Pattern Recognition*, IEEE CS Press, Los Alamitos, Calif., 1990, pp. 83-87.

Jain, R.C., S. Bartlett, and N. O'Brien, "Motion Stereo Using Ego-Motion Complex Logarithmic Mapping," *IEEE Trans. Pattern Analysis and Machine Intelligence*, Vol. 9, No. 3, 1987, pp. 356-369.

Jamison, T.A. and R.J. Schalkoff, "Image Labeling: A Neural Network Approach," *Image and Vision Computing*, Vol. 6, 1988, pp. 203-214.

Jau, Y.C. and R.T. Chin, "Shape from Texture Using the Wigner Distribution," *Proc. IEEE Conf. Computer Vision and Pattern Recognition*, IEEE CS Press, Los Alamitos, Calif., 1988, pp. 515-523.

Jepson, A.D. and M.R.M. Jenkin, "The Fast Computation of Disparity from Phase Differences," *Proc. IEEE Conf. Computer Vision and Pattern Recognition*, IEEE CS Press, Los Alamitos, Calif. 1989, pp. 398-403.

Jou, J.Y. and A.C. Bovik, "Improved Initial Approximation and Intensity-Guided Discontinuity Detection in Visible-Surface Reconstruction," *Computer Vision, Graphics and Image Processing*, Vol. 47, 1989, pp. 292-326.

Kanade, T., "A Theory of Origami World," *Artificial Intelligence*, Vol. 13, Vol. 1-3, 1980, pp. 279-311.

Kanade, T., "Recovering of the Three-Dimensional Shape of an Object from a Single View," *Artificial Intelligence*, Vol. 17, 1981, pp. 409-460.

Kanade, T., "Geometrical Aspects of Interpreting Images as a Three-Dimensional Scene," *Proc. IEEE*, Vol. 71, No. 7, IEEE Press, New York, N.Y., 1983, pp. 789-802.

Kanade, T. and J.P. Kender, "Mapping Image Properties into Shape Constraints: Skewed Symmetry, Affine-Transformable Patterns, and the Shape-from-Texture Paradigm," in *Human and Machine Vision*, J. Beck, B. Hope, A. Rosenfeld, eds., Academic Press, New York, N.Y., 1983.

Kanatani, K., "Camera Rotation Invariance of Image Characteristics," *Computer Vision, Graphics and Image Processing*, Vol. 39, No. 3, 1987, pp. 328-354.

Kanatani, K., "Constraint on Length and Angle," *Computer Vision, Graphics and Image Processing*, Vol. 41, No. 1, 1988, pp. 28-42.

Kanatani, K., "Reconstruction of Consistent Shape from Inconsistent Data: Optimization of 2 1/2 D Sketches," *Int'l J. Computer Vision*, Vol. 3, No. 4, 1989, pp. 261-291.

Kass, M., "Linear Image Features in Stereopsis," *Int'l J. Computer Vision*, Vol. 1, 1988, pp. 357-368.

Kass, M. and A. Witkin, "Analyzing Oriented Patterns," *Computer Vision, Graphics and Image Processing*, Vol. 37, 1987, pp. 362-385.

Kayaalp, A., A.R. Rao, and R.C. Jain, "Scanning Electron Microscope-Based Stereo Analysis," *Machine Vision and Applications*, Vol. 3, No. 4, 1990, pp. 231-246.

Kehtarnavaz, N. and R.J.P. deFigueiredo, "A Framework for Surface Reconstruction from 3-D Contours," *Computer Vision, Graphics and Image Processing*, Vol. 42, No. 1, 1988, pp. 32-47.

Kender, J.R, *Shape from Texture*, PhD thesis, Carnegie-Mellon Univ., 1980.

Kender, J.R., "Surface Constraints from Linear Extents," *Proc. DARPA Image Understanding Workshop*, 1983, pp. 49-53.

Kim, B. and P. Burger, "Calculation of Surface Position and Orientation Using the Photometric Stereo Method," *Proc. IEEE Conf. Computer Vision and Pattern Recognition*, IEEE CS Press, Los Alamitos, Calif., 1988, pp. 492-497.

Kim, Y.C. and J.K. Aggarwal, "Positioning 3-D Objects Using Stereo Images," *IEEE Trans. Robotics and Automation*, Vol. 3, No. 4, 1987, pp. 361-373.

Kittler, J. and E.R. Hancock, "Combining Evidence in Probabilistic Relaxation," *Int'l. J. Pattern Recognition and Artificial Intelligence*, Vol. 3, No. 1, 1989, pp. 29-51.

Kittler, J. and J. Illingworth, "Relaxation Labeling Algorithms - A Review," *Image and Vision Computing*, Vol. 3, No. 4, 1985, pp. 206-216.

Koenderink, J.J. and A.J. van Doorn, "Photometric Invariants Related to Solid Shape," *Optica Acta*, Vol. 27, No. 7, 1980, pp. 981-996.

Koenderink, J.J. and A.J. van Doorn, "The Shape of Smooth Objects and the Way Contours End," *Perception*, Vol. 11, Pion Limited, London, U.K., 1982, pp. 129-137.

Krotkov, E.P., *Active Computer Vision by Cooperative Focus and Stereo*, Springer-Verlag, New York, N.Y., 1989.

Krotkov, E., E. Henriksen, and R. Kories, "Nonlinear Multiresolution: A Shape-from Shading Example," *IEEE Trans. Pattern Analysis and Machine Intelligence*, Vol. 12, No. 12, 1990, pp. 1206-1210.

Le Bras-Mehlman, et al., "How the Delaunay Triangulation Can Be Used for Representing Stereo Data," *Proc. Second Int'l Conf. Computer Vision*, IEEE CS Press, Los Alamitos, Calif., 1988, pp. 54-59.

Lee, D., "Algorithms for Shape from Shading and Occluding Boundaries," *Proc. IEEE Conf. Computer Vision and Pattern Recognition*, IEEE CS Press, Los Alamitos, Calif., 1988, pp. 478-485.

Lee, D., "Some Computational Aspects of Low-Level Computer Vision," *Proc. IEEE*, Vol. 76, No. 8, IEEE Press, New York, N.Y., 1988, pp. 890-898.

Lee, D. and T. Pavlidis, "One-Dimensional Regularization with Discontinuities," *IEEE Trans. Pattern Analysis and Machine Intelligence*, Vol. 10, No. 6, 1988, pp. 822-829.

Lee, S.J., R.M. Haralick, and L.G. Shapiro, "Understanding Objects with Curved Surfaces from a Single Perspective View of Boundaries," *Artificial Intelligence*, Vol. 26, 1985, pp. 145-169.

Li, S.Z., "Reconstruction without Discontinuities," *Proc. Third Int'l Conf. Computer Vision*, IEEE CS Press, Los Alamitos, Calif., 1990, pp. 709-712.

Liu, H.H., T.Y. Young, and A. Das, "A Multilevel Parallel Processing Approach to Scene Labeling," *IEEE Trans. Pattern Analysis and Machine Intelligence*, Vol. 10, No. 4, 1988, pp. 586-590.

Lucas, B.D. and T. Kanade, "Optical Navigation by the Method of Differences," *Proc. Int'l Joint Conf. Artificial Intelligence*, Morgan Kaufmann Publishers, Inc., San Mateo, Calif., 1985, pp. 981-984.

Luo, R.C., M.H. Lin, and R.S. Scherp, "Dynamic Multi-Sensor Data Fusion Systems for Intelligent Robots," *IEEE Trans. Robotics and Automation*, Vol. 4, No. 4, 1988, pp. 386-396.

Luo, W. and H. Matre, "Using Surface Model to Correct and Fit Disparity Data in Stereovision," *Proc. Tenth Int'l Conf. Pattern Recognition*, IEEE CS Press, Los Alamitos, Calif., 1990, pp. 60-64.

Mackworth, A.K., "Interpreting Pictures of Polyhedral Scenes," *Artificial Intelligence*, Vol. 4, No. 1, 1973, pp. 121-137.

Mackworth, A.K., "Consistency in Networks of Relations," *Artificial Intelligence*, Vol. 8, No. 1, 1977, pp. 121-137.

Mackworth, A.K. and E.C. Freuder, "The Complexity of Some Polynomial Network Consistency Algorithms for Constraint Satisfaction Problems," *Artificial Intelligence*, Vol. 25, No. 1, 1985, pp. 65-74.

Malik, J., "Interpreting Line Drawings of Curved Objects," *Int'l J. Computer Vision*, Vol. 1, 1987, pp. 73-103.

Malik, J. and D. Maydan, "Recovering Three-Dimensional Shape from a Single Image of Curved Objects," *IEEE Trans. Pattern Analysis and Machine Intelligence*, Vol. 11, No. 6, 1989, pp. 555-566.

Malik, J. and P. Perona, "Preattentive Texture Discrimination with Early Vision Mechanisms," *J. Opt. Soc. Am. A*, Vol. 7, No. 5, 1990, pp. 923-932.

March, R., "A Regularization Model for Stereo Vision with Controlled Continuity," *Pattern Recognition Letters*, Vol. 10, 1989, pp. 259-263.

Marinos, C. and A. Blake, "Shape from texture: The Homogeneity Hypothesis," *Proc. Third Int'l Conf. Computer Vision*, IEEE CS Press, Los Alamitos, Calif., 1990, pp. 350-353.

Marr, D. and T. Poggio, "Analysis of a Cooperative Stereo Algorithm," *Biological Cybernetics*, Vol. 28, 1978, pp. 223-239.

Marroquin, J., S. Mitter, and T. Poggio, "Probabilistic Solution of Ill-Posed Problems in Computational Vision," *J. American Statistical Assoc.*, Vol. 82, (397) 1987, pp. 76-89.

Matthies, L. and S.A. Shafer, "Error Modeling in Stereo Navigation," *IEEE Trans. Robotics and Automation*, Vol. 3, No. 3, 1987, pp. 239-248.

Mayhew, J.E.W. and J.P. Frisby, "Psychophysical and Computational Studies Towards a Theory of Human Stereopsis," *Artificial Intelligence*, Vol. 17, 1981, pp. 349-385.

McKeown Jr., D.M., "Building Knowledge-Based System for Detecting Man-Made Structures from Remotely Sensed Imagery," *Proc. Royal Soc. Lond. B*, Vol. A324, 1988, pp. 423-435.

Mingolla, E. and J.T. Todd, "Perception of Solid Shape from Shading," *Biological Cybernetics*, Vol. 53, 1986, pp. 137-151.

Mitiche, A. and J.K. Aggarwal, "Multiple Sensor Integration/Fusion Through Image Processing: A Review," *Optical Eng.*, Vol. 25, No. 3, 1986, pp. 379-386.

Moerdler, M.L., "Multiple Shape-from-Texture into Texture Analysis and Surface Segmentation," *Proc. Second Int'l Conf. Computer Vision*, IEEE CS Press, Los Alamitos, Calif., 1988, pp. 316-320.

Moerdler, M.L. and T.E. Boult, "The Integration of Information from Stereo and Multiple Shape-from-Texture Cues," *Proc. IEEE Conf. Computer Vision and Pattern Recognition*, IEEE CS Press, Los Alamitos, Calif., 1988, pp. 524-529.

Mohan, R., G. Medioni, and R. Nevatia, "Stereo Error Detection, Correction, and Evaluation," *IEEE Trans. Pattern Analysis and Machine Intelligence*, Vol. 11, No. 2, 1989, pp. 113-120.

Mulgaonkar, P.G., L.G. Shapiro, and R.M. Haralick, "Shape from Perspective: A Rule-Based Approach," *Computer Vision, Graphics and Image Processing*, Vol. 36, 1986, pp. 298-320.

Naeve, A. and J.-O. Eklundh, "On Projective Geometry and the Recovery of 3-D Structure," *Proc. First Int'l Conf. Computer Vision*, IEEE CS Press, Los Alamitos, Calif., 1987, pp. 128-135.

Naito, S. and A. Rosenfeld, "Shape from Random Planar Features," *Computer Vision, Graphics and Image Processing*, Vol. 42, No. 3, 1988, pp. 345-370.

Nalwa, V.S., "Line-Drawing Interpretation: Straight Lines and Conic Sections," *IEEE Trans. Pattern Analysis and Machine Intelligence*, Vol. 10, No. 4, 1988, pp. 514-529.

Nalwa, V.S., "Line-Drawing Interpretation: A Mathematical Framework," *Int'l J. Computer Vision*, Vol. 2, 1988, pp. 103-124.

Nalwa, V.S., "Line-Drawing Interpretation: Bilateral Symmetry," *IEEE Trans. Pattern Analysis and Machine Intelligence*, Vol. 11, No. 10, 1989, pp. 1117-1120.

Nayar, S.K., K. Ikeuchi, and T. Kanade, "Shape from Interreflections," *Proc. Third Int'l Conf. Computer Vision*, IEEE CS Press, Los Alamitos, Calif., 1990, pp. 2-11.

Nishihara, H.K., "Practical Real-Time Imaging Stereo Matcher," *Optical Eng.*, Vol. 23, 1984, pp. 536-545.

Ohta, Y., M. Watanabe, and K. Ikeda, "Improving Depth Map by Trinocular Stereo," *Proc. Eighth Int'l Conf. Pattern Recognition*, IEEE CS Press, Los Alamitos, Calif., 1986, pp. 519-521.

Oliensis, J., "Existence and Uniqueness in Shape from Shading," *Proc. Tenth Int'l Conf. Pattern Recognition*, IEEE CS Press, Los Alamitos, Calif., 1990, pp. 341-345.

Olsen, S.I., "Stereo Correspondence by Surface Reconstruction," *IEEE Trans. Pattern Analysis and Machine Intelligence*, Vol. 12, No. 3, 1990, pp. 309-314.

Olsen, T.J. and R.D. Potter, "Real-Time Vergence Control," *Proc. IEEE Conf. Computer Vision and Pattern Recognition*, IEEE CS Press, Los Alamitos, Calif., 1989, pp. 404-409.

Onn, R. and A. Bruckstein, "Integrability Disambiguates Surface Recovery in Two-Image Photometric Stereo," *Int'l J. Computer Vision*, Vol. 5, No. 1, 1990, pp. 105-113.

Parent, P. and S.W. Zucker, "Radial Projection: An Efficient Update Rule for Relaxation Labeling," *IEEE Trans. Pattern Analysis and Machine Intelligence*, Vol. 11, No. 8, 1989, pp. 886-889.

Park, J.-S. and J.T. Tou, "Highlight Separation and Surface Orientations for 3-D Specular Objects," *Proc. Tenth Int'l Conf. Pattern Recognition*, IEEE CS Press, Los Alamitos, Calif., 1990, pp. 331-335.

Penna, M.A., "A Shape from Shading Analysis for a Single Perspective Image of a Polyhedron," *IEEE Trans. Pattern Analysis and Machine Intelligence*, Vol. 11, No. 6, 1989, pp. 545-554.

Penna, M.A., "Local and Semi-Local Shape from Shading for a Single Perspective Image of a Smooth Object," *Computer Vision, Graphics and Image Processing*, Vol. 46, No. 3, 1989, pp. 346-366.

Pentland, A.P., "Local Shading Analysis," *IEEE Trans. Pattern Analysis and Machine Intelligence*, Vol. 6, No. 2, 1984, pp. 170-187.

Pentland, A.P., "Shading into Texture," *Artificial Intelligence*, Vol. 29, No. 2, 1986, pp. 147-170.

Pentland, A.P., "Shape Information from Shading: A Theory About Human Perception," *Proc. Second Int'l Conf. Computer Vision*, IEEE CS Press, Los Alamitos, Calif., 1988, pp. 404-413.

Pentland, A.P., "A Possible Neural Mechanism for Computing Shape from Shading," *Neural Computation*, Vol. 1, No. 2, 1989, pp. 208-217.

Poggio, T., V. Torre, and C. Koch, "Computational Vision and Regularization Theory," *Nature*, Vol. 317, No. 26, 1985, pp. 314-319.

Pong, T.C. and B.G. Kaiser, "A Hierarchical Approach to the Correspondence Problem," *IEEE Trans. Systems, Man, and Cybernetics*, Vol. 19, 1989, pp. 271-276.

Pong, T.C., R.M. Haralick, and L.G. Shapiro, "Matching Topographic Structures in Stereo Vision," *Pattern Recognition Letters*, Vol. 9, 1989, pp. 127-136.

Porrill, J., S.B. Pollard, and J.E.W. Mayhew, "Optimal Combination of Multiple Sensors Including Stereo Vision," *Image and Vision Computing*, Vol. 5, 1987, pp. 174-180.

Price, K.E., "Relaxation Matching Techniques: A Comparison," *IEEE Trans. Pattern Analysis and Machine Intelligence*, Vol. 7, No. 5, 1985, pp. 617-623.

Quam, L.H., "Hierarchical Warp Stereo," *Proc. DARPA Image Understanding Workshop*, 1984, pp. 149-155.

Quan, L. and R. Mohr, "Matching Perspective Images Using Geometric Constraints and Perceptual Grouping," *Proc. Second Int'l Conf. Computer Vision*, IEEE CS Press, Los Alamitos, Calif., 1988, pp. 679-684.

Rao, A.R. and B.G. Schunck, "Computing Oriented Texture Fields," *Proc. IEEE Conf. Computer Vision and Pattern Recognition,* IEEE CS Press, Los Alamitos, Calif., 1989, pp. 61-69.

Rao, A.R. and R.C. Jain, "Analyzing Oriented Textures Through Phase Portraits," *Proc. Tenth Int'l Conf. Pattern Recognition,* IEEE CS Press, Los Alamitos, Calif., 1990, pp. 336-340.

Richards, W. and D.D. Hoffman, "Codon Constraints on Closed 2D Shapes," *Computer Vision, Graphics and Image Processing,* Vol. 31, No. 3, 1985, pp. 265-281.

Richards, W.A., J.J. Koenderink, and D.D. Hoffman, "Inferring Three-Dimensional Shapes from Two-Dimensional Silhouettes," *J. Opt. Soc. Am. A,* Vol. 4, No. 7, 1987, pp. 1168-1175.

Roan, S.J., J.K. Aggarwal, and W.N. Martin, "Multiple Resolution Imagery and Texture Analysis," *Pattern Recognition,* Vol. 20, No. 1, 1987, pp. 17-31.

Ron, G. and S. Peleg, "Multiresolution Shape from Shading," *Proc. IEEE Conf. Computer Vision and Pattern Recognition,* IEEE CS Press, Los Alamitos, Calif., 1989, pp. 350-355.

Samal, A. and T. Henderson, "Parallel Split-Level Relaxation," *Int'l J. Pattern Recognition and Artificial Intelligence,* Vol. 2, 1988, pp. 425-442.

Sato, H., S.K. Nayar, and K. Ikeuchi, "Extracting Shape and Reflectance of Glossy Surfaces by Using 3-D Photometric Sampling Method," *IAPR Workshop on Machine Vision Applications,* 1990, pp. 133-136.

Saund, E., "Representation and the Dimensions of Shape Deformation," *Proc. Third Int'l Conf. Computer Vision,* IEEE CS Press, Los Alamitos, Calif., 1990, pp. 684-689.

Shafer, S.A. and T. Kanade, "Using Shadows in Finding Surface Orientations," *Computer Vision, Graphics and Image Processing,* Vol. 22, 1983, pp. 145-176.

Shafer, S.A., T. Kanade, and J. Kender, "Gradient Space Under Orthography and Perspective," *Computer Vision, Graphics and Image Processing,* Vol. 24, 1983, pp. 182-199.

Shah, Y.C., R. Chapman, and R.B. Mahani, "A New Technique to Extract Range Information from Stereo Images," *IEEE Trans. Pattern Analysis and Machine Intelligence,* Vol. 11, No. 7, 1989, pp. 768-773.

Shakunaga, T. and H. Kaneko, "Perspective Angle Transform: Principle of Shape from Angles," *Int'l J. Computer Vision,* Vol. 3, No. 3, 1989, pp. 239-254.

Shao, M., T. Simchony, and R. Chellappa, "New Algorithms for Reconstruction of a 3-D Depth Map from One or More Images," *Proc. IEEE Conf. Computer Vision and Pattern Recognition,* IEEE CS Press, Los Alamitos, Calif., 1988, pp. 530-535.

Shapira, R., "The Use of Objects Faces in Interpreting Line Drawings," *IEEE Trans. Pattern Analysis and Machine Intelligence,* Vol. 6, No. 6, 1984, pp. 789-794.

Shapira, R., "More About Polyhedra - Interpretation Through Constructions in the Image Plane," *IEEE Trans. Pattern Analysis and Machine Intelligence,* Vol. 7, No. 1, 1985, pp. 1-16.

Sherman, D. and S. Peleg, "Stereo by Incremental Matching of Contours," *IEEE Trans. Pattern Analysis and Machine Intelligence,* Vol. 12, No. 11, 1990, pp. 1102-1106.

Shrikhande, N. and G. Stockman, "Surface Orientation from a Projected Grid," *IEEE Trans. Pattern Analysis and Machine Intelligence,* Vol. 11, No. 6, 1988, pp. 650-655.

Silverman, J.F. and D.B. Cooper, "Bayesian Clustering for Unsupervised Estimation of Surface and Texture Models," *IEEE Trans. Pattern Analysis and Machine Intelligence,* Vol. 10, No. 4, 1988, pp. 482-495.

Skifstad, K. and R.C. Jain, "Range Estimation from Intensity Gradient Analysis," *Machine Vision and Applications,* Vol. 2, No. 1, 1989, pp. 81-102.

Smith, G.B., "Stereo Integral Equations," *Proc. Nat'l Conf. Artificial Intelligence,* MIT Press, Cambridge, Mass., 1986, pp. 689-694.

Stevens, K.A., "The Visual Interpretation of Surface Contours," *Artificial Intelligence,* Vol. 17, No. 1, 1981, pp. 47-73.

Stevens, K.A. and A. Brookes, "Depth Reconstruction from Stereopsis," *Proc. First Int'l Conf. Computer Vision,* IEEE CS Press, Los Alamitos, Calif., 1987, pp. 682-686.

Stevens, K. A. and A. Brookes, "Integrating Stereopsis with Monocular Interpretations of Planar Surfaces," *Vision Research,* Vol. 28, No. 3, 1988, pp. 371-386.

Stevenson, R.L. and E.J. Delp, "Invariant Reconstruction of Visual Surfaces," *Proc. IEEE Workshop on Interpretation of 3-D Scenes,* IEEE CS Press, Los Alamitos, Calif., 1989, pp. 131-137.

Stevenson, R.L. and E.J. Delp, "Viewpoint Invariant Recovery of Visual Surfaces from Sparse Data," *Proc. Third Int'l Conf. Computer Vision,* IEEE CS Press, Los Alamitos, Calif., 1990, pp. 309-312.

Stewart, C.V. and C.R. Dyer, "The Trinocular General Support Algorithm: A Three-Camera Stereo Algorithm for Overcoming Binocular Matching Errors," *Proc. Second Int'l Conf. Computer Vision,* IEEE CS Press, Los Alamitos, Calif., 1988, pp. 134-138.

Strat, T.M. and M.A. Fischler, "One-Eyed Stereo: A General Approach to Modeling Scene Geometry," *IEEE Trans. Pattern Analysis and Machine Intelligence,* Vol. 8, No. 6, 1986, pp. 730-741.

Subbarao, M., "Parallel Depth Recovery by Changing Camera Parameters," *Proc. Second Int'l Conf. Computer Vision,* IEEE CS Press, Los Alamitos, Calif., 1988, pp. 149-155.

Subirana, B., S. Vilanova, and J. Brian, "Curved Inertia Frames and the Skeleton Sketch: Finding Salient Frames of Reference," *Proc. Third Int'l Conf. Computer Vision,* IEEE CS Press, Los Alamitos, Calif., 1990, pp. 702-708.

Sugihara, K., "Mathematical Structures of Line Drawings of Polyhedrons - Toward Man-Machine Communication by Means of Line Drawings," *IEEE Trans. Pattern Analysis and Machine Intelligence,* Vol. 4, No. 5, 1982, pp. 458-469.

Sugihara, K., "An Algebraic Approach to Shape-from-Image Problems," *Artificial Intelligence,* Vol. 23, No. 1, 1984, pp. 59-95.

Tagare, H.D. and R.J.P. deFigueiredo, "A Theory of Photometric Stereo for General Class of Reflectance Maps," *Proc. IEEE Conf. Computer Vision and Pattern Recognition,* IEEE CS Press, Los Alamitos, Calif., 1989, pp. 38-45.

Tagare, H.D. and R.J.P. de Figueiredo, "Simultaneous Estimation of Shape and Reflectance Maps from Photometric Stereo," *Proc. Third Int'l Conf. Computer Vision,* IEEE CS Press, Los Alamitos, Calif., 1990, pp. 340-343.

Terzopoulos, D., "Multilevel Computational Processes for Visual Surface Reconstruction," *Computer Vision, Graphics and Image Processing,* Vol. 24, No. 1, 1983, pp. 52-96.

Terzopoulos, D., "Image Analysis Using Multigrid Relaxation Methods," *IEEE Trans. Pattern Analysis and Machine Intelligence,* Vol. 8, No. 2, 1986, pp. 129-139.

Terzopoulos, D., "Regularization of Inverse Visual Problems Involving Discontinuities," *IEEE Trans. Pattern Analysis and Machine Intelligence,* Vol. 8, No. 4, 1986, pp. 413-424.

Terzopoulos, D., "The Computation of Visible Surface Representations," *IEEE Trans. Pattern Analysis and Machine Intelligence,* Vol. 10, No. 4, 1988, pp. 417-438.

Terzopoulos, D. and K. Waters, "Analysis of Facial Images Using Physical and Anatomical Models," *Proc. Third Int'l Conf. Computer Vision,* IEEE CS Press, Los Alamitos, Calif., 1990, pp. 727-732.

Terzopoulos, D. and A. Witkin, "Physically Based Models with Rigid and Deformable Components," *IEEE Computer Graphics and Applications,* Vol. 8, No. 6, 1988, pp. 41-51.

Terzopoulos, D., A. Witkin, and M. Kass, "Symmetry-Seeking Models and 3-D Object Reconstruction," *Int'l J. Computer Vision,* Vol. 1, No. 3, 1987, pp. 211-221.

Thirion, E. and L. Quan, "Geometrical Learning from Multiple Stereo Views Through Monocular Based Feature Grouping," *Proc. Third Int'l Conf. Computer Vision,* IEEE CS Press, Los Alamitos, Calif., 1990, pp. 481-484.

Tirumalai, A.P., B.G. Schunck, and R.C. Jain, "Dynamic Stereo with Self-Calibration," *Proc. Third Int'l Conf. Computer Vision,* IEEE CS Press, Los Alamitos, Calif., 1990, pp. 466-470.

Treisman, A., "Preattentive Processing in Vision," *Computer Vision, Graphics and Image Processing,* Vol. 31, No. 2, 1985, pp. 156-177.

Tsotsos, J.K., "A Complexity Level Analysis of Immediate Vision," *Int'l J. Computer Vision,* Vol. 1, 1988, pp. 303-320.

Ullman, S., "Visual Routines," *Cognition,* Vol. 18, 1984, pp. 97-159.

Ulupinar, F. and R. Nevatia, "Using Symmetries for Analysis for Shape from Contours," *Proc. Second Int'l Conf. Computer Vision,* IEEE CS Press, Los Alamitos, Calif., 1988, pp. 414-426.

Ulupinar, F. and R. Nevatia, "Inferring Shape from Contour for Curved Surfaces," *Proc. Tenth Int'l Conf. Pattern Recognition,* IEEE CS Press, Los Alamitos, Calif., 1990, pp. 147-154.

Ulupinar, F. and R. Nevatia, "Shape from Contour: Straight Homogeneous Generalized Cones," *Proc. Third Int'l Conf. Computer Vision,* IEEE CS Press, Los Alamitos, Calif., 1990, pp. 582-586.

Vaillant, R. and O.D. Faugeras, "Using Occluding Contours for Recovering Shape Properties of Objects," *Proc. IEEE Workshop on Interpretation of 3-D Scenes,* IEEE CS Press, Los Alamitos, Calif., 1989, pp. 26-32.

Van Gool, L., P. Dewaele, and O. Oosterlinck, "Texture Analysis Anno 1983," *Computer Vision, Graphics, and Image Processing,* Vol. 29, 1985, pp. 336-357.

Verri, A. and A. Yuille, "Some Perspective Projection Invariants," *J. Opt. Soc. Am. A,* Vol. 5, No. 3, 1988, pp. 426-431.

Walker, E.L. and M. Herman, "Geometric Reasoning for Constructing 3-D Scene Descriptions from Images," *Artificial Intelligence,* Vol. 37, 1988, pp. 275-290.

Waltz, D., "Understanding Line Drawing of Scenes with Shadows," in *The Psychology of Computer Vision,* P. H. Winston, ed., McGraw-Hill, New York, N.Y., 1975.

Wang, Y.F. and J.K. Aggarwal, "Surface Reconstruction and Representation of 3-D Scenes," *Pattern Recognition,* Vol. 19, No. 3, 1986, pp. 197-207.

Wang, Y.-F. and J.-F. Wang, "Surface Reconstruction Using Deformable Models with Interior and Boundary Constraints," *Proc. Third Int'l Conf. Computer Vision,* IEEE CS Press, Los Alamitos, Calif., 1990, pp. 300-303.

Wang, Y.F., A. Mitiche, and J.K. Aggarwal, "Computation of Surface Orientation and Structure of Objects Using Grid Coding," *IEEE Trans. Pattern Analysis and Machine Intelligence,* Vol. 9, No. 1, 1987, pp. 129-137.

Watanabe, M. and Y. Ohta, "Cooperative Integration of Multiple Stereo Algorithms," *Proc. Third Int'l Conf. Computer Vision,* IEEE CS Press, Los Alamitos, Calif., 1990, pp. 476-480.

Weinshall, D., "Application of Qualitative Depth and Shape from Stereo," *Proc. Second Int'l Conf. Computer Vision,* IEEE CS Press, Los Alamitos, Calif., 1988, pp. 144-148.

Weymouth, T.E. and S. Moezzi, "Wide Base-Line Dynamic Stereo: Approximation and Refinement," *Proc. IEEE Conf. Computer Vision and Pattern Recognition,* IEEE CS Press, Los Alamitos, Calif., 1988, pp. 183-188.

Whaite, P. and E.P. Ferrie, "From Uncertainty to Visual Exploration," *Proc. Third Int'l Conf. Computer Vision,* IEEE CS Press, Los Alamitos, Calif., 1990, pp. 690-697.

Wildes, R.P., "An Analysis of Stereo Disparity for the Recovery of Three-Dimensional Scene Geometry," *Proc. IEEE Workshop on Interpretation of 3-D Scenes,* IEEE CS Press, Los Alamitos, Calif., 1989, pp. 2-8.

Witkin, A.P., "Recovering Surface Shape and Orientation from Texture," *Artificial Intelligence,* Vol. 17, No. 1, 1981, pp. 17-45.

Witkin, A.P. and J.M. Tenenbaum, "On the Role of Structure in Vision," in *Human and Machine Vision,* J. Beck, B. Hope, and A. Rosenfeld, eds., Academic Press, New York, N.Y., 1983, pp. 481-543,

Wolff, L.B., "Shape Understanding from Lambertian Photometric Flow Fields," *Proc. IEEE Conf. Computer Vision and Pattern Recognition,* IEEE CS Press, Los Alamitos, Calif., 1989, pp. 46-52.

Wolff, L.B., "Using Polarization to Separate Reflection Components," *Proc. IEEE Conf. Computer Vision and Pattern Recognition,* IEEE CS Press, Los Alamitos, Calif., 1989, pp. 363-369.

Wolff, L.B., "A Photometric Invariant and Shape Constraints at Parabolic Points," *Proc. Third Int'l Conf. Computer Vision,* IEEE CS Press, Los Alamitos, Calif., 1990, pp. 344-349.

Wolff, L.B. and T.E. Boult, "Polarization/Radiometric Based Material Classification," *Proc. IEEE Conf. Computer Vision and Pattern Recognition,* IEEE CS Press, Los Alamitos, Calif., 1989, pp. 387-396.

Wolff, L.B. and T.E. Boult, "Using Line Correspondence Stereo to Measure Surface Orientation," *Proc. Int'l Joint Conf. Artificial Intelligence,* Morgan Kaufmann Publishers, Inc., San Mateo, Calif., 1989, pp. 1655-1660.

Woodham, R.J., "Analyzing Images of Curved Surfaces," *Artificial Intelligence,* Vol. 17, 1981, pp. 117-140.

Worrall, A.D., K.D. Baker, and G.D. Sullivan, "Roll Angle Consistency Constraints," *Image and Vision Computing,* Vol. 8 , No. 1, 1990, pp. 78-84.

Xu, J. and Y.-H. Yang, "Generalized Multidimensional Orthogonal Polynomials with Applications to Shape Analysis," *IEEE Trans. Pattern Analysis and Machine Intelligence,* Vol. 12, No. 9, 1990, pp. 906-913.

Yachida, M., Y. Kitamura, and M. Kimachi, "Trinocular Vision: New Approach for Correspondence Problem," *Proc. Eighth Int'l Conf. Pattern Recognition,* IEEE CS Press, Los Alamitos, Calif., 1986, pp. 1041-1044.

Zheng, Y., et al., "SWITCHER: A Stereo Algorithm for Ground Plane Obstacle Detection," *Image and Vision Computing,* Vol. 8, 1990, pp. 57-62.

Zhuang, X., R.M. Haralick, and H. Joo, "A Simplex-Like Algorithm for the Relaxation Labeling Process," *IEEE Trans. Pattern Analysis and Machine Intelligence,* Vol. 11, No. 12, 1989, pp. 1316-1321.

Zucker, S.W., "Early Orientation Selection: Tangent Fields and the Dimensionality of Their Support," *Computer Vision, Graphics and Image Processing,* Vol. 32, 1985, pp. 74-103.

Chapter 5: Three-Dimensional Object Recognition
Selected Bibliography

Acampora, A.S. and J.H. Winters, "Three-Dimensional Ultrasonic Vision for Robotic Applications," *IEEE Trans. Pattern Analysis and Machine Intelligence,* Vol. 11, No. 3, 1989, pp. 291-303.

Arbter, K., et al., "Application of Affine-Invariant Fourier Descriptors to Recognition of 3-D Objects," *IEEE Trans. Pattern Analysis and Machine Intelligence,* Vol. 12, No. 7, 1990, pp. 640-647.

Bajcsy, R. and F. Solina, "Three Dimensional Object Representation Revisited," *Proc. First Int'l Conf. Computer Vision,* IEEE CS Press, Los Alamitos, Calif., 1987, pp. 231-240.

Ballard, D.H. and D. Sabbah, "Viewer Independent Recognition," *IEEE Trans. Pattern Analysis and Machine Intelligence,* Vol. 5, No. 6, 1983, pp. 653-660.

Barr, A.H., "Superquadrics and Angle-Preserving Transformations," *IEEE Computer Graphics and Applications,* Vol. 1, No. 1, 1981, pp. 11-23.

Barr, A.H., "Global and Local Deformations of Solid Primitives," *ACM Computer Graphics, SIGGRAPH,* Vol. 18, No. 3, ACM, Inc., New York, N.Y., 1984, pp. 21-30.

Barry, M., et al., "A Multi-Level Geometric Reasoning System for Vision," *Artificial Intelligence,* Vol. 37, 1989, pp. 291-332.

Basri, R. and S. Ullman, "The Alignment of Objects with Smooth Surfaces," *Proc. Second Int'l Conf. Computer Vision,* IEEE CS Press, Los Alamitos, Calif., 1988, pp. 482-488.

Bastuscheck, C.M., et al., "Object Recognition by Three-Dimensional Curve Matching," *Int'l J. of Intelligence Systems,* Vol. 1, 1986, pp. 105-132.

Beausmans, J.M.H., D.D. Hoffman, and B.M. Bennett, "Description of Solid Shape and its Inference from Occluding Contours," *J. Opt. Soc. Am. A,* Vol. 4, No. 7, 1987, pp. 1155-1167.

Ben-Arie, J., "The Probabilistic Peaking Effect of Viewed Angles and Distances with Applications to 3-D Object Recognition," *IEEE Trans. Pattern Analysis and Machine Intelligence,* Vol. 12, No. 8, 1990, pp. 760-774.

Ben-Arie, J. and A. Zvi Meiri, "3-D Objects Recognition by Optimal Matching Search of Multinary Relations Graph," *Computer Vision, Graphics and Image Processing,* Vol. 37, 1987, pp. 345-361.

Besl, P.J., "Geometric Modeling and Computer Vision," *Proc. IEEE,* Vol. 76, No. 8, IEEE Press, New York, N.Y., 1988, pp. 936-958.

Besl, P. and R.C. Jain, "Invariant Surface Characteristics for 3-D Object Recognition in Range Images," *Computer Vision, Graphics and Image Processing,* Vol. 33, No. 1, 1986, pp. 33-79.

Bhanu, B. and C. Ho, "CAD-based 3-D Object Representation for Robot Vision," *Computer,* Vol. 20, No. 8, 1987, pp. 19-36.

Bhanu, B. and J.C. Ming, "Recognition of Occluded Objects: A Cluster-Structure Algorithm," *Pattern Recognition,* Vol. 20, No. 2, 1987, pp. 199-211.

Bhanu, B. and L.A. Nuttall, "Recognition of 3-D Objects in Range Images Using a Butterfly Multiprocessor," *Pattern Recognition,* Vol. 22, No. 1, 1989, pp. 49-64.

Biederman, I., "Human Image Understanding: Recent Research and Theory," *Computer Vision, Graphics and Image Processing,* Vol. 32, No. 1, 1985, pp. 29-73.

Biederman, I., "Recognition-by-Components: A Theory of Human Image Understanding," *Psychological Review,* Vol. 94, No. 2, 1987, pp. 115-147.

Binford, T.O., "Survey of Model-Based Image Analysis," *Int'l J. Robotics Research,* Vol. 1, No. 1, 1982, pp. 18-64.

Boissonnat, J., "Geometric Structures for Three-Dimensional Shape Representation," *ACM Trans. on Graphics,* Vol. 3, No. 4, 1984, pp. 266-286.

Bolle, R.M. and D.B. Cooper, "On Optimally Combining Pieces of Information, with Application to Estimating 3-D Complex-Object Position from Range Data," *IEEE Trans. Pattern Analysis and Machine Intelligence,* Vol. 8, No. 5, 1986, pp. 619-638.

Bolle, R.M., et al., "Active 3-D Object Models," *Proc. Third Int'l Conf. Computer Vision,* IEEE CS Press, Los Alamitos, Calif., 1990, pp. 329-333.

Bolle, R.M., et al., "Visual Recognition Using Concurrent and Layered Parameter Networks," *Proc. IEEE Conf. Computer Vision and Pattern Recognition,* IEEE CS Press, Los Alamitos, Calif., 1989, pp. 625-631.

Bolles, R.C. and P. Horaud, "3DPO: A Three-Dimensional Part Orientation System," *Int'l J. Robotics Research,* Vol. 5, 1986, pp. 3-26.

Bowyer, K., et al., "Developing the Aspect Graph Representation for Use in Image Understanding," *Proc. DARPA Image Understanding Workshop,* 1989, pp. 831-849.

Brady, J.P., N. Nandhakumar, and J.K. Aggarwal, "Recent Progress in the Recognition of Objects from Range Data," *Image and Vision Computing,* 1988, 295-307.

Bresler, Y., J.A. Fessler, and A. Macovski, "A Bayesian Approach to Reconstruction from Incomplete Projections of a Multiple Objects 3-D Domain," *IEEE Trans. Pattern Analysis and Machine Intelligence,* Vol. 11, No. 8, 1989, pp. 840-858.

Breuel, T.M., "Adaptive Model Base Indexing," *Proc. DARPA Image Understanding Workshop,* 1989, pp. 805-814.

Brooks, R.A., "Model-Based Three-Dimensional Interpretations of Two-Dimensional Images," *IEEE Trans. Pattern Analysis and Machine Intelligence,* Vol. 5, No. 2, 1983, pp. 140-150.

Brou, P., "Using the Gaussian Image to Find the Orientations of Objects," *Int'l J. Robotics Research,* Vol. 3, No. 4, 1984, pp. 89-125.

Burns, B.J. and L.J. Kitchen, "Recognition in 2-D Images of 3-D Objects from Large Model Bases Using Prediction Hierarchies," *Proc. Int'l Joint Conf. Artificial Intelligence,* Morgan Kaufmann Publishers, Inc., San Mateo, Calif., 1987, pp. 763-766.

Burns, J.B. and L.J. Kitchen, "Rapid Object Recognition from a Large Model Based Using Prediction Hierarchies," *Proc. of DARPA Image Understanding Workshop,* 1988, pp. 711-719.

Callahan, J. and R. Weiss, "A Model for Describing Surface Shape," *Proc. IEEE Conf. Computer Vision and Pattern Recognition*, IEEE CS Press, Los Alamitos, Calif., 1985, pp. 240-245.

Canny, J., Z. Gigus, and R. Seidel, "Efficiently Computing and Representing Aspect Graphs of Polyhedral Objects," *Proc. Second Int'l Conf. Computer Vision*, IEEE CS Press, Los Alamitos, Calif., 1988, pp. 30-39.

Cappellini, V., et al., "From Multiple Views to Object Recognition," *IEEE Trans. Circuits and Systems*, Vol. 34, 1987, pp. 1344-1350.

Cernuschi-Frias, B., et al., "Toward a Model-Based Bayesian Theory for Estimating and Recognizing Parameterized 3-D Objects Using Two or More Images Taken from Different Positions," *IEEE Trans. Pattern Analysis and Machine Intelligence*, Vol. 11, No. 10, 1989, pp. 1028-1052.

Chen, C.H. and A.C. Kak, "A Robot Vision System for Recognizing 3-D Objects in Low-Order Polynomial Time," *IEEE Trans. Systems, Man, and Cybernetics*, Vol. 19, No. 6, 1989, pp. 1564-1575.

Chen, H.H., "Pose Determination from Line-to-Plane Correspondences: Existence Condition and Closed-Form Solutions," *Proc. Third Int'l Conf. Computer Vision*, IEEE CS Press, Los Alamitos, Calif., 1990 pp. 374-379.

Chen, S.W. and G. Stockman, "Object Wings - 2 1/2-D Primitives for 3-D Recognition," *Proc. IEEE Conf. Computer Vision and Pattern Recognition*, IEEE CS Press, Los Alamitos, Calif., 1989, pp. 535-440.

Chen, S.W. and G. Stockman, "Wing Representation for Rigid 3-D Objects," *Proc. Tenth Int'l Conf. Pattern Recognition*, IEEE CS Press, Los Alamitos, Calif., 1990, pp. 398-402.

Chien, C.H. and J.K. Aggarwal, "Identification of 3-D Objects from Multiple Silhouettes Using Quadtrees/Octrees," *Computer Vision, Graphics and Image Processing*, Vol. 36, 1986, pp. 256-273.

Chien, C.H and J.K. Aggarwal, "Model Construction and Shape Recognition from Occluding Contours," *IEEE Trans. Pattern Analysis and Machine Intelligence*, Vol. 11, No. 4, 1989, pp. 372-389.

Chin, R.T. and C.R. Dyer, "Model-Based Recognition in Robot Vision," *ACM Computing Surveys*, Vol. 18, No. 1, 1986, pp. 67-108.

Chu, N.T. and L.G. Shapiro, "Experiments in Model-Based Matching Using a Relational Pyramid Representation," *Proc. SPIE/IEEE Applications of Artificial Intelligence Conference VIII*, Vol. 1293, 1990, 236-247.

Cohen, L.D. and I. Cohen, "A Finite Element Method Applied to New Active Contour Models and 3-D Reconstruction from Cross Sections," *Proc. Third Int'l Conf. Computer Vision*, IEEE CS Press, Los Alamitos, Calif., 1990, pp. 587-591.

Connell, J.H. and M. Brady, "Generating and Generalizing Models of Visual Objects," *Artificial Intelligence*, Vol. 31, No. 2, 1987, pp. 159-183.

Cooper, P.R., "Parallel Structure Recognition with Uncertainty: Coupled Segmentation and Matching," *Proc. Third Int'l Conf. Computer Vision*, IEEE CS Press, Los Alamitos, Calif., 1900, pp. 287-291.

Dhome, M., et al., "Determination of the Attitude of 3-D Objects from a Single Perspective View," *IEEE Trans. Pattern Analysis and Machine Intelligence*, Vol. 11, No. 12, 1989, pp. 1265-1278.

Dickinson, S.J., A.P. Pentland, and A. Rosenfeld, "Qualitative 3-D Shape Reconstruction Using Distributed Aspect Graph Matching," *Proc. Third Int'l Conf. Computer Vision*, IEEE CS Press, Los Alamitos, Calif., 1990, pp. 257-262.

Draper, B.A. and E.M. Riseman, "Learning 3-D Object Recognition Strategies," *Proc. Third Int'l Conf. Computer Vision*, IEEE CS Press, Los Alamitos, Calif., 1990, pp. 320-324.

Ettinger, G.J., "Large Hierarchical Object Recognition in Robot Vision," *Proc. IEEE Conf. Computer Vision and Pattern Recognition*, IEEE CS Press, Los Alamitos, Calif., 1988, pp. 32-41.

Fan, T.J., G. Medioni, and R. Nevatia, "Recognizing 3-D Objects Using Surface Descriptions," *IEEE Trans. Pattern Analysis and Machine Intelligence*, Vol. 11, No. 11, 1989, pp. 1140-1157.

Faugeras, O.D. and M. Hebert, "The Representation, Recognition, and Locating of 3-D Objects," *Int'l J. Robotics Research*, Vol. 5, 1986, pp. 27-52.

Feldman, J.A., "Connectionist Models and Parallelism in High Level Vision," *Computer Vision, Graphics and Image Processing*, Vol. 31, 1985, pp. 178-200.

Fisher, R.B., "Using Surfaces and Object Models to Recognize Partially Obscured Pbjects," *Proc. Int'l Joint Conf. Artificial Intelligence*, Morgan Kaufmann Publishers, Inc., San Mateo, Calif., 1983, pp. 989-995.

Fisher, R.B., "Determining Back-Facing Curved Model Surfaces by Analysis at the Boundary," *Proc. Third Int'l Conf. Computer Vision*, IEEE CS Press, Los Alamitos, Calif., 1990, pp. 296-299.

Flynn, P.J. and A.K. Jain, "Bonsai: 3-D Object Recognition Using Constrained Search," *Proc. Third Int'l Conf. Computer Vision*, IEEE CS Press, Los Alamitos, Calif., 1990, pp. 263-267.

Flynn, P.J. and A.K. Jain, "CAD-Based Vision," *IEEE Trans. Pattern Analysis and Machine Intelligence*, Vol. 13, No. 2, 1991, 114-132.

Forsyth, D., et al., "Invariance - A New Framework for Vision," *Proc. Third Int'l Conf. Computer Vision*, IEEE CS Press, Los Alamitos, Calif., 1990, pp. 598-605.

Ganapathy, S., "Decomposition of Transformation Matrices for Robot Vision," *Proc. IEEE Int'l Conf. Robotics*, IEEE CS Press, Los Alamitos, Calif., 1984, pp. 130-139.

Gerig, G., "Linking Image-Space and Accumulator-Space: A New Approach for Object-Recognition," *Proc. First Int'l Conf. Computer Vision*, IEEE CS Press, Los Alamitos, Calif., 1987, pp. 112-117.

Goad, C., "Fast 3-D Model Based Vision," in *From Pixels to Predicates: Recent Advances in Computational and Robot Vision*, Ablex, Norwood, N.J., 1986, pp. 371-391

Grimson, W.E.L., "Sensing Strategies for Disambiguating Among Multiple Objects in Known Poses," *IEEE Trans. Robotics and Automation*, Vol. 2, No. 4, 1986, pp. 196-213.

Grimson, W.E.L., "The Combinatorics of Local Constraints in Model-Based Recognition and Localization from Sparse Data," *J. Assoc. of Computing Machinery*, Vol. 33, No. 4, 1986, pp. 658-686.

Grimson, W.E.L., "The Combinatorics of Object Recognition in Clustered Environments Using Constrained Search," *Proc. Second Int'l Conf. Computer Vision*, IEEE CS Press, Los Alamitos, Calif., 1988, pp. 218-227.

Grimson, W.E.L., "On the Recognition of Curved Objects," *IEEE Trans. Pattern Analysis and Machine Intelligence,* Vol. 11, No. 6, 1989, pp. 632-643.

Grimson, W.E.L., "On the Recognition of Parameterized 2-D Pbjects," *Int'l J. Computer Vision,* Vol. 2, No. 2, 1989, pp. 353-371.

Grimson, W.E.L., "The Effect of Indexing on the Complexity of Object Recognition," *Proc. Third Int'l Conf. Computer Vision,* IEEE CS Press, Los Alamitos, Calif., 1990, pp. 644-653.

Grimson, W.E.L. and D.P. Huttenlocher, "On the Sensitivity of the Hough Transform for Object Recognition," *IEEE Trans. Pattern Analysis and Machine Intelligence,* Vol. 12, No. 3, 1990, pp. 255-274.

Grimson, W.E.L. and D.P. Huttenlocher, "On the Sensitivity of Geometric Hashing," *Proc. Third Int'l Conf. Computer Vision,* IEEE CS Press, Los Alamitos, Calif., 1990, pp. 334-339.

Grimson, W.E.L. and T. Lozano-Perez, "Localizing Overlapping Parts by Searching the Interpretation Tree," *IEEE Trans. Pattern Analysis and Machine Intelligence,* Vol. 9, No. 4, 1987, pp. 469-482.

Gupta, A., L. Bogoni, and R. Bajcsy, "Quantitative and Qualitative Measures for the Evaluation of the Superquadric Models," *Proc. IEEE Workshop on Interpretation of 3-D Scenes,* IEEE CS Press, Los Alamitos, Calif., 1989, pp. 162-169.

Hanson, A.J., "Hyperquadrics: Smoothly Deformable Shapes with Convex Polyhedral Bounds," *Computer Vision, Graphics and Image Processing,* Vol. 44, 1988, pp. 191-210.

Haralick, R.M., et al., "Pose Estimation from Correspondence Point Data," *IEEE Trans. Systems, Man, and Cybernetics,* Vol. 19, No. 6, 1989, pp. 1426-1446.

Heel, J., "Temporally Integrated Surface Reconstruction," *Proc. Third Int'l Conf. Computer Vision,* IEEE CS Press, Los Alamitos, Calif., 1990, pp. 292-295.

Herman, M., "Matching Three-Dimensional Symbolic Descriptions Obtained from Multiple Views of a Scene," *Proc. IEEE Conf. Computer Vision and Pattern Recognition,* IEEE CS Press, Los Alamitos, Calif., 1985, pp. 585-590.

Hoffman, D.D. and W. Richards, "Parts of Recognition," *Cognition,* Vol. 18, 1984, pp. 65-96.

Hoffman, R. and A.K. Jain, "Learning Rules for 3-D Object Recognition," *Proc. IEEE Conf. Computer Vision and Pattern Recognition,* IEEE CS Press, Los Alamitos, Calif., 1988, pp. 885-892.

Hoffman, R., H.R. Keshavan, and F. Towfiq, "CAD-Driven Machine Vision," *IEEE Trans. Systems, Man, and Cybernetics,* Vol. 19, No. 6, 1989, pp. 1477-1488.

Hong, L. and D. Brzakovic, "An Approach to 3-D Scene Reconstruction from Noisy Binocular Image Sequences Using Information Fusion," *Proc. Third Int'l Conf. Computer Vision,* IEEE CS Press, Los Alamitos, Calif., 1990, pp. 658-661.

Hong, K.S., K. Ikeuchi, and K.D. Gremban, "Minimum Cost Aspect Classification: A Module of a Vision Algorithm Compiler," *Proc. Tenth Int'l Conf. Pattern Recognition,* IEEE CS Press, Los Alamitos, Calif., 1990, pp. 65-69.

Horaud, R., "New Methods for Matching 3-D Objects with Single Perspective Views," *IEEE Trans. Pattern Analysis and Machine Intelligence,* Vol. 9, No. 3, 1987, pp. 401-412.

Horn, B.K.P., "Extended Gaussian Images," *Proc. IEEE,* Vol. 72, No. 11, IEEE Press, New York, N.Y., 1984, pp. 1656-1678.

Huang, C.L., "Contour Generation and Shape Restoration of the Straight Homogeneous Generalized Cylinder," *Proc. Tenth Int'l Conf. Pattern Recognition,* IEEE CS Press, Los Alamitos, Calif., 1990, pp. 409-413.

Hutchinson, S.A., R.I. Cromwell, and A.C. Kak, "Applying Uncertainty Reasoning to Model Based Object Recognition," *Proc. IEEE Conf. Computer Vision and Pattern Recognition,* IEEE CS Press, Los Alamitos, Calif., 1989, pp. 541-548.

Huttenlocher, D.P. and S. Ullman, "Object Recognition Using Alignment," *Proc. First Int'l Conf. Computer Vision,* IEEE CS Press, Los Alamitos, Calif., 1987, pp. 102-111.

Huttenlocher, D.P. and S. Ullman, "Recognizing Solid Objects by Alignment with an Image," *Int'l J. Computer Vision,* Vol. 5, No. 2, 1990, pp. 195-212.

Idesawa, M., "Multi-Precision Position Measuring Method with r-hpsd Scheme," *IAPR Workshop on Machine Vision Applications,* 1990, pp. 129-132.

Ikeuchi, K. and K.S. Hong, "Determining Linear Shape Change: Toward Automatic Generation of Object Recognition Programs," *Proc. IEEE Conf. Computer Vision and Pattern Recognition,* IEEE CS Press, Los Alamitos, Calif., 1989, pp. 450-457.

Ikeuchi, K. and T. Kanade, "Modeling Sensors: Toward Automatic Generation of Object Recognition Program," *Computer Vision, Graphics and Image Processing,* Vol. 48, No. 1, 1989, pp. 50-79.

Jain, A.K. and R. Hoffman, "Evidence-Based Recognition of 3-D Objects," *IEEE Trans. Pattern Analysis and Machine Intelligence,* Vol. 10, No. 6, 1988, pp. 783-802.

Jain, R.C. and A.K. Jain, "Report on Range Image Understanding Workshop, East Lansing, Michigan, March 21-23, 1988," *Machine Vision and Applications,* Vol. 2, 1989, pp. 5-60.

Kanatani, K., "Hypothesizing and Testing Geometric Attributes of Image Data," *Proc. Third Int'l Conf. Computer Vision,* IEEE CS Press, Los Alamitos, Calif., 1990, pp. 370-373.

Kapur, D. and J.L. Mundy, " Wu's Method and its Application to Perspective Viewing," *Artificial Intelligence,* Vol. 37, No. 1, 1988, pp. 15-36.

Kender, J.R. and D.G. Freudenstein, "What is a `Degenerate' View?," *Proc. Int'l Joint Conf. Artificial Intelligence,* Morgan Kaufmann Publishers, Inc., San Mateo, Calif., 1987, pp. 801-804.

Kim, Y.C. and J.K. Aggarwal, "Rectangular Parallelepiped Coding: A Volumetric Representation of Three-Dimensional Objects," *J. Opt. Soc. Am. A,* Vol. 2, No. 3, 1986, pp. 127-134.

Kim, Y.C. and J.K. Aggarwal, "Positioning Three-Dimensional Objects Using Stereo Images," *IEEE Trans. Robotics and Automation,* Vol. 3, No. 4, 1987, pp. 361-373.

Knoll, T. and R.C. Jain, "Recognizing Partially Visible Objects Using Feature Indexed Hypotheses," *IEEE Trans. Robotics and Automation,* Vol. 2, No. 1, 1986, pp. 3-13.

Koch, M.W. and R.L. Kashyap, "Using Polygons to Recognize and Locate Partially Occluded Objects," *IEEE Trans. Pattern Analysis and Machine Intelligence,* Vol. 9, No. 4, 1987, pp. 483-494.

Koenderink, J.J., *Solid Shape,* MIT Press, Cambridge, Mass., 1989.

Kriegman, D.J. and J. Ponce, "On Recognizing and Positioning Curved 3-D Objects from Image Contours," *IEEE Trans. Pattern Analysis and Machine Intelligence,* Vol. 12, No. 12, 1990, pp. 1127-1137.

Krishnapuram, R. and D. Casasent, "Determination of Three-Dimensional Object Location and Orientation from Range Images," *IEEE Trans. Pattern Analysis and Machine Intelligence,* Vol. 11, No. 11, 1989, pp. 1158-1167.

Kuno, Y., Y. Okamoto, and S. Okada, "Object Recognition Using a Feature Search Strategy Generated from a 3-D Model," *Proc. Third Int'l Conf. Computer Vision,* IEEE CS Press, Los Alamitos, Calif., 1990, pp. 626-635.

Lamdan, Y., J.T. Schwartz, and H.J. Wolfson, "Object Recognition by Affine Invariant Matching," *Proc. IEEE Conf. Computer Vision and Pattern Recognition,* IEEE CS Press, Los Alamitos, Calif., 1988, pp. 335-344.

Lee, S. and H.S. Hahn, "Object Recognition and Localization Using Optical Proximity Sensor System: Polyhedral Case," *Proc. IEEE Workshop on Interpretation of 3-D Scenes,* IEEE CS Press, Los Alamitos, Calif., 1989, pp. 75-81.

Lin, W.C. and K.S. Fu, "A Syntactic Approach to 3-D Object Representation," *IEEE Trans. Pattern Analysis and Machine Intelligence,* Vol. 6, No. 3, 1984, pp. 351-364.

Linnainmaa, S., D. Harwood, and L.S. Davis, "Pose Determination of a Three-Dimensional Object Using Triangle Pairs," *IEEE Trans. Pattern Analysis and Machine Intelligence,* Vol. 10, No. 5, 1988, pp. 634-647.

Lowe, D.G., "The Viewpoint Consistency Constraint," *Int'l J. Computer Vision,* Vol. 1, 1987, pp. 57-72.

Lu, H., L.G. Shapiro, and O.I. Camps, "A Relational Pyramid Approach to View Class Determination," *Proc. IEEE Workshop on Interpretation of 3-D Scenes,* IEEE CS Press, Los Alamitos, Calif., 1989, pp. 177-183.

Lysak, D.B. Jr. and R. Kasturi, "Interpretation of Line Drawings with Multiple Views," *Proc. Tenth Int'l Conf. Pattern Recognition,* IEEE CS Press, Los Alamitos, Calif., 1990, pp. 220-222.

Magee, M. and M. Nathan, "A Viewpoint Independent Modeling Approach to Object Recognition," *IEEE Trans. Robotics and Automation,* Vol. 3, 1987, pp. 351-356.

Magee, M. and M. Nathan, "Spatial Reasoning, Sensor Repositioning and Disambiguation in 3-D Model Based Recognition," *Workshop Spatial Reasoning and Multi-Sensor Fusion,* Morgan Kaufmann Publishers, Inc., San Mateo, Calif., 1987, pp. 262-271.

Magee, M.J., et al., "Experiments in Intensity Guided Range Sensing Recognition of Three-Dimensional Objects," *IEEE Trans. Pattern Analysis and Machine Intelligence,* Vol. 7, No. 6, 1985, pp. 629-637.

Marefat, M. and R.L. Kashyap, "Geometric Reasoning for Recognition of Three-Dimensional Object Features," *IEEE Trans. Pattern Analysis and Machine Intelligence,* Vol. 12, No. 10, 1990, pp. 949-965.

Martin, W.N. and J.K. Aggarwal, "Volumetric Description of Objects from Multiple Views," *IEEE Trans. Pattern Analysis and Machine Intelligence,* Vol. 5, No. 2, 1983, pp. 150-158.

Mundy, J.L. and A.J. Heller, "The Evolution and Testing of a Model-Based Object Recognition System," *Proc. Third Int'l Conf. Computer Vision,* IEEE CS Press, Los Alamitos, Calif., 1990, pp. 268-282.

Mundy, J., A.J. Heller, and D.W. Thompson, "The Concept of an Effective Viewpoint," *Proc. DARPA Image Understanding Workshop,* 1988, pp. 651-659.

Murase, H., "Surface Shape Reconstruction of an Undulating Transparent Object," *Proc. Third Int'l Conf. Computer Vision,* IEEE CS Press, Los Alamitos, Calif., 1990, pp. 313-319.

Murray, D.W. and D.B. Cook, "Using the Orientation of Fragmentary 3-D Edge Segments for Polyhedral Object Recognition," *Int'l J. Computer Vision,* Vol. 2, No. 2, 1988, pp. 153-169.

Nackman, L.R., "Two-Dimensional Critical Point Configuration Graphs," *IEEE Trans. Pattern Analysis and Machine Intelligence,* Vol. 6, No. 4, 1984, pp. 442-450.

Nasrabadi, N.M., W. Li, and C.Y. Choo, "Object Recognition by a Hopfield Neural Network," *Proc. Third Int'l Conf. Computer Vision,* IEEE CS Press, Los Alamitos, Calif., 1990, pp. 325-328.

Nitzan, D., "Three-Dimensional Vision Structure for Robot Applications," *IEEE Trans. Pattern Analysis and Machine Intelligence,* Vol. 10, No. 3, 1988, pp. 291-309.

Oh, C., N. Nandhakumar, and J.K. Aggarwal, "Integrated Modeling of Thermal and Visual Image Generation," *Proc. IEEE Conf. Computer Vision and Pattern Recognition,* IEEE CS Press, Los Alamitos, Calif., 1989, pp. 356-362.

Oshima, M. and Y. Shirai, "Object Recognition Using Three-Dimensional Information," *IEEE Trans. Pattern Analysis and Machine Intelligence,* Vol. 5, No. 4, 1983, pp. 353-361.

Pasquariello, G., et al., "A System for 3-D Workpiece Recognition," *Proc. Second Int'l Conf. Computer Vision,* IEEE CS Press, Los Alamitos, Calif., 1988, pp. 280-284.

Pentland, A.P., "On Describing Complex Surface Shapes," *Image and Vision Computing,* Vol. 3, 1986, 153-162.

Pentland, A.P., "Perceptual Organization and the Representation of Natural Form," *Artificial Intelligence,* Vol. 28, No. 3, 1986, pp. 293-331.

Pinker, S., "Visual Cognition: An Introduction," *Cognition,* 1984, pp. 1-63.

Plantinga, H. and C.R. Dyer, "Visibility, Occlusion and the Aspect Graph," *Int'l J. Computer Vision,* Vol. 5, No. 2, 1990, pp. 137-160.

Pollard, S.B., et al., "Matching Geometrical Descriptions in Three-Space," *Image and Vision Computing,* Vol. 5, 1987, pp. 73-78.

Ponce, J. and O. Faugeras, "An Object Centered Hierarchical Representation for 3-D Objects: The Prism Tree," *Computer Vision, Graphics and Image Processing,* Vol. 38, 1987, pp. 1-28.

Ponce, J. and D. Kriegman, "On Recognizing and Positioning Curved 3-D Objects from Image Contours," *Proc. IEEE Workshop on Interpretation of 3-D Scenes,* IEEE CS Press, Los Alamitos, Calif., 1989, pp. 61-67.

Ponce, J., D. Chelberg, and W.B. Mann, "Invariant Properties of Straight Homogeneous Generalized Cylinders and Their Contours," *IEEE Trans. Pattern Analysis and Machine Intelligence,* Vol. 11, No. 9, 1989, pp. 951-966.

Potmesil, M., "Generating Octree Models of 3-D Objects from Their Silhouettes in a Sequence of Images," *Computer Vision, Graphics and Image Processing,* Vol. 40, No. 1, 1987, pp. 1-29.

Reeves, A.P. and R.W. Taylor, "Identification of Three-Dimensional Objects Using Range Information," *IEEE Trans. Pattern Analysis and Machine Intelligence,* Vol. 11, No. 4, 1989, pp. 403-410.

Richetim, M., M. Dhome, and J.T. Lapreste, "Inverse Perspective Transform from Zero-Curvature Curve Points Application to the Location of Some Generalized Cylinders," *Proc. IEEE Conf. Computer Vision and Pattern Recognition*, IEEE CS Press, Los Alamitos, Calif., 1989, pp. 517-522.

Rosenfeld, A., "Recognizing Unexpected Objects: A Proposed Approach," *Int'l J. Pattern Recognition and Artificial Intelligence*, Vol. 1, 1987, pp. 71-84.

Sabata, B., F. Arman, and J.K. Aggarwal, "Segmentation of 3-D Range Images Using Pyramidal Data Structures," *Proc. Third Int'l Conf. Computer Vision*, IEEE CS Press, Los Alamitos, Calif., 1990, pp. 662-666.

Sakaguchi, Y., et al., "Generation of 3-D Models Based on Image Fusion of Range Data," *IAPR Workshop on Machine Vision Applications*, 1990, pp. 147-150,.

Sallam, M., J. Stewman, and K. Bowyer, "Computing the Visual Potential of an Articulated Assembly of Parts," *Proc. Third Int'l Conf. Computer Vision*, IEEE CS Press, Los Alamitos, Calif., 1990, pp. 636-643.

Schwartz, J.T. and M. Sharir, "Identification of Partially Obscured Objects in Two and Three Dimensions by Matching Noisy Characteristic Curves," *Int'l J. Robotics Research*, Vol. 6, No. 2, 1987, pp. 29-44.

Seales, W.B. and C.R. Dyer, "Modeling the Rim Appearance," *Proc. Third Int'l Conf. Computer Vision*, IEEE CS Press, Los Alamitos, Calif., 1990, pp. 698-701.

Shapiro, L.G. and R.M. Haralick, "A Metric for Comparing Relational Descriptions," *IEEE Trans. Pattern Analysis and Machine Intelligence*, Vol. 7, No. 1, 1985, pp. 90-94.

Shapiro, L.G. and H. Lu, "Accumulator-Based Inexact Matching Using Relational Summaries," *Machine Vision and Applications*, Vol. 3, No. 3, 1990, pp. 143-158.

Shoham, D. and S. Ullman, "Aligning a Model to an Image Using Minimal Information," *Proc. Second Int'l Conf. Computer Vision*, IEEE CS Press, Los Alamitos, Calif., 1988, pp. 259-263.

Shvaytser, H., "Towards a Computational Theory of Model Based Vision and Perception," *Proc. Third Int'l Conf. Computer Vision*, IEEE CS Press, Los Alamitos, Calif., 1990, pp. 283-286.

Stark, L., D. Eggert, and K. Bowyer, "Aspect Graphs and Nonlinear Optimization in 3-D Object Recognition," *Proc. Second Int'l Conf. Computer Vision*, IEEE CS Press, Los Alamitos, Calif., 1988, pp. 501-507.

Stockman, G., "Object Recognition and Localization via Pose Clustering," *Computer Vision, Graphics and Image Processing*, Vol. 40, 1987, pp. 361-387.

Stockman, G.C. and B. Flinchbaugh, "Recognition via Alignment Using Aspect Models," *Proc. SPIE/IEEE Applications of Artificial Intelligence Conference VIII*, Vol. 1293, 1990, 224-235.

Subrahmonia, J., Y.P. Hung, and D.B. Cooper, "Model-based Segmentation and Estimation of 3-D Surfaces from Two or More Intensity Images Using Markov Random Fields," *Proc. Tenth Int'l Conf. Pattern Recognition*, IEEE CS Press, Los Alamitos, Calif., 1990, pp. 390-397.

Suenaga, Y. and Y. Watanabe, "A Method for the Synchronized Acquisition of Cylindrical Range and Color Data," *IAPR Workshop on Machine Vision Applications*, 1990, pp. 137-142.

Taylor, R.W. and A.P. Reeves, "Classification Quality Assessment for a Generalized Model-Based Object Identification System," *IEEE Trans. Systems, Man, and Cybernetics*, Vol. 19, 1989, pp. 846-853.

Terzopoulos, D. and D. Metaxas, "Dynamic 3-D Models with Local and Global Deformations: Deformable Superquadrics," *Proc. Third Int'l Conf. Computer Vision*, IEEE CS Press, Los Alamitos, Calif., 1990, pp. 606-615.

Trivedi, M.M., C. Chen, and D.H. Cress, "Object Detection by Step-Wise Analysis of Spectral, Spatial and Topographic Features," *Computer Vision, Graphics and Image Processing*, Vol. 51, 1990, pp. 235-255.

Umeyama, S., T. Kasvand, and M. Hospital, "Recognition and Positioning of Three-Dimensional Objects by Combining Matchings of Primitive Local Patterns," *Computer Vision, Graphics and Image Processing*, Vol. 44, No. 1, 1988, pp. 58-76.

Verly, J.G. and R.L. Delanoy, "Appearance-Model-Based Representation and Matching of 3-D Objects," *Proc. Third Int'l Conf. Computer Vision*, IEEE CS Press, Los Alamitos, Calif., 1990, pp. 248-256.

Vermuri, B.C. and J.K. Aggarwal, "Representation and Recognition of Objects from Dense Range Maps," *IEEE Trans. Circuits and Systems*, Vol. 34, 1987, pp. 1351-1363.

Vermuri, B.C., A. Mitiche,, and J.K. Aggarwal, "Curvature-Based Representations of Objects from Range Data," *Image and Vision Computing*, Vol. 4, No. 2, 1986, 107-114.

Wesley, G. and M.A. Markowsky, "Fleshing Out Projections," *IBM J. Research and Development*, Vol. 25, No. 6, 1981, pp. 934-954.

Wong, A.K.C., S.W. Lu, and M. Rioux, "Recognition and Shape Synthesis of 3-D Objects Based on Attributed Hypergraphs," *IEEE Trans. Pattern Analysis and Machine Intelligence*, Vol. 11, No. 3, 1989, pp. 279-290.

Yang, H.S. and A.C. Kak, "Determination of the Identity, Position and Orientation of the Topmost Object in a Pile," *Computer Vision, Graphics and Image Processing*, Vol. 36, 1986, pp. 229-255.

Yokoya, N. and M.D. Levine, "Volumetric Description of Solids of Revolution in a Range Image," *Proc. Tenth Int'l Conf. Pattern Recognition*, IEEE CS Press, Los Alamitos, Calif., 1990, pp. 303-308.

Chapter 6: Dynamic Vision
Selected Bibliography

Abidi, M.A. and R.C. Gonzalez, "Motion Detection in Radar Images," *Proc. Seventh Int'l Conf. Pattern Recognition*, IEEE CS Press, Los Alamitos, Calif., 1984, pp. 787-790.

Adelson, E.H. and J.R. Bergen, "Spatiotemporal Energy Models for the Perception of Motion," *Optical Society of America*, Vol. 2, No. 2, 1985, pp. 284-299.

Adiv, G., "Determining 3-D Motion and Structure from Optical Flow Generated by Several Moving Objects," *IEEE Trans. Pattern Analysis and Machine Intelligence*, Vol. 7, No. 4, 1985, pp. 384-401.

Adiv, G., "Inherent Ambiguities in Recovering 3-D Motion and Structure from a Noisy Flow Field," *IEEE Trans. Pattern Analysis and Machine Intelligence*, Vol. 11, No. 5, 1989, pp. 477-489.

Aggarwal, J.K., "Motion and Time-Varying Imagery," *Computer Graphics*, 1984, pp. 20-21.

Aggarwal, J.K. and M.J. Magee, "Determining Motion Parameters Using Intensity Guided Range Sensing," *Pattern Recognition*, Vol. 19, No. 2, 1986, pp. 169-180.

Aggarwal, J.K. and A. Mitiche, "Structure and Motion from Images: Fact and Fiction," *Proc. Third IEEE Workshop on Computer Vision: Representation and Control*, IEEE CS Press, Los Alamitos, Calif., 1985, pp. 127-128.

Aggarwal, J.K., L.S. Davis, and W.N. Martin, "Correspondence Processes in Dynamic Scene Analysis," *Proc. IEEE*, Vol. 69, No. 5, IEEE Press, New York, N.Y., 1981, pp. 562-572.

Ahuja, N. and C. Nash, "Octree Representations of Moving Objects," *Computer Vision, Graphics and Image Processing*, Vol. 26, 1984, pp. 207-216.

Aisbett, J., "An Iterated Estimation of Motion Parameters of a Rigid Body from Noisy Displacement Vectors," *IEEE Trans. Pattern Analysis and Machine Intelligence*, Vol. 12, No. 11, 1990, pp. 1092-1098.

Allmen, M. and C.R. Dyer, "Cyclic Motion Detection using Spatiotemporal Surfaces and Curves," *Proc. Tenth Int'l Conf. Pattern Recognition*, IEEE CS Press, Los Alamitos, Calif., 1990, pp. 365-370.

Allmen, M. and C.R. Dyer, "Computing Spatiotemporal Surface Flow," *Proc. Third Int'l Conf. Computer Vision*, IEEE CS Press, Los Alamitos, Calif., 1990, pp. 47-51.

Aloimonos, J., "Purposive and Qualitative Active Vision," *Proc. Tenth Int'l Conf. Pattern Recognition*, IEEE CS Press, Los Alamitos, Calif., 1990, pp. 346-360.

Aloimonos, J.Y. and C.M. Brown, "The Relationship Between Optical Flow and Surface Orientation," *Proc. Seventh Int'l Conf. Pattern Recognition*, IEEE CS Press, Los Alamitos, Calif., 1984, pp. 542-545.

Aloimonos, J.Y. and C.M. Brown, "On the Kinetic Depth Effect," *Biological Cybernetics*, Vol. 60, 1989, pp. 445-455.

Anandan, P., "A Computational Framework and an Algorithm for the Measurement of Visual Motion," *Int'l J. Computer Vision*, Vol. 2, No. 3, 1989, pp. 283-310.

Anstis, S.M., "The Perception of Apparent Movement," *Phil. Trans. Royal Soc. London B*, Vol 290, 1980, pp. 153-168.

Aoki, M., "Detection of Moving Objects Using Line Image Sequence," *Proc. Seventh Int'l Conf. Pattern Recognition*, IEEE CS Press, Los Alamitos, Calif., 1984, pp. 784-786.

Arnspang, J., "Optic Acceleration," *Proc. Second Int'l Conf. Computer Vision*, IEEE CS Press, Los Alamitos, Calif., 1988, pp. 364-373.

Arnspang, J., "Direct Determination of a Non Accelerating Greylevel Scene," *Proc. Tenth Int'l Conf. Pattern Recognition*, IEEE CS Press, Los Alamitos, Calif., 1990, pp. 319-323.

Asada, M., M. Kimura, and Y. Shirai, "Dynamic Integration of Height Maps into a 3-D World Representation From Range Image Sequences," *Proc. Third Int'l Conf. Computer Vision*, IEEE CS Press, Los Alamitos, Calif., 1990, pp. 548-557.

Baker, H. H., "Surface Reconstruction from Image Sequences," *Proc. Second Int'l Conf. Computer Vision*, IEEE CS Press, Los Alamitos, Calif., 1988, pp. 334-343.

Baker, H. H. and R.C. Bolles, "Generalizing Epipolar-Plane Image Analysis on the Spatiotemporal Surface," *Int'l J. Computer Vision*, Vol. 3, No. 1, 1989, pp. 33-49.

Ballard, D.H. and C.M. Brown, *Computer Vision*, Prentice-Hall, Englewood Cliffs, N.J., 1982.

Ballard, D.H. and O.A. Kimball, "Rigid Body Motion from Depth and Optical Flow," *Computer Vision, Graphics and Image Processing*, Vol. 22, 1983, pp. 95-115.

Barron, J.L., et al., "Determination of Egomotion and Environmental Layout from Noisy Time-Varying Image Velocity in Binocular Image Sequences," *Proc. Int'l Joint Conf. Artificial Intelligence*, Morgan Kaufmann Publishers, Inc., San Mateo, Calif., 1987, pp. 822-825.

Barron, J.L., A.D. Jepson, and J.K. Tsotsos, "The Sensitivity of Motion and Structure Computations," *Proc. Nat'l Conf. on Artificial Intelligence*, MIT Press, Cambridge, Mass., 1987, pp. 700-705.

Barron, J.L., A.D. Jepson, and J.K. Tsotsos, "The Feasibility of Motion and Structure Computations," *Proc. Second Int'l Conf. Computer Vision*, IEEE CS Press, Los Alamitos, Calif., 1988, pp. 651-657.

Bergen, J.R. et al, "Computing Two Motions from Three Frames," *Proc. Third Int'l Conf. Computer Vision*, IEEE CS Press, Los Alamitos, Calif., 1990, pp. 27-32.

Bergholm, F., "A Theory on Optical Velocity Fields and Ambiguous Motion of Curves," *Proc. Second Int'l Conf. Computer Vision*, IEEE CS Press, Los Alamitos, Calif., 1988, pp. 165-176.

Bergholm, F., "Motion from Flow Along Contours: A Note on Robustness and Ambiguous Cases," *Int'l J. Computer Vision*, Vol. 2, No. 4, pp. 395-415.

Bergholm, G., "Decomposition Theory and Transformations of Visual Directions," *Proc. Third Int'l Conf. Computer Vision*, IEEE CS Press, Los Alamitos, Calif., 1990, pp. 85-90.

Bhanu, B. and W. Burger, "Approximation of Displacement Fields Using Wavefront Region Growing," *Computer Vision, Graphics and Image Processing*, Vol. 41, 1988, pp. 306-322.

Black, M.J. and P. Anandan, "A Model for the Detection of Motion Over Time," *Proc. Third Int'l Conf. Computer Vision*, IEEE CS Press, Los Alamitos, Calif., 1990, pp. 33-37.

Bolles, R.C., H.H. Baker, and D.H. Marimont, "Epipolar-Plane Image Analysis: An Approach to Determining Structure from Motion," *Int'l J. Computer Vision*, Vol. 1, pp. 7-55.

Bouthemy, P., "A Maximum Likelihood Framework for Determining Moving Edges," *IEEE Trans. Pattern Analysis and Machine Intelligence*, Vol. 11, No. 5, 1989, pp. 499-511.

Bray, A.J., "Tracking Objects Using Image Disparities," *Image and Vision Computing*, Vol. 8, No. 1, 1990, pp. 4-9.

Broida, T.J. and R. Chellappa, "Estimation of Object Motion Parameters from Noisy Images," *IEEE Trans. Pattern Analysis and Machine Intelligence*, Vol. 8, No. 1, 1986, pp. 90-99.

Broida, T.J. and R. Chellappa, "Performance Bounds for Estimating Three-Dimensional Motion Parameters from a Sequence of Noisy Images," *J. Opt. Soc. Am. A*, Vol. 6, No. 6, 1989.

Broida, T.J. and R. Chellappa, "Experiments and Uniqueness Results on Object Structure and Kinematics from a Sequence of Monocular Images," *Proc. Workshop on Visual Motion*, IEEE CS Press, Los Alamitos, Calif, 1989, pp. 21-30.

Burger, W. and B. Bhanu, "Qualitative Motion Understanding," *Proc. Int'l Joint Conf. Artificial Intelligence*, Morgan Kaufmann Publishers, Inc., San Mateo, Calif., 1987, pp. 819-821.

Burger, W. and B. Bhanu, "Estimating 3-D Egomotion from Perspective Image Sequences," *IEEE Trans. Pattern Analysis and Machine Intelligence*, Vol. 12, No. 11, 1990, pp. 1040-1058.

Burt, P.J. et al, "Object Tracking with a Moving Camera," *Proc. Workshop on Visual Motion*, IEEE CS Press, Los Alamitos, Calif., 1989, pp. 2-12.

Buxton, B.F. and H. Buxton, "Monocular Depth Perception from Optical Flow by Space Time Signal Processing," *Proc. Royal Soc. London B*, 1983, pp. 27-47.

Buxton, B.F and H. Buxton, "Computation of Optical Flow from the Motion of Edge Features in Image Sequences," *Image & Vision Computing*, Vol. 2, No. 2, 1984, pp. 59-75.

Campani, M. and A. Verri, "Computing Optical Flow from an Overconstrained System of Linear Algebraic Equations," *Proc. Third Int'l Conf. Computer Vision*, IEEE CS Press, Los Alamitos, Calif., 1990, pp. 22-26.

Cappelini, V., A. del Bimbo, and P. Nesi, "Object Motion Identification for Object Recognition," *IAPR Workshop on Machine Vision Applications*, 1990, pp. 189-194.

Carlsson, S., "Information in the Geometric Structure of Retinal Flow Fields," *Proc. Second Int'l Conf. Computer Vision*, IEEE CS Press, Los Alamitos, Calif., 1988, pp. 629-633.

Chang, Y.-L. and J.K. Aggarwal, "Reconstructing 3-D Lines from a Sequence of 2-D Projections: Representation and Estimation," *Proc. Third Int'l Conf. Computer Vision*, IEEE CS Press, Los Alamitos, Calif., 1990. pp. 101-105.

Charnley, D. and R. Blissett, "Surface Reconstruction from Outdoor Image Sequences," *Image and Vision Computing*, Vol. 7, 1989, pp. 10-16.

Chen, C.W. and T.S. Huang, "Epicardial Motion and Deformation Estimation from Coronary Artery Bifurcation Points," *Proc. Third Int'l Conf. Computer Vision*, IEEE CS Press, Los Alamitos, Calif., 1990, pp. 456-459.

Chen, H.H., "Motion and Depth from Binocular Orthographic Views," *Proc. Second Int'l Conf. Computer Vision*, IEEE CS Press, Los Alamitos, Calif., 1988, pp. 634-640.

Chen, H.H. and T.S. Huang, "Matching 3-D Line Segments with Applications to Multiple-Object Motion Estimation," *IEEE Trans. Pattern Analysis and Machine Intelligence*, Vol. 12, No. 10, 1990, pp. 1002-1008.

Chharbra, A.K. and T.A. Grogan, "Uniqueness, the Minimum Norm Constraint, and Analog Networks for Optical Flow Along Contours," *Proc. Third Int'l Conf. Computer Vision*, IEEE CS Press, Los Alamitos, Calif., 1990, pp. 80-84.

Chu, H.C. and E.J. Delp, "Estimating Displacement Vectors from an Image Sequence," *J. Opt. Soc. Am. A*, Vol. 6, No. 6, 1989.

Cipolla, R. and M. Yamamoto, "Stereoscopic Tracking of Bodies in Motion," *Image and Vision Computing*, Vol. 8, No. 1, 1990, pp. 85-90.

Costabile, M.F., C. Guerra, and G.G. Pieroni, "Matching Shapes: A Case Study in Time-Varying Images," *Computer Vision, Graphics and Image Processing*, Vol. 29, 1985, pp. 296-310.

Crowley, J.L., P. Stelmaszyk, and C. Discours, "Measuring Image Flow by Tracking Edge-Lines," *Proc. Second Int'l Conf. Computer Vision*, IEEE CS Press, Los Alamitos, Calif., 1988, pp. 658-664.

Cui, N., J. Weng, and P. Cohen, "Extended Structure and Motion Analysis from Monocular Image Sequences," *Proc. Third Int'l Conf. Computer Vision*, IEEE CS Press, Los Alamitos, Calif., 1990, pp. 222-229.

D'Haeyer, J., "Determining Motion of Image Curves from Local Pattern Changes," *Computer Vision, Graphics and Image Processing*, Vol. 34, 1986, pp. 166-188.

Daugman, J.G., "Pattern and Motion Vision Without Laplacian Zero Crossings," *J. Opt. Soc. Am. A*, Vol. 5, No. 7, 1988, pp. 1142-1148.

Davis, L.S., Z. Wu, and H. Sun, "Contour-Based Motion Estimation," *Computer Vision, Graphics and Image Processing*, Vol. 23, 1983, pp. 313-326.

Debrunner, C.H. and N. Ahuja, "A Direct Data Approximation Based Motion Estimation Algorithm," *Proc. Tenth Int'l Conf. Pattern Recognition*, IEEE CS Press, Los Alamitos, Calif., 1990, pp. 384-389.

Dickmanns, E.D., "Object Recognition and Real-Time Relative State Estimation Under Egomotion," in *Real-Time Object Measurement and Classification*, A.K. Jain, ed., Springer-Verlag, Berlin, 1988.

Dickmanns, E.D. and V. Graefe, "Dynamic Monocular Machine Vision," *Machine Vision and Applications*, Vol. 1, No. 4, 1988, pp. 223-240.

Dickmanns, E.D. and V. Graefe, "Applications of Dynamic Monocular Machine Vision," *Machine Vision and Applications*, Vol. 1, No. 4, 1988, pp. 241-261.

Dickmanns, E.D., B. Mysliwetz, and T. Christians, "An Integrated Spatio-Temporal Approach for Automatic Visual Guidance of Autonomous Vehicles," *IEEE Trans. on Systems, Man, and Cybernetics*, Vol. 20, No. 6, 1990, pp. 1273-1284.

Dietz, T.E., K.R. Diller, and J.K. Aggarwal, "Automated Computer Evaluation of Time-Varying Cryomicroscopical Images," *Cryobiology*, Vol. 21, 1984, pp. 200-208.

Duncan, J.H. and T.C. Chou, "Temporal Edges: The Detection of Motion and the Computation of Optical Flow," *Proc. Second Int'l Conf. Computer Vision*, IEEE CS Press, Los Alamitos, Calif., 1988, pp. 374-382.

Dutta, R. and M.A. Snyder, "Robustness of Correspondence-Based Structure from Motion," *Proc. Third Int'l Conf. Computer Vision*, IEEE CS Press, Los Alamitos, Calif., 1990, pp. 106-110.

Fang, J.-Q. and T.S. Huang, "Some Experiments on Estimating the 3-D Motion Parameters of a Rigid Body from Two Consecutive Image Frames," *IEEE Trans. Pattern Analysis and Machine Intelligence*, Vol. 6, No. 5, 1984, pp. 545-554.

Fang, J.Q. and T.S. Huang, "Solving Three-Dimensional Small-Rotation Motion Equations: Uniqueness, Algorithms, and Numerical Results," *Computer Vision, Graphics and Image Processing*, Vol. 26, 1984, pp. 183-206.

Fleet, D.J. and A.D. Jepson, "Computation of Component Image Velocity from Local Phase Information," *Int'l J. Computer Vision*, Vol. 5, No. 1, 1990, pp.77-104.

Fogel, S.V., "A Nonlinear Approach to the Motion Correspondence Problem," *Proc. Second Int'l Conf. Computer Vision*, IEEE CS Press, Los Alamitos, Calif., 1988, pp. 619-628.

Fogel, S.V., "Implementation of a Nonlinear Approach to the Motion Correspondence Problem," *Proc. IEEE Workshop on Visual Motion*, IEEE CS Press, Los Alamitos, Calif., 1989, pp. 87-98.

Fuh, C.S. and P. Maragos, "Region-Based Optical Flow Estimation," *Proc. IEEE Conf. Computer Vision and Pattern Recognition*, IEEE CS Press, Los Alamitos, Calif., 1989, pp. 130-35.

Girosi, F., A. Verri, and V. Torre, "Constraints for the Computation of Optical Flow," *Proc. IEEE Workshop on Visual Motion*, IEEE CS Press, Los Alamitos, Calif., 1989, pp. 116-124.

Giusto, D.D. and G. Vernazza, "Optical Flow Calculation from Feature Space Analysis Through an Automatic Segmentation Process," *Signal Processing*, Vol. 16, 1989, pp. 41-51.

Gould, K. and M. Shah, "The Trajectory Primal Sketch: A Multi-Scale Scheme for Representing Motion Characteristics," *Proc. IEEE Conf. Computer Vision and Pattern Recognition*, IEEE CS Press, Los Alamitos, Calif., 1989, pp. 79-85.

Goutsias, J. and J.M. Mendel, "Simultaneous Optimal Segmentation and Model Estimation of Nonstationary Noisy Images," *IEEE Trans. Pattern Analysis and Machine Intelligence*, Vol. 11, No. 9, 1989, pp. 990-998.

Grzywacz, N.M. and E.C. Hildreth, "Incremental Rigidity Scheme for Recovering Structure from Motion: Position-Based Versus Velocity-Based Formulations," *J. Opt. Soc. Am. A*, Vol. 4, No. 3, 1987, pp. 503-518.

Hadani, I. and E. Barta, "The Hybrid Constraint Equation for Motion Extraction," *Image and Vision Computing*, Vol. 7, 1989, pp. 217-224.

Haralick, R.M. and X. Zhuang, "A Note on 'Rigid Body Motion from Depth and Optical Flow'," *Computer Vision, Graphics and Image Processing*, Vol. 34, 1986, pp. 372-387.

Hayashi, B.Y. and S. Negahdaripour, "Direct Motion Stereo: Recovery of Observer Motion and Scene Structure," *Proc. Third Int'l Conf. Computer Vision*, IEEE CS Press, Los Alamitos, Calif., 1990, pp. 446-450.

Haynes, S.M. and R.C. Jain, "Time-Varying Edge Detection," *Computer Graphics and Image Processing*, Vol. 21, 1983, pp. 345-367.

Haynes, S.M. and R.C. Jain, "Event Detection and Correspondence," *Optical Engineering*, Vol. 25, No. 3, 1986, pp. 387-393.

Haynes, S.M. and R.C. Jain, "A Qualitative Approach for Recovering Depths in Dynamic Scenes," *IEEE Workshop on Computer Vision*, IEEE CS Press, Los Alamitos, Calif., 1987, pp. 66-71.

Heeger, D.J., "Model for the Extraction of Image Flow," *J. Opt. Soc. Am. A*, Vol. 4, No. 8, 1987, pp. 1455-1471.

Heeger, D.J. and G. Hager, "Egomotion and the Stabilized World," *Proc. Second Int'l Conf. Computer Vision*, IEEE CS Press, Los Alamitos, Calif., 1988, pp. 435-440.

Heeger, D.J. and A. Jepson, "Simple Method for Computing 3-D Motion and Depth," *Proc. Third Int'l Conf. Computer Vision*, IEEE CS Press, Los Alamitos, Calif., 1990, pp. 96-100.

Heitz, F. and P. Bouthemy, "Multimodal Motion Estimation and Segmentation Using Markov Random Fields," *Proc. Tenth Int'l Conf. Pattern Recognition*, IEEE CS Press, Los Alamitos, Calif., 1990, pp. 378-383.

Herman, M. and T. Kanade, "Incremental Reconstruction of 3-D Scenes from Multiple, Complex Images," *Artificial Intelligence*, Vol. 30, 1986, pp. 289-341.

Hoffman, D.D. and B.M. Bennett, "Inferring the Relative Three-Dimensional Positions of Two Moving Points," *J. Opt. Soc. Am. A*, Vol. 2, No. 2, 1985, pp. 350-353.

Hoffman, D.D. and B.M. Bennett, "The Computation of Structure from Fixed-Axis Motion: Rigid Structures," *Biological Cybernetics*, Vol. 54, 1986, pp. 71-83.

Horn, B.K.P., "Motion Fields are Hardly Ever Ambiguous," *Int'l J. Computer Vision*, Vol. 1, 1987, pp. 259-274.

Horn, B.K.P., "Relative Orientation," *Int'l J. Computer Vision*, Vol. 4, No. 1, 1990, pp. 59-78.

Horn, B.K.P. and B.G. Schunck, "Determining Optical Flow," *Artificial Intelligence*, Vol. 17, 1981, pp. 185-203.

Horn, B.K.P. and E.J. Weldon, "Direct Methods for Recovering Motion," *Int'l J. Computer Vision*, Vol. 2, No. 1, 1988, pp. 151-75.

Huang, T.S., "Modeling Analysis, and Visalization of Nonrigid Object Motion," *Proc. Tenth Int'l Conf. Pattern Recognition*, IEEE CS Press, Los Alamitos, Calif., 1990, pp. 361-364.

Huang, T.S. and O.D. Faugeras, "Some Properties of the E Matrix in Two-View Motion Estimation," *IEEE Trans. Pattern Analysis and Machine Intelligence*, Vol. 11, No. 12, 1989, pp. 1310-1312.

Huang, T.S. and C.H. Lee, "Motion and Structure from Orthographic Projection," *IEEE Trans. Pattern Analysis and Machine Intelligence*, Vol. 11, No. 5, 1989, pp. 536-540.

Hutchinson, J., et al., "Computing Motion Using Analog and Binary Resistive Networks," *Computer*, Vol. 21, No. 3, 1988, pp. 52-63.

Jacobson, L. and H. Wechsler, "Derivation of Optical Flow Using a Spatiotemporal-Frequency Approach," *Computer Vision, Graphics and Image Processing*, Vol. 38, No. 1, 1987, pp. 29-65.

Jain, R.C., "Extraction of Motion Information from Peripheral Processes," *IEEE Trans. Pattern Analysis and Machine Intelligence*, Vol. 3, No. 5, 1981, pp. 489-503.

687

Jain, R.C., "Dynamic Vision," *Proc. Ninth Int'l Conf. Pattern Recognition*, IEEE CS Press, Los Alamitos, Calif., 1988, pp. 226-235.

Jain, R.C., S. Bartlett, and N. O'Brien, "Motion Stereo Using Ego-Motion Complex Logarithmic Mapping," *IEEE Trans. Pattern Analysis and Machine Intelligence*, Vol. 9, No. 3, 1987, pp. 356-369.

Jain, R.C., Y. Roth-Tabak, and K. Skifstad, "Hyperpyramids for Vision-Driven Navigation," *Proc. SPIE Conf. on Applications of Artificial Intelligence VI*, Vol. 937, 1988, pp. 630-637.

Jasinschi, R.S., "Space-Time Sampling with Motion Uncertainty: Constraints on Space-Time Filtering," *Proc. Second Int'l Conf. Computer Vision*, IEEE CS Press, Los Alamitos, Calif., 1988, pp. 428-434.

Jasinschi, R. and A. Yuille, "Nonrigid Motion and Regge Calculus," *J. Opt. Soc. Am. A*, Vol. 6, 1989, pp. 1088-1095.

Jayaramamurthy, S.N. and R.C. Jain, "An Approach to the Segmentation of Textured Dynamic Scenes," *Computer Vision, Graphics and Image Processing*, Vol. 21, No. 2, 1983, pp. 239-261.

Jezouin, J.L. and N. Ayache, "3-D Structure from a Monocular Sequence of Images," *Proc. Third Int'l Conf. Computer Vision*, IEEE CS Press, Los Alamitos, Calif., 1990, pp. 441-445.

Kanatani, K., "Tracing Planar Surface Motion from a Projection without Knowing the Correspondence," *Computer Vision, Graphics and Image Processing*, Vol. 29, No. 1, 1985, pp. 1-12.

Kanatani, K., "Structure and Motion from Optical Flow Under Perspective Projection," *Computer Vision, Graphics and Image Processing*, Vol. 38, No. 2, 1987, pp. 122-146.

Kanatani, K., "Transformation of Optical Flow by Camera Rotation," *IEEE Trans. Pattern Analysis and Machine Intelligence*, Vol. 10, No. 2, 1988, pp. 131-143.

Kearney, J.K., W.B. Thompson, and D.L. Boley, "Optical Flow Estimation: An Error Analysis of Gradient-Based Methods with Local Optimization," *IEEE Trans. Pattern Analysis and Machine Intelligence*, Vol. 9, No. 2, 1987, pp. 229-244.

Kehtarnavaz, N. and S. Mohan, "A Framework for Estimation of Motion Parameters from Range Images," *Computer Vision, Graphics and Image Processing*, Vol. 46, 1989, pp. 88-105.

Kim, Y.C. and J.K. Aggarwal, "Determining Object Motion in a Sequence of Stereo Images," *IEEE Trans. Robotics and Automation*, Vol. 3, No. 6, 1987, pp. 599-614.

Koenderink, J.J. and A.J. van Doorn, "Facts on Optic Flow," *Biological Cybernetics*, Vol. 56, 1987, pp. 247-254.

Koenderink, J.J., A.J. van Doorn, and W.A. van de Grind, "Spatial and Temporal Parameters of Motion Detection in the Peripheral Visual Field," *J. Opt. Soc. Am. A*, Vol. 2, No. 2, 1985, pp. 252-259.

Konrad, J. and E. Dubois, "Multigrid Bayesian and Estimation of Image Motion Fields Using Stochastic Relaxation," *Proc. Second Int'l Conf. Computer Vision*, IEEE CS Press, Los Alamitos, Calif., 1988, pp. 354-362.

Landy, M.S., "Parallel Model of the Kinetic Depth Effect Using Local Computations," *J. Opt. Soc. Am. A*, Vol. 4, No. 5, 1987, pp. 864-877.

Lawton, D.T., "Processing Translational Motion Sequences," *Computer Graphics and Image Processing*, Vol. 22, No. 1, 1983, pp. 116-144.

Lee, C.H., "Structure and Motion from Two Perspective Views Via Planar Patch," *Proc. Second Int'l Conf. Computer Vision*, IEEE CS Press, Los Alamitos, Calif., 1988, pp. 158-164.

Lee, D., A. Papageorgiou, and G.W. Wasilkowski, "Computing Optical Flow," *Proc. Workshop on Visual Motion*, IEEE CS Press, Los Alamitos, Calif., 1989, pp. 99-106.

Lee, S. and Y. Kay, "A Kalman Filter Approach for Accurate 3-D Motion Estimation from a Sequence of Stereo Images," *Proc. Tenth Int'l Conf. Pattern Recognition*, IEEE CS Press, Los Alamitos, Calif., 1990, pp. 104-108.

Legters, G.R. and T.Y. Young, "A Mathematical Model for Computer Image Tracking," *IEEE Trans. Pattern Analysis and Machine Intelligence*, Vol. 4, No. 6, 1982, pp. 583-594.

Levine, M.D., P.B. Noble, and Y.M. Youssef, "Understanding Blood Cell Motion," *Computer Vision, Graphics and Image Processing*, Vol. 21, No. 1, 1983, pp. 58-84.

Lin, X. and Z. Zhu, "Detecting Height from Constrained Motion," *Proc. Third Int'l Conf. Computer Vision*, IEEE CS Press, Los Alamitos, Calif., 1990, pp. 503-506.

Little, J.J. and A. Verri, "Analysis of Differential and Matching Methods for Optical Flow," *Proc. Workshop on Visual Motion*, IEEE CS Press, Los Alamitos, Calif., 1989, pp. 173-180.

Little, J.J., H.H. Bulthoff, and T. Poggio, "Parallel Optical Flow Using Local Voting," *Proc. Second Int'l Conf. Computer Vision*, IEEE CS Press, Los Alamitos, Calif., 1988, pp. 454-459.

Loomis, J.M. and D.W. Eby, "Perceiving Structure from Motion: Failure of Shape Constancy," *Proc. Second Int'l Conf. Computer Vision*, IEEE CS Press, Los Alamitos, Calif., 1988, pp. 383-391.

Lowe, D.G., "Integrated Treatment of Matching and Measurement Errors for Robust Model-Based Motion Tracking," *Proc. Third Int'l Conf. Computer Vision*, IEEE CS Press, Los Alamitos, Calif., 1990, pp. 436-440.

Magee, M.J. and J.K. Aggarwal, "Determining Vanishing Points from Perspective Images," *Computer Vision, Graphics and Image Processing*, Vol. 26, 1984, pp. 256-267.

Markandey, V. and B.E. Flinchbaugh, "Multispectral Constraints for Optical Flow Computation," *Proc. Third Int'l Conf. Computer Vision*, IEEE CS Press, Los Alamitos, Calif., 1990, pp. 38-41.

Mase, K., "An Application of Optical Flow - Extraction of Facial Expression" *IAPR Workshop on Machine Vision Applications*, 1990, pp. 195-198.

Matthies, L., R. Szeliski, and T. Kanade, "Kalman Filter-Based Algorithms for Estimating Depth from Image Sequences," *Int'l J. Computer Vision*, Vol. 3, No. 3, 1989, pp. 209-237.

Maybank, S.J., "Rigid Velocities Compatible with Five Image Velocity Vectors," *Image and Vision Computing*, Vol. 8 , No. 1, 1990, pp. 18-23.

McIvor, A.M., "Edge Recognition in Dynamic Vision," *Proc. IEEE Conf. Computer Vision and Pattern Recognition*, IEEE CS Press, Los Alamitos, Calif., 1989, pp. 118-123.

Mecocci, A., "Moving Object Recognition and Classification in External Environments," *Signal Processing*, Vol. 18, 1989, pp. 183-194.

Meygret, A. and M. Thonnat, "Segmentation of Optical Flow and 3-D Data for the Interpretation of Mobile Objects," *Proc. Third Int'l Conf. Computer Vision*, IEEE CS Press, Los Alamitos, Calif., 1990, pp. 238-245.

Mitiche, A., "On Lineopsis and Computation of Structure and Motion," *IEEE Trans. Pattern Analysis and Machine Intelligence*, Vol. 8, No. 1, 1986, pp. 109-112.

Mitiche, A., "Three-Dimensional Space From Optical Flow Correspondence," *Computer Vision, Graphics and Image Processing*, Vol. 42, 1988, pp. 306-317.

Mitiche, A. and P. Bouthemy, "Tracking Modeled Objects Using Binocular Images," *Computer Vision, Graphics and Image Processing*, Vol. 32, 1985, pp. 384-396.

Mitiche, A., S. Seida, and J.K. Aggarwal, "Using Constancy of Distance to Estimate Position and Displacement in Space," *IEEE Trans. Pattern Analysis and Machine Intelligence*, Vol. 10, No. 4, 1988, pp. 594-599.

Mori, T., "An Active Method of Extracting Egomotion Parameters from Optical Flow," *Biological Cybernetics*, Vol. 52, 1985, pp. 405-407.

Mukawa, N., "Estimation of Shape, Reflection Coefficients, and Illuminant Direction from Image Sequence," *Proc. Third Int'l Conf. Computer Vision*, IEEE CS Press, Los Alamitos, Calif., 1990, pp. 507-512.

Murray, D.W., "Algebraic Polyhedral Constraints and 3-D Structure from Motion," *Image and Vision Computing*, Vol. 8, No. 1, 1990, pp. 24-31.

Murray, D.W. and B.F. Buxton, "Scene Segmentation from Visual Motion Using Global Optimization," *IEEE Trans. Pattern Analysis and Machine Intelligence*, Vol. 9, No. 2, 1987, pp. 220-228.

Murray, D.W., D.A. Castelow, and B.F. Buxton, "From Image Sequences to Recognized Moving Polyhedral Objects," *Int'l J. Computer Vision*, Vol. 3, No. 3, 1989, pp. 181-207.

Mutch, K.M. and W.B. Thompson, "Analysis of Accretion and Deletion at Boundaries in Dynamic Scenes," *IEEE Trans. Pattern Analysis and Machine Intelligence*, Vol. 7, No. 2, 1985, pp. 133-138.

Nagel, H.H., "On a Constraint Equation for the Estimation of Displacement Rates in Image Sequences," *IEEE Trans. Pattern Analysis and Machine Intelligence*, Vol 11, No. 1, 1989, pp. 13-30.

Nagel, H.H. and W. Enkelmann, "An Investigation of Smoothness Constraints for the Estimation of Displacement Vector Fields from Image Sequences," *IEEE Trans. Pattern Analysis and Machine Intelligence*, Vol. 8, No. 5, 1986, pp. 565-593.

Navab, N., R. Deriche, and O.D. Faugeras, "Recovering 3-D Motion and Structure from Stereo and 2-D Token Tracking Cooperation," *Proc. Third Int'l Conf. Computer Vision*, IEEE CS Press, Los Alamitos, Calif., 1990, pp. 513-516.

Negahdaripour, S., "Critical Surface Pairs and Triplets," *Int'l J. Computer Vision*, Vol. 3, No. 4, 1989, pp. 293-311.

Negahdaripour, S., "Multiple Interpretations of the Shape and Motion of Objects from Two Perspective Images," *IEEE Trans. Pattern Analysis and Machine Intelligence*, Vol. 12, No. 11, 1990, pp. 1025-1039.

Nelson, R.C. and J.Y. Aloimonos, "Obstacle Avoidance Using Flow Field Divergence," *IEEE Trans. Pattern Analysis and Machine Intelligence*, Vol. 11, No. 10, 1989, pp. 1102-1106.

Nevatia, R., "Depth Measurement by Motion Stereo," *Computer Graphics and Image Processing*, Vol. 5, 1976, pp. 203-214.

Ohta, N., "Movement Vector Detection with Reliability," *IAPR Workshop on Machine Vision Applications*, 1990, pp. 177-180.

Peleg, S. and H. Rom, "Motion Based Segmentation," *Proc. Tenth Int'l Conf. Pattern Recognition*, IEEE CS Press, Los Alamitos, Calif., 1990, pp. 109-113.

Pentland, A., "Photometric Motion," *Proc. Third Int'l Conf. Computer Vision*, IEEE CS Press, Los Alamitos, Calif., 1990, pp. 178-189.

Prager, J.M. and M.A. Arbib, "Computing the Optic Flow: The Match Algorithm and Prediction," *Computer Vision, Graphics and Image Processing*, Vol. 24, 1983, pp. 271-304.

Prazdny, K., "Egomotion and Relative Depth Map from Optical Flow," *Biological Cybernetics*, Vol. 36, 1980, pp. 87-102.

Prazdny, K., "On the Information in Optical Flows," *Computer Vision, Graphics and Image Processing*, Vol. 22, 1983, pp. 239-259.

Prazdny, K., "Detection of Binocular Disparities," *Biological Cybernetics*, Vol. 52, 1985, pp. 93-99.

Prazdny, K., "Studies of Some New Phenomena of Motion Perception," *Biological Cybernetics*, Vol. 52, 1985, pp. 187-194.

Price, K., "Multi-Frame Feature-Based Motion Analysis," *Proc. Tenth Int'l Conf. Pattern Recognition*, IEEE CS Press, Los Alamitos, Calif., 1990, pp. 114-118.

Reiger, J.H. and D.T. Lawton, "Processing Differential Image Motion," *J. Opt. Soc. Am. A*, Vol. 2, No. 2, 1985, pp. 354-359.

Richards, W., "Structure from Stereo and Motion," *J. Opt. Soc. Am. A*, Vol. 2, No. 2, 1985, pp. 343-349.

Rink, R.E., T.M. Caelli, and V.G. Gourishankar, "Recovery of the 3-D Location and Motion of a Rigid Object Through Camera Image (An Extended Kalman Filter Approach)," *Int'l J. Computer Vision*, Vol. 2, No. 4, 1989, pp. 373-393.

Sawhney, H.S., J. Oliensis, and A.R. Hanson, "Description and Reconstruction from Image Trajectories of Rotational Motion," *Proc. Third Int'l Conf. Computer Vision*, IEEE CS Press, Los Alamitos, Calif., 1990, pp. 494-498.

Schalkoff, R.J., "Dynamic Imagery Modeling and Motion Estimation Using Weak Formulations," *IEEE Trans. Pattern Analysis and Machine Intelligence*, Vol. 9, No. 4, 1987, pp. 578-584.

Schunck, B.G., "Image Flow: Fundamentals and Algorithms," in *Motion Understanding: Robot and Human Vision*, W. N. Martin and J. K. Aggarwal, eds., Kluwer, 1988.

Schunck, B.G., "Motion Segmentation and Estimation by Constraint Line Clustering," *IEEE Trans. Pattern Analysis and Machine Intelligence*, Vol. 11, No. 10, 1989, pp. 1010-1027.

Scott, G.L., "Four-Line' Method of Locally Estimating Optic Flow," *Image and Vision Computing*, Vol. 5, 1987, pp. 67-72.

Sethi, I.K. and R.C. Jain, "Finding Trajectories of Feature Points in a Monocular Image Sequences," *IEEE Trans. Pattern Analysis and Machine Intelligence*, Vol. 9, No. 1, 1987, pp. 56-73.

Shahraray, B. and M.K. Brown, "Robust Depth Estimation from Optical Flow," *Proc. Second Int'l Conf. Computer Vision*, IEEE CS Press, Los Alamitos, Calif., 1988, pp. 641-650.

Shigang, L., S. Tsuji, and M. Imai, "Determining of Camera Rotation from Vanishing Points of Lines on Horizontal Planes," *Proc. Third Int'l Conf. Computer Vision*, IEEE CS Press, Los Alamitos, Calif., 1990, pp. 499-502.

689

Shiraishi, K., M. Terauchi, and K. Onaga, "Recognition of Human Motion Based on Interpretation of 2-D Pattern Deformation," *IAPR Workshop on Machine Vision Applications*, 1990, pp. 185-189.

Shulman, D. and J.Y. Herve, "Regularization of Discontinuous Flow Fields," *Proc. Workshop on Visual Motion*, IEEE CS Press, Los Alamitos, Calif., 1989, pp. 81-86.

Silven, O., "Estimating the Pose and Motion of a Known Object for Real-Time Robotic Tracking," *IAPR Workshop on Machine Vision Applications*, 1990, pp. 357-361.

Singh, A., "An Estimation-Theoretic Framework for Image-Flow Computation," *Proc. Third Int'l Conf. Computer Vision*, IEEE CS Press, Los Alamitos, Calif., 1990, pp. 168-177.

Spetsakis, M. and J.Y. Aloimonos, "Optimal Computing of Structure from Motion Using Point Correspondences in Two Frames," *Proc. Second Int'l Conf. Computer Vision*, IEEE CS Press, Los Alamitos, Calif., 1988, pp. 449-453.

Spetsakis, M.E. and J.Y. Aloimonos, "Structure from Motion Using Line Correspondences," *Int'l J. Computer Vision*, Vol. 4, No. 3, 1990, pp. 171-183.

Spoerri, A. and S. Ullman, "The Early Detection of Motion Boundaries," *Proc. First Int'l Conf. Computer Vision*, IEEE CS Press, Los Alamitos, Calif., 1987, pp. 209-218.

Stephens, R.S., "Real-Time 3-D Object Tracking," *Image and Vision Computing*, Vol. 8, No. 1, 1990.

Subbarao, M., "Interpretation of Image Flow: Rigid Curved Surfaces in Motion," *Int'l J. Computer Vision*, Vol. 2, No. 1, 1988, pp. 77-96.

Subbarao, M. and A.M. Waxman, "Closed Form Solutions to Image Flow Equations for Planar Surfaces in Motion," *Computer Vision, Graphics and Image Processing*, Vol. 36, 1986, pp. 208-228.

Szeliski, R., "Estimating Motion from Sparse Range Data Without Correspondence," *Proc. Second Int'l Conf. Computer Vision*, IEEE CS Press, Los Alamitos, Calif., 1988, pp. 207-216.

Taalebinezhaad, M.A., "Direct Recovery of Motion and Shape in the General Case by Fixation," *Proc. Third Int'l Conf. Computer Vision*, IEEE CS Press, Los Alamitos, Calif., 1990, pp. 451-455.

Tan, C.L. and W.N. Martin, "A Distributed System for Analyzing Time-Varying Multiresolution Imagery," *Computer Vision, Graphics and Image Processing*, Vol. 36, 1986, pp. 162-174.

Terzopoulos, D., A.P. Witkin, and M. Kass, "Constraints on Deformable Models: Recovering 3-D Shape and Nonrigid Motion," *Artificial Intelligence*, Vol. 36, 1988, pp. 91-123.

Thompson, W.B., "Dynamic Occlusion Analysis in Optical Flow Fields," *IEEE Trans. Pattern Analysis and Machine Intelligence*, Vol. 7, No. 4, 1985, pp. 374-383.

Tomasi, C. and T. Kanade, "Shape and Motion Without Depth," *Proc. Third Int'l Conf. Computer Vision*, IEEE CS Press, Los Alamitos, Calif., 1990, pp. 91-95.

Topa, L.C. and R.J. Schalkoff, "Edge Detection and Thinning in Time-Varying Image Sequences Using Spatio-Temporal Templates," *Pattern Recognition*, Vol. 22, 1989, pp 143-154.

Tsai, R.Y. and T.S. Huang, "Estimating Three-Dimensional Motion Parameters of a Rigid Planar Patch," *IEEE Trans. Acoustics, Speech, and Signal Processing*, Vol. 29, No. 6, 1981, pp. 1147-1152.

Tsai, R.Y. and T.S. Huang, "Uniqueness and Estimation of 3-D Motion Parameters of Rigid Objects with Curved Surfaces," *IEEE Trans. Pattern Analysis and Machine Intelligence*, Vol. 6, No. 1, 1984, pp. 13-27.

Tsai, R.Y., T.S. Huang, and W.L Zhu, "Estimating Three-Dimensional Motion Parameters of a Rigid Planar Patch, II: Singular Value Decomposition," *IEEE Trans. Acoustics, Speech, and Signal Processing*, Vol. 30, No. 4, 1982, pp. 525-534.

Tseng, G. and A.K. Sood, "Analysis of Long Image Sequence for Structure and Motion Estimation," *IEEE Trans. Systems, Man, and Cybernetics*, Vol. 19, 1989, pp. 1511-1526.

Tsukune, H. and J.K. Aggarwal, "Analyzing Orthographic Projection of Multiple 3-D Velocity Vector Fields in Optical Flow," *Computer Vision, Graphics, And Image Processing*, Vol. 42, 1988, pp. 157-191.

Tziritas, G., "Recursive And/Or Iterative Estimation of the Two-Dimensional Velocity Field and Reconstruction of Three-Dimensional Motion," *Signal Processing*, Vol. 16, 1989, pp. 53-72.

Ullman, S., "Analysis of Visual Motion by Biological and Computer Systems," *Computer*, Vol. 14, No. 8, 1984, pp. 97-160.

Verri, A. and T. Poggio, "Against Quantitative Optical Flow," *Proc. First Int'l Conf. Computer Vision*, IEEE CS Press, Los Alamitos, Calif., 1987, pp. 171-180.

Vieville, T. and O.D. Faugeras, "Feed-Forward Recovery of Motion and Structure from a Sequence of 2D-Lines Matches," *Proc. Third Int'l Conf. Computer Vision*, IEEE CS Press, Los Alamitos, Calif., 1990. pp. 517-521.

Wang, G., R.M. Inigo, and E.S. McVey, "A Single-Pixel Target Detection & Tracking System," *Proc. Tenth Int'l Conf. Pattern Recognition*, IEEE CS Press, Los Alamitos, Calif., 1990, pp. 99-103.

Waxman, A.M. and J.H. Duncan, "Binocular Image Flows: Steps Toward Stereo-Motion Fusion," *IEEE Trans. Pattern Analysis and Machine Intelligence*, Vol. 8, No. 6, 1986, pp. 715-729.

Waxman, A.M. and S.S. Sinha, "Dynamic Stereo: Passive Ranging to Moving Objects from Relative Image Flows," *IEEE Trans. Pattern Analysis and Machine Intelligence*, Vol. 8, No. 4, 1986, pp. 406-412.

Waxman, A.M. and K. Wohn, "Contour Evolution, Neighborhood Deformation and Image Flow: Textured Surfaces in Motion," in *Image Understanding*, W. Richards and S. Ullman, eds., Chap. 4, 1985-86, Ablex, 1987.

Waxman, A.M. and K. Wohn, "Image Flow Theory: A Framework for 3-D Inference from Time-Varying Imagery," in *Advances in Computer Vision*, C.M. Brown, ed., Lawrence Erlbaum, Hillsdale, N.J., 1988.

Waxman, A.M., B. Kamgar-Parsi, and M. Subbarao, "Closed-Form Solutions to Image Flow Equations for 3-D Structure and Motion," *Int'l J. Computer Vision*, Vol. 1, 1987, pp. 239-258.

Waxman, A.M., J. Wu, and F. Bergholm, "Convected Activation Profiles and the Measurement of Visual Motion," *Proc. IEEE Conf. Computer Vision and Pattern Recognition*, IEEE CS Press, Los Alamitos, Calif., 1988, pp. 717-723.

Weinshall, D., "Direct Computation of Qualitative 3-D Shape and Motion Invariants," *Proc. Third Int'l Conf. Computer Vision*, IEEE CS Press, Los Alamitos, Calif., 1990, pp. 230-237.

Weng, J., T.S. Huang, and N. Ahuja, "Motion and Structure from Two Perspective Views: Algorithms, Error Analysis, and Error Estimation," *IEEE Trans. Pattern Analysis and Machine Intelligence*, Vol. 11, No. 5, 1989, pp. 451-476.

Weng, J., T.S. Huang, and N. Ahuja, "Estimating Motion and Structure from Line Matches: Performance Obtained and Beyond," *Proc. Tenth Int'l Conf. Pattern Recognition*, IEEE CS Press, Los Alamitos, Calif., 1990, pp. 168-172.

Werkhoven, P., A. Toet, and J.J. Koenderink, "Displacement Estimates Through Adaptive Affinities," *IEEE Trans. Pattern Analysis and Machine Intelligence*, Vol. 12, No. 7, 1990, pp. 658-663.

Westphal, H. and H.H. Nagel, "Toward the Derivation of Three-Dimensional Descriptions from Image Sequences for Nonconvex Moving Objects," *Computer Vision, Graphics and Image Processing*, Vol. 34, 1986, pp. 302-320.

Williams, L.R. and A.R. Hanson, "Translating Optical Flow into Token Matching and Depth from Looming," *Proc. Second Int'l Conf. Computer Vision*, IEEE CS Press, Los Alamitos, Calif., 1988, pp. 441-448.

Woodham, R.J., "Multiple Light Source Optical Flow," *Proc. Third Int'l Conf. Computer Vision*, IEEE CS Press, Los Alamitos, Calif., 1990, pp. 42-46.

Wu, J., R. Brockett, and K. Wohn, "A Contour-Based Recovery of Image Flow: Iterative Method," *Proc. IEEE Conf. Computer Vision and Pattern Recognition*, IEEE CS Press, Los Alamitos, Calif., 1989, pp. 124-129.

Xu, G., S. Tsuji, and M. Asada, "A Motion Stereo Method Based on Coarse-To-Fine Control Strategy," *IEEE Trans. Pattern Analysis and Machine Intelligence*, Vol. 9, No. 2, 1987, pp. 332-336.

Yamamoto, M., "A General Aperture Problem for Direct Estimation of 3-D Motion Parameters," *IEEE Trans. Pattern Analysis and Machine Intelligence*, Vol. 11, No. 5, 1989, pp. 528-536.

Yamamoto, M. et al, "Direct Estimation of Deformable Motion Parameters from Range Image Sequence," *Proc. Third Int'l Conf. Computer Vision*, IEEE CS Press, Los Alamitos, Calif., 1990, pp. 460-465.

Young, G.-S. and R. Chellappa, "Statistical Analysis of Inherent Ambiguities in Recovering 3-D Motion from a Noisy Flow Field," *Proc. Tenth Int'l Conf. Pattern Recognition*, IEEE CS Press, Los Alamitos, Calif., 1990, pp. 371-377.

Young, G.-S. J. and R. Chellappa, "3-D Motion Estimation Using a Sequence of Noisy Stereo Images: Models, Estimation, and Uniqueness Results," *IEEE Trans. Pattern Analysis and Machine Intelligence*, Vol. 12, No. 8, 1990, pp. 735-759.

Yuille, A.L. and N. Grzywacz, "A Mathematical Analysis of the Motion Coherence Theory," *Int'l J. Computer Vision*, Vol. 3, No. 2, 1989, pp. 155-175.

Zhang, Z. and O.D. Faugeras, "Tracking and Grouping 3-D Line Segments," *Proc. Third Int'l Conf. Computer Vision*, IEEE CS Press, Los Alamitos, Calif., 1990, pp. 577-581.

Zhang, Z., O.D. Faugeras, and N. Ayache, "Analysis of a Sequence of Stereo Scenes Containing Multiple Moving Objects Using Rigidity Constraints," *Proc. Second Int'l Conf. Computer Vision*, IEEE CS Press, Los Alamitos, Calif., 1988, pp. 177-186.

Zhao, W.Z., F.H. Qi, and T.Y. Young, "Dynamic Estimation of Optical Flow Field Using Objective Functions," *Image and Vision Computing*, Vol. 7, No. 4, 1989, pp. 259-267.

Zheng, J.Y. and S. Tsuji, "Panoramic Representation of Scenes for Route Understanding," *Proc. Tenth Int'l Conf. Pattern Recognition*, IEEE CS Press, Los Alamitos, Calif., 1990, pp. 161-167.

Zucker, S.W. and L. Iverson, "From Orientation Selection to Optical Flow," *Computer Vision, Graphics and Image Processing*, Vol. 37, 1987, pp. 196-220.

Chapter 7: Knowledge-based Vision
Selected Bibliography

Alexandrov, V.V. and N.D. Gorsky, "Expert Systems Simulating Human Visual Perception," *Int'l J. Pattern Recognition and Artificial Intelligence*, Vol. 3, 1989, pp. 19-28.

Ballard, D.H., C.M. Brown, and J.A. Feldman, "An Approach to Knowledge-Directed Image Analysis," in *Computer Vision Systems*, A.R. Hanson and E.M. Riseman, eds., Academic Press, New York, N.Y., 1978, pp. 271-281.

Barr, A. and E.A. Feigenbaum, *The Handbook of Artificial Intelligence*, William Kaufmann, Los Altos, Calif., 1982.

Bobick, A.F. and R.C. Bolles, "Representation Space: An Approach to the Integration of Visual Information," *Proc. IEEE Conf. Computer Vision and Pattern Recognition*, IEEE CS Press, Los Alamitos, Calif., 1989, pp. 492-499.

Bogdanowicz, J.F., "An Evolving System for Image Understanding," *Proc. SPIE Conf. Digital Image Processing*, Vol. 528, 1985, pp. 110-116.

Bolle, R.M., A. Califano, and R. Kjeldsen, "Data and Model Driven Focus of Foveation," *Proc. Tenth Int'l Conf. Pattern Recognition*, IEEE CS Press, Los Alamitos, Calif., 1990, pp. 1-7.

Edelman, S. and T. Poggio, "Representations in High-Level Vision: Reasessing the Inverse Optics Paradigm," *Proc. DARPA Image Understanding Workshop*, 1989, pp. 944-949.

Hanson, A. and E. Riseman, "The VISIONS Image Understanding System," in *Advances in Computer Vision*, C. Brown, ed., 1988, Erlbaum, Hillsdale, N.J., pp. 1-114.

Herman, M. and T. Kanade, "The 3-D MOSAIC Scene Understanding System: Incremental Reconstruction of 3-D Scenes from Multiple Complex Images," *Artificial Intelligence*, Vol. 30, No. 3, 1986, pp. 289-341.

Hopkins, S., G.J. Michaelson, and A.M. Wallace, "Parallel Imperative and Functional Approaches to Visual Scene Labeling," *Image and Vision Computing*, Vol. 7, No. 3, 1989, pp. 178-193.

Kak, A.C., "Spatial Reasoning," *AI Magazine*, Vol. 9, No. 2, 1988, pp. 23.

Koons, D.B. and B.H. McCormick, "A Model of Visual Knowledge Representation," *Proc. First Int'l Conf. Computer Vision*, IEEE CS Press, Los Alamitos, Calif., 1987, pp. 365-372.

Kuan, D. et al, "A Constraint-Based System for Interpretation of Aerial Imagery," *Proc. Second Int'l Conf. Computer Vision*, IEEE CS Press, Los Alamitos, Calif., 1988, pp. 601-609.

Lawton, D.T. and T.S. Levitt, "Knowledge Based Vision for Terrestrial Robots," *Proc. DARPA Image Understanding Workshop*, 1989, pp. 128-133.

Levine, M.D. and A.M. Nazif, "Dynamic Measurement of Computer Generated Image Segmentations," *IEEE Trans. Pattern Analysis and Machine Intelligence*, Vol. 7, No. 2, 1985, pp. 155-164.

Levitt, T.S. et al, "Probability-Based Control for Computer Vision," *Proc. DARPA Image Understanding Workshop*, 1989, pp. 355-369.

Marefat, M. and R.L. Kashyap, "Geometric Reasoning for Recognition of Three-Dimensional Object Features," *IEEE Trans. Pattern Analysis and Machine Intelligence*, Vol. 12, No. 10, Oct. 1990, pp. 949-965.

McKeown Jr., D.M., "Building Knowledge-Based System for Detecting Man-Made Structures from Remotely Sensed Imagery," *Proc. Royal Soc. London B*, Vol. A324, 1988, pp. 423-435.

McKeown Jr., D.M., W.A. Harvey Jr., and J. McDermott, "Rule-Based Interpretation of Aerial Imagery," *IEEE Trans. Pattern Analysis and Machine Intelligence*, Vol. 7, No. 5, 1985, pp. 570-585.

Modestino, J.W. and J. Zhang, "A Markov Random Field Model-Based Approach to Image Interpretation," *Proc. IEEE Conf. Computer Vision and Pattern Recognition*, IEEE CS Press, Los Alamitos, Calif., 1989, pp. 458-465.

Morris, D.T. and A. Narendra-Nathan, "A Rule-Based System for Dimensional Analysis of Glass Containers," *Image and Vision Computing*, Vol. 7, No. 4, 1989, pp. 274-280.

Mulder, J.A., A.K. Mackworth, and W.S. Havens, "Knowledge Structuring and Constraint Satisfaction: The Mapsee Approach," *IEEE Trans. Pattern Analysis and Machine Intelligence*, Vol. 10, No. 6, 1988, pp. 866-879.

Nandhakumar, N. and J.K. Aggarwal, "Integrated Analysis of Thermal and Visual Images for Scene Interpretation," *IEEE Trans. Pattern Analysis and Machine Intelligence*, Vol. 10, No. 4, 1988, pp. 469-481.

Nazif, A.M. and M.D. Levine, "Low Level Image Segmentation: An Expert System," *IEEE Trans. Pattern Analysis and Machine Intelligence*, Vol. 6, No. 5, 1984, pp. 555-577.

Niemann, H. et al, "A Knowledge-Based Vision System for Industrial Applications," *Machine Vision and Applications*, Vol. 3, No. 4, 1990, pp. 201-229.

Niemann, H. et al, "Ernest: A Semantic Network System for Pattern Understanding," *IEEE Trans. Pattern Analysis and Machine Intelligence*, Vol. 12, No. 9, 1990, pp. 883-905.

Oh, C., N. Nandhakumar, and J.K. Aggarwal, "Integrated Modeling of Thermal and Visual Image Generation," *Proc. IEEE Conf. Computer Vision and Pattern Recognition*, IEEE CS Press, Los Alamitos, Calif., 1989, pp. 356-362.

Olin, K.E., et al., "Knowledge-Based Vision Technology Overview for Obstacle Detection and Avoidance," *Proc. DARPA Image Understanding Workshop*, 1989, pp. 134-143.

Pentland, A.P., "Perceptual Organization and the Representation of Natural Form," *Artificial Intelligence*, Vol. 28, No. 3, 1986, pp. 293-331.

Provan, G.M., "The Visual Constraint Recognition System: Analyzing the Role of Reasoning in High Level Vision," *Proc. Workshop on Computer Vision*, IEEE CS Press, Los Alamitos, Calif., 1987, pp. 170-175.

Reiter, R. and A.K. Mackworth, "A Logical Framework for Depiction and Image Interpretation," *Artificial Intelligence*, Vol. 41, No. 2, 1989, pp. 125-156.

Rich, E., *Artificial Intelligence*, McGraw-Hill, New York, N.Y., 1983.

Rosenfeld, A., "'Expert' Vision Systems: Some Issues," *Computer Vision, Graphics and Image Processing*, Vol. 34, No. 1, 1986, pp. 99-117.

Shvaytser, H., "Towards a Computational Theory of Model Based Vision and Perception," *Proc. Third Int'l Conf. Computer Vision*, IEEE CS Press, Los Alamitos, Calif., 1990, pp. 283-286.

Srihari, S.N. and Z. Xiang, "Spatial Knowledge Representation," *Int'l J. Pattern Recognition and Artificial Intelligence*, Vol. 3, 1989, pp. 67-84.

Tehrani, S., T.E. Weymouth, and G.B.L. Mancini, "Knowledge-Guided Left Ventricular Boundary Detection," *Proc. IEEE Conf. Computer Vision and Pattern Recognition*, IEEE CS Press, Los Alamitos, Calif., 1989, pp. 342-347.

Trivedi, M.M., "Analysis of High Resolution Aerial Images," in *Image Analysis Applications*, R. Kasturi and M.M. Trivedi, eds., Marcel Dekker, New York, N.Y., 1990, pp. 281-305.

Tsotsos, J.K., "Knowledge and the Visual Process: Content, Form and Use," *Pattern Recognition*, Vol. 17, No. 1, 1984, pp. 13-27.

Tsotsos, J.K., "Knowledge Organization and Its Role in Representation and Interpretation for Time-Varying Data: The ALVEN System," *Computational Intelligence*, Vol. 1, 1985, pp. 16-32.

Wallace, A.M., "A Comparison of Approaches to High-Level Image Interpretation," *Pattern Recognition*, Vol. 21, 1988, pp. 241-259.

Wesley, L.P., "Evidential Knowledge-Based Computer Vision," *J. Opt. Soc. Am. A*, Vol. 25, No. 3, 1986, pp. 363-379.

Woods, P.W., D. Pycock, and C.J. Taylor, "A Frame-Based System for Modeling and Executing Visual Tasks," *Image and Vision Computing*, Vol. 7, No. 2, 1989, pp. 102-108.

Zhang, J. and J.W. Modestino, "A Model-Fitting Approach to Cluster Validation with Application to Stochastic Model-Based Image Segmentation," *IEEE Trans. Pattern Analysis and Machine Intelligence*, Vol. 12, No. 10, 1990, pp. 1009-1017.

Chapter 8: Applications
Selected Bibliography

Aerial Image Analysis:

Conners, R.W., M.M. Trivedi, and C.A. Harlow, "Segmentation of a Complex Urban Scene Using Texture Operators," *Computer Vision, Graphics, and Image Processing,* Vol. 25, 1984, pp. 273-310.

Fischler, M.A., J.M. Tenenbaum, and H.C. Wolf, "Detection of Roads and Linear Structures in Low-Resolution Aerial Imagery Using a Multisource Knowledge Integration Technique," *Computer Graphics and Image Processing,* Vol. 15, No. 3, 1981, pp. 201-223.

Harlow, C.A., R.W. Conners, and M.M. Trivedi, "Developing a Computer Vision System for the Analysis of Aerial Scenes," *Proc. Seventh Int'l Conf. Pattern Recognition,* IEEE, CS Press, Los Alamitos, Calif., 1984, pp. 407-410.

Harlow, C.A. et al, "Scene Analysis of High Resolution Aerial Scenes," *Optical Engineering,* Vol. 25, No. 3, 1986, pp. 347-355.

Hsieh, Y.C., F. Perlant, and D.M. McKeown, "Recovering 3-D Information from Complex Aerial Imagery," *Proc. Tenth Int'l Conf. Pattern Recognition,* IEEE, CS Press, Los Alamitos, Calif., 1990, pp. 136-146.

Huertas, A. and R. Nevatia., "Detecting Buildings in Aerial Images," *Computer Vision, Graphics, and Image Processing,* Vol. 41, 1988, pp. 131-152.

Kuan, D. et al, "A Constraint-Based System for Interpretation of Aerial Imagery," *Proc. Second Int'l Conf. Computer Vision,* IEEE CS Press, Los Alamitos, Calif., 1988, pp. 601-609.

Landgrabe, D.A., "Analysis Technology for Land Remote Sensing," *Proc. IEEE,* Vol. 69, No. 5, IEEE Press, New York, N.Y., 1981, pp. 628-642.

Laprade, R.H., "Split-and-Merge Segmentation of Aerial Photographs," *Computer Vision, Graphics, and Image Processing,* Vol. 44, No. 1, 1988, pp. 77-86.

Matsuyama, T., "Knowledge-Based Aerial Image Understanding Systems and Expert Systems for Image Processing," *IEEE Trans. on Geoscience and Remote Sensing,* Vol. 25, No. 3, 1987, pp. 305-316.

McKeown, D.M., "Toward Automatic Cartographic Feature Extraction," in *Mapping and Spatial Modeling for Navigation,* L.F. Pau, ed., NATO ASI Series, Vol. F 65, Springer-Verlag, Berlin, Heidelberg, 1990, pp. 149-180.

McKeown, D.M., W.A. Harvey, and J.M. McDermott., "Rule-Based Interpretation of Aerial Imagery," *IEEE Trans. Pattern Analysis and Machine Intelligence,* Vol. 7, No. 5, 1985, pp. 570-584.

Sevingny, L.G. et al, "Discrimination and Classification of Vehicles in Natural Scenes from Thermal Imagery," *Computer Vision, Graphics, and Image Processing,* Vol. 24, 1983, pp. 229-243.

Trivedi, M.M., "Analysis of High Resolution Aerial Images," in *Image Analysis Applications,* R. Kasturi and M.M. Trivedi, eds., Marcel Dekker, New York, N.Y., 1990, pp. 281-305.

Document Image Analysis:

Abdulla, W.H., A.O.M. Saleh, and A.H. Morad, "A Preprocessing Algorithm for Hand-Written Character Recognition Letters," *Pattern Recognition,* Vol. 7, No. 1, 1988, pp. 13-18.

Ahmed, P. and C.Y. Suen, "Computer Recognition of Totally Unconstrained Handwritten Zip Codes," *Int'l J. Pattern Recognition and Artificial Intelligence,* Vol. 1, 1987, pp. 1-15.

Akiyama, T. and N. Hagita, "Automated Entry System for Printed Documents," *Pattern Recognition,* Vol. 23, 1990, pp. 141-154.

Al-Emami, S. and M. Usher, "On-Line Recognition of Handwritten Arabic Characters," *IEEE Trans. Pattern Analysis and Machine Intelligence,* Vol. 12, No. 7, 1990, pp. 704-710.

Almuallim, H. and S. Yamaguchi, "A Method of Recognition of Arabic Cursive Handwriting," *IEEE Trans. Pattern Analysis and Machine Intelligence,* Vol. 9, No. 5, 1987, pp. 715-722.

Ammar, M., Y. Yoshida, and T. Fukumura, "Off-Line Preprocessing and Verification of Signatures," *Int'l J. Pattern Recognition and Artificial Intelligence,* Vol. 2, 1988, pp. 589-602.

Amin, T.J. and R. Kasturi, "Map Data Processing: Recognition of Lines and Symbols," *Optical Engineering,* Vol. 26, 1987, pp. 354-358.

Antoine, D., S. Collin, and K. Tombre, "Analysis of Technical Documents: The REDRAW System," *Proc. IAPR Workshop on Syntactic and Structural Pattern Recognition,* Murray Hill, N.J., 1990, pp. 1-20.

Baird, H.S., "Feature Identification for Hybrid Structural/Statistical Pattern Classification," *Computer Vision, Graphics, and Image Processing,* Vol. 42, 1988, pp. 318-33.

Baird, H.S., "Document Image Defect Models," *Proc. IAPR Workshop on Syntactic and Structural Pattern Recognition,* Murray Hill, N.J., 1990, pp. 38-46.

Baird, H.S., "Anatomy of a Page Reader," *Proc. IAPR Workshop on Machine Vision Applications,* 1990, pp. 483-486.

Baird, H.S. and K. Thompson, "Reading Chess," *IEEE Trans. Pattern Analysis and Machine Intelligence,* Vol. 12, No. 6, 1990, pp. 552-559.

Bapista, G. and K.M. Kulkarni, "A High Accuracy Algorithm for Recognition of Handwritten Numerals," *Pattern Recognition,* Vol. 21, 1988, pp. 287-291.

Belaid, A., J.J. Brault, and Y. Chenevoy, "Knowledge-Based System for Structured Document Recognition," *Proc. IAPR Workshop on Machine Vision Applications,* 1990, pp. 465-469.

Bixler, J.P. and J.P. Sanford, "A Technique for Encoding Lines and Regions in Engineering Drawings," *Pattern Recognition,* Vol. 18, 1985, pp. 367-377.

Bixler, J.P., L.T. Watson, and J.P. Sanford, "Spline-Based Recognition of Straight Lines and Curves in Engineering Line Drawings," *Image and Vision Computing,* Vol.6, 1988, pp. 262-269.

Bow, S.T. and R. Kasturi, "A Graphics Recognition System for Interpretation of Line Drawings," in *Image Analysis Applications,* Marcel Dekker, 1990, pp. 37-72.

Bozinovic, R.M. and S.N. Srihari, "Off-Line Cursive Script Word Recognition," *IEEE Trans. Pattern Analysis and Machine Intelligence,* Vol. 11, No. 1, 1989, pp. 68-83.

Brossman, C. and G.R. Cross, "Model-Based Recognition of Characters in Trademark Artwork," *Pattern Recognition Letters,* Vol. 11, 1990, pp. 363-370.

Brown, R.M., T.H. Fay, and C.L. Walker, "Handprinted Symbol Recognition System," *Pattern Recognition,* Vol. 21, 1988, pp. 91-118.

Cabrelli, C.A. and U.M. Molter, "Automatic Representation of Binary Images," *IEEE Trans. Pattern Analysis and Machine Intelligence,* Vol. 12, No. 11, 1990, pp. 1190-1196.

Campbell-Grant, I.R. and P.J. Robinson, "An Introduction to ISO DIS 8613, 'Office Document Architecture', and Its Application to Computer Graphics," *Computer & Graphics,* Vol. 11, 1987, pp. 325-341.

Casey, R.G. and D.R. Ferguson, "Intelligent Forms Processing," *IBM Systems Journal,* Vol. 29, 1990, pp. 435-450.

Cash, G.L. and M. Hatamian, "Optical Character Recognition by the Method of Moments," *Computer Vision, Graphics, and Image Processing,* Vol. 39, 1987, pp. 29-310.

Chen, K.J., K.C. Li, and Y.L. Chang, "A System for On-Line Recognition of Chinese Characters," *Int'l J. Pattern Recognition and Artificial Intelligence,* Vol. 2, 1988, pp. 139-148.

Chen, P.N., Y.S. Chen, and W.H. Hsu, "Stroke Relation Coding - A New Approach to the Recognition of Multi-Font Printed Chinese Characters," *Int'l J. Pattern Recognition and Artificial Intelligence,* Vol. 2, 1988, pp. 149-160.

Cheng, F.H., W.H. Hsu, and M.Y. Chen, "Recognition of Handwritten Chinese Characters by Modified Hough Transform Techniques," *IEEE Trans. Pattern Analysis and Machine Intelligence,* Vol. 11, No. 4, 1989, pp. 429-439.

Cheng, Y.Q., Y.L. Cao, and J.Y. Yang, "An Automatic Recognition System of Assembly Drawings," *Proc. IAPR Workshop on Machine Vision Applications,* 1990, pp. 211-214.

Collin, S. and D. Colnet, "Analysis of Dimension in Mechanical Engineering Drawings," *Proc. IAPR Workshop on Machine Vision Applications,* 1990, pp. 105-108.

Davis, R.H. and J. Lyall, "Recognition of Handwritten Characters - A Review," *Image and Vision Computing,* Vol. 4, 1986, pp. 208-218.

de Jesus, E.O., "High Level Loader and Recognizer of Electrical and Electronic Images Diagrams," *Proc. IAPR Workshop on Machine Vision Applications,* 1990, pp. 101-103.

Dengel, A., "Document Image Analysis - Expectation-Driven Text Recognition," *Proc. IAPR Workshop on Syntactic and Structural Pattern Recognition,* 1990, pp. 78-87.

Dengel, A. and G. Barth, "High Level Document Analysis Guided by Geometric Aspects," *Int'l J. Pattern Recognition and Artificial Intelligence,* Vol. 2, 1988, pp. 641-655.

Dinan, R.F., L.D. Painter, and R.R. Rodite, "Image Plus High Performance Transaction System," *IBM Systems Journal,* Vol. 29, 1990, pp. 421-434.

Dori, D., "Self Structural Syntax Directed Pattern Recognition of Dimensioning Components in Engineering Drawings," *Proc. IAPR Workshop on Syntactic and Structural Pattern Recognition,* 1990, pp. 88-112.

Dori, D. and A. Pnueli, "The Grammar of Dimensions in Machine Drawings," *Computer Vision, Graphics, and Image Processing,* Vol. 42, No. 1, 1988, pp. 1-18.

Downton, A.C. and C.G. Leedham, "Preprocessing and Presorting of Envelope Images for Automatic Sorting Using OCR," *Pattern Recognition,* Vol. 23, 1990, pp. 347-362.

El-Dabi, S.S., R. Ramis, and A. Kamel, "Arabic Character Recognition System: A Statistical Approach for Recognizing Cursive Typewritten Text," *Pattern Recognition,* Vol. 23, 1990, pp. 485-495.

El-Khaly, and M.A.Sid-Ahmed, "Machine Recognition of Optically Captured Machine Printed Arabic Text," *Pattern Recognition,* Vol. 23, 1990, pp. 1207-1214.

El-Sheikh, T.S. and S.G. El-Taweel, "Real-Time Arabic Handwritten Character Recognition," *Pattern Recognition,* Vol. 23, 1990, pp. 1323-1332.

Elliman, D.G. and I.T. Lancaster, "A Review of Segmentation and Contextual Analysis Techniques for Text Recognition," *Pattern Recognition,* Vol. 23, 1990, pp. 337-346.

Espelid, R. et al, "Automatic Digitizing of the Colour-Layer of Thematic Maps," *Proc. IAPR Workshop on Machine Vision Applications,* 1990, pp. 299-302.

Fahn, C.S., J.F. Wang, and J.Y. Lee, "A Topology-Based Component Extractor for Understanding Electronic Circuit Diagrams," *Computer Vision, Graphics, and Image Processing,* Vol. 44, 1988, pp. 119-138.

Fletcher, L.A. and R. Kasturi, "A Robust Algorithm for Text String Separation from Mixed Text/Graphics Images," *IEEE Trans. Pattern Analysis and Machine Intelligence,* Vol. 10, No. 6, 1988, pp. 910-918.

Freeman, H. and J. Ahn, "On the Problem of Placing Names in a Geographic Map," *Int'l J. Pattern Recognition and Artificial Intelligence,* Vol. 1, 1987, pp. 121-140.

Fujisawa, H. and Y. Nakano, "A Top-Down Approach for the Analysis of Document Images," *Proc. IAPR Workshop on Syntactic and Structural Pattern Recognition,* 1990, pp. 113-122.

Futatsumata, T. et al, "Development of an Automatic Recognition System for Plant Diagrams," *Proc. IAPR Workshop on Machine Vision Applications,* 1990, pp. 207-210.

Futrelle, R.P., "Strategies for Diagram Understanding: Generalized Equivalence, Spatial/Object Pyramids, and Animate Vision," *Proc. Tenth Int'l Conf. Pattern Recognition,* IEEE CS Press, Los Alamitos, Calif., 1990, pp. 403-408.

Goodson, K.J. and P.H. Lewis, "A Knowledge-Based Line Recognition System," *Pattern Recognition Letters,* Vol. 11, 1990, pp. 295-304.

Govindan, V.K. and A.P. Shivaprasad, "Character Recognition - A Review," *Pattern Recognition,* Vol. 23, 1990, pp. 671-683.

Groen, F.C.A., A.C. Sanderson, and J.F. Schlag, "Symbol Recognition in Electrical Diagrams Using Probabilistic Graph Matching," *Pattern Recognition,* Vol. 3, 1985, pp. 343-350.

Hayakawa, T. et al, "Recognition of Roads in an Urban Map by Using the Topological Road-Network," *Proc. IAPR Workshop on Machine Vision Applications,* 1990, pp. 215-221.

Ho, T.K., J.J. Hull, and S.N. Srihari, "Combination of Structural Classifiers," *Proc. IAPR Workshop on Syntactic and Structural Pattern Recognition,* 1990, pp. 123-136.

Hori, O. and A. Okazaki, "High Quality Vectorization Based on a Generic Object Model," *Proc. IAPR Workshop on Syntactic and Structural Pattern Recognition,* 1990, pp. 137-153.

Hrechak, A.K. and J.A. McHugh, "Automated Fingerprint Recognition Using Structural Matching," *Pattern Recognition,* Vol. 23, 1990, pp. 893-904.

Ilg, M. and R. Ogniewicz, "Knowledge-Based Interpretation of Road Maps Based on Symmetrical Skeletons," *Proc. IAPR Workshop on Machine Vision Applications,* 1990, pp. 161-164.

Joseph. S.H., "Processing of Engineering Line Drawings for Automatic Input to CAD," *Pattern Recognition,* Vol. 22, 1989, pp. 1-11.

Joseph, S.H. and T.P. Pridmore, "A System for the Interpretation of Images of Graphics," *Proc. IAPR Workshop on Syntactic and Structural Pattern Recognition,* 1990, pp. 154-164.

Kanai, J., "Text-Line Extraction Using Character Prototypes," *Proc. IAPR Workshop on Syntactic and Structural Pattern Recognition,* 1990, pp. 182-191.

Kasturi, R., "Image Analysis Techniques for Geographic Information Systems", in *Image Analysis Applications,* Marcel Dekker, 1990, pp. 127-163.

Kasturi, R. and J. Alemany, "Information Extraction from Images of Paper-based Maps for Query Processing," *IEEE Trans. Software Engineering* (special section on Image Databases), Vol. 14, 1988, pp. 671-675.

Kasturi, R., S. Siva, and L. O'Gorman, "Techniques for Line Drawing Interpretation: An Overview," *Proc. IAPR Workshop on Machine Vision Applications,* 1990, pp. 151-160.

Kasturi, R. et al, "Map Data Processing in Geographical Information Systems," *Computer,* Vol. 22, No. 12, 1989, pp. 10-21.

Kasturi, R. et al, "Document Image Analysis: An Overview of Techniques for Graphics Recognition," *Proc. IAPR Workshop on Syntactic and Structural Pattern Recognition,* 1990, pp. 192-230.

Kasturi, R. et al, "A System for Interpretation of Line Drawings," *IEEE Trans. Pattern Analysis and Machine Intelligence,* Vol. 12, No. 10, 1990, pp. 978-992.

Kato, H. and S. Inokuchi, "The Recognition System for Printed Piano Music Using Musical Knowledge and Constraints," *Proc. IAPR Workshop on Syntactic and Structural Pattern Recognition,* 1990, pp. 231-248.

Kerrick, D.D. and A.C. Bovik, "Microprocessor-Based Recognition of Handprinted Characters from a Tablet Input," *Pattern Recognition,* Vol. 21, 1988, pp. 525-537.

Kise, K., et al., "Model Based Understanding of Document Images," *Proc. IAPR Workshop on Machine Vision Applications,* 1990, pp. 471-474.

Kita, N., "Handwriting Model Adjustable to Writers," *Proc. IAPR Workshop on Machine Vision Applications,* 1990, pp. 431-440.

Kultanen, P., E. Oja, and L. Xu, "Randomized Hough Transform (RHT) in Engineering Drawing Vectorization System," *Proc. IAPR Workshop on Machine Vision Applications,* 1990, pp. 173-180.

Kumar, R.E., A. Agarwal, and A.K. Pujari, "Off-Line Shorthand Recognition System," *Proc. IAPR Workshop on Machine Vision Applications,* 1990, pp. 437-444.

Kurtzberg, J.M., "Feature Analysis for Symbol Recognition by Elastic Matching," *IBM J. Res. Develop.,* Vol. 31, No. 1, 1987, pp. 91-95.

Lam, L. and C.Y. Suen, "Structural Classification and Relaxation Matching of Totally Unconstrained Handwritten Zip-code Numbers," *Pattern Recognition,* Vol. 21, No. 1, 1988, pp. 19-31.

Lee, D.S., S.W. Lam, and S.N. Srihari, "A Structural Approach to Recognize Hand-printed and Degraded Machine-printed Characters," *Proc. IAPR Workshop on Syntactic and Structural Pattern Recognition,* 1990, pp. 256-272.

Lee, S.W., J.H. Kim, and F.C.A. Groen, "Translation-, Rotation-, and Scale-Invariant Recognition of Hand-Drawn Electrical Circuit Symbols with Attributed Graph Matching," *Proc. IAPR Workshop on Syntactic and Structural Pattern Recognition,* 1990, pp. 273-292.

Lee, S.W., J.H. Kim, and F.C.A. Groen, "Translation-, Rotation-, and Scale- Invariant Recognition of Hand-Drawn Symbols in Schematic Diagrams," *Int'l J. Pattern Recognition and Artificial Intelligence,* Vol. 4, 1990, pp. 1-25.

Leedham, C.G. and A.C. Downton, "Automatic Recognition and Transcription of Pitman's Handwritten Shorthand - An Approach to Shortforms," *Pattern Recognition,* Vol. 20, 1987, pp. 341-348.

Leung, C.H., Y.S. Cheung, and Y.L. Wong, "A Knowledge-Based Stroke-Matching Method for Chinese Character Recognition," *IEEE Trans. Systems, Man, and Cybernetics,* Vol. 17, No. 6, 1987, pp. 993-1003.

Li, H.F., R. Jayakumar and M. Youssef, "Parallel Algorithms for Recognizing Handwritten Characters Using Shape Features," *Pattern Recognition,* Vol. 22, 1989, pp. 641-652.

Luo, Q., et al., "Recognition of Document Structure on the Basis of Spatial and Geometric Relationships between Document Items," *Proc. IAPR Workshop on Machine Vision Applications,* 1990, pp. 461-464.

Lysak, D.B. Jr. and R. Kasturi, "Interpretation of Line Drawings with Multiple Views," *Proc. Tenth Int'l Conf. on Pattern Recognition,* IEEE CS Press, Los Alamitos, Calif., 1990, pp. 220-222.

Maderlechner, G., " 'Symbolic Subtraction' of Fixed Formatted Graphics and Text from Filled-in Forms," *Proc. IAPR Workshop on Machine Vision Applications,* 1990, pp. 457-459.

Mantas, J., "An Overview of Character Recognition Methodologies," *Pattern Recognition,* Vol. 19, 1986, pp. 425-430.

Marukawa, K. et al, "A High Speed Word Matching Algorithm for Handwritten Chinese Character Recognition," *Proc. IAPR Workshop on Machine Vision Applications,* 1990, pp. 445-449.

Mehtre, B.M. and B. Chatterjee, "Segmentation of Fingerprint Images - A Composite Method," *Pattern Recognition,* Vol. 22, 1989, pp. 381-385.

Mehtre, B.M. and A.K. Jain, "Automatic Classification of Fingerprint Images," *IAPR Workshop on Machine Vision Applications,* 1990, pp. 287-290.

Mehtre, B.M., N.N. Murthy, and S. Kapoor, "Segmentation of Fingerprint Images Using the Directional Image," *Pattern Recognition,* Vol. 20, 1987, pp. 429-435.

Miligram, M., M. Jobert, and B. Lamy, "A Segmentation Free Approach to Symbol Extraction and Recognition from Image Document," *Proc. IAPR Workshop on Machine Vision Applications,* 1990, pp. 475-478.

Mitchell, B.T. and A.M. Gillies, "A Model-Based Computer Vision System for Recognizing Handwritten ZIP Codes," *Machine Vision and Applications,* Vol. 2, No. 4, 1989, pp. 231-243.

Moon, Y.S. and W.K. Hui, "High Quality Chinese Fonts Generation for Desktop Publishing - A Computer Vision Approach," *Pattern Recognition Letters,* Vol. 9, 1989, pp. 147-151.

Morishita, T., M. Ooura, and Y. Ishii, "A Kanji Recognition Method which Detects Writing Errors," *Int'l J. Pattern Recognition and Artificial Intelligence,* Vol. 2, 1988, 181-195.

Murase, H. and T. Wakahara, "Online Hand-Sketched Figure Recognition," *Pattern Recognition,* Vol. 19, 1986, pp. 147-160.

Musavi, M.T. et al, "A Vision-Based Method to Automate Map Processing," *Pattern Recognition,* Vol. 21, 1988, pp. 319-326.

Nagasamy, V. and N.A. Langrana, "Engineering Drawing Processing and Vectorization System," *Computer Vision, Graphics, and Image Processing,* Vol. 49, 1990, pp. 379-397.

Nagy, G. "Towards a Structured-Document-Image Utility," *Proc. IAPR Workshop on Syntactic and Structural Pattern Recognition,* 1990, pp. 293-309.

Nakano, Y. et al, "An Algorithm for the Skew Normalization of Document Image," *Proc. Tenth Int'l Conf. Pattern Recognition,* IEEE CS Press, Los Alamitos, Calif., 1990, pp. 8-13.

Namane, A. and M.A. Sid-Ahmed, "Character Scaling by Contour Method," *IEEE Trans. Pattern Analysis and Machine Intelligence,* Vol. 12, No. 6, 1990, pp. 600-606.

Nouboud, F. and R. Plamondon, "On-Line Recognition of Handprinted Characters: Survey and Beta Tests," *Pattern Recognition,* Vol. 23, 1990, pp. 1031-1044.

Okamoto, M. and A. Miyazawa, "An Experimental Implementation of Document Recognition System for Papers Containing Mathematical Expressions," *Proc. IAPR Workshop on Syntactic and Structural Pattern Recognition,* 1990, pp. 335-350.

Okazaki, A. et al, "An Automatic Circuits Diagram Reader with Loop-Structure-Based Symbol Recognition," *IEEE Trans. Pattern Analysis and Machine Intelligence,* Vol. 10, No. 3, 1988, pp. 331-341.

Parizeau, M. and R. Plamondon, "A Comparative Analysis of Regional Correlation, Dynamic Time Warping, and Skeletal Tree Matching for Signature Verification," *IEEE Trans. Pattern Analysis and Machine Intelligence,* Vol. 12, No. 7, 1990, pp. 710-716.

Pavlidis, T., "A Vectorizer and Feature Extractor from Document Recognition," *Computer Vision, Graphics, and Image Processing,* Vol. 35, 1986, pp. 111-127.

Pham, B., "Conic B-Splines for Curve Fitting: A Unifying Approach," *Computer Vision, Graphics, and Image Processing,* Vol. 45, 1989, pp. 117-125.

Plamondon, R. and G. Lorette, "Automatic Signature Verification and Writer Identification - The State of the Art," *Pattern Recognition,* Vol. 22, 1989, pp. 107-131.

Plesums, C.A. and R.W. Bartels, "Large-Scale Image Systems: USAA Case Study," *IBM Systems Journal,* Vol. 29, 1990, pp. 343-355.

Rao, P.V.S., "Word-Based Recognition of Cursive Script," *Proc. IAPR Workshop on Machine Vision Applications,* 1990, pp. 441-445.

Risse, T., "Hough Transform for Line Recognition: Complexity of Evidence Accumulation and Cluster Detection," *Computer Vision, Graphics, and Image Processing,* Vol. 46, 1989, pp. 327-345.

Roach, J.W. and J.E. Tatem, "Using Domain Knowledge in Low-Level Visual Processing to Interpret Handwritten Music: An Experiment," *Pattern Recognition,* Vol. 21, No. 1, 1988, pp. 33-44.

Sabourin, R., R. Plamondon, and G. Lorette, "Off-Line Identification with Handwritten Signature Images: Survey and Perspectives," *Proc. IAPR Workshop on Syntactic and Structural Pattern Recognition,* 1990, pp. 377-391.

Satoh, S. and M. Sakauchi, "Descriptive Ability of Drawing Image Understanding Framework Using State Transition Models," *Proc. IAPR Workshop on Machine Vision Applications,* 1990, pp. 199-202.

Seemuller, W.W., "The Extraction of Ordered Vector Drainage Networks from Elevation Data," *Computer Vision, Graphics, and Image Processing,* Vol. 47, No. 1, 1989, pp. 45-58.

Shih, C-C. and R. Kasturi, "Extraction of Graphic Primitives from Images of Paper-based Drawings," *Machine Vision and Applications,* Vol. 2, 1989, pp. 103-113.

Shlien, S., "Multifont Character Recognition for Typeset Documents," *Int'l J. Pattern Recognition and Artificial Intelligence,* Vol. 2, 1988, pp. 603-620.

Shridhar, M. and A. Badreldin, "Recognition of Isolated and Simply Connected Handwritten Numerals," *Pattern Recognition,* Vol. 19, 1986.

Simon, J.C. and O. Baret, "Regularities and Singularities in Line Pictures," *Proc. IAPR Workshop on Syntactic and Structural Pattern Recognition,* 1990, pp. 423-439.

Sinha, R.M.K., "Rule Based Contextual Post-Processing for Devanagari Text Recognition," *Pattern Recognition,* Vol. 20, 1987, pp. 475-485.

Sinha, R.M.K. and B. Prasada, "Visual Text Recognition Through Contextual Processing," *Pattern Recognition,* Vol. 21, 1988, pp. 463-479.

Sinha, R.M.K. and H.C. Karnick, "Plang Based Specification of Patterns with Variations for Pictorial Data Bases," *Computer Vision, Graphics, and Image Processing,* Vol. 43, 1988, pp. 98-110.

Srihari, S.N. and V. Govindaraju, "Analysis of Textual Images Using the Hough Transform," *Machine Vision and Application,* Vol. 2, 1989, pp. 141-153.

Srinivasan, V.S., "Identification of Core and Delta Points in Fingerprint Images," *Proc. IAPR Workshop on Machine Vision Applications,* 1990, pp. 263-266.

Stringa, L, "Efficient Classification of Totally Unconstrained Handwritten Numerals with a Trainable Multilayer Network," *Pattern Recognition Letters,* Vol. 10, 1989, pp. 273-280.

697

Suzuki, S. and T. Yamada, "Maris: Map Recognition Input System," *Pattern Recognition*, Vol. 23, 1990, pp. 919-933.

Tappert, C.C., C.Y. Suen, and T. Wakahara, "The State of the Art in On-Line Handwriting Recognition," *IEEE Trans. Pattern Analysis and Machine Intelligence*, Vol. 12, No. 8, 1990, pp. 787-808.

Taxt, T., P.J. Flynn, and A.K. Jain, "Segmentation of Document Images," *IEEE Trans. Pattern Analysis and Machine Intelligence*, Vol. 11, No. 12, 1989, pp. 1322-1329.

Taxt, T., J.B. Olafsdottir, and M. Dehlen, "Recognition of Handwritten Symbols," *Pattern Recognition*, Vol. 23, 1990, pp. 1155-1166.

Thibadeau, R.H. and D.M. McNulty, "Two Systems for Converting Raster Data to Numerical Control Data," *Proc. IAPR Workshop on Machine Vision Applications*, 1990, pp. 227-231.

Tsuji, Y. et al, "Document Recognition System with Layout Structure Generator," *Proc. IAPR Workshop on Machine Vision Applications*, 1990, pp. 479-482.

Vaxiviere, P. and K. Tombre, "Interpretation of Mechanical Engineering Drawings for Paper-CAD Conversion," *Proc. IAPR Workshop on Machine Vision Applications*, 1990, pp. 203-205.

Viseshsin, S. and S. Murai, "Automated Height Information Acquisition from Topographic Map," *Proc. IAPR Workshop on Machine Vision Applications*, 1990, pp. 219-221.

Viswanathan, M., "Analysis of Scanned Documents - A Syntactic Approach," *Proc. IAPR Workshop on Syntactic and Structural Pattern Recognition*, 1990, pp. 450-459.

Wang, C.H. and S.N. Srihari, "A Framework for Object Recognition in a Visually Complex Environment and its Application to Locating Address Blocks on Mail Pieces," *Int'l J. Computer Vision*, Vol. 2, 1988, pp. 125-151.

Wolberg, G., "A Syntactic Omni-Font Character Recognition System," *Int'l J. Pattern Recognition and Artificial Intelligence*, Vol. 1, 1987, pp. 303-322.

Xia, Y. and C. Sun, "Recognizing Restricted Handwritten Chinese Characters by Structure Similarity Method," *Pattern Recognition Letters*, Vol. 11, No. 1, 1990, pp. 67-73.

Yeh, P.S. et al, "Address Location on Envelopes," *Pattern Recognition*, Vol. 20, 1987, pp. 213- 227.

Yong, Y., "Handprinted Chinese Character Recognition Via Neural Networks," *Pattern Recognition Letters*, Vol. 7, No. 1, 1988, pp. 19-25.

Medical Image Analysis:

Abdel, A., O. Hasekioglu, and J.J. Bloomer, "Image Segmentation via Motion Vector Estimates," *SPIE Medical Imaging IV*, 1990, pp. 366-373.

Adam, D., O. Hareuveni, and S. Sideman, "Semiautomated Border Tracking of Cine-Echocardiographic Ventricular Images," *IEEE Trans. on Medical Imaging*, 1987, pp. 266-271.

Ahn, C.B. and Z.H. Cho, "A New Phase Correction Method in NMR Imaging Based on Autocorrection and Histogram Analysis," *IEEE Trans. on Medical Imaging*, 1987, pp. 32-36.

Amamoto, D.Y., R. Kasturi and A. Mamourian, "Tissue-type Discrimination in Magnetic Resonance Images," *Proc. Tenth Int'l Conf. Pattern Recognition*, IEEE CS Press, Los Alamitos, Calif., 1990, pp. 603-607.

Apicella, A., J.S. Kippenhan, and J.H. Nagel, "Fast Multi-Modality Image Matching," *Proc. SPIE Medical Imaging III*, Vol. 1090, 1989, pp. 252-263.

Armadillo, R. et al, "Modeling and Shape Decomposition of Anatomical Organs by Using Superquadric Primitives," *Eleventh Ann. IEEE Engineering in Medical and Biology Conf.*, 1989, pp. 610-611.

Barth, K.L., B. Eicker, and J. Seissl, "Automated Biplane Vessel Recognition in Digital Coronary Angiograms," *Proc. of SPIE Medical Imaging I*, 1990, pp. 266-277.

Bartoo, G.T., "Multi-Modality Image Registration Using Centroid Mapping," *Eleventh Ann. IEEE Engineering in Medical and Biology Conf.*, 1989, pp. 550-552.

Besson, G.M., "Vascular Segmentation Using Snake Transforms and Region Growing," *Proc. SPIE Medical Imaging III*, Vol. 1090, 1989, pp. 429-435.

Biederman, "Human Visual Pattern Recognition," *Proc. SPIE Medical Imaging IV*, Vol. 1231, 1990, pp. 2-9.

Bow, S.T. and X.-F. Wang, "Applications of Pattern Recognition and AI Technique to the Cytoscreening of Vaginal Smears by Computer," *Proc. SPIE Medical Imaging III*, Vol. 1090, 1989, pp. 551-555.

Chaudhuri, S. et al, "Detection of Blood Vessels in Retinal Images Using Two-Dimensional Matched Filters," *IEEE Trans. on Medical Imaging*, 1989, pp. 263-269.

Chen, C.-T., "Edge and Surface Searching in Medical Images," *Proc. of SPIE Medical Imaging II*, Vol. 914, 1988, pp. 594-599.

Chen, S.Y., "Sensor Integration for Tomographic Image Segmentation," *Eleventh Ann. IEEE Engineering in Medical and Biology Conf.*, 1988, pp. 1387-1388.

Chen, S.Y. and W.-C. Lin, "Expert Vision System for Medical Image Segmentation," *Proc. SPIE Medical Imaging III*, Vol. 1090, 1989, pp. 162-172.

Chu, C.H., E.J. Delp, and A.J. Buda, "Detecting Left Ventricular Endocardial and Epicardial Boundaries by Digital 2-D Echocardiography," *IEEE Trans. Medical Imaging*, 1988, pp. 81-90.

Cios, K.J. and A. Sarieh, "An Edge Extraction Technique for Noisy Images," *IEEE Trans. on Biomedical Engineering*, 1990, pp. 520-524.

Dalton, B.L. and G. du Boulay, "Medical Image Matching," *Proceeding of SPIE Medical Imaging II*, Vol. 914, 1988, pp. 456-464.

Dann, R. and J. Hoford, "3-D Computerized Brain Atlas for Elastic Matching: Creation and Initial Evaluation," *Proc. of SPIE Medical Imaging II*, Vol. 914, 1988, pp. 600-608.

Davis, D.H., D.R. Dance, and C.H. Jones, "Automatic Detection of Microcalcifications in Digital Mammograms," *Proc. SPIE Medical Imaging IV*, Vol. 1231, 1990, pp. 185-193.

Dhawan, A.P. and S. Juvvadi, "Knowledge-Based Analysis and Understanding of 3-D Medical Images," *Proc. of SPIE Medical Imaging II,* Vol. 914, 1988, pp. 422-428.

Dunn, S.M., "Biological Image Understanding," *Proc. SPIE Medical Imaging III,* Vol. 1090, 1989, pp. 480-491.

Egbert, D.D., V.G. Kaburlasos, and P.H. Goodman, "Invariant Feature Extraction for Neurocomputer Analysis of Biomedical Images," *Second IEEE Symp. Computer-Based Medical Systems,* IEEE CS Press, Los Alamitos, Calif., 1989, pp. 69-75.

Ehricke, H., "Problems and Approaches for Tissue Segmentation in 3-D MR Imaging," *Proc. SPIE Medical Imaging IV,* Vol. 1231, 1990, pp. 128-137.

Evans, A.C. et al, "Anatomical-Functional Correlative Analysis of the Human Brain Using 3-D Imaging System," *Proc. SPIE Medical Imaging III,* Vol. 1090, 1989, pp. 264-274.

Faber, T.L. and E.M. Stokely, "Feature Detection in 3-D Medical Images Using Shape Information," *IEEE Trans. on Medical Imaging,* 1987, pp. 8-13.

Friendland, N. and D. Adam, "Automatic Ventricular Cavity Boundary Detection from Sequential Ultrasound Images Using Simulated Annealing," *IEEE Trans. on Medical Imaging,* 1989, pp. 344-353.

Giger, M.L., K. Doi, and H. MacMahon, "Computerized Detection of Lung Nodules in Digital Chest Radiographs," *Proc. of SPIE Medical Imaging II,* Vol. 914, 1987, pp. 384-386.

Gordon, D. and J.K. Udupa, "Fast Surface Tracking in Three-Dimensional Binary Images," *Computer Vision, Graphics, and Image Processing,* Vol. 45, 1989, pp. 196-214.

Hibbard, L.S. et al, "Three-Dimensional Representation and Analysis of Brain Energy Metabolism," *Science,* Vol. 236, 1987, pp. 1641-1646.

Ji, Z. and J. Yang, "The Development of Automatic Recognition System for DNA," *Tenth Ann. IEEE Engineering in Medical and Biology Conf.,* 1988, pp. 366-367.

Kennedy, D.N., P.A. Filipek, and V.S. Caviness, Jr, "Anatomic Segmentation and Volumetric Calculations in Nuclear Magnetic Resonance Imaging," *IEEE Trans. on Medical Imaging,* 1989, pp. 1-7.

Kim, N.H., A.C. Bovik, and S.J. Aggarwal, "Shape Description of Biological Objects vis Stereo Light Microscopy," *IEEE Trans. on Systems, Man, and Cybernetics,* Vol. 20, No. 2, 1990, pp. 475-489.

Klingler Jr., J.W. et al, "Segmentation of Echocardiographic Image Using Mathematical Morphology," *IEEE Trans. Biomedical Engineering,* 1988, pp. 925-934.

Kowarski, D., "Expert System and Image and Text Database," *Third IEEE Symp. Computer-Based Medical Systems,* IEEE CS Press, Los Alamitos, Calif., 1990, pp. 298-305.

Lee, R.H. and R.M. Leahy, "Multispectral Tissue Classification of MR Images Using Sensor Fusion Approaches," *Proc. SPIE Medical Imaging IV,* Vol. 1231, 1990, pp. 149-159.

Lifshitz, L.M. and S.M. Pizer, "A Multiresolution Hierarchical Approach to Image Segmentation Based on Intensity Extrema," *IEEE Trans. Pattern Analysis and Machine Intelligence,* Vol. 12, No. 6, June, 1990, pp. 529-540.

Lilly, P., J. Jenkins, and P. Bourdillon, "Automatic Contour Definition on Left Ventriculograms by Image Evidence and a Multiple Template-Based Model," *IEEE Trans. on Medical Imaging,* 1989, pp. 173-185.

Luo, R.C. and Y. Kim, "Representation and Recognition of 3-D Curved Objects Using Complete 3-D Range Data," *Proc. SPIE Medical Imaging IV,* Vol. 1231, 1990, pp. 103-115.

McGlone, J.S. et al, "A Computerized System for Measuring Cerebral Metabolism," *IEEE Trans. Bio-Medical Engineering,* Vol. 34, 1987, pp. 704-712.

Merickel, M.B. et. al, "Multi-Dimensional MRI Pattern Recognition of Atherosclerosis," *Eighth Ann. IEEE Engineering in Medical and Biology Conf.,* 1986, pp. 1142-1145.

Michael, D.J. and A.C. Nelson, "Handx: A Model-Based System for Automatic Segmentation of Bones from Digital Hand Radiographs," *IEEE Trans. on Medical Imaging,* 1989, pp. 64-69.

Minato, K et al, "Automatic Contour Detection Using a 'Fixed-Point Hachimura-Kuwahara Filter' for Spect Attenuation," *IEEE Trans. on Medical Imaging,* 1987, pp. 126-133.

Prasad, B. et al, "A Knowledge-Based System for Tutoring Bronchial Asthma Diagnosis," *Second IEEE Symp. Computer-Based Medical Systems,* IEEE CS Press, Los Alamitos, Calif., 1989, pp. 40-45.

Ro, D.W. et al, "Computed Masks in Coronary Subtraction Imaging," *IEEE Trans. on Medical Imaging,* 1987, pp. 297-300.

Smets, C., P. Suetens, and A.J. Oosterlinck, "Knowledge-Based System for the Delineation of the Coronary Arteries," *Proc. SPIE Medical Imaging III,* Vol. 1090, 1989, pp. 214-219.

Sun, Y., "Automated Identification of Vessel Contours in Coronary Arteriograms by an Adaptive Tracking Algorithm," *IEEE Trans. on Medical Imaging,* 1989, pp. 78-88.

Sun, Y., "Automated Biplane Vessel Recognition in Digital Coronary Angiograms," *Proc. SPIE Medical Imaging IV,* Vol. 1231, 1990, pp. 257-265.

Tehrani, S., T.E. Weymouth, and G.B.J. Mancini, "Knowledge-Guided Left Ventricular Boundary Detection," *Proc. IEEE Conf. Computer Vision and Pattern Recognition,* IEEE CS Press, Los Alamitos, Calif., 1989, pp. 342-347.

Trivedi, S.S., G.T. Herman, and J.K. Udupa, "Segmentation into Three Classes Using Gradients," *IEEE Trans. on Medical Imaging,* 1986, pp. 116-119.

Unser, M. et al, "Automated Extraction of Serial Myocardial Borders from M-mode Echocardiograms," *IEEE Trans. on Medical Imaging,* 1989, pp. 96-103.

van der Stelt, P.F. and W.G.M. Geraets, "Automated Recognition of Bone Structure in Osteoporotic Patients," *Proc. SPIE Medical Imaging III,* Vol. 1090, 1989, pp. 376-382.

Vandermeulen, D. et al, "Knowledge-Based 3-D Segmentation of Blood Vessels on a Spatial Sequence of MRI and Ultrasound Images," *Proc. SPIE Medical Imaging III,* Vol. 1090, 1989, pp. 142-152.

Watson, A.B. and A.J. Ahumada, "A Hexagonal Orthogonal-Oriented Pyramid as a Model of Image Representation on Visual Cortex," *IEEE Trans. Biomedical Engineering,* 1989, pp. 97-106.

Yan, H. and J.C. Gore, "Optimized MR Image Segmentation for Tissue Characterization," *Tenth Ann. IEEE Engineering in Medical and Biology Conf.*, 1988, pp. 338-339.

Industrial Inspection and Robotics:

Barnett, K. and M.M. Trivedi, "Analysis of Thermal and Visual Images for Industrial Inspection Tasks," *Proc. Applications of Artificial Intelligence,* VII, 1989, 482-488.

Bartlett, S.J. et al, "Automatic Solder Joint Inspection," *IEEE Trans. Pattern Analysis and Machine Intelligence,* Vol. 10, No. 1, 1988, pp. 31-43.

Boerner, H. and H. Strecker, "Automated X-Ray Inspection of Aluminum Castings," *IEEE Trans. Pattern Analysis and Machine Intelligence,* Vol. 10, No. 1, 1988, pp. 79-91.

Chen, C., M.M. Trivedi, and C. Bidlack, "Design and Implementation of Autonomous Spill Cleaning Robotic System," *Proc. SPIE/IEEE Applications of Artificial Intelligence Conf. VIII,* Vol. 1293, 1990, pp. 691-703.

Chen, C., M.M. Trivedi, and S.B. Marapane, "Extending Capabilities of a Robotic Vision System," *Proc. SPIE/IEEE Applications of Artificial Intelligence Conf. VII,* Vol. 1095, 1989, pp. 579-580.

Chin, R.T., *Algorithms and Techniques for Automated Visual Inspection,* Academic Press, New York, N.Y., 1986, pp. 587-612.

Chin, R.T. and C.A. Harlow, "Automated Visual Inspection: A Survey," *IEEE Trans. Pattern Analysis and Machine Intelligence,* Vol. 4, No. 6, 1982, pp. 557-573.

Courtney, J.W., M.J. Magee, and J.K. Aggarwal, "Robot Guidance Using Computer Vision," *Pattern Recognition,* Vol. 17, No. 6, 1984, pp. 585-592.

Darwish, A.M. and A.K. Jain, "A Rule-Based Approach for Visual Pattern Inspection," *IEEE Trans. Pattern Analysis and Machine Intelligence,* Vol. 10, No. 1, 1988, pp. 56-68.

He, S., N. Abe, and T. Kitahashi, "Understanding Assembly Illustrations in an Assembly Manual without any Model of Mechanical Parts," *Proc. Third Int'l Conf. Computer Vision,* IEEE CS Press, Los Alamitos, Calif., 1990, pp. 573-576.

Jarvis, J.F., "A Method for Automating the Visual Inspection of Printed Wiring Boards," *IEEE Trans. Pattern Analysis and Machine Intelligence,* Vol. 2, No. 1, 1980, pp. 77-82.

Kak, A.C. et al, "A Knowledge-Based Robotic Assembly Cell," *IEEE EXPERT,* Vol. 1, No. 1, 1986, pp. 63-83.

Lavin, M.A. and L.I. Lieberman, "AML/V: An Industrial Machine Vision Programming System," *Int'l J. Robotics Research,* Vol. 1, No. 3, 1982, pp. 42-56.

Lougheed, R.M. and R.E. Sampson, "3-D Imaging Systems and High-Speed Processing for Robot Control," *Machine Vision and Applications,* Vol. 1, 1988, pp. 41-57.

Mandeville, J.R., "Novel Method for Analysis of Printed Circuit Images," *IBM J. Res. Develop.,* Vol. 29, No. 1, 1985, pp. 73-86.

Maruyama, T. et al, "Hand-Eye System with Three-Dimensional Vision and Microgripper for Handling Flexible Wire," *Machine Vision and Applications,* Vol. 3, No. 4, 1990, pp. 189-199.

McIntosh, W.E., "Automating the Inspection of Printed Circuit Boards," *Robotics Today,* 1983, pp. 75-100.

Niemann, H. et al, "Interpretation of Industrial Scenes by Semantic Networks," *IAPR Workshop on Machine Vision Applications,* 1990, pp. 39-42.

Nishihara, K.H. and P.A. Crossley, "Measuring Photolithographic Overlay Accuracy and Critical Dimensions by Correlating Binarized Laplacian of Gaussian Convolutions," *IEEE Trans. Pattern Analysis and Machine Intelligence,* Vol. 10, No. 1, 1988, pp. 17-30.

Pau, L.F., "Integrated Testing and Algorithms for Visual Inspection of Integrated Circuits," *IEEE Trans. Pattern Analysis and Machine Intelligence,* Vol. 5, No. 6, 1983, pp. 602-608.

Piironen, T. et al, "Automated Visual Inspection of Rolled Metal Surfaces," *Machine Vision and Applications,* Vol. 3, No. 4, 1990, pp. 247-254.

Rosenfeld, A., "Machine Vision for Industry: Tasks, Tools, and Techniques," *Image and Vision Computing,* Vol. 3, 1985, pp. 122-135.

Sanderson, A.C., L.E. Weiss, and S.K. Nayar, "Structured Highlight Inspection of Specular Surfaces," *IEEE Trans. Pattern Analysis and Machine Intelligence,* Vol. 10, No. 1, 1988, pp. 44-55.

Sanz, J.L.C. and D. Petkovic, "Machine Vision Algorithms for Automated Inspection of Thin-Film Disk Heads," *IEEE Trans. Pattern Analysis and Machine Intelligence,* Vol. 10, No. 6, 1988, pp. 830-848.

Sanz, J.L.C., F. Merkle, and K.Y. Wong, "Automated Digital Visual Inspection with Dark-Field Microscopy," *J. Opt. Soc. Am. A,* Vol. 2, 1985, pp. 1857-1862.

Shneier, M.O., R. Lunia, and M. Herman, "Prediction-Based Vision for Robot Control," *Computer,* Vol. 20, No. 8, 1987, pp. 46-55.

Shu, D.B. et al, "A Line Extraction Method for Automated SEM Inspection of VLSI Resist," *IEEE Trans. Pattern Analysis and Machine Intelligence,* Vol. 10, No. 1, 1988, pp. 117-121.

Shuttleworth, P.J. and M. Robinson, "3-D Vision for Robot Manipulator Control," *Proc. SPIE/IEEE Applications of Artificial Intelligence Conf. VIII,* Vol. 1293, 1990, pp. 344-353.

Sood, R.K. and E. Al-Hujazi, "An Integrated Approach to Segmentation of Range Images of Industrial Parts," *IAPR Workshop on Machine Vision Applications,* 1990, pp. 27-30.

Trivedi, M.M. and C. Chen, "Sensor-Driven Intelligent Robotics," *Advances in Computers,* Vol. 32, 1991, pp. 173-216.

Trivedi, M.M., C. Chen, and S.B. Marapane, "A Vision System for Robotic Inspection and Manipulation," *Computer,* Vol. 22, No. 6, 1989, pp. 91-97.

Trivedi, M.M. et al, "Developing Robotic Systems with Multiple Sensors," *IEEE Trans. on Systems, Man, and Cybernetics,* Vol. 20, No. 6, 1990, pp. 1285-1300.

Urban, J.-P., G. Motyle, and J. Gallice, "A Visual Servoing Approach Applied to Robotic Tasks," *IAPR Workshop on Machine Vision Applications,* 1990, pp. 351-356.

Yoda, H. et al, "An Automatic Wafer Inspection System Using Pipelined Image Processing Techniques," *IEEE Trans. Pattern Analysis and Machine Intelligence,* Vol. 10, No. 1, 1988, pp. 4-16.

Autonomous Navigation:

Bares, J. et al, "Ambler- An Autonomous Rover for Planetary Exploration," *Computer,* Vol. 22, No. 6, 1989, pp. 18-26.

Brooks, R.A., "Visual Map Making for a Mobile Robot," *Proc. IEEE Int'l Conf. Robotics and Automation,* IEEE CS Press, Los Alamitos, Calif., 1985, pp. 824-829.

Bruss, A.R. and B.K.P. Horn, "Passive Navigation," *Computer Vision, Graphics, and Image Processing,* Vol. 21, No. 1, 1983, pp. 3-20.

Chattergy, R., "Some Heuristics for the Navigation of a Robot," *Int'l J. Robotics Research,* Vol. 4, No. 1, 1985, pp. 59-66.

Dhome, M. et al, "Localization of Autonomous Mobile Robots by Monocular Vision in Modelled Sites: Application to a Nuclear Power Plant," *IAPR Workshop on Machine Vision Applications,* 1990, pp. 337-342.

Dickmanns, E.D. and V. Graefe, "Dynamic Monocular Machine Vision," *Machine Vision and Applications,* Vol. 1, No. 4, 1988, pp. 223-240.

Dickmanns, E.D. and V. Graefe, "Applications of Dynamic Monocular Machine Vision," *Machine Vision and Applications,* Vol. 1, No. 4, 1988, pp. 241-261.

Dickmanns, E.D., B. Mysliwetz, and T. Christians, "An Integrated Spatio-Temporal Approach for Automatic Visual Guidance of Autonomous Vehicles," *IEEE Trans. on Systems, Man, and Cybernetics,* Vol. 20, No. 6, 1990, pp. 1273-1284.

Elfes, A., "Sonar-Based Real-World Mapping and Navigation," *IEEE Trans. Robotics and Automation,* Vol. 3, No. 3, 1987, pp. 249-265.

Fennema, C., A. Hanson, and E. Riseman, "Towards Autonomous Mobile Robot Navigation," *Proc. DARPA Image Understanding Workshop,* 1989, pp. 219-231.

Flynn, A.M., "Combining Sonar and Infrared Sensors for Mobile Robot Navigation," *Int'l J. Robotics Research,* Vol. 7, No. 6, 1988, pp. 5-14.

Hanson, A.R. and C. Fennema, "Experiments in Autonomous Navigation," *Proc. Tenth Int'l Conf. Pattern Recognition,* IEEE CS Press, Los Alamitos, Calif., 1990, pp 24-31.

Hoshino, J., T. Uemura, and I. Masuda., "Region-Based Reconstruction of an Indoor Scene Using an Integration of Active and Passive Sensing Techniques," *Proc. Third Int'l Conf. Computer Vision,* IEEE CS Press, Los Alamitos, Calif., 1990, pp. 568-572.

Ishiguro, H., M. Yamamoto, and S. Tsuji, "Omni-Directional Stereo for Making Global Map," *Proc. Third Int'l Conf. Computer Vision,* IEEE CS Press, Los Alamitos, Calif., 1990, pp. 540-547.

Kahn, P., L. Kitchen, and E.M. Riseman, "A Fast Line Finder for Vision-Guided Navigation," *IEEE Trans. Pattern Analysis and Machine Intelligence,* Vol. 12, No. 11, 1990, pp. 1098-1102.

Keirsey, D. et al, "Autonomous Vehicle Control Using AI Technique," *IEEE Trans. on Software Engineering,* Vol. 11, 1985, pp. 986-992.

Koch, E. et al, "Simulation of Path Planning for a System with Vision and Map Updating," *Proc. IEEE Int'l Conf. on Robotics and Automation,* IEEE CS Press, Los Alamitos, Calif., 1985, pp. 1-15.

Kriegman, D.J., E. Triendl, and T.O. Binford, "Stereo Vision and Navigation in Buildings for Mobile Robots," *IEEE Trans. Robotics and Automation,* Vol. 5, 1989, pp. 792-804.

Kuan, D., G. Phipps, and A.C. Hsueh, "Autonomous Robotic Vehicle Road Following," *IEEE Trans. Pattern Analysis and Machine Intelligence,* Vol. 10, No. 5, 1988, pp. 648-658.

McDermott, D. and E. Davis, "Planning Routes through Uncertain Territory," *Artificial Intelligence,* Vol. 22, 1984, pp. 107-156.

McVey, E.S., K.C. Drake, and R.M. Inigo, "Range Measurements by a Mobile Robot Using a Navigation Line," *IEEE Trans. Pattern Analysis and Machine Intelligence,* Vol. 8, No. 1, 1986, pp. 105-109.

Miller, D.P. et al, "Robot Navigation," *Proc. Int'l Joint Conf. Artificial Intelligence,* 1989, pp. 1672-1674.

Rao, N.S.V., "Algorithmic Framework for Learned Robot Navigation in Unknown Terrains," *Computer,* Vol. 22, No. 6, 1989, pp. 37-43.

Rodriguez, J.J. and J.K. Aggarwal, "Navigation Using Image Sequence Analysis and 3-D Terrain Matching," *Proc. IEEE Workshop on Interpretation of 3-D Scenes,* IEEE CS Press, Los Alamitos, Calif., 1989, pp. 200-207.

Rosenfeld, A. and L.S. Davis, "Image Understanding Techniques for Autonomous Vehicle Navigation," *Proc. DARPA Image Understanding Workshop,* 1985, pp. 1-3.

Roth-Tabak, Y. and T. Weymouth, "Using and Generating Environment Models for Indoor Mobile Robots," *IAPR Workshop on Machine Vision Applications,* 1990, pp. 343-346.

Sharma, U.K. and D. Kuan, "Real-Time Model-Based Geometric Reasoning for Vision-Guided Navigation," *Machine Vision and Applications,* Vol. 2, 1989, pp. 31-44.

Sugihara, K., "Some Location Properties for Robot Navigation Using Single Camera," *Computer Vision, Graphics, and Image Processing,* Vol. 42, 1988, pp. 112-129.

Thorpe, C. et al, "Vision and Navigation for the Carnegie-Mellon Navlab," *IEEE Trans. Pattern Analysis and Machine Intelligence,* Vol. 10, No. 3, 1988, pp. 362-373.

Thorpe, C. and T. Kanade, "Carnegie Mellon Navlab Vision," *Proc. DARPA Image Understanding Workshop,* 1989, pp. 273-282.

Turk, M.A. et al, "VITS - A Vision System for Autonomous Land Vehicle Navigation," *IEEE Trans. Pattern Analysis and Machine Intelligence,* Vol. 10, No. 3, 1988, pp. 342-360.

Weisbin, C.R. et al, "Autonomous Mobile Robot Navigation and Learning," *Computer,* Vol. 22, No. 6, 1989, pp. 29-35.

Zhang, Z. and O. Faugeras, "Building a 3-D World Model with a Mobile Robot: 3-D Line Segment Representation and Integration," *Proc. Tenth Int'l Conf. Pattern Recognition,* IEEE CS Press, Los Alamitos, Calif., 1990, pp. 38-42.

Zheng, J.Y., M. Barth, and S. Tsuji, "Qualitative Route Scene Description Using Autonomous Landmark Detection," *Proc. Third Int'l Conf. Computer Vision,* IEEE CS Press, Los Alamitos, Calif., 1990, pp. 558-562.

The following list of books, special issues, and conferences are relevant to computer vision. We have limited the selections to those published since 1980.

Books and Edited Volumes

Ahuja, N. and B.J. Schachter, *Pattern Models,* John Wiley & Sons, New York, N.Y., 1983.

Allen, P.K., *Robotic Object Recognition Using Vision and Touch,* Kluwer, Boston, 1987.

Aloimonos, J.Y. and D. Shulman, *Integration of Visual Modules: An Extension of the Marr Paradigm,* Academic Press, Boston, Mass., 1989.

Arbib, M.A. and A.R. Hanson, eds., *Vision, Brain, and Cooperative Computation,* MIT Press, Cambridge, Mass., 1987.

Baird, H.S., *Model-Based Image Matching Using Location,* MIT Press, Cambridge, Mass., 1984.

Ballard, D.H. and C.M. Brown, *Computer Vision,* Prentice-Hall, Englewood Cliffs, N.J., 1982.

Barr, A. and E.A. Feigenbaum, *The Handbook of Artificial Intelligence,* William Kaufmann, Los Altos, Calif., 1982.

Baxes, G.A., *Digital Image Processing: A Practical Primer,* Prentice-Hall, Englewood Cliffs, N.J., 1984.

Beck, J., B. Hope, and A. Rosenfeld, eds., *Human and Machine Vision,* Academic Press, New York, N.Y., 1983.

Besl, P., *Surfaces in Range Image Understanding,* Springer-Verlag, New York, N.Y., 1988.

Blake, A. and T. Troscianko, eds., *AI and the Eye,* John Wiley & Sons, New York, N.Y., 1990.

Blake, A. and A. Zisserman, *Visual Reconstruction,* MIT Press, Cambridge, Mass., 1987.

Bow, S.T., *Pattern Recognition: Applications to Large Data-Set Problems,* Marcel-Dekker, New York, N.Y., 1984.

Boyle, R. and R.C. Thomas, *Computer Vision: A First Course,* Blackwell Scientific Publications, Boston, Mass., 1988.

Braddick, O.J. and A.C. Sleigh, *Physical and Biological Processing of Images,* Springer-Verlag, Berlin, 1983.

Brady, J.M., ed., *Computer Vision,* North-Holland Publishing Co., Amsterdam, 1981.

Brady, J.M. and R. Paul, eds., *Robotics Research: The First Int'l Symposium,* MIT Press, Cambridge, Mass., 1984.

Brooks, R., *Model-Based Computer Vision,* UMI Research Press, Ann Arbor, Mich., 1984.

Brown, C., ed., *Advances in Computer Vision,* Erlbaum Lawrence Associates, Hillsdale, N.J., 1988, (2 volumes).

Cappellini, V., ed., *Time-Varying Image Processing and Moving Object Recognition,* Elsevier Science Publishing, New York, N.Y., 1987.

Cappellini, V., ed., *Time-Varying Image Processing and Moving Object Recognition* (2), Elsevier Science Publishing, New York, N.Y., 1990.

Chang, S.K., *Principles of Pictorial Information Systems Design,* Prentice-Hall, Englewood Cliffs, N.J., 1989.

Chellappa, R. and A.A. Sawchuk, eds., *Digital Image Processing and Analysis: Volume I: Digital Image Processing,* IEEE CS Press, Los Alamitos, Calif., 1985.

Chellappa, R. and A.A. Sawchuk, eds., *Digital Image Processing and Analysis: Volume II: Digital Image Analysis,* IEEE CS Press, Los Alamitos, Calif., 1986.

Chen, S.S., ed., *Image Understanding in Unstructured Environment,* (Erice-Trapani, Sicily, January 5-25, 1987), World Scientific, Singapore, 1988.

Devijver, P.A. and J. Kittler, eds., "Pattern Recognition Theory and Applications", *Proc. NATO Advanced Study Institute,* 1986, Springer-Verlag, Berlin, 1987.

Dew, P.M., R.A. Earnshaw, and T.R. Heywood, eds., *Parallel Processing for Computer Vision and Display,* Addison-Wesley, Reading, Mass., 1989.

Dougherty, E.R. and C.R. Giardina, *Image Processing - Continuous to Discrete,* Prentice-Hall, Englewood Cliffs, N.J., 1987.

Dougherty, E.R. and C.R. Giardina, *Matrix Structured Image Processing,* Prentice-Hall, Englewood Cliffs, N.J., 1986.

Dougherty, E.R. and C.R. Giardina, *Morphological Methods in Image and Signal Processing,* Prentice-Hall, Englewood Cliffs, N.J., 1987.

Duff, M.J.B. and S. Levialdi, *Languages and Architectures for Image Processing,* Academic Press, New York, N.Y., 1981.

Ekstorm, M.P., *Digital Image Processing Techniques,* Academic Press, Orlando, Florida, 1984.

Fairhurst, M., *Computer Vision for Robotic Systems - An Introduction,* Prentice-Hall, New York, N.Y., 1988.

Fan, T.-J., *Describing and Recognizing 3-D Objects Using Surface Properties,* Springer-Verlag, New York, N.Y., 1990.

Faugeras, O.D., ed., *Fundamentals in Computer Vision,* Cambridge Univ. Press, Cambridge, Mass., 1983.

Fischler, M.A. and O. Firschein, eds., *Readings in Computer Vision: Issues, Problems, Principles, and Paradigms,* Morgan Kaufmann, Publishers, Inc., San Mateo, Calif., 1987.

Fisher, R.B., *From Surfaces to Objects: Computer Vision and Three Dimensional Scene Analysis,* John Wiley & Sons, New York, N.Y., 1989.

Freeman, H. and G.G. Pieroni, eds., "Map Data Processing," *Proc. NATO Advanced Study Institute,* 1979, Academic Press, New York, N.Y., 1980.

Freeman, H., ed., "Machine Vision - Algorithms, Architectures, and Systems," *Proc. Workshop Machine Vision: Where are we Going?,* 1987, Academic Press, Boston, Mass., 1988.

Freeman, H., ed., *Machine Vision for Inspection & Measurement,* Academic Press, San Diego, Calif., 1989.

Freeman, H., ed., *Machine Vision for Three-dimensional Scenes,* Academic Press, Boston, Mass., 1990.

Frisby, J., *Seeing: Illusion, Brain, and Mind,* Oxford Univ. Press, Oxford, UK, 1980.

Fu, K.S., *Applications of Pattern Recognition,* CRC Press, Boca Raton, Florida, 1982.

Fu, K.S., *Syntactic Pattern Recognition and Applications,* Prentice-Hall, Englewood Cliffs, N.J., 1982.

Fu, K.S., R.C. Gonzalez, and C.S.G. Lee, *Robotics: Control, Sensing, Vision, and Intelligence,* McGraw Hill, 1987.

Fu, K.S. and T.L. Kunii, eds., *Picture Eng.,* Springer-Verlag, New York, N.Y., 1982.

Galbiati Jr., L.J., *Machine Vision and Digital Image Processing Fundamentals,* Prentice-Hall, Englewood Cliffs, N.J., 1990.

Gale, A.G., M.H. Freeman, C.M. Haslegrave, P. Smith, and S.P. Taylor, eds., *Vision in Vehicles II,* North-Holland, Amsterdam, 1988.

Gelsema, E.S. and L.N. Kanal, eds., "Pattern Recognition in Practice," *Proc. of an Int'l Workshop,* North-Holland, Amsterdam, 1980.

Gelsema, E.S. and L.N. Kanal, eds., Pattern Recognition in Practice II," *Proc. of an Int'l Workshop*, North-Holland, Amsterdam, 1986.

Gonzalez, R.C. and P. Wintz, *Digital Image Processing*, Addison-Wesley, Reading, Mass., Second edition, 1987.

Green, W.B., *Digital Image Processing: A Systems Approach*, Van Nostrand Reinhold, New York, N.Y., Second edition, 1989.

Grimson, W.E.L., *From Images to Surfaces: A Computational Study of the Human Early Visual System*, MIT Press, Cambridge, Mass., 1981.

Grossberg, N., *Neural Networks and Natural Intelligence*, MIT Press, Cambridge, Mass., 1988.

Haralick, R.M., ed., "Pictorial Data Analysis," *Proc. NATO Advanced Study Institute on Pictorial Data Analysis*, Springer-Verlag, Berlin, 1983.

Haralick, R.M. and J.C. Simon, eds., Issues in Digital Image Processing," *Proc. NATO Advanced Study Institute on Digital Image Processing and Analysis*, Sijthoff & Noordoff, Groningen, 1980.

Henderson, T.C., *Discrete Relaxation Techniques*, Oxford Univ. Press, New York, N.Y., 1989.

Hildreth, E.C., *The Measurement of Visual Motion*, MIT Press, Cambridge, Mass., 1983.

Hord, R.M., *Remote Sensing - Methods and Applications*, John Wiley & Sons, New York, N.Y., 1986.

Horn, B.K.P., *Robot Vision*, McGraw-Hill, New York, N.Y., 1986.

Horn, B.K.P. and M.J. Brooks, eds., *Shape from Shading*, MIT Press, Cambridge, Mass., 1989.

Huang, T.S., ed., *Image Sequence Processing and Dynamic Scene Analysis*, Springer-Verlag, New York, N.Y., 1983.

Huang, T.S., ed., *Advances in Computer Vision and Image Processing: Image Reconstruction from Incomplete Observation*, JAI Press, Greenwich, Conn., 1984.

Huang, T.S., ed., *Advances in Computer Vision and Image Processing: Image Enhancement and Restoration*, JAI Press, Greenwich, Conn., 1986.

Huang, T.S., ed., *Advances in Computer Vision and Image Processing: Time-Varying Imagery Analysis*, JAI Press, Greenwich, Conn., 1987.

Ingle, D.J., M.A. Goodale, and R.J.W. Mansfield, eds., *Analysis of Visual Behavior*, MIT Press, Cambridge, Mass., 1982.

Jain, A.K., *Fundamentals of Digital Image Processing*, Prentice-Hall, Englewood Cliffs, N.J., 1989.

Jain, A.K., ed., *Real-Time Object Measurement and Classification*, Springer-Verlag, Berlin, 1988.

Jain, R.C. and A.K. Jain, eds., *Analysis and Interpretation of Range Images*, Springer-Verlag, New York, N.Y., 1990.

Kak, A. and S.S. Chen, eds., Spatial Reasoning and Multi-Sensor Fusion," *Proc. 1987 Workshop*, Morgan Kaufmann Publishers, Inc., San Mateo, Calif., 1987.

Kak, A.C. and M. Slaney, eds., *Principles of Computerized Tomographic Imaging*, IEEE Press, New York, N.Y., 1988.

Kanade, T., ed., *Three-Dimensional Machine Vision*, Kluwer Academic, Norwell, Mass., 1987.

Kanal, L.N. and A. Rosenfeld, eds., *Progress in Pattern Recognition*, Vol. 1, North Holland, New York, N.Y., 1981.

Kanal, L.N. and A. Rosenfeld, eds., *Progress in Pattern Recognition 2*, Noth Holland, New York, N.Y., 1985.

Kasturi, R. and M.M. Trivedi, eds., *Image Analysis Applications*, Marcel Dekker Inc., New York, N.Y., 1990.

Kender, J., *Shape from Texture*, Morgan Kaufman, Los Altos, Calif., 1986.

Kittler, J., K.S. Fu, and L.F. Pau, eds., "Pattern Recognition Theory and Applications," *Proc. NATO Advanced Study Institute*, D. Reidel, Dordrecht, Holland, 1982.

Koenderink, J.J., *Solid Shape*, MIT Press, Cambridge, Mass., 1989.

Kovalevsky, V.A., *Image Pattern Recognition*, Springer-Verlag, New York, N.Y., 1980.

Krotkov, E.P., *Active Computer Vision by Cooperative Focus and Stereo*, Springer-Verlag, New York, N.Y., 1989.

Krzyzak, A., T. Kasvand, and C.Y. Suen, eds., "Computer Vision and Shape Recognition," *Canadian Conf. Pattern Recognition and Picture Processing: Vision Interface '88*, World Scientific, Singapore, 1989.

Kumar, V., P.S. Gopalakrishnan, and L.N. Kanal, eds., *Parallel Algorithms for Machine Intelligence and Vision*, Springer-Verlag, New York, N.Y., 1990.

Lancaster, P. and K.S.Salkaukas, *Curve & Surface Fitting: An Introduction*, Academic Press, London, U.K., 1986.

Levialdi, S., ed., *Multicomputer Vision*, Academic Press, San Diego, Calif., 1988.

Levine, M.D., *Vision in Man and Machine*, McGraw-Hill, New York, N.Y., 1985.

Lowe, D., *Perceptual Organization and Visual Recognition*, Kluwer, Boston, Mass., 1985.

Marr, D., *Vision: A Computational Investigation into the Human Representation and Processing of Visual Information*, W. H. Freeman & Co., San Francisco, Calif., 1982.

Martin, W.N., J.K. Aggarwal, *Motion Understanding: Robot & Human Vision*, Kluwer, Boston, Mass., 1988.

McCafferty, J.D., *Human and Computer Vision: Computing Perceptual Organisation*, Ellis Horwood, New York, N.Y., 1990.

Murray, D.W. and B.F. Buxton, *Experiments in the Machine Interpretation of Visual Motion*, MIT Press, Cambridge, Mass., 1990.

Nagao, M. and T. Matsuyama, *A Structural Analysis of Complex Aerial Photographs*, Plenum Press, New York, N.Y., 1980.

Nevatia, R., Machine *Perception*, Prentice-Hall, Englewood Cliffs, N.J., 1982.

Nilblack, W., *An Introduction to Digital Image Processing*, Prentice-Hall, Englewood Cliffs, N.J., 1986.

Ohta, Y., *Knowledge-Based Interpretation of Outdoor Natural Color Scenes*, Pitman, Mass., 1985.

Offen, R.J., *VLSI Image Processing*, McGraw-Hill, New York, N.Y., 1985.

Page, I., ed., *Parallel Architectures and Computer Vision*, Oxford Univ. Press, New York, N.Y., 1988.

Pao, Y.H. and G.W. Ernst, eds., *Context-Directed Pattern Recognition and Machine Intelligence Techniques for Information Processing*, IEEE Press, New York, N.Y., 1982.

Pau, L.F., *Computer Vision for Electronics Manufacturing*, Plenum Press, New York, N.Y., 1989.

Pavlidis, T., *Algorithms for Graphics and Image Processing*, Computer Science Press, Rockville, Maryland, 1982.

Pentland, A.P., ed., *From Pixels to Predicates: Recent Advances in Computational and Robot Vision*, Ablex, Norwood, N.J., 1986.

Pieroni, G.G., ed., *Issues on Machine Vision*, Springer-Verlag, New York, N.Y., 1989.

Pratt, W.K., *Digital Image Processing*, Second Edition, John Wiley & Sons, New York, N.Y., 1991.

Pugh, A., ed., *Robot Vision*, IFS (Publications) Ltd., U.K., 1983.

Rao, A.R., *Taxonomy for Texture Description and Identification,* Springer-Verlag, New York, N.Y., 1990.

Rich, E., *Artificial Intelligence,* McGraw-Hill, New York, N.Y., 1983.

Richards, W. and S. Ullman, eds., *Image Understanding 1985-1986,* Ablex, Norwood, N.J., 1987.

Rioux, M. and L. Cournoyer, *The NRCC Three-Dimensional Image Data Files,* Nat'l Research Council Canada, Ottawa, Canada, 1989.

Rock, I., *The Logic of Perception,* MIT Press, Cambridge, Mass., 1983.

Ronse, C. and P.A. Devijver, *Connected Components in Binary Images: The Detection Problem,* Research Studies Press, Letchworth, Hertfordshire, England, 1984.

Rosenfeld, A., ed., *Multiresolution Image Processing & Analysis,* Springer-Verlag, New York, N.Y., 1984.

Rosenfeld, A., ed., *Techniques for 3-D Machine Perception,* Elsevier Science Publisher, Amsterdam, Holland, 1986.

Rosenfeld, A. and A. Kak, *Digital Picture Processing,* Volumes 1 & 2, Academic Press, New York, N.Y., Second edition, 1982.

Sanz, J.L.C., ed., *Advances in Machine Vision,* Springer-Verlag, New York, N.Y., 1989.

Sanz, J.L.C., E.B. Hinkle, and A.K. Jain, *Radon and Projection Transform-based Computer Vision: Algorithms, a Pipeline Architecture, and Industrial Applications,* Springer-Verlag, New York, N.Y., 1988.

Schalkoff, R.J., *Digital Image Processing and Computer Vision,* John Wiley & Sons, New York, N.Y., 1989.

Serra, J., *Image Analysis and Mathematical Morphology,* Academic Press, New York, N.Y., 1982.

Serra, J., ed., *Image Analysis and Mathematical Morphology 2: Technical Advances,* Academic Press, New York, N.Y., 1988.

Shafer, S.A., *Shadows and Silhouettes in Computer Vision,* Kluwer Academic Press, Boston, Mass., 1985.

Shani, U., *Understanding Three-Dimensional Images: Recognition of Abdominal Anatomy from CAT Scans,* UMI Research Press, Ann Arbor, Mich., 1984.

Shirai, Y., *Three-Dimensional Computer Vision,* Springer-Verlag, New York, N.Y., 1987.

Simon, J.C., "From Pixels to Features", *Proc. of a Workshop,* North Holland, Amsterdam, 1989.

Simon, J.C. and R.M. Haralick, eds., Digital Image Processing," *Proc. NATO Advanced Study Institute,* D. Reidel, Dordrecht, Holland, 1981.

Suen, C.Y. and R. DeMori, eds., *Computer Analysis and Perception,* Vol. 1, Visual Signals, CRC Press, Boca Raton, Florida, 1982.

Sugihara, K., *Machine Interpretation of Line Drawings,* MIT Press, Cambridge, Mass., 1986.

Szeliski, R., *Bayesian Modeling of Uncertainty in Low-level Vision,* Kluwer, Boston, Mass., 1989.

Tanimoto, S.L., *Elements of Artificial Intelligence,* Computer Science Press, 1990.

Tanimoto, S. and A. Klinger, eds., *Structured Computer Vision: Machine Perception through Hierarchical Computational Structures,* Academic Press, New York, N.Y., 1980.

Trivedi, M.M., ed., *Selected Papers on Digital Image Processing,* Milestone series Vol. 17, SPIE Press, 1990.

Uhr, L., ed., *Parallel Computer Vision,* Academic Press, Boston, Mass., 1987.

Vogt, R.C., *Automatic Generation of Morphological Set Recognition Algorithms,* Springer-Verlag, New York, N.Y., 1989.

Watanabe, S., *Pattern Recognition: Human and Mechanical,* John Wiley & Sons, New York, N.Y., 1985.

Wechsler, H., *Computational Vision,* Academic Press, Boston, Mass., 1990.

Wilson, R. and M. Spann, *Image Segmentation and Uncertainty,* John Wiley & Sons, New York, N.Y., 1988.

Winston, P.H., *Artificial Intelligence,* second edition, Addison-Wesley, Reading, Mass., 1984.

Wong, A.K.C. and A. Pugh, eds., *Machine Intelligence and Knowledge Eng. for Robotic Applications,* Springer-Verlag, Berlin, 1987.

Woodwark, J., ed., *Geometric Reasoning,* Oxford Univ. Press, New York, N.Y., 1989.

Yaroslavsky, L.P., *Digital Picture Processing, An Introduction,* Springer-Verlag, Berlin, 1985.

Yaroslavsky, L.P., A. Rosenfeld, and W. Wilhelmi, eds., "Computer Analysis of Images and Patterns," *Proc. of CAIP '87, Second Conf. on Automatic Image Processing,* Akademie-Verlag, Berlin, 1987.

Young, T.Y. and K.S. Fu, eds., *Handbook of Pattern Recognition and Image Processing,* Academic Press, Orlando, FL, 1986.

Zuech, N. and R.K. Miller, *Machine Vision,* Fairmont Press, Lilburn, GA, 1987.

Conference and Workshop Proceedings

IEEE Conference on Computer Vision and Pattern Recognition, 1983-1991, published by IEEE Computer Society Press.

IEEE International Conference on Computer Vision, 1987-1990, published by IEEE Computer Society Press.

First European Conference on Computer Vision, published by Springer-Verlag, New York, N.Y.

International Conference on Pattern Recognition, 1980-1990, published by IEEE Computer Society Press.

Annual DARPA Image Understanding Workshop, 1980-1989, sponsored by Defense Advanced Research Projects Agency, Information Science and Technology Office.

Scandinavian Conference on Image Analysis (SCIA), 1980-1989,

International Joint Conference on Artificial Intelligence, 1981-1991, sponsored by International Joint Conferences on Artificial Intelligence, Inc., published by Morgan Kaufmann Publishers, Inc., San Mateo, California.

National Conference on Artificial Intelligence, 1980-1990, sponsored by The American Association for Artificial Intelligence, published by Morgan Kaufmann Publishers, Inc., San Mateo, California.

IEEE Conference on Artificial Intelligence Applications (CAIA), 1984-1989, published by the IEEE Computer Society Press.

International Conference on Image Analysis and Processing (ICIAP), 1980-1989.

IEEE International Conference on Image Processing 1989.

IEEE International Conference on Robotics and Automation, 1984-1990, sponsored by IEEE Council on Robotics and Automation, published by IEEE Computer Society Press.

International Conference on Robot Vision and Sensory Controls (ICRVSC), 1981-1988, organized by IFS (Conferences) Ltd., Bedford, U.K. and other co-sponsors.

IEEE Workshop on Computer Vision: Representation and Control, 1982-1987.

IEEE Workshop on Motion: Representation and Analysis, 1986.

IEEE Workshop on Visual Motion, 1989.

IEEE Workshop on Interpretation of 3D Scenes, 1989.

IEEE Workshop on Robust Computer Vision, 1990.

IEEE Workshop on Directions in Automated CAD-Based Vision, 1991.

IAPR Workshop on Computer Vision - Special Hardware and Industrial Applications, 1988.

IAPR Workshop on Machine Vision Applications, proceedings published for IAPR by M. Takagi, Univ. of Tokyo, Japan, 1990.

IAPR Workshop on Syntactic and Structural Pattern Recognition, 1990, proceedings edited by H. Baird, AT&T Bell Laboratories.

SPIE Conference on Applications of Artificial Intelligence, 1984-1990, published by SPIE-The International Society for Optical Eng., Bellingham, Washington, U.S.A.

SPIE Conference on Intelligent Robots and Computer Vision, 1984-1989, published by SPIE-The International Society for Optical Eng., Bellingham, Washington, U.S.A.

SPIE Conference on Medical Imaging, 1987-1990, published by SPIE-The International Society for Optical Eng., Bellingham, Washington, U.S.A.

SPIE Conference on Mobile Robots, 1986-1989, published by SPIE-The International Society for Optical Eng., Bellingham, Washington, U.S.A.

SPIE Conference on Optics, Illumination, and Image Sensing for Machine Vision, 1986-1990, published by SPIE-The International Society for Optical Eng., Bellingham, Washington, U.S.A.

SPIE Conference on Visual Communications and Image Processing, 1986-1990, published by SPIE-The International Society for Optical Eng., Bellingham, Washington, U.S.A.

SPIE Conference on Applications of Digital Image Processing, 1982-1990, A.G. Tescher, editor, published by SPIE-The International Society for Optical Eng., Bellingham, Washington, U.S.A.

SPIE Critical Review Series Conferences, published by SPIE-The International Society for Optical Eng., Bellingham, Washington, U.S.A.:
Robotics and Robot Sensing Systems, Vol. 442, D. Casasent and E.L. Hall, editors, 1983.
Remote Sensing, Vol. 475, P.N. Slater, editor, 1984.
Digital Image Processing, Vol. 528, A.G. Tescher, editor, 1985.
Image Pattern Recognition, Vol. 755, F.J. Corbett, editor, 1987.

SPIE Conference on Techniques and Applications of Image Understanding, Vol. 281, J.J. Pearson, editor, 1981, published by SPIE-The International Society for Optical Eng., Bellingham, Washington, U.S.A.

SPIE Conference on 3-D Machine Perception, Vol. 283, B.R. Altschuler, editor, D.C., 1981, published by SPIE-The International Society for Optical Eng., Bellingham, Washington, U.S.A.

SPIE Conference on Processing of Images and Data from Optical Sensors, Vol. 292, W.H. Carter, editor, 1981, published by SPIE-The International Society for Optical Eng., Bellingham, Washington, U.S.A.

SPIE Conference on Design of Digital Image Processing Systems, Vol. 301, J.L. Mannos, editor, 1981, published by SPIE-The International Society for Optical Eng., Bellingham, Washington, U.S.A.

SPIE Conference on Robot Vision, Vol. 336, A. Rosenfeld, editor, 1982, published by SPIE-The International Society for Optical Eng., Bellingham, Washington, U.S.A.

SPIE Conference on Image Understanding and Man-Machine Interface, Vol. 758, J.J. Pearson and E. Barrett, editors, 1987, published by SPIE-The International Society for Optical Eng., Bellingham, Washington, U.S.A.

SPIE Parallel Architectures for Image Processing, Vol. 1246, J. Ghosh and C.G. Harrison, editors, 1990, published by SPIE-The International Society for Optical Eng., Bellingham, Washington, U.S.A.

Special issues

Advances in mathematical morphology, J. Serra, ed., *Signal Processing*, Vol. 16, April 1989.

Advances in syntactic pattern recognition, H. Bunke and A. Sanfeliu, eds., *Pattern Recognition*, Vol. 19, 1986.

Artificial intelligence and signal processing in underwater acoustics and geophysics problems, C.H. Chen, ed., *Pattern Recognition*, Vol. 18, No. 6, 1985.

Autonomous intelligent machines, S.S. Iyengar and R.L. Kashyap, eds., *Computer*, Vol. 22, June 1989.

CAD-based robot vision, B. Bhanu, ed., *Computer*, Vol. 20, August 1987.

Computer analysis of time-varying images, W.E. Snyder, ed., *Computer*, Vol. 14, August 1981.

Computational geometry, R. Forrest, L. Guibas, and J. Nievergelt, eds., *ACM Trans. Graphics*, Vol. 3, October 1984.

Computational geometry, C.K. Yap, ed., *Algorithmica*, Vol. 4, 1989.

Computational geometry, C. K. Yap, ed., *Journal of Computer and System Sciences*, Vol. 39, October 1989.

Computer graphics in medicine and biology, J.M.S. Prewitt, ed., *IEEE Computer Graphics and Applications*, Vol. 3, August 1983.

Computer vision, R.M. Haralick, ed., *Computer Vision, Graphics and Image Processing*, 22, April 1983.

Computer vision, M. Brady, ed., *Artificial Intelligence*, Vol. 17, No. 1 and No. 3, 1981.

Computer vision, H. Li and J.R. Kender, eds., *Proceedings of the IEEE*, Vol. 76, August 1988.

Computer vision, M.M. Trivedi and A. Rosenfeld, eds., *IEEE Trans. Systems, Man, and Cybernetics*, Vol. 19, December 1989.

Computerized tomography, G.T. Herman, ed., *Proceedings of the IEEE*, Vol. 71, March 1983.

Connectionist models and their applications, J.A. Feldman, ed., *Cognitive Science*, 9, January-March 1985.

Current issues and trends in computer vision, L. Shapiro and A. Kak, eds., *Computer Vision, Graphics and Image Processing*, 36, November-December 1986.

Digital image processing and application, A.N. Venetsanopoulos, ed., *IEEE Trans. Circuits and Systems*, Vol. 34, November 1987.

Factory automation and robotics (special section), H.J. Bernstein, ed., *Comm. ACM*, Vol. 29, June 1986.

Frontier in computer graphics and applications: selections from intergraphics '83, T.L. Kunii, ed., *IEEE Computer Graphics and Applications*, Vol. 3, December 1983.

Geometric reasoning, D. Kapur and J. Mundy, eds., *Artificial Intelligence*, Vol. 37, December 1988.

Human and machine vision, A. Rosenfeld, ed., *Computer Vision, Graphics and Image Processing*, 31-32, August-October 1985.

Image analysis and processing, S. Levialdi, ed., *Signal Processing*, Vol. 3, July 1981.

Image database management (special section), S.S. Iyengar and R.L. Kashyap, eds., *IEEE Trans. Software Engineering*, Vol. 14, May 1988.

Image database management, Grosky W. and R. Mehrotra, eds., *Computer*, Vol. 22, December 1989.

Image processing, H. Freitag, ed., *Proceedings of the IEEE*, Vol. 69, May 1981.

Image restoration & reconstruction, M.I. Sezan and A.M. Tekalp, eds., *Optical Eng.*, Vol. 29, May 1990.

Industrial machine vision and computer vision technology part I and II, J.L.C. Sanz, ed., *IEEE Trans. Pattern Analysis and Machine Intelligence*, January and May 1988.

Knowledge based image analysis, N. Niemann and Y.T. Chien, eds., *Pattern Recognition*, Vol. 17, August 1984.

Machine Vision mensuration, R.M. Haralick, ed., *Computer Vision, Graphics and Image Processing*, Vol. 40, December 1987.

Machine vision and image understanding, O. Firschein, ed., *IEEE Control Systems Magazine*, Vol. 8, June 1988.

Memorial issue for Professor King-Sun Fu, T. Pavlidis, ed., *IEEE Trans. Pattern Analysis and Machine Intelligence*, Vol. 8, No. 3, May 1986.

Modeling of natural phenomena, A. Fournier and W.T. Reeves, eds., *ACM Trans. Graphics*, Vol. 6, July 1987.

Multiresolution representation (special section), S.L. Tanimoto, ed., *IEEE Trans. Pattern Analysis and Machine Intelligence*, Vol. 11, July 1989.

Optical pattern recognition, B.V.K.V. Kumar, ed., *Optical Eng.*, Vol. 29, September 1990.

Papers from Third International Conference on Pattern Recognition of the British Pattern Recognition Assoc., D. Rutovitz, ed., *Pattern Recognition Letters*, Vol. 5, No. 2, Feb. 1987, Vol. 6, No. 1 and No. 2, June, July 1987.

Pattern recognition of cell images, J.W. Bacus and P.H. Bartels, eds., *Pattern Recognition*, Vol. 13, No. 1 and No. 4, 1981.

Perceiving Earth's resources from space, D.A. Landgrebe, ed., *Proceedings of the IEEE*, Vol. 73, June 1985.

Sensor data fusion, J.M. Brady, ed., *Int'l J. of Robotic Research*, Vol. 6, December 1988.

Shape analysis in image processing, *Pattern Recognition*, Vol. 13, No. 2, 1981.

Spatial reasoning, A. Kak, ed., *AI Magazine*, Vol. 9, Summer 1988.

Time-varying imagery, J.K. Aggarwal, ed., *Computer Vision, Graphics and Image Processing*, 21, January 1983.

Visual communications systems, A.N. Netravali and B. Prasada, ed., *Proceedings of the IEEE*, Vol. 73, April 1985.

Visual motion, W.B. Thompson, ed., *IEEE Trans. Pattern Analysis and Machine Intelligence*, Vol. 11, May 1989.

INDEX

The following index was created by searching for terms in the chapter introductions and in the titles and abstracts of reprinted papers; terms in the main body of the papers are not indexed.

About the authors

Rangachar Kasturi was born in Bangalore, India in 1949. He received his BE degree in electrical engineering from Bangalore University in 1968 and his MSEE and PhD from Texas Tech University, Lubbock, in 1980 and 1982, respectively.

Professor Kasturi is an associate professor of electrical and computer engineering at the Pennsylvania State University, where he was an assistant professor from 1982 to 1986. From 1989 to 1990, he was a visiting scholar at the Artificial Intelligence Laboratory of the University of Michigan. From 1978 to 1982, he was a research assistant at Texas Tech University in the areas of multiplex holography and digital image processing. From 1976 to 1978, he was the engineering officer at the Visvesvaraya Industrial and Technological Museum, Bangalore, and from 1969 to 1976 he was with Bharat Electronics Ltd., Bangalore, as a research and development engineer.

Professor Kasturi's current research interests are in the applications of image analysis and computer vision techniques. He is a contributing author and a co-editor of the book, *Image Analysis Applications*, Marcel Dekker, 1990. He is a senior member of the IEEE, and a member of the Optical Society of America, the International Society for Optical Engineering (SPIE), American Society for Photogrammetry and Remote Sensing, Eta Kappa Nu, and Sigma Xi. He is the chairman of the Technical Committee on Graphics Recognition (TC-10) of the International Association for Pattern Recognition (IAPR). He was a general chairman of the 1990 IAPR Workshop on Machine Vision Applications. He is an associate editor of *IEEE Transactions on Pattern Analysis and Machine Intelligence*. During 1987-1990, Professor Kasturi delivered lectures on his research at many chapters of the IEEE Computer Society through its Distinguished Visitor Program.

Ramesh Jain received his BE from Nagpur University, India in 1969 and his PhD from IIT, Kharagpur, India, in 1975. He is currently a Professor of electrical engineering and computer science and the Director of the Artificial Intelligence Laboratory at the University of Michigan. He has been affiliated with Stanford University, IBM Alamaden Research Labs, General Motors Research Labs, Wayne State University, University of Texas at Austin, University of Hamburg, West Germany, and Indian Institute of Technology, Kharagpur, India.

Professor Jain's current research interests are in computer vision and artificial intelligence. Some of the projects he has completed include: semiconductor wafer inspection using scanning electron microscopes and optical microscopes, automatic visual inspection of solder joints for IBM, laser range image processing for CAD-based vision systems, robotic navigation and rotorcraft navigation using machine vision, and applications of expert systems in inspection systems. He is a consultant in the areas of computer vision, artificial intelligence, and computer graphics.

Professor Jain is a senior member of IEEE and a member of ACM, AAAI, Pattern Recognition Society, Cognitive Science Society, Optical Society of America, the International Society for Optical Engineering (SPIE), and the Society of Manufacturing Engineers. He has been involved in organizing several professional conferences and workshops. Currently, he is on the editorial boards of *IEEE Expert, Machine Vision and Applications, Computer Vision Graphics and Image Processing*, the *Bulletin of Approximate Reasoning*, and *Image and Vision Computing*.

IEEE Computer Society Press Titles

For further information call toll-free 1-800-CS-BOOKS or write:

IEEE Computer Society Press, 10662 Los Vaqueros Circle, PO Box 3014,
Los Alamitos, California 90720-1264, USA

IEEE Computer Society, 13, avenue de l'Aquilon,
B-1200 Brussels, BELGIUM

IEEE Computer Society, Ooshima Building, 2-19-1 Minami-Aoyama,
Minato-ku, Tokyo 107, JAPAN

Knowledge-Based Systems:
Fundamentals and Tools
Edited by Oscar N. Garcia and Yi-Tzuu Chien
(ISBN 0-8186-1924-4); 512 pages

Local Network Technology (Third Edition)
Edited by William Stallings
(ISBN 0-8186-0825-0); 512 pages

Nearest Neighbor Pattern Classification Techniques
Edited by Belur V. Dasarathy
(ISBN 0-8186-8930-7); 464 pages

Object-Oriented Computing,
Volume 1: Concepts
Edited by Gerald E. Petersen
(ISBN 0-8186-0821-8); 214 pages

Object-Oriented Computing,
Volume 2: Implementations
Edited by Gerald E. Petersen
(ISBN 0-8186-0822-6); 324 pages

Real-Time Systems
Abstractions, Languages, and Design Methodologies
Edited by Krishna M. Kavi
(ISBN 0-8186-3152-X); 550 pages

Reduced Instruction Set Computers (RISC)
(Second Edition)
Edited by William Stallings
(ISBN 0-8186-8943-9); 448 pages

Software Design Techniques (Fourth Edition)
Edited by Peter Freeman and Anthony I. Wasserman
(ISBN 0-8186-0514-6); 730 pages

Software Engineering Project Management
Edited by Richard H. Thayer
(ISBN 0-8186-0751-3); 512 pages

Software Maintenance and Computers
Edited by David H. Longstreet
(ISBN 0-8186-8898-X); 304 pages

Software Management
(Fourth Edition)
Edited by Donald J. Reifer
(ISBN 0-8186-3342-5); 656 pages

Software Reengineering
Edited by Robert S. Arnold
(ISBN 0-8186-3272-0); 688 pages

Software Reuse — Emerging Technology
Edited by Will Tracz
(ISBN 0-8186-0846-3); 400 pages

Software Risk Management
Edited by Barry W. Boehm
(ISBN 0-8186-8906-4); 508 pages

Standards, Guidelines and Examples on System
and Software Requirements Engineering
Edited by Merlin Dorfman and Richard H. Thayer
(ISBN 0-8186-8922-6); 626 pages

System and Software Requirements Engineering
Edited by Richard H. Thayer and Merlin Dorfman
(ISBN 0-8186-8921-8); 740 pages

Systems Network Architecture
Edited by Edwin R. Coover
(ISBN 0-8186-9131-X); 464 pages

Test Access Port and Boundary-Scan Architecture
Edited by Colin M. Maunder and Rodham E. Tulloss
(ISBN 0-8186-9070-4); 400 pages

Visual Programming Environments: Paradigms and Systems
Edited by Ephraim Glinert
(ISBN 0-8186-8973-0); 680 pages

Visual Programming Environments: Applications and Issues
Edited by Ephraim Glinert
(ISBN 0-8186-8974-9); 704 pages

Visualization in Scientific Computing
Edited by G. M. Nielson, B. Shriver, and L. Rosenblum
(ISBN 0-8186-8979-X); 304 pages

Volume Visualization
Edited by Arie Kaufman
(ISBN 0-8186-9020-8); 494 pages

REPRINT COLLECTIONS

Distributed Computing Systems:
Concepts and Structures
Edited by A. L. Ananda and B. Srinivasan
(ISBN 0-8186-8975-0); 416 pages

Expert Systems:
A Software Methodology for Modern Applications
Edited by Peter G. Raeth
(ISBN 0-8186-8904-8); 476 pages

Milestones in Software Evolution
Edited by Paul W. Oman and Ted G. Lewis
(ISBN 0-8186-9033-X); 332 pages

Object-Oriented Databases
Edited by Ez Nahouraii and Fred Petry
(ISBN 0-8186-8929-3); 256 pages

Validating and Verifying Knowledge-Based Systems
Edited by Uma G. Gupta
(ISBN 0-8186-8995-1); 400 pages

ARTIFICIAL NEURAL NETWORKS TECHNOLOGY SERIES

Artificial Neural Networks —
Concept Learning
Edited by Joachim Diederich
(ISBN 0-8186-2015-3); 160 pages

Artificial Neural Networks —
Electronic Implementation
Edited by Nelson Morgan
(ISBN 0-8186-2029-3); 144 pages

Artificial Neural Networks —
Theoretical Concepts
Edited by V. Rao Vemuri
(ISBN 0-8186-0855-2); 160 pages

SOFTWARE TECHNOLOGY SERIES

Bridging Faults and IDDQ Testing
Edited by Yashwant K. Malaiya and Rochit Rajsuman
(ISBN 0-8186-3215-1); 128 pages

Computer-Aided Software Engineering (CASE)
(2nd Edition)
Edited by Elliot Chikofsky
(ISBN 0-8186-3590-8); 184 pages

Fault-Tolerant Software Systems:
Techniques and Applications
Edited by Hoang Pham
(ISBN 0-8186-3210-0); 128 pages

Software Reliability Models:
Theoretical Development, Evaluation, and Applications
Edited by Yashwant K. Malaiya and Pradip K. Srimani
(ISBN 0-8186-2110-9); 136 pages

MATHEMATICS TECHNOLOGY SERIES

Computer Algorithms
Edited by Jun-ichi Aoe
(ISBN 0-8186-2123-0); 154 pages

Distributed Mutual Exclusion Algorithms
Edited by Pradip K. Srimani and Sunil R. Das
(ISBN 0-8186-3380-8); 168 pages

Genetic Algorithms
Edited by Bill P. Buckles and Frederick E. Petry
(ISBN 0-81862935-5); 120 pages

Multiple-Valued Logic in VLSI Design
Edited by Jon T. Butler
(ISBN 0-8186-2127-3); 128 pages